JEEP WAGONEER/COMANCHE/CHEROKEE
1984-96 REPAIR MANUAL

CHILTON'S™

President	Dean F. Morgantini, S.A.E.
Vice President–Finance	Barry L. Beck
Vice President–Sales	Glenn D. Potere
Executive Editor	Kevin M. G. Maher
Production Manager	Ben Greisler, S.A.E.
Project Managers	Michael Abraham, George B. Heinrich III, Will Kessler, A.S.E., Richard Schwartz
Editors	Will Kessler, A.S.E., Thomas A. Mellon

CHILTON™ Automotive Books
PUBLISHED BY **W. G. NICHOLS, INC.**

Manufactured in USA
© 1996 Chilton Book Company
1020 Andrew Drive
West Chester, PA 19380
ISBN 0-8019-8674-5
Library of Congress Catalog Card No. 96-85120
3456789012 7654321098

Contents

Contents

SAFETY NOTICE

Proper service and repair procedures are vital to the safe, reliable operation of all motor vehicles, as well as the personal safety of those performing repairs. This manual outlines procedures for servicing and repairing vehicles using safe, effective methods. The procedures contain many NOTES, CAUTIONS and WARNINGS which should be followed along with standard procedures to eliminate the possibility of personal injury or improper service which could damage the vehicle or compromise its safety.

It is important to note that the repair procedures and techniques, tools and parts for servicing motor vehicles, as well as the skill and experience of the individual performing the work vary widely. It is not possible to anticipate all of the conceivable ways or conditions under which vehicles may be serviced, or to provide cautions as to all of the possible hazards that may result. Standard and accepted safety precautions and equipment should be used when handling toxic or flammable fluids, and safety goggles or other protection should be used during cutting, grinding, chiseling, prying, or any other process that can cause material removal or projectiles.

Some procedures require the use of tools specially designed for a specific purpose. Before substituting another tool or procedure, you must be completely satisfied that neither your personal safety, nor the performance of the vehicle will be endangered.

Although information in this manual is based on industry sources and is complete as possible at the time of publication, the possibility exists that some vehicle manufacturers made later changes which could not be included here. While striving for total accuracy, W. G. Nichols, Inc. cannot assume responsibility for any errors, changes or omissions that may occur in the compilation of this data.

PART NUMBERS

Part numbers listed in this reference are not recommendations by Chilton for any product by brand name. They are references that can be used with interchange manuals and aftermarket supplier catalogs to locate each brand supplier's discrete part number.

SPECIAL TOOLS

Special tools are recommended by the vehicle manufacturer to perform their specific job. Use has been kept to a minimum, but where absolutely necessary, they are referred to in the text by the part number of the tool manufacturer. These tools can be purchased, under the appropriate part number, from your local dealer or regional distributor, or an equivalent tool can be purchased locally from a tool supplier or parts outlet. Before substituting any tool for the one recommended, read the SAFETY NOTICE at the top of this page.

ACKNOWLEDGMENTS

W. G. Nichols, Inc. expresses appreciation to Chrysler Corporation for their generous assistance.

1

GENERAL INFORMATION AND MAINTENANCE

HOW TO USE THIS BOOK

Chilton's Total Car Care manual for the Wagoneer, Cherokee, Comanche and Grand Cherokee/Wagoneer models from 1984 through 1996 is intended to help you learn more about the inner workings of your vehicle while saving you money on its upkeep and operation.

The beginning of the book will likely be referred to the most, since that is where you will find information for maintenance and tune-up. The other sections deal with the more complex systems of your vehicle. Operating systems from engine through brakes are covered to the extent that the average do-it-yourselfer becomes mechanically involved. This book will not explain such things as rebuilding a differential for the simple reason that the expertise required and the investment in special tools make this task uneconomical. It will, however, give you detailed instructions to help you change your own brake pads and shoes, replace spark plugs, and perform many more jobs that can save you money, give you personal satisfaction and help you avoid expensive problems.

A secondary purpose of this book is a reference for owners who want to understand their vehicle and/or their mechanics better. In this case, no tools at all are required.

Where to Begin

Before removing any bolts, read through the entire procedure. This will give you the overall view of what tools and supplies will be required. There is nothing more frustrating than having to walk to the bus stop on Monday morning because you were short one bolt on Sunday afternoon. So read ahead and plan ahead. Each operation should be approached logically and all procedures thoroughly understood before attempting any work.

All sections contain adjustments, maintenance, removal and installation procedures, and in some cases, repair or overhaul procedures. When repair is not considered practical, we tell you how to remove the part and then how to install the new or rebuilt replacement. In this way, you at least save the labor costs. Backyard repair of some components is just not practical.

Avoiding Trouble

Many procedures in this book require you to "label and disconnect . . ." a group of lines, hoses or wires. Don't be lulled into thinking you can remember where everything goes — you won't. If you hook up vacuum or fuel lines incorrectly, the vehicle will run poorly, if at all. If you hook up electrical wiring incorrectly, you may instantly learn a very expensive lesson.

You don't need to know the official or engineering name for each hose or line. A piece of masking tape on the hose and a piece on its fitting will allow you to assign your own label such as the letter A or a short name. As long as you remember your own code, the lines can be reconnected by matching similar letters or names. Do remember that tape will dissolve in gasoline or other fluids; if a component is to be washed or cleaned, use another method of identification. A permanent felt-tipped marker can be very handy for marking metal parts. Remove any tape or paper labels after assembly.

Maintenance or Repair?

It's necessary to mention the difference between maintenance and repair. Maintenance includes routine inspections, adjustments, and replacement of parts which show signs of normal wear. Maintenance compensates for wear or deterioration. Repair implies that something has broken or is not working. A need for repair is often caused by lack of maintenance. Example: draining and refilling the automatic transmission fluid is maintenance recommended by the manufacturer at specific mileage intervals. Failure to do this can ruin the transmission/transaxle, requiring very expensive repairs. While no maintenance program can prevent items from breaking or wearing out, a general rule can be stated: MAINTENANCE IS CHEAPER THAN REPAIR.

Two basic mechanic's rules should be mentioned here. First, whenever the left side of the vehicle or engine is referred to, it is meant to specify the driver's side. Conversely, the right side of the vehicle means the passenger's side. Second, most screws and bolts are removed by turning counterclockwise, and tightened by turning clockwise.

Safety is always the most important rule. Constantly be aware of the dangers involved in working on an automobile and take the proper precautions. See the information in this section regarding SERVICING YOUR VEHICLE SAFELY and the SAFETY NOTICE on the acknowledgment page.

Avoiding the Most Common Mistakes

Pay attention to the instructions provided. There are 3 common mistakes in mechanical work:

1. Incorrect order of assembly, disassembly or adjustment. When taking something apart or putting it together, performing steps in the wrong order usually just costs you extra time; however, it CAN break something. Read the entire procedure before beginning disassembly. Perform everything in the order in which the instructions say you should, even if you can't immediately see a reason for it. When you're taking apart something that is very intricate, you might want to draw a picture of how it looks when assembled at one point in order to make sure you get everything back in its proper position. We will supply exploded views whenever possible. When making adjustments, perform them in the proper order; often, one adjustment affects another, and you cannot expect even satisfactory results unless each adjustment is made only when it cannot be changed by any other.

2. Overtorquing (or undertorquing). While it is more common for overtorquing to cause damage, undertorquing may allow a fastener to vibrate loose causing serious damage. Especially when dealing with aluminum parts, pay attention to torque specifications and utilize a torque wrench in assembly. If a torque figure is not available, remember that if you are using the right tool to perform the job, you will probably not have to strain yourself to get a fastener tight enough. The pitch of most threads is so slight that the tension you put on

the wrench will be multiplied many times in actual force on what you are tightening. A good example of how critical torque is can be seen in the case of spark plug installation, especially where you are putting the plug into an aluminum cylinder head. Too little torque can fail to crush the gasket, causing leakage of combustion gases and consequent overheating of the plug and engine parts. Too much torque can damage the threads or distort the plug, changing the spark gap.

There are many commercial products available for ensuring that fasteners won't come loose, even if they are not torqued just right (a very common brand is Loctite®). If you're worried about getting something together tight enough to hold, but loose enough to avoid mechanical damage during assembly, one of these products might offer substantial insurance. Before choosing a threadlocking compound, read the label on the package and make sure the product is compatible with the materials, fluids, etc. involved.

3. Crossthreading. This occurs when a part such as a bolt is screwed into a nut or casting at the wrong angle and forced. Crossthreading is more likely to occur if access is difficult. It helps to clean and lubricate fasteners, then to start threading with the part to be installed positioned straight in. Then, start the bolt, spark plug, etc. with your fingers. If you encounter resistance, unscrew the part and start over again at a different angle until it can be inserted and turned several times without much effort. Keep in mind that many parts, especially spark plugs, have tapered threads, so that gentle turning will automatically bring the part you're threading to the proper angle, but only if you don't force it or resist a change in angle. Don't put a wrench on the part until it's been tightened a couple of turns by hand. If you suddenly encounter resistance, and the part has not seated fully, don't force it. Pull it back out to make sure it's clean and threading properly.

Always take your time and be patient; once you have some experience, working on your vehicle may well become an enjoyable hobby.

TOOLS AND EQUIPMENT

▶ **See Figures 1, 2, 3, 4, 5, 6, 7, 8, 9, 10, 11, 12, 13 and 14**

Naturally, without the proper tools and equipment it is impossible to properly service your vehicle. It would also be virtually impossible to catalog every tool that you would need to perform all of the operations in this book. Of course, It would be unwise for the amateur to rush out and buy an expensive set of tools on the theory that he/she may need one or more of them at some time.

The best approach is to proceed slowly, gathering a good quality set of those tools that are used most frequently. Don't be misled by the low cost of bargain tools. It is far better to spend a little more for better quality. Forged wrenches, 6 or 12-point sockets and fine tooth ratchets are by far preferable to their less expensive counterparts. As any good mechanic can tell you, there are few worse experiences than trying to work on a vehicle with bad tools. Your monetary savings will be far outweighed by frustration and mangled knuckles.

Begin accumulating those tools that are used most frequently: those associated with routine maintenance and tune-up. In addition to the normal assortment of screwdrivers and pliers, you should have the following tools:

• Wrenches/sockets and combination open end/box end wrenches in sizes from ⅛-¾ in. or 3-19mm (depending on whether your vehicle uses standard or metric fasteners) and a ¹³⁄₁₆ in. or ⅝ in. spark plug socket (depending on plug type).

➡**If possible, buy various length socket drive extensions. Universal-joint and wobble extensions can be extremely useful, but be careful when using them, as they can change the amount of torque applied to the socket.**

• Jackstands for support.
• Oil filter wrench.
• Spout or funnel for pouring fluids.
• Grease gun for chassis lubrication (unless your vehicle is not equipped with any grease fittings — for details, please refer to information on Fluids and Lubricants found later in this section).

• Hydrometer for checking the battery (unless equipped with a sealed, maintenance-free battery).
• A container for draining oil and other fluids.
• Rags for wiping up the inevitable mess.

In addition to the above items there are several others that are not absolutely necessary, but handy to have around. These include Oil Dry® (or an equivalent oil absorbent gravel — such as cat litter) and the usual supply of lubricants, antifreeze and fluids, although these can be purchased as needed. This is a basic list for routine maintenance, but only your personal needs and desire can accurately determine your list of tools.

After performing a few projects on the vehicle, you'll be amazed at the other tools and non-tools on your workbench. Some useful household items are: a large turkey baster or siphon, empty coffee cans and ice trays (to store parts), ball of twine, electrical tape for wiring, small rolls of colored tape for tagging lines or hoses, markers and pens, a note pad, golf tees (for plugging vacuum lines), metal coat hangers or a roll

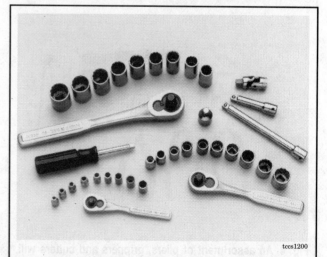

tccs1200

Fig. 1 All but the most basic procedures will require an assortment of ratchets and sockets

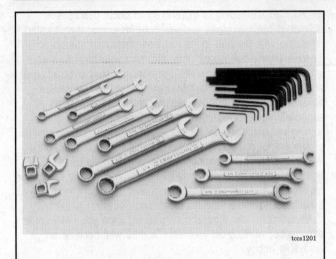

Fig. 2 In addition to ratchets, a good set of wrenches and hex keys will be necessary

Fig. 3 A hydraulic floor jack and a set of jackstands are essential for lifting and supporting the vehicle

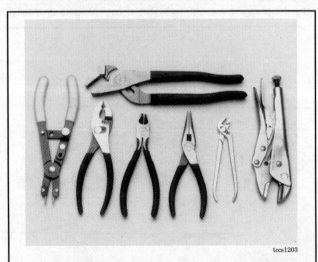

Fig. 4 An assortment of pliers, grippers and cutters will be handy, for old rusted parts and stripped bolt heads

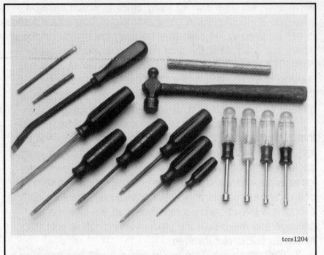

Fig. 5 Various drivers, chisels and prybars are great tools to have in your toolbox

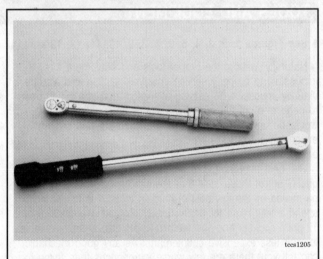

Fig. 6 Many repairs will require the use of a torque wrench to assure the components are properly fastened

of mechanics's wire (to hold things out of the way), dental pick or similar long, pointed probe, a strong magnet, and a small mirror (to see into recesses and under manifolds).

A more advanced set of tools, suitable for tune-up work, can be drawn up easily. While the tools are slightly more sophisticated, they need not be outrageously expensive. There are several inexpensive tach/dwell meters on the market that are every bit as good for the average mechanic as a professional model. Just be sure that it goes to a least 1200-1500 rpm on the tach scale and that it works on 4, 6 and 8-cylinder engines. (If you have one or more vehicles with a diesel engine, a special tachometer is required since diesels don't use spark plug ignition systems). The key to these purchases is to make them with an eye towards adaptability and wide range. A basic list of tune-up tools could include:

- Tach/dwell meter.
- Spark plug wrench and gapping tool.
- Feeler gauges for valve or point adjustment. (Even if your vehicle does not use points or require valve adjustments, a feeler gauge is helpful for many repair/overhaul procedures).

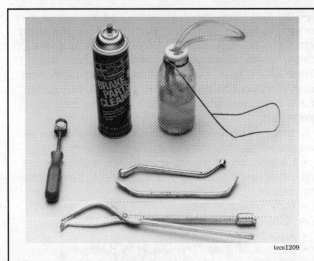

tccs1209

Fig. 7 Although not always necessary, using specialized brake tools will save time

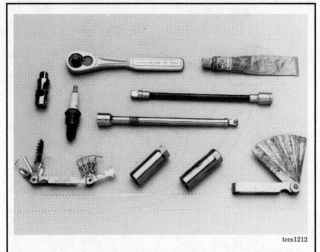

tccs1212

Fig. 10 A variety of tools and gauges should be used for spark plug gapping and installation

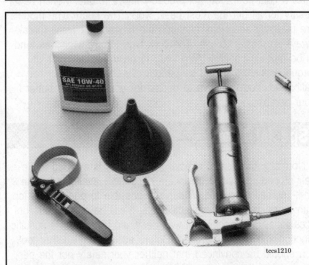

tccs1210

Fig. 8 A few inexpensive lubrication tools will make maintenance easier

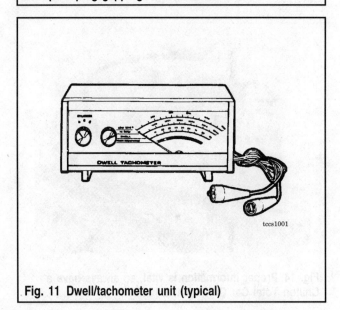

tccs1001

Fig. 11 Dwell/tachometer unit (typical)

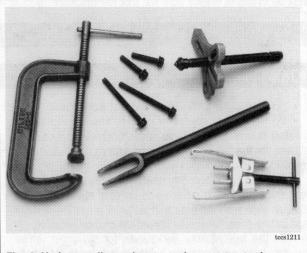

tccs1211

Fig. 9 Various pullers, clamps and separator tools are needed for many larger, more complicated repairs

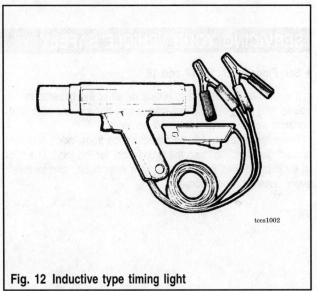

tccs1002

Fig. 12 Inductive type timing light

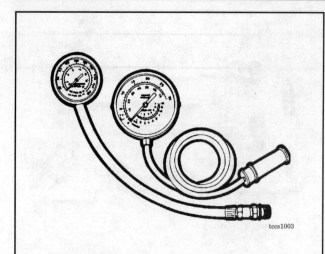

Fig. 13 Compression gauge and a combination vacuum/fuel pressure test gauge

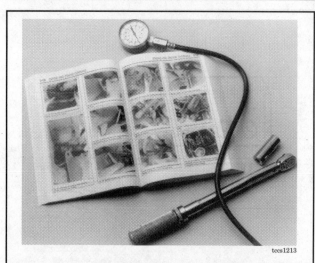

Fig. 14 Proper information is vital, so always have a Chilton Total Car Care manual handy

A tachometer/dwell meter will ensure accurate tune-up work on vehicles without electronic ignition. The choice of a timing light should be made carefully. A light which works on the DC current supplied by the vehicle's battery is the best choice; it should have a xenon tube for brightness. On any vehicle with an electronic ignition system, a timing light with an inductive pickup that clamps around the No. 1 spark plug cable is preferred.

In addition to these basic tools, there are several other tools and gauges you may find useful. These include:

- Compression gauge. The screw-in type is slower to use, but eliminates the possibility of a faulty reading due to escaping pressure.
- Manifold vacuum gauge.
- 12V test light.
- A combination volt/ohmmeter
- Induction Ammeter. This is used for determining whether or not there is current in a wire. These are handy for use if a wire is broken somewhere in a wiring harness.

As a final note, you will probably find a torque wrench necessary for all but the most basic work. The beam type models are perfectly adequate, although the newer click types (breakaway) are easier to use. The click type torque wrenches tend to be more expensive. Also keep in mind that all types of torque wrenches should be periodically checked and/or re-calibrated. You will have to decide for yourself which better fits your purpose.

Special Tools

Normally, the use of special factory tools is avoided for repair procedures, since these are not readily available for the do-it-yourself mechanic. When it is possible to perform the job with more commonly available tools, it will be pointed out, but occasionally, a special tool was designed to perform a specific function and should be used. Before substituting another tool, you should be convinced that neither your safety nor the performance of the vehicle will be compromised.

Special tools can usually be purchased from an automotive parts store or from your dealer. In some cases special tools may be available directly from the tool manufacturer.

SERVICING YOUR VEHICLE SAFELY

▶ **See Figures 15, 16, 17 and 18**

It is virtually impossible to anticipate all of the hazards involved with automotive maintenance and service, but care and common sense will prevent most accidents.

The rules of safety for mechanics range from "don't smoke around gasoline," to "use the proper tool for the job." The trick to avoiding injuries is to develop safe work habits and to take every possible precaution.

Do's

- Do keep a fire extinguisher and first aid kit handy.
- Do wear safety glasses or goggles when cutting, drilling, grinding or prying, even if you have 20-20 vision. If you wear glasses for the sake of vision, wear safety goggles over your regular glasses.
- Do shield your eyes whenever you work around the battery. Batteries contain sulfuric acid. In case of contact with the eyes or skin, flush the area with water or a mixture of water and baking soda, then seek immediate medical attention.
- Do use safety stands (jackstands) for any under vehicle service. Jacks are for raising vehicles; jackstands are for making sure the vehicle stays raised until you want it to come down. Whenever the vehicle is raised, block the wheels remaining on the ground and set the parking brake.

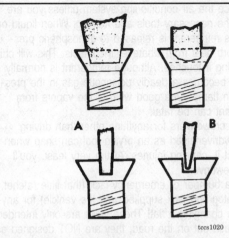

Fig. 15 Screwdrivers should be kept in good condition to prevent injury or damage which could result if the blade slips from the screw

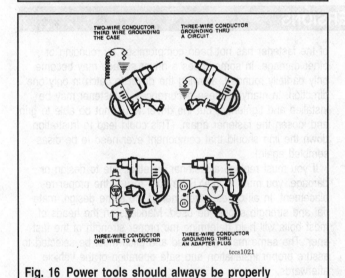

Fig. 16 Power tools should always be properly grounded

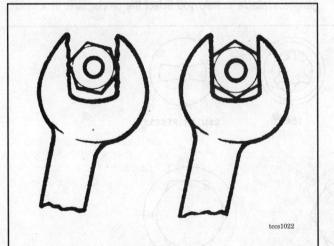

Fig. 17 Using the correct size wrench will help prevent the possibility of rounding off a nut

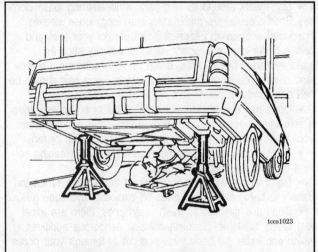

Fig. 18 NEVER work under a vehicle unless it is supported using safety stands (jackstands)

• Do use adequate ventilation when working with any chemicals or hazardous materials. Like carbon monoxide, the asbestos dust resulting from some brake lining wear can be hazardous in sufficient quantities.

• Do disconnect the negative battery cable when working on the electrical system. The secondary ignition system contains EXTREMELY HIGH VOLTAGE. In some cases it can even exceed 50,000 volts.

• Do follow manufacturer's directions whenever working with potentially hazardous materials. Most chemicals and fluids are poisonous if taken internally.

• Do properly maintain your tools. Loose hammerheads, mushroomed punches and chisels, frayed or poorly grounded electrical cords, excessively worn screwdrivers, spread wrenches (open end), cracked sockets, slipping ratchets, or faulty droplight sockets can cause accidents.

• Likewise, keep your tools clean; a greasy wrench can slip off a bolt head, ruining the bolt and often harming your knuckles in the process.

• Do use the proper size and type of tool for the job at hand. Do select a wrench or socket that fits the nut or bolt. The wrench or socket should sit straight, not cocked.

• Do, when possible, pull on a wrench handle rather than push on it, and adjust your stance to prevent a fall.

• Do be sure that adjustable wrenches are tightly closed on the nut or bolt and pulled so that the force is on the side of the fixed jaw.

• Do strike squarely with a hammer; avoid glancing blows.

• Do set the parking brake and block the drive wheels if the work requires a running engine.

Don'ts

• Don't run the engine in a garage or anywhere else without proper ventilation — EVER! Carbon monoxide is poisonous; it takes a long time to leave the human body and you can build up a deadly supply of it in your system by simply breathing in a little every day. You may not realize you are slowly poisoning yourself. Always use power vents, windows, fans and/or open the garage door.

• Don't work around moving parts while wearing loose clothing. Short sleeves are much safer than long, loose sleeves. Hard-toed shoes with neoprene soles protect your toes and give a better grip on slippery surfaces. Jewelry such as watches, fancy belt buckles, beads or body adornment of any kind is not safe working around a vehicle. Long hair should be tied back under a hat or cap.

• Don't use pockets for toolboxes. A fall or bump can drive a screwdriver deep into your body. Even a rag hanging from your back pocket can wrap around a spinning shaft or fan.

• Don't smoke when working around gasoline, cleaning solvent or other flammable material.

• Don't smoke when working around the battery. When the battery is being charged, it gives off explosive hydrogen gas.

• Don't use gasoline to wash your hands; there are excellent soaps available. Gasoline contains dangerous additives which can enter the body through a cut or through your pores. Gasoline also removes all the natural oils from the skin so that bone dry hands will suck up oil and grease.

• Don't service the air conditioning system unless you are equipped with the necessary tools and training. When liquid or compressed gas refrigerant is released to atmospheric pressure it will absorb heat from whatever it contacts. This will chill or freeze anything it touches. Although refrigerant is normally non-toxic, R-12 becomes a deadly poisonous gas in the presence of an open flame. One good whiff of the vapors from burning refrigerant can be fatal.

• Don't use screwdrivers for anything other than driving screws! A screwdriver used as an prying tool can snap when you least expect it, causing injuries. At the very least, you'll ruin a good screwdriver.

• Don't use a bumper or emergency jack (that little ratchet, scissors, or pantograph jack supplied with the vehicle) for anything other than changing a flat! These jacks are only intended for emergency use out on the road; they are NOT designed as a maintenance tool. If you are serious about maintaining your vehicle yourself, invest in a hydraulic floor jack of at least a 1½ ton capacity, and at least two sturdy jackstands.

FASTENERS, MEASUREMENTS AND CONVERSIONS

Bolts, Nuts and Other Threaded Retainers

▶ See Figures 19, 20, 21 and 22

Although there are a great variety of fasteners found in the modern car or truck, the most commonly used retainer is the threaded fastener (nuts, bolts, screws, studs, etc). Most threaded retainers may be reused, provided that they are not damaged in use or during the repair. Some retainers (such as stretch bolts or torque prevailing nuts) are designed to deform when tightened or in use and should not be reinstalled.

Whenever possible, we will note any special retainers which should be replaced during a procedure. But you should always inspect the condition of a retainer when it is removed and replace any that show signs of damage. Check all threads for rust or corrosion which can increase the torque necessary to achieve the desired clamp load for which that fastener was originally selected. Additionally, be sure that the driver surface of the fastener has not been compromised by rounding or other damage. In some cases a driver surface may become only partially rounded, allowing the driver to catch in only one direction. In many of these occurrences, a fastener may be installed and tightened, but the driver would not be able to grip and loosen the fastener again. (This could lead to frustration down the line should that component ever need to be disassembled again).

If you must replace a fastener, whether due to design or damage, you must ALWAYS be sure to use the proper replacement. In all cases, a retainer of the same design, material and strength should be used. Markings on the heads of most bolts will help determine the proper strength of the fastener. The same material, thread and pitch must be selected to assure proper installation and safe operation of the vehicle afterwards.

Thread gauges are available to help measure a bolt or stud's thread. Most automotive and hardware stores keep gauges available to help you select the proper size. In a pinch,

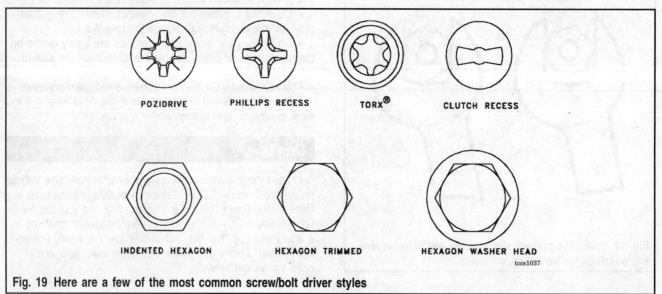

POZIDRIVE   PHILLIPS RECESS   TORX®   CLUTCH RECESS

INDENTED HEXAGON   HEXAGON TRIMMED   HEXAGON WASHER HEAD

tccs1037

Fig. 19 Here are a few of the most common screw/bolt driver styles

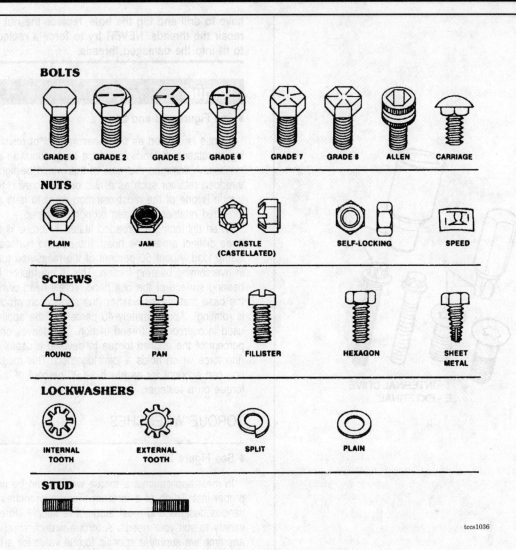

Fig. 20 There are many different types of threaded retainers found on vehicles

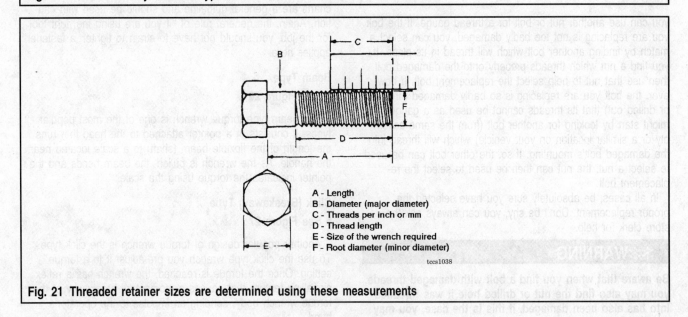

A - Length
B - Diameter (major diameter)
C - Threads per inch or mm
D - Thread length
E - Size of the wrench required
F - Root diameter (minor diameter)

tccs1038

Fig. 21 Threaded retainer sizes are determined using these measurements

have to drill and tap the hole, replace the nut or otherwise repair the threads. NEVER try to force a replacement bolt to fit into the damaged threads.

Torque

▶ See Figures 23 and 24

Torque is defined as the measurement of resistance to turning or rotating. It tends to twist a body about an axis of rotation. A common example of this would be tightening a threaded retainer such as a nut, bolt or screw. Measuring torque is one of the most common ways to help assure that a threaded retainer has been properly fastened.

When tightening a threaded fastener, torque is applied in three distinct areas, the head, the bearing surface and the clamp load. About 50 percent of the measured torque is used in overcoming bearing friction. This is the friction between the bearing surface of the bolt head, screw head or nut face and the base material or washer (the surface on which the fastener is rotating). Approximately 40 percent of the applied torque is used in overcoming thread friction. This leaves only about 10 percent of the applied torque to develop a useful clamp load (the force which holds a joint together). This means that friction can account for as much as 90 percent of the applied torque on a fastener.

TORQUE WRENCHES

▶ See Figure 25

In most applications, a torque wrench can be used to assure proper installation of a fastener. Torque wrenches come in various designs and most automotive supply stores will carry a variety to suit your needs. A torque wrench should be used any time we supply a specific torque value for a fastener. A torque wrench can also be used if you are following the general guidelines in the accompanying charts. Keep in mind that because there is no worldwide standardization of fasteners, the charts are a general guideline and should be used with caution. Again, the general rule of "if you are using the right tool for the job, you should not have to strain to tighten a fastener" applies here.

Beam Type
▶ See Figure 26

The beam type torque wrench is one of the most popular types. It consists of a pointer attached to the head that runs the length of the flexible beam (shaft) to a scale located near the handle. As the wrench is pulled, the beam bends and the pointer indicates the torque using the scale.

Click (Breakaway) Type
▶ See Figure 27

Another popular design of torque wrench is the click type. To use the click type wrench you pre-adjust it to a torque setting. Once the torque is reached, the wrench has a reflex signalling feature that causes a momentary breakaway of the torque wrench body, sending an impulse to the operator's hand.

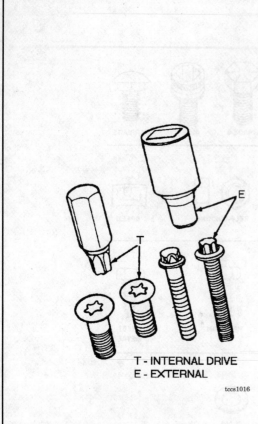

T - INTERNAL DRIVE
E - EXTERNAL

tccs1016

Fig. 22 Special fasteners such as these Torx® head bolts are used by manufacturers to discourage people from working on vehicles without the proper tools

you can use another nut or bolt for a thread gauge. If the bolt you are replacing is not too badly damaged, you can select a match by finding another bolt which will thread in its place. If you find a nut which threads properly onto the damaged bolt, then use that nut to help select the replacement bolt. If however, the bolt you are replacing is so badly damaged (broken or drilled out) that its threads cannot be used as a gauge, you might start by looking for another bolt (from the same assembly or a similar location on your vehicle) which will thread into the damaged bolt's mounting. If so, the other bolt can be used to select a nut; the nut can then be used to select the replacement bolt.

In all cases, be absolutely sure you have selected the proper replacement. Don't be shy, you can always ask the store clerk for help.

❊❊WARNING

Be aware that when you find a bolt with damaged threads, you may also find the nut or drilled hole it was threaded into has also been damaged. If this is the case, you may

	Mark	Class		Mark	Class
Hexagon head bolt	 4 — 5 — Bolt head No. 6 — 7 — 8 9 — 10 — 11 —	4T 5T 6T 7T 8T 9T 10T 11T	Stud bolt	No mark 	4T
	 No mark	4T			
Hexagon flange bolt w/ washer hexagon bolt	 No mark	4T		Grooved 	6T
Hexagon head bolt	 Two protruding lines	5T			
Hexagon flange bolt w/ washer hexagon bolt	 Two protruding lines	6T	Welded bolt	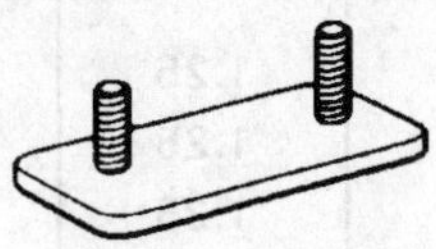	4T
Hexagon head bolt	 Three protruding lines	7T			
Hexagon head bolt	 Four protruding lines	8T			

tccs1240

Fig. 23 Determining bolt strength of metric fasteners — NOTE: this is a typical bolt marking system, but there is not a worldwide standard

Class	Diameter mm	Pitch mm	Specified torque					
			Hexagon head bolt			Hexagon flange bolt		
			N·m	kgf·cm	ft·lbf	N·m	kgf·cm	ft·lbf
4T	6	1	5	55	48 in.·lbf	6	60	52 in.·lbf
	8	1.25	12.5	130	9	14	145	10
	10	1.25	26	260	19	29	290	21
	12	1.25	47	480	35	53	540	39
	14	1.5	74	760	55	84	850	61
	16	1.5	115	1,150	83	—	—	—
5T	6	1	6.5	65	56 in.·lbf	7.5	75	65 in.·lbf
	8	1.25	15.5	160	12	17.5	175	13
	10	1.25	32	330	24	36	360	26
	12	1.25	59	600	43	65	670	48
	14	1.5	91	930	67	100	1,050	76
	16	1.5	140	1,400	101	—	—	—
6T	6	1	8	80	69 in.·lbf	9	90	78 in.·lbf
	8	1.25	19	195	14	21	210	15
	10	1.25	39	400	29	44	440	32
	12	1.25	71	730	53	80	810	59
	14	1.5	110	1,100	80	125	1,250	90
	16	1.5	170	1,750	127	—	—	—
7T	6	1	10.5	110	8	12	120	9
	8	1.25	25	260	19	28	290	21
	10	1.25	52	530	38	58	590	43
	12	1.25	95	970	70	105	1,050	76
	14	1.5	145	1,500	108	165	1,700	123
	16	1.5	230	2,300	166	—	—	—
8T	8	1.25	29	300	22	33	330	24
	10	1.25	61	620	45	68	690	50
	12	1.25	110	1,100	80	120	1,250	90
9T	8	1.25	34	340	25	37	380	27
	10	1.25	70	710	51	78	790	57
	12	1.25	125	1,300	94	140	1,450	105
10T	8	1.25	38	390	28	42	430	31
	10	1.25	78	800	58	88	890	64
	12	1.25	140	1,450	105	155	1,600	116
11T	8	1.25	42	430	31	47	480	35
	10	1.25	87	890	64	97	990	72
	12	1.25	155	1,600	116	175	1,800	130

tccs1241

Fig. 24 Typical bolt torques for metric fasteners — WARNING: use only as a guide

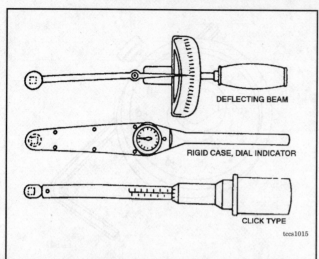

Fig. 25 Various styles of torque wrenches are usually available at your local automotive supply store

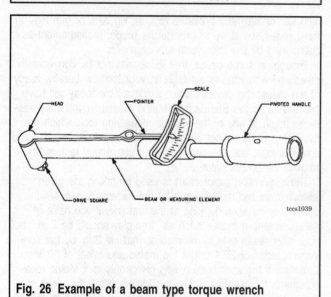

Fig. 26 Example of a beam type torque wrench

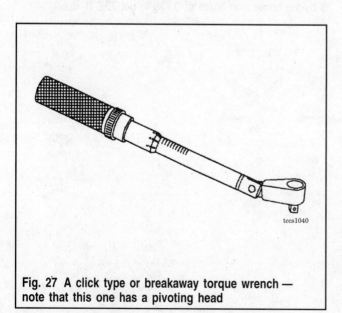

Fig. 27 A click type or breakaway torque wrench — note that this one has a pivoting head

Pivot Head Type
▸ **See Figures 27 and 28**

Some torque wrenches (usually of the click type) may be equipped with a pivot head which can allow it to be used in areas of limited access. BUT, it must be used properly. To hold a pivot head wrench, grasp the handle lightly, and as you pull on the handle, it should be floated on the pivot point. If the handle comes in contact with the yoke extension during the process of pulling, there is a very good chance the torque readings will be inaccurate because this could alter the wrench loading point. The design of the handle is usually such as to make it inconvenient to deliberately misuse the wrench.

➡ **It should be mentioned that the use of any U-joint, wobble or extension will have an effect on the torque readings, no matter what type of wrench you are using. For the most accurate readings, install the socket directly on the wrench driver. If necessary, straight extensions (which hold a socket directly under the wrench driver) will have the least effect on the torque reading. Avoid any extension that alters the length of the wrench from the handle to the head/driving point (such as a crow's foot). U-joint or Wobble extensions can greatly affect the readings; avoid their use at all times.**

Rigid Case (Direct Reading)
▸ **See Figure 29**

A rigid case or direct reading torque wrench is equipped with a dial indicator to show torque values. One advantage of these wrenches is that they can be held at any position on the wrench without affecting accuracy. These wrenches are often preferred because they tend to be compact, easy to read and have a great degree of accuracy.

TORQUE ANGLE METERS

▸ **See Figure 30**

Because the frictional characteristics of each fastener or threaded hole will vary, clamp loads which are based strictly

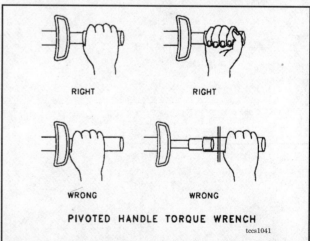

Fig. 28 Torque wrenches with pivoting heads must be grasped and used properly to prevent an incorrect reading

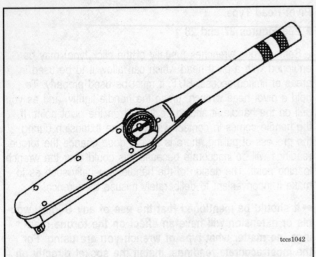

Fig. 29 The rigid case (direct reading) torque wrench uses a dial indicator to show torque

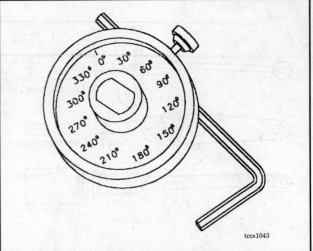

Fig. 30 Some specifications require the use of a torque angle meter (mechanical protractor)

on torque will vary as well. In most applications, this variance is not significant enough to cause worry. But, in certain applications, a manufacturer's engineers may determine that more precise clamp loads are necessary (such is the case with many aluminum cylinder heads). In these cases, a torque angle method of installation would be specified. When installing fasteners which are torque angle tightened, a predetermined seating torque and standard torque wrench are usually used first to remove any compliance from the joint. The fastener is then tightened the specified additional portion of a turn measured in degrees. A torque angle gauge (mechanical protractor) is used for these applications.

Standard and Metric Measurements

▶ See Figure 31

Throughout this manual, specifications are given to help you determine the condition of various components on your vehicle, or to assist you in their installation. Some of the most common measurements include length (in. or cm/mm), torque (ft. lbs.,

inch lbs. or Nm) and pressure (psi, in. Hg, kPa or mm Hg). In most cases, we strive to provide the proper measurement as determined by the manufacturer's engineers.

Though, in some cases, that value may not be conveniently measured with what is available in your toolbox. Luckily, many of the measuring devices which are available today will have two scales so the Standard or Metric measurements may easily be taken. If any of the various measuring tools which are available to you do not contain the same scale as listed in the specifications, use the accompanying conversion factors to determine the proper value.

The conversion factor chart is used by taking the given specification and multiplying it by the necessary conversion factor. For instance, looking at the first line, if you have a measurement in inches such as "free-play should be 2 in." but your ruler reads only in millimeters, multiply 2 in. by the conversion factor of 25.4 to get the metric equivalent of 50.8mm. Likewise, if the specification was given only in a Metric measurement, for example in Newton Meters (Nm), then look at the center column first. If the measurement is 100 Nm, multiply it by the conversion factor of 0.738 to get 73.8 ft. lbs.

CONVERSION FACTORS

LENGTH–DISTANCE

Inches (in.)	x 25.4	= Millimeters (mm)	x .0394	= Inches
Feet (ft.)	x .305	= Meters (m)	x 3.281	= Feet
Miles	x 1.609	= Kilometers (km)	x .0621	= Miles

VOLUME

Cubic Inches (in3)	x 16.387	= Cubic Centimeters	x .061	= in3
IMP Pints (IMP pt.)	x .568	= Liters (L)	x 1.76	= IMP pt.
IMP Quarts (IMP qt.)	x 1.137	= Liters (L)	x .88	= IMP qt.
IMP Gallons (IMP gal.)	x 4.546	= Liters (L)	x .22	= IMP gal.
IMP Quarts (IMP qt.)	x 1.201	= US Quarts (US qt.)	x .833	= IMP qt.
IMP Gallons (IMP gal.)	x 1.201	= US Gallons (US gal.)	x .833	= IMP gal.
Fl. Ounces	x 29.573	= Milliliters	x .034	= Ounces
US Pints (US pt.)	x .473	= Liters (L)	x 2.113	= Pints
US Quarts (US qt.)	x .946	= Liters (L)	x 1.057	= Quarts
US Gallons (US gal.)	x 3.785	= Liters (L)	x .264	= Gallons

MASS–WEIGHT

Ounces (oz.)	x 28.35	= Grams (g)	x .035	= Ounces
Pounds (lb.)	x .454	= Kilograms (kg)	x 2.205	= Pounds

PRESSURE

Pounds Per Sq. In. (psi)	x 6.895	= Kilopascals (kPa)	x .145	= psi
Inches of Mercury (Hg)	x .4912	= psi	x 2.036	= Hg
Inches of Mercury (Hg)	x 3.377	= Kilopascals (kPa)	x .2961	= Hg
Inches of Water (H_2O)	x .07355	= Inches of Mercury	x 13.783	= H_2O
Inches of Water (H_2O)	x .03613	= psi	x 27.684	= H_2O
Inches of Water (H_2O)	x .248	= Kilopascals (kPa)	x 4.026	= H_2O

TORQUE

Pounds–Force Inches (in–lb)	x .113	= Newton Meters (N·m)	x 8.85	= in–lb
Pounds–Force Feet (ft–lb)	x 1.356	= Newton Meters (N·m)	x .738	= ft–lb

VELOCITY

Miles Per Hour (MPH)	x 1.609	= Kilometers Per Hour (KPH)	x .621	= MPH

POWER

Horsepower (Hp)	x .745	= Kilowatts	x 1.34	= Horsepower

FUEL CONSUMPTION*

Miles Per Gallon IMP (MPG)	x .354	= Kilometers Per Liter (Km/L)
Kilometers Per Liter (Km/L)	x 2.352	= IMP MPG
Miles Per Gallon US (MPG)	x .425	= Kilometers Per Liter (Km/L)
Kilometers Per Liter (Km/L)	x 2.352	= US MPG

*It is common to covert from miles per gallon (mpg) to liters/100 kilometers (1/100 km), where mpg (IMP) x 1/100 km = 282 and mpg (US) x 1/100 km = 235.

TEMPERATURE

Degree Fahrenheit (°F)	= (°C x 1.8) + 32
Degree Celsius (°C)	= (°F – 32) x .56

tccs1044

Fig. 31 Standard and metric conversion factors chart

HISTORY AND MODEL IDENTIFICATION

In 1984 a new, redesigned, downsized version of the Wagoneer/ Cherokee line was introduced. These smaller, fuel efficient models incorporated features such as a standard 4-cylinder, 2.5L engine, with a V6-2.8L engine as an option, new transfer case/transmission combinations, and for the first time, integrated frames.

For 1985, the Jeep line up remained unchanged.

For 1986, Jeep introduced the Comanche. The Comanche is a pick-up version of the downsized Wagoneer and is available in both 2 and 4 wheel drive. The engine selection for the Wagoneer/Cherokee/Comanche remains the same as previous years, with the exception of an optional 4-cylinder, 126 cu. in. turbocharged, Renault-made diesel. Throttle body fuel injection replaced the carburetor on the 2.5L.

The line up continued unchanged in 1987, with one notable exception. The V6-2.8L engine made by General Motors was no longer offered. In its place was a 4.0L, inline engine made by AMC. The engine is mechanically similar to the older 258 AMC engines with a redesigned cylinder head and Multi-point Fuel Injection.

In 1988 Chrysler Corporation bought the Jeep division from AMC. The model line-up remained unchanged but the diesel engine was discontinued.

For 1989, Jeep introduced a four-wheel anti-lock brake system on Cherokee and Wagoneer models equipped with the 4.0L 6-cylinder engine and Selec-Trac full-time four wheel drive system. This was a first for the light truck industry.

In 1990, the Jeep line continued unchanged.

In 1991 the familiar Wagoneer name has been dropped and replaced with the Cherokee Briarwood. The Grand Wagoneer is still offered.

In 1992 the 5.2L engine was introduced in the Grand Cherokee and Grand Wagoneer.

In 1993 Sequential MultiPort Fuel Injection (SMPI) was introduced on the 2.5L engine.

In 1994 R-134a air conditioning refrigerant was introduced and in 1995, a driver's side air bag was introduced.

In 1996 OBD II On-Board Diagnostics was introduced for all powertrains.

SERIAL NUMBER IDENTIFICATION

Vehicle

▶ See Figures 32, 33, 34 and 35

The Vehicle Identification Number (VIN) plate is located on the left side of the instrument panel pad, visible through the windshield.

In addition to the VIN plate, the vehicle is equipped with a Vehicle Identification Plate affixed to the left side of the firewall in the engine compartments. Pre-1990 model vehicles may have the plate attached to the left side of the radiator support. The VIN plate and the Vehicle Identification plate can be interpreted by the accompanying illustrations.

A metal identification plate is riveted to the driver side of the dash panel in the engine compartment.

1. Order number
2. Paint gun number
3. Vehicle identification number (VIN)
4. Vehicle deviation or special sales request and order (SSR & O)
5. Trim option number
6. Paint option number

86741g01

Fig. 33 Pre-1990 Vehicle Identification Number (VIN)

Engine

2.1L TURBO DIESEL

▶ See Figure 36

The serial number for the Renault-built diesel is found on a machined pad located at the front of the block.

86741p01

Fig. 32 The VIN plate is usually located on the left side of the instrument panel, visible through the windshield

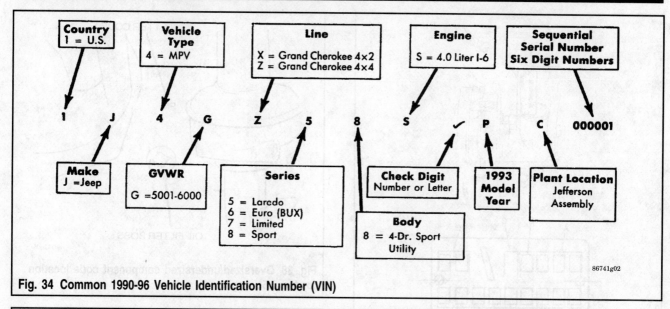

Fig. 34 Common 1990-96 Vehicle Identification Number (VIN)

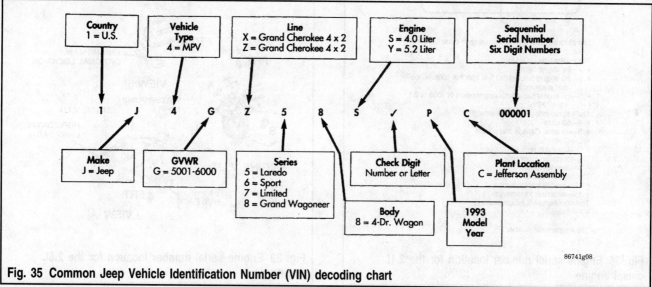

Fig. 35 Common Jeep Vehicle Identification Number (VIN) decoding chart

2.5L ENGINE

▶ See Figures 37 and 38

The serial number for the American-Motors built 2.5L engine is located on a machined pad on the rear right side of the block, between cylinders number 3 and 4.

Also on the block, just above the oil filter, is the oversized/undersized component code. The codes are explained as follows:

B: cylinder bores 0.010 in. over
C: camshaft bearing bores 0.010 in. over
M: main bearing journals 0.010 in. under
P: connecting rod journals 0.010 in. under

2.8L ENGINE

▶ See Figure 39

The serial number for the Chevrolet built 2.8L engine is located on an upward facing, machined surface on the right side of the block, just below the cylinder head and above the water pump.

4.0L ENGINE

▶ See Figure 40

The serial number is found on a machined surface on the right side of the engine block between number 2 and 3 cylinders. For further identification, the displacement is cast into the side of the block. The letter in the code identifies the engine by displacement (cu. in.), carburetor type and compression ratio.

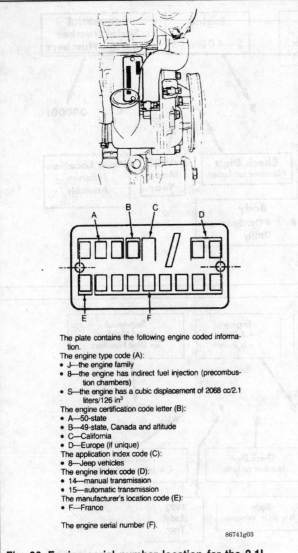

The plate contains the following engine coded information.

The engine type code (A):
- J—the engine family
- 8—the engine has indirect fuel injection (precombustion chambers)
- S—the engine has a cubic displacement of 2068 cc/2.1 liters/126 in³

The engine certification code letter (B):
- A—50-state
- B—49-state, Canada and altitude
- C—California
- D—Europe (if unique)

The application index code (C):
- 8—Jeep vehicles

The engine index code (D):
- 14—manual transmission
- 15—automatic transmission

The manufacturer's location code (E):
- F—France

The engine serial number (F).

86741g03

Fig. 36 Engine serial number location for the 2.1L diesel engine

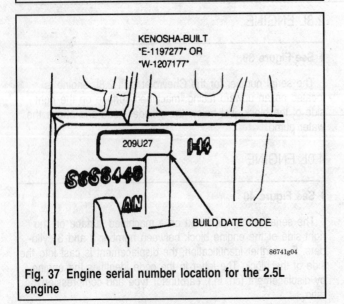

KENOSHA-BUILT
"E-1197277" OR
"W-1207177"

209U27

BUILD DATE CODE

86741g04

Fig. 37 Engine serial number location for the 2.5L engine

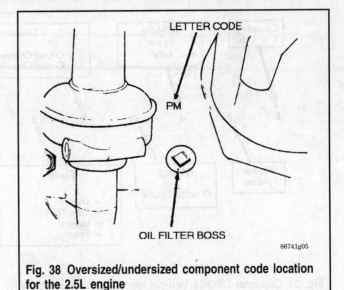

86741g05

Fig. 38 Oversized/undersized component code location for the 2.5L engine

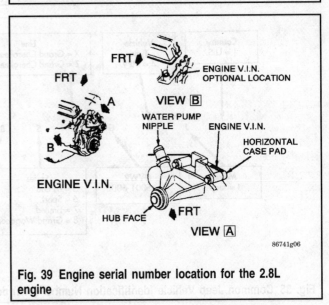

86741g06

Fig. 39 Engine serial number location for the 2.8L engine

The undersize/oversize bearing letter codes, located on the boss directly above the oil filter, are as follows:
Letter B indicates 0.010 in. oversized cylinder bore.
Letter C indicates 0.010 in. oversized camshaft block bores.
Letter M indicates 0.010 in. undersized main bearings.
Letter P indicates 0.010 in. undersized connecting rod bearings.

5.2L ENGINE

The serial number is found on a machined surface on the left, front corner of the cylinder block.

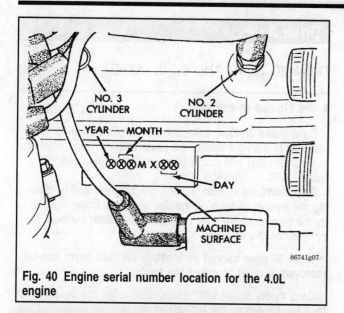

Fig. 40 Engine serial number location for the 4.0L engine

Transmission

MANUAL TRANSMISSIONS

Aisin AX4, AX5 and AX15 Transmissions
▶ See Figures 41 and 42

The AX4 is a 4-speed synchromesh manual transmission. The AX5 and AX15 are 5-speed synchromesh manual transmissions. The shift mechanism in all is integral and mounted in the shift tower portion of the housing. The transmission identification code for the Aisin AX4/5/15 transmissions is located on the bottom of the transmission case near the filler plug. The first three numbers identify the date of manufacture (for example, 902 = 1989, February). The next series of numbers is the serial number.

BA10/5 Transmission
▶ See Figure 43

The BA10/5 is a 5-speed, synchromesh manual transmission. The shifter is mounted in the transmission's intermediate case. The BA10/5 identification code is located on a tag, riveted to the left side of the transmission. The plate provides build date, part number, and serial number identification.

AUTOMATIC TRANSMISSIONS

AW-4 Transmission
▶ See Figure 44

The AW-4 is a 4-speed, electronically controlled automatic transmission. The identification plate is attached to the right side of the transmission case.

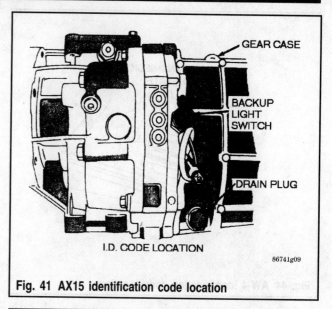

Fig. 41 AX15 identification code location

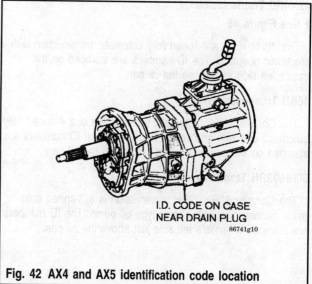

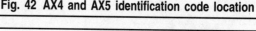

Fig. 42 AX4 and AX5 identification code location

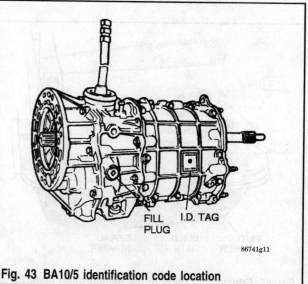

Fig. 43 BA10/5 identification code location

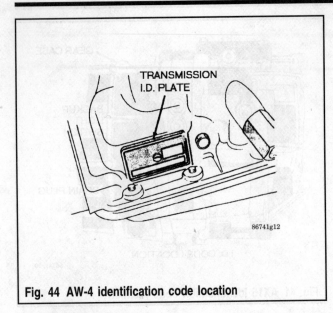

Fig. 44 AW-4 identification code location

42/44RE Transmission

▶ See Figure 45

The 42/44RE is a 4-speed fully automatic transmission with electronic governor. The ID numbers are stamped on the case's left side just above the oil pan.

46RH Transmission

The Chrysler 46RH automatic transmission is a 4-speed fully automatic unit with an overdrive 4th gear. The ID numbers are stamped on the case's left side just above the oil pan.

30RH/32RH Transmission

The Chrysler 30RH/32RH transmission is a 3-speed automatic transmission with a gear type oil pump. The ID numbers are stamped on case's left side just above the oil pan.

Drive Axles

DANA 30, 35, 44 AND 8¼ IN. AXLE

▶ See Figures 46 and 47

Dana model 30 drive axles can be identified by an ID plate attached to the right side of the cover housing. Tag information tag includes ring and pinion gear, production date and manufacturer's ID.

Gear ratio for the Dana 30 axle can be computed by dividing the number of teeth on the ring gear (the larger number) by the number of teeth on the pinion gear. Both numbers are provided on the ID plate.

➡ If the ID plate cannot be located, the rear cover can be removed in order to count the teeth.

Dana model 35, 44 and 8¼ in. drive axles can be identified by a tag located on the left side of the housing cover. The tag lists part number and gear ratio. The production date and manufacturer's ID are stamped into the right side axle shaft.

AMC 7⁹/₁₆ IN.

▶ See Figure 48

The ID code for the AMC 7⁹/₁₆ in. axle is stamped in the right side axle tube boss. Code "S" indicates a 3.73:1 ratio. Code "T" indicates a 3.31:1 ratio. Code "SS" or "TT" indicates the rear axle has a Trac-Lok® differential.

Transfer Case

▶ See Figure 49

The ID plate for all New Process transfer cases is attached to the rear of the case. The ID plate provides model, assembly and serial numbers along with low range ratio. The serial number is also the build date (for example, 8-10-89 = August 10, 1989).

Fig. 45 Common location of the identification code for the 42/44RE, 46/30RH and 32RH transmissions

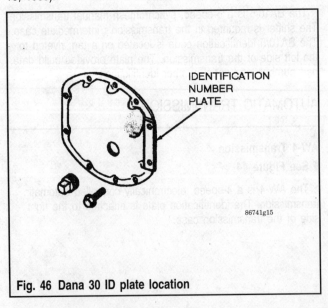

Fig. 46 Dana 30 ID plate location

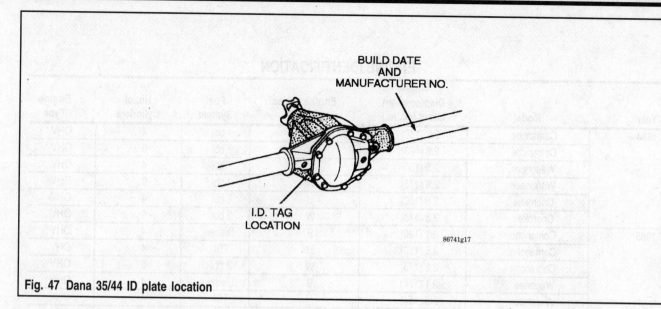

BUILD DATE
AND
MANUFACTURER NO.

I.D. TAG
LOCATION

86741g17

Fig. 47 Dana 35/44 ID plate location

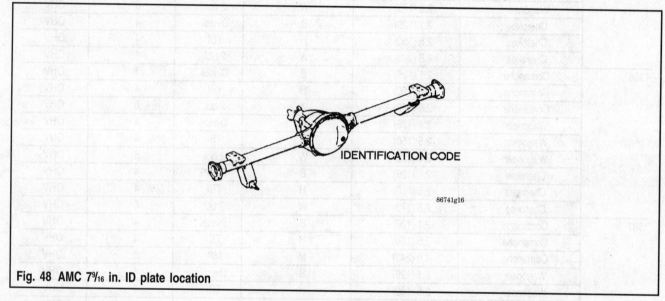

IDENTIFICATION CODE

86741g16

Fig. 48 AMC 7⁹/₁₆ in. ID plate location

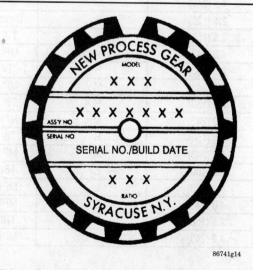

NEW PROCESS GEAR

MODEL

X X X

X X X X X X X

ASS'Y NO

SERIAL NO

SERIAL NO./BUILD DATE

X X X

RATIO

SYRACUSE N.Y.

86741g14

Fig. 49 The identification plate for all New Process transfer cases is attached to the rear of the case

ENGINE IDENTIFICATION

Year	Model	Engine Displacement Liters (cu. in.)	Engine Series (ID/VIN)	Fuel System	No. of Cylinders	Engine Type
1984	Comanche	2.5 (150)	U	1 bbl	4	OHV
	Comanche	2.8 (173)	W	2 bbl	6	OHV
	Wagoneer	2.5 (150)	U	1 bbl	4	OHV
	Wagoneer	2.8 (173)	W	2 bbl	6	OHV
	Cherokee	2.5 (150)	U	1 bbl	4	OHV
	Cherokee	2.8 (173)	W	2 bbl	6	OHV
1985	Comanche	2.1 (126)	B	Diesel	4	OHV
	Comanche	2.5 (150)	H	TBI	4	OHV
	Comanche	2.8 (173)	W	2 bbl	6	OHV
	Wagoneer	2.1 (126)	B	Diesel	4	OHV
	Wagoneer	2.5 (150)	H	TBI	4	OHV
	Wagoneer	2.8 (173)	W	2 bbl	6	OHV
	Cherokee	2.1 (126)	B	Diesel	4	OHV
	Cherokee	2.5 (150)	H	TBI	4	OHV
	Cherokee	2.8 (173)	W	2 bbl	6	OHV
1986	Comanche	2.1 (126)	B	Diesel	4	OHV
	Comanche	2.5 (150)	H	TBI	4	OHV
	Comanche	2.8 (173)	W	2 bbl	6	OHV
	Wagoneer	2.1 (126)	B	Diesel	4	OHV
	Wagoneer	2.5 (150)	H	TBI	4	OHV
	Wagoneer	2.8 (173)	W	2 bbl	6	OHV
	Cherokee	2.1 (126)	B	Diesel	4	OHV
	Cherokee	2.5 (150)	H	TBI	4	OHV
	Cherokee	2.8 (173)	W	2 bbl	6	OHV
1987	Comanche	2.1 (126)	B	Diesel	4	OHV
	Comanche	2.5 (150)	H	TBI	4	OHV
	Comanche	4.0 (243)	M	MPI	6	OHV
	Wagoneer	2.1 (126)	B	Diesel	4	OHV
	Wagoneer	2.5 (150)	H	TBI	4	OHV
	Wagoneer	4.0 (243)	M	MPI	6	OHV
	Cherokee	2.1 (126)	B	Diesel	4	OHV
	Cherokee	2.5 (150)	H	TBI	4	OHV
	Cherokee	4.0 (243)	M	MPI	6	OHV
1988	Comanche	2.5 (150)	H	TBI	4	OHV
	Comanche	4.0 (243)	M	MPI	6	OHV
	Wagoneer	2.5 (150)	H	TBI	4	OHV
	Wagoneer	4.0 (243)	M	MPI	6	OHV
	Cherokee	2.5 (150)	H	TBI	4	OHV
	Cherokee	4.0 (243)	M	MPI	6	OHV
1989	Comanche	2.5 (150)	E	TBI	4	OHV
	Comanche	4.0 (243)	L	MPI	6	OHV
	Wagoneer	4.0 (243)	L	MPI	6	OHV
	Cherokee	2.5 (150)	E	TBI	4	OHV
	Cherokee	4.0 (243)	L	MPI	6	OHV

86741CA4

ENGINE IDENTIFICATION

Year	Model	Engine Displacement Liters (cu. in.)	Engine Series (ID/VIN)	Fuel System	No. of Cylinders	Engine Type
1990	Comanche	2.5 (150)	E	TBI	4	OHV
	Comanche	4.0 (243)	L	MPI	6	OHV
	Wagoneer	4.0 (243)	L	MPI	6	OHV
	Cherokee	2.5 (150)	E	TBI	4	OHV
	Cherokee	4.0 (243)	L	MPI	6	OHV
1991	Comanche	2.5 (150)	P	MPI	4	OHV
	Comanche	4.0 (243)	S	MPI	6	OHV
	Cherokee	2.5 (150)	P	MPI	4	OHV
	Cherokee	4.0 (243)	S	MPI	6	OHV
1992	Comanche	2.5 (150)	P	MPI	4	OHV
	Comanche	4.0 (243)	S	MPI	6	OHV
	Cherokee	2.5 (150)	P	MPI	4	OHV
	Cherokee	4.0 (243)	S	MPI	6	OHV
1993	Cherokee	2.5 (150)	P	MPI	4	OHV
	Cherokee	4.0 (243)	S	MPI	6	OHV
	Grand Cherokee	4.0 (243)	S	MPI	6	OHV
	Grand Cherokee	5.2 (318)	Y	MPI	8	OHV
	Grand Wagoneer	5.2 (318)	Y	MPI	8	OHV
1994	Cherokee	2.5 (150)	P	MPI	4	OHV
	Cherokee	4.0 (243)	S	MPI	6	OHV
	Grand Cherokee	4.0 (243)	S	MPI	6	OHV
	Grand Cherokee	5.2 (318)	Y	MPI	8	OHV
1995	Cherokee	2.5 (150)	P	MPI	4	OHV
	Cherokee	4.0 (243)	S	MPI	6	OHV
	Grand Cherokee	4.0 (243)	S	MPI	6	OHV
	Grand Cherokee	5.2 (318)	Y	MPI	8	OHV
1996	Cherokee	2.5 (150)	P	MPI	4	OHV
	Cherokee	4.0 (243)	S	MPI	6	OHV
	Grand Cherokee	4.0 (243)	S	MPI	6	OHV
	Grand Cherokee	5.2 (318)	Y	MPI	8	OHV

TBI - Throttle Body Injection

MPI - Multi Port Injection

OHV - Over Head Valve

86741CA5

VEHICLE IDENTIFICATION CHART

Engine Code						Model Year	
Code	Liters	Cu. In.	Cyl.	Fuel Sys.	Eng. Mfg.	Code	Year
B	2.1	126	4	Diesel	Renault	E	1984
U	2.5	150	4	1 bbl	AMC	F	1985
H	2.5	150	4	TBI	AMC	G	1986
W	2.8	173	6	2 bbl	Chevrolet	H	1987
M	4.0	243	6	MPI	Chrysler	J	1988
E	2.5	150	4	TBI	AMC	K	1989
L	4.0	243	6	MPI	Chrysler	L	1990
P	2.5	150	4	MPI	AMC	M	1991
S	4.0	243	6	MPI	Chrysler	N	1992
Y	5.2	318	8	MPI	Chrysler	P	1993
						R	1994
						S	1995
						T	1996

TBI - Throttle Body Injection

MPI - Multi Port Injection

86741CA3

MANUAL TRANSMISSION IDENTIFICATION

Year	Engine	Model	Transmission
1984	2.5L	All	T4
	All	All	T5
	2.5L	All	AX4
	All	All	AX5
1985	2.5L	All	AX4
	All	All	AX5
1986	2.5L	All	AX4
	All	All	AX5
1987	2.5L	All	AX4
	All	All	AX5
	All	All	BA 10/5
1988	All	All	AX5
	All	All	BA 10/5
1989	All	All	AX5
	All	All	BA 10/5
	4.0L	All	AX15
1990	All	All	AX5
	4.0L	All	AX15
1991	All	All	AX5
	4.0L	All	AX15
1992	All	All	AX15
1993	All	All	AX15
1994	All	All	AX15
1995	All	All	AX15
1996	All	All	AX15

86741CB2

REAR AXLE IDENTIFICATION

Year	Engine	Model	Axle
1984	All	All	AMC
1985	All	All	AMC
1986	All	All	AMC
1987	All	All	Model 35
	All	Metric Ton Package	Model 44
1988	All	All	Model 35
	All	Metric Ton Package	Model 44
1989	All	All	Model 35
	All	Metric Ton Package	Model 44
1990	All	All	Model 35
	All	Metric Ton Package	Model 44
1991	All	All	Model 35
	All	Metric Ton Package	Model 44
1992	All	All	Model 35
	All	Metric Ton Package	Model 44
1993	All	All	Model 35
	All	All, except ABS equipped	Model 44
1994	All	All	Model 35
	All	All, except ABS equipped	Model 44
1995	All	All	Model 35
	All	All, except ABS equipped	Model 44
1996	All	All	Model 35
	All	All, except ABS equipped	Model 44

86741CB4

AUTOMATIC TRANSMISSION IDENTIFICATION

Year	Engine	Model	Transmission
1984	All	All	904
1985	All	All	904
1986	All	All	904
1987	All	All	AW4
1988	All	All	AW4
1989	All	All	AW4
1990	All	All	AW4
1991	All	All	AW4
1992	All	All	AW4
1993	4.0L	Grand Cherokee/Wagoneer	AW4
	All	Cherokee	AW4
	5.2L	Grand Cherokee/Wagoneer	46RH
1994	2.5L	Cherokee	30RH
	4.0L	Cherokee	32RH/AW4
	4.0L	Grand Cherokee	42RE/42RH
	5.2L	Grand Cherokee	46RH
1995	2.5L	Cherokee	30RH
	4.0L	Cherokee	AW4
	4.0L	Grand Cherokee	42RE
	5.2L	Grand Cherokee	46RH
1996	2.5L	Cherokee	30RH
	4.0L	Cherokee	AW4
	All	Grand Cherokee	42/44RE

86741CB1

FRONT AXLE IDENTIFICATION

Year	Engine	Model	Axle
1984	All	All	Model 30
1985	All	All	Model 30
1986	All	All	Model 30
1987	All	All	Model 30
1988	All	All	Model 30
1989	All	All	Model 30
1990	All	All	Model 30
1991	All	All	Model 30
1992	All	All	Model 30
1993	All	All	Model 30
1994	All	All	Model 30
1995	All	All	Model 30
1996	All	All	Model 30

86741CB3

TRANSFER CASE IDENTIFICATION

Year	Transmission	Model	Transfer Case
1984	Automatic	All	NP229
	All	All	NP207
1985	All	All	NP207
	Automatic	All	NP225
1986	All	All	NP207
	Automatic	All	NP225
1987	All	All	NP207
	Automatic	All	NP225
1988	All	All	NP231
	All	All	NP242
1989	All	All	NP231
	All	All	NP242
1990	All	All	NP231
	All	All	NP242
1991	All	All	NP231
	All	All	NP242
1992	All	All	NP231
	All	All	NP242
1993	All	All	NP231
	All	All	NP242
	All	All	NP249
1994	All	All	NP231
	All	All	NP242
	All	All	NP249
1995	All	All	NP231
	All	All	NP242
	All	All	NP249
1996	All	All	NP231
	All	All	NP249

86741CB5

ROUTINE MAINTENANCE

▶ **See Figures 50 and 51**

Proper maintenance and tune-up is the key to long and trouble-free vehicle life, and the work can yield its own rewards. Studies have shown that a properly tuned and maintained vehicle can achieve better gas mileage than an out-of-tune vehicle. As a conscientious owner and driver, set aside a Saturday morning, say once a month, to check or replace items which could cause major problems later. Keep your own personal log to jot down which services you performed, how much the parts cost you, the date, and the exact odometer reading at the time. Keep all receipts for such items as engine oil and filters, so that they may be referred to in case of related problems or to determine operating expenses. As a do-it-yourselfer, these receipts are the only proof you have that the required maintenance was performed. In the event of a warranty problem, these receipts will be invaluable.

The literature provided with your vehicle when it was originally delivered includes the factory recommended maintenance schedule. If you no longer have this literature, replacement copies are usually available from the dealer. A maintenance schedule is provided later in this section, in case you do not have the factory literature.

Air Cleaner

SERVICING

Engines with the dry paper type filter should have the filter replaced every 30,000 miles (48,000 km). Under dusty conditions, the element should be checked weekly, or more often if conditions warrant and should be replaced at the first signs of clogging.

On engines using a dry paper filter with the polyurethane wrap the wrap should be carefully removed every 6,000 miles

MAINTENANCE COMPONENT LOCATIONS - 1987 WAGONEER SHOWN

1. Coolant recovery tank
2. Engine oil dipstick
3. Crankcase ventilation fitting (CCV)
4. Brake master cylinder
5. Windshield washer fluid reservoir
6. Air filter housing
7. Power steering pump
8. Serpentine drive belt
9. CCV system fresh air hose
10. Engine oil filler cap
11. Idler pulley
12. Air conditioning compressor
13. Radiator hose
14. Battery
15. Air conditioning hose
16. Engine oil filter

Fig. 50 Engine compartment component locations — 1987 Wagoneer shown

86741pZ1

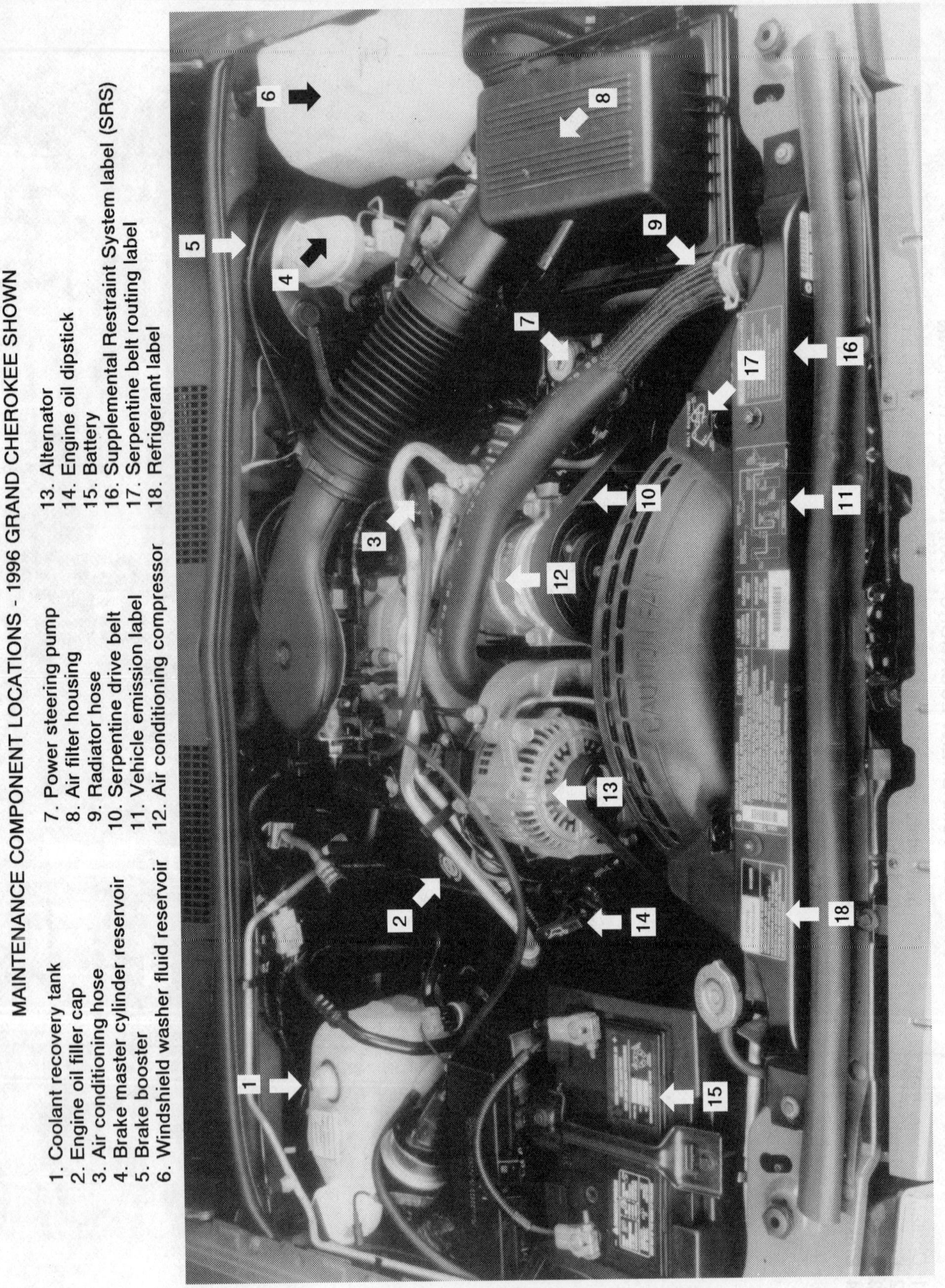

MAINTENANCE COMPONENT LOCATIONS - 1996 GRAND CHEROKEE SHOWN

1. Coolant recovery tank
2. Engine oil filler cap
3. Air conditioning hose
4. Brake master cylinder reservoir
5. Brake booster
6. Windshield washer fluid reservoir
7. Power steering pump
8. Air filter housing
9. Radiator hose
10. Serpentine drive belt
11. Vehicle emission label
12. Air conditioning compressor
13. Alternator
14. Engine oil dipstick
15. Battery
16. Supplemental Restraint System label (SRS)
17. Serpentine belt routing label
18. Refrigerant label

Fig. 51 Engine compartment component locations — 1996 Grand Cherokee shown

86741pZ2

(9600 km). Shake, the dirt from the wrap, DO NOT WASH IT, squeeze the old oil out by pressing it flat between two rags, then liberally soak it with SAE 10W-30 engine oil. Squeeze it flat to remove excess oil. At the same time, direct compressed air at the inside of the paper element to remove dirt. Replace the paper element every 30,000 miles (48,000 km) or sooner if necessary.

REMOVAL & INSTALLATION

▶ See Figures 52, 53, 54 and 55

1. Remove the air cleaner cover and filter element.
2. Clean the filter element by gently blowing trapped debris from the filter with compressed air. Direct the air in the opposite direction of normal flow. Keep the air nozzle at least two inches (50 mm) away from the filter to avoid damage to the filter.

3. If the filter element has become saturated with oil, replace it and inspect the crankcase ventilating system for proper operation.
4. Clean the air cleaner cover and body.
5. Install the air cleaner element and cover.

Fuel Filter

SERVICING

The inline fuel filter should be cleaned or replaced every 30,000 miles (48,000km). If the vehicle is driven in abnormally dirty conditions or if contaminated gasoline was put in the gas tank, the filter could become clogged before 30,000 miles (48,000 km). The fuel sediment bowl type filter need not be serviced unless there is evidence of foreign matter (such as water or dirt) visible in the bowl. If there is, remove and empty the bowl, wipe it dry with a clean cloth and replace it. The

Fig. 52 Remove the air cleaner cover — 1987 model shown

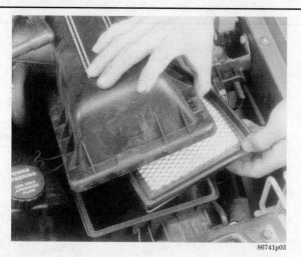

Fig. 53 Remove the filter element from the housing — 1987 model shown

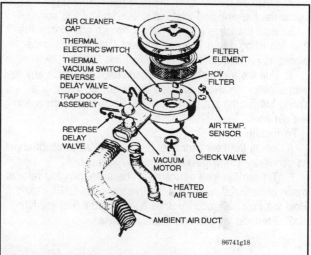

Fig. 54 Exploded view of the carbureted engine air cleaner assembly

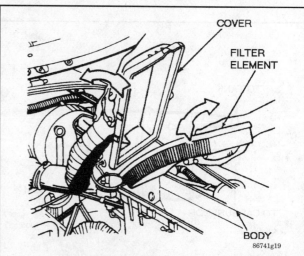

Fig. 55 Removing the air cleaner on a fuel injected engine — 1991 model shown

paper element filter cannot be serviced. These filters must be replaced at the suggested intervals.

REMOVAL & INSTALLATION

Carbureted Engines

2.5L ENGINES

▶ See Figure 56

1. Remove and discard the fuel filter, hoses and clamps.
2. Install the new fuel filter with arrows on the casing pointing toward the carburetor and fuel return nipple facing upward.
3. Secure the filter with new hoses and clamps.

2.8L ENGINES

▶ See Figure 57

1. Remove the air cleaner assembly to gain access to the carburetor inlet nut.
2. Clean all debris away from the manifold and place rags below the fuel line and inlet nut to absorb any fuel spillage.
3. Hold the large inlet nut with a wrench and loosen the fuel line fitting with a flare nut wrench. (This wrench is designed to prevent stripping of the fuel line fitting).
4. Pull the fuel pipe from the carburetor and catch any fuel with a clean rag. Next, unscrew the large nut. There is a spring behind the nut, so be careful. Remove the spring and the old filter.

To install:

5. Install the new filter and, if you are at all in doubt about its condition, a new gasket behind the inlet nut.
6. Tighten the inlet nut carefully, because the carburetor is made of very soft metal and the threads could EASILY strip. Hold the inlet nut securely while tightening the fuel line fitting.
7. Start the vehicle and check for leaks.

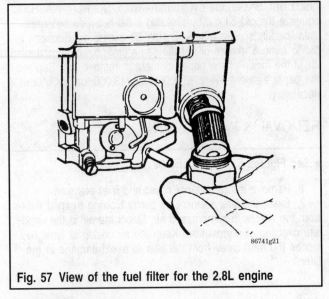

Fig. 57 View of the fuel filter for the 2.8L engine

Fuel Injectioned Engines

▶ See Figure 58

The fuel filter on the 2.5L, 4.0L and 5.2L engines is located under the vehicle, mounted on the frame rail on the driver's side.

2.5L ENGINES

1. Disconnect the battery ground cable.
2. Remove the fuel tank filler cap.
3. Raise and support the rear end on jackstands.
4. Remove the hoses and clamps from the filter.
5. Remove the filter strap bolt and remove the filter.

To install:

➡ **The filter is marked for installation. IN goes towards the fuel tank, OUT towards the engine.**

6. Place the new filter on the frame rail and tighten the strap bolt to 106 inch lbs. (12 Nm).
7. Install and securely clamp the hoses.
8. Start the vehicle and check for leaks.

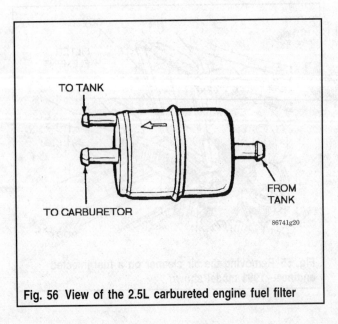

Fig. 56 View of the 2.5L carbureted engine fuel filter

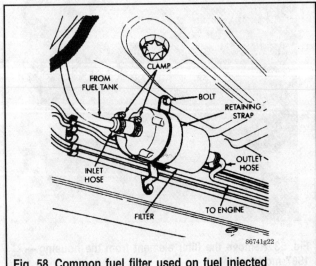

Fig. 58 Common fuel filter used on fuel injected engines

4.0L AND 5.2L ENGINES

▶ See Figures 59 and 60

1. Disconnect the battery ground cable.
2. Remove the fuel tank filler cap.

✳✳CAUTION

DON'T ALLOW FUEL TO SPRAY OR SPILL ON THE ENGINE OR EXHAUST MANIFOLD! PLACE HEAVY SHOP TOWELS UNDER THE PRESSURE PORT TO ABSORB ANY ESCAPED FUEL!

3. Relieve the fuel system pressure. Refer to Section 5 for the proper procedure.
4. Raise and safely support the rear end on jackstands.
5. Remove the hoses and clamps from the filter.
6. Remove the filter strap bolt and remove the filter.

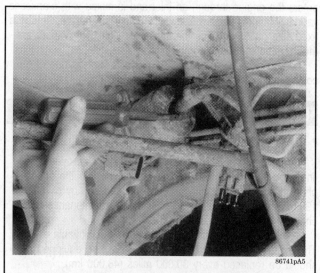
Fig. 59 Remove the hoses and clamps from the filter

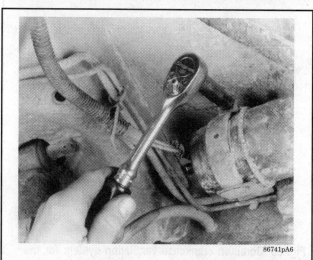
Fig. 60 Remove the filter strap bolt and then remove the filter

To install:

➡**The filter is marked for installation. IN goes towards the fuel tank OUT towards the engine.**

7. Place the new filter on the frame rail and tighten the strap bolt to 106 inch lbs. (12 Nm).
8. Install and securely clamp the hoses.
9. Lower the vehicle and connect the negative battery cable.
10. Start the vehicle and check for leaks.

Diesel Engines

▶ See Figure 61

1. Attach one end of a piece of flexible tubing to the filter draincock. Run the other end into a one quart container.
2. Open the filter vent valve and open the draincock. Drain the filter completely.
3. Remove the filter.
4. Discard the filter. Install the new filter, close the vent and drain cock.

Positive Crankcase Ventilation (PCV) System

▶ See Figures 62 and 63

The PCV valve, which is the heart of the positive crankcase ventilation system, should be changed every 30,000 miles (48,000 km). The main thing to keep in mind is that the valve must be free of dirt and residue to stay in working order. As long as the valve is clean and is not showing signs of becoming damaged or clogged, it should perform its function properly. When the valve becomes sticky and will not operate freely, it should be replaced.

The PCV valve is used to control the rate at which crankcase vapors are returned to the intake manifold. The action of the valve plunger is controlled by intake manifold vacuum and the spring. During deceleration and idle, when manifold vacuum is high, it overcomes the tension of the valve spring and the plunger bottoms in the manifold end of the valve housing. Because of the valve construction, it reduces, but does not

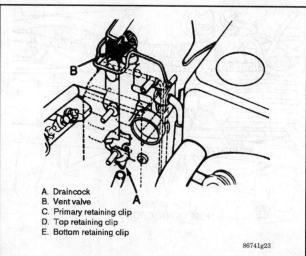

A. Draincock
B. Vent valve
C. Primary retaining clip
D. Top retaining clip
E. Bottom retaining clip

Fig. 61 View of the diesel engine fuel filter and related components

stop, the passage of vapors to the intake manifold. When the engine is lightly accelerated, or operated at constant speed, spring tension matches intake manifold vacuum pull and the plunger takes a mid-position in the valve body, allowing more vapors to flow into the manifold.

REMOVAL & INSTALLATION

▶ See Figure 64

1. Remove the PCV valve from cylinder head.
2. Remove the PCV valve from PCV hose.
3. Installation is the reverse of removal.

Crankcase Ventilation (CCV) System

▶ See Figures 65 and 66

The Crankcase Ventilation (CCV) System performs the same function as the conventional PCV system, but without the use

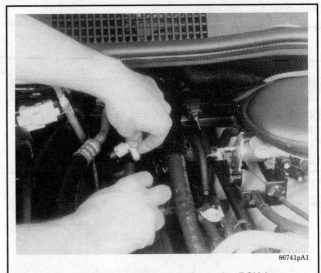
Fig. 64 Removing the PCV valve from the PCV hose

of a vacuum controlled valve. When in operation, fresh air enters the engine through an inlet and is mixed with crankcase vapors. Manifold vacuum draws the vapor/air mixture through a fixed size orifice and into the intake manifold. The vapors are then burned off during combustion.

There is no servicing to the CCV system unless one of the components gets clogged or fails.

Evaporative Canister

▶ See Figures 67 and 68

The function of the Evaporative canister is to prevent gasoline vapors from the fuel tank from escaping into the atmosphere. Periodic maintenance is not required on any of the 1988-96 models (on all vehicles a sealed, maintenance-free, charcoal canister is used).

Some older model vehicles may have a removable air filter. The air filter in the bottom of the canister, if so equipped, should be replaced every 30,000 miles (48,000 km).

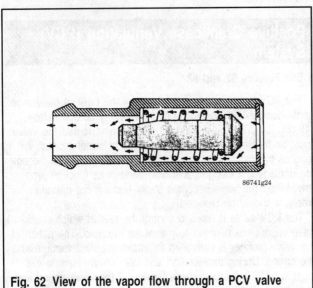
Fig. 62 View of the vapor flow through a PCV valve

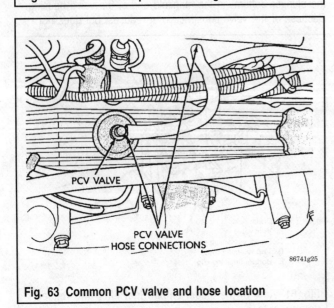
Fig. 63 Common PCV valve and hose location

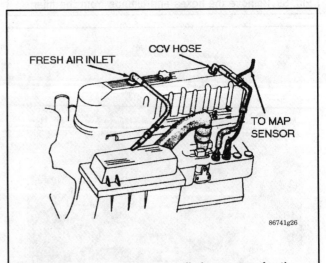
Fig. 65 Common crankcase ventilation system for the 4.0L engine

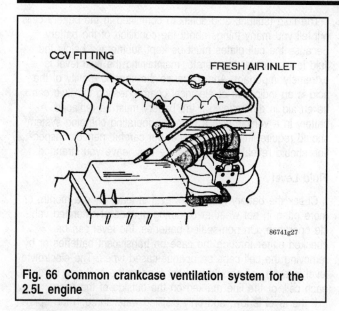

Fig. 66 Common crankcase ventilation system for the 2.5L engine

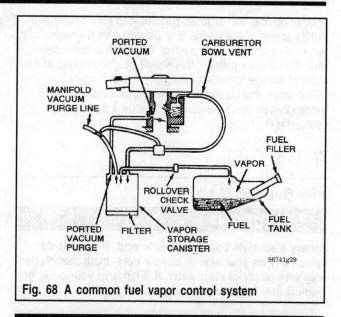

Fig. 68 A common fuel vapor control system

To determine if your vehicle has a cannister filter, remove the canister from the vehicle and inspect the bottom of the canister for a filter.

In spite of the fact that this system requires no periodic maintenance, it is a good idea to quickly look over the hoses when servicing the PCV system. If any of these hoses is cracked, torn, or rotted, the result could be vacuum leaks and consequent poor engine operation, or an annoying smell of fuel vapor. If any of these hoses should require replacement, make sure to use a high quality replacement hose of a material approved for use in fuel bearing applications. Ordinary vacuum type rubber hose will not give satisfactory life or reliable performance.

Battery

GENERAL MAINTENANCE

All batteries, regardless of type, should be carefully secured by a battery hold-down device. If this is not done, the battery terminals or casing may crack from stress applied to the battery during vehicle operation. A battery which is not secured may allow acid to leak out, making it discharge faster; such leaking corrosive acid can also eat away components under the hood. A battery that is not sealed must be checked periodically for electrolyte level. You cannot add water to a sealed maintenance-free battery (although not all maintenance-free batteries are sealed), but a sealed battery must also be checked for proper electrolyte level as indicated by the color of the built-in hydrometer "eye."

Keep the top of the battery clean, as a film of dirt can help completely discharge a battery that is not used for long periods. A solution of baking soda and water may be used for cleaning, but be careful to flush this off with clear water. DO NOT let any of the solution into the filler holes. Baking soda neutralizes battery acid and will de-activate a battery cell.

❉❉CAUTION

Always use caution when working on or near the battery. Never allow a tool to bridge the gap between the negative and positive battery terminals. Also, be careful not to allow a tool to provide a ground between the positive cable/terminal and any metal component on the vehicle. Either of these conditions will cause a short circuit leading to sparks and possible personal injury.

Batteries in vehicles which are not operated on a regular basis can fall victim to parasitic loads (small current drains which are constantly drawing current from the battery). Normal parasitic loads may drain a battery on a vehicle that is in storage and not used for 6-8 weeks. Vehicles that have additional accessories such as a cellular phone, an alarm system

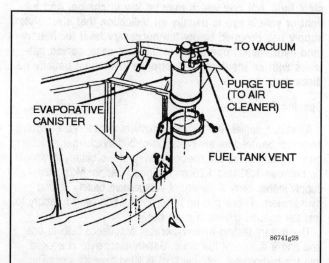

Fig. 67 Exploded view of a common evaporative canister and related components

or other devices that increase parasitic load may discharge a battery sooner. If the vehicle is to be stored for 6-8 weeks in a secure area and the alarm system, if present, is not necessary, the negative battery cable should be disconnected at the onset of storage to protect the battery charge.

Remember that constantly discharging and recharging will shorten battery life. Take care not to allow a battery to be needlessly discharged.

BATTERY FLUID

▶ See Figures 69, 70 and 71

�֍✖CAUTION

Battery electrolyte contains sulfuric acid. If you should splash any on your skin or in your eyes, flush the affected area with plenty of clear water. If it lands in your eyes, get medical help immediately.

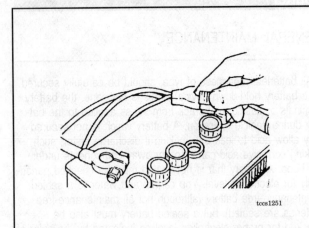

Fig. 69 On non-maintenance free batteries, the level can be checked through the case on translucent batteries; the cell caps must be removed on other models

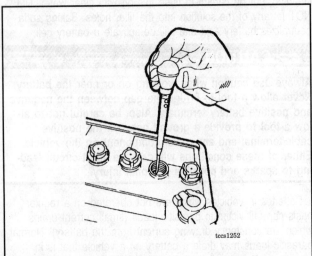

Fig. 70 Check the specific gravity of the battery's electrolyte with a hydrometer

The fluid (sulfuric acid solution) contained in the battery cells will tell you many things about the condition of the battery. Because the cell plates must be kept submerged below the fluid level in order to operate, maintaining the fluid level is extremely important. And, because the specific gravity of the acid is an indication of electrical charge, testing the fluid can be an aid in determining if the battery must be replaced. A battery in a vehicle with a properly operating charging system should require little maintenance, but careful, periodic inspection should reveal problems before they leave you stranded.

Fluid Level

Check the battery electrolyte level at least once a month, or more often in hot weather or during periods of extended vehicle operation. On non-sealed batteries, the level can be checked either through the case on translucent batteries or by removing the cell caps on opaque-cased types. The electrolyte level in each cell should be kept filled to the split ring inside each cell, or the line marked on the outside of the case.

If the level is low, add only distilled water through the opening until the level is correct. Each cell is separate from the others, so each must be checked and filled individually. Distilled water should be used, because the chemicals and minerals found in most drinking water are harmful to the battery and could significantly shorten its life.

If water is added in freezing weather, the vehicle should be driven several miles to allow the water to mix with the electrolyte. Otherwise, the battery could freeze.

Although some maintenance-free batteries have removable cell caps for access to the electrolyte, the electrolyte condition and level on all sealed maintenance-free batteries must be checked using the built-in hydrometer "eye." The exact type of eye varies between battery manufacturers, but most apply a sticker to the battery itself explaining the possible readings. When in doubt, refer to the battery manufacturer's instructions to interpret battery condition using the built-in hydrometer.

➡**Although the readings from built-in hydrometers found in sealed batteries may vary, a green eye usually indicates a properly charged battery with sufficient fluid level. A dark eye is normally an indicator of a battery with sufficient fluid, but one which may be low in charge. And a light or yellow eye is usually an indication that electrolyte supply has dropped below the necessary level for battery (and hydrometer) operation. In this last case, sealed batteries with an insufficient electrolyte level must usually be discarded.**

Specific Gravity

As stated earlier, the specific gravity of a battery's electrolyte level can be used as an indication of battery charge. At least once a year, check the specific gravity of the battery. It should be between 1.20 and 1.26 on the gravity scale. Most auto supply stores carry a variety of inexpensive battery testing hydrometers. These can be used on any non-sealed battery to test the specific gravity in each cell.

The battery testing hydrometer has a squeeze bulb at one end and a nozzle at the other. Battery electrolyte is sucked into the hydrometer until the float is lifted from its seat. The specific gravity is then read by noting the position of the float. If gravity is low in one or more cells, the battery should be slowly charged and checked again to see if the gravity has

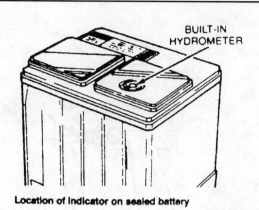

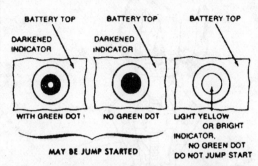

BATTERY TOP · BATTERY TOP · BATTERY TOP

DARKENED INDICATOR · DARKENED INDICATOR

WITH GREEN DOT · NO GREEN DOT · LIGHT YELLOW OR BRIGHT INDICATOR, NO GREEN DOT DO NOT JUMP START

MAY BE JUMP STARTED

Check the appearance of the charge indicator on top of the battery before attempting a jump start; if it's not green or dark, do not jump start the car

tccs1253

Fig. 71 A typical sealed (maintenance-free) battery with a built-in hydrometer — NOTE that the hydrometer eye may vary between battery manufacturers; always refer to the battery's label

come up. Generally, if after charging, the specific gravity between any two cells varies more than 50 points (0.50), the battery should be replaced as it can no longer produce sufficient voltage to guarantee proper operation.

On sealed batteries, the built-in hydrometer is the only way of checking specific gravity. Again, check with your battery's manufacturer for proper interpretation of its built-in hydrometer readings.

CABLES

▶ **See Figures 72, 73, 74, 75, 76 and 77**

Once a year (or as necessary), the battery terminals and the cable clamps should be cleaned. Loosen the clamps and remove the cables, negative cable first. On batteries with posts on top, the use of a puller specially made for this purpose is recommended. These are inexpensive and available in most auto parts stores. Side terminal battery cables are secured with a small bolt.

tccs1207

Fig. 73 The underside of this special battery tool has a wire brush to clean post terminals

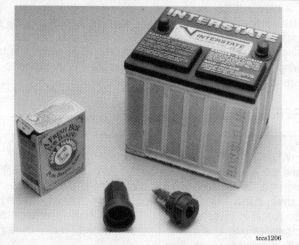

tccs1206

Fig. 72 Maintenance is performed with household items and with special tools like this post cleaner

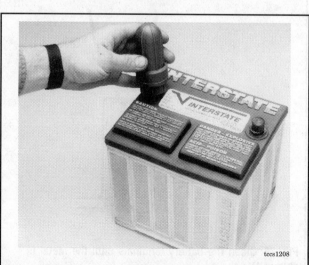

tccs1208

Fig. 74 Place the tool over the terminals and twist to clean the post

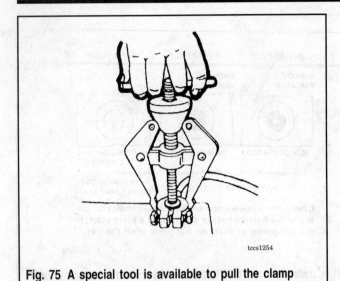

Fig. 75 A special tool is available to pull the clamp from the post

Clean the cable clamps and the battery terminal with a wire brush, until all corrosion, grease, etc., is removed and the metal is shiny. It is especially important to clean the inside of the clamp (an old knife is useful here) thoroughly, since a small deposit of foreign material or oxidation there will prevent a sound electrical connection and inhibit either starting or charging. Special tools are available for cleaning these parts, one type for conventional top post batteries and another type for side terminal batteries.

Before installing the cables, loosen the battery hold-down clamp or strap, remove the battery and check the battery tray. Clear it of any debris, and check it for soundness (the battery tray can be cleaned with a baking soda and water solution). Rust should be wire brushed away, and the metal given a couple coats of anti-rust paint. Install the battery and tighten the hold-down clamp or strap securely. Do not overtighten, as this can crack the battery case.

After the clamps and terminals are clean, reinstall the cables, negative cable last; DO NOT hammer the clamps onto

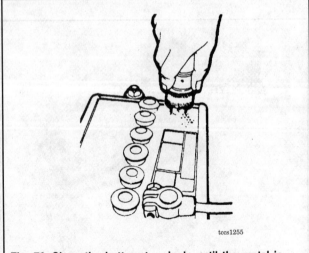

Fig. 76 Clean the battery terminals until the metal is shiny

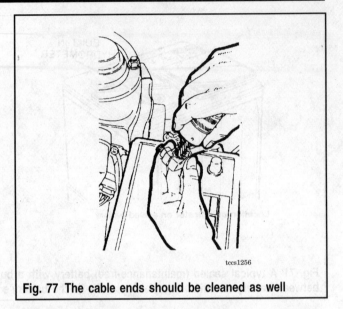

Fig. 77 The cable ends should be cleaned as well

post batteries. Tighten the clamps securely, but do not distort them. Give the clamps and terminals a thin external coating of grease after installation, to retard corrosion.

Check the cables at the same time that the terminals are cleaned. If the cable insulation is cracked or broken, or if the ends are frayed, the cable should be replaced with a new cable of the same length and gauge.

CHARGING

✳✳CAUTION

The chemical reaction which takes place in all batteries generates explosive hydrogen gas. A spark can cause the battery to explode and splash acid. To avoid serious personal injury, be sure there is proper ventilation and take appropriate fire safety precautions when connecting, disconnecting, or charging a battery and when using jumper cables.

A battery should be charged at a slow rate to keep the plates inside from getting too hot. However, if some maintenance-free batteries are allowed to discharge until they are almost "dead," they may have to be charged at a high rate to bring them back to "life." Always follow the charger manufacturer's instructions on charging the battery.

REPLACEMENT

When it becomes necessary to replace the battery, select one with a rating equal to or greater than the battery originally installed. Deterioration and just plain aging of the battery cables, starter motor, and associated wires makes the battery's job harder in successive years. The slow increase in electrical resistance over time makes it prudent to install a new battery with a greater capacity than the old.

V-Belts

INSPECTION

▶ See Figures 78, 79, 80, 81 and 82

Inspect the belts for signs of glazing or cracking. A glazed belt will be perfectly smooth from slippage, while a good belt will have a slight texture of fabric visible. Cracks will usually start at the inner edge of the belt and run outward. All worn or damaged drive belts should be replaced immediately. It is best to replace all drive belts at one time, as a preventive mainte-nance measure, during this service operation.

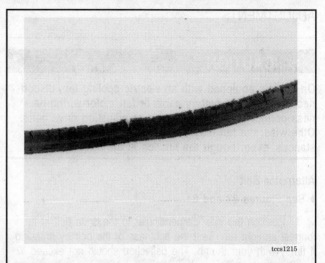

Fig. 80 Deep cracks in this belt will cause flex, building up heat that will eventually lead to belt failure

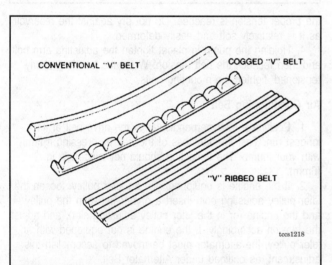

Fig. 78 There are typically 3 types of accessory drive belts found on vehicles today

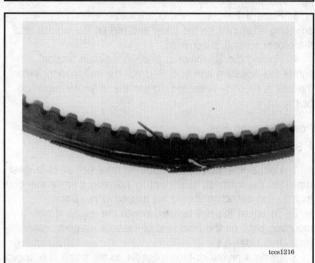

Fig. 81 The cover of this belt is worn, exposing the critical reinforcing cords to excessive wear

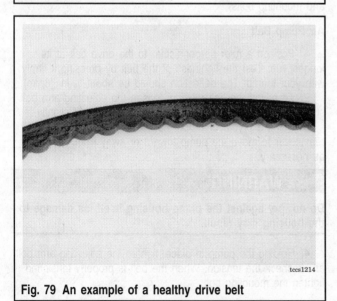

Fig. 79 An example of a healthy drive belt

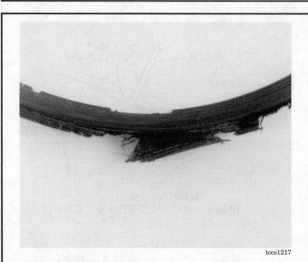

Fig. 82 Installing too wide a belt can result in serious belt wear and/or breakage

ADJUSTMENTS

Alternator Belt

▶ See Figures 83 and 84

1. Position the ruler perpendicular to the drive belt at its longest straight run. Test the tightness of the belt by pressing it firmly with your thumb. The deflection should not exceed ¼ in. (6mm).
2. If the deflection exceeds ¼ in. (6mm), loosen the alternator mounting and adjusting arm bolts.
3. Place a 1 in. open-end or adjustable wrench on the adjusting ridge cast on the body, and pull on the wrench until the proper tension is achieved.
4. Holding the alternator in place to maintain tension, tighter the adjusting arm bolt. Recheck the belt tension. When the belt is properly tensioned, tighten the alternator mounting bolt.

Power Steering Belt

▶ See Figure 85

1. Hold a ruler perpendicular to the drive belt at its longest run. Test the tightness of the belt by pressing it firmly with you thumb. The deflection should not exceed ¼ in. (6mm).
2. To adjust the belt tension, loosen the adjusting and mounting bolts on the front face of the steering pump cover plate (hub side).
3. Using a prybar or broom handle on the pump hub, move the power steering pump toward or away from the engine until

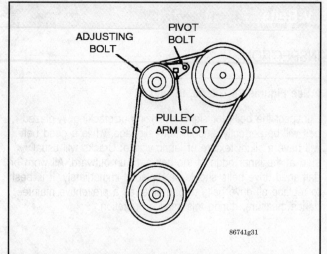

Fig. 84 Some pulleys have a rectangular slot to aid in moving the accessories to be tightened

the proper tension is reached. Do not pry against the reservoir as it is relatively soft and easily deformed.
4. Holding the pump in place, tighten the adjusting arm bolt and then recheck the belt tension. When the belt is properly tensioned, tighten the mounting bolts.

Air Conditioning Belt

1. Position a ruler perpendicular to the drive belt at its longest run. Test the tightness of the belt by pressing it firmly with your thumb. The deflection should not exceed ¼ in. (6mm).
2. If the engine is equipped with an idler pulley, loosen the idler pulley adjusting bolt, insert a prybar between the pulley and the engine (or in the idler pulley adjusting slot), and adjust the tension accordingly. If the engine is not equipped with an idler pulley, the alternator must be moved to accomplish this adjustment, as outlined under Alternator Belt.
3. When the proper tension is reached, tighten the idler pulley adjusting bolt (if so equipped) or the alternator adjusting and mounting bolts.

Air Pump Belt

1. Position a ruler perpendicular to the drive belt at its longest run. Test the tightness of the belt by pressing it firmly with your thumb. The deflection should be about ¼ in. (6mm).
2. To adjust the belt tension, loosen the adjusting arm bolt slightly. If necessary, also loosen the mounting bolt slightly.
3. Using a prybar or broom handle, pry against the pump rear cover to move the pump toward or away from the engine as necessary.

4. Holding the pump in place, tighten the adjusting arm bolt and recheck the tension. When the belt is properly tensioned tighten the mounting bolt.

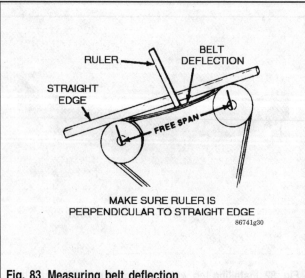

Fig. 83 Measuring belt deflection

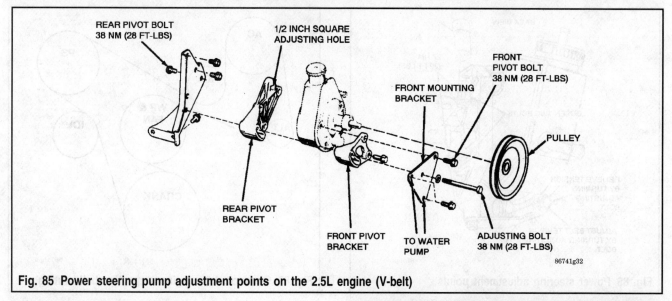

REAR PIVOT BOLT
38 NM (28 FT-LBS)

1/2 INCH SQUARE
ADJUSTING HOLE

FRONT
PIVOT
BOLT
38 NM (28 FT-LBS)

FRONT MOUNTING
BRACKET

PULLEY

REAR PIVOT
BRACKET

FRONT PIVOT
BRACKET

TO WATER
PUMP

ADJUSTING BOLT
38 NM (28 FT-LBS)

86741g32

Fig. 85 Power steering pump adjustment points on the 2.5L engine (V-belt)

REMOVAL & INSTALLATION

Alternator Belt

1. Loosen the alternator mounting and adjusting arm bolts.
2. Pivot the alternator inward and remove the belt from the vehicle.
   To install:
3. Install a new belt.
4. Holding the alternator in place to maintain tension, tighten the alternator mounting and adjusting arm bolts.

Power Steering Belt

1. Loosen the adjusting and mounting bolts on the front face of the steering pump cover plate (hub side).
2. Pivot the power steering pump inward and remove the drive belt.
   To install:
3. Install the drive belt.
4. Holding the pump in place, tighten the adjusting arm bolt and the mounting bolts.

Air Conditioning Compressor Belt

1. If the engine is equipped with an idler pulley, loosen the idler pulley adjusting bolt and remove the belt.
2. If not equipped with an idler pulley, loosen the adjusting and mounting bolts.
3. Pivot the air conditioning compressor inward and remove the drive belt.
4. Installation is the reverse of removal.

Air Pump Drive Belt

1. Loosen the adjusting arm bolt slightly. If necessary, also loosen the mounting bolt slightly and remove the drive belt.
   To install:
2. Holding the pump in place, install the drive belt, then tighten the adjusting arm bolt and the mounting bolt.

Serpentine Belt

INSPECTION

When inspecting serpentine drive belts, small cracks that run across the ribbed surface of the belt from rib to rib are considered normal. If the the cracks are running along the rib (rather across), this is not normal and the belt(s) must be replaced.

ADJUSTMENT

It is not necessary to adjust the tension on the 5.2L engine. The engine is equipped with an automatic tensioner. The tensioner maintains correct tension at all times.

2.5L and 4.0L Engines

▶ See Figures 86, 87 and 88

➡If the vehicle is not equipped with power steering, it will be equipped with an idler pulley. If equipped with an idler pulley, refer to and follow the 5.2L belt removal and installation procedure.

1. Loosen the rear power steering pump mounting bolts.
2. Loosen the pump upper pivot bolt, lower locknut and pump adjusting bolt.
3. Use a belt tension gauge placed in the middle of the belt being tested. Proper tension for a new belt is 180-200 lbs. (800-900 N) and 140-160 lbs. (623-712 N) for a used belt.
4. Tighten the pump adjusting bolt to achieve proper tension and recheck the belt tension.

REMOVAL & INSTALLATION

2.5L and 4.0L Engines

▶ See Figures 89 and 90

1. Loosen the rear power steering pump mounting bolts.

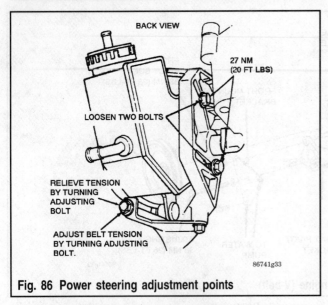

Fig. 86 Power steering adjustment points

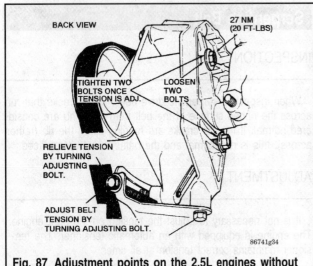

Fig. 87 Adjustment points on the 2.5L engines without power steering (rear view)

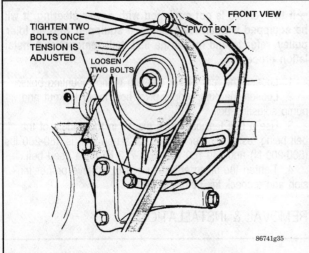

Fig. 88 Adjustment points on the 2.5L engine (front view)

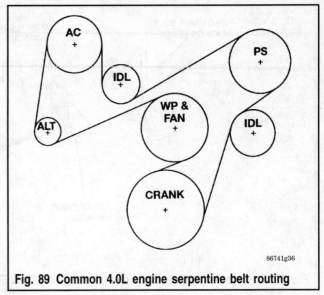

Fig. 89 Common 4.0L engine serpentine belt routing

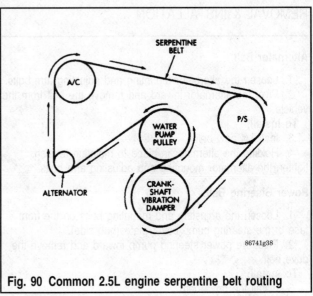

Fig. 90 Common 2.5L engine serpentine belt routing

2. Loosen the pump upper pivot bolt, lower locknut and the pump adjusting bolt.

3. Remove the belt.

To install:

4. Install the belt.

5. Tighten the pump adjusting bolt to achieve proper tension.

6. Install the pump rear mounting bolts, pivot bolt and locknut. Tighten the bolts to 20. ft. lbs. (27 Nm).

7. Check the belt for proper tension. If tension is incorrect, refer to the adjustment procedure in this section.

5.2L Engines

▶ See Figures 91, 92, 93, 94 and 95

1. Attach a socket or wrench to the pulley mounting bolt on the automatic tensioner and rotate the tensioner assembly clockwise until the tension has been removed from the belt.

2. Remove the belt from the idler pulley first and then from the vehicle.

To install:

→The tensioner is equipped with an indexing arrow on the back of the tensioner and an indexing mark on the tensioner housing. If a new belt is being installed, ensure the arrow is within 1/8 in. (3mm) of the indexing mark.

3. Position the belt over all the pulleys except the idler pulley.

4. Attach a socket or wrench to the pulley mounting bolt on the automatic tensioner and rotate the tensioner assembly clockwise and place the belt over the idler pulley.

5. Let the tensioner rotate back into place and remove the socket or wrench.

6. Ensure that the belt is properly seated.

7. Check the belt indexing marks.

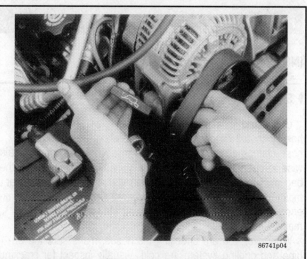

Fig. 94 Rotate the assembly clockwise until the tension has been removed from the belt — 1996 model shown

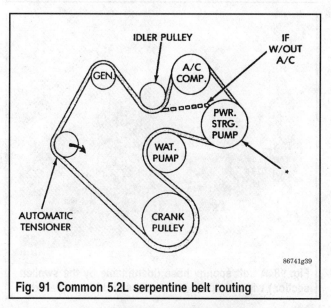

Fig. 91 Common 5.2L serpentine belt routing

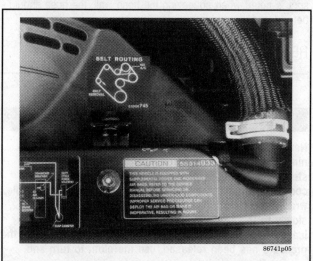

Fig. 95 A belt routing label may be found on the fan shroud in later model vehicles — 1996 model shown

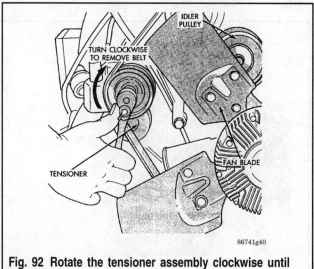

Fig. 92 Rotate the tensioner assembly clockwise until the tension has been removed from the belt

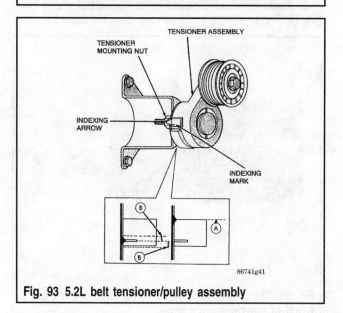

Fig. 93 5.2L belt tensioner/pulley assembly

Hoses

INSPECTION

▶ See Figures 96, 97, 98 and 99

Upper and lower radiator hoses, along with the heater hoses, should be checked for deterioration, leaks and loose hose clamps at least every 15,000 miles (24,000 km). It is also wise to check the hoses periodically in early spring and at the beginning of the fall or winter when you are performing other maintenance. A quick visual inspection could discover a weakened hose which might have left you stranded if it had remained unrepaired.

Whenever you are checking the hoses, make sure the engine and cooling system are cold. Visually inspect for cracking, rotting or collapsed hoses, and replace as necessary. Run your hand along the length of the hose. If a weak or swollen spot is noted when squeezing the hose wall, the hose should be replaced.

REMOVAL & INSTALLATION

1. Remove the radiator pressure cap.

✳✳CAUTION

Never remove the pressure cap while the engine is running, or personal injury from scalding hot coolant or steam may result. If possible, wait until the engine has cooled to remove the pressure cap. If this is not possible, wrap a thick cloth around the pressure cap and turn it slowly to the stop. Step back while the pressure is released from the cooling system. When you are sure all the pressure has been released, use the cloth to turn and remove the cap.

2. Position a clean container under the radiator and/or engine draincock or plug, then open the drain and allow the

tccs1220

Fig. 97 A hose clamp that is too tight can cause older hoses to separate and tear on either side of the clamp

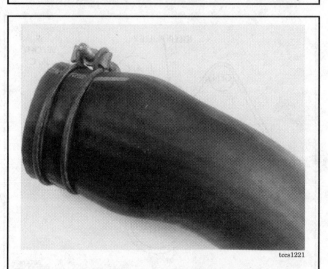
tccs1221

Fig. 98 A soft spongy hose (identifiable by the swollen section) will eventually burst and should be replaced

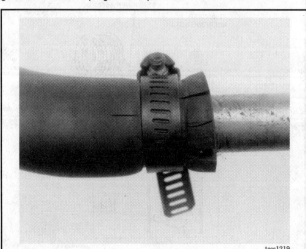
tccs1219

Fig. 96 The cracks developing along this hose are a result of age-related hardening

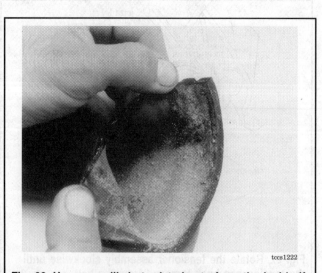
tccs1222

Fig. 99 Hoses are likely to deteriorate from the inside if the cooling system is not periodically flushed

cooling system to drain to an appropriate level. For some upper hoses, only a little coolant must be drained. To remove hoses positioned lower on the engine, such as a lower radiator hose, the entire cooling system must be emptied.

❊❊CAUTION

When draining coolant, keep in mind that cats and dogs are attracted by ethylene glycol antifreeze, and are quite likely to drink any that is left in an uncovered container or in puddles on the ground. This will prove fatal in sufficient quantity. Always drain coolant into a sealable container. Coolant may be reused unless it is contaminated or several years old.

3. Loosen the hose clamps at each end of the hose requiring replacement. Clamps are usually either of the spring tension type (which require pliers to squeeze the tabs and loosen) or of the screw tension type (which require screw or hex drivers to loosen). Pull the clamps back on the hose away from the connection.

4. Twist, pull and slide the hose off the fitting, taking care not to damage the neck of the component from which the hose is being removed.

➡**If the hose is stuck at the connection, do not try to insert a screwdriver or other sharp tool under the hose end in an effort to free it, as the connection and/or hose may become damaged. Heater connections especially may be easily damaged by such a procedure. If the hose is to be replaced, use a single-edged razor blade to make a slice along the portion of the hose which is stuck on the connection, perpendicular to the end of the hose. Do not cut deep so as to prevent damaging the connection. The hose can then be peeled from the connection and discarded.**

5. Clean both hose mounting connections. Inspect the condition of the hose clamps and replace them, if necessary.

To install:

6. Dip the ends of the new hose into clean engine coolant to ease installation.

7. Slide the clamps over the replacement hose, then slide the hose ends over the connections into position.

8. Position and secure the clamps at least ¼ in. (6mm) from the ends of the hose. Make sure they are located beyond the raised bead of the connector.

9. Close the radiator and/or engine drains and properly refill the cooling system with the clean drained engine coolant or a suitable mixture of coolant and water.

10. If available, install a pressure tester and check for leaks. If a pressure tester is not available, run the engine until normal operating temperature is reached (allowing the system to naturally pressurize), then check for leaks.

❊❊CAUTION

If you are checking for leaks with the system at normal operating temperature, BE EXTREMELY CAREFUL not to touch any moving or hot engine parts. Once temperature has been reached, shut the engine OFF, and check for leaks around the hose fittings and connections which were removed earlier.

CV-Boots

INSPECTION

▶ **See Figures 100 and 101**

The CV (Constant Velocity) boots should be checked for damage each time the oil is changed and any other time the vehicle is raised for service. These boots keep water, grime, dirt and other damaging matter from entering the CV-joints. Any of these could cause early CV-joint failure which can be expensive to repair. Heavy grease thrown around the inside of the front wheel(s) and on the brake caliper/drum can be an indication of a torn boot. Thoroughly check the boots for missing clamps and tears. If the boot is damaged, it should be replaced immediately. Please refer to Section 7 for procedures.

Spark Plugs

▶ **See Figure 102**

A typical spark plug consists of a metal shell surrounding a ceramic insulator. A metal electrode extends downward through the center of the insulator and protrudes a small distance. Located at the end of the plug and attached to the side of the outer metal shell is the side electrode. The side electrode bends in at a 90° angle so that its tip is just past and parallel to the tip of the center electrode. The distance between these two electrodes (measured in thousandths of an inch or hundredths of a millimeter) is called the spark plug gap.

The spark plug does not produce a spark but instead provides a gap across which the current can arc. The coil produces anywhere from 20,000 to 50,000 volts (depending on the type and application) which travels through the wires to the spark plugs. The current passes along the center electrode and jumps the gap to the side electrode, and in doing so, ignites the air/fuel mixture in the combustion chamber.

tccs1011

Fig. 100 CV-boots must be inspected periodically for damage

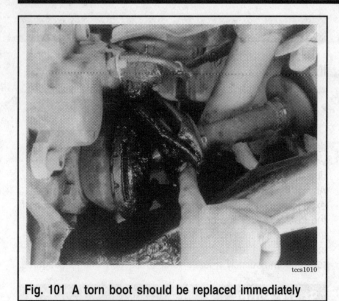

Fig. 101 A torn boot should be replaced immediately

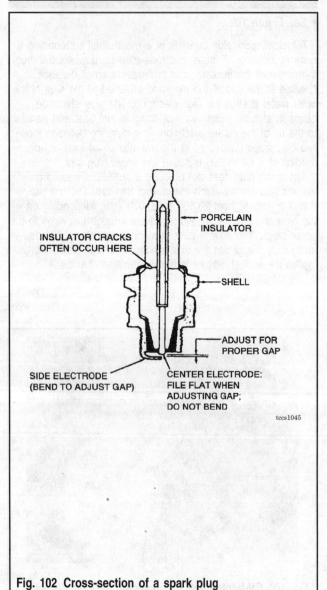

PORCELAIN INSULATOR

INSULATOR CRACKS OFTEN OCCUR HERE

SHELL

ADJUST FOR PROPER GAP

SIDE ELECTRODE (BEND TO ADJUST GAP)

CENTER ELECTRODE: FILE FLAT WHEN ADJUSTING GAP; DO NOT BEND

tccs1045

Fig. 102 Cross-section of a spark plug

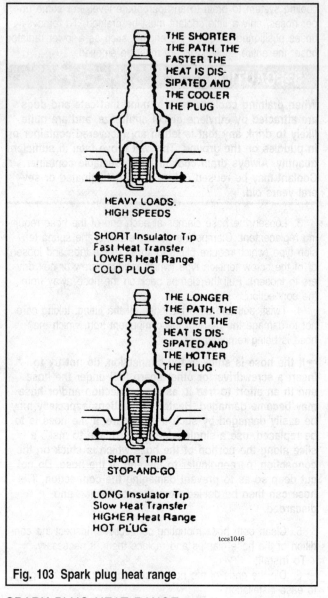

THE SHORTER THE PATH, THE FASTER THE HEAT IS DIS-SIPATED AND THE COOLER THE PLUG

HEAVY LOADS. HIGH SPEEDS

SHORT Insulator Tip
Fast Heat Transfer
LOWER Heat Range
COLD PLUG

THE LONGER THE PATH, THE SLOWER THE HEAT IS DIS-SIPATED AND THE HOTTER THE PLUG

SHORT TRIP STOP-AND-GO

LONG Insulator Tip
Slow Heat Transfer
HIGHER Heat Range
HOT PLUG

tccs1046

Fig. 103 Spark plug heat range

SPARK PLUG HEAT RANGE

◆ See Figure 103

Spark plug heat range is the ability of the plug to dissipate heat. The longer the insulator (or the farther it extends into the engine), the hotter the plug will operate; the shorter the insulator (the closer the electrode is to the block's cooling passages) the cooler it will operate. A plug that absorbs little heat and remains too cool will quickly accumulate deposits of oil and carbon since it is not hot enough to burn them off. This leads to plug fouling and consequently to misfiring. A plug that absorbs too much heat will have no deposits but, due to the excessive heat, the electrodes will burn away quickly and might possibly lead to preignition or other ignition problems. Preignition takes place when plug tips get so hot that they glow sufficiently to ignite the air/fuel mixture before the actual spark occurs. This early ignition will usually cause a pinging during low speeds and heavy loads.

The general rule of thumb for choosing the correct heat range when picking a spark plug is: if most of your driving is long distance, high speed travel, use a colder plug; if most of your driving is stop and go, use a hotter plug. Original equipment plugs are generally a good compromise between the 2 styles and most people never have the need to change their plugs from the factory-recommended heat range.

REMOVAL & INSTALLATION

▶ **See Figures 104, 105, 106 and 107**

A set of spark plugs usually requires replacement after about 20,000-30,000 miles (32,000-48,000 km), depending on your style of driving. In normal operation, plug gap increases about 0.001 in. (0.025mm) for every 2,500 miles (4000 km). As the gap increases, the plug's voltage requirement also increases. It requires a greater voltage to jump the wider gap and about two to three times as much voltage to fire the plug at high speeds than at idle. The improved air/fuel ratio control of modern fuel injection combined with the higher voltage output of modern ignition systems will often allow an engine to run sig-

nificantly longer on a set of standard spark plugs, but keep in mind that efficiency will drop as the gap widens (along with fuel economy and power).

When you're removing spark plugs, work on one at a time. Don't start by removing the plug wires all at once, because, unless you number them, they may become mixed up. Take a minute before you begin and number the wires with tape.

1. Disconnect the negative battery cable, and if the vehicle has been run recently, allow the engine to thoroughly cool.

2. Carefully twist the spark plug wire boot to loosen it, then pull upward and remove the boot from the plug. Be sure to pull on the boot and not on the wire, otherwise the connector located inside the boot may become separated.

3. Using compressed air, blow any water or debris from the spark plug well to assure that no harmful contaminants are allowed to enter the combustion chamber when the spark plug is removed. If compressed air is not available, use a rag or a brush to clean the area.

➡ **Remove the spark plugs when the engine is cold, if possible, to prevent damage to the threads. If removal of the plugs is difficult, apply a few drops of penetrating oil or silicone spray to the area around the base of the plug, and allow it a few minutes to work.**

4. Using a spark plug socket that is equipped with a rubber insert to properly hold the plug, turn the spark plug counterclockwise to loosen and remove the spark plug from the bore.

✳✳WARNING

Be sure not to use a flexible extension on the socket. Use of a flexible extension may allow a shear force to be applied to the plug. A shear force could break the plug off in the cylinder head, leading to costly and frustrating repairs.

To install:

5. Inspect the spark plug boot for tears or damage. If a damaged boot is found, the spark plug wire must be replaced.

6. Using a wire feeler gauge, check and adjust the spark plug gap. When using a gauge, the proper size should pass between the electrodes with a slight drag. The next larger size

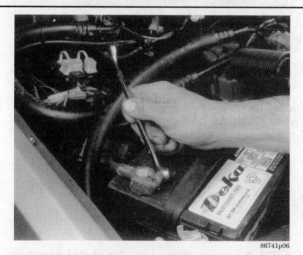

Fig. 104 Disconnect the negative battery cable before replacing or repairing any electrically related component

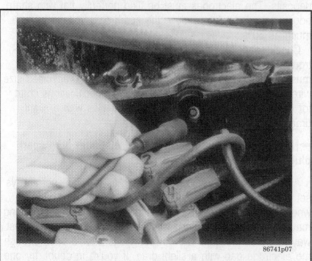

Fig. 105 Tag and disengage the spark plug wire from the spark plug

Fig. 106 Using a spark plug socket, remove the spark plug from the bore

should not be able to pass while the next smaller size should pass freely.

7. Carefully thread the plug into the bore by hand. If resistance is felt before the plug is almost completely threaded, back the plug out and begin threading again. In small, hard to reach areas, an old spark plug wire and boot could be used as a threading tool. The boot will hold the plug while you twist the end of the wire and the wire is supple enough to twist before it would allow the plug to crossthread.

✳✳WARNING

Do not use the spark plug socket to thread the plugs. Always carefully thread the plug by hand or using an old plug wire to prevent the possibility of crossthreading and damaging the cylinder head bore.

8. Carefully tighten the spark plug. If the plug you are installing is equipped with a crush washer, seat the plug, then tighten about ¼ turn to crush the washer. If you are installing a tapered seat plug, tighten the plug to specifications provided by the vehicle or plug manufacturer.

9. Apply a small amount of silicone dielectric compound to the end of the spark plug or inside the spark plug boot to prevent sticking, then install the boot to the spark plug and push until it clicks into place. The click may be felt or heard, then gently pull back on the boot to assure proper contact.

INSPECTION & GAPPING

▶ **See Figures 108, 109, 110, 111, 112, 113, 114, 115, 116, 117 and 118**

Check the plugs for deposits and wear. If they are not going to be replaced, clean the plugs thoroughly. Remember that any kind of deposit will decrease the efficiency of the plug. Plugs can be cleaned on a spark plug cleaning machine, which can sometimes be found in service stations, or you can do an acceptable job of cleaning with a stiff brush. If the plugs are cleaned, the electrodes must be filed flat. Use an ignition points file, not an emery board or the like, which will leave

Fig. 108 A normally worn spark plug should have light tan or gray deposits on the firing tip

deposits. The electrodes must be filed perfectly flat with sharp edges; rounded edges reduce the spark plug voltage by as much as 50%.

Check spark plug gap before installation. The ground electrode (the L-shaped one connected to the body of the plug) must be parallel to the center electrode, and the specified size wire gauge (please refer to the Tune-Up Specifications chart for details) must pass between the electrodes with a slight drag.

➡ **NEVER adjust the gap on a used platinum type spark plug.**

Always check the gap on new plugs as they are not always set correctly at the factory. Do not use a flat feeler gauge when measuring the gap on a used plug, because the reading may be inaccurate. A round-wire type gapping tool is the best way to check the gap. The correct gauge should pass through the electrode gap with a slight drag. If you're in doubt, try one size smaller and one larger. The smaller gauge should go through easily, while the larger one shouldn't go through at all. Wire gapping tools usually have a bending tool attached. Use

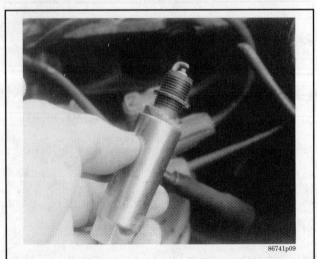

Fig. 107 Inspect the spark plug for signs of damage, deposits and wear

Fig. 109 A carbon fouled plug, identified by soft, sooty, black deposits, may indicate an improperly tuned vehicle. Check the air cleaner, ignition components and engine control system

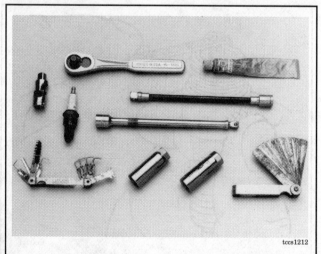

Fig. 110 A variety of tools and gauges is needed for spark plug service

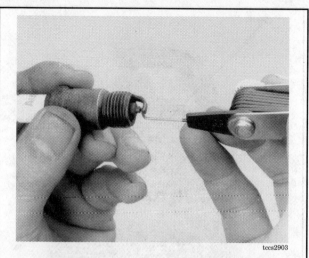

Fig. 111 Checking the spark plug gap with a feeler gauge

Fig. 112 A physically damaged spark plug may be evidence of severe detonation in that cylinder. Watch that cylinder carefully between services, as a continued detonation will not only damage the plug, but could also damage the engine

Fig. 113 An oil fouled spark plug indicates an engine with worn piston rings and/or bad valve seals allowing excessive oil to enter the chamber

Fig. 115 This spark plug has been left in the engine too long, as evidenced by the extreme gap — Plugs with such an extreme gap can cause misfiring and stumbling accompanied by a noticeable lack of power

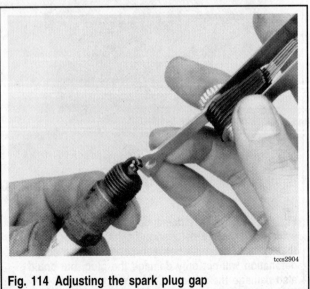

Fig. 114 Adjusting the spark plug gap

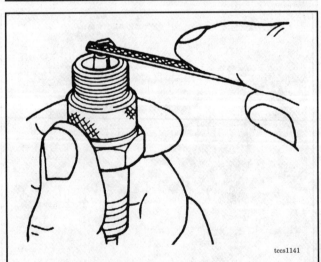

Fig. 116 If the plug is in good condition, the electrode may be filed flat and reused

Tracking Arc
High voltage arcs between a fouling deposit on the insulator tip and spark plug shell. This ignites the fuel/air mixture at some point along the insulator tip, retarding the ignition timing which causes a power and fuel loss.

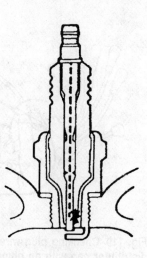

Wide Gap
Spark plug electrodes are worn so that the high voltage charge cannot arc across the electrodes. Improper gapping of electrodes on new or "cleaned" spark plugs could cause a similar condition. Fuel remains unburned and a power loss results.

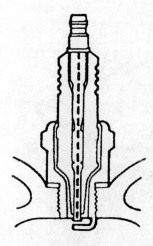

Flashover
A damaged spark plug boot, along with dirt and moisture, could permit the high voltage charge to short over the insulator to the spark plug shell or the engine. A buttress insulator design helps prevent high voltage flashover.

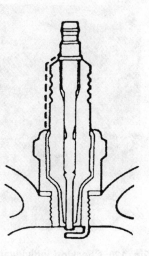

Fouled Spark Plug
Deposits that have formed on the insulator tip may become conductive and provide a "shunt" path to the shell. This prevents the high voltage from arcing between the electrodes. A power and fuel loss is the result.

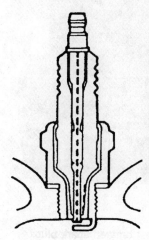

Bridged Electrodes
Fouling deposits between the electrodes "ground out" the high voltage needed to fire the spark plug. The arc between the electrodes does not occur and the fuel air mixture is not ignited. This causes a power loss and exhausting of raw fuel.

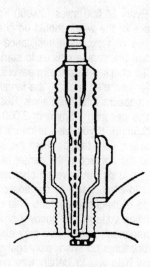

Cracked Insulator
A crack in the spark plug insulator could cause the high voltage charge to "ground out." Here, the spark does not jump the electrode gap and the fuel air mixture is not ignited. This causes a power loss and raw fuel is exhausted.

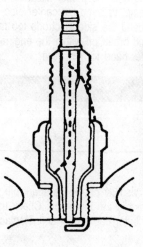

tccs201A

Fig. 117 Used spark plugs which show damage may indicate engine problems

Fig. 118 A bridged or almost bridged spark plug, identified by a build-up between the electrodes caused by excessive carbon or oil build-up on the plug

that to adjust the side electrode until the proper distance is obtained. Absolutely never attempt to bend the center electrode. Also, be careful not to bend the side electrode too far or too often as it may weaken and break off within the engine, requiring removal of the cylinder head to retrieve it.

Spark Plug Wires

TESTING

▶ **See Figures 119 and 120**

At every tune-up/inspection, visually check the spark plug cables for burns, cuts, or breaks in the insulation. Check the boots and nipples on the distributor cap and/or coil. Replace any damaged wiring.

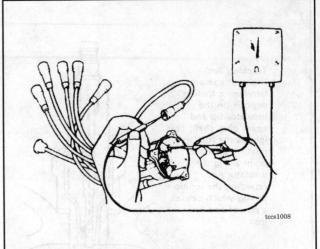

Fig. 119 Checking plug wire resistance through the distributor cap with an ohmmeter

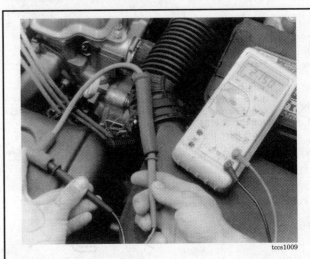

Fig. 120 Checking individual plug wire resistance with a digital ohmmeter

Every 50,000 miles (80,000 Km) or 60 months, the resistance of the wires should be checked with an ohmmeter. Wires with excessive resistance will cause misfiring, and may make the engine difficult to start in damp weather.

To check resistance, measure the length of each wire with a ruler and then multiply the length by the figures given, in order to measure total resistance. Resistance must be 250-1,000 ohms per inch (25mm) or 3,000-12,000 ohms per foot (30.5mm). If you wish to check the cap at the same time, you can run your test between the spark plug end of the plug wire and the contact at the center of the inside of the cap.

If you do not have an ohmmeter, you may want to take your car to a mechanic or diagnostic center with an oscilloscope type of diagnosis system. This unit will read the curve of ignition voltage and uncover problems with wires, or any other component, easily. You may also want to refer to the previous procedures on spark plug analysis, as looking at the plugs may help you to identify wire problems.

Distributor Cap and Rotor

REMOVAL & INSTALLATION

▶ See Figures 121, 122, 123 and 124

1. Unplug the distributor connector from the wiring harness connector.
2. Loosen the distributor cap retaining screws.
3. Label, and if necessary, disconnect the spark plug wires from the distributor cap.
4. Lift the cap off of the distributor.
5. Note in which direction the distributor spark pick-up is pointing, then pull the rotor off of the distributor shaft.

To install:

6. Push the new rotor onto the distributor shaft. Make certain it is pointing in the same direction.
7. Set the distributor cap back onto the distributor.

8. Tighten the distributor cap retaining screws until they are snug.
9. Connect the spark plug wires back onto the distributor cap.
10. Plug the distributor connector into the wiring harness connector.

INSPECTION

Remove the distributor cap and inspect the inside for flashover, cracking of the carbon button, lack of spring tension on the carbon button, cracking of the cap, and burned, worn terminals. Also check for broken distributer cap towers. If any of these conditions are present, the distributor cap and/or cables should be replaced.

When replacing the distributor cap, transfer cables from the original cap to the new cap one at a time. Ensure that each cable is installed into the corresponding tower of the new cap.

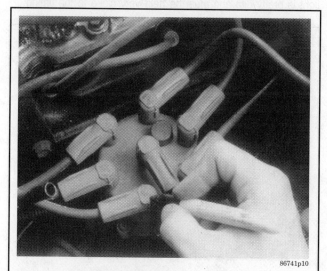

Fig. 121 Label the spark plug wires

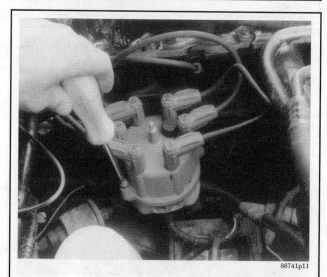

Fig. 122 Loosen the distributor retaining screws

Fig. 123 Remove the distributor cap

Fig. 124 Remove the rotor from the distributor shaft

Fully seat the wires into the towers. If necessary, refer to the appropriate engine firing order diagram.

Light scaling of the terminals can be cleaned with a sharp knife. If the terminals are heavily scaled, replace the distributor cap.

A cap that is greasy, dirty or has a powder-like substance on the inside should be cleaned with a solution of warm water and mild detergent. Scrub the cap with a soft brush. Thoroughly rinse the cap and dry it with a clean soft cloth.

Replace the rotor with a new one if it is cracked, or if the tip is excessively burned or heavily scaled. If the spring terminal does not have adequate tension, replace the rotor with a new one.

Ignition Timing

Ignition timing is the measurement, in degrees of crankshaft rotation, of the point at which the spark plugs fire in each of the cylinders. It is measured in degrees before or after Top Dead Center (TDC) of the compression stroke. Ignition timing is controlled by turning the distributor body in the engine.

Ideally, the air/fuel mixture in the cylinder will be ignited by the spark plug just as the piston passes TDC of the compression stroke. If this happens, the piston will be beginning its downward motion of the power stroke just as the compressed and ignited air/fuel mixture starts to expand. The expansion of the air/fuel mixture then forces the piston down on the power stroke and turns the crankshaft.

Because it takes a fraction of a second for the spark plug to ignite the mixture in the cylinder, the spark plug must fire a little before the piston reaches TDC. Otherwise, the mixture will not be completely ignited as the piston passes TDC and the full power of the explosion will not be used by the engine.

The timing measurement is given in degrees of crankshaft rotation before the piston reaches TDC (BTDC). If the setting for the ignition timing is 5° BTDC, the spark plug must fire 5° before each piston reaches TDC. This only holds true, however, when the engine is at idle speed.

As the engine speed increases, the pistons go faster. The spark plugs have to ignite the fuel even sooner if it is to be completely ignited when the piston reaches TDC. To do this, the distributor has a means to advance the timing of the spark as the engine speed increases. This is accomplished by input from the electronic ignition control module and other computer sources. If the distributor is equipped with a vacuum advance unit, it is necessary to disconnect the vacuum line from the diaphragm when the ignition timing is being set.

If the ignition is set too far advanced (BTDC), the ignition and expansion of the fuel in the cylinder will occur too soon and tend to force the piston down while it is still traveling up. This causes engine ping. If the ignition spark is set too far retarded, after TDC (ATDC), the piston will have already passed TDC and started on its way down when the fuel is ignited. This will cause the piston to be forced down for only a portion of its travel. This will result in poor engine performance and lack of power.

The timing is best checked with a timing light. This device is connected in series with the No. 1 spark plug. The current that fires the spark plug also causes the timing light to flash.

When the engine is running, the timing light is aimed at the timing marks on the engine and crankshaft pulley.

ADJUSTMENT

▶ **See Figures 125, 126, 127, 128 and 129**

Timing is adjustable on 1984-92 vehicles only. On 1993 and later vehicles, the timing is controlled by the Powertrain Control Module (PCM) and is not adjustable.

On 1984-92 models, timing should be checked at each tune-up and any time components are replaced in the ignition system. The timing marks consist of a notch on the rim of the crankshaft pulley and a graduated scale attached to the engine front (timing) cover. A stroboscopic flash (dynamic) timing light must be used, as a static light is too inaccurate for emission controlled engines.

There are three basic types of timing lights available. The first is a simple neon bulb with two wire connections. One wire connects to the spark plug terminal and the other plugs into the end of the spark plug wire for the No. 1 cylinder, thus connecting the light in series with the spark plug. This type of light is pretty dim and must be held very close to the timing

Fig. 125 Common location of the marks — 1987 model shown

Fig. 126 Using a timing light to adjust ignition timing

marks to be seen. Sometimes a dark corner has to be sought out to see the flash at all. This type of light is very inexpensive. The second type operates from the vehicle's battery — two alligator clips connect to the battery terminals, while an adapter enables a third clip to be connected to the No. 1 spark plug and wire. This type provides a nice bright flash that you can see even in bright sunlight. It is the type most often seen in professional shops. The third type replaces the battery power source with 110 volt current.

1. Warm up the engine to normal operating temperature. Stop the engine and connect the timing light to the No. 1 spark plug wire and a tachometer to the Tach terminal on the distributor cap.

➡Most tachometers require a special clip to attach the meter to the distributor. This clip may or may not be included with the tachometer.

2. Clean off the timing marks and mark the pulley notch and timing scale with white chalk.

3. Disconnect and plug the vacuum hose from the vacuum advance unit (if equipped).

4. Start the engine and aim the timing light at the pointer marks. Be careful not to touch the fan, because it may appear to be standing still. If the pulley notch isn't aligned with the proper timing mark (refer to the Tune-Up Specifications chart), the timing will have to be adjusted.

5. Loosen the distributor clamp locknut. Turn the distributor slowly to adjust the timing, holding it by the base and not the cap. Turn it counterclockwise to advance timing (toward BTDC), and clockwise to retard (toward TDC or ATDC).

6. Tighten the locknut. Check the timing again, in case the distributor moved slightly as you tightened it.

7. Unplug and connect the distributor vacuum line if applicable, and correct the idle speed to that specified in the Tune-Up Specifications chart.

8. Stop the engine and disconnect the timing light.

Valve Lash

Valve adjustment determines how far the valves enter the cylinder and how long they stay open and closed.

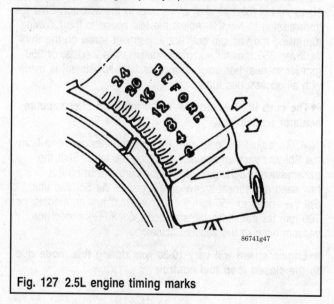

Fig. 127 2.5L engine timing marks

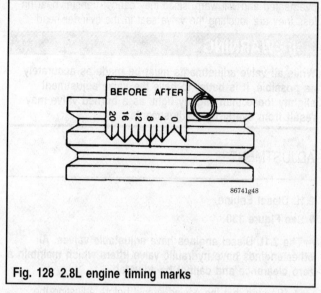

Fig. 128 2.8L engine timing marks

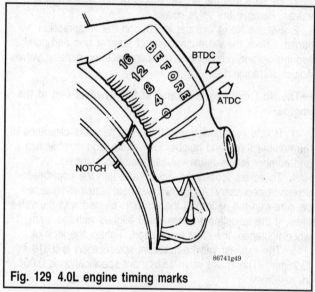

Fig. 129 4.0L engine timing marks

If the valve clearance is too large, part of the lift of the camshaft will be used in removing the excessive clearance. Consequently, the valve will not be opening as far as it should. This condition has two effects: the valve train components will emit a tapping sound as they take up the excessive clearance, and the engine will perform poorly because the valves don't open fully and allow the proper amount of gases to flow into and out of the engine.

If the valve clearance is too small, the intake valves and the exhaust valves will open too far and they will not fully seat on the cylinder head when they close. When a valve seats itself on the cylinder head, it does two things: it seals the combustion chamber so that none of the gases in the cylinder escape and it cools itself by transferring some of the heat it absorbs from the combustion in the cylinder to the cylinder head and to the engine's cooling system. If the valve clearance is too small, the engine will run poorly because of the gases escaping from the combustion chamber. The valves will also become overheated and will warp, since they cannot transfer heat unless they are touching the valve seat in the cylinder head.

✳✳WARNING

While all valve adjustments must be made as accurately as possible, it is better to have the valve adjustment slightly loose than slightly tight, as a burned valve may result from overly tight adjustments.

ADJUSTMENT

2.1L Diesel Engine

▶ See Figure 130

➡The 2.1L Diesel engines have adjustable valves. All other engines have hydraulic valve lifters which maintain a zero clearance and cannot be adjusted.

1. Be sure that the engine is cold before adjusting the valves. Remove the valve cover.
2. Set the No. 1 cylinder to TDC on the compression stroke. Check the valve clearance of number one and number two intake, and number one and number three exhaust valves. Adjust as required.

➡The No.1 cylinder is located at the flywheel end of the engine.

3. Rotate the crankshaft 360°, then check the clearance of the number three and number four intake, and number two and number four exhaust valves. Adjust as required.
4. To adjust, loosen the locknut and turn the adjustment screw as necessary. As each adjustment screw is tightened, be sure that the bottom of the screw is aligned with the valve stem. If the adjustment screw is not aligned with the stem when tightened, the stem could bend. Tighten the locknut.
5. The exhaust valve adjustment specification is 0.010 in. (0.25mm). The intake valve adjustment specification is 0.008 in. (0.20mm)

Idle Speed and Mixture Adjustments

This section contains only tune-up adjustment procedures for fuel systems. Descriptions, adjustments, and overhaul procedures for fuel system components can be found in Section 5.

1984-85 MODELS

2.5L Engine

1. Fully warm up the engine.
2. Check the choke fast idle adjustment: Disconnect and plug the EGR valve vacuum hose. Position the fast idle adjustment screw on the second step of the fast idle cam with the transmission in Neutral. Adjust the fast idle speed to 2,000 rpm for manual transmission models, or 2,300 rpm for automatic transmission models. Allow the throttle to return to normal curb idle and reconnect the EGR vacuum.
3. To adjust the Sol-Vac Vacuum Actuator: Remove the vacuum hose from the vacuum actuator and plug the hose.

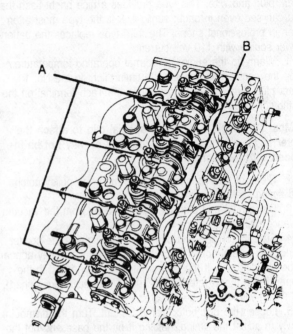

A. Intake valve rocker arms
B. Exhaust valve rocker arms

86741g42

Fig. 130 Valve arrangement on the 2.1L diesel engine

Connect an external vacuum source to the actuator and apply 10-15 in. Hg (68-103 kPa) of vacuum to the actuator. Shift the transmission to Neutral. Adjust the idle speed to the following rpm using the vacuum actuator adjustment screw on the throttle lever: 850 rpm for automatic transmission models, or 950 rpm for manual transmission models. The adjustment is made with all accessories turned off.

➡The curb idle should always be adjusted after vacuum actuator adjustment.

4. To adjust the curb idle: Remove the vacuum hose from the Sol-Vac vacuum actuator and plug the hose. Shift the transmission into Neutral. Adjust the curb idle using the ¼ in. hex head adjustment screw on the end of the Sol-Vac unit. Set the speed to 750 rpm for manual transmission models, or 700 rpm for automatic transmission models. Reconnect the vacuum hose to the vacuum actuator.

➡Engine speed will vary 10-30 rpm during this mode due to the closed loop fuel control.

5. To adjust the TRC: The TRC screw is preset at the factory and should not require adjustment. However, to check adjustment, the screw should be ¾ turn from the closed throttle position.

2.8L Engine

EXCEPT CALIFORNIA

1. Connect a tachometer to the ignition coil negative terminal or to the pigtail wire connector above the heater blower motor.

2. Disconnect and plug the vacuum hose at the distributor vacuum advance.

3. If necessary, adjust the ignition timing with the engine speed at or below specifications.

4. Unplug and reconnect the vacuum hose to the distributor vacuum advance unit.

5. Disconnect the deceleration valve hose and canister purge hose. Plug the hose and remove the air cleaner assembly.

6. If equipped with air conditioning, turn the control switch to the ON position and open the throttle momentarily to insure the solenoid armature is fully extended. Adjust the solenoid idle speed adjusting screw to obtain the specified engine curb idle speed rpm. Turn the air conditioning control switch to the OFF position.

7. If not equipped with air conditioning, adjust the engine idle speed rpm with the solenoid idle speed adjusting screw. Disconnect the solenoid wire and adjust the curb idle.

8. Install the air cleaner assembly. Connect all hoses and other connections.

CALIFORNIA MODELS

▶ See Figures 131 and 132

➡Some California Jeeps with the V6 engine are equipped with a 2,200 hour engine timer. The timer activates a solenoid to control operation of the carburetor secondary vacuum break after 2,200 hours of vehicle operation. The timer is not a serviceable component and must not be disassembled. In the event of a timer malfunction, the complete engine wiring harness must be replaced.

1. Connect a tachometer to the ignition system. Start the engine and operate to normal operating temperature.

2. Turn off all accessories including the air conditioning system.

3. Put the manual transmission equipped vehicles in Neutral, and the automatic transmission equipped vehicles in Drive with the parking brake locked and the wheels chocked.

4. Adjust the curb idle speed adjusting screw to obtain the specified rpm of 700 for both manual and automatic transmission equipped vehicles.

5. Disconnect the vacuum hose from the idle kick actuator and connect an outside vacuum source to the actuator. Apply 15 in. Hg. (51 kPa) of vacuum to the actuator.

6. Adjust the actuator hex head adjustment screw for the specified 1,200 rpm with both types of transmissions in the Neutral position.

7. Stop the engine, remove the tachometer and vacuum pump. Install the vacuum hose to the actuator.

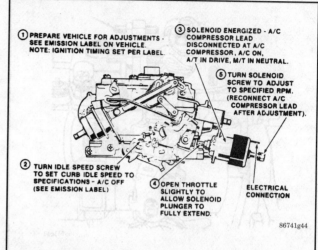

Fig. 131 E2SE carburetor idle speed adjustment — without A/C

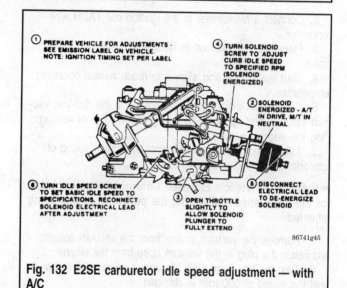

Fig. 132 E2SE carburetor idle speed adjustment — with A/C

1985-87 MODELS

2.1L Diesel Engine

▶ See Figure 133

1. Connect a tachometer to the ignition system. The idle speed is adjusted on the injection pump linkage.

2. Loosen the screw locknut, adjust the idle speed to 750-850 rpm with the adjusting screw and tighten the locknut.

3. Stop the engine and remove the tachometer.

2.5L Engine

WITH YFA CARBURETOR

1. The Throttlle Return Control TRC (anti-diesel) adjustment screw is statically set at ¾ turn from the throttle valve closed position during factory assembly and does not normally require readjustment. Should this adjustment be required, turn the adjustment screw counterclockwise to the throttle plate closed position and then turn the screw clockwise ¾ turn.

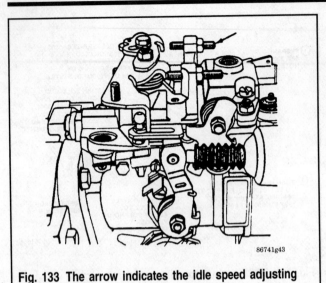

Fig. 133 The arrow indicates the idle speed adjusting screw

2. Connect a tachometer to the ignition coil TACH wire connector.

3. Place the transmission in Neutral and set the parking brake.

4. Start the engine and allow it to reach normal operating temperature.

5. Connect an external vacuum source to the Sol-Vac vacuum actuator and apply 10-15 in. Hg (34-51 kPa) of vacuum. Plug the engine vacuum hose.

6. Adjust the vacuum actuator until an engine speed of approximately 1,000 rpm is achieved.

➡Refer to the Vehicle Emission Control Information Label for the latest specifications for the particular engine being adjusted.

7. Remove the vacuum source from the vacuum actuator and retain the plug in the vacuum hose from the engine.

8. Turn the hex-head curb idle speed adjustment screw until the speed of 500 rpm is obtained.

➡Refer to the Vehicle Emission Control Label for the latest specifications for the particular engine being adjusted.

9. Stop the engine, then unplug and connect the engine vacuum hose to the vacuum actuator.

10. Remove the tachometer from the engine.

WITH THROTTLE BODY FUEL INJECTION

Adjustments are not possible on this unit, as all functions are computer controlled.

2.8L Engines

EXCEPT CALIFORNIA

1. Connect a tachometer to the ignition coil negative terminal or to the pigtail wire connector above the heater blower motor.

2. Disconnect and plug the vacuum hose at the distributor vacuum advance.

3. If necessary, adjust the ignition timing with the engine speed at or below specifications.

4. Unplug and reconnect the vacuum hose to the distributor vacuum advance unit.

5. Disconnect the deceleration valve hose and canister purge hose. Plug the hose and remove the air cleaner assembly.

6. If equipped with air conditioning, turn the control switch to the ON position and open the throttle momentarily to insure the solenoid armature is fully extended. Adjust the solenoid idle speed adjusting screw to obtain the specified engine curb idle speed rpm. Turn the air conditioning control switch to the OFF position.

7. If not equipped with air conditioning, adjust the engine idle speed rpm with the solenoid idle speed adjusting screw. Disconnect the solenoid wire and adjust the curb idle.

8. Install the air cleaner assembly. Connect all hoses and other connections.

CALIFORNIA MODELS

➡Some California Jeeps with the V6 engine are equipped with a 2,200 hour engine timer. The timer activates a solenoid to control operation of the carburetor secondary vacuum break after 2,200 hours of vehicle operation. The timer is not a serviceable component and must not be disassembled. In the event of a timer malfunction, the complete engine wiring harness must be replaced.

1. Connect a tachometer to the ignition system. Start the engine and operate to normal operating temperature.

2. Turn off all accessories including the air conditioning system.

3. Put the manual transmission equipped vehicles in Neutral and the automatic transmission equipped vehicles in Drive with the parking brake set and the wheels chocked.

4. Adjust the curb idle speed adjusting screw to obtain the specified rpm of 700 for both manual and automatic transmission equipped vehicles.

5. Disconnect the vacuum hose from the idle kick actuator and connect an outside vacuum source to the actuator. Apply 15 in. Hg (68 kPa) of vacuum to the actuator.

6. Adjust the actuator hex head adjustment screw for the specified 1,200 rpm with both types of transmissions in the Neutral position.

7. Stop the engine, remove the tachometer and vacuum pump. Install the vacuum hose to the actuator.

1988-96 MODELS

The 2.5L TBI, 2.5L MFI, 4.0L MFI and 5.2L MFI are all fuel injected. Routine adjustments are computer controlled. No routine idle speed adjustments are possible.

Air Conditioning

➡Be sure to consult the laws in your area before servicing the air conditioning system. In most areas, it is illegal to perform repairs involving refrigerant unless the work is done by a certified technician. Also, it is quite likely that you will not be able to purchase refrigerant without proof of certification.

GASOLINE ENGINE TUNE-UP SPECIFICATIONS

Year	Engine ID/VIN	Engine Displacement Liters (c.i.d)	Spark Plugs Gap (in.)	Ignition Timing (deg.) MT	AT	Fuel Pump (psi)	Idle Speed (rpm) MT	AT	Valve Clearance In.	Ex.
1984	U	2.5 (150)	0.035	12B	12B	6.5-8	750	750	Hyd.	Hyd.
	W	2.8 (173)	0.041	10B	10B	6.5-8	750	750	Hyd.	Hyd.
1985	H	2.5 (150)	0.035	12B	12B	14-15	750	750	Hyd.	Hyd.
	W	2.8 (173)	0.041	10B	10B	6.5-8	750	750	Hyd.	Hyd.
1986	H	2.5 (150)	0.035	12B	12B	14-15	750	750	Hyd.	Hyd.
	W	2.8 (173)	0.041	10B	10B	6.5-8	750	750	Hyd.	Hyd.
1987	H	2.5 (150)	0.035	1	1	14-15	750	750	Hyd.	Hyd.
	M	4.0 (242)	0.035	1	1	31	1	1	Hyd.	Hyd.
1988	H	2.5 (150)	0.035	1	1	14-15	1	1	Hyd.	Hyd.
	M	4.0 (242)	0.035	1	1	31	1	1	Hyd.	Hyd.
1989	E	2.5 (150)	0.035	1	1	14-15	1	1	Hyd.	Hyd.
	L	4.0 (242)	0.035	1	1	31	1	1	Hyd.	Hyd.
1990	E	2.5 (150)	0.035	1	1	14-15	1	1	Hyd.	Hyd.
	L	4.0 (242)	0.035	1	1	31	1	1	Hyd.	Hyd.
1991	P	2.5 (150)	0.035	1	1	39-41	1	1	Hyd.	Hyd.
	S	4.0 (242)	0.035	1	1	39-41	1	1	Hyd.	Hyd.
1992	P	2.5 (150)	0.035	1	1	39-41	1	1	Hyd.	Hyd.
	S	4.0 (242)	0.035	1	1	39-41	1	1	Hyd.	Hyd.
1993	P	2.5 (150)	0.035	1	1	39-41	1	1	Hyd.	Hyd.
	S	4.0 (242)	0.035	1	1	39-41	1	1	Hyd.	Hyd.
	Y	5.2 (5211)	0.035	1	1	39-41	1	1	Hyd.	Hyd.
1994	P	2.5 (150)	0.035	1	1	39-41	1	1	Hyd.	Hyd.
	S	4.0 (242)	0.035	1	1	39-41	1	1	Hyd.	Hyd.
	Y	5.2 (5211)	0.035	1	1	39-41	1	1	Hyd.	Hyd.
1995	P	2.5 (150)	0.035	1	1	39-41	1	1	Hyd.	Hyd.
	S	4.0 (242)	0.035	1	1	39-41	1	1	Hyd.	Hyd.
	Y	5.2 (5211)	0.035	1	1	39-41	1	1	Hyd.	Hyd.
1996	P	2.5 (150)	0.035	1	1	39-41	1	1	Hyd.	Hyd.
	S	4.0 (242)	0.035	1	1	39-41	1	1	Hyd.	Hyd.
	Y	5.2 (5211)	0.035	1	1	39-41	1	1	Hyd.	Hyd.

NOTE: The Vehicle Emission Control Information label often reflects specification changes made during production. The label figures must be used if they differ from those in this chart.

1: Not adjustable

86741cA1

DIESEL ENGINE TUNE-UP SPECIFICATIONS

Year	Engine ID/VIN	Engine Displacement Liters (cu. in.)	Valve Clearance Intake (in.)	Exhaust (in.)	Intake Valve Opens (deg.)	Injection Pump Setting (deg.)	Injection Nozzle Pressure (psi) New	Used	Idle Speed (rpm)	Cranking Compression Pressure (psi)
1985	B	2.1 (126)	0.008	0.010	14B	8B	1885	NA	800 1	2
1986	B	2.1 (126)	0.008	0.010	14B	8B	1885	NA	800 1	2
1987	B	2.1 (126)	0.008	0.010	14B	8B	1885	NA	800 1	2

NOTE: The Vehicle Emission Control Information label often reflects specification changes made during production. The label figures must be used if they differ from those in this chart.

1: Without solenoid. 1100 with solenoid

2: Check all cylinders. The difference between cylinders should not be more than 25%.

86741CA2

SAFETY PRECAUTIONS

There are two major hazards associated with air conditioning systems and they both relate to the refrigerant gas. First, the refrigerant gas (R-12 or R-134a) is an extremely cold substance. When exposed to air, it will instantly freeze any surface it comes in contact with, including your eyes. The other hazard relates to fire (if your vehicle is equipped with R-12). Although normally non-toxic, the R-12 gas becomes highly poisonous in the presence of an open flame. One good whiff of the vapor formed by burning R-12 can be fatal. Keep all forms of fire (including cigarettes) well clear of the air conditioning system.

Because of the inherent dangers involved with working on air conditioning systems, these safety precautions must be strictly followed.

• Avoid contact with a charged refrigeration system, even when working on another part of the air conditioning system or vehicle. If a heavy tool comes into contact with a section of tubing or a heat exchanger, it can easily cause the relatively soft material to rupture.

• When it is necessary to apply force to a fitting which contains refrigerant, as when checking that all system couplings are securely tightened, use a wrench on both parts of the fitting involved, if possible. This will avoid putting torque on refrigerant tubing. (It is also advisable to use tube or line wrenches when tightening these flare nut fittings.)

➡**R-12 refrigerant is a chlorofluorocarbon which, when released into the atmosphere, can contribute to the depletion of the ozone layer in the upper atmosphere. Ozone filters out harmful radiation from the sun.**

• Do not attempt to discharge the system without the proper tools. Precise control is possible only when using the service gauges and a proper A/C refrigerant recovery station. Wear protective gloves when connecting or disconnecting service gauge hoses.

• Discharge the system only in a well ventilated area, as high concentrations of the gas which might accidentally escape can exclude oxygen and act as an anesthetic. When leak testing or soldering, this is particularly important, as toxic gas is formed when R-12 contacts any flame.

• Never start a system without first verifying that both service valves are properly installed, and that all fittings throughout the system are snugly connected.

• Avoid applying heat to any refrigerant line or storage vessel. Charging may be aided by using water heated to less than 125°F (50°C) to warm the refrigerant container. Never allow a refrigerant storage container to sit out in the sun, or near any other source of heat, such as a radiator or heater.

• Always wear goggles to protect your eyes when working on a system. If refrigerant contacts the eyes, it is advisable in all cases to consult a physician immediately.

• Frostbite from liquid refrigerant should be treated by first gradually warming the area with cool water, and then gently applying petroleum jelly. A physician should be consulted.

• Always keep refrigerant drum fittings capped when not in use. If the container is equipped with a safety cap to protect the valve, make sure the cap is in place when the can is not being used. Avoid sudden shock to the drum, which might occur from dropping it, or from banging a heavy tool against it.

Never carry a drum in the passenger compartment of a vehicle.

• Always completely discharge the system into a suitable recovery unit before painting the vehicle (if the paint is to be baked on), or before welding anywhere near refrigerant lines.

• When servicing the system, minimize the time that any refrigerant line or fitting is open to the air in order to prevent moisture or dirt from entering the system. Contaminants such as moisture or dirt can damage internal system components. Always replace O-rings on lines or fittings which are disconnected. Prior to installation coat, but do not soak, replacement O-rings with suitable compressor oil.

GENERAL SERVICING PROCEDURES

➡**It is recommended, and possibly required by law, that a qualified technician perform the following services.**

✳✳WARNING

Some of the vehicles covered by this manual may be equipped with R-134a refrigerant systems, rather than R-12. Be ABSOLUTELY SURE what type of system you are working on before attempting to add refrigerant. Use of the wrong refrigerant or oil will cause damage to the system.

The most important aspect of air conditioning service is the maintenance of a pure and adequate charge of refrigerant in the system. A refrigeration system cannot function properly if a significant percentage of the charge is lost. Leaks are common because the severe vibration encountered underhood in an automobile can easily cause a sufficient cracking or loosening of the air conditioning fittings; allowing, the extreme operating pressures of the system to force refrigerant out.

The problem can be understood by considering what happens to the system as it is operated with a continuous leak. Because the expansion valve regulates the flow of refrigerant to the evaporator, the level of refrigerant there is fairly constant. The receiver/drier stores any excess refrigerant, and so a loss will first appear there as a reduction in the level of liquid. As this level nears the bottom of the vessel, some refrigerant vapor bubbles will begin to appear in the stream of liquid supplied to the expansion valve. This vapor decreases the capacity of the expansion valve very little as the valve opens to compensate for its presence. As the quantity of liquid in the condenser decreases, the operating pressure will drop there and throughout the high side of the system. As the refrigerant continues to be expelled, the pressure available to force the liquid through the expansion valve will continue to decrease, and, eventually, the valve's orifice will prove to be too much of a restriction for adequate flow even with the needle fully withdrawn.

At this point, low side pressure will start to drop, and a severe reduction in cooling capacity, marked by freeze-up of the evaporator coil, will result. Eventually, the operating pressure of the evaporator will be lower than the pressure of the atmosphere surrounding it, and air will be drawn into the system wherever there are leaks in the low side.

Because all atmospheric air contains at least some moisture, water will enter the system mixing with the refrigerant and oil.

Trace amounts of moisture will cause sludging of the oil, and corrosion of the system. Saturation and clogging of the filter/drier, and freezing of the expansion valve orifice will eventually result. As air fills the system to a greater and greater extent, it will interfere more and more with the normal flows of refrigerant and heat.

From this description, it should be obvious that much of the repairman's focus in on detecting leaks, repairing them, and then restoring the purity and quantity of the refrigerant charge. A list of general rules should be followed in addition to all safety precautions:

- Keep all tools as clean and dry as possible.
- Thoroughly purge the service gauges/hoses of air and moisture before connecting them to the system. Keep them capped when not in use.
- Thoroughly clean any refrigerant fitting before disconnecting it, in order to minimize the entrance of dirt into the system.
- Plan any operation that requires opening the system beforehand, in order to minimize the length of time it will be exposed to open air. Cap or seal the open ends to minimize the entrance of foreign material.
- When adding oil, pour it through an extremely clean and dry tube or funnel. Keep the oil capped whenever possible. Do not use oil that has not been kept tightly sealed.
- Purchase refrigerant intended for use only in automatic air conditioning systems.
- Completely evacuate any system that has been opened for service, or that has leaked sufficiently to draw in moisture and air. This requires evacuating air and moisture with a good vacuum pump for at least one hour. If a system has been open for a considerable length of time it may be advisable to evacuate the system for up to 12 hours (overnight).
- Use a wrench on both halves of a fitting that is to be disconnected, so as to avoid placing torque on any of the refrigerant lines.
- When overhauling a compressor, pour some of the oil into a clean glass and inspect it. If there is evidence of dirt, metal particles, or both, flush all refrigerant components with clean refrigerant before evacuating and recharging the system. In addition, if metal particles are present, the compressor should be replaced.
- Schrader valves may leak only when under full operating pressure. Therefore, if leakage is suspected but cannot be located, operate the system with a full charge of refrigerant and look for leaks from all Schrader valves. Replace any faulty valves.

Additional Preventive Maintenance

USING THE SYSTEM

The easiest and most important preventive maintenance for your A/C system is to be sure that it is used on a regular basis. Running the system for five minutes each month (no matter what the season) will help assure that the seals and all internal components remain lubricated.

ANTIFREEZE

▶ See Figure 134

In order to prevent heater core freeze-up during A/C operation, it is necessary to maintain a proper antifreeze protection. Use a hand-held antifreeze tester (hydrometer) to periodically check the condition of the antifreeze in your engine's cooling system.

➡**Antifreeze should not be used longer than the manufacturer specifies.**

RADIATOR CAP

For efficient operation of an air conditioned vehicle's cooling system, the radiator cap should have a holding pressure which meets manufacturer's specifications. A cap which fails to hold these pressures should be replaced.

CONDENSER

Any obstruction of or damage to the condenser configuration will restrict the air flow which is essential to its efficient operation. It is therefore a good rule to keep this unit clean and in proper physical shape.

➡**Bug screens which are mounted in front of the condenser (unless they are original equipment) are regarded as obstructions.**

CONDENSATION DRAIN TUBE

This single molded drain tube expels the condensation, which accumulates on the bottom of the evaporator housing, into the engine compartment. If this tube is obstructed, the air conditioning performance can be restricted and condensation buildup can spill over onto the vehicle's floor.

SYSTEM INSPECTION

➡**R-12 refrigerant is a chlorofluorocarbon which, when released into the atmosphere, can contribute to the depletion of the ozone layer in the upper atmosphere. Ozone filters out harmful radiation from the sun.**

The easiest and often most important check for the air conditioning system consists of a visual inspection of the system components. Visually inspect the air conditioning system for refrigerant leaks, damaged compressor clutch, compressor drive belt tension and condition, plugged evaporator drain tube,

tccs1233

Fig. 134 Use an antifreeze tester to determine the freezing and boiling level of the coolant in your vehicle

blocked condenser fins, disconnected or broken wires, blown fuses, corroded connections and poor insulation.

A refrigerant leak will usually appear as an oily residue at the leakage point In the system. The oily residue soon picks up dust or dirt particles from the surrounding air and appears greasy. Through time, this will build up and appear to be a heavy dirt impregnated grease. Most leaks are caused by damaged or missing O-ring seals at the component connections, damaged charging valve cores or missing service gauge port caps.

For a thorough visual and operational inspection, check the following:

1. Check the surface of the radiator and condenser for dirt, leaves or other material which might block air flow.

2. Check for kinks in hoses and lines. Check the system for leaks.

3. Make sure the drive belt is under the proper tension. When the air conditioning is operating, make sure the drive belt is free of noise or slippage.

4. Make sure the blower motor operates at all appropriate positions, then check for distribution of the air from all outlets with the blower on **HIGH**.

➡**Keep in mind that under conditions of high humidity, air discharged from the A/C vents may not feel as cold as expected, even if the system is working properly. This is because the vaporized moisture in humid air retains heat more effectively than does dry air, making the humid air more difficult to cool.**

5. Make sure the air passage selection lever is operating correctly. Start the engine and warm it to normal operating temperature, then make sure the hot/cold selection lever is operating correctly.

DISCHARGING, EVACUATING AND CHARGING

Discharging, evacuating and charging the air conditioning system must be performed by a properly trained and certified mechanic in a facility equipped with refrigerant recovery/recycling equipment that meets SAE standards for the type of system to be serviced.

If you don't have access to the necessary equipment, we recommend that you take your vehicle to a reputable service station to have the work done. If you still wish to perform repairs on the vehicle, have them discharge the system, then take your vehicle home and perform the necessary work. When you are finished, return the vehicle to the station for evacuation and charging. Just be sure to cap ALL A/C system fittings immediately after opening them and keep them protected until the system is recharged.

Windshield Wipers

ELEMENT (REFILL) CARE AND REPLACEMENT

▶ **See Figures 135, 136, 137, 138, 139, 140, 141, 142, 144, 143, 145 and 146**

For maximum effectiveness and longest element life, the windshield and wiper blades should be kept clean. Dirt, tree sap, road tar and so on will cause streaking, smearing and blade deterioration if left on the glass. It is advisable to wash the windshield carefully with a commercial glass cleaner at least once a month. Wipe off the rubber blades with the wet rag afterwards. Do not attempt to move wipers across the windshield by hand; damage to the motor and drive mechanism will result.

To inspect and/or replace the wiper blade elements, place the wiper switch in the **LOW** speed position and the ignition switch in the **ACC** position. When the wiper blades are approximately vertical on the windshield, turn the ignition switch to **OFF**.

Examine the wiper blade elements. If they are found to be cracked, broken or torn, they should be replaced immediately. Replacement intervals will vary with usage, although ozone deterioration usually limits element life to about one year. If the wiper pattern is smeared or streaked, or if the blade chatters across the glass, the elements should be replaced. It is easiest and most sensible to replace the elements in pairs.

If your vehicle is equipped with aftermarket blades, there are several different types of refills and your vehicle might have any kind. Aftermarket blades and arms rarely use the exact same type blade or refill as the original equipment. Here are some typical aftermarket blades; not all may be available for your vehicle:

The Anco® type uses a release button that is pushed down to allow the refill to slide out of the yoke jaws. The new refill slides back into the frame and locks in place.

Some Trico® refills are removed by locating where the metal backing strip or the refill is wider. Insert a small screwdriver blade between the frame and metal backing strip. Press down to release the refill from the retaining tab.

Other types of Trico® refills have two metal tabs which are unlocked by squeezing them together. The rubber filler can then be withdrawn from the frame jaws. A new refill is installed by inserting the refill into the front frame jaws and sliding it rearward to engage the remaining frame jaws. There are usually four jaws; be certain when installing that the refill is engaged in all of them. At the end of its travel, the tabs will lock into place on the front jaws of the wiper blade frame.

Another type of refill is made from polycarbonate. The refill has a simple locking device at one end which flexes downward out of the groove into which the jaws of the holder fit, allowing easy release. By sliding the new refill through all the jaws and pushing through the slight resistance when it reaches the end of its travel, the refill will lock into position.

To replace the Tridon® refill, it is necessary to remove the wiper blade. This refill has a plastic backing strip with a notch about 1 in. (25mm) from the end. Hold the blade (frame) on a hard surface so that the frame is tightly bowed. Grip the tip of the backing strip and pull up while twisting counterclockwise.

The backing strip will snap out of the retaining tab. Do this for the remaining tabs until the refill is free of the blade. The length of these refills is molded into the end and they should be replaced with identical types.

Regardless of the type of refill used, be sure to follow the part manufacturer's instructions closely. Make sure that all of the frame jaws are engaged as the refill is pushed into place and locked. If the metal blade holder and frame are allowed to touch the glass during wiper operation, the glass will be scratched.

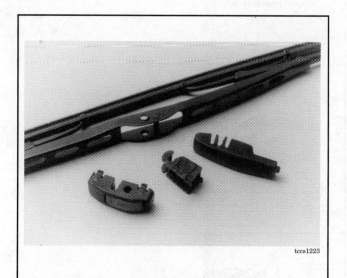

tccs1223

Fig. 135 Bosch® wiper blade and fit kit

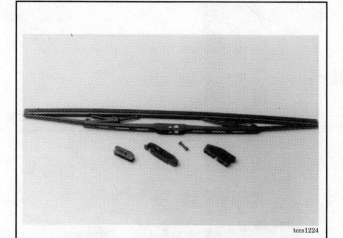

tccs1224

Fig. 136 Lexor® wiper blade and fit kit

tccs1225

Fig. 137 Pylon® wiper blade and adaptor

tccs1226

Fig. 138 Trico® wiper blade and fit kit

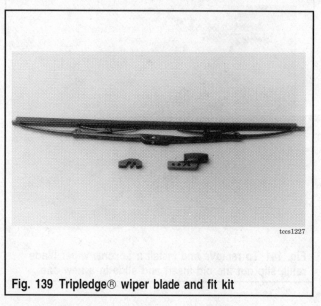

tccs1227

Fig. 139 Tripledge® wiper blade and fit kit

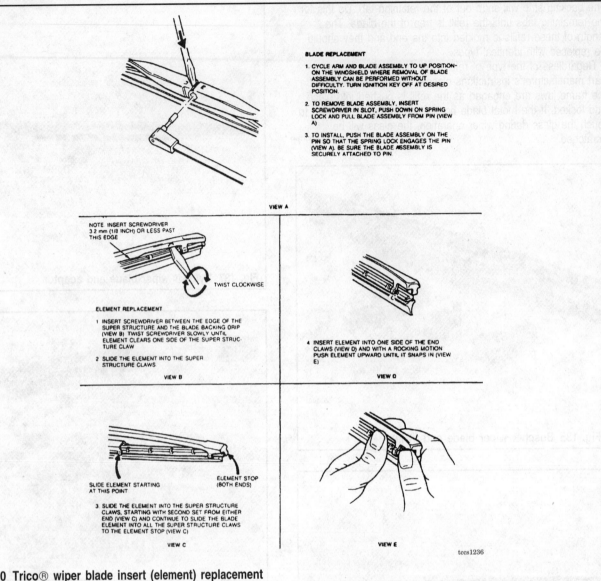

BLADE REPLACEMENT

1. CYCLE ARM AND BLADE ASSEMBLY TO UP POSITION-
ON THE WINDSHIELD WHERE REMOVAL OF BLADE
ASSEMBLY CAN BE PERFORMED WITHOUT
DIFFICULTY. TURN IGNITION KEY OFF AT DESIRED
POSITION.

2. TO REMOVE BLADE ASSEMBLY, INSERT
SCREWDRIVER IN SLOT, PUSH DOWN ON SPRING
LOCK AND PULL BLADE ASSEMBLY FROM PIN (VIEW
A)

3. TO INSTALL, PUSH THE BLADE ASSEMBLY ON THE
PIN SO THAT THE SPRING LOCK ENGAGES THE PIN
(VIEW A). BE SURE THE BLADE ASSEMBLY IS
SECURELY ATTACHED TO PIN.

VIEW A

NOTE: INSERT SCREWDRIVER
3.2 mm (1/8 INCH) OR LESS PAST
THIS EDGE

TWIST CLOCKWISE

ELEMENT REPLACEMENT

1 INSERT SCREWDRIVER BETWEEN THE EDGE OF THE
SUPER STRUCTURE AND THE BLADE BACKING DRIP
(VIEW B) TWIST SCREWDRIVER SLOWLY UNTIL
ELEMENT CLEARS ONE SIDE OF THE SUPER STRUC-
TURE CLAW

2 SLIDE THE ELEMENT INTO THE SUPER
STRUCTURE CLAWS

VIEW B

4 INSERT ELEMENT INTO ONE SIDE OF THE END
CLAWS (VIEW D) AND WITH A ROCKING MOTION
PUSH ELEMENT UPWARD UNTIL IT SNAPS IN (VIEW
E)

VIEW D

SLIDE ELEMENT STARTING
AT THIS POINT

ELEMENT STOP
(BOTH ENDS)

3. SLIDE THE ELEMENT INTO THE SUPER STRUCTURE
CLAWS, STARTING WITH SECOND SET FROM EITHER
END (VIEW C) AND CONTINUE TO SLIDE THE BLADE
ELEMENT INTO ALL THE SUPER STRUCTURE CLAWS
TO THE ELEMENT STOP (VIEW C)

VIEW C

VIEW E

tccs1236

Fig. 140 Trico® wiper blade insert (element) replacement

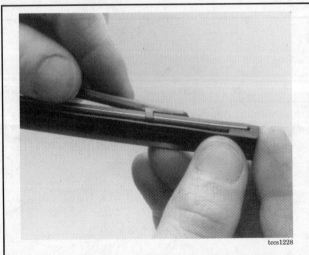

tccs1228

Fig. 141 To remove and install a Lexor® wiper blade refill, slip out the old insert and slide in a new one

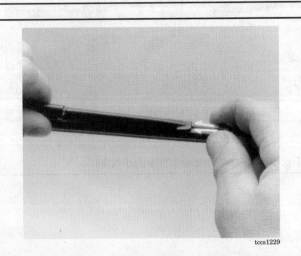

tccs1229

Fig. 142 On Pylon® inserts, remove the clip at the end prior to sliding the insert off. Don't forget to reinstall the clip

BLADE REPLACEMENT

1. Cycle arm and blade assembly to a position on the windshield where removal of blade assembly can be performed without difficulty. Turn ignition key off at desired position.
2. To remove blade assembly from wiper arm, pull up on spring lock and pull blade assembly from pin (View A). Be sure spring lock is not pulled excessively or it will become distorted.
3. To install, push the blade assembly onto the pin so that the spring lock engages the pin (View A). Be sure the blade assembly is securely attached to pin.

ELEMENT REPLACEMENT

1. In the plastic backing strip which is part of the rubber blade assembly, there is an 11.11mm (7/16 inch) long notch located approximately one inch from either end. Locate either notch.
2. Place the frame of the wiper blade assembly on a firm surface with either notched end of the backing strip visible.
3. Grasp the frame portion of the wiper blade assembly and push down until the blade assembly is tightly bowed.
4. With the blade assembly in the bowed position, grasp the tip of the backing strip firmly, pulling up and twisting C.C.W. at the same time. The backing strip will then snap out of the retaining tab on the end of the frame.
5. Lift the wiper blade assembly from the surface and slide the backing strip down the frame until the notch lines up with the next retaining tab, twist slightly, and the backing strip will snap out. Continue this operation with the remaining tabs until the blade element is completely detached from the frame.
6. To install blade element, reverse the above procedure, making sure all six (6) tabs are locked to the backing strip before installing blade to wiper arm.

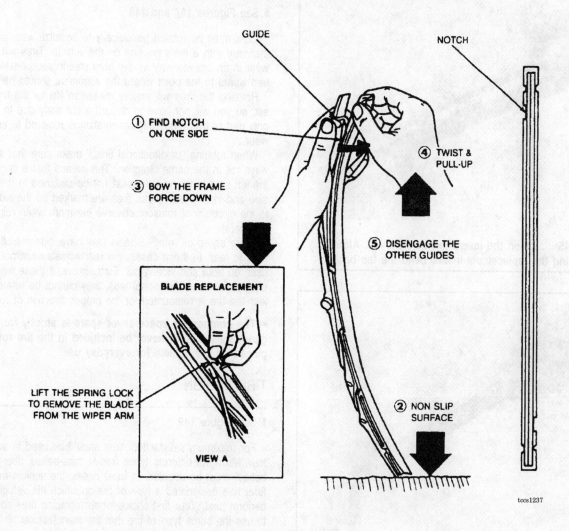

Fig. 143 Tridon® wiper blade insert (element) replacement

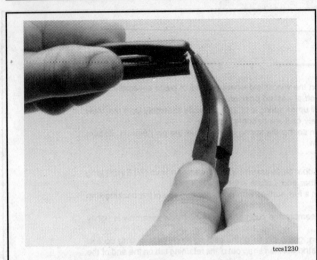

Fig. 144 On Trico® wiper blades, the tab at the end of the blade must be turned up . . .

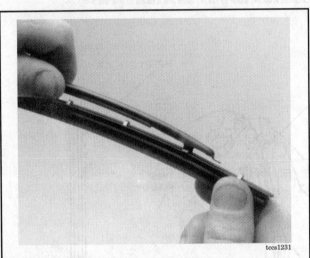

Fig. 145 . . . then the insert can be removed. After installing the replacement insert, bend the tab back

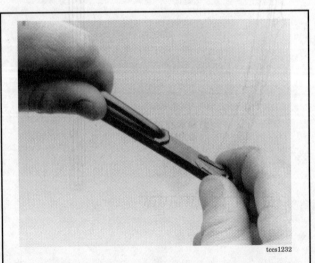

Fig. 146 The Tripledge® wiper blade insert is removed and installed using a securing clip

Tires and Wheels

Common sense and good driving habits will afford maximum tire life. Fast starts, sudden stops and hard cornering are hard on tires and will shorten their useful life span. Make sure that you don't overload the vehicle or run with incorrect pressure in the tires. Both of these practices will increase tread wear.

➡**For optimum tire life, keep the tires properly inflated, rotate them often and have the wheel alignment checked periodically.**

Inspect your tires frequently. Be especially careful to watch for bubbles in the tread or sidewall, deep cuts or underinflation. Replace any tires with bubbles in the sidewall. If cuts are so deep that they penetrate to the cords, discard the tire. Any cut in the sidewall of a radial tire renders it unsafe. Also look for uneven tread wear patterns that may indicate the front end is out of alignment or that the tires are out of balance.

TIRE ROTATION

▶ **See Figures 147 and 148**

Tires must be rotated periodically to equalize wear patterns that vary with a tire's position on the vehicle. Tires will also wear in an uneven way as the front steering/suspension system wears to the point where the alignment should be reset.

Rotating the tires will ensure maximum life for the tires as a set, so you will not have to discard a tire early due to wear on only part of the tread. Regular rotation is required to equalize wear.

When rotating "unidirectional tires," make sure that they always roll in the same direction. This means that a tire used on the left side of the vehicle must not be switched to the right side and vice-versa. These tires are marked on the sidewall as to the direction of rotation; observe the mark when reinstalling the tire(s).

Some styled or "mag" wheels may have different offsets front to rear. In these cases, the rear wheels must not be used up front and vice-versa. Furthermore, if these wheels are equipped with unidirectional tires, they cannot be rotated unless the tire is remounted for the proper direction of rotation.

➡**The compact or space-saver spare is strictly for emergency use. It must never be included in the tire rotation or placed on the vehicle for everyday use.**

TIRE DESIGN

▶ **See Figure 149**

For maximum satisfaction, tires should be used in sets of four. Mixing of different types (radial, bias-belted, fiberglass belted) must be avoided. In most cases, the vehicle manufacturer has designated a type of tire on which the vehicle will perform best. Your first choice when replacing tires should be to use the same type of tire that the manufacturer recommends.

When radial tires are used, tire sizes and wheel diameters should be selected to maintain ground clearance and tire load

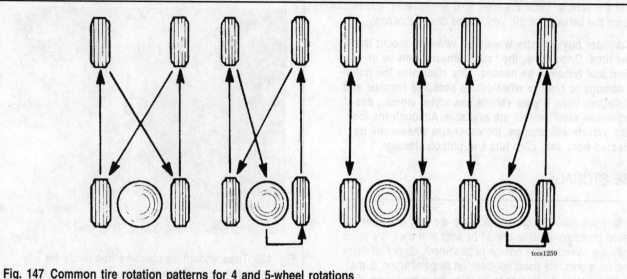

Fig. 147 Common tire rotation patterns for 4 and 5-wheel rotations

Fig. 148 Unidirectional tires, identified by an arrow or the word "rotation" can only be rotated on the same side of the vehicle (front-to-rear).

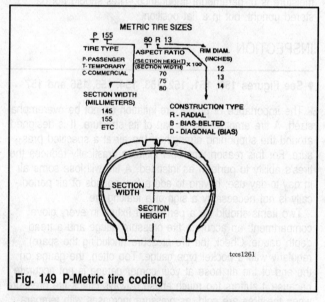

Fig. 149 P-Metric tire coding

capacity equivalent to the original specified tire. Radial tires should always be used in sets of four.

❊❊CAUTION

Radial tires should never be used on only the front axle.

When selecting tires, pay attention to the original size as marked on the tire. Most tires are described using an industry size code sometimes referred to as P-Metric. This allows the exact identification of the tire specifications, regardless of the manufacturer. If selecting a different tire size or brand, remember to check the installed tire for any sign of interference with the body or suspension while the vehicle is stopping, turning sharply or heavily loaded.

Snow Tires

Good radial tires can produce a big advantage in slippery weather, but in snow, a street radial tire does not have suffi-

cient tread to provide traction and control. The small grooves of a street tire quickly pack with snow and the tire behaves like a billiard ball on a marble floor. The more open, chunky tread of a snow tire will self-clean as the tire turns, providing much better grip on snowy surfaces.

To satisfy municipalities requiring snow tires during weather emergencies, most snow tires carry either an M + S designation after the tire size stamped on the sidewall, or the designation "all-season." In general, no change in tire size is necessary when buying snow tires.

Most manufacturers strongly recommend the use of 4 snow tires on their vehicles for reasons of stability. If snow tires are fitted only to the drive wheels, the opposite end of the vehicle may become very unstable when braking or turning on slippery surfaces. This instability can lead to unpleasant endings if the driver can't counteract the slide in time.

Note that snow tires, whether 2 or 4, will affect vehicle handling in all non-snow situations. The stiffer, heavier snow tires will noticeably change the turning and braking characteristics of the vehicle. Once the snow tires are installed, you must re-learn the behavior of the vehicle and drive accordingly.

➡Consider buying extra wheels on which to mount the snow tires. Once done, the "snow wheels" can be installed and removed as needed. This eliminates the potential damage to tires or wheels from seasonal removal and installation. Even if your vehicle has styled wheels, see if inexpensive steel wheels are available. Although the look of the vehicle will change, the expensive wheels will be protected from salt, curb hits and pothole damage.

TIRE STORAGE

If they are mounted on wheels, store the tires at proper inflation pressure. All tires should be kept in a cool, dry place. If they are stored in the garage or basement, do not let them stand on a concrete floor; set them on strips of wood, a mat or a large stack of newspaper. Keeping them away from direct moisture is of paramount importance. Tires should not be stored upright, but in a flat position.

INSPECTION

▶ **See Figures 150, 151, 152, 153, 154, 155, 156 and 157**

The importance of proper tire inflation cannot be overemphasized. A tire employs air as part of its structure. It is designed around the supporting strength of the air at a specified pressure. For this reason, improper inflation drastically reduces the tires's ability to perform as intended. A tire will lose some air in day-to-day use; having to add a few pounds of air periodically is not necessarily a sign of a leaking tire.

Two items should be a permanent fixture in every glove compartment: an accurate tire pressure gauge and a tread depth gauge. Check the tire pressure (including the spare) regularly with a pocket type gauge. Too often, the gauge on the end of the air hose at your corner garage is not accurate because it suffers too much abuse. Always check tire pressure when the tires are cold, as pressure increases with temperature. If you must move the vehicle to check the tire inflation, do not drive more than a mile before checking. A cold tire is generally one that has not been driven for more than three hours.

A plate or sticker is normally provided somewhere in the vehicle (door post, hood, tailgate or trunk lid) which shows the proper pressure for the tires. Never counteract excessive pressure build-up by bleeding off air pressure (letting some air out). This will cause the tire to run hotter and wear quicker.

✳✳CAUTION

Never exceed the maximum tire pressure embossed on the tire! This is the pressure to be used when the tire is at maximum loading, but it is rarely the correct pressure for everyday driving. Consult the owner's manual or the tire pressure sticker for the correct tire pressure.

Once you've maintained the correct tire pressures for several weeks, you'll be familiar with the vehicle's braking and handling personality. Slight adjustments in tire pressures can fine-

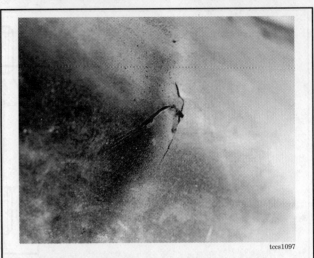

Fig. 150 Tires should be checked frequently for any sign of puncture or damage

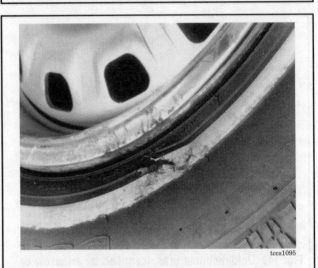

Fig. 151 Tires with deep cuts, or cuts which show bulging should be replaced immediately

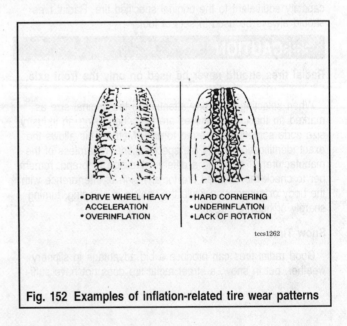

- DRIVE WHEEL HEAVY ACCELERATION
- OVERINFLATION

- HARD CORNERING
- UNDERINFLATION
- LACK OF ROTATION

Fig. 152 Examples of inflation-related tire wear patterns

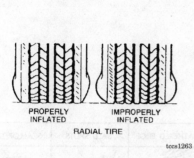

Fig. 153 Radial tires have a characteristic sidewall bulge; don't try to measure pressure by looking at the tire. Use a quality air pressure gauge

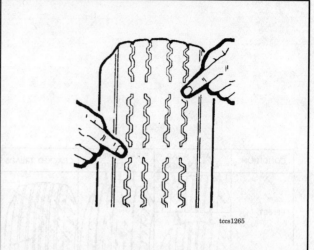

Fig. 155 Tread wear indicators will appear when the tire is worn

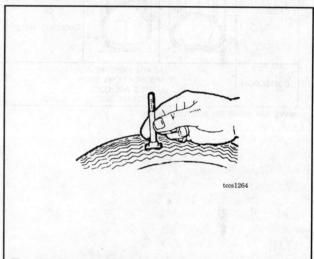

Fig. 156 Accurate tread depth indicators are inexpensive and handy

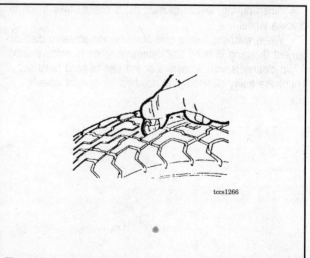

Fig. 157 A penny works well for a quick check of tread depth

tune these characteristics, but never change the cold pressure specification by more than 2 psi. A slightly softer tire pressure will give a softer ride but also yield lower fuel mileage. A slightly harder tire will give crisper dry road handling but can cause skidding on wet surfaces. Unless you're fully attuned to the vehicle, stick to the recommended inflation pressures.

All tires made since 1968 have built-in tread wear indicator bars that show up as 1/2 in. (13mm) wide smooth bands across the tire when 1/16 in. (1.5mm) of tread remains. The appearance of tread wear indicators means that the tires should be replaced. In fact, many states have laws prohibiting the use of tires with less than this amount of tread.

You can check your own tread depth with an inexpensive gauge or by using a Lincoln head penny. Slip the Lincoln penny (with Lincoln's head upside-down) into several tread grooves. If you can see the top of Lincoln's head in 2 adjacent grooves, the tire has less than 1/16 in. (1.5mm) tread left and should be replaced. You can measure snow tires in the same manner by using the "tails" side of the Lincoln penny. If you can see the top of the Lincoln memorial, it's time to replace the snow tire(s).

CARE OF SPECIAL WHEELS

If you have invested money in magnesium, aluminum alloy or sport wheels, special precautions should be taken to make sure your investment is not wasted and that your special wheels look good for the life of the vehicle.

Special wheels are easily damaged and/or scratched. Occasionally check the rims for cracking, impact damage or air leaks. If any of these are found, replace the wheel. But in order to prevent this type of damage and the costly replacement of a special wheel, observe the following precautions:

• Use extra care not to damage the wheels during removal, installation, balancing, etc. After removal of the wheels from the vehicle, place them on a mat or other protective surface. If they are to be stored for any length of time, support them on strips of wood. Never store tires and wheels upright; the tread may develop flat spots.

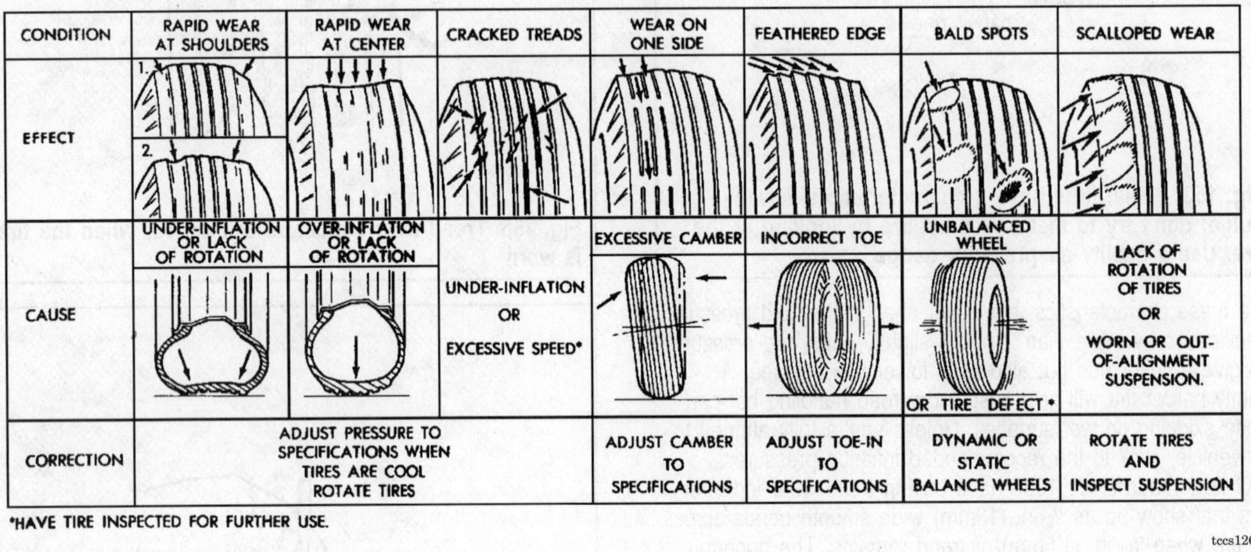

CONDITION	RAPID WEAR AT SHOULDERS	RAPID WEAR AT CENTER	CRACKED TREADS	WEAR ON ONE SIDE	FEATHERED EDGE	BALD SPOTS	SCALLOPED WEAR
EFFECT							
CAUSE	UNDER-INFLATION OR LACK OF ROTATION	OVER-INFLATION OR LACK OF ROTATION	UNDER-INFLATION OR EXCESSIVE SPEED*	EXCESSIVE CAMBER	INCORRECT TOE	UNBALANCED WHEEL OR TIRE DEFECT*	LACK OF ROTATION OF TIRES OR WORN OR OUT-OF-ALIGNMENT SUSPENSION.
CORRECTION		ADJUST PRESSURE TO SPECIFICATIONS WHEN TIRES ARE COOL ROTATE TIRES		ADJUST CAMBER TO SPECIFICATIONS	ADJUST TOE-IN TO SPECIFICATIONS	DYNAMIC OR STATIC BALANCE WHEELS	ROTATE TIRES AND INSPECT SUSPENSION

*HAVE TIRE INSPECTED FOR FURTHER USE.

tccs1267

Fig. 154 Common tire wear patterns and causes

• When driving, watch for hazards; it doesn't take much to crack a wheel.

• When washing, use a mild soap or non-abrasive dish detergent (keeping in mind that detergent tends to remove wax). Avoid cleansers with abrasives or the use of hard brushes. There are many cleaners and polishes for special wheels.

• If possible, remove the wheels during the winter. Salt and sand used for snow removal can severely damage the finish of a wheel.

• Make certain the recommended lug nut torque is never exceeded or the wheel may crack. Never use snow chains on special wheels; severe scratching will occur.

Troubleshooting Basic Wheel Problems

Problem	Cause	Solution
The car's front end vibrates at high speed	• The wheels are out of balance • Wheels are out of alignment	• Have wheels balanced • Have wheel alignment checked/adjusted
Car pulls to either side	• Wheels are out of alignment • Unequal tire pressure • Different size tires or wheels	• Have wheel alignment checked/adjusted • Check/adjust tire pressure • Change tires or wheels to same size
The car's wheel(s) wobbles	• Loose wheel lug nuts • Wheels out of balance • Damaged wheel • Wheels are out of alignment • Worn or damaged ball joint • Excessive play in the steering linkage (usually due to worn parts) • Defective shock absorber	• Tighten wheel lug nuts • Have tires balanced • Raise car and spin the wheel. If the wheel is bent, it should be replaced • Have wheel alignment checked/adjusted • Check ball joints • Check steering linkage • Check shock absorbers
Tires wear unevenly or prematurely	• Incorrect wheel size • Wheels are out of balance • Wheels are out of alignment	• Check if wheel and tire size are compatible • Have wheels balanced • Have wheel alignment checked/adjusted

86741c01

Troubleshooting Basic Tire Problems

Problem	Cause	Solution
The car's front end vibrates at high speeds and the steering wheel shakes	• Wheels out of balance • Front end needs aligning	• Have wheels balanced • Have front end alignment checked
The car pulls to one side while cruising	• Unequal tire pressure (car will usually pull to the low side) • Mismatched tires • Front end needs aligning	• Check/adjust tire pressure • Be sure tires are of the same type and size • Have front end alignment checked
Abnormal, excessive or uneven tire wear See "How to Read Tire Wear"	• Infrequent tire rotation • Improper tire pressure • Sudden stops/starts or high speed on curves	• Rotate tires more frequently to equalize wear • Check/adjust pressure • Correct driving habits
Tire squeals	• Improper tire pressure • Front end needs aligning	• Check/adjust tire pressure • Have front end alignment checked

86741c02

Tire Size Comparison Chart

"Letter" sizes			Inch Sizes	Metric-inch Sizes		
"60 Series"	"70 Series"	"78 Series"	1965–77	"60 Series"	"70 Series"	"80 Series"
			5.50-12, 5.60-12	165/60-12	165/70-12	155-12
		Y78-12	6.00-12			
		W78-13	5.20-13	165/60-13	145/70-13	135-13
		Y78-13	5.60-13	175/60-13	155/70-13	145-13
			6.15-13	185/60-13	165/70-13	155-13, P155/80-13
A60-13	A70-13	A78-13	6.40-13	195/60-13	175/70-13	165-13
B60-13	B70-13	B78-13	6.70-13	205/60-13	185/70-13	175-13
			6.90-13			
C60-13	C70-13	C78-13	7.00-13	215/60-13	195/70-13	185-13
D60-13	D70-13	D78-13	7.25-13			
E60-13	E70-13	E78-13	7.75-13			195-13
			5.20-14	165/60-14	145/70-14	135-14
			5.60-14	175/60-14	155/70-14	145-14
			5.90-14			
A60-14	A70-14	A78-14	6.15-14	185/60-14	165/70-14	155-14
	B70-14	B78-14	6.45-14	195/60-14	175/70-14	165-14
	C70-14	C78-14	6.95-14	205/60-14	185/70-14	175-14
D60-14	D70-14	D78-14				
E60-14	E70-14	E78-14	7.35-14	215/60-14	195/70-14	185-14
F60-14	F70-14	F78-14, F83-14	7.75-14	225/60-14	200/70-14	195-14
G60-14	G70-14	G77-14, G78-14	8.25-14	235/60-14	205/70-14	205-14
H60-14	H70-14	H78-14	8.55-14	245/60-14	215/70-14	215-14
J60-14	J70-14	J78-14	8.85-14	255/60-14	225/70-14	225-14
L60-14	L70-14		9.15-14	265/60-14	235/70-14	
	A70-15	A78-15	5.60-15	185/60-15	165/70-15	155-15
B60-15	B70-15	B78-15	6.35-15	195/60-15	175/70-15	165-15
C60-15	C70-15	C78-15	6.85-15	205/60-15	185/70-15	175-15
	D70-15	D78-15				
E60-15	E70-15	E78-15	7.35-15	215/60-15	195/70-15	185-15
F60-15	F70-15	F78-15	7.75-15	225/60-15	205/70-15	195-15
G60-15	G70-15	G78-15	8.15-15/8.25-15	235/60-15	215/70-15	205-15
H60-15	H70-15	H78-15	8.45-15/8.55-15	245/60-15	225/70-15	215-15
J60-15	J70-15	J78-15	8.85-15/8.90-15	255/60-15	235/70-15	225-15
	K70-15		9.00-15	265/60-15	245/70-15	230-15
L60-15	L70-15	L78-15, L84-15	9.15-15			235-15
	M70-15	M78-15				255-15
		N78-15				

Note: Every size tire is not listed and many size comparisons are approximate, based on load ratings. Wider tires than those supplied new with the vehicle, should always be checked for clearance.

86741c03

FLUIDS AND LUBRICANTS

Fluid Disposal

Used fluids such as engine oil, transmission fluid, antifreeze and brake fluid are hazardous wastes and must be disposed of properly. Before draining any fluids, consult with your local authorities; in many areas, waste oil, antifreeze, etc. is being accepted as a part of recycling programs. A number of service stations and auto parts stores are also accepting waste fluids for recycling.

Be sure of the recycling center's policies before draining any fluids, as many will not accept different fluids that have been mixed together.

Oil and Fuel Recommendations

OIL

▶ See Figure 158

Jeep recommends the use of what are called "multigrade" oils. These are specially formulated to change their viscosity with a change in temperature, unlike straight grade oils. The oils are designated by the use of two numbers, the first referring to the thickness of the oil, relative to straight mineral oils, at a low temperature such as 0°F (-18°C). The second number refers to the thickness, also relative to straight mineral oils, at high temperatures typical of highway driving (200°F 93°C). These numbers are preceded by the designation "SAE," representing the Society of Automotive Engineers which sets the viscosity standards. For example, use of an SAE 10W-40 oil would give nearly ideal engine operation under almost all operating conditions. The oil would be as thin as a straight 10 weight oil at cold cranking temperatures, and as thick as a straight 40 weight oil at hot running conditions.

SYNTHETIC OIL

There are excellent synthetic and fuel-efficient oils available that, under the right circumstances, can help provide better fuel mileage and better engine protection. However, these advantages come at a price, which can be more than the cost per quart of conventional motor oils.

Before pouring any synthetic oils into your vehicle's engine, you should consider the condition of the engine and the type of driving you do. Also, check the manufacturer's warranty conditions regarding the use of synthetics.

Generally, it is best to avoid the use of synthetic oil in both brand new and older, high mileage engines. New engines require a proper break-in, and the synthetics are so slippery that they can hinder this. Most manufacturers recommend that you wait at least 5,000 miles (8,000 km) before switching to a synthetic oil. Conversely, older engines are looser and tend to use more oil. Synthetics will slip past worn parts more readily than regular oil. If your truck already leaks oil (due to worn parts and bad seals or gaskets), it will leak more with a slippery synthetic inside.

Consider your type of driving. If most of your accumulated mileage is on the highway at higher, steadier speeds, a synthetic oil will reduce friction and probably help deliver better fuel mileage. Under such ideal highway conditions, the oil change interval can be extended, as long as the oil filter will operate effectively for the extended life of the oil. If the filter can't do its job for this extended period, dirt and sludge will build up in your engine's crankcase, sump, oil pump and lines, no matter what type of oil is used. If using synthetic oil in this manner, you should continue to change the oil filter at the recommended intervals.

Vehicles used under harder, stop-and-go, short hop circumstances should always be serviced more frequently, and for these vehicles, synthetic oil may not be a wise investment. Because of the necessary shorter change interval needed for this type of driving, you cannot take advantage of the long recommended change interval of most synthetic oils.

GASOLINE

A prime requirement for gasoline is the use of unleaded fuel only. All the vehicles covered in this manual require the use of unleaded fuel exclusively, to protect the catalytic converter. Failure to follow this recommendation will result in failure of the catalyst and consequent failure to pass the emission test many states now require. The use of unleaded fuel also prolongs the life of spark plugs, the engine as a whole, and the exhaust system.

Fuels of the same octane rating have varying anti-knock qualities. Thus, if your engine knocks or pings, try switching brands of gasoline before trying a more expensive higher octane fuel. Fuel should be selected for the brand and octane which performs without pinging.

Your engine's fuel requirements can change with time, due to carbon buildup which changes the compression ratio. If switching brands or grades of gas doesn't work, check the ignition timing. If it is necessary to retard timing from specifications, don't change it more than about 4°. Retarded timing will reduce power output and fuel mileage, and will also increase engine temperature.

Basic engine octane requirements, to be used in your initial choice of fuel, are 87 octane, unleaded. This rating is an average of Research and Motor methods of determination: (R+M)/2. For increased vehicle performance and gas mileage, use a premium unleaded fuel, that is, one with a rating of at least 91 octane. More octane results in better performance and economy in these engines because the ignition system will compensate for its characteristics by advancing the timing.

Gasohol consisting of 10% ethanol and 90% gasoline may be used in your vehicle, but gasolines containing methanol (wood alcohol) are not approved. They can damage fuel system parts and cause operating problems.

DIESEL

The diesel engine in your Jeep is designed to run on No. 2 diesel fuel with a cetane rating of 40. For operation when the outdoor air temperature is consistently below freezing, the use of No.1 diesel fuel or the addition of a cold weather additive is recommended.

Fuel makers produce two grades of diesel fuel, No. 1 and No. 2, for use in automotive diesel engines. Generally speaking, No. 2 fuel is recommended over No. 1 for driving in temperatures above 20°F (-7°C). In fact, in many areas, No. 2 diesel is the only fuel available. By comparison, No. 2 diesel fuel is less volatile than No. 1 fuel, and gives better fuel economy. No. 2 fuel is also a better injection pump lubricant.

Two important characteristics of diesel fuel are its cetane number and its viscosity.

The cetane number of a diesel fuel refers to the ease with which a diesel fuel ignites. High cetane numbers mean that the fuel will ignite with relative ease or that it ignites well at

Fig. 158 Look for the API oil identification label when choosing your engine oil

low temperatures. Naturally, the lower the cetane number, the higher the temperature must be to ignite the fuel. Most commercial fuels have cetane numbers that range from 35 to 65. No. 1 diesel fuel generally has a higher cetane rating than No. 2 fuel.

Viscosity is the ability of a liquid, in this case diesel fuel, to flow. Using straight No. 2 diesel fuel below 20°F (-7°C) can cause problems, because this fuel tends to become cloudy, meaning wax crystals begin forming in the fuel. 20°F (-7°C) is often called the cloud point for No. 2 fuel. In extremely cold weather No. 2 fuel can stop flowing altogether. In either case, fuel flow is restricted, which can result in a no-start condition or poor engine performance. Fuel manufacturers often winterize No. 2 diesel fuel by using various fuel additives and blends (No. 1 diesel fuel, kerosene, etc.) to lower its wintertime viscosity. Generally speaking, though, No. 1 diesel fuel is more satisfactory in extremely cold weather.

➡No. 1 and No. 2 diesel fuels will mix and burn with no ill effects, although the engine manufacturer will undoubtedly recommend one or the other. Consult the owner's manual for information.

Depending on local climate, most fuel manufacturers make winterized No. 2 fuel available seasonally.

Many automobile manufacturers publish pamphlets giving the locations of diesel fuel stations nationwide. Contact the local dealer for information.

Do not substitute home heating oil for automotive diesel fuel. While in some cases, home heating oil refinement levels equal those of diesel fuel, many times they are far below diesel engine requirements. The result of using dirty home heating oil will be a clogged fuel system, in which case the entire system may have to be dismantled and cleaned.

One more word on diesel fuels. Don't thin diesel fuel with gasoline in cold weather. The lighter gasoline, which is more explosive, will cause rough running at the very least, and may cause extensive damage to the fuel system if enough is used.

Engine

✳✳CAUTION

The EPA warns that prolonged contact with used engine oil may cause a number of skin disorders, including cancer! You should make every effort to minimize your exposure to used engine oil. Protective gloves should be worn when changing the oil. Wash your hands and any other exposed skin areas as soon as possible after exposure to used engine oil. Soap and water, or waterless hand cleaner, should be used.

OIL LEVEL CHECK

▶ See Figures 159, 160 and 161

1. With the engine **OFF**. Park your vehicle is on a level surface to ensure an accurate reading.
2. Let the engine cool for a few moments to allow the oil to drain into the crankcase.

3. Raise the hood and position the hold-up rod, if so equipped.
4. Remove the oil dipstick from the right side of 4-cylinder engines or on the left of 6-cylinder engines and wipe it clean.
5. Reinstall the dipstick until it is firmly seated in the tube.
6. Remove the dipstick and take the oil level reading.
7. Add oil through the valve cover filler hole if the oil level is below the add mark on the dipstick.
8. Allow sufficient time for all the oil to drain into the crankcase after you have added it and recheck the oil level.

OIL AND FILTER CHANGE

▶ See Figures 162, 163, 164, 165 and 166

✳✳CAUTION

The EPA warns that prolonged contact with used engine oil may cause a number of skin disorders, including cancer! You should make every effort to minimize your exposure to used engine oil. Protective gloves should be worn when changing the oil. Wash your hands and any other exposed skin areas as soon as possible after exposure to used engine oil. Soap and water, or waterless hand cleaner should be used.

The engine oil is to be changed every 7,500 miles (1,200 km). The oil should be changed more frequently, however, under conditions such as:

- Driving in dusty conditions
- Continuous trailer pulling or RV use
- Extensive or prolonged idling
- Extensive short trip operation in freezing temperatures (when the engine is not thoroughly warmed up)
- Frequent long runs at high speeds and high ambient temperatures
- Stop-and-go service, such as delivery vehicles

If any of these conditions exist, the recommended oil and filter change interval should be reduced to every 3,000 miles (4,800 km). Operation of the engine in severe conditions such

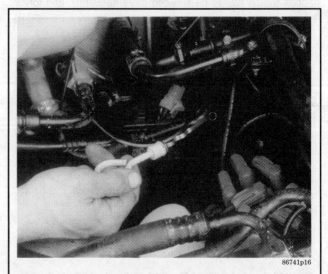

86741p16

Fig. 159 Remove the engine oil dipstick

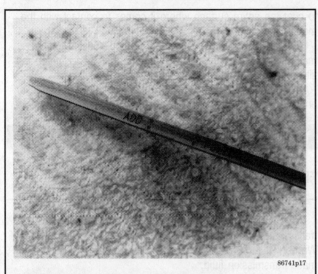

Fig. 160 After removing the dipstick check the oil level

Fig. 161 If needed, add the proper amount and grade of oil

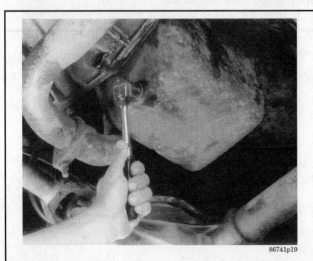

Fig. 162 Loosen the oil pan drain plug using a socket and rachet

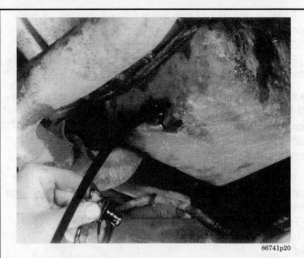

Fig. 163 Remove the oil pan drain plug and let the engine oil completely drain

as a dust storm, volcanic ash or deep water may require an immediate oil and filter change.

1. Before draining the oil, make sure that the engine is at operating temperature. Hot oil will hold more impurities in suspension and will flow better, allowing it to remove more oil and dirt.

2. Raise the vehicle and support it safely with jackstands, then remove the oil filler cap.

3. Place a suitable drain pan under the oil pan.

4. Using the proper size socket and rachet, loosen the oil pan drain plug.

5. Unscrew the plug with your fingers using a rag to shield your fingers from the heat. Push in on the plug as you unscrew it so you can feel when all of the screw threads are out of the hole. You can then remove the plug quickly with the minimum amount of oil running down your arm. You will also have the plug in your hand and not in the bottom of a pan of hot oil. Be careful of the oil. If it is at operating temperatures, it is hot enough to burn you or at least make you uncomfortable.

Fig. 164 Remove the old oil filter using a suitable oil filter wrench

6. When the oil has completely drained from the oil pan, reinstall the drain plug.

7. Place a suitable drain pan under the filter.

8. Using a suitable oil filter wrench, loosen and remove the filter by turning it counterclockwise.

➡When using a band type oil filter wrench to remove an oil filter, place the wrench as high up on the filter as possible (closest to the filter mounting pad). This will reduce the chance of crushing the oil filter and making it very difficult to remove.

9. With a rag wrapped around the filter, unscrew the filter from the oil pump housing. Be careful of hot oil that might run down the side of the filter.

To install:

10. Wipe the base of the mounting pad with a clean, dry cloth.

11. Before you install the new filter, smear a small amount of clean oil on the oil filter gasket with your finger, just enough to coat the entire surface where it comes in contact with the mounting pad.

12. Install the oil filter onto the oil pump housing until it makes contact with the sealing surface, then hand-tighten the filter one full turn, do not overtighten.

13. Fill the crankcase with the proper amount and grade of engine oil.

Manual Transmissions

FLUID RECOMMENDATIONS

Recommended lubricant for AX4/5/15 and BA10/5 manual transmissions is SAE 75W-90, API Grade GL-5 gear lubricant. Warner T4 & T5 manual transmissions use DEXRON®II automatic transmission fluid.

LEVEL CHECK

▶ **See Figures 167 and 168**

The level of lubricant in the transmission should be maintained at the filler hole on all manual transmissions. This hole may be located on either side of the transmission case.

1. Raise and safely support the vehicle using jackstands.

2. Remove the filler hole plug.

3. Being careful of sharp edges, insert your finger into the filler hole. The lube should be within ¼ in. (6mm) of the bottom edge pf the hole.

4. After checking the level, make sure to reinstall the filler hole plug.

5. Lower the vehicle.

DRAIN AND REFILL

The lubricant in the manual transmission should be changed every 30,000 miles (48,000 km).

1. Raise the vehicle and safely support it with jackstands.

Fig. 165 Before installing a new oil filter, lightly coat the rubber gasket with clean oil

Fig. 166 Fill the crankcase with proper amount and grade of engine oil

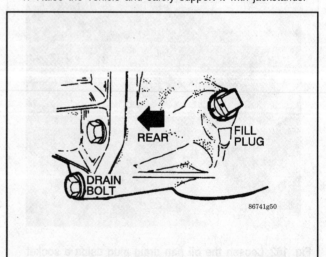

Fig. 167 Manual transmission fill and drain plugs, using a tailshaft bolt as the drain plug

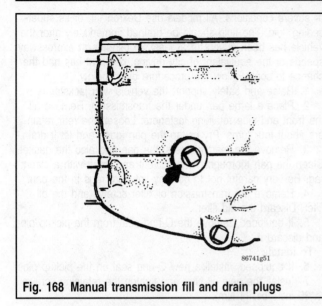

Fig. 168 Manual transmission fill and drain plugs

2. Remove the filler hole plug from the transmission case.

3. Place a container to collect the fluid under the drain hole.

4. Remove the drain plug which is located at the bottom of the transmission or on either side near the bottom, and allow all the fluid to drain into the container.

5. Reinstall the drain plug.

6. Refill the transmission with the recommended lubricant added in small amounts through the filler hole.

7. After the proper fluid level has been reached, install the filler hole plug and lower the vehicle.

Automatic Transmission

FLUID RECOMMENDATIONS

Use only DEXRON®II or its superceding automatic transmission fluid.

LEVEL CHECK

▶ **See Figures 169, 170, 171 and 172**

The fluid level in automatic transmissions is checked with a dipstick located in the filler pipe at the right rear of the engine. The fluid level should be maintained between the ADD and FULL marks on the end of the dipstick, with the automatic transmission fluid at normal operating temperature. To raise the level from the ADD mark to the FULL mark requires the addition of one pint of fluid. The fluid level with the fluid at room temperature (75°F or 24°C) should be approximately 4¼ in. (10.8cm) below the ADD mark.

➡**In checking the automatic transmission fluid, insert the dipstick in the filler tube with the markings toward the center of the truck. Also, remember that the FULL mark on the dipstick is the indication of the level of the automatic**

Fig. 169 Remove the automatic transmission dipstick

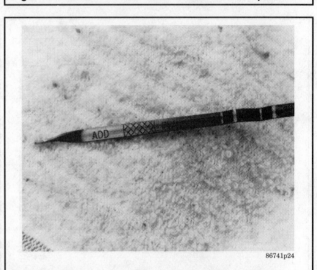

Fig. 170 Wipe the dipstick off with a clean rag and reinsert it in the tube to obtain a correct reading

transmission fluid when it is at operating temperature. This temperature is only obtained after at least 15 miles of expressway driving or the equivalent of city driving.

To check the automatic transmission fluid level, follow the procedure given below. This procedure is applicable either when the fluid is at room temperature or at operating temperature.

1. With the transmission in Park, the engine running at idle speed, the foot brake applied and the vehicle resting on level ground, move the transmission gear selector through each of the gear positions, including Reverse, allowing time for the transmission to engage.

2. Return the shift selector to the Park position and apply the parking brake. Do not turn the engine off, but leave it running at idle speed.

3. Clean all dirt from around the transmission dipstick cap and the end of the filler tube.

4. Pull the dipstick out of the tube, wipe it off with a clean cloth, and push it back into the tube all the way, making sure that it seats completely.

5. Pull the dipstick out of the tube again and read the level of the fluid.

6. The level should be between the ADD and FULL marks. Do not overfill the transmission because this will cause foaming, loss of fluid through the vent and malfunctioning of the transmission.

➡**Transmission fluid should be light red and free of foreign material. If the fluid is dark brown or black in color and smells burnt, the fluid has been overheated and should be replaced.**

FLUID AND FILTER CHANGE

▶ **See Figures 173, 174, 175, 176, 177 and 178**

The transmission fluid in an automatic transmission should be changed every 30,000 miles (48,000 km) of normal driving or every 15,000 miles (24,000 km) of driving under abnormal or severe conditions. All models use Dexron®II, or its superceding fluid. The fluid should be drained immediately after the vehicle has been driven for at least 20 minutes at expressway speeds or the equivalent of city driving, before it has had the chance to cool. Follow the procedure given below:

1. Raise and safely support the vehicle with jackstands.

2. Place a large pan under the transmission. Remove all the front and side retaining fasteners. Loosen the rear retainers about four turns. Pry or tap the pan loose and let it drain.

3. Remove the rear retainers, the pan and also the gasket. Clean the pan thoroughly with solvent and dry it with a clean rag. Be very careful not to get any lint from rags in the pan.

4. Remove the transmission oil filter screws and the oil filter. Discard the old filter.

5. If equipped, remove the O-ring seal from the pickup pipe and discard it.

   To install:

6. If equipped, install a new O-ring seal on the pickup pipe.

7. Install the new oil filter and tighten the retaining screws to 35 inch lbs. (4 Nm).

Fig. 171 If necessary, add the proper type and amount of transmission fluid

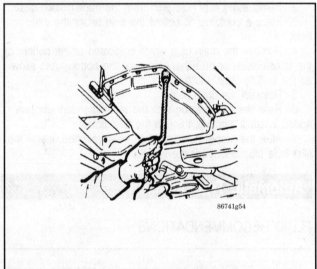

Fig. 173 Remove the transmission pan bolts

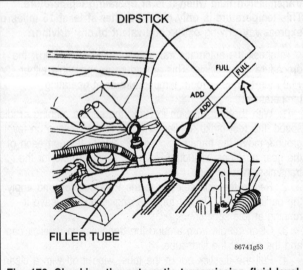

Fig. 172 Checking the automatic transmission fluid level

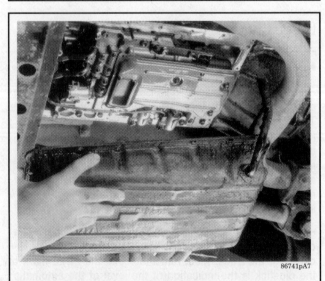

Fig. 174 Remove the transmission pan

8. Position a new gasket on the pan mating surface. Install the pan and secure it with the retaining fasteners. Tighten the retainers to 150 inch lbs. (17 Nm).

9. Lower the vehicle and remove the transmission dipstick.

10. Insert a clean transmission fluid funnel in the transmission dipstick tube.

11. Pour about 4 quarts (3.79L) of automatic transmission fluid in the filler pipe.

12. Start the engine. Do not race it. Allow the engine to idle for a few minutes.

13. Move the transmission gear selector through each of the gear positions, including Reverse, allowing time for the transmission to engage.

14. Return the shift selector to the Park position and apply the parking brake. Do not turn the engine off, but leave it running at idle speed.

15. Insert the dipstick into the tube.

16. Pull the dipstick out of the tube again and read the level of the fluid on the stick.

17. Add fluid as necessary. Do not overfill the transmission.

18. Drive the vehicle long enough to thoroughly warm up the transmission. Recheck the fluid level and add fluid as necessary.

Transfer Case

FLUID RECOMMENDATION

All transfer cases covered by this manual use Dexron®II automatic transmission fluid.

LEVEL CHECK

▶ **See Figures 179 and 180**

Fluid should be maintained at the level of the filler plug hole. When you check the lubricant, make sure that the vehicle is level so that you get a true reading. When the filler plug is removed, the lubricant should run out of the hole. If there is

Fig. 175 Remove the filter retaining bolts

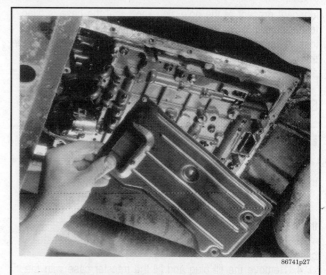

Fig. 176 Remove the filter from the transmission

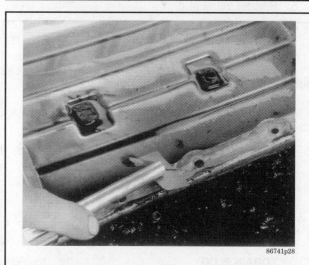

Fig. 177 Clean the pan thoroughly with solvent and dry it with a clean rag

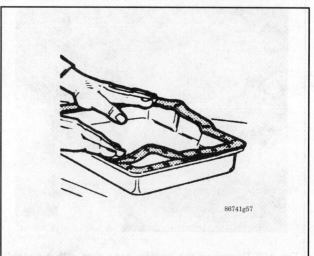

Fig. 178 Position a new gasket on the pan mating surface

lubricant present at the hole, you know that the case is filled to the proper level. Replace the plug quickly for a minimum loss of lubricant. If lubricant does not run out of the hole when the plug is removed, lubricant should be added. Replace the plug as soon as the lubricant reaches the level of the hole.

DRAIN AND REFILL

▶ **See Figures 181 and 182**

All transfer cases are to be serviced at the same time and in the same manner as the manual transmissions.
1. Raise the vehicle and safely support it with jackstands.
2. Place a large pan under the transfer case and remove the transfer case drain plug.
3. Let all of the fluid drain completely from the transfer case, then reinstall the drain plug.
4. Remove the fill plug and fill the transfer case with the proper type and amount of fluid.
5. Reinstall the fill plug.

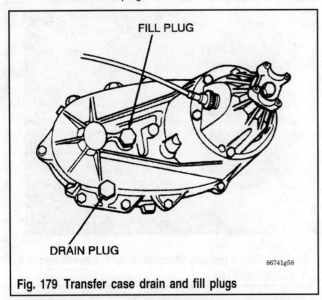

Fig. 179 Transfer case drain and fill plugs

Fig. 180 Removing the transfer case plug with a socket and rachet

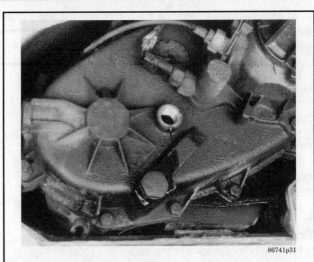

Fig. 181 Remove the transfer case drain plug and let the fluid completely drain

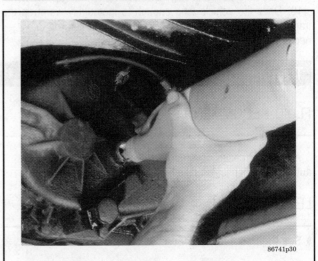

Fig. 182 Fill the transfer case with the proper type and amount of fluid

Front and Rear Axle

FLUID RECOMMENDATIONS

The standard front and rear axle differentials use SAE 75W/90, API grade GL 5 hypoid gear lubricant. SAE 80W-140 API grade GL 5 hypoid gear lubricant is recommended when trailer towing. With Trac-Lok® (limited slip) differentials, add a container of Trac-Lok® lubricant additive.

FLUID LEVEL CHECK

▶ **See Figures 183, 184, 185, 186, 187, 188, 189 and 190**

Check the level of the oil in the differential housing every 7,500 miles (12,000 km) under normal driving conditions, and every 3,000 miles (4,800 km) if the vehicle is used in severe

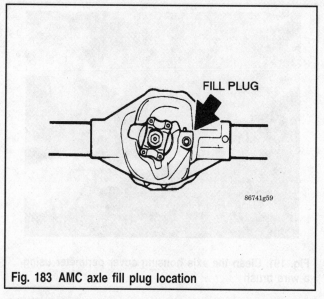

Fig. 183 AMC axle fill plug location

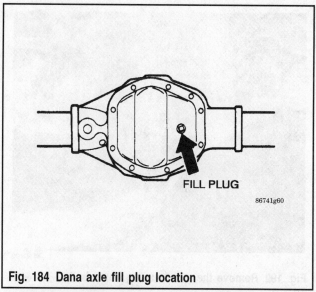

Fig. 184 Dana axle fill plug location

Fig. 185 Loosen the front axle drain plug

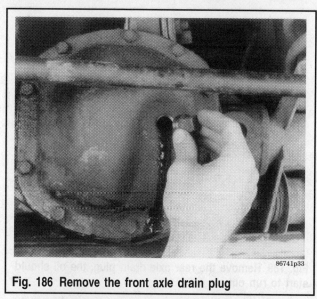

Fig. 186 Remove the front axle drain plug

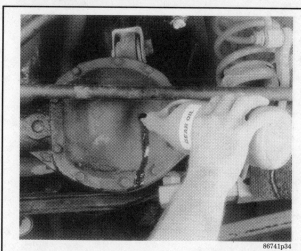

Fig. 187 If necessary, add the proper amount of gear oil

Fig. 188 Loosen the rear axle drain plug

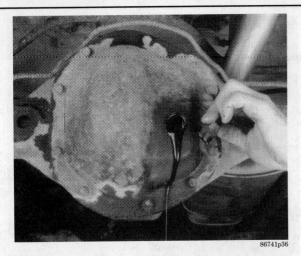

Fig. 189 Remove the rear axle drain plug, the oil should start to run out

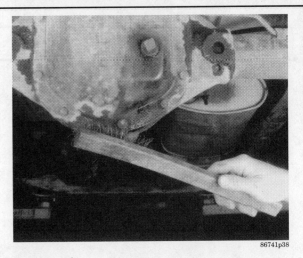

Fig. 191 Clean the axle housing cover perimeter using a wire brush

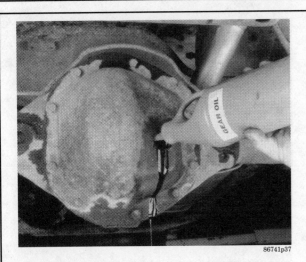

Fig. 190 If necessary, add the proper amount of gear oil

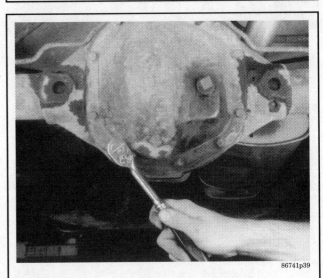

Fig. 192 Remove the axle housing cover bolts

driving conditions. The level should be up to the filler hole. When you remove the filler plug, the oil should start to run out. If it does not, add fluid to obtain an acceptable level.

DRAIN AND REFILL

▶ **See Figures 191, 192 and 193**

The lubricant should be changed every 30,000 miles (48,000 km). Under severe conditions, the lubricant should be changed every 15,000 miles (24,000 km). If running in deep water, change the lubricant daily.

Follow the procedure given below for changing the lubricant in the front and rear axle differentials:

1. Raise the vehicle and safely support it with jackstands.

2. Remove the axle differential housing cover and allow the lubricant to drain out into a proper container.

3. Install the differential housing cover with a new gasket.

➡**Some rear axle covers are not equipped with a gasket. If a gasket is not used, seal the cover using RTV sealant.**

4. Tighten the cover attaching bolts to 15-25 ft. lbs. (20-33 Nm).

5. Remove the fill plug and add new lubricant to the fill hole level.

6. Replace the fill plug.

7. Lower the vehicle.

➡**Trac-Lok® (limited-slip) differentials may be cleaned only by disassembling the unit and wiping with clean, lint-free rags. Use no chemical solvents or compressed air**

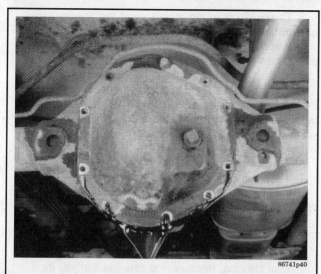

Fig. 193 Let the fluid drain completely from the axle

Cooling Systems

FLUID RECOMMENDATIONS

▶ See Figures 194 and 195

The cooling system was filled at the factory with a high quality coolant solution that is good for year-round operation, which protects the system from freezing. If coolant is needed, a 50/50 mix of ethylene glycol or other suitable antifreeze and water should be used. Alcohol or methanol base coolants are specifically not recommended. Antifreeze solution should be used all year, even in summer, to prevent rust and to take advantage of the solution's higher boiling point compared to plain water. This is imperative on air conditioned models; the heater core can freeze if it isn't protected.

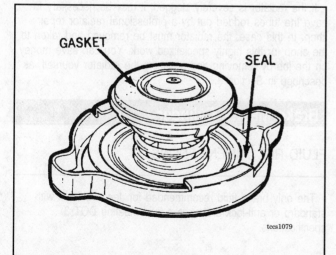

Fig. 194 Be sure the rubber gasket on the radiator cap has a tight seal

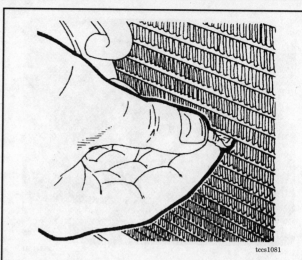

Fig. 195 Periodically remove all debris from the radiator fins

LEVEL CHECK

▶ See Figures 196 and 197

The coolant should be checked at each fuel stop, to prevent the possibility of overheating and serious engine damage. To check the coolant level simply look into the expansion tank.

✳✳CAUTION

The radiator coolant is under pressure when hot. To avoid the danger of physical injury, coolant should be checked or replenished only when cool. To remove the cap, slowly rotate it counterclockwise to the stop, but do not press down. Wait until all pressure is released (indicated when the hissing sound stops), then press down on the cap while continuing to rotate it counterclockwise. Wear eye protection and use a glove or a thick rag to prevent burns.

✳✳WARNING

Never add large quantities of cold coolant to a hot engine. A cracked engine block may result. If it is absolutely necessary to add coolant to a hot engine, do so only with the engine idling and add only small quantities at a time.

If the level is low, simply add coolant mixture to the tank until the upper level line is reached. If the system shows signs of overheating and, possibly, a small leak, you may want to check the level in the radiator when the engine is **cold**.

Each year, the cooling system should be serviced as follows:
1. Wash the radiator cap and filler neck with clean water.
2. Check the coolant for proper level and freeze protection.
3. Pressure test the cooling system using a cooling system pressure tester and follow the tool manufacturers instructions. If a replacement cap is installed, be sure that it conforms to the original specifications.
4. Tighten the hose clamps and inspect all hoses. Replace hoses that are swollen, cracked or otherwise deteriorated.

Fig. 196 After the engine has cooled, remove the radiator cap to check the coolant level

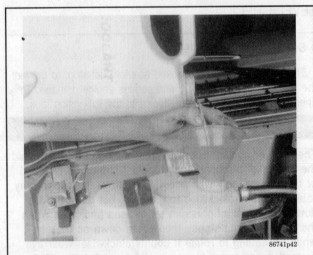

Fig. 197 Coolant may be added to the coolant recovery tank or to the radiator

5. Clean the frontal area of the radiator core, and the air conditioning condenser, if so equipped.

DRAIN AND REFILL

♦ See Figures 198 and 199

Every 3 years or 52,000 miles (84,000 km) whichever comes first, the system should be serviced as follows:

1. Run the engine with the cap removed and the heater **ON** until operating temperature is reached (indicated by heat in the upper radiator hose).

2. With the engine stopped, open the radiator draincock located at the bottom of the radiator, and the cylinder block drain plug(s) located on the side(s) of the cylinder block.

3. Completely drain the coolant, close the draincock and drain plug(s).

4. Add sufficient clean water to fill the system. Run the engine, then drain and refill the system as often as necessary until the drain water is as close to colorless as possible.

5. Add sufficient coolant to provide the required freezing and corrosion protection (at least a 50% solution of antifreeze and water). Fill the radiator to the cold level. Run the engine with the cap removed until normal operating temperature is reached.

6. Check the hot level.

7. Install the cap and fill the overflow tank to the HOT line.

FLUSHING AND CLEANING THE SYSTEM

A well maintained system should never require aggressive flushing or cleaning. However, you may find that you (or a previous owner) have neglected to change the antifreeze often enough to fully protect the system. It may have obviously accumulated rust inside, or there may be visible clogging of the radiator tubes.

There are two basic means of rectifying this situation for the do-it-yourselfer. One is to purchase a kit designed to allow you to reverse-flush the system with the pressure available from a garden hose. This kit comes with special fittings which allow you to force water downward inside the engine block and upward (or in reverse of normal flow) in the radiator. The kit will have complete instructions.

The other means is to purchase a chemical cleaner. The cleaner is installed after the system is flushed and filled with fresh water, and cleans the system as you drive a short distance or idle the engine hot. In all cases, the cleaner must be flushed completely from the system after use. In some cases, it may be necessary to follow up with the use of a neutralizer. Make sure to follow the instructions very carefully. These cleaners are quite potent, chemically, and work very well; because of that fact, you must be careful to flush and, if necessary, neutralize the effect of the cleaner to keep it from damaging your cooling system.

If the radiator is severely clogged, it may be necessary to have the tubes rodded out by a professional radiator repair shop. In this case, the radiator must be removed and taken to the shop for this highly specialized work. You can save money on the job by removing and replacing the radiator yourself, as described in Section 3.

Brake Master Cylinder

FLUID RECOMMENDATIONS

The only brake fluid recommended for Jeep vehicles with standard or anti-lock brakes is a fluid meeting DOT 3 specifications.

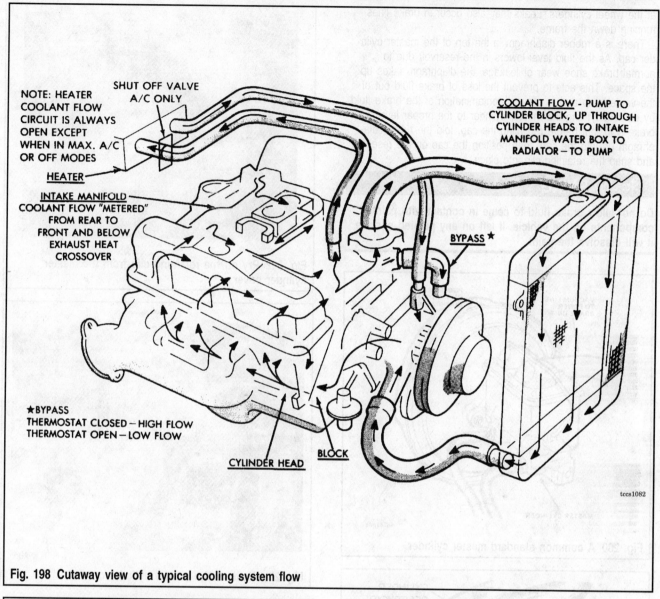

NOTE: HEATER COOLANT FLOW CIRCUIT IS ALWAYS OPEN EXCEPT WHEN IN MAX. A/C OR OFF MODES

SHUT OFF VALVE A/C ONLY

HEATER

INTAKE MANIFOLD COOLANT FLOW "METERED" FROM REAR TO FRONT AND BELOW EXHAUST HEAT CROSSOVER

COOLANT FLOW - PUMP TO CYLINDER BLOCK, UP THROUGH CYLINDER HEADS TO INTAKE MANIFOLD WATER BOX TO RADIATOR – TO PUMP

BYPASS ★

★**BYPASS**
THERMOSTAT CLOSED – HIGH FLOW
THERMOSTAT OPEN – LOW FLOW

CYLINDER HEAD   **BLOCK**

tccs1082

Fig. 198 Cutaway view of a typical cooling system flow

TOOL C-4080

tccs1083

Fig. 199 Cooling systems should be pressure tested for leaks periodically

FLUID LEVEL CHECK

Standard Power Brake System
◆ **See Figures 200, 201, 202 and 203**

The master cylinder reservoir is located under the hood, on the left side of the firewall.

1. Before removing the master cylinder reservoir cap, make sure the vehicle is resting on level ground and clean all dirt away from the top of the master cylinder.

2. Pry off the retaining clip and remove the cap. The fluid level should be within ¼ in. (6mm) of the top of the reservoir on both single and dual master cylinders.

3. Use new brake fluid only when adding fluid to the reservoir.

4. Add the fluid and bring it to the proper level.

If the level of the fluid is less than half the volume of the reservoir, it is advised that you check the brake system for leaks. Leak in a hydraulic brake system most commonly occur at the wheel cylinders. Leaks may also occur in brake lines running down the frame.

There is a rubber diaphragm in the top of the master cylinder cap. As the fluid level lowers in the reservoir due to normal brake shoe wear or leakage, the diaphragm takes up the space. This acts to prevent the loss of brake fluid out of the vented cap and to prevent contamination of the brake fluid by dirt. After filling the master cylinder to the proper level with brake fluid, but before replacing the cap, fold the rubber diaphragm up into the cap, then position the cap on the reservoir and snap the retaining clip into place.

✳✳WARNING

Do not allow brake fluid to come in contact with painted components on the vehicle. If left on any painted surface, it will dissolve the paint.

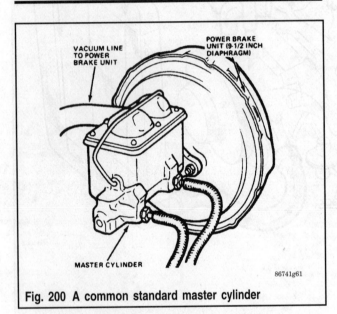

Fig. 200 A common standard master cylinder

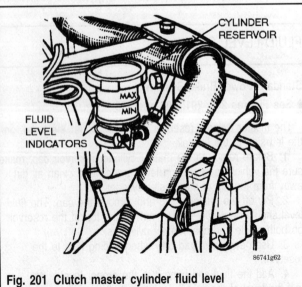

Fig. 201 Clutch master cylinder fluid level

Fig. 202 Pry off the retaining clip from the master cylinder cover

Fig. 203 Remove the master cylinder cover

Anti-Lock Brake System

The anti-lock brake system reservoir is located next to the windshield washer fluid reservoir.

1. Before removing the master cylinder reservoir cap, make sure the vehicle is resting on level ground and clean all dirt away from the top of the master cylinder.

2. Remove the reservoir cap. The fluid level should be within 1/4 in. (6mm) of the top of the reservoir, or at the MAX mark on both single and dual master cylinders.

3. If the level is low, add clean, fresh brake fluid.

4. Replace the reservoir cap when the system has been replenished.

✳✳WARNING

Overfilling could cause fluid overflow and possible reservoir damage when the pump begins cycling.

Clutch Master Cylinder

FLUID RECOMMENDATIONS

The only fluid recommended for Jeep vehicles with a clutch master cylinder is a fluid meeting DOT 3 specifications.

FLUID LEVEL CHECK

The master cylinder reservoir is located under the hood, on the left side of the firewall.

1. Before removing the master cylinder reservoir cap, make sure the vehicle is resting on level ground and clean all dirt away from the top of the master cylinder.
2. Pry off the retaining clip and remove the cap. The fluid level should be within ¼ in. (6mm) of the top of the reservoir on both single and dual master cylinders.
3. Use new brake fluid only when adding fluid to the reservoir.
4. Add the fluid and bring it to the proper level.

✳✳WARNING

Do not allow brake fluid to come in contact with painted components on the vehicle. If left on any painted surface, it will dissolve the paint.

Power Steering Pump

FLUID RECOMMENDATIONS

Use only Mopar Power Steering Fluid, or its equivalent.

LEVEL CHECK

▶ See Figures 204, 205 and 206

On models with power steering, check the fluid in the power steering pump every 7,500 miles. (12,000 km). The fluid level can be checked with the fluid either hot or cold. Fluid level should be at the correct point (FULL HOT or FULL COLD) on the dipstick attached to the inside of the lid of the power steering pump. Fill the unit with power steering fluid. If the pump is low on fluid, check all the power steering hoses and connections, and the hydraulic cylinder for possible leaks.

Chassis Greasing

▶ See Figure 207

The lubrication chart indicates where the grease fittings are located. The vehicle should be greased according to the intervals in the Preventive Maintenance Schedule at the end of this section.

Water resistant EP chassis lubricant (grease) should be used for all chassis grease points.

Fig. 204 Remove the dipstick from the power steering pump

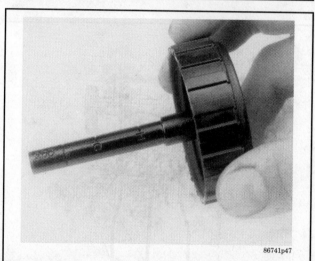

Fig. 205 Check the fluid level on the power steering pump dipstick

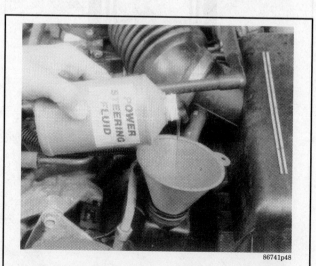

Fig. 206 If necessary, add the proper amount of power steering fluid and replace the dipstick

Every year or 7,500 miles (12,000 km), the front suspension ball joints, both upper and lower on each side of the vehicle, must be greased. Many vehicles covered in this manual are equipped with grease nipples on the ball joints, although some may have plugs which must be removed and nipples fitted. Some late model vehicles have lifetime lubricated chassis components which cannot be serviced.

❋❋WARNING

Do not pump so much grease into the ball joint that excess grease squeezes out of the rubber boot. This destroys the watertight seal.

Jack up the front end of the vehicle and safely support it with jackstands. Block the rear wheels and firmly apply the parking brake. If the vehicle has been parked in temperatures below 20°F (-7°C) for any length of time, park it in a heated garage for an hour or so until the ball joints loosen up enough to accept the grease.

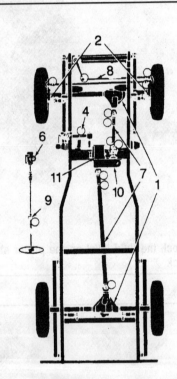

1. Differentials
2. Front wheel bearings
3. Nut used
4. Clutch lever and linkage
6. Manual steering gear
7. Driveshafts
8. Steering linkage
9. Steering shaft U-joint
10. Transfer case
11. Transmission

86741g63

Fig. 207 Common lubrication points on many Jeep vehicles

Depending on which front wheel you work on first, turn the wheel and tire outward, either full-lock right or full-lock left. You will then have the ends of the upper and lower suspension control arms in front of you, with the grease nipples visible. The upper ball joint nipples point up (top ball joint) and the lower ball joint nipples point down, through the end of each control arm. If the nipples are not accessible enough, remove the wheel and tire. Wipe all debris from the nipples or from around the plugs (if installed). If plugs are on the vehicle, remove them and install grease nipples in the holes (nipples are available in various thread sizes at most auto parts stores). Using a hand operated, low pressure grease gun loaded with a quality chassis grease, grease the ball joint only until the rubber joint boot begins to swell out.

STEERING LINKAGE

The steering linkage should be greased at the same interval as the ball joints. Grease nipples are installed on the steering tie rod ends on most models. Wipe all dirt from around the fittings at each tie rod end. Using a hand operated, low pressure grease gun loaded with a suitable chassis grease, grease the linkage until the old grease begins to squeeze out around the tie rod ends. Wipe off the nipples and any excess grease. Also grease the nipples on the steering idler arms.

PARKING BRAKE LINKAGE

Use chassis grease on the parking brake cable where it contacts the cable guides, levers and linkage.

AUTOMATIC TRANSMISSION LINKAGE

Apply a small amount of clean engine oil to the kickdown and shift linkage points at 7,500 mile (12,077 km) intervals.

Body Lubrication and Maintenance

CARE OF YOUR VEHICLE

Glass Surfaces

All glass surfaces should be kept clean at all times for safe driving. Use the same type of cleaner you use on windows in your home. Never use abrasive cleaners, as they will scratch the window surfaces.

Exterior Care

Your vehicle is exposed to all kinds of corrosive effects from nature and chemicals. Some of these are road salt, oils, rain, hail and sleet, just to name a few. To protect not only the paint and trim, but also the many exposed mounts and fixtures, it is important to wash your vehicle often and thoroughly. After washing, allow all surfaces to drain and dry before parking in a closed garage. Washing may not clean all deposits off your vehicle, so you may need additional cleaners. When using professional cleaners, make sure they are suitable for enamel/acrylic painted surfaces, chrome, tires etc. These supplies can be purchased in your local auto parts store. You also should wax and polish your vehicle every few months to keep the paint in good shape.

LOCK CYLINDERS

Apply graphite lubricant sparingly through the key slot. Insert the key and operate the lock several times to be sure that the lubricant is worked into the lock cylinder.

DOOR HINGES AND HINGE CHECKS

Spray a white lubricant on the hinge pivot points to eliminate any binding conditions. Open and close the door several times to be sure that the lubricant is evenly and thoroughly distributed.

TAILGATE

Spray a white lubricant on all of the pivot and friction surfaces to eliminate any squeaks or binds. Work the tailgate to distribute the lubricant.

BODY DRAIN HOLES

Be sure that the drain holes in the doors and rocker panels are open. A small screwdriver can be used to clear them of any debris.

Front Wheel Bearings

REMOVAL, REPACKING & INSTALLATION

➡Sodium-based grease is not compatible with lithium-based grease. Read the package labels and be careful not to mix the two types. If there is any doubt as to the type of grease used, completely clean the old grease from the bearing and hub before replacing.

Before handling the bearings, there are a few things that you should remember to do and not to do.

Remember to DO the following:
• Remove all outside dirt from the housing before exposing the bearing.
• Treat a used bearing as gently as you would a new one.
• Work with clean tools in clean surroundings.
• Use clean, dry canvas gloves, or at least clean, dry hands.
• Clean solvents and flushing fluids are a must.
• Use clean paper when laying out the bearings to dry.
• Protect disassembled bearings from rust and dirt. Cover them up.
• Use clean rags to wipe bearings.

• Keep the bearings in oil-proof paper when they are to be stored or are not in use.
• Clean the inside of the housing before replacing the bearing.

Do NOT do the following:
• Don't work in dirty surroundings.
• Don't use dirty, chipped or damaged tools.
• Try not to work on wooden work benches or use wooden mallets.
• Don't handle bearings with dirty or moist hands.
• Do not use gasoline for cleaning; use a safe solvent.
• Do not spin-dry bearings with compressed air. They will be damaged.
• Do not spin dirty bearings.
• Avoid using cotton waste or dirty cloths to wipe bearings.
• Try not to scratch or nick bearing surfaces.
• Do not allow the bearing to come in contact with dirt or rust at any time.

2-Wheel Drive

▶ **See Figures 208, 209, 210, 211, 212, 213, 214, 215, 216, 217, 218, 219, 220, 221 and 222**

1. Raise and safely support the front end on jackstands.
2. Remove the wheels.
3. Remove the caliper without disconnecting the brake line. Suspend it out of the way using a piece of wire to prevent damage.
4. Remove the grease cap, cotter pin, nut cap, nut, and washer from the spindle. Discard the cotter pin.
5. Slowly remove the hub and rotor; catch the outer bearing as it falls.
6. Carefully drive out the inner bearing and seal from the hub using a wood block.

To install:
7. Inspect the bearing races for excessive wear, pitting or grooves. If they are cracked or grooved, or if pitting and excess wear is present, drive them out with a drift or punch.
8. Check the bearing for excess wear, pitting or cracks, or excessive looseness.

➡If it is necessary to replace either the bearing or the race, replace both. Never replace just a bearing or a race. These parts wear in a mating pattern. If just one is replaced, premature failure of the new part will result.

9. If the old parts are retained, thoroughly clean them in a safe solvent and allow them to dry on a clean towel. Never spin them dry with compressed air.
10. On vehicles with drum brakes, cover the spindle with a cloth and thoroughly brush all dirt from the brakes. Never blow the dirt off the brakes, due to the potential presence of asbestos in the dirt, which is harmful to your health when inhaled.
11. Remove the cloth, then thoroughly clean the spindle and the inside of the hub.
12. Pack the inside of the hub with EP wheel bearing grease. Add grease to the hub until it is flush with the inside diameter of the bearing cup.
13. Pack the bearing with the same grease. A needle-shaped wheel bearing packer is best for this operation. If one is not available, place a large amount of grease in the palm of your hand and slide the edge of the bearing cage through the

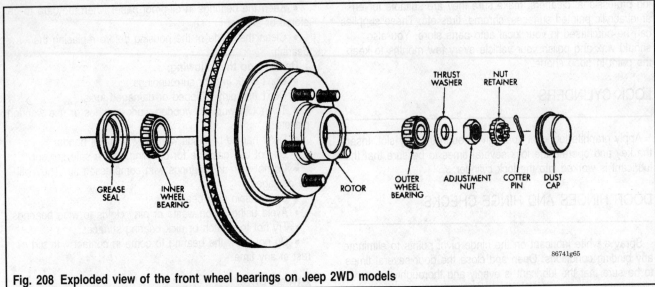

Fig. 208 Exploded view of the front wheel bearings on Jeep 2WD models

GREASE SEAL — INNER WHEEL BEARING — ROTOR — OUTER WHEEL BEARING — ADJUSTMENT NUT — THRUST WASHER — NUT RETAINER — COTTER PIN — DUST CAP

86741g65

Fig. 209 Pry the dust cap from the hub taking care not to distort or damage its flange

TCCS8024

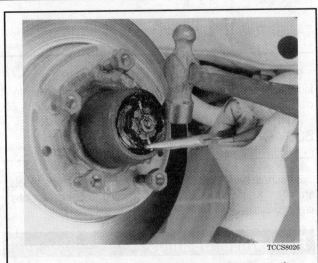

Fig. 211 If difficulty is encountered, gently tap on the pliers with a hammer to help free the cotter pin

TCCS8026

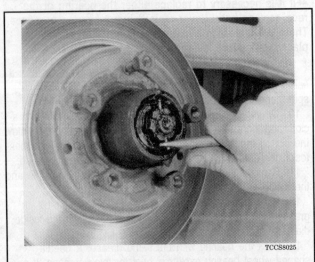

Fig. 210 Once the bent ends are cut, grasp the cotter pin and pull or pry it free of the spindle

TCCS8025

grease to pick up as much as possible, then work the grease in as best you can with your fingers.

14. If a new race is being installed, very carefully drive it into position until it bottoms all around, using a brass drift. Be careful to avoid scratching the surface.

15. Place the inner bearing in the race and install a new grease seal.

16. Clean the rotor contact surface if necessary.

17. Position the hub and rotor on the spindle and install the outer bearing.

18. Install the washer and nut.

19. While turning the rotor, torque the nut to 25 ft. lbs. (33 Nm) to seat the bearings.

20. Back off the nut ½ turn, and, while turning the rotor, torque the nut to 19 inch lbs. (2 Nm).

21. Install the nut cap and a new cotter pin. Install the grease cap.

22. Install the caliper.

23. Repeat Steps 3-23 for the other front wheel.

24. Install the wheels.

Fig. 212 Loosen and remove the castellated nut from the spindle

Fig. 213 Remove the washer from the spindle

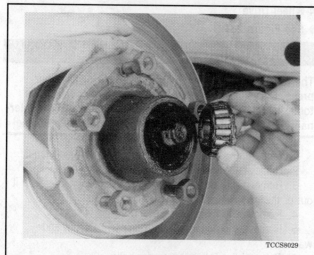

Fig. 214 With the nut and washer out of the way, the outer bearings may be removed from the hub

Fig. 215 Pull the hub and inner bearing assembly from the spindle

Fig. 216 Use a small prytool to remove the old inner bearing seal

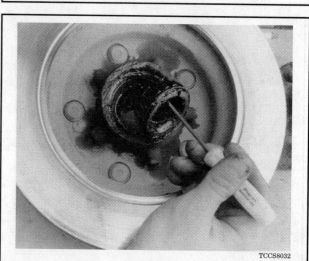

Fig. 217 With the seal removed, the inner bearing may be withdrawn from the hub

Fig. 218 Thoroughly pack the bearing with fresh, high temperature wheel-bearing grease before installation

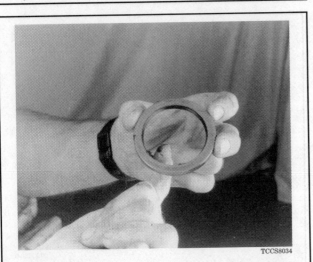

Fig. 219 Apply a thin coat of fresh grease to the new inner bearing seal lip

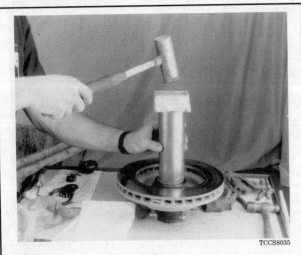

Fig. 220 Use a suitably sized driver to install the inner bearing seal to the hub

Fig. 221 Tighten the nut to 12 ft. lbs. while gently spinning the wheel, then adjust the bearings

Fig. 222 Install the dust cap by gently tapping on the flange — DO NOT hammer on the center

4-Wheel Drive

▶ See Figure 223

✳✳WARNING

The following procedure requires the use of an arbor press. Chrysler Corp. notes that only the special press tools listed below should be used, or damage to the internal machined shoulder of the bearing carrier is probable!

1. Raise and safely support the front end on jackstands.
2. Remove the wheels.
3. Remove, but do not disconnect, the caliper. Suspend it out of the way.
4. Remove the rotor. See Section 9.
5. Remove the cotter pin, nut retainer, axle nut and washer.
6. Remove the 3 bearing carrier bolts.
7. Remove the hub/bearing carrier and the rotor shield.

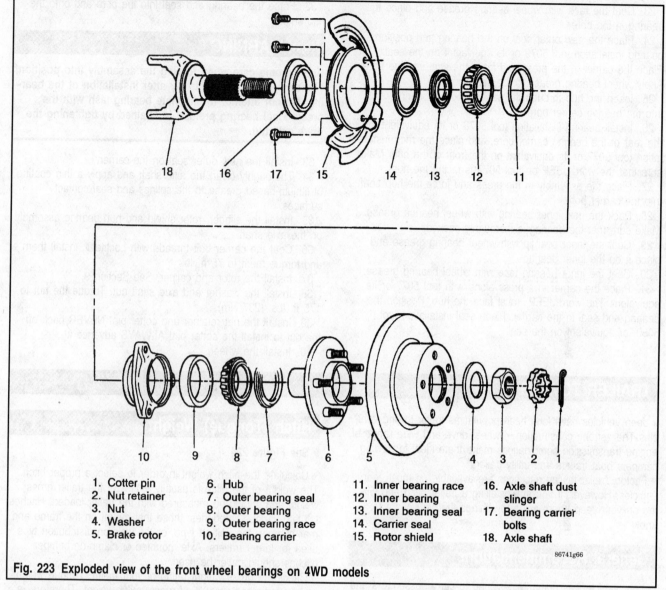

1. Cotter pin
2. Nut retainer
3. Nut
4. Washer
5. Brake rotor
6. Hub
7. Outer bearing seal
8. Outer bearing
9. Outer bearing race
10. Bearing carrier
11. Inner bearing race
12. Inner bearing
13. Inner bearing seal
14. Carrier seal
15. Rotor shield
16. Axle shaft dust slinger
17. Bearing carrier bolts
18. Axle shaft

86741g66

Fig. 223 Exploded view of the front wheel bearings on 4WD models

8. Using an arbor press, press the hub out of the bearing carrier. Special tools 5073 and 5074 or their equivalents are available for this job. Secure the carrier to the press plate with M12 x 1.75mm x 40mm bolts.

9. Cut and remove the plastic cage from the hub inner bearing. Using diagonal pliers or tin snips, cut the bearing cage. Discard the rollers after removing the cage.

10. Remove what remains of the inner bearing as follows:
    a. Install a bearing separator tool on the inner bearing.
    b. Position the separator tool and hub in an arbor press.
    c. Force the hub out of the inner bearing with press pin tool 5074 or its equivalent.

11. Remove the bearing carrier outer seal and discard it.

12. Drive the inner bearing seal out and discard it. If you're using tool 5078 or its equivalent, make sure that the word JEEP faces downward.

13. Attach press plate tool 5073 or its equivalent, to the rear of the carrier. Secure it in the press using M12 x 1.75mm x 40mm bolts.

14. Position bearing race remover 5076, or its equivalent, in the carrier bore between the inner and outer bearing races.

15. Position the press pin tool 5074 on tool 5076.

16. Place the bearing carrier in the press and force the inner bearing race from the carrier bore. Reverse the position of the carrier and tools, and force the outer bearing race from the bore.

To install:

17. Thoroughly clean all reusable parts with a safe solvent. Discard any parts that appear worn or damaged.

18. Attach press plate tool 5073 or its equivalent on the bearing carrier. Secure it in the press using M12 x 1.75mm x 40mm bolts.

19. Position the new outer bearing race in the bore.

20. Position bearing race installation tool 5077 or its equivalent on the race. Make sure that the word JEEP faces downward. Press the race into the bore. The race should be flush with the machined shoulder of the carrier.

21. Position the new inner bearing race in the carrier bore. Reverse the position of the carrier and tools, and force the inner race into the bore.

22. Thoroughly pack the new outer bearing with wheel bearing grease. Make sure that the bearing is fully packed.

23. Coat the race with wheel bearing grease and place the bearing in the bore.

24. Place the new outer seal on the bearing and position bearing installation tool 5079 or its equivalent on the seal. Place the carrier in the press and force the seal into the bore. Apply wheel bearing grease to the seal lip.

25. Insert the hub through the seal and outer bearing, and into the bearing carrier bore.

26. Install bearing installation tool 5078 or its equivalent into the rear of the bearing carrier bore, and place the race installation tool 5077 or its equivalent on the front of the hub. Make sure that the word JEEP on tool 5077 is facing the hub.

27. Place the assembly in the press and force the hub shaft into the carrier bore.

28. Pack the new inner bearing with wheel bearing grease. Make sure that the bearing is thoroughly packed.

29. Coat the inner seal lip with wheel bearing grease and place it on the inner bearing.

30. Coat the inner bearing race with wheel bearing grease.

31. Place the carrier in a press along with tool 5077 or its equivalent. The word JEEP must face the hub. Position the bearing and seal in the carrier. Place seal installation tool 5080, or equivalent on the seal.

32. Force the bearing and seal into the bore and onto the hub shaft.

✳✳WARNING

Use extreme care when forcing the assembly into position! The carrier must rotate freely after installation of the bearing! Do not attempt to eliminate bearing lash with the press. Final bearing preload is attained by tightening the drive axle nut.

33. Install the new outer seal on the carrier.

34. Thoroughly clean the axle shaft and apply a thin coating of lithium-based grease to the splines and seal contact surfaces.

35. Install the slinger, rotor shield and hub bearing assembly on the axle shaft.

36. Coat the carrier bolt threads with Loctite®, install them and torque them to 75 ft. lbs.

37. Install the rotor and caliper. See Section 9.

38. Install the washer and axle shaft nut. Torque the nut to 175 ft. lbs. (237 Nm).

39. Install the nut retainer and cotter pin. NEVER back off the nut to install the cotter pin! ALWAYS advance it!

40. Install the wheel.

TRAILER TOWING

Jeep vehicles have long been popular as trailer towing vehicles. Their strong construction, 4-wheel drive and wide range of engine transmission combinations make them ideal for towing campers boat trailers and utility trailers.

Factory trailer towing packages are available on most Jeep vehicles. However, if you are installing a trailer hitch and wiring on your Jeep, there are a few things that you ought to know.

General Recommendations

Your vehicle was primarily designed to carry passengers and cargo. It is important to remember that towing a trailer will place additional loads on your vehicle's engine, drive train, steering, braking and other systems. However, if you decide to tow a trailer, using the proper equipment is a must.

Local laws may require specific equipment such as trailer brakes or fender mounted mirrors. Check your local laws.

Trailer Weight

The weight of the trailer is the most important factor. A good weight-to-horsepower ratio is about 35:1, that is 35 lbs. of Gross Combined Weight (GCW) for every horsepower your engine develops. Multiply the engine's rated horsepower by 35 and subtract the weight of the vehicle passengers and luggage. The number remaining is the approximate ideal maximum weight you should tow, although a numerically higher axle ratio can help compensate for heavier weight.

Hitch (Tongue) Weight

▶ **See Figure 224**

Calculate the hitch weight in order to select a proper hitch. The weight of the hitch is usually 9-11% of the trailer gross weight and should be measured with the trailer loaded. Hitches fall into various categories: those that mount on the frame and rear bumper, the bolt-on type, or the weld-on distribution type used for larger trailers. Axle mounted or clamp-on bumper hitches should never be used.

Check the gross weight rating of your trailer. Tongue weight is usually figured as 10% of gross trailer weight. Therefore, a

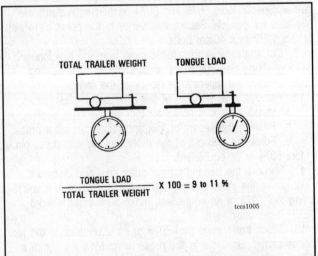

Fig. 224 Calculating proper tongue weight for your trailer

trailer with a maximum gross weight of 2000 lbs. will have a maximum tongue weight of 200 lbs. (90 kg) Class I trailers fall into this category. Class II trailers are those with a gross weight rating of 2000-3000 lbs. (928-1362 kg), while Class III trailers fall into the 3500-6000 lbs. (1589-2724 kg) category. Class IV trailers are those over 6000 lbs. (2724 kg) and are for use with fifth wheel vehicles, only.

When you've determined the hitch that you'll need, follow the manufacturer's installation instructions, exactly, especially when it comes to fastener torques. The hitch will subjected to a lot of stress and good hitches come with hardened bolts. Never substitute an inferior bolt for a hardened bolt.

Cooling

ENGINE

Overflow Tank

One of the most common, if not THE most common, problems associated with trailer towing is engine overheating. If you have a cooling system without an expansion tank, you'll definitely need to get an aftermarket expansion tank kit, preferably one with at least a 2 quart capacity. These kits are easily installed on the radiator's overflow hose, and come with a pressure cap designed for expansion tanks.

Flex Fan

Another helpful accessory for vehicles using a belt-driven radiator fan is a flex fan. These fans are large diameter units designed to provide more airflow at low speeds, by using fan blades that have deeply cupped surfaces. The blades then flex, or flatten out, at high speed, when less cooling air is needed. These fans are far lighter in weight than stock fans, requiring less horsepower to drive them. Also, they are far quieter than stock fans. If you do decide to replace your stock fan with a flex fan, note that if your vehicle has a fan clutch, a spacer will be needed between the flex fan and water pump hub.

Oil Cooler

Aftermarket engine oil coolers are helpful for prolonging engine oil life and reducing overall engine temperatures. Both of these factors increase engine life. While not absolutely neces-sary in towing Class I and some Class II trailers, they are recommended for heavier Class II and all Class III towing. Engine oil cooler systems usually consist of an adapter, screwed on in place of the oil filter, a remote filter mounting and a multi-tube, finned heat exchanger, which is mounted in front of the radiator or air conditioning condenser.

TRANSMISSION

An automatic transmission is usually recommended for trailer towing. Modern automatics have proven reliable and, of course, easy to operate, in trailer towing. The increased load of a trailer, however, causes an increase in the temperature of the automatic transmission fluid. Heat is the worst enemy of an automatic transmission. As the temperature of the fluid increases, the life of the fluid decreases.

It is essential, therefore, that you install an automatic transmission cooler. The cooler, which consists of a multi-tube, finned heat exchanger, is usually installed in front of the radiator or air conditioning compressor, and hooked in-line with the transmission cooler tank inlet line. Follow the cooler manufacturer's installation instructions.

Select a cooler of at least adequate capacity, based upon the combined gross weights of the vehicle and trailer.

Cooler manufacturers recommend that you use an aftermarket cooler in addition to, and not instead of, the present cooling tank in your radiator. If you do want to use it in place of the radiator cooling tank, get a cooler at least two sizes larger than normally necessary.

➡**A transmission cooler can, sometimes, cause slow or harsh shifting in the transmission during cold weather, until the fluid has a chance to come up to normal operating temperature. Some coolers can be purchased with, or retrofitted with, a temperature bypass valve which will allow fluid flow through the cooler only when the fluid has reached a certain operating temperature.**

Handling A Trailer

Towing a trailer with ease and safety requires a certain amount of experience. It's a good idea to learn the feel of a trailer by practicing turning, stopping and backing in an open area such as an empty parking lot.

TOWING THE VEHICLE

If your Jeep has to be towed by a tow vehicle, it can be towed forward for any distance, as long as it is done fairly slowly. If your Jeep has to be towed backward, remove the front axle drive flanges to prevent the front differential from rotating. If the drive flanges are removed, improvise a cover to keep out dust and dirt.

JUMP STARTING A DEAD BATTERY

▶ **See Figure 225**

Whenever a vehicle is jump started, precautions must be followed in order to prevent the possibility of personal injury.

Remember that batteries contain a small amount of explosive hydrogen gas which is a by-product of battery charging. Sparks should always be avoided when working around batteries, especially when attaching jumper cables. To minimize the possibility of accidental sparks, follow the procedure carefully.

✳✳CAUTION

NEVER hook the batteries up in a series circuit or the entire electrical system will go up in smoke, including the starter!

Vehicles equipped with a diesel engine may utilize two 12 volt batteries. If so, the batteries are connected in a parallel circuit (positive terminal to positive terminal, negative terminal to negative terminal). Hooking the batteries up in parallel circuit increases battery cranking power without increasing total battery voltage output. Output remains at 12 volts. On the other hand, hooking two 12 volt batteries up in a series circuit (positive terminal to negative terminal, positive terminal to negative terminal) increases total battery output to 24 volts (12 volts plus 12 volts).

Jump Starting Precautions

- Be sure that both batteries are of the same voltage. Vehicles covered by this manual and most vehicles on the road today utilize a 12 volt charging system.
- Be sure that both batteries are of the same polarity (have the same terminal, in most cases NEGATIVE grounded).
- Be sure that the vehicles are not touching or a short could occur.
- On serviceable batteries, be sure the vent cap holes are not obstructed.
- Do not smoke or allow sparks anywhere near the batteries.
- In cold weather, make sure the battery electrolyte is not frozen. This can occur more readily in a battery that has been in a state of discharge.
- Do not allow electrolyte to contact your skin or clothing.

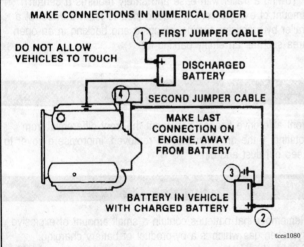

MAKE CONNECTIONS IN NUMERICAL ORDER

DO NOT ALLOW VEHICLES TO TOUCH

① FIRST JUMPER CABLE

DISCHARGED BATTERY

SECOND JUMPER CABLE

MAKE LAST CONNECTION ON ENGINE, AWAY FROM BATTERY

BATTERY IN VEHICLE WITH CHARGED BATTERY

③

②

tccs1080

Fig. 225 Connect the jumper cables to the batteries and engine in the order shown

Jump Starting Procedure

GASOLINE ENGINE VEHICLES

1. Make sure that the voltages of the 2 batteries are the same. Most batteries and charging systems are of the 12 volt variety.
2. Pull the jumping vehicle (with the good battery) into a position so the jumper cables can reach the dead battery and that vehicle's engine. Make sure that the vehicles do NOT touch.
3. Place the transmissions/transaxles of both vehicles in **Neutral** (MT) or **P** (AT), as applicable, then firmly set their parking brakes.

➡**If necessary for safety reasons, the hazard lights on both vehicles may be operated throughout the entire procedure without significantly increasing the difficulty of jumping the dead battery.**

4. Turn all lights and accessories OFF on both vehicles. Make sure the ignition switches on both vehicles are turned to the **OFF** position.
5. Cover the battery cell caps with a rag, but do not cover the terminals.
6. Make sure the terminals on both batteries are clean and free of corrosion or proper electrical connection will be impeded. If necessary, clean the battery terminals before proceeding.
7. Identify the positive (+) and negative (-) terminals on both batteries.
8. Connect the first jumper cable to the positive (+) terminal of the dead battery, then connect the other end of that cable to the positive (+) terminal of the booster (good) battery.
9. Connect one end of the other jumper cable to the negative (-) terminal on the booster battery and the final cable clamp to an engine bolt head, alternator bracket or other solid, metallic point on the engine with the dead battery. Try to pick a ground on the engine that is positioned away from the battery in order to minimize the possibility of the 2 clamps touching should one loosen during the procedure. DO NOT connect this clamp to the negative (-) terminal of the bad battery.

✳✳CAUTION

Be very careful to keep the jumper cables away from moving parts (cooling fan, belts, etc.) on both engines.

10. Check to make sure that the cables are routed away from any moving parts, then start the donor vehicle's engine. Run the engine at moderate speed for several minutes to allow the dead battery a chance to receive some initial charge.
11. With the donor vehicle's engine still running slightly above idle, try to start the vehicle with the dead battery. Crank the engine for no more than 10 seconds at a time and let the starter cool for at least 20 seconds between tries. If the vehicle does not start in 3 tries, it is likely that something else is also wrong or that the battery needs additional time to charge.
12. Once the vehicle is started, allow it to run at idle for a few seconds to make sure that it is operating properly.

13. Turn ON the headlights, heater blower and, if equipped, the rear defroster of both vehicles in order to reduce the severity of voltage spikes and subsequent risk of damage to the vehicles' electrical systems when the cables are disconnected. This step is especially important to any vehicle equipped with computer control modules.

14. Carefully disconnect the cables in the reverse order of connection. Start with the negative cable that is attached to the engine ground, then the negative cable on the donor battery. Disconnect the positive cable from the donor battery and finally, disconnect the positive cable from the formerly dead battery. Be careful when disconnecting the cables from the positive terminals not to allow the alligator clips to touch any metal on either vehicle or a short and sparks will occur.

DUAL-BATTERY DIESEL VEHICLES

Vehicles equipped with the diesel engine utilize two 12 volt batteries, one on either side of the engine compartment. The batteries are connected in a parallel circuit (positive terminal to positive terminal, negative terminal to negative terminal). Hooking the batteries up in parallel circuit increases battery cranking power without increasing total battery voltage output. Output remains at 12 volts.

❋❋CAUTION

NEVER hook the batteries up in a series circuit or the entire electrical system will go up in smoke, including the starter.

On the other hand, hooking two 12 volt batteries up in a series circuit (positive terminal to negative terminal, positive terminal to negative terminal) increases total battery output to 24 volts (12 volts plus 12 volts).

In the event that a diesel needs to be jump started, use the following procedure.

1. Turn all lights off.
2. Turn on the heater blower motor to remove residual voltage.
3. Connect one jumper cable to the passenger side battery positive (+) terminal and the other cable clamp to the positive (+) terminal of the booster (good) battery.
4. Connect one end of the other jumper cable to the negative (-) terminal of the booster (good) battery and the other cable clamp to an engine bolt head, alternator bracket or other solid, metallic point on the diesel engine. DO NOT connect this clamp to the negative (-) terminal of the bad battery.

❋❋CAUTION

Be very careful to keep the jumper cables away from moving part (cooling fan, belts, etc.) on both engines.

5. Start the engine of the donor vehicle and run at moderate speed.
6. Start the engine of the diesel.
7. When the diesel starts, remove the cable from the engine block before disconnecting the positive terminal.

JACKING

▶ **See Figures 226 and 227**

Your Jeep was supplied with a jack for emergency road repairs. This jack is fine for changing a flat tire or other short-term procedures not requiring you to go beneath the vehicle. If it is used in an emergency situation, carefully follow the instructions provided either with the jack or in your owner's manual. Do not attempt to use the jack on any portions of the vehicle other than specified by the vehicle manufacturer. Always block the diagonally opposite wheel when using a jack.

A more convenient way of jacking is the use of a garage or floor jack. You may use the floor jack at the specified points in following the illustrations.

Never place the jack under the radiator, engine or transmission components. Severe and expensive damage will result when the jack is raised. Additionally, never jack under the floorpan or bodywork; the metal will deform.

Whenever you plan to work under the vehicle, you must support it on jackstands or ramps. Never use cinder blocks or stacks of wood to support the vehicle, even if you're only going to be under it for a few minutes. Never crawl under the vehicle when it is supported only by the tire-changing jack or other floor jack.

➡**Always position a block of wood or small rubber pad on top of the jack or jackstand to protect the lifting point's finish when lifting or supporting the vehicle.**

Small hydraulic, screw, or scissors jacks are satisfactory for raising the vehicle. Drive-on trestles or ramps are also a handy and safe way to both raise and support the vehicle. Be careful though, some ramps may be too steep to drive your vehicle onto without scraping the front bottom panels. Never support the vehicle on any suspension member (unless specifically instructed to do so by a repair manual) or by an underbody panel.

Jacking Precautions

The following safety points cannot be overemphasized:
• Always block the opposite wheel or wheels to keep the vehicle from rolling off the jack.
• When raising the front of the vehicle, firmly apply the parking brake.
• When the drive wheels are to remain on the ground, leave the vehicle in gear to help prevent it from rolling.
• Always use jackstands to support the vehicle when you are working underneath. Place the stands beneath the vehicle's jacking brackets. Before climbing underneath, rock the vehicle a bit to make sure it is firmly supported.

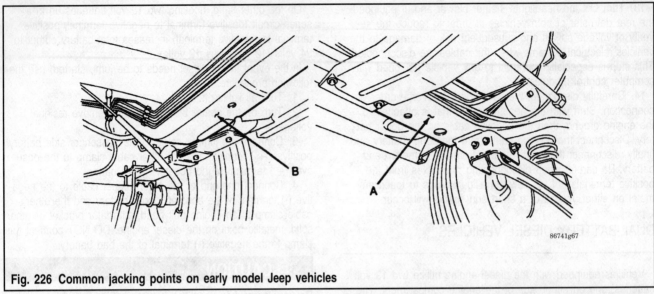

Fig. 226 Common jacking points on early model Jeep vehicles

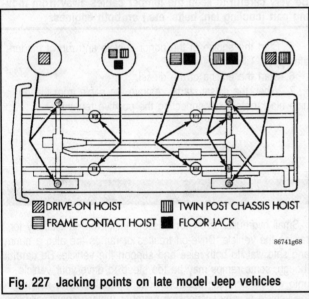

DRIVE-ON HOIST   TWIN POST CHASSIS HOIST
FRAME CONTACT HOIST   FLOOR JACK

Fig. 227 Jacking points on late model Jeep vehicles

Jacking Procedure

Scissors jacks or hydraulic jacks are recommended for all Jeep vehicles. To change a tire, place the jack beneath the spring plate below the axle, near the wheel to be changed.

Make sure that you are on level ground, that the transmission is in Reverse with manual transmissions (or in Park with automatic transmissions), the parking brake is set, and the tire diagonally opposite to the one to be changed is blocked so that it will not roll. Loosen the lug nut before you jack the wheel to be changed completely free of the ground.

HOW TO BUY A USED VEHICLE

Many people believe that a two or three year old used car or vehicle is a better buy than a new vehicle. This may be true as most new vehicles suffer the heaviest depreciation in the first two years and, at three years old, a vehicle is usually not old enough to present a lot of costly repair problems. But keep in mind, when buying a non-warranted automobile, there are no guarantees. Whatever the age of the used vehicle you might want to purchase, this section and a little patience should increase your chances of selecting one that is safe and dependable.

Tips

1. First decide what model you want, and how much you want to spend.

2. Check the used car lots and your local newspaper ads. Privately owned vehicles are usually less expensive, however, you may not get a warranty that, in many cases, comes with a used vehicle purchased from a lot. Of course, some aftermarket warranties may not be worth the extra money, so this is a point you will have to debate and consider based on your priorities.

3. Never shop at night. The glare of the lights make it easy to miss faults on the body caused by accident or rust repair.

4. Try to get the name and phone number of the previous owner. Contact him/her and ask about the vehicle. If the owner of a lot refuses this information, look for a vehicle somewhere else.

A private seller can tell you about the vehicle and maintenance. But remember, there's no law requiring honesty from private citizens selling used vehicles. There is a law that forbids tampering with or turning back the odometer mileage. This includes both the private citizen and the lot owner. The law also requires that the seller or anyone transferring ownership of the vehicle must provide the buyer with a signed statement indicating the mileage on the odometer at the time of transfer.

5. You may wish to contact the National Highway Traffic Safety Administration (NHTSA) to find out if the vehicle has ever been included in a manufacturer's recall. Write down the year, model and serial number before you buy the vehicle, then contact NHTSA (there should be a 1-800 number that your phone company's information line can supply). If the vehicle was listed for a recall, make sure the needed repairs were made.

6. Refer to the Used Vehicle Checklist in this section and check all the items on the vehicle you are considering. Some items are more important than others. Only you know how much money you can afford for repairs, and depending on the price of the vehicle, may consider performing any needed work yourself. Beware, however, of trouble in areas that will affect operation, safety or emission. Problems in the Used Vehicle Checklist break down as follows:

• Numbers 1-8: Two or more problems in these areas indicate a lack of maintenance. You should beware.

• Numbers 9-13: Problems here tend to indicate a lack of proper care, however, these can usually be corrected with a tune-up or relatively simple parts replacement.

• Numbers 14-17: Problems in the engine or transmission can be very expensive. Unless you are looking for a project, walk away from any vehicle with problems in 2 or more of these areas.

7. If you are satisfied with the apparent condition of the vehicle, take it to an independent diagnostic center or mechanic for a complete check. If you have a state inspection program, have it inspected immediately before purchase, or specify on the bill of sale that the sale is conditional on passing state inspection.

8. Road test the vehicle — refer to the Road Test Checklist in this section. If your original evaluation and the road test agree — the rest is up to you.

USED VEHICLE CHECKLIST

▶ See Figure 228

➡The numbers on the illustrations refer to the numbers on this checklist.

1. Mileage: Average mileage is about 12,000-15,000 miles (19,300-24,100 km) per year. More than average mileage may indicate hard usage or could indicate many highway miles (which could be less detrimental than half as many tough around town miles).

2. Paint: Check around the tailpipe, molding and windows for overspray indicating that the vehicle has been repainted.

3. Rust: Check fenders, doors, rocker panels, window moldings, wheelwells, floorboards, under floormats, and in the trunk for signs of rust. Any rust at all will be a problem. There is no way to permanently stop the spread of rust, except to replace the part or panel.

➡If rust repair is suspected, try using a magnet to check for body filler. A magnet should stick to the sheet metal parts of the body, but will not adhere to areas with large amounts of filler.

4. Body appearance: Check the moldings, bumpers, grille, vinyl roof, glass, doors, trunk lid and body panels for general overall condition. Check for misalignment, loose hold-down clips, ripples, scratches in glass, welding in the trunk, severe misalignment of body panels or ripples, any of which may indicate crash work.

5. Leaks: Get down and look under the vehicle. There are no normal leaks, other than water from the air conditioner condenser.

6. Tires: Check the tire air pressure. One old trick is to pump the tire pressure up to make the vehicle roll easier. Check the tread wear, open the trunk and check the spare too. Uneven wear is a clue that the front end may need an alignment.

7. Shock absorbers: Check the shock absorbers by forcing downward sharply on each corner of the vehicle. Good shocks will not allow the vehicle to bounce more than once after you let go.

8. Interior: Check the entire interior. You're looking for an interior condition that agrees with the overall condition of the vehicle. Reasonable wear is expected, but be suspicious of new seat covers on sagging seats, new pedal pads, and worn armrests. These indicate an attempt to cover up hard use. Pull back the carpets and look for evidence of water leaks or flooding. Look for missing hardware, door handles, control knobs, etc. Check lights and signal operations. Make sure all accessories (air conditioner, heater, radio, etc.) work. Check windshield wiper operation.

9. Belts and Hoses: Open the hood, then check all belts and hoses for wear, cracks or weak spots.

10. Battery: Low electrolyte level, corroded terminals and/or cracked case indicate a lack of maintenance.

11. Radiator: Look for corrosion or rust in the coolant indicating a lack of maintenance.

12. Air filter: A severely dirty air filter would indicate a lack of maintenance.

13. Ignition wires: Check the ignition wires for cracks, burned spots, or wear. Worn wires will have to be replaced.

14. Oil level: If the oil level is low, chances are the engine uses oil or leaks. Beware of water in the oil (there is probably a cracked block or bad head gasket), excessively thick oil (which is often used to quiet a noisy engine), or thin, dirty oil with a distinct gasoline smell (this may indicate internal engine problems).

15. Automatic Transmission: Pull the transmission dipstick out when the engine is running. The level should read FULL, and the fluid should be clear or bright red. Dark brown or black fluid that has distinct burnt odor, indicates a transmission in need of repair or overhaul.

16. Exhaust: Check the color of the exhaust smoke. Blue smoke indicates, among other problems, worn rings. Black smoke can indicate burnt valves or carburetor problems. Check the exhaust system for leaks; it can be expensive to replace.

17. Spark Plugs: Remove one or all of the spark plugs (the most accessible will do, though all are preferable). An engine

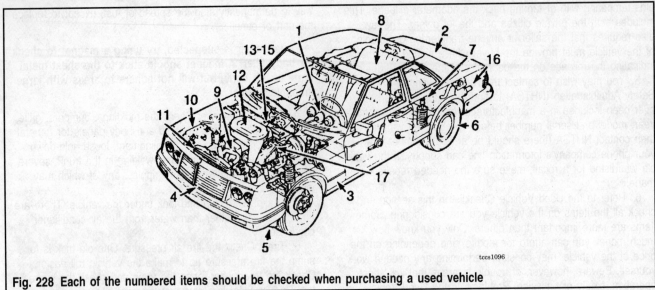

Fig. 228 Each of the numbered items should be checked when purchasing a used vehicle

tccs1096

in good condition will show plugs with a light tan or gray deposit on the firing tip.

ROAD TEST CHECKLIST

1. **Engine Performance:** The vehicle should be peppy whether cold or warm, with adequate power and good pickup. It should respond smoothly through the gears.

2. **Brakes:** They should provide quick, firm stops with no noise, pulling or brake fade.

3. **Steering:** Sure control with no binding harshness, or looseness and no shimmy in the wheel should be expected. Noise or vibration from the steering wheel when turning the vehicle means trouble.

4. **Clutch (Manual Transmission):** Clutch action should give quick, smooth response with easy shifting. The clutch pedal should have free-play before it disengages the clutch. Start the engine, set the parking brake, put the transmission in first gear and slowly release the clutch pedal. The engine should begin to stall when the pedal is $1/2$-$3/4$ of the way up.

5. **Automatic Transmission:** The transmission should shift rapidly and smoothly, with no noise, hesitation, or slipping.

6. **Differential:** No noise or thumps should be present. Differentials have no normal leaks.

7. **Driveshaft/Universal Joints:** Vibration and noise could mean driveshaft problems. Clicking at low speed or coast conditions means worn U-joints.

8. **Suspension:** Try hitting bumps at different speeds. A vehicle that bounces excessively has weak shock absorbers or struts. Clunks mean worn bushings or ball joints.

9. **Frame/Body:** Wet the tires and drive in a straight line. Tracks should show two straight lines, not four. Four tire tracks indicate a frame/body bent by collision damage. If the tires can't be wet for this purpose, have a friend drive along behind you and see if the vehicle appears to be traveling in a straight line.

CAPACITIES

Year	Model	Engine ID/VIN	Engine Displacement Liters (cu. in.)	Engine Oil with Filter (qts.)	Transmission (pts.)			Drive Axle (pts.)	Fuel Tank (gal.)	Cooling System (qts.)
					4-Spd	5-Spd	Auto.			
1984	Comanche	U	2.5 (150)	4	4 [1]	4.5	15.8	2.5 [3]	13.5 [2]	9
	Comanche	W	2.8 (173)	5	4 [1]	4.5	15.8	2.5 [3]	13.5 [2]	9
	Wagoneer	U	2.5 (150)	4	4 [1]	4.5	15.8	2.5 [3]	13.5 [2]	9
	Wagoneer	W	2.8 (173)	5	4 [1]	4.5	15.8	2.5 [3]	13.5 [2]	9
	Cherokee	U	2.5 (150)	4	4 [1]	4.5	15.8	2.5 [3]	13.5 [2]	9
	Cherokee	W	2.8 (173)	5	4 [1]	4.5	15.8	2.5 [3]	13.5	9
1985	Comanche	B	2.1 (126)	6.3	4 [1]	4.5	15.8	2.5 [3]	13.5 [2]	9
	Comanche	H	2.5 (150)	4	4 [1]	4.5	15.8	2.5 [3]	13.5 [2]	9
	Comanche	W	2.8 (173)	5	4 [1]	4.5	15.8	2.5 [3]	13.5 [2]	9
	Wagoneer	B	2.1 (126)	6.3	4 [1]	4.5	15.8	2.5 [3]	13.5 [2]	9
	Wagoneer	H	2.5 (150)	4	4 [1]	4.5	15.8	2.5 [3]	13.5 [2]	9
	Wagoneer	W	2.8 (173)	5	4 [1]	4.5	15.8	2.5 [3]	13.5	9
	Cherokee	B	2.1 (126)	6.3	4 [1]	4.5	15.8	2.5 [3]	13.5 [2]	9
	Cherokee	H	2.5 (150)	4	4 [1]	4.5	15.8	2.5 [3]	13.5 [2]	9
	Cherokee	W	2.8 (173)	5	4 [1]	4.5	15.8	2.5 [3]	13.5 [2]	9
1986	Comanche	B	2.1 (126)	6.3	4 [1]	4.5	15.8	2.5 [3]	13.5 [2]	9
	Comanche	H	2.5 (150)	4	4 [1]	4.5	15.8	2.5 [3]	13.5 [2]	9
	Comanche	W	2.8 (173)	5	4 [1]	4.5	15.8	2.5 [3]	13.5 [2]	9
	Wagoneer	B	2.1 (126)	6.3	4 [1]	4.5	15.8	2.5 [3]	13.5 [2]	9
	Wagoneer	H	2.5 (150)	4	4 [1]	4.5	15.8	2.5 [3]	13.5 [2]	9
	Wagoneer	W	2.8 (173)	5	4 [1]	4.5	15.8	2.5 [3]	13.5 [2]	9
	Cherokee	B	2.1 (126)	6.3	4 [1]	4.5	15.8	2.5 [3]	13.5 [2]	9
	Cherokee	H	2.5 (150)	4	4 [1]	4.5	15.8	2.5 [3]	13.5 [2]	9
	Cherokee	W	2.8 (173)	5	4 [1]	4.5	15.8	2.5 [3]	13.5 [2]	9
1987	Comanche	B	2.1 (126)	6.3	4 [1]	4.5	15.8	2.5 [3]	13.5 [2]	9
	Comanche	H	2.5 (150)	4	4 [1]	4.5	15.8	2.5 [3]	13.5 [2]	9
	Comanche	M	4.0 (243)	6	3.9 [1]	4.5	15.8	2.5 [3]	13.5 [2]	12
	Wagoneer	B	2.1 (126)	6.3	4 [1]	4.5	15.8	2.5 [3]	13.5 [2]	9
	Wagoneer	H	2.5 (150)	4	4 [1]	4.5	15.8	2.5 [3]	13.5 [2]	9
	Wagoneer	M	4.0 (243)	6	3.9 [1]	4.5	15.8	2.5 [3]	13.5 [2]	12
	Cherokee	B	2.1 (126)	6.3	4 [1]	4.5	15.8	2.5 [3]	13.5 [2]	9
	Cherokee	H	2.5 (150)	4	4 [1]	4.5	15.8	2.5 [3]	13.5 [2]	9
	Cherokee	M	4.0 (243)	6	3.9 [1]	4.5	15.8	2.5 [3]	13.5 [2]	12
1988	Comanche	H	2.5 (150)	4	4 [1]	4.9	17	2.5 [3]	13.5 [2]	9
	Comanche	M	4.0 (243)	6	4 [1]	4.9	17	2.5 [3]	13.5 [2]	12
	Wagoneer	H	2.5 (150)	4	4 [1]	4.9	17	2.5 [3]	13.5 [2]	9
	Wagoneer	M	4.0 (243)	6	4 [1]	4.9	17	2.5 [3]	13.5 [2]	12
	Cherokee	H	2.5 (150)	4	4 [1]	4.9	17	2.5 [3]	13.5 [2]	9
	Cherokee	M	4.0 (243)	6	4 [1]	4.9	17	2.5 [3]	13.5 [2]	12
1989	Comanche	E	2.5 (150)	4	4 [1]	4.9	17	2.5 [3]	18.5	9
	Comanche	L	4.0 (243)	6	4 [1]	4.9	17	2.5 [3]	18.5	12
	Wagoneer	L	4.0 (243)	6	4 [1]	4.9	17	2.5 [3]	20	12
	Cherokee	E	2.5 (150)	4	4 [1]	4.9	17	2.5 [3]	20	9
	Cherokee	L	4.0 (243)	6	4 [1]	4.9	17	2.5 [3]	20	12
1990	Comanche	E	2.5 (150)	4	4 [1]	4.9	17	2.5 [3]	18.5	9
	Comanche	L	4.0 (243)	6	4 [1]	4.9	17	2.5 [3]	18.5	12

86741CA7

CAPACITIES

Year	Model	Engine ID/VIN	Engine Displacement Liters (cu. in.)	Engine Oil with Filter (qts.)	Transmission (pts.)			Drive Axle (pts.)	Fuel Tank (gal.)	Cooling System (qts.)
					4-Spd	5-Spd	Auto.			
1990	Cherokee	E	2.5 (150)	4	4 [1]	4.9	17	2.5 [3]	20	9
	Cherokee	L	4.0 (243)	6	4 [1]	4.9	17	2.5 [3]	20	12
1991	Comanche	P	2.5 (150)	4	7	7.4	17	2.5 [3]	18.5	10
	Comanche	S	4.0 (243)	6	7	6.7	17	2.5 [3]	18.5	12
	Cherokee	P	2.5 (150)	4	-	7.4	17	2.5 [3]	20	10
	Cherokee	S	4.0 (243)	6	-	6.7	17	2.5 [3]	20	12
1992	Comanche	P	2.5 (150)	4	7	7.4	17	2.5 [3]	18.5	10
	Comanche	S	4.0 (243)	6	7	6.7	17	2.5 [3]	18.5	12
	Cherokee	P	2.5 (150)	4	-	7.4	17	2.5 [3]	20	10
	Cherokee	S	4.0 (243)	6	-	6.7	17	2.5 [3]	20	12
1993	Cherokee	P	2.5 (150)	4	-	7.4	17	2.5 [3]	20	10
	Cherokee	S	4.0 (243)	6	-	6.7	17	2.5 [3]	20	12
	Grand Cherokee	S	4.0 (243)	6	-	6.5	17	3.4	23	9.3
	Grand Cherokee	Y	5.2 (318)	5	-	6.5	17	3.4	23.0	14.9
	Grand Wagoneer	Y	5.2 (318)	5	-	-	17	3.4	23.0	14.9
1994	Cherokee	P	2.5 (150)	4	-	7.4	17	2.5 [3]	20	10
	Cherokee	S	4.0 (243)	6	-	6.7	17	2.5 [3]	20	12
	Grand Cherokee	S	4.0 (243)	6	-	6.5	17	3.4	23	9.3
	Grand Cherokee	Y	5.2 (318)	5	-	6.5	17	3.4	23.0	14.9
1995	Cherokee	P	2.5 (150)	4	-	7.4	17	2.5 [4]	20	10
	Cherokee	S	4.0 (243)	6	-	6.7	17	2.5 [4]	20	12
	Grand Cherokee	S	4.0 (243)	6	-	6.5	17	3.4	23	9.3
	Grand Cherokee	Y	5.2 (318)	5	-	6.5	17	3.4	23.0	14.9
1996	Cherokee	P	2.5 (150)	4	-	7.4	17	2.5 [4]	20	10
	Cherokee	S	4.0 (243)	6	-	6.7	17	2.5 [4]	20	12
	Grand Cherokee	S	4.0 (243)	6	-	6.5	17	3.4	23	9.3
	Grand Cherokee	Y	5.2 (318)	5	-	6.5	17	3.4	23.0	14.9

1: Aisian Warner Transmission 7.4 pts.

2: Optional 20 gallon tank available

3: Heavy Duty: 3 pts.

4: 8 1/4 axle: 4.4 pts. When equipped with TRAC-LOK, add 2 oz. od friction modifier

86741CA8

PREVENTIVE MAINTENANCE CHART

Interval	Item	Service
Every 7,500 miles	Engine oil and filter	Change
	Oil filler cap	Clean
	Steering gear	Check level
	Power steering reservoir	Check level
	Differentials	Check level
	Manual transmission	Check level
	Transfer case	Check level
	Automatic transmission	Check level
	Steering Linkage	EP chassis lube
	Universal joints	EP chassis lube
	Exhaust system	Check
Every 30,000 miles	Automatic transmission	Change fluid/filter
	Manual transmission	Change fluid
	Transfer case	Change fluid
	Spark plugs	Replace
	Air filter	Replace
	Drive belts	Inspect/adjust
	Fuel filter	Replace
	Coolant ①	Replace
	PCV valve	Replace
	Brakes	Check
	Wheel bearings	Clean/repack
Every 60,000 miles	Drive belts	Replace
	Ignition wires	Replace
	Distributor cap/rotor	Replace
	Battery	Replace

① or 36 months (24 months thereafter)

86741c96

ENGLISH TO METRIC CONVERSION: MASS (WEIGHT)

Current mass measurement is expressed in pounds and ounces (lbs. & ozs.). The metric unit of mass (or weight) is the kilogram (kg). Even although this table does not show conversion of masses (weights) larger than 15 lbs, it is easy to calculate larger units by following the data immediately below.

To convert ounces (oz.) to grams (g): multiply th number of ozs. by 28
To convert grams (g) to ounces (oz.): multiply the number of grams by .035

To convert pounds (lbs.) to kilograms (kg): multiply the number of lbs. by .45
To convert kilograms (kg) to pounds (lbs.): multiply the number of kilograms by 2.2

lbs	kg	lbs	kg	oz	kg	oz	kg
0.1	0.04	0.9	0.41	0.1	0.003	0.9	0.024
0.2	0.09	1	0.4	0.2	0.005	1	0.03
0.3	0.14	2	0.9	0.3	0.008	2	0.06
0.4	0.18	3	1.4	0.4	0.011	3	0.08
0.5	0.23	4	1.8	0.5	0.014	4	0.11
0.6	0.27	5	2.3	0.6	0.017	5	0.14
0.7	0.32	10	4.5	0.7	0.020	10	0.28
0.8	0.36	15	6.8	0.8	0.023	15	0.42

ENGLISH TO METRIC CONVERSION: TEMPERATURE

To convert Fahrenheit (°F) to Celsius (°C): take number of °F and subtract 32; multiply result by 5; divide result by 9

To convert Celsius (°C) to Fahrenheit (°F): take number of °C and multiply by 9; divide result by 5; add 32 to total

Fahrenheit (F)		Celsius (C)		Fahrenheit (F)		Celsius (C)		Fahrenheit (F)		Celsius (C)	
°F	°C	°C	°F	°F	°C	°C	°F	°F	°C	°C	°F
−40	−40	−38	−36.4	80	26.7	18	64.4	215	101.7	80	176
−35	−37.2	−36	−32.8	85	29.4	20	68	220	104.4	85	185
−30	−34.4	−34	−29.2	90	32.2	22	71.6	225	107.2	90	194
−25	−31.7	−32	−25.6	95	35.0	24	75.2	230	110.0	95	202
−20	−28.9	−30	−22	100	37.8	26	78.8	235	112.8	100	212
−15	−26.1	−28	−18.4	105	40.6	28	82.4	240	115.6	105	221
−10	−23.3	−26	−14.8	110	43.3	30	86	245	118.3	110	230
−5	−20.6	−24	−11.2	115	46.1	32	89.6	250	121.1	115	239
0	−17.8	−22	−7.6	120	48.9	34	93.2	255	123.9	120	248
1	−17.2	−20	−4	125	51.7	36	96.8	260	126.6	125	257
2	−16.7	−18	−0.4	130	54.4	38	100.4	265	129.4	130	266
3	−16.1	−16	3.2	135	57.2	40	104	270	132.2	135	275
4	−15.6	−14	6.8	140	60.0	42	107.6	275	135.0	140	284
5	−15.0	−12	10.4	145	62.8	44	112.2	280	137.8	145	293
10	−12.2	−10	14	150	65.6	46	114.8	285	140.6	150	302
15	−9.4	−8	17.6	155	68.3	48	118.4	290	143.3	155	311
20	−6.7	−6	21.2	160	71.1	50	122	295	146.1	160	320
25	−3.9	−4	24.8	165	73.9	52	125.6	300	148.9	165	329
30	−1.1	−2	28.4	170	76.7	54	129.2	305	151.7	170	338
35	1.7	0	32	175	79.4	56	132.8	310	154.4	175	347
40	4.4	2	35.6	180	82.2	58	136.4	315	157.2	180	356
45	7.2	4	39.2	185	85.0	60	140	320	160.0	185	365
50	10.0	6	42.8	190	87.8	62	143.6	325	162.8	190	374
55	12.8	8	46.4	195	90.6	64	147.2	330	165.6	195	383
60	15.6	10	50	200	93.3	66	150.8	335	168.3	200	392
65	18.3	12	53.6	205	96.1	68	154.4	340	171.1	205	401
70	21.1	14	57.2	210	98.9	70	158	345	173.9	210	410
75	23.9	16	60.8	212	100.0	75	167	350	176.7	215	414

ENGLISH TO METRIC CONVERSION: LENGTH

To convert inches (ins.) to millimeters (mm): multiply number of inches by 25.4

To convert millimeters (mm) to inches (ins.): multiply number of millimeters by .04

Inches		Decimals	Milli-meters	Inches to millimeters		Inches		Decimals	Milli-meters	Inches to millimeters	
				inches	mm					inches	mm
	1/64	0.051625	0.3969	0.0001	0.00254		33/64	0.515625	13.0969	0.6	15.24
1/32		0.03125	0.7937	0.0002	0.00508	17/32		0.53125	13.4937	0.7	17.78
	3/64	0.046875	1.1906	0.0003	0.00762		35/64	0.546875	13.8906	0.8	20.32
1/16		0.0625	1.5875	0.0004	0.01016	9/16		0.5625	14.2875	0.9	22.86
	5/64	0.078125	1.9844	0.0005	0.01270		37/64	0.578125	14.6844	1	25.4
3/32		0.09375	2.3812	0.0006	0.01524	19/32		0.59375	15.0812	2	50.8
	7/64	0.109375	2.7781	0.0007	0.01778		39/64	0.609375	15.4781	3	76.2
1/8		0.125	3.1750	0.0008	0.02032	5/8		0.625	15.8750	4	101.6
	9/64	0.140625	3.5719	0.0009	0.02286		41/64	0.640625	16.2719	5	127.0
5/32		0.15625	3.9687	0.001	0.0254	21/32		0.65625	16.6687	6	152.4
	11/64	0.171875	4.3656	0.002	0.0508		43/64	0.671875	17.0656	7	177.8
3/16		0.1875	4.7625	0.003	0.0762	11/16		0.6875	17.4625	8	203.2
	13/64	0.203125	5.1594	0.004	0.1016		45/64	0.703125	17.8594	9	228.6
7/32		0.21875	5.5562	0.005	0.1270	23/32		0.71875	18.2562	10	254.0
	15/64	0.234375	5.9531	0.006	0.1524		47/64	0.734375	18.6531	11	279.4
1/4		0.25	6.3500	0.007	0.1778	3/4		0.75	19.0500	12	304.8
	17/64	0.265625	6.7469	0.008	0.2032		49/64	0.765625	19.4469	13	330.2
9/32		0.28125	7.1437	0.009	0.2286	25/32		0.78125	19.8437	14	355.6
	19/64	0.296875	7.5406	0.01	0.254		51/64	0.796875	20.2406	15	381.0
5/16		0.3125	7.9375	0.02	0.508	13/16		0.8125	20.6375	16	406.4
	21/64	0.328125	8.3344	0.03	0.762		53/64	0.828125	21.0344	17	431.8
11/32		0.34375	8.7312	0.04	1.016	27/32		0.84375	21.4312	18	457.2
	23/64	0.359375	9.1281	0.05	1.270		55/64	0.859375	21.8281	19	482.6
3/8		0.375	9.5250	0.06	1.524	7/8		0.875	22.2250	20	508.0
	25/64	0.390625	9.9219	0.07	1.778		57/64	0.890625	22.6219	21	533.4
13/32		0.40625	10.3187	0.08	2.032	29/32		0.90625	23.0187	22	558.8
	27/64	0.421875	10.7156	0.09	2.286		59/64	0.921875	23.4156	23	584.2
7/16		0.4375	11.1125	0.1	2.54	15/16		0.9375	23.8125	24	609.6
	29/64	0.453125	11.5094	0.2	5.08		61/64	0.953125	24.2094	25	635.0
15/32		0.46875	11.9062	0.3	7.62	31/32		0.96875	24.6062	26	660.4
	31/64	0.484375	12.3031	0.4	10.16		63/64	0.984375	25.0031	27	690.6
1/2		0.5	12.7000	0.5	12.70						

ENGLISH TO METRIC CONVERSION: TORQUE

To convert foot-pounds (ft. lbs.) to Newton-meters: multiply the number of ft. lbs. by 1.3

To convert inch-pounds (in. lbs.) to Newton-meters: multiply the number of in. lbs. by .11

in lbs	N-m	in lbs	N-m	in lbs	N-m	in lbs	N-m	in lbs	N-m
0.1	0.01	1	0.11	10	1.13	19	2.15	28	3.16
0.2	0.02	2	0.23	11	1.24	20	2.26	29	3.28
0.3	0.03	3	0.34	12	1.36	21	2.37	30	3.39
0.4	0.04	4	0.45	13	1.47	22	2.49	31	3.50
0.5	0.06	5	0.56	14	1.58	23	2.60	32	3.62
0.6	0.07	6	0.68	15	1.70	24	2.71	33	3.73
0.7	0.08	7	0.78	16	1.81	25	2.82	34	3.84
0.8	0.09	8	0.90	17	1.92	26	2.94	35	3.95
0.9	0.10	9	1.02	18	2.03	27	3.05	36	4.0/

ENGLISH TO METRIC CONVERSION: TORQUE

Torque is now expressed as either foot-pounds (ft./lbs.) or inch-pounds (in./lbs.). The metric measurement unit for torque is the Newton-meter (Nm). This unit—the Nm—will be used for all SI metric torque references, both the present ft./lbs. and in./lbs.

ft lbs	N-m	ft lbs	N-m	ft lbs	N-m	ft lbs	N-m
0.1	0.1	33	44.7	74	100.3	115	155.9
0.2	0.3	34	46.1	75	101.7	116	157.3
0.3	0.4	35	47.4	76	103.0	117	158.6
0.4	0.5	36	48.8	77	104.4	118	160.0
0.5	0.7	37	50.7	78	105.8	119	161.3
0.6	0.8	38	51.5	79	107.1	120	162.7
0.7	1.0	39	52.9	80	108.5	121	164.0
0.8	1.1	40	54.2	81	109.8	122	165.4
0.9	1.2	41	55.6	82	111.2	123	166.8
1	1.3	42	56.9	83	112.5	124	168.1
2	2.7	43	58.3	84	113.9	125	169.5
3	4.1	44	59.7	85	115.2	126	170.8
4	5.4	45	61.0	86	116.6	127	172.2
5	6.8	46	62.4	87	118.0	128	173.5
6	8.1	47	63.7	88	119.3	129	174.9
7	9.5	48	65.1	89	120.7	130	176.2
8	10.8	49	66.4	90	122.0	131	177.6
9	12.2	50	67.8	91	123.4	132	179.0
10	13.6	51	69.2	92	124.7	133	180.3
11	14.9	52	70.5	93	126.1	134	181.7
12	16.3	53	71.9	94	127.4	135	183.0
13	17.6	54	73.2	95	128.8	136	184.4
14	18.9	55	74.6	96	130.2	137	185.7
15	20.3	56	75.9	97	131.5	138	187.1
16	21.7	57	77.3	98	132.9	139	188.5
17	23.0	58	78.6	99	134.2	140	189.8
18	24.4	59	80.0	100	135.6	141	191.2
19	25.8	60	81.4	101	136.9	142	192.5
20	27.1	61	82.7	102	138.3	143	193.9
21	28.5	62	84.1	103	139.6	144	195.2
22	29.8	63	85.4	104	141.0	145	196.6
23	31.2	64	86.8	105	142.4	146	198.0
24	32.5	65	88.1	106	143.7	147	199.3
25	33.9	66	89.5	107	145.1	148	200.7
26	35.2	67	90.8	108	146.4	149	202.0
27	36.6	68	92.2	109	147.8	150	203.4
28	38.0	69	93.6	110	149.1	151	204.7
29	39.3	70	94.9	111	150.5	152	206.1
30	40.7	71	96.3	112	151.8	153	207.4
31	42.0	72	97.6	113	153.2	154	208.8
32	43.4	73	99.0	114	154.6	155	210.2

tccs1c03

ENGLISH TO METRIC CONVERSION: FORCE

Force is presently measured in pounds (lbs.). This type of measurement is used to measure spring pressure, specifically how many pounds it takes to compress a spring. Our present force unit (the pound) will be replaced in SI metric measurements by the Newton (N). This term will eventually see use in specifications for electric motor brush spring pressures, valve spring pressures, etc.

To convert pounds (lbs.) to Newton (N): multiply the number of lbs. by 4.45

lbs	N	lbs	N	lbs	N	oz	N
0.01	0.04	21	93.4	59	262.4	1	0.3
0.02	0.09	22	97.9	60	266.9	2	0.6
0.03	0.13	23	102.3	61	271.3	3	0.8
0.04	0.18	24	106.8	62	275.8	4	1.1
0.05	0.22	25	111.2	63	280.2	5	1.4
0.06	0.27	26	115.6	64	284.6	6	1.7
0.07	0.31	27	120.1	65	289.1	7	2.0
0.08	0.36	28	124.6	66	293.6	8	2.2
0.09	0.40	29	129.0	67	298.0	9	2.5
0.1	0.4	30	133.4	68	302.5	10	2.8
0.2	0.9	31	137.9	69	306.9	11	3.1
0.3	1.3	32	142.3	70	311.4	12	3.3
0.4	1.8	33	146.8	71	315.8	13	3.6
0.5	2.2	34	151.2	72	320.3	14	3.9
0.6	2.7	35	155.7	73	324.7	15	4.2
0.7	3.1	36	160.1	74	329.2	16	4.4
0.8	3.6	37	164.6	75	333.6	17	4.7
0.9	4.0	38	169.0	76	338.1	18	5.0
1	4.4	39	173.5	77	342.5	19	5.3
2	8.9	40	177.9	78	347.0	20	5.6
3	13.4	41	182.4	79	351.4	21	5.8
4	17.8	42	186.8	80	355.9	22	6.1
5	22.2	43	191.3	81	360.3	23	6.4
6	26.7	44	195.7	82	364.8	24	6.7
7	31.1	45	200.2	83	369.2	25	7.0
8	35.6	46	204.6	84	373.6	26	7.2
9	40.0	47	209.1	85	378.1	27	7.5
10	44.5	48	213.5	86	382.6	28	7.8
11	48.9	49	218.0	87	387.0	29	8.1
12	53.4	50	224.4	88	391.4	30	8.3
13	57.8	51	226.9	89	395.9	31	8.6
14	62.3	52	231.3	90	400.3	32	8.9
15	66.7	53	235.8	91	404.8	33	9.2
16	71.2	54	240.2	92	409.2	34	9.4
17	75.6	55	244.6	93	413.7	35	9.7
18	80.1	56	249.1	94	418.1	36	10.0
19	84.5	57	253.6	95	422.6	37	10.3
20	89.0	58	258.0	96	427.0	38	10.6

tccs1c04

ENGLISH TO METRIC CONVERSION: LIQUID CAPACITY

Liquid or fluid capacity is presently expressed as pints, quarts or gallons, or a combination of all of these. In the metric system the liter (l) will become the basic unit. Fractions of a liter would be expressed as deciliters, centiliters, or most frequently (and commonly) as milliliters.

To convert pints (pts.) to liters (l): multiply the number of pints by .47
To convert liters (l) to pints (pts.): multiply the number of liters by 2.1
To convert quarts (qts.) to liters (l): multiply the number of quarts by .95

To convert liters (l) to quarts (qts.): multiply the number of liters by 1.06
To convert gallons (gals.) to liters (l): multiply the number of gallons by 3.8
To convert liters (l) to gallons (gals.): multiply the number of liters by .26

gals	liters	qts	liters	pts	liters
0.1	0.38	0.1	0.10	0.1	0.05
0.2	0.76	0.2	0.19	0.2	0.10
0.3	1.1	0.3	0.28	0.3	0.14
0.4	1.5	0.4	0.38	0.4	0.19
0.5	1.9	0.5	0.47	0.5	0.24
0.6	2.3	0.6	0.57	0.6	0.28
0.7	2.6	0.7	0.66	0.7	0.33
0.8	3.0	0.8	0.76	0.8	0.38
0.9	3.4	0.9	0.85	0.9	0.43
1	3.8	1	1.0	1	0.5
2	7.6	2	1.9	2	1.0
3	11.4	3	2.8	3	1.4
4	15.1	4	3.8	4	1.9
5	18.9	5	4.7	5	2.4
6	22.7	6	5.7	6	2.8
7	26.5	7	6.6	7	3.3
8	30.3	8	7.6	8	3.8
9	34.1	9	8.5	9	4.3
10	37.8	10	9.5	10	4.7
11	41.6	11	10.4	11	5.2
12	45.4	12	11.4	12	5.7
13	49.2	13	12.3	13	6.2
14	53.0	14	13.2	14	6.6
15	56.8	15	14.2	15	7.1
16	60.6	16	15.1	16	7.6
17	64.3	17	16.1	17	8.0
18	68.1	18	17.0	18	8.5
19	71.9	19	18.0	19	9.0
20	75.7	20	18.9	20	9.5
21	79.5	21	19.9	21	9.9
22	83.2	22	20.8	22	10.4
23	87.0	23	21.8	23	10.9
24	90.8	24	22.7	24	11.4
25	94.6	25	23.6	25	11.8
26	98.4	26	24.6	26	12.3
27	102.2	27	25.5	27	12.8
28	106.0	28	26.5	28	13.2
29	110.0	29	27.4	29	13.7
30	113.5	30	28.4	30	14.2

ENGLISH TO METRIC CONVERSION: PRESSURE

The basic unit of pressure measurement used today is expressed as pounds per square inch (psi). The metric unit for psi will be the kilopascal (kPa). This will apply to either fluid pressure or air pressure, and will be frequently seen in tire pressure readings, oil pressure specifications, fuel pump pressure, etc.

To convert pounds per square inch (psi) to kilopascals (kPa): multiply the number of psi by 6.89

Psi	kPa	Psi	kPa	Psi	kPa	Psi	kPa
0.1	0.7	37	255.1	82	565.4	127	875.6
0.2	1.4	38	262.0	83	572.3	128	882.5
0.3	2.1	39	268.9	84	579.2	129	889.4
0.4	2.8	40	275.8	85	586.0	130	896.3
0.5	3.4	41	282.7	86	592.9	131	903.2
0.6	4.1	42	289.6	87	599.8	132	910.1
0.7	4.8	43	296.5	88	606.7	133	917.0
0.8	5.5	44	303.4	89	613.6	134	923.9
0.9	6.2	45	310.3	90	620.5	135	930.8
1	6.9	46	317.2	91	627.4	136	937.7
2	13.8	47	324.0	92	634.3	137	944.6
3	20.7	48	331.0	93	641.2	138	951.5
4	27.6	49	337.8	94	648.1	139	958.4
5	34.5	50	344.7	95	655.0	140	965.2
6	41.4	51	351.6	96	661.9	141	972.2
7	48.3	52	358.5	97	668.8	142	979.0
8	55.2	53	365.4	98	675.7	143	985.9
9	62.1	54	372.3	99	682.6	144	992.8
10	69.0	55	379.2	100	689.5	145	999.7
11	75.8	56	386.1	101	696.4	146	1006.6
12	82.7	57	393.0	102	703.3	147	1013.5
13	89.6	58	399.9	103	710.2	148	1020.4
14	96.5	59	406.8	104	717.0	149	1027.3
15	103.4	60	413.7	105	723.9	150	1034.2
16	110.3	61	420.6	106	730.8	151	1041.1
17	117.2	62	427.5	107	737.7	152	1048.0
18	124.1	63	434.4	108	744.6	153	1054.9
19	131.0	64	441.3	109	751.5	154	1061.8
20	137.9	65	448.2	110	758.4	155	1068.7
21	144.8	66	455.0	111	765.3	156	1075.6
22	151.7	67	461.9	112	772.2	157	1082.5
23	158.6	68	468.8	113	779.1	158	1089.4
24	165.5	69	475.7	114	786.0	159	1096.3
25	172.4	70	482.6	115	792.9	160	1103.2
26	179.3	71	489.5	116	799.8	161	1110.0
27	186.2	72	496.4	117	806.7	162	1116.9
28	193.0	73	503.3	118	813.6	163	1123.8
29	200.0	74	510.2	119	820.5	164	1130.7
30	206.8	75	517.1	120	827.4	165	1137.6
31	213.7	76	524.0	121	834.3	166	1144.5
32	220.6	77	530.9	122	841.2	167	1151.4
33	227.5	78	537.8	123	848.0	168	1158.3
34	234.4	79	544.7	124	854.9	169	1165.2
35	241.3	80	551.6	125	861.8	170	1172.1
36	248.2	81	558.5	126	868.7	171	1179.0

tccs1c06

ENGLISH TO METRIC CONVERSION: PRESSURE

The basic unit of pressure measurement used today is expressed as pounds per square inch (psi). The metric unit for psi will be the kilopascal (kPa). This will apply to either fluid pressure or air pressure, and will be frequently seen in tire pressure readings, oil pressure specifications, fuel pump pressure, etc.

To convert pounds per square inch (psi) to kilopascals (kPa): multiply the number of psi by 6.89

Psi	kPa	Psi	kPa	Psi	kPa	Psi	kPa
172	1185.9	216	1489.3	260	1792.6	304	2096.0
173	1192.8	217	1496.2	261	1799.5	305	2102.9
174	1199.7	218	1503.1	262	1806.4	306	2109.8
175	1206.6	219	1510.0	263	1813.3	307	2116.7
176	1213.5	220	1516.8	264	1820.2	308	2123.6
177	1220.4	221	1523.7	265	1827.1	309	2130.5
178	1227.3	222	1530.6	266	1834.0	310	2137.4
179	1234.2	223	1537.5	267	1840.9	311	2144.3
180	1241.0	224	1544.4	268	1847.8	312	2151.2
181	1247.9	225	1551.3	269	1854.7	313	2158.1
182	1254.8	226	1558.2	270	1861.6	314	2164.9
183	1261.7	227	1565.1	271	1868.5	315	2171.8
184	1268.6	228	1572.0	272	1875.4	316	2178.7
185	1275.5	229	1578.9	273	1882.3	317	2185.6
186	1282.4	230	1585.8	274	1889.2	318	2192.5
187	1289.3	231	1592.7	275	1896.1	319	2199.4
188	1296.2	232	1599.6	276	1903.0	320	2206.3
189	1303.1	233	1606.5	277	1909.8	321	2213.2
190	1310.0	234	1613.4	278	1916.7	322	2220.1
191	1316.9	235	1620.3	279	1923.6	323	2227.0
192	1323.8	236	1627.2	280	1930.5	324	2233.9
193	1330.7	237	1634.1	281	1937.4	325	2240.8
194	1337.6	238	1641.0	282	1944.3	326	2247.7
195	1344.5	239	1647.8	283	1951.2	327	2254.6
196	1351.4	240	1654.7	284	1958.1	328	2261.5
197	1358.3	241	1661.6	285	1965.0	329	2268.4
198	1365.2	242	1668.5	286	1971.9	330	2275.3
199	1372.0	243	1675.4	287	1978.8	331	2282.2
200	1378.9	244	1682.3	288	1985.7	332	2289.1
201	1385.8	245	1689.2	289	1992.6	333	2295.9
202	1392.7	246	1696.1	290	1999.5	334	2302.8
203	1399.6	247	1703.0	291	2006.4	335	2309.7
204	1406.5	248	1709.9	292	2013.3	336	2316.6
205	1413.4	249	1716.8	293	2020.2	337	2323.5
206	1420.3	250	1723.7	294	2027.1	338	2330.4
207	1427.2	251	1730.6	295	2034.0	339	2337.3
208	1434.1	252	1737.5	296	2040.8	240	2344.2
209	1441.0	253	1744.4	297	2047.7	341	2351.1
210	1447.9	254	1751.3	298	2054.6	342	2358.0
211	1454.8	255	1758.2	299	2061.5	343	2364.9
212	1461.7	256	1765.1	300	2068.4	344	2371.8
213	1468.7	257	1772.0	301	2075.3	345	2378.7
214	1475.5	258	1778.8	302	2082.2	346	2385.6
215	1482.4	259	1785.7	303	2089.1	347	2392.5

tccs1c07

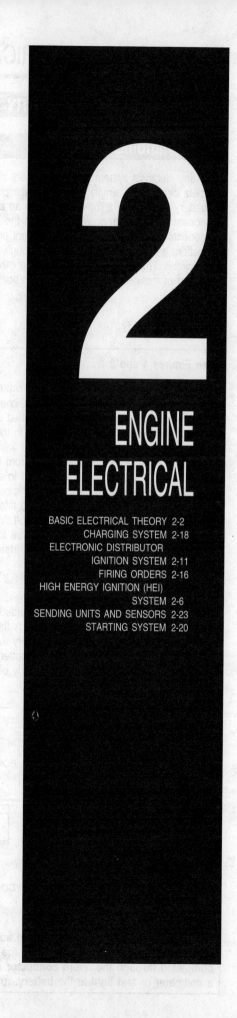

2

ENGINE
ELECTRICAL

BASIC ELECTRICAL THEORY

Understanding Electricity

For any electrical system to operate, there must be a complete circuit. This simply means that the power flow from the battery must make a full circle. When an electrical component is operating, power flows from the battery to the components, passes through the component (load) causing it to function, and returns to the battery through the ground path of the circuit. This ground may be either another wire or a metal part of the vehicle (depending upon how the component is designed).

BASIC CIRCUITS

▶ See Figures 1 and 2

Perhaps the easiest way to visualize a circuit is to think of connecting a light bulb (with two wires attached to it) to the battery. If one of the two wires was attached to the negative post (-) of the battery and the other wire to the positive post (+), the circuit would be complete and the light bulb would illuminate. Electricity could follow a path from the battery to the bulb and back to the battery. It's not hard to see that with longer wires on our light bulb, it could be mounted anywhere on the vehicle. Further, one wire could be fitted with a switch so that the light could be turned on and off. Various other items could be added to our primitive circuit to make the light flash, become brighter or dimmer under certain conditions, or advise the user that it's burned out.

Ground

Some automotive components are grounded through their mounting points. The electrical current runs through the chassis of the vehicle and returns to the battery through the ground (-) cable; if you look, you'll see that the battery ground cable connects between the battery and the body of the vehicle.

Load

Every complete circuit must include a "load" (something to use the electricity coming from the source). If you were to connect a wire between the two terminals of the battery (DON'T do this, but take our word for it) without the light bulb, the battery would attempt to deliver its entire power supply from one pole to another almost instantly. This is a short circuit. The electricity is taking a short cut to get to ground and is not being used by any load in the circuit. This sudden and uncontrolled electrical flow can cause great damage to other components in the circuit and can develop a tremendous amount of heat. A short in an automotive wiring harness can develop sufficient heat to melt the insulation on all the surrounding wires and reduce a multiple wire cable to one sad lump of plastic and copper. Two common causes of shorts are broken insulation (thereby exposing the wire to contact with surrounding metal surfaces or other wires) or a failed switch (the pins inside the switch come out of place and touch each other).

Switches and Relays

Some electrical components which require a large amount of current to operate also have a relay in their circuit. Since these circuits carry a large amount of current (amperage or amps), the thickness of the wire in the circuit (wire gauge) is also greater. If this large wire were connected from the load to the control switch on the dash, the switch would have to carry the high amperage load and the dash would be twice as large to accommodate wiring harnesses as thick as your wrist. To prevent these problems, a relay is used. The large wires in the circuit are connected from the battery to one side of the relay and from the opposite side of the relay to the load. The relay is normally open, preventing current from passing through the circuit. An additional, smaller wire is connected from the relay to the control switch for the circuit. When the control switch is turned on, it grounds the smaller wire to the relay and completes its circuit. The main switch inside the relay closes, sending power to the component without routing the main

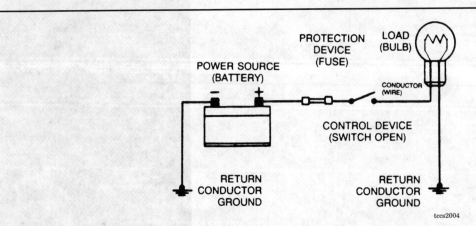

Fig. 1 Here is an example of a simple automotive circuit. When the switch is closed, power from the positive battery terminal flows through the fuse, then the switch and to the load (light bulb), the light illuminates and then, the circuit is completed through the return conductor and the vehicle ground. If the light did not work, the tests could be made with a voltmeter or test light at the battery, fuse, switch or bulb socket

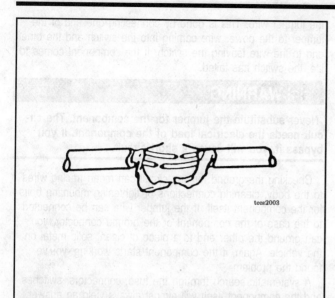

Fig. 2 Damaged insulation can allow wires to break (causing an open circuit) or touch (causing a short)

power through the inside of the vehicle. Some common circuits which may use relays are the horn, headlights, starter and rear window defogger systems.

Protective Devices

It is possible for larger surges of current to pass through the electrical system of your vehicle. If this surge of current were to reach the load in the circuit, it could burn it out or severely damage it. To prevent this, fuses, circuit breakers and/or fusible links are connected into the supply wires of the electrical system. These items are nothing more than a built-in weak spot in the system. It's much easier to go to a known location (the fusebox) to see why a circuit is inoperative than to dissect 15 feet of wiring under the dashboard, looking for what happened.

When an electrical current of excessive power passes through the fuse, the fuse blows (the conductor melts) and breaks the circuit, preventing the passage of current and protecting the components.

A circuit breaker is basically a self repairing fuse. It will open the circuit in the same fashion as a fuse, but when either the short is removed or the surge subsides, the circuit breaker resets itself and does not need replacement.

A fuse link (fusible link or main link) is a wire that acts as a fuse. One of these is normally connected between the starter relay and the main wiring harness under the hood. Since the starter is usually the highest electrical draw on the vehicle, an internal short during starting could direct about 130 amps into the wrong places. Consider the damage potential of introducing this current into a system whose wiring is rated at 15 amps and you'll understand the need for protection. Since this link is very early in the electrical path, it's the first place to look if nothing on the vehicle works, but the battery seems to be charged and is properly connected.

TROUBLESHOOTING

▶ See Figures 3, 4 and 5

Electrical problems generally fall into one of three areas:
• The component that is not functioning is not receiving current.
• The component is receiving power but is not using it or is using it incorrectly (component failure).
• The component is improperly grounded.

The circuit can be can be checked with a test light and a jumper wire. The test light is a device that looks like a pointed screwdriver with a wire on one end and a bulb in its handle. A jumper wire is simply a piece of wire with alligator clips or special terminals on each end. If a component is not working,

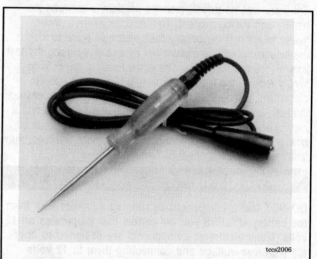

Fig. 3 A 12 volt test light is useful when checking parts of a circuit for power

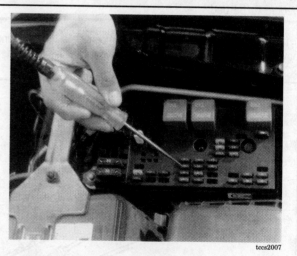

Fig. 4 Here, someone is checking a circuit by making sure there is power to the component's fuse

you must follow a systematic plan to determine which of the three causes is the villain.

1. Turn ON the switch that controls the item not working.

➡**Some items only work when the ignition switch is turned ON.**

2. Disconnect the power supply wire from the component.

3. Attach the ground wire of a test light or a voltmeter to a good metal ground.

4. Touch the end probe of the test light (or the positive lead of the voltmeter) to the power wire; if there is current in the wire, the light in the test light will come on (or the voltmeter will indicate the amount of voltage). You have now established that current is getting to the component.

5. Turn the ignition or dash switch **OFF** and reconnect the wire to the component.

If there was no power, then the problem is between the battery and the component. This includes all the switches, fuses, relays and the battery itself. The next place to look is the fusebox; check carefully either by eye or by using the test light across the fuse clips. The easiest way to check is to simply replace the fuse. If the fuse is blown, and upon replacement, immediately blows again, there is a short between the fuse and the component. This is generally (not always) a sign of an internal short in the component. Disconnect the power wire at the component again and replace the fuse; if the fuse holds, the component is the problem.

✳✳WARNING

DO NOT test a component by running a jumper wire from the battery UNLESS you are certain that it operates on 12 volts. Many electronic components are designed to operate with less voltage and connecting them to 12 volts could destroy them. Jumper wires are best used to bypass a portion of the circuit (such as a stretch of wire or a switch) that DOES NOT contain a resistor and is suspected to be bad.

If all the fuses are good and the component is not receiving power, find the switch for the circuit. Bypass the switch with

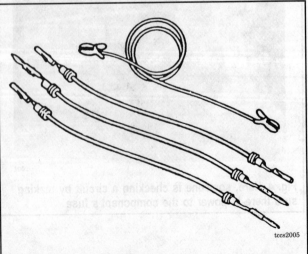

tccs2005

Fig. 5 Jumper wires with various connectors are handy for quick electrical testing

the jumper wire. This is done by connecting one end of the jumper to the power wire coming into the switch and the other end to the wire leaving the switch. If the component comes to life, the switch has failed.

✳✳WARNING

Never substitute the jumper for the component. The circuit needs the electrical load of the component. If you bypass it, you will cause a short circuit.

Checking the ground for any circuit can mean tracing wires to the body, cleaning connections or tightening mounting bolts for the component itself. If the jumper wire can be connected to the case of the component or the ground connector, you can ground the other end to a piece of clean, solid metal on the vehicle. Again, if the component starts working, you've found the problem.

A systematic search through the fuse, connectors, switches and the component itself will almost always yield an answer. Loose and/or corroded connectors, particularly in ground circuits, are becoming a larger problem in modern vehicles. The computers and on-board electronic (solid state) systems are highly sensitive to improper grounds and will change their function drastically if one occurs.

Remember that for any electrical circuit to work, ALL the connections must be clean and tight.

➡**For more information on Understanding and Troubleshooting Electrical Systems, please refer to Section 6 of this manual.**

Battery, Starting and Charging Systems

BASIC OPERATING PRINCIPLES

Battery

The battery is the first link in the chain of mechanisms which work together to provide cranking of the automobile engine. In most modern vehicles, the battery is a lead/acid electrochemical device consisting of six 2v subsections (cells) connected in series so the unit is capable of producing approximately 12v of electrical pressure. Each subsection consists of a series of positive and negative plates held a short distance apart in a solution of sulfuric acid and water.

The two types of plates are of dissimilar metals. This sets-up a chemical reaction, and it is this reaction which produces current flow from the battery when its positive and negative terminals are connected to an electrical accessory such as a lamp or motor. The continued transfer of electrons would eventually convert the sulfuric acid to water, and make the two plates identical in chemical composition. As electrical energy is removed from the battery, its voltage output tends to drop. Thus, measuring battery voltage and battery electrolyte composition are two ways of checking the ability of the unit to supply power. During engine cranking, electrical energy is removed from the battery. However, if the charging circuit is in good condition and the operating conditions are normal, the power removed from the battery will be replaced by the alternator which will force electrons back through the battery, reversing the normal flow, and restoring the battery to its original chemical state.

Starting System

The battery and starting motor are linked by very heavy electrical cables designed to minimize resistance to the flow of current. Generally, the major power supply cable that leaves the battery goes directly to the starter, while other electrical system needs are supplied by a smaller cable. During starter operation, power flows from the battery to the starter and is grounded through the vehicle's frame/body or engine and the battery's negative ground strap.

The starter is a specially designed, direct current electric motor capable of producing a great amount of power for its size. One thing that allows the motor to produce a great deal of power is its tremendous rotating speed. It drives the engine through a tiny pinion gear (attached to the starter's armature), which drives the very large flywheel ring gear at a greatly reduced speed. Another factor allowing it to produce so much power is that only intermittent operation is required of it. Thus, little allowance for air circulation is necessary, and the windings can be built into a very small space.

The starter solenoid is a magnetic device which employs the small current supplied by the start circuit of the ignition switch. This magnetic action moves a plunger which mechanically engages the starter and closes the heavy switch connecting it to the battery. The starting switch circuit usually consists of the starting switch contained within the ignition switch, a neutral safety switch or clutch pedal switch, and the wiring necessary to connect these in series with the starter solenoid or relay.

The pinion, a small gear, is mounted to a one way drive clutch. This clutch is splined to the starter armature shaft. When the ignition switch is moved to the **START** position, the solenoid plunger slides the pinion toward the flywheel ring gear via a collar and spring. If the teeth on the pinion and flywheel match properly, the pinion will engage the flywheel immediately. If the gear teeth butt one another, the spring will be compressed and will force the gears to mesh as soon as the starter turns far enough to allow them to do so. As the solenoid plunger reaches the end of its travel, it closes the contacts that connect the battery and starter, then the engine is cranked.

As soon as the engine starts, the flywheel ring gear begins turning fast enough to drive the pinion at an extremely high rate of speed. At this point, the one-way clutch begins allowing the pinion to spin faster than the starter shaft so that the starter will not operate at excessive speed. When the ignition switch is released from the starter position, the solenoid is de-energized, and a spring pulls the gear out of mesh interrupting the current flow to the starter.

Some starters employ a separate relay, mounted away from the starter, to switch the motor and solenoid current on and off. The relay replaces the solenoid electrical switch, but does not eliminate the need for a solenoid mounted on the starter used to mechanically engage the starter drive gears. The relay is used to reduce the amount of current the starting switch must carry.

Charging System

The automobile charging system provides electrical power for operation of the vehicle's ignition system, starting system and all electrical accessories. The battery serves as an electrical surge or storage tank, storing (in chemical form) the energy originally produced by the engine driven generator. The system also provides a means of regulating output to protect the battery from being overcharged and to avoid excessive voltage to the accessories.

The storage battery is a chemical device incorporating parallel lead plates in a tank containing a sulfuric acid/water solution. Adjacent plates are slightly dissimilar, and the chemical reaction of the two dissimilar plates produces electrical energy when the battery is connected to a load such as the starter motor. The chemical reaction is reversible, so that when the generator is producing a voltage (electrical pressure) greater than that produced by the battery, electricity is forced into the battery, and the battery is returned to its fully charged state.

Newer automobiles use alternating current generators or alternators, because they are more efficient, can be rotated at higher speeds, and have fewer brush problems. In an alternator, the field usually rotates while all the current produced passes only through the stator winding. The brushes bear against continuous slip rings. This causes the current produced to periodically reverse the direction of its flow. Diodes (electrical one way valves) block the flow of current from traveling in the wrong direction. A series of diodes is wired together to permit the alternating flow of the stator to be rectified back to 12 volts DC for use by the vehicle's electrical system.

The voltage regulating function is performed by a regulator. The regulator is often built in to the alternator; this system is termed an integrated or internal regulator.

HIGH ENERGY IGNITION (HEI) SYSTEM

Description And Operation

The HEI system, used on 2.5L, 2.8L and 4.0L engines, is a pulse-triggered, transistorized controlled, inductive discharge ignition system. The entire HEI system (except for the ignition coil on fuel injected engines) is contained within the distributor cap.

The distributor, in addition to housing the mechanical and vacuum advance mechanisms, contains the electronic control module, and the magnetic triggering device. The magnetic pick-up assembly contains a permanent magnet, a pole piece with internal teeth, and a pick-up coil (not to be confused with the ignition coil).

In the HEI system, as in other electronic ignition systems, the breaker points have been replaced with an electronic switch — a transistor — which is located within the control module. This switching transistor performs the same function the points did in an conventional ignition system. It simply turns coil primary current on and off at the correct time. Essentially then, electronic and conventional ignition systems operate on the same principle.

The module which houses the switching transistor is controlled (turned on and off) by a magnetically generated impulse induced in the pick-up coil. When the teeth of the rotating timer align with the teeth of the pole piece, the induced voltage in the pick-up coil signals the electronic module to open the coil primary circuit. The primary current then decreases, and a high voltage is induced in the ignition coil secondary windings which is then directed through the rotor and high voltage leads (spark plug wires) to fire the spark plugs.

In essence then, the pick-up coil module system simply replaces the conventional breaker points and condenser. The condenser found within the distributor is for radio suppression purposes only and has nothing to do with the ignition process. The module automatically controls the dwell period, increasing it with increasing engine speed. Since dwell is automatically controlled, it cannot be adjusted. The module itself is non-adjustable and non-repairable and must be replaced if found defective.

HEI SYSTEM PRECAUTIONS

Before going on to troubleshooting, it might be a good idea to take note of the following precautions:

Timing Light Use

Inductive pick-up timing lights are the best kind to use if your truck is equipped with HEI. Timing lights which connect between the spark plug and the spark plug wire occasionally (not always) give false readings.

Spark Plug Wires

The plug wires used with HEI systems are of a different construction than conventional wires. When replacing them, make sure you get the correct wires, since conventional wires won't carry the voltage. Also, handle them carefully to avoid cracking or splitting them and never pierce them.

Tachometer Use

Not all tachometers will operate or indicate correctly when used on a HEI system. While some tachometers may give a reading, this does not necessarily mean the reading is correct. In addition, some tachometers hook up differently from others. If you can't figure out whether or not your tachometer will work on your truck, check with the tachometer manufacturer.

HEI Systems Testers

▶ See Figure 6

Instruments designed specifically for testing HEI systems are available from several tool manufacturers. Some of these will even test the module itself. However, the tests given in the following section will require only an ohmmeter and a voltmeter.

Diagnosis and Testing

▶ See Figures 7, 8 and 9

The symptoms of a defective component within the HEI system are exactly the same as those you would encounter in a conventional system. Some of these symptoms are:
- Hard or no Starting
- Rough Idle
- Fuel Poor Economy
- Engine misses under load or while accelerating

If you suspect a problem in the ignition system, there are certain preliminary checks which you should carry out before you begin to check the electronic portions of the system. First, it is extremely important to make sure the vehicle battery is in a good state of charge. A defective or poorly charged battery will cause the various components of the ignition system to read incorrectly when they are being tested. Second, make sure all wiring connections are clean and tight, not only at the battery, but also at the distributor cap, ignition coil, and at the electronic control module.

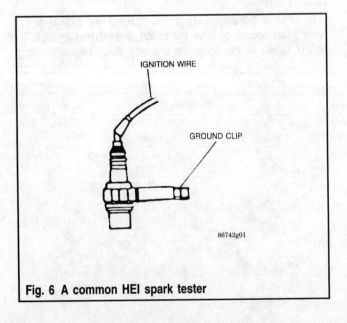

86742g01

Fig. 6 A common HEI spark tester

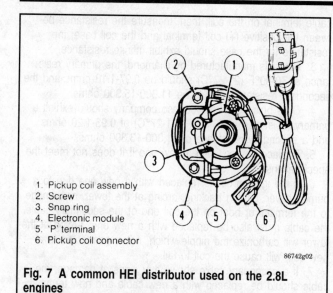

1. Pickup coil assembly
2. Screw
3. Snap ring
4. Electronic module
5. 'P' terminal
6. Pickup coil connector

86742g02

Fig. 7 A common HEI distributor used on the 2.8L engines

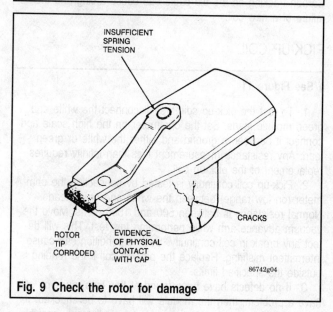

INSUFFICIENT SPRING TENSION

CRACKS

ROTOR TIP CORRODED

EVIDENCE OF PHYSICAL CONTACT WITH CAP

86742g04

Fig. 9 Check the rotor for damage

SECONDARY SPARK TEST

Since the only change between electronic and conventional ignition systems is in the distributor component area, it is imperative to check the secondary ignition circuit first. If the secondary circuit checks out properly, then the engine condition is probably not the fault of the ignition system. To check the secondary ignition system, perform a simple spark test.

1. Remove one of the plug wires and insert some sort of extension in the plug socket. An old spark plug with the ground electrode removed makes a good extension.

2. Hold the wire and extension about ¼ in. (6mm) away from the block and crank the engine. If a normal spark occurs, then the problem is most likely not in the ignition system.

3. Check for fuel system problems, or fouled spark plugs.

4. If, however, there is no spark or a weak spark, then further ignition system testing will have to be done. Troubleshooting techniques fall into two categories, depending on the nature of the problem. The categories are (1) Engine cranks, but won't start or (2) Engine runs, but runs rough or cuts out.

Engine Fails to Start

1. If the engine won't start, perform a spark test as described earlier. If no spark occurs, check for the presence of normal battery voltage at the battery (**BAT**) terminal in the distributor cap. The ignition switch must be in the **ON** position for this test.

2. If battery voltage is not present, this indicates an open circuit in the ignition primary wiring leading to the distributor. In this case, you will have to check wiring continuity back to the ignition switch using a test light.

3. If there is battery voltage at the **BAT** terminal, but no spark at the plugs, then the problem lies within the distributor assembly. Go on to test the ignition coil.

Engine Runs, but Runs Roughly or Cuts Out

1. Make sure the plug wires are in good shape first. There should be no obvious cracks or breaks. You can check the

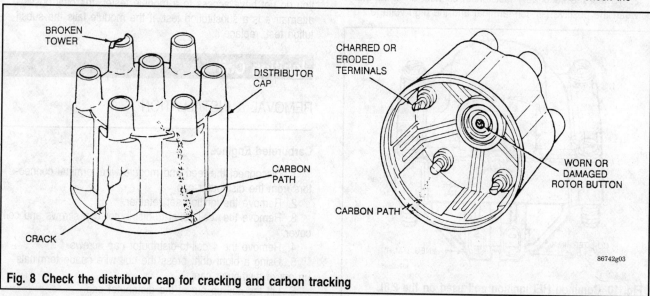

BROKEN TOWER

DISTRIBUTOR CAP

CARBON PATH

CRACK

CHARRED OR ERODED TERMINALS

WORN OR DAMAGED ROTOR BUTTON

CARBON PATH

86742g03

Fig. 8 Check the distributor cap for cracking and carbon tracking

plug wires with an ohmmeter, but do not pierce the wires with a probe.

2. If the plug wires are OK, remove the cap assembly, and check for moisture, cracks, chips, or carbon tracks, or any other high voltage leaks or failures.

3. Replace the cap if you find any defects. Make sure the timer wheel rotates when the engine is cranked. If everything is all right so far, go on to test the ignition coil.

IGNITION COIL

Carbureted Engines
▶ See Figure 10

1. Connect an ohmmeter between the **TACH** and **BAT** terminals in the distributor cap. The primary coil resistance should be less than one ohm (zero or nearly zero).

2. To check the coil secondary resistance, connect an ohmmeter between the rotor button and the **BAT** terminal. Then connect the ohmmeter between the ground terminal and the rotor button. The resistance in both cases should be between 6000 and 30,000 ohms.

3. Replace the coil only if the readings in Step 1 and 2 are infinite.

➡These resistance checks will not disclose shorted coil windings. This condition can be detected only with scope analysis or a suitably designed coil tester. If these instruments are unavailable, replace the coil with a known good coil as a final coil test.

Fuel Injected Engines

The ignition coil is designed to operate without an external ballast resistor. Inspect the coil for arcing. Test the coil primary and secondary resistance.

Measure the primary resistance as follows:

1. Connect an ohmmeter between the positive (+) and negative (-) terminals (the terminals which are connected to the engine wiring harness) on the coil.

2. To test the secondary resistance, connect an ohmmeter between the positive (+) coil terminal and the high voltage

cable terminal on the coil, then, measure the resistance between the positive (+) coil terminal and the coil case; the resistance for the case should exhibit infinite resistance.

3. For coils manufactured by Diamond, the primary resistance at 70-80°F (21-27°C) should be 0.97-1.18 ohms and the secondary resistance should be 11,300-15,300 ohms.

4. Coils built by the Toyodenso company should exhibit a primary resistance at 70-80°F (21-27°C) of 0.95-1.20 ohms and a secondary resistance of 11,300-13,300 ohms.

5. Replace any coil with a new one if it does not meet the specifications.

6. If the ignition coil is replaced with a new one due to a burned tower, carbon tracking, arcing at the tower, or damage to the terminal or boot on the coil end of the secondary cable, the cable must also be replaced with a new one. Arcing at the tower will carbonize the nipple which, if it is connected to a new coil, will cause the coil to fail.

7. If a secondary cable shows any signs of damage, the cable should be replaced with a new cable and new terminal. Carbon tracking on the old cable can cause arcing and the failure of a new coil.

PICK-UP COIL

▶ See Figure 11

1. To test the pick-up coil, first disconnect the white and green module leads. Set the ohmmeter on the high scale and connect it between a ground and either the white or green lead. Any resistance measurement less than infinity requires replacement of the pick-up coil.

2. Pick-up coil continuity is tested by connecting the ohmmeter (on low range) between the white and green leads. Normal resistance is between 500 and 1500 ohms. Move the vacuum advance arm while performing this test. This will detect any break in coil continuity. Such a condition can cause intermittent misfiring. Replace the pick-up coil if the reading is outside the specified limits.

3. If no defects have been found at this time, and you still have a problem, then the module will have to be checked. If you do not have access to a module tester, the only possible alternative is a substitution test. If the module fails the substitution test, replace it.

Ignition Coil

REMOVAL & INSTALLATION

Carbureted Engines

1. Disconnect the feed and module wire terminal connectors from the distributor cap.

2. Remove the ignition set retainer.

3. Remove the coil cover-to-distributor cap screws and coil cover.

4. Remove the 4 coil-to-distributor cap screws.

5. Using a blunt drift, press the coil wire spade terminals up out of distributor cap.

6. Lift the coil up out of the distributor cap.

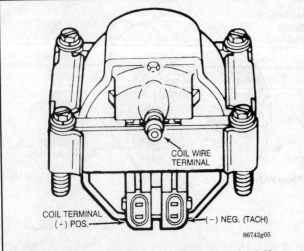

COIL WIRE TERMINAL

COIL TERMINAL (+) POS.

(−) NEG. (TACH)

86742g05

Fig. 10 Common HEI ignition coil used on the 2.8L engine

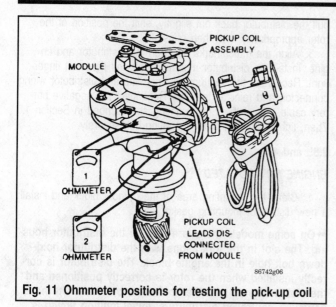

Fig. 11 Ohmmeter positions for testing the pick-up coil

7. Remove and clean the coil spring, rubber seal washer and coil cavity of the distributor cap.

8. Coat the rubber seal with a dielectric lubricant furnished in the replacement ignition coil package.

9. Reverse the above procedures to install.

Fuel Injected Engines

1. Make sure that the ignition switch is in the **OFF** position.

2. Tag and disconnect the coil wire and the connector on the side of the coil.

3. Remove the nuts holding the coil and bracket assembly to the engine and lift out the coil. The coil may be riveted to the bracket, to remove it will require drilling the rivets and punching them out.

4. Position the coil on the engine and tighten the nuts.

5. Engage the coil wire and electrical connectors.

Vacuum Advance Unit

REMOVAL & INSTALLATION

1. Remove the distributor cap and rotor as previously described.

2. Disconnect the vacuum hose from the vacuum advance unit.

3. Remove the two vacuum advance retaining screws, pull the advance unit outward, rotate and disengage the operating rod from its tang.

4. Reverse the above procedure to install.

Ignition Module

REMOVAL & INSTALLATION

▶ See Figure 12

1. Remove the distributor cap and rotor.

2. Disconnect the harness connector and pick-up coil spade connectors from the module. Be careful not to damage the wires when removing the connector.

3. Remove the two screws and module from the distributor housing.

4. Coat the bottom of the new module with dielectric silicone lubricant. This is usually supplied with the new module. Reverse the above procedure to install.

Distributor

REMOVAL

1. Remove the high-tension wires from the distributor cap terminal towers, noting their positions to assure correct reassembly.

2. Remove the primary lead from the terminal post at the side of the distributor.

3. Disconnect the vacuum line if equipped.

4. Remove the distributor cap retaining hooks or screws and remove the distributor cap.

5. Note the position of the rotor in relation to the base. Scribe a mark on the base of the distributor and on the engine to facilitate reinstallation. Align the marks with the direction the metal tip of the rotor is pointing.

6. Remove the bolt that hold the distributor to the engine.

7. Lift the distributor assembly from the engine.

INSTALLATION

2.8L Engine

ENGINE NOT ROTATED

1. Insert the distributor shaft and assembly into the engine. Line up the mark on the distributor and the one on the engine with the metal tip of the rotor. Make sure that the vacuum advance diaphragm is pointed in the same direction as it was

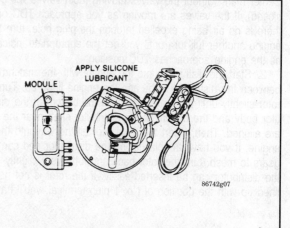

Fig. 12 Ensure the mating surfaces are coated with dielectric compound before installing the module

pointed originally. This will be done automatically if the marks on the engine and the distributor are line up with the rotor.

2. Install the distributor hold-down bolt and clamp. Leave the screw loose enough so that you can move the distributor with heavy hand pressure.

3. Connect the primary wire to the distributor side of the coil. Install the distributor cap on the distributor housing. Secure the distributor cap with the spring clips or the screw type retainers, whichever is used.

4. Install the spark plug wires. Make sure that the wires are pressed all of the way into the top of the distributor cap and firmly onto the spark plugs.

➡ Design of the V6 engine requires a special form of distributor cam. The distributor may be serviced in the regular way and should cause no more problems than any other distributor, if the firing plan is thoroughly understood. The distributor cam is not ground to standard 6-cylinder indexing intervals. This particular form requires that the original pattern of spark plug wiring be used. The engine will not run in balance if No. 1 spark plug wire is inserted into No. 6 distributor cap tower, even though each wire in the firing sequence is advanced to the next distributor tower. There is a difference between the firing intervals of each succeeding cylinder through the 720° engine cycle.

5. Set the ignition timing.

ENGINE ROTATED

➡ If the engine has been turned while the distributor has been removed, or if the marks were not drawn, it will be necessary to initially time the engine.

1. If the engine has been rotated while the distributor was out, you'll have to first put the engine at Top Dead Center firing position on No. 1 cylinder. You can either remove the valve cover or No. 1 spark plug to determine engine position. Rotate the engine with a socket wrench on the nut at the center of the front pulley in the normal direction of rotation. Either feel for air being expelled forcefully through the spark plug hole or watch for the engine to rotate up to the Top Center mark without the valves moving (both valves will be closed). If the valves are moving as you approach TDC or there is no air being expelled through the plug hole, turn the engine another full turn until you get the appropriate indication as the engine approaches TDC position.

2. Start the distributor into the engine with the matchmarks between the distributor body and the engine lined up. Turn the rotor slightly until the matchmarks on the bottom of the distributor body and the bottom of the distributor shaft near the gear are aligned. Then, insert the distributor all the way into the engine. If you have trouble getting the distributor and camshaft gears to mesh, turn the rotor back and forth very slightly until the distributor can be inserted easily. If the rotor is not now lined up with the position of No. 1 plug terminal, you'll have to

pull the distributor back out slightly, shift the position of the rotor appropriately, and then reinstall it.

3. Align the matchmarks between the distributor and engine. Install the distributor mounting bolt and tighten it finger-tight. Reconnect the vacuum advance line and distributor wiring connector, and reinstall the cap. Reconnect the negative battery cable. Adjust the ignition timing as described in Section 1. Then, tighten the distributor mounting bolt securely.

2.5L and 4.0L

ENGINE NOT ROTATED

1. Clean the mounting area of the cylinder block and install a new distributor mounting gasket.

➡ On some models there is a fork on the distributor housing. The slot in the fork aligns with the distributor hold-down bolt hole in the engine block. The distributor is correctly installed when the rotor is correctly positioned and the slot is aligned with the hold-down bolt hole. On these computer controlled distributors, initial ignition timing is not adjustable.

2. Align the rotor tip with the scribe mark on the distributor housing during removal, then turn the rotor approximately ⅛ turn counterclockwise past the scribe mark.

3. Slide the distributor shaft down into the engine. It may be necessary to move the rotor and shaft slightly to engage the distributor shaft with the oil pump slot. Align the scribe mark on the distributor housing with the mark on the cylinder block.

➡ Ensure that the distributor is fully seated against the cylinder block. It may be necessary to slightly rotate (bump) the engine while applying light downward force to fully engage the distributor shaft with the oil pump drive gear shaft.

4. Install the distributor shaft hold-down and bolt. Tighten the bolt to 17 ft. lbs. (23 Nm).

5. Install distributor cap and ignition wires. Insure that the wires are routed correctly before attempting to start engine.

ENGINE ROTATED

1. Rotate the engine until the No.1 piston is at TDC compression.

2. Using a flat-bladed screwdriver, in the distributor hole, rotate the oil pump gear so that the slot in the oil pump shaft is in the correct position (see illustration).

3. With the distributor cap removed, install the distributor so that the rotor is positioned correctly (see illustration). Insure that the distributor is fully seated against the cylinder block. If not, remove the distributor and perform the entire procedure again.

4. Tighten the hold-down bolt.

5. Install distributor cap and ignition wires. Insure that the wires are routed correctly before attempting to start engine.

ELECTRONIC DISTRIBUTOR IGNITION SYSTEM

General Information

The ignition system consists of:
- an ignition coil
- an ignition distributor containing a rotor and camshaft position sensor
- The Electronic Control Unit (ECU), also known as the Powertrain Control Module (PCM)
- Crankshaft position, throttle position and MAP sensors

The amount of spark advance provided by the engine controller is based on five input factors. The factors are coolant temperature, manifold absolute pressure, engine speed, manifold air temperature and throttle position.

Base ignition timing is not adjustable. The controller opens and closes the ignition coil ground circuit to adjust ignition timing for changing engine operating conditions.

Diagnosis and Testing

SECONDARY SPARK TEST

▶ See Figure 13

Since the only change between electronic and conventional ignition systems is in the distributor component area, it is imperative to check the secondary ignition circuit first. If the secondary circuit checks out properly, then the engine condition is probably not the fault of the ignition system. To check the secondary ignition system, perform a simple spark test.

1. Remove one of the plug wires and insert some sort of extension in the plug socket. An old spark plug with the ground electrode removed makes a good extension.

2. Hold the wire and extension about ¼ in. (6mm) away from the block and crank the engine. If a normal spark occurs, then the problem is most likely not in the ignition system. Check for fuel system problems, or fouled spark plugs.

IGNITION COIL TEST

▶ See Figures 14 and 15

The ignition coil is designed to operate without an external ballast resistor. Inspect the coil for arcing. Test the coil primary and secondary resistance.

Measure the primary resistance as follows:

1. Connect an ohmmeter between the positive (+) and negative (-) terminals (the terminals which are connected to the engine wiring harness) on the coil.

2. To test the secondary resistance, connect an ohmmeter between the positive (+) coil terminal and the high voltage cable terminal on the coil, then measure the resistance between the positive (+) coil terminal and the coil case; the resistance for the case should exhibit infinite resistance.

3. For coils manufactured by Diamond, the primary resistance at 70-80°F (21-27°C) should be 0.97-1.18 ohms and the secondary resistance should be 11,300-15,300 ohms.

4. Coils built by the Toyodenso company should exhibit a primary resistance at 70-80°F (21-27°C) of 0.95-1.20 ohms and a secondary resistance of 11,300-13,300 ohms.

5. Replace any coil with a new one if it does not meet the specifications.

VACUUM ADVANCE

➡ **This is used on carbureted models only**

1. Bring the engine to operating temperature.

2. Disconnect the three-wire connector to the vacuum input switches, and disconnect and plug the vacuum hose from the distributor vacuum advance.

3. Connect a vacuum pump (available through local tool distributors) to the vacuum advance unit.

4. Connect a timing light to the No. 1 spark plug wire, and a tachometer to the negative terminal on the coil.

5. Start engine and increase engine speed.

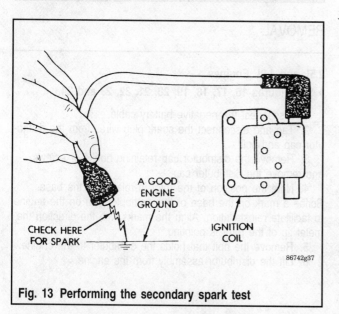

Fig. 13 Performing the secondary spark test

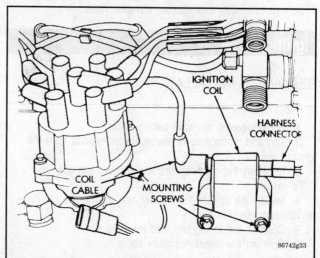

Fig. 14 Ignition coil and related components — 1993 4.0L model shown

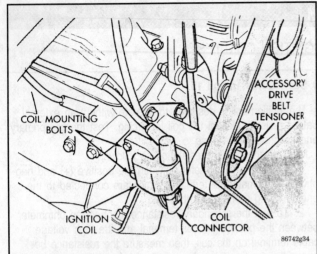

Fig. 15 Ignition coil and related components — 1993 5.2L model shown

6. While observing the timing degree scale with a timing light, apply vacuum to the distributor vacuum advance unit. If timing advances, the unit is functioning properly. If timing does not advance, replace the vacuum advance unit.

7. Stop engine, remove all test equipment, replace the three-wire connector and vacuum advance hose.

CENTRIFUGAL ADVANCE

➡**This is used on carbureted models only**

1. Bring the engine to operating temperature.
2. Disconnect the three-wire connector to the vacuum input switches, and disconnect and plug the vacuum hose from the distributor vacuum advance.
3. Connect a timing light to the No. 1 spark plug wire.
4. With the engine idling, slowly increase the speed and observe the timing mark. Timing should advance smoothly as engine speed increases. If timing advances unevenly, check and repair the centrifugal advance unit.
5. Stop engine, remove all test equipment, replace the three-wire connector and vacuum advance hose.

Ignition Coil

REMOVAL & INSTALLATION

1. Disengage the negative battery cable.
2. Tag and disengage all electrical connections from the ignition coil.
3. Unfasten the coil retainers and remove the coil.
To install:
4. Install the coil on the bracket and tighten the retainers to 100 inch. lbs. (11 Nm).
5. Connect the wiring removed from the coil.
6. Connect the negative battery cable.

Vacuum Advance Unit

REMOVAL & INSTALLATION

1. Remove the distributor cap and rotor.
2. Disconnect the vacuum hose from the vacuum advance unit.
3. Remove the two vacuum advance retaining screws.
4. Tilt the vacuum advance unit to disengage the link from the pick-up coil pin. It may be necessary to loosen the base plate screws for necessary clearance.
5. Insert an Allen wrench into the vacuum hose tube of the old unit and count the number of clockwise turns necessary to bottom the adjusting screw.
6. Turn the adjusting screw of the new unit clockwise to bottom, then counter clockwise the same number of turns in the above step.
7. When installing the new unit, insure that the link is engaged on the pin of the pick-up coil.
8. Install and tighten all screws. Replace the rotor and cap.
9. Check ignition timing and adjust if required, then connect the vacuum advance hose to the unit.

Automatic Shutdown (ASD) Relay

REMOVAL & INSTALLATION

The Automatic Shutdown (ASD) Relay is located in the Power Distribution Center (PDC). The PDC is located in the engine compartment.
1. Refer to the label on the PDC cover to determine the relay location.
2. Gently pull the relay from the PDC.
3. Installation is the reverse of removal.

Distributor

REMOVAL

2.5L and 4.0L Engines
▶ **See Figures 16, 17, 18, 19, 20, 21, 22, 23 and 24**

1. Disconnect the negative battery cable.
2. Tag and disconnect the spark plug wires from the distributor cap and coil
3. Remove the distributor cap retaining hooks or screws and remove the distributor cap.
4. Note the position of the rotor in relation to the base. Scribe a mark on the base of the distributor and on the engine to facilitate reinstallation. Align the marks with the direction the metal tip of the rotor is pointing.
5. Remove the bolt that holds the distributor to the engine.
6. Lift the distributor assembly from the engine.

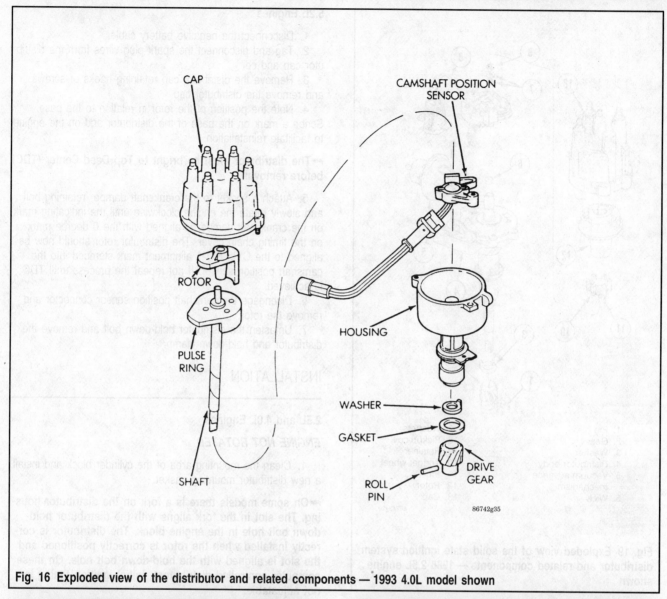

CAP

CAMSHAFT POSITION SENSOR

ROTOR

PULSE RING

SHAFT

HOUSING

WASHER

GASKET

ROLL PIN

DRIVE GEAR

86742g35

Fig. 16 Exploded view of the distributor and related components — 1993 4.0L model shown

86742p01

Fig. 17 Disconnect the negative battery cable

86742p02

Fig. 18 Tag and disconnect the spark plug wires

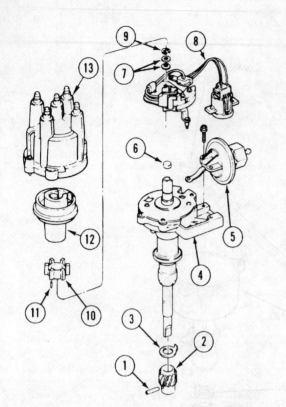

1. Pin
2. Gear
3. Washer
4. Distributor body
5. Vacuum advance mechanism
6. Wick
7. Washers
8. Pickup coil
9. Retainer
10. Trigger wheel
11. Pin
12. Rotor
13. Cap

86742g20

Fig. 19 Exploded view of the solid state ignition system distributor and related components — 1988 2.5L engine shown

5.2L Engines

1. Disconnect the negative battery cable.
2. Tag and disconnect the spark plug wires from the distributor cap and coil
3. Remove the distributor cap retaining hooks or screws and remove the distributor cap.
4. Note the position of the rotor in relation to the base. Scribe a mark on the base of the distributor and on the engine to facilitate reinstallation.

➡**The distributor must be bright to Top Dead Center (TDC) before removal.**

5. Attach a socket to the crankshaft damper retaining bolt and slowly rotate the engine clockwise until the indicating mark on the crankshaft damper is aligned with the 0 degree mark on the timing chain cover. The distributor rotor should now be aligned to the CYL. NO 1 alignment mark stamped into the camshaft position sensor. If not repeat the process until TDC is achieved.
6. Disengage the camshaft position sensor connector and remove the rotor.
7. Unfasten the distributor hold-down bolt and remove the distributor and hold-down clamp.

INSTALLATION

2.5L and 4.0L Engines

ENGINE NOT ROTATED

1. Clean the mounting area of the cylinder block and install a new distributor mounting gasket.

➡**On some models there is a fork on the distributor housing. The slot in the fork aligns with the distributor hold-down bolt hole in the engine block. The distributor is correctly installed when the rotor is correctly positioned and the slot is aligned with the hold-down bolt hole. On these computer controlled distributors, initial ignition timing is not adjustable.**

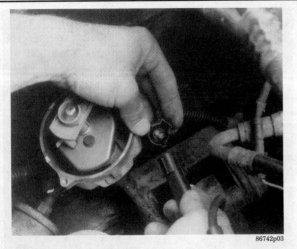

86742p03

Fig. 20 Tag and disengage any distributor electrical connections

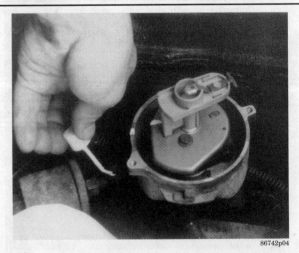

86742p04

Fig. 21 Scribe a mark on the base of the distributor and on the engine to facilitate reinstallation

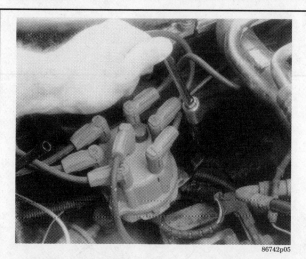

Fig. 22 Using a distributor wrench, loosen the distributor hold-down bolt

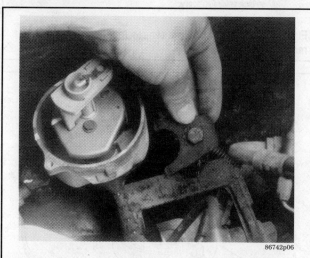

Fig. 23 Remove the distributor hold-down bolt and clamp

Fig. 24 Remove the distributor from the vehicle

2. Align the rotor tip with the scribe mark on the distributor housing during removal, then turn the rotor approximately 1/8 turn counterclockwise past the scribe mark.

3. Slide the distributor shaft down into the engine. It may be necessary to move the rotor and shaft slightly to engage the distributor shaft with the oil pump slot. Align the scribe mark on the distributor housing with the mark on the cylinder block.

➡**Ensure that the distributor is fully seated against the cylinder block. It may be necessary to slightly rotate (bump) the engine while applying light downward force to fully engage the distributor shaft with the oil pump drive gear shaft.**

4. Install the distributor shaft hold-down and bolt. Tighten the bolt to 17 ft. lbs.. (23 Nm).

5. Install distributor cap and ignition wires. Insure that the wires are routed correctly before attempting to start engine.

ENGINE ROTATED

1. Remove the No. 1 cylinder spark plug. Turn the engine using a socket wrench on the large bolt on the front of the crankshaft pulley. Place a finger near the No. 1 spark plug hole and turn the crankshaft until the piston reaches Top Dead Center (TDC). As the engine approaches TDC, you will feel air being expelled by the No. 1 cylinder. If the position is not being met, turn the engine another full turn (360 degree). Once the engine's position is correct, install the spark plug.

2. Using a flat-bladed screwdriver, in the distributor hole, rotate the oil pump gear so that the slot in the oil pump shaft is in the correct position.

3. With the distributor cap removed, install the distributor so that the rotor is positioned correctly. Insure that the distributor is fully seated against the cylinder block. If not, remove the distributor and perform the entire procedure again.

4. Tighten the hold-down bolt.

5. Install distributor cap and ignition wires. Insure that the wires are routed correctly before attempting to start engine.

5.2L Engines

ENGINE NOT ROTATED

1. Clean the mounting area of the cylinder block and install a new distributor mounting gasket.

2. Lightly oil the O-ring seal on the distributor housing and install the rotor.

3. Slide the distributor shaft down into the engine. It may be necessary to move the rotor and shaft slightly to engage the distributor shaft with the oil pump slot. Ensure the rotor is aligned with the CYL. NO. 1 alignment mark on the camshaft position sensor.

➡**Ensure that the distributor is fully seated against the cylinder block. It may be necessary to slightly rotate (bump) the engine while applying light downward force to fully engage the distributor shaft with the oil pump drive gear shaft.**

4. Install the distributor shaft hold-down and bolt. Tighten the bolt to 200 inch. lbs. (22.5 Nm)

5. Install distributor cap and engage all electrical wires and connections. Insure that the wires are routed correctly before attempting to start the vehicle.

ENGINE ROTATED

1. Remove the No. 1 cylinder spark plug. Turn the engine using a socket wrench on the large bolt on the front of the crankshaft pulley. Place a finger near the No. 1 spark plug hole and turn the crankshaft until the piston reaches Top Dead Center (TDC). As the engine approaches TDC, you will feel air being expelled by the No. 1 cylinder. If the position is not being met, turn the engine another full turn (360 degree). Once the engine's position is correct, install the spark plug.

2. Using a flat-bladed screwdriver, in the distributor hole, rotate the oil pump gear so that the slot in the oil pump shaft is in the correct position.

3. Clean the mounting area of the cylinder block and install a new distributor mounting gasket.

4. Lightly oil the O-ring seal on the distributor housing and install the rotor.

5. Slide the distributor shaft down into the engine. It may be necessary to move the rotor and shaft slightly to engage the distributor shaft with the oil pump slot. Ensure the rotor is aligned with the CYL. NO. 1 alignment mark on the camshaft position sensor.

➡ **Ensure that the distributor is fully seated against the cylinder block. It may be necessary to slightly rotate (bump) the engine while applying light downward force to fully engage the distributor shaft with the oil pump drive gear shaft.**

6. Install the distributor shaft hold-down and bolt. Tighten the bolt to 200 inch. lbs. (22.5 Nm)

7. Install distributor cap and engage all electrical wires and connections. Insure that the wires are routed correctly before attempting to start the vehicle.

Crankshaft Position Sensor

▶ **See Figures 25 and 26**

Refer to Section 4 under Electronic Engine Controls for removal, installation and testing of the crankshaft position sensor.

Camshaft Position Sensor

Refer to Section 4 under Electronic Engine Controls for removal, installation and testing of the camshaft position sensor.

FIRING ORDERS

▶ **See Figures 27, 28, 29, 30 and 31**

➡ **To avoid confusion, tag and remove the wires one at a time, for replacement**

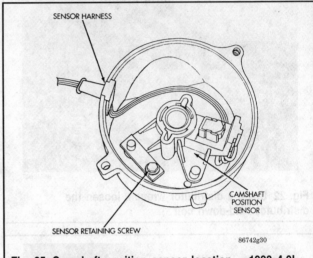

Fig. 25 Camshaft position sensor location — 1993 4.0L model shown

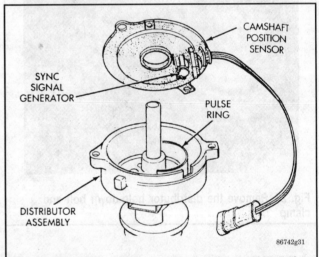

Fig. 26 Camshaft position sensor location — 1993 5.2L model shown

If a distributor is not keyed for installation with only one orientation, it could have been removed previously and rewired. The resultant wiring would hold the correct firing order, but could change the relative placement of the plug towers in relation to the engine. For this reason alone you should ALWAYS tag the wires before removal.

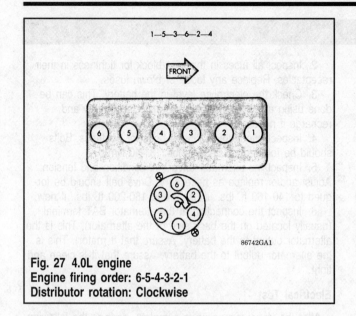

Fig. 27 4.0L engine
Engine firing order: 6-5-4-3-2-1
Distributor rotation: Clockwise

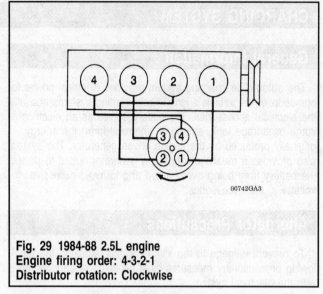

Fig. 29 1984-88 2.5L engine
Engine firing order: 4-3-2-1
Distributor rotation: Clockwise

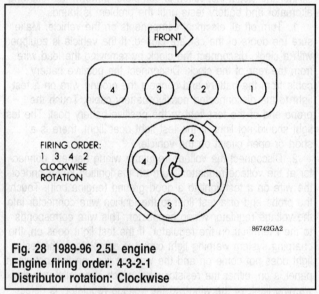

Fig. 28 1989-96 2.5L engine
Engine firing order: 4-3-2-1
Distributor rotation: Clockwise

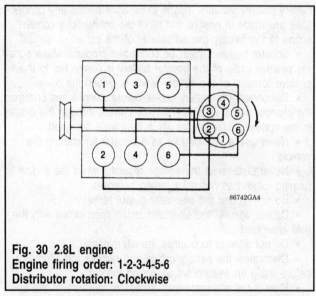

Fig. 30 2.8L engine
Engine firing order: 1-2-3-4-5-6
Distributor rotation: Clockwise

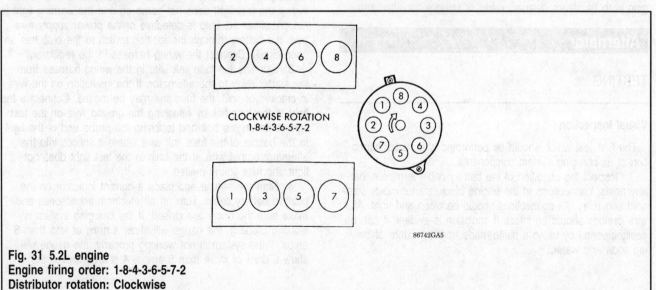

Fig. 31 5.2L engine
Engine firing order: 1-8-4-3-6-5-7-2
Distributor rotation: Clockwise

CHARGING SYSTEM

General Information

The automobile charging system provides electrical power for operation of the vehicle's ignition and starting systems and all the electrical accessories. The battery serves as an electrical surge or storage tank, storing (in chemical form) the energy originally produced by the engine driven generator. The system also provides a means of regulating generator output to protect the battery from being overcharged and to avoid excessive voltage to the accessories.

Alternator Precautions

To prevent damage to the alternator and regulator, the following precautionary measures must be taken when working with the electrical system.

- Never reverse the battery connections. Always check the battery polarity visually. This is to be done before any connections are made to ensure that all of the connections correspond to the battery ground polarity of the car
- Booster batteries must be connected properly. Make sure the positive cable of the booster battery is connected to the positive terminal of the battery which is getting the boost
- Disconnect the battery cables before using a fast charger; the charger has a tendency to force current through the diodes in the opposite direction for which they were designed.
- Never use a fast charger as a booster for starting the vehicle
- Never disconnect the voltage regulator while the engine is running, unless as noted for testing purposes.
- Do not ground the alternator output terminal
- Do not operate the alternator on an open circuit with the field energized
- Do not attempt to polarize the alternator
- Disconnect the battery cables and remove the alternator before using an electric arc welder on the car
- Protect the alternator from excessive moisture. If the engine is to be steam cleaned, cover or remove the alternator

Alternator

TESTING

Visual Inspection

The first test which should be performed is a visual inspection of all charging system components.

1. Inspect the condition of the battery cable terminals, battery posts, connections at the engine block, starter motor solenoid and relay. All connections should be clean and tight. All wire casings should be intact. If corrosion is evident, it can be easily cleaned by using a paste made from a mixture of baking soda and water.

2. Inspect all fuses in the fuse block for tightness in their receptacles. Replace any loose or blown fuses.

3. Check the electrolyte level in the battery. This can be done using a hydrometer. Add water to the battery and recharge if necessary.

4. Inspect alternator mounting bolts for tightness. Bolts should be torqued to 23-30 ft. lbs. (31-40 Nm).

5. Inspect the alternator drive belt condition and tension. Adjust and/or replace as necessary. Drive belt should be torqued to 140-160 ft. lbs.. if used, and 180-200 ft. lbs.. if new.

6. Inspect the connection at the alternator BAT terminal (usually located on the back side of the alternator). This is the alternator output to the battery. Assure that it rnator). This is the alternator output to the battery. Assure that it is clean and tight.

Electrical Test

After the visual inspection is complete, perform the following alternator and battery tests until the problem is found.

1. Turn off all electrical components on the vehicle. Make sure the doors of the car are closed. If the vehicle is equipped with a clock, disconnect the clock by removing the lead wire from the rear of the clock. Disconnect the positive battery cable from the battery and connect the ground wire on a test light to the disconnected positive battery cable. Touch the probe end of the test light to the positive battery post. The test light should not light. If the test light does light, there is a short or open circuit on the vehicle.

2. Disconnect the voltage regulator wiring harness connector at the voltage regulator. Turn on the ignition key. Connect the wire on a test light to a good ground (engine bolt). Touch the probe end of a test light to the ignition wire connector into the voltage regulator wiring connector. This wire corresponds to the I terminal on the regulator. If the test light goes on, the charging system warning light circuit is complete. If the test light does not come on and the warning light on the instrument panel is on, either the resistor wire, which is parallel with the warning light, or the wiring to the voltage regulator, is defective. If the test light does not come on and the warning light is not on, either the bulb is defective or the power supply wire from the battery through the ignition switch to the bulb has an open circuit. Connect the wiring harness to the regulator.

3. Examine the fuse link wire in the wiring harness from the starter relay to the alternator. If the insulation on the wire is cracked or split, the fuse link may be melted. Connect a test light to the fuse link by attaching the ground wire on the test light to an engine bolt and touching the probe end of the light to the bottom of the fuse link wire where it splices into the alternator output wire. If the bulb in the test light does not light, the fuse link is melted.

4. Start the engine and place a current indicator on the positive battery cable. Turn off all electrical accessories and make sure the doors are closed. If the charging system is working properly, the gauge will show a draw of less than 5 amps. If the system is not working properly, the gauge will show a draw of more than 5 amps. A charge moves the

needle toward the battery, a draw moves the needle away from the battery. Turn the engine **OFF**.

➡In order for the current indicator to give a valid reading, the car must be equipped with battery cables which are of the same gauge size and quality as original equipment battery cables.

5. Disconnect the wiring harness from the voltage regulator at the regulator. Connect a male spade terminal (solderless connector) to each end of a jumper wire. Insert one end of the wire into the wiring harness connector which corresponds to the A terminal on the regulator. Insert the other end of the wire into the wiring harness connector which corresponds to the F terminal on the regulator. Position the connector with the jumper wire installed so that it cannot contact any metal surface under the hood. Position a current indicator gauge on the positive battery cable. Have an assistant start the engine. Observe the reading on the current indicator. Have your assistant slowly raise the speed of the engine to about 2000 rpm or until the current indicator needle stops moving, whichever comes first. Do not run the engine for more than a short period of time in this condition. If the wiring harness connector or jumper wire becomes excessively hot during this test turn off the engine and check for a grounded wire in the regulator wiring harness. If the current indicator shows a charge of about three amps less than the output of the alternator, the alternator is working properly. If the previous tests showed a draw, the voltage regulator is defective. If the gauge does not show the proper charging rate, the alternator is defective.

Once the determination is made that the alternator is at fault, off vehicle testing can be used to determine the defective component inside the alternator.

REMOVAL & INSTALLATION

▶ **See Figures 32 and 33**

1. Disconnect the negative battery cable.
2. Remove the drive belt.
3. Tag and disengage the alternator wiring.
4. Unfasten the alternator mounting and pivot bolts and remove the alternator.

To install:

5. Mount the alternator to the brackets with the nuts and bolts. Tighten the two mounting bolts and nuts to 40 ft. lbs.. (54 Nm).
6. Engage the alternator electrical connections.
7. Install the drive belt and attach the negative battery cable.

Regulator

Regulators used with Jeep alternators are transistorized (in most cases they are internally mounted in the alternator) and cannot be serviced. If one of these units proves defective, the alternator must be replaced.

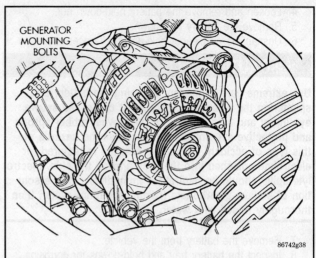

Fig. 32 View of the alternator mounting bolts — 1996 model shown

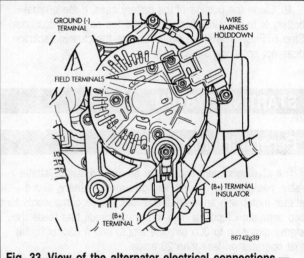

Fig. 33 View of the alternator electrical connections — 1996 model shown

Battery

REMOVAL & INSTALLATION

✳✳CAUTION

If you get battery acid in your eyes or on your skin, rinse it off immediately with lots of water. Go to a doctor if it gets in your eyes. The gases formed inside the battery cells are highly explosive. Never check the level of the electrolyte in the presence of flame or when smoking. Never charge a battery in an unventilated area.

1. Loosen the battery terminal clamp bolts.
2. Use a battery terminal puller to remove the battery negative (-) cable clamp first.
3. Use the battery terminal puller to remove the battery positive (+) cable clamp.

4. Loosen and remove the battery hold-down nut.
5. Remove the battery hold-down.
6. Unsnap the air cleaner hold-downs, if necessary.

✳✳CAUTION

Use extreme care to prevent dropping the battery and splattering the electrolyte, because it can cause severe eye injury and skin burns. Rubber gloves, rubber aprons and protective eye shields will decrease the hazards of this type of accident. Immediate first aid is required for electrolyte splashed into the eyes and on the skin. Electrolyte spills should be neutralized immediately with a solution of sodium bicarbonate (baking soda) and water, then thoroughly rinsed with water.

7. Remove the battery from the vehicle.
8. Inspect the battery tray and hold-downs for corrosion. Remove corrosion using a stiff bristle brush and a baking soda and warm water solution. Paint any exposed bare metal. Replace damaged components with new ones.
9. Clean the outside of the battery case, if the original battery is to be reinstalled. Clean the top cover as described in Step 8. Flush with clean water. Ensure the cleaning solution does not enter the battery cells.

10. Inspect the case for cracks or other damage that would result in leakage of electrolyte.
11. Remove the corrosion from the battery posts and clamps with a suitable battery terminal cleaning tool.
   To install:
12. Position the battery in the tray. Ensure that the positive and negative terminals (posts) are correctly located. The cables must reach their respective posts without stretching.
13. Ensure that the tab at the battery base is positioned in the tray properly before tightening the hold-down.
14. Install the battery hold-down and secure with the hold-down nut.
15. Place a new felt grease washer on the positive (+) terminal post.

✳✳WARNING

It is important that the cables are connected to the proper battery posts. Be sure to connect the positive (+) cable to the positive terminal and the negative (-) cable to the negative terminal. Reverse polarity will damage the alternator diodes and the radio.

16. Connect and tighten the positive cable terminal clamp first.
17. Connect and tighten the negative cable terminal clamp.

STARTING SYSTEM

General Information

The starting system consists of an ignition switch, starter relay, neutral safety switch, wiring harness, battery, and a starter motor with an integral solenoid. These components form two separate circuits: a high amperage circuit that feeds the starter motor up to 300 or more amps, and a control circuit that operates on less than 20 amps.

Starter

TESTING

Testing Preparation

Before commencing with the starting system diagnostics, verify:
   • The battery top posts, and terminals are clean.
   • The alternator drive belt tension and condition is correct.
   • The battery state-of-charge is correct.
   • The battery cable connections at the starter and engine block are clean and free from corrosion.
   • The wiring harness connectors and terminals are clean and free from corrosion.
   • Proper circuit grounding.

Starter Feed Circuit

✳✳CAUTION

The ignition system must be disabled to prevent engine start while performing the following tests.

1. Connect a volt-ampere tester (multimeter) to the battery terminals.
2. Disable the ignition system.
3. Verify that all lights and accessories are Off, and the transaxle shift selector is in Park (automatic) or Neutral (manual). Set the parking brake.
4. Rotate and hold the ignition switch in the **START** position. Observe the volt-ampere tester:
   • If the voltage reads above 9.6 volts, and the amperage draw reads above 250 amps, go to the starter feed circuit resistance test (following this test).
   • If the voltage reads 12.4 volts or greater and the amperage reads 0-10 amps, refer to the starter solenoid and relay tests.

✳✳WARNING

Do not overheat the starter motor or draw the battery voltage below 9.6 volts during cranking operations.

5. After the starting system problems have been corrected, verify the battery state of charge and charge the battery if necessary. Disconnect all of the testing equipment and connect the ignition coil cable or ignition coil connector. Start the vehicle several times to assure the problem was corrected.

Starter Feed Circuit Resistance

Before proceeding with this test, refer to the battery tests and starter feed circuit test. The following test will require a voltmeter, which is capable of accuracy to 0.1 volt.

✳✳CAUTION

The ignition system must be disabled to prevent engine start while performing the following tests.

1. Disable the ignition system.
2. With all wiring harnesses and components (except for the coils) properly connected, perform the following:

    a. Connect the negative (-) lead of the voltmeter to the negative battery post, and the positive (+) lead to the negative (-) battery cable clamp. Rotate and hold the ignition switch in the **START** position. Observe the voltmeter. If the voltage is detected, correct the poor contact between the cable clamp and post.

    b. Connect the positive (+) lead of the voltmeter to the positive battery post, and the negative (-) to the positive battery cable clamp. Rotate and hold the ignition switch key in the **START** position. Observe the voltmeter. If voltage is detected, correct the poor contact between the cable clamp and post.

    c. Connect the negative lead of the voltmeter to the negative (-) battery terminal, and positive lead to the engine block near the battery cable attaching point. Rotate and hold the ignition switch in the **START** position. If the voltage reads above 0.2 volt, correct the poor contact at ground cable attaching point. If the voltage reading is still above 0.2 volt after correcting the poor contact, replace the negative ground cable with a new one.

3. Remove the heater shield. Refer to removal and installation procedures to gain access to the starter motor and solenoid connections. Perform the following steps:

    a. Connect the positive (+) voltmeter lead to the starter motor housing and the negative (-) lead to the negative battery terminal. Hold the ignition switch key in the **START** position. If the voltage reads above 0.2 volt, correct the poor starter to engine ground.

    b. Connect the positive (+) voltmeter lead to the positive battery terminal, and the negative lead to the battery cable terminal on the starter solenoid. Rotate and hold the ignition key in the **START** position. If the voltage reads above 0.2 volt, correct poor contact at the battery cable to the solenoid connection. If the reading is still above 0.2 volt after correcting the poor contacts, replace the positive battery cable with a new one.

    c. If the resistance tests did not detect feed circuit failures, refer to the starter solenoid test.

Starter Solenoid

ON VEHICLE

1. Before testing, assure the parking brake is set, the transmission is in Park (automatic) or Neutral (manual), and the battery is fully charged and in good condition.
2. Connect a voltmeter from the (S) terminal on the solenoid to ground. Turn the ignition switch to the **START** position and test for battery voltage. If battery voltage is not found,

inspect the ignition switch circuit. If battery voltage is found, proceed to next step.

3. Connect an ohmmeter between the battery negative post and the starter solenoid mounting plate (manual) or the ground terminal (automatic). Turn the ignition switch to the **START** position. The ohmmeter should read zero (0). If not, repair the faulty ground.

4. If both tests are performed and the solenoid still does not energize, replace the solenoid.

BENCH TEST

1. Remove the starter from the vehicle.
2. Disconnect the field coil wire from the field coil terminal.
3. Check for continuity between the solenoid terminal and field coil terminal with a continuity tester. Continuity (resistance) should be present.
4. Check for continuity between the solenoid terminal and solenoid housing. Continuity should be detected. If continuity is detected, the solenoid is good.
5. If continuity is not detected in either test, the solenoid has an open circuit and is defective and must be replaced.

Cold Cranking Test

➡**The battery must be fully charged and in good condition before starting this test.**

1. Connect a volt meter across the positive and negative terminals of the battery. Connect an induction meter to the positive battery cable.
2. Fully engage parking brake, place manual transmission in Neutral, automatic transmission in Park.
3. Disconnect the ignition coil wire from the distributor cap and connect a suitable jumper wire between the coil cable and a good body ground.
4. Have an assistant crank the engine by turning the ignition switch (key) to the **START** position. Observe the voltmeter and induction meter.
5. Replace or rebuild the starter motor if not within specifications. A cold motor will increase starter motor current.

Starter/Ground Cable Test

When performing these tests, it is important that the voltmeter be connected to the terminals, not the cables themselves.

Before testing, assure that the ignition control module (if equipped) is disconnected, the parking brake is set, the transmission is in Park (automatic) or Neutral (manual), and the battery is fully charged and in good condition.

1. Check voltage between the positive battery post and the center of the B + terminal on the starter solenoid stud.
2. Check voltage between the negative battery post and the engine block.
3. Disconnect the ignition coil wire from the distributor cap and connect a suitable jumper wire between the coil cable and a good body ground.
4. Have an assistant crank the engine and measure voltage again. Voltage drop should not exceed 0.5 volts.
5. If voltage drop is greater than 0.5 volts, clean metal surfaces. Apply a thick layer of silicone grease. Install a new cadmium plated bolt and star washer on the battery terminal and a new brass nut on the starter solenoid. Retest and replace cable not within specifications.

Starter Relay

1984-90 VEHICLES

1. Insure that the transmission is in Park (automatic) or Neutral (manual) and that the parking brake is applied.

2. Turn the ignition switch to the **START** position and listen for the starter relay to click. If a click is heard, the relay functioning correctly. If not, go to next step.

3. Connect a jumper wire from pin G on the relay to ground. Turn the ignition switch to **START** and listen for a click. If a click is heard, repair the short to ground. If not, go to next step.

4. With starter solenoid terminal (S) disconnected (prevent terminal from touching metal parts), test for battery voltage. If battery voltage is found, replace the relay. If battery voltage is not found, repair the short to the relay terminal (SOL).

1991-96 VEHICLES

1. Remove the relay from the power distribution center, located near the coolant overflow tank in the engine compartment.

2. Check continuity between terminals 87A and 30. If an open circuit is found, replace the relay.

3. Check resistance between terminals 85 and 86. If resistance is not 70-80 ohms, replace the relay.

4. Check continuity between terminals 30 and 87 with a battery connected between terminals 85 and 86. If an open circuit is found, replace the relay.

REMOVAL & INSTALLATION

Except 2.1L Diesel

◆ **See Figures 34, 35 and 36**

1. Disconnect the battery ground.

2. Raise and support the vehicle on jackstands.

3. On 1989-91 models equipped with a 2.5L engine, it is necessary to remove the exhaust clamp and bracket, and the transmission brace rod before removing the starter.

4. Remove all wires from the starter and tag them for installation.

➡ **It may be easier to remove the solenoid wires after lowering the starter. Support the starter before removing the wires. DO NOT LET THE STARTER HANG BY THE WIRES.**

5. On 4.0L and 5.2L engine it may be necessary to remove the oil cooler line bracket and the exhaust brace.

6. Remove all but one attaching bolt, support the starter (it's heavier than it looks) and remove the last bolt.

7. Lower the starter from the engine.

To install:

8. Install the starter in the engine and hand-tighten the retaining bolts.

9. Engage any electrical connections that were removed from the starter.

10. Tighten the retaining bolts and engage any cooler lines, braces and brackets that were removed. Lower the vehicle.

11. Connect the negative battery cable and check for proper starter operation.

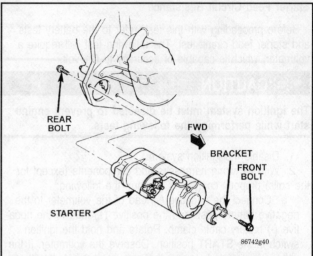

Fig. 34 Exploded view of the starter — 1996 4.0L model shown

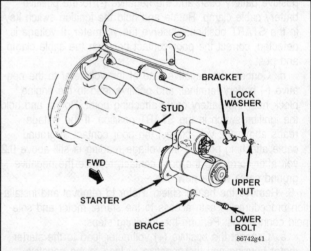

Fig. 35 Exploded view of the starter — 1996 5.2L model shown

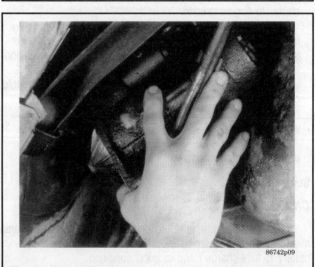

Fig. 36 Removing the starter from the vehicle — 1987 model shown

2.1L Diesel

1. Disconnect the battery ground.
2. Remove all wires from the starter and tag them for installation.
3. Raise and support the vehicle on jackstands.
4. Remove the starter upper bracket.
5. Take up the weight of the engine with a floor jack and remove the left side engine mount.
6. Remove the starter lower support bracket.
7. Support the starter (it's heavier than it looks) and re-move the attaching bolts. Remove the starter.
   To install:
8. Install the starter and HAND-TIGHTEN ONLY, the at-taching bolts. Insure locating dowel is properly seated in hole.
9. Install the upper and lower support bracket, hand tighten only.
10. Tighten the starter attaching bolts to 37 ft. lbs.. (50 Nm). Tighten the upper bracket bolts to 37 ft. lbs.. (50 Nm), and then the lower bracket bolts to 37 ft. lbs.. (50 Nm).
11. Install the engine mount. Tighten the engine mount-to-block bolt to 40 ft. lbs.. (54 Nm)., the engine mount-to-frame bolt to 48 ft. lbs.. (65 Nm).; the engine mount-to-bell housing bolt to 35 ft. lbs.. (47 Nm).
12. Connect all wires and lower the vehicle.

Starter Solenoid

REMOVAL & INSTALLATION

Starter Mounted

➡**On most engines it is necessary to remove the starter. See starter removal/installation procedures.**

SENDING UNITS AND SENSORS

General Information

The sending units and sensors covered in this section are not related to engine control. For the sensors and sending units which help control the engine, refer to Section 4.

Oil Pressure Sending Unit

OPERATION

▶ **See Figure 37**

The low oil pressure/check gauges warning lamp (fed by the oil pressure sending unit) will illuminate when the ignition key is turned to the **ON** position without starting the vehicle. In cluster assemblies without tachometers, the low oil pressure lamp will illuminate if the sending unit indicates that the engine oil pressure has dropped below a safe oil pressure level. The sending unit alters resistance in its circuit depending on the amount of oil pressure detected. (The resistance is raised as the oil pressure is increased). Therefore, the range of various

1. Disconnect negative battery cable.
2. Label and remove all wires from the solenoid. Remove the "M" terminal bolt (Delco-Remy).
3. Remove the solenoid mounting screws. Hold the Sole-noid tight, there is a spring inside.
4. Remove the solenoid (by twisting on Delco-Remy units) with the armature and return spring.
5. Installation is the reverse of removal. Assure mounting surface is clean to provide a good ground.

Remotely Mounted

1. Disconnect negative battery cable.
2. Label and remove all wires from the solenoid. Remove the solenoid mounting screws.
3. Installation is the reverse of removal. Assure mounting surface is clean to provide a good ground.

Starter Relay

REMOVAL & INSTALLATION

1984-90 Models

1. Disconnect the negative battery cable.
2. Identify, tag and disconnect relay wires. Remove relay attaching screws.
3. Replace the relay and reconnect all wires.
4. Replace negative battery cable and test relay operation.

1991-96 Models

1. Remove the relay from the power distribution center, lo-cated in the engine compartment.
2. Installation is the reverse of removal.

resistances is read by the oil pressure/check gauge and trans-lated into a needle position of the oil pressure gauge. When the oil sending unit receives pressure which below a factory set level, the oil pressure warning light illuminates.

TESTING

1. To test the normally closed oil lamp circuit, disengage the locking connector and measure the resistance between the switch terminal (terminal for the wire to the warning lamp) and the metal housing. The ohmmeter should read 0 ohms.
2. To test the sending unit, measure the resistance be-tween the sending unit terminal and the metal housing. The ohmmeter should read an open circuit (infinite resistance).
3. Start the engine.
4. Once again, test each terminal against the metal housing:
   a. The oil switch terminal-to-housing circuit should read an open circuit if there is oil pressure present.
   b. The sending unit-to-housing circuit should read be-tween 15-80 ohms, depending on the engine speed, oil tem-perature and oil viscosity.

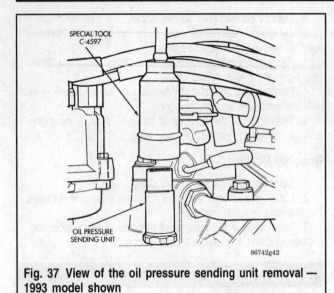

Fig. 37 View of the oil pressure sending unit removal — 1993 model shown

5. To test the oil pressure sender only, rev the engine and watch the ohms reading, which should fluctuate slightly (within the range of 15-80 ohms) as rpm increases.

6. If the above results were not obtained, replace the sending unit/switch with a new one.

REMOVAL & INSTALLATION

1. Disconnect the negative battery cable from the battery.
2. Unplug the oil pressure sending unit wiring harness connector from the sending unit.
3. Unscrew the sending unit from the engine block.

To install:

4. Install and tighten the new sending unit.
5. Plug the electrical wiring harness into the sending unit.
6. Attach the negative battery cable.

Coolant Temperature Sender

OPERATION

▶ See Figure 38

The engine coolant temperature sending unit, not to be confused with the engine temperature sensor used for the fuel injection system, is a variable resistor. The sending unit decreases its resistance as the engine coolant temperature rises.

TESTING

Perform this test on a cold or cool engine.

1. Disconnect the negative (-) battery cable.
2. Unplug the electrical wiring from the sending unit.
3. Using an ohmmeter, measure the resistance between the terminal and the sending unit's metal body

a. Infinite resistance or zero resistance: the sending unit is bad, replace the sender with a new one.

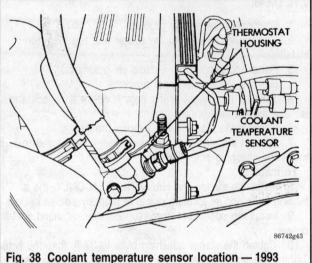

Fig. 38 Coolant temperature sensor location — 1993 4.0L model shown

b. Other than infinite or zero resistance: continue test.

4. Remove the temperature sender from the engine.

5. Position the sending unit so the metal shaft (opposite end from the electrical connectors) is in a pot of water. Make sure that the electrical connector is not submerged and only the tip of the sending unit's body is in the water.

6. Heat the pot of water at a medium rate. While the water is warming, continue to measure the resistance of the terminal and the metal body of the sending unit:

a. As the water warms up, the resistance goes down in a steady manner: the sending unit is good.

b. As the water warms up, the resistance does not change or changes in erratic jumps: the sender is bad, replace it with a new one.

7. Install the good or new sending unit into the engine, then connect the negative battery cable.

REMOVAL & INSTALLATION

✳✳CAUTION

When draining the coolant, keep in mind that cats and dogs are attracted by ethylene glycol antifreeze, and are quite likely to drink any that is left in an uncovered container or in puddles on the ground. This will prove fatal in sufficient quantity. Always drain the coolant into a sealable container. Coolant should be reused unless it is contaminated or several years old.

1. Disconnect the negative battery cable.
2. Drain the cooling system to a level is below the sensor.
3. Detach the electrical connector from the sensor.
4. Remove the sensor from the engine. On some applications, the coolant sensor threads into the thermostat housing.
5. Installation is the reverse of the removal procedure. Fill and bleed the cooling system.

ENGINE
AND
ENGINE
OVERHAUL

ENGINE MECHANICAL

Engine Overhaul Tips

Most engine overhaul procedures are fairly standard. In addition to specific parts replacement procedures and specifications for your individual engine, this section is also a guide to acceptable rebuilding procedures. Examples of standard rebuilding practice are given and should be used along with specific details concerning your particular engine.

Competent and accurate machine shop services will ensure maximum performance, reliability and engine life. In most instances it is more profitable for the do-it-yourself mechanic to remove, clean and inspect the component, buy the necessary parts and deliver these to a shop for actual machine work.

On the other hand, much of the rebuilding work (crankshaft, block, bearings, piston rods, and other components) is well within the scope of the do-it-yourself mechanic's tools and abilities. You will have to decide for yourself the depth of involvement you desire in an engine repair or rebuild.

TOOLS

The tools required for an engine overhaul or parts replacement will depend on the depth of your involvement. With a few exceptions, they will be the tools found in a mechanic's tool kit (see Section 1 of this manual). More in-depth work will require some or all of the following:

- A dial indicator (reading in thousandths) mounted on a universal base
- Micrometers and telescope gauges
- Jaw and screw-type pullers
- Scraper
- Valve spring compressor
- Ring groove cleaner
- Piston ring expander and compressor
- Ridge reamer
- Cylinder hone or glaze breaker
- Plastigage®
- Engine stand

The use of most of these tools is illustrated in this section. Many can be rented for a one-time use from a local parts jobber or tool supply house specializing in automotive work.

Occasionally, the use of special tools is called for. See the information on Special Tools and the Safety Notice in the front of this book before substituting another tool.

INSPECTION TECHNIQUES

Procedures and specifications are given in this chapter for inspecting, cleaning and assessing the wear limits of most major components. Other procedures such as Magnaflux® and Zyglo® can be used to locate material flaws and stress cracks. Magnaflux® is a magnetic process applicable only to ferrous materials. The Zyglo® process coats the material with a fluorescent dye penetrant and can be used on any material.

Checking for suspected surface cracks can be more readily made using spot check dye. The dye is sprayed onto the suspected area, wiped off and the area sprayed with a developer. Cracks will show up brightly.

OVERHAUL TIPS

Aluminum has become extremely popular for use in engines, due to its low weight. Observe the following precautions when handling aluminum parts:
- Never hot tank aluminum parts (the caustic hot tank solution will eat the aluminum.
- Remove all aluminum parts (identification tag, etc.) from engine parts prior to the tanking.
- Always coat threads lightly with engine oil or anti-seize compounds before installation, to prevent seizure.
- Never overtorque bolts or spark plugs especially in aluminum threads.

Stripped threads in any component can be repaired using any of several commercial repair kits (Heli-Coil®, Microdot®, Keenserts®, etc.).

When assembling the engine, any parts that will be exposed to frictional contact must be prelubed to provide lubrication at initial start-up. Any product specifically formulated for this purpose can be used, but engine oil is not recommended as a prelube in most cases.

When semi-permanent (locked, but removable) installation of bolts or nuts is desired, threads should be cleaned and coated with Loctite® or another similar, commercial non-hardening sealant.

REPAIRING DAMAGED THREADS

▶ **See Figures 1, 2, 3, 4 and 5**

Several methods of repairing damaged threads are available. Heli-Coil® (shown here), Keenserts® and Microdot® are among the most widely used. All involve basically the same principle — drilling out stripped threads, tapping the hole and installing a prewound insert — making welding, plugging and oversize fasteners unnecessary.

Two types of thread repair inserts are usually supplied: a standard type for most inch coarse, inch fine, metric course and metric fine thread sizes and a spark lug type to fit most spark plug port sizes. Consult the individual tool manufacturer's catalog to determine exact applications. Typical thread repair kits will contain a selection of prewound threaded inserts, a tap (corresponding to the outside diameter threads of the insert) and an installation tool. Spark plug inserts usually differ because they require a tap equipped with pilot threads and a combined reamer/tap section. Most manufacturers also supply blister-packed thread repair inserts separately in addition to a master kit containing a variety of taps and inserts plus installation tools.

Before attempting to repair a threaded hole, remove any snapped, broken or damaged bolts or studs. Penetrating oil can be used to free frozen threads. The offending item can usually be removed with locking pliers or using a screw/stud extractor. After the hole is clear, the thread can be repaired,

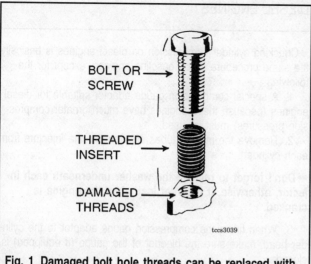

Fig. 1 Damaged bolt hole threads can be replaced with thread repair inserts

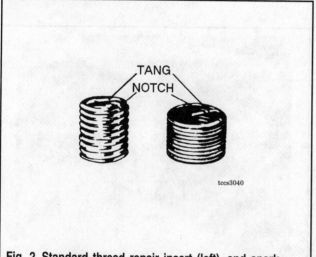

Fig. 2 Standard thread repair insert (left), and spark plug thread insert

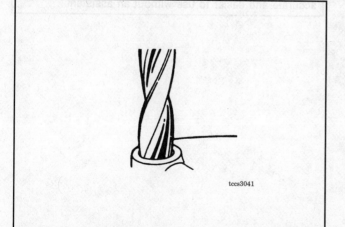

Fig. 3 Drill out the damaged threads with the specified size bit. Be sure to drill completely through the hole or to the bottom of a blind hole

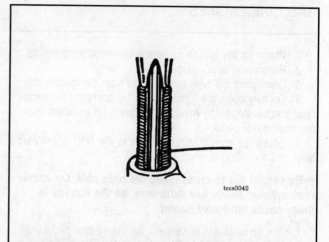

Fig. 4 Using the kit, tap the hole in order to receive the thread insert. Keep the tap well oiled and back it out frequently to avoid clogging the threads

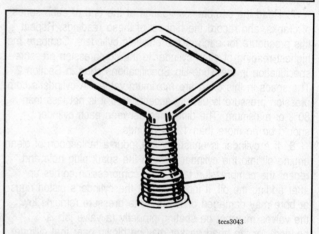

Fig. 5 Screw the insert onto the installer tool until the tang engages the slot. Thread the insert into the hole until it is 1/4-1/2 turn below the top surface, then remove the tool and break off the tang using a punch

as shown in the series of accompanying illustrations and in the kit manufacturer's instructions.

Checking Engine Compression

▶ See Figure 6

A noticeable lack of engine power, excessive oil consumption and/ or poor fuel mileage measured over an extended period are all indicators of internal engine war. Worn piston rings, scored or worn cylinder bores, blown head gaskets, sticking or burnt valves and worn valve seats are all possible culprits here. A check of each cylinder's compression will help you locate the problems.

As mentioned in the Tools and Equipment section of Section 1, a screw-in type compression gauge is more accurate that the type you simply hold against the spark plug hole, although it takes slightly longer to use. It's worth it to obtain a more accurate reading. Follow the procedures below for gasoline and diesel engines trucks.

GASOLINE ENGINES

1. Warm up the engine to normal operating temperature.
2. Remove all spark plugs.
3. Disconnect the high tension lead from the ignition coil.
4. On fully open the throttle either by operating the carburetor throttle linkage by hand or by having an assistant floor the accelerator pedal.
5. Screw the compression gauge into the No.1 spark plug hole until the fitting is snug.

➡Be careful not to crossthread the plug hole. On aluminum cylinder heads use extra care, as the threads in these heads are easily ruined.

6. Ask an assistant to depress the accelerator pedal fully on both carbureted and fuel injected trucks. Then, while you read the compression gauge, ask the assistant to crank the engine two or three times in short bursts using the ignition switch.

7. Read the compression gauge at the end of each series of cranks, and record the highest of these readings. Repeat this procedure for each of the engine's cylinders. Compare the highest reading of each cylinder to the compression pressure specification in the Tune-Up Specifications chart in Section 2. The specs in this chart are maximum values. A cylinder's compression pressure is usually acceptable if it is not less than 80% of maximum. The difference between each cylinder should be no more than 12-14 pounds.

8. If a cylinder is unusually low, pour a tablespoon of clean engine oil into the cylinder through the spark plug hole and repeat the compression test. If the compression comes up after adding the oil, it indicates that the cylinder's piston rings or bore may damaged or worn. If the pressure remains low, the valves may not be seating properly (a valve job is needed), or the head gasket may be blown near that cylinder. If compression in any two adjacent cylinders is low, and if the addition of oil doesn't help the compression, there is leakage past the head gasket. Oil and coolant water in the combustion chamber can result from this problem. There may be evidence of water droplets on the engine dipstick when a head gasket has blown.

DIESEL ENGINES

Checking cylinder compression on diesel engines is basically the same procedure as on gasoline engines, except for the following:

1. A special compression gauge adaptor suitable for diesel engines (because these engines have much greater compression pressures) must be used.
2. Remove the injector tubes and remove the injectors from each cylinder.

➡Don't forget to remove the washer underneath each injector, otherwise, it may get lost when the engine is cranked.

3. When fitting the compression gauge adaptor to the cylinder head, make sure the bleeder of the gauge (if equipped) is closed.
4. When reinstalling the injector assemblies, install new washers underneath each injector.

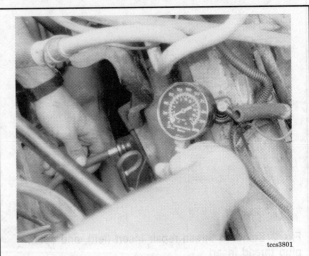

tccs3801

Fig. 6 A screw-in type compression gauge is more accurate and easier to use without an assistant

GENERAL ENGINE SPECIFICATIONS

Year	Engine ID/VIN	Engine Displacement Liters (cu. in.)	Fuel System Type	Net Horsepower @ rpm	Net Torque @ rpm (ft. lbs.)	Bore x Stroke (in.)	Compression Ratio	Oil Pressure @ rpm
1984	U	2.5 (150)	1 bbl	83 @ 4200	116 @ 2600	3.876 x 3.188	9.2:1	40 @ 2000
	W	2.8 (173)	2 bbl	115 @ 4800	150 @ 3500	3.500 x 2.990	8.5:1	45 @ 2000
1985	B	2.1 (126)	Diesel	85 @ 3750	132 @ 2750	3.503 x 3.358	21.5:1	43 @ 2000
	H	2.5 (150)	TBI	117 @ 5000	135 @ 3000	3.876 x 3.188	9.2:1	40 @ 2000
	W	2.8 (173)	2 bbl	115 @ 4800	150 @ 3500	3.500 x 2.990	8.5:1	45 @ 2000
1986	B	2.1 (126)	Diesel	85 @ 3750	132 @ 2750	3.503 x 3.358	21.5:1	43 @ 2000
	H	2.5 (150)	TBI	117 @ 5000	135 @ 3000	3.876 x 3.188	9.2:1	40 @ 2000
	W	2.8 (173)	2 bbl	115 @ 4800	150 @ 3500	3.500 x 2.990	8.5:1	45 @ 2000
1987	B	2.1 (126)	Diesel	85 @ 3750	132 @ 2750	3.503 x 3.358	21.5:1	43 @ 2000
	H	2.5 (150)	TBI	117 @ 5000	135 @ 3000	3.876 x 3.188	9.2:1	40 @ 2000
	M	4.0 (243)	MPI	150 @ 4300	210 @ 2100	3.874 x 3.441	8.8:1	40 @ 2000
1988	H	2.5 (150)	TBI	117 @ 5000	135 @ 3000	3.876 x 3.188	9.2:1	40 @ 2000
	M	4.0 (243)	MPI	150 @ 4300	210 @ 2100	3.874 x 3.441	8.8:1	40 @ 2000
1989	E	2.5 (150)	TBI	121 @ 5250	141 @ 3250	3.876 x 3.188	9.2:1	37 @ 1600
	L	4.0 (243)	MPI	177 @ 4500	224 @ 2500	3.874 x 3.441	8.8:1	37 @ 1600
1990	E	2.5 (150)	TBI	121 @ 5250	141 @ 3250	3.876 x 3.188	9.2:1	37 @ 1600
	L	4.0 (243)	MPI	177 @ 4500	224 @ 2500	3.874 x 3.441	8.8:1	37 @ 1600
1991	P	2.5 (150)	MPI	130 @ 5250	149 @ 3250	3.876 x 3.188	9.1.:1	37 @ 1600
	S	4.0 (243)	MPI	190 @ 4750	225 @ 4000	3.874 x 3.441	8.8:1	37 @ 1600
1992	P	2.5 (150)	MPI	130 @ 5250	149 @ 3250	3.876 x 3.188	9.1.:1	37 @ 1600
	S	4.0 (243)	MPI	190 @ 4750	225 @ 4000	3.874 x 3.441	8.8:1	37 @ 1600
1993	P	2.5 (150)	MPI	130 @ 5250	149 @ 3250	3.876 x 3.188	9.1.:1	37 @ 1600
	S	4.0 (243)	MPI	190 @ 4750	225 @ 4000	3.874 x 3.441	8.8:1	37 @ 1600
	Y	5.2 (318)	MPI	220 @ 4800	285 @ 3600	3.91 x 3.31	9.1:1	30 @ 3000
1994	P	2.5 (150)	MPI	130 @ 5250	149 @ 3250	3.876 x 3.188	9.1.:1	37 @ 1600
	S	4.0 (243)	MPI	190 @ 4750	225 @ 4000	3.874 x 3.441	8.8:1	37 @ 1600
	Y	5.2 (318)	MPI	220 @ 4800	285 @ 3600	3.91 x 3.31	9.1:1	30 @ 3000
1995	P	2.5 (150)	MPI	130 @ 5250	149 @ 3250	3.876 x 3.188	9.1.:1	37 @ 1600
	S	4.0 (243)	MPI	190 @ 4750	225 @ 4000	3.874 x 3.441	8.8:1	37 @ 1600
	Y	5.2 (318)	MPI	220 @ 4800	285 @ 3600	3.91 x 3.31	9.1:1	30 @ 3000
1996	P	2.5 (150)	MPI	130 @ 5250	149 @ 3250	3.876 x 3.188	9.1.:1	37 @ 1600
	S	4.0 (243)	MPI	190 @ 4750	225 @ 4000	3.874 x 3.441	8.8:1	37 @ 1600
	Y	5.2 (318)	MPI	220 @ 4800	285 @ 3600	3.91 x 3.31	9.1:1	30 @ 3000

86743c01

VALVE SPECIFICATIONS

Year	Engine ID/VIN	Engine Displacement Liters (ci)	Seat Angle (deg.)	Face Angle (deg.)	Spring Test Pressure (lbs. @ in.)	Spring Installed Height (in.)	Stem-to-Guide Clearance (in.) Intake	Stem-to-Guide Clearance (in.) Exhaust	Stem Diameter (in.) Intake	Stem Diameter (in.) Exhaust
1984	U	2.5 (150)	44.5	44	212 @ 1.203	1.625	0.0010-0.0030	0.0010-0.0030	0.3110-0.3120	0.3110-0.3120
	W	2.8 (173)	46	45	195 @ 1.180	1.570	0.0010-0.0027	0.0010-0.0027	0.3410-0.3416	0.3410-0.3416
1985	B	2.1 (126)	45	45	135 @ 1.173	1.547	0.0010-0.0030	0.0010-0.0030	0.3140	0.3140
	H	2.5 (150)	44.5	44	212 @ 1.203	1.625	0.0010-0.0030	0.0010-0.0030	0.3110-0.3120	0.3110-0.3120
	W	2.8 (173)	46	45	195 @ 1.180	1.570	0.0010-0.0027	0.0010-0.0027	0.3410-0.3416	0.3410-0.3416
1986	B	2.1 (126)	45	45	135 @ 1.173	1.547	0.0010-0.0030	0.0010-0.0030	0.3140	0.3140
	H	2.5 (150)	44.5	45	200 @ 1.216	1.640	0.0010-0.0030	0.0010-0.0030	0.3110-0.3120	0.3110-0.3120
	W	2.8 (173)	46	45	195 @ 1.180	1.570	0.0010-0.0027	0.0010-0.0027	0.3410-0.3416	0.3410-0.3416
1987	B	2.1 (126)	45	45	135 @ 1.173	1.547	0.0010-0.0030	0.0010-0.0030	0.3140	0.3140
	H	2.5 (150)	44.5	45	200 @ 1.216	1.640	0.0010-0.0030	0.0010-0.0030	0.3110-0.3120	0.3110-0.3120
	M	4.0 (243)	44.5	45	210 @ 1.200	1.625	0.0010-0.0030	0.0010-0.0030	0.3110-0.3120	0.3110-0.3120
1988	H	2.5 (150)	44.5	45	200 @ 1.216	1.640	0.0010-0.0030	0.0010-0.0030	0.3110-0.3120	0.3110-0.3120
	M	4.0 (243)	44.5	45	210 @ 1.200	1.625	0.0010-0.0030	0.0010-0.0030	0.3110-0.3120	0.3110-0.3120
1989	E	2.5 (150)	44.5	45	200 @ 1.216	1.640	0.0010-0.0030	0.0010-0.0030	0.3110-0.3120	0.3110-0.3120
	L	4.0 (243)	44.5	45	210 @ 1.200	1.625	0.0010-0.0030	0.0010-0.0030	0.3110-0.3120	0.3110-0.3120
1990	E	2.5 (150)	44.5	45	200 @ 1.216	1.640	0.0010-0.0030	0.0010-0.0030	0.3110-0.3120	0.3110-0.3120
	L	4.0 (243)	44.5	45	210 @ 1.200	1.625	0.0010-0.0030	0.0010-0.0030	0.3110-0.3120	0.3110-0.3120
1991	P	2.5 (150)	44.5	45	200 @ 1.216	1.640	0.0010-0.0030	0.0010-0.0030	0.3110-0.3120	0.3110-0.3120
	S	4.0 (243)	44.5	45	210 @ 1.200	1.625	0.0010-0.0030	0.0010-0.0030	0.3110-0.3120	0.3110-0.3120
1992	P	2.5 (150)	44.5	45	200 @ 1.216	1.640	0.0010-0.0030	0.0010-0.0030	0.3110-0.3120	0.3110-0.3120
	S	4.0 (243)	44.5	45	210 @ 1.200	1.625	0.0010-0.0030	0.0010-0.0030	0.3110-0.3120	0.3110-0.3120

86743c02

VALVE SPECIFICATIONS

Year	Engine ID/VIN	Engine Displacement Liters (ci)	Seat Angle (deg.)	Face Angle (deg.)	Spring Test Pressure (lbs. @ in.)	Spring Installed Height (in.)	Stem-to-Guide Clearance (in.)		Stem Diameter (in.)	
							Intake	Exhaust	Intake	Exhaust
1993	P	2.5 (150)	44.5	45	200 @ 1.216	1.640	0.0010-0.0030	0.0010-0.0030	0.3110-0.3120	0.3110-0.3120
	S	4.0 (243)	44.5	45	210 @ 1.200	1.625	0.0010-0.0030	0.0010-0.0030	0.3110-0.3120	0.3110-0.3120
	Y	5.2 (318)	44.25-44.75	43.25-43.75	200 @ 1.212	1.640	0.0010-0.0030	0.0010-0.0030	0.3110-0.3120	0.3110-0.3120
1994	P	2.5 (150)	44.5	45	200 @ 1.216	1.640	0.0010-0.0030	0.0010-0.0030	0.3110-0.3120	0.3110-0.3120
	S	4.0 (243)	44.5	45	210 @ 1.200	1.625	0.0010-0.0030	0.0010-0.0030	0.3110-0.3120	0.3110-0.3120
	Y	5.2 (318)	44.25-44.75	43.25-43.75	200 @ 1.212	1.640	0.0010-0.0030	0.0010-0.0030	0.3110-0.3120	0.3110-0.3120
1995	P	2.5 (150)	44.5	45	200 @ 1.216	1.640	0.0010-0.0030	0.0010-0.0030	0.3110-0.3120	0.3110-0.3120
	S	4.0 (243)	44.5	45	210 @ 1.200	1.625	0.0010-0.0030	0.0010-0.0030	0.3110-0.3120	0.3110-0.3120
	Y	5.2 (318)	44.25-44.75	43.25-43.75	200 @ 1.212	1.640	0.0010-0.0030	0.0010-0.0030	0.3110-0.3120	0.3110-0.3120
1996	P	2.5 (150)	44.5	45	200 @ 1.216	1.640	0.0010-0.0030	0.0010-0.0030	0.3110-0.3120	0.3110-0.3120
	S	4.0 (243)	44.5	45	210 @ 1.200	1.625	0.0010-0.0030	0.0010-0.0030	0.3110-0.3120	0.3110-0.3120
	Y	5.2 (318)	44.25-44.75	43.25-43.75	200 @ 1.212	1.640	0.0010-0.0030	0.0010-0.0030	0.3110-0.3120	0.3110-0.3120

86743c03

CAMSHAFT SPECIFICATIONS

All measurements given in inches.

Year	Engine ID/VIN	Engine Displacement Liters (ci)	Journal Diameter 1	2	3	4	5	Elevation In.	Ex.	Bearing Clearance	Camshaft End Play
1984	U	2.5 (150)	2.0300-2.0290	2.0200-2.0190	2.0100-2.0090	2.0000-1.9990	-	0.2650	0.2650	0.0010-0.0030	0
	W	2.8 (173)	1.8690-1.8670	1.8690-1.8670	1.8690-1.8670	-	-	0.2311	0.2625	0.0010-0.0039	0
1985	B	2.1 (126)	NA	NA	NA	NA	NA	NA	NA	NA	0.001-0.005
	H	2.5 (150)	2.0300-2.0290	2.0200-2.0190	2.0100-2.0090	2.0000-1.9990	-	0.2650	0.2650	0.0010-0.0030	0
	W	2.8 (173)	1.8690-1.8670	1.8690-1.8670	1.8690-1.8670	-	-	0.2311	0.2625	0.0010-0.0039	0
1986	B	2.1 (126)	NA	NA	NA	NA	NA	NA	NA	NA	0.001-0.005
	H	2.5 (150)	2.0300-2.0290	2.0200-2.0190	2.0100-2.0090	2.0000-1.9990	-	0.2650	0.2650	0.0010-0.0030	0
	W	2.8 (173)	1.8690-1.8670	1.8690-1.8670	1.8690-1.8670	-	-	0.2311	0.2625	0.0010-0.0039	0
1987	B	2.1 (126)	NA	NA	NA	NA	NA	NA	NA	NA	0.001-0.005
	H	2.5 (150)	2.0300-2.0290	2.0200-2.0190	2.0100-2.0090	2.0000-1.9990	-	0.2650	0.2650	0.0010-0.0030	0
	M	4.0 (243)	2.0300-2.0290	2.0200-2.0190	2.0100-2.0090	2.0000-1.9990	-	0.2530	0.2530	0.0010-0.0030	0
1988	H	2.5 (150)	2.0300-2.0290	2.0200-2.0190	2.0100-2.0090	2.0000-1.9990	-	0.2650	0.2650	0.0010-0.0030	0
	M	4.0 (243)	2.0300-2.0290	2.0200-2.0190	2.0100-2.0090	2.0000-1.9990	-	0.2530	0.2530	0.0010-0.0030	0
1989	E	2.5 (150)	2.0300-2.0290	2.0200-2.0190	2.0100-2.0090	2.0000-1.9990	-	0.2650	0.2650	0.0010-0.0030	0
	L	4.0 (243)	2.0300-2.0290	2.0200-2.0190	2.0100-2.0090	2.0000-1.9990	-	0.2530	0.2530	0.0010-0.0030	0
1990	E	2.5 (150)	2.0300-2.0290	2.0200-2.0190	2.0100-2.0090	2.0000-1.9990	-	0.2650	0.2650	0.0010-0.0030	0
	L	4.0 (243)	2.0300-2.0290	2.0200-2.0190	2.0100-2.0090	2.0000-1.9990	-	0.2530	0.2530	0.0010-0.0030	0
1991	P	2.5 (150)	2.0300-2.0290	2.0200-2.0190	2.0100-2.0090	2.0000-1.9990	-	0.2650	0.2650	0.0010-0.0030	0
	S	4.0 (243)	2.0300-2.0290	2.0200-2.0190	2.0100-2.0090	2.0000-1.9990	-	0.2530	0.2530	0.0010-0.0030	0
1992	P	2.5 (150)	2.0300-2.0290	2.0200-2.0190	2.0100-2.0090	2.0000-1.9990	-	0.2650	0.2650	0.0010-0.0030	0
	S	4.0 (243)	2.0300-2.0290	2.0200-2.0190	2.0100-2.0090	2.0000-1.9990	-	0.2530	0.2530	0.0010-0.0030	0

86743c04

CAMSHAFT SPECIFICATIONS
All measurements given in inches.

Year	Engine ID/VIN	Engine Displacement Liters (ci)	Journal Diameter					Elevation		Bearing Clearance	Camshaft End Play
			1	2	3	4	5	In.	Ex.		
1993	P	2.5 (150)	2.0300-2.0290	2.0200-2.0190	2.0100-2.0090	2.0000-1.9990	-	0.2650	0.2650	0.0010-0.0030	0
	S	4.0 (243)	2.0300-2.0290	2.0200-2.0190	2.0100-2.0090	2.0000-1.9990	-	0.2530	0.2530	0.0010-0.0030	0
	Y	5.2 (318)	1.9990-1.9980	1.9830-1.9820	1.9680-1.9670	1.9520-1.9510	1.5615-1.5605	NA	NA	0.0010-0.0030	0.0020-0.01
1994	P	2.5 (150)	2.0300-2.0290	2.0200-2.0190	2.0100-2.0090	2.0000-1.9990	-	0.2650	0.2650	0.0010-0.0030	0
	S	4.0 (243)	2.0300-2.0290	2.0200-2.0190	2.0100-2.0090	2.0000-1.9990	-	0.2530	0.2530	0.0010-0.0030	0
	Y	5.2 (318)	1.9990-1.9980	1.9830-1.9820	1.9680-1.9670	1.9520-1.9510	1.5615-1.5605	NA	NA	0.0010-0.0030	0.0020-0.01
1995	P	2.5 (150)	2.0300-2.0290	2.0200-2.0190	2.0100-2.0090	2.0000-1.9990	-	0.2650	0.2650	0.0010-0.0030	0
	S	4.0 (243)	2.0300-2.0290	2.0200-2.0190	2.0100-2.0090	2.0000-1.9990	-	0.2530	0.2530	0.0010-0.0030	0
	Y	5.2 (318)	1.9990-1.9980	1.9830-1.9820	1.9680-1.9670	1.9520-1.9510	1.5615-1.5605	NA	NA	0.0010-0.0030	0.0020-0.01
1996	P	2.5 (150)	2.0300-2.0290	2.0200-2.0190	2.0100-2.0090	2.0000-1.9990	-	0.2650	0.2650	0.0010-0.0030	0
	S	4.0 (243)	2.0300-2.0290	2.0200-2.0190	2.0100-2.0090	2.0000-1.9990	-	0.2530	0.2530	0.0010-0.0030	0
	Y	5.2 (318)	1.9990-1.9980	1.9830-1.9820	1.9680-1.9670	1.9520-1.9510	1.5615-1.5605	NA	NA	0.0010-0.0030	0.0020-0.01

86743c05

CRANKSHAFT AND CONNECTING ROD SPECIFICATIONS

All measurements are given in inches.

Year	Engine ID/VIN	Engine Displacement Liters (ci)	Crankshaft				Connecting Rod		
			Main Brg. Journal Dia.	Main Brg. Oil Clearance	Shaft End-play	Thrust on No.	Journal Diameter	Oil Clearance	Side Clearance
1984	U	2.5 (150)	2.4996-2.5001	0.0010-0.0025	0.0015-0.0065	2	2.0934-2.0955	0.0010-0.0030	0.0100-0.0190
	W	2.8 (173)	①	0.0016-0.0030	0.0020-0.0060	3	1.9980-1.9990	0.0010-0.0030	0.006-0.0170
1985	B	2.1 (126)	2.4750	0.0098	0.0055-0.0090	3	2.2163	0.0098	0.012-0.0190
	H	2.5 (150)	2.4996-2.5001	0.0010-0.0025	0.0015-0.0065	2	2.0934-2.0955	0.0010-0.0030	0.0100-0.0190
	W	2.8 (173)	①	0.0016-0.0030	0.0020-0.0060	3	1.9980-1.9990	0.0010-0.0030	0.006-0.0170
1986	B	2.1 (126)	2.4750	0.0098	0.0055-0.0090	3	2.2163	0.0098	0.012-0.0190
	H	2.5 (150)	2.4996-2.5001	0.0010-0.0025	0.0015-0.0065	2	2.0934-2.0955	0.0010-0.0025	0.0100-0.0190
	W	2.8 (173)	①	0.0016-0.0030	0.0020-0.0060	3	1.9980-1.9990	0.0010-0.0030	0.006-0.0170
1987	B	2.1 (126)	2.4750	0.0098	0.0055-0.0090	3	2.2163	0.0098	0.012-0.0190
	H	2.5 (150)	2.4996-2.5001	0.0010-0.0025	0.0015-0.0065	2	2.0934-2.0955	0.0010-0.0025	0.0100-0.0190
	M	4.0 (243)	2.4996-2.5001	0.0010-0.0025	0.0015-0.0065	3	2.0934-2.0955	0.0010-0.0030	0.0100-0.0190
1988	H	2.5 (150)	2.4996-2.5001	0.0010-0.0025	0.0015-0.0065	2	2.0934-2.0955	0.0010-0.0025	0.0100-0.0190
	M	4.0 (243)	2.4996-2.5001	0.0010-0.0025	0.0015-0.0065	3	2.0934-2.0955	0.0010-0.0030	0.0100-0.0190
1989	E	2.5 (150)	2.4996-2.5001	0.0010-0.0025	0.0015-0.0065	2	2.0934-2.0955	0.0010-0.0025	0.0100-0.0190
	L	4.0 (243)	2.4996-2.5001	0.0010-0.0025	0.0015-0.0065	3	2.0934-2.0955	0.0010-0.0030	0.0100-0.0190
1990	E	2.5 (150)	2.4996-2.5001	0.0010-0.0025	0.0015-0.0065	2	2.0934-2.0955	0.0010-0.0025	0.0100-0.0190
	L	4.0 (243)	2.4996-2.5001	0.0010-0.0025	0.0015-0.0065	3	2.0934-2.0955	0.0010-0.0030	0.0100-0.0190
1991	P	2.5 (150)	2.4996-2.5001	0.0010-0.0025	0.0015-0.0065	2	2.0934-2.0955	0.0010-0.0025	0.0100-0.0190
	S	4.0 (243)	2.4996-2.5001	0.0010-0.0025	0.0015-0.0065	3	2.0934-2.0955	0.0010-0.0030	0.0100-0.0190
1992	P	2.5 (150)	2.4996-2.5001	0.0010-0.0025	0.0015-0.0065	2	2.0934-2.0955	0.0010-0.0025	0.0100-0.0190
	S	4.0 (243)	2.4996-2.5001	0.0010-0.0025	0.0015-0.0065	3	2.0934-2.0955	0.0010-0.0030	0.0100-0.0190

86743c06

CRANKSHAFT AND CONNECTING ROD SPECIFICATIONS
All measurements are given in inches.

Year	Engine ID/VIN	Engine Displacement Liters (ci)	Crankshaft				Connecting Rod		
			Main Brg. Journal Dia.	Main Brg. Oil Clearance	Shaft End-play	Thrust on No.	Journal Diameter	Oil Clearance	Side Clearance
1993	P	2.5 (150)	2.4996-2.5001	0.0010-0.0025	0.0015-0.0065	2	2.0934-2.0955	0.0010-0.0025	0.0100-0.0190
	S	4.0 (243)	2.4996-2.5001	0.0010-0.0025	0.0015-0.0065	3	2.0934-2.0955	0.0010-0.0030	0.0100-0.0190
	Y	5.2 (318)	2.4995-2.5005	②	0.0020-0.0100	3	2.1240-2.1250	0.0005-0.0022	0.0060-0.0140
1994	P	2.5 (150)	2.4996-2.5001	0.0010-0.0025	0.0015-0.0065	2	2.0934-2.0955	0.0010-0.0025	0.0100-0.0190
	S	4.0 (243)	2.4996-2.5001	0.0010-0.0025	0.0015-0.0065	3	2.0934-2.0955	0.0010-0.0030	0.0100-0.0190
	Y	5.2 (318)	2.4995-2.5005	②	0.0020-0.0100	3	2.1240-2.1250	0.0005-0.0022	0.0060-0.0140
1995	P	2.5 (150)	2.4996-2.5001	0.0010-0.0025	0.0015-0.0065	2	2.0934-2.0955	0.0010-0.0025	0.0100-0.0190
	S	4.0 (243)	2.4996-2.5001	0.0010-0.0025	0.0015-0.0065	3	2.0934-2.0955	0.0010-0.0030	0.0100-0.0190
	Y	5.2 (318)	2.4995-2.5005	②	0.0020-0.0100	3	2.1240-2.1250	0.0005-0.0022	0.0060-0.0140
1996	P	2.5 (150)	2.4996-2.5001	0.0010-0.0025	0.0015-0.0065	2	2.0934-2.0955	0.0010-0.0025	0.0100-0.0190
	S	4.0 (243)	2.4996-2.5001	0.0010-0.0025	0.0015-0.0065	3	2.0934-2.0955	0.0010-0.0030	0.0100-0.0190
	Y	5.2 (318)	2.4995-2.5005	②	0.0020-0.0100	3	2.1240-2.1250	0.0005-0.0022	0.0060-0.0140

1: Nos.1, 2, 4: 2.4930-2.24940
   No. 3: 2.4920-2.4930
2: No. 1: 0.0005-0.0015
   Except No. 1: 0.0005-0.0025

86743c07

PISTON AND RING SPECIFICATIONS

All measurements are given in inches.

Year	Engine ID/VIN	Engine Displacement Liters (ci)	Piston Clearance	Ring Gap			Ring Side Clearance		
				Top Compression	Bottom Compression	Oil Control	Top Compression	Bottom Compression	Oil Control
1984	U	2.5 (150)	0.0006-0.0016	0.0100-0.0200	0.0100-0.0200	0.0100-0.0250	0.0017-0.0032	0.0017-0.0032	0.0010-0.008
	W	2.8 (173)	0.0006-0.0016	0.0098-0.0196	0.0098-0.0196	0.0200-0.0550	0.0010-0.0027-	0.0015-0.0037	0.0078 max.
1985	H	2.5 (150)	0.0006-0.0016	0.0100-0.0200	0.0100-0.0200	0.0100-0.0250	0.0017-0.0032	0.0017-0.0032	0.0010-0.008
	W	2.8 (173)	0.0006-0.0016	0.0098-0.0196	0.0098-0.0196	0.0200-0.0550	0.0010-0.0027-	0.0015-0.0037	0.0078 max.
1986	H	2.5 (150)	0.0006-0.0016	0.0100-0.0200	0.0100-0.0200	0.0100-0.0250	0.0017-0.0032	0.0017-0.0032	0.0010-0.008
	W	2.8 (173)	0.0006-0.0016	0.0098-0.0196	0.0098-0.0196	0.0200-0.0550	0.0010-0.0027-	0.0015-0.0037	0.0078 max.
1987	H	2.5 (150)	0.0013-0.0021	0.0100-0.0200	0.0100-0.0200	0.0150-0.0550	0.0010-0.0032	0.0010-0.0032	0.0010-0.0021
	M	4.0 (243)	0.0009-0.0017	0.0100-0.0200	0.0100-0.0200	0.0100-0.0250	0.0017-0.0032	0.0017-0.0032	0.0010-0.008
1988	H	2.5 (150)	0.0013-0.0021	0.0100-0.0200	0.0100-0.0200	0.0150-0.0550	0.0010-0.0032	0.0010-0.0032	0.0010-0.0021
	M	4.0 (243)	0.0009-0.0017	0.0100-0.0200	0.0100-0.0200	0.0100-0.0250	0.0017-0.0032	0.0017-0.0032	0.0010-0.008
1989	E	2.5 (150)	0.0013-0.0021	0.0100-0.0200	0.0100-0.0200	0.0150-0.0550	0.0010-0.0032	0.0010-0.0032	0.0010-0.0021
	L	4.0 (243)	0.0009-0.0017	0.0100-0.0200	0.0100-0.0200	0.0100-0.0250	0.0017-0.0032	0.0017-0.0032	0.0010-0.008
1990	E	2.5 (150)	0.0013-0.0021	0.0100-0.0200	0.0100-0.0200	0.0150-0.0550	0.0010-0.0032	0.0010-0.0032	0.0010-0.0021
	L	4.0 (243)	0.0009-0.0017	0.0100-0.0200	0.0100-0.0200	0.0100-0.0250	0.0017-0.0032	0.0017-0.0032	0.0010-0.008
1991	P	2.5 (150)	0.0013-0.0021	0.0100-0.0200	0.0100-0.0200	0.0150-0.0550	0.0010-0.0032	0.0010-0.0032	0.0010-0.0021
	S	4.0 (243)	0.0009-0.0017	0.0100-0.0200	0.0100-0.0200	0.0100-0.0250	0.0017-0.0032	0.0017-0.0032	0.0010-0.008
1992	P	2.5 (150)	0.0013-0.0021	0.0100-0.0200	0.0100-0.0200	0.0150-0.0550	0.0010-0.0032	0.0010-0.0032	0.0010-0.0021
	S	4.0 (243)	0.0009-0.0017	0.0100-0.0200	0.0100-0.0200	0.0100-0.0250	0.0017-0.0032	0.0017-0.0032	0.0010-0.008
1993	P	2.5 (150)	0.0013-0.0021	0.0100-0.0200	0.0100-0.0200	0.0150-0.0550	0.0010-0.0032	0.0010-0.0032	0.0010-0.0021
	S	4.0 (243)	0.0009-0.0017	0.0100-0.0200	0.0100-0.0200	0.0100-0.0250	0.0017-0.0032	0.0017-0.0032	0.0010-0.008
	Y	5.2 (318)	0.0005-0.0015	0.0100-0.0200	0.0100-0.0200	0.0100-0.0500	0.0015-0.0030	0.0015-0.0030	0.0020-0.008

86743c08

PISTON AND RING SPECIFICATIONS

All measurements are given in inches.

Year	Engine ID/VIN	Engine Displacement Liters (ci)	Piston Clearance	Ring Gap			Ring Side Clearance		
				Top Compression	Bottom Compression	Oil Control	Top Compression	Bottom Compression	Oil Control
1994	P	2.5 (150)	0.0013-0.0021	0.0100-0.0200	0.0100 0.0200	0.0150-0.0550	0.0010-0.0032	0.0010-0.0032	0.0010-0.0021
	S	4.0 (243)	0.0009-0.0017	0.0100-0.0200	0.0100-0.0200	0.0100-0.0250	0.0017-0.0032	0.0017-0.0032	0.0010-0.008
	Y	5.2 (318)	0.0005-0.0015	0.0100-0.0200	0.0100-0.0200	0.0100-0.0500	0.0015-0.0030	0.0015-0.0030	0.0020-0.008
1995	P	2.5 (150)	0.0013-0.0021	0.0100-0.0200	0.0100-0.0200	0.0150-0.0550	0.0010-0.0032	0.0010-0.0032	0.0010-0.0021
	S	4.0 (243)	0.0009-0.0017	0.0100-0.0200	0.0100-0.0200	0.0100-0.0250	0.0017-0.0032	0.0017-0.0032	0.0010-0.008
	Y	5.2 (318)	0.0005-0.0015	0.0100-0.0200	0.0100-0.0200	0.0100-0.0500	0.0015-0.0030	0.0015-0.0030	0.0020-0.008
1996	P	2.5 (150)	0.0013-0.0021	0.0100-0.0200	0.0100-0.0200	0.0150-0.0550	0.0010-0.0032	0.0010-0.0032	0.0010-0.0021
	S	4.0 (243)	0.0009-0.0017	0.0100-0.0200	0.0100-0.0200	0.0100-0.0250	0.0017-0.0032	0.0017-0.0032	0.0010-0.008
	Y	5.2 (318)	0.0005-0.0015	0.0100-0.0200	0.0100-0.0200	0.0100-0.0500	0.0015-0.0030	0.0015-0.0030	0.0020-0.008

NOTE: For the 2.1L diesel, the pistons, rings, and cylinder liners are installed as a matched set. Specifications for individual parts are not applicable.

86743c09

TORQUE SPECIFICATIONS
All readings in ft. lbs.

Year	Engine ID/VIN	Engine Displacement Liters (cc)	Cylinder Head Bolts	Main Bearing Bolts	Rod Bearing Bolts	Crankshaft Damper Bolts	Flywheel Bolts	Manifold Intake	Manifold Exhaust	Spark Plugs	Lug Nut
1984	U	2.5 (150)	[7]	80	33	80	50 [1]	23	[6]	27	75
	W	2.8 (173)	70	63-74	34-40	66-84	45-55	23	25	20	75
1985	B	2.1 (126)	[8]	69	48	96	44	20	31	-	75
	H	2.5 (150)	[7]	80	33	80	50 [1]	[2]	[6]	27	75
	W	2.8 (173)	70	63-74	34-40	66-84	44-55	23	25	20	75
1986	B	2.1 (126)	[8]	69	48	96	44	20	31	-	75
	H	2.5 (150)	[7]	80	33	80	50 [1]	[2]	[6]	27	75
	W	2.8 (173)	70	63-74	34-40	66-84	44-55	23	25	20	75
1987	B	2.1 (126)	[8]	69	48	96	44	20	31	-	75
	H	2.5 (150)	[7]	80	33	80	50 [1]	[2]	[6]	27	75
	M	4.0 (243)	[9]	80	33	80	105	[3]	[3]	27	75
1988	H	2.5 (150)	[7]	80	33	80	50 [1]	[2]	[6]	27	75
	M	4.0 (243)	[9]	80	33	80	105	[3]	[3]	27	75
1989	E	2.5 (150)	[10]	80	33	80	50 [1]	[2]	[6]	27	75
	L	4.0 (243)	[9]	80	33	80	105	[3]	[3]	27	75
1990	E	2.5 (150)	[10]	80	33	80	50 [1]	[4]	[6]	27	75
	L	4.0 (243)	[9]	80	33	80	105	[3]	[3]	27	75
1991	P	2.5 (150)	[10]	80	33	80	50 [1]	[4]	[6]	27	75
	S	4.0 (243)	[9]	80	33	80	105	[3]	[3]	27	75
1992	P	2.5 (150)	[10]	80	33	80	50 [1]	[4]	[6]	27	75
	S	4.0 (243)	[9]	80	33	80	105	[3]	[3]	27	75
1993	P	2.5 (150)	[10]	80	33	80	50 [1]	[4]	[6]	27	75
	S	4.0 (243)	[9]	80	33	80	105	[3]	[3]	27	75
	Y	5.2 (318)	[11]	85	45	135	105	[5]	20	30	75
1994	P	2.5 (150)	[10]	80	33	80	105	[4]	[6]	27	75
	S	4.0 (243)	[9]	80	33	80	105	[3]	[3]	27	75
	Y	5.2 (318)	[11]	85	45	135	105	[5]	20	30	75
1995	P	2.5 (150)	[10]	80	33	80	105	[4]	[6]	27	75
	S	4.0 (243)	[9]	80	33	80	105	[3]	[3]	27	75
	Y	5.2 (318)	[11]	85	45	135	105	[5]	20	30	75
1996	P	2.5 (150)	[10]	80	33	80	105	[4]	[6]	27	75
	S	4.0 (243)	[9]	80	33	80	105	[3]	[3]	27	75
	Y	5.2 (318)	[11]	85	45	135	105	[5]	20	30	75

NOTE: Always refer to the text for proper procedures and sequence illustrations.

1: Plus turn an additional 60 degrees

2: Bolts 1, 6, 7 and 8 to 30 ft. lbs.
Bolts 2, 3, 4 and 5 to 23 ft. lbs.
Bolts 9 and 10 to 14 ft. lbs.

3: Bolts 1 and 5 to 23 ft. lbs.
Bolts 6 and 7 to 17 ft. lbs.
Bolts 8 through 11 to 23 ft. lbs.

4: Bolt 1 to 30 ft. lbs.
Bolts 2, 3, 4, and 5 to 23 ft. lbs.
Bolts 6 and 7 to 30 ft. lbs.

5: Bolts 1 through 4 to 72 inch lbs.
Bolts 5 through 12 to 72 inch lbs.
All to 12 ft. lbs.

6: Bolt 1 to 30 ft. lbs.
Bolts 2 and 5 to 23 ft. lbs.
Bolts 6 and 7 to 23 ft. lbs.

7: All except bolt 8 to 85 ft. lbs.
Bolt 8 to 75 ft. lbs.

8: First pass to 22 ft. lbs.
Second pass to 37 ft. lbs.
Third pass to 70-77 ft. lbs.

9: First pass to 22 ft. lbs.
Second pass to 45 ft. lbs.
Except bolt 11 to 110 ft. lbs.
Bolt 11 to 100 ft. lbs.

10: First pass to 22 ft. lbs.
Second pass to 45 ft. lbs.
Bolts 1 through 6 to 110 ft. lbs.
Bolt 7 to 100 ft. lbs.
Bolts 8 through 10 to 110 ft. lbs.

11: All to 50 ft. lbs.
All to 105 ft. lbs.

86743c10

Engine

REMOVAL & INSTALLATION

In the process of removing the engine, you will come across a number of steps which call for the removal of a separate component or system, such as "disconnect the exhaust system" or "remove the radiator." In most instances, a detailed removal procedure can be found elsewhere in this manual.

It is virtually impossible to list each individual wire and hose which must be disconnected, simply because so many different model and engine combinations have been manufactured. Careful observation and common sense are the best possible additions to any repair procedure. Be absolutely sure to tag and wire or hose before it is disconnected, so that you can be assured of proper reconnection during installation.

2.1L Diesel Engines

▶ **See Figures 7 and 8**

1. Disconnect the battery cables and remove the battery. Remove the hood.
2. If equipped, remove the skid plate.
3. Drain the radiator. Remove the air cleaner assembly.

✳✳CAUTION

When draining the coolant, keep in mind that cats and dogs are attracted by ethylene glycol antifreeze, and are quite likely to drink any that is left in an uncovered container or in puddles on the ground. This will prove fatal in sufficient quantity. Always drain the coolant into a sealable container. Coolant should be reused unless it is contaminated or several years old.

➡**The air conditioning system must only be discharged using an approved recovery/recycling machine. Please refer to Section 1 for more information.**

4. If equipped, discharge the air conditioning compressor. Be sure to observe all safety precautions.
5. Disconnect the radiator hoses and remove the E-clip from the bottom of the radiator.
6. Raise and support the vehicle safely. If the vehicle is equipped with automatic transmission disconnect the oil cooler lines at the radiator.
7. Remove the splash shield from the oil pan. Lower the vehicle.
8. Loosen the radiator shroud and remove the radiator fan assembly. Remove the shroud and the splash shield.
9. Remove the radiator and the condenser assembly from the vehicle. Remove the inner cooler.
10. Remove the exhaust shield from the manifold. Disconnect the hoses at the remote oil filter. Remove the oil filter.
11. Tag and disconnect all vacuum hoses and electrical connections. Disconnect and plug the fuel inlet and outlet lines at the fuel pump.
12. If equipped with automatic transmission, remove the left motor mount through bolt retaining nut.
13. Remove the motor mount retaining bolts. Disconnect the accelerator cable. Raise and support the vehicle safely.

14. Disconnect and drain the power steering hoses at the power steering pump.
15. Disconnect the exhaust pipe at the exhaust manifold. Remove the motor mount retaining nuts.
16. Support the engine. Remove the left motor mount bolts. On automatic transmission equipped vehicles, remove the left motor mount.
17. Remove the starter.
18. If the vehicle is equipped with automatic transmission, mark and remove the converter-to-drive plate bolts through the starter opening. Install the left motor mount and retaining bolts finger-tight. Install the motor mount cushion through bolt. Remove the engine support.
19. Remove the accessible transmission-to-engine retaining bolts.
20. Lower the vehicle. Remove the remaining engine-to-transmission retaining bolts.
21. Remove the power steering pump from the engine. Remove the oil separator and disconnect the hoses. Disconnect the heater hoses.

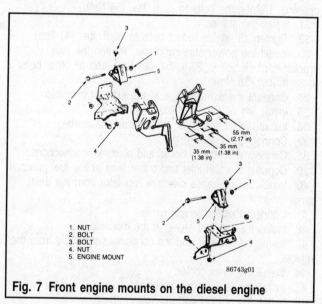

1. NUT
2. BOLT
3. BOLT
4. NUT
5. ENGINE MOUNT

55 mm (2.17 in)
35 mm (1.38 in)
35 mm (1.38 in)

86743g01

Fig. 7 Front engine mounts on the diesel engine

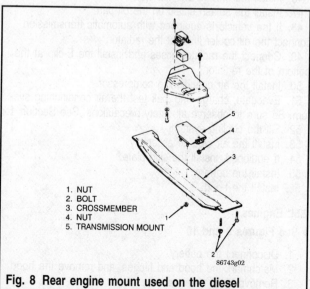

1. NUT
2. BOLT
3. CROSSMEMBER
4. NUT
5. TRANSMISSION MOUNT

86743g02

Fig. 8 Rear engine mount used on the diesel

22. Remove the reference pressure regulator from the dash panel. Install the engine lifting device and position a jack under the transmission.
23. Remove the engine from the vehicle.

To install:

24. Lower the engine into the vehicle.

➡It may be necessary to remove the engine mount cushions to ease alignment of the engine.

25. On trucks with a manual transmission, slide the transmission input shaft into the clutch splines, align the flywheel housing bolt holes and install the lower bolts finger-tight.
26. On trucks with an automatic transmission, align the torque converter housing and engine and install the lower bolts finger-tight.
27. Install all remaining bolts. Tighten all bolts to 30 ft. lbs. (41 Nm).
28. Install any engine mount cushions previously removed.
29. Remove the engine lifting device.
30. If the vehicle is equipped with automatic transmission, install the converter-to-drive plate bolts through the starter opening. Tighten the bolts to 40 ft. lbs. (54 Nm).
31. Install the starter.
32. Tighten all engine mount bolts to 30 ft. lbs. (41 Nm).
33. Install the power steering pump. Tighten the rear bracket-to-block bolt to 20 ft. lbs. (27 Nm), and all other bolts to 28 ft. lbs. (38 Nm).
34. Connect the exhaust pipe at the exhaust manifold.
35. Install the oil filter and lines.
36. Install the oil separator and connect the hoses.
37. Connect the heater hoses.
38. Connect all vacuum hoses and electrical connections.
39. Connect the fuel inlet and outlet lines at the fuel pump.
40. Install the reference pressure regulator from the dash panel.
41. Connect the accelerator cable.
42. Install the exhaust shield at the manifold.
43. Install the radiator and the condenser assembly from the vehicle.
44. Install the inner cooler.
45. Install the radiator fan assembly.
46. Install the shroud and the splash shield.
47. Install the splash shield on the oil pan.
48. If the vehicle is equipped with automatic transmission connect the oil cooler lines at the radiator.
49. Connect the radiator hoses and install the E-clip at the bottom of the radiator.
50. Install the air conditioning compressor.
51. Evacuate, charge and leak test the air conditioning system. Be sure to observe all safety precautions. See Section 1.
52. Fill the cooling system.
53. Install the air cleaner assembly.
54. If equipped, install the skid plate.
55. Install the battery.
56. Install the hood.

2.5L Engines

♦ **See Figures 9 and 10**

1. Disconnect the battery.
2. Matchmark the hood and hinges, and remove the hood.
3. Remove the air cleaner.

4. Drain the coolant and engine oil.

✳✳CAUTION

When draining the coolant, keep in mind that cats and dogs are attracted by ethylene glycol antifreeze, and are quite likely to drink any that is left in an uncovered container or in puddles on the ground. This will prove fatal in sufficient quantity. Always drain the coolant into a sealable container. Coolant should be reused unless it is contaminated or several years old.

5. Remove the radiator hoses.
6. Remove the fan shroud and transmission cooler lines.

➡The air conditioning system must only be discharged using an approved recovery/recycling machine. Please refer to Section 1 for more information.

7. If equipped, discharge the air conditioning compressor. Be sure to observe all safety precautions.
8. Remove the condenser and radiator.
9. Remove the fan and install a 5/16 in. x 1/5 in. capscrew through the pulley and into the water pump flange to maintain pulley alignment.
10. Disconnect the heater hoses.
11. Disconnect and tag all wires, hoses, and cables connected to the engine.
12. Remove the service ports from the air conditioning compressor and cap the openings.
13. Drain the power steering reservoir.
14. Remove the power steering hoses at the gear.
15. Remove the check valve from the power brake vacuum hose.
16. Raise and support the front end on jackstands.
17. Remove the starter.
18. Disconnect the exhaust pipe at the manifold.
19. Remove the bell housing access plate.
20. On trucks equipped with automatic transmission, match-mark the torque converter and flywheel. Remove the attaching bolts.
21. Remove the upper flywheel housing-to-engine bolts; loosen the lower ones.
22. Take up the weight of the engine with a shop crane.
23. Remove the engine mount bolts.
24. Raise the engine off the mounts.
25. Support the transmission with a floor jack.
26. Remove the remaining engine-to-flywheel housing bolts.
27. Move the engine forward to clear the transmission, and lift it from the vehicle.

To install:

28. Lower the engine into the vehicle.

➡It may be easier to align the engine and transmission if you remove the engine mount cushions from the brackets.

29. On trucks with a manual transmission, engage the transmission input shaft with the clutch splines. Align the flywheel housing bolt holes and install the lower engine-to-transmission bolts finger-tight.
30. On trucks with an automatic transmission, align the torque converter housing and engine. Loosely install the 4 lower transmission-to-engine bolts.
31. Install the engine mount cushions.

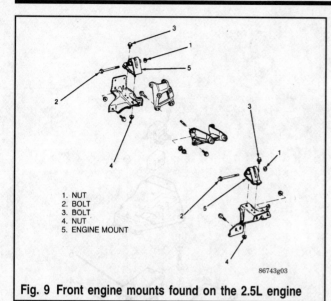

Fig. 9 Front engine mounts found on the 2.5L engine

1. NUT
2. BOLT
3. BOLT
4. NUT
5. ENGINE MOUNT

86743g03

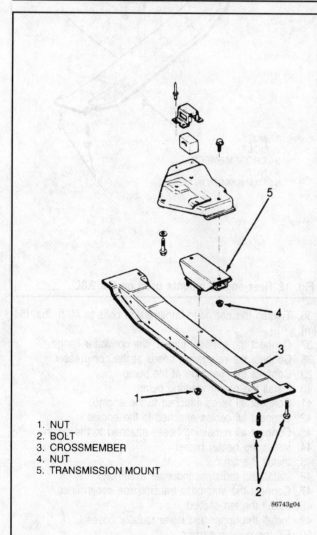

Fig. 10 Rear engine mount on the 2.5L engine

1. NUT
2. BOLT
3. CROSSMEMBER
4. NUT
5. TRANSMISSION MOUNT

86743g04

32. Lower the engine onto the mounts.
33. Remove the shop crane.
34. On trucks equipped with automatic transmission, install the torque converter-to-flywheel bolts. Tighten the bolts to 40 ft. lbs. (54 Nm).
35. Install the converter housing access plate.
36. Install the remaining engine-to-flywheel housing bolts. Tighten the upper bolts to 27 ft. lbs. (37 Nm); the lower bolts to 43 ft. lbs. (58 Nm).
37. Install the engine mount bolts. Tighten the bolts to 48 ft. lbs. (65 Nm).
38. Connect the exhaust pipe at the manifold. Tighten the bolts to 23 ft. lbs. (31 Nm).
39. Install the starter.
40. Install the check valve on the power brake vacuum hose.
41. Install the power steering hoses at the gear.
42. Fill the power steering reservoir.
43. Install the service ports on the air conditioning compressor.
44. Connect all wires, hoses, and cables to the engine.
45. Connect the heater hoses.
46. Install the fan and pulley.
47. Install the condenser and radiator.
48. Install the fan shroud and transmission cooler lines.
49. Install the radiator hoses.
50. Fill the cooling system.
51. Fill the crankcase.
52. Install the air cleaner.
53. Install the hood.
54. Connect the battery.
55. Evacuate, charge and leak test the refrigerant system.

2.8L Engines

▶ See Figures 11 and 12

1. Remove the battery cables.
2. Remove the air cleaner.
3. Remove the hood.
4. Drain the cooling system.

✳✳CAUTION

When draining the coolant, keep in mind that cats and dogs are attracted by ethylene glycol antifreeze, and are quite likely to drink any that is left in an uncovered container or in puddles on the ground. This will prove fatal in sufficient quantity. Always drain the coolant into a sealable container. Coolant should be reused unless it is contaminated or several years old.

5. Remove the upper and lower radiator hoses.
6. Remove the fan shroud.
7. Disconnect the automatic transmission cooler lines.

➡The air conditioning system must only be discharged using an approved recovery/recycling machine. Please refer to Section 1 for more information.

8. If equipped, discharge the air conditioning compressor. Be sure to observe all safety precautions.
9. Remove the radiator/condenser assembly.

10. Remove the fan. If equipped with a fan clutch, do not lay the fan on its back or front. This will cause the clutch to leak and be irreversibly damaged.

11. Remove the heater hoses.

12. Disconnect and tag all remaining hoses attached to the engine.

13. Disconnect and tag all cables attached to the engine.

14. Disconnect and tag all wires attached to the engine.

15. Remove the power steering pump.

16. Disconnect the fuel pipe at the pump.

17. Disconnect the refrigerant hoses at the compressor and cap the openings.

18. Raise and support the truck on jackstands.

19. Disconnect the exhaust pipe at the converter flange.

20. Remove the flywheel housing access plate.

21. On vehicles equipped with automatic transmission, matchmark the converter-to-flywheel and remove the bolts.

22. Remove the flywheel housing-to-engine bolts.

23. Lower the vehicle.

24. Place a floor jack under the transmission.

25. Attach a shop crane to the engine lifting eyes.

26. Remove the engine mount bolts.

27. Lift the engine from the truck.

To install:

28. Lift the engine from the truck.

➡**It will be easier to align the engine if you remove the engine support cushions.**

29. Install the flywheel housing-to-engine bolts finger-tight.

30. Install the support cushions and lower the engine onto the mounts.

31. Install the engine mount bolts. Tighten the through-bolts to 92 ft. lbs. (125 Nm).

32. Remove the shop crane.

33. Remove the floor jack under the transmission.

34. On vehicles equipped with automatic transmission, install the converter-to-flywheel bolts. Tighten the bolts to 25 ft. lbs. (34 Nm).

35. Install the flywheel housing access plate.

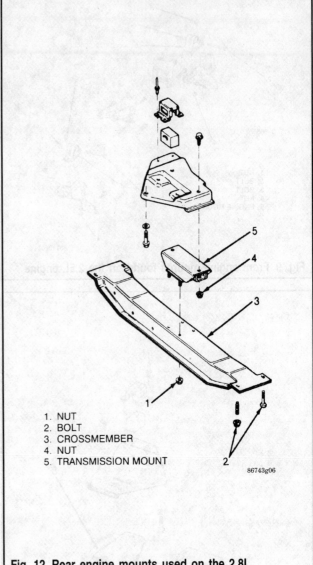

1. NUT
2. BOLT
3. CROSSMEMBER
4. NUT
5. TRANSMISSION MOUNT

86743g06

Fig. 12 Rear engine mounts used on the 2.8L

36. Tighten the engine-to-transmission bolts to 40 ft. lbs. (54 Nm).

37. Connect the exhaust pipe at the converter flange.

38. Connect the refrigerant hoses at the compressor.

39. Connect the fuel pipe at the pump.

40. Install the power steering pump.

41. Connect all wires attached to the engine.

42. Connect all cables attached to the engine.

43. Connect all remaining hoses attached to the engine.

44. Install the heater hoses.

45. Install the fan.

46. Install the radiator/condenser assembly.

47. Connect the automatic transmission cooler lines.

48. Install the fan shroud.

49. Install the upper and lower radiator hoses.

50. Fill the cooling system.

51. Install the hood.

52. Install the air cleaner.

53. Install the battery cables.

54. Evacuate, charge and leak test the refrigerant system.

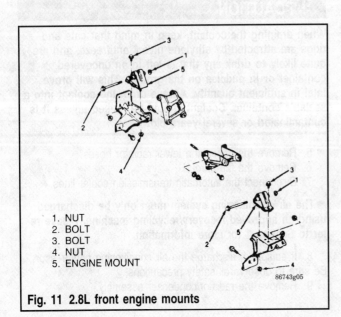

1. NUT
2. BOLT
3. BOLT
4. NUT
5. ENGINE MOUNT

86743g05

Fig. 11 2.8L front engine mounts

4.0L Engines

COMANCHE AND CHEROKEE

▶ See Figures 13, 14 and 15

1. Disconnect the negative battery cable.
2. Properly relieve the fuel system pressure.

➡The air conditioning system must only be discharged using an approved recovery/recycling machine. Please refer to Section 1 for more information.

3. If equipped, discharge the air conditioning compressor. Be sure to observe all safety precautions.
4. Matchmark the hood and hinges and remove the hood.
5. Drain the cooling system.

➡Label all electrical connectors and vacuum lines prior to disconnecting them, so they can be reinstalled in their proper locations.

6. Remove the upper, lower and coolant recovery hoses.
7. Remove the fan shroud.
8. If equipped with an automatic transmission, disconnect the fluid cooler lines.
9. Remove the radiator and if equipped, A/C condenser.
10. Remove the engine cooling fan and install a $5/16$ x $1/2$ inch capscrew through the fan pulley into the water pump flange. This will maintain the pulley and water pump in alignment when the crankshaft is rotated.
11. Disconnect the heater hoses.
12. Disconnect the throttle linkages, speed control cable, if equipped and throttle valve rod.
13. Disconnect the oxygen sensor electrical connector.
14. Disconnect the fuel injection harness connectors.
15. Disconnect the quick-connection fuel lines at the fuel rail and return line.
16. Remove the fuel line bracket from the intake manifold.
17. Remove the air cleaner assembly.
18. If equipped with A/C, remove the service valves and cap the compressor ports.
19. Remove the power brake vacuum check valve from the booster, if equipped.
20. If equipped with power steering, perform the following:
    a. Disconnect the steering hoses from the fittings at the steering gear.
    b. Drain the pump reservoir.
    c. Cap all fittings once removed.
21. Disconnect the coolant hoses from the rear of the intake manifold.
22. Identify, tag and disconnect all necessary wires and vacuum lines.
23. Raise and support the vehicle safely.
24. Remove the oil filter.
25. Remove the starter.
26. Disconnect the exhaust pipe from the manifold.
27. Remove the flywheel/converter housing access cover.
28. If equipped with an automatic transmission, matchmark the converter to the driveplate and remove the bolts.
29. Remove the upper flywheel/converter housing bolts and loosen the bottoms bolts.
30. Remove the engine mount-to-engine compartment bracket bolts.
31. Remove the engine shock damper bracket from the sill.

32. Lower the vehicle.
33. Attach a lifting device to the engine.
34. Raise the engine slightly off the front supports.
35. Place a support stand under the transmission housing.
36. Remove the remaining flywheel bolts.
37. Lift the engine out of the vehicle.
38. Install the oil filter to keep foreign material out of the engine.

To install:

39. Remove the oil filter.
40. Lower the engine into the vehicle. To ease installation, remove the engine mounts to aid in engine-to-transmission alignment.
41. If equipped with a manual transmission, perform the following.
    a. Insert the transmission shaft into the clutch spline.
    b. Align the flywheel housing with the engine.
    c. Install and tighten the flywheel housing bolts finger-tight.
42. If equipped with an automatic transmission, perform the following.
    a. Align the torque converter housing with the engine.
    b. Loosely install the converter housing lower bolts and install the next higher nut and bolt on each side.
    c. Tighten all 4 bolts finger-tight.
43. If removed, install the engine mounts.
44. Lower the engine into place and remove the lifting device.
45. Raise and support the vehicle safely.
46. If equipped with an automatic transmission, perform the following.
    a. Align the torque converter to the driveplate.
    b. Install the bolts and torque them to 40 ft. lbs. (54 Nm).
    c. Install the access cover.
    d. Install the exhaust pipe support.
47. Install the remaining converter/flywheel bolts finger-tight.
48. Install the starter.
49. Tighten the engine support cushion bolts/nuts.
50. Tighten the loose converter/flywheel bolts to 28 ft. lbs. (38 Nm).
51. Install the oil filter.
52. Connect the exhaust pipe to the manifold.
53. Lower the vehicle.
54. Connect the coolant hoses and tighten the clamps.
55. If equipped with power steering, perform the following:
    a. Unplug the lines and connect them to the steering gear. Tighten the fittings to 38 ft. lbs. (52 Nm).
    b. Fill the pump reservoir with fluid.
56. Remove the alignment cap screw and install the fan.
57. Install the radiator, condenser, if equipped and fan shroud.
58. Connect the radiator hoses.
59. If equipped with an automatic transmission, connect the cooling lines.
60. Connect the oxygen sensor electrical connector.
61. Connect the throttle valve rod and retainer. Connect the throttle cable and install the rod and spring.
62. If equipped, connect the cruise control cable.
63. Connect the fuel lines to the throttle body.
64. Connect all vacuum lines and electrical connectors disconnected during removal.

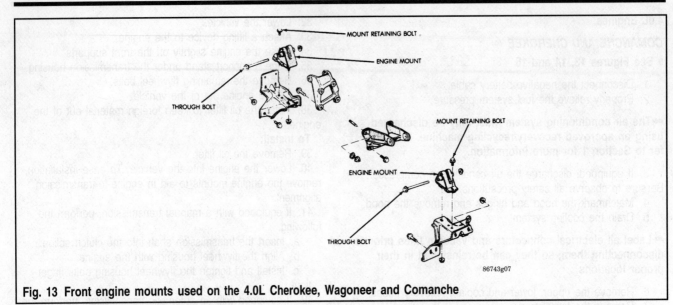

Fig. 13 Front engine mounts used on the 4.0L Cherokee, Wagoneer and Comanche

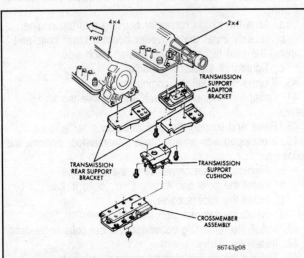

Fig. 14 Rear engine mount used on 4.0L Cherokee, Wagoneer and Comanche with automatic transmissions

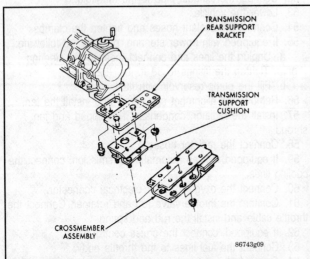

Fig. 15 Rear engine mount used on 4.0L Cherokee, Wagoneer and Comanche with manual transmissions

65. If equipped with A/C, connect the service valves to the compressor ports.
66. Install the air cleaner.
67. Install the hood.
68. Connect the battery cables.
69. Fill the cooling system.
70. Start the engine and check for leaks.
71. If equipped, evacuate, recharge and leak test the A/C system.
72. Check and top off fluid levels.

1993-96 GRAND CHEROKEE

▶ **See Figures 16, 17 and 18**

1. Matchmark the hood to the hinges and remove the hood.
2. Remove the battery.
3. Properly relieve the fuel system pressure.
4. Drain the cooling system.
5. Remove the air cleaner and tube.
6. Remove the radiator.
7. Remove the heater hoses.
8. Label and disconnect the necessary vacuum lines.
9. Remove the distributor cap and wiring.
10. Disconnect the accelerator linkage.
11. Remove the air duct from the throttle body.
12. Label and disconnect the Manifold Absolute Pressure (MAP) sensor, Idle Air Control (IAC) motor and Throttle Position Sensor (TPS) electrical connectors from the throttle body.
13. Disconnect the vacuum line from the throttle body.
14. Disconnect (unsnap) the control cables from the throttle body (lever) arm.
15. Remove the throttle body from the intake manifold. Discard the gasket.
16. Disconnect the oil pressure electrical connector.

➡ **The air conditioning system must only be discharged using an approved recovery/recycling machine. Please refer to Section 1 for more information.**

17. If equipped, discharge the air conditioning compressor. Be sure to observe all safety precautions.
18. Disconnect the A/C lines from the compressor.

19. If equipped with power steering, disconnect the lines from the pump.
20. Remove the starter.
21. Remove the alternator.
22. Raise and support the vehicle safely.
23. Disconnect the fuel line connections coming from the fuel rail.
24. Disconnect the exhaust pipe from the manifold.
25. Support the transmission with a stand.
26. Remove the bell housing bolts and inspection plate.
27. Attach a C-clamp to the bottom of the torque converter housing to prevent the torque converter from coming out.
28. Matchmark the torque converter to the driveplate and remove the bolts.
29. Disconnect the engine from the torque converter driveplate.

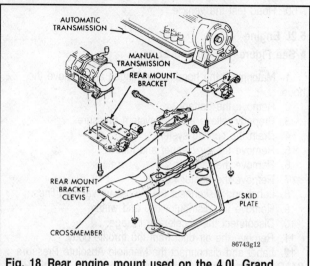

Fig. 18 Rear engine mount used on the 4.0L Grand Cherokee

30. Install a suitable lifting device to the engine.

✳✳WARNING

Do not lift the engine by the intake manifold.

31. Remove the front engine mount through-bolts.
32. Lower the vehicle.
33. Remove the engine from the vehicle and mount on a suitable workstand.

To install:
34. Remove the engine from the workstand and position it in the engine compartment.
35. Raise and support the vehicle.
36. Position the torque converter and driveplate. Tighten the bolts to 271 inch lbs. (31 Nm).
37. Install the front engine mount through-bolts.
38. Install the bell housing bolts and torque them to 30 ft. lbs. (41 Nm).
39. Remove the C-clamp and install the inspection plate. Remove the stand from the transmission.
40. Connect the exhaust pipe to the manifold.
41. Connect the fuel rail lines.
42. Lower the vehicle.
43. Install the starter.
44. Install the alternator.
45. If equipped, install the power steering hoses.
46. If equipped, connect the A/C hoses.
47. Connect the accelerator linkage.
48. Connect the starter wires.
49. Connect the oil pressure electrical connector.
50. Install the distributor cap and wires.
51. Connect the vacuum lines.
52. Install the radiator, radiator hoses and heater hoses.
53. Install the fan shroud into position.
54. Install the air cleaner.
55. Install the battery.
56. Fill the cooling system.
57. Start the engine and check for leaks.
58. If equipped, evacuate, recharge and leak test the A/C system.
59. Install the hood.

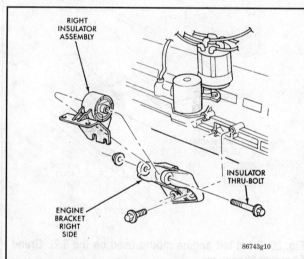

Fig. 16 Front right engine mount used on the 4.0L Grand Cherokee

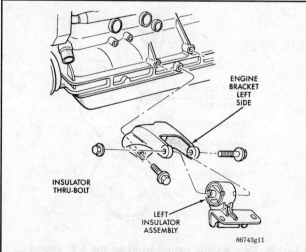

Fig. 17 Front left engine mount used on the 4.0L Grand Cherokee

60. Road test the vehicle.

5.2L Engine

▶ **See Figures 19, 20 and 21**

1. Matchmark the hood to the hinges and remove the hood.
2. Remove the battery.
3. Properly relieve the fuel system pressure.
4. Drain the cooling system.
5. Remove the air cleaner and tube.
6. Remove the radiator.
7. Remove the heater hoses.
8. Label and disconnect the necessary vacuum lines.
9. Remove the distributor cap and wiring.
10. Disconnect the accelerator linkage.
11. Remove the air duct from the throttle body.
12. Label and disconnect the Manifold Absolute Pressure (MAP) sensor, Idle Air Control (IAC) motor and Throttle Position Sensor (TPS) electrical connectors from the throttle body.
13. Disconnect the vacuum line from the throttle body.
14. Disconnect (unsnap) the control cables from the throttle body (lever) arm.
15. Remove the throttle body from the intake manifold. Discard the gasket.
16. Disconnect the oil pressure electrical connector.

➡**The air conditioning system must only be discharged using an approved recovery/recycling machine. Please refer to Section 1 for more information.**

17. If equipped, discharge the air conditioning compressor. Be sure to observe all safety precautions.
18. Disconnect the A/C lines from the compressor.
19. If equipped with power steering, disconnect the lines from the pump.
20. Remove the starter.
21. Remove the alternator.
22. Raise and support the vehicle safely.
23. Disconnect the fuel line connections coming from the fuel rail.
24. Disconnect the exhaust pipe from the manifold.
25. Support the transmission with a stand.
26. Remove the bell housing bolts and inspection plate.
27. Attach a C-clamp to the bottom of the torque converter housing to prevent the torque converter from coming out.
28. Matchmark the torque converter to the driveplate and remove the bolts.
29. Disconnect the engine from the torque converter driveplate.
30. Install a suitable lifting device to the engine.

❉❉WARNING

Do not lift the engine by the intake manifold.

31. Remove the front engine mount through-bolts.
32. Lower the vehicle.
33. Remove the engine from the vehicle and mount on a suitable workstand.

   To install:
34. Remove the engine from the workstand and position it in the engine compartment.

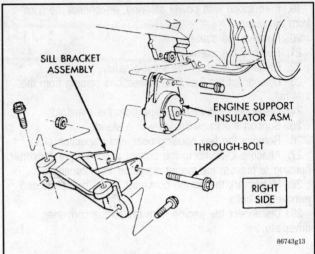

Fig. 19 Front right engine mount used on the 5.2L Grand Cherokee/Wagoneer

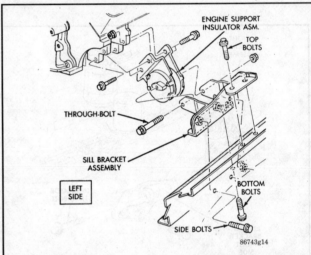

Fig. 20 Front left engine mount used on the 5.2L Grand Cherokee/Wagoneer

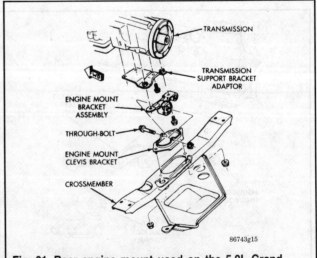

Fig. 21 Rear engine mount used on the 5.2L Grand Cherokee/Wagoneer

35. Raise and support the vehicle.
36. Position the torque converter and driveplate. Tighten the bolts to 271 inch lbs. (31 Nm).
37. Install the front engine mount through-bolts.
38. Install the bell housing bolts and tighten them to 30 ft. lbs. (41 Nm).
39. Remove the C-clamp and install the inspection plate. Remove the stand from the transmission.
40. Connect the exhaust pipe to the manifold.
41. Connect the fuel rail lines.
42. Lower the vehicle.
43. Install the starter.
44. Install the alternator.
45. If equipped, install the power steering hoses.
46. If equipped, connect the A/C hoses.
47. Connect the accelerator linkage.
48. Connect the starter wires.
49. Connect the oil pressure electrical connector.
50. Install the distributor cap and wires.
51. Connect the vacuum lines.
52. Install the radiator, radiator hoses and heater hoses.
53. Install the fan shroud into position.
54. Install the air cleaner.
55. Install the battery.
56. Fill the cooling system.
57. Start the engine and check for leaks.
58. If equipped, evacuate, recharge and leak test the A/C system.
59. Install the hood.
60. Road test the vehicle.

Rocker Arm (Valve) Cover

REMOVAL & INSTALLATION

2.1L Diesel Engines

1. Disconnect the negative battery cable
2. Disconnect vacuum and oil breather hoses that route over the rocker arm cover.
3. Remove the rocker arm cover retaining bolts. Remove the cover.
4. Remove the cover gasket, clean the mating surfaces and install the new gasket.
5. Install the retaining bolts and tighten them to 35 inch lbs. (4 Nm). Reconnect vacuum and oil breather hoses that were disconnected during removal.

2.5L Engines

▶ See Figures 22, 23, 24, 25, 26 and 27

1. Remove the air cleaner and the PCV valve molded hose.
2. Disconnect the fuel line at the fuel pump and swivel to allow removal of the rocker arm cover (carbureted engines).
3. Disconnect or remove any vacuum or air hoses to provide access to the rocker arm cover.

➡To avoid damaging the rocker arm cover, DO NOT pry the cover upward until the RTV seal has been broken.

Fig. 24 Remove the bolts securing the cover to the head

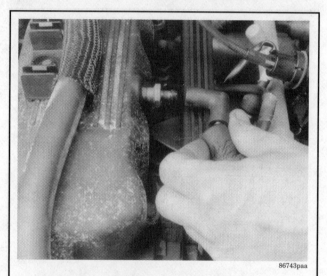
Fig. 22 Disconnect the PCV hose from the cover

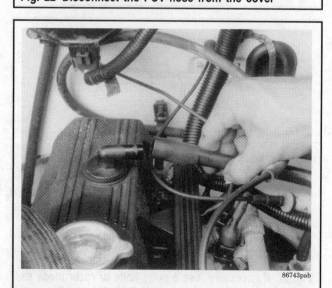
Fig. 23 Unplug the fresh air hose from the valve cover

Fig. 25 Lift the vacuum pipe from the studs

Fig. 26 Remove the valve cover from the head

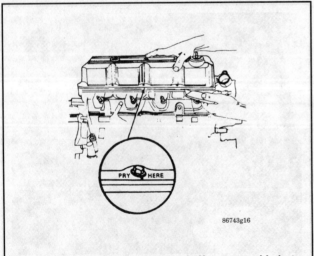

Fig. 27 If necessary, use a putty knife or razor blade to break the seal. Pry only where indicated

4. Remove the rocker arm cover retaining bolts. Break the RTV seal by gently tapping the cover.

5. Thoroughly clean old sealer from head and cover. Examine rocker arm cover for cracks or bent rails.

To install:

6. Apply a ⅛ in. (3mm) bead of RTV sealant along the entire length of the rocker arm cover rail. Allow the sealant to set-up for a few seconds.

7. While the sealant is still fluid, install the rocker arm cover on the cylinder head. Take care not to get any sealant on the rocker arms or valve train components.

8. Install rocker arm cover retaining bolts and tighten to 55 inch lbs. (6 Nm).

9. Reposition and connect all previously disconnected vacuum and air hoses. Install the PCV valve and hose. Install the air cleaner.

2.8L Engines
▶ **See Figures 28 and 29**

LEFT SIDE

1. Disconnect the battery cables.

2. Disconnect the hoses, wire connectors and pipe bracket Remove the spark plug wires and clips from the retaining stud.

3. Remove the rocker arm cover retaining bolts. Break the RTV seal by gently tapping the cover.

4. Thoroughly clean old sealer from head and cover. Examine rocker arm cover for cracks or bent rails.

To install:

5. Apply a ⅛ in. (3mm) bead of RTV sealant along the entire length of the rocker arm cover rail. Allow the sealant to set-up for a few seconds.

6. While the sealant is still fluid, install the rocker arm cover on the cylinder head. Take care not to get any sealant on the rocker arms or valve train components.

7. Install rocker arm cover retaining bolts and tighten to 8 ft. lbs. (11 Nm).

8. Connect all previously disconnected wires, hoses and brackets. Reconnect the battery cables.

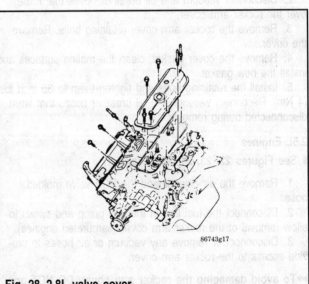

Fig. 28 2.8L valve cover

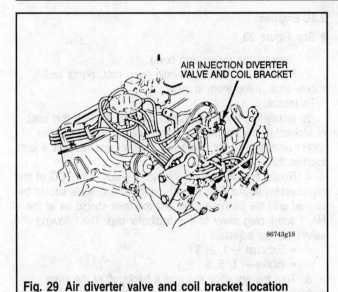

Fig. 29 Air diverter valve and coil bracket location

RIGHT SIDE

1. Disconnect the battery cables.
2. Remove the air cleaner, air injection diverter and coil bracket.
3. Disconnect the air hose from the air injection manifold, wire connectors and vacuum hoses.
4. Remove the spark plug wires and clip from the retaining stud.
5. Disconnect the carburetor controls and remove from the bracket.
6. Remove the rocker arm cover retaining bolts. Break the RTV seal by gently tapping on the cover.
7. Thoroughly clean old sealer from head and cover. Examine rocker arm cover for cracks or bent rails.

To install:

8. Apply a ⅛ in. (3mm) bead of RTV sealant along the entire length of the rocker arm cover rail. Allow the sealant to set-up for a few seconds.
9. While the sealant is still fluid, install the rocker arm cover on the cylinder head. Take care not to get any sealant on the rocker arms or valve train components.
10. Install rocker arm cover retaining bolts and tighten to 8 ft. lbs. (11 Nm).
11. Connect all previously disconnected wires, hoses and brackets. Reconnect the carburetor controls, air injection diverter valve and coil bracket. Install the air cleaner and reconnect the battery cables.

4.0L Engines

1. Remove the hoses and cruise control servo (if equipped).
2. Remove the rocker arm cover retaining bolts. Break the RTV seal by gently tapping on the cover.
3. Thoroughly clean old sealer from head and cover. Examine rocker arm cover for cracks or bent rails.

To install:

4. Apply a ⅛ in. (3mm) bead of RTV sealant along the entire length of the rocker arm cover rail. Allow the sealant to set-up for a few seconds.

5. While the sealant is still fluid, install the rocker arm cover on the cylinder head. Take care not to get any sealant on the rocker arms or valve train components.
6. Install rocker arm cover retaining bolts and tighten to 55 inch lbs. (6 Nm).
7. Install the PCV molded hoses and cruise control servo (if equipped).

5.2L Engine

1. Disconnect the negative battery cable.
2. Label and disconnect the necessary hoses from the cylinder head cover.
3. If removing the left cylinder head cover, remove the coolant tube bracket.
4. Remove the spark plug wires from the holders and disconnect them from the spark plugs.
5. Loosen the bolts, then remove the cylinder head cover and gasket. The steel backed silicon gasket can be used again if not damaged.

To install:

6. Install the cylinder head cover and gasket. On the left cover, install the coolant tube bracket. Tighten the cylinder head cover retaining bolts to 96 inch lbs. (11 Nm).
7. Connect the spark plug wires to the spark plugs and install the wires in the holders.
8. Connect all hoses that were disconnected during the removal procedure.
9. Connect the negative battery cable.

Rocker Arms/Shafts

REMOVAL & INSTALLATION

2.1L Diesel Engines

1. Disconnect the negative battery cable. Remove the rocker arm cover and gasket.
2. Remove the rocker shaft retaining bolts. Remove the rocker arm shaft assembly from the vehicle.
3. Installation is the reverse of the removal procedure. Be sure to use new gaskets and adjust the valves as required. Tighten the bolts to 20 ft. lbs. (27 Nm).

2.5L and 4.0L Engines

▶ See Figures 30, 31 and 32

1. Remove the rocker arm cover.
2. Remove the two capscrews at each bridge and pivot assembly. Alternately loosen the bolts one turn at a time to avoid damaging the bridges.
3. Remove the bridges, pivots and rocker arms. Keep them in order.
4. While the rocker arm is removed, inspect the pivot surface area. Replace any rocker arms that are scuffed, pitted or excessively worn.
5. Inspect the valve stem tip contact surface. Replace any rocker arm that is pitted or excessively worn.
6. Installation is the reverse of removal. Loosely install the capscrews then alternately tighten to 19 ft. lbs. (26 Nm).
7. Install the rocker arm cover.

Fig. 30 Loosen and capscrews at each bridge and pivot assembly

Fig. 31 Remove the pivot assembly . . .

Fig. 32 . . . then the rocker arms

2.8L Engines

▶ See Figure 33

1. Remove the rocker arm cover.
2. Remove the rocker arm hold-down nuts, pivots and rocker arms. Keep them in order.

To install:

3. Installation is the reverse of removal. Apply a thin coat of Molykote®, or equivalent, to the bearing surfaces of the rocker arms and pivots. Tighten the rocker arm nut until it just touches the valve stem.
4. Rotate the engine until the No. 1 piston is at TDC of the compression stroke. The **0** mark on the timing scale should be aligned with the timing pointer and the rotor should be at the No. 1 spark plug tower of the distributor cap. The following valves can be adjusted:
   - Exhaust — 1, 2, 3
   - Intake — 1, 5, 6
5. Turn the adjusting nut until it backs off of the stem slightly, then tighten it until it just touches the stem. Then, turn the nut $1\frac{1}{8}$ turns more to center the tappet plunger.
6. Rotate the engine one complete revolution more. This will bring No. 4 piston to TDC compression. At this point, the following valves may be adjusted:
   - Exhaust — 4, 5, 6
   - Intake — 2, 3, 4
7. Install rocker arm covers. Start engine and check ignition timing and idle speed.

5.2L Engines

▶ See Figure 34

1. Disconnect the negative battery cable.
2. Remove the cylinder head cover and gasket.
3. Remove the rocker arm bolts and remove the rocker arm pivots and rocker arms. Keep the rocker arm assemblies in order so they can be reinstalled in their original locations.
4. Remove the pushrods, keeping them in order so they can be reinstalled in their original locations.

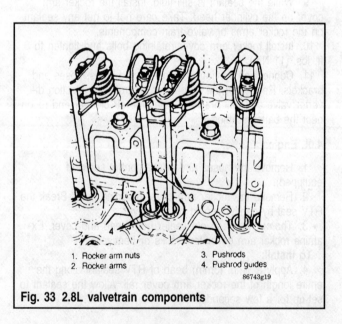

1. Rocker arm nuts
2. Rocker arms
3. Pushrods
4. Pushrod guides

86743g19

Fig. 33 2.8L valvetrain components

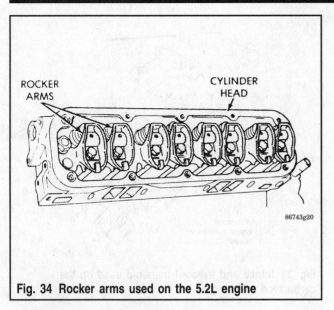

Fig. 34 Rocker arms used on the 5.2L engine

To install:

5. Rotate the crankshaft until the **V8** mark lines up with the TDC mark on the timing chain cover (located 17.5° ATDC from the No. 1 firing mark).

✳✳WARNING

Do not rotate or crank the engine during or immediately after rocker arm installation. Allow about 5 minutes for the hydraulic lifters to bleed down.

6. Install the pushrods in their original locations. Make sure they are seated in the lifters.
7. Lubricate the pushrod tips, rocker arm bearing surfaces and rocker arm pivots with clean engine oil.
8. Install the rocker arm and pivot assemblies in their original locations. Tighten the bolts to 21 ft. lbs. (28 Nm).
9. Install the cylinder head cover and gasket.
10. Connect the negative battery cable.

Thermostat

REMOVAL & INSTALLATION

▶ **See Figures 35, 36 and 37**

1. Disconnect the negative battery cable.
2. If necessary, disconnect the coolant temperature sensor electrical connector.
3. Remove the attaching bolts and lift the housing from the engine.
4. Remove the thermostat and gasket.
   To install:
5. Clean all gasket surfaces thoroughly.
6. Place the thermostat in the housing with the spring inside the engine.
7. Install a new gasket with a small amount of sealing compound applied to both sides.
8. Install the water outlet and tighten the attaching bolts to 30 ft. lbs. (41 Nm).

Fig. 36 . . . then remove the housing from the engine

Fig. 37 Remove the thermostat from the engine

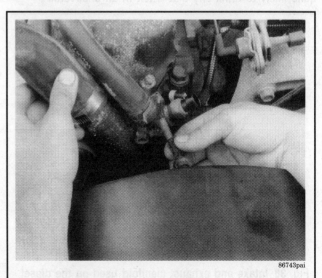

Fig. 35 Remove the attaching bolts . . .

9. Connect the coolant temperature sensor connector to the housing.

10. Refill the cooling system.

Intake Manifold

REMOVAL & INSTALLATION

2.1L Diesel Engines

▶ See Figure 38

1. Disconnect the negative battery cable. Disconnect the air inlet hose at the intake manifold.

2. Tag and remove all hoses and/or wires as necessary in order to gain access to the intake manifold retaining bolts.

3. Tag and remove all vacuum hoses and electrical connections that are attached to the intake manifold.

4. Remove the intake manifold retaining bolts. Remove the assembly from the vehicle. Discard the intake manifold gaskets.

   To install:

5. Clean mating surfaces of all gasket material. Install new gasket.

6. Installation is the reverse of removal. Tighten bolts from center to outside of manifold in steps to 20 ft. lbs. (27 Nm).

2.5L Engines

CARBURETED

▶ See Figures 39 and 40

➡It may be necessary to remove the carburetor from the intake manifold before the manifold is removed.

1. Disconnect the negative battery cable. Drain the radiator.

✳✳CAUTION

When draining the coolant, keep in mind that cats and dogs are attracted by ethylene glycol antifreeze, and are quite likely to drink any that is left in an uncovered

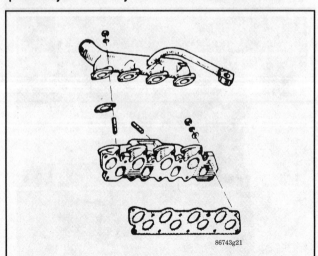

Fig. 38 Intake and exhaust manifold used on the diesel engine

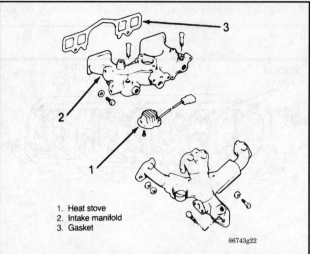

1. Heat stove
2. Intake manifold
3. Gasket

86743g22

Fig. 39 Intake and exhaust manifold used on the carbureted 2.5L engine

container or in puddles on the ground. This will prove fatal in sufficient quantity. Always drain the coolant into a sealable container. Coolant should be reused unless it is contaminated or several years old.

2. Remove the air cleaner. Disconnect the fuel pipe. Remove the carburetor.

3. Disconnect the coolant hoses from the intake manifold.

4. Disconnect the throttle cable from the bellcrank.

5. Disconnect the PCV valve vacuum hose from the intake manifold.

6. If equipped, remove the vacuum advance CTO valve vacuum hoses.

7. Disconnect the system coolant temperature sender wire connector (located on the intake manifold). Disconnect the air temperature sensor wire, if equipped.

8. Disconnect the vacuum hose from the EGR valve.

9. On vehicles equipped with power steering remove the power steering pump and its mounting bracket. Do not detach the power steering pump hoses.

10. Disconnect the intake manifold electric heater wire connector, as required.

11. Disconnect the throttle valve linkage, if equipped with automatic transmission.

12. Disconnect the EGR valve tube from the intake manifold.

13. Remove the intake manifold attaching screws, nuts and clamps. Remove the intake manifold. Discard the gasket.

14. Clean the mating surfaces of the manifold and cylinder head.

➡If the manifold is being replaced, ensure all fittings, etc., are transferred to the replacement manifold.

   To install:

15. Clean the mating surfaces of the manifold and cylinder head.

16. Install the intake manifold, with a new gasket. Install intake manifold attaching screws, nuts and clamps. Using the sequence shown in the illustration, tighten the bolts in steps to 23 ft. lbs. (31 Nm).

17. Connect the EGR valve tube.

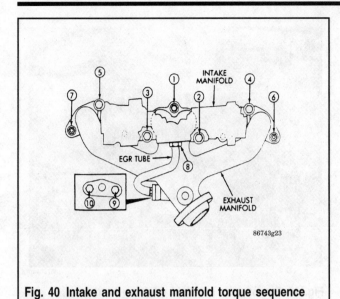

Fig. 40 Intake and exhaust manifold torque sequence

18. Connect the throttle valve linkage, if equipped with automatic transmission.

19. Connect the intake manifold electric heater wire connector, as required.

20. On vehicles equipped with power steering install the power steering pump and its mounting bracket.

21. Connect the vacuum hose to the EGR valve.

22. Connect the system coolant temperature sender wire connector (located on the intake manifold).

23. Connect the air temperature sensor wire, if equipped.

24. If equipped, install the vacuum advance CTO valve vacuum hoses.

25. Connect the PCV valve vacuum hose at the intake manifold.

26. Connect the throttle cable at the bellcrank.

27. Connect the coolant hoses at the intake manifold.

28. Install the carburetor and working in a crisscross pattern, tighten the nuts to 14 ft. lbs. (19 Nm).

29. Connect the fuel pipe.

30. Install the air cleaner.

31. Connect the negative battery cable.

32. Fill the cooling system.

FUEL INJECTED

▶ **See Figures 41, 42, 43, 44, 45, 46 and 47**

1. Disconnect negative battery cable.

2. Remove the air cleaner inlet hose.

3. Loosen the accessory drive belt tension and remove the drive belt.

4. Remove the power steering pump and brackets. Support them from the radiator support with wire.

5. Remove the fuel tank filler cap to relieve the fuel tank pressure. Relieve the fuel system pressure.

6. Disconnect the fuel supply tube from the fuel rail by squeezing the tabs of the quick connector and pulling. When disconnected, the retainer will stay on the fuel tube and the O-rings and spacer will remain in the connector. Use an "L" shaped paper clip to remove the O-rings and spacer.

➡ **Whenever a fuel system disconnect fitting is disconnected the O-rings, spacer and retainer must be replaced.**

7. Follow the instructions on the O-ring replacement kit package to install the new O-rings and spacer.

8. Disconnect the accelerator cable from the throttle body and hold-down bracket. Disconnect the cruise control connector (if equipped) by loosening it with your hands. DO NOT attempt to pry off.

9. Disconnect all necessary electrical connectors:
   • the throttle position sensor
   • Idle speed motor
   • Coolant temperature sensor at the thermostat
   • Manifold air temperature sensor at the intake manifold
   • Fuel injectors
   • Oxygen sensor

10. Disconnect the crankcase ventilation vacuum hose and manifold absolute pressure sensor vacuum hose at the intake manifold. Disconnect the crankcase ventilation hose on the rocker arm cover.

11. Disconnect the vacuum hose at the EGR transducer and solenoid (if necessary).

12. Disconnect the molded vacuum harness.

Fig. 41 Disengage the accelerator cable from the throttle body

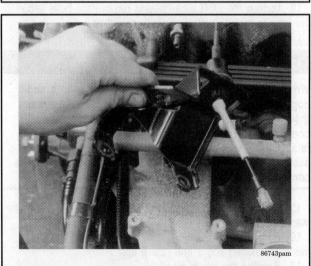

Fig. 42 Remove the cable hold-down bracket from the manifold

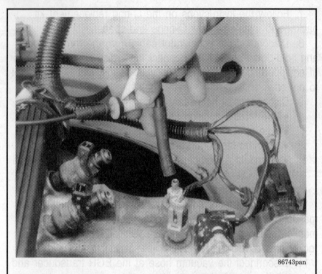

Fig. 43 Unplug the necessary vacuum hoses . . .

Fig. 45 Remove the manifold retaining hardware . . .

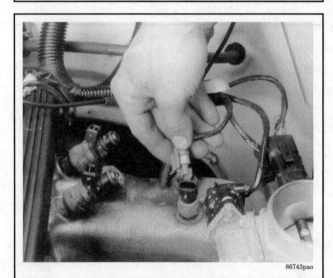

Fig. 44 . . . and electrical connectors from the manifold

Fig. 46 . . . then remove the manifold from the engine

13. Loosen the EGR tube nut and remove the bolts securing the tube to the exhaust manifold (if necessary).

14. Drain the cooling system.

✲✲CAUTION

When draining the coolant, keep in mind that cats and dogs are attracted by ethylene glycol antifreeze, and are quite likely to drink any that is left in an uncovered container or in puddles on the ground. This will prove fatal in sufficient quantity. Always drain the coolant into a sealable container. Coolant should be reused unless it is contaminated or several years old.

15. Disconnect the vacuum brake booster hose at the intake manifold.

16. Remove bolts number 2 through 5 securing the intake manifold. Loosen bolt 1 and nuts 6 and 7.

17. Remove the intake manifold.

To install:

18. Clean the intake manifold and cylinder head mating surfaces. DO NOT allow foreign material to enter the intake manifold or cylinder head ports. Install the new intake manifold gasket over the locating dowels.

19. Position the intake manifold in place and finger-tighten bolts.

20. Use a new EGR tube gasket and attach the EGR tube to the exhaust manifold. Finger-tighten bolts 9 and 10. Leave the EGR tube nut at the intake manifold finger-tight.

21. Tighten the fasteners in sequence and to the specified torque.

Models Through 1990
- Fasteners 1, 6, 7, and 8: 30 ft. lbs. (40 Nm)
- Fasteners 2, 3, 4, and 5: 23 ft. lbs. (31 Nm)
- Fasteners 9 and 10: 14 ft. lbs. (19 Nm)

1991-96 Models
- Fastener 1: 30 ft. lbs. (40 Nm)
- Fasteners 2, 3, 4, and 5: 23 ft. lbs. (31 Nm)
- Fasteners 6 and 7: 30 ft. lbs. (40 Nm)

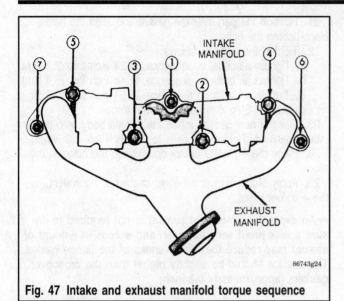

Fig. 47 Intake and exhaust manifold torque sequence

22. Connect the fuel return and supply tube to the connector next to the fuel rail. Don't forget to install the new O-rings. Push them into the fitting until a click is heard. Verify correct installation by first ensuring only the retainer tabs protrude from the connectors and second by pulling out on the fuel tubes to ensure they are locked in place.

23. Attach heater hoses to manifold (if necessary), connect the molded vacuum hoses to the intake manifold, the EGR transducer, the EGR solenoid and the rocker arm cover.

24. Connect electrical connectors previously disconnected.

25. Connect the crankcase ventilation vacuum hose and manifold absolute pressure sensor vacuum hose.

26. Install the power steering pump and bracket assembly to the water pump and intake manifold.

27. Connect the accelerator cable and cruise control cable (if equipped) to the hold-down bracket and throttle arm.

28. Install and tension the accessory drive belt.

➡**Ensure that the accessory drive belt is routed correctly. Failure to do so can cause the water pump to turn in the wrong direction resulting in engine overheating.**

29. Connect the negative battery cable. Start the engine and check for leaks.

2.8L Engines

▶ **See Figure 48**

➡**It may be necessary to remove the carburetor from the intake manifold before the manifold is removed.**

1. Disconnect the negative battery cable. Remove the air cleaner and rocker arm covers. Drain the coolant.

✳✳CAUTION

When draining the coolant, keep in mind that cats and dogs are attracted by ethylene glycol antifreeze, and are quite likely to drink any that is left in an uncovered container or in puddles on the ground. This will prove fatal in sufficient quantity. Always drain the coolant into a sealable container. Coolant should be reused unless it is contaminated or several years old.

2. If equipped with air conditioning disconnect the compressor and move it to one side. Disconnect the spark plugs wires at the spark plugs. Disconnect the wires at the ignition coil.

3. If equipped, remove the air pump and bracket.

4. Remove the distributor cap. Mark the position of the ignition rotor in relation to the distributor body and remove the distributor. Do not crank the engine with the distributor removed.

5. Remove the EGR valve. Remove the air hose. Disconnect the charcoal canister hoses. Remove the pipe bracket from the left cylinder head, if equipped.

6. Remove the diverter valve. Remove the power brake vacuum hose. Remove the heater and radiator hoses from the intake manifold.

7. Disconnect and label the vacuum hoses. If equipped, remove the EFE pipe from the rear of the manifold. Disconnect the coolant temperature switches.

8. Remove the carburetor linkage. Disconnect and plug the fuel line.

9. Remove the manifold retaining bolts and nuts.

10. Remove the intake manifold. Remove and discard the gaskets, and scrape off the old silicone seal from the front and rear ridges.

To install:

11. The gaskets are marked for right and left side installation; do not interchange them. Clean the sealing surface of the engine block, and apply a 0.19 in. (5mm) wide bead of silicone sealer to each ridge.

12. Install the new gaskets onto the heads. The gaskets will have to be cut slightly to fit past the center pushrods. Do not cut any more material than necessary. Hold the gaskets in place by extending the ridge bead of sealer 1/4 in. (6mm) onto the gasket ends.

13. Install the intake manifold. The area between the ridges and the manifold should be completely sealed.

14. Install the retaining bolts and nuts, and tighten in sequence to 23 ft. lbs. (31 Nm). Do not overtighten the manifold. It is made of aluminum, and can be warped or cracked with excessive force.

15. Connect the fuel line.

16. Install the carburetor linkage.

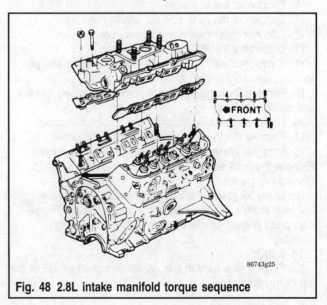

Fig. 48 2.8L intake manifold torque sequence

17. Connect the vacuum hoses.
18. Install the EFE pipe at the rear of the manifold.
19. Connect the coolant temperature switches.
20. Install the diverter valve.
21. Install the power brake vacuum hose.
22. Install the heater and radiator hoses.
23. Install the EGR valve.
24. Install the air hose.
25. Connect the charcoal canister hoses.
26. Install the pipe bracket at the left cylinder head, if equipped.
27. Install the distributor.
28. Install the distributor cap.
29. Install the air pump and bracket.
30. Connect the air conditioning compressor.
31. Install the rocker arm covers.
32. Connect the spark plugs wires at the spark plugs.
33. Connect the wires at the ignition coil.
34. Connect the negative battery cable.
35. Install the air cleaner.
36. Fill the cooling system.

4.0L Engines

The intake and exhaust manifold are mounted externally on the left side of the engine and are attached to the cylinder head. They are removed as a unit. Please refer to the combination manifold procedure.

5.2L Engines

▶ See Figures 49 and 50

1. Disconnect the negative battery cable.
2. Properly relieve the fuel system pressure.
3. Drain the cooling system.
4. Remove the air cleaner.
5. Remove the alternator.
6. Remove the fuel lines and fuel rail.
7. Disconnect the accelerator linkage and, if equipped, the cruise control and transmission kickdown cables.
8. Remove the return spring.
9. Remove the distributor cap and wires.
10. Disconnect the coil wires.
11. Disconnect the heat indicator sending unit wire.
12. Disconnect the heater and bypass hoses.
13. Disconnect the PCV and EVAP lines.
14. If equipped with A/C, remove the compressor and position it aside with the lines attached.
15. Remove the support bracket from the mounting bracket and intake manifold.
16. Remove the intake manifold and discard the gaskets.
17. Remove the throttle body and discard the gasket.
18. Turn the intake manifold upside down and support it. Remove the bolts and lift the plenum pan off the manifold. Discard the gasket.
19. Clean all gasket mating surfaces. Clean the intake manifold with solvent and blow dry with compressed air. The plenum pan rail must be clean, dry and free of all foreign material.

To install:

20. Place a new plenum pan gasket onto the seal rail of the intake manifold.

21. Position the pan over the gasket and align the holes. Hand-tighten the bolts.
22. Tighten the bolts as follows:
    a. Tighten all bolts, in sequence, to 24 inch lbs. (2.7 Nm).
    b. Tighten all bolts, in sequence, to 48 inch lbs. (5.4 Nm).
    c. Tighten all bolts, in sequence, to 84 inch lbs. (9.5 Nm).
    d. Repeat Step c to ensure proper torque.
23. Using a new gasket, install the throttle body onto the intake manifold. Tighten the bolts to 200 inch lbs. (23 Nm).
24. Place the 4 plastic locator dowels into the holes in the block.
25. Apply Mopar rubber adhesive sealant or equivalent, to the 4 corner joints.

➡**An excessive amount of sealant is not required to ensure a leak proof seal, however, and excessive amount of sealant may reduce the effectiveness of the flange gasket. The sealant should be slightly higher than the crossover gaskets (approximately 0.2 inch).**

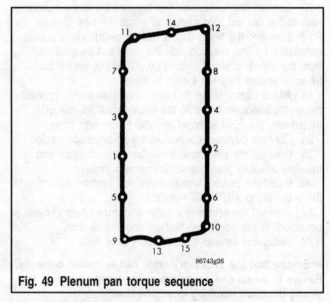

Fig. 49 Plenum pan torque sequence

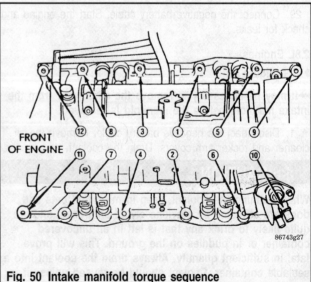

Fig. 50 Intake manifold torque sequence

26. Install the front and rear crossover gaskets onto the dowels.

27. Install the flange gaskets. Ensure the vertical port alignment tab is resting on the deck face of the block. Also, the horizontal mating alignment tabs must be in position with the mating cylinder head gasket tabs. The words MANIFOLD SIDE should be visible on the center of each flange gasket.

28. Carefully lower the intake manifold into place. Use the alignment dowels in the crossover gaskets to position the manifold. Once in place ensure the gaskets are still in position.

29. Tighten the manifold bolts in sequence to the following specifications:

    a. Bolts 1-4 — 72 inch lbs. (8 Nm) in 12 inch lbs. (1.4 Nm) Intervals

    b. Bolts 5-12 — 72 inch lbs. (8 Nm)

    c. Repeat Steps a and b to ensure proper torque.

    d. All bolts — 12 ft. lbs. (16 Nm)

    e. Repeat Step d to ensure proper torque.

30. Connect the PCV and EVAP lines.

31. Install the coil wires.

32. Connect the heat indicator sending unit wire.

33. Connect the heater and bypass hoses.

34. Install the distributor cap and wires.

35. Hook up the return spring.

36. Connect the accelerator linkage and, if equipped, cruise control and transmission kick down cables.

37. Install the fuel lines and fuel rail.

38. Install the support bracket.

39. Install the alternator and drive belt.

40. If equipped with A/C, install the compressor.

41. Install the air cleaner.

42. Fill the cooling system.

43. Connect the negative battery cable.

44. Start the engine and check for leaks.

Exhaust Manifold

REMOVAL & INSTALLATION

2.1L Diesel Engines

▶ See Figure 38

1. Disconnect the negative battery cable. Remove the intake manifold.

2. Disconnect the exhaust pipe from the adapter.

3. Remove the oil supply pipe and the oil return hose from the turbocharger assembly.

4. Disconnect the turbocharger air inlet and outlet hoses.

5. Remove the turbocharger retaining bolts. Remove the turbocharger from the vehicle.

6. Remove the exhaust manifold retaining bolts. Remove the exhaust manifold and gasket. Discard the gasket.

To install:

7. Position the exhaust manifold and gasket on the head.

8. Install the exhaust manifold retaining bolts and tighten them to 31 ft. lbs. (42 Nm).

9. Install the turbocharger.

10. Connect the turbocharger air inlet and outlet hoses.

11. Install the oil supply pipe and the oil return hose at the turbocharger assembly.

12. Connect the exhaust pipe at the adapter.

13. Install the intake manifold.

14. Connect the negative battery cable.

2.5L Engines

▶ See Figures 39, 40, 47, 51 and 52

1. Disconnect the negative battery cable.

2. Remove the intake manifold.

3. Disconnect the exhaust pipe at the manifold.

4. Remove the fasteners and exhaust manifold.

To install:

5. Clean the intake manifold and cylinder head mating surfaces.

6. Using a new intake manifold gasket, position the intake and exhaust manifolds on the cylinder head and place spacers over the end studs to center the exhaust manifold. Install the end stud nuts and washer clamps but do not tighten.

7. Install washer clamp and bolt at position 1 and tighten to 30 ft. lbs. (41 Nm).

Fig. 51 Remove the fasteners from the exhaust manifold . . .

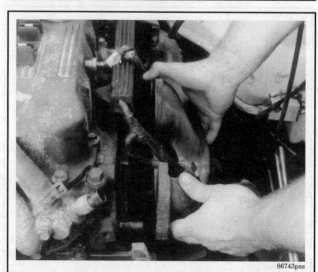

Fig. 52 . . . then remove the manifold from the engine

8. Install bolts and washers at positions 2-5 and tighten to 23 ft. lbs. (31 Nm).

9. Tighten end stud nuts (positions 6 and 7) to 23 ft. lbs. (31 Nm).

10. Install all components removed from the intake manifold.

11. Connect the exhaust pipe and tighten the bolts to 23 ft. lbs. (31 Nm).

2.8L Engines

▶ See Figure 53

LEFT SIDE

1. Disconnect the negative battery cable. Remove the air cleaner.

2. Remove the air injection hose and manifold (if equipped).

3. Remove the power steering bracket.

4. Raise and support the vehicle safely. Unbolt and remove the exhaust pipe at the manifold.

5. Unbolt and remove the manifold.

To install:

6. Clean the mating surfaces of the cylinder head and manifold. Install the manifold onto the head, and install the retaining bolts finger-tight.

7. Tighten the manifold bolts in a circular pattern, working from the center to the ends, to 25 ft. lbs. (34 Nm) in two stages.

8. Connect the exhaust pipe to the manifold.

9. The remainder of installation is the reverse of removal.

RIGHT SIDE

1. Disconnect the negative battery cable. Raise and support the vehicle safely.

2. Disconnect the exhaust pipe from the exhaust manifold.

3. Lower the vehicle. Remove the spark plug wires from the plugs. Number them first if they are not already labeled. Remove the cruise control servo from the right inner fender panel, if equipped.

4. Remove the air supply pipes from the manifold. Remove the Pulsair bracket bolt from the rocker cover, on models so equipped, then remove the pipe assembly.

5. Remove the manifold retaining bolts and remove the manifold.

To install:

6. Clean the mating surfaces of the cylinder head and manifold. Position the manifold against the head and install the retaining bolts finger-tight.

7. Tighten the bolts in a circular pattern, working from the center to the ends, to 25 ft. lbs. (34 Nm) in two stages.

8. Install the air supply system. Install the spark plug wires. If equipped install the cruise control servo.

9. Raise and support the vehicle safely. Connect the exhaust pipe to the manifold.

4.0L Engines

The intake and exhaust manifolds of the 4.0L must be removed together. Please refer to the combination manifold procedure in this section.

5.2L Engines

▶ See Figure 54

1. Disconnect the negative battery cable.

2. Remove the exhaust manifold heat shields.

3. Remove the spark plug wire loom and cables from the mounting stud at the rear of the valve cover and position the cables at the top of the valve cover.

4. Label and disconnect the 2 hoses from the EGR valve.

5. Disconnect the electrical connector and hoses from the EGR transducer.

6. Remove the EGR valve and discard the gasket.

7. Disconnect the oil pressure sending unit electrical connector.

8. Using oil pressure sending unit remover C-4597 or equivalent, remove the sending unit.

9. Loosen the EGR mounting nut from the intake manifold.

10. Remove the mounting bolts and EGR tube. Discard the gasket.

11. Raise and safely support the vehicle.

12. Disconnect the exhaust pipes from the manifolds.

13. Lower the vehicle.

14. Remove the fasteners and exhaust manifold.

To install:

➡If the manifold mounting studs came out with the fasteners, replace the studs.

15. Position the manifold and install the conical washers on the studs.

16. Install new bolt and washer assemblies into the remaining holes. Working from the center outward, tighten the fasteners to 20 ft. lbs. (27 Nm).

17. Raise and support the vehicle safely.

18. Connect the exhaust pipes to the manifolds and tighten the fasteners to 23 ft. lbs. (31 Nm).

19. Lower the vehicle.

20. Clean the EGR and tube gasket mating surfaces.

21. Install a new gasket onto the exhaust manifold ends of the EGR tube and install the tube. Tighten the tube nut to the intake manifold and tighten the tube-to-exhaust manifold bolts to 204 inch lbs. (14 Nm).

22. Coat the threads of the oil pressure sending unit with sealer taking care not to apply sealant to the opening. Install

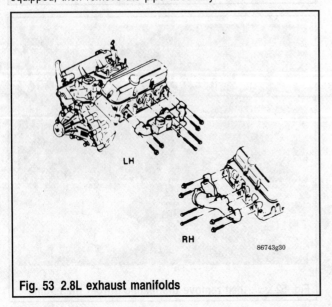

Fig. 53 2.8L exhaust manifolds

LH

RH

86743g30

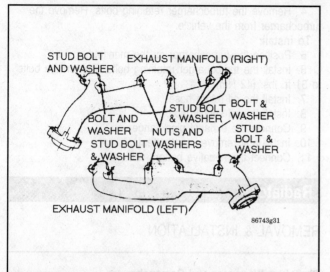

Fig. 54 Exhaust manifolds used on the 5.2L engine

the sending unit and tighten it to 130 inch lbs. (14 Nm) and connect the electrical connector.

23. Install the EGR valve and new gasket to the intake manifold and tighten the bolts to 200 inch lbs. (23 Nm).

24. Position the EGR transducer and connect the vacuum lines and electrical connector.

25. Position the spark plug cables and loom into place and connect the cables.

26. Install the exhaust heat shields and tighten the bolts to 20 ft. lbs. (27 Nm).

27. Connect the negative battery cable.

Combination Manifold

REMOVAL & INSTALLATION

♦ **See Figures 55 and 56**

➡This procedure applies only to the 4.0L engine. The intake and exhaust manifold are mounted externally on the left side of the engine and are attached to the cylinder head. They are removed as a unit.

1. Disconnect the negative battery cable.
2. Remove the air cleaner assembly.
3. Disconnect the accelerator cable, cruise control cable, if equipped and transmission line pressure cable.
4. Disconnect all electrical connectors on the intake manifold.
5. Disconnect and remove the fuel supply and return lines from the fuel rail assembly.
6. Remove the fuel rail and injectors.
7. Loosen the accessory drive belts.
8. Remove the power steering pump.
9. Disconnect the exhaust pipe from the manifold and discard the seal.
10. Remove the intake and exhaust manifold attaching nuts and bolts.
11. Remove the manifold assembly and gasket.

To install:

12. Clean the gasket mating surfaces thoroughly. Install a new gasket over the alignment dowels and position the exhaust manifold to the cylinder head. Install bolt No. 3 finger-tight.

13. Install the intake manifold and the remaining bolts and washers.

14. Tighten bolts, in sequence, to the following torque specifications:
   a. Bolts 1-5 — 23 ft. lbs. (31 Nm)
   b. Bolts 6 and 7 — 17 ft. lbs. (23 Nm)
   c. Bolts 8-11 — 23 ft. lbs. (31 Nm)

15. Install the fuel rail and injectors.

16. Install the power steering pump and tension the accessory belt to specification.

17. Using new O-rings, install the fuel supply and return lines.

18. Connect all electrical connectors, vacuum connectors, throttle cable, cruise control cable and transmission lines pressure cable.

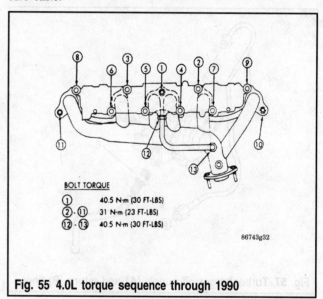

Fig. 55 4.0L torque sequence through 1990

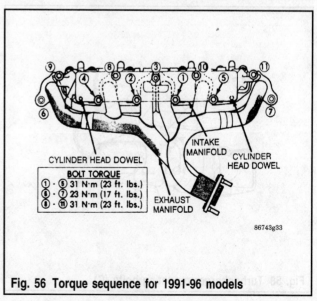

Fig. 56 Torque sequence for 1991-96 models

19. Install the air cleaner assembly.
20. Using a new seal, connect the exhaust pipe to the manifold and tighten the bolts to 23 ft. lbs. (31 Nm).
21. Connect the negative battery cable.
22. Start the engine and check for leaks.

Turbocharger

REMOVAL & INSTALLATION

▶ **See Figures 57 and 58**

➡ This procedure applies to the 2.1L diesel engine only.

1. Disconnect the negative battery cable.
2. Remove all the necessary components in order to gain access to the turbocharger retaining bolts.
3. Disconnect the exhaust pipe flange. Remove the oil supply pipe. Remove the oil return hose.

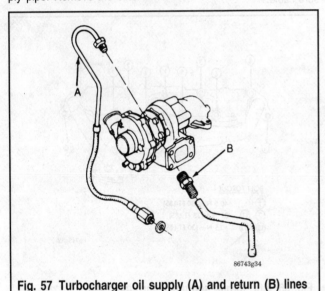

Fig. 57 Turbocharger oil supply (A) and return (B) lines

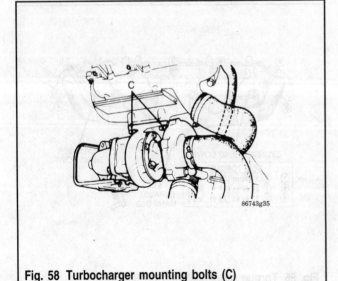

Fig. 58 Turbocharger mounting bolts (C)

4. Remove the turbocharger retaining bolts. Remove the turbocharger from the vehicle.

To install:
5. Position the turbocharger on the manifold.
6. Install the turbocharger retaining bolts. Tighten the bolts to 31 ft. lbs. (42 Nm).
7. Install the oil return hose.
8. Install the oil supply pipe.
9. Connect the exhaust pipe flange.
10. Install any removed components.
11. Connect the negative battery cable.

Radiator

REMOVAL & INSTALLATION

Cherokee, Wagoneer and Comanche

▶ **See Figures 59, 60, 61, 62, 63, 64, 65 and 66**

1. Disconnect the negative battery cable.
2. Remove the grille reinforcement panel, as necessary.
3. Drain the cooling system.
4. Remove the radiator upper and lower hoses.
5. If equipped, remove the transmission cooler lines.
6. Unplug any electrical connections.
7. Remove the fan shroud mounting bolts and pull the fan shroud back to the engine.
8. Remove the alignment dowel E-clip from the lower radiator mounting bracket.
9. Disconnect the overflow tube from the radiator.
10. Remove all attaching bolts and screws that secure the radiator to the radiator support.
11. Remove the condenser-to-radiator mounting bolts and pull the radiator out of the vehicle.

➡ Take care not to damage the radiator fins.

12. Empty the remaining coolant in the radiator.

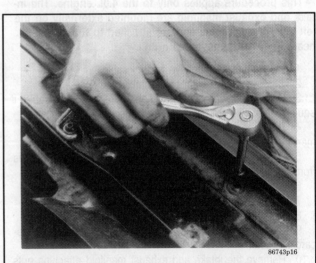

Fig. 59 Remove the bolts securing the grille reinforcement panel . . .

Fig. 60 . . . then remove the panel

Fig. 63 Remove the radiator support bolts . . .

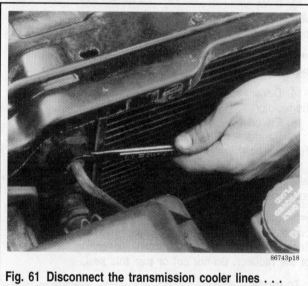

Fig. 61 Disconnect the transmission cooler lines . . .

Fig. 64 . . . then remove the support

Fig. 62 . . . and unplug any electrical connections

Fig. 65 Remove the radiator attaching bolts . . .

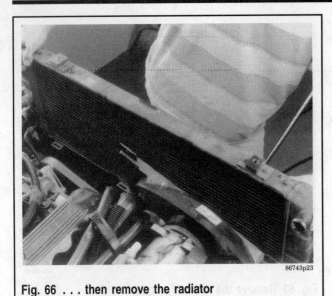

Fig. 66 . . . then remove the radiator

To install:

13. Slide the radiator into position behind the condenser, if equipped.

14. Align the dowel pin with the bottom mounting bracket and install the E-clip.

15. Tighten the condenser-to-radiator bolts to 55 inch lbs. (6.2 Nm).

16. Install and tighten the radiator mounting bolts.

17. Install the grille.

18. Connect the transmission cooler lines, if equipped.

19. Install the fan shroud.

20. Connect the radiator hoses.

21. Connect the negative battery cable.

22. Fill the cooling system to the correct level.

1993-96 Grand Cherokee/Wagoneer

♦ See Figure 67

1. Disconnect the negative battery cable.
2. Open the radiator valve and drain the cooling system.
3. Remove the fan and shroud assembly.

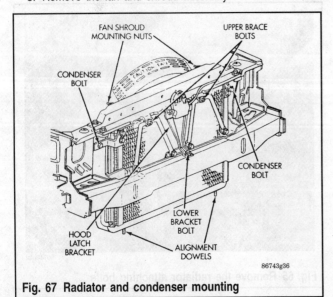

Fig. 67 Radiator and condenser mounting

4. If equipped, disconnect the automatic transmission cooling line quick-fit connections.

5. Matchmark the upper radiator crossmember and adjust the crossmember to the left or right.

6. Eight clips are used to retain a rubber seal to the body. Gently pry up the outboard clips (2 per side) until the rubber seal can be removed. Do not remove the seals entirely. Fold back the seal on both sides to access the grille opening reinforcement mounting bolts and remove the bolts.

7. Remove the grille.

8. Remove the upper brace bolt from each of the 2 radiator braces.

9. Remove the crossmember-to-radiator mounting nuts.

10. Working through the grille opening, remove the lower bracket bolt securing the lower part of the hood latch or hood latch cable from the crossmember.

11. Lift the crossmember straight up and position it aside.

12. If equipped with A/C, remove the 2 A/C condenser-to-radiator mounting bolts which also retain the side mounted rubber air seals.

13. If not equipped with A/C, remove the bolts retaining the side mounted rubber air seals compressed between the radiator and crossmember.

➡**Note the location of the air seals. To prevent overheating, they must be installed in their original position.**

14. Disconnect the coolant reservoir/overflow tank hose from the radiator.

15. Disconnect the upper hose from the radiator.

16. Carefully lift the radiator a slight amount and disconnect the lower hose from the radiator.

17. Lift the radiator up and out of the engine compartment, take care not to scrape the fins or disturb the A/C condenser if equipped.

➡**If equipped with an auxiliary automatic transmission oil cooler, use caution during radiator removal. The oil cooler lines are routed through a rubber air seal on the left side of the radiator. Do not cut or tear this seal.**

To install:

18. Lower the radiator into the vehicle. Guide the alignment dowels into the hoses in the rubber air seals and then through the A/C support brackets, if equipped. Continue to guide the radiator through the rubber grommets located in the lower crossmember.

➡**If equipped with A/C, the L-shaped brackets, located on the bottom of the condenser, must be positioned between the bottom of the rubber air seals and top of rubber grommets.**

19. Connect the lower radiator hose to the radiator.

20. Connect the upper radiator hose to the radiator.

21. If equipped with A/C, install the bolts condenser-to-radiator mounting bolts.

22. If not equipped with A/C, install the rubber air seal retaining bolts.

23. Connect the reservoir/overflow tank hose to the radiator.

24. If the radiator-to-upper crossmember rubber insulators were removed, install them.

25. Install the hood latch support bracket-to-lower frame crossmember bolt.

26. Install the bolts securing the upper radiator crossmember to the body.

27. Install the radiator-to-upper crossmember nuts.

28. Install a bolt to each upper radiator brace.

29. Install the grille.

30. Position the rubber seal and push down on the clips until seated.

31. If equipped, connect the transmission cooling lines.

32. Install the fan shroud with the fan.

33. Install the fan and shroud.

34. Rotate the fan blades and ensure they do not interfere with the shroud and at least 1 in. (25mm) of clearance is allowed. Correct as necessary.

35. Fill the cooling system.

Engine Fan

REMOVAL & INSTALLATION

Except 5.2L Engines

VISCOUS DRIVE FAN

▶ See Figures 68, 69 and 70

1. Remove the upper fan shroud bolts and lift the shroud from its lower securing tabs.

2. Remove the accessory drive belts.

3. Remove the fan flange-to-pulley mounting nuts.

4. Remove the fan and viscous drive as an assembly.

5. Remove the fan blade-to-viscous drive bolts and separate the assembly.

To install:

6. Position the fan on the viscous drive. Install the bolts and tighten them to 187 inch lbs. (24 Nm).

7. Position the mounting flange of the viscous drive assembly onto the pulley. Install the nuts and tighten them to 18 ft. lbs. (24 Nm).

8. Install the accessory drive belts.

9. Insert the shroud into its retaining tabs and install the upper bolts.

Fig. 68 Remove the fan shroud

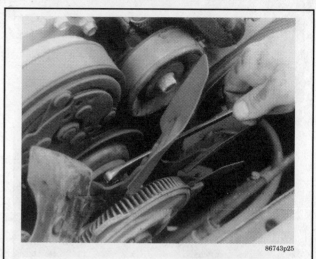

Fig. 69 Remove the fan flange-to-pulley mounting nuts . . .

Fig. 70 . . . then remove the fan assembly

ELECTRIC FAN

▶ See Figures 71, 72 and 73

1. Disconnect the negative battery cable.

2. Disconnect the electrical connector.

3. Remove the upper fan shroud bolts.

4. Lift the fan assembly up and out of the engine compartment.

To install:

5. Insert the shroud into its retaining tabs and install the upper bolts.

6. Connect the electrical connector.

7. Connect the negative battery cable.

5.2L Engines

▶ See Figure 74

1. Disconnect the negative battery cable.

2. The viscous fan drive and blade assembly is threaded into the water pump hub shaft. Remove the fan drive and blade assembly from the water pump by turning the mounting

Fig. 71 Unplug the electrical connection

Fig. 72 Remove the shroud attaching bolts . . .

Fig. 73 . . . then remove the fan assembly

nut counterclockwise as viewed from the front while securing the water pump pulley. Do not remove or unbolt the fan drive and blade at this time. *1 7/16 NUT*

➡**The threads on the viscous fan drive are right hand threaded.**

3. Remove the 2 fan shroud-to-upper crossmember nuts.
4. Remove the fan drive, blade and shroud as an assembly.

✳✳WARNING

Do not place the viscous fan drive in a horizontal position. If stored horizontally, silicone fluid in the viscous fan drive could drain into its bearing assembly and the assembly would have to be replaced.

✳✳CAUTION

Do not remove the water pump pulley-to-water pump bolts. The pulley is under spring tension.

5. Remove the 4 bolts securing the fan blade assembly to the viscous fan drive.
   To install:
6. Install the fan blade on the viscous drive. Install the bolts and tighten them to 17 ft. lbs. (23 Nm).
7. Position the fan shroud, viscous fan and blade into the engine compartment as an assembly.
8. Position the fan shroud to the radiator. Insert the lower slots of the shroud into the crossmember. Install the upper attaching nuts.

➡**Ensure the upper and lower portions of the fan shroud are firmly connected. All air must flow through the radiator.**

9. Install the fan drive and blade assembly to the water pump shaft and tighten the nut.

➡**Ensure there is at least 1 inch (25mm) between the tips of the fan blades and shroud.**

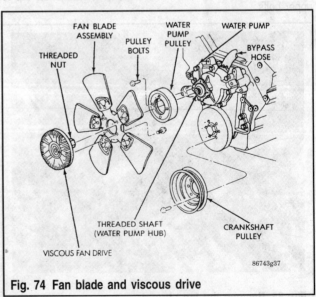

Fig. 74 Fan blade and viscous drive

10. Connect the negative battery cable.

Water Pump

REMOVAL & INSTALLATION

2.1L Diesel Engines

▶ See Figures 75 and 76

1. Disconnect the negative battery cable. Drain the engine coolant.

✳✳CAUTION

When draining the coolant, keep in mind that cats and dogs are attracted by ethylene glycol antifreeze, and are quite likely to drink any that is left in an uncovered container or in puddles on the ground. This will prove fatal in sufficient quantity. Always drain the coolant into a sealable container. Coolant should be reused unless it is contaminated or several years old.

2. Remove the coolant hose from the water pump.
3. Remove the drive belts.
4. Remove the fan and hub assembly.
5. It is not necessary to remove the timing belt tensioner. Use a long strap and clip in order to retain the timing belt tensioner plunger in place.
6. Remove the water pump retaining bolts. Remove the water pump assembly from the vehicle.

To install:

7. Clean the mating surfaces of all gasket material.
8. Do not use sealer on the new gasket. Position the gasket and pump on the engine and install the bolts. Tighten the bolts to 15 ft. lbs. (20 Nm).
9. Re-tension the timing belt.
10. Install the fan and hub, drive belts and coolant hoses.
11. Fill the cooling system.
12. Connect the battery.

2.5L, 2.8L and 4.0L Engines

▶ See Figures 77, 78 and 79

➡Some vehicles use a serpentine drive belt and have a reverse rotating water pump coupled with a viscous fan drive assembly. The components are identified by the words REVERSE stamped on the cover of the viscous drive and on the inner side of the fan. The word REV is also cast into the body of the water pump.

1. Disconnect the negative battery cable.
2. Drain the cooling system.
3. Disconnect the hoses at the pump.
4. Remove the drive belts.
5. Remove the power steering pump bracket.
6. Remove the fan and shroud.
7. If equipped, remove the idler pulley to gain clearance for pump removal.
8. Unbolt and remove the pump.

To install:

9. Clean the mating surfaces thoroughly.

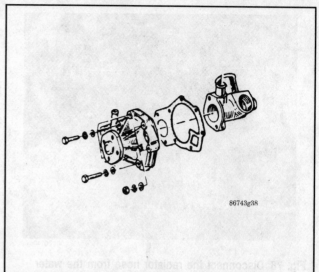

Fig. 75 Water pump mounting on the diesel engine

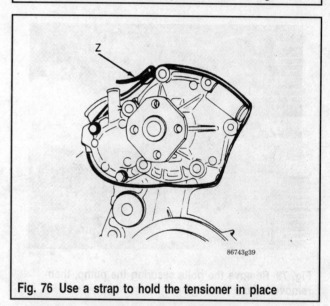

Fig. 76 Use a strap to hold the tensioner in place

Fig. 77 Remove the power steering pump and bracket, then move it aside

Fig. 78 Disconnect the radiator hose from the water pump

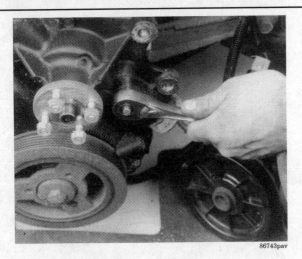

Fig. 79 Remove the bolts securing the pump, then remove it from the engine

10. Using a new gasket, install the pump and tighten the bolts to 13 ft. lbs. (18 Nm).

11. If removed, install the idler pulley.

12. Reconnect the hoses at the pump and install accessory drive belt.

13. Install the power steering pump bracket. Install the fan and shroud.

14. Adjust the belt tension and fill the cooling system to the correct level.

15. Operate the engine with the heater control valve in the **HEAT** position until the thermostat opens to purge air from the system. Check coolant level and fill as required.

5.2L Engines

♦ See Figure 80

1. Disconnect the negative battery cable.

2. Open the radiator valve and drain the cooling system.

3. Remove the cooling fan and shroud as an assembly.

4. Remove the accessory drive belt.

5. Remove the water pump pulley from the hub.

6. Disconnect the hoses from the water pump.

7. Loosen the heater hose coolant return tube mounting bolt and nut and remove the tube. Discard the O-ring.

8. Remove the water pump mounting bolts.

9. Loosen the clamp at the water pump end of the bypass hose. Slip the bypass hose from the water pump while removing the pump from the engine. Discard the gasket.

To install:

10. Clean all gasket mating surfaces.

11. Guide the water pump and new gasket into position while connecting the bypass hose to the pump. Tighten the water pump bolts to 30 ft. lbs. (40 Nm).

12. Install the bypass hose clamp.

13. Spin the water pump to ensure the pump impeller does not rub against the timing chain cover.

14. Coat a new O-ring with coolant and install it to the heater hose coolant return tube.

15. Install the coolant return tube to the engine. Ensure the slot in the tube bracket is bottomed to the mounting bolt. This will properly position the return tube.

16. Connect the radiator hose to the water pump.

17. Connect the heater hose and clamp to the return tube.

18. Install the water pump pulley and tighten the bolts to 20 ft. lbs. (27 Nm).

19. Install the accessory drive belt.

20. Install the cooling fan and shroud.

21. Fill the cooling system.

22. Connect the negative battery cable.

23. Start the engine and check for leaks.

Cylinder Head

REMOVAL & INSTALLATION

➡It is important to note that each engine has its own head bolt torque sequence and tightening specification. Incorrect tightening procedure may cause head warpage and compression loss. Correct sequence and torque for each engine model is shown in this section.

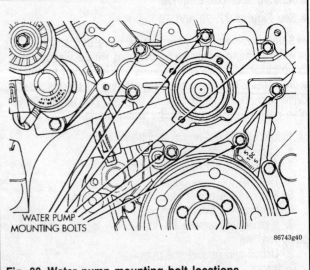

WATER PUMP
MOUNTING BOLTS

Fig. 80 Water pump mounting bolt locations

2.1L Diesel Engines

▶ **See Figures 81, 82, 83, 84, 85, 86, 87 and 88**

1. Disconnect the negative battery cable.
2. Remove the intake manifold. Remove the exhaust manifold.
3. Remove the rocker arm cover. Drain the engine coolant. Remove the timing belt cover.

✳✳CAUTION

When draining the coolant, keep in mind that cats and dogs are attracted by ethylene glycol antifreeze, and are quite likely to drink any that is left in an uncovered container or in puddles on the ground. This will prove fatal in sufficient quantity. Always drain the coolant into a sealable container. Coolant should be reused unless it is contaminated or several years old.

4. Install sprocket holding tool MOT-854 or equivalent and remove the camshaft sprocket retaining bolt. Remove the special tool.
5. Loosen the bolts and move the tensioner away from the timing belt. Retighten the tensioner bolts.
6. Remove the timing belt from the sprockets.

➡ **If it is necessary to remove the fuel injection pump sprocket use special tool BVI-28-01 or BVI-859 to accomplish this procedure.**

7. Disconnect the fuel pipe fittings from the injectors. Plug them in order to prevent dirt from entering the system.
8. Disconnect the fuel pipe fittings from the fuel injection pump. Plug them in order to prevent dirt from entering the system.
9. Remove the fuel pipes from their mountings on the engine. Remove all hoses and connectors from the fuel injection pump.
10. Remove the injection pump retaining bolts. Remove the fuel injection pump and its mounting brackets, as an assembly, from the vehicle.
11. Remove the retaining bolts and nuts from the cylinder head. Loosen pivot bolt but do not remove it. Remove the remaining cylinder head bolts.
12. Place a block of wood against the cylinder head and tap it with a hammer in order to loosen the cylinder head gasket. The pivot movement will be minimal due to the small clearance between the studs and the cylinder head. Remove the pivot bolt from the cylinder head.
13. Remove the retaining bolts and the rocker arm shaft assembly from the cylinder head.

➡ **Do not lift the cylinder head from the cylinder block until the gasket is completely loosened from the cylinder liners. Otherwise, the liner seals could be broken.**

14. Remove the cylinder head and the gasket from the engine block. While the head is off, install liner clamp tool MOT 521-01 to hold the liners in place in the block.

To install:

15. Remove liner clamp tool MOT 521-01.
16. Position cylinder head locating tool MOT 720 on the block to insure proper alignment.

17. Position the cylinder head and the new gasket from the engine block. Be sure that the new cylinder head gasket is positioned properly on the cylinder head and that it is the correct thickness for piston protrusion. Whenever major components, such as pistons, liners, crankshaft, etc., have been replaced, the piston protrusion must be measured to determine proper replacement head gasket thickness. Measure the protrusion as follows:

   a. Rotate the crankshaft one complete revolution clockwise and bring No. 1 piston to a point just below and before TDC.
   b. Place thrust plate tool MOT 252-01 on top of the piston.
   c. Assemble a dial indicator in the block gauge MOT 25101 and place this assembly on one side of the thrust plate.
   d. Zero the indicator with the stem on the cylinder block face.
   e. Place the stem on the top of the piston and rotate the crankshaft clockwise to TDC of the piston. Record the piston travel.
   f. Repeat the procedure with the dial indicator on the opposite side of the block. Record the piston travel.
   g. Add the two figures together and divide by two. Repeat the protrusion measurement for the three remaining pistons. The piston with the greatest protrusion should be the basis for determining gasket thickness. For example, if the amount of greatest piston protrusion is:

   • Less than 0.96mm, use a gasket 1.6mm thick
   • Between 0.96mm and 1.04mm, use a 1.7mm thick gasket
   • More than 1.04mm, use a 1.8mm thick gasket

18. Install the head bolts. Tighten the cylinder head retaining bolts to 22 ft. lbs. (30 Nm), then to 37 ft. lbs. (50 Nm), then to 70-77 ft. lbs. (95-104 Nm). Once all the bolts are tightened, recheck the torque.

➡ **The cylinder head bolts must be retightened after the cylinder head is installed in the vehicle. Operate the engine for a minimum of twenty minutes. Allow the engine to cool for a minimum of two and one half hours. Loosen each cylinder head bolt in sequence about ⅛ turn. Then retighten in the proper sequence and tighten to 70-77 ft. lbs. (95-104 Nm). For the final tightening, tighten the bolts again, in sequence, without loosening them to 70-77 ft. lbs. (95-104 Nm).**

19. Remove tool MOT 720.
20. Install the rocker arm shaft assembly.
21. Install the fuel injection pump and its mounting brackets, as an assembly. See Section 5.
22. Install the fuel pipes on their mountings on the engine. Install all hoses and connectors on the fuel injection pump.
23. Connect the fuel pipe fittings to the fuel injection pump.
24. Connect the fuel pipe fittings from the injectors.
25. Install the timing belt.
26. Re-tension the timing belt.
27. Install the camshaft sprocket retaining bolt.
28. Install the valve cover.
29. Install the timing belt cover.
30. Install the intake manifold.
31. Install the exhaust manifold.
32. Fill the cooling system.

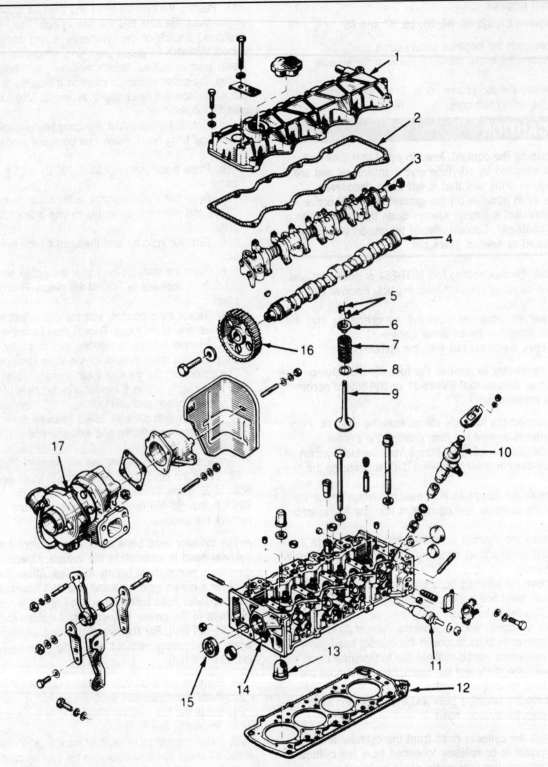

1. Cylinder head cover
2. Cylinder head cover gasket
3. Rocker arm and shaft assembly
4. Camshaft
5. Valve spring locks
6. Valve spring retainer
7. Valve spring
8. Valve spring washer
9. Valve
10. Injector
11. Glow plug
12. Cylinder head gasket
13. Pre-combustion chamber
14. Cylinder head
15. Camshaft oil seal
16. Camshaft sprocket
17. Turbocharger

86743g41

Fig. 81 Exploded view of the diesel cylinder head

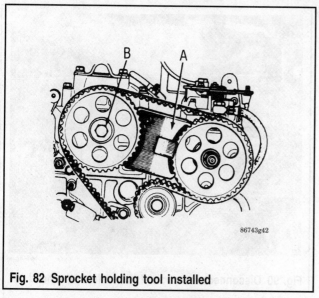

Fig. 82 Sprocket holding tool installed

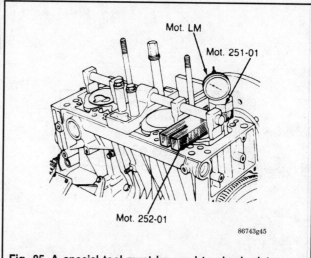

Fig. 85 A special tool must be used to check piston protrusion

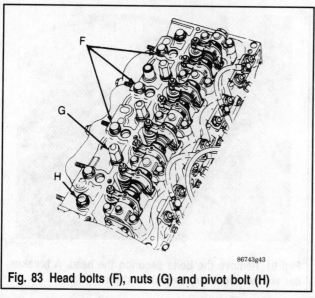

Fig. 83 Head bolts (F), nuts (G) and pivot bolt (H)

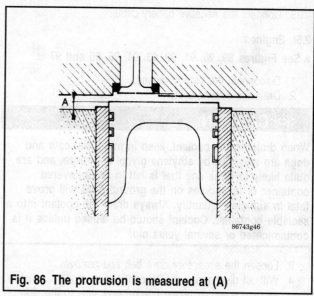

Fig. 86 The protrusion is measured at (A)

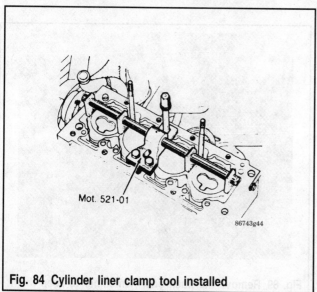

Fig. 84 Cylinder liner clamp tool installed

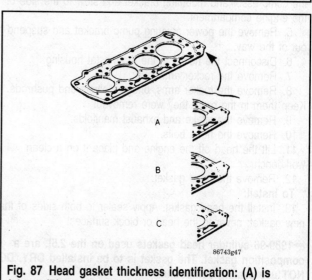

Fig. 87 Head gasket thickness identification: (A) is 1.6mm (B) is 1.7mm (C) is 1.8mm

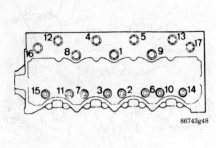

Fig. 88 Head bolt torque sequence

33. Connect the negative battery cable.

2.5L Engines

▶ See Figures 89, 90, 91, 92, 93, 94, 95, 96 and 97

1. Disconnect the battery ground.
2. Drain the cooling system.

✳✳CAUTION

When draining the coolant, keep in mind that cats and dogs are attracted by ethylene glycol antifreeze, and are quite likely to drink any that is left in an uncovered container or in puddles on the ground. This will prove fatal in sufficient quantity. Always drain the coolant into a sealable container. Coolant should be reused unless it is contaminated or several years old.

3. Loosen the accessory drive belt and remove.
4. Without discharging the air conditioning system, remove the compressor and mounting bracket and stow to the side of the engine compartment.
5. Remove the power steering pump bracket and suspend out of the way.
6. Disconnect the hoses at the thermostat housing.
7. Remove the rocker arm cover.
8. Remove the rocker arms, bridges, pivots and pushrods. Keep them in the order they were removed!
9. Remove the intake and exhaust manifolds.
10. Remove the head bolts.
11. Lift the head off the engine and place it on a clean workbench.
12. Remove the head gasket.
   To install:
13. Install the head gasket. Apply sealer to both sides of the new gasket; never to the head or block surfaces!

➡**1989-96 cylinder head gaskets used on the 2.5L are a composition gasket. The gasket is to be installed DRY. DO NOT use sealing compound.**

14. Fabricate two cylinder head alignment dowels from used head bolts. Use the longest head bolts. Cut the bolt off below

Fig. 90 Disconnect the coolant hoses from the head

Fig. 91 Remove the bolts securing the head. A breaker bar will be necessary to loosen them

Fig. 89 Remove the pushrods. Remember to keep them in order

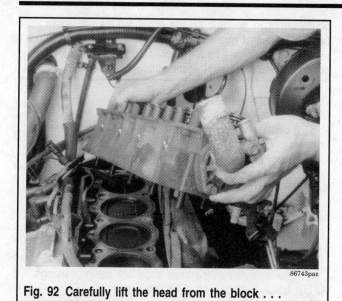

Fig. 92 Carefully lift the head from the block . . .

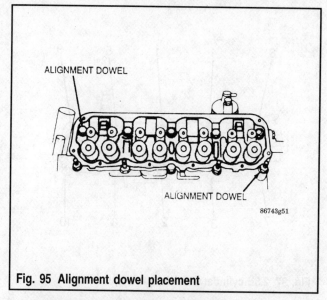

Fig. 95 Alignment dowel placement

Fig. 93 . . . then remove and discard the old gasket

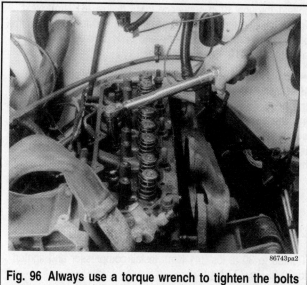

Fig. 96 Always use a torque wrench to tighten the bolts

the hex head. Next cut a slot in the top of the dowel to allow easier removal.

15. Install cylinder head alignment dowels. Install head gasket (manufacturer number up) and cylinder head.

➡Cylinder head bolts should be reused only once. Replace head bolts which were previously used or are marked with paint. If head bolts are to be reused, mark each head with paint for later reference.

16. Install cylinder head bolts replacing alignment dowels with cylinder head bolts as you go. Coat cylinder head bolt 8 (1984-88) or bolt 7 (1989-96) with Permatex® No. 2 sealant, or equivalent, and install.

17. Tighten cylinder head bolts in the correct sequence, to the following torque specifications:
  • On 1984-88 models, using three steps, tighten all bolts in sequence (except bolt 8) to 85 ft. lbs. (115 Nm); tighten bolt 8 to 75 ft. lbs. (101 Nm)
  • On 1989-96 models, using three steps, tighten bolts 1 through 10 in sequence to 22 ft. lbs. (30 Nm), then tighten

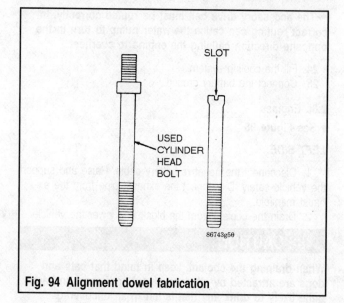

Fig. 94 Alignment dowel fabrication

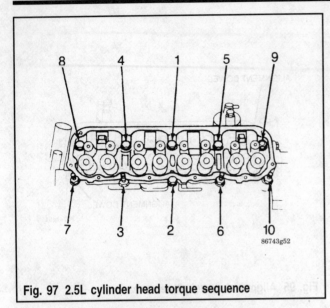

Fig. 97 2.5L cylinder head torque sequence

bolts 1 through 10 in sequence to 45 ft. lbs. (61 Nm). Next, tighten bolts 1 through 6 in sequence to 110 ft. lbs. (150 Nm), bolt 7 to 100 ft. lbs. (136 Nm), and bolts 8 through 10 in sequence to 110 ft. lbs. (150 Nm)

➡Some head bolts used on the spark plug side of the 1984 2.5L were improperly hardened and may break under the head during service or at head installation while torquing the bolts. Engines with the defective bolts are serial numbers 310U06 through 310U14. Whenever a broken bolt is found, replace all bolts on the spark plug side of the head with bolt number 400 6593.

18. Install the rocker arm cover.
19. Install the intake and exhaust manifolds.
20. Connect the hoses at the thermostat housing.
21. Install power steering pump bracket and pump.
22. Install air conditioning compressor mounting bracket. Tighten to 30 ft. lbs. (41 Nm). Install compressor and tighten to 20 ft. lbs. (27 Nm).
23. Install the accessory drive belt.

➡The accessory drive belt must be routed correctly. Incorrect routing can cause the water pump to turn in the opposite direction causing the engine to overheat.

24. Fill the cooling system.
25. Connect the battery ground.

2.8L Engines
▶ See Figure 98

LEFT SIDE

1. Disconnect the negative battery cable. Raise and support the vehicle safely. Disconnect the exhaust pipe from the exhaust manifold.
2. Drain the coolant from the block and lower the vehicle.

✳✳CAUTION

When draining the coolant, keep in mind that cats and dogs are attracted by ethylene glycol antifreeze, and are quite likely to drink any that is left in an uncovered container or in puddles on the ground. This will prove fatal in sufficient quantity. Always drain the coolant into a sealable container. Coolant should be reused unless it is contaminated or several years old.

3. Remove the intake manifold.
4. Remove the exhaust manifold.
5. If equipped, remove the power steering pump and bracket.
6. Remove the dipstick tube.
7. Loosen the rocker arm bolts and remove the pushrods. Keep the pushrods in the same order as removed.
8. Remove the cylinder head bolts in stages and in the reverse order of the tightening sequence.
9. Remove the cylinder head. Do not pry on the head to loosen.

To install:
10. Thoroughly clean the head and block mating surfaces. All bolt holes must be free of foreign material.
11. Place a new head gasket on the block with the words "This Side Up" facing upward.
12. Position the cylinder head on the block.
13. Coat the cylinder head bolts with RTV silicone sealant and install them. Tighten the bolts, in sequence, in three equal stages. The final stage should be 70 ft. lbs. (95 Nm).
14. Install the pushrods, keeping them in the same order as removed.
15. Install the rocker arms.
16. Install the dipstick tube.
17. Install the power steering pump and bracket.
18. Install the exhaust manifold.
19. Install the intake manifold.
20. Connect the exhaust pipe from the exhaust manifold.
21. Fill the cooling system.
22. Connect the negative battery cable.
23. Adjust the valves.

RIGHT SIDE

1. Disconnect the negative battery cable. Raise and support the vehicle safely. Drain the coolant from the block.

✳✳CAUTION

When draining the coolant, keep in mind that cats and dogs are attracted by ethylene glycol antifreeze, and are quite likely to drink any that is left in an uncovered container or in puddles on the ground. This will prove fatal in sufficient quantity. Always drain the coolant into a sealable container. Coolant should be reused unless it is contaminated or several years old.

2. Disconnect the exhaust pipe and lower the vehicle.
3. If equipped, remove the cruise control servo bracket.
4. Remove the alternator and air pump bracket assembly.
5. Remove the intake manifold.
6. Loosen the rocker arm nuts and remove the pushrods. Keep the pushrods in the order in which they were removed.
7. Remove the cylinder head bolts in stages and in the reverse order of the tightening sequence.
8. Remove the cylinder head. Do not pry on the cylinder head to loosen it.

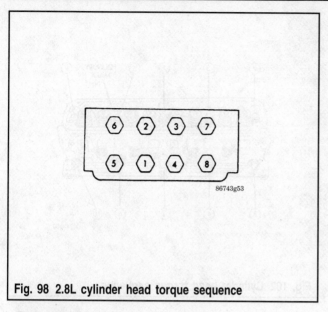

Fig. 98 2.8L cylinder head torque sequence

To install:

9. Thoroughly clean the head and block mating surfaces. All bolt holes must be free of foreign material.

10. Place a new head gasket on the block with the words "This Side Up" facing upward.

11. Position the cylinder head on the block.

12. Coat the cylinder head bolts with RTV silicone sealant and install them. Tighten the bolts, in sequence, in three equal stages. The final stage should be 70 ft. lbs. (95 Nm).

13. Install the pushrods, keeping them in the same order as removed.

14. Install the rocker arms.

15. Install the exhaust manifold.

16. Install the intake manifold.

17. Connect the exhaust pipe from the exhaust manifold.

18. Fill the cooling system.

19. Connect the negative battery cable.

20. Adjust the valve lash.

4.0L Engines

▶ **See Figure 99**

1. Disconnect the negative battery cable.
2. Drain the cooling system.
3. Disconnect the hoses at the thermostat housing.
4. Properly relieve the fuel system pressure.
5. Remove the cylinder head cover.
6. Loosen the rocker arms.
7. Remove the pushrods.

➡️**The valvetrain components must be replaced in their original positions.**

8. Remove the intake and exhaust manifold from the cylinder head.

9. Disconnect the spark plug wires and remove the spark plugs.

10. Disconnect the temperature sending unit wire, ignition coil and bracket assembly from the engine.

11. Remove the accessory drive belt(s).

12. Unbolt and set aside the power steering pump and bracket. Do not disconnect the hoses.

13. Remove the intake and exhaust manifold assembly.

14. If equipped with A/C, perform the following:

   a. Remove the compressor and position it aside with the lines attached.

   b. Remove the compressor bracket bolts from the cylinder head.

   c. Loosen the through bolt at the bottom of the bracket.

15. Remove the alternator.

16. Remove the cylinder head bolts, the cylinder head and gasket from the block.

➡️**Bolt No. 14 cannot be removed until the head is moved forward. Pull the bolt out as far as it will go and suspend in place by wrapping with tape.**

17. Discard the gasket. Thoroughly clean the head and block mating surfaces. Check them for warpage with a straight-edge. Deviation should not exceed 0.002 in. (0.05mm) in a 6 in. (152mm) span.

To install:

18. Coat a new head gasket with suitable sealing compound and place it on the block. Most replacement gaskets will have the word **TOP** stamped on them.

➡️**Apply sealing compound only to the cylinder head gasket. Do not allow sealing compound to enter the cylinder bore.**

19. Install the cylinder head and bolts. The threads of bolt No. 11 must be coated with Loctite® 592 sealant before installation. Tighten the bolts in 3 steps, using the correct sequence:

   a. Tighten all bolts to 22 ft. lbs. (30 Nm).

   b. Tighten all bolts to 45 ft. lbs. (61 Nm).

   c. Retighten all bolts to 45 ft. lbs. (61 Nm).

   d. Tighten all bolts, except bolt 11, in sequence to 110 ft. lbs. (150 Nm).

   e. Tighten bolt 11 to 100 ft. lbs. (136 Nm)

➡️**Cylinder head bolts should be reused only once. Replace the head bolts which were previously used or are marked with paint. If head bolts are to be reused, mark each head bolt with paint for future reference. Head bolts should be installed using sealer.**

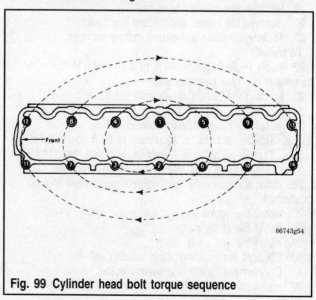

Fig. 99 Cylinder head bolt torque sequence

20. Install the ignition coil.
21. Install the air conditioning compressor.
22. Install the alternator.
23. Install the intake and exhaust manifold assembly.
24. Install the power steering pump and bracket.
25. Install the accessory drive belt(s).
26. Connect the temperature sending unit wire, ignition coil and bracket.
27. Install the spark plugs and wires.
28. Install the pushrods, rocker arm assembly, gasket and cylinder head cover.
29. Connect the hoses at the thermostat housing.
30. Fill the cooling system.
31. Connect the negative battery cable.
32. Run the engine to normal operating temperature and check for leaks.

5.2L Engines

▶ See Figures 100, 101 and 102

1. Disconnect the negative battery cable.
2. Properly relieve the fuel system pressure.
3. Drain the cooling system.
4. Remove the alternator.
5. Disconnect the PCV valve.
6. Disconnect the EVAP fuel lines.
7. Remove the air cleaner and disconnect the fuel lines.
8. Disconnect the accelerator linkage, speed control cable, if equipped, and transmission kickdown cables.
9. Remove the return spring.
10. Remove the distributor cap and wires.
11. Disconnect the coil wires.
12. Disconnect the heat indicator sending unit wire.
13. Disconnect the heater and bypass hoses.
14. Remove the cylinder head covers, discard the gaskets.
15. Remove the intake manifold and throttle body.
16. Remove the exhaust manifolds.
17. Remove the rocker arm assemblies and pushrods.

➡Identify the rocker arms and pushrods for installation purposes.

18. Remove the spark plugs.
19. Remove the cylinder head bolts.
20. Remove the heads and discard the gaskets.
21. Thoroughly clean the gasket mating surfaces.

To install:
22. Apply Perfect Sealer No. 5 or equivalent, to the inner corners of the new head gaskets.
23. Position the head gaskets onto the block.
24. Position the cylinder heads onto the cylinder block.
25. Install the cylinder head bolts as follows:
   a. Tighten all bolts, in sequence, to 50 ft. lbs. (68 Nm).
   b. Tighten all bolts, in sequence, to 105 ft. lbs. (143 Nm).
   c. Repeat Step b to ensure the torque is correct.
26. Install the pushrods and rocker arms to their original positions.
27. Install the intake and exhaust manifolds.
28. Install the spark plugs.
29. Install the coil wires.
30. Connect the heat indicating sending unit wire.
31. Connect the heater and bypass hoses.
32. Install the distributor cap and wires.

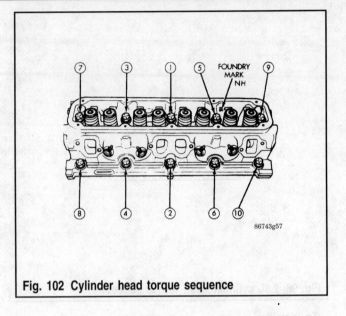

Fig. 102 Cylinder head torque sequence

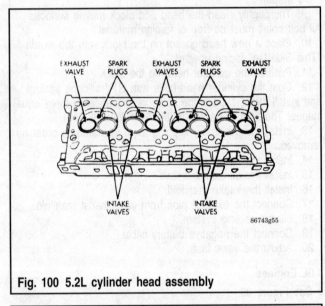

Fig. 100 5.2L cylinder head assembly

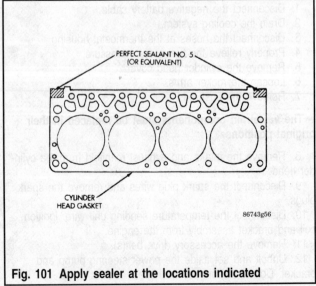

Fig. 101 Apply sealer at the locations indicated

33. Hook up the return spring.

34. Connect the accelerator linkage, speed control cable, if equipped and transmission kickdown cables.

35. Install the fuel lines.

36. Install the alternator.

37. Install the intake manifold-to-alternator bracket support rod.

38. Place new cylinder head cover gaskets into position and install the cylinder head covers.

39. Install the PCV valve.

40. Connect the EVAP lines.

41. Install the air cleaner.

42. Fill the cooling system.

43. Connect the negative battery cable. Start the engine and check for leaks.

CLEANING AND INSPECTION

▶ See Figures 103 and 104

1. With the valves installed to protect the valve seats, remove deposits from the combustion chambers and valve heads with a scraper and a wire brush. Be careful not to damage the cylinder head gasket surface. After the valves are removed, clean the valve guide bores with a valve guide cleaning tool or a bristle brush. Using cleaning solvent to remove dirt, grease and other deposits, clean all bolts holes; be sure the oil passage is clean (V6 engines).

2. Remove all deposits from the valves with a fine wire brush or buffing wheel.

3. Inspect the cylinder heads for cracks or excessively burned areas in the ports and bowl (below the valve) area. Check gasket surface for burrs and nicks. Replace the head if it is cracked.

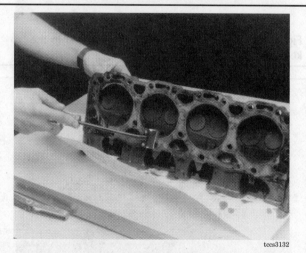

Fig. 103 Use a gasket scraper to remove the bulk of the old head gasket

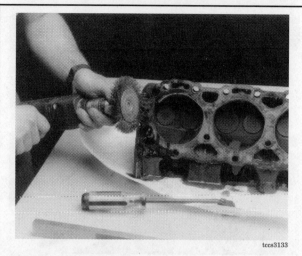

Fig. 104 An electric drill equipped with a wire wheel will expedite gasket removal

RESURFACING

Cylinder Head Flatness
▶ See Figures 105 and 106

When the cylinder head is removed, check the flatness of the cylinder head gasket surfaces.

1. Place a straightedge across the gasket surface of the cylinder head. Using feeler gauges, determine the clearance at the center of the straightedge.

2. If warpage exceeds 0.003 in. (0.076mm) in a 6 in. (152mm) span, or 0.006 in. (0.15mm); 0.008 in. (0.20mm) for the diesel, over the total length, the cylinder head must be resurfaced.

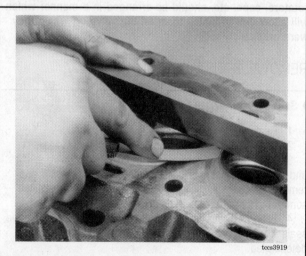

Fig. 105 Check the cylinder head for warpage along the center . . .

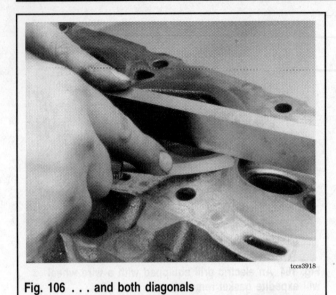

Fig. 106 . . . and both diagonals

3. If necessary to refinish the cylinder head gasket surface, do not plane or grind off more than 0.010 in. (0.25mm); 0.002 in. (0.05mm) for the diesel, from the original gasket surface.

➡When milling the cylinder heads of V6 or V8 engines, the intake manifold mounting position is altered, and must be corrected by milling the manifold flange a proportionate amount. Consult an experienced machinist about this.

Valves

➡Fabricate a valve arrangement board to use when you remove the valves, which will indicate the port in which each valve was originally installed (and which cylinder head on V6 or V8 models). Also note that the valve keys, rotators, caps, etc. should be arranged in a manner which will allow you to install them on the valve on which they were originally used.

REMOVAL & INSTALLATION

▶ **See Figures 107, 108 and 109**

1. Remove the cylinder head.
2. Remove the rocker arm assemblies.
3. Using a spring compressor, compress the valve springs and remove the keepers (locks). Relax the compressor and remove the rotators, the springs and the lower washers (on some engines). Keep all parts in order.
4. Slide the valve seals from the stems. Replace the valve seals when service is performed or when seals have deteriorated.
5. Remove any burrs from the top of the valve stem with jewelers file and slide the valves from the head, keeping them in order for installation.
   To install:
6. Thoroughly clean the valve stems and guides. Lightly lubricate the stem with oil and install the valve in its respective valve guide.

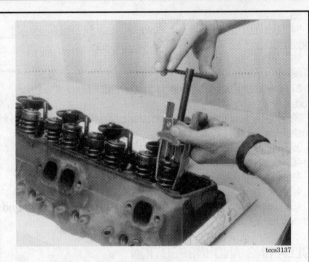

Fig. 107 Use a spring compressor tool to relieve the spring tension

Fig. 108 A small magnet will help in removal to the keepers

Fig. 109 Once the spring has been removed, the seal can be removed from the stem

7. Install replacement valve stem oil seals (marked INT for intake and EXH for exhaust) over the stems and onto valve guide boss.

➡**If valves with oversized stems are used, oversize oil seals are required.**

8. Position the valve spring and retainer on the cylinder head and compress the valve spring (with an appropriate valve spring compressor). Install valve locks and release the tool.

9. Lightly tap valve spring with a rubber hammer to ensure the spring is seated properly.

10. Install cylinder head on cylinder block.

INSPECTION

▶ **See Figure 110**

1. Clean all carbon deposits from the combustion chambers, valve ports, valve stems valve guides and head.

2. Inspect the combustion chambers and valve ports for cracks. Inspect for cracks on the exhaust seat and the gasket surface at each coolant passage.

3. Inspect valves for burned, cracked or warped heads. Inspect for scuffed or bent valve stems.

4. Install each valve into its respective guide bore of the cylinder head.

5. Mount a dial indicator so that the stem is at 90° to the valve stem, as close to the valve guide as possible.

6. Move the valve off its seat, and measure the valve guide-to-stem clearance by rocking the stem back and forth to actuate the dial indicator. The correct clearance is 0.001-0.003 in. (0.025-0.076mm).

7. The valve guide, if worn, must be repaired before the valve seats can be resurfaced. Valves with oversize stems are available to fit valve guides that are reamed oversize for repair.

REFACING

Valve refacing should only be handled by a reputable machine shop, as the experience and equipment needed to do the job are beyond that of the average owner/mechanic. During the course of a normal valve job, refacing is necessary when simply lapping the valves into their seats will not correct the seat and face wear. When the valves are reground (resurfaced), the valve seats must also be recut, again requiring special equipment and experience.

VALVE LAPPING

▶ **See Figure 111**

After machine work has been performed on the valves, it may be necessary to lap the valve to assure proper contact. For this, you should first contact your machine shop to determine if lapping is necessary. Some machine shops will perform this for you as part of the service, but the precision machining which is available today often makes lapping unnecessary. Additionally, the hardened valves/seats used in modern automobiles may make lapping difficult or impossible. If your machine shop recommends that you lap the valves, proceed as follows:

1. Set the cylinder head on the workbench, combustion chamber side up. Rest the head on wooden blocks on either end, so there are two or three inches between the tops of the valve guides and the bench.

2. Lightly lube the valve stem with clean engine oil. Coat the valve seat completely with valve grinding compound. Use just enough compound that the full width and circumference of the seat are covered.

3. Install the valve in its proper location in the head. Attach the suction cup end of the valve lapping tool to the valve head. It usually helps to put a small amount of saliva into the suction cup to aid it sticking to the valve.

4. Rotate the tool between the palms, changing position and lifting the tool often to prevent grooving. Lap the valve in until a smooth, evenly polished seat and valve face are evident.

Fig. 110 A dial gauge may be used to check valve stem-to-guide clearance

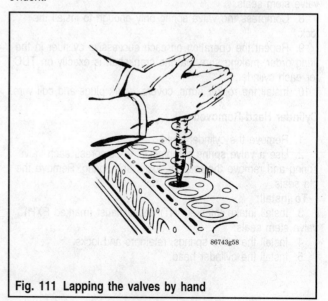

Fig. 111 Lapping the valves by hand

5. Remove the valve from the head. Wipe away all traces of grinding compound from the valve face and seat. Wipe out the port with a solvent soaked rag, and swab out the valve guide with a piece of solvent soaked rag to make sure there are no traces of compound grit inside the guide. This cleaning is important.

6. Proceed through the remaining valves, one at a time. Make sure the valve faces, seats, cylinder ports and valve guides are clean before reassembling the valvetrain.

Valve Stem Oil Seal

REMOVAL & INSTALLATION

Cylinder Head Installed

▶ **See Figures 112, 113 and 114**

If valve stem oil seals are found to be the cause of excessive oil consumption, they may be replaced without removing the cylinder block.

➡**Compressed air is required to perform this procedure. Only one valve may be serviced at a time.**

1. Remove spark plug wires and spark plugs from cylinder head.
2. Remove rocker arm cover. Remove rocker arms, pivots, bridges and capscrews.
3. Detach the coil wire from the distributor.
4. Turn the engine so that No.1 cylinder is at Top Dead Center on the compression stroke. Both valves for No. 1 cylinder should be fully closed and the crankshaft damper timing mark at TDC. The distributor rotor will point at the No. 1 spark plug wire location in the cap.
5. Apply 90-100 psi air pressure to No.1 cylinder, using a spark plug air hold adaptor.
6. Use a valve spring compressor to compress each No. 1 cylinder valve spring and remove the retainer, locks and spring. Remove the old seals.
7. Install intake (marked INT) and exhaust (marked EXH) valve stem seals.
8. Compress the valve spring only enough to install the lock.
9. Repeat the operation on each successive cylinder in the firing order, making sure that the crankshaft is exactly on TDC for each cylinder.
10. Install the rocker arms, covers, spark plugs and coil wire.

Cylinder Head Removed

1. Remove the cylinder head.
2. Use a valve spring compressor to compress each valve spring and remove the retainer, locks and spring. Remove the old seals.
   To install:
3. Install intake (marked INT) and exhaust (marked EXH) valve stem seals.
4. Install the valve springs, retainers and locks.
5. Install the cylinder head.

Fig. 112 Compress the spring using a suitable compressor

Fig. 113 A magnet will prevent loss of the keepers

Fig. 114 With the spring removed, the seals can be accessed

Valve Springs

REMOVAL & INSTALLATION

The valve spring removal and installation procedure is part of the valves removal and installation procedure.

INSPECTION

▶ **See Figures 115, 116 and 117**

1. Use a valve spring tester (J-22738-02) and a torque wrench to test valve spring tension. Replace any springs that are not within 1 lb. of all other springs.

2. Install valve spring retainer and locks on valve stem. Use a telescopic gauge to measure the installed height of the spring (from the bottom of the spring cup in the head to the bottom of the retainer). If not within specifications use valve spring shims to bring spring into specification.

➡**If a valve spring requires more than 0.090 in. (2.28mm) in spacers, replace the spring. Use only one shim of correct thickness per spring.**

3. Place the spring on a flat surface next to a square. Measure the height of the spring, and rotate it against the edge of the square to measure distortion. If spring height varies (by comparison) by more than 0.06 in. (1.5mm) or if distortion exceeds 0.06 in. (1.5mm), replace the spring.

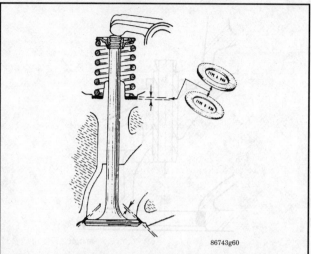

Fig. 116 Using shims to correct valve spring installed height

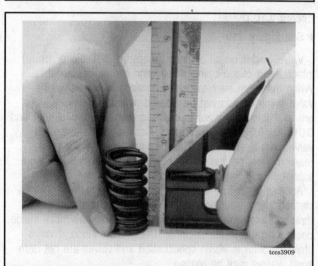

Fig. 117 The spring must also be checked for squareness

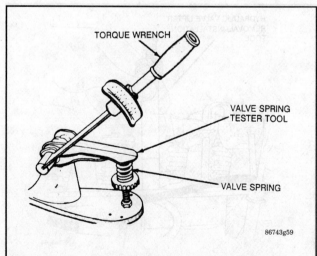

Fig. 115 The springs should be checked for proper tension

Valve Guides

REMOVAL & INSTALLATION

2.1L Diesel

▶ **See Figure 118**

➡**A press is used for removal and installation of guides. It is recommended for this procedure to be performed by a machine shop.**

1. Remove and disassemble the cylinder head.

2. Place the head in the press and press the old guide out through the bottom and the new one in through the top.

3. Once the new guide is in place, check its protrusion. The distance from the bottom end of the guide to the head mating surface should be 1.27 in. (32.5mm).

4. After the guides are in place, they must be reamed to 0.31 in. (8mm).

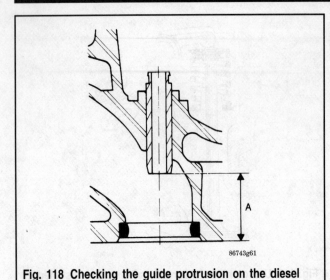

Fig. 118 Checking the guide protrusion on the diesel engine

Except 2.1L Diesel

▶ **See Figure 119**

Valve guides on all engines except the 2.1L diesel are an integral part of the cylinder head and are not replaceable. When the valve stem-to-guide clearance is excessive, the valve guide bores must be reamed oversize. Service valves are available with oversize stems in 0.003 in. (0.0762mm) and 0.015 in. (0.381mm) increments. Corresponding oversized valve stem seals must be used. If the valve guides are reamed oversize, the valve seats must be refaced to ensure valve seat concentricity to the valve guide.

Another procedure available to bring valve stem-to-guide clearance into specification is knurling. A special tool is threaded into the valve guide which displaces the metal inside, decreasing the inside diameter. Using this method, if valve stem diameter is within specification and valves are not damaged, valves may be reused.

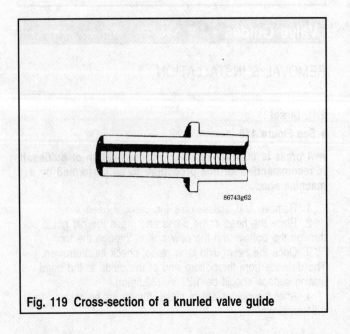

Fig. 119 Cross-section of a knurled valve guide

Valve Lifters

REMOVAL & INSTALLATION

▶ **See Figures 120 and 121**

1. Remove the rocker arm cover.
2. Remove the rocker arm bridge and pivot assembly by alternately loosening the capscrews 1 turn at a time. Remove the pushrods. Keep all components in order.
3. On 2.8L and 5.2L engines, remove the intake manifold. On the 5.2L engine, remove the yoke retainer and aligning yokes. Remove the lifters.
4. On all other engines, remove the lifters through the pushrod opening in the cylinder head using a lifter removal tool.
   To install:
5. Dip each lifter in MOPAR engine oil supplement and install into lifter bore using lifter tool.

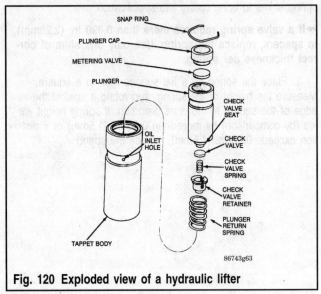

Fig. 120 Exploded view of a hydraulic lifter

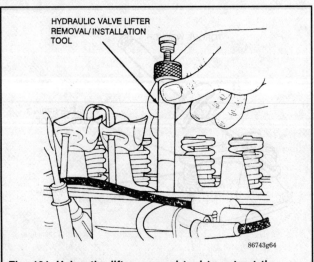

Fig. 121 Using the lifter removal tool to extract the lifters

6. Install all components (in their original positions) in reverse order of removal. On 5.2L engines, install the yoke retainers and tighten the bolts to 200 inch lbs. (23 Nm).

7. Pour remaining engine oil supplement in engine. The engine oil supplement must remain in the engine for at least 1000 miles but need not be drained until the next scheduled oil change.

Oil Pan

REMOVAL & INSTALLATION

2.1L Diesel Engines

▶ See Figure 122

1. Disconnect the negative battery cable. Raise and support the vehicle safely. Remove the converter housing shield as required.

2. Drain the engine oil. This engine has two oil drain plugs both must be opened.

✳✳CAUTION

The EPA warns that prolonged contact with used engine oil may cause a number of skin disorders, including cancer! You should make every effort to minimize your exposure to used engine oil. Protective gloves should be worn when changing the oil. Wash your hands and any other exposed skin areas as soon as possible after exposure to used engine oil. Soap and water, or waterless hand cleaner should be used.

3. Remove all the necessary components in order to gain access to the oil pan retaining bolts.

4. Remove the oil pan retaining bolts. Remove the oil pan from the engine.

To install:

5. Clean all gasket surfaces thoroughly. Be careful to avoid bending the oil pan mating flanges.

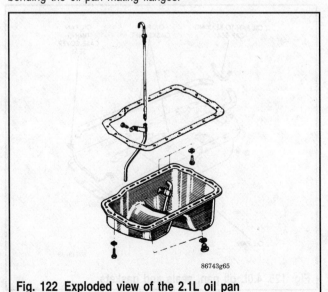

Fig. 122 Exploded view of the 2.1L oil pan

6. If the oil pan was assembled with RTV gasket material, run a 0.23 in. (6mm) bead of new sealer around the oil pan flanges, outboard of the mounting holes. The sealer sets in 15 minutes, so work quickly! If a gasket was used, coat the oil pan flanges with gasket sealer and place the gasket on the pan. Coat the engine block mounting surfaces with sealer.

7. Position the pan on the block and install the bolts. Tighten the bolts to 79 inch lbs. (9 Nm).

8. Install the drain plugs, fill the crankcase, run the engine and check for leaks.

2.5L Engines

▶ See Figure 123

1. Disconnect the battery ground.
2. Raise and support the vehicle safely.
3. Drain the oil

✳✳CAUTION

The EPA warns that prolonged contact with used engine oil may cause a number of skin disorders, including cancer! You should make every effort to minimize exposure to used engine oil. Protective gloves should be worn when changing the oil. Wash your hands and any other exposed skin areas as soon as possible after exposure to used engine oil. Soap and water, or waterless hand cleaner should be used.

4. Disconnect the exhaust pipe at the manifold and the exhaust hanger at the catalytic converter. Lower the exhaust.
5. Remove the starter.
6. Remove the bellhousing access plate.
7. If necessary, remove the engine mount and raise the engine to gain clearance.
8. Unbolt and remove the oil pan.

To install:

9. Clean the gasket surfaces thoroughly. Remove all sludge and dirt from the oil pan sump.
10. Install a replacement seal at the bottom of the timing case cover and at the rear bearing cap.
11. Using new gaskets coated with sealer, install the oil pan and tighten the 1/4 bolts to 80 inch lbs. (9 Nm); the 5/16 bolts to 11 ft. lbs. (15 Nm).
12. Lower the engine until it is properly located on the engine mounts. Tighten engine mount bolts to 48 ft. lbs. (65 Nm).
13. Tighten oil pan drain plug to 25 ft. lbs. (34 Nm).
14. Install the bellhousing access plate.
15. Install the starter.
16. Connect the exhaust pipe at the manifold and the exhaust hanger at the catalytic converter.
17. Fill the crankcase.
18. Connect the battery ground.
19. Start engine and inspect for leaks.

2.8L Engines

▶ See Figure 124

1. Disconnect the battery ground.
2. Raise the support the vehicle safely.

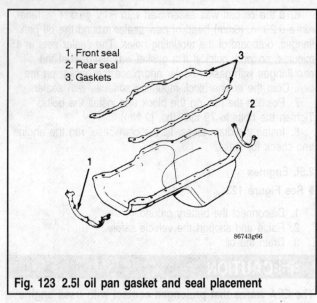

1. Front seal
2. Rear seal
3. Gaskets

86743g66

Fig. 123 2.5l oil pan gasket and seal placement

3. Drain the oil.

> ❊❊**CAUTION**
>
> The EPA warns that prolonged contact with used engine oil may cause a number of skin disorders, including cancer! You should make every effort to minimize your exposure to used engine oil. Protective gloves should be worn when changing the oil. Wash your hands and any other exposed skin areas as soon as possible after exposure to used engine oil. Soap and water, or waterless hand cleaner should be used.

4. Remove the bellhousing access cover.
5. Disconnect the exhaust pipes at the manifold.
6. Remove the starter.
7. Disconnect the exhaust pipe at the converter flange and lower the exhaust so that the "Y" portion rests on the axle upper control arms.
8. Unbolt and remove the pan.

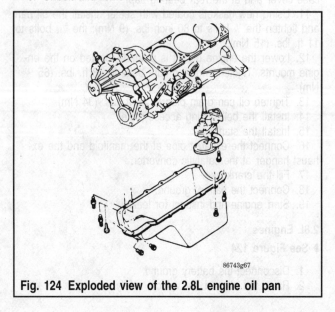

86743g67

Fig. 124 Exploded view of the 2.8L engine oil pan

To install:

9. Remove all RTV gasket material. Remove all sludge and dirt from the oil pan sump.
10. Install a new rear pan seal.
11. Apply a 1/8 in. (3mm) bead of RTV gasket material all the way around the pan sealing surface.
12. Install the pan and tighten the bolts to 12 ft. lbs. (16 Nm).
13. Connect the exhaust pipe at the converter flange.
14. Install the starter.
15. Connect the exhaust pipes at the manifold.
16. Install the bellhousing access cover.
17. Fill the crankcase.
18. Connect the battery ground.

4.0L Engines

▶ **See Figures 125, 126, 127 and 128**

1. Disconnect the battery ground.
2. Raise and support the vehicle safely.
3. Drain the oil.

> ❊❊**CAUTION**
>
> The EPA warns that prolonged contact with used engine oil may cause a number of skin disorders, including cancer! You should make every effort to minimize your exposure to used engine oil. Protective gloves should be worn when changing the oil. Wash your hands and any other exposed skin areas as soon as possible after exposure to used engine oil. Soap and water, or waterless hand cleaner should be used.

4. Disconnect the exhaust pipe at the manifold and the exhaust hanger at the catalytic converter. Lower the exhaust.
5. Remove the starter.
6. Remove the bellhousing access plate.
7. If necessary, remove the engine mount and raise the engine to gain clearance.
8. Unbolt and remove the oil pan.

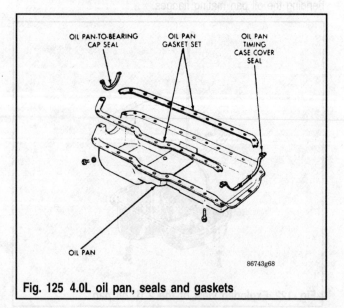

OIL PAN-TO-BEARING CAP SEAL

OIL PAN GASKET SET

OIL PAN TIMING CASE COVER SEAL

OIL PAN

86743g68

Fig. 125 4.0L oil pan, seals and gaskets

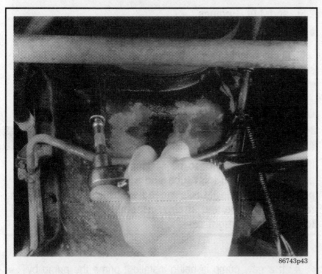

86743p43

Fig. 126 Use an extension to access the retaining bolts

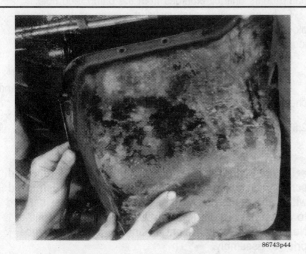

86743p44

Fig. 127 With the retaining bolts removed, lower the pan from the engine

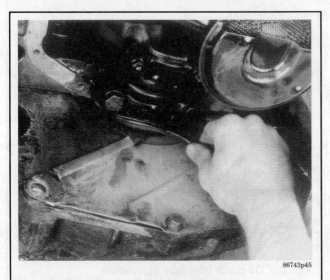

86743p45

Fig. 128 Remove all of the old gaskets

To install:

9. Clean the gasket surfaces thoroughly. Remove all sludge and dirt from the oil pan sump.

10. When installing the front oil pan seal to the timing chain cover, apply a generous amount of Permatex® No. 2 or equivalent sealer to the end tabs. Also, cement the oil pan side gaskets to the mating surface on the bottom of the engine block. Coat the inside curved surface of the new oil pan rear seal with soap and apply a generous amount of Permatex® No. 2 or equivalent to the gasket contacting surface of the seal end tabs.

11. Install the seal in the recess of the rear main bearing cap, making certain that it is fully seated.

12. Apply engine oil to the oil pan contacting surface of the front and rear oil pan seals.

13. Install the oil pan. Tighten the 1/4 bolts to 80 inch lbs. (9 Nm); the 5/16 bolts to 11 ft. lbs. (15 Nm); the oil pan drain plug to 30 ft. lbs. (41 Nm).

14. Lower the engine and install the engine mount.

15. Install the bellhousing access plate.

16. Install the starter.

17. Connect the exhaust pipe at the manifold and the exhaust hanger at the catalytic converter.

18. Fill the crankcase.

19. Connect the battery ground.

5.2L Engine

1. Disconnect the negative battery cable.

2. Raise and safely support the vehicle.

3. Remove the oil pan drain plug and drain the engine oil.

4. Remove the oil filter.

5. Remove the starter.

6. If equipped, disconnect the oil level sensor.

7. Position the oil cooler lines out of the way.

8. Disconnect the oxygen sensor and remove the exhaust pipe.

9. Remove the oil pan bolts and carefully slide the oil pan to the rear. If equipped, be careful not to damage the oil level sensor.

10. Clean all sealant and old gasket material from the oil pan and cylinder block mating surfaces. Thoroughly clean the oil pan.

To install:

11. Fabricate 4 alignment dowels from 1 1/2 x 5/16 in. bolts. Cut the heads off the bolts and cut a slot in the dowel to allow installation/removal with a screwdriver.

12. Install the dowels in the cylinder block. Apply a small amount of silicone sealant in the corner of the cap and cylinder block.

13. Slide the one-piece gasket over the dowels and onto the block. Position the oil pan over the dowels and onto the gasket. If equipped, be careful not to damage the oil level sensor.

14. Install the oil pan bolts and tighten to 215 inch lbs. (24 Nm). Remove the dowels and install the remaining bolts. Tighten to 215 inch lbs. (24 Nm).

15. Install the drain plug and tighten to 25 ft. lbs. (34 Nm).

16. Install the exhaust pipe and connect the oxygen sensor.

17. Install the oil filter. If equipped, connect the oil level sensor.

18. Install the starter. Move the oil cooler lines back into position.

19. Lower the vehicle and connect the negative battery cable.

20. Fill the engine with the proper type and quantity of oil. Start the engine and check for leaks.

Oil Pump

REMOVAL & INSTALLATION

2.1L Diesel Engines

1. Disconnect the negative battery cable.

2. Remove the vacuum pump along with the oil pump drive gear.

3. Remove the timing belt cover. Loosen the intermediate shaft drive sprocket using tool MOT 855 or equivalent.

4. Remove the intermediate shaft bolt, sprocket, cover, clamp plate and intermediate shaft.

5. Raise and support the vehicle safely. Drain the engine oil. Remove the oil pan.

✳✳CAUTION

The EPA warns that prolonged contact with used engine oil may cause a number of skin disorders, including cancer! You should make every effort to minimize your exposure to used engine oil. Protective gloves should be worn when changing the oil. Wash your hands and any other exposed skin areas as soon as possible after exposure to used engine oil. Soap and water, or waterless hand cleaner should be used.

6. Remove the piston skirt cooling oil jet assembly to oil pump pipe.

7. Remove the oil pump retaining bolts. Remove the oil pump.

8. Be sure that the oil pump locating dowels are in place on the pump.

9. Inspect the gears for abnormal wear, chips, looseness on the shafts, galling, and scoring.

10. Inspect the cover and cavity for breaks, cracks, distortion, and abnormal wear.

11. Install the gears into the pump cavity, and with the use of a straight edge and feeler gauge, check the gear to housing clearance.

12. Repair or replace defective components as required.

13. Install the oil pump and retaining bolts. Use a new gasket. Tighten the bolts to 33 ft. lbs. (45 Nm).

14. Install the piston skirt cooling oil jet assembly on oil pump pipe.

15. Install the oil pan.

16. Install the intermediate shaft and sprocket.

17. Install the timing belt cover.

18. Install the vacuum pump and oil pump drive gear.

19. Connect the negative battery cable.

20. Fill the crankcase.

2.5L and 4.0L Engines

▶ See Figure 129

1. Disconnect the negative battery cable. Raise and safely support the vehicle.

2. Drain the engine oil and remove the oil pan.

3. Unbolt and remove the pump assembly from the block. Discard the gasket.

✳✳WARNING

If the oil pump is not to be serviced, do not disturb the position of the oil inlet tube and strainer assembly in the pump body. If the tube is moved within the pump body, a replacement tube and strainer assembly must be installed to assure an airtight seal.

To install:

4. If a new pump is being installed, prime the pump by submerging the strainer in clean engine oil and turning the pump gears until oil emerges from the pump feed hole.

5. Using a new gasket, install the pump on the cylinder block. Tighten the short bolt to 10 ft. lbs. (14 Nm) and the long bolt to 17 ft. lbs. (23 Nm).

6. Install the oil pan and lower the vehicle.

7. Fill the engine with the proper type and quantity of oil.

8. Connect the negative battery cable. Start the engine and check for proper oil pressure.

2.8L Engines

1. Remove the oil pan.

➡Do not disturb the position of the oil pick-up tube and screen assembly in the pump body. If the tube is moved within the pump body, a new assembly must be installed to assure an airtight seal. Apply a thin film of Permatex® No. 2 sealant or equivalent around the end of the tube prior to assembly.

2. Unbolt and remove the pump assembly from the block. Discard any gaskets.

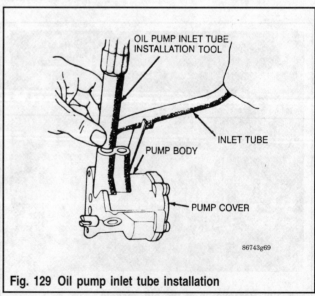

Fig. 129 Oil pump inlet tube installation

To install:

3. Install the pump on the block, using a new gasket (if one was removed).

4. Tighten the bolt to 25-30 ft. lbs. (34-41 Nm).

5. Install the pan.

5.2L Engines

▶ See Figure 130

1. Disconnect the negative battery cable.

2. Raise and safely support the vehicle.

3. Drain the engine oil and remove the oil pan.

4. Unbolt and remove the pump assembly from the rear main bearing cap.

To install:

5. If a new pump is being installed, prime the pump by submerging the pickup in clean engine oil and turning the pump gears until oil emerges from the pump feed hole.

6. Install the oil pump. During installation, slowly rotate the pump body to ensure driveshaft-to-pump rotor shaft engagement.

7. Hold the oil pump base flush against the mating surface of the rear main bearing cap and finger-tighten the pump mounting bolts. Tighten the mounting bolts to 30 ft. lbs. (41 Nm).

8. Install the oil pan and lower the vehicle. Fill the engine with the proper type and quantity of oil.

9. Connect the negative battery cable. Start the engine and check for proper oil pressure.

INSPECTION

Gear End Clearance

▶ See Figure 131

1. Remove the cover retaining screws and cover from the pump body.

2. Place a straightedge across the ends of the gears and the pump body.

3. Measure the clearance between the gears and the straight edge. A 0.002-0.006 in. (0.05-0.15mm) feeler gauge should fit snugly but freely.

➡ It is recommended that all oil pumps, even new replacement pumps, be checked for proper clearance.

4. If gear clearance is excessive, replace the pump assembly.

Gear-to-Body Clearance

▶ See Figure 132

1. With both gears in place, measure the gear to body clearance by inserting a feeler gauge between a gear tooth and the pump wall directly opposite the point of gear mesh.

2. Correct clearance is 0.002-0.004 in. (0.05-0.10mm). Rotate and check all gears in the same manner. Replace pump if clearance is excessive.

3. Install idler and drive gear into pump housing. Spin gears to assure that a binding condition does not exist.

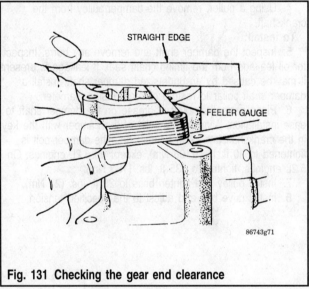

Fig. 131 Checking the gear end clearance

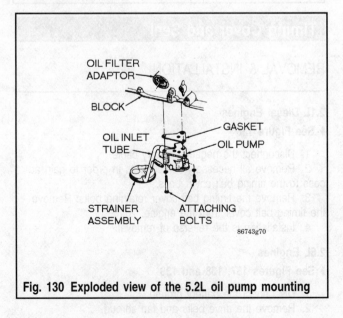

Fig. 130 Exploded view of the 5.2L oil pump mounting

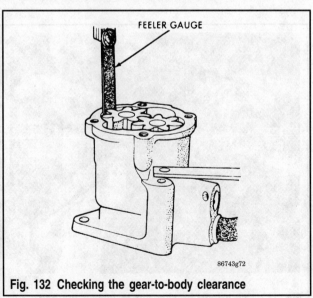

Fig. 132 Checking the gear-to-body clearance

4. To assure self priming of the oil pump, fill the gear cavity with petroleum jelly before installing the pump cover. DO NOT use grease.

5. Apply a thin bead of Loctite® 515 or equivalent to the top of the pump housing. Install pump screws and tighten to 70 inch lbs. (8 Nm).

Crankshaft Pulley (Vibration Damper)

REMOVAL & INSTALLATION

▶ See Figures 133, 134 and 135

1. Remove the fan shroud, as required.
2. On those engines with a separate pulley, remove the retaining bolts and separate the pulley from the vibration damper.
3. Remove the vibration damper/pulley retaining bolt from the crankshaft end.
4. Using a puller, remove the damper/pulley from the crankshaft.

To install:

5. Inspect the damper shaft and remove any burrs. Inspect for oil leakage from the timing chain seal. If leakage is present it may be caused by an undersized damper shaft. Install a damper shaft collar to restore correct outside diameter.
6. Place a small amount of grease on the damper shaft to ease installation. Align the key slot of the damper with the key in the crankshaft and push damper on. The damper bolt is tightened to 80 ft. lbs. (108 Nm), except on 5.2L engines. On 5.2L engines, tighten to 135 ft. lbs. (183 Nm).
7. Install pulley and tighten bolts to 20 ft. lbs. (27 Nm).
8. Install drive belt and adjust to the specified tension.

Fig. 134 . . . then remove it from the crankshaft

Fig. 135 A puller must be used to extract the damper from the engine

Fig. 133 Use a long breaker bar to loosen the bolt . . .

Timing Cover and Seal

REMOVAL & INSTALLATION

2.1L Diesel Engines
▶ See Figure 136

1. Disconnect the negative battery cable.
2. Remove all necessary components in order to gain access to the timing belt cover bolts.
3. Remove the timing belt cover retaining bolts. Remove the timing belt cover from the engine.
4. Installation is the reverse of removal.

2.5L Engines
▶ See Figures 137, 138 and 139

1. Disconnect the battery ground.
2. Remove the drive belts and fan shroud.

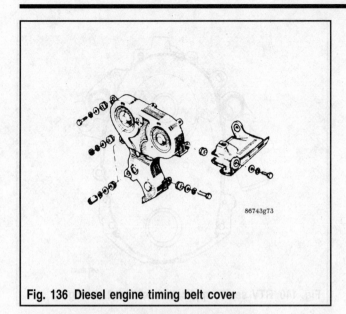

Fig. 136 Diesel engine timing belt cover

3. Unscrew the vibration damper bolts and washer.

4. Using a puller, remove the vibration damper.

5. Remove the fan assembly. If the fan is equipped with a fan clutch DO NOT LAY IT DOWN! If you lay it down, the fluid will leak out of the clutch and irreversibly damage the fan.

6. Remove the air conditioning compressor/alternator bracket assembly and lay it out of the way. DO NOT DISCONNECT THE REFRIGERANT LINES!

7. Unbolt the cover from the block and oil pan. Remove the cover and front seal.

8. Cut off the oil pan side gasket end tabs and oil pan front seal tabs.

9. Clean all gasket mating surfaces thoroughly.

10. Remove the seal from the cover.

To install:

11. Apply sealer to both sides of the new case cover gasket and position it on the block.

12. Cut the end tabs off the new oil pan side gaskets corresponding to those cut off the original gasket and attach the tabs to the oil pan with gasket cement.

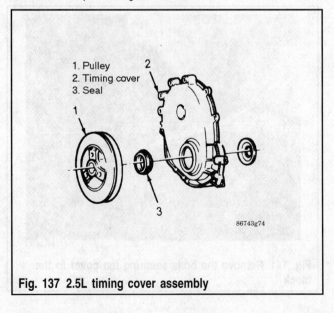

1. Pulley
2. Timing cover
3. Seal

Fig. 137 2.5L timing cover assembly

13. Coat the front cover seal end tab recesses generously with RTV sealant and position the side seal in the cover.

14. Apply engine oil to the seal-to-pan contact surface.

15. Position the cover on the block.

16. Insert alignment tool J-22248 into the crankshaft opening in the cover.

17. Install the cover bolts. Tighten the cover-to-block bolts to 5 ft. lbs. (7 Nm); the cover-to-pan bolts to 11 ft. lbs. (15 Nm).

18. Remove the alignment tool and position the new front seal on the tool with the seal lip facing outward. Apply a light film of sealer to the outside diameter of the seal. Lightly coat the crankshaft with clean engine oil.

19. Position the tool and seal over the end of the crankshaft and insert the Draw Screw J-9163-2 into the installation tool.

20. Tighten the nut until the tool just contacts the cover.

21. Remove the tools and apply a light film of engine oil on the vibration damper hub contact surface of the seal.

22. With the key inserted in the keyway in the crankshaft install the vibration damper, washer and bolt. Lubricate the bolt and tighten it to 108 ft. lbs. (146 Nm).

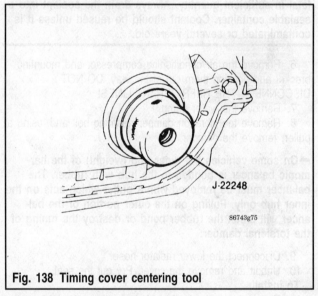

Fig. 138 Timing cover centering tool

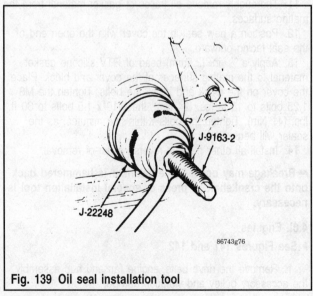

Fig. 139 Oil seal installation tool

23. If equipped with a serpentine belt, tighten the pulley-to-damper bolts to 20 ft. lbs. (27 Nm). Install all other parts in reverse order of removal.

2.8L Engines

▶ See Figure 140

1. Disconnect the battery ground.
2. Remove the drive belts.
3. Remove the fan shroud.
4. Remove the fan and pulley. If the fan is equipped with a fan clutch, DO NOT LAY IT ON ITS SIDE! If you do, the fluid will leak out and the fan clutch will have to be replaced.
5. Drain the cooling system.

✴✴CAUTION

When draining the coolant, keep in mind that cats and dogs are attracted by ethylene glycol antifreeze, and are quite likely to drink any that is left in an uncovered container or in puddles on the ground. This will prove fatal in sufficient quantity. Always drain the coolant into a sealable container. Coolant should be reused unless it is contaminated or several years old.

6. Remove the air conditioning compressor and mounting bracket and position them out of the way. DO NOT DISCONNECT THE REFRIGERANT LINES!
7. Remove the water pump.
8. Remove the vibration damper retaining bolt and, using a puller, remove the damper.

➡On some vehicles the outer ring (weight) of the harmonic balancer is bonded to the hub with rubber. The balancer must be removed with a puller which acts on the inner hub only. Pulling on the outer portion of the balancer will break the rubber bond or destroy the tuning of the torsional damper.

9. Disconnect the lower radiator hose.
10. Unbolt and remove the cover. Pry out the seal.

To install:

11. Thoroughly remove all traces of gasket material from the mating surfaces.
12. Position a new seal in the cover with the open end of the seal facing outward.
13. Apply a $3/32$ in. (2.5mm) bead of RTV silicone gasket material to the mating surfaces of the cover and block. Place the cover on the block and install the bolts. Tighten the M8 x 1.25 bolts to 18 ft. lbs. (24 Nm); the M10 x 1.5 bolts to 30 ft. lbs. (41 Nm). Tighten the bolts within five minutes, as the sealer will begin to set.
14. Install all other parts in reverse order of removal.

➡Breakage may occur if the balancer is hammered back onto the crankshaft. A press or special installation tool is necessary.

4.0L Engines

▶ See Figures 141 and 142

1. Remove the drive belts, engine fan and hub assembly, the accessory pulley and vibration damper.

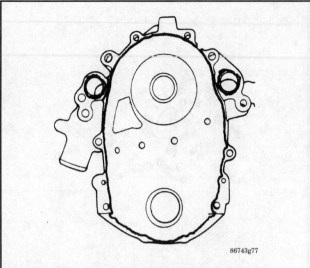

Fig. 140 RTV sealer application for the 2.8L engine

2. Remove the air conditioning compressor and alternator bracket assembly and set it aside. Don't disconnect the refrigerant lines.
3. Remove the oil pan to timing chain cover screws and the screws that attach the cover to the block.
4. Raise the timing chain cover just high enough to detach the retaining nibs of the oil pan neoprene seal from the bottom side of the cover. This must be done to prevent pulling the seal end tabs away from the tongues of the oil pan gaskets, which would cause a leak.
5. Remove the timing chain cover and gasket from the engine. Make sure the timing chain tensioner spring and thrust pin do not fall out of the preload bolt.
6. Use a razor blade to cut off the oil pan seal end tabs flush with the front face of the cylinder block and remove the seal. Clean the timing chain cover, oil pan, and cylinder block surfaces.
7. Remove the crankshaft oil seal from the timing chain cover. Thoroughly clean the mating surfaces.

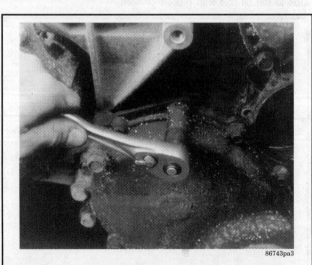

Fig. 141 Remove the bolts securing the cover to the block

86743pa4

Fig. 142 Carefully remove the cover from the engine

To install:

8. Apply RTV gasket material to both sides of the new gasket and position the gasket on the block.

9. Cut the end tabs off of the replacement oil pan side gaskets, corresponding to those cut off of the original gasket. Cement the end tabs to the oil pan.

10. Coat the front cover end tab recesses with a generous amount of RTV gasket sealant and position the seal on the timing case cover. Apply a coat of clean engine oil to the seal-to-pan contact surfaces.

11. Make sure the tension spring and thrust pin are in place in the preload bolt. Position the case cover on the block.

12. Place cover alignment tool (J-22248) in the crankshaft opening of the cover.

13. Install the cover-to-block bolts and the oil pan-to-cover bolts. Tighten the cover-to-block bolts to 62 inch lbs. (7 Nm); the cover-to-pan bolts to 11 ft. lbs. (15 Nm).

14. Remove the alignment tool and position the seal on the tool with the lip facing outward.

15. Apply a light coat of sealer on the outside diameter of the seal.

16. Lightly coat the crankshaft with clean engine oil.

17. Position the tool and seal over the end of the crankshaft and insert a screw tool into the seal installation tool.

18. Tighten the nut against the tool until it contacts the cover.

19. Remove the tools and apply a light coating of engine oil on the vibration damper hub contact surface of the seal.

20. Install the damper.

21. Install all other parts in reverse order of removal. tighten the damper pulley bolts to 20 ft.lbs.

5.2L Engines

1. Disconnect the negative battery cable.
2. Properly relieve the fuel system pressure.
3. Drain the cooling system.
4. Remove the serpentine belt.
5. Remove the cooling fan shroud and position it on the engine.
6. Remove the water pump.
7. Remove the power steering pump.

8. Remove the vibration damper using puller C-3688 or equivalent.

9. Disconnect the fuel lines.

10. Loosen the oil pan bolts and remove the front bolt at each side.

11. Remove the timing chain cover bolts. Remove the chain cover and gasket using extreme caution to avoid damaging the oil pan gasket.

To install:

12. Install a new timing chain cover gasket to the chain cover. Apply a small amount of Mopar silicone rubber adhesive sealant or equivalent, at the joint where the chain cover and oil pan gasket meet.

13. Install the timing chain cover taking care not to damage to oil pan. Tighten the timing chain cover bolts to 30 ft. lbs. (41 Nm) and oil pan bolts to 215 inch lbs. (24 Nm).

14. Install the vibration damper.

15. Connect the fuel lines.

16. Install the water pump.

17. Install the power steering pump.

18. Install the serpentine belt.

19. Install the cooling fan shroud.

20. Fill the cooling system.

21. Connect the negative battery cable.

Timing Belt

REMOVAL & INSTALLATION

▶ **See Figures 143, 144, 145 and 146**

➡**This applies to 2.1L diesel engines only.**

1. Disconnect the negative battery cable.

2. Remove the timing belt cover.

3. Install sprocket holding tool MOT 854 or equivalent and remove the camshaft sprocket retaining bolt. Remove the special tool.

4. Loosen the bolts and move the chain tensioner away from the timing belt. Tighten the tensioner bolts.

5. Remove the timing belt from the sprockets. Inspect the belt, using the accompanying diagnosis chart.

6. If it is necessary to remove the fuel injection pump sprocket, use tools BVI 28-01 and BVI 859, or equivalent.

➡**The following installation steps must be followed, exactly!**

7. Remove the access plug in the block, on the left side, and install the holding tool, MOT 861 in the hole. Rotate the crankshaft slowly, clockwise, until the tool drops into the TDC locating slot in the crankshaft counterweight.

➡**Don't use this tool as a crankshaft holding tool. When tightening or loosening geartrain fasteners, use a flywheel holding tool, such as tool MOT 582.**

8. Install sprocket holding tool, MOT 854 to retain the camshaft and injection pump sprockets. Make sure that the timing marks are positioned as shown.

9. Install the timing belt. There should be a total of 19 belt teeth between the camshaft and injection pump timing marks.

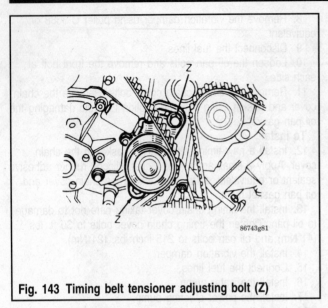

Fig. 143 Timing belt tensioner adjusting bolt (Z)

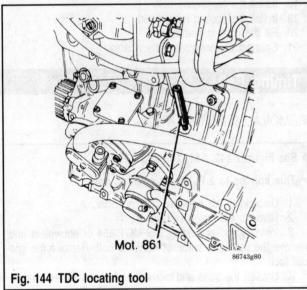

Mot. 861

Fig. 144 TDC locating tool

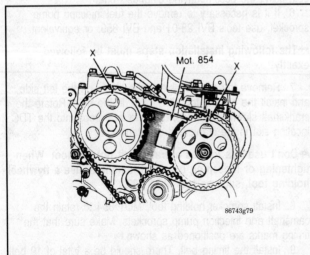

Mot. 854

Fig. 145 Camshaft and injection pump timing marks aligned

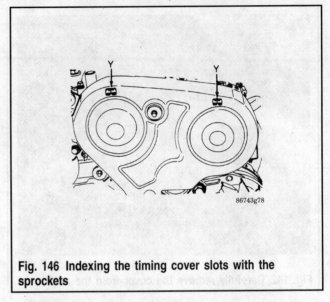

Fig. 146 Indexing the timing cover slots with the sprockets

10. Temporarily position the timing cover over the sprockets. The camshaft and injection pump timing marks must index with the pointers in the cover's timing slots.

11. Remove the cover.

12. Remove the holding tool, MOT 854.

13. Make sure that the timing belt tensioner bolts are 1/2 turn loose, maximum.

14. The tensioner should, automatically, bear against the belt giving the proper belt tension. Tighten the tensioner bolts.

15. Remove the TDC locating tool and install the plug.

16. Rotate the crankshaft, slowly, CLOCKWISE, two complete revolutions.

➡NEVER rotate the crankshaft counterclockwise while adjusting belt tension.

17. Loosen the tensioner bolts 1/8 turn, maximum, then tighten them again.

18. Check the belt deflection at a point midway between the camshaft and injection pump sprockets. The belt should deflect 1.37 in. (35mm).

19. Install the timing belt cover.

Timing Chain and Gears

REMOVAL & INSTALLATION

2.5L Engines

▶ See Figures 147 and 148

1. Disconnect the negative battery cable.

2. Remove the fan and shroud, the accessory drive belts, vibration damper and pulley.

3. Remove the timing case cover.

4. Rotate the crankshaft so that the timing marks on the cam and crank sprockets align next to each other.

5. Remove the oil slinger from the crankshaft.

6. Remove the cam sprocket retaining bolt and remove the sprocket and chain. The crank sprocket may also be removed at this time. If the tensioner is to be removed, the oil pan must be removed first.

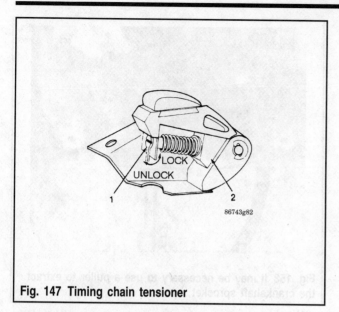

Fig. 147 Timing chain tensioner

To install:

7. Prior to installation, turn the tensioner lever to the unlock (down) position.

8. Pull the tensioner block toward the tensioner to compress the spring. Hold the block and turn the tensioner lever to the lock (up) position.

9. Install the camshaft/crankshaft sprocket and timing chain together, as a unit. Ensure timing marks are aligned properly. The camshaft sprocket bolt should be tightened to 50 ft. lbs. (68 Nm) on 1984-88 models or 80 ft. lbs. (108 Nm) on 1989-96 models.

10. Install all other components in the reverse order of removal.

2.8L Engines

1. Disconnect the negative battery cable.
2. Remove the timing cover.
3. Turn the crankshaft to bring the No. 1 piston to TDC of its compression stroke. The timing marks on the crankshaft and camshaft sprockets should be aligned as shown with the No. 4 cylinder in firing position.

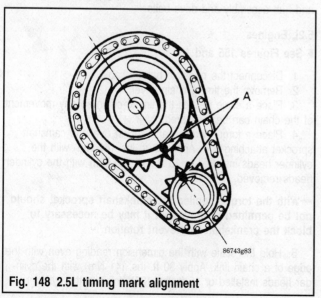

Fig. 148 2.5L timing mark alignment

4. Remove the camshaft sprocket and chain. If the sprocket is stuck, you can remove it by tapping it lightly with a plastic or wood mallet.

5. Lubricate the chain and sprockets with Molykote®, or equivalent. Install the cam sprocket and chain, with the timing marks aligned and the dowel in the camshaft aligned with the hole in the sprocket.

6. Install the sprocket on the camshaft and tighten the cam sprocket bolts to 20 ft. lbs. (27 Nm).

7. Install the timing cover. Reconnect the negative battery cable.

4.0L Engines

▶ **See Figures 149, 150, 151, 152, 153 and 154**

1. Remove the drive belts, engine fan and hub assembly, accessory pulley, vibration damper and timing chain cover.

2. Remove the tension spring and thrust pin from the preload bolt, if equipped.

3. Remove the oil seal from the timing chain cover.

4. Remove the camshaft sprocket retaining bolt and washer.

5. Rotate the crankshaft until the timing mark on the crankshaft sprocket is closest to and in a center line with the timing pointer of the camshaft sprocket.

6. Remove the camshaft sprocket and timing chain as an assembly. Disassemble the chain and sprockets. If necessary, remove the crankshaft sprocket.

To install:

7. Assemble the timing chain, crankshaft sprocket and camshaft sprocket with the timing marks aligned.

8. Install the assembly to the crankshaft and the camshaft. Install the camshaft sprocket retaining bolt and washer and tighten to 80 ft. lbs. (108 Nm).

9. Check the alignment of the chain and sprockets by counting the number of links or pins with the sprockets positioned as illustrated. There must be 15 pins between the marks on the sprockets.

10. Lubricate the tension spring, thrust pin and pin bore with MOPAR engine oil supplement, or equivalent, and install.

11. Install the timing chain cover and a new oil seal.

Fig. 149 Remove the oil deflector

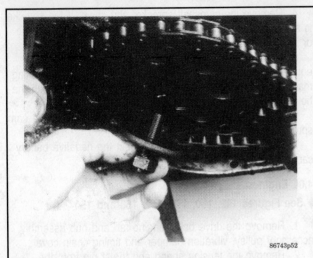

Fig. 150 Remove the camshaft retaining bolt and washer

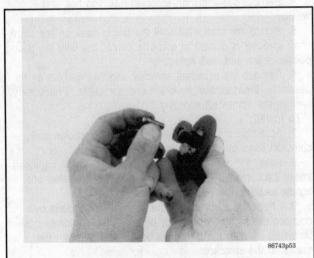

Fig. 151 Be careful not to lose the thrust pin and spring

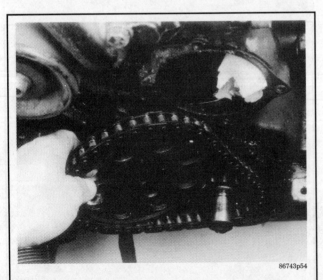

Fig. 152 Remove the camshaft sprocket and chain

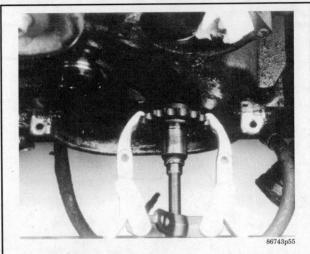

Fig. 153 It may be necessary to use a puller to extract the crankshaft sprocket

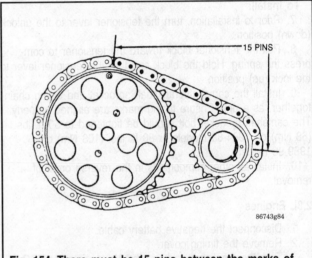

15 PINS

Fig. 154 There must be 15 pins between the marks of the sprockets

12. Install the vibration damper, accessory pulley, engine fan and hub assembly and drive belts.

5.2L Engines

▶ **See Figures 155 and 156**

1. Disconnect the negative battery cable.
2. Remove the timing chain cover.
3. Place a scale next to the timing chain so any movement of the chain can be measured.
4. Place a torque wrench and socket over the camshaft sprocket attaching bolt. Apply 30 ft. lbs. (41 Nm) with the cylinder heads installed or 15 ft. lbs. (20 Nm) with the cylinder heads removed.

➡**With the torque applied the crankshaft sprocket should not be permitted to move, but it may be necessary to block the crankshaft to prevent rotation.**

5. Hold the scale with the dimension reading even with the edge of a chain link. Apply 30 ft. lbs. (41 Nm) with the cylinder heads installed or 15 ft. lbs. (20 Nm) with the cylinder

heads removed, in the reverse direction. Note the amount of chain movement.

6. Install a new timing chain if the movement exceeds 1/8 inch (3.175mm).

7. Remove the camshaft sprocket retaining bolt.

8. Remove the timing chain and sprockets.

To install:

9. Position the camshaft and crankshaft sprockets on a bench with the timing marks facing each other.

10. Position the timing chain onto the sprockets.

11. Turn the crankshaft and camshaft to align with the keyway location in the crankshaft and camshaft sprockets.

12. Keeping tension on the chain, slide the sprocket and chain assembly onto the engine.

13. Ensure the timing marks are still aligned by using a straightedge.

14. Install the camshaft bolt and tighten it to 50 ft. lbs. (68 Nm).

15. Install the timing chain cover.

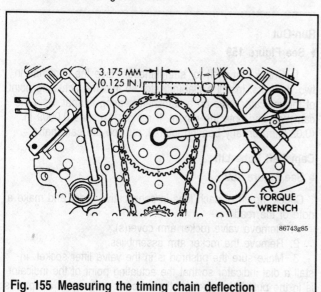

Fig. 155 Measuring the timing chain deflection

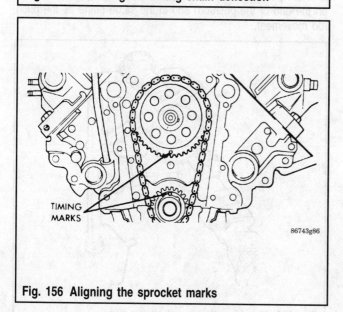

Fig. 156 Aligning the sprocket marks

16. Connect the negative battery cable.

Camshaft and Bearings

REMOVAL & INSTALLATION

2.1L Diesel Engines

▶ See Figure 157

1. Disconnect the negative battery cable.

2. Drain the cooling system.

❊❊CAUTION

When draining the coolant, keep in mind that cats and dogs are attracted by ethylene glycol antifreeze, and are quite likely to drink any that is left in an uncovered container or in puddles on the ground, This will prove fatal in sufficient quantity. Always drain the coolant into a sealable container. Coolant should be reused unless it is contaminated or several years old.

3. Remove the valve cover and timing chain cover.

4. Remove the cylinder head.

5. Remove the camshaft gear using tool BVI 28-01.

6. Remove the oil seal from the cylinder head by prying it out using a suitable tool.

7. Remove the camshaft from the cylinder head.

To install:

8. Coat the camshaft with an engine oil supplement.

9. Carefully install the camshaft in the cylinder head.

10. Install the oil seal in the cylinder.

11. Install the camshaft gear. Hold the sprocket with tool MOT 855 while tightening to 37 ft. lbs. (50 Nm).

12. Install the cylinder head.

13. Install the valve cover and timing chain cover.

14. Fill the cooling system.

15. Connect the negative battery cable.

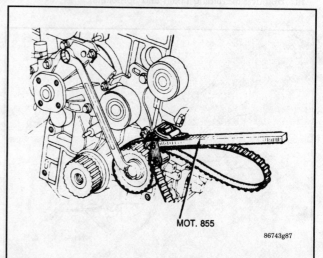

Fig. 157 Hold the camshaft gear while tightening the bolt

2.5L, 2.8L, 4.0L and 5.2L Engines

▶ See Figure 158

1. Disconnect the battery ground.
2. Drain the cooling system.

❋❋CAUTION

When draining the coolant, keep in mind that cats and dogs are attracted by ethylene glycol antifreeze, and are quite likely to drink any that is left in an uncovered container or in puddles on the ground. This will prove fatal in sufficient quantity. Always drain the coolant into a sealable container. Coolant should be reused unless it is contaminated or several years old.

➡ The air conditioning system must be discharged using an approved recovery/recycling machine only. Please refer to Section 1 for more information.

3. Discharge the air conditioning system, remove the radiator and air conditioning condenser.
4. On carbureted engines, remove the fuel pump.
5. Matchmark the distributor and engine for installation. Note the rotor position by marking it on the distributor body. Unbolt and remove the distributor and wires.
6. Remove the rocker arm cover.
7. Remove the rocker arm assemblies.
8. Remove the pushrods.

➡ Keep everything in order for installation. If a replacement camshaft is to be installed, replace hydraulic lifters to ensure durability of camshaft lobes and lifter bottoms.

9. Using a tool J-21884, or equivalent, remove the hydraulic lifters.
10. Remove the vibration damper and timing chain cover.

➡ If the camshaft sprocket appears to have been rubbing against the cover, check the oil pressure relief holes in the rear cam journal for debris.

11. Remove the timing chain and sprockets.

12. Slide the camshaft from the engine. If necessary, remove front bumper and/or grille to allow removal of camshaft through front of vehicle.
13. Inspect the cam lobes, bearing journals, bearings and distributor drive gear for wear. Replace if necessary.

To install:

14. Lubricate all moving parts with engine oil supplement prior to installation.
15. Install camshaft and tighten camshaft sprocket retaining bolts.
16. Remainder of installation procedure is reverse of removal.

➡ Run engine for at least 30 minutes at varying rpm's (between 1000-2000 rpm) to allow camshaft and lifters to break-in. Change oil and filter immediately after break-in period.

INSPECTION

Run-Out

▶ See Figure 159

1. Check camshaft for straightness. Place the camshaft in two V-blocks. Install a dial indicator so that the actuating point of the indicator rests on a camshaft bearing journal. Spin the camshaft and note the runout. If run-out exceeds 0.0009 in. (0.023mm) on any bearing journal, replace the camshaft.

Camshaft Lobe Lift

▶ See Figure 160

Check the lift of each lobe in consecutive order and make a note of the reading.

1. Remove valve rocker arm cover(s).
2. Remove the rocker arm assemblies.
3. Make sure the pushrod is in the valve lifter socket. Install a dial indicator so that the actuating point of the indicator is in the pushrod socket (or the indicator ball socket adaptor is on the end of the pushrod) and in the same plane as the push rod movement.

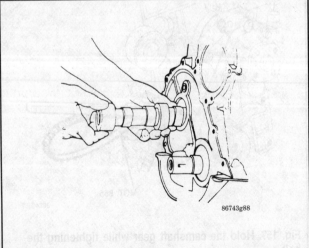

86743g88

Fig. 158 Be careful not to damage the bearings when removing or installing the camshaft

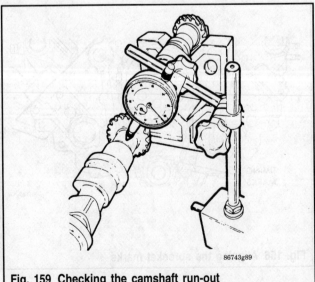

86743g89

Fig. 159 Checking the camshaft run-out

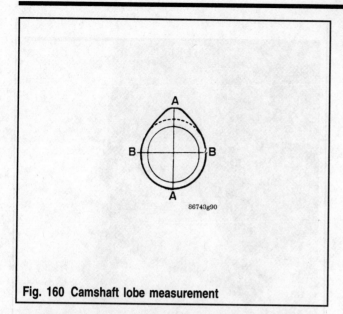

Fig. 160 Camshaft lobe measurement

4. Install an auxiliary starter switch Crank the engine with the ignition switch **OFF**. Turn the crankshaft over until the tappet is on the base circle of the camshaft lobe. At this position, the pushrod will be in its lowest position.

5. Zero the dial indicator. Continue to rotate the crankshaft slowly until the pushrod is in the fully raised position.

6. Compare the total lift recorded on the dial indicator with the specification shown on the Camshaft Specification chart.

7. Check the accuracy of the original indicator reading by continuing to rotate the crankshaft and noting the highest lift recorded on the dial indicator. If the lift on any lobe is below specified wear limits listed, the camshaft and the valve lifters must be replaced.

8. Remove the dial indicator and auxiliary starter switch.

9. Install the rocker arm assemblies. Check the valve clearance. Adjust if required (refer to procedure in this section).

10. Install the rocker arm cover(s).

Camshaft End-Play

➡On engines with an aluminum or nylon camshaft sprocket, prying against the sprocket, with the valve train load on the camshaft, can break or damage the sprocket. Therefore, the rocker arm adjusting nuts must be backed off, or the rocker arm and shaft assembly must be loosened sufficiently to free the camshaft. After checking the camshaft end-play, check the valve clearance. Adjust if required (refer to procedure in this section).

1. Push the camshaft toward the rear of the engine. Install a dial indicator so that the indicator point is on the camshaft sprocket attaching screw.

2. Zero the dial indicator. Position a prybar between the camshaft gear and the block. Pull the camshaft forward and release it. Compare the dial indicator reading with the specifications.

3. If the end play is excessive, check the spacer for correct installation before it is removed. If the spacer is correctly installed, replace the thrust plate.

4. Remove the dial indicator.

BEARING REPLACEMENT

1. Remove the engine following the procedures in this section and install it on an engine stand.

2. Remove the camshaft, flywheel and crankshaft, following the appropriate procedures. Push the pistons to the top of the cylinder.

3. Remove the camshaft rear bearing bore plug. Remove the camshaft bearings with a bearing removal tool.

4. Select the proper size expanding collet and back-up nut and assemble on the mandrel. With the expanding collet collapsed, install the collet assembly in the camshaft bearing and tighten the back-up nut on the expanding mandrel until the collet fits the camshaft bearing.

5. Assemble the puller screw and extension (if necessary) and install on the expanding mandrel. Wrap a cloth around the threads of the puller screw to protect the front bearing or journal. Tighten the pulling nut against the thrust bearing and pulling plate to remove the camshaft bearing. Be sure to hold a wrench on the end of the puller screw to prevent it from turning.

6. To remove the front bearing, install the puller from the rear of the cylinder block.

7. Position the new bearings at the bearing bores, and press them in place. Be sure to center the pulling plate and puller screw to avoid damage to the bearing. Failure to use the correct expanding collet can cause severe bearing damage. Align the oil holes in the bearings with the oil holes in the cylinder block before pressing bearings into place.

8. Install the camshaft rear bearing bore plug.

9. Install the camshaft, crankshaft, flywheel and related parts, following the appropriate procedures.

10. Install the engine in the truck, following procedures described earlier in this section.

Pistons and Connecting Rods

➡Use care at all times when handling and servicing rods and pistons. To prevent possible damage to these units, DO NOT allow rods or pistons to strike hard objects or one another.

REMOVAL

▶ See Figures 161, 162, 163 and 164

➡To ease the removal and installation of internal engine components, it is recommended that the engine be removed for servicing.

1. Remove the head(s).

2. Remove the oil pan.

3. Rotate the engine to bring each piston, in turn, to the bottom of its stroke. With the piston bottomed, remove the ridge at the top of the cylinder. DO NOT CUT TOO DEEPLY!

4. Matchmark the rods and caps. If the pistons are to be removed from the connecting rod, mark the cylinder number on the piston with a silver pencil or quick drying paint for proper cylinder identification and cap-to-rod location. Remove the connecting rod capnuts and lift off the rod caps, keeping them in

order. Install a guide hose over the rod bolt threads to prevent damage to the bearing journal and rod bolt threads.

5. Using a hammer handle, push the piston and rod assemblies up out of the block.

➡On diesel engines, remove each connecting rod, cylinder liner and piston as a complete assembly. Each piston and cylinder liner are matched as a set, so, be sure that they are marked properly for installation.

CLEANING AND INSPECTION

▶ **See Figures 165, 166 and 167**

Clean varnish from piston skirts and pins with a cleaning solvent. DO NOT WIRE BRUSH ANY PART OF THE PISTON. Remove old piston rings and clean the ring grooves with a groove cleaner. Make sure oil ring holes and slots are clean.

Inspect the piston for cracked ring lands, skirts or pin bosses, wavy or worn ring lands, scuffed or damaged skirts,

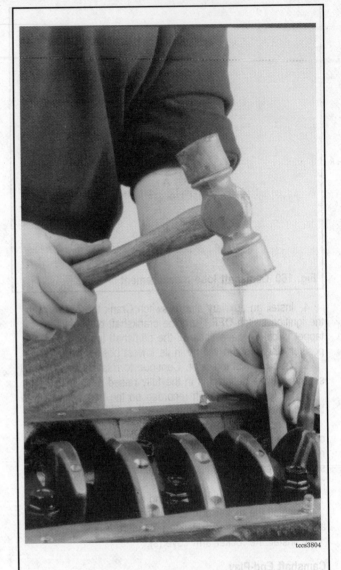
Fig. 163 Carefully tap the piston out of the bore

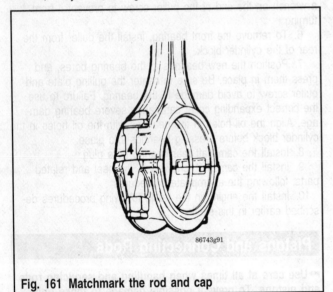
Fig. 161 Matchmark the rod and cap

Fig. 162 Place rubber hose over the studs to prevent damage to the crankshaft and cylinders

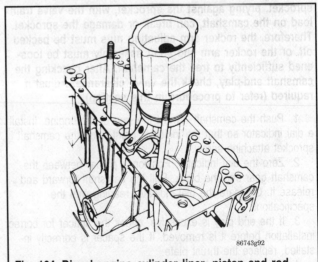
Fig. 164 Diesel engine cylinder liner, piston and rod assembly

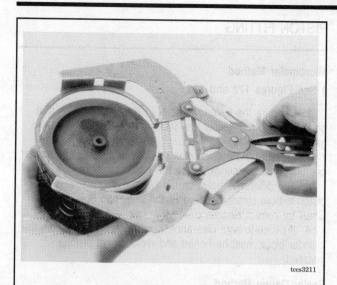

Fig. 165 Use a ring expander to remove the rings

Fig. 166 Clean the grooves using a ring groove cleaner

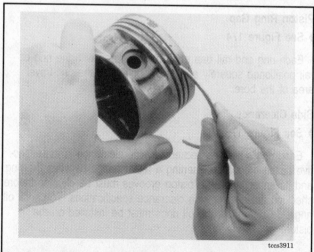

Fig. 167 You can use a piece of an old ring to clean the grooves, BUT be careful the ring is sharp

eroded areas at the top of the piston. Replace pistons that are damaged or show signs of excessive wear. Inspect the grooves for nicks or burrs that might cause the rings to hang up.

Inspect connecting rod bearings for scoring and bent alignment tabs. Also check for grooving, fatigue or any sign of abnormal wear. Inspect connecting rod journals for signs of scoring, nicks burrs or abnormal wear. Any of these conditions signal problems which should be investigated.

Using a straightedge, check the connecting rods for straightness. It is advisable to have connecting rods Magnafluxed® for cracks.

RIDGE REMOVAL AND HONING

▶ **See Figures 168 and 169**

➡Cylinder honing and/or boring should be performed by a reputable, professional machine shop with the proper equipment. In some cases, clean-up honing can be done with the cylinder block in the vehicle, but most extensive honing and all cylinder boring must be done with the block stripped and removed from the vehicle.

As the cylinder bore wears, a ridge is formed at the top of the cylinder where the rings never scrape. Removing this ridge makes piston removal easier and prevents damage to the rings. A ridge reamer is installed into the cylinder, tightened, then the cutters of the reamer are moved upward as the threaded portion of the reamer is rotated.

When new piston rings are installed in an engine, the cylinder bore must have a cross-hatch pattern finish. This allows the rings and bore wear together and provide better oil control and compression. This cross-hatch pattern is achieved by honing. No more than 0.0008 in (0.02 mm) should be removed during this process, since the finished roundness of the cylinder will be destroyed.

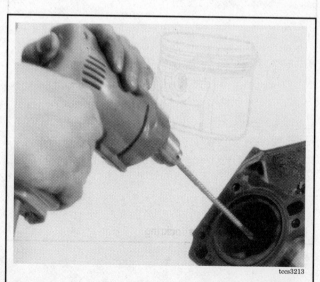

Fig. 168 Using a flexible hone to remove bore glazing

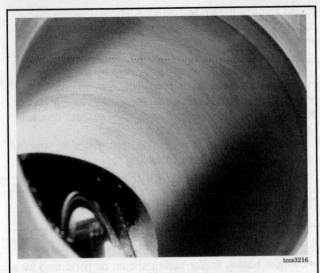

Fig. 169 A properly cross-hatched cylinder bore

PISTON PIN REPLACEMENT

▶ **See Figures 170 and 171**

1. If replacement pistons are to be used, remove the piston pin lockring (if used). Install the guide bushing of the piston pin removal/installation tool.

2. Place the piston and connecting rod assembly on a support, and place the assembly in an arbor press. Press the pin out of the connecting rod, using the appropriate piston pin tool.

3. Assemble the rod with a new piston. Using the piston pin tool, install the new piston pin. Install new lockrings.

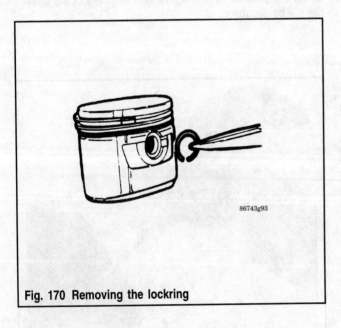

Fig. 170 Removing the lockring

PISTON FITTING

Micrometer Method

▶ **See Figures 172 and 173**

1. Measure the inside diameter of the cylinder bore at a point 2 in. (50mm) below the deck surface using a dial bore gauge.

2. Measure the outside diameter of the piston at the piston centerline and perpendicular to the piston pin bore.

3. The difference between the two measurements is the piston-to-bore clearance. See Piston and Ring Specifications Chart for correct clearance.

4. If piston-to-bore clearance is not within specification, the cylinder block must be honed and replacement pistons installed.

Feeler Gauge Method

1. Remove the rings from the piston.

2. Insert a long 0.001 in. (0.025mm) feeler gauge into the cylinder bore.

3. Insert the piston, top first, into the bore along side the feeler gauge. With the entire piston inserted into the bore, the piston should not bind against the feeler gauge.

4. Repeat Steps 2 and 3 with a 0.002 in. (0.05mm) feeler gauge. The piston should bind.

5. If the piston binds using the 0.001 in. (0.025mm) feeler gauge or does not bind using the 0.002 in. (0.05mm) feeler gauge, the piston is not the correct size for the bore. Replace the piston and/or hone the bore to gain proper piston-to-bore clearance.

PISTON RING REPLACEMENT

For service ring specifications and detailed installation procedures, refer to the ring manufacturer's instructions. When installing new rings, gap and side clearance should be checked as follows.

Piston Ring Gap

▶ **See Figure 174**

Each ring and rail gap must be measured with the ring or rail positioned squarely and at the bottom of the ring-travel area of the bore.

Side Clearance

▶ **See Figure 175**

Each ring must be checked for side clearance in its respective piston groove by inserting a feeler gauge between the ring and its upper land. The piston grooves must be cleaned before checking the ring for side clearance specifications. To check oil ring side clearance, the oil rings must be installed on the piston.

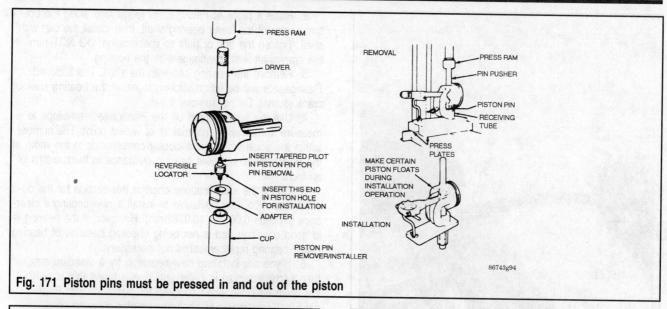

Fig. 171 Piston pins must be pressed in and out of the piston

Fig. 172 Measure the inside of the bore with a telescoping gauge

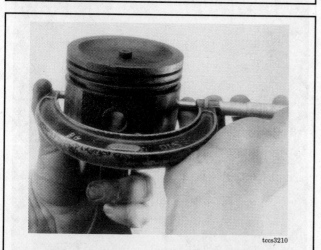

Fig. 173 Measure the outside diameter of the piston at the piston centerline and perpendicular to the piston pin

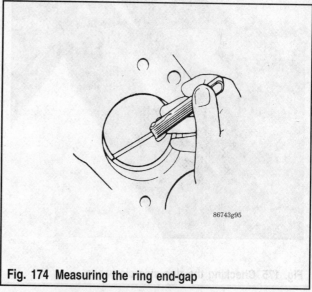

Fig. 174 Measuring the ring end-gap

ROD BEARING REPLACEMENT

▶ **See Figures 176 and 177**

Connecting rod bearings for the engine covered in this manual consist of two halves or shells which are interchangable in the rod and cap. When the shells are placed in position, the ends extend slightly beyond the rod and cap surfaces. As the rod bolts are tightened, the shells will be capped tightly in place to insure positive seating and to prevent turning. A tang holds the shells in place.

If a rod bearing becomes noisy or is worn so that its clearance on the crank journal is sloppy, a new bearing of the correct undersize must be selected and installed since there is a provision for adjustment.

➡**Under no circumstances should the rod end or cap be filed to adjust the bearing clearance, nor should shims of any kind be used.**

Fig. 175 Checking the ring side clearance

Inspect the rod bearings while the rod assemblies are out of the engine. If the shells are scored or show flaking, they should be replaced. If they are in good shape check for proper clearance on the crank journal. Any scoring or ridges on the crank journal means the crankshaft must be replaced, or reground and fitted with undersized bearings.

➡**Make sure connecting rods and their caps are kept together, and that the caps are installed in the proper direction.**

Replacement bearings are available in standard size, and in undersizes for reground crankshafts. Connecting rod-to-crankshaft bearing clearance is checked using Plastigage® at either the top or bottom of each crank journal. The Plastigage® has a range of 0.001-0.003 in. (0.0254-0.0762mm).

1. Remove the rod cap with the bearing shell. Completely clean the bearing shell and the crank journal, and blow any oil from the oil hole in the crankshaft; Plastigage® is soluble in oil.

2. Place a piece of Plastigage® lengthwise along the bottom center of the lower bearing shell, then install the cap with shell. Tighten the bolt or nuts to specification. DO NOT turn the crankshaft with Plastigage® in the bearing.

3. Remove the bearing cap with the shell. The flattened Plastigage® will be found sticking to either the bearing shell or crank journal. Do not remove it yet.

4. Use the scale printed on the Plastigage® envelope to measure the flattened material at its widest point. The number within the scale which most closely corresponds to the width of the Plastigage® indicates bearing clearance in thousandths of an inch.

5. Check the specifications chart in this section for the desired clearance. It is advisable to install a new bearing if clearance exceeds 0.003 in. (0.0762mm). However, if the bearing is in good condition and is not being checked because of bearing noise, bearing replacement is not necessary.

6. If you are installing new bearings, try a standard size, then each undersize in order until one is found that is within the specified limits when checked for clearance with Plastigage®. Each undersize shell has its size stamped on it.

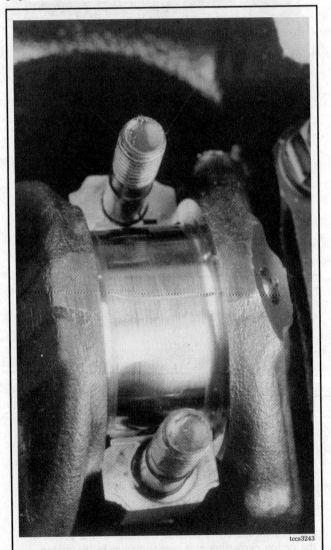

Fig. 176 Apply a strip of gauging material to the bearing journal, then install and tighten the cap

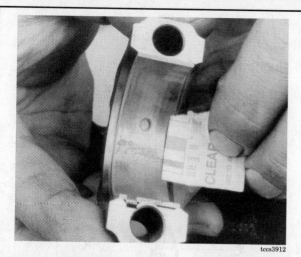

Fig. 177 After the cap is removed, use the scale to check the clearance

7. When the proper size shell is found, clean off the Plasti-gage®, oil the bearing thoroughly, reinstall the cap with its shell and tighten the rod bolt nuts to specification.

➡**With the proper bearing selected and the nuts tightened, it should be possible to move the connecting rod back and forth freely on the crank journal as allowed by the specified connecting rod and clearance. If the rod cannot be moved, either the rod bearing is too far undersize or the rod is misaligned.**

ASSEMBLY AND INSTALLATION

◆ **See Figures 178, 179 and 180**

1. Using a ring expander, install properly gapped piston rings in the grooves, with their gaps staggered.
2. Coat the pistons with clean engine oil and apply a ring compressor. Position the rod and piston assembly (don't forget to install the rod bearing) over the cylinder bore and slide the piston into the cylinder bore until the rod bottoms on the crank journal. Take care to avoid nicking the cylinder walls.

➡**The pistons will have a mark on the crown, such as a groove or notch or stamped symbol. This mark indicates the side of the piston which should face front.**

3. Install the bearing caps with the stamped numbers matched.
4. Tighten the cap bolts (nuts) to specification.

Cylinder Liners and Seals

REMOVAL & INSTALLATION

◆ **See Figures 181 and 182**

➡**This applies to the 2.1L diesel engine only.**

1. Remove the engine from the vehicle.
2. Remove the cylinder head.
3. Remove the oil pan.

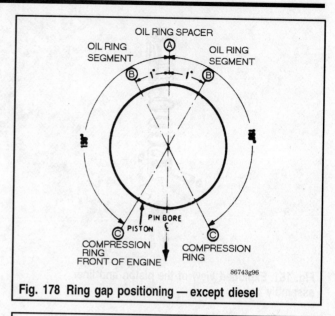

Fig. 178 Ring gap positioning — except diesel

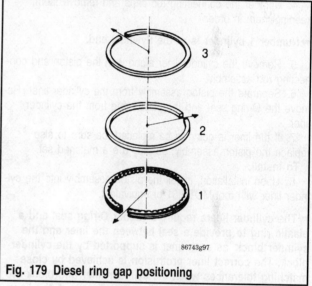

Fig. 179 Diesel ring gap positioning

Fig. 180 Installing the piston in the block using a ring compressor

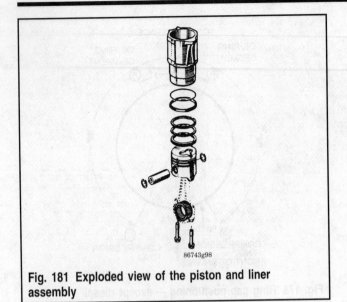

Fig. 181 Exploded view of the piston and liner assembly

4. Number the connecting rod caps and remove them, keeping them in order.

➡**Number 1 cylinder is at the flywheel end.**

5. Remove the cylinder liner along with the piston and connecting rod assembly.

6. Separate the piston assembly from the cylinder liner. Remove the O-ring seal and the plastic ring from the cylinder liner.

7. If the liner is going to be replaced, be sure to also replace the piston assembly, as they are a matched set.

To install:

8. Upon installation, install the piston assembly into the cylinder liner with tool MOT 851 or equivalent.

➡**The cylinder liners require a rubber O-ring seal and a plastic ring to provide a seal between the liner and the cylinder block, as each liner is supported by the cylinder block. The correct liner protrusion is achieved by close matching tolerances when the cylinder liner and block are manufactured. If replacement liners are required, the liner protrusions above the cylinder block must be measured and all the cylinder liners rearranged according to the results of the measurements.**

CYLINDER LINER PROTRUSION MEASUREMENT

◆ **See Figure 183**

1. Insert each reusable cylinder liner in its original position in the cylinder block. If applicable, insert the replacement liner in the cylinder block.

2. Install tool MOT-LM and MOT 251-01 or equivalent, on the engine block and tighten the screw clamp. Position tool MOT 25201 or equivalent, across each cylinder liner, in turn, and secure it with tool MOT 853 or equivalent. Tighten the tool retaining bolts gradually and tighten them to 37 ft. lbs. (50 Nm). This will assure that each cylinder liner will be firmly in contact with the cylinder block.

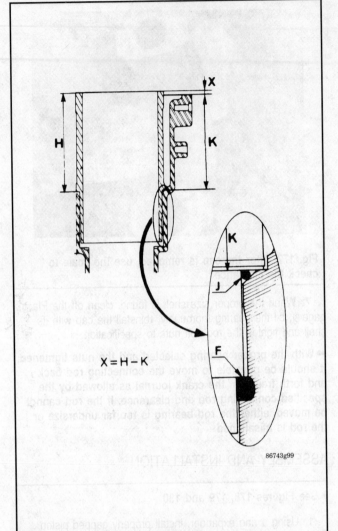

$$X = H - K$$

Fig. 182 Cylinder liner installation. (X) is the liner protrusion, (J) is the rubber O-ring and (F) is the plastic O-ring

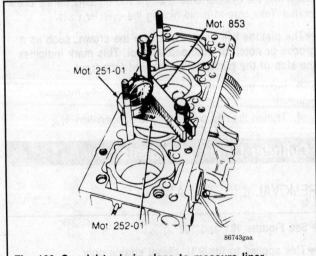

Fig. 183 Special tools in place to measure liner protrusion

3. Measure the protrusion, X, of each cylinder liner above the cylinder block using the dial indicator and block gauge. The correct specification is 0.0019-0.0048 in. (0.050-0.120mm).

4. If an out-of-specification cylinder liner protrusion is measured, install a replacement liner. Measure the protrusion to determine if the cylinder block or the cylinder liner is defective.

5. With all cylinder liner protrusions within specification arrange them so that the difference in protrusion between any two adjacent liners does not exceed 0.015 in. (0.040mm).

6. The protrusions are stepped down from the number one cylinder to the number four cylinder or from the number four cylinder to the number one cylinder.

7. When the correct cylinder liner protrusion arrangement has been determined, match each piston and connecting rod assembly with its original liner and remark each according to the new position in the cylinder block.

Freeze Plugs and Block Heater

REMOVAL & INSTALLATION

▶ See Figures 184, 185 and 186

Freeze plugs are located on the side of the engine block and the front or side of the cylinder heads. Unless you are rebuilding your engine or a freeze plug starts to leak, they require no maintenance.

Block heaters are used to warm the engine coolant prior to initial start up of the engine. They are also used to prevent coolant freeze up in severe climates. The block heater replaces one of the freeze plugs and is plugged into 110v house current via an extension cord routed from the engine compartment.

Installation and removal of freeze plugs is fairly simple. Set aside all components which impede removal of the plug. Use a hammer and punch to remove the freeze plug from the block. Coat the new plug with sealer and install, using a brass drift (a large socket works well too), until the plug is flush with the block.

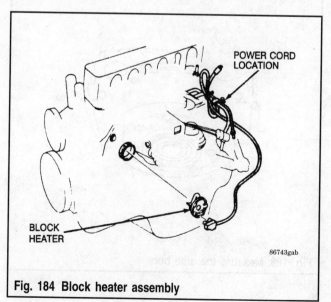

Fig. 184 Block heater assembly

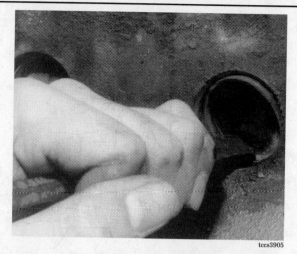

Fig. 185 Using a punch and hammer, the freeze plug can be loosened in the block

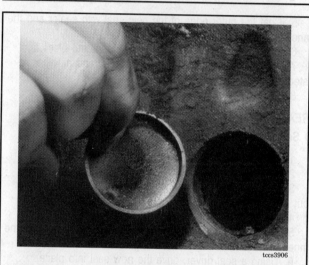

Fig. 186 Once the freeze plug has been loosened, it can be removed from the block

Crankshaft Main Oil Seal

REMOVAL & INSTALLATION

2.1L Diesel Engines

If the end seals are being replaced, remove the engine and place it on an engine stand. If the side seals are being replaced, remove the oil pan. It advisable to replace the end seals if the side seals are leaking.

FRONT END MAIN SEAL

▶ See Figure 187

1. Remove the engine.
2. Remove the timing chain and sprockets.
3. Using a sharp awl, punch a hole in the seal and pry it out of its bore.
4. Thoroughly clean the bore.

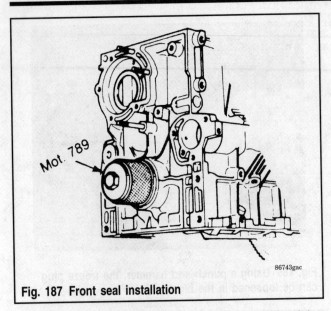

Fig. 187 Front seal installation

5. Coat the outer edge of the new seal with sealer and the inner sealing surface with clean engine oil.

6. Using a seal driver, drive the new seal into place.

7. Install the timing chain and sprockets, and all other related parts.

8. Install the engine.

REAR END MAIN SEAL

▶ See Figure 188

1. Remove the engine.
2. Remove the flywheel.
3. Using a sharp awl, punch a hole in the seal and pry it out of its bore.
4. Thoroughly clean the bore.
5. Coat the outer edge of the new seal with sealer and the inner sealing surface with clean engine oil.
6. Using a seal driver, drive the new seal into place.
7. Install the flywheel.

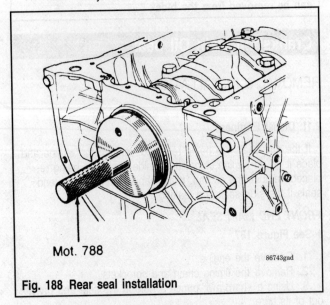

Fig. 188 Rear seal installation

8. Install the engine.

SIDE SEALS

▶ See Figures 189 and 190

➡ **Depending on working clearance, it may be necessary to remove the engine.**

1. Remove the oil pan.
2. Remove the main bearing cap.
3. Remove the side seals.
4. Thoroughly clean the seal surfaces in the block and cap.
5. Install the cap.
6. Measure the width of the seal bore.
7. If the seal bore is 0.196 in. (5mm) or less, use a 0.20 in. (5.1mm) thick seal; if it is more than 0.196 in. (5mm), use a 0.25 in. (5.4mm) thick seal.
8. Remove the bearing cap.
9. Insert the proper side seals in the cap grooves with the grooves in the seals facing outward. Each seal should stick out from the cap about 0.007 in. (0.2mm).
10. Lightly coat the seals with clean engine oil.
11. Cover the length of each seal with a strip of aluminum foil and install the cap and seals in the block. Don't install the cap bolts. Remove the foil.
12. Measure the side seal protrusion above the cap. Protrusion should be greater than 0.027 in. (0.7mm).
13. Tighten the bearing cap bolts to 72 ft. lbs. (98 Nm).
14. Cut the side seals to within 0.019-0.027 in. (0.5-0.7mm) protrusion.
15. Install the oil pan.

2.5L Engines

▶ See Figure 191

1. Remove the transmission.
2. Remove the flywheel.
3. Pry out the seal from around the crankshaft flange.

To install:

4. Coat the inner lip of the new seal with clean engine oil.

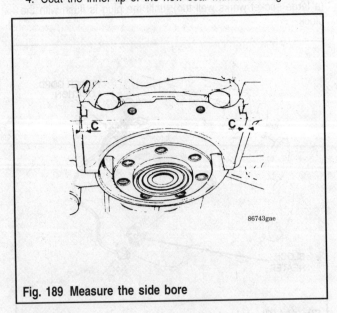

Fig. 189 Measure the side bore

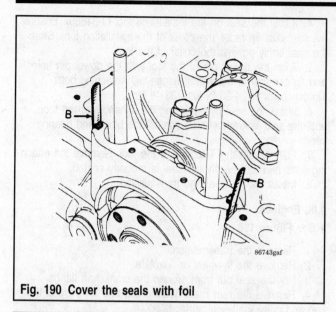

Fig. 190 Cover the seals with foil

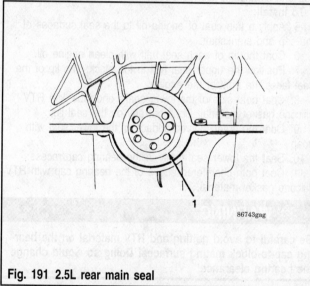

Fig. 191 2.5L rear main seal

5. Gently tap the new seal into place, flush with the block, using a rear main seal installer tool.

➡ **The felt lip must be located inside the flywheel mounting surface. If the lip is not positioned correctly, the flywheel could damage the seal.**

6. Install all parts in reverse order of removal.

2.8L Engines

The General Motors built 2.8L will have one of two different rear main seal assemblies: either a 1-piece or 2-piece seal. The 2-piece type requires removal of the rear main bearing cap for servicing. The wide, 1-piece seal, used on later model engines, requires the removal of the transmission and flywheel.

2-PIECE

▶ See Figures 192 and 193

1. Remove the oil pan and pump.

2. Remove the rear main bearing cap.

3. Gently pack the upper seal into the groove approximate ¼ in. (6mm) on each side.

4. Measure the amount the seal was driven in on one side and add ¹⁄₁₆ in. (1.5mm). Cut this length from the old lower cap seal. Be sure to get a sharp cut. Repeat for the other side.

5. Place the piece of cut seal into the groove and pack the seal into the block. Do this for each side.

➡ **GM makes a guide tool (J-29114-1) which bolts to the block via an oil pan bolt hole, and a packing tool (J29114-2) which are machined to provide a built-in stop for the installation of the short cut pieces. Using the packing tool, work the short pieces of seal onto the guide tool, then pack them into the block with the packing tool.**

6. Install a new lower seal in the rear main cap.

7. Install a piece of Plastigage® or the equivalent on the bearing journal. Install the rear cap and tighten to 70 ft. lbs. (95 Nm). Remove the cap and check the gauge for bearing clearance. If out of specification, the ends of the seal may be frayed or not flush, preventing the cap from proper sealing. Correct as required.

8. Clean the journal, and apply a thin film of RTV silicone sealer to the mating surfaces of the cap and block. Do not allow any sealer to get onto the journal or bearing. Install the bearing cap and tighten to 70 ft. lbs. (95 Nm). Install the pan and pump.

1-PIECE

▶ See Figures 194 and 195

1. Remove transmission and flywheel.

2. Using an appropriate tool, pry the seal from around the crankshaft flange. Insert the prytool under the seal dust lip and pry up and out.

➡ **DO NOT allow the prytool to contact the crankshaft journal surface.**

To install:

3. Clean and lubricate the inner and outer surfaces of the replacement seal thoroughly with engine oil.

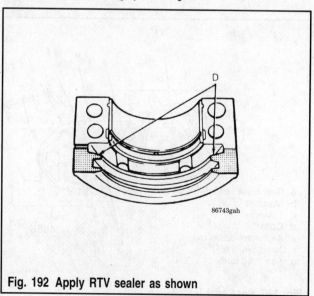

Fig. 192 Apply RTV sealer as shown

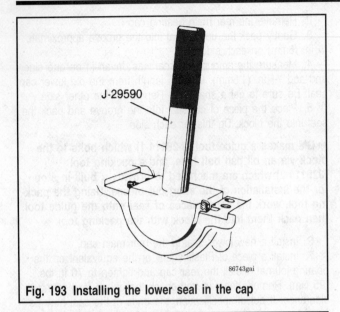

Fig. 193 Installing the lower seal in the cap

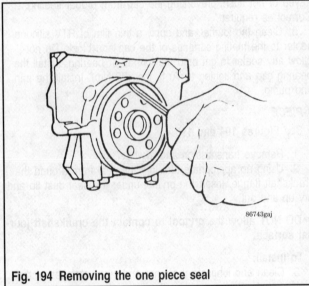

Fig. 194 Removing the one piece seal

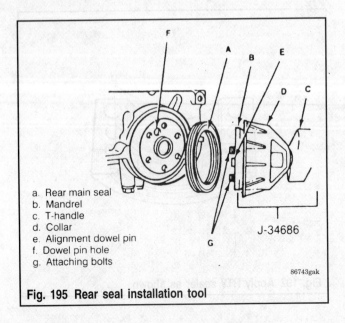

a. Rear main seal
b. Mandrel
c. T-handle
d. Collar
e. Alignment dowel pin
f. Dowel pin hole
g. Attaching bolts

Fig. 195 Rear seal installation tool

4. Install the seal on the installation tool (J-34686). Ensure the seal dust lip faces the collar of the installation tool. Seat the seal firmly against the collar of the tool.

5. Align the dowel pin of the tool with the dowel pin hole and tighten tool to crankshaft flange with attaching bolts. Tighten bolts to 24-36 ft. lbs. (33-49 Nm).

6. Install the seal by tightening the T-handle of the tool until the seal is firmly seated against the block and bearing cap.

7. Fully retract the T-handle of the tool. Remove the attaching bolts and tool. Verify the seal is properly seated.

8. Install the flywheel and transmission.

4.0L Engines

▶ See Figure 196

1. Remove the transmission.
2. Remove the flywheel or flexplate.
3. Pry the seal out from around the crankshaft flange.
4. Remove the rear main bearing cap and wipe clean the cap and crankshaft seal surfaces.

To install:

5. Apply a thin coat of engine oil to the seal surfaces of the cap and crankshaft.

6. Coat the lip of each seal half with clean engine oil.

7. Position the upper seal half in the block. The lip of the seal faces the front of the engine.

8. Coat both side of the lower seal's end tabs with RTV silicone gasket material. Don't get any on the seal lip.

9. Coat the outer, curved surface of the lower seal with soap.

10. Seat the lower seal firmly in the bearing cap recess.

11. Coat both chamfered edges of the bearing cap with RTV silicone gasket material.

✳✳WARNING

Be careful to avoid getting and RTV material on the bearing cap-to-block mating surfaces! Doing so would change the bearing clearance!

12. Install the bearing cap.

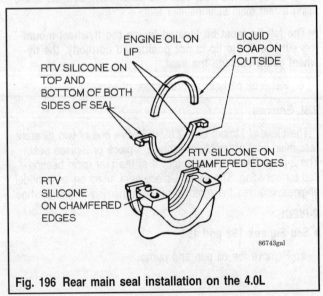

ENGINE OIL ON LIP

LIQUID SOAP ON OUTSIDE

RTV SILICONE ON TOP AND BOTTOM OF BOTH SIDES OF SEAL

RTV SILICONE ON CHAMFERED EDGES

RTV SILICONE ON CHAMFERED EDGES

Fig. 196 Rear main seal installation on the 4.0L

13. Tighten all the main bearing caps to 80 ft. lbs. (108 Nm).

5.2L Engines

1. Remove the oil pan.
2. Remove the oil pump.
3. Remove the rear bearing cap. Remove and discard the old lower seal.
4. Carefully remove and discard the the upper seal.
5. Lightly oil the new upper seal lips with engine oil. To allow ease of installation of the seal, loosen at least 2 main bearing caps.
6. Rotate the new upper seal into the cylinder block being careful not to shave or cut the outer surface of the seal. Install the new seal with the yellow paint facing towards the rear of the engine.
7. Install the new lower seal with the yellow paint facing the rear of the engine.
8. Apply a 0.20 in. (5mm) drop of Loctite® 515 or equivalent on each side of the rear main bearing cap. Do not allow sealant to contact the seal. Assemble the cap immediately.
9. Install the cap with cleaned and oiled bolts. Alternately tighten all cap bolts to 85 ft. lbs. (115 Nm).
10. Install the oil pump.
11. Install the oil pan.

Crankshaft and Main Bearings

REMOVAL & INSTALLATION

1. With the engine removed from the vehicle and placed on an engine stand, disconnect the spark plug wires from the spark plugs and remove the wires and bracket assembly from the attaching stud on the rocker arm cover(s) if so equipped. Disconnect the coil to distributor high tension lead at the coil. Remove the distributor cap and spark plug wires as an assembly. Remove the spark plugs to allow easy rotation of the crankshaft.
2. Remove the fuel pump and oil filter. Slide the water pump by-pass hose clamp (if so equipped) toward the water pump. Remove the alternator and mounting brackets.
3. Remove the crankshaft pulley from the crankshaft vibration damper. Remove the capscrew and washer from the end of the crankshaft. Install a universal puller on the crankshaft vibration damper and remove the damper.
4. Remove the timing chain belt cover and crankshaft sprockets/gears and chain/belt.
5. Invert the engine on the work stand. Remove the clutch pressure plate and disc (manual shift transmission). Remove the flywheel and engine rear cover plate (automatic transmission). Remove the oil pan and gasket. Remove the oil pump.
6. Make sure all bearing caps (main and connecting rod) are marked so that they can be installed in their original locations. Turn the crankshaft until the connecting rod from which the cap is being removed is down, and remove the bearing cap. Push the connecting rod and piston assembly up into the cylinder. Repeat this procedure until all the connecting rod bearing caps are removed.

7. Remove the main bearings caps.
8. Carefully lift the crankshaft out of the block so that the thrust bearing surfaces are not damaged. Handle the crankshaft with care to avoid possible damage to the finished surfaces.

➡If the engine is equipped with a one piece rear main seal, remove the seal prior to removing the crankshaft.

9. Remove the rear main seal from the block and rear main bearing cap.
10. Remove the main bearing inserts from the block and bearing caps.
11. Remove the connecting rod bearing inserts from the connecting rods and caps.

To install:

12. If the crankshaft main bearing journals have been refinished to a definite undersize, install the correct undersize bearings. Be sure the bearing inserts and bearing bores are clean. Foreign material under the inserts will distort the bearing and cause a failure.
13. Place the upper main bearing inserts in position in the bores with the tang fitting in the slot. Be sure the oil holes in the bearing inserts are aligned with the oil holes in the cylinder block.
14. Install the lower main bearing inserts in the bearing caps.
15. Check all bearing clearances with Plastigage®. If clearance is not within specification, check the crankshaft and crankshaft bearing bore for correct size. Recondition as necessary.
16. Clean the rear main oil seal groove and the mating surfaces of the block and rear main bearing cap.
17. Dip the lip-type seal halves in clean engine oil. Install the seals in the bearing cap and block with the undercut side of the seal toward the front of the engine.

➡This procedure applies only to engines with two-piece rear main bearing oil seals. those having one-piece seals will be installed after the crankshaft is in place.

18. Carefully lower the crankshaft into place. Be careful not to damage the bearing surfaces.
19. Install all the bearing caps except the thrust bearing cap. Be sure the main bearing caps are installed in their original locations. Tighten the bearing cap bolts to specifications.
20. Install the thrust bearing cap with the bolts finger-tight.
21. Pry the crankshaft forward against the thrust surface of the upper half of the bearing.
22. Hold the crankshaft forward and pry the thrust bearing cap to the rear. This will align the thrust surfaces of both halves of the bearing.
23. Retain the forward pressure on the crankshaft. Tighten the cap bolts to specifications.
24. Check the crankshaft end-play.
25. On engines with one piece rear main bearing oil seal, coat a new crankshaft rear oil seal with oil and install using a seal driver. Inspect the seal to be sure it was not damaged during installation.
26. Install new bearing inserts in the connecting rods and caps. Check the clearance of each bearing. If clearance is not within specification, check the size of the crankshaft journal and connecting rod bore. Recondition as necessary.

27. After the connecting rod bearings have been fitted, apply a light coat of engine oil to the journals and bearings.

28. Turn the crankshaft throw to the bottom of its stroke. Push the piston all the way down until the rod bearing seats on the crankshaft journal.

29. Install the connecting rod cap using a feeler gauge to keep cap and rod aligned. Tighten the nuts to specification.

30. After the piston and connecting rod assemblies have been installed, check the side clearance with a feeler gauge between the connecting rods on each connecting rod crankshaft journal. Refer to Crankshaft and Connecting Rod specifications chart in this section.

31. Install all other components in reverse order of removal.

CLEANING AND INSPECTION

Crankshaft

➡**Handle the crankshaft carefully to avoid damage to the finish surfaces.**

1. Clean the crankshaft with solvent, and blow out all oil passages with compressed air.

2. Use crocus cloth to remove any sharp edges, burrs or other imperfections which might damage the oil seal during installation or cause premature seal wear.

➡**Do not use crocus cloth to polish the seal surfaces. A finely polished surface may produce poor sealing or cause premature seal wear.**

3. Inspect the main and connecting rod journals for cracks, scratches, grooves or scores.

4. Measure the diameter of each journal at least four places to determine out-of-round, taper or undersize condition.

5. On an engine with a manual transmission, check the fit of the clutch pilot bearing in the bore of the crankshaft. A needle roller bearing and adapter assembly is used as a clutch pilot bearing. It is inserted directly into the engine crank shaft. The bearing and adapter assembly cannot be serviced separately. A new bearing must be installed whenever a bearing is removed.

Main Bearings

1. Check the clearance of each main bearing by using the following procedure:

   a. Place a piece of Plastigage® or its equivalent, on bearing surface across full width of bearing cap and about ¼ in. (6mm) off-center.

   b. Install cap and tighten bolts to specifications. Do not turn crankshaft while Plastigage® is in place.

   c. Remove the cap. Using Plastigage® scale, check width of Plastigage® at widest point to get the minimum clearance. Check at narrowest point to get maximum clearance. Difference between readings is taper of journal.

   d. If clearance exceeds specified limits, try a 0.001 in. (0.0254mm) or 0.002 in. (0.051mm) undersize bearing in combination with the standard bearing. Bearing clearance must be within specified limits. If standard and 0.002 in. (0.051mm) undersize bearing does not bring clearance within desired limits, refinish crankshaft journal, then install undersize bearings.

2. Install all the bearing caps except the thrust bearing cap. Be sure the main bearing caps are installed in their original locations. Tighten the bearing cap bolts to specifications.

3. Install the thrust bearing cap with the bolts finger-tight.

4. Pry the crankshaft forward against the thrust surface of the upper half of the bearing.

5. Hold the crankshaft forward and pry the thrust bearing cap to the rear. This will align the thrust surfaces of both halves of the bearing.

6. Retain the forward pressure on the crankshaft. Tighten the cap bolts to specifications.

Crankshaft End-Play
▶ **See Figures 197 and 198**

1. Check the crankshaft end-play after installing all main bearing caps and aligning thrust bearing inserts.

2. Force the crankshaft forward and then toward the rear of the engine.

3. Install a dial indicator so that the contact point rests against the crankshaft flange and the indicator axis is parallel to the crankshaft axis.

4. Zero the dial indicator. Push the crankshaft forward and note the reading on the dial.

5. If the end-play exceeds the wear limit listed in the Crankshaft and Connecting Rod Specifications chart, replace the thrust bearing. If the end-play is less than the minimum limit, inspect the thrust bearing faces for scratches, burrs, nicks, or dirt. If the thrust faces are not damaged or dirty, then they probably were not aligned properly.

Flywheel and Ring Gear

REMOVAL & INSTALLATION

1. Remove the transmission and transfer case.

2. Remove the clutch or torque converter, from the flywheel. The flywheel bolts should be loosened a little at a time in a cross pattern to avoid warping the flywheel. On trucks

tccs3805

Fig. 197 A dial gauge may be used to check crankshaft end-play

Fig. 198 Carefully pry the shaft back and forth while reading the dial gauge for play

with manual transmission, replace the pilot bearing in the end of the crankshaft if removing the flywheel.

EXHAUST SYSTEM

General Information

➡Safety glasses should be worn at all times when working on or near the exhaust system. Older exhaust systems will almost always be covered with loose rust particles which will shower you when disturbed. These particles are more than a nuisance and could injure your eye.

Whenever working on the exhaust system always keep the following in mind:
• Check the complete exhaust system for open seams, holes loose connections, or other deterioration which could permit exhaust fumes to seep into the passenger compartment.
• The exhaust system is usually supported by free-hanging rubber mountings which permit some movement of the exhaust system, but does not permit transfer of noise and vibration into the passenger compartment. Do not replace the rubber mounts with solid ones.
• Before removing any component of the exhaust system, ALWAYS squirt a liquid rust dissolving agent onto the fasteners for ease of removal. A lot of knuckle skin will be saved by following this rule. It may even be wise to spray the fasteners and allow them to sit overnight.

✳✳CAUTION

Allow the exhaust system to cool sufficiently before spraying a solvent exhaust fasteners. Some solvents are highly flammable and could ignite when sprayed on hot exhaust components.

• Annoying rattles and noise vibrations in the exhaust system are usually caused by misalignment of the parts. When

3. The flywheel should be checked for cracks and glazing. It can be resurfaced by a machine shop.

4. Installation is the reverse of removal. Tighten the bolts a little at a time in a cross pattern, to the torque figure shown in the Torque Specifications Chart.

RING GEAR REPLACEMENT

➡The ring gear is replaceable only on engines mated with a manual transmission. Engines with automatic transmissions have ring gears which are welded to the flexplate.

1. If the ring gear is to be replaced, drill a hole in the gear between two teeth, being careful not to contact the flywheel surface. Using a cold chisel at this point, crack the ring gear and remove it.
2. Polish the inner surface of the new ring gear and heat it in an oven to about 600°F (315°C). Chill the flywheel in the freezer for a few minutes. Quickly place the ring gear on the flywheel and tap it into place, making sure that it is fully seated.

➡Never heat the ring gear past 800°F (426°C), or the tempering will be destroyed.

aligning the system, leave all bolts and nuts loose until all parts are properly aligned, then tighten, working from front to rear.
• When installing exhaust system parts, make sure there is enough clearance between the hot exhaust parts and pipes and hoses that would be adversely affected by excessive heat. Also make sure there is adequate clearance from the floor pan to avoid possible overheating of the floor.

COMPONENT REPLACEMENT

▶ See Figure 199

Exhaust Downpipe
▶ See Figure 200

1. Raise and safely suppport the vehicle on jackstands.
2. Saturate all bolts and nuts with penetrating lubricant.
3. Disconnect the downpipe from the manifold and discard the seal.
4. Support the transmission with a floor jack and remove the rear crossmember.
5. Remove the pipe-to-flywheel housing bracket.
6. Support the catalytic converter and disconnect the downpipe. Discard the gasket.
7. Installation is the reverse of removal. Use new gaskets and seals. Tighten all fasteners to 23 ft. lbs. (31 Nm).

Catalytic Converter
▶ See Figures 201 and 202

1. Raise and safely support the vehicle on jackstands.
2. Saturate all bolts and nuts with penetrating lubricant.
3. Remove the converter-to-muffler clamp.

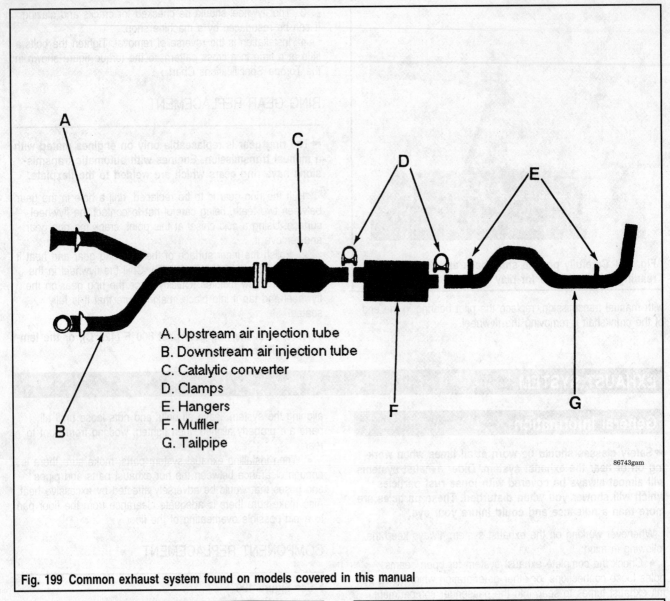

A. Upstream air injection tube
B. Downstream air injection tube
C. Catalytic converter
D. Clamps
E. Hangers
F. Muffler
G. Tailpipe

86743gam

Fig. 199 Common exhaust system found on models covered in this manual

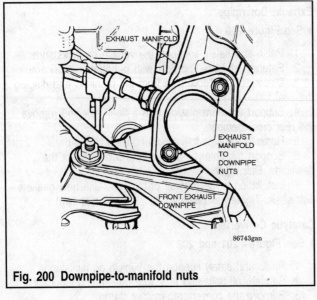

86743gan

Fig. 200 Downpipe-to-manifold nuts

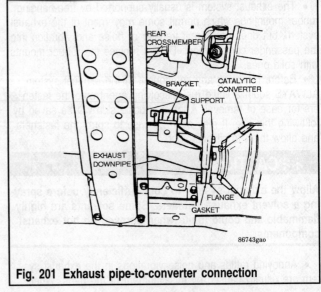

86743gao

Fig. 201 Exhaust pipe-to-converter connection

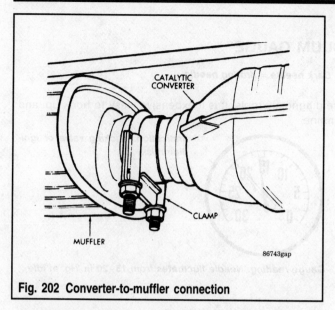

Fig. 202 Converter-to-muffler connection

4. Heat the converter-to-muffler connection with a torch until it becomes cherry red.

5. Remove all muffler hangers and twist the muffler back-and-forth to free it from the converter.

6. Disconnect the downpipe from the converter. Discard the gasket.

7. Installation is the reverse of removal. Use new gaskets. Tighten the downpipe connection to 23 ft. lbs. (31 Nm); the muffler clamp to 45 ft. lbs. (61 Nm).

Muffler and Tailpipe

▶ **See Figure 203**

1. Raise and safely support the vehicle on jackstands.

2. Saturate all bolts and nuts with penetrating lubricant.

3. Remove the converter-to-muffler clamp.

4. Heat the converter-to-muffler connection with a torch until it becomes cherry red.

5. Remove all muffler hangers and twist the muffler back-and-forth to free it from the converter.

➡**Original equipment mufflers are welded to the tailpipe. Replacement mufflers and tailpipes clamp together.**

6. Installation is the reverse of removal. Tighten the muffler-to-converter clamp bolt to 45 ft. lbs. (61 Nm).

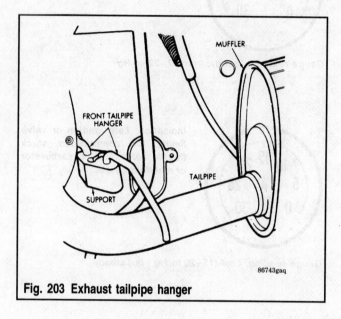

Fig. 203 Exhaust tailpipe hanger

USING A VACUUM GAUGE

White needle = steady needle   *Dark needle = drifting needle*

The vacuum gauge is one of the most useful and easy-to-use diagnostic tools. It is inexpensive, easy to hook up, and provides valuable information about the condition of your engine.

Indication: Normal engine in good condition

Gauge reading: Steady, from 17–22 in./Hg.

Indication: Sticking valve or ignition miss

Gauge reading: Needle fluctuates from 15–20 in./Hg. at idle

Indication: Late ignition or valve timing, low compression, stuck throttle valve, leaking carburetor or manifold gasket.

Gauge reading: Low (15–20 in./Hg.) but steady

Indication: Improper carburetor adjustment, or minor intake leak at carburetor or manifold

NOTE: Bad fuel injector O-rings may also cause this reading.

Gauge reading: Drifting needle

Indication: Weak valve springs, worn valve stem guides, or leaky cylinder head gasket (vibrating excessively at all speeds).

NOTE: A plugged catalytic converter may also cause this reading.

Gauge reading: Needle fluctuates as engine speed increases

Indication: Burnt valve or improper valve clearance. The needle will drop when the defective valve operates.

Gauge reading: Steady needle, but drops regularly

Indication: Choked muffler or obstruction in system. Speed up the engine. Choked muffler will exhibit a slow drop of vacuum to zero.

Gauge reading: Gradual drop in reading at idle

Indication: Worn valve guides

Gauge reading: Needle vibrates excessively at idle, but steadies as engine speed increases

Troubleshooting Engine Mechanical Problems

Problem	Cause	Solution
External oil leaks	• Cylinder head cover RTV sealant broken or improperly seated	• Replace sealant; inspect cylinder head cover sealant flange and cylinder head sealant surface for distortion and cracks
	• Oil filler cap leaking or missing	• Replace cap
	• Oil filter gasket broken or improperly seated	• Replace oil filter
	• Oil pan side gasket broken, improperly seated or opening in RTV sealant	• Replace gasket or repair opening in sealant; inspect oil pan gasket flange for distortion
	• Oil pan front oil seal broken or improperly seated	• Replace seal; inspect timing case cover and oil pan seal flange for distortion
	• Oil pan rear oil seal broken or improperly seated	• Replace seal; inspect oil pan rear oil seal flange; inspect rear main bearing cap for cracks, plugged oil return channels, or distortion in seal groove
	• Timing case cover oil seal broken or improperly seated	• Replace seal
	• Excess oil pressure because of restricted PCV valve	• Replace PCV valve
	• Oil pan drain plug loose or has stripped threads	• Repair as necessary and tighten
	• Rear oil gallery plug loose	• Use appropriate sealant on gallery plug and tighten
	• Rear camshaft plug loose or improperly seated	• Seat camshaft plug or replace and seal, as necessary
Excessive oil consumption	• Oil level too high	• Drain oil to specified level
	• Oil with wrong viscosity being used	• Replace with specified oil
	• PCV valve stuck closed	• Replace PCV valve
	• Valve stem oil deflectors (or seals) are damaged, missing, or incorrect type	• Replace valve stem oil deflectors
	• Valve stems or valve guides worn	• Measure stem-to-guide clearance and repair as necessary
	• Poorly fitted or missing valve cover baffles	• Replace valve cover
	• Piston rings broken or missing	• Replace broken or missing rings
	• Scuffed piston	• Replace piston
	• Incorrect piston ring gap	• Measure ring gap, repair as necessary
	• Piston rings sticking or excessively loose in grooves	• Measure ring side clearance, repair as necessary
	• Compression rings installed upside down	• Repair as necessary
	• Cylinder walls worn, scored, or glazed	• Repair as necessary

tccs3c02

Troubleshooting Engine Mechanical Problems

Problem	Cause	Solution
Excessive oil consumption (cont.)	• Piston ring gaps not properly staggered	• Repair as necessary
	• Excessive main or connecting rod bearing clearance	• Measure bearing clearance, repair as necessary
No oil pressure	• Low oil level	• Add oil to correct level
	• Oil pressure gauge, warning lamp or sending unit inaccurate	• Replace oil pressure gauge or warning lamp
	• Oil pump malfunction	• Replace oil pump
	• Oil pressure relief valve sticking	• Remove and inspect oil pressure relief valve assembly
	• Oil passages on pressure side of pump obstructed	• Inspect oil passages for obstruction
	• Oil pickup screen or tube obstructed	• Inspect oil pickup for obstruction
	• Loose oil inlet tube	• Tighten or seal inlet tube
Low oil pressure	• Low oil level	• Add oil to correct level
	• Inaccurate gauge, warning lamp or sending unit	• Replace oil pressure gauge or warning lamp
	• Oil excessively thin because of dilution, poor quality, or improper grade	• Drain and refill crankcase with recommended oil
	• Excessive oil temperature	• Correct cause of overheating engine
	• Oil pressure relief spring weak or sticking	• Remove and inspect oil pressure relief valve assembly
	• Oil inlet tube and screen assembly has restriction or air leak	• Remove and inspect oil inlet tube and screen assembly. (Fill inlet tube with lacquer thinner to locate leaks.)
	• Excessive oil pump clearance	• Measure clearances
	• Excessive main, rod, or camshaft bearing clearance	• Measure bearing clearances, repair as necessary
High oil pressure	• Improper oil viscosity	• Drain and refill crankcase with correct viscosity oil
	• Oil pressure gauge or sending unit inaccurate	• Replace oil pressure gauge
	• Oil pressure relief valve sticking closed	• Remove and inspect oil pressure relief valve assembly
Main bearing noise	• Insufficient oil supply	• Inspect for low oil level and low oil pressure
	• Main bearing clearance excessive	• Measure main bearing clearance, repair as necessary
	• Bearing insert missing	• Replace missing insert
	• Crankshaft end-play excessive	• Measure end-play, repair as necessary
	• Improperly tightened main bearing cap bolts	• Tighten bolts with specified torque
	• Loose flywheel or drive plate	• Tighten flywheel or drive plate attaching bolts
	• Loose or damaged vibration damper	• Repair as necessary

Troubleshooting Engine Mechanical Problems

Problem	Cause	Solution
Connecting rod bearing noise	• Insufficient oil supply	• Inspect for low oil level and low oil pressure
	• Carbon build-up on piston	• Remove carbon from piston crown
	• Bearing clearance excessive or bearing missing	• Measure clearance, repair as necessary
	• Crankshaft connecting rod journal out-of-round	• Measure journal dimensions, repair or replace as necessary
	• Misaligned connecting rod or cap	• Repair as necessary
	• Connecting rod bolts tightened improperly	• Tighten bolts with specified torque
Piston noise	• Piston-to-cylinder wall clearance excessive (scuffed piston)	• Measure clearance and examine piston
	• Cylinder walls excessively tapered or out-of-round	• Measure cylinder wall dimensions, rebore cylinder
	• Piston ring broken	• Replace all rings on piston
	• Loose or seized piston pin	• Measure piston-to-pin clearance, repair as necessary
	• Connecting rods misaligned	• Measure rod alignment, straighten or replace
	• Piston ring side clearance excessively loose or tight	• Measure ring side clearance, repair as necessary
	• Carbon build-up on piston is excessive	• Remove carbon from piston
Valve actuating component noise	• Insufficient oil supply	• Check for: (a) Low oil level (b) Low oil pressure (c) Wrong hydraulic tappets (d) Restricted oil gallery (e) Excessive tappet to bore clearance
	• Rocker arms or pivots worn	• Replace worn rocker arms or pivots
	• Foreign objects or chips in hydraulic tappets	• Clean tappets
	• Excessive tappet leak-down	• Replace valve tappet
	• Tappet face worn	• Replace tappet; inspect corresponding cam lobe for wear
	• Broken or cocked valve springs	• Properly seat cocked springs; replace broken springs
	• Stem-to-guide clearance excessive	• Measure stem-to-guide clearance, repair as required
	• Valve bent	• Replace valve
	• Loose rocker arms	• Check and repair as necessary
	• Valve seat runout excessive	• Regrind valve seat/valves
	• Missing valve lock	• Install valve lock
	• Excessive engine oil	• Correct oil level

tccs3c04

Troubleshooting Engine Performance

Problem	Cause	Solution
Hard starting (engine cranks normally)	• Faulty engine control system component • Faulty fuel pump • Faulty fuel system component • Faulty ignition coil • Improper spark plug gap • Incorrect ignition timing • Incorrect valve timing	• Repair or replace as necessary • Replace fuel pump • Repair or replace as necessary • Test and replace as necessary • Adjust gap • Adjust timing • Check valve timing; repair as necessary
Rough idle or stalling	• Incorrect curb or fast idle speed • Incorrect ignition timing • Improper feedback system operation • Faulty EGR valve operation • Faulty PCV valve air flow • Faulty TAC vacuum motor or valve • Air leak into manifold vacuum • Faulty distributor rotor or cap • Improperly seated valves • Incorrect ignition wiring • Faulty ignition coil • Restricted air vent or idle passages • Restricted air cleaner	• Adjust curb or fast idle speed (If possible) • Adjust timing to specification • Refer to Chapter 4 • Test EGR system and replace as necessary • Test PCV valve and replace as necessary • Repair as necessary • Inspect manifold vacuum connections and repair as necessary • Replace rotor or cap (Distributor systems only) • Test cylinder compression, repair as necessary • Inspect wiring and correct as necessary • Test coil and replace as necessary • Clean passages • Clean or replace air cleaner filter element
Faulty low-speed operation	• Restricted idle air vents and passages • Restricted air cleaner • Faulty spark plugs • Dirty, corroded, or loose ignition secondary circuit wire connections • Improper feedback system operation • Faulty ignition coil high voltage wire • Faulty distributor cap	• Clean air vents and passages • Clean or replace air cleaner filter element • Clean or replace spark plugs • Clean or tighten secondary circuit wire connections • Refer to Chapter 4 • Replace ignition coil high voltage wire (Distributor systems only) • Replace cap (Distributor systems only)
Faulty acceleration	• Incorrect ignition timing • Faulty fuel system component • Faulty spark plug(s) • Improperly seated valves • Faulty ignition coil	• Adjust timing • Repair or replace as necessary • Clean or replace spark plug(s) • Test cylinder compression, repair as necessary • Test coil and replace as necessary

tccs3c05

Troubleshooting Engine Performance

Problem	Cause	Solution
Faulty acceleration (cont.)	• Improper feedback system operation	• Refer to Chapter 4
Faulty high speed operation	• Incorrect ignition timing • Faulty advance mechanism	• Adjust timing (if possible) • Check advance mechanism and repair as necessary (Distributor systems only)
	• Low fuel pump volume • Wrong spark plug air gap or wrong plug	• Replace fuel pump • Adjust air gap or install correct plug
	• Partially restricted exhaust manifold, exhaust pipe, catalytic converter, muffler, or tailpipe	• Eliminate restriction
	• Restricted vacuum passages • Restricted air cleaner	• Clean passages • Cleaner or replace filter element as necessary
	• Faulty distributor rotor or cap	• Replace rotor or cap (Distributor systems only)
	• Faulty ignition coil • Improperly seated valve(s)	• Test coil and replace as necessary • Test cylinder compression, repair as necessary
	• Faulty valve spring(s)	• Inspect and test valve spring tension, replace as necessary
	• Incorrect valve timing	• Check valve timing and repair as necessary
	• Intake manifold restricted	• Remove restriction or replace manifold
	• Worn distributor shaft	• Replace shaft (Distributor systems only)
	• Improper feedback system operation	• Refer to Chapter 4
Misfire at all speeds	• Faulty spark plug(s) • Faulty spark plug wire(s) • Faulty distributor cap or rotor	• Clean or relace spark plug(s) • Replace as necessary • Replace cap or rotor (Distributor systems only)
	• Faulty ignition coil • Primary ignition circuit shorted or open intermittently	• Test coil and replace as necessary • Troubleshoot primary circuit and repair as necessary
	• Improperly seated valve(s)	• Test cylinder compression, repair as necessary
	• Faulty hydraulic tappet(s) • Improper feedback system operation	• Clean or replace tappet(s) • Refer to Chapter 4
	• Faulty valve spring(s)	• Inspect and test valve spring tension, repair as necessary
	• Worn camshaft lobes • Air leak into manifold	• Replace camshaft • Check manifold vacuum and repair as necessary
	• Fuel pump volume or pressure low • Blown cylinder head gasket • Intake or exhaust manifold passage(s) restricted	• Replace fuel pump • Replace gasket • Pass chain through passage(s) and repair as necessary
Power not up to normal	• Incorrect ignition timing • Faulty distributor rotor	• Adjust timing • Replace rotor (Distributor systems only)

Troubleshooting Engine Performance

Problem	Cause	Solution
Power not up to normal (cont.)	• Incorrect spark plug gap	• Adjust gap
	• Faulty fuel pump	• Replace fuel pump
	• Faulty fuel pump	• Replace fuel pump
	• Incorrect valve timing	• Check valve timing and repair as necessary
	• Faulty ignition coil	• Test coil and replace as necessary
	• Faulty ignition wires	• Test wires and replace as necessary
	• Improperly seated valves	• Test cylinder compression and repair as necessary
	• Blown cylinder head gasket	• Replace gasket
	• Leaking piston rings	• Test compression and repair as necessary
	• Improper feedback system operation	• Refer to Chapter 4
Intake backfire	• Improper ignition timing	• Adjust timing
	• Defective EGR component	• Repair as necessary
	• Defective TAC vacuum motor or valve	• Repair as necessary
Exhaust backfire	• Air leak into manifold vacuum	• Check manifold vacuum and repair as necessary
	• Faulty air injection diverter valve	• Test diverter valve and replace as necessary
	• Exhaust leak	• Locate and eliminate leak
Ping or spark knock	• Incorrect ignition timing	• Adjust timing
	• Distributor advance malfunction	• Inspect advance mechanism and repair as necessary (Distributor systems only)
	• Excessive combustion chamber deposits	• Remove with combustion chamber cleaner
	• Air leak into manifold vacuum	• Check manifold vacuum and repair as necessary
	• Excessively high compression	• Test compression and repair as necessary
	• Fuel octane rating excessively low	• Try alternate fuel source
	• Sharp edges in combustion chamber	• Grind smooth
	• EGR valve not functioning properly	• Test EGR system and replace as necessary
Surging (at cruising to top speeds)	• Low fuel pump pressure or volume	• Replace fuel pump
	• Improper PCV valve air flow	• Test PCV valve and replace as necessary
	• Air leak into manifold vacuum	• Check manifold vacuum and repair as necessary
	• Incorrect spark advance	• Test and replace as necessary
	• Restricted fuel filter	• Replace fuel filter
	• Restricted air cleaner	• Clean or replace air cleaner filter element
	• EGR valve not functioning properly	• Test EGR system and replace as necessary
	• Improper feedback system operation	• Refer to Chapter 4

tccs3c07

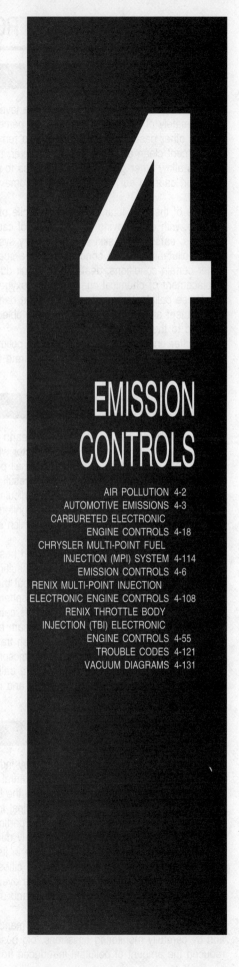

4

EMISSION
CONTROLS

AIR POLLUTION

The earth's atmosphere, at or near sea level, consists approximately of 78 percent nitrogen, 21 percent oxygen and 1 percent other gases. If it were possible to remain in this state, 100 percent clean air would result. However, many varied sources allow other gases and particulates to mix with the clean air, causing our atmosphere to become unclean or polluted.

Some of these pollutants are visible while others are invisible, with each having the capability of causing distress to the eyes, ears, throat, skin and respiratory system. Should these pollutants become concentrated in a specific area and under certain conditions, death could result due to the displacement or chemical change of the oxygen content in the air. These pollutants can also cause great damage to the environment and to the many man made objects that are exposed to the elements.

To better understand the causes of air pollution, the pollutants can be categorized into 3 separate types, natural, industrial and automotive.

Natural Pollutants

Natural pollution has been present on earth since before man appeared and continues to be a factor when discussing air pollution, although it causes only a small percentage of the overall pollution problem. It is the direct result of decaying organic matter, wind born smoke and particulates from such natural events as plain and forest fires (ignited by heat or lightning), volcanic ash, sand and dust which can spread over a large area of the countryside.

Such a phenomenon of natural pollution has been seen in the form of volcanic eruptions, with the resulting plume of smoke, steam and volcanic ash blotting out the sun's rays as it spreads and rises higher into the atmosphere. As it travels into the atmosphere the upper air currents catch and carry the smoke and ash, while condensing the steam back into water vapor. As the water vapor, smoke and ash travel on their journey, the smoke dissipates into the atmosphere while the ash and moisture settle back to earth in a trail hundreds of miles long. In some cases, lives are lost and millions of dollars of property damage result.

Industrial Pollutants

Industrial pollution is caused primarily by industrial processes, the burning of coal, oil and natural gas, which in turn produce smoke and fumes. Because the burning fuels contain large amounts of sulfur, the principal ingredients of smoke and fumes are sulfur dioxide and particulate matter. This type of pollutant occurs most severely during still, damp and cool weather, such as at night. Even in its less severe form, this pollutant is not confined to just cities. Because of air movements, the pollutants move for miles over the surrounding countryside, leaving in its path a barren and unhealthy environment for all living things.

Working with Federal, State and Local mandated regulations and by carefully monitoring emissions, big business has greatly reduced the amount of pollutant introduced from its industrial sources, striving to obtain an acceptable level. Because of the mandated industrial emission clean up, many land areas and streams in and around the cities that were formerly barren of vegetation and life, have now begun to move back in the direction of nature's intended balance.

Automotive Pollutants

The third major source of air pollution is automotive emissions. The emissions from the internal combustion engines were not an appreciable problem years ago because of the small number of registered vehicles and the nation's small highway system. However, during the early 1950's, the trend of the American people was to move from the cities to the surrounding suburbs. This caused an immediate problem in transportation because the majority of suburbs were not afforded mass transit conveniences. This lack of transportation created an attractive market for the automobile manufacturers, which resulted in a dramatic increase in the number of vehicles produced and sold, along with a marked increase in highway construction between cities and the suburbs. Multi-vehicle families emerged with a growing emphasis placed on an individual vehicle per family member. As the increase in vehicle ownership and usage occurred, so did pollutant levels in and around the cities, as suburbanites drove daily to their businesses and employment, returning at the end of the day to their homes in the suburbs.

It was noted that a smoke and fog type haze was being formed and at times, remained in suspension over the cities, taking time to dissipate. At first this "smog," derived from the words "smoke" and "fog," was thought to result from industrial pollution but it was determined that automobile emissions shared the blame. It was discovered that when normal automobile emissions were exposed to sunlight for a period of time, complex chemical reactions would take place.

It is now known that smog is a photo chemical layer which develops when certain oxides of nitrogen (NOx) and unburned hydrocarbons (HC) from automobile emissions are exposed to sunlight. Pollution was more severe when smog would become stagnant over an area in which a warm layer of air settled over the top of the cooler air mass, trapping and holding the cooler mass at ground level. The trapped cooler air would keep the emissions from being dispersed and diluted through normal air flows. This type of air stagnation was given the name "Temperature Inversion."

TEMPERATURE INVERSION

In normal weather situations, surface air is warmed by heat radiating from the earth's surface and the sun's rays. This causes it to rise upward, into the atmosphere. Upon rising it will cool through a convection type heat exchange with the cooler upper air. As warm air rises, the surface pollutants are carried upward and dissipated into the atmosphere.

When a temperature inversion occurs, we find the higher air is no longer cooler, but is warmer than the surface air, causing the cooler surface air to become trapped. This warm air blanket can extend from above ground level to a few hundred or even a few thousand feet into the air. As the surface air is trapped, so are the pollutants, causing a severe smog condition. Should this stagnant air mass extend to a few thousand feet high, enough air movement with the inversion takes place to allow the smog layer to rise above ground level but the pollutants still cannot dissipate. This inversion can remain for days over an area, with the smog level only rising or lowering from ground level to a few hundred feet high. Meanwhile, the pollutant levels increase, causing eye irritation, respiratory problems, reduced visibility, plant damage and in some cases, even disease.

This inversion phenomenon was first noted in the Los Angeles, California area. The city lies in terrain resembling a basin and with certain weather conditions, a cold air mass is held in the basin while a warmer air mass covers it like a lid.

Because this type of condition was first documented as prevalent in the Los Angeles area, this type of trapped pollution was named Los Angeles Smog, although it occurs in other areas where a large concentration of automobiles are used and the air remains stagnant for any length of time.

HEAT TRANSFER

Consider the internal combustion engine as a machine in which raw materials must be placed so a finished product comes out. As in any machine operation, a certain amount of wasted material is formed. When we relate this to the internal combustion engine, we find that through the input of air and

fuel, we obtain power during the combustion process to drive the vehicle. The by-product or waste of this power is, in part, heat and exhaust gases with which we must dispose.

The heat from the combustion process can rise to over 4000°F (2204°C). The dissipation of this heat is controlled by a ram air effect, the use of cooling fans to cause air flow and a liquid coolant solution surrounding the combustion area to transfer the heat of combustion through the cylinder walls and into the coolant. The coolant is then directed to a thin-finned, multi-tubed radiator, from which the excess heat is transferred to the atmosphere by 1 of the 3 heat transfer methods, conduction, convection or radiation.

The cooling of the combustion area is an important part in the control of exhaust emissions. To understand the behavior of the combustion and transfer of its heat, consider the air/fuel charge. It is ignited and the flame front burns progressively across the combustion chamber until the burning charge reaches the cylinder walls. Some of the fuel in contact with the walls is not hot enough to burn, thereby snuffing out or quenching the combustion process. This leaves unburned fuel in the combustion chamber. This unburned fuel is then forced out of the cylinder and into the exhaust system, along with the exhaust gases.

Many attempts have been made to minimize the amount of unburned fuel in the combustion chambers due to quenching, by increasing the coolant temperature and lessening the contact area of the coolant around the combustion area. However, design limitations within the combustion chambers prevent the complete burning of the air/fuel charge, so a certain amount of the unburned fuel is still expelled into the exhaust system, regardless of modifications to the engine.

AUTOMOTIVE EMISSIONS

Before emission controls were mandated on internal combustion engines, other sources of engine pollutants were discovered along with the exhaust emissions. It was determined that engine combustion exhaust produced approximately 60 percent of the total emission pollutants, fuel evaporation from the fuel tank and carburetor vents produced 20 percent, with the final 20 percent being produced through the crankcase as a by-product of the combustion process.

Exhaust Gases

The exhaust gases emitted into the atmosphere are a combination of burned and unburned fuel. To understand the exhaust emission and its composition, we must review some basic chemistry.

When the air/fuel mixture is introduced into the engine, we are mixing air, composed of nitrogen (78 percent), oxygen (21 percent) and other gases (1 percent) with the fuel, which is 100 percent hydrocarbons (HC), in a semi-controlled ratio. As the combustion process is accomplished, power is produced to move the vehicle while the heat of combustion is transferred to the cooling system. The exhaust gases are then composed of nitrogen, a diatomic gas (N_2), the same as was introduced in the engine, carbon dioxide (CO_2), the same gas that is used in beverage carbonation, and water vapor (H_2O). The nitrogen (N_2), for the most part, passes through the engine unchanged, while the oxygen (O_2) reacts (burns) with the hydrocarbons

(HC) and produces the carbon dioxide (CO_2) and the water vapors (H_2O). If this chemical process would be the only process to take place, the exhaust emissions would be harmless. However, during the combustion process, other compounds are formed which are considered dangerous. These pollutants are hydrocarbons (HC), carbon monoxide (CO), oxides of nitrogen (NOx) oxides of sulfur (SOx) and engine particulates.

HYDROCARBONS

Hydrocarbons (HC) are essentially fuel which was not burned during the combustion process or which has escaped into the atmosphere through fuel evaporation. The main sources of incomplete combustion are rich air/fuel mixtures, low engine temperatures and improper spark timing. The main sources of hydrocarbon emission through fuel evaporation on most vehicles used to be the vehicle's fuel tank and carburetor float bowl.

To reduce combustion hydrocarbon emission, engine modifications were made to minimize dead space and surface area in the combustion chamber. In addition, the air/fuel mixture was made more lean through the improved control which feedback carburetion and fuel injection offers and by the addition of external controls to aid in further combustion of the hydrocarbons outside the engine. Two such methods were the addition of air injection systems, to inject fresh air into the exhaust manifolds and the installation of catalytic converters, units that are able to burn traces of hydrocarbons without affecting the internal combustion process or fuel economy.

To control hydrocarbon emissions through fuel evaporation, modifications were made to the fuel tank to allow storage of the fuel vapors during periods of engine shut-down. Modifications were also made to the air intake system so that at specific times during engine operation, these vapors may be purged and burned by blending them with the air/fuel mixture.

CARBON MONOXIDE

Carbon monoxide is formed when not enough oxygen is present during the combustion process to convert carbon (C) to carbon dioxide (CO_2). An increase in the carbon monoxide (CO) emission is normally accompanied by an increase in the hydrocarbon (HC) emission because of the lack of oxygen to completely burn all of the fuel mixture.

Carbon monoxide (CO) also increases the rate at which the photo chemical smog is formed by speeding up the conversion of nitric oxide (NO) to nitrogen dioxide (NO_2). To accomplish this, carbon monoxide (CO) combines with oxygen (O_2) and nitric oxide (NO) to produce carbon dioxide (CO_2) and nitrogen dioxide (NO_2). ($CO + O_2 + NO = CO_2 + NO_2$).

The dangers of carbon monoxide, which is an odorless and colorless toxic gas are many. When carbon monoxide is inhaled into the lungs and passed into the blood stream, oxygen is replaced by the carbon monoxide in the red blood cells, causing a reduction in the amount of oxygen supplied to the many parts of the body. This lack of oxygen causes headaches, lack of coordination, reduced mental alertness and, should the carbon monoxide concentration be high enough, death could result.

NITROGEN

Normally, nitrogen is an inert gas. When heated to approximately 2500°F (1371°C) through the combustion process, this gas becomes active and causes an increase in the nitric oxide (NO) emission.

Oxides of nitrogen (NOx) are composed of approximately 97-98 percent nitric oxide (NO). Nitric oxide is a colorless gas but when it is passed into the atmosphere, it combines with oxygen and forms nitrogen dioxide (NO_2). The nitrogen dioxide then combines with chemically active hydrocarbons (HC) and when in the presence of sunlight, causes the formation of photo-chemical smog.

Ozone

To further complicate matters, some of the nitrogen dioxide (NO_2) is broken apart by the sunlight to form nitric oxide and oxygen. ($NO_2 + sunlight = NO + O$). This single atom of oxygen then combines with diatomic (meaning 2 atoms) oxygen (O_2) to form ozone (O_3). Ozone is one of the smells associated with smog. It has a pungent and offensive odor, irritates the eyes and lung tissues, affects the growth of plant life and causes rapid deterioration of rubber products. Ozone

can be formed by sunlight as well as electrical discharge into the air.

The most common discharge area on the automobile engine is the secondary ignition electrical system, especially when inferior quality spark plug cables are used. As the surge of high voltage is routed through the secondary cable, the circuit builds up an electrical field around the wire, which acts upon the oxygen in the surrounding air to form the ozone. The faint glow along the cable with the engine running that may be visible on a dark night, is called the "corona discharge." It is the result of the electrical field passing from a high along the cable, to a low in the surrounding air, which forms the ozone gas. The combination of corona and ozone has been a major cause of cable deterioration. Recently, different and better quality insulating materials have lengthened the life of the electrical cables.

Although ozone at ground level can be harmful, ozone is beneficial to the earth's inhabitants. By having a concentrated ozone layer called the "ozonosphere," between 10 and 20 miles (16-32 km) up in the atmosphere, much of the ultra violet radiation from the sun's rays are absorbed and screened. If this ozone layer were not present, much of the earth's surface would be burned, dried and unfit for human life.

OXIDES OF SULFUR

Oxides of sulfur (SOx) were initially ignored in the exhaust system emissions, since the sulfur content of gasoline as a fuel is less than $1/10$ of 1 percent. Because of this small amount, it was felt that it contributed very little to the overall pollution problem. However, because of the difficulty in solving the sulfur emissions in industrial pollutions and the introduction of catalytic convertor to the automobile exhaust systems, a change was mandated. The automobile exhaust system, when equipped with a catalytic converter, changes the sulfur dioxide (SO_2) into the sulfur trioxide (SO_3).

When this combines with water vapors (H_2O), a sulfuric acid mist (H_2SO_4) is formed and is a very difficult pollutant to handle since it is extremely corrosive. This sulfuric acid mist that is formed, is the same mist that rises from the vents of an automobile battery when an active chemical reaction takes place within the battery cells.

When a large concentration of vehicles equipped with catalytic converters are operating in an area, this acid mist may rise and be distributed over a large ground area causing land, plant, crop, paint and building damage.

PARTICULATE MATTER

A certain amount of particulate matter is present in the burning of any fuel, with carbon constituting the largest percentage of the particulates. In gasoline, the remaining particulates are the burned remains of the various other compounds used in its manufacture. When a gasoline engine is in good internal condition, the particulate emissions are low but as the engine wears internally, the particulate emissions increase. By visually inspecting the tail pipe emissions, a determination can be made as to where an engine defect may exist. An engine with light gray or blue smoke emitting from the tail pipe normally indicates an increase in the oil consumption through burning due to internal engine wear. Black smoke would indicate a defective fuel delivery system, causing the engine to operate in a rich mode. Regardless of the color of the smoke, the internal part of the engine or the fuel delivery system should be repaired to prevent excess particulate emissions.

Diesel and turbine engines emit a darkened plume of smoke from the exhaust system because of the type of fuel used. Emission control regulations are mandated for this type of emission and more stringent measures are being used to prevent excess emission of the particulate matter. Electronic components are being introduced to control the injection of the fuel at precisely the proper time of piston travel, to achieve the optimum in fuel ignition and fuel usage. Other particulate after-burning components are being tested to achieve a cleaner emission.

Good grades of engine lubricating oils should be used, which meet the manufacturers specification. Cut-rate oils can contribute to the particulate emission problem because of their low flash or ignition temperature point. Such oils burn prematurely during the combustion process causing emission of particulate matter.

The cooling system is an important factor in the reduction of particulate matter. The optimum combustion will occur, with the cooling system operating at a temperature specified by the manufacturer. The cooling system must be maintained in the same manner as the engine oiling system, as each system is required to perform properly in order for the engine to operate efficiently for a long time.

Crankcase Emissions

Crankcase emissions are made up of water, acids, unburned fuel, oil fumes and particulates. These emissions are classified as hydrocarbons (HC) and are formed by the small amount of unburned, compressed air/fuel mixture entering the crankcase from the combustion area (between the cylinder walls and piston rings) during the compression and power strokes. The head of the compression and combustion help to form the remaining crankcase emissions.

Since the first engines, crankcase emissions were allowed into the atmosphere through a road draft tube, mounted on the lower side of the engine block. Fresh air came in through an open oil filler cap or breather. The air passed through the crankcase mixing with blow-by gases. The motion of the vehicle and the air blowing past the open end of the road draft tube caused a low pressure area (vacuum) at the end of the tube. Crankcase emissions were simply drawn out of the road draft tube into the air.

To control the crankcase emission, the road draft tube was deleted. A hose and/or tubing was routed from the crankcase to the intake manifold so the blow-by emission could be burned with the air/fuel mixture. However, it was found that

intake manifold vacuum, used to draw the crankcase emissions into the manifold, would vary in strength at the wrong time and not allow the proper emission flow. A regulating valve was needed to control the flow of air through the crankcase.

Testing, showed the removal of the blow-by gases from the crankcase as quickly as possible, was most important to the longevity of the engine. Should large accumulations of blow-by gases remain and condense, dilution of the engine oil would occur to form water, soots, resins, acids and lead salts, resulting in the formation of sludge and varnishes. This condensation of the blow-by gases occurs more frequently on vehicles used in numerous starting and stopping conditions, excessive idling and when the engine is not allowed to attain normal operating temperature through short runs.

Evaporative Emissions

Gasoline fuel is a major source of pollution, before and after it is burned in the automobile engine. From the time the fuel is refined, stored, pumped and transported, again stored until it is pumped into the fuel tank of the vehicle, the gasoline gives off unburned hydrocarbons (HC) into the atmosphere. Through the redesign of storage areas and venting systems, the pollution factor was diminished, but not eliminated, from the refinery standpoint. However, the automobile still remained the primary source of vaporized, unburned hydrocarbon (HC) emissions.

Fuel pumped from an underground storage tank is cool but when exposed to a warmer ambient temperature, will expand. Before controls were mandated, an owner might fill the fuel tank with fuel from an underground storage tank and park the vehicle for some time in warm area, such as a parking lot. As the fuel would warm, it would expand and should no provisions or area be provided for the expansion, the fuel would spill out of the filler neck and onto the ground, causing hydrocarbon (HC) pollution and creating a severe fire hazard. To correct this condition, the vehicle manufacturers added overflow plumbing and/or gasoline tanks with built in expansion areas or domes.

However, this did not control the fuel vapor emission from the fuel tank. It was determined that most of the fuel evaporation occurred when the vehicle was stationary and the engine not operating. Most vehicles carry 5-25 gallons (19-95 liters) of gasoline. Should a large concentration of vehicles be parked in one area, such as a large parking lot, excessive fuel vapor emissions would take place, increasing as the temperature increases.

To prevent the vapor emission from escaping into the atmosphere, the fuel systems were designed to trap the vapors while the vehicle is stationary, by sealing the system from the atmosphere. A storage system is used to collect and hold the fuel vapors from the carburetor (if equipped) and the fuel tank when the engine is not operating. When the engine is started, the storage system is then purged of the fuel vapors, which are drawn into the engine and burned with the air/fuel mixture.

EMISSION CONTROLS

Crankcase Ventilation Systems

OPERATION

▶ See Figure 1

Crankcase emission control equipment is separated into two different systems: Positive Crankcase Ventilation (PVC) and Crankcase Ventilation System (CCV). The systems perform the same function, differing only in the way the exhaust gases are metered. The PVC system uses a valve, containing spring loaded plunger, which meters the amount of crankcase vapors routed to the combustion chamber based on manifold vacuum. The CCV system contains a metered orifice of a calibrated size which meters the amount of crankcase vapors drawn from the engine based on manifold vacuum.

When the engine is running, a small portion of the gases which are formed in the combustion chamber during combustion leak by the piston rings and enter the crankcase. Since these gases are under pressure, they tend to escape from the crankcase and enter into the atmosphere. If these gases were allowed to remain the the crankcase for any length of time, they would contaminate the engine oil and cause sludge to build up. If the gases are allowed to escape into the atmosphere, they would pollute the air, as they contain unburned hydrocarbons. The crankcase emission control equipment recycles these gases back into the engine combustion chamber where they are burned.

While the engine is running, clean filtered air is drawn into the crankcase either directly through the oil filler cap, or through a filter mounted in the air cleaner assembly and connected to the oil filler cap. As the air passes through the crankcase it picks up combustion gases, carries them out of the crankcase, through the PCV valve, and into the intake manifold. After entering the intake manifold gases are drawn into the combustion chamber and burned.

The most critical component in the system is the metering device — the PCV valve in the PVC system, or the metered orifice in the CCV system — which controls the amount of gases recycled into the combustion chamber. If the metering device should become clogged, gases will be prevented from escaping the crankcase by the normal route. Since the gases are under pressure, they will find a point of least resistance, usually a weak oil seal or gasket, and create an oil leak. In addition to creating oil leaks, clogged ventilation systems also allow gases to remain in the crankcase for an extended period of time. This promotes the formation of sludge in the engine and ultimately leads to decreased engine life.

COMPONENT TESTING

PCV Valve

▶ See Figure 2

To inspect the PCV valve, remove the valve from the rocker arm cover hose, then shake it. If the valve rattles, it is probably fine; if there is no sound, it must be replaced and the PCV hose cleaned by spraying solvent (such as a carburetor cleaner type of solvent) through it.

If the valve rattles, you should still check the PCV valve with the engine idling. Pull it out of the vent module and place your finger or thumb over the end to stop air flow. You should feel some suction, and the engine speed should drop slightly. If there is no suction, or if the engine idle speeds up and smooths out considerably, replace the valve. Remove the PCV hose from the engine, then inspect it and, if the inside is coated with gum and varnish, clean it by spraying solvent through it.

Check the vacuum at the PCV inlet (from the rocker arm cover to the air cleaner) tube, as well. Disconnect this tube from the air cleaner and loosely hold a piece of paper over the tube. After a few seconds (10-15 seconds), enough vacuum should build up to cause the paper to be sucked against the

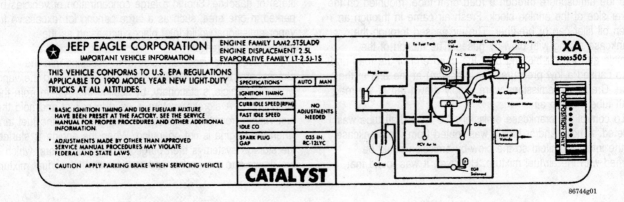

Fig. 1 View of a common federal vehicle emission control information label

opening with a noticeable amount of force. This test proves whether or not the suction side of the system is clear.

CCV Fitting

▶ See Figures 3 and 4

1. With the engine running, remove the CCV fitting.

a. If the fitting is not plugged, a hissing noise will be heard as air passes through the valve. A strong vacuum should also be felt when a finger is placed over the fitting.

b. Install the CCV fitting.

c. Remove the fresh air hose from the air cleaner assembly and loosely hold a piece of paper over the open end of the hose. After allowing about one minute for the crankcase pressure to reduce, the paper should be sucked against the opening with a noticeable amount of force.

2. Turn the engine **OFF**. Remove the metered orifice fitting, and check for a plugged condition. A clicking noise should be heard to indicate that the valve mechanism is free.

3. If the crankcase ventilation system meets the tests in Steps 1 and 2 above, no further service is required. If not, the CCV fitting must be cleaned and the system checked again.

4. If Step 1c fails when the CCV fitting is cleaned, it will be necessary to replace the molded vacuum hose with a new one, and to clean the metered orifice port.

5. Clean or replace the engine air cleaner filter element with a new one — for more details, refer to the air cleaner procedure located in Section 1.

Evaporative Emission Control System

OPERATION

The evaporative emission control system prevents the release of unburned hydrocarbons, from gasoline or gasoline vapor, into the atmosphere. When pressure in the fuel tank is below 3 psi (20 kPa), the pressure relief/rollover valves open allowing fuel vapors to flow to the evaporative canister where they are absorbed by a charcoal mixture. This prevents exces-

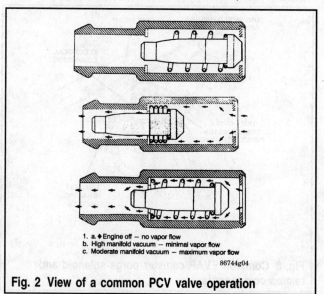

1. a. ◆ Engine off — no vapor flow
b. High manifold vacuum — minimal vapor flow
c. Moderate manifold vacuum — maximum vapor flow

86744g04

Fig. 2 View of a common PCV valve operation

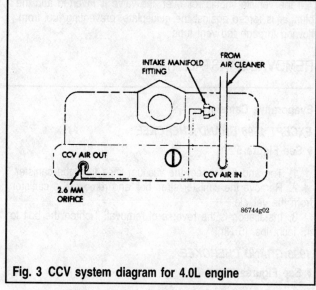

86744g02

Fig. 3 CCV system diagram for 4.0L engine

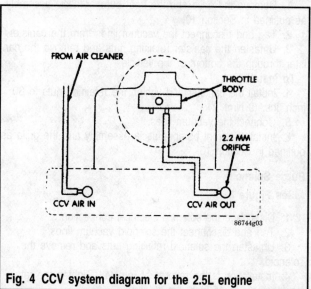

86744g03

Fig. 4 CCV system diagram for the 2.5L engine

sive pressure build-up in the fuel system. Most canisters are equipped with a calibrated orifice at the inlet to the canister.

The evaporative canister is mounted to the passenger side frame rail. Inlet ports on the canister are connected to the rollover/pressure relief valves, the air cleaner, and the fuel tank vent through hoses and tubes.

Canister purge operation is activated by the purge shutoff switch. An air cleaner venturi provides the vacuum to open the switch which allows vapors collected in the canister to be drawn into the airstream. The vapors then pass through the intake manifold and are burned in the combustion process.

The fuel tanks of all vehicles are equipped with two pressure relief/rollover valves. The valves relieve fuel tank pressure and prevent fuel flow through the fuel tank vent hoses in the event of vehicle rollover.

The valves consist of a plunger, spring, orifice and guide plate. The valve is normally open allowing fuel vapor to vent to the canister. If the bottom of the plunger is contacted by sloshing fuel, the plunger seats in the guide plate preventing fuel from reaching the canister.

If the vehicle should roll over, the valve is inverted and the plunger is forced against the guideplate, preventing fuel from flowing through the vent tube.

REMOVAL & INSTALLATION

Evaporative Canister

EXCEPT 1996 GRAND CHEROKEE

▶ See Figure 5

1. Tag and disconnect the vacuum lines from the canister.
2. Remove the canister strap bolt and remove the canister from the vehicle.
3. Installation is the reverse of removal. Tighten the bolt to 45 inch. lbs. (5 Nm).

1996 GRAND CHEROKEE

▶ See Figures 6 and 7

1. Remove the grille and the front bumper/fascia assembly as outlined in Section 10.
2. Tag and disconnect the vacuum lines from the canister.
3. Unfasten the canister retaining nuts and remove the canister through the bottom of the vehicle.

To install:

4. Install the canister and tighten the retaining nuts to 80 inch. lbs. (9 Nm).
5. Connect the vacuum lines.
6. Install the front bumper/fascia assembly and the grille as outlined in Section 10.

Purge Solenoid

▶ See Figure 0

1. Disengage the solenoid electrical connection.
2. Tag and disconnect the solenoid vacuum lines.
3. Unfasten the solenoid retaining nuts and remove the solenoid.
4. Installation is the reverse of removal. Tighten the retaining fasteners to 45 inch. lbs. (5 Nm).

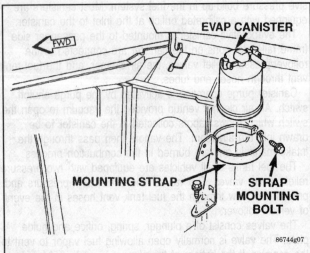

Fig. 5 Exploded view of the EVAP cannister and related components — 1996 Cherokee model shown

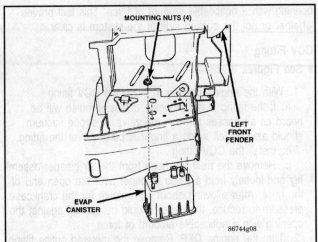

Fig. 6 Exploded view of the cannister location for the 4.0L California emission package — 1996 Grand Cherokee model

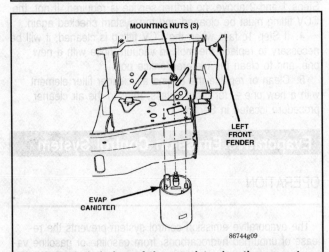

Fig. 7 Exploded view of the cannister location except the California emission package — 1996 Grand Cherokee model

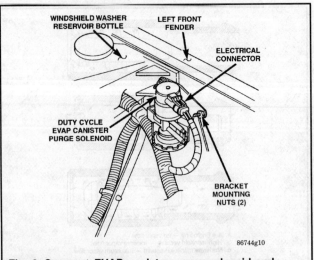

Fig. 8 Common EVAP canister purge solenoid and related components

Pressure Relief/Rollover Valve

♦ **See Figures 9 and 10**

1. Disconnect the battery negative cable.
2. Relieve the fuel system as outlined in Section 5.

➡**DO NOT allow fuel to spill on the intake or exhaust manifolds. Use shop rags to absorb any spilled fuel.**

3. Drain the fuel tank dry using a siphon pump.
4. Raise and support the vehicle with jackstands.
5. Remove the fuel tank. See appropriate procedure in Section 5.
6. If equipped, remove the vapor hose at the valve.
7. The rollover valve is seated in a grommet. Pry one side of the valve up and twist to remove the grommet from the tank.

To install:

8. Start one side of the grommet into the fuel tank opening and using finger pressure only, press the valve grommet into position.
9. Engage the vapor hose, if equipped.
10. Install the tank as outlined in Section 5.
11. Fill the tank and connect the negative battery cable.
12. Start the vehicle and check for leaks.

Thermostatically Controlled Air Cleaner System (TAC)

OPERATION

♦ **See Figures 11 and 12**

The TAC system consists of a heat shroud which is integral with the right side exhaust manifold, a hot air hose and a special air cleaner assembly equipped with an air temperature sensor, a vacuum motor and air valve assembly.

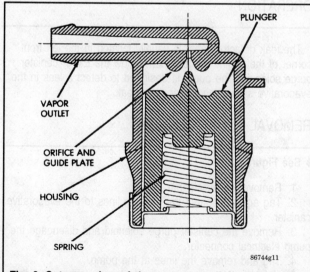

Fig. 9 Cutaway view of the pressure relief/rollover valve

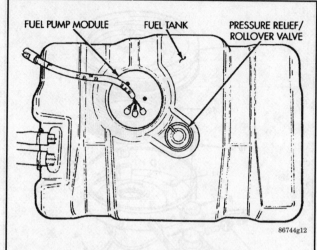

Fig. 10 View of the pressure relief/rollover valve location

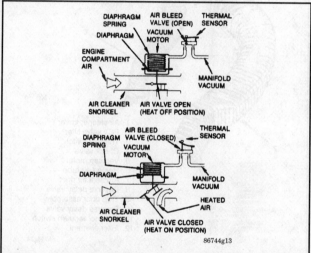

Fig. 11 Thermostatically controlled air cleaner operation (upper open, lower closed)

The air temperature sensor incorporates an air bleed valve which regulates the amount of vacuum applied to the vacuum motor, controlling the air valve position to supply either heated air from the exhaust manifold or cool air from the engine compartment.

During the warm-up period when underhood temperatures are low, the air bleed valve is closed and sufficient vacuum is applied to the vacuum motor to hold the air valve in the closed (heat on) position.

As the temperature of the air entering the air cleaner approaches approximately 115°F (46°C), the air bleed valve opens to decrease the amount of vacuum applied to the vacuum motor. The diaphragm spring in the vacuum motor then moves the air valve into the open (heat off) position, allowing only underhood air to enter the air cleaner.

The air valve in the air cleaner will also open, regardless of air temperature, during heavy acceleration to obtain maximum air flow through the air cleaner.

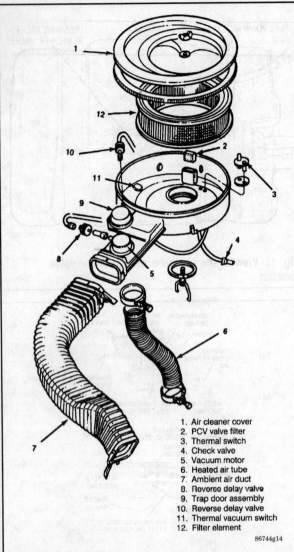

1. Air cleaner cover
2. PCV valve filter
3. Thermal switch
4. Check valve
5. Vacuum motor
6. Heated air tube
7. Ambient air duct
8. Reverse delay valve
9. Trap door assembly
10. Reverse delay valve
11. Thermal vacuum switch
12. Filter element

86744g14

Fig. 12 Exploded view of the thermostatically controlled air cleaner

COMPONENT TESTING

Vacuum Motor

1. With the engine **OFF**, observe the position of the air valve. It can be observed by looking down the air snorkle with a mirror. The valve should be fully open (allowing in only cool air from the snorkle).

2. Start the engine and observe the position of the air valve. It should be fully closed (allowing in only hot air from the exhaust manifold) below operating temperature.

3. Depress the throttle rapidly and release. The air valve should briefly remain stationary and then move toward the closed and then back toward the open position.

4. Warm the engine to normal operating temperature. The air valve should be fully open.

5. Stop the engine.

6. If the air valve does not function properly, inspect for mechanical binding in the snorkle or vacuum leaks in the hoses, vacuum motor, air temperature sensor or intake manifold.

7. If air valve manually operates freely and no vacuum leaks are found, connect a vacuum hose from an intake manifold vacuum source directly to the vacuum motor.

   a. On 2.5L engines: If the valve closes, the TAC sensor, thermal check valve or delay valve is defective. If the valve does not close, the vacuum motor is defective.

   b. On 4.0L engines: If the valve closes, the air temperature sensor is defective. If the valve does not close, the vacuum motor is defective.

Reverse Delay Valve

The reverse delay valve provides approximately 100 seconds of delay before allowing the air valve to fully close.

1. Remove the vacuum hose from the end of the valve that is not black in color (usually facing away from the vacuum motor). Using a hand powered vacuum pump, apply 2-4 in. Hg (13-27 kPa) of vacuum.

2. Note the time required for the vacuum to bleed off. Specification is 4.5-13.2 seconds. If not within specifications, replace the valve.

3. Install replacement valve with the black end toward the vacuum motor.

Air Temperature Switch

1. Disconnect vacuum hoses from thermal switch.

2. Connect a hand operated vacuum pump to vacuum source side of the sensor and a vacuum gauge to the vacuum motor side of the switch.

3. Apply 14 in. Hg (96 kPa) of vacuum to the switch.

4. With the switch below normal operating temperature, vacuum should be maintained.

5. Heat the switch to operating temperature. The air vent valve should open and decrease the vacuum to zero. Replace switch if defective.

Leak Detection Pump

OPERATION

The leak detector pump is usually located in the left front corner of the engine compartment below the EVAP canister purge solenoid. The pump is designed to detect a leak in the evaporative system and to seal the leak.

REMOVAL & INSTALLATION

▶ **See Figure 13**

1. Remove the air cleaner.

2. Tag and disconnect the vacuum lines to the evaporative canister.

3. Remove the canister purge solenoid and disengage the pump electrical connector.

4. Tag and remove the lines at the pump.

5. Unfasten the pump retaining fasteners and remove the pump.

To install:

6. Install the pump and tighten the retaining fasteners to 60 inch. lbs. (7 Nm).

7. Engage the lines at the pump and install the canister purge solenoid.

8. Engage the pump electrical connection and install the canister.

9. Engage the canister vacuum lines and install the air cleaner.

Exhaust Gas Recirculation (EGR) System

OPERATION

♦ See Figure 14

NOx (oxides of nitrogen) is a tailpipe emission caused by the oxidation of nitrogen in the combustion chamber. When the peak combustion temperatures go over 2500°F (1371°C) NOx is formed in excessive amounts. To keep the combustion temperatures down, exhaust gas is recirculated.

Recirculation of the exhaust gases is accomplished by having a movable valve between the exhaust and intake manifolds. Upon a predetermined demand, engine vacuum is routed to the valve, opening the connecting port and allowing exhaust gases to enter the intake tract.

The EGR valves used on Jeep vehicles fall into three categories:

• An EGR valve with no backpressure sensor which is controlled by ported vacuum only. 2.5L and 2.8L engines are equipped with this type of EGR valve.

• An EGR valve with an external backpressure sensor which is controlled by ported vacuum and backpressure. 4.0L engines are equipped with this type of EGR valve.

• An EGR valve with an electric EGR transducer is found on 5.2L engines.

Thermal vacuum switches, which control the amount of vacuum available to the EGR valve based on air or water temperature, are used to disable the EGR system before the vehicle reaches operating temperature.

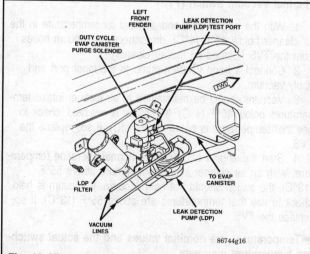

Fig. 13 View of a leak detection pump and related components

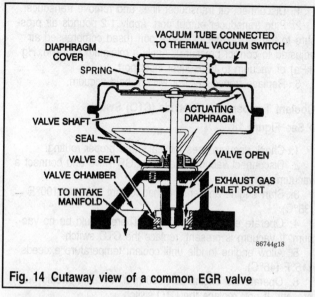

Fig. 14 Cutaway view of a common EGR valve

COMPONENT TESTING

EGR Solenoid

1. Start engine and bring to normal operating temperature. Allow engine to idle while performing tests.

2. Check vacuum at solenoid vacuum source hose. Disconnect the hose and attach a vacuum gauge.

3. Vacuum should be 15 in. Hg. (103 kPa), If low, check for leaks, loose fittings or kinks in the line.

4. Check vacuum at solenoid port. Disconnect the line and attach a vacuum gauge.

5. If vacuum reading is zero, go to Step 6. If vacuum is present, check solenoid operation with the Diagnostic Readout Box (DRB II) service tester and repair as necessary.

6. Disengage electrical connector at solenoid. If vacuum is present, proceed to EGR valve test. If not, replace the solenoid.

EGR Valve

1. Leave solenoid electrical connector disengaged. Bypass the vacuum transducer, if equipped, and connect EGR valve solenoid output hose directly to the nipple on the EGR valve.

2. The engine should run roughly or stall. If this occurs, the valve is good. Proceed to the transducer test, for 4.0L engines. If engine rpm does not change, disconnect hose from EGR and connect a hand vacuum pump.

3. Apply 12 in. Hg (82 kPa) of vacuum. If engine runs rough or stalls, inspect vacuum lines in EGR system for leaks and repair as necessary. If no leaks are found, go to transducer test for the 4.0L engine; Step 4 for the other engines.

4. If engine idle still does not change, remove the EGR valve and inspect for a blockage in the intake manifold passage. Repair as necessary. If no blockage is found, replace the EGR valve.

Vacuum Transducer

♦ See Figures 15, 16 and 17

➡ This is used on 4.0L engines only.

1. Disconnect all transducer lines and remove transducer.

2. Plug transducer output port. Apply 1-2 pounds air pressure to transducer backpressure port (used compressed air adjusted to correct pressure). Apply a minimum of 12 in. Hg (kPa) of vacuum to transducer input port.

3. Replace transducer if it will not hold vacuum.

Coolant Temperature Override (CTO) Switch

▶ See Figure 18

1. Check vacuum lines for leaks and proper routing.

2. Disconnect vacuum line from EGR valve and connect a vacuum gauge.

3. Start engine and ensure that coolant is below 100°F (38°C).

4. Operate engine a 1,500 rpm. There should be no vacuum. If vacuum is present, replace the CTO switch.

5. Allow engine to idle until coolant temperature exceeds 115°F (46°C).

6. Operate the engine at 1,500 rpm. Vacuum should be present. If not, replace the CTO switch.

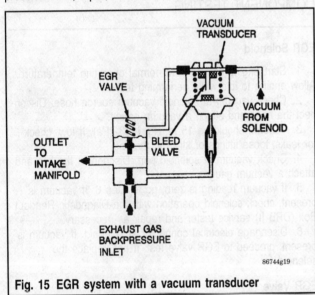

Fig. 15 EGR system with a vacuum transducer

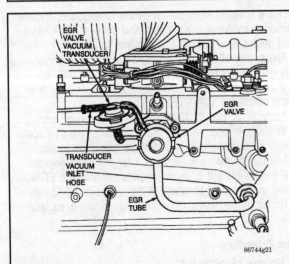

Fig. 16 View of a 4.0L engine with an EGR valve and a vacuum transducer

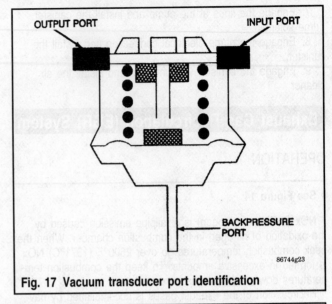

Fig. 17 Vacuum transducer port identification

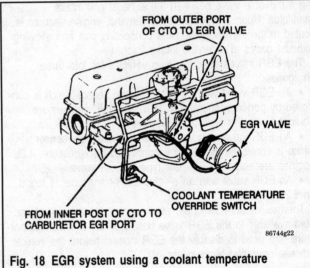

Fig. 18 EGR system using a coolant temperature override switch

Thermal Vacuum Switch (TVS)

1. With the engine cold and ambient air temperature in the air cleaner below 40°F (4°C), disconnect the vacuum hoses from the TVS (located on the air cleaner).

2. Connect a hand vacuum pump to the inner port and apply vacuum.

3. Vacuum should be maintained at air cleaner intake temperatures below 40°F (4°C). If vacuum is not held, check to see that temperature is below 40°F (4°C). If so, replace the TVS.

4. Start the engine and warm to normal operating temperature. With an air cleaner intake temperature above 55°F (13°C), the switch should not hold vacuum. If vacuum is held, check to see that temperatures are above 55°F (13°C). If so, replace the TVS.

➡Temperatures are nominal values and the actual switching temperature may vary.

REMOVAL & INSTALLATION

EGR Valve

▶ See Figures 19, 20 and 21

1. Tag and disengage the vacuum hoses to the EGR valve and the valve control.
2. Remove the EGR retaining bolts, then the valve and gasket.

To install:

3. Clean both mating surfaces and install a new gasket.
4. Install the EGR valve and tighten the retaining bolts to 200 inch. lbs. (23 Nm).
5. Engage the vacuum hoses.

EGR Tube

▶ See Figures 22 and 23

EXCEPT 5.2L ENGINES

1. Remove EGR tube-to-exhaust manifold bolts.
2. Unscrew EGR tube line nut at intake manifold. Remove EGR tube.
3. Install EGR tube with a new gasket. Tighten line nut to 30 ft. lbs. (40 Nm) and exhaust manifold bolts to 14 ft. lbs. (18 Nm).

5.2L ENGINES

▶ See Figure 24

1. Remove the spark plug wire loom and wires from the valve cover. Position the wires to one side.
2. Remove the right exhaust manifold heat shield retainers and the shield.
3. Remove the EGR valve. Refer to the proper procedure in this section.
4. Disengage the oil pressure sending unit electrical connection and remove the sending unit using tool C-4597 or its equivalent.
5. Unfasten the EGR tube nut at the intake manifold and the tube mounting bolts at the exhaust manifold.

86744p01

Fig. 20 Removing the EGR valve

86744p02

Fig. 21 Remove and discard the old EGR valve gasket

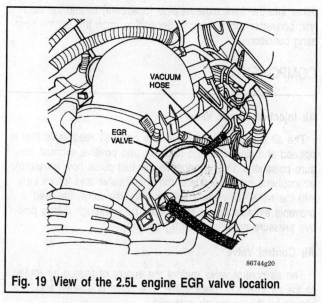
86744g20

Fig. 19 View of the 2.5L engine EGR valve location

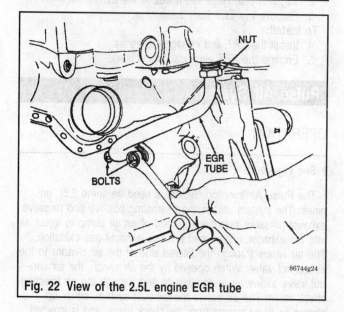
86744g24

Fig. 22 View of the 2.5L engine EGR tube

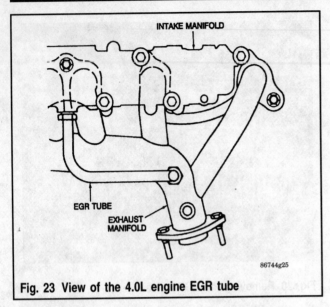

Fig. 23 View of the 4.0L engine EGR tube

6. Remove the EGR tube and gasket. Discard the old gasket.

To install:

7. Clean the EGR tube and exhaust manifold mating surfaces and install a new gasket.

8. Install the EGR tube and engage it to both manifolds. Fasten the nut at the intake manifold and tighten the bolts at the exhaust manifold to 204 inch. lbs. (23 Nm).

9. Coat the threads of the oil pressure sender with a thread sealant and install the sender. Tighten the sender to 130 inch. lbs. (14 Nm).

10. Engage the sender electrical connection.

11. Install the EGR valve. Refer to the proper procedure in this section.

12. Install the right exhaust shield and tighten the retainers.

13. Install the spark plug loom and wires.

Electric EGR Transducer (EET)

1. Disengage the EET electrical connector.

2. Tag and disengage the hoses to the EET.

3. Remove the EET from the engine.

To install:

4. Install the EET and engage the hoses.

5. Engage the EET electrical connections.

Pulse Air System

OPERATION

▶ See Figure 25

The Pulse Air Injection System is used on some 2.5L engines. The system utilizes the alternating positive and negative exhaust pressure pulsations instead of an air pump to inject air into the exhaust system and produce exhaust gas oxidation. The air enters through the filtered side of the air cleaner to the air control valve. When opened by the air switch, the air control valve allows air to continue to and through the air injection check valve. The air enters the exhaust system, either upstream or down stream from the check valve, and is injected

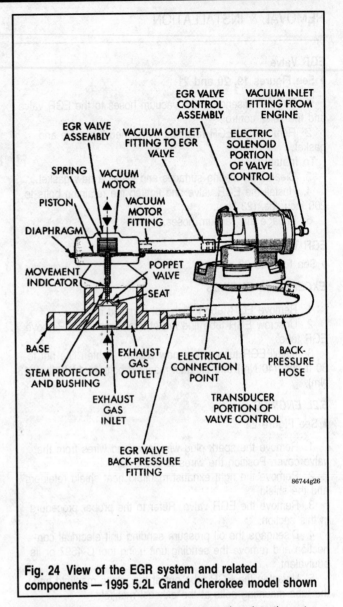

Fig. 24 View of the EGR system and related components — 1995 5.2L Grand Cherokee model shown

either into the front exhaust pipe (upstream) or into the catalytic converter (downstream), depending upon the engine operating conditions.

COMPONENTS

Air Injection Check Valve

The air injection check valve is a one-way reed valve that is opened and closed by the negative and positive exhaust pressure pulsations. During negative exhaust pulse (low pressure), atmospheric pressure opens the check valve and forces air into the exhaust system. Being a one-way valve, the reed prevents exhaust from being forced back through during positive pressure pulsations (high pressure).

Air Control Valve

The air control valve meters the supply of filtered air routed to the air injection check valve. The valve is opened and closed by the air switch solenoid.

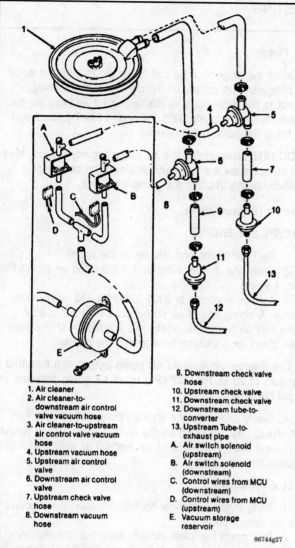

1. Air cleaner
2. Air cleaner-to-downstream air control valve vacuum hose
3. Air cleaner-to-upstream air control valve vacuum hose
4. Upstream vacuum hose
5. Upstream air control valve
6. Downstream air control valve
7. Upstream check valve hose
8. Downstream vacuum hose
9. Downstream check valve hose
10. Upstream check valve
11. Downstream check valve
12. Downstream tube-to-converter
13. Upstream Tube-to-exhaust pipe
A. Air switch solenoid (upstream)
B. Air switch solenoid (downstream)
C. Control wires from MCU (downstream)
D. Control wires from MCU (upstream)
E. Vacuum storage reservoir

86744g27

Fig. 25 Exploded view of the pulse air system and related components

Air Switch Solenoid

The air switch solenoid controls the air control valve by alternating vacuum on and off. The solenoid is controlled by the Micro Computer Unit (MCU).

Vacuum Storage Tank

Engine vacuum is stored in a reservoir tank until released by the air switch solenoid.

Micro Computer Unit (MCU)

The MCU switches air injection either upstream or downstream, depending on the engines operating conditions, by energizing and de-energizing the air switch solenoid.

Air Injection System

OPERATION

▶ **See Figure 26**

The air pump air injection system, used on some engines, incorporates a belt driven air pump, a vacuum controlled diverter (bypass) valve, two air injection manifolds with check valves, and the necessary connecting hoses. This system provides for air injection into the exhaust system at the exhaust manifolds.

COMPONENTS

Air Pump

▶ **See Figure 27**

The air injection pump is a positive displacement vane type which is permanently lubricated and requires little periodic maintenance. The only serviceable parts on the air pump are the filter, exhaust tube, and relief valve. The relief valve relieves the air flow when the pump pressure reaches a preset level. This occurs at high engine rpm. This serves to prevent damage to the pump and to limit maximum exhaust manifold temperatures.

Pump Air Filter

Some air pumps are equipped with a replaceable element type air filter. The filter should be replaced every 12,000 miles (19,300 km) under normal conditions and sooner under off-road use. Other models draw their air supply through the carburetor air filter.

Diverter (Bypass) Valve

▶ **See Figure 28**

The diverter valve has two outlets; one for each air injection tube.

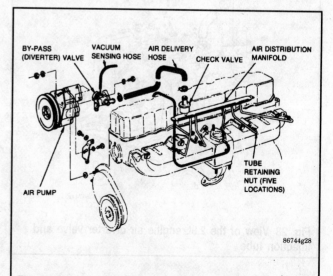

BY-PASS (DIVERTER) VALVE
VACUUM SENSING HOSE
AIR DELIVERY HOSE
CHECK VALVE
AIR DISTRIBUTION MANIFOLD
AIR PUMP
TUBE RETAINING NUT (FIVE LOCATIONS)

86744g28

Fig. 26 View of the air pump system on the 4.0L engine

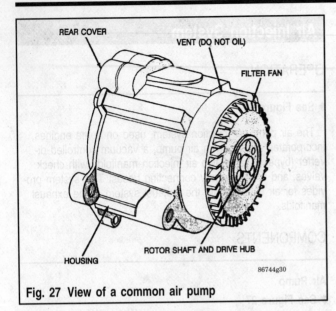

Fig. 27 View of a common air pump

The valve momentarily diverts air pump output from the tubes and vents it to atmosphere during rapid deceleration. In addition, the valve functions as a pressure release for excessive air pump output.

Air Injection Tubes

The air injection tubes distribute air via the diverter valve to each of the exhaust ports. The ends of the tubes project into the ports near the exhaust valve seat.

A check valve, incorporating a stainless steel spring plunger and an asbestos seat, is integral with each air injection tube. The check valve functions to prevent the reverse flow of exhaust gas into the air pump during a malfunction of the pump or diverter valve.

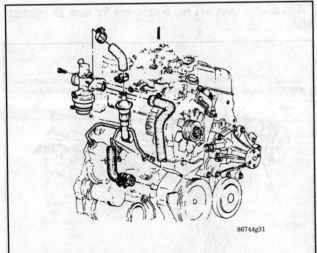

Fig. 28 View of the 2.8L engine air diverter valve and injection tube

TESTING

Air Pump

Check the air pump drive belt for proper tension and adjust as necessary. Do not pry on the die cast pump housing. Check to see if the pump is discharging air. Remove the air outlet hose at the pump. With the engine running, air should be felt at the pump outlet opening.

➡**DO NOT disassemble the air pump for any reason. Internal components are not serviceable. If the air pump is malfunctioning, replace the pump as a unit.**

Diverter (Bypass) Valve

EXCEPT 2.8L ENGINE

1. Start the engine and operate at idle speed.
2. Check the diverter valve vent. Little or no air should flow from the vent.
3. Accelerate engine to 2000-3000 rpm and rapidly close throttle. A strong flow of air should pass from the diverter valve vent for 3 seconds. If air does not flow or engine backfires, check for a vacuum hose leak at the diverter.

➡**The diverter valve vents air pump output at a manifold vacuum of 20 in. Hg (137 kPa) or an air pump pressure of 5 psi (34 kPa).**

4. Slowly accelerate the engine between 2500-3500 rpm. Air should begin to flow from the diverter valve vent. If vacuum is present and the valve does not function as described above, replace the valve.

2.8L ENGINE

1. Bring engine to normal operating temperature. Remove the air cleaner cover.
2. Disconnect the lower vacuum hose from the diverter valve. Air pump output should be directed to the air cleaner.
3. Connect the vacuum hose to the diverter valve. Air pump output should be directed to the exhaust manifolds.
4. If air is not directed as described above, check to see that the vacuum source is drawing vacuum. If so, replace the diverter.

➡**California emissions diverter valves also function as vacuum switches. They are controlled directly by the Electric Control Module (ECM) so that air is diverted to the air cleaner during closed throttle deceleration, high electrical load on the engine control system, the first five seconds of start up and when the engine is off.**

Check Valves

1. Disconnect air hoses at the air tubes.
2. With the engine operating above idle, listen and feel for exhaust gas leakage from the check valves and tubes.

➡**A slight leak from the check valves is normal.**

3. Replace components which are rusted through or leak excessively.

REMOVAL & INSTALLATION

Air Pump

▶ See Figure 29

1. Disconnect the output hose from the pump.
2. Loosen the mount bracket-to-pump bolts.
3. Remove the drive belt, pivot bolt and brace bolts. Remove the pump.
4. Installation is the reverse of removal. Tighten the mounting bolts to 20 ft. lbs. (27 Nm).

Air Injection Tubes

1. Disconnect the air hoses at the check valve.
2. Remove the air tube fittings from the exhaust manifolds. Some resistance may be encountered due to a build-up of carbon on the threads. Remove the air injection tubes.
3. Installation is the reverse of removal. Be sure to use new gaskets. Tighten the injection tubes to 38 ft. lbs. (51 Nm).

Catalytic Converter

OPERATION

▶ See Figure 30

The catalytic converter, standard equipment in most newer vehicles, has the job of altering pollutants in the vehicle's exhaust gas. The catalytic converters do this by chemically altering the harmful chemicals present in exhaust gases, such as oxides of nitrogen (NO_x), unburned hydrocarbons (HC), carbon monoxide (CO) and oxides of sulfur (SO_x) into harmless variants of these chemicals, such as carbon dioxide (CO_2) and water (H_2O). For a more in-depth description of the chemical reactions in exhaust gases, refer to the beginning of this section.

Two things can to destroy the catalyst: the use of leaded gas and excessive heat. The use of leaded fuel was the most common cause of catalyst destruction. The lead coats the thin layer of platinum and palladium (that actually promotes final combustion of the almost completely burned hydrocarbons that enter the catalytic converter). The coating keeps the mixture from actually contacting the noble metals. The lead may also cause the passages of the "substrate" — the material that carries the noble metal coating — to clog. This would cause the vehicle to run at reduced power or even stop altogether.

Excessive heat results in the converter when raw fuel and air with a high oxygen content enter the catalytic converter, which greatly accelerates the combustion process. This most often occurs when a spark plug wire is disconnected. Excessive heat during misfiring due to poor vehicle maintenance and prolonged testing with the ignition system wires disconnected are two common ways a catalyst may be rendered ineffective. Test procedures should be accomplished as-quickly-as possible. The vehicle should be shut off whenever misfiring is noted. Misfiring due to extremely lean or extremely rich mixtures will also damage the catalyst.

While the catalyst itself is a maintenance-free item, it should be understood that long life depends completely on proper fueling and good maintenance. The vehicle should be tuned as required, and the fuel and air filters, as well as the oxygen sensor, should be changed as specified. Ignition wires and the distributor cap and rotor should be inspected/tested and replaced if necessary to prevent misfire.

REMOVAL & INSTALLATION

For the removal and installation of the catalytic converter, refer to the end of Section 3.

Emissions Maintenance Reminder Light

▶ See Figures 31 and 32

Some Jeep vehicles are equipped with an Emissions Maintenance Reminder (EMR) light. The EMR light comes on after the vehicle has reached 82,500 miles (132,767 km) and informs the owner when oxygen sensor and other related emissions service is required. The light is located in the instrument cluster.

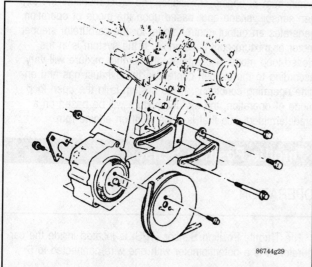

86744g29

Fig. 29 View of the 2.5L engine air pump mounting

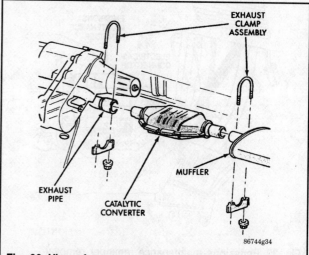

86744g34

Fig. 30 View of a commonly used catalytic converter — 1995 vehicle shown

The oxygen sensor and EMR module are interdependent. When the reminder light illuminates, the oxygen sensor and EMR module should be replaced simultaneously. This is important in ensuring proper engine performance.

RESETTING

The maintenance reminder cannot be reset after reaching the specified mileage, the unit must be replaced. The unit is mounted on the dash panel to the right of the steering column. To replace the reminder module:

1. Remove the attaching screws and disengage the reminder electrical connector.

2. Install the connector to the new EMR and replace the attaching screws.

➡ On vehicles equipped with cruise control, the cruise control module may need to be moved to gain access to the EMR.

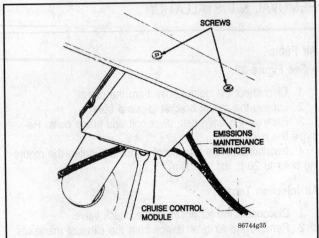

Fig. 31 On earlier model vehicles it is sometimes necessary to remove the cruise control module to gain access to the emissions maintenance reminder

CARBURETED ELECTRONIC ENGINE CONTROLS

General Information

◆ **See Figures 33, 34 and 35**

There are two primary modes of operation of the Computerized Emission Control (CEC) feedback system: open loop and closed loop. The system will be in the open loop mode of operation (or a variation of it) whenever the engine operating conditions do not meet the programmed criteria for closed loop operation. During open loop operation, the air/fuel mixture is maintained at a programmed ratio that is dependent on the type of engine operation involved. The oxygen sensor data is not accepted by the system during this mode of operation.

When all input data meets the programmed criteria for closed loop operation, the exhaust gas oxygen content signal from the oxygen sensor is accepted by the computer. This results in an air/fuel mixture that will be optimum for the engine operating condition and also will correct any pre-existing mixture condition which is too lean or too rich.

➡ **A high oxygen content in the exhaust gas indicates a lean air/fuel mixture. A low oxygen content indicates a rich air/fuel mixture. The optimum air/fuel mixture ratio is 14.7:1.**

Micro Computer Unit (MCU)

OPERATION

The Micro Computer Unit, or MCU, is the heart of the electronic control system. The MCU receives signals from various engine sensors to constantly monitor the engine operating conditions, then it uses this information to make adjustments in order to achieve the optimum performance and economy with a minimum of engine emissions. The MCU monitors the oxygen sensor voltage and, based upon the mode of operation, generates an output control signal for the carburetor stepper motor or mixture control solenoid. If the system is in the closed loop mode of operation, the air/fuel mixture will vary according to the oxygen content in the exhaust gas and engine operating conditions. If the system is in the open loop mode of operation, the air/fuel mixture will be based on a predetermined ratio that is dependent on engine rpm.

Throttle Position Sensor

OPERATION

The Throttle Position Sensor (TPS) is located inside the carburetor. It is a potentiometer with one wire connected to 5

Fig. 32 Emissions maintenance reminder removal

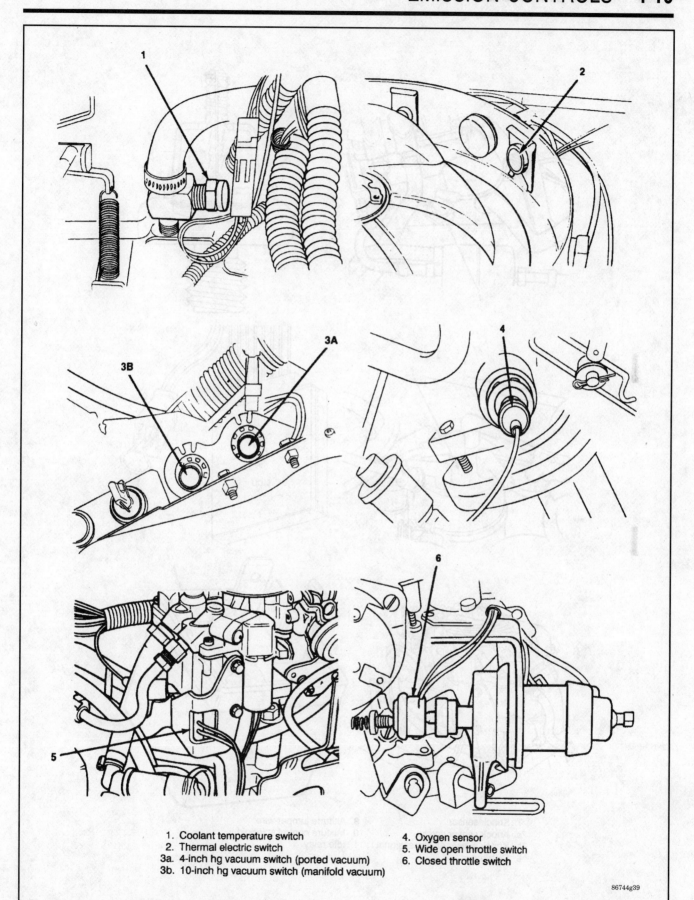

1. Coolant temperature switch
2. Thermal electric switch
3a. 4-inch hg vacuum switch (ported vacuum)
3b. 10-inch hg vacuum switch (manifold vacuum)
4. Oxygen sensor
5. Wide open throttle switch
6. Closed throttle switch

86744g39

Fig. 33 A view of some CEC system components

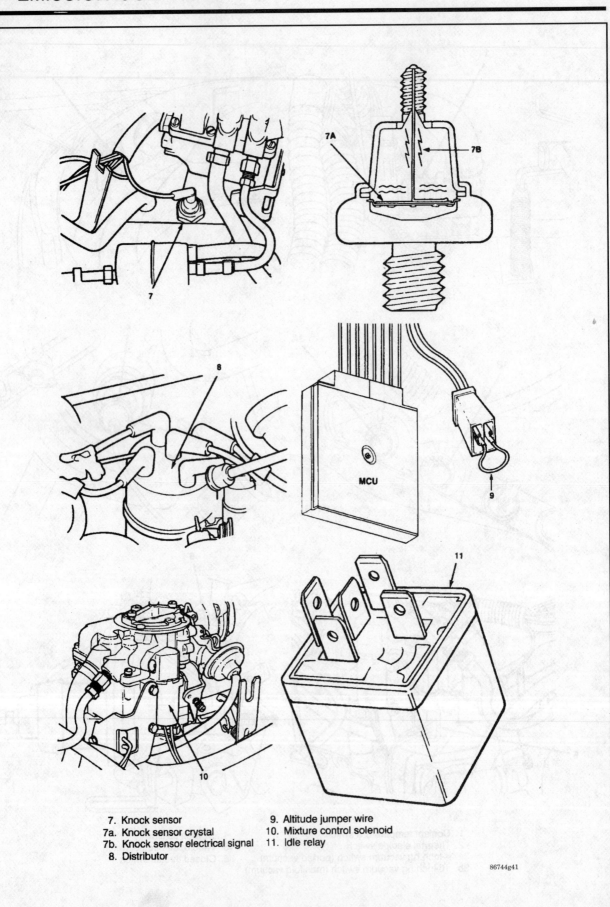

7. Knock sensor
7a. Knock sensor crystal
7b. Knock sensor electrical signal
8. Distributor
9. Altitude jumper wire
10. Mixture control solenoid
11. Idle relay

86744g41

Fig. 34 A view of some CEC system components

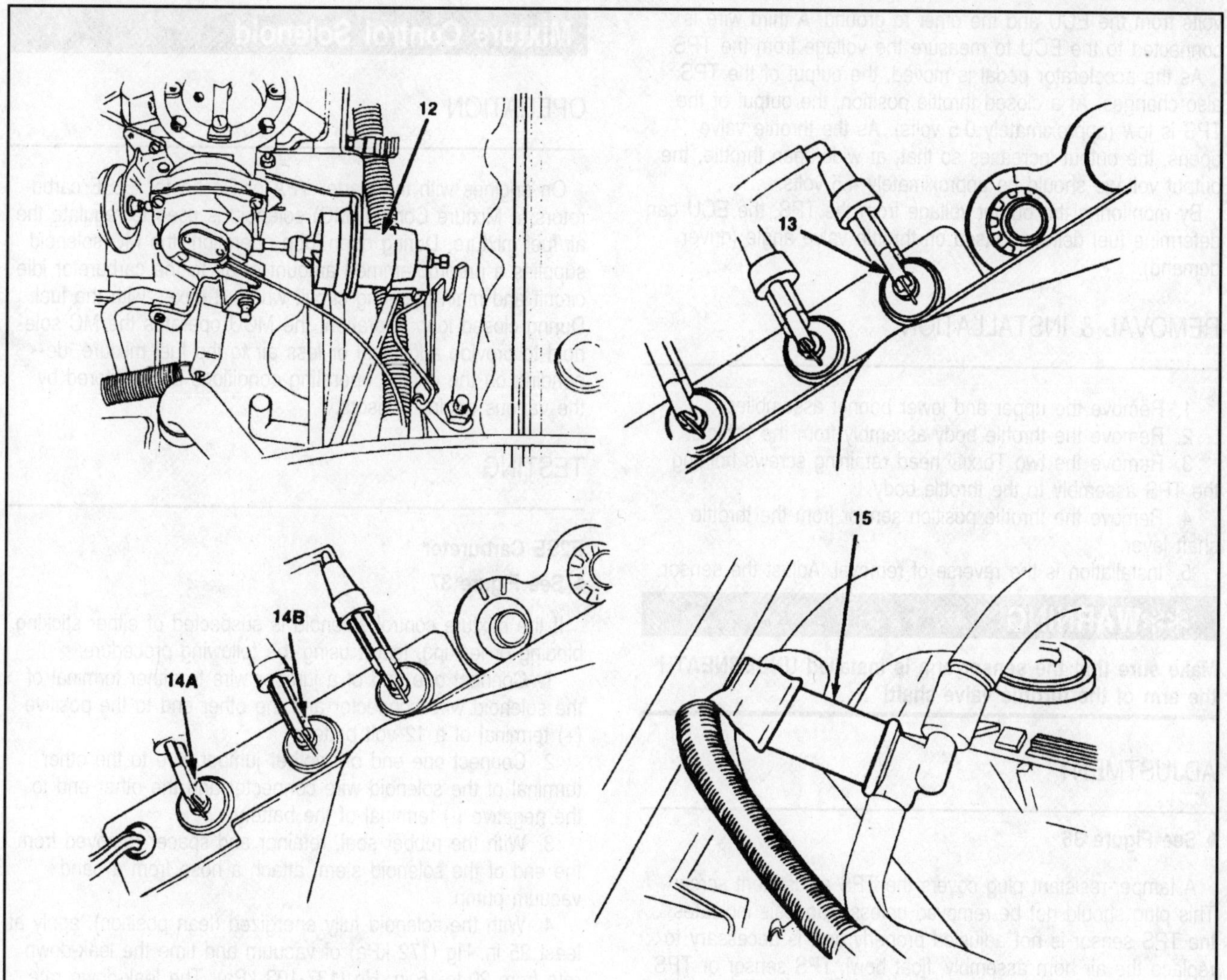

12. Sole-vac throttle positioner
13. Idle solenoid
14a. Upstream solenoid
14b. Downstream solenoid

15. PCV solenoid
16. Bowl vent solenoid
17. Intake manifold heater switch

86744g40

Fig. 35 A view of some CEC system components

volts from the ECU and the other to ground. A third wire is connected to the ECU to measure the voltage from the TPS.

As the accelerator pedal is moved, the output of the TPS also changes. At a closed throttle position, the output of the TPS is low (approximately 0.5 volts). As the throttle valve opens, the output increases so that, at wide-open throttle, the output voltage should be approximately 4.5 volts.

By monitoring the output voltage from the TPS, the ECU can determine fuel delivery based on throttle valve angle (driver demand).

REMOVAL & INSTALLATION

1. Remove the upper and lower bonnet assemblies.
2. Remove the throttle body assembly from the vehicle.
3. Remove the two Torx® head retaining screws holding the TPS assembly to the throttle body.
4. Remove the throttle position sensor from the throttle shaft lever.
5. Installation is the reverse of removal. Adjust the sensor.

❊❊WARNING

Make sure that the sensor arm is installed UNDERNEATH the arm of the throttle valve shaft!

ADJUSTMENT

▶ **See Figure 36**

A tamper-resistant plug covers the TPS adjustment screw. This plug should not be removed unless diagnosis indicates the TPS sensor is not adjusted properly or it is necessary to replace the air horn assembly, float bowl, TPS sensor or TPS adjustment screw. This is a critical adjustment that must be performed accurately and carefully to ensure proper engine performance and emission control. If TPS adjustment is indicated, proceed as follows:

1. Use a $5/64$ in. (2mm) drill bit to drill a hole in the steel cup plug covering the TPS adjustment screw. Use care in drilling to prevent damage to the adjustment screw head.
2. Use a small slide hammer to remove the steel plug from the air horn.
3. Unplug the TPS connector and use jumper wires to connect all three terminals.
4. Connect a digital voltmeter between the TPS connector center terminal B and the bottom terminal C (ground).
5. With the ignition **ON** (engine **OFF**), turn the TPS adjustment screw to obtain 0.26 volts (260 mv) at the curb idle throttle position with the A/C off.
6. After all adjustments are complete, a new tamper-proof plug (supplied in service kits) or silicone RTV rubber sealant must be inserted into the TPS adjustment screw hole to seal the adjustment. If a plug is used, it should be installed with the cup facing outward and flush with the top of the casting.

Mixture Control Solenoid

OPERATION

On engines with the Carter YFA or Rochester E2SE carburetors, a Mixture Control (MC) solenoid is used to regulate the air/fuel mixture. During open loop operation, the MC solenoid supplies a preprogrammed amount of air to the carburetor idle circuit and main metering circuit where it mixes with the fuel. During closed loop operation, the MCU operates the MC solenoid to provide additional or less air to the fuel mixture, depending on the engine operating conditions as monitored by the various engine sensors.

TESTING

E2SE Carburetor
▶ **See Figure 37**

If the mixture control solenoid is suspected of either sticking, binding or leaking, test it using the following procedure:

1. Connect one end of a jumper wire to either terminal of the solenoid wire connector and the other end to the positive (+) terminal of a 12 volt battery.
2. Connect one end of another jumper wire to the other terminal of the solenoid wire connector and the other end to the negative (-) terminal of the battery.
3. With the rubber seal, retainer and spacer removed from the end of the solenoid stem, attach a hose from a hand vacuum pump.
4. With the solenoid fully energized (lean position), apply at least 25 in. Hg (172 kPa) of vacuum and time the leak-down rate from 20-to-15 in. Hg (137-103 kPa). The leak-down rate should not exceed 5 in. Hg (34 kPa) in 5 seconds. If the leak-down rate exceeds that amount, replace the solenoid.
5. To test the solenoid for sticking in the down (de-energized) position, remove the jumper wire to the 12 volt battery and observe the hand vacuum pump gauge. It should move to zero in less than one second.

REMOVAL & INSTALLATION

1. Remove three (3) mixture control solenoid screws in the horn, then using a slight twisting motion, carefully lift solenoid out of air horn. Remove and discard solenoid gasket.
2. Remove seal retainer and rubber seal from end of solenoid stem being careful not to damage or nick end of solenoid stem. Discared seal and retainer.
   To install:
3. Install spacer and new rubber seal on new mixture control solenoid stem making sure seal is up against the spacer. Then, using a suitable socket and hammer, carefully drive retainer on stem. Drive retainer on stem only far enough to retain rubber seal on stem leaving a slight clearance between the retainer and seal to allow for seal expansion.

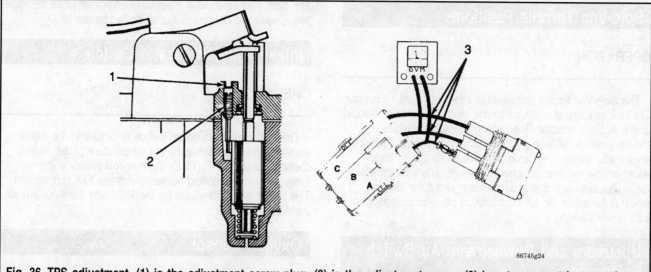

Fig. 36 TPS adjustment. (1) is the adjustment screw plug; (2) is the adjustment screw; (3) how to connect jumper wires

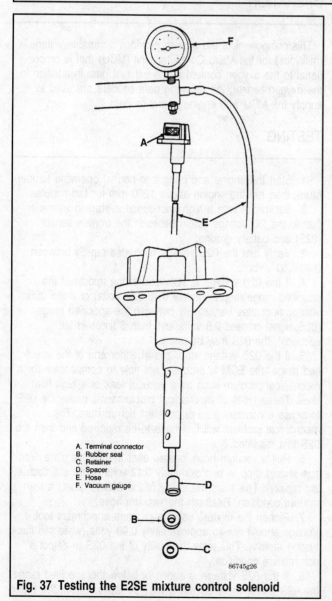

A. Terminal connector
B. Rubber seal
C. Retainer
D. Spacer
E. Hose
F. Vacuum gauge

86745g26

Fig. 37 Testing the E2SE mixture control solenoid

4. Prior to installing a replacement mixture control solenoid, lightly coat the rubber seal on the end of the solenoid stem with a automatic transmission fluid or light engine oil.

5. Using a new mounting gasket, install mixture control solenoid on air horn, carefully aligning solenoid stem with recess in bottom of bowl.

6. Use a slight twisting motion of the solenoid during installation to ensure rubber seal on stem is guided into recess in the bottom of the bowl to prevent distortion or damage to the rubber seal.

7. Install the three solenoid attaching screws and tighten securely.

8. Install mixture control solenoid connector, and check for proper latching. The latch may require filing. Check colors of wires in connector for proper position. Pink wire must be on right hand terminal of connector, as viewed from harness end. If incorrect, use Tool J-28742, BT 8234-A or equivalent to remove wires from connector and replace.

Idle Relay and Solenoid

OPERATION

The idle relay is energized by the MCU to control the vacuum actuator portion of the Sole-Vac throttle positioner by providing a ground for the idle relay. The relay energizes the idle solenoid, which allows vacuum to operate the Sole-Vac vacuum actuator. This, in turn, opens the throttle and increases engine speed. The idle solenoid is located on a bracket on the left front inner fender panel and can be identified by the red connecting wires.

Sole-Vac Throttle Positioner

OPERATION

The Sole-Vac throttle positioner is attached to the carburetor. The unit consists of a closed throttle switch, a holding solenoid and a vacuum actuator. The holding solenoid maintains the throttle position, while the vacuum actuator provides additional engine idle speed when accessories such as the air conditioner or rear window defogger are in use. The vacuum actuator is also activated during deceleration and if the steering wheel is turned to the full stop position on vehicles equipped with power steering.

Upstream and Downstream Air Switch Solenoids

OPERATION

The upstream and downstream solenoids of the pulse air system distribute air to the exhaust pipe and catalytic converter. Both solenoids are energized by the MCU to route air into the the exhaust pipe at a point after the oxygen sensor. When energized, the downstream solenoid routes air into the second bed of the dual-bed catalytic converter. This additional air reacts with the exhaust gases to reduce engine emissions.

The solenoids are located on a bracket attached to the left inner front fender panel. The idle solenoid is also located on this same bracket.

PCV Shutoff Solenoid

OPERATION

The positive crankcase ventilation shutoff solenoid is installed in the PCV valve hose and is energized by the MCU to turn off the crankcase ventilation system when the engine is at idle speed. An anti-diesel relay system on 4-cylinder engines, consisting of an anti-diesel relay and a delay relay, prevents engine run-on when the ignition is switched off by momentarily energizing the PCV valve solenoid when the ignition is switched **OFF** to prevent air entering below the throttle plate.

Bowl Vent Solenoid

OPERATION

The bowl vent solenoid is located in the hose between the carburetor bowl vent and the canister. The bowl vent solenoid is closed and allows no fuel vapor to flow when the engine is operating. When the engine is not operating, the solenoid is open and allows vapor to flow to the charcoal canister to control hydrocarbon emissions from the carburetor float bowl.

The bowl vent solenoid is electrically energized when the ignition is switched **ON** and is not controlled by the MCU.

Intake Manifold Heater Switch

OPERATION

The intake manifold heater switch is located in the intake manifold and is controlled by the temperature of the engine coolant. Below 160°F (71°C) the manifold heater switch activates the intake manifold heater to improve fuel vaporization. The switch is not controlled by the MCU and does not provide input information to it.

Oxygen Sensor

OPERATION

This component of the system provides a variable voltage (millivolts) for the Micro Computer Unit (MCU) that is proportional to the oxygen content in the exhaust gas. In addition to the oxygen sensor, the following data senders are used to supply the MCU with engine operation data.

TESTING

1. Start the engine and bring it to normal operating temperature, then run the engine above 1200 rpm for two minutes.
2. Backprobe with a high impedance averaging voltmeter (set to the DC voltage scale) between the oxygen sensor (02S) and battery ground.
3. Verify that the 02S voltage fluctuates rapidly between 0.40-0.60 volts.
4. If the 02S voltage is stabilized at the middle of the specified range (approximately 0.45-0.55 volts) or if the 02S voltage fluctuates very slowly between the specified range (02S signal crosses 0.5 volts less than 5 times in ten seconds), the 02S may be faulty.
5. If the 02S voltage stabilizes at either end of the specified range, the ECM is probably not able to compensate for a mechanical problem such as a vacuum leak or a high float level. These types of mechanical problems will cause the 02S to sense a constant lean or constant rich mixture. The mechanical problem will first have to be repaired and then the 02S test repeated.
6. Pull a vacuum hose located after the throttle plate. Voltage should drop to approximately 0.12 volts (while still fluctuating rapidly). This tests the ability of the 02S to detect a lean mixture condition. Reattach the vacuum hose.
7. Richen the mixture using a propane enrichment tool. Voltage should rise to approximately 0.90 volts (while still fluctuating rapidly). This tests the ability of the 02S to detect a rich mixture condition.
8. If the 02S voltage is above or below the specified range, the 02S and/or the O2S wiring may be faulty. Check the wiring for any breaks, repair as necessary and repeat the test.

REMOVAL & INSTALLATION

✳✳WARNING

The sensor uses a permanently attached pigtail and connector. This pigtail should not be removed from the sensor. Damage or removal of the pigtail or connector could affect the proper operation of the sensor. Keep the electrical connector and louvered end of the sensor clean and free of grease. NEVER use cleaning solvents of any type on the sensor!

➡**The oxygen sensor may be difficult to remove when the temperature of the engine is below 120°F (49°C). Excessive force may damage the threads in the exhaust manifold or exhaust pipe.**

1. Unplug the electrical connector and any attaching hardware.
2. Remove the sensor using an appropriate sized wrench or special socket.
   To install:
3. Coat the threads of the sensor with an anti-seize compound before installation. New sensors are usually precoated with this compound.

➡**DO NOT use a conventional anti-seize paste. The use of a regular paste may electrically insulate the sensor, rendering it useless. The threads MUST be coated with the proper electrically conductive anti-seize compound.**

4. Install the sensor and tighten to 30 ft. lbs. (40 Nm). Use care in making sure the silicone boot is in the correct position to avoid melting it during operation.
5. Engage the electrical connector and attaching hardware if used.

Knock Sensor

OPERATION

The knock sensor is a tuned piezoelectric crystal transducer that is located in the cylinder head. The knock sensor provides the MCU with an electrical signal that is created by vibrations that correspond to its center frequency (5550 Hz). Vibrations from engine knock (detonation) cause the crystal inside the sensor to vibrate and produce an electrical signal that is used by the MCU to selectively retard the ignition timing of any single cylinder or combination of cylinders to eliminate the knock condition.

Vacuum Switches

OPERATION

Two vacuum-operated electrical switches (ported and manifold) are used to detect and send throttle position data to the MCU for idle (closed), partial and Wide Open Throttle (WOT).

These switches are located together in a bracket attached to the dash panel in the engine compartment. The 4 in. Hg (27 kPa) vacuum switch can be identified by its natural (beige) color, while the 10 in. Hg (68 kPa) vacuum switch is green in color. The 4 in. Hg (27 kPa) switch is controlled by ported vacuum and its electrical contact is normally in the open position when the vacuum level is less than 4 in. Hg (27 kPa). When the vacuum exceeds 4 in. Hg (27 kPa), the switch closes. The 4 in. Hg (27 kPa) vacuum switch tells the MCU when either a closed or deep throttle condition exists.

The 10 in. Hg (68 kPa) vacuum switch is controlled by manifold vacuum. Its electrical contact is normally closed when the vacuum level is less than 10 in. Hg (68 kPa); if the vacuum level exceeds 10 in. Hg (68 kPa), the switch opens. This switch tells the MCU that either a partial or medium throttle condition exists.

Coolant Temperature Switch

OPERATION

The temperature switch supplies engine coolant temperature data to the MCU. Until the engine is sufficiently warmed (above 135°F/57°C), the system remains in the open loop mode of operation (i.e., a fixed air/fuel mixture based upon engine rpm).

Thermal Electric Switch

OPERATION

The thermal electric switch is located inside the air cleaner to sense the incoming air temperature and indicate a cold weather start-up condition to the MCU when the air temperature is below 50°F (10°C). Above 65°F (18°C), the switch opens to indicate a normal engine start-up condition to the MCU.

Wide Open Throttle (WOT) Switch

OPERATION

The wide open throttle switch is attached to the base of the carburetor by a mounting bracket. It is a mechanically operated electrical switch that is controlled by the position of the throttle. When the throttle is placed in the wide-open position, a cam on the throttle shaft actuates the switch about 15 degrees before the wide-open position to indicate a full-throttle demand to the MCU.

REMOVAL & INSTALLATION

1. Remove the air cleaner assembly.
2. Disconnect the throttle return spring.
3. Disconnect the throttle cable.

4. Disengage the wire harness connector to the WOT switch.

5. Remove the two WOT switch-to-bracket mounting screws.

6. Remove the WOT switch.

To install:

7. Install the WOT switch and tighten the retainers.

8. Engage the wire harness connector to the switch.

9. Connect the throttle cable and the throttle return spring.

10. Install the air cleaner assembly.

Altitude Jumper Wire

OPERATION

The altitude jumper wire connector is located next to the MCU. The jumper wire provides the MCU with an indication of whether the vehicle is being operated above or below a 4000 ft. elevation (high altitude operation). The connector normally has no jumper wire installed. If a vehicle is to be operated in a designated high altitude area, a jumper wire must be installed.

Diagnosis and Testing

♦ See Figures 38, 39 and 40

➡The CEC system should be considered as a possible source of trouble only after normal tests, that would apply to a vehicle without the system, have been performed.

The CEC Fuel Feedback System incorporates a diagnostic connector to provide a means for systematic evaluation of each component that could cause an operational failure. Electronic Fuel Feedback testers, ET-501-82 and ET-501-84 or equivalent, are available to aid in the system diagnosis. When a tester is not available, other test equipment can be substituted.

The equipment required to perform the checks and tests includes a tachometer, a hand vacuum pump and a digital volt-ohmmeter (DVOM) with a minimum ohms per volt of 10 megaohms.

❊❊WARNING

The use of a voltmeter with less than 10 megaohms per volt input impedance can destroy the oxygen sensor. Since it is necessary to look inside the carburetor with the engine running, observe the following precautions.

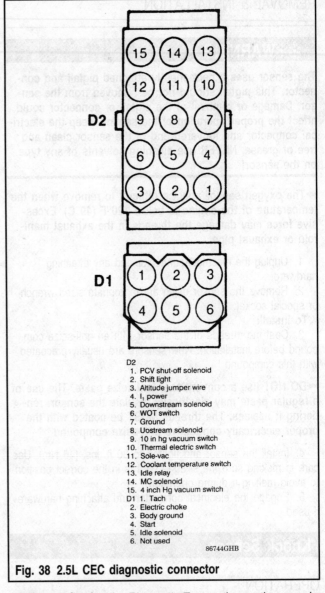

D2
1. PCV shut-off solenoid
2. Shift light
3. Altitude jumper wire
4. I, power
5. Downstream solenoid
6. WOT switch
7. Ground
8. Uostream solenoid
9. 10 in hg vacuum switch
10. Thermal electric switch
11. Sole-vac
12. Coolant temperature switch
13. Idle relay
14. MC solenoid
15. 4 inch Hg vacuum switch
D1 1. Tach
2. Electric choke
3. Body ground
4. Start
5. Idle solenoid
6. Not used

86744GHB

Fig. 38 2.5L CEC diagnostic connector

Before performing the Diagnostic Tests, other engine associated systems that can affect air/fuel mixture, combustion efficiency or exhaust gas composition should be tested for faults. These systems include:

1. Basic carburetor adjustments.
2. Mechanical engine operation (spark plugs, valves, rings, etc.).
3. Ignition system components and operation.
4. Gaskets (intake manifold, carburetor or base plate); loose vacuum hoses or fittings, or loose electrical connections.

CEC SYSTEM

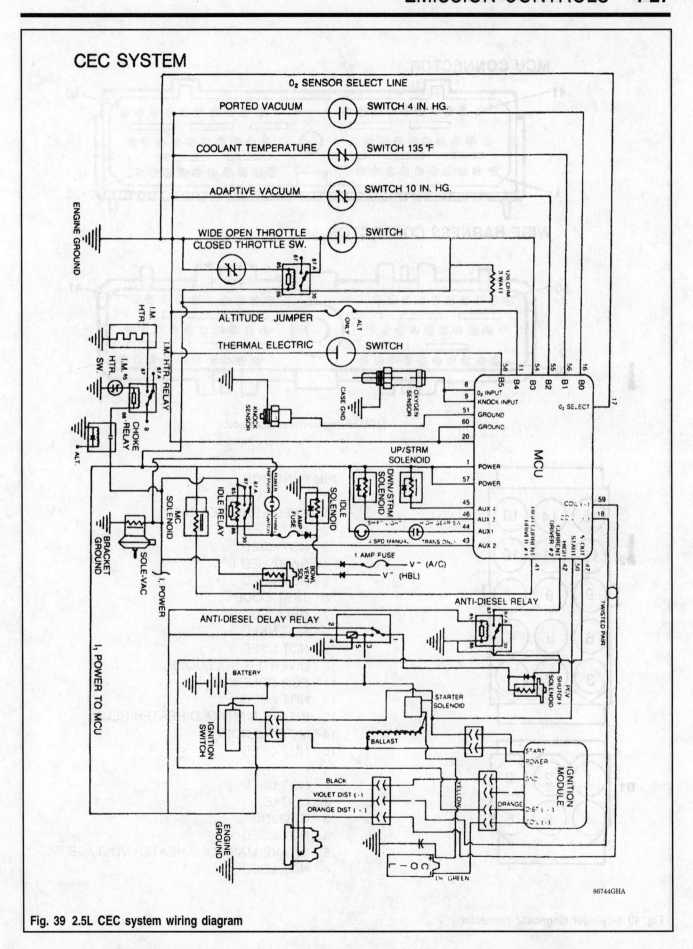

Fig. 39 2.5L CEC system wiring diagram

86744GHA

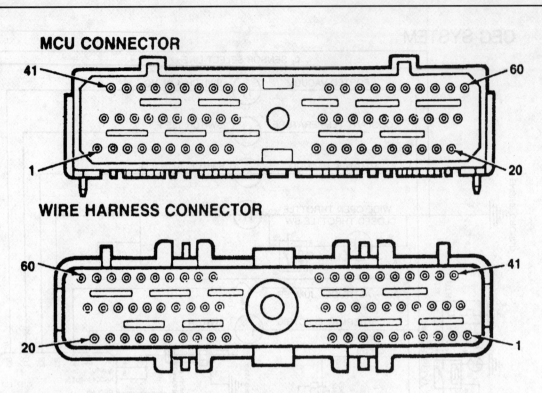

MCU CONNECTOR

41 → 60

1 → 20

WIRE HARNESS CONNECTOR

60 → 41

20 → 1

MCU wiring harness connector

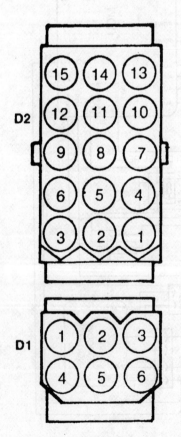

PIN FUNCTION

D2

1	CHECK ENGINE LIGHT
2	NOT USED
3	NOT USED
4	SWITCHED B+
5	NOT USED
6	TEST CODE
7	GROUND
8	NOT USED
9	NOT USED
10	DIVERTER SOLENOID
11	EGR SOLENOID
12	NOT USED
13	INTAKE MANIFOLD HEATER RELAY
14	MC SOLENOID
15	NOT USED

D1

1	NOT USED
2	CHOKE
3	GROUND
4	NOT USED
5	INTAKE MANIFOLD HEATER VOLTAGE
6	NOT USED

86744GHC

Fig. 40 6-cylinder diagnostic connector

FOUR CYLINDER CEC SYSTEM DIAGNOSTIC CHARTS

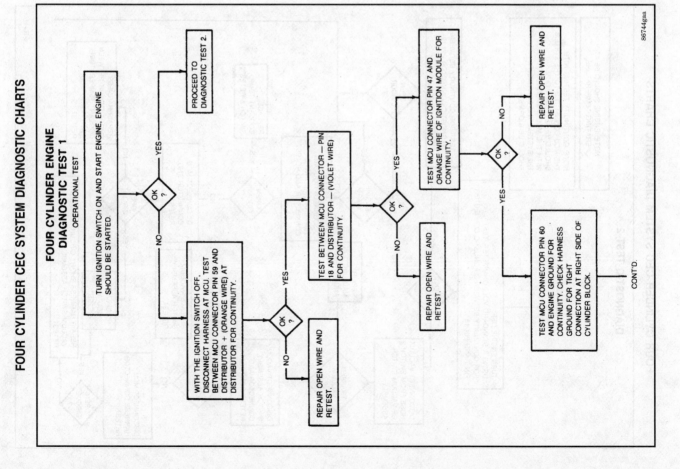

CONTINUED FROM PREVIOUS PAGE

OK ?
NO → REPAIR OPEN WIRE AND RETEST.

YES

TURN IGNITION SWITCH TO ON POSITION WITHOUT STARTING ENGINE. TEST MCU CONNECTOR PIN 1 AND GROUND FOR BATTERY VOLTAGE. TURN SWITCH OFF.

OK ?
NO → REPAIR OPEN WIRE AND RETEST.

YES

TEST MCU CONNECTOR PIN 50 AND THE S TERMINAL OF THE STARTER SOLENOID FOR CONTINUITY.

OK ?
YES → REPLACE MCU AND RETEST.*
NO → REPAIR OPEN WIRE AND RETEST.

*NOTE: BEFORE REPLACING MCU, IF ENGINE FAILS TO START, CHECK FOR FAILURE OF IGNITION MODULE, COIL, DISTRIBUTOR, ETC. SEE IGNITION SYSTEMS.

86744gab

FOUR CYLINDER CEC SYSTEM DIAGNOSTIC CHARTS

FOUR CYLINDER ENGINE DIAGNOSTIC TEST 1
OPERATIONAL TEST

TURN IGNITION SWITCH ON AND START ENGINE. ENGINE SHOULD BE STARTED.

OK ?
YES → PROCEED TO DIAGNOSTIC TEST 2.

NO

WITH THE IGNITION SWITCH OFF, DISCONNECT HARNESS AT MCU. TEST BETWEEN MCU CONNECTOR PIN 59 AND DISTRIBUTOR + (ORANGE WIRE) AT DISTRIBUTOR FOR CONTINUITY.

OK ?
NO → REPAIR OPEN WIRE AND RETEST.

YES

TEST BETWEEN MCU CONNECTOR — PIN 18 AND DISTRIBUTOR — (VIOLET WIRE) FOR CONTINUITY.

OK ?
NO → REPAIR OPEN WIRE AND RETEST.

YES

TEST MCU CONNECTOR PIN 47 AND ORANGE WIRE OF IGNITION MODULE FOR CONTINUITY.

OK ?
NO → REPAIR OPEN WIRE AND RETEST.

YES

TEST MCU CONNECTOR PIN 60 AND ENGINE GROUND FOR CONTINUITY. CHECK HARNESS GROUND FOR TIGHT CONNECTION AT RIGHT SIDE OF CYLINDER BLOCK.

CONT'D.

86744gaa

FOUR CYLINDER CEC SYSTEM DIAGNOSTIC CHARTS

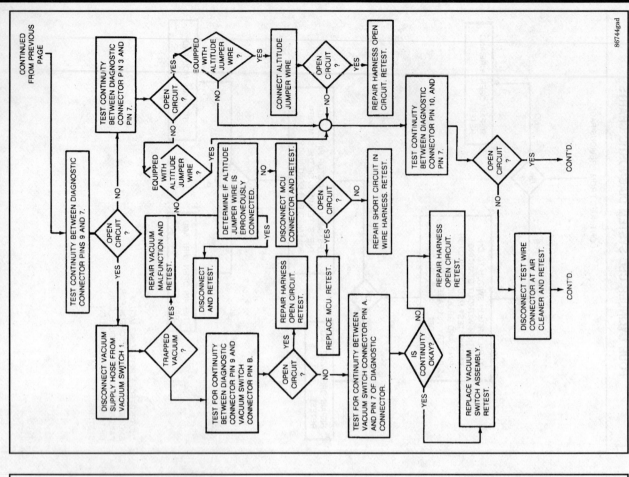

FOUR CYLINDER CEC SYSTEM DIAGNOSTIC CHARTS

DIAGNOSTIC TEST 2

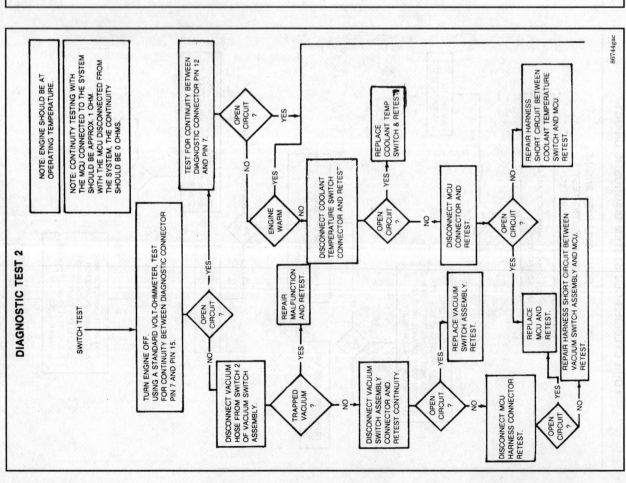

FOUR CYLINDER CEC SYSTEM DIAGNOSTIC CHARTS

86744gaf

TEST FOR CONTINUITY BETWEEN PIN 6 AND PIN 7 OF DIAGNOSTIC CONNECTOR.

OPEN CIRCUIT?

TURN IGNITION SWITCH TO THE ON POSITION. DEPRESS ACCELERATOR PEDAL TO HALF THROTTLE POSITION WHILE MONITORING CONTINUITY BETWEEN PIN 6 AND PIN 7 OF DIAGNOSTIC CONNECTOR.

OPEN CIRCUIT?

REPEAT SEVERAL TIMES UNTIL SATISFIED SWITCH AND RELAY ARE FUNCTIONING NORMALLY.

CONT'D.

REMOVE CLOSED THROTTLE SWITCH RELAY FROM CONNECTOR. INSERT A JUMPER BETWEEN HARNESS TERMINALS 87A AND 30/51. TEST FOR CONTINUITY BETWEEN PIN 6 AND PIN 7 OF DIAGNOSTIC CONNECTOR.

OPEN CIRCUIT?

REPLACE CLOSED THROTTLE RELAY. RETEST.

REPAIR OPEN CIRCUIT IN CLOSED THROTTLE RELAY HARNESS. RETEST.

TURN IGNITION OFF. REMOVE CLOSED THROTTLE RELAY FROM CONNECTOR. TURN IGNITION SWITCH ON. CHECK FOR 12V BETWEEN TERMINAL 86 ON WIRE HARNESS AND GROUND.

IS 12 VOLTS PRESENT?

REPAIR OPEN IN POWER LINE FEED TO CLOSED THROTTLE RELAY. RETEST.

TURN OFF IGNITION. CHECK FOR A SHORT BETWEEN 87A AND 30/51 TERMINALS ON WIRE HARNESS.

IS A SHORT PRESENT?

REPAIR SHORT IN CLOSED THROTTLE RELAY HARNESS. RETEST.

CHECK FOR CONTINUITY BETWEEN TERMINAL 85 ON WIRE HARNESS AND PIN 7 OF DIAGNOSTIC CONNECTOR WHILE DEPRESSING ACCELERATOR PEDAL.

OPEN CIRCUIT?

REPLACE RELAY (CLOSED THROTTLE) RETEST.

DISCONNECT CLOSED THROTTLE SWITCH, INSERT JUMPER BETWEEN HARNESS TERMINALS. CHECK FOR CONTINUITY BETWEEN TERMINAL 85 OR WIRE HARNESS AND PIN 7 OF DIAGNOSTIC CONNECTOR.

OPEN CIRCUIT?

REPLACE CLOSED THROTTLE SWITCH. RETEST.

REPAIR OPEN IN WIRE HARNESS. RETEST.

FOUR CYLINDER CEC SYSTEM DIAGNOSTIC CHARTS

86744gae

CONTINUED FROM PREVIOUS PAGE

DISCONNECT CLOSED THROTTLE SWITCH RELAY. TEST FOR CONTINUITY BETWEEN PIN 6 AND PIN 7 ON DIAGNOSTIC CONNECTOR.

OPEN CIRCUIT?

DISCONNECT WOT SWITCH CONNECTOR AT CARBURETOR AND RETEST.

DEPRESS ACCELERATOR PEDAL TO WIDE OPEN THROTTLE POSITION MONITORING CONTINUITY BETWEEN PIN 6 AND PIN 7 OF DIAGNOSTIC CONN.

OPEN CIRCUIT?

REPEAT SEVERAL TIMES UNTIL SATISFIED SWITCH IS FUNCTIONING NORMALLY.

RECONNECT CLOSED THROTTLE SWITCH RELAY. DISCONNECT WOT SWITCH CONNECTOR AT CARBURETOR.

CONT'D.

OPEN CIRCUIT?

REPLACE WOT SWITCH AND RETEST.

DISCONNECT MCU AND RETEST.

OPEN CIRCUIT?

REPLACE MCU AND RETEST.

*NOTE THE WOT SWITCH IS DIFFICULT TO REPLACE BEFORE REMOVING THE SWITCH CONNECT A REPLACEMENT SWITCH TO THE WIRE HARNESS CONNECTOR AND RETEST TO ENSURE ORIGINAL SWITCH IS FAULTY.

CONTINUED FROM PREVIOUS PAGE

OPEN CIRCUIT?

IS AIR CLEANER AIR TEMP ABOVE 55°F?

ALLOW AIR CLEANER AIR TEMPERATURE TO HEAT TO 65°F AND RETEST.

REPLACE TES AND RETEST.

DISCONNECT MCU CONNECTOR AND RETEST.

OPEN CIRCUIT?

REPLACE MCU AND RETEST.

REPAIR SHORT CIRCUIT IN TES WIRES AND RETEST.

REPAIR SHORT CIRCUIT IN WOT SWITCH OR CLOSED THROTTLE SW HARNESS RETEST.

DISCONNECT WOT SWITCH CONNECTOR AND CONNECT JUMPER WIRE BETWEEN WIRE HARNESS CONNECTOR TERMINALS. RETEST FOR CONTINUITY.

INSPECT CARBURETOR LINKAGE AND ENSURE SWITCH IS BEING ENGAGED.

OK?

REPAIR AND RETEST

OPEN CIRCUIT?

REPAIR OPEN CIRCUIT IN WOT SWITCH WIRE HARNESS. ENSURE THERE IS CONTINUITY BETWEEN WOT SWITCH AND MCU CONNECTOR PIN 54

REPLACE WOT SWITCH AND RETEST.

FOUR CYLINDER CEC SYSTEM DIAGNOSTIC CHARTS

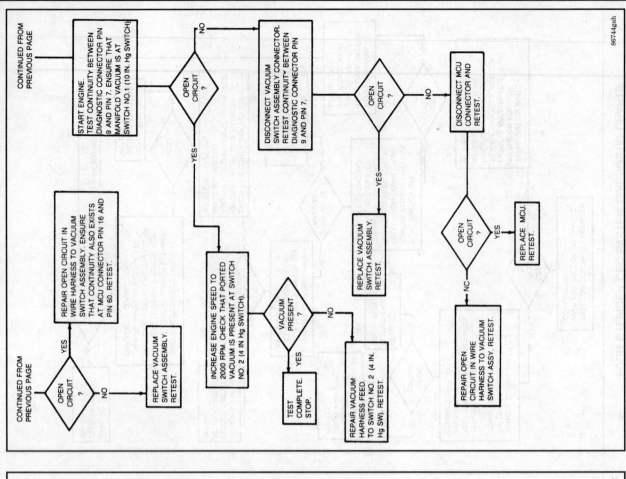

86744gah

FOUR CYLINDER CEC SYSTEM DIAGNOSTIC CHARTS

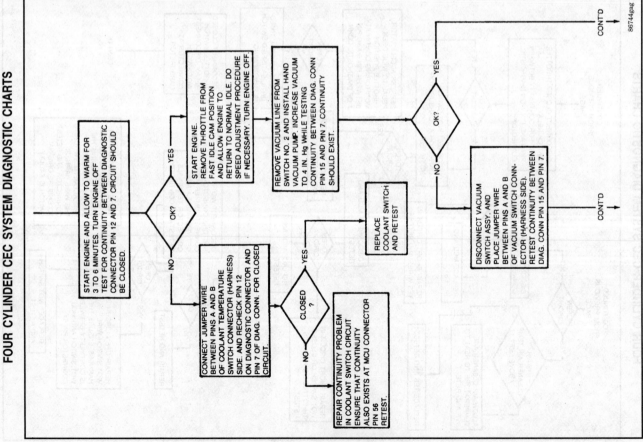

86744gag

FOUR CYLINDER CEC SYSTEM DIAGNOSTIC CHARTS

DIAGNOSTIC TEST 4.

KNOCK SENSOR TEST

86744gai

WARM ENGINE TO NORMAL OPERATING TEMPERATURE. CHECK ENGINE TIMING (SET TO SPECS IF NECESSARY).

CONNECT TIMING LIGHT AND TACHOMETER. START ENGINE. DISCONNECT AND PLUG VACUUM LINE TO 10 IN. Hg SWITCH (SWITCH NO. 1). INCREASE ENGINE RPM TO 1600 AND HOLD. KNOCK ON INTAKE MANIFOLD NEXT TO KNOCK SENSOR WITH METALLIC OBJECT WHILE WATCHING TIMING MARKS.

DOES TIMING RETARD ?

YES → TURN OFF ENGINE TEST COMPLETE.

NO ↓

IS TIMING LESS THAN 12° (OR SET VALUE) ?

YES → TURN ENGINE OFF. DISCONNECT MCU CONNECTOR. USING OHMMETER TEST FOR A SHORT BETWEEN MCU PIN 51 AND ALL OTHER PINS IN MCU CONNECTOR.

SHORT CIRCUIT ?

YES → REPAIR SHORT CIRCUIT WIRE HARNESS RETEST.

NO → REPLACE MCU. RETEST.

NO (from IS TIMING LESS) → TURN OFF ENGINE. DISCONNECT MCU CONNECTOR AND TERMINAL FROM KNOCK SENSOR. USING OHMMETER TEST FOR CONTINUITY BETWEEN MCU-PIN 51 AND KNOCK SENSOR TERMINAL LUG.

OPEN CIRCUIT ?

YES → REPAIR OPEN CIRCUIT IN WIRE HARNESS BETWEEN KNOCK SENSOR AND MCU. RETEST.

NO → CHECK FOR SHORT BETWEEN MCU PIN 51 AND MCU PIN 60

IS SHORT CIRCUIT PRESENT ?

YES → REPAIR SHORT CIRCUIT IN WIRE HARNESS RETEST.

NO → REPLACE KNOCK SENSOR. RETEST IF STILL NOT FUNCTIONING REPLACE MCU.

FOUR CYLINDER CEC SYSTEM DIAGNOSTIC CHARTS

DIAGNOSTIC TEST 3

CLOSED LOOP OPERATIONAL TEST.

86744gai

CONNECT THE LEAD (+) OF A DWELL METER TO PIN NO. 14 ON THE DIAGNOSTIC CONNECTOR - SET METER ON THE 6-CYLINDER DWELL SCALE. CONNECT THE LEAD (−) OF DWELL METER TO GROUND. START ENGINE AND WARM UNTIL COOLANT TEMPERATURE HAS STABILIZED. INCREASE ENGINE SPEED TO 2000 RPM AND MAINTAIN WHILE OBSERVING THE DWELL METER POINTER.

DOES DWELL METER POINTER MOVE TOWARD FULL SCALE OR ZERO POSITION ?

YES → PROCEED TO TEST 5.

NO ↓

DOES DWELL METER POINTER OSCILLATE AROUND A FIXED POINT?

YES → NEAR FULL RICH OR LEAN POSITION ?

NO → PROCEED TO TEST 5.

NEAR FULL RICH OR LEAN POSITION ?

YES → PROCEED TO TEST 5.

NO → IF DWELL METER POINTER IS OSCILLATING NEAR MIDPOINT. CLOSED LOOP CIRCUIT IS FUNCTIONING NORMALLY. TEST COMPLETE.

FOUR CYLINDER CEC SYSTEM DIAGNOSTIC CHARTS

FOUR CYLINDER CEC SYSTEM DIAGNOSTIC CHARTS

DIAGNOSTIC TEST 5
OXYGEN SENSOR AND CLOSED LOOP TEST.

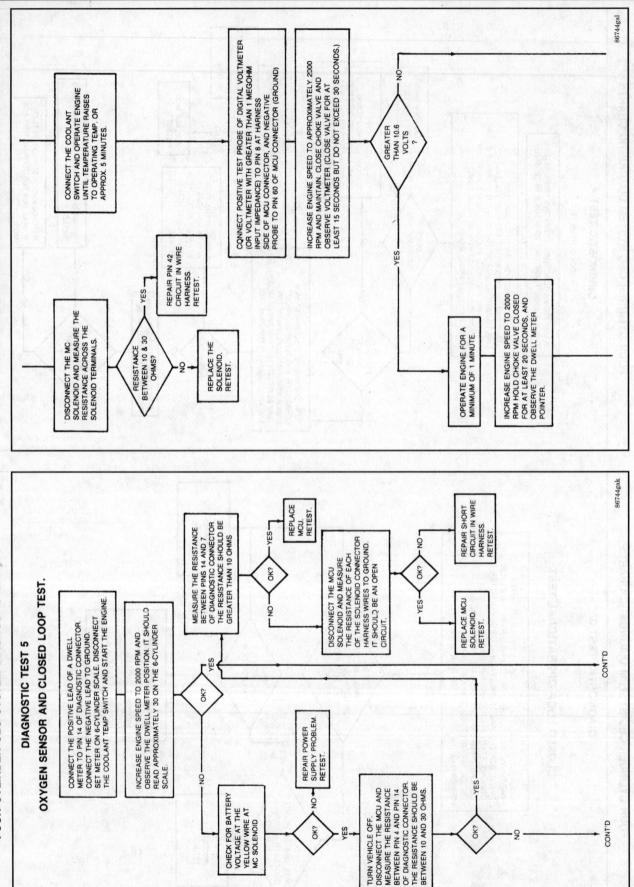

FOUR CYLINDER CEC SYSTEM DIAGNOSTIC CHARTS

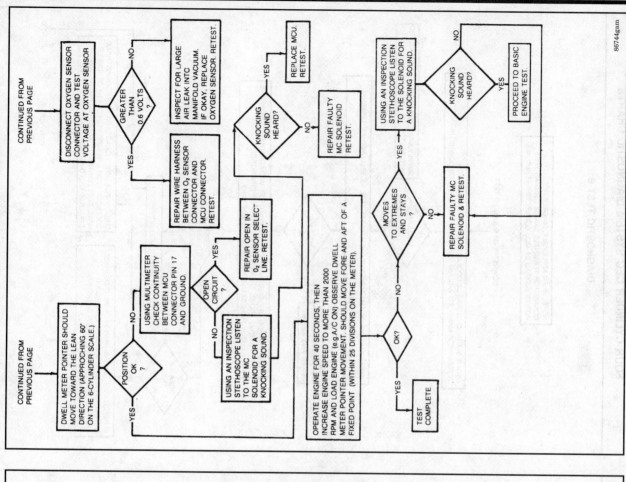

FOUR CYLINDER CEC SYSTEM DIAGNOSTIC CHARTS

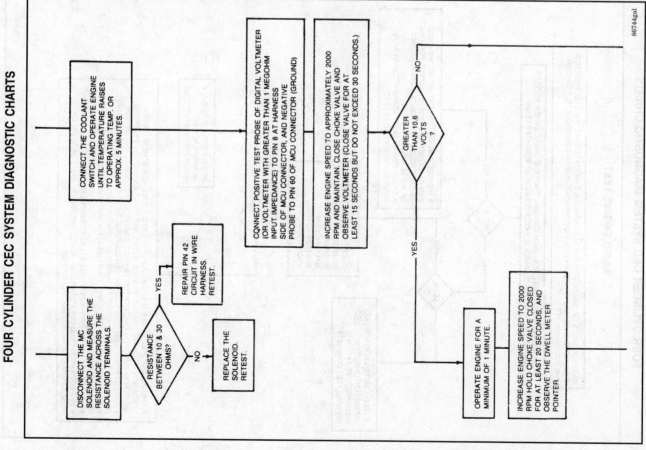

FOUR CYLINDER CEC SYSTEM DIAGNOSTIC CHARTS

DIAGNOSTIC TEST 6

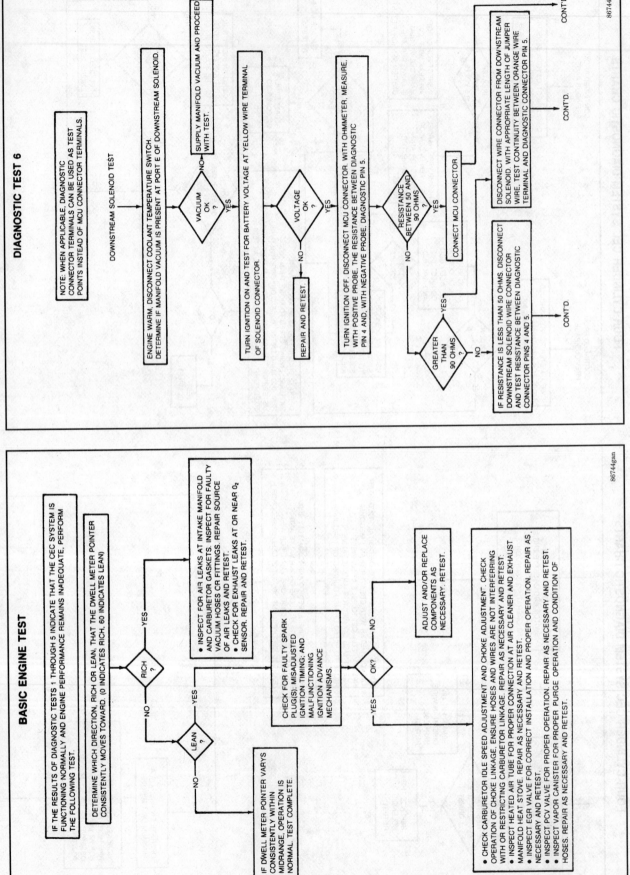

NOTE: WHEN APPLICABLE, DIAGNOSTIC CONNECTOR TERMINALS CAN BE USED AS TEST POINTS INSTEAD OF MCU CONNECTOR TERMINALS.

DOWNSTREAM SOLENOID TEST

ENGINE WARM. DISCONNECT COOLANT TEMPERATURE SWITCH. DETERMINE IF MANIFOLD VACUUM IS PRESENT AT PORT E OF DOWNSTREAM SOLENOID.

VACUUM OK? — NO → SUPPLY MANIFOLD VACUUM AND PROCEED WITH TEST.

YES

TURN IGNITION ON AND TEST FOR BATTERY VOLTAGE AT YELLOW WIRE TERMINAL OF SOLENOID CONNECTOR.

VOLTAGE OK? — NO → REPAIR AND RETEST.

YES

TURN IGNITION OFF. DISCONNECT MCU CONNECTOR. WITH OHMMETER, MEASURE, WITH POSITIVE PROBE, THE RESISTANCE BETWEEN DIAGNOSTIC PIN 4 AND, WITH NEGATIVE PROBE, DIAGNOSTIC PIN 5.

RESISTANCE BETWEEN 50 AND 90 OHMS? — YES → CONNECT MCU CONNECTOR → DISCONNECT WIRE CONNECTOR FROM DOWNSTREAM SOLENOID. WITH APPROPRIATE LENGTH OF JUMPER WIRE, TEST CONTINUITY BETWEEN ORANGE WIRE TERMINAL AND DIAGNOSTIC CONNECTOR PIN 5. → CONT'D

NO

GREATER THAN 90 OHMS? — YES → (up to CONNECT MCU CONNECTOR)

NO → IF RESISTANCE IS LESS THAN 50 OHMS. DISCONNECT DOWNSTREAM SOLENOID WIRE CONNECTOR AND TEST RESISTANCE BETWEEN DIAGNOSTIC CONNECTOR PINS 4 AND 5 → CONT'D.

CONT'D

FOUR CYLINDER CEC SYSTEM DIAGNOSTIC CHARTS

BASIC ENGINE TEST

IF THE RESULTS OF DIAGNOSTIC TESTS 1 THROUGH 5 INDICATE THAT THE CEC SYSTEM IS FUNCTIONING NORMALLY AND ENGINE PERFORMANCE REMAINS INADEQUATE, PERFORM THE FOLLOWING TEST.

DETERMINE WHICH DIRECTION, RICH OR LEAN, THAT THE DWELL METER POINTER CONSISTENTLY MOVES TOWARD. (0 INDICATES RICH, 60 INDICATES LEAN)

RICH? — YES → • INSPECT FOR AIR LEAKS AT INTAKE MANIFOLD AND CARBURETOR GASKETS. INSPECT FOR FAULTY VACUUM HOSES CR FITTINGS. REPAIR SOURCE OF AIR LEAKS AND RETEST.
• CHECK FOR EXHAUST LEAKS AT OR NEAR 0₂ SENSOR. REPAIR AND RETEST.

NO

LEAN? — NO → IF DWELL METER POINTER VARYS CONSISTENTLY WITHIN MIDRANGE, OPERATION IS NORMAL. TEST COMPLETE.

YES

CHECK FOR FAULTY SPARK PLUG(S): MISADJUSTED IGNITION TIMING; AND MALFUNCTIONING IGNITION ADVANCE MECHANISMS.

OK? — NO → ADJUST AND/OR REPLACE COMPONENTS AS NECESSARY. RETEST.

YES

• CHECK CARBURETOR IDLE SPEED ADJUSTMENT AND CHOKE ADJUSTMENT. CHECK OPERATION OF CHOKE LINKAGE, ENSURE HOSES AND WIRES ARE NOT INTERFERING WITH OR RESTRICTING CARBURETOR LINKAGE. REPAIR AS NECESSARY AND RETEST.
• INSPECT HEATED AIR TUBE FOR PROPER CONNECTION AT AIR CLEANER AND EXHAUST MANIFOLD HEAT STOVE. REPAIR AS NECESSARY AND RETEST.
• INSPECT EGR VALVE FOR CORRECT INSTALLATION AND PROPER OPERATION. REPAIR AS NECESSARY AND RETEST.
• INSPECT PCV VALVE FOR PROPER OPERATION. REPAIR AS NECESSARY AND RETEST.
• INSPECT VAPOR CANISTER FOR PROPER PURGE OPERATION AND CONDITION OF HOSES. REPAIR AS NECESSARY AND RETEST.

86744gao

86744gan

FOUR CYLINDER CEC SYSTEM DIAGNOSTIC CHARTS

DIAGNOSTIC TEST 7

NOTE: WHEN APPLICABLE, DIAGNOSTIC CONNECTOR TERMINALS CAN BE USED AS TEST POINTS INSTEAD OF MCU CONNECTOR TERMINALS.

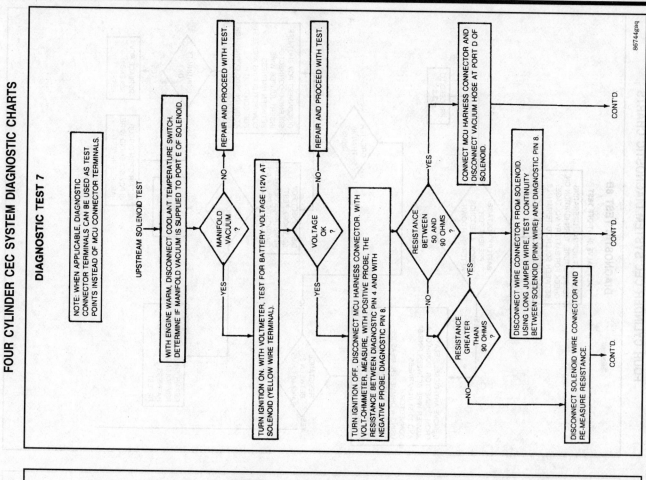

FOUR CYLINDER CEC SYSTEM DIAGNOSTIC CHARTS

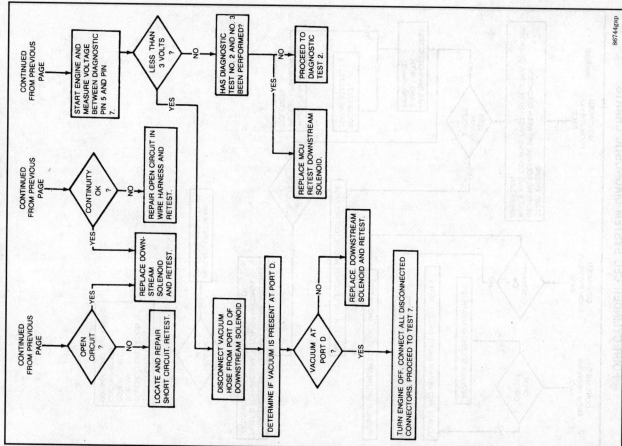

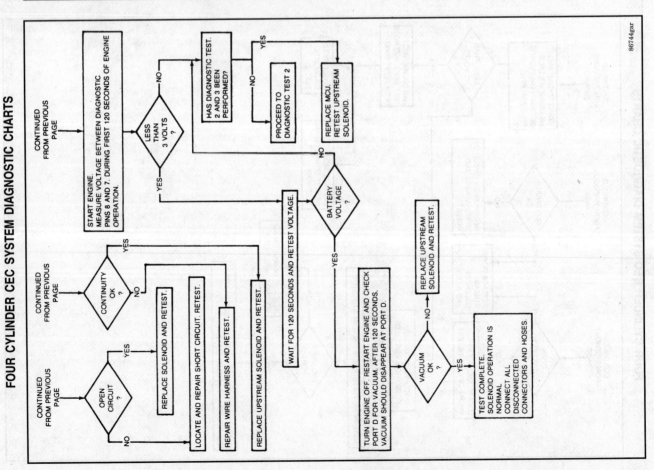

FOUR CYLINDER CEC SYSTEM DIAGNOSTIC CHARTS

DIAGNOSTIC TEST 8B

PCV VALVE SHUT-OFF TEST

ENGINE AT NORMAL OPERATING TEMPERATURE. TURN IGNITION ON. CHECK FOR BATTERY VOLTAGE BETWEEN SOLENOID TERMINALS WHILE TURNING IGNITION OFF.

BATTERY VOLTAGE PRESENT FOR APPROX. 4 SECONDS AFTER SHUTDOWN?

NO → PROCEED TO 8B1

YES → REMOVE ANTI-DIESEL RELAY FROM CONNECTOR. CONNECT A JUMPER WIRE BETWEEN PINS 87 AND 30/51 IN HARNESS CONNECTOR. USING A OHMMETER, MEASURE THE RESISTANCE OF SOLENOID WITH RED PROBE (POS.) ON DIAGNOSTIC PIN 4 AND BLACK (NEG.) PROBE ON DIAGNOSTIC PIN 1.

RESISTANCE BETWEEN 20 AND 40 OHMS?

YES →

NO → GREATER THAN 40 OHMS?

GREATER THAN 40 OHMS? — YES → DISCONNECT PCV SHUT-OFF SOLENOID CONNECTOR. INSERT JUMPER WIRE BETWEEN HARNESS CONNECTOR PINS AND TEST FOR CONTINUITY AT DIAGNOSTIC CONNECTOR PIN 4 AND PIN 1

NO → DISCONNECT PCV SOLENOID. TEST RESISTANCE BETWEEN DIAGNOSTIC PINS 4 & 1

CONTINUITY OK? — YES → REPLACE PCV SOLENOID. RETEST.

NO → REPAIR OPEN CIRCUIT IN PCV SOLENOID WIRE HARNESS RETEST

OPEN CIRCUIT? — YES → REPLACE PCV SOLENOID. RETEST.

NO → REPAIR SHORT CIRCUIT IN PCV SOLENOID WIRE HARNESS. RETEST.

86744gas

FOUR CYLINDER CEC SYSTEM DIAGNOSTIC CHARTS

CONTINUED FROM PREVIOUS PAGE → START ENGINE. MEASURE VOLTAGE BETWEEN DIAGNOSTIC PINS 8 AND 7. DURING FIRST 120 SECONDS OF ENGINE OPERATION.

LESS THAN 3 VOLTS?

NO → HAS DIAGNOSTIC TEST 2 AND 3 BEEN PERFORMED?

YES → REPLACE MCU. RETEST UPSTREAM SOLENOID.

NO → PROCEED TO DIAGNOSTIC TEST 2

YES → BATTERY VOLTAGE?

NO → WAIT FOR 120 SECONDS AND RETEST VOLTAGE.

YES → TURN ENGINE OFF. RESTART ENGINE AND CHECK PORT D FOR VACUUM. AFTER 120 SECONDS, VACUUM SHOULD DISAPPEAR AT PORT D.

VACUUM OK? — NO → REPLACE UPSTREAM SOLENOID AND RETEST.

YES → TEST COMPLETE. SOLENOID OPERATION IS NORMAL. CONNECT ALL DISCONNECTED CONNECTORS AND HOSES.

CONTINUED FROM PREVIOUS PAGE → CONTINUITY OK?

YES →

NO → REPAIR WIRE HARNESS AND RETEST.

CONTINUED FROM PREVIOUS PAGE → OPEN CIRCUIT?

YES → REPLACE SOLENOID AND RETEST.

NO → LOCATE AND REPAIR SHORT CIRCUIT. RETEST.

REPLACE UPSTREAM SOLENOID AND RETEST.

86744gar

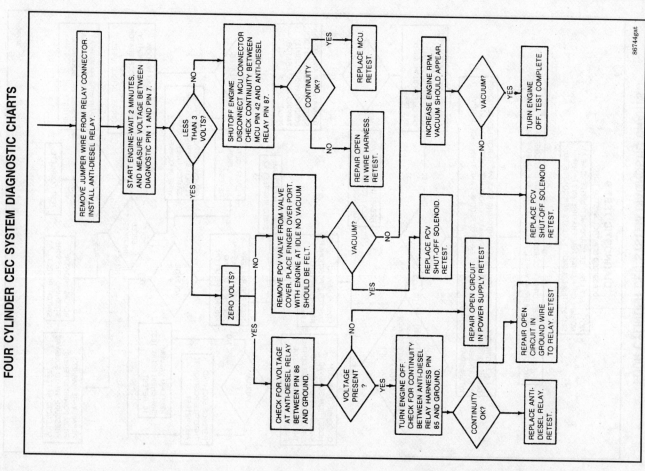

FOUR CYLINDER CEC SYSTEM DIAGNOSTIC CHARTS

DIAGNOSTIC TEST 8B

PCV VALVE SHUT-OFF TEST

86744gau

FOUR CYLINDER CEC SYSTEM DIAGNOSTIC CHARTS

86744gat

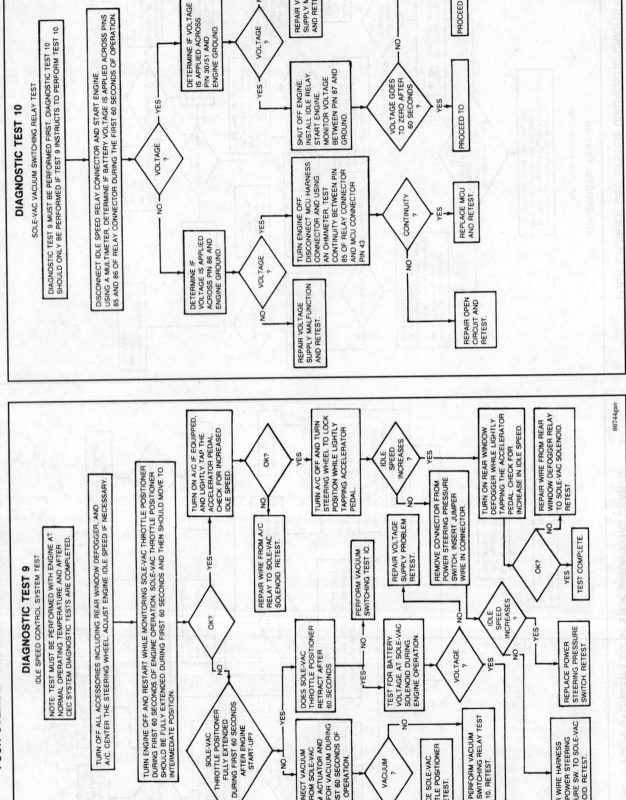

FOUR CYLINDER CEC SYSTEM DIAGNOSTIC CHARTS

DIAGNOSTIC TEST 10

SOLE-VAC VACUUM SWITCHING RELAY TEST

DIAGNOSTIC TEST 9 MUST BE PERFORMED FIRST. DIAGNOSTIC TEST 10 SHOULD ONLY BE PERFORMED IF TEST 9 INSTRUCTS TO PERFORM TEST 10.

FOUR CYLINDER CEC SYSTEM DIAGNOSTIC CHARTS

DIAGNOSTIC TEST 9

IDLE SPEED CONTROL SYSTEM TEST

NOTE: TEST MUST BE PERFORMED WITH ENGINE AT NORMAL OPERATING TEMPERATURE AND AFTER CEC SYSTEM DIAGNOSTIC TESTS ARE COMPLETED.

FOUR CYLINDER CEC SYSTEM DIAGNOSTIC CHARTS

DIAGNOSTIC TEST 10 (CONT'D)

SOLE-VAC VACUUM SWITCHING RELAY TEST (CONT'D)

FOUR CYLINDER CEC SYSTEM DIAGNOSTIC CHARTS

DIAGNOSTIC TEST 10 (CONT'D)

SOLE-VAC VACUUM SWITCHING RELAY TEST (CONT'D)

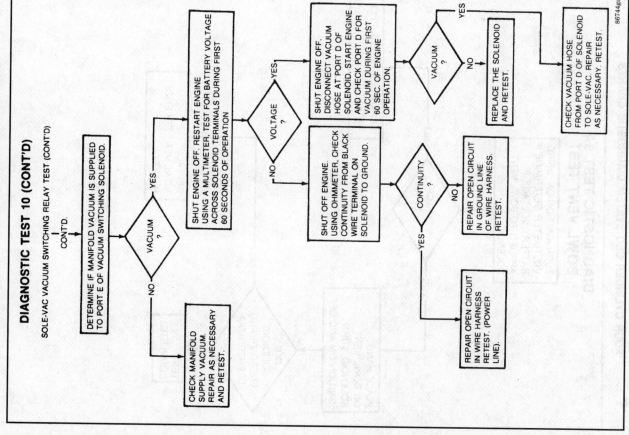

FOUR CYLINDER CEC SYSTEM DIAGNOSTIC CHARTS

INTAKE MANIFOLD HEATER TEST — 49 STATE

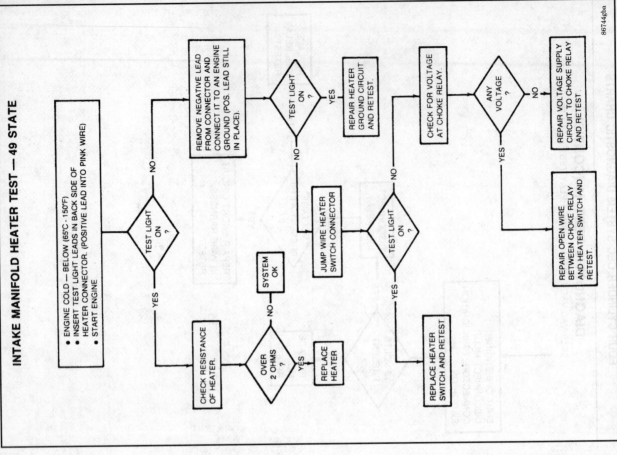

86744gba

FOUR CYLINDER CEC SYSTEM DIAGNOSTIC CHARTS

DIAGNOSTIC TEST 8A BOWL VENT TEST

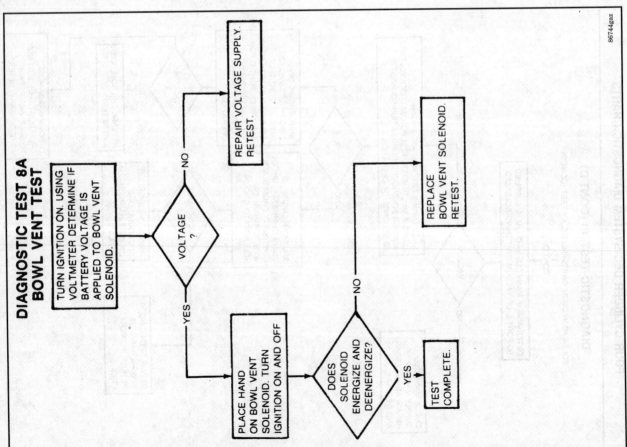

86744gaz

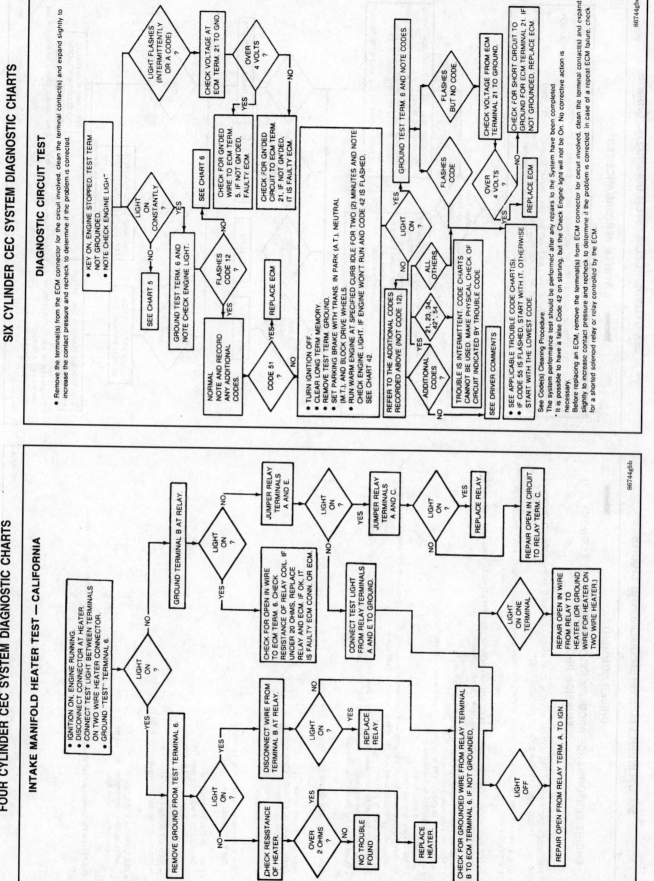

SIX CYLINDER CEC SYSTEM DIAGNOSTIC CHARTS

DIAGNOSTIC CIRCUIT TEST

- Remove the terminal(s) from the ECM connector for the circuit involved, clean the terminal contact(s) and expand slightly to increase the contact pressure and recheck to determine if the problem is corrected.

FOUR CYLINDER CEC SYSTEM DIAGNOSTIC CHARTS

INTAKE MANIFOLD HEATER TEST — CALIFORNIA

SIX CYLINDER CEC SYSTEM DIAGNOSTIC CHARTS

SYSTEM PERFORMANCE TEST

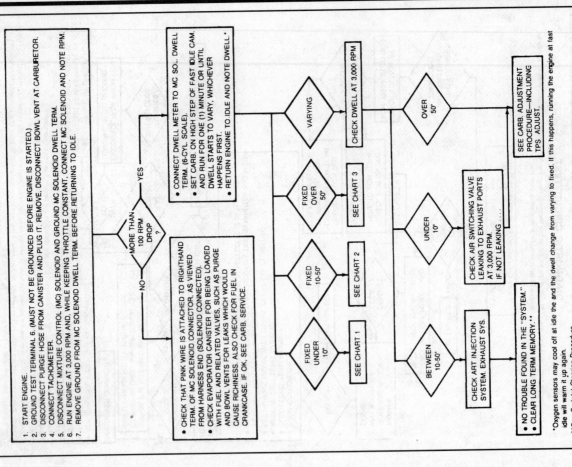

1. START ENGINE.
2. GROUND TEST TERMINAL 6. (MUST NOT BE GROUNDED BEFORE ENGINE IS STARTED.)
3. DISCONNECT PURGE HOSE FROM CANISTER AND PLUG IT. REMOVE, DISCONNECT BOWL VENT AT CARBURETOR.
4. CONNECT TACHOMETER.
5. DISCONNECT MIXTURE CONTROL (MC) SOLENOID AND GROUND MC SOLENOID DWELL TERM.
6. RUN ENGINE AT 3,000 RPM AND, WHILE KEEPING THROTTLE CONSTANT, CONNECT MC SOLENOID AND NOTE RPM.
7. REMOVE GROUND FROM MC SOLENOID DWELL TERM. BEFORE RETURNING TO IDLE.

SIX CYLINDER CEC SYSTEM DIAGNOSTIC CHARTS

DRIVER COMMENTS

ENGINE PERFORMANCE PROBLEM (ODOR, SURGE, FUEL ECONOMY ...) EMISSION PROBLEM

IF THE CHECK ENGINE LIGHT IS NOT ON, NORMAL CHECKS THAT WOULD BE PERFORMED ON THE VEHICLE WITHOUT THE SYSTEM SHOULD BE DONE FIRST.

IF THE ALTERNATOR OR COOLANT LIGHT IS ON WITH THE CHECK ENGINE LIGHT, THEY SHOULD BE DIAGNOSED FIRST.

INSPECT FOR POOR CONNECTIONS AT COOLANT SENSOR, MC SOLENOID, ETC., AND POOR OR LOOSE VACUUM HOSES AND CONNECTIONS. REPAIR AS NECESSARY.

- Intermittent Check Engine light but no trouble code stored.
  Check for intermittent connection in circuit from:
  - Ignition coil to ground and arcing at spark plug wires or plugs.
  - ECM Voltage Supply Terminals.
  - ECM Ground Terminals.
  - Loss of long-term memory.

  Grounding dwell lead for 10 seconds with test lead ungrounded should give Code 23, which should be retained after the engine is stopped and the ignition turned to RUN position. If it is not, ECM is defective.
  EST wires should be kept away from the spark plug wires, distributor housing, coil and alternator. Wires from ECM Term. 13 to dist. and the shield around EST wires should have a good ground.
  - Open diode across A/C compressor clutch.

- Stalling, Rough Idle, Dieseling or Improper Idle Speed.

- Detonation (spark knock)
  Check: MAP or Vacuum Sensor output.
  EGR operation.
  TPS enrichment operation.
  HEI operation.

- Poor Performance and/or Fuel Economy.
  See EST diagnosis.

- Poor Full Throttle Performance
  See Chart 4 if equipped with TPS.

- Intermittent No-start
  - Incorrect pickup coil or ignition coil.
  - Intermittent ground connections on ECM.

- ALL OTHER COMPLAINTS
  Make system performance test on warm engine.
  (upper radiator hose hot).

The System Performance Test should be performed after any repairs to the system has been made.

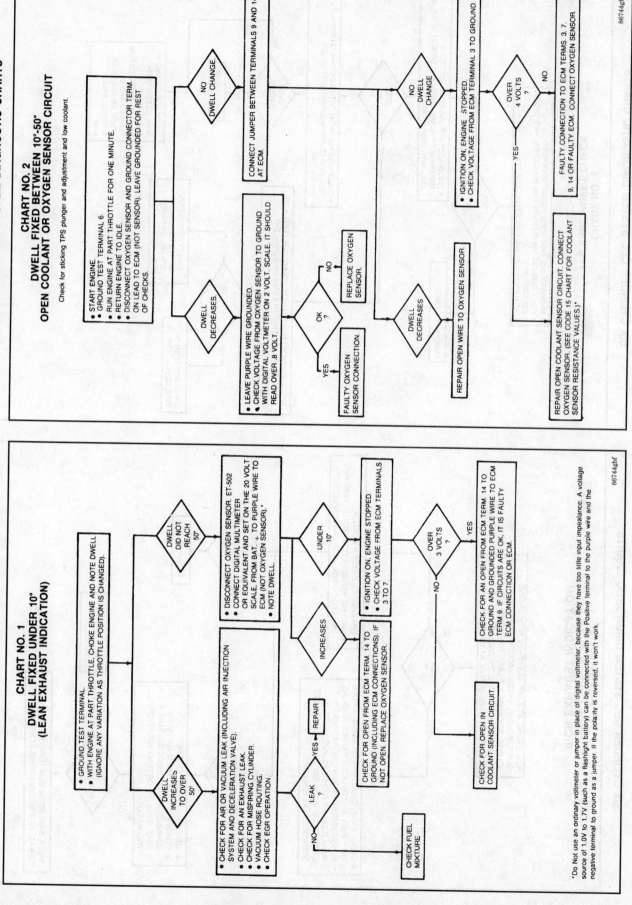

SIX CYLINDER CEC SYSTEM DIAGNOSTIC CHARTS

CHART NO. 4
TPS ENRICHMENT CHECK

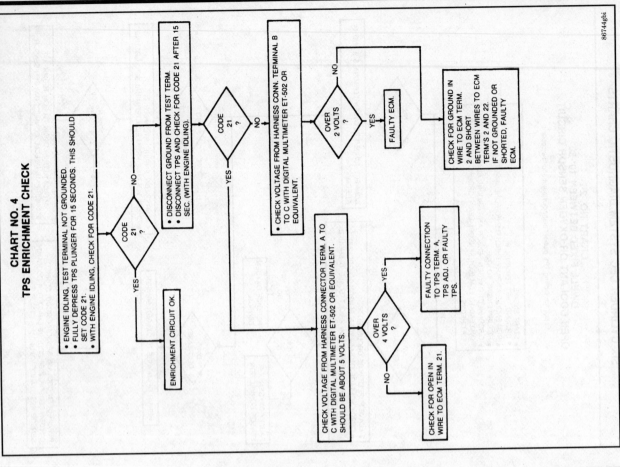

SIX CYLINDER CEC SYSTEM DIAGNOSTIC CHARTS

CHART NO. 3
DWELL FIXED OVER 50°
RICH EXHAUST INDICATION

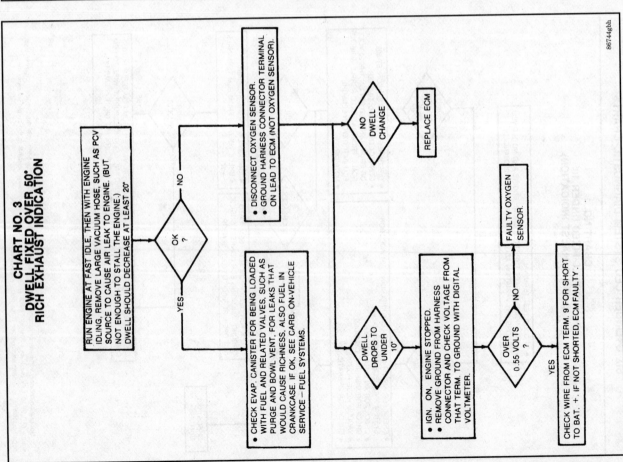

SIX CYLINDER CEC SYSTEM DIAGNOSTIC CHARTS

CHART NO. 6
CODE 12 DOES NOT FLASH
(REMOTE LAMP DRIVER IN HARNESS)

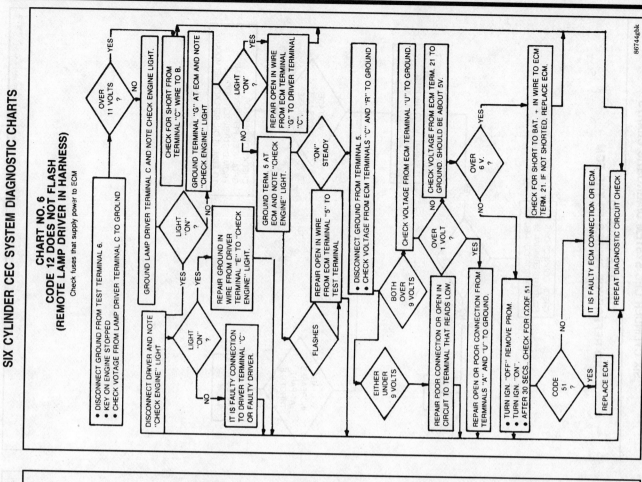

SIX CYLINDER CEC SYSTEM DIAGNOSTIC CHARTS

CHART NO. 5
CHECK ENGINE LIGHT INOPERATIVE

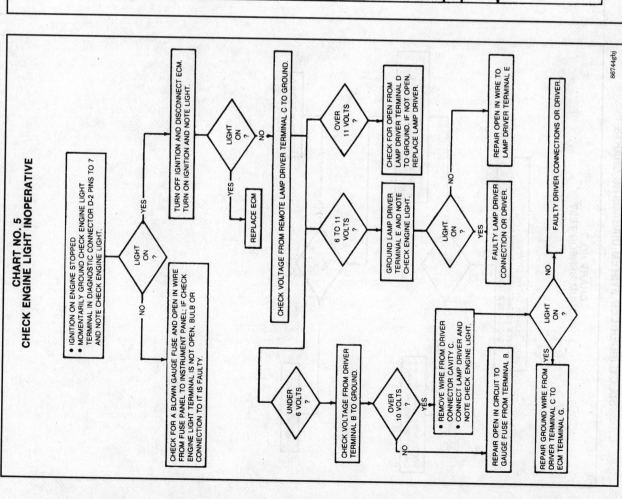

SIX CYLINDER CEC SYSTEM DIAGNOSTIC CHARTS

TROUBLE CODE 12
NO REFERENCE PULSES TO THE ECM

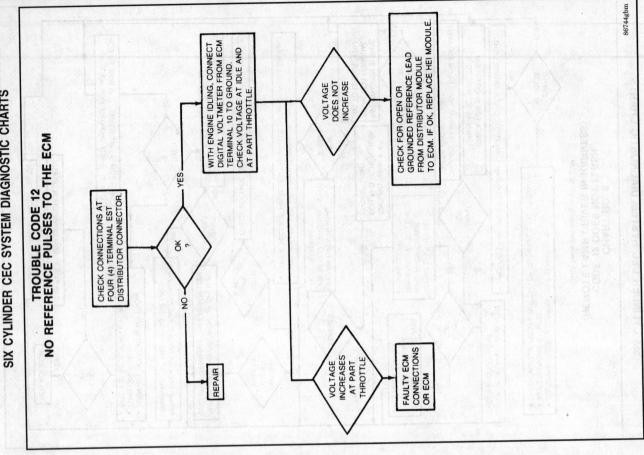

CHECK CONNECTIONS AT FOUR (4) TERMINAL EST DISTRIBUTOR CONNECTOR.

OK ?

NO → REPAIR

YES → WITH ENGINE IDLING, CONNECT DIGITAL VOLTMETER FROM ECM TERMINAL 10 TO GROUND. CHECK VOLTAGE AT IDLE AND AT PART THROTTLE.

VOLTAGE DOES NOT INCREASE → CHECK FOR OPEN OR GROUNDED REFERENCE LEAD FROM DISTRIBUTOR MODULE TO ECM. IF OK, REPLACE HEI MODULE.

VOLTAGE INCREASES AT PART THROTTLE → FAULTY ECM CONNECTIONS OR ECM

86744gbm

SIX CYLINDER CEC SYSTEM DIAGNOSTIC CHARTS

CHART NO.7
VACUUM SENSOR TEST

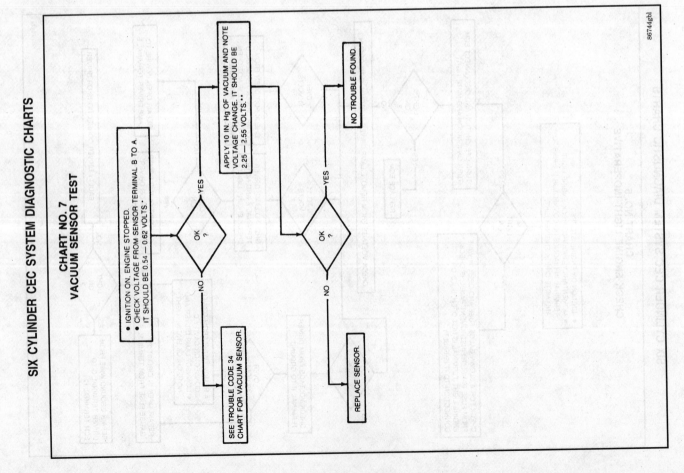

- IGNITION ON, ENGINE STOPPED.
- CHECK VOLTAGE FROM SENSOR TERMINAL B TO A. IT SHOULD BE 0.54 — 0.62 VOLTS.

OK ?

NO → SEE TROUBLE CODE 34 CHART FOR VACUUM SENSOR.

YES → APPLY 10 IN. Hg OF VACUUM AND NOTE VOLTAGE CHANGE. IT SHOULD BE 2.25 — 2.55 VOLTS.**

OK ?

NO → REPLACE SENSOR.

YES → NO TROUBLE FOUND.

86744ghl

SIX CYLINDER CEC SYSTEM DIAGNOSTIC CHARTS

TROUBLE CODE 14
SHORTED COOLANT SENSOR CIRCUIT

If the engine coolant light is on, check for overheating condition first.

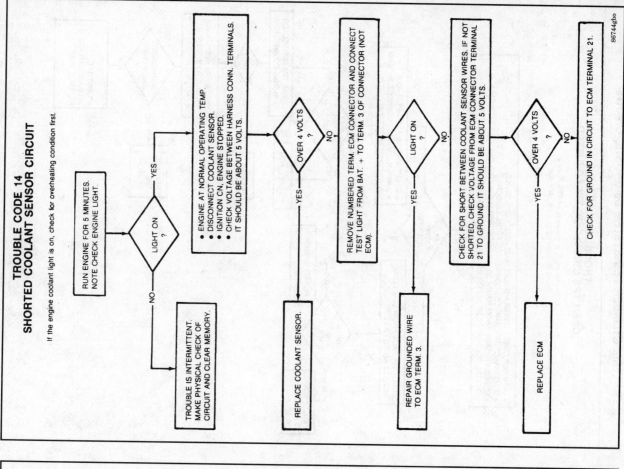

SIX CYLINDER CEC SYSTEM DIAGNOSTIC CHARTS

TROUBLE CODE 13
OPEN OXYGEN SENSOR CIRCUIT

Checking for sticking or misadjusted throttle position sensor.
If codes 13 and 21 are displayed, go to code 21 first.

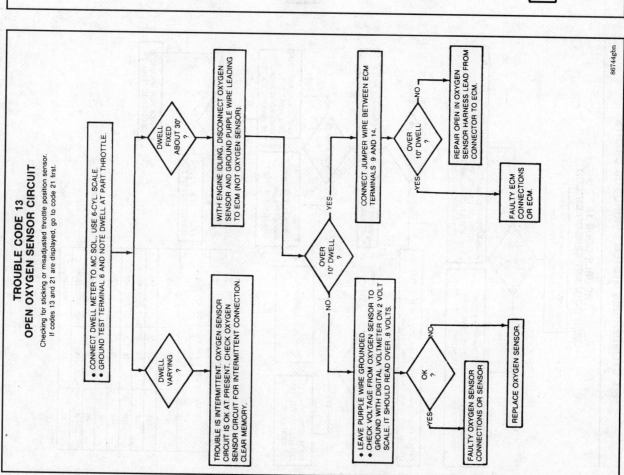

SIX CYLINDER CEC SYSTEM DIAGNOSTIC CHARTS

TROUBLE CODE 21
OPEN TPS CIRCUIT OR MISADJUSTED

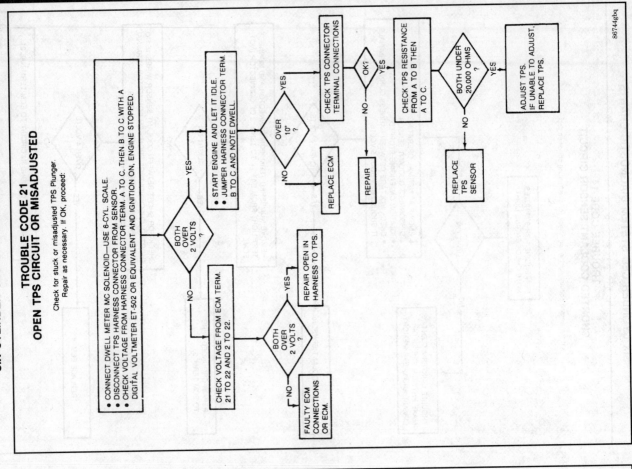

SIX CYLINDER CEC SYSTEM DIAGNOSTIC CHARTS

TROUBLE CODE 15
OPEN COOLANT SENSOR CIRCUIT

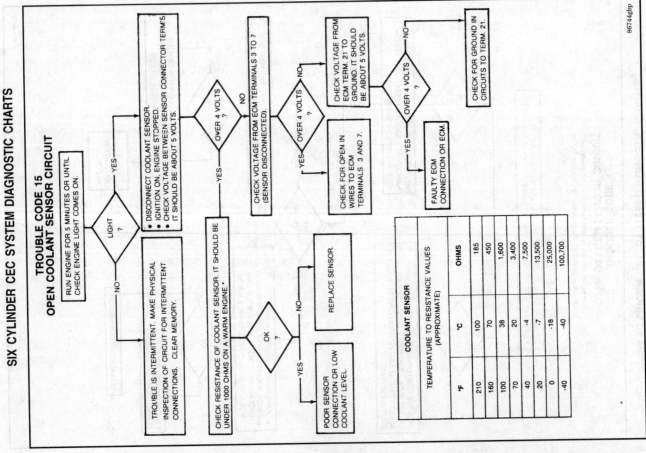

COOLANT SENSOR

TEMPERATURE TO RESISTANCE VALUES
(APPROXIMATE)

°F	°C	OHMS
210	100	185
160	70	450
100	38	1,600
70	20	3,400
40	-4	7,500
20	-7	13,500
0	-18	25,000
-40	-40	100,700

SIX CYLINDER CEC SYSTEM DIAGNOSTIC CHARTS

TROUBLE CODE 34
VACUUM SENSOR VOLTAGE TOO HIGH OR LOW

Check for over 34 kPa (10 inches Hg) of vacuum at sensor with engine idling. If OK, repair.

SIX CYLINDER CEC SYSTEM DIAGNOSTIC CHARTS

TROUBLE CODE 23
OPEN OR GROUNDED MC SOLENOID CIRCUIT

Check connections at MC solenoid. If O.K.: Clear memory* and recheck for code(s). If no code 23, circuit is OK.

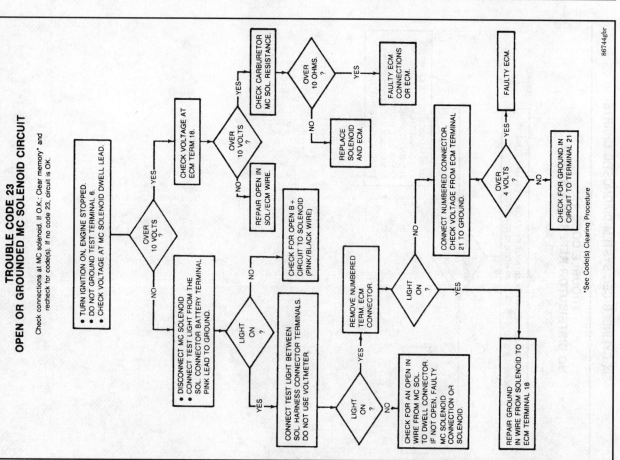

*This requires use of three jumpers between the sensor and the connector.

*See Code(s) Clearing Procedure

86744gbs

86744gbr

SIX CYLINDER CEC SYSTEM DIAGNOSTIC CHARTS

TROUBLE CODE 42
BYPASS OR EST PROBLEM

If vehicle will not start and run, check for grounded EST wire to ECM terminal 12.

WITH ENGINE AT FAST IDLE, NOTE TIMING. GROUND TEST TERMINAL 6 AND NOTE TIMING; IT SHOULD CHANGE.

CHANGE ?

YES → NO TROUBLE FOUND

NO

- DISCONNECT 4 TERMINAL EST CONNECTOR FROM DISTRIBUTOR
- WITH ENGINE STOPPED, CONNECT JUMPER FROM A TO B IN DISTRIBUTOR SIDE OF EST CONNECTOR.
- START ENGINE, GROUND TEST TERMINAL 6 AND CONNECT TEST LIGHT FROM BATTERY + TO TERM. C OR 4 TERM. EST CONN.

ENGINE STOPPED ?

YES → CHECK FOR OPEN EST WIRE TO TERMINAL E OF HEI MODULE. IF WIRE IS OK, FAULTY HEI MODULE CONNECTION OR MODULE.

NO

WITH TEST LIGHT STILL CONNECTED, REMOVE JUMPER BETWEEN TERMINALS A AND B.

ENGINE STOPPED ?

YES → CHECK FOR CORRECT HEI MODULE.
CHECK FOR OPEN WIRE FROM:
- EST CONNECTOR TERMINAL A TO ECM TERMINAL 12 AND OPEN OR GROUND WIRE FROM EST CONNECTOR TERMINAL C TO ECM TERMINAL 11. IF NOT GROUNDED OR OPEN, FAULTY ECM CONNECTION OR ECM.

NO

CHECK DISTRIBUTOR WIRES FOR:
- OPEN OR GROUND TO MODULE TERMINAL B.
- SHORT BETWEEN MODULE TERMINALS R AND E. IF WIRES ARE OK, FAULTY HEI MODULE CONNECTION OR MODULE.

86744gbu

SIX CYLINDER CEC SYSTEM DIAGNOSTIC CHARTS

TROUBLE CODE 41
NO DISTRIBUTOR REFERENCE SIGNAL

WITH ENGINE IDLING, CHECK OUTPUT OF VACUUM OR MAP SENSOR TERMINALS B TO A AS VACUUM HOSE IS REMOVED.

MORE THAN .5 VOLT CHANGE ?

YES → MAKE PHYSICAL CHECK OF WIRES AND CONNECTIONS FOR GROUNDS AND BAD CONNECTIONS. ALSO CHECK DISTRIBUTOR PICK-UP COIL RESISTANCE AND CONNECTIONS. TROUBLE IS INTERMITTENT.

NO

SEE TROUBLE CODE 34 CHART

86744gbt

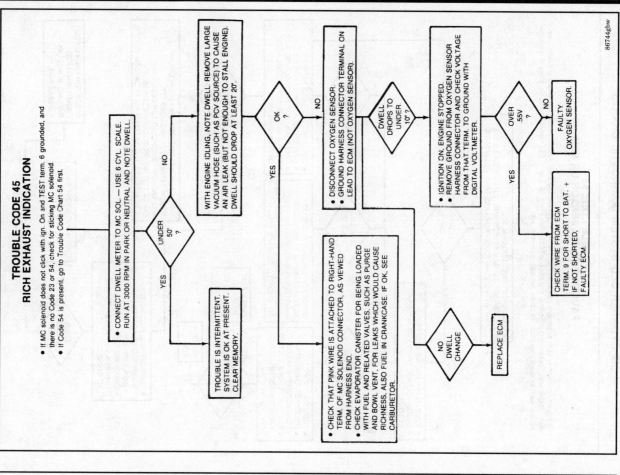

SIX CYLINDER CEC SYSTEM DIAGNOSTIC CHARTS

TROUBLE CODE 45
RICH EXHAUST INDICATION

- If MC solenoid does not click with ign. On and TEST term. 6 grounded, and there is no Code 23 or 54, check for sticking MC solenoid.
- If Code 54 is present, go to Trouble Code Chart 54 first.

CONNECT DWELL METER TO MC SOL. — USE 6 CYL. SCALE. RUN AT 3000 RPM IN PARK OR NEUTRAL AND NOTE DWELL.

UNDER 50°?

YES → TROUBLE IS INTERMITTENT. SYSTEM IS OK AT PRESENT. CLEAR MEMORY.

NO → WITH ENGINE IDLING, NOTE DWELL. REMOVE LARGE VACUUM HOSE (SUCH AS PCV SOURCE) TO CAUSE AN AIR LEAK (BUT NOT ENOUGH TO STALL ENGINE). DWELL SHOULD DROP AT LEAST 20°.

OK?

NO → DISCONNECT OXYGEN SENSOR. GROUND HARNESS CONNECTOR TERMINAL ON LEAD TO ECM (NOT OXYGEN SENSOR).

DWELL DROPS TO UNDER 10°?

YES → CHECK THAT PINK WIRE IS ATTACHED TO RIGHT-HAND TERM. OF MC SOLENOID CONNECTOR, AS VIEWED FROM HARNESS END. CHECK EVAPORATOR CANISTER FOR BEING LOADED WITH FUEL AND RELATED VALVES, SUCH AS PURGE AND BOWL VENT, FOR LEAKS WHICH WOULD CAUSE RICHNESS. ALSO FUEL IN CRANKCASE. IF OK, SEE CARBURETOR.

NO → IGNITION ON, ENGINE STOPPED. REMOVE GROUND FROM OXYGEN SENSOR HARNESS CONNECTOR AND CHECK VOLTAGE FROM THAT TERM. TO GROUND WITH DIGITAL VOLTMETER.

OVER .55V?

YES → CHECK WIRE FROM ECM TERM. 9 FOR SHORT TO BAT. + IF NOT SHORTED, FAULTY ECM.

NO → FAULTY OXYGEN SENSOR.

NO DWELL CHANGE → REPLACE ECM

86744gbw

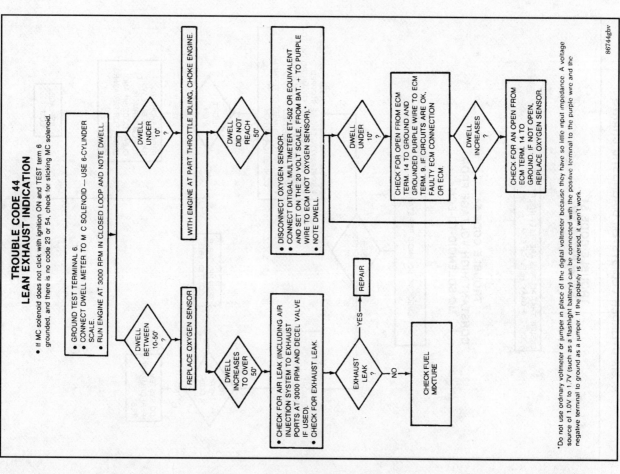

SIX CYLINDER CEC SYSTEM DIAGNOSTIC CHARTS

TROUBLE CODE 44
LEAN EXHAUST INDICATION

- If MC solenoid does not click with ignition ON and TEST term 6 grounded, and there is no code 23 or 54, check for sticking MC solenoid.

- GROUND TEST TERMINAL 6
- CONNECT DWELL METER TO M C SOLENOID — USE 6-CYLINDER SCALE.
- RUN ENGINE AT 3000 RPM IN CLOSED LOOP AND NOTE DWELL.

DWELL BETWEEN 10-50°?

REPLACE OXYGEN SENSOR

DWELL INCREASES TO OVER 50°?

CHECK FOR AIR LEAK (INCLUDING AIR INJECTION SYSTEM TO EXHAUST PORTS AT 3000 RPM AND DECEL VALVE IF USED). CHECK FOR EXHAUST LEAK.

EXHAUST LEAK?

YES → REPAIR

NO → CHECK FUEL MIXTURE

DWELL UNDER 10°?

WITH ENGINE AT PART THROTTLE IDLING, CHOKE ENGINE.

DWELL DID NOT REACH 50°?

- DISCONNECT OXYGEN SENSOR.
- CONNECT DITIGAL MULTIMETER ET-502 OR EQUIVALENT AND SET ON THE 20 VOLT SCALE, FROM BAT. + TO PURPLE WIRE TO ECM (NOT OXYGEN SENSOR).*
- NOTE DWELL.

DWELL UNDER 10°?

CHECK FOR OPEN FROM ECM TERM. 14 TO GROUND AND GROUNDED PURPLE WIRE TO ECM TERM. 9. IF CIRCUITS ARE OK, FAULTY ECM CONNECTION OR ECM.

DWELL INCREASES?

CHECK FOR AN OPEN FROM ECM TERM. 14 TO GROUND. IF NOT OPEN, REPLACE OXYGEN SENSOR.

*Do not use ordinary voltmeter or jumper in place of the digital voltmeter because they have so little input impedance. A voltage source of 1.0V to 1.7V (such as a flashlight battery) can be connected with the positive terminal to the purple wire and the negative terminal to ground as a jumper. If the polarity is reversed, it won't work.

86744gbv

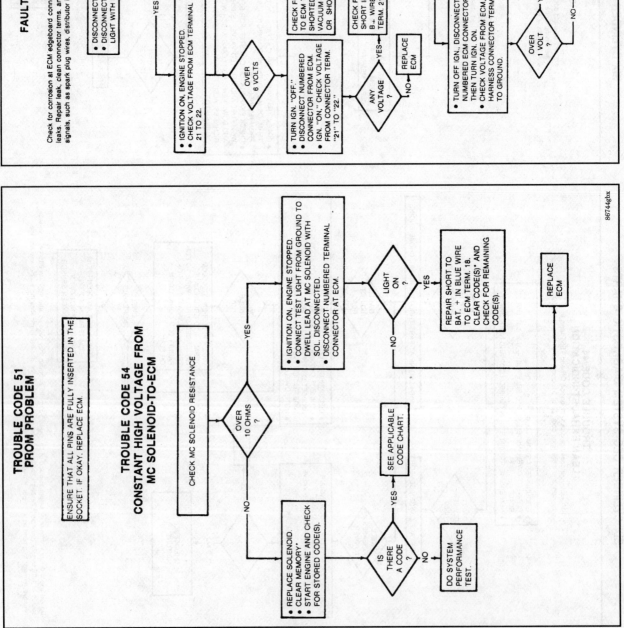

SIX CYLINDER CEC SYSTEM DIAGNOSTIC CHARTS

**TROUBLE CODE 55
FAULTY OXYGEN SENSOR OR ECM**

Check for corrosion at ECM edgeboard connectors and terms. If present, check for coolant sensor, windshield or heater core leaks. Repair leak, clean connector terms. and replace ECM. Also, check for 4 term. EST harness being too close to electrical signals, such as spark plug wires, distributor housing, generator, etc.

- DISCONNECT TEST TERMINAL 6.
- DISCONNECT OXYGEN SENSOR AND NOTE CHECK ENGINE LIGHT WITH ENGINE IDLING FOR LESS THAN ONE MINUTE.

LIGHT ON ?

NO → 4 TO 6 VOLTS → DISCONNECT OXYGEN SENSOR. IGNITION ON. ENGINE STOPPED. CHECK VOLTAGE FROM CONNECTOR OF PURPLE WIRE DISCONNECTED FROM OXYGEN SENSOR.

OVER 1 VOLT ?

NO → CHECK FOR INTERMITTENT GROUND IN CIRCUIT TO ECM TERMINAL 21 (INCLUDES TPS, AND VACUUM SENSORS). CLEAR CODES AND CHECK FOR RECURRENCE OF CODE 55. F IT REAPPEARS, IT COULD BE FAULTY OXYGEN SENSOR.

CHECK FOR OPEN CIRCUIT FROM TERM. 14 TO GROUND. IF NOT OPEN, REPLACE ECM.

YES → UNDER 4 VOLTS → CHECK FOR GROUND IN CIRCUIT TO ECM TERMINAL 21 (INCLUDES SHORTED OR GROUNDED OR TPS VACUUM SENSOR). IF NOT GROUNDED OR SHORTED, REPLACE ECM.

YES → CHECK FOR SHORT IN B+ WIRE TO TERM. 21.

- IGNITION ON. ENGINE STOPPED.
- CHECK VOLTAGE FROM ECM TERMINAL 21 TO 22.

OVER 6 VOLTS → TURN IGN. "OFF." DISCONNECT NUMBERED CONNECTOR FROM ECM. IGN. "ON." CHECK VOLTAGE FROM CONNECTOR TERM. "21" TO "22."

ANY VOLTAGE ?

YES → CHECK FOR SHORT IN B.+ WIRE TO TERM. 21.

NO → REPLACE ECM

- TURN OFF IGN., DISCONNECT NUMBERED ECM CONNECTOR AND THEN TURN IGN. ON.
- CHECK VOLTAGE FROM ECM, HARNESS CONNECTOR TERM. 9 TO GROUND.

OVER 1 VOLT ?

YES → CHECK FOR SHORT FROM WIRE TO ECM TERM. 9 TO BAT.

NO →

SIX CYLINDER CEC SYSTEM DIAGNOSTIC CHARTS

**TROUBLE CODE 51
PROM PROBLEM**

ENSURE THAT ALL PINS ARE FULLY INSERTED IN THE SOCKET. IF OKAY, REPLACE ECM.

**TROUBLE CODE 54
CONSTANT HIGH VOLTAGE FROM
MC SOLENOID-TO-ECM**

CHECK MC SOLENOID RESISTANCE

OVER 10 OHMS ?

YES →
- IGNITION ON. ENGINE STOPPED.
- CONNECT TEST LIGHT FROM GROUND TO DWELL LEAD AT MC SOLENOID WITH SOL. DISCONNECTED.
- DISCONNECT NUMBERED TERMINAL CONNECTOR AT ECM.

LIGHT ON ?

YES → REPAIR SHORT TO BAT. + IN BLUE WIRE TO ECM TERM. 18. CLEAR CODE(S)* AND CHECK FOR REMAINING CODE(S).

NO → REPLACE ECM

NO →
- REPLACE SOLENOID.
- CLEAR MEMORY*
- START ENGINE AND CHECK FOR STORED CODE(S).

IS THERE A CODE ?

YES → SEE APPLICABLE CODE CHART.

NO → DO SYSTEM PERFORMANCE TEST.

8674gbx

RENIX THROTTLE BODY INJECTION (TBI) ELECTRONIC ENGINE CONTROLS

General Information

The Renix throttle body fuel injection system is a "pulse time" system that uses a single solenoid-type injector to meter fuel into the throttle body above the throttle blade. Fuel is metered to the engine by an Electronic Control Unit (ECU), which controls the amount of fuel delivery according to input from various engine sensors that monitor exhaust gas oxygen content, coolant temperature, manifold absolute pressure, crankshaft position and throttle position. These sensors provide an electronic signal by varying resistance within the sensor itself. By reading the difference in resistance, the ECU can determine engine operating conditions and calculate the correct air/fuel mixture, and ignition timing under varying engine loads and temperatures. In addition, the ECU controls idle speed, emission control and fuel pump operation, the upshift indicator lamp and the A/C compressor clutch.

Renix TBI fuel injection has two main subsystems; a fuel subsystem and a control subsystem. The fuel subsystem consists of an electric fuel pump (mounted in the fuel tank), a fuel filter, a pressure regulator and the fuel injector. The control subsystem consists of a Manifold Air Temperature (MAT) sensor, a Coolant Temperature Sensor (CTS), a Manifold Absolute Pressure (MAP) sensor, a knock sensor, an exhaust gas oxygen (O_2) sensor, an Electronic Control Unit (ECU), a gear position indicator (automatic transmission only), a Throttle Position Sensor (TPS) and power steering pressure switch with a load swap relay. In addition to these sensors which send signals to the ECU, there are various devices which receive signals from the ECU to control different functions such as exhaust gas recirculation, idle speed control, air conditioner operation, etc.

Electronic Control Unit (ECU)

REMOVAL & INSTALLATION

The ECU is located underneath the instrument panel between the steering column and the heater A/C housing.
1. Disconnect the negative battery cable.
2. Unfasten the locknuts securing the ECU and bracket to the dash.
3. Unfasten the ECU-to-bracket retainer.
4. Disengage the connectors from the ECU.
5. Remove the ECU.
To install:
6. Install the ECU into the bracket and tighten the retainer.
7. Engage the ECU electrical connections.
8. Install the ECU and bracket in position and fasten the retainers.
9. Connect the negative battery cable.

Throttle Position Sensor (TPS)

OPERATION

The throttle position sensor is mounted on the throttle plate assembly and provides the ECU with an input signal of up to 5 volts to indicate throttle position. At minimum throttle opening (idle speed), a signal input of approximately 1 volt is transmitted to the ECU. As the throttle opening increases, voltage increases to a maximum of approximately 5 volts at the wide open throttle position.

A dual TPS is used on models equipped with automatic transmission. This dual TPS not only provides the ECU with input voltages, but also supplies the Transmission Control Unit (TCU) with an input of throttle position.

Coolant Temperature Sensor (CTS)

OPERATION

The coolant temperature sensor is located on the left side of the cylinder block, just below the exhaust manifold. The CTS provides an engine coolant temperature input to the ECU, which will then enrich the air/fuel mixture delivered by the injectors when the engine coolant is cold. Based on the CTS signal, the ECU will also control engine warmup idle speed, increase ignition advance and inhibit EGR operation when the coolant is cold.

Manifold Absolute Pressure (MAP) Sensor

OPERATION

The manifold absolute pressure sensor is mounted on the dash panel behind the engine. The MAP sensor reacts to absolute pressure in the intake manifold and provides an input voltage to the ECU. Manifold pressure is used to supply mixture density information and ambient barometric pressure information to the ECU. A hose from the intake manifold provides the input pressure.

Manifold Air Temperature (MAT) Sensor

OPERATION

The manifold air temperature sensor is located in the intake manifold. The MAT sensor reacts to the temperature of the air in the intake manifold and provides an input to the ECU to allow it to compensate for air density changes during high temperature operation.

Knock Sensor

OPERATION

The knock sensor is located on the lower left side of the cylinder block, just above the oil pan. The knock sensor provides and input to the ECU that indicates detonation (knock) during engine operation. When detonation occurs, the ECU retards the ignition timing advance to eliminate the detonation at the applicable cylinder.

Heated Oxygen (HO2S) Sensor

OPERATION

The heated oxygen sensor, or HO2S sensor is located at the exhaust system, usually near the catalytic converter. It produces a voltage signal of 0.1-1.0 volts based on the amount of oxygen in the exhaust gas. When a low amount of oxygen is present (caused by a rich air/fuel mixture), the sensor produces a low voltage. When a high amount of oxygen is present (caused by a lean air/fuel mixture), the sensor produces a high voltage. Because an accurate voltage signal is only produced if the sensor temperature is above approximately 600°F, a fast acting heating element is built into its body.

The ECU uses the HO2S sensor voltage signal to constantly adjust the amount of fuel injected which keeps the engine at its peek efficiency.

TESTING

1. Start the engine and bring it to normal operating temperature, then run the engine above 1200 rpm for two minutes.
2. Backprobe with a high impedance averaging voltmeter (set to the DC voltage scale) between the HO2S sensor signal wire and battery ground.
3. Verify that the sensor voltage fluctuates rapidly between 0.40-0.60 volts.
4. If the sensor voltage is stabilized at the middle of the specified range (approximately 0.45-0.55 volts) or if the voltage fluctuates very slowly between the specified range (HO2S signal crosses 0.5 volts less than 5 times in ten seconds), the sensor may be faulty.
5. If the sensor voltage stabilizes at either end of the specified range, the ECU is probably not able to compensate for a mechanical problem such as a vacuum leak. These types of mechanical problems will cause the sensor to report a constant lean or constant rich mixture. The mechanical problem will first have to be repaired and then the HO2S sensor test repeated.
6. Pull a vacuum hose located after the throttle plate. Voltage should drop to approximately 0.12 volts (while still fluctuating rapidly). This tests the ability of the sensor to detect a lean mixture condition. Reattach the vacuum hose.
7. Richen the mixture using a propane enrichment tool. Sensor voltage should rise to approximately 0.90 volts (while still fluctuating rapidly). This tests the ability of the sensor to detect a rich mixture condition.
8. If the sensor voltage is above or below the specified range, the sensor and/or the sensor wiring may be faulty. Check the wiring for any breaks, repair as necessary and repeat the test.
9. Further sensor operational testing requires the use of a special tester M.S.1700, or equivalent.

Testing

▶ **See Figures 41, 42, 43, 44 and 45**

Follow the accompanying diagnostic charts to test the Renix TBI system.

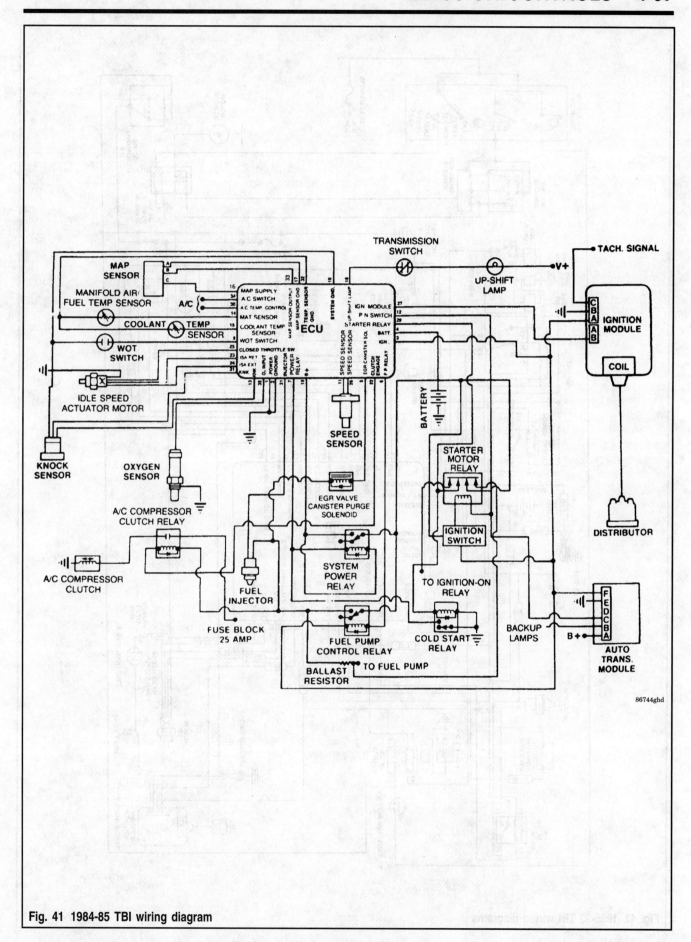

Fig. 41 1984-85 TBI wiring diagram

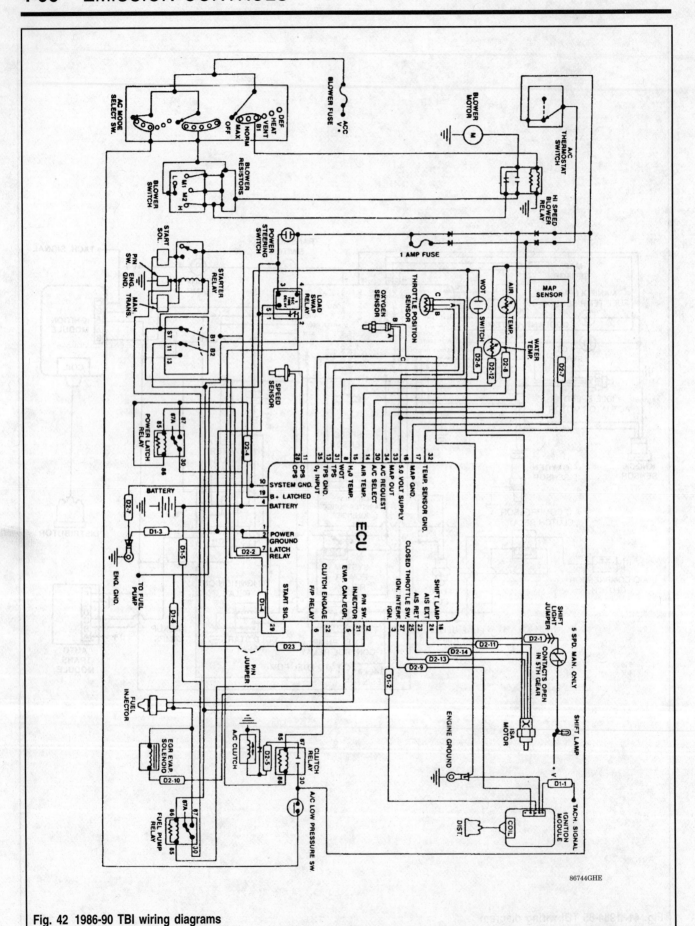

Fig. 42 1986-90 TBI wiring diagrams

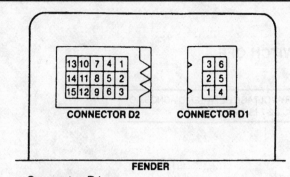

Connector D1
1. Tach (rpm) Voltage (Input)
2. Ignition
3. Ground
4. Starter Motor Relay
5. Battery
6. Fuel Pump

Connector D2
1. ECU Data Output
2. System Power Relay
3. Park/Neutral Switch
4. System Power (B+)
5. A/C Clutch
6. WOT Switch
7. Ground
8. Air/Fuel Temperature Sensor
9. Ignition Power Module
10. EGR Valve/Canister Purge Solenoid
11. ISA Motor Forward
12. Coolant Temperature Sensor
13. Closed Throttle Switch
14. ISA Motor Reverse
15. Automatic Transmission Diagnosis

86744GB2

Fig. 43 1984-85 TBI diagnostic connector

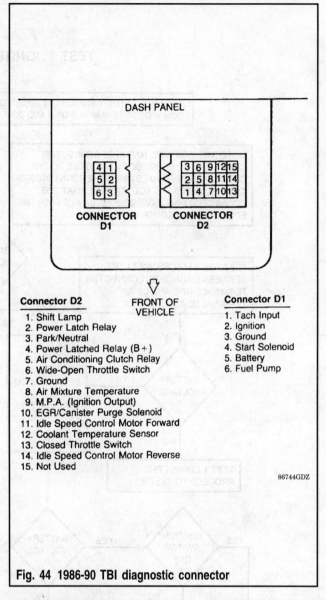

Connector D2
1. Shift Lamp
2. Power Latch Relay
3. Park/Neutral
4. Power Latched Relay (B+)
5. Air Conditioning Clutch Relay
6. Wide-Open Throttle Switch
7. Ground
8. Air Mixture Temperature
9. M.P.A. (Ignition Output)
10. EGR/Canister Purge Solenoid
11. Idle Speed Control Motor Forward
12. Coolant Temperature Sensor
13. Closed Throttle Switch
14. Idle Speed Control Motor Reverse
15. Not Used

Connector D1
1. Tach Input
2. Ignition
3. Ground
4. Start Solenoid
5. Battery
6. Fuel Pump

86744GDZ

Fig. 44 1986-90 TBI diagnostic connector

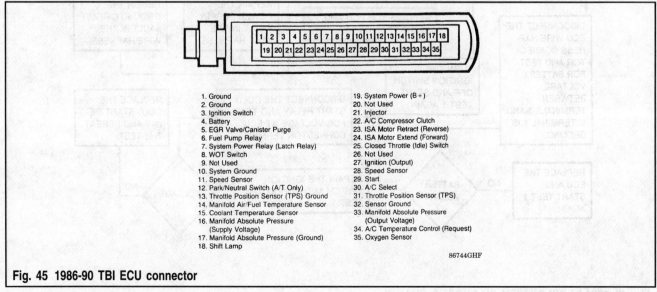

1. Ground
2. Ground
3. Ignition Switch
4. Battery
5. EGR Valve/Canister Purge
6. Fuel Pump Relay
7. System Power Relay (Latch Relay)
8. WOT Switch
9. Not Used
10. System Ground
11. Speed Sensor
12. Park/Neutral Switch (A/T Only)
13. Throttle Position Sensor (TPS) Ground
14. Manifold Air/Fuel Temperature Sensor
15. Coolant Temperature Sensor
16. Manifold Absolute Pressure (Supply Voltage)
17. Manifold Absolute Pressure (Ground)
18. Shift Lamp
19. System Power (B+)
20. Not Used
21. Injector
22. A/C Compressor Clutch
23. ISA Motor Retract (Reverse)
24. ISA Motor Extend (Forward)
25. Closed Throttle (Idle) Switch
26. Not Used
27. Ignition (Output)
28. Speed Sensor
29. Start
30. A/C Select
31. Throttle Position Sensor (TPS)
32. Sensor Ground
33. Manifold Absolute Pressure (Output Voltage)
34. A/C Temperature Control (Request)
35. Oxygen Sensor

86744GHF

Fig. 45 1986-90 TBI ECU connector

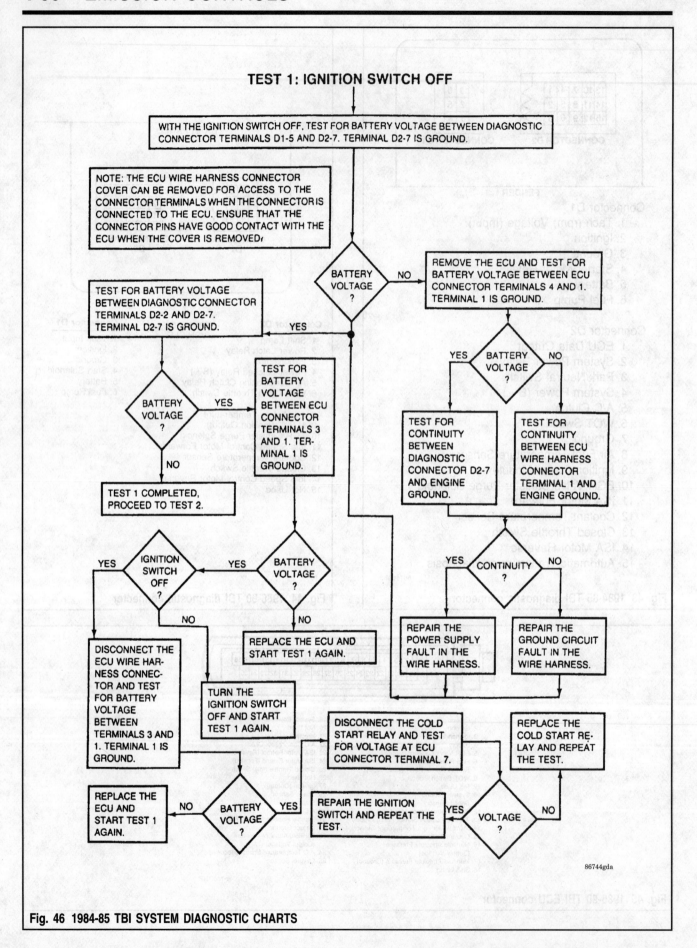

TEST 1: IGNITION SWITCH OFF

WITH THE IGNITION SWITCH OFF, TEST FOR BATTERY VOLTAGE BETWEEN DIAGNOSTIC CONNECTOR TERMINALS D1-5 AND D2-7. TERMINAL D2-7 IS GROUND.

NOTE: THE ECU WIRE HARNESS CONNECTOR COVER CAN BE REMOVED FOR ACCESS TO THE CONNECTOR TERMINALS WHEN THE CONNECTOR IS CONNECTED TO THE ECU. ENSURE THAT THE CONNECTOR PINS HAVE GOOD CONTACT WITH THE ECU WHEN THE COVER IS REMOVED.

BATTERY VOLTAGE?

NO → REMOVE THE ECU AND TEST FOR BATTERY VOLTAGE BETWEEN ECU CONNECTOR TERMINALS 4 AND 1. TERMINAL 1 IS GROUND.

YES

TEST FOR BATTERY VOLTAGE BETWEEN DIAGNOSTIC CONNECTOR TERMINALS D2-2 AND D2-7. TERMINAL D2-7 IS GROUND.

BATTERY VOLTAGE?

YES → TEST FOR BATTERY VOLTAGE BETWEEN ECU CONNECTOR TERMINALS 3 AND 1. TERMINAL 1 IS GROUND.

NO

TEST 1 COMPLETED, PROCEED TO TEST 2.

BATTERY VOLTAGE?

YES → BATTERY VOLTAGE?

YES → IGNITION SWITCH OFF?

NO

NO → REPLACE THE ECU AND START TEST 1 AGAIN.

YES → DISCONNECT THE ECU WIRE HARNESS CONNECTOR AND TEST FOR BATTERY VOLTAGE BETWEEN TERMINALS 3 AND 1. TERMINAL 1 IS GROUND.

NO → TURN THE IGNITION SWITCH OFF AND START TEST 1 AGAIN.

BATTERY VOLTAGE?

NO → REPLACE THE ECU AND START TEST 1 AGAIN.

YES → REPAIR THE IGNITION SWITCH AND REPEAT THE TEST.

BATTERY VOLTAGE?

YES → TEST FOR CONTINUITY BETWEEN DIAGNOSTIC CONNECTOR D2-7 AND ENGINE GROUND.

NO → TEST FOR CONTINUITY BETWEEN ECU WIRE HARNESS CONNECTOR TERMINAL 1 AND ENGINE GROUND.

CONTINUITY?

YES → REPAIR THE POWER SUPPLY FAULT IN THE WIRE HARNESS.

NO → REPAIR THE GROUND CIRCUIT FAULT IN THE WIRE HARNESS.

DISCONNECT THE COLD START RELAY AND TEST FOR VOLTAGE AT ECU CONNECTOR TERMINAL 7.

REPLACE THE COLD START RELAY AND REPEAT THE TEST.

VOLTAGE?

YES → REPAIR THE IGNITION SWITCH AND REPEAT THE TEST.

NO → REPLACE THE COLD START RELAY AND REPEAT THE TEST.

86744gda

Fig. 46 1984-85 TBI SYSTEM DIAGNOSTIC CHARTS

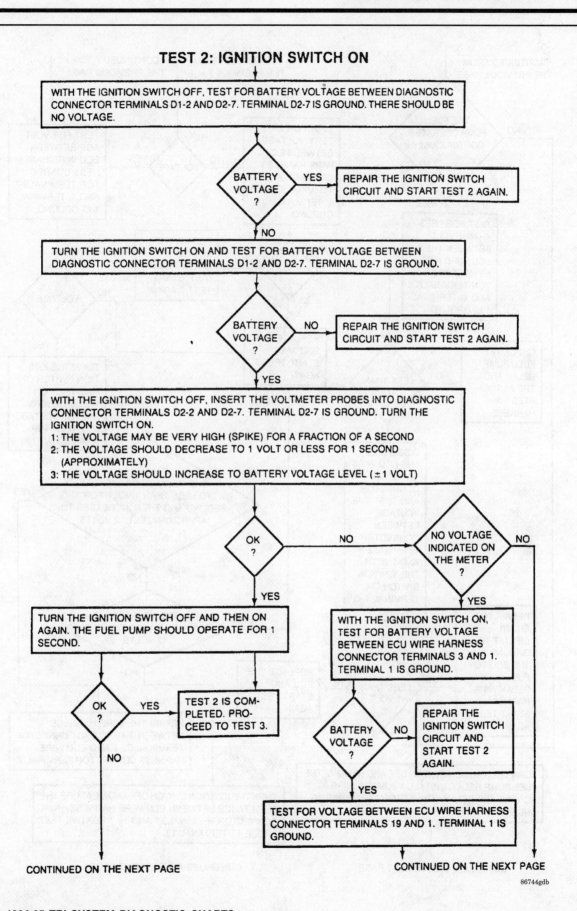

TEST 2: IGNITION SWITCH ON

WITH THE IGNITION SWITCH OFF, TEST FOR BATTERY VOLTAGE BETWEEN DIAGNOSTIC CONNECTOR TERMINALS D1-2 AND D2-7. TERMINAL D2-7 IS GROUND. THERE SHOULD BE NO VOLTAGE.

BATTERY VOLTAGE ?

YES → REPAIR THE IGNITION SWITCH CIRCUIT AND START TEST 2 AGAIN.

NO

TURN THE IGNITION SWITCH ON AND TEST FOR BATTERY VOLTAGE BETWEEN DIAGNOSTIC CONNECTOR TERMINALS D1-2 AND D2-7. TERMINAL D2-7 IS GROUND.

BATTERY VOLTAGE ?

NO → REPAIR THE IGNITION SWITCH CIRCUIT AND START TEST 2 AGAIN.

YES

WITH THE IGNITION SWITCH OFF, INSERT THE VOLTMETER PROBES INTO DIAGNOSTIC CONNECTOR TERMINALS D2-2 AND D2-7. TERMINAL D2-7 IS GROUND. TURN THE IGNITION SWITCH ON.
1: THE VOLTAGE MAY BE VERY HIGH (SPIKE) FOR A FRACTION OF A SECOND
2: THE VOLTAGE SHOULD DECREASE TO 1 VOLT OR LESS FOR 1 SECOND (APPROXIMATELY)
3: THE VOLTAGE SHOULD INCREASE TO BATTERY VOLTAGE LEVEL (±1 VOLT)

OK ?

NO → NO VOLTAGE INDICATED ON THE METER ? — NO

YES

TURN THE IGNITION SWITCH OFF AND THEN ON AGAIN. THE FUEL PUMP SHOULD OPERATE FOR 1 SECOND.

YES (from NO VOLTAGE INDICATED ON THE METER)

WITH THE IGNITION SWITCH ON, TEST FOR BATTERY VOLTAGE BETWEEN ECU WIRE HARNESS CONNECTOR TERMINALS 3 AND 1. TERMINAL 1 IS GROUND.

OK ?

YES → TEST 2 IS COMPLETED. PROCEED TO TEST 3.

NO

BATTERY VOLTAGE ?

NO → REPAIR THE IGNITION SWITCH CIRCUIT AND START TEST 2 AGAIN.

YES

TEST FOR VOLTAGE BETWEEN ECU WIRE HARNESS CONNECTOR TERMINALS 19 AND 1. TERMINAL 1 IS GROUND.

CONTINUED ON THE NEXT PAGE

CONTINUED ON THE NEXT PAGE

86744gdb

Fig. 47 1984-85 TBI SYSTEM DIAGNOSTIC CHARTS

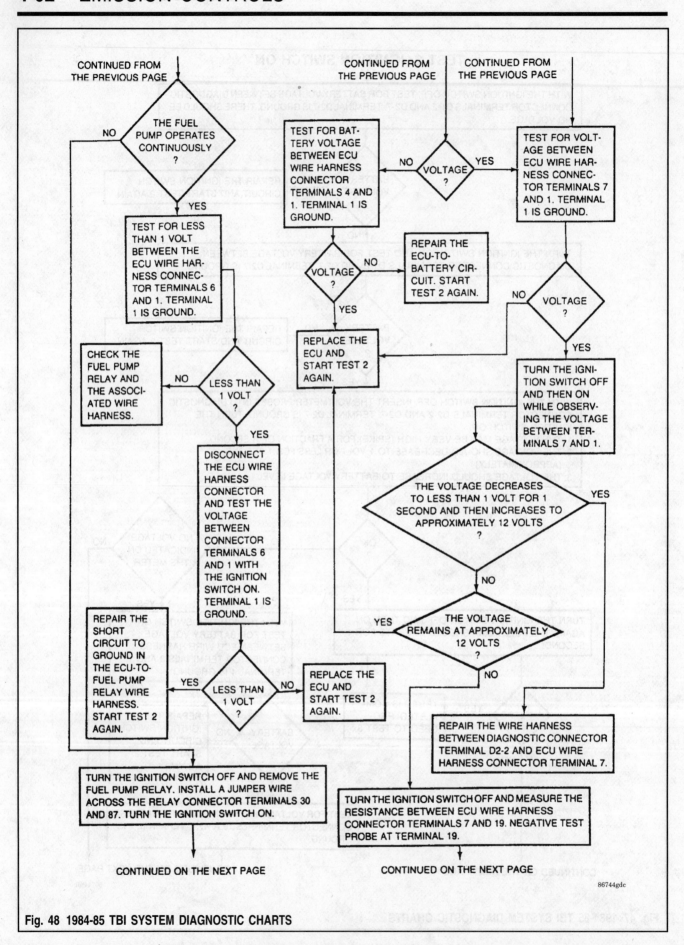

Fig. 48 1984-85 TBI SYSTEM DIAGNOSTIC CHARTS

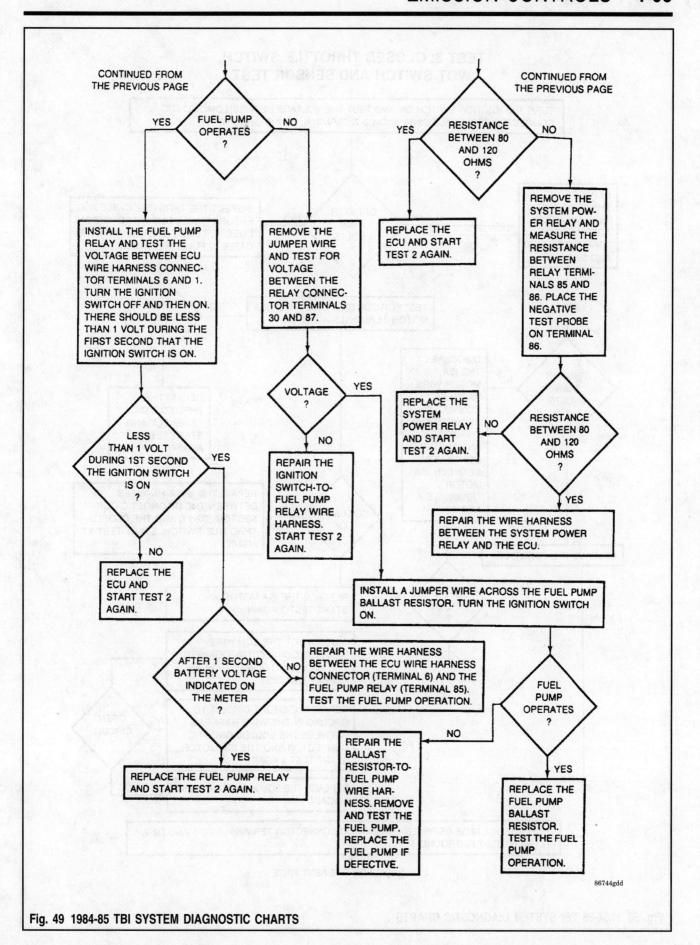

Fig. 49 1984-85 TBI SYSTEM DIAGNOSTIC CHARTS

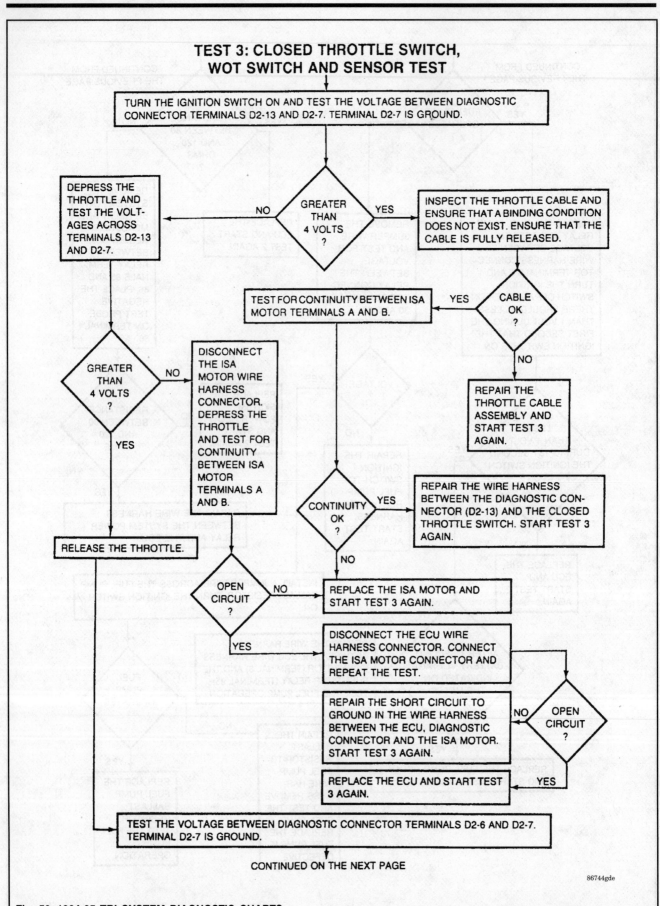

TEST 3: CLOSED THROTTLE SWITCH, WOT SWITCH AND SENSOR TEST

TURN THE IGNITION SWITCH ON AND TEST THE VOLTAGE BETWEEN DIAGNOSTIC CONNECTOR TERMINALS D2-13 AND D2-7. TERMINAL D2-7 IS GROUND.

GREATER THAN 4 VOLTS ?

NO — DEPRESS THE THROTTLE AND TEST THE VOLTAGES ACROSS TERMINALS D2-13 AND D2-7.

YES — INSPECT THE THROTTLE CABLE AND ENSURE THAT A BINDING CONDITION DOES NOT EXIST. ENSURE THAT THE CABLE IS FULLY RELEASED.

CABLE OK ?

YES — TEST FOR CONTINUITY BETWEEN ISA MOTOR TERMINALS A AND B.

NO — REPAIR THE THROTTLE CABLE ASSEMBLY AND START TEST 3 AGAIN.

GREATER THAN 4 VOLTS ?

NO — DISCONNECT THE ISA MOTOR WIRE HARNESS CONNECTOR. DEPRESS THE THROTTLE AND TEST FOR CONTINUITY BETWEEN ISA MOTOR TERMINALS A AND B.

YES — RELEASE THE THROTTLE.

CONTINUITY OK ?

YES — REPAIR THE WIRE HARNESS BETWEEN THE DIAGNOSTIC CONNECTOR (D2-13) AND THE CLOSED THROTTLE SWITCH. START TEST 3 AGAIN.

OPEN CIRCUIT ?

NO — REPLACE THE ISA MOTOR AND START TEST 3 AGAIN.

YES — DISCONNECT THE ECU WIRE HARNESS CONNECTOR. CONNECT THE ISA MOTOR CONNECTOR AND REPEAT THE TEST.

OPEN CIRCUIT ?

NO — REPAIR THE SHORT CIRCUIT TO GROUND IN THE WIRE HARNESS BETWEEN THE ECU, DIAGNOSTIC CONNECTOR AND THE ISA MOTOR. START TEST 3 AGAIN.

YES — REPLACE THE ECU AND START TEST 3 AGAIN.

TEST THE VOLTAGE BETWEEN DIAGNOSTIC CONNECTOR TERMINALS D2-6 AND D2-7. TERMINAL D2-7 IS GROUND.

CONTINUED ON THE NEXT PAGE

86744gde

Fig. 50 1984-85 TBI SYSTEM DIAGNOSTIC CHARTS

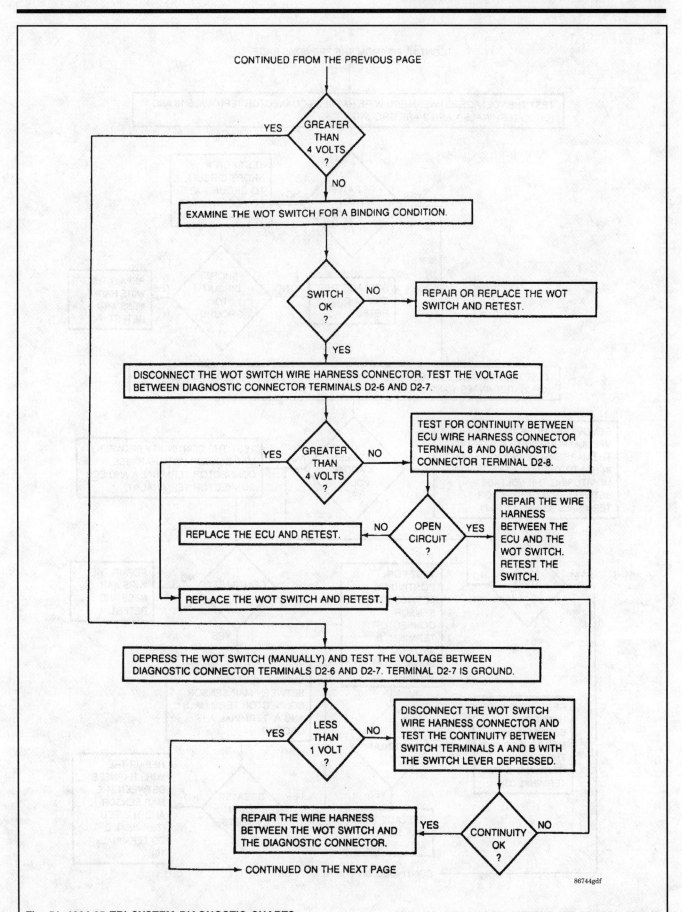

CONTINUED FROM THE PREVIOUS PAGE

GREATER THAN 4 VOLTS ?

YES

NO

EXAMINE THE WOT SWITCH FOR A BINDING CONDITION.

SWITCH OK ?

NO

REPAIR OR REPLACE THE WOT SWITCH AND RETEST.

YES

DISCONNECT THE WOT SWITCH WIRE HARNESS CONNECTOR. TEST THE VOLTAGE BETWEEN DIAGNOSTIC CONNECTOR TERMINALS D2-6 AND D2-7.

GREATER THAN 4 VOLTS ?

YES

NO

TEST FOR CONTINUITY BETWEEN ECU WIRE HARNESS CONNECTOR TERMINAL 8 AND DIAGNOSTIC CONNECTOR TERMINAL D2-8.

OPEN CIRCUIT ?

NO

YES

REPLACE THE ECU AND RETEST.

REPAIR THE WIRE HARNESS BETWEEN THE ECU AND THE WOT SWITCH. RETEST THE SWITCH.

REPLACE THE WOT SWITCH AND RETEST.

DEPRESS THE WOT SWITCH (MANUALLY) AND TEST THE VOLTAGE BETWEEN DIAGNOSTIC CONNECTOR TERMINALS D2-6 AND D2-7. TERMINAL D2-7 IS GROUND.

LESS THAN 1 VOLT ?

YES

NO

DISCONNECT THE WOT SWITCH WIRE HARNESS CONNECTOR AND TEST THE CONTINUITY BETWEEN SWITCH TERMINALS A AND B WITH THE SWITCH LEVER DEPRESSED.

REPAIR THE WIRE HARNESS BETWEEN THE WOT SWITCH AND THE DIAGNOSTIC CONNECTOR.

YES

CONTINUITY OK ?

NO

CONTINUED ON THE NEXT PAGE

86744gdf

Fig. 51 1984-85 TBI SYSTEM DIAGNOSTIC CHARTS

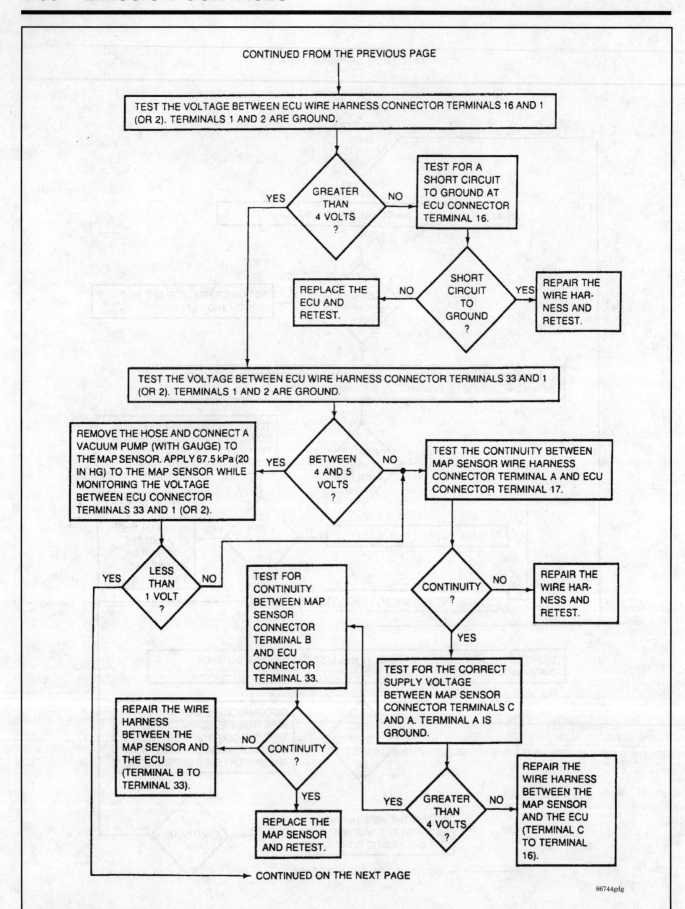

CONTINUED FROM THE PREVIOUS PAGE

TEST THE VOLTAGE BETWEEN ECU WIRE HARNESS CONNECTOR TERMINALS 16 AND 1 (OR 2). TERMINALS 1 AND 2 ARE GROUND.

GREATER THAN 4 VOLTS ?

YES

NO

TEST FOR A SHORT CIRCUIT TO GROUND AT ECU CONNECTOR TERMINAL 16.

REPLACE THE ECU AND RETEST.

NO

SHORT CIRCUIT TO GROUND ?

YES

REPAIR THE WIRE HARNESS AND RETEST.

TEST THE VOLTAGE BETWEEN ECU WIRE HARNESS CONNECTOR TERMINALS 33 AND 1 (OR 2). TERMINALS 1 AND 2 ARE GROUND.

REMOVE THE HOSE AND CONNECT A VACUUM PUMP (WITH GAUGE) TO THE MAP SENSOR. APPLY 67.5 kPa (20 IN HG) TO THE MAP SENSOR WHILE MONITORING THE VOLTAGE BETWEEN ECU CONNECTOR TERMINALS 33 AND 1 (OR 2).

YES

BETWEEN 4 AND 5 VOLTS ?

NO

TEST THE CONTINUITY BETWEEN MAP SENSOR WIRE HARNESS CONNECTOR TERMINAL A AND ECU CONNECTOR TERMINAL 17.

LESS THAN 1 VOLT ?

YES

NO

TEST FOR CONTINUITY BETWEEN MAP SENSOR CONNECTOR TERMINAL B AND ECU CONNECTOR TERMINAL 33.

CONTINUITY ?

NO

REPAIR THE WIRE HARNESS AND RETEST.

YES

TEST FOR THE CORRECT SUPPLY VOLTAGE BETWEEN MAP SENSOR CONNECTOR TERMINALS C AND A. TERMINAL A IS GROUND.

REPAIR THE WIRE HARNESS BETWEEN THE MAP SENSOR AND THE ECU (TERMINAL B TO TERMINAL 33).

NO

CONTINUITY ?

YES

REPLACE THE MAP SENSOR AND RETEST.

YES

GREATER THAN 4 VOLTS ?

NO

REPAIR THE WIRE HARNESS BETWEEN THE MAP SENSOR AND THE ECU (TERMINAL C TO TERMINAL 16).

CONTINUED ON THE NEXT PAGE

86744gdg

Fig. 52 1984-85 TBI SYSTEM DIAGNOSTIC CHARTS

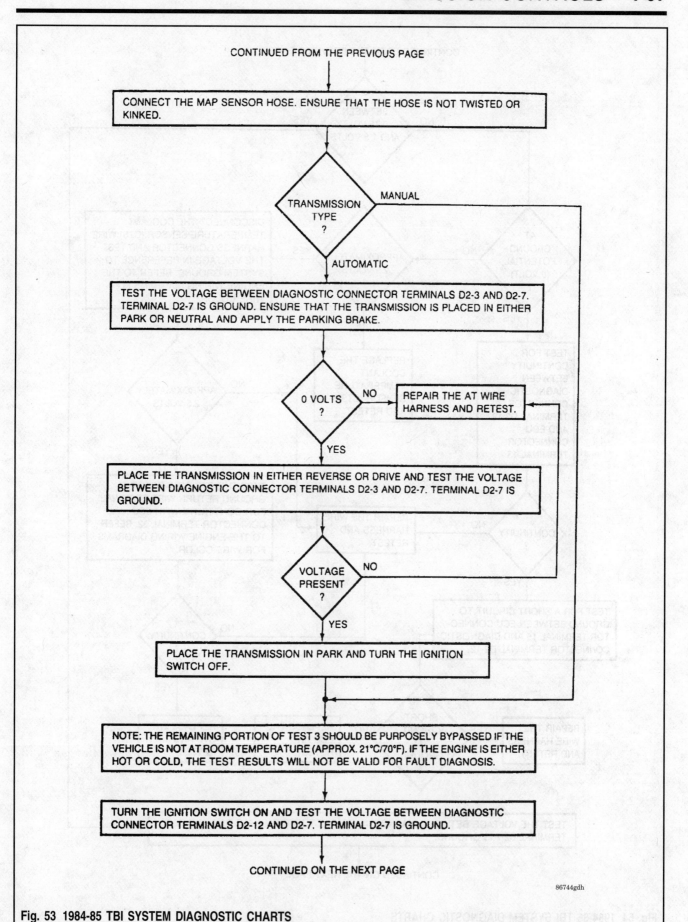

CONTINUED FROM THE PREVIOUS PAGE

CONNECT THE MAP SENSOR HOSE. ENSURE THAT THE HOSE IS NOT TWISTED OR KINKED.

TRANSMISSION TYPE ?

MANUAL

AUTOMATIC

TEST THE VOLTAGE BETWEEN DIAGNOSTIC CONNECTOR TERMINALS D2-3 AND D2-7. TERMINAL D2-7 IS GROUND. ENSURE THAT THE TRANSMISSION IS PLACED IN EITHER PARK OR NEUTRAL AND APPLY THE PARKING BRAKE.

0 VOLTS ?

NO

REPAIR THE AT WIRE HARNESS AND RETEST.

YES

PLACE THE TRANSMISSION IN EITHER REVERSE OR DRIVE AND TEST THE VOLTAGE BETWEEN DIAGNOSTIC CONNECTOR TERMINALS D2-3 AND D2-7. TERMINAL D2-7 IS GROUND.

VOLTAGE PRESENT ?

NO

YES

PLACE THE TRANSMISSION IN PARK AND TURN THE IGNITION SWITCH OFF.

NOTE: THE REMAINING PORTION OF TEST 3 SHOULD BE PURPOSELY BYPASSED IF THE VEHICLE IS NOT AT ROOM TEMPERATURE (APPROX. 21°C/70°F). IF THE ENGINE IS EITHER HOT OR COLD, THE TEST RESULTS WILL NOT BE VALID FOR FAULT DIAGNOSIS.

TURN THE IGNITION SWITCH ON AND TEST THE VOLTAGE BETWEEN DIAGNOSTIC CONNECTOR TERMINALS D2-12 AND D2-7. TERMINAL D2-7 IS GROUND.

CONTINUED ON THE NEXT PAGE

86744gdh

Fig. 53 1984-85 TBI SYSTEM DIAGNOSTIC CHARTS

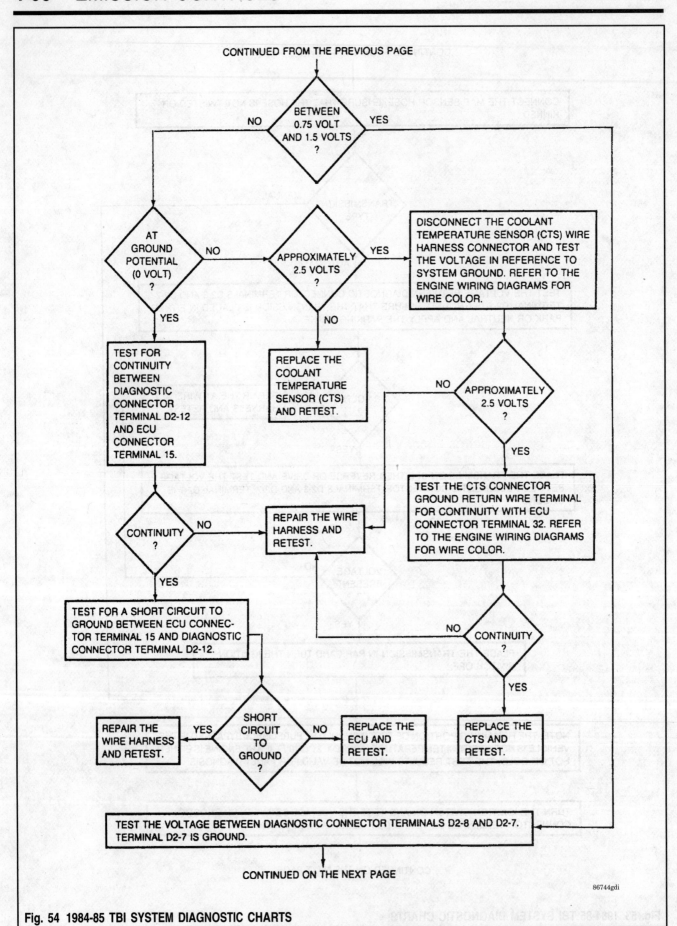

Fig. 54 1984-85 TBI SYSTEM DIAGNOSTIC CHARTS

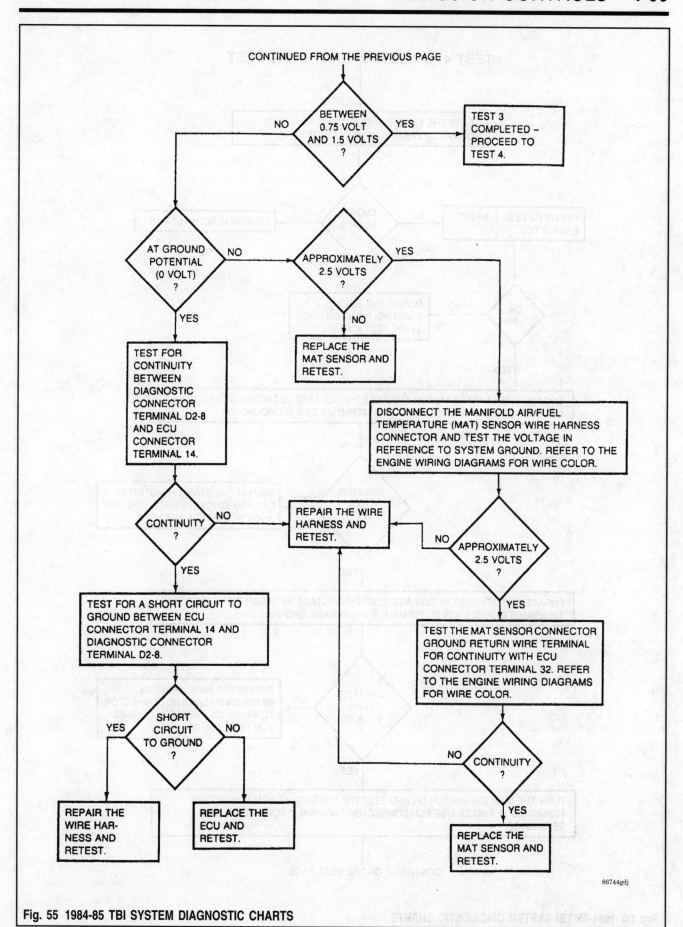

CONTINUED FROM THE PREVIOUS PAGE

BETWEEN 0.75 VOLT AND 1.5 VOLTS ? — YES → TEST 3 COMPLETED – PROCEED TO TEST 4.

NO

AT GROUND POTENTIAL (0 VOLT) ? — NO → APPROXIMATELY 2.5 VOLTS ? — YES

YES

APPROXIMATELY 2.5 VOLTS ? — NO → REPLACE THE MAT SENSOR AND RETEST.

TEST FOR CONTINUITY BETWEEN DIAGNOSTIC CONNECTOR TERMINAL D2-8 AND ECU CONNECTOR TERMINAL 14.

DISCONNECT THE MANIFOLD AIR/FUEL TEMPERATURE (MAT) SENSOR WIRE HARNESS CONNECTOR AND TEST THE VOLTAGE IN REFERENCE TO SYSTEM GROUND. REFER TO THE ENGINE WIRING DIAGRAMS FOR WIRE COLOR.

CONTINUITY ? — NO → REPAIR THE WIRE HARNESS AND RETEST.

YES

APPROXIMATELY 2.5 VOLTS ? — NO → REPAIR THE WIRE HARNESS AND RETEST.

YES

TEST FOR A SHORT CIRCUIT TO GROUND BETWEEN ECU CONNECTOR TERMINAL 14 AND DIAGNOSTIC CONNECTOR TERMINAL D2-8.

TEST THE MAT SENSOR CONNECTOR GROUND RETURN WIRE TERMINAL FOR CONTINUITY WITH ECU CONNECTOR TERMINAL 32. REFER TO THE ENGINE WIRING DIAGRAMS FOR WIRE COLOR.

SHORT CIRCUIT TO GROUND ? — YES / NO

CONTINUITY ? — NO / YES

REPAIR THE WIRE HAR-NESS AND RETEST.

REPLACE THE ECU AND RETEST.

REPLACE THE MAT SENSOR AND RETEST.

86744gdj

Fig. 55 1984-85 TBI SYSTEM DIAGNOSTIC CHARTS

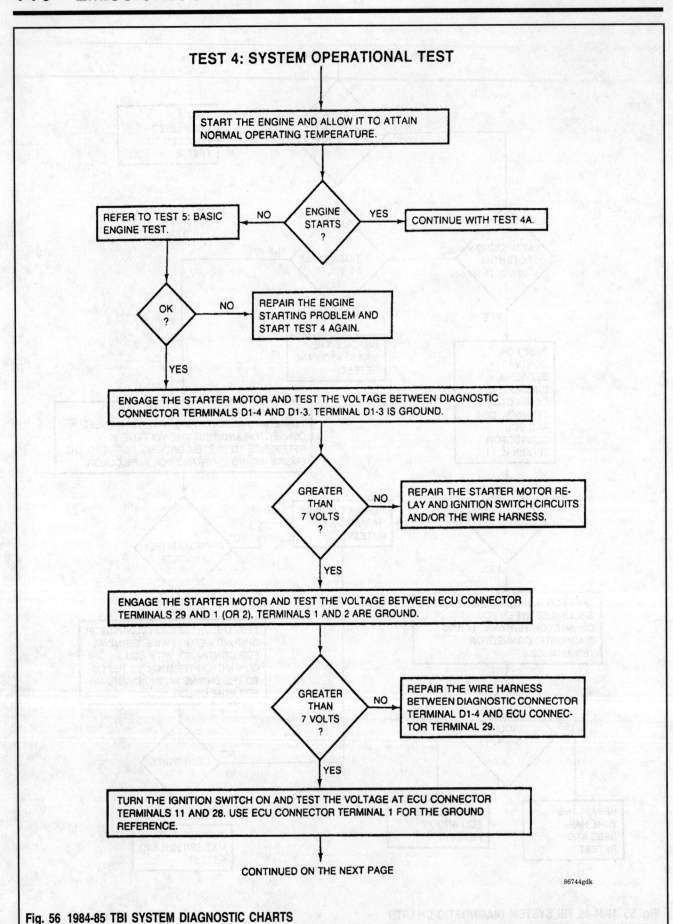

TEST 4: SYSTEM OPERATIONAL TEST

START THE ENGINE AND ALLOW IT TO ATTAIN NORMAL OPERATING TEMPERATURE.

ENGINE STARTS ?

NO → REFER TO TEST 5: BASIC ENGINE TEST.

YES → CONTINUE WITH TEST 4A.

OK ?

NO → REPAIR THE ENGINE STARTING PROBLEM AND START TEST 4 AGAIN.

YES

ENGAGE THE STARTER MOTOR AND TEST THE VOLTAGE BETWEEN DIAGNOSTIC CONNECTOR TERMINALS D1-4 AND D1-3. TERMINAL D1-3 IS GROUND.

GREATER THAN 7 VOLTS ?

NO → REPAIR THE STARTER MOTOR RELAY AND IGNITION SWITCH CIRCUITS AND/OR THE WIRE HARNESS.

YES

ENGAGE THE STARTER MOTOR AND TEST THE VOLTAGE BETWEEN ECU CONNECTOR TERMINALS 29 AND 1 (OR 2). TERMINALS 1 AND 2 ARE GROUND.

GREATER THAN 7 VOLTS ?

NO → REPAIR THE WIRE HARNESS BETWEEN DIAGNOSTIC CONNECTOR TERMINAL D1-4 AND ECU CONNECTOR TERMINAL 29.

YES

TURN THE IGNITION SWITCH ON AND TEST THE VOLTAGE AT ECU CONNECTOR TERMINALS 11 AND 28. USE ECU CONNECTOR TERMINAL 1 FOR THE GROUND REFERENCE.

CONTINUED ON THE NEXT PAGE

86744gdk

Fig. 56 1984-85 TBI SYSTEM DIAGNOSTIC CHARTS

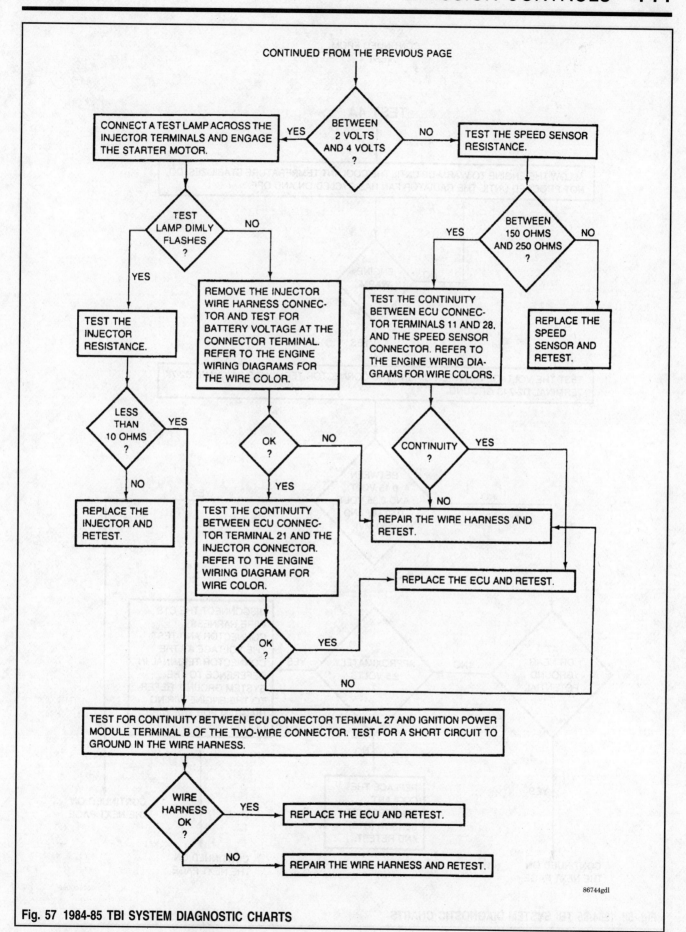

Fig. 57 1984-85 TBI SYSTEM DIAGNOSTIC CHARTS

86744gdl

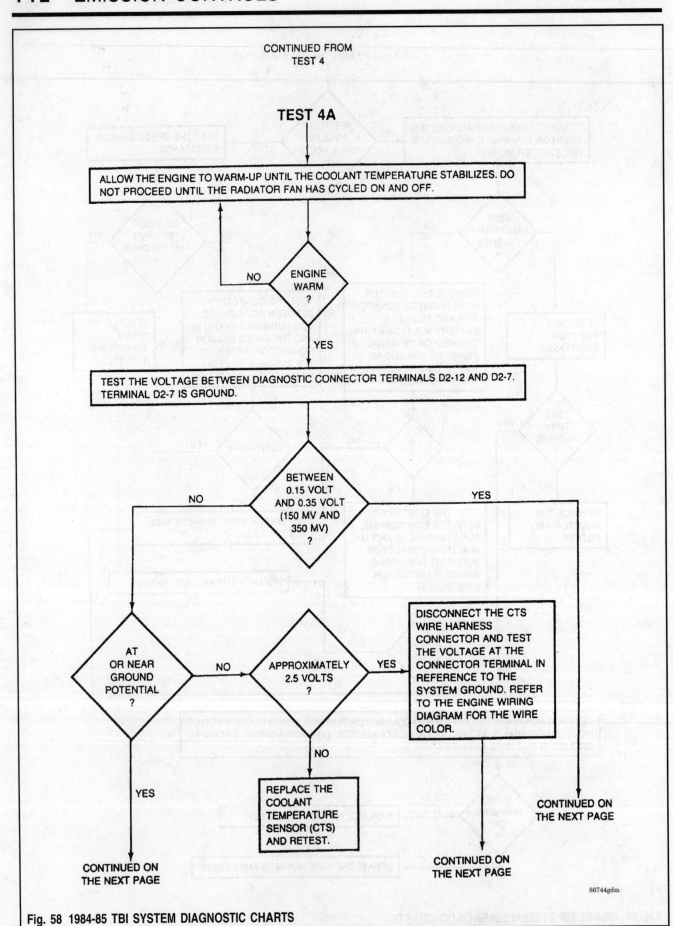

Fig. 58 1984-85 TBI SYSTEM DIAGNOSTIC CHARTS

CONTINUED FROM
TEST 4

TEST 4A

ALLOW THE ENGINE TO WARM-UP UNTIL THE COOLANT TEMPERATURE STABILIZES. DO
NOT PROCEED UNTIL THE RADIATOR FAN HAS CYCLED ON AND OFF.

ENGINE
WARM
?

NO

YES

TEST THE VOLTAGE BETWEEN DIAGNOSTIC CONNECTOR TERMINALS D2-12 AND D2-7.
TERMINAL D2-7 IS GROUND.

BETWEEN
0.15 VOLT
AND 0.35 VOLT
(150 MV AND
350 MV)
?

NO

YES

AT
OR NEAR
GROUND
POTENTIAL
?

NO

APPROXIMATELY
2.5 VOLTS
?

YES

DISCONNECT THE CTS
WIRE HARNESS
CONNECTOR AND TEST
THE VOLTAGE AT THE
CONNECTOR TERMINAL IN
REFERENCE TO THE
SYSTEM GROUND. REFER
TO THE ENGINE WIRING
DIAGRAM FOR THE WIRE
COLOR.

NO

REPLACE THE
COOLANT
TEMPERATURE
SENSOR (CTS)
AND RETEST.

YES

CONTINUED ON
THE NEXT PAGE

CONTINUED ON
THE NEXT PAGE

CONTINUED ON
THE NEXT PAGE

86744gdm

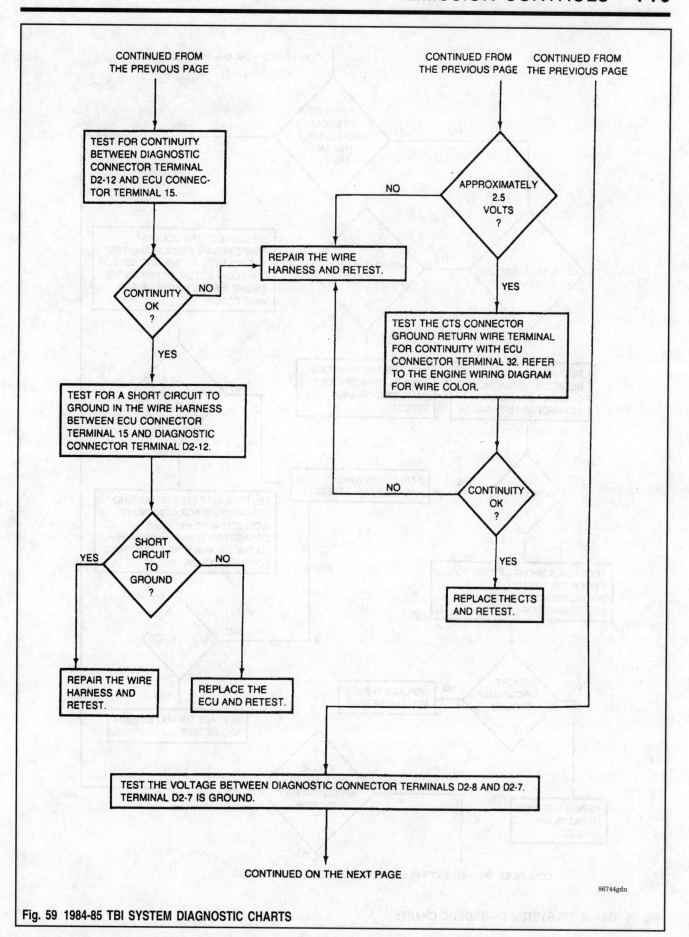

CONTINUED FROM THE PREVIOUS PAGE

TEST FOR CONTINUITY BETWEEN DIAGNOSTIC CONNECTOR TERMINAL D2-12 AND ECU CONNECTOR TERMINAL 15.

CONTINUITY OK ?

NO → REPAIR THE WIRE HARNESS AND RETEST.

YES

TEST FOR A SHORT CIRCUIT TO GROUND IN THE WIRE HARNESS BETWEEN ECU CONNECTOR TERMINAL 15 AND DIAGNOSTIC CONNECTOR TERMINAL D2-12.

SHORT CIRCUIT TO GROUND ?

YES → REPAIR THE WIRE HARNESS AND RETEST.

NO → REPLACE THE ECU AND RETEST.

CONTINUED FROM THE PREVIOUS PAGE   CONTINUED FROM THE PREVIOUS PAGE

APPROXIMATELY 2.5 VOLTS ?

NO → REPAIR THE WIRE HARNESS AND RETEST.

YES

TEST THE CTS CONNECTOR GROUND RETURN WIRE TERMINAL FOR CONTINUITY WITH ECU CONNECTOR TERMINAL 32. REFER TO THE ENGINE WIRING DIAGRAM FOR WIRE COLOR.

CONTINUITY OK ?

NO → (to REPAIR THE WIRE HARNESS AND RETEST)

YES

REPLACE THE CTS AND RETEST.

TEST THE VOLTAGE BETWEEN DIAGNOSTIC CONNECTOR TERMINALS D2-8 AND D2-7. TERMINAL D2-7 IS GROUND.

CONTINUED ON THE NEXT PAGE

86744gdn

Fig. 59 1984-85 TBI SYSTEM DIAGNOSTIC CHARTS

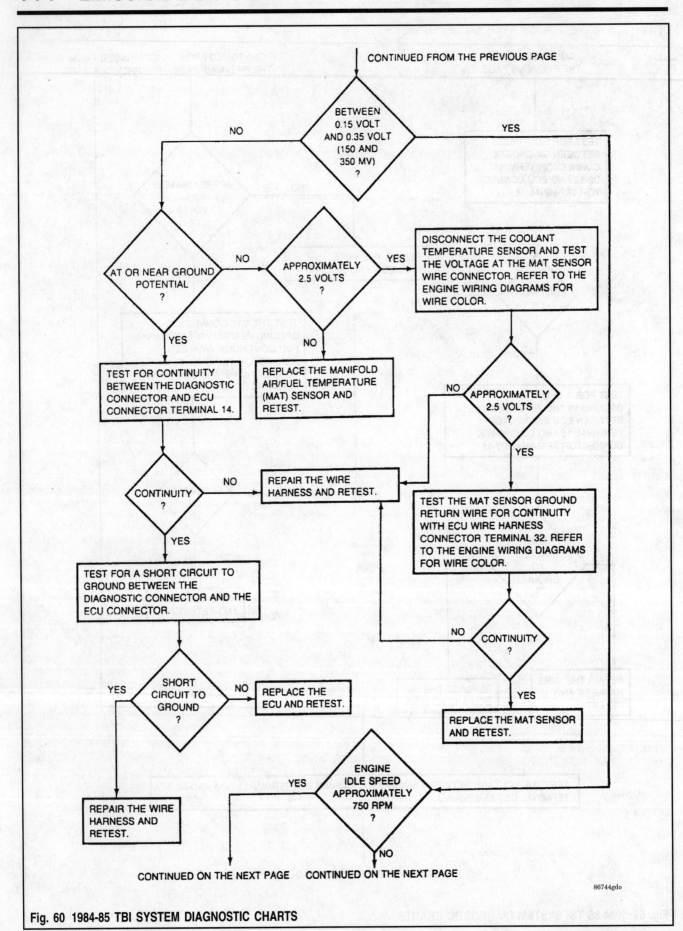

CONTINUED FROM THE PREVIOUS PAGE

BETWEEN 0.15 VOLT AND 0.35 VOLT (150 AND 350 MV) ?

NO — YES

AT OR NEAR GROUND POTENTIAL ?

NO — APPROXIMATELY 2.5 VOLTS ?

YES — DISCONNECT THE COOLANT TEMPERATURE SENSOR AND TEST THE VOLTAGE AT THE MAT SENSOR WIRE CONNECTOR. REFER TO THE ENGINE WIRING DIAGRAMS FOR WIRE COLOR.

NO — REPLACE THE MANIFOLD AIR/FUEL TEMPERATURE (MAT) SENSOR AND RETEST.

YES — TEST FOR CONTINUITY BETWEEN THE DIAGNOSTIC CONNECTOR AND ECU CONNECTOR TERMINAL 14.

APPROXIMATELY 2.5 VOLTS ?

NO — YES

CONTINUITY ?

NO — REPAIR THE WIRE HARNESS AND RETEST.

YES — TEST FOR A SHORT CIRCUIT TO GROUND BETWEEN THE DIAGNOSTIC CONNECTOR AND THE ECU CONNECTOR.

TEST THE MAT SENSOR GROUND RETURN WIRE FOR CONTINUITY WITH ECU WIRE HARNESS CONNECTOR TERMINAL 32. REFER TO THE ENGINE WIRING DIAGRAMS FOR WIRE COLOR.

SHORT CIRCUIT TO GROUND ?

YES — NO — REPLACE THE ECU AND RETEST.

CONTINUITY ?

NO — YES — REPLACE THE MAT SENSOR AND RETEST.

REPAIR THE WIRE HARNESS AND RETEST.

ENGINE IDLE SPEED APPROXIMATELY 750 RPM ?

YES — NO

CONTINUED ON THE NEXT PAGE   CONTINUED ON THE NEXT PAGE

86744gdo

Fig. 60 1984-85 TBI SYSTEM DIAGNOSTIC CHARTS

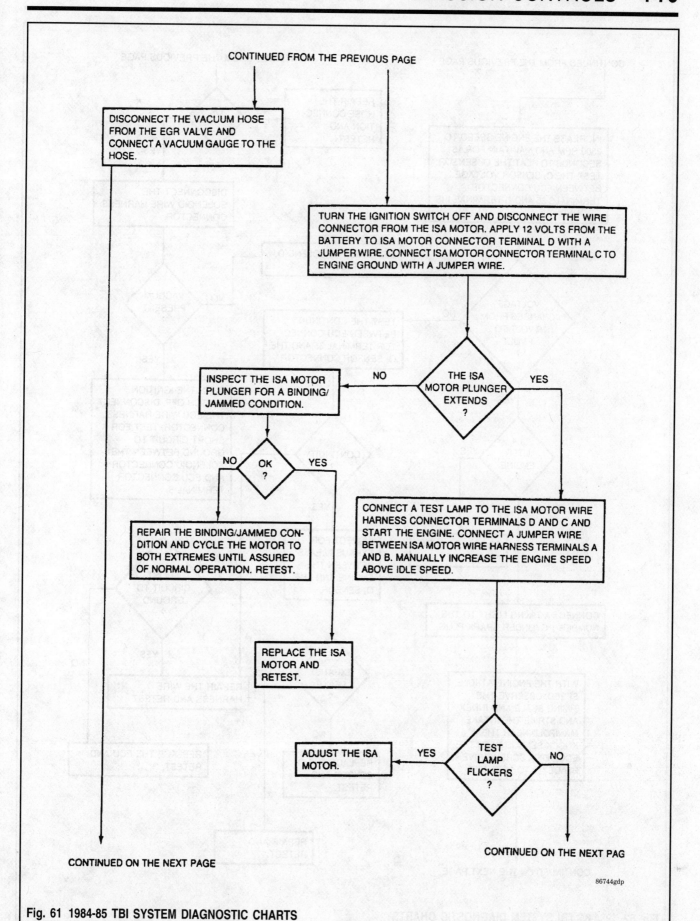

CONTINUED FROM THE PREVIOUS PAGE

DISCONNECT THE VACUUM HOSE FROM THE EGR VALVE AND CONNECT A VACUUM GAUGE TO THE HOSE.

TURN THE IGNITION SWITCH OFF AND DISCONNECT THE WIRE CONNECTOR FROM THE ISA MOTOR. APPLY 12 VOLTS FROM THE BATTERY TO ISA MOTOR CONNECTOR TERMINAL D WITH A JUMPER WIRE. CONNECT ISA MOTOR CONNECTOR TERMINAL C TO ENGINE GROUND WITH A JUMPER WIRE.

INSPECT THE ISA MOTOR PLUNGER FOR A BINDING/JAMMED CONDITION. ← NO — THE ISA MOTOR PLUNGER EXTENDS ? — YES →

OK ? — NO / YES

REPAIR THE BINDING/JAMMED CONDITION AND CYCLE THE MOTOR TO BOTH EXTREMES UNTIL ASSURED OF NORMAL OPERATION. RETEST.

CONNECT A TEST LAMP TO THE ISA MOTOR WIRE HARNESS CONNECTOR TERMINALS D AND C AND START THE ENGINE. CONNECT A JUMPER WIRE BETWEEN ISA MOTOR WIRE HARNESS TERMINALS A AND B. MANUALLY INCREASE THE ENGINE SPEED ABOVE IDLE SPEED.

REPLACE THE ISA MOTOR AND RETEST.

ADJUST THE ISA MOTOR. ← YES — TEST LAMP FLICKERS ? — NO →

CONTINUED ON THE NEXT PAGE

CONTINUED ON THE NEXT PAG

86744gdp

Fig. 61 1984-85 TBI SYSTEM DIAGNOSTIC CHARTS

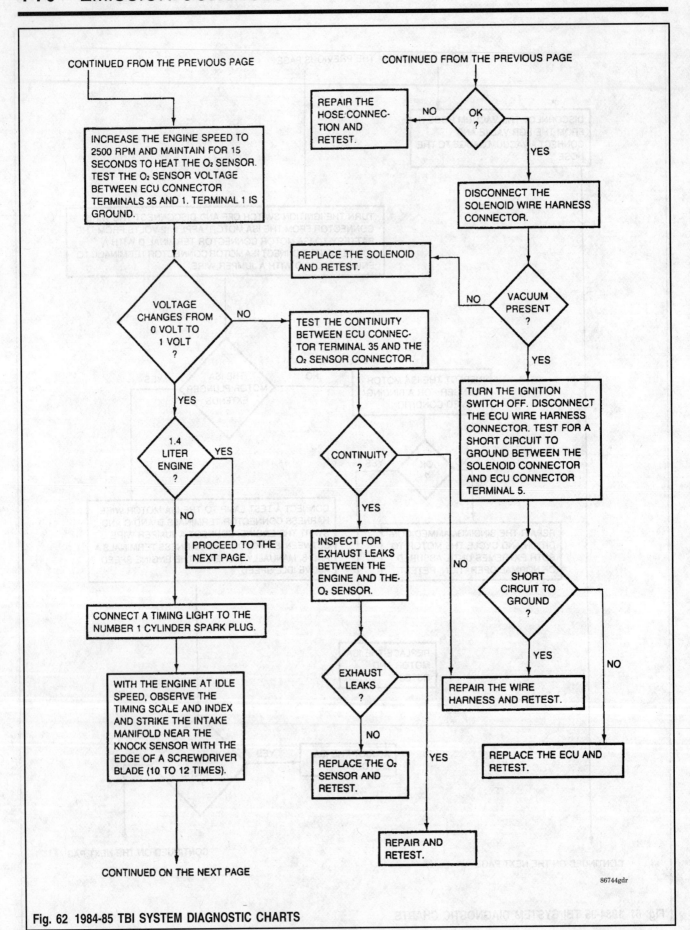

Fig. 62 1984-85 TBI SYSTEM DIAGNOSTIC CHARTS

86744gdr

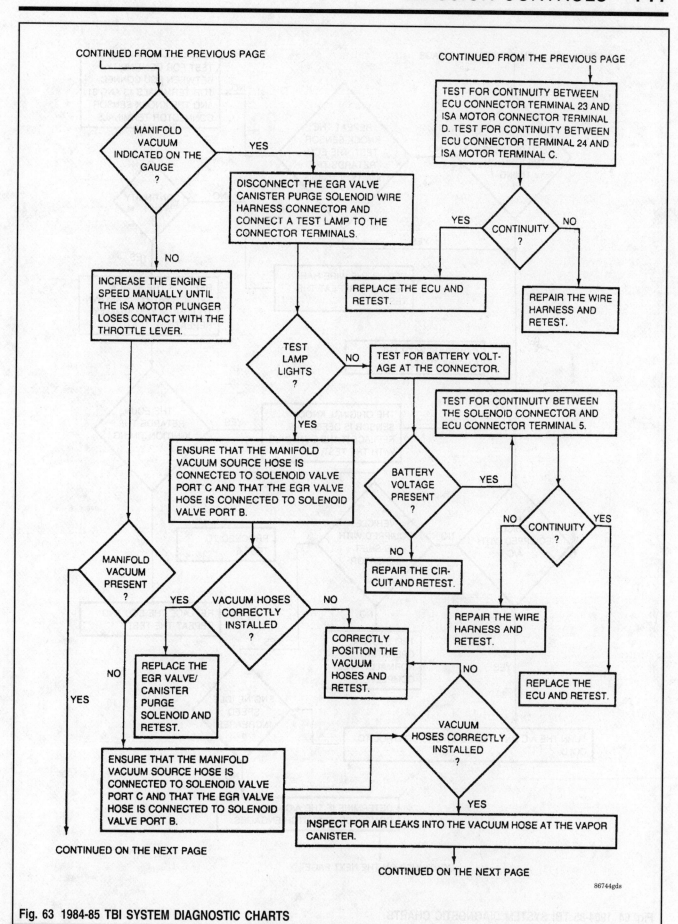

Fig. 63 1984-85 TBI SYSTEM DIAGNOSTIC CHARTS

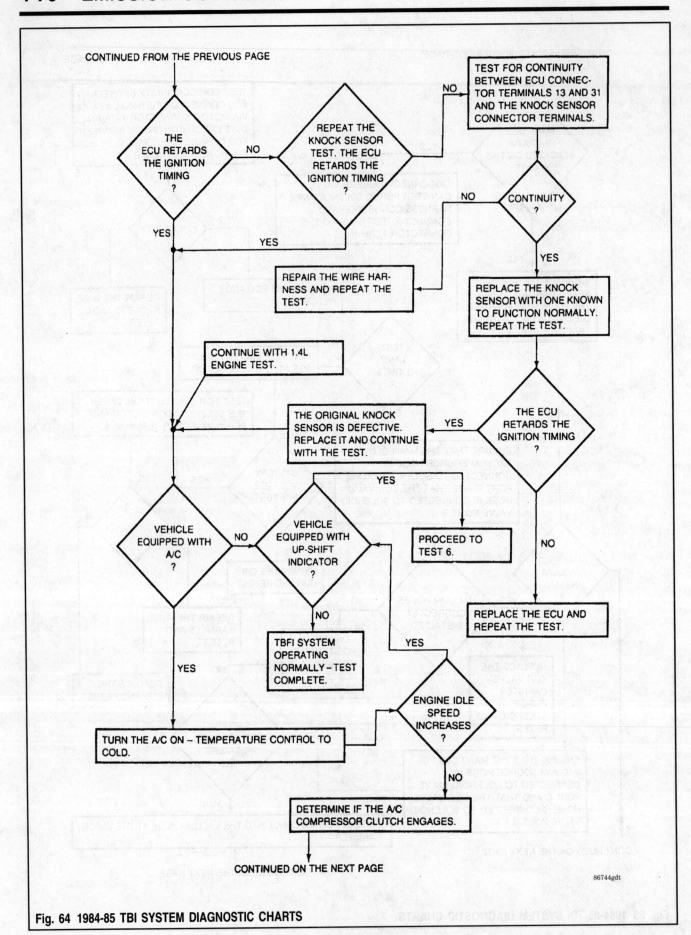

Fig. 64 1984-85 TBI SYSTEM DIAGNOSTIC CHARTS

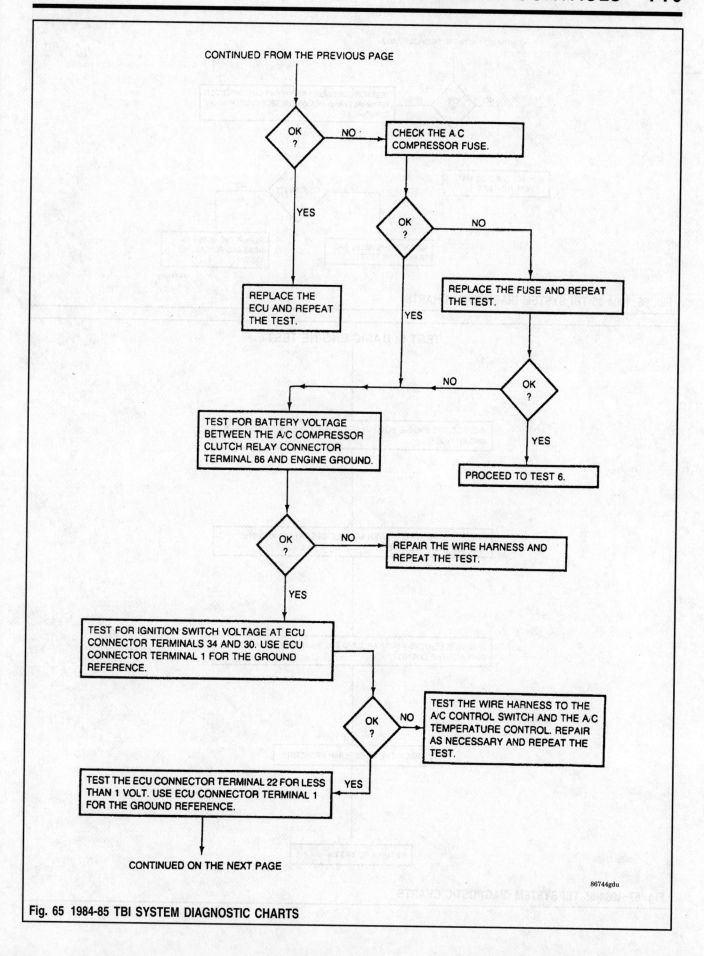

CONTINUED FROM THE PREVIOUS PAGE

OK
?

NO → CHECK THE A.C COMPRESSOR FUSE.

YES

OK
?

NO

YES

REPLACE THE ECU AND REPEAT THE TEST.

REPLACE THE FUSE AND REPEAT THE TEST.

OK
?

NO

YES

PROCEED TO TEST 6.

TEST FOR BATTERY VOLTAGE BETWEEN THE A/C COMPRESSOR CLUTCH RELAY CONNECTOR TERMINAL 86 AND ENGINE GROUND.

OK
?

NO → REPAIR THE WIRE HARNESS AND REPEAT THE TEST.

YES

TEST FOR IGNITION SWITCH VOLTAGE AT ECU CONNECTOR TERMINALS 34 AND 30. USE ECU CONNECTOR TERMINAL 1 FOR THE GROUND REFERENCE.

OK
?

NO → TEST THE WIRE HARNESS TO THE A/C CONTROL SWITCH AND THE A/C TEMPERATURE CONTROL. REPAIR AS NECESSARY AND REPEAT THE TEST.

YES

TEST THE ECU CONNECTOR TERMINAL 22 FOR LESS THAN 1 VOLT. USE ECU CONNECTOR TERMINAL 1 FOR THE GROUND REFERENCE.

CONTINUED ON THE NEXT PAGE

86744gdu

Fig. 65 1984-85 TBI SYSTEM DIAGNOSTIC CHARTS

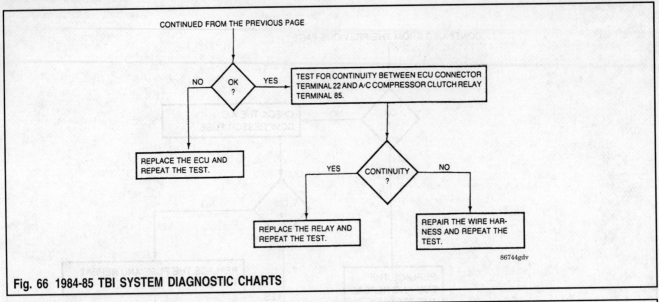

CONTINUED FROM THE PREVIOUS PAGE

OK ?

NO → REPLACE THE ECU AND REPEAT THE TEST.

YES → TEST FOR CONTINUITY BETWEEN ECU CONNECTOR TERMINAL 22 AND A/C COMPRESSOR CLUTCH RELAY TERMINAL 85.

CONTINUITY ?

YES → REPLACE THE RELAY AND REPEAT THE TEST.

NO → REPAIR THE WIRE HARNESS AND REPEAT THE TEST.

86744gdv

Fig. 66 1984-85 TBI SYSTEM DIAGNOSTIC CHARTS

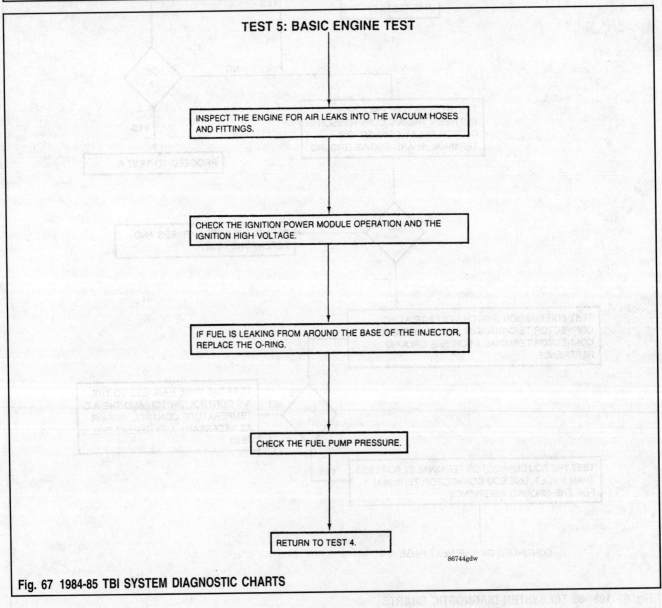

TEST 5: BASIC ENGINE TEST

INSPECT THE ENGINE FOR AIR LEAKS INTO THE VACUUM HOSES AND FITTINGS.

CHECK THE IGNITION POWER MODULE OPERATION AND THE IGNITION HIGH VOLTAGE.

IF FUEL IS LEAKING FROM AROUND THE BASE OF THE INJECTOR, REPLACE THE O-RING.

CHECK THE FUEL PUMP PRESSURE.

RETURN TO TEST 4.

86744gdw

Fig. 67 1984-85 TBI SYSTEM DIAGNOSTIC CHARTS

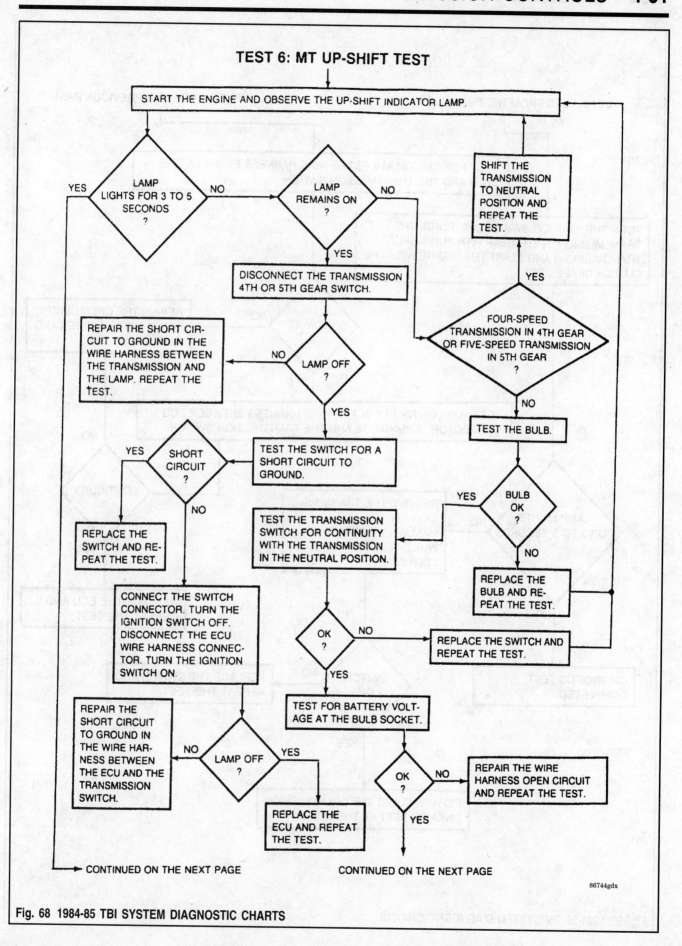

TEST 6: MT UP-SHIFT TEST

START THE ENGINE AND OBSERVE THE UP-SHIFT INDICATOR LAMP.

LAMP LIGHTS FOR 3 TO 5 SECONDS ?

LAMP REMAINS ON ?

SHIFT THE TRANSMISSION TO NEUTRAL POSITION AND REPEAT THE TEST.

DISCONNECT THE TRANSMISSION 4TH OR 5TH GEAR SWITCH.

FOUR-SPEED TRANSMISSION IN 4TH GEAR OR FIVE-SPEED TRANSMISSION IN 5TH GEAR ?

REPAIR THE SHORT CIR-CUIT TO GROUND IN THE WIRE HARNESS BETWEEN THE TRANSMISSION AND THE LAMP. REPEAT THE TEST.

LAMP OFF ?

TEST THE BULB.

SHORT CIRCUIT ?

TEST THE SWITCH FOR A SHORT CIRCUIT TO GROUND.

BULB OK ?

REPLACE THE SWITCH AND RE-PEAT THE TEST.

TEST THE TRANSMISSION SWITCH FOR CONTINUITY WITH THE TRANSMISSION IN THE NEUTRAL POSITION.

REPLACE THE BULB AND RE-PEAT THE TEST.

CONNECT THE SWITCH CONNECTOR. TURN THE IGNITION SWITCH OFF. DISCONNECT THE ECU WIRE HARNESS CONNEC-TOR. TURN THE IGNITION SWITCH ON.

OK ?

REPLACE THE SWITCH AND REPEAT THE TEST.

REPAIR THE SHORT CIRCUIT TO GROUND IN THE WIRE HAR-NESS BETWEEN THE ECU AND THE TRANSMISSION SWITCH.

TEST FOR BATTERY VOLT-AGE AT THE BULB SOCKET.

LAMP OFF ?

OK ?

REPAIR THE WIRE HARNESS OPEN CIRCUIT AND REPEAT THE TEST.

REPLACE THE ECU AND REPEAT THE TEST.

CONTINUED ON THE NEXT PAGE

CONTINUED ON THE NEXT PAGE

86744gdx

Fig. 68 1984-85 TBI SYSTEM DIAGNOSTIC CHARTS

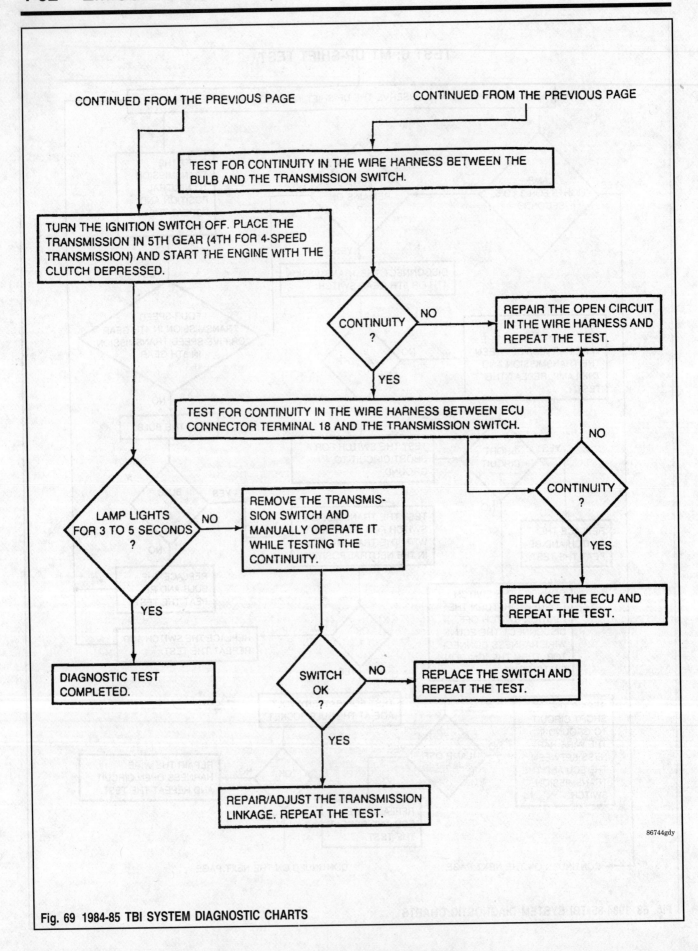

CONTINUED FROM THE PREVIOUS PAGE

CONTINUED FROM THE PREVIOUS PAGE

TEST FOR CONTINUITY IN THE WIRE HARNESS BETWEEN THE BULB AND THE TRANSMISSION SWITCH.

TURN THE IGNITION SWITCH OFF. PLACE THE TRANSMISSION IN 5TH GEAR (4TH FOR 4-SPEED TRANSMISSION) AND START THE ENGINE WITH THE CLUTCH DEPRESSED.

CONTINUITY ? — NO → REPAIR THE OPEN CIRCUIT IN THE WIRE HARNESS AND REPEAT THE TEST.

YES

TEST FOR CONTINUITY IN THE WIRE HARNESS BETWEEN ECU CONNECTOR TERMINAL 18 AND THE TRANSMISSION SWITCH.

NO

CONTINUITY ?

LAMP LIGHTS FOR 3 TO 5 SECONDS ? — NO → REMOVE THE TRANSMISSION SWITCH AND MANUALLY OPERATE IT WHILE TESTING THE CONTINUITY.

YES

REPLACE THE ECU AND REPEAT THE TEST.

DIAGNOSTIC TEST COMPLETED.

SWITCH OK ? — NO → REPLACE THE SWITCH AND REPEAT THE TEST.

YES

REPAIR/ADJUST THE TRANSMISSION LINKAGE. REPEAT THE TEST.

86744gdy

Fig. 69 1984-85 TBI SYSTEM DIAGNOSTIC CHARTS

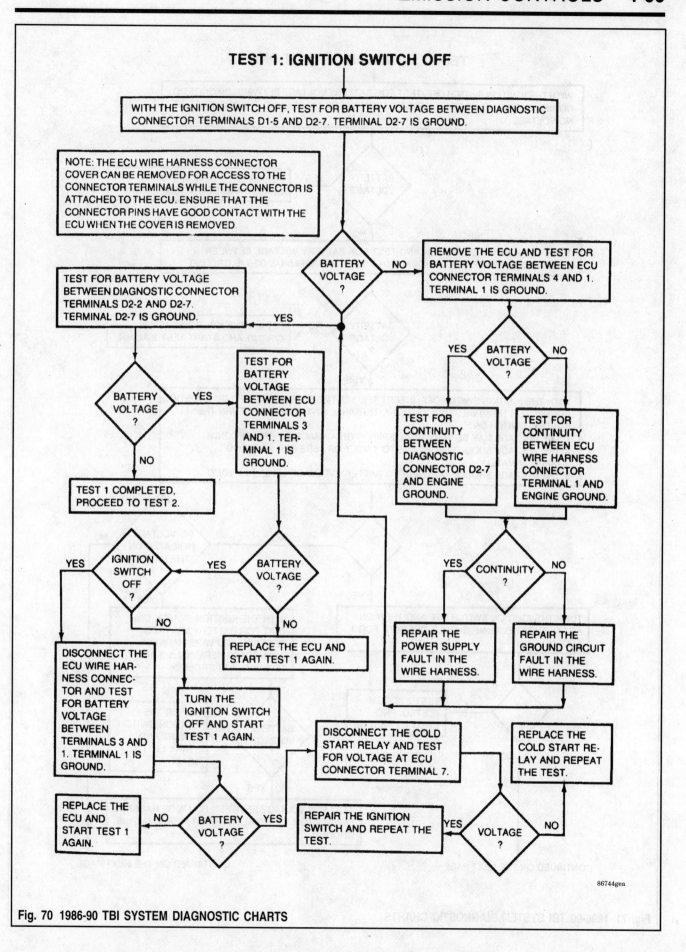

TEST 1: IGNITION SWITCH OFF

WITH THE IGNITION SWITCH OFF, TEST FOR BATTERY VOLTAGE BETWEEN DIAGNOSTIC CONNECTOR TERMINALS D1-5 AND D2-7. TERMINAL D2-7 IS GROUND.

NOTE: THE ECU WIRE HARNESS CONNECTOR COVER CAN BE REMOVED FOR ACCESS TO THE CONNECTOR TERMINALS WHILE THE CONNECTOR IS ATTACHED TO THE ECU. ENSURE THAT THE CONNECTOR PINS HAVE GOOD CONTACT WITH THE ECU WHEN THE COVER IS REMOVED.

BATTERY VOLTAGE?

TEST FOR BATTERY VOLTAGE BETWEEN DIAGNOSTIC CONNECTOR TERMINALS D2-2 AND D2-7. TERMINAL D2-7 IS GROUND.

NO — REMOVE THE ECU AND TEST FOR BATTERY VOLTAGE BETWEEN ECU CONNECTOR TERMINALS 4 AND 1. TERMINAL 1 IS GROUND.

YES

BATTERY VOLTAGE?

BATTERY VOLTAGE?

YES — TEST FOR BATTERY VOLTAGE BETWEEN ECU CONNECTOR TERMINALS 3 AND 1. TERMINAL 1 IS GROUND.

NO — TEST 1 COMPLETED, PROCEED TO TEST 2.

YES — TEST FOR CONTINUITY BETWEEN DIAGNOSTIC CONNECTOR D2-7 AND ENGINE GROUND.

NO — TEST FOR CONTINUITY BETWEEN ECU WIRE HARNESS CONNECTOR TERMINAL 1 AND ENGINE GROUND.

IGNITION SWITCH OFF?

YES — BATTERY VOLTAGE?

NO — REPLACE THE ECU AND START TEST 1 AGAIN.

CONTINUITY?

YES — REPAIR THE POWER SUPPLY FAULT IN THE WIRE HARNESS.

NO — REPAIR THE GROUND CIRCUIT FAULT IN THE WIRE HARNESS.

YES — DISCONNECT THE ECU WIRE HARNESS CONNECTOR AND TEST FOR BATTERY VOLTAGE BETWEEN TERMINALS 3 AND 1. TERMINAL 1 IS GROUND.

NO — TURN THE IGNITION SWITCH OFF AND START TEST 1 AGAIN.

DISCONNECT THE COLD START RELAY AND TEST FOR VOLTAGE AT ECU CONNECTOR TERMINAL 7.

REPLACE THE COLD START RELAY AND REPEAT THE TEST.

REPLACE THE ECU AND START TEST 1 AGAIN.

NO — BATTERY VOLTAGE? — YES

REPAIR THE IGNITION SWITCH AND REPEAT THE TEST.

YES — VOLTAGE? — NO

Fig. 70 1986-90 TBI SYSTEM DIAGNOSTIC CHARTS

86744gea

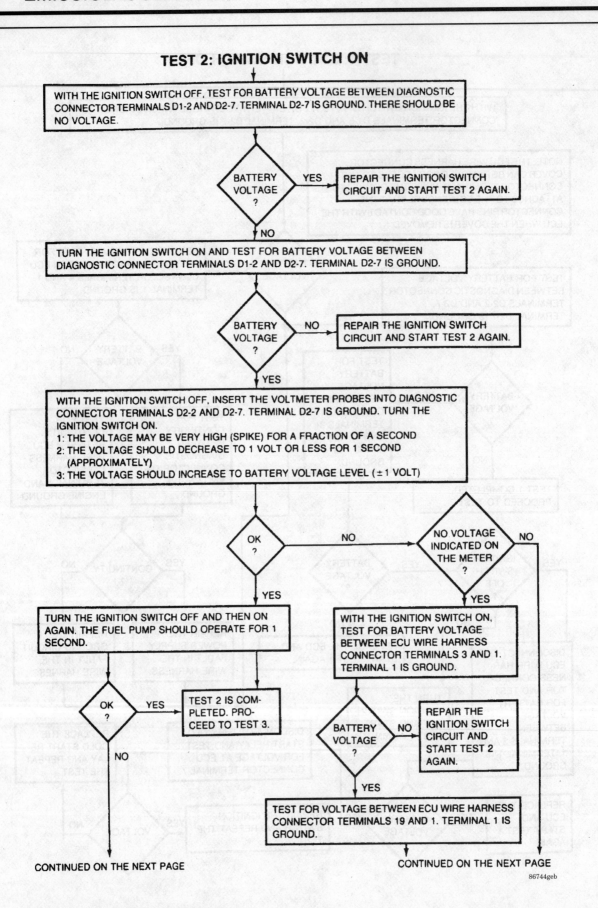

TEST 2: IGNITION SWITCH ON

WITH THE IGNITION SWITCH OFF, TEST FOR BATTERY VOLTAGE BETWEEN DIAGNOSTIC CONNECTOR TERMINALS D1-2 AND D2-7. TERMINAL D2-7 IS GROUND. THERE SHOULD BE NO VOLTAGE.

BATTERY VOLTAGE ? — YES → REPAIR THE IGNITION SWITCH CIRCUIT AND START TEST 2 AGAIN.

NO

TURN THE IGNITION SWITCH ON AND TEST FOR BATTERY VOLTAGE BETWEEN DIAGNOSTIC CONNECTOR TERMINALS D1-2 AND D2-7. TERMINAL D2-7 IS GROUND.

BATTERY VOLTAGE ? — NO → REPAIR THE IGNITION SWITCH CIRCUIT AND START TEST 2 AGAIN.

YES

WITH THE IGNITION SWITCH OFF, INSERT THE VOLTMETER PROBES INTO DIAGNOSTIC CONNECTOR TERMINALS D2-2 AND D2-7. TERMINAL D2-7 IS GROUND. TURN THE IGNITION SWITCH ON.
1: THE VOLTAGE MAY BE VERY HIGH (SPIKE) FOR A FRACTION OF A SECOND
2: THE VOLTAGE SHOULD DECREASE TO 1 VOLT OR LESS FOR 1 SECOND (APPROXIMATELY)
3: THE VOLTAGE SHOULD INCREASE TO BATTERY VOLTAGE LEVEL (± 1 VOLT)

OK ? — NO → NO VOLTAGE INDICATED ON THE METER ? — NO →

YES

YES

TURN THE IGNITION SWITCH OFF AND THEN ON AGAIN. THE FUEL PUMP SHOULD OPERATE FOR 1 SECOND.

WITH THE IGNITION SWITCH ON, TEST FOR BATTERY VOLTAGE BETWEEN ECU WIRE HARNESS CONNECTOR TERMINALS 3 AND 1. TERMINAL 1 IS GROUND.

OK ? — YES → TEST 2 IS COMPLETED. PROCEED TO TEST 3.

NO

BATTERY VOLTAGE ? — NO → REPAIR THE IGNITION SWITCH CIRCUIT AND START TEST 2 AGAIN.

YES

TEST FOR VOLTAGE BETWEEN ECU WIRE HARNESS CONNECTOR TERMINALS 19 AND 1. TERMINAL 1 IS GROUND.

CONTINUED ON THE NEXT PAGE

CONTINUED ON THE NEXT PAGE

86744geb

Fig. 71 1986-90 TBI SYSTEM DIAGNOSTIC CHARTS

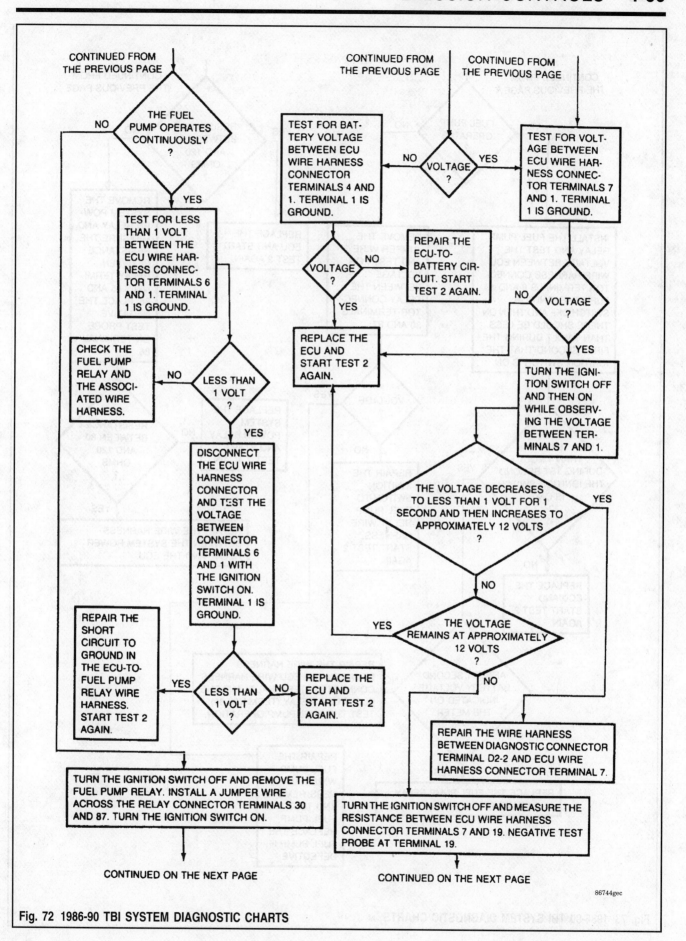

CONTINUED FROM THE PREVIOUS PAGE

THE FUEL PUMP OPERATES CONTINUOUSLY ? — NO →

YES ↓

TEST FOR LESS THAN 1 VOLT BETWEEN THE ECU WIRE HARNESS CONNECTOR TERMINALS 6 AND 1. TERMINAL 1 IS GROUND.

LESS THAN 1 VOLT ? — NO → CHECK THE FUEL PUMP RELAY AND THE ASSOCIATED WIRE HARNESS.

YES ↓

DISCONNECT THE ECU WIRE HARNESS CONNECTOR AND TEST THE VOLTAGE BETWEEN CONNECTOR TERMINALS 6 AND 1 WITH THE IGNITION SWITCH ON. TERMINAL 1 IS GROUND.

LESS THAN 1 VOLT ? — YES → REPAIR THE SHORT CIRCUIT TO GROUND IN THE ECU-TO-FUEL PUMP RELAY WIRE HARNESS. START TEST 2 AGAIN.

— NO → REPLACE THE ECU AND START TEST 2 AGAIN.

TURN THE IGNITION SWITCH OFF AND REMOVE THE FUEL PUMP RELAY. INSTALL A JUMPER WIRE ACROSS THE RELAY CONNECTOR TERMINALS 30 AND 87. TURN THE IGNITION SWITCH ON.

CONTINUED ON THE NEXT PAGE

CONTINUED FROM THE PREVIOUS PAGE

TEST FOR BATTERY VOLTAGE BETWEEN ECU WIRE HARNESS CONNECTOR TERMINALS 4 AND 1. TERMINAL 1 IS GROUND.

VOLTAGE ? — NO → VOLTAGE ? — YES →

VOLTAGE ? — NO → REPAIR THE ECU-TO-BATTERY CIRCUIT. START TEST 2 AGAIN.

YES ↓

REPLACE THE ECU AND START TEST 2 AGAIN.

CONTINUED FROM THE PREVIOUS PAGE

TEST FOR VOLTAGE BETWEEN ECU WIRE HARNESS CONNECTOR TERMINALS 7 AND 1. TERMINAL 1 IS GROUND.

VOLTAGE ? — NO →

YES ↓

TURN THE IGNITION SWITCH OFF AND THEN ON WHILE OBSERVING THE VOLTAGE BETWEEN TERMINALS 7 AND 1.

THE VOLTAGE DECREASES TO LESS THAN 1 VOLT FOR 1 SECOND AND THEN INCREASES TO APPROXIMATELY 12 VOLTS ? — YES →

NO ↓

THE VOLTAGE REMAINS AT APPROXIMATELY 12 VOLTS ? — YES →

— NO →

REPAIR THE WIRE HARNESS BETWEEN DIAGNOSTIC CONNECTOR TERMINAL D2-2 AND ECU WIRE HARNESS CONNECTOR TERMINAL 7.

TURN THE IGNITION SWITCH OFF AND MEASURE THE RESISTANCE BETWEEN ECU WIRE HARNESS CONNECTOR TERMINALS 7 AND 19. NEGATIVE TEST PROBE AT TERMINAL 19.

CONTINUED ON THE NEXT PAGE

86744gec

Fig. 72 1986-90 TBI SYSTEM DIAGNOSTIC CHARTS

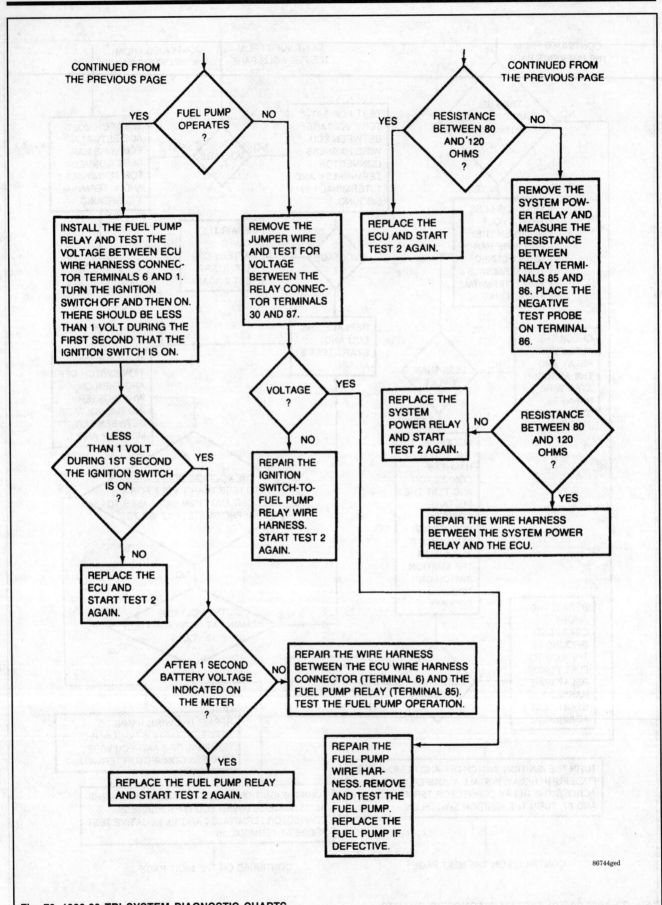

Fig. 73 1986-90 TBI SYSTEM DIAGNOSTIC CHARTS

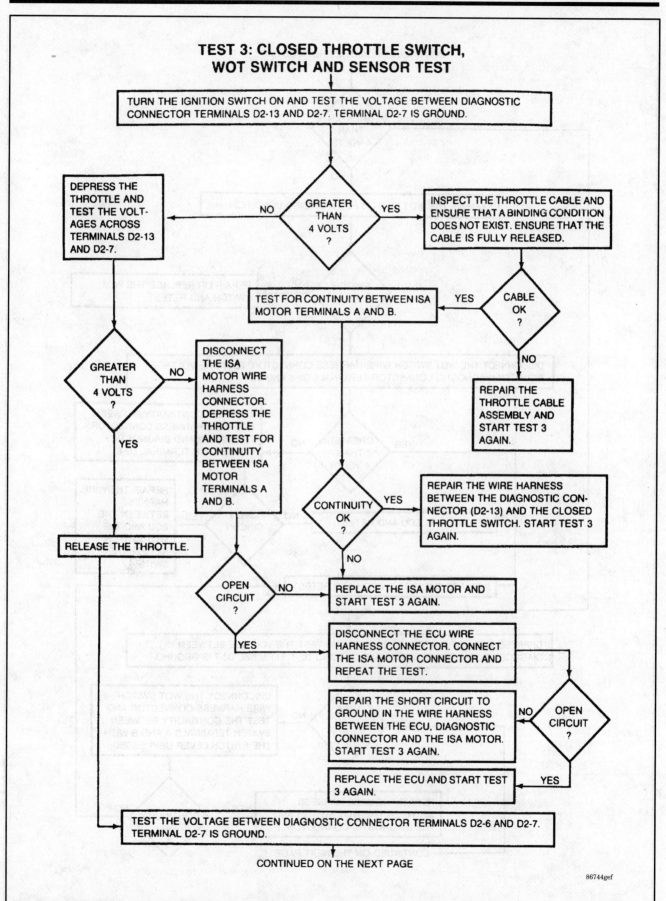

**TEST 3: CLOSED THROTTLE SWITCH,
WOT SWITCH AND SENSOR TEST**

TURN THE IGNITION SWITCH ON AND TEST THE VOLTAGE BETWEEN DIAGNOSTIC CONNECTOR TERMINALS D2-13 AND D2-7. TERMINAL D2-7 IS GROUND.

GREATER THAN 4 VOLTS ?

NO — DEPRESS THE THROTTLE AND TEST THE VOLTAGES ACROSS TERMINALS D2-13 AND D2-7.

YES — INSPECT THE THROTTLE CABLE AND ENSURE THAT A BINDING CONDITION DOES NOT EXIST. ENSURE THAT THE CABLE IS FULLY RELEASED.

CABLE OK ?

YES — TEST FOR CONTINUITY BETWEEN ISA MOTOR TERMINALS A AND B.

NO — REPAIR THE THROTTLE CABLE ASSEMBLY AND START TEST 3 AGAIN.

GREATER THAN 4 VOLTS ?

NO — DISCONNECT THE ISA MOTOR WIRE HARNESS CONNECTOR. DEPRESS THE THROTTLE AND TEST FOR CONTINUITY BETWEEN ISA MOTOR TERMINALS A AND B.

YES — RELEASE THE THROTTLE.

CONTINUITY OK ?

YES — REPAIR THE WIRE HARNESS BETWEEN THE DIAGNOSTIC CONNECTOR (D2-13) AND THE CLOSED THROTTLE SWITCH. START TEST 3 AGAIN.

NO

OPEN CIRCUIT ?

NO — REPLACE THE ISA MOTOR AND START TEST 3 AGAIN.

YES — DISCONNECT THE ECU WIRE HARNESS CONNECTOR. CONNECT THE ISA MOTOR CONNECTOR AND REPEAT THE TEST.

REPAIR THE SHORT CIRCUIT TO GROUND IN THE WIRE HARNESS BETWEEN THE ECU, DIAGNOSTIC CONNECTOR AND THE ISA MOTOR. START TEST 3 AGAIN.

OPEN CIRCUIT ?

NO

YES — REPLACE THE ECU AND START TEST 3 AGAIN.

TEST THE VOLTAGE BETWEEN DIAGNOSTIC CONNECTOR TERMINALS D2-6 AND D2-7. TERMINAL D2-7 IS GROUND.

CONTINUED ON THE NEXT PAGE

86744gef

Fig. 74 1986-90 TBI SYSTEM DIAGNOSTIC CHARTS

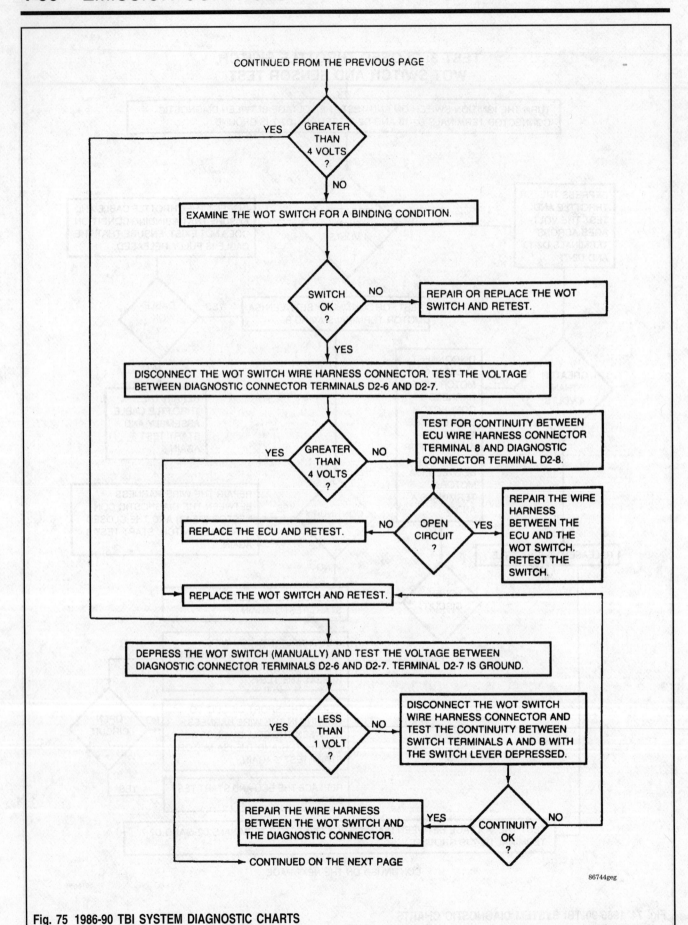

Fig. 75 1986-90 TBI SYSTEM DIAGNOSTIC CHARTS

86744geg

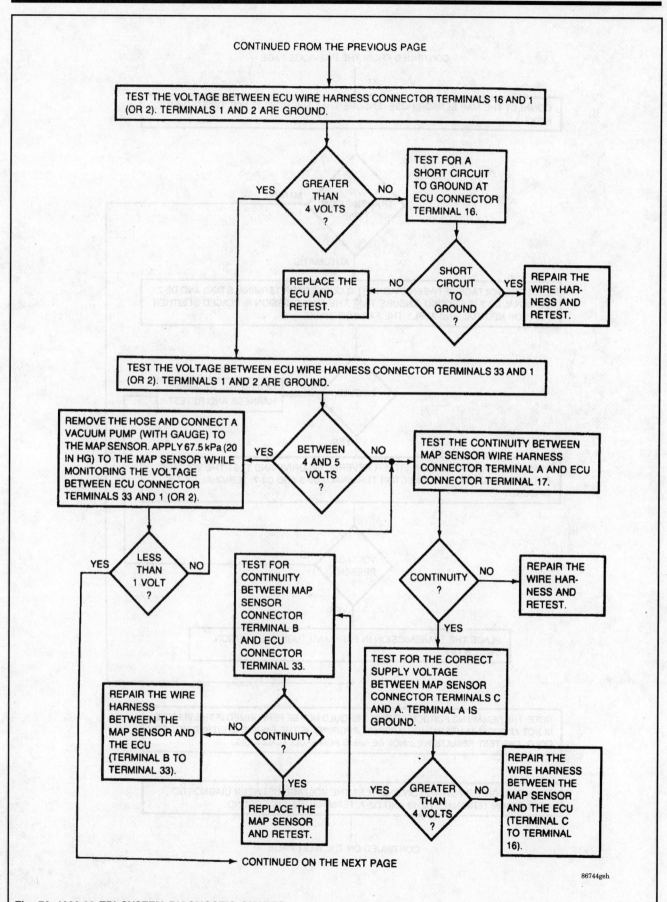

CONTINUED FROM THE PREVIOUS PAGE

TEST THE VOLTAGE BETWEEN ECU WIRE HARNESS CONNECTOR TERMINALS 16 AND 1 (OR 2). TERMINALS 1 AND 2 ARE GROUND.

GREATER THAN 4 VOLTS ?

YES

NO — TEST FOR A SHORT CIRCUIT TO GROUND AT ECU CONNECTOR TERMINAL 16.

SHORT CIRCUIT TO GROUND ?

NO — REPLACE THE ECU AND RETEST.

YES — REPAIR THE WIRE HARNESS AND RETEST.

TEST THE VOLTAGE BETWEEN ECU WIRE HARNESS CONNECTOR TERMINALS 33 AND 1 (OR 2). TERMINALS 1 AND 2 ARE GROUND.

BETWEEN 4 AND 5 VOLTS ?

YES — REMOVE THE HOSE AND CONNECT A VACUUM PUMP (WITH GAUGE) TO THE MAP SENSOR. APPLY 67.5 kPa (20 IN HG) TO THE MAP SENSOR WHILE MONITORING THE VOLTAGE BETWEEN ECU CONNECTOR TERMINALS 33 AND 1 (OR 2).

NO — TEST THE CONTINUITY BETWEEN MAP SENSOR WIRE HARNESS CONNECTOR TERMINAL A AND ECU CONNECTOR TERMINAL 17.

LESS THAN 1 VOLT ?

YES

NO — TEST FOR CONTINUITY BETWEEN MAP SENSOR CONNECTOR TERMINAL B AND ECU CONNECTOR TERMINAL 33.

CONTINUITY ?

NO — REPAIR THE WIRE HARNESS AND RETEST.

YES — TEST FOR THE CORRECT SUPPLY VOLTAGE BETWEEN MAP SENSOR CONNECTOR TERMINALS C AND A. TERMINAL A IS GROUND.

CONTINUITY ?

NO — REPAIR THE WIRE HARNESS BETWEEN THE MAP SENSOR AND THE ECU (TERMINAL B TO TERMINAL 33).

YES — REPLACE THE MAP SENSOR AND RETEST.

GREATER THAN 4 VOLTS ?

YES

NO — REPAIR THE WIRE HARNESS BETWEEN THE MAP SENSOR AND THE ECU (TERMINAL C TO TERMINAL 16).

CONTINUED ON THE NEXT PAGE

86744geh

Fig. 76 1986-90 TBI SYSTEM DIAGNOSTIC CHARTS

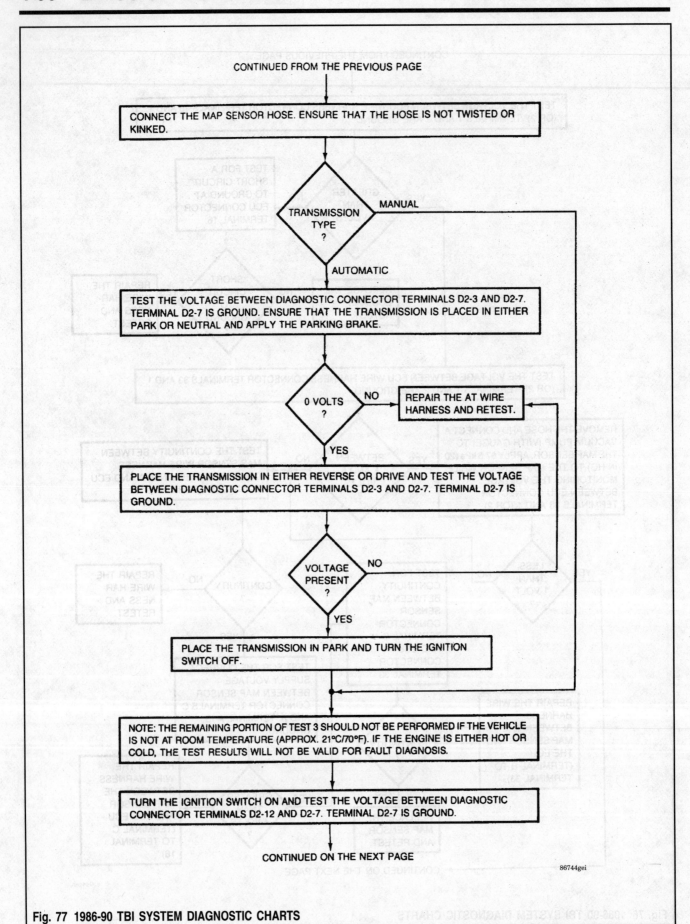

CONTINUED FROM THE PREVIOUS PAGE

CONNECT THE MAP SENSOR HOSE. ENSURE THAT THE HOSE IS NOT TWISTED OR KINKED.

TRANSMISSION TYPE ? — MANUAL

AUTOMATIC

TEST THE VOLTAGE BETWEEN DIAGNOSTIC CONNECTOR TERMINALS D2-3 AND D2-7. TERMINAL D2-7 IS GROUND. ENSURE THAT THE TRANSMISSION IS PLACED IN EITHER PARK OR NEUTRAL AND APPLY THE PARKING BRAKE.

0 VOLTS ? — NO → REPAIR THE AT WIRE HARNESS AND RETEST.

YES

PLACE THE TRANSMISSION IN EITHER REVERSE OR DRIVE AND TEST THE VOLTAGE BETWEEN DIAGNOSTIC CONNECTOR TERMINALS D2-3 AND D2-7. TERMINAL D2-7 IS GROUND.

VOLTAGE PRESENT ? — NO

YES

PLACE THE TRANSMISSION IN PARK AND TURN THE IGNITION SWITCH OFF.

NOTE: THE REMAINING PORTION OF TEST 3 SHOULD NOT BE PERFORMED IF THE VEHICLE IS NOT AT ROOM TEMPERATURE (APPROX. 21°C/70°F). IF THE ENGINE IS EITHER HOT OR COLD, THE TEST RESULTS WILL NOT BE VALID FOR FAULT DIAGNOSIS.

TURN THE IGNITION SWITCH ON AND TEST THE VOLTAGE BETWEEN DIAGNOSTIC CONNECTOR TERMINALS D2-12 AND D2-7. TERMINAL D2-7 IS GROUND.

CONTINUED ON THE NEXT PAGE

86744gei

Fig. 77 1986-90 TBI SYSTEM DIAGNOSTIC CHARTS

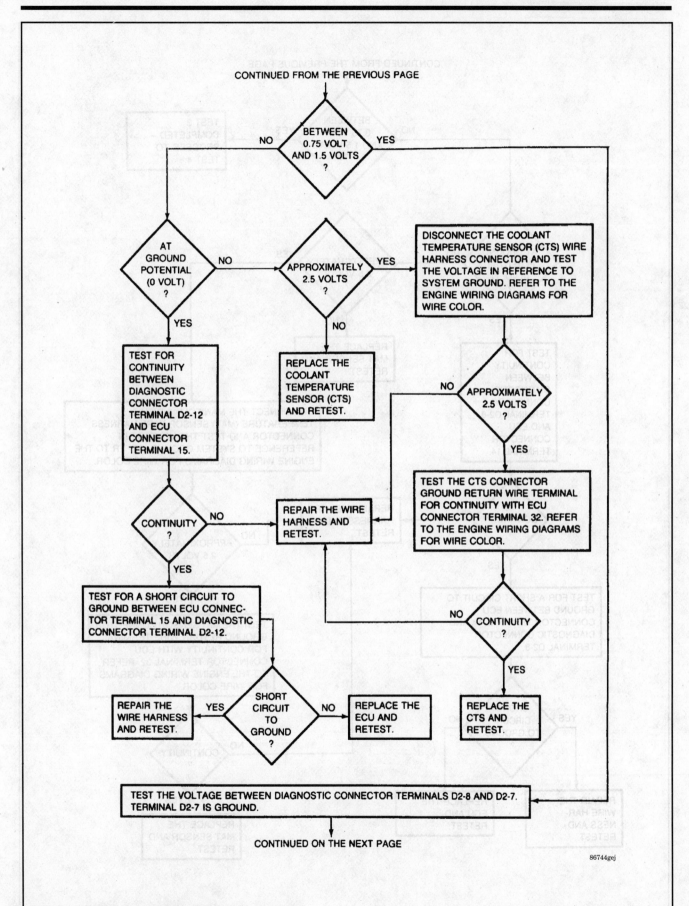

CONTINUED FROM THE PREVIOUS PAGE

BETWEEN 0.75 VOLT AND 1.5 VOLTS ?

NO — YES

AT GROUND POTENTIAL (0 VOLT) ?

NO — APPROXIMATELY 2.5 VOLTS ?

YES — DISCONNECT THE COOLANT TEMPERATURE SENSOR (CTS) WIRE HARNESS CONNECTOR AND TEST THE VOLTAGE IN REFERENCE TO SYSTEM GROUND. REFER TO THE ENGINE WIRING DIAGRAMS FOR WIRE COLOR.

YES

NO

TEST FOR CONTINUITY BETWEEN DIAGNOSTIC CONNECTOR TERMINAL D2-12 AND ECU CONNECTOR TERMINAL 15.

REPLACE THE COOLANT TEMPERATURE SENSOR (CTS) AND RETEST.

NO — APPROXIMATELY 2.5 VOLTS ?

YES

TEST THE CTS CONNECTOR GROUND RETURN WIRE TERMINAL FOR CONTINUITY WITH ECU CONNECTOR TERMINAL 32. REFER TO THE ENGINE WIRING DIAGRAMS FOR WIRE COLOR.

CONTINUITY ?

NO — REPAIR THE WIRE HARNESS AND RETEST.

YES

TEST FOR A SHORT CIRCUIT TO GROUND BETWEEN ECU CONNECTOR TERMINAL 15 AND DIAGNOSTIC CONNECTOR TERMINAL D2-12.

NO — CONTINUITY ?

YES

SHORT CIRCUIT TO GROUND ?

YES — REPAIR THE WIRE HARNESS AND RETEST.

NO — REPLACE THE ECU AND RETEST.

REPLACE THE CTS AND RETEST.

TEST THE VOLTAGE BETWEEN DIAGNOSTIC CONNECTOR TERMINALS D2-8 AND D2-7. TERMINAL D2-7 IS GROUND.

CONTINUED ON THE NEXT PAGE

86744gej

Fig. 78 1986-90 TBI SYSTEM DIAGNOSTIC CHARTS

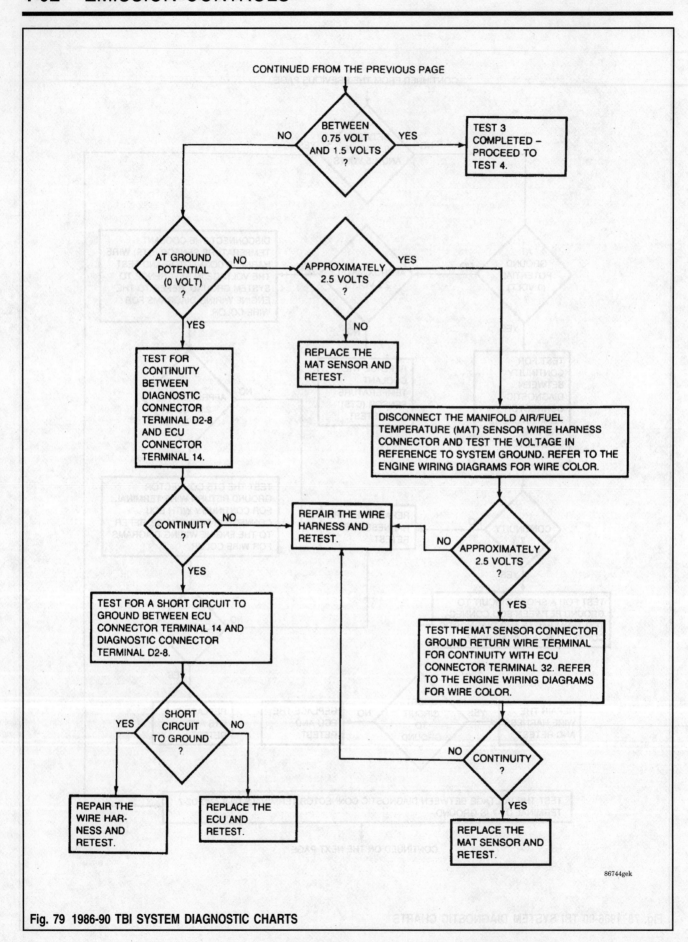

Fig. 79 1986-90 TBI SYSTEM DIAGNOSTIC CHARTS

86744gek

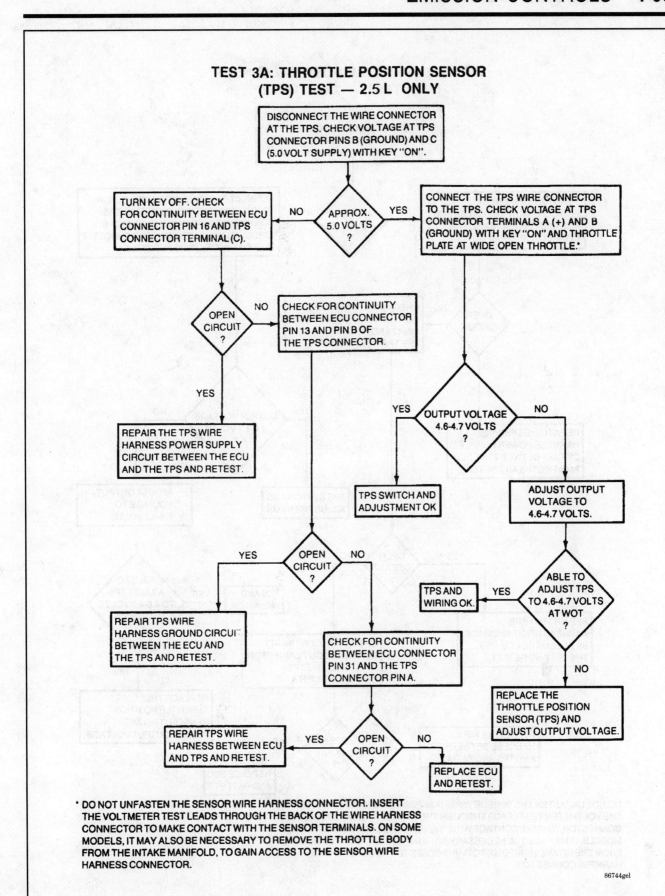

TEST 3A: THROTTLE POSITION SENSOR (TPS) TEST — 2.5 L ONLY

DISCONNECT THE WIRE CONNECTOR AT THE TPS. CHECK VOLTAGE AT TPS CONNECTOR PINS B (GROUND) AND C (5.0 VOLT SUPPLY) WITH KEY "ON".

APPROX. 5.0 VOLTS ?

NO → TURN KEY OFF. CHECK FOR CONTINUITY BETWEEN ECU CONNECTOR PIN 16 AND TPS CONNECTOR TERMINAL (C).

YES → CONNECT THE TPS WIRE CONNECTOR TO THE TPS. CHECK VOLTAGE AT TPS CONNECTOR TERMINALS A (+) AND B (GROUND) WITH KEY "ON" AND THROTTLE PLATE AT WIDE OPEN THROTTLE.*

OPEN CIRCUIT ?

NO → CHECK FOR CONTINUITY BETWEEN ECU CONNECTOR PIN 13 AND PIN B OF THE TPS CONNECTOR.

YES → REPAIR THE TPS WIRE HARNESS POWER SUPPLY CIRCUIT BETWEEN THE ECU AND THE TPS AND RETEST.

OUTPUT VOLTAGE 4.6-4.7 VOLTS ?

YES → TPS SWITCH AND ADJUSTMENT OK

NO → ADJUST OUTPUT VOLTAGE TO 4.6-4.7 VOLTS.

OPEN CIRCUIT ?

YES → REPAIR TPS WIRE HARNESS GROUND CIRCUIT BETWEEN THE ECU AND THE TPS AND RETEST.

NO → CHECK FOR CONTINUITY BETWEEN ECU CONNECTOR PIN 31 AND THE TPS CONNECTOR PIN A.

ABLE TO ADJUST TPS TO 4.6-4.7 VOLTS AT WOT ?

YES → TPS AND WIRING OK.

NO → REPLACE THE THROTTLE POSITION SENSOR (TPS) AND ADJUST OUTPUT VOLTAGE.

OPEN CIRCUIT ?

YES → REPAIR TPS WIRE HARNESS BETWEEN ECU AND TPS AND RETEST.

NO → REPLACE ECU AND RETEST.

* DO NOT UNFASTEN THE SENSOR WIRE HARNESS CONNECTOR. INSERT THE VOLTMETER TEST LEADS THROUGH THE BACK OF THE WIRE HARNESS CONNECTOR TO MAKE CONTACT WITH THE SENSOR TERMINALS. ON SOME MODELS, IT MAY ALSO BE NECESSARY TO REMOVE THE THROTTLE BODY FROM THE INTAKE MANIFOLD, TO GAIN ACCESS TO THE SENSOR WIRE HARNESS CONNECTOR.

86744gel

Fig. 80 1986-90 TBI SYSTEM DIAGNOSTIC CHARTS

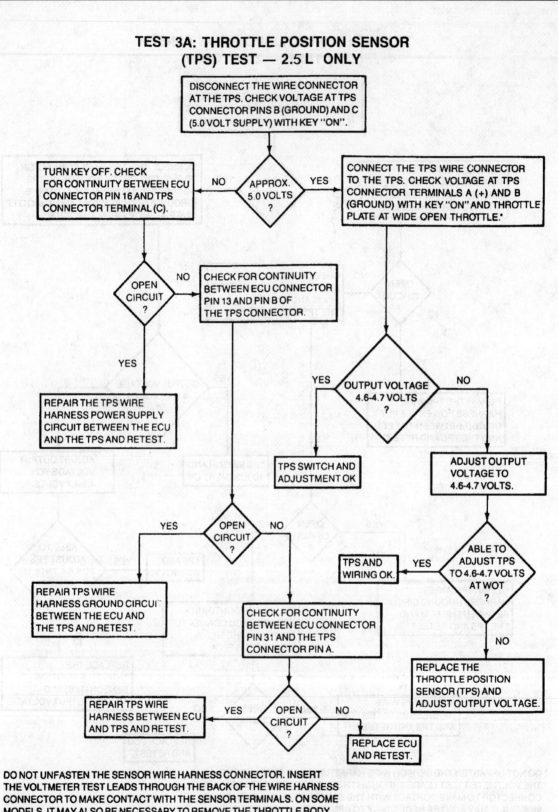

**TEST 3A: THROTTLE POSITION SENSOR
(TPS) TEST — 2.5 L ONLY**

DISCONNECT THE WIRE CONNECTOR AT THE TPS. CHECK VOLTAGE AT TPS CONNECTOR PINS B (GROUND) AND C (5.0 VOLT SUPPLY) WITH KEY "ON".

APPROX. 5.0 VOLTS ?

NO — TURN KEY OFF. CHECK FOR CONTINUITY BETWEEN ECU CONNECTOR PIN 16 AND TPS CONNECTOR TERMINAL (C).

YES — CONNECT THE TPS WIRE CONNECTOR TO THE TPS. CHECK VOLTAGE AT TPS CONNECTOR TERMINALS A (+) AND B (GROUND) WITH KEY "ON" AND THROTTLE PLATE AT WIDE OPEN THROTTLE.*

OPEN CIRCUIT ?

NO — CHECK FOR CONTINUITY BETWEEN ECU CONNECTOR PIN 13 AND PIN B OF THE TPS CONNECTOR.

YES — REPAIR THE TPS WIRE HARNESS POWER SUPPLY CIRCUIT BETWEEN THE ECU AND THE TPS AND RETEST.

OUTPUT VOLTAGE 4.6-4.7 VOLTS ?

YES — TPS SWITCH AND ADJUSTMENT OK

NO — ADJUST OUTPUT VOLTAGE TO 4.6-4.7 VOLTS.

OPEN CIRCUIT ?

YES — REPAIR TPS WIRE HARNESS GROUND CIRCUIT BETWEEN THE ECU AND THE TPS AND RETEST.

NO — CHECK FOR CONTINUITY BETWEEN ECU CONNECTOR PIN 31 AND THE TPS CONNECTOR PIN A.

ABLE TO ADJUST TPS TO 4.6-4.7 VOLTS AT WOT ?

YES — TPS AND WIRING OK.

NO — REPLACE THE THROTTLE POSITION SENSOR (TPS) AND ADJUST OUTPUT VOLTAGE.

OPEN CIRCUIT ?

YES — REPAIR TPS WIRE HARNESS BETWEEN ECU AND TPS AND RETEST.

NO — REPLACE ECU AND RETEST.

* DO NOT UNFASTEN THE SENSOR WIRE HARNESS CONNECTOR. INSERT THE VOLTMETER TEST LEADS THROUGH THE BACK OF THE WIRE HARNESS CONNECTOR TO MAKE CONTACT WITH THE SENSOR TERMINALS. ON SOME MODELS, IT MAY ALSO BE NECESSARY TO REMOVE THE THROTTLE BODY FROM THE INTAKE MANIFOLD, TO GAIN ACCESS TO THE SENSOR WIRE HARNESS CONNECTOR.

86744gel

Fig. 81 1986-90 TBI SYSTEM DIAGNOSTIC CHARTS

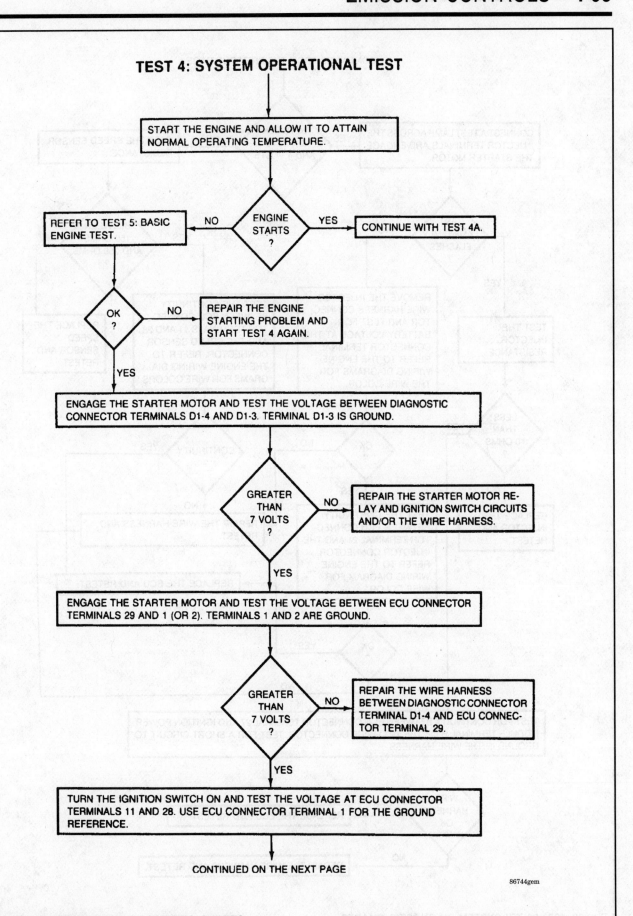

TEST 4: SYSTEM OPERATIONAL TEST

START THE ENGINE AND ALLOW IT TO ATTAIN NORMAL OPERATING TEMPERATURE.

ENGINE STARTS ?

NO → REFER TO TEST 5: BASIC ENGINE TEST.

YES → CONTINUE WITH TEST 4A.

OK ?

NO → REPAIR THE ENGINE STARTING PROBLEM AND START TEST 4 AGAIN.

YES

ENGAGE THE STARTER MOTOR AND TEST THE VOLTAGE BETWEEN DIAGNOSTIC CONNECTOR TERMINALS D1-4 AND D1-3. TERMINAL D1-3 IS GROUND.

GREATER THAN 7 VOLTS ?

NO → REPAIR THE STARTER MOTOR RELAY AND IGNITION SWITCH CIRCUITS AND/OR THE WIRE HARNESS.

YES

ENGAGE THE STARTER MOTOR AND TEST THE VOLTAGE BETWEEN ECU CONNECTOR TERMINALS 29 AND 1 (OR 2). TERMINALS 1 AND 2 ARE GROUND.

GREATER THAN 7 VOLTS ?

NO → REPAIR THE WIRE HARNESS BETWEEN DIAGNOSTIC CONNECTOR TERMINAL D1-4 AND ECU CONNECTOR TERMINAL 29.

YES

TURN THE IGNITION SWITCH ON AND TEST THE VOLTAGE AT ECU CONNECTOR TERMINALS 11 AND 28. USE ECU CONNECTOR TERMINAL 1 FOR THE GROUND REFERENCE.

CONTINUED ON THE NEXT PAGE

86744gem

Fig. 82 1986-90 TBI SYSTEM DIAGNOSTIC CHARTS

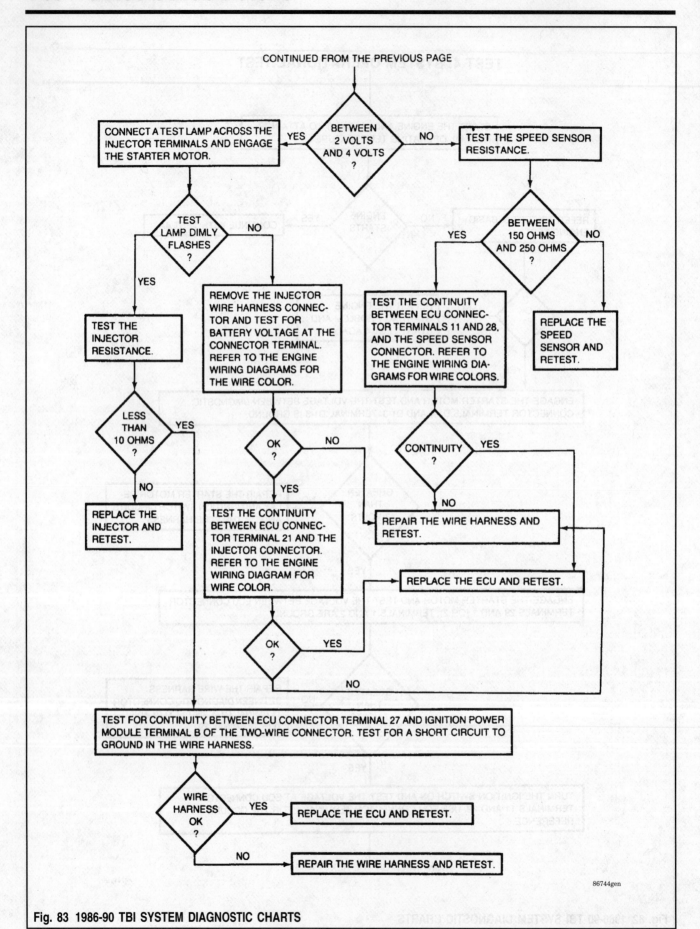

Fig. 83 1986-90 TBI SYSTEM DIAGNOSTIC CHARTS

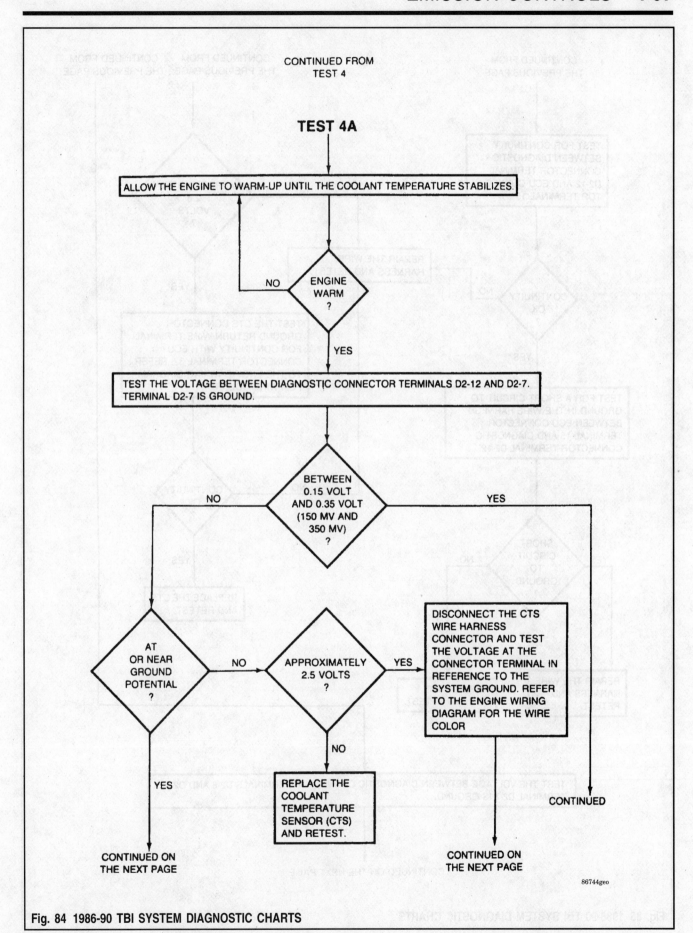

Fig. 84 1986-90 TBI SYSTEM DIAGNOSTIC CHARTS

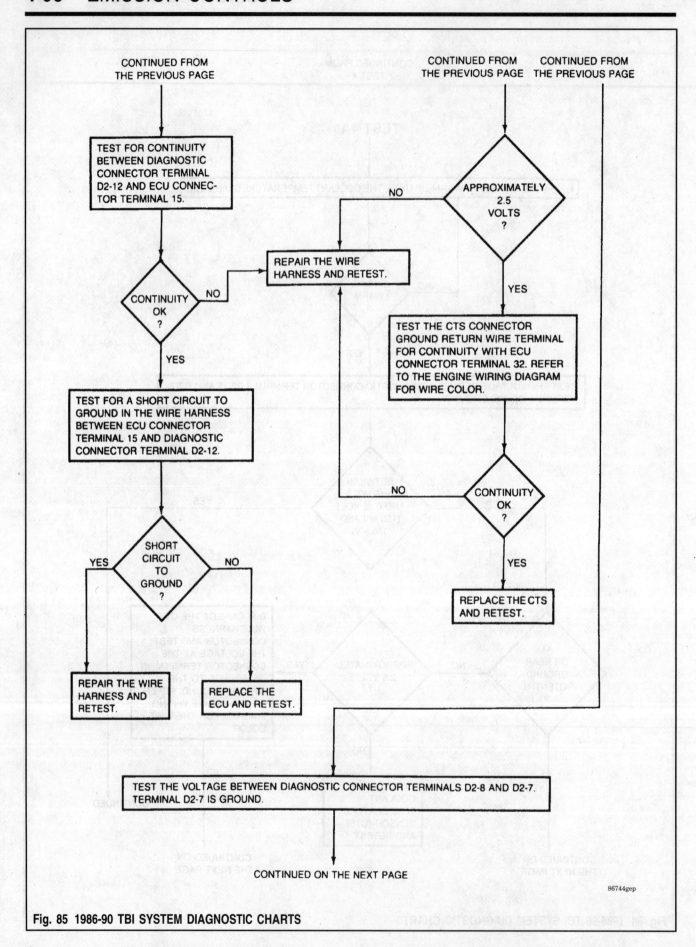

Fig. 85 1986-90 TBI SYSTEM DIAGNOSTIC CHARTS

CONTINUED FROM THE PREVIOUS PAGE

CONTINUED FROM THE PREVIOUS PAGE

CONTINUED FROM THE PREVIOUS PAGE

TEST FOR CONTINUITY BETWEEN DIAGNOSTIC CONNECTOR TERMINAL D2-12 AND ECU CONNECTOR TERMINAL 15.

APPROXIMATELY 2.5 VOLTS ?

NO

CONTINUITY OK ?

NO → REPAIR THE WIRE HARNESS AND RETEST.

YES

YES

TEST THE CTS CONNECTOR GROUND RETURN WIRE TERMINAL FOR CONTINUITY WITH ECU CONNECTOR TERMINAL 32. REFER TO THE ENGINE WIRING DIAGRAM FOR WIRE COLOR.

TEST FOR A SHORT CIRCUIT TO GROUND IN THE WIRE HARNESS BETWEEN ECU CONNECTOR TERMINAL 15 AND DIAGNOSTIC CONNECTOR TERMINAL D2-12.

NO

CONTINUITY OK ?

SHORT CIRCUIT TO GROUND ?

YES

YES

REPLACE THE CTS AND RETEST.

NO

REPAIR THE WIRE HARNESS AND RETEST.

REPLACE THE ECU AND RETEST.

TEST THE VOLTAGE BETWEEN DIAGNOSTIC CONNECTOR TERMINALS D2-8 AND D2-7. TERMINAL D2-7 IS GROUND.

CONTINUED ON THE NEXT PAGE

86744gep

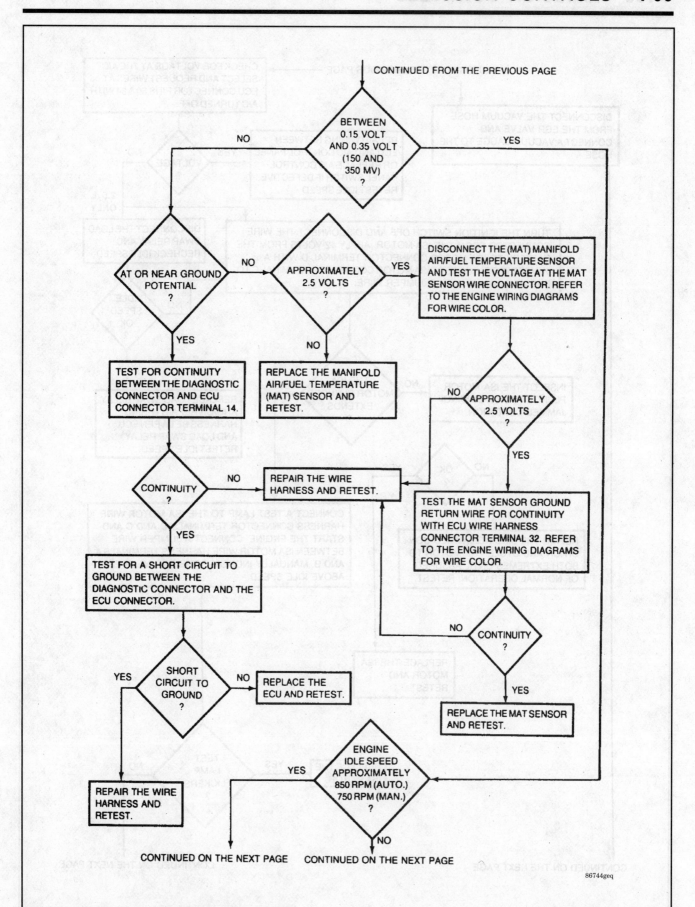

CONTINUED FROM THE PREVIOUS PAGE

BETWEEN 0.15 VOLT AND 0.35 VOLT (150 AND 350 MV) ?

NO → AT OR NEAR GROUND POTENTIAL ?

YES → DISCONNECT THE VACUUM HOSE FROM THE EGR VALVE AND CONNECT A VACUUM GAGE TO THE

NO → APPROXIMATELY 2.5 VOLTS ?

YES → DISCONNECT THE (MAT) MANIFOLD AIR/FUEL TEMPERATURE SENSOR AND TEST THE VOLTAGE AT THE MAT SENSOR WIRE CONNECTOR. REFER TO THE ENGINE WIRING DIAGRAMS FOR WIRE COLOR.

AT OR NEAR GROUND POTENTIAL ? — YES → TEST FOR CONTINUITY BETWEEN THE DIAGNOSTIC CONNECTOR AND ECU CONNECTOR TERMINAL 14.

APPROXIMATELY 2.5 VOLTS ? — NO → REPLACE THE MANIFOLD AIR/FUEL TEMPERATURE (MAT) SENSOR AND RETEST.

APPROXIMATELY 2.5 VOLTS ? — NO →

APPROXIMATELY 2.5 VOLTS ? — YES → TEST THE MAT SENSOR GROUND RETURN WIRE FOR CONTINUITY WITH ECU WIRE HARNESS CONNECTOR TERMINAL 32. REFER TO THE ENGINE WIRING DIAGRAMS FOR WIRE COLOR.

CONTINUITY ? — NO → REPAIR THE WIRE HARNESS AND RETEST.

CONTINUITY ? — YES → TEST FOR A SHORT CIRCUIT TO GROUND BETWEEN THE DIAGNOSTIC CONNECTOR AND THE ECU CONNECTOR.

CONTINUITY ? — NO →

CONTINUITY ? — YES → REPLACE THE MAT SENSOR AND RETEST.

SHORT CIRCUIT TO GROUND ? — NO → REPLACE THE ECU AND RETEST.

SHORT CIRCUIT TO GROUND ? — YES → REPAIR THE WIRE HARNESS AND RETEST.

ENGINE IDLE SPEED APPROXIMATELY 850 RPM (AUTO.) 750 RPM (MAN.) ? — YES →

ENGINE IDLE SPEED APPROXIMATELY 850 RPM (AUTO.) 750 RPM (MAN.) ? — NO →

CONTINUED ON THE NEXT PAGE   CONTINUED ON THE NEXT PAGE

86744geq

Fig. 86 1986-90 TBI SYSTEM DIAGNOSTIC CHARTS

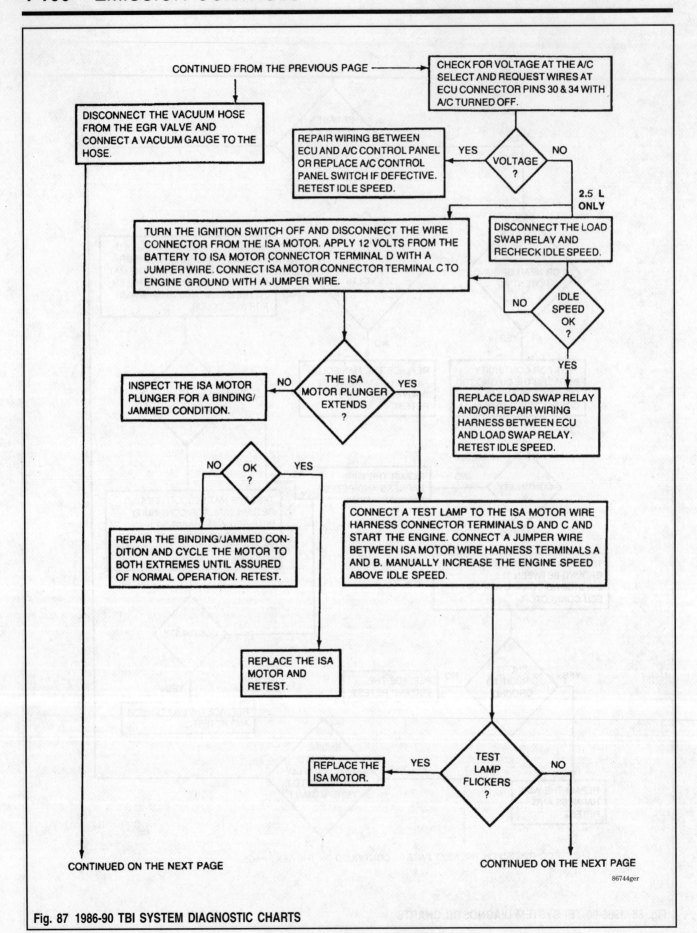

CONTINUED FROM THE PREVIOUS PAGE

CHECK FOR VOLTAGE AT THE A/C SELECT AND REQUEST WIRES AT ECU CONNECTOR PINS 30 & 34 WITH A/C TURNED OFF.

DISCONNECT THE VACUUM HOSE FROM THE EGR VALVE AND CONNECT A VACUUM GAUGE TO THE HOSE.

VOLTAGE ?

YES — REPAIR WIRING BETWEEN ECU AND A/C CONTROL PANEL OR REPLACE A/C CONTROL PANEL SWITCH IF DEFECTIVE. RETEST IDLE SPEED.

NO

2.5 L ONLY

DISCONNECT THE LOAD SWAP RELAY AND RECHECK IDLE SPEED.

TURN THE IGNITION SWITCH OFF AND DISCONNECT THE WIRE CONNECTOR FROM THE ISA MOTOR. APPLY 12 VOLTS FROM THE BATTERY TO ISA MOTOR CONNECTOR TERMINAL D WITH A JUMPER WIRE. CONNECT ISA MOTOR CONNECTOR TERMINAL C TO ENGINE GROUND WITH A JUMPER WIRE.

IDLE SPEED OK ?

NO

INSPECT THE ISA MOTOR PLUNGER FOR A BINDING/JAMMED CONDITION.

NO — THE ISA MOTOR PLUNGER EXTENDS ? — YES

REPLACE LOAD SWAP RELAY AND/OR REPAIR WIRING HARNESS BETWEEN ECU AND LOAD SWAP RELAY. RETEST IDLE SPEED.

YES

OK ?

NO

YES

REPAIR THE BINDING/JAMMED CONDITION AND CYCLE THE MOTOR TO BOTH EXTREMES UNTIL ASSURED OF NORMAL OPERATION. RETEST.

CONNECT A TEST LAMP TO THE ISA MOTOR WIRE HARNESS CONNECTOR TERMINALS D AND C AND START THE ENGINE. CONNECT A JUMPER WIRE BETWEEN ISA MOTOR WIRE HARNESS TERMINALS A AND B. MANUALLY INCREASE THE ENGINE SPEED ABOVE IDLE SPEED.

REPLACE THE ISA MOTOR AND RETEST.

REPLACE THE ISA MOTOR. — YES — TEST LAMP FLICKERS ? — NO

CONTINUED ON THE NEXT PAGE

CONTINUED ON THE NEXT PAGE

86744ger

Fig. 87 1986-90 TBI SYSTEM DIAGNOSTIC CHARTS

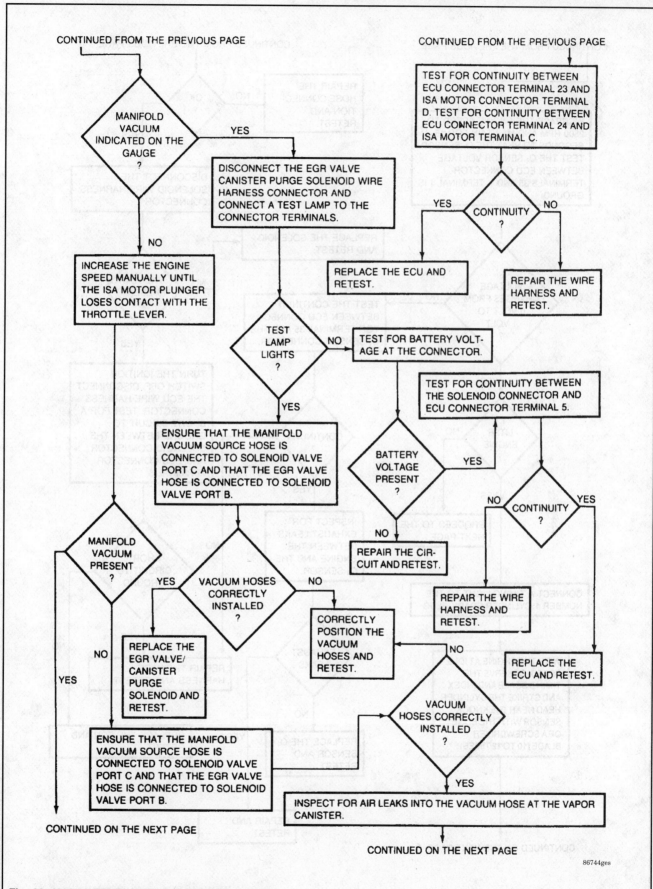

CONTINUED FROM THE PREVIOUS PAGE

CONTINUED FROM THE PREVIOUS PAGE

MANIFOLD VACUUM INDICATED ON THE GAUGE ?

YES

NO

DISCONNECT THE EGR VALVE CANISTER PURGE SOLENOID WIRE HARNESS CONNECTOR AND CONNECT A TEST LAMP TO THE CONNECTOR TERMINALS.

INCREASE THE ENGINE SPEED MANUALLY UNTIL THE ISA MOTOR PLUNGER LOSES CONTACT WITH THE THROTTLE LEVER.

TEST FOR CONTINUITY BETWEEN ECU CONNECTOR TERMINAL 23 AND ISA MOTOR CONNECTOR TERMINAL D. TEST FOR CONTINUITY BETWEEN ECU CONNECTOR TERMINAL 24 AND ISA MOTOR TERMINAL C.

CONTINUITY ?

YES

NO

REPLACE THE ECU AND RETEST.

REPAIR THE WIRE HARNESS AND RETEST.

TEST LAMP LIGHTS ?

NO

TEST FOR BATTERY VOLTAGE AT THE CONNECTOR.

YES

ENSURE THAT THE MANIFOLD VACUUM SOURCE HOSE IS CONNECTED TO SOLENOID VALVE PORT C AND THAT THE EGR VALVE HOSE IS CONNECTED TO SOLENOID VALVE PORT B.

TEST FOR CONTINUITY BETWEEN THE SOLENOID CONNECTOR AND ECU CONNECTOR TERMINAL 5.

BATTERY VOLTAGE PRESENT ?

YES

NO

CONTINUITY ?

NO

YES

MANIFOLD VACUUM PRESENT ?

YES

VACUUM HOSES CORRECTLY INSTALLED ?

NO

REPAIR THE CIRCUIT AND RETEST.

REPAIR THE WIRE HARNESS AND RETEST.

REPLACE THE ECU AND RETEST.

NO

YES

REPLACE THE EGR VALVE/ CANISTER PURGE SOLENOID AND RETEST.

CORRECTLY POSITION THE VACUUM HOSES AND RETEST.

NO

ENSURE THAT THE MANIFOLD VACUUM SOURCE HOSE IS CONNECTED TO SOLENOID VALVE PORT C AND THAT THE EGR VALVE HOSE IS CONNECTED TO SOLENOID VALVE PORT B.

VACUUM HOSES CORRECTLY INSTALLED ?

YES

INSPECT FOR AIR LEAKS INTO THE VACUUM HOSE AT THE VAPOR CANISTER.

CONTINUED ON THE NEXT PAGE

CONTINUED ON THE NEXT PAGE

86744ges

Fig. 88 1986-90 TBI SYSTEM DIAGNOSTIC CHARTS

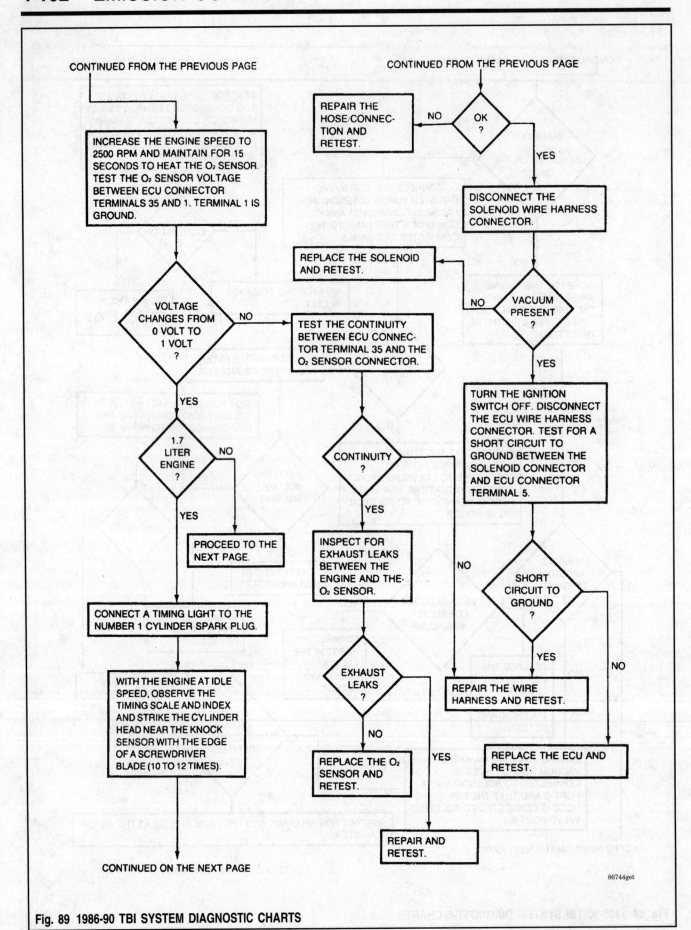

CONTINUED FROM THE PREVIOUS PAGE

CONTINUED FROM THE PREVIOUS PAGE

INCREASE THE ENGINE SPEED TO 2500 RPM AND MAINTAIN FOR 15 SECONDS TO HEAT THE O_2 SENSOR. TEST THE O_2 SENSOR VOLTAGE BETWEEN ECU CONNECTOR TERMINALS 35 AND 1. TERMINAL 1 IS GROUND.

VOLTAGE CHANGES FROM 0 VOLT TO 1 VOLT ?

— NO →

1.7 LITER ENGINE ? — NO →

YES

PROCEED TO THE NEXT PAGE.

CONNECT A TIMING LIGHT TO THE NUMBER 1 CYLINDER SPARK PLUG.

WITH THE ENGINE AT IDLE SPEED, OBSERVE THE TIMING SCALE AND INDEX AND STRIKE THE CYLINDER HEAD NEAR THE KNOCK SENSOR WITH THE EDGE OF A SCREWDRIVER BLADE (10 TO 12 TIMES).

CONTINUED ON THE NEXT PAGE

REPAIR THE HOSE/CONNECTION AND RETEST.

← NO —

OK ?

YES

DISCONNECT THE SOLENOID WIRE HARNESS CONNECTOR.

REPLACE THE SOLENOID AND RETEST.

← NO —

VACUUM PRESENT ?

YES

TURN THE IGNITION SWITCH OFF. DISCONNECT THE ECU WIRE HARNESS CONNECTOR. TEST FOR A SHORT CIRCUIT TO GROUND BETWEEN THE SOLENOID CONNECTOR AND ECU CONNECTOR TERMINAL 5.

TEST THE CONTINUITY BETWEEN ECU CONNECTOR TERMINAL 35 AND THE O_2 SENSOR CONNECTOR.

CONTINUITY ?

YES

INSPECT FOR EXHAUST LEAKS BETWEEN THE ENGINE AND THE O_2 SENSOR.

SHORT CIRCUIT TO GROUND ?

NO

YES — NO →

EXHAUST LEAKS ?

NO

REPLACE THE O_2 SENSOR AND RETEST.

YES

REPAIR THE WIRE HARNESS AND RETEST.

REPLACE THE ECU AND RETEST.

REPAIR AND RETEST.

86744get

Fig. 89 1986-90 TBI SYSTEM DIAGNOSTIC CHARTS

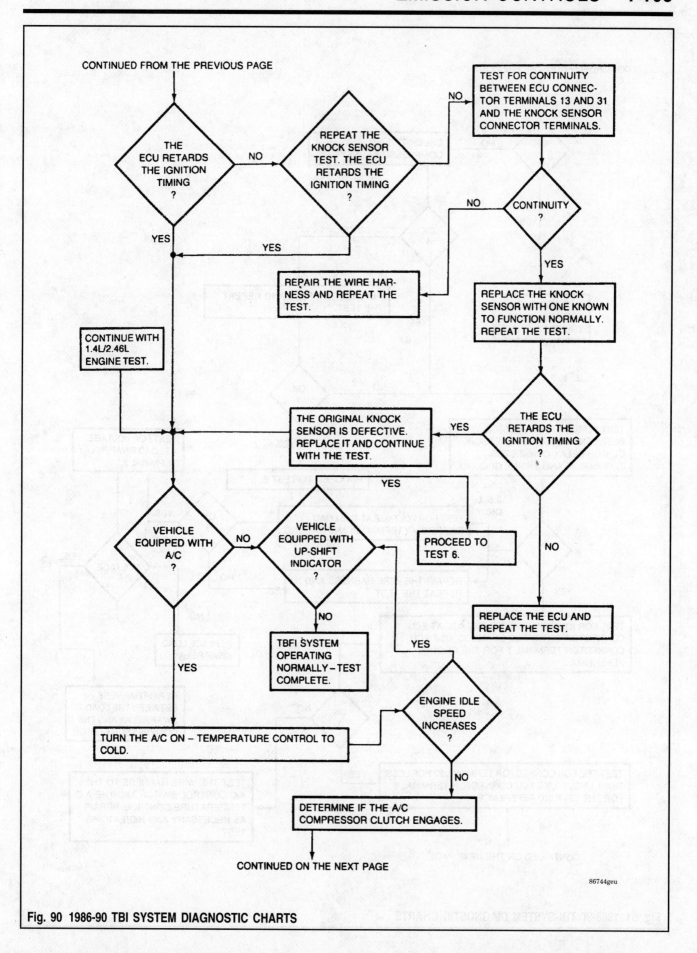

Fig. 90 1986-90 TBI SYSTEM DIAGNOSTIC CHARTS

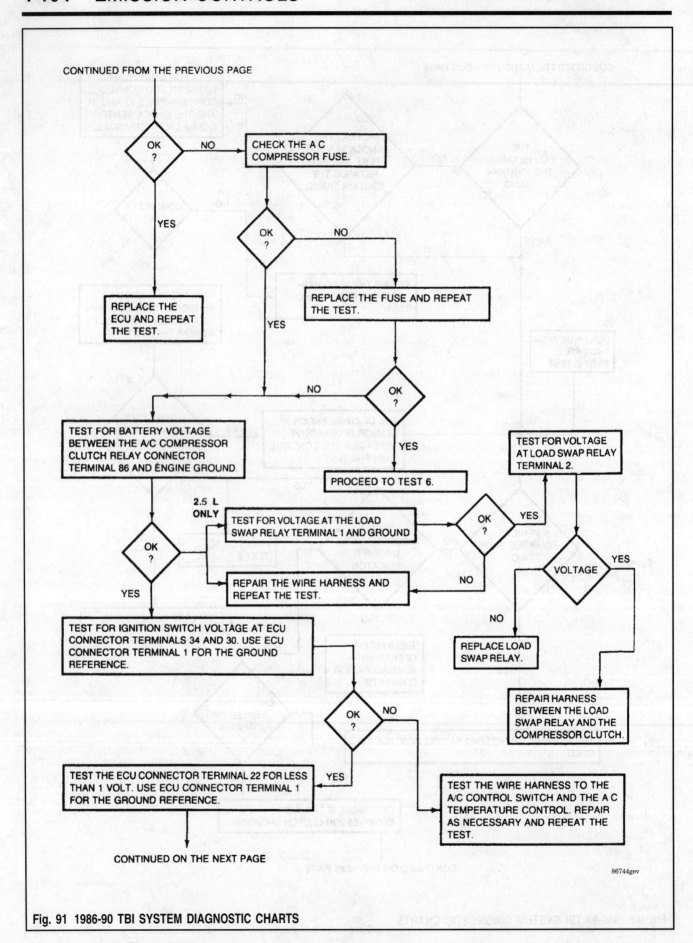

CONTINUED FROM THE PREVIOUS PAGE

OK ? — NO → CHECK THE A C COMPRESSOR FUSE.

YES → REPLACE THE ECU AND REPEAT THE TEST.

OK ? — NO → REPLACE THE FUSE AND REPEAT THE TEST.

YES

OK ? — YES → PROCEED TO TEST 6.

NO → TEST FOR BATTERY VOLTAGE BETWEEN THE A/C COMPRESSOR CLUTCH RELAY CONNECTOR TERMINAL 86 AND ENGINE GROUND.

2.5 L ONLY

TEST FOR VOLTAGE AT THE LOAD SWAP RELAY TERMINAL 1 AND GROUND

OK ? — YES → TEST FOR VOLTAGE AT LOAD SWAP RELAY TERMINAL 2.

NO → REPAIR THE WIRE HARNESS AND REPEAT THE TEST.

VOLTAGE — YES → REPAIR HARNESS BETWEEN THE LOAD SWAP RELAY AND THE COMPRESSOR CLUTCH.

NO → REPLACE LOAD SWAP RELAY.

OK ? — YES → TEST FOR IGNITION SWITCH VOLTAGE AT ECU CONNECTOR TERMINALS 34 AND 30. USE ECU CONNECTOR TERMINAL 1 FOR THE GROUND REFERENCE.

OK ? — NO → TEST THE WIRE HARNESS TO THE A/C CONTROL SWITCH AND THE A C TEMPERATURE CONTROL. REPAIR AS NECESSARY AND REPEAT THE TEST.

YES → TEST THE ECU CONNECTOR TERMINAL 22 FOR LESS THAN 1 VOLT. USE ECU CONNECTOR TERMINAL 1 FOR THE GROUND REFERENCE.

CONTINUED ON THE NEXT PAGE

86744gev

Fig. 91 1986-90 TBI SYSTEM DIAGNOSTIC CHARTS

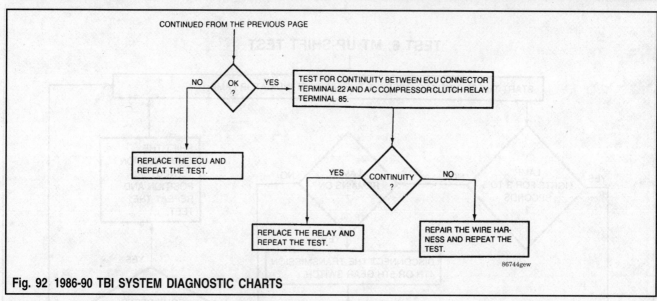

Fig. 92 1986-90 TBI SYSTEM DIAGNOSTIC CHARTS

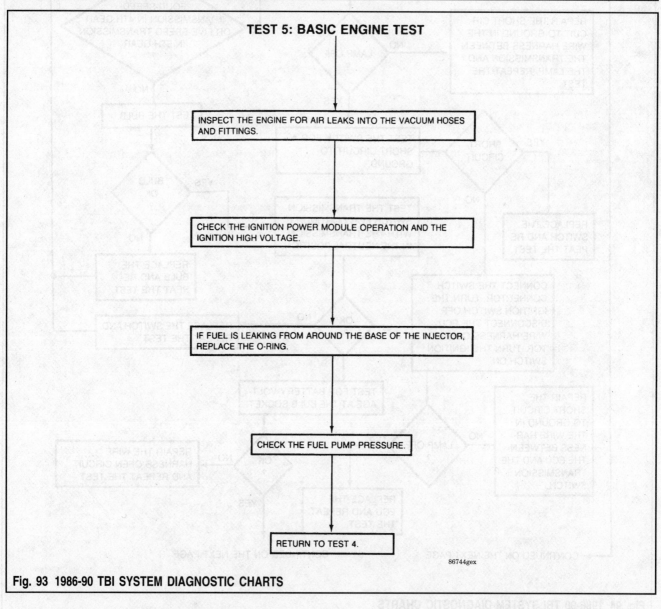

Fig. 93 1986-90 TBI SYSTEM DIAGNOSTIC CHARTS

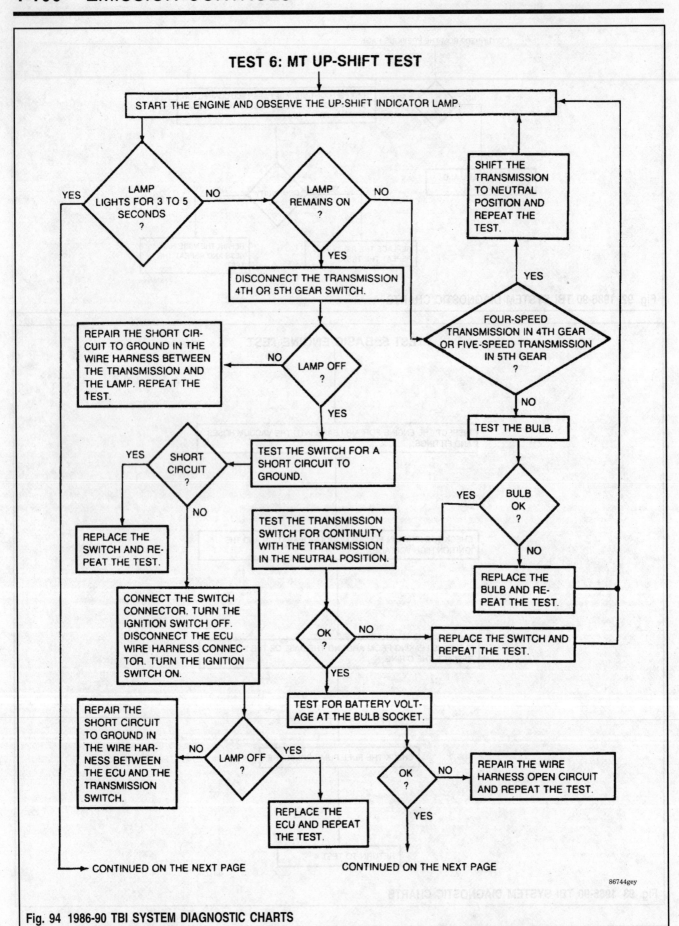

TEST 6: MT UP-SHIFT TEST

START THE ENGINE AND OBSERVE THE UP-SHIFT INDICATOR LAMP.

LAMP LIGHTS FOR 3 TO 5 SECONDS ?

LAMP REMAINS ON ?

SHIFT THE TRANSMISSION TO NEUTRAL POSITION AND REPEAT THE TEST.

DISCONNECT THE TRANSMISSION 4TH OR 5TH GEAR SWITCH.

FOUR-SPEED TRANSMISSION IN 4TH GEAR OR FIVE-SPEED TRANSMISSION IN 5TH GEAR ?

REPAIR THE SHORT CIRCUIT TO GROUND IN THE WIRE HARNESS BETWEEN THE TRANSMISSION AND THE LAMP. REPEAT THE TEST.

LAMP OFF ?

TEST THE BULB.

TEST THE SWITCH FOR A SHORT CIRCUIT TO GROUND.

SHORT CIRCUIT ?

BULB OK ?

REPLACE THE SWITCH AND RE-PEAT THE TEST.

TEST THE TRANSMISSION SWITCH FOR CONTINUITY WITH THE TRANSMISSION IN THE NEUTRAL POSITION.

REPLACE THE BULB AND RE-PEAT THE TEST.

CONNECT THE SWITCH CONNECTOR. TURN THE IGNITION SWITCH OFF. DISCONNECT THE ECU WIRE HARNESS CONNEC-TOR. TURN THE IGNITION SWITCH ON.

OK ?

REPLACE THE SWITCH AND REPEAT THE TEST.

REPAIR THE SHORT CIRCUIT TO GROUND IN THE WIRE HAR-NESS BETWEEN THE ECU AND THE TRANSMISSION SWITCH.

LAMP OFF ?

TEST FOR BATTERY VOLT-AGE AT THE BULB SOCKET.

OK ?

REPAIR THE WIRE HARNESS OPEN CIRCUIT AND REPEAT THE TEST.

REPLACE THE ECU AND REPEAT THE TEST.

CONTINUED ON THE NEXT PAGE

CONTINUED ON THE NEXT PAGE

86744gey

Fig. 94 1986-90 TBI SYSTEM DIAGNOSTIC CHARTS

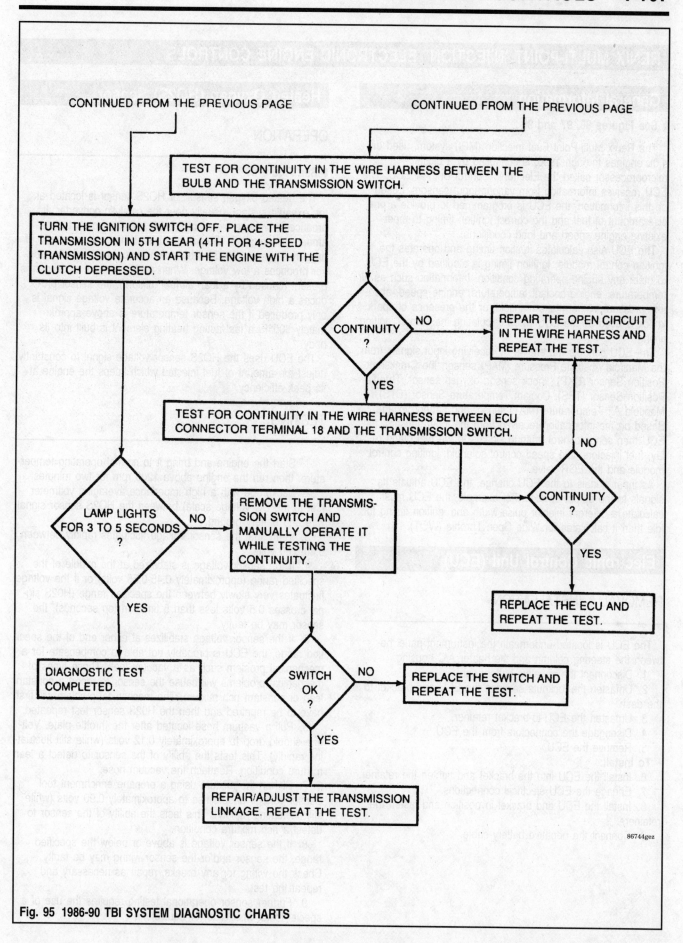

CONTINUED FROM THE PREVIOUS PAGE

CONTINUED FROM THE PREVIOUS PAGE

TEST FOR CONTINUITY IN THE WIRE HARNESS BETWEEN THE BULB AND THE TRANSMISSION SWITCH.

TURN THE IGNITION SWITCH OFF. PLACE THE TRANSMISSION IN 5TH GEAR (4TH FOR 4-SPEED TRANSMISSION) AND START THE ENGINE WITH THE CLUTCH DEPRESSED.

CONTINUITY ?

NO → REPAIR THE OPEN CIRCUIT IN THE WIRE HARNESS AND REPEAT THE TEST.

YES

TEST FOR CONTINUITY IN THE WIRE HARNESS BETWEEN ECU CONNECTOR TERMINAL 18 AND THE TRANSMISSION SWITCH.

CONTINUITY ?

NO

YES → REPLACE THE ECU AND REPEAT THE TEST.

LAMP LIGHTS FOR 3 TO 5 SECONDS ?

NO → REMOVE THE TRANSMISSION SWITCH AND MANUALLY OPERATE IT WHILE TESTING THE CONTINUITY.

YES

DIAGNOSTIC TEST COMPLETED.

SWITCH OK ?

NO → REPLACE THE SWITCH AND REPEAT THE TEST.

YES

REPAIR/ADJUST THE TRANSMISSION LINKAGE. REPEAT THE TEST.

Fig. 95 1986-90 TBI SYSTEM DIAGNOSTIC CHARTS

86744gez

RENIX MULTI-POINT INJECTION ELECTRONIC ENGINE CONTROLS

General Information

▶ See Figures 96, 97 and 98

The Renix Multi-Point Fuel Injection (MPI) system, used on 4.0L engines through 1990, is controlled by a digital microprocessor called the Electronic Control Unit, or ECU. The ECU receives information from various input sensors. Based on this information, the ECU is programmed to provide a precise amount of fuel and the correct ignition timing to meet existing engine speed and load conditions.

The ECU also calculates ignition timing and operates the ignition control module. Ignition timing is modified by the ECU to meet any engine operating condition. Information such as air temperature, engine coolant temperature, engine speed, absolute pressure in the intake manifold, or the presence of spark knock is used by the ECU when calculating the correct ignition timing.

The ECU controls the engine by receiving input signals from the Manifold Absolute Pressure (MAP) sensor, the Crankshaft Position Sensor (CKP), knock sensor, oxygen sensor, Throttle Position Sensor (TPS), Coolant Temperature Sensor (CTS), Manifold Air Temperature (MAT) sensor and battery voltage. Based on the information received from the input sensors, the ECU then sends control (output) signals to the fuel pump relay, fuel injectors, idle speed control solenoid, ignition control module and the EGR valve.

As input signals to the ECU change, the ECU adjusts its signals to the output devices. For example, the ECU must calculate a different injector pulse width and ignition timing for idle than it calculates for Wide Open Throttle (WOT).

Electronic Control Unit (ECU)

REMOVAL & INSTALLATION

The ECU is located underneath the instrument panel between the steering column and the heater A/C housing.

1. Disconnect the negative battery cable.
2. Unfasten the locknuts securing the ECU and bracket to the dash.
3. Unfasten the ECU-to-bracket retainer.
4. Disengage the connectors from the ECU.
5. Remove the ECU.

To install:

6. Install the ECU into the bracket and tighten the retainer.
7. Engage the ECU electrical connections.
8. Install the ECU and bracket in position and fasten the retainers.
9. Connect the negative battery cable.

Heated Oxygen (HO2S) Sensor

OPERATION

▶ See Figure 99

The heated oxygen sensor, or HO2S sensor is located at the exhaust system, usually near the catalytic converter. It produces a voltage signal of 0.1-1.0 volts based on the amount of oxygen in the exhaust gas. When a low amount of oxygen is present (caused by a rich air/fuel mixture), the sensor produces a low voltage. When a high amount of oxygen is present (caused by a lean air/fuel mixture), the sensor produces a high voltage. Because an accurate voltage signal is only produced if the sensor temperature is above approximately 600°F, a fast acting heating element is built into its body.

The ECU uses the HO2S sensor voltage signal to constantly adjust the amount of fuel injected which keeps the engine at its peek efficiency.

TESTING

1. Start the engine and bring it to normal operating temperature, then run the engine above 1200 rpm for two minutes.
2. Backprobe with a high impedance averaging voltmeter (set to the DC voltage scale) between the HO2S sensor signal wire and battery ground.
3. Verify that the sensor voltage fluctuates rapidly between 0.40-0.60 volts.
4. If the sensor voltage is stabilized at the middle of the specified range (approximately 0.45-0.55 volts) or if the voltage fluctuates very slowly between the specified range (HO2S signal crosses 0.5 volts less than 5 times in ten seconds), the sensor may be faulty.
5. If the sensor voltage stabilizes at either end of the specified range, the ECU is probably not able to compensate for a mechanical problem such as a vacuum leak. These types of mechanical problems will cause the sensor to report a constant lean or constant rich mixture. The mechanical problem will first have to be repaired and then the HO2S sensor test repeated.
6. Pull a vacuum hose located after the throttle plate. Voltage should drop to approximately 0.12 volts (while still fluctuating rapidly). This tests the ability of the sensor to detect a lean mixture condition. Reattach the vacuum hose.
7. Richen the mixture using a propane enrichment tool. Sensor voltage should rise to approximately 0.90 volts (while still fluctuating rapidly). This tests the ability of the sensor to detect a rich mixture condition.
8. If the sensor voltage is above or below the specified range, the sensor and/or the sensor wiring may be faulty. Check the wiring for any breaks, repair as necessary and repeat the test.
9. Further sensor operational testing requires the use of a special tester M.S.1700, or equivalent.

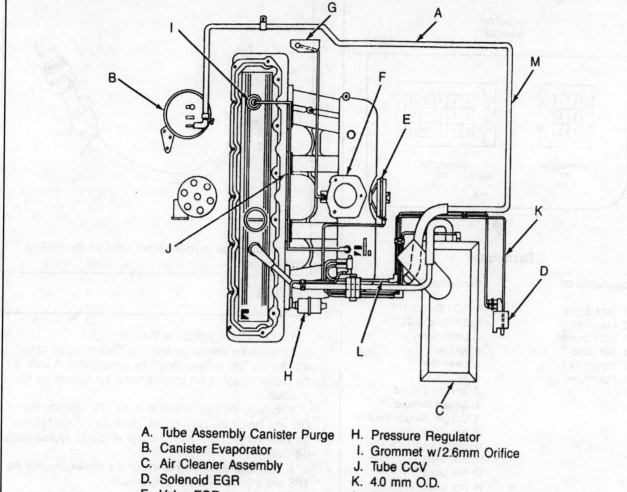

A. Tube Assembly Canister Purge
B. Canister Evaporator
C. Air Cleaner Assembly
D. Solenoid EGR
E. Valve EGR
F. Throttle Body Assembly
G. Map Sensor

H. Pressure Regulator
I. Grommet w/2.6mm Orifice
J. Tube CCV
K. 4.0 mm O.D.
L. 6.4 mm O.D.
M. 14.3 mm O.D.

86744g49

Fig. 96 Exploded view of the Renix Multi-Point Fuel Injection (MPI) system

REMOVAL & INSTALLATION

1. Raise the vehicle and support it with jackstands.
2. Disengage the HO2S sensor wiring connector and remove it using tool YA 8875, or its equivalent.
To install:
3. Inspect the threads of the HO2S sensor. Apply an anti-seize compound only if there is none visible on the threads. Be careful not to contaminate the sensor tip with any foreign compounds.
4. Install the sensor using tool YA 8875, or its equivalent and engage the wiring connector.
5. Carefully lower the vehicle.

Throttle Position Sensor (TPS)

OPERATION

♦ **See Figure 100**

The throttle position sensor is mounted on the throttle plate assembly and provides the ECU with an input signal of up to 5 volts to indicate throttle position. At minimum throttle opening (idle speed), a signal input of approximately 1 volt is transmitted to the ECU. As the throttle opening increases, voltage increases to a maximum of approximately 5 volts at the wide open throttle position.

A dual TPS is used on models equipped with automatic transmission. This dual TPS not only provides the ECU with input voltages, but also supplies the Transmission Control Unit (TCU) with an input of throttle position.

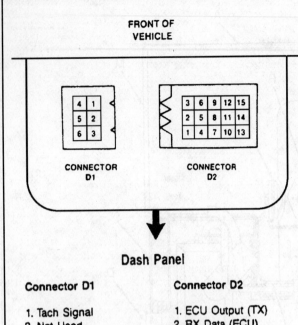

Dash Panel

Connector D1

1. Tach Signal
2. Not Used
3. ECU Ground
4. Not Used
5. Battery (+)
6. Fuel Pump (+)

Connector D2

1. ECU Output (TX)
2. RX Data (ECU)
3. Latch Relay
4. Ignition
5. Latch B +
6. A/C Clutch
7. Ignition Ground
8. Sensor Ground
9. Oxygen Sensor Heater
10. Not Used
11. Shift Lamp
12. Not Used
13. Not Used
14. Not Used
15. Automatic Transmission Diagnosis

86744g50

Fig. 97 Renix MPI system diagnostic connector

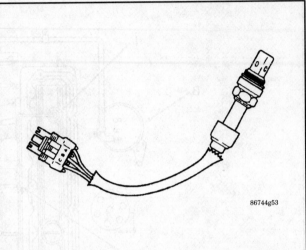

86744g53

Fig. 99 Common oxygen sensor used on the 1989-90 MPI system

TESTING

1. Unplug the connector at the TPS.
2. Check the voltage between the black and grey wires with the key **ON**. Voltage should be approximately 5 volts. If the proper voltage is not present, check the harness for shorts or opens.
3. Engage the wire connector to the TPS. With the key **ON**, and the throttle plate closed, check the voltage between the blue and the black wires. Voltage should be approximately 0.8 volts.
4. If voltage is not correct, loosen the screws securing the TPS and adjust until 0.8 volts is present.
5. If adjusting does not bring sensor voltage to specification, replace the TPS.

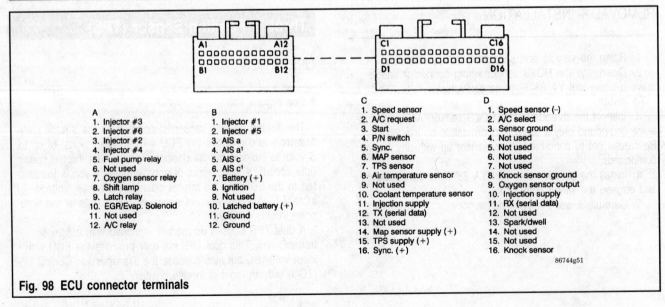

A

1. Injector #3
2. Injector #6
3. Injector #2
4. Injector #4
5. Fuel pump relay
6. Not used
7. Oxygen sensor relay
8. Shift lamp
9. Latch relay
10. EGR/Evap. Solenoid
11. Not used
12. A/C relay

B

1. Injector #1
2. Injector #5
3. AIS a
4. AIS a¹
5. AIS c
6. AIS c¹
7. Battery (+)
8. Ignition
9. Not used
10. Latched battery (+)
11. Ground
12. Ground

C

1. Speed sensor
2. A/C request
3. Start
4. P/N switch
5. Sync.
6. MAP sensor
7. TPS sensor
8. Air temperature sensor
9. Not used
10. Coolant temperature sensor
11. Injection supply
12. TX (serial data)
13. Not used
14. Map sensor supply (+)
15. TPS supply (+)
16. Sync. (+)

D

1. Speed sensor (–)
2. A/C select
3. Sensor ground
4. Not used
5. Not used
6. Not used
7. Not used
8. Knock sensor ground
9. Oxygen sensor output
10. Injection supply
11. RX (serial data)
12. Not used
13. Spark/dwell
14. Not used
15. Not used
16. Knock sensor

86744g51

Fig. 98 ECU connector terminals

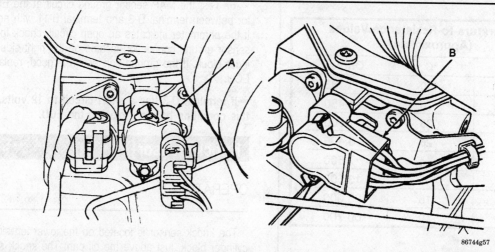

Fig. 100 Throttle position switch (A) used on vehicles with manual transmissions and (B) used on vehicles with automatic transmissions

Coolant Temperature Sensor (CTS)

OPERATION

The coolant temperature sensor is located on the left side of the cylinder block, just below the exhaust manifold. The CTS provides an engine coolant temperature input to the ECU, which will then enrich the air/fuel mixture delivered by the injectors when the engine coolant is cold. Based on the CTS signal, the ECU will also control engine warmup idle speed, increase ignition advance and inhibit EGR operation when the coolant is cold.

TESTING

▶ See Figure 101

Disconnect the wire harness connector from the CTS and measure the resistance of the sensor with a high input impedance (digital) volt-ohmmeter. The resistance should be less than 1000 ohms with the engine warm. Refer to the resistance chart and replace the sensor if it is not within the range of resistance specified in the chart. Measure the resistance of the wire harness between ECU wire harness connector terminal D-3 and the sensor connector terminal, and terminal C-10 to the sensor connector terminal and repair the wire harness if an open circuit is indicated.

Manifold Air Temperature (MAT) Sensor

OPERATION

The manifold air temperature sensor is located in the intake manifold. The MAT sensor reacts to the temperature of the air

Temperature-to-Resistance Values (Approximate)		
°F	°C	Ohms
212	100	185
160	70	450
100	38	1,600
70	20	3,400
40	4	7,500
20	-7	13,500
0	-18	25,000
-40	-40	100,700

Fig. 101 CTS sensor resistance test chart — 1989-90 vehicles

in the intake manifold and provides an input to the ECU to allow it to compensate for air density changes during high temperature operation.

TESTING

▶ See Figure 102

Disconnect the wire harness connector from the MAT and measure the resistance of the sensor with a high input impedance (digital) volt-ohmmeter. The resistance should be less than 1000 ohms with the engine warm. Refer to the resistance chart and replace the sensor if it is not within the range of resistance specified in the chart. Measure the resistance of the wire harness between ECU wire harness connector terminal D-3 and the sensor connector terminal, and terminal C-8 to the sensor connector terminal. Repair the wire harness if the resistance is greater than 1 ohm.

Temperature-to-Resistance Values (Approximate)		
°F	°C	Ohms
212	100	185
160	70	450
100	38	1,600
70	20	3,400
40	4	7,500
20	-7	13,500
0	-18	25,000
-40	-40	100,700

86744g58

Fig. 102 MAT sensor resistance test chart — 1989-90 vehicles

Manifold Absolute Pressure (MAP) Sensor

OPERATION

▶ **See Figure 103**

The manifold absolute pressure sensor is mounted on the dash panel behind the engine. The MAP sensor reacts to absolute pressure in the intake manifold and provides an input voltage to the ECU. Manifold pressure is used to supply mixture density information and ambient barometric pressure information to the ECU. A hose from the intake manifold provides the input pressure.

TESTING

1. Inspect the MAP sensor vacuum hose connection at the throttle body and sensor and repair as necessary.
2. Test the MAP sensor output voltage at the MAP sensor connector terminal B (as marked on the sensor body) with the ignition switch and the engine **OFF**. The output voltage should be 4-5 volts.

➡ **The voltage should drop to 0.5-1.5 volts with a hot, neutral idle speed condition.**

3. Test ECU terminal C-6 for the same voltage as in Step 2 to verify the wire harness condition and repair as necessary.
4. Test the MAP sensor supply voltage at the sensor connector terminal C with the ignition **ON**. The voltage should be 4.5-5.5 volts. The same voltage should be present at terminal C-14 of the ECU wire harness connector. Repair or replace the wire harness as necessary. If the ECU is suspect, use Diagnostic Tester M.S.1700, or equivalent, to test ECU function. Follow the manufactures instructions.
5. Test the MAP sensor ground circuit at the sensor connector terminal A and ECU connector terminal D-3. Repair the wire harness as necessary.

6. Test the MAP sensor ground circuit at the ECU connector between terminal D-3 and terminal B-11 with an ohmmeter. If the ohmmeter indicates an open circuit, check for a defective sensor ground connection located on the right side of the cylinder block. If the ground connection is good, replace the ECU.

➡ **If terminal D-3 has a short circuit to 12 volts, correct this condition before replacing the ECU.**

Knock Sensor

OPERATION

The knock sensor is located on the lower left side of the cylinder block, just above the oil pan. The knock sensor provides and input to the ECU that indicates detonation (knock) during engine operation. When detonation occurs, the ECU retards the ignition timing advance to eliminate the detonation at the applicable cylinder.

TESTING

➡ **This procedure requires the use of a special tool M.S.1700, or an equivalent knock sensor tester.**

1. Connect diagnostic tester M.S.1700, or equivalent, to the vehicle according to the manufacturer's instructions.
2. Proceed to state display mode.
3. Start the engine.
4. Observe and note the knock unit value.
5. Using the tip of a screwdriver or a small hammer, gently tap on the cylinder block near the knock sensor and watch the knock value. The knock value should increase while tapping on the block.
6. If the knock value does not increase while tapping on the block, check the sensor connector. If the connection is good, replace the knock sensor.

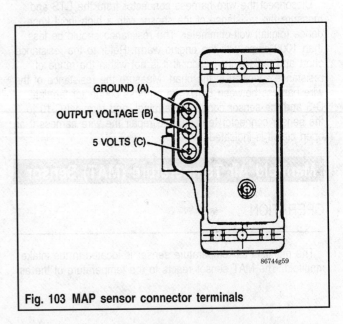

86744g59

Fig. 103 MAP sensor connector terminals

Crankshaft Position Sensor (CKP)

OPERATION

▶ **See Figure 104**

The Crankshaft Position Sensor (CKP) is secured by special shouldered bolts to the flywheel/drive plate housing. It is preset in its mounting at the factory and is non-adjustable in the field. The sensor senses TDC and engine speed by detecting the flywheel teeth as they pass during engine operation.

The flywheel has a large trigger tooth and notch located 12 small teeth before each Top Dead Center (TDC) position. When a small tooth and notch pass the magnet core in the sensor, the concentration and then collapse of the magnetic flux induces a small voltage spike into the sensor pickup coil winding. These small voltage spikes enable the ECU to count the teeth as they pass the sensor.

When a large trigger tooth and notch pass the magnet core in the sensor, the increased concentration/collapse of the magnetic flux induces a higher voltage spike into the pickup coil winding. This higher voltage spike indicates to the ECU that a piston will soon be at the TDC position 12 teeth later. The ignition timing for the cylinder is either advanced or retarded as necessary by the ECU according to the sensor inputs.

TESTING

Unplug the sensor connector from the ignition control module and connect an ohmmeter between terminals **A** and **B** as marked on the connector. The ohmmeter should read 125-275 ohms on a hot engine. Replace the sensor if the readings are not as stated.

Latch Relay

OPERATION

▶ **See Figures 105 and 106**

The latch relay is located on the right inner fender panel. This relay is initially energized during engine startup and remains energized until 3-5 seconds after the engine is stopped. This enables the ECU to extend the idle speed stepper motor for the next startup, then cease operation.

TESTING

A relay in the de-energized position should have continuity between terminals 87A and 30. Resistance values between terminals 85 and 86 is 70-80 ohms for resistor relays and 81-91 ohms for diode relays. Not all relays have battery voltage connected to terminal 30. Some may have battery voltage connected to terminals 87 or 87A.

Camshaft Position Sensor (CMP)

OPERATION

The camshaft position sensor, or CMP sensor is located inside the distributor. The ECU uses the CMP signal to determine the position of the No. 1 cylinder piston during its power stroke. The ECU uses this information in conjunction with the crankshaft position sensor to determine spark timing among other things.

The CMP sensor contains a Hall effect device which sends either a 0.0 volt or a 5.0 volt signal to the ECU depending on the position of the distributor shaft.

If the cam signal is lost while the engine is running, the ECU will calculate spark timing based on the last CMP signal

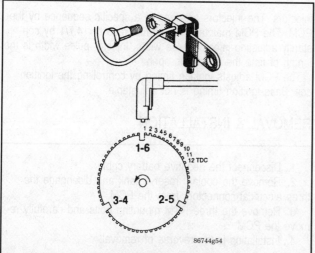

86744g54

Fig. 104 View of the Crankshaft Position Sensor (CKP) and flywheel used on the Renix MPI system

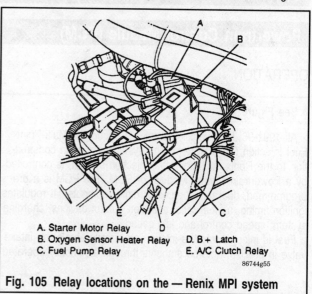

A. Starter Motor Relay
B. Oxygen Sensor Heater Relay
C. Fuel Pump Relay
D. B + Latch
E. A/C Clutch Relay

86744g55

Fig. 105 Relay locations on the — Renix MPI system

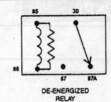 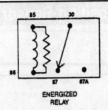

BOTTOM VIEW OF RELAY   RELAY CONNECTOR   DE-ENERGIZED RELAY   ENERGIZED RELAY

TERMINAL NUMBER

30 = usually connected to battery voltage — can be switched or B+ at all times.

87A = connected to 30 in the de-energized position.

87 = connected to 30 in the energized position which supplies battery voltage to the operated device.

86 = connected to the electromagnet and usually connected to a switched power source.

85 = also is connected to the electromagnet and is usually grounded by a switch or ECU.

86744g56

Fig. 106 Relay terminal identification — Renix MPI system

and the engine will continue to run. However, the engine will not run after it is shut off.

TESTING

1. Insert the positive (+) lead of a voltmeter into the blue wire at the distributor connector and the negative (-) lead into the gray/white wire at the distributor connector.

➡**Do not unplug the distributor connector from the distributor. Insert the voltmeter leads into the back side of the connector to make contact with the terminals.**

2. Set the voltmeter on the 15 volt AC scale and turn the ignition switch **ON**. The voltmeter should read approximately 5 volts. If there is no voltage, check the voltmeter leads for a good connection.

3. If there is still no voltage, remove the ECU and check for voltage at pin C-16 and ground with the harness connected. If there is still no voltage present, perform a vehicle test using tester M.S.1700, or equivalent.

4. If voltage is present, check for continuity between the blue wire at the distributor connector and pin C-16 at the ECU. If there is no continuity, repair the wire harness as necessary.

5. Check for continuity between the gray/white wire at the distributor connector and pin C-5 at the ECU. If there is no continuity, repair the wire harness as necessary.

6. Check for continuity between the black wire at the distributor connector and ground. If there is no continuity, repair the wire harness as necessary.

7. Crank the engine while observing the voltmeter; the needle should fluctuate back and forth while the engine is cranking. This verifies that the stator in the distributor is operating properly. If there is no sync pulse, stator replacement is necessary.

CHRYSLER MULTI-POINT FUEL INJECTION (MPI) SYSTEM

Powertrain Control Module (PCM)

OPERATION

▶ **See Figure 107**

All 1991-96 Jeep vehicles employ a sequential Multi-Point Fuel Injection (MPI) System. The system, similar in construction to the Renix multi-point fuel injection system, is controlled by a Powertrain Control Module, or PCM. The PCM is a pre-programmed, dual microprocessor digital computer. It regulates ignition timing, air-fuel ratio, emission control devices, charging system, speed control and idle speed.

Fuel is injected into the intake port directly above the intake valve in precise metered amounts through electrically operated injectors. The injectors are fired in a specific sequence by the PCM. The PCM maintains an air/fuel ratio of 14.7/1 by constantly adjusting injector pulse width. Injector pulse width is the length of time the injector is open.

The PCM adjusts ignition timing by controlling the ignition coil. Base ignition timing is not adjustable.

REMOVAL & INSTALLATION

1. Disconnect the negative battery cable.

2. Remove the coolant reserve tank and disengage the three electrical connectors from the PCM.

3. Remove the three PCM mounting bolts and carefully remove the PCM.

4. Installation is the reverse of removal.

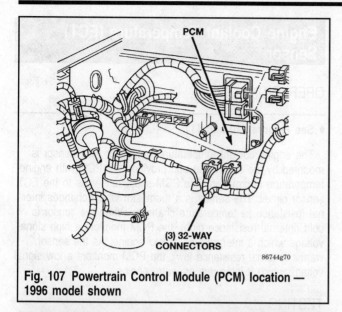

**Fig. 107 Powertrain Control Module (PCM) location —
1996 model shown**

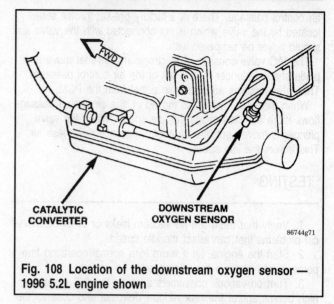

**Fig. 108 Location of the downstream oxygen sensor —
1996 5.2L engine shown**

Heated Oxygen (HO2S) Sensor

OPERATION

▶ **See Figure 108**

The heated oxygen sensor, or HO2S sensor is located at
the exhaust system, usually near the catalytic converter. It
produces a voltage signal of 0.1-1.0 volts based on the
amount of oxygen in the exhaust gas. When a low amount of
oxygen is present (caused by a rich air/fuel mixture), the sensor produces a low voltage. When a high amount of oxygen is
present (caused by a lean air/fuel mixture), the sensor produces a high voltage. Because an accurate voltage signal is
only produced if the sensor temperature is above approximately 600°F, a fast acting heating element is built into its
body.

The PCM uses the HO2S sensor voltage signal to constantly
adjust the amount of fuel injected which keeps the engine at
its peek efficiency. 1996 vehicles are equipped with a second
HO2S sensor which is used to monitor the efficiency of the
catalytic converter.

TESTING

1. Start the engine and bring it to normal operating temperature, then run the engine above 1200 rpm for two minutes.
2. Backprobe with a high impedance averaging voltmeter
(set to the DC voltage scale) between the HO2S sensor signal
wire and battery ground.
3. Verify that the sensor voltage fluctuates rapidly between
0.40-0.60 volts.
4. If the sensor voltage is stabilized at the middle of the
specified range (approximately 0.45-0.55 volts) or if the voltage
fluctuates very slowly between the specified range (HO2S signal crosses 0.5 volts less than 5 times in ten seconds), the
sensor may be faulty.
5. If the sensor voltage stabilizes at either end of the specified range, the PCM is probably not able to compensate for a

mechanical problem such as a vacuum leak. These types of
mechanical problems will cause the sensor to report a constant
lean or constant rich mixture. The mechanical problem will first
have to be repaired and then the HO2S sensor test repeated.
6. Pull a vacuum hose located after the throttle plate. Voltage should drop to approximately 0.12 volts (while still fluctuating rapidly). This tests the ability of the sensor to detect a lean
mixture condition. Reattach the vacuum hose.
7. Richen the mixture using a propane enrichment tool.
Sensor voltage should rise to approximately 0.90 volts (while
still fluctuating rapidly). This tests the ability of the sensor to
detect a rich mixture condition.
8. If the sensor voltage is above or below the specified
range, the sensor and/or the sensor wiring may be faulty.
Check the wiring for any breaks, repair as necessary and
repeat the test.

REMOVAL & INSTALLATION

1. Raise the vehicle and support it with jackstands.
2. Disengage the HO2S sensor wiring connector and remove it using tool YA 8875, or its equivalent.
To install:
3. Inspect the threads of the HO2S sensor. Apply an anti-
seize compound only if there is none visible on the threads.
Be careful not to contaminate the sensor tip with any foreign
compounds.
4. Install the sensor using tool YA 8875, or its equivalent
and engage the wiring connector.
5. Carefully lower the vehicle.

Idle Air Control (IAC) Valve

OPERATION

The Idle Air Control valve, or IAC valve is mounted on the
back of the throttle body. The valve controls the idle speed of
the engine by controlling the amount of air flowing through the

air control passage. There is a factory pre-set throttle screw located by the valve which is not connected with the valve and should never be tampered with.

The IAC valve consists of electronic motors that move a pintle shaped plunger in and out of the air control passage. The valve receives an electronic signal from the PCM.

When the valve plunger is moved in, the air control passage flows more air. This raises the idle speed. When the valve plunger is moved out, the air control passage flows less air. This lowers the idle speed.

TESTING

1. Verify that there are no vacuum leaks or other mechanical problems that can affect the idle speed.
2. Start the engine, let it warm to a normal operating temperature and observe the idle speed.
3. Turn on various consumers such as the A/C system, high beams and/or the rear window defroster and observe the idle speed.
4. With the brake pedal firmly depressed, place the vehicle in gear (automatic transmission) or place the vehicle in fourth gear and slightly disengage the clutch (manual transmission). Observe the idle speed. Return the transmission to park or neutral.
5. If the idle speed does not immediately return to specification, the IAC valve may be faulty.

REMOVAL & INSTALLATION

▶ See Figure 109

1. Remove the air intake duct at the throttle body.
2. Disengage the IAC valve wiring connector, remove the two mounting screws and carefully pull the valve from the throttle body.
3. Installation is the reverse of removal.

Engine Coolant Temperature (ECT) Sensor

OPERATION

▶ See Figures 110 and 111

The engine coolant temperature sensor, or ECT sensor is mounted by the thermostat and provides the PCM with engine temperature information. The PCM supplies 5 volts to the ECT sensor circuit. The sensor is a thermistor which changes internal resistance as temperature changes. When the sensor is cold (internal resistance high), the PCM monitors a high signal voltage which it interprets as a cold engine. As the sensor warms (internal resistance low), the PCM monitors a low signal voltage which it interprets as warm engine.

TESTING

▶ See Figure 112

1. With the engine cold, remove the ECT sensor.
2. Immerse the tip of the sensor in container of water.
3. Connect a digital ohmmeter to the two terminals of the sensor.
4. Using a calibrated thermometer, compare the resistance of the sensor to the temperature of the water. Refer to the sensor resistance illustration.
5. Repeat the test at two other temperature points, heating or cooling the water as necessary.
6. If the sensor does not meet specification, it must be replaced.

REMOVAL & INSTALLATION

1. With the engine cold, partially drain the cooling system. Record the amount of coolant drained.
2. Carefully disengage the ECT sensor wiring connector.

Fig. 109 Removing the IAC valve from the throttle body

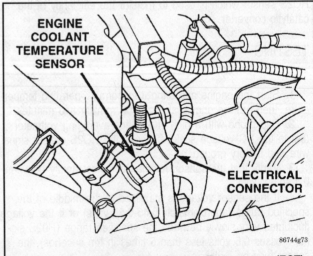

Fig. 110 View of the Engine Coolant Temperature (ECT) Sensor — 1996 4.0L engine shown

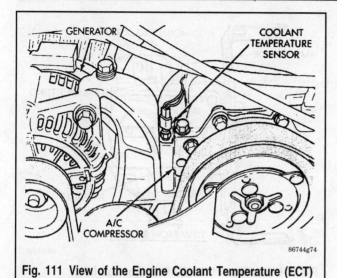

Fig. 111 View of the Engine Coolant Temperature (ECT) Sensor — 1996 5.2L engine shown

3. Unscrew the sensor.

To install:

4. Coat the threads of the ECT sensor with sealant and install it into the block. Tighten the sensor to 8 ft. lbs. (11 Nm).

5. Engage the sensor wiring connector.

6. Fill the system with the same amount of coolant as was drained and check for leaks.

Intake Manifold Air Temperature (MAT) Sensor

OPERATION

▶ **See Figures 113 and 114**

The intake manifold air temperature sensor, or MAT sensor is mounted on the intake manifold and provides the PCM with intake air temperature information. The sensor is a temperature dependent resistor. As the temperature of the air rises, the sensor resistance drops and as the temperature of the air drops, the sensor resistance rises.

TESTING

1. Remove the MAT sensor from the intake manifold.

2. Connect a digital ohmmeter to the two terminals of the sensor.

3. Using a calibrated thermometer, compare the resistance of the sensor to the temperature of the ambient air. Refer to the Sensor Resistance Chart.

4. Repeat the test at two other temperature points, heating or cooling the air as necessary with a hair dryer or other suitable tool.

5. If the sensor does not meet specification, it must be replaced.

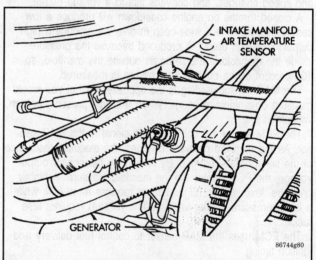

Fig. 113 Intake Manifold Air Temperature (MAT) Sensor — 1996 5.2L engine shown

TEMPERATURE		RESISTANCE (OHMS)	
C	F	MIN	MAX
-40	-40	291,490	381,710
-20	-4	85,850	108,390
-10	14	49,250	61,430
0	32	29,330	35,990
10	50	17,990	21,810
20	68	11,370	13,610
25	77	9,120	10,880
30	86	7,370	8,750
40	104	4,900	5,750
50	122	3,330	3,880
60	140	2,310	2,670
70	158	1,630	1,870
80	176	1,170	1,340
90	194	860	970
100	212	640	720
110	230	480	540
120	248	370	410

86744gKD

Fig. 112 Temperature-to-resistance relationship of the ECT and MAT sensors

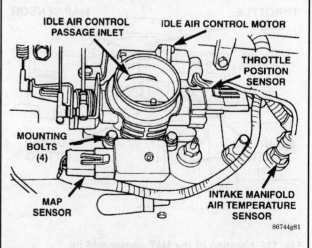

Fig. 114 Intake Manifold Air Temperature (MAT) Sensor — 1996 4.0L engine shown

REMOVAL & INSTALLATION

1. Disengage the MAT sensor wiring harness and unscrew the sensor.

To install:

2. Screw in the sensor and tighten it to 20 ft. lbs. (28 Nm).
3. Engage the sensor wiring connector.

Manifold Air Pressure (MAP) Sensor

OPERATION

▶ **See Figures 115 and 116**

The Manifold Absolute Pressure sensor, or MAP sensor is mounted on the throttle body. It measures the changes in intake manifold pressure, which result from the engine load and speed changes, and converts this to a voltage output.

A closed throttle on engine coastdown will produce a low sensor output, while a wide-open throttle will produce a high output. This high output is produced because the pressure inside the manifold is the same as outside the manifold, so 100 percent of the outside air pressure is measured.

The MAP sensor reading is the opposite of what you would measure on a vacuum gauge. When manifold pressure is high, vacuum is low.

The PCM sends a 5 volt reference signal to the MAP sensor. As the manifold pressure changes, the electrical resistance of the sensor also changes. By monitoring the sensor output voltage, the PCM knows the the manifold pressure. A higher pressure, low vacuum (high voltage) requires more fuel, while a lower pressure, higher vacuum (low voltage) requires less fuel.

The PCM uses the MAP sensor to control fuel delivery and ignition timing.

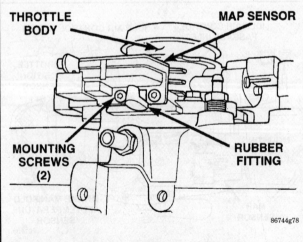

Fig. 115 Location of the MAP sensor and its retainers — 1996 4.0L engine shown

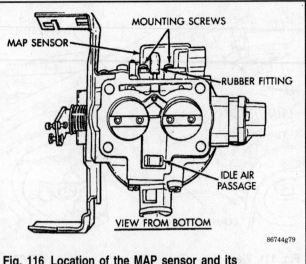

Fig. 116 Location of the MAP sensor and its retainers — 1996 5.2L engine shown

TESTING

1. Backprobe with a high impedance voltmeter at MAP sensor terminal Nos. 1 and 3.
2. With the key **ON** and engine off, the voltmeter reading should be approximately 5.0 volts.
3. If the voltage is not as specified, either the wiring to the MAP sensor or the PCM may be faulty. Correct any wiring or PCM faults before continuing test.
4. Backprobe with the high impotence voltmeter at MAP sensor terminal Nos. 1 and 2.
5. Start the vehicle and verify that the sensor voltage is 0.5-1.8 volts with the engine at a normal idling speed.
6. Verify that the sensor voltage reaches 3.9-4.8. volts at Wide Open Throttle (WOT).
7. If the sensor voltage is not as specified, check the sensor and the sensor vacuum source for a leak or a restriction. If no leaks or restrictions are found, the sensor may be faulty.

REMOVAL & INSTALLATION

1. If the MAP sensor is mounted on the front of the throttle body, the throttle body must first be removed from the engine.
2. If the sensor is mounted on the side of the throttle body, the intake air tube must first be removed.
3. Remove the two sensor mounting screws and carefully pull the sensor away from the throttle body. Be careful not to lose the rubber L-shaped fitting that attaches the sensor to the throttle body.

To install:

4. Install rubber L-shaped fitting to the sensor.
5. Place the sensor into position being careful to guide the fitting onto the throttle body nipple.
6. Install the sensor mounting screws. Tighten the screws to 25 inch. lbs. (3 Nm).
7. Install the intake air tube or the throttle body as necessary.

Throttle Position (TPS) Sensor

OPERATION

▶ See Figure 117

The Throttle Position Sensor, or TPS is connected to the throttle shaft on the throttle body. It sends throttle valve angle information to the PCM. The PCM uses this information to determine fuel delivery volume.

The TPS is a potentiometer with one end connected to 5 volts from the PCM and the other to ground. A third wire is connected to the PCM to measure the voltage from the TPS.

As the throttle valve angle is changed (accelerator pedal moved), the output of the TPS also changes. At a closed throttle position, the output of the TPS is low (approximately .5 volts). As the throttle valve opens, the output increases so that, at wide-open throttle, the output voltage should be above 3.9 volts.

By monitoring the output voltage from the TPS, the PCM can determine fuel delivery based on throttle valve angle (driver demand).

TESTING

1. With the key **ON** and engine **OFF**, backprobe with a high impedance voltmeter at the two end terminals of the TPS connector and battery ground. Verify that one terminal reads approximately 5.0 volts.

2. Backprobe with a high impedance ohmmeter between the end terminal that did not have the 5.0 volt signal and battery ground. Verify that the resistance is less than 5 ohms.

3. If the voltages are not as specified, either the wiring to the TPS or the PCM may be faulty. Correct any wiring or PCM faults before continuing test.

4. With the key **ON** and engine off and the throttle closed, the TPS voltage should be approximately 0.5-1.2 volts.

5. Verify that the TPS voltage increases or decreases smoothly as the throttle is opened or closed. Make sure to open and close the throttle very slowly in order to detect any abnormalities in the TPS voltage reading.

6. If the sensor voltage is not as specified, replace the sensor.

REMOVAL & INSTALLATION

▶ See Figures 118 and 119

1. Remove the air intake tube at the throttle body.
2. Disengage the TPS wiring connector and remove the two mounting screws.
3. Carefully remove the TPS from the throttle body.
To install:
4. The throttle shaft end has a tang that can be fitted into the TPS two different ways. Only one of the installed positions is correct. When correctly positioned, the TPS can be rotated a few degrees. To determine correct positioning, place the TPS onto the throttle body with the throttle shaft tang on one side of the TPS socket. Verify that the TPS can be rotated. If the TPS cannot be rotated, place the TPS on the throttle body with the throttle shaft tang on the other side.
5. Tighten the two TPS mounting bolts to 60 inch lbs. (7 Nm) and engage the wiring connector.
6. Manually operate the throttle and check for any binding.
7. Install the air intake tube.

Camshaft Position (CMP) Sensor

OPERATION

▶ See Figure 120

The Camshaft Position Sensor, or CMP sensor is located inside the distributor. The PCM uses the CMP signal to determine the position of the No. 1 cylinder piston during its power stroke. The PCM uses this information in conjunction with the crankshaft position sensor to determine spark timing among other things.

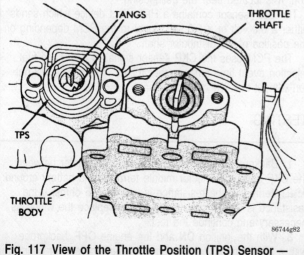

Fig. 117 View of the Throttle Position (TPS) Sensor — 1996 4.0L engine

Fig. 118 Remove the throttle position sensor retainers . . .

Fig. 119 . . . then, remove the throttle position sensor

The CMP sensor contains a Hall effect device which sends either a 0.0 volt or a 5.0 volt signal to the PCM depending on the position of the distributor shaft.

If the cam signal is lost while the engine is running, the PCM will calculate spark timing based on the last CMP signal and the engine will continue to run. However, the engine will not run after it is shut off.

TESTING

1. Make sure that the ignition is **OFF**, remove the distributor cap and turn the engine over by hand.
2. Verify that the distributor shaft turns. If the distributor shaft does not turn, the engine must be checked for proper mechanical operation.
3. Backprobe with a high impedance ohmmeter between the CMP sensor connector middle terminal and battery ground.
4. Verify that the resistance is less than 5 ohms. If the resistance is not as specified, repair or replace the wiring as necessary and continue the test.

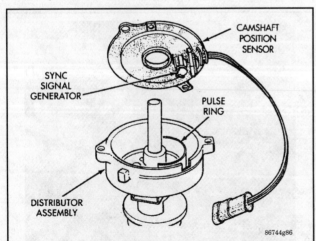

Fig. 120 Exploded view of a common camshaft position sensor and related components — 1996 5.2L engine shown

5. With the ignition **ON** and the engine **OFF**, backprobe with a high impedance voltmeter between the sensor connector middle terminal and either of the end terminals.
6. Verify that a 5 volt or greater signal is present at one of the two terminals. If not as specified, repair or replace the wiring as necessary and continue the test.
7. With the ignition **ON** and the engine **OFF**, backprobe with a high impedance voltmeter between the sensor connector middle terminal and the end terminal that did not have the 5 volt or greater signal.
8. Crank the engine by hand and verify that the voltage reading alternates between 0.0 or 5.0 volts.
9. Install the distributor cap and crank the engine with starter. Verify that the voltage reading is 2.5 volts (averaging voltmeters only).
10. If the voltage readings are not as specified, the sensor may be faulty.

REMOVAL & INSTALLATION

1. Disconnect the negative battery cable and remove the intake air tube if necessary.
2. Remove the distributor cap and the rotor.
3. Disengage the CMP sensor wiring connector and carefully lift the sensor out of the distributor.

To install:

4. Carefully place the sensor into the distributor. Make sure that any alignment notches or tabs line up properly.
5. Install the distributor rotor and cap.
6. Engage the sensor wiring connector and connect the negative battery cable.

Crankshaft Position (CKP) Sensor

OPERATION

▶ See Figures 121 and 122

The Crankshaft Position Sensor, or CKP sensor provides the PCM with information about engine speed and crankshaft position. It is located near the bellhousing.

The CKP sensor contains a Hall effect device which sends either a 0.0 volt or a 5.0 volt signal to the PCM depending on the position of the distributor shaft.

The PCM uses the CKP sensor signal to determine fuel injection event time among other things. The engine will not run without the CKP sensor signal.

TESTING

1. Backprobe with a high impedance ohmmeter between the CKP sensor connector middle terminal and battery ground.
2. Verify that the resistance is less than 5 ohms. If the resistance is not as specified, repair or replace the wiring as necessary and continue the test.
3. With the ignition **ON** and the engine **OFF**, backprobe with a high impedance voltmeter between the sensor connector middle terminal and either of the end terminals.

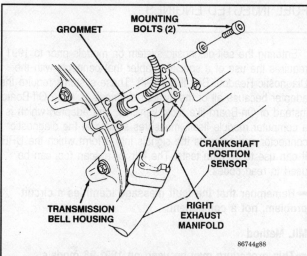

Fig. 121 View of the crankshaft position sensor and its location — 1996 5.2L engine shown

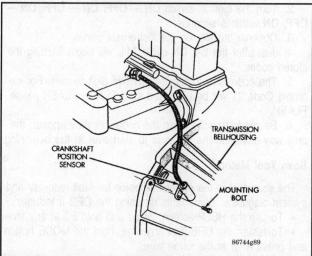

Fig. 122 View of the crankshaft position sensor and its location — 1996 4.0L engine shown

4. Verify that a 5 volt or greater signal is present at one of the two terminals. If not as specified, repair or replace the wiring as necessary and continue the test.

5. With the ignition **ON** and the engine **OFF**, backprobe with a high impedance voltmeter between the sensor connector middle terminal and the end terminal that did not have the 5 volt or greater signal.

6. Crank the engine and verify that the voltage reading alternates between 0.0 and 5.0 volts or verify that the voltage reading is 2.5 volts (averaging voltmeters only).

7. If the voltage readings are not as specified, the sensor may be faulty.

REMOVAL & INSTALLATION

4.0L Engine

1. The CKP sensor is located on the transmission bellhousing. Disengage the sensor wiring connector and remove the sensor wiring hold-down clip from the fuel rail.

2. Remove the sensor mounting bolt and carefully pull the sensor out of the bellhousing.

3. Installation is the reverse of removal.

5.2L Engine

1. The CKP sensor is bolted to the top of the cylinder block near the rear of the right cylinder head. Disengage the sensor wiring connector and remove the two sensor mounting bolts.

2. Carefully pull the sensor out of the cylinder block.

3. Installation is the reverse of removal.

TROUBLE CODES

General Information

The self-diagnostic system is designed to detect problems most likely to occur within the various system components. When the engine is started, the CHECK ENGINE/POWER LOSS light will remain on momentarily and then be turned off. This light is also known as the Malfunction Indicator Lamp (MIL). If the MIL remains on, the self-diagnostic system has detected a problem.

Fuel injected engines and the carbureted 2.8L six cylinder engine with the California emissions package have a self-diagnostic system with a MIL mounted in the instrument panel.

VISUAL INSPECTIONS

This is possibly the most critical step of diagnosis. A detailed examination of connectors, wiring and vacuum hoses can often lead to a repair without further diagnosis. A careful inspector will check the undersides of hoses as well as the integrity of hard-to-reach hoses blocked by the air cleaner or other component. Wiring should be checked carefully for any sign of strain, burning, crimping, or terminals pulled-out from a connector. Checking connectors at components or in harnesses is required; usually, pushing them together will reveal a loose fit.

Reading Codes

CARBURETED ENGINES

When a jumper wire is connected between the trouble code test terminals 6 and 7 of the 15-terminal diagnostic connector (D2), the CHECK ENGINE light will flash a trouble code or codes that indicate a problem area. For a bulb and system check, the CHECK ENGINE light will illuminate when the ignition switch is ON and the engine not started. If the test terminals are then grounded, the light will flash a code 12 that indicates the self-diagnostic system is operational. A code 12 consists of one flash, followed by a short pause, then two more flashes in quick succession. After a longer pause, the code will repeat two more times. If more than one trouble code is stored, each will be flashed three more times in numerical order, from the lowest to the highest numbered code.

➡ Remember that the fault message identifies a circuit problem, not a component.

CODE 12: No distributor reference pulses to the ECM. This code is not stored in memory and will only flash while the trouble exists. This code is normal when the ignition is switched ON with the engine not running.

CODE 13: Oxygen sensor circuit. The engine must operate for up to 5 minutes at part throttle, under road load, before this code will be set.

CODE 14: Shorted coolant sensor circuit. The engine must operate for up to 5 minutes before this code will be set.

CODE 15: Open coolant sensor circuit. The engine must operate for up to 5 minutes before this code will be set.

CODE 21: Throttle position sensor circuit. The engine must operate for at least 25 seconds at curb idle speed before this code will be set.

CODE 23: Mixture control solenoid circuit is shorted or open.

CODE 34: Vacuum sensor circuit. The engine must operate for up to 5 minutes at curb idle speed before this code will be set.

CODE 41: No distributor reference pulses to the ECM at the specified engine manifold vacuum. This code will be stored in memory.

CODE 42: Electronic Spark Timing (EST) bypass circuit or EST circuit has short circuit to ground or an open circuit.

CODE 44: Lean exhaust indication. The engine must operate for up to 5 minutes, be in closed loop operation and at part throttle before this code will be set.

CODE 44 & 45: If these two codes appear at the same time, it indicates a problem in the oxygen sensor circuit.

CODE 45: Rich exhaust indication. The engine must operate for up to 5 minutes, be in closed loop and at part throttle before this code will be set.

CODE 51: Faulty calibration unit (PROM) or installation. It requires up to 30 seconds for this code to be set.

CODE 54: Mixture Control (MC) solenoid circuit is shorted or the ECM is faulty.

CODE 55: Voltage reference has short circuit to ground (terminal 21), faulty oxygen sensor or faulty ECM.

FUEL INJECTED ENGINES

Entering the self-diagnostic system on models prior to 1991 requires the use of a special adapter that connects with the Diagnostic Readout Box II (DRB-II). These systems require the adapter because all of the system diagnosis is done Off-Board instead of On-Board like most vehicles. The adapter, which is a computer module itself, measures signals at the diagnostic connector and converts the signals into a form which the DRB-II can use to perform tests. The MIL or a scan tool can be used to read codes.

➡ Remember that the fault message identifies a circuit problem, not a component.

MIL Method

➡ This procedure may be used on 1991-96 models.

1. Start the engine, if possible, cycle the transmission selector and the A/C switch if applicable. Shut off the engine.
2. Turn the ignition switch ON — OFF, ON — OFF, ON — OFF, ON within 5 seconds.
3. Observe the MIL on the instrument panel.
4. Just after the last ON cycle, MIL will begin flashing the stored codes.
5. The codes are transmitted as two digit flashes. For example Code 21 will be displayed as a FLASH FLASH pause FLASH.
6. Be ready to write down the codes as they appear; the only way to repeat the codes is to start over at the beginning.

Scan Tool Method

The scan tool is the preferred choice for fault recovery and system diagnosis. Some hints on using the DRB-II include:

• To use the HELP screen, press and hold F3 at any time.
• To restart the DRB-II at any time, hold the MODE button and press ATM at the same time.
• Pressing the up or down arrows will move forward or backward one item within a menu.
• To select an item, either press the number of the item or move the cursor arrow to the selection, then press ENTER.
• To return to the previous display (screen), press ATM.
• Some test screens display multiple items. To view only one, move the cursor arrow to the desired item, then press ENTER.

To read stored faults with the DRB-II:

1. With the ignition switch OFF, connect the tool to the diagnostic connector near the engine controller under the hood. Turn the ignition ON.
2. Start the engine if possible. Cycle the transmission from P to a forward gear, then back to P, Cycle the air conditioning on and off. Turn the ignition switch OFF.
3. Turn the ignition switch ON but do not start the engine. The DRB-II will begin its power-up sequence; do not touch any keys on the scan tool during this sequence.
4. Reading faults must be selected from the FUEL/IGN MENU. To reach this menu on the DRB-II:

   a. When the initial menu is displayed after the power-up sequence, use the down arrow to display choice 4) SELECT SYSTEM and select this choice.

b. Once on the — SELECT SYSTEM — screen, choose 1) ENGINE. This will enter the engine diagnostics section of the program.

c. The screen will momentarily display the engine family and SBEC identification numbers. After a few seconds the screen displays the choices 1) With A/C and 2) Without A/C. Select and enter the correct choice for the vehicle.

d. When the — ENGINE SYSTEM — screen appears, select 1) FUEL/IGNITION from the menu.

e. On the next screen, select 2) READ FAULTS

5. If any faults are stored, the display will show how many are stored (1 of 4 faults, etc.) and issue a text description of the problem, such as COOLANT SENSOR VOLTAGE TOO LOW. The last line of the display shows the number of engine starts since the code was set. If the number displayed is 0 starts, this indicates a hard or current fault. Faults are displayed in reverse order of occurrence; the first fault shown is the most current and the last fault shown is the oldest.

6. Press the down arrow to read each fault after the first. Record the screen data carefully for easy reference.

7. If no faults are stored in the controller, the display will state NO FAULTS DETECTED and show the number of starts since the system memory was last erased.

8. After all faults have been read and recorded, press ATM.

Except 1991-96 Models

Code 1000 — Ignition line low.
Code 1001 — Ignition line high.
Code 1002 — Oxygen heater line.
Code 1004 — Battery voltage low.
Code 1005 — Sensor ground line out of limits.
Code 1010 — Diagnostic enable line low.
Code 1011 — Diagnostic enable line high.
Code 1012 — MAP line low.
Code 1013 — MAP line high.
Code 1014 — Fuel pump line low.
Code 1015 — Fuel pump line high.
Code 1016 — Charge air temperature sensor low.
Code 1017 — Charge air temperature sensor high.
Code 1018 — No serial data from the ECU.
Code 1021 — Engine failed to start due to mechanical, fuel, or ignition problem.
Code 1022 — Start line low.
Code 1024 — ECU does not see start signal.
Code 1025 — Wide open throttle circuit low.
Code 1027 — ECU sees wide open throttle.
Code 1028 — ECU does not see wide open throttle.
Code 1031 — ECU sees closed throttle.
Code 1032 — ECU does not see closed throttle.
Code 1033 — Idle speed increase line low.
Code 1034 — Idle speed increase line high.
Code 1035 — Idle speed decrease line low.
Code 1036 — Idle speed decrease line high.
Code 1037 — Throttle position sensor reads low.
Code 1038 — Park/Neutral line high.
Code 1040 — Latched B+ line low.
Code 1041 — Latched B+ line high.
Code 1042 — No Latched B+ ½ volt drop.
Code 1047 — Wrong ECU.
Code 1048 — Manual vehicle equipped with automatic ECU.
Code 1049 — Automatic vehicle equipped with manual ECU.

Code 1050 — Idle RPM's less than 500.
Code 1051 — Idle RPM's greater than 2000.
Code 1052 — MAP sensor out of limits.
Code 1053 — Change in MAP reading out of limits.
Code 1054 — Coolant temperature sensor line low.
Code 1055 — Coolant temperature sensor line high.
Code 1056 — Inactive coolant temperature sensor.
Code 1057 — Knock circuit shorted.
Code 1058 — Knock value out of limits.
Code 1059 — A/C request line low.
Code 1060 — A/C request line high.
Code 1061 — A/C select line low.
Code 1062 — A/C select line high.
Code 1063 — A/C clutch line low.
Code 1064 — A/C clutch line high.
Code 1065 — Oxygen reads rich.
Code 1066 — Oxygen reads lean.
Code 1067 — Latch relay line low.
Code 1068 — Latch relay line high.
Code 1070 — A/C cutout line low.
Code 1071 — A/C cutout line high.
Code 1073 — ECU does not see speed sensor signal.
Code 1200 — ECU defective.
Code 1202 — Injector shorted to ground.
Code 1209 — Injector open.
Code 1218 — No voltage at ECU from power latch relay.
Code 1220 — No voltage at ECU from EGR solenoid.
Code 1221 — No injector voltage.
Code 1222 — MAP not grounded.
Code 1223 — No ECU tests run.

1991-95 Models

Code 88 — Display used for start of test.
Code 11 — Camshaft signal or Ignition signal — no reference signal detected during engine cranking.
Code 12 — Memory to controller has been cleared within 50-l00 engine starts.
Code 13 — MAP sensor pneumatic signal — no variation in MAP sensor signal is detected or no difference is recognized between the engine MAP reading and the stored barometric pressure reading..
Code 14 — MAP voltage too high or too low.
Code 15 — Vehicle speed sensor signal — no distance sensor signal detected during road load conditions.
Code 16 — Knock sensor circuit — Open or short has been detected in the knock sensor circuit.
Code 16 — Battery input sensor — battery voltage sensor input below 4 volts with engine running.
Code 17 — Low engine temperature — engine coolant temperature remains below normal operating temperature during vehicle travel; possible thermostat problem.
Code 21 — Oxygen sensor signal — neither rich or lean condition is detected from the oxygen sensor input.
Code 22 — Coolant voltage low — coolant temperature sensor input below the minimum acceptable voltage/Coolant voltage high — coolant temperature sensor input above the maximum acceptable voltage.
Code 23 — Air Charge or Throttle Body temperature voltage HIGH/LOW — charge air temperature sensor input is above or below the acceptable voltage limits.
Code 24 — Throttle Position sensor voltage high or low.

Code 25 — Automatic Idle Speed (AIS) motor driver circuit — short or open detected in 1 or more of the AIS control circuits.

Code 26 — Injectors No. 1, 2, or 3 peak current not reached, high resistance in circuit.

Code 27 — Injector control circuit — bank output driver stage does not respond properly to the control signal.

Code 27 — Injectors No. 1, 2, or 3 control circuit and peak current not reached.

Code 31 — Purge solenoid circuit — open or short detected in the purge solenoid circuit.

Code 32 — Exhaust Gas Recirculation (EGR) solenoid circuit — open or short detected in the EGR solenoid circuit/EGR system failure — required change in fuel/air ratio not detected during diagnostic test.

Code 33 — Air conditioner clutch relay circuit — open or short detected in the air conditioner clutch relay circuit. If vehicle doesn't have air conditioning ignore this code.

Code 34 — Speed control servo solenoids or MUX speed control circuit HIGH/LOW — open or short detected in the vacuum or vent solenoid circuits or speed control switch input above or below allowable voltage.

Code 35 — Radiator fan control relay circuit — open or short detected in the radiator fan relay circuit.

Code 35 — Idle switch shorted — switch input shorted to ground — some 1993 vehicles.

Code 37 — Part Throttle Unlock (PTU) circuit for torque converter clutch — open or short detected in the torque converter part throttle unlock solenoid circuit.

Code 37 — Baro Reed Solenoid — solenoid does not turn off when it should.

Code 37 — Shift indicator circuit (manual transaxle).

Code 41 — Charging system circuit — output driver stage for generator field does not respond properly to the voltage regulator control signal.

Code 42 — Fuel pump or no Autoshut-down (ASD) relay voltage sense at controller.

Code 43 — Ignition control circuit — peak primary circuit current not respond properly with maximum dwell time.

Code 43 — Ignition coil #1, 2, or 3 primary circuits — peak primary was not achieved within the maximum allowable dwell time.

Code 44 — Battery temperature voltage — problem exists in the PCM battery temperature circuit or there is an open or short in the engine coolant temperature circuit.

Code 44 — Fused J2 circuit in not present in the logic board; used on the single engine module controller system.

Code 44 — Overdrive solenoid circuit — open or short in overdrive solenoid circuit.

Code 46 — Battery voltage too high — battery voltage sense input above target charging voltage during engine operation.

Code 47 — Battery voltage too low — battery voltage sense input below target charging voltage.

Code 51 — Air/fuel at limit — oxygen sensor signal input indicates LEAN air/fuel ratio condition during engine operation.

Code 52 — Air/fuel at limit — oxygen sensor signal input indicates RICH air/fuel ratio condition during engine operation.

Code 53 — Internal controller failure — internal engine controller fault condition detected during self test.

Code 54 — Camshaft or (distributor sync.) reference circuit — No camshaft position sensor signal detected during engine rotation.

Code 55 — End of message.

Code 61 — Baro read solenoid — open or short detected in the baro read solenoid circuit.

Code 62 — EMR mileage not stored — unsuccessful attempt to update EMR mileage in the controller EEPROM.

Code 63 — EEPROM write denied — unsuccessful attempt to write to an EEPROM location by the controller.

Code 64 — Flex fuel sensor — Flex fuel sensor signal out of range — (new in 1993) — CNG Temperature voltage out of range — CN gas pressure out of range.

Code 66 — No CCD messages or no BODY CCD messages or no EATX CCD messages — messages from the CCD bus or the BODY CCD or the EATX CCD were not received by the PCM.

Code 76 — Ballast bypass relay — open or short in fuel pump relay circuit.

Code 77 — Speed control relay — an open or short has been detected in the speed control relay.

Code 88 — Display used for start of test.

Code Error — Fault code error — Unrecognized fault ID received by DRBII.

1996 *DIAGNOSTIC TROUBLE CODES*

MIL CODE'	GENERIC SCAN TOOL CODE	HEX CODE	DRB SCAN TOOL DISPLAY	DESCRIPTION OF DIAGNOSTIC TROUBLE CODE
11	P1391**	9D	Intermittent Loss of CMP or CKP	Intermittent loss of either camshaft or crankshaft position sensor
	or	28	No Crank Reference Signal at PCM	No crank reference signal detected during engine cranking.
	or P1398**	BA	Misfire Adaptive Numerator at Limit	CKP sensor target windows have too much variation
12*			Battery Disconnect	Direct battery input to PCM was disconnected within the last 50 Key-on cycles.
13**	P1297	27	No Change in MAP From Start to Run	No difference recognized between the engine MAP reading and the barometric (atmospheric) pressure reading from start-up.
14**	P0107	24	MAP Sensor Voltage Too Low	MAP sensor input below minimum acceptable voltage.
	or P0108	25	MAP Sensor Voltage Too High	MAP sensor input above maximum acceptable voltage.
	or P1296	87	No 5 Volts To MAP Sensor	5 Volt output to MAP sensor open
15**	P0500	23	No Vehicle Speed Sensor Signal	No vehicle speed sensor signal detected during road load conditions.
	or P0720	A6	Low Output Spd Sensr RPM, Above 15 MPH	Output Speed Sensor Circuit
17**	P0125	80	Closed Loop Temp Not Reached	Engine does not reach 50°F within 5 minutes with a vehicle speed signal.
17	or	21	Engine Is Cold Too Long	Engine did not reach operating temperature within acceptable limits.

86744gIA

DESCRIPTION AND OPERATION (Continued)

MIL CODE'	GENERIC SCAN TOOL CODE	HEX CODE	DRB SCAN TOOL DISPLAY	DESCRIPTION OF DIAGNOSTIC TROUBLE CODE
21**	P0131	9B	Upstream O2s Voltage Shorted to Ground	Tested after key off and at start to run.
	or			
	P0132	3E	Left O2 Sensor Shorted to Voltage	Left oxygen sensor input voltage maintained above the normal operating range.
	or			
	P0133	66	Upstream O2 Sensor Slow Response	Upstream oxygen sensor response slower than minimum required switching frequency or value does not go above .65 volts.
	or			
	P0135	67	Upstream O2 Sensor Heater Failure	Upstream oxygen sensor heating element circuit malfunction
	or			
	P0137	9C	Downstream O2s Voltage Shorted to Ground	Tested after key off and at start to run.
	or			
	P0138	7E	Downstream O2 Sensor Shorted to Voltage	Downstream oxygen sensor input voltage maintained above the normal operating range.
	or			
	P0141	69	Downstream O2 Sensor Heater Failure	Downstream oxygen sensor heating element circuit malfunction
22**	P0117	1E	ECT Sensor Voltage Too Low	Engine coolant temperature sensor input below minimum acceptable voltage.
	or			
	P0118	1F	ECT Sensor Voltage Too High	Engine coolant temperature sensor input above maximum acceptable voltage.
23**	P0112	39	Intake Air Temp Sensor Voltage Low	Intake air temperature sensor input below the maximum acceptable voltage.
	or			
	P0113	3A	Intake Air Temp Sensor Voltage High	Intake air temperature sensor input above the minimum acceptable voltage.
24**	P0121	84	TPS Voltage Does Not Agree With MAP	TPS signal does not correlate to MAP sensor
	or			
	P0122	1A	Throttle Position Sensor Voltage Low	Throttle position sensor input below the minimum acceptable voltage
	or			
	P0123	1B	Throttle Position Sensor Voltage High	Throttle position sensor input above the maximum acceptable voltage.
25**	P0505	19	Idle Air Control Motor Circuits	A shorted or open condition detected in one or more of the idle air control motor circuits.
	or			
	P1294	8A	Target Idle Not Reached	Actual idle speed does not equal target idle speed.
27**	P0201	15	Injector #1 Control Circuit	Injector #1 output driver does not respond properly to the control signal.
	or			

86744gIB

DESCRIPTION AND OPERATION (Continued)

MIL CODE'	GENERIC SCAN TOOL CODE	HEX CODE	DRB SCAN TOOL DISPLAY	DESCRIPTION OF DIAGNOSTIC TROUBLE CODE
	P0202	14	Injector #2 Control Circuit	Injector #2 output driver does not respond properly to the control signal.
	or			
	P0203	13	Injector #3 Control Circuit	Injector #3 output driver does not respond properly to the control signal.
	or			
	P0204	3D	Injector #4 Control Circuit	Injector #4 output driver does not respond properly to the control signal.
	or			
	P0205	45	Injector #5 Control Circuit	Injector #5 output driver does not respond properly to the control signal.
	or			
	P0206	46	Injector #6 Control Circuit	Injector #6 output driver does not respond properly to the control signal.
	or			
	P0207	4F	Injector #7 Control Circuit	Injector #7 output driver does not respond properly to the control signal. (5.2L only)
	or			
	P0208	50	Injector #8 Control Circuit	Injector #8 output driver does not respond properly to the control signal. (5.2L only)
31*	P0441	71	Evap Purge Flow Monitor Failure	Insufficient or excessive vapor flow detected during evaporative emission system operation.
	or			
	P0442	A0	Evap Sys Small Leak	Hole smaller than .040 in system.
	or			
	P0443	12	EVAP Purge Solenoid Circuit	An open or shorted condition detected in the duty cycle purge solenoid circuit.
	or			
	P0455	A1	Evap Sys Gross Leak	Hole larger than .040 in system.
	or			
	P01494	B7	Leak Detection Pump Pressure Switch	
	or			
	P01495	B8	Leak Detection Pump Solenoid Circuit	
	or			
	P1486	BB	Evap Hose Pinched	Pinched hose in EVAP circuit.
33*		10	A/C Clutch Relay Circuit	An open or shorted condition detected in the A/C clutch relay circuit.
34*		0F	Speed Control Solenoid Circuits	An open or shorted condition detected in the Speed Control vacuum or vent solenoid circuits.
	or			
		57	Speed Control Switch Always Low	MUX speed control switch below rated volts.
37**	P0711	A4	Trans Temp Sensor, No Temp Rise After Start	Transmission temperature sensor

86744gIC

DESCRIPTION AND OPERATION (Continued)

MIL CODE'	GENERIC SCAN TOOL CODE	HEX CODE	DRB SCAN TOOL DISPLAY	DESCRIPTION OF DIAGNOSTIC TROUBLE CODE
	or P0712	4A	Trans Temp Sensor Voltage too Low	Transmission temperature sensor
	or P0713	4B	Trans Temp Sensor Voltage too High	Transmission temperature sensor
	or P0740	94	Torq Conv Clu, No RPM Drop At Lockup	Relationship between engine speed and vehicle speed indicates no torque converter clutch engagement.
	or P0743	0C	Torque Converter Clutch Soleniod CKT	An open or shorted condition detected in the torque converter part throttle unlock solenoid control circuit.
	or P1899	72	P/N switch Stuck In Park Or In Gear	Park/Neutral Switch Performance
41***		0B	Generator Field Not Switching Properly	An open or shorted condition detected in the generator field control circuit.
42*	or	65	Fuel Pump Relay Control Circuit	An open or shorted condition detected in the fuel pump relay control circuit.
	or	0A	Auto Shutdown Relay Control Circuit	An open or shorted condition detected in the auto shutdown relay circuit.
	or	2C	No ASD Relay Output Voltage at PCM	An Open condition Detected In The ASD Relay Output Circuit.
	or	95	Fuel Level Sending Unit Volts Too Low	Open circuit between BCM and fuel gauge sending unit.
	or	96	Fuel Level Sending Unit Volts Too High	Circuit shorted to voltage between BCM and fuel gauge sending unit.
	or	97	Fuel Level Unit No Change Over Miles	No movement of fuel level sender detected.
43**	P0300 or	6A	Multiple Cylinder Misfire	Misfire detected in multiple cylinders.
	P0301 or	6B	Cylinder #1 Misfire	Misfire detected in cylinder #1.
	P0302 or	6C	Cylinder #2 Misfire	Misfire detected in cylinder #2.
	P0303 or	6D	Cylinder #3 Misfire	Misfire detected in cylinder #3.
	P0304 or	6E	Cylinder #4 Misfire	Misfire detected in cylinder #4.
	P0305 or	AE	Cylinder #5 Misfire	Misfire detected in cylinder #5.

86744gID

DESCRIPTION AND OPERATION (Continued)

MIL CODE'	GENERIC SCAN TOOL CODE	HEX CODE	DRB SCAN TOOL DISPLAY	DESCRIPTION OF DIAGNOSTIC TROUBLE CODE
	P0306 or	AF	Cylinder #6 Misfire	Misfire detected in cylinder #6.
	P0307 or	B0	Cylinder #7 Misfire	Misfire detected in cylinder #7. (5.2L only)
	P0308 or	B1	Cylinder #8 Misfire	Misfire detected in cylinder #8. (5.2L only)
	P0351	2B	Ignition Coil #1 Primary Circuit	Peak primary circuit current not achieved with maximum dwell time.
44**	P1492 or	9A	Battery Temp Sensor Voltage Too High	Battery temperature sensor input voltage above an acceptable range.
	P1493	99	Battery Temp Sensor Voltage Too Low	Battery temperature sensor input voltage below an acceptable range.
45**	P0748 or	AB	Governor Pressure Solenoid Control Circuit	Governor pressure solenoid circuit
	P0753 or	32	Trans 3-4 Solenoid Circuit	Overdrive Solenoid Circuit
	P1756 or	8D	Gov Press Not Equal To Target @ 15-20 PSI	Governor mid-pressure malfunction
	P1763 or	A8	Governor Pressure Sensr Volts Too Hi	Governor pressure sensor volts above rated volts.
	P1764 or	A7	Governor Pressure Sensr Volts Too Lo	Governor pressure sensor volts below rated volts.
	P1765 or	AD	Trans 12 Volt Supply Relay Cntrl Circuit	Transmission relay circuit
	P0783 or	A5	3-4 Shift Sol, No RPM Drop @ 3-4 Shift	3-4 Shift Malfunction
	P1757 or	8E	Gov Pres Above 3 PSI In Gear With 0 MPH	Governor low pressure malfunction
	P1762 or	A9	Gov Press Sen Offset Volts Too Lo Or Hi	Governor pressure sensor
		BC	O/D Switch Pressed (LO) More than 5 Min	Overdrive switch low
46***		06	Charging System Voltage Too High	Battery voltage sense input above target charging voltage during engine operation.
47***		05	Charging System Voltage Too Low	Battery voltage sense input below target charging during engine operation. Also, no significant change detected in battery voltage during active test of generator output circuit.

86744gIE

DESCRIPTION AND OPERATION (Continued)

MIL CODE'	GENERIC SCAN TOOL CODE	HEX CODE	DRB SCAN TOOL DISPLAY	DESCRIPTION OF DIAGNOSTIC TROUBLE CODE
51**	P0171	77	Fuel System Lean	A lean air/fuel mixture has been indicated by an abnormally rich correction factor.
52**	P0172	76	Fuel System Rich	A rich air/fuel mixture has been indicated by an abnormally lean correction factor.
53**	P0600 or	44	SPI Communication	PCM Internal fault condition detected.
	P0601	02	Internal Controller Failure	PCM Internal fault condition detected.
54**	P0340	01	No Cam Signal at PCM	No camshaft signal detected during engine cranking.
55*				Completion of fault code display on Check Engine lamp.
63**	P1698	31	PCM Failure EEPROM Write Denied	Unsuccessful attempt to write to an EEPROM location by the PCM.
72**	P0420	70	Catalytic Converter Efficency Failure	Catalyst efficiency below required level.
77		52	S/C Power Relay Circuit	Malfuntion detected with power feed to speed control servo soleniod

* Check Engine Lamp (MIL) will not illuminate if this Diagnostic Trouble Code was recorded. Cycle Ignition key as described in manual and observe code flashed by Check Engine lamp.

** Check Engine Lamp (MIL) will illuminate during engine operation if this Diagnostic Trouble Code was recorded.

*** Generator Lamp illuminated

86744gIF

Clearing Codes

Stored faults should only be cleared by use of the DRB-II or similar scan tool. Disconnecting the battery will clear codes but is not recommended as doing so will also clear all other memories on the vehicle and may affect drive ability. Unplugging the PCM connector will also clear codes, but on newer models it may store a power loss code and will affect driveability until the vehicle is driven and the PCM can relearn its driveability memory.

The — ERASE — screen will appear when ATM is pressed at the end of the stored faults. Select the desired action from ERASE or DON'T ERASE. If ERASE is chosen, the display asks ARE YOU SURE? Pressing ENTER erases stored faults and displays the message FAULTS ERASED. After the faults are erased, press ATM to return the FUEL/IGN MENU.

VACUUM DIAGRAMS

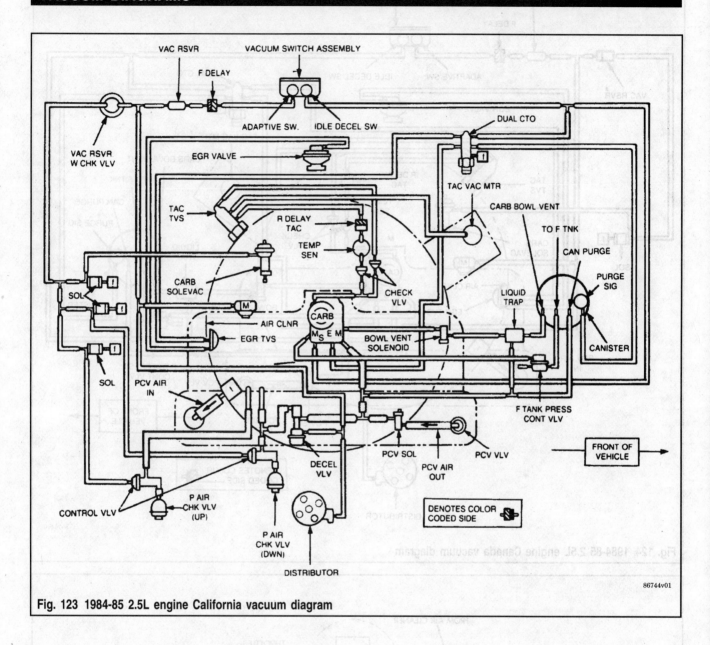

Fig. 123 1984-85 2.5L engine California vacuum diagram

86744v01

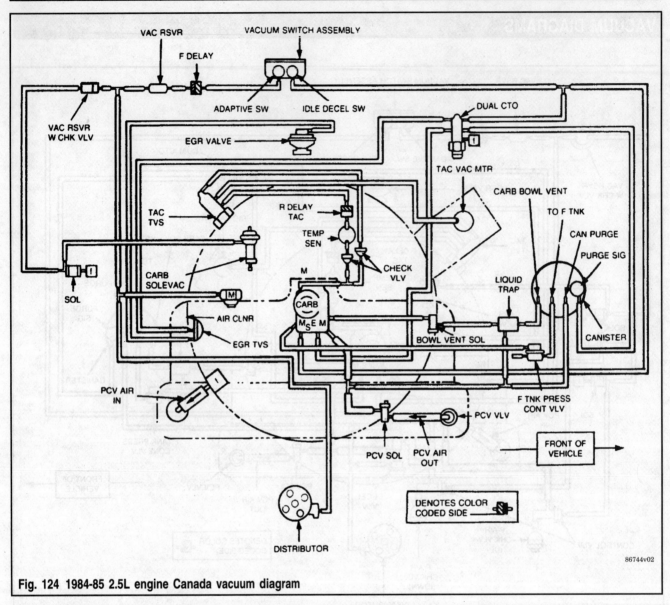

Fig. 124 1984-85 2.5L engine Canada vacuum diagram

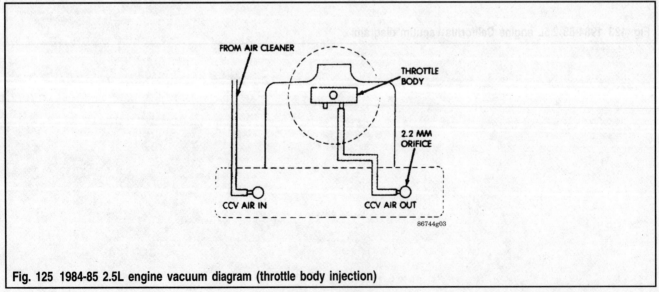

Fig. 125 1984-85 2.5L engine vacuum diagram (throttle body injection)

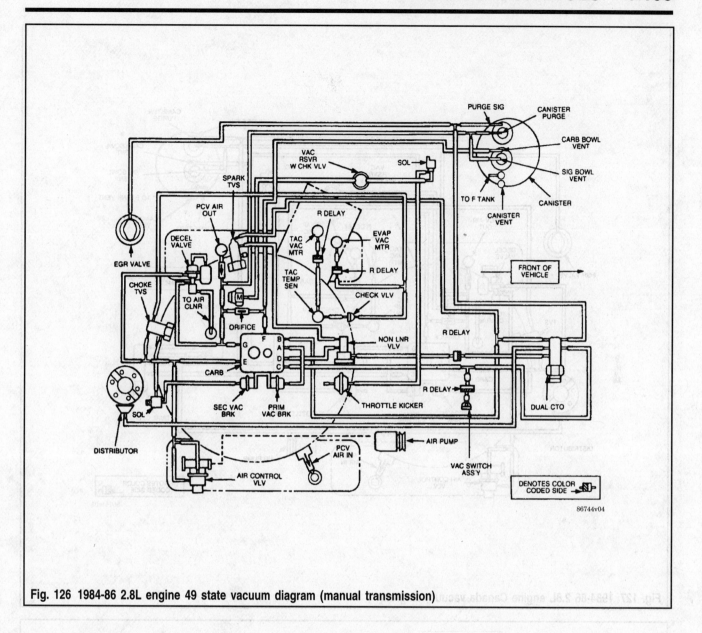

Fig. 126 1984-86 2.8L engine 49 state vacuum diagram (manual transmission)

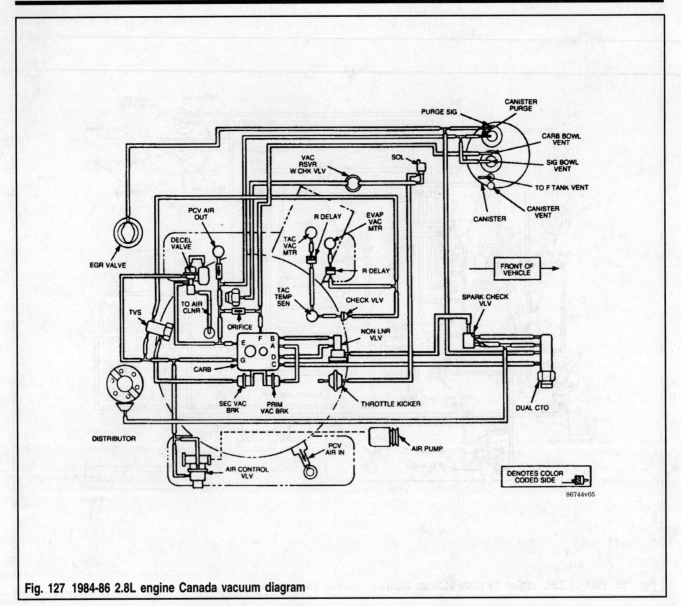

Fig. 127 1984-86 2.8L engine Canada vacuum diagram

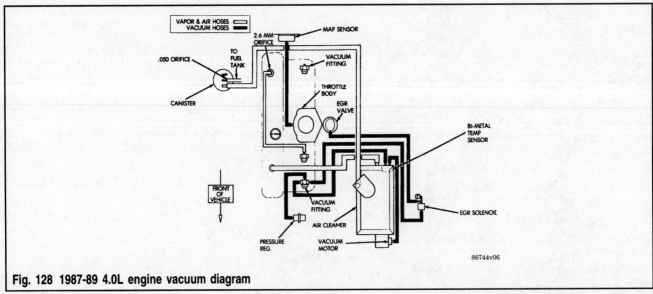

Fig. 128 1987-89 4.0L engine vacuum diagram

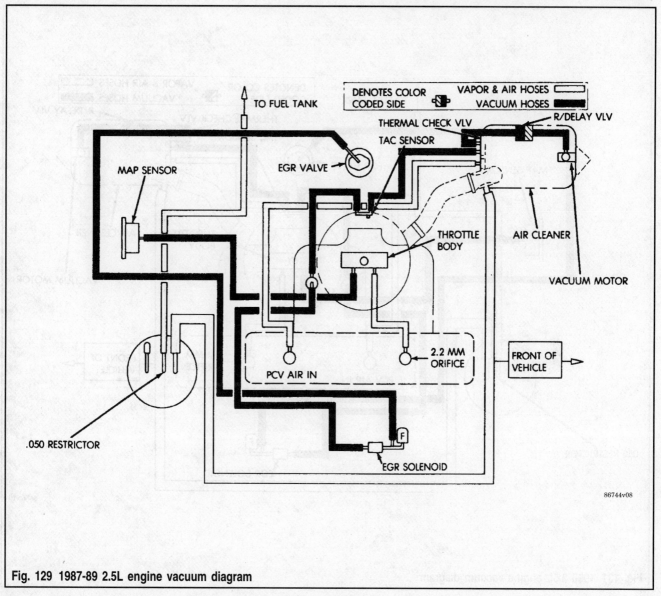

Fig. 129 1987-89 2.5L engine vacuum diagram

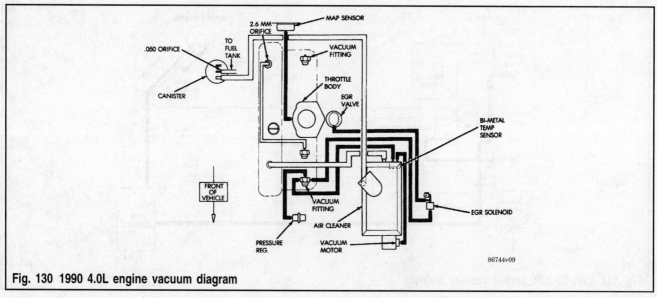

Fig. 130 1990 4.0L engine vacuum diagram

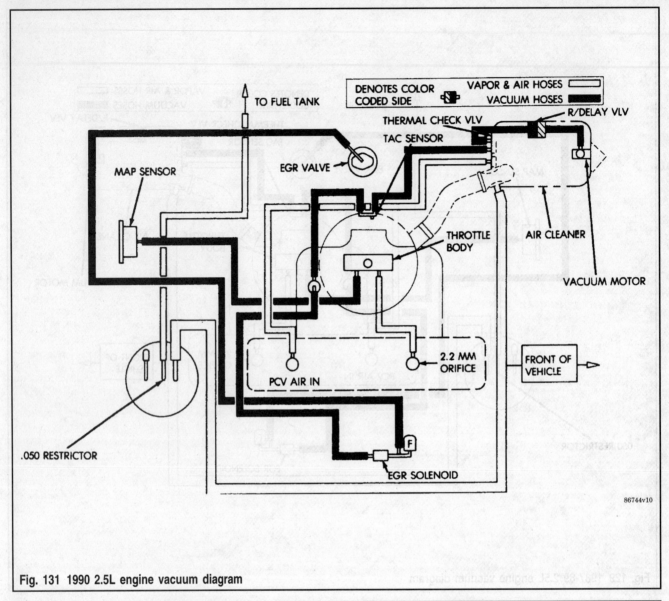

Fig. 131 1990 2.5L engine vacuum diagram

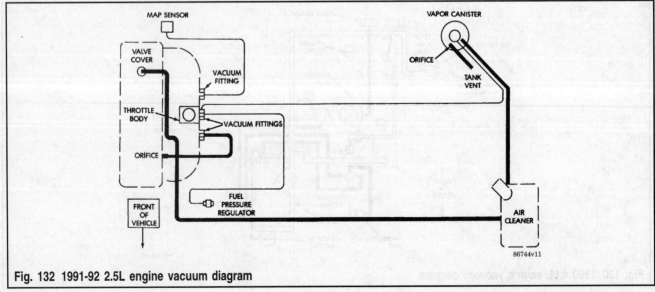

Fig. 132 1991-92 2.5L engine vacuum diagram

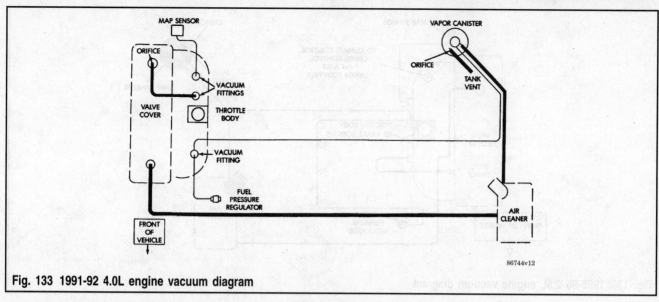

Fig. 133 1991-92 4.0L engine vacuum diagram

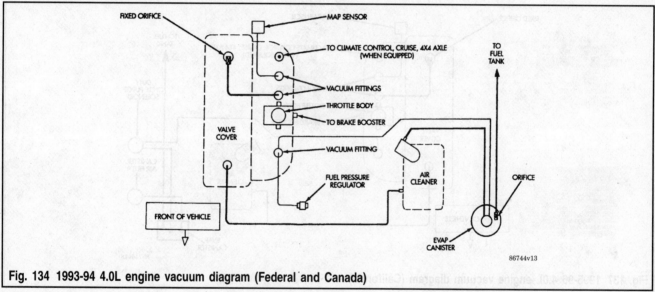

Fig. 134 1993-94 4.0L engine vacuum diagram (Federal and Canada)

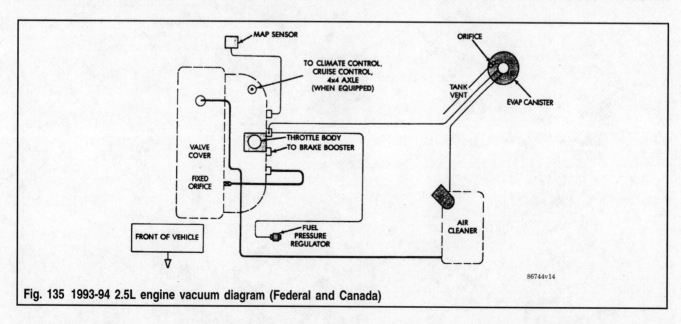

Fig. 135 1993-94 2.5L engine vacuum diagram (Federal and Canada)

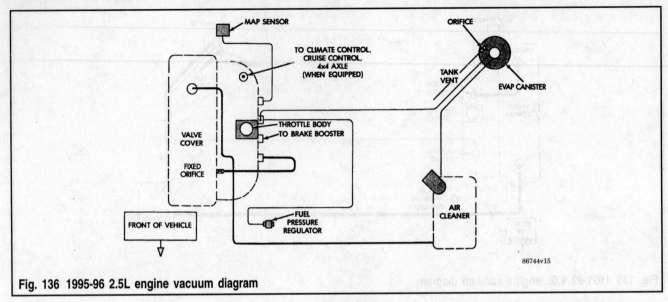

Fig. 136 1995-96 2.5L engine vacuum diagram

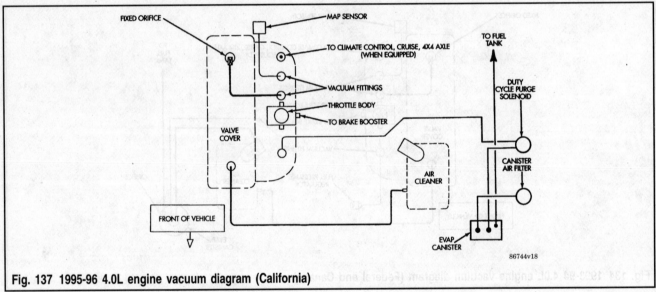

Fig. 137 1995-96 4.0L engine vacuum diagram (California)

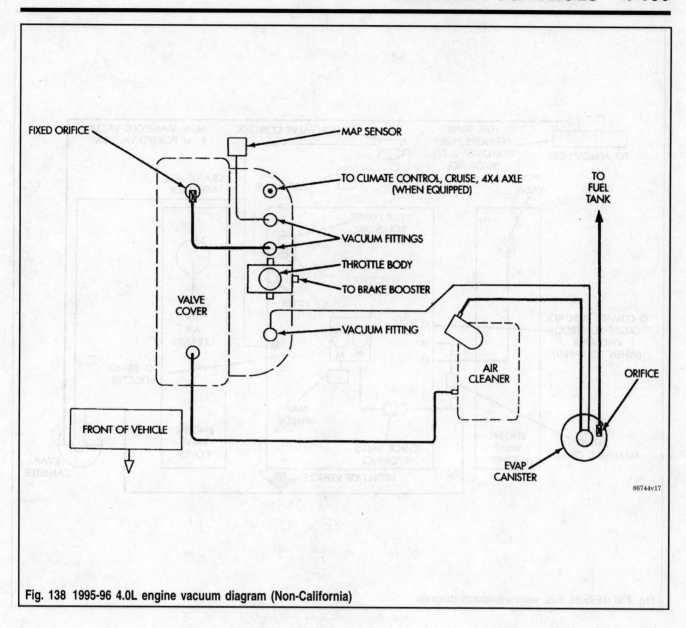

Fig. 138 1995-96 4.0L engine vacuum diagram (Non-California)

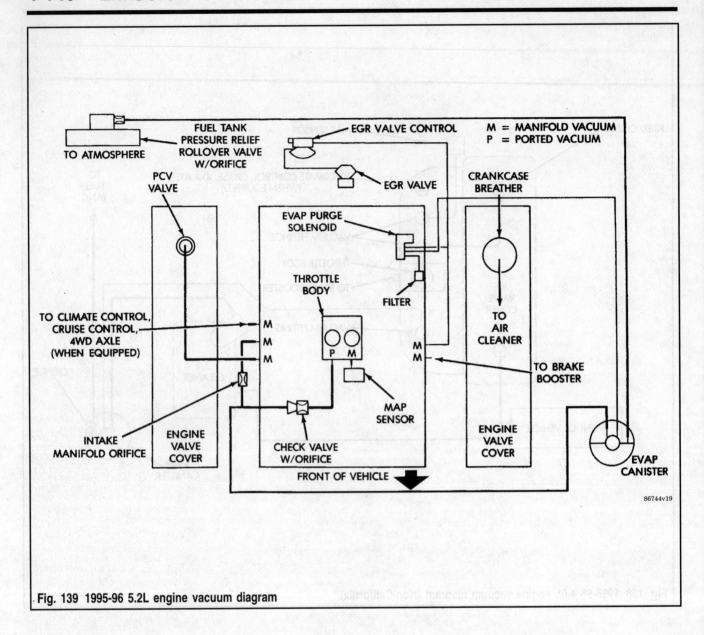

Fig. 139 1995-96 5.2L engine vacuum diagram

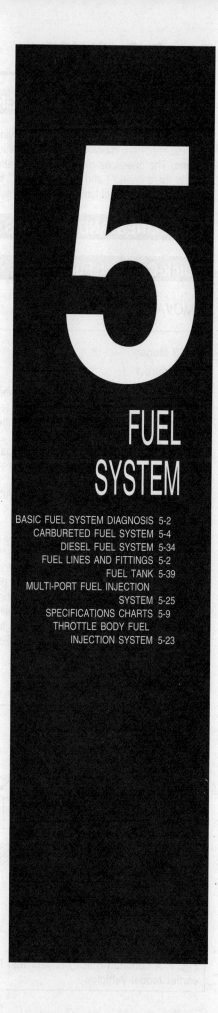

5

FUEL SYSTEM

BASIC FUEL SYSTEM DIAGNOSIS

When there is a problem starting or driving a vehicle, two of the most important checks involve the ignition and the fuel systems. The questions most mechanics attempt to answer first, "is there spark?" and "is there fuel?" will often lead to solving most basic problems. For ignition system diagnosis and testing, please refer to the information on engine electrical components and ignition systems found earlier in this manual. If the ignition system checks out (there is spark), then you must determine if the fuel system is operating properly (is there fuel?).

FUEL LINES AND FITTINGS

Quick-Connect Fuel Line

REMOVAL & INSTALLATION

1988-93 Models
▶ See Figure 1

1. Release the fuel system pressure, then separate the quick-connect fuel line tubes at the inner fender panel by squeezing the two retaining tabs against the fuel line. Pull the tube and retainer from the fitting.
2. Remove the two O-rings and the spacer from the fitting. This can be accomplished by using a paper clip or piece of heavy wire bent into an L-shape.
3. Remove the retainer from the fuel tube and discard the O-rings, spacer and retainer.

To install:
4. Install the new retainer assembly by pushing it into the quick-connect fitting until it clicks.
5. Grasp the disposable plastic plug and remove it from the replacement fitting. By removing only the plastic plug, the O-rings, spacer and retainer will remain in the fitting.
6. Push the fuel line into the fitting until a click is heard and the connection is complete. Give the fuel line connection a firm tug to verify that it is seated and locked properly.

1994-96 Models

SINGLE TAB TYPE
▶ See Figures 2 and 3

❉❉CAUTION

The O-rings and spacers of this type of fitting are not serviced separately. Do not attempt to repair damaged fuel lines or fittings. If the lines, fittings and O-rings are defective the complete fuel line assembly must be replaced.

1. Disconnect the negative battery cable.
2. Relieve the fuel system pressure as outlined in this section.
3. Clean the fitting of any dirt and grime and press the release on the side of the fitting to release the tab.
4. While pressing the release tab, pry up the pull tab with a screwdriver.
5. Raise the tab until it separates from the fitting and discard the old tab. Disconnect the fitting from the component or line being serviced.

To install:
6. Inspect the line for damage and clean the fitting and lubricate with clean engine oil.
7. Engage the fitting to the line or component it was removed from.
8. Using a new pull tab, push the tab down until it locks into place in the fitting.
9. Verify the fitting is locked in place by pulling on the tube and fitting.

86745g01

Fig. 1 A common quick connect fuel line used on earlier model vehicles

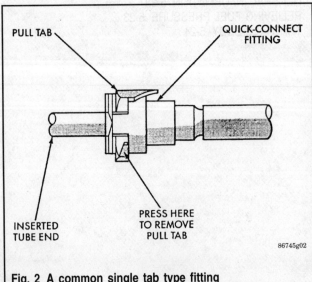

86745g02

Fig. 2 A common single tab type fitting

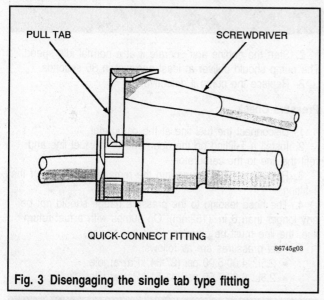

Fig. 3 Disengaging the single tab type fitting

10. Connect the negative battery cable, start the vehicle and check for leaks.

TWO-TAB TYPE

▶ See Figure 4

✵✵CAUTION

The O-rings and spacers of this type of fitting are not serviced separately. Do not attempt to repair damaged fuel lines or fittings. If the lines, fittings and O-rings are defective the complete fuel line assembly must be replaced.

1. Disconnect the negative battery cable.
2. Relieve the fuel system pressure as outlined in this section.
3. Clean the fitting of any dirt and grime.
4. Squeeze the release tabs against the sides of the fitting and pull the fitting from the component or line being serviced.

➡**The plastic retainer will stay on the component being serviced after the fitting has been disconnected.**

To install:

5. Inspect the line for damage and clean the fitting and lubricate with clean engine oil.
6. Engage the fitting to the line or component it was removed from. The connection has been made when a click is heard.
7. Verify the fitting is locked in place by pulling on the tube and fitting.
8. Connect the negative battery cable, start the vehicle and check for leaks.

PLASTIC RETAINER TYPE

▶ See Figure 5

This type of fitting can be identified by the use of a full round plastic retainer ring usually black in color.
1. Disconnect the negative battery cable.
2. Relieve the fuel system pressure as outlined in this section.

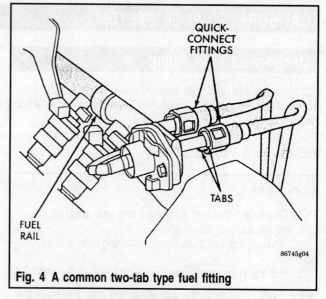

Fig. 4 A common two-tab type fuel fitting

3. Clean the fitting of any dirt and grime.
4. Release the fitting from the component or line being serviced by pushing the fitting towards the component while pushing the plastic retaining into the fitting. With the plastic ring fully depressed, pull the fitting from the component.
   To install:

➡**The plastic retainer will stay on the component being serviced after the fitting has been disconnected.**

5. Inspect the line for damage and clean the fitting and lubricate with clean engine oil.
6. Engage the fitting to the line or component it was removed from. The connection has been made when a click is felt.
7. Verify the fitting is locked in place by pulling on the tube and fitting.
8. Connect the negative battery cable, start the vehicle and check for leaks.

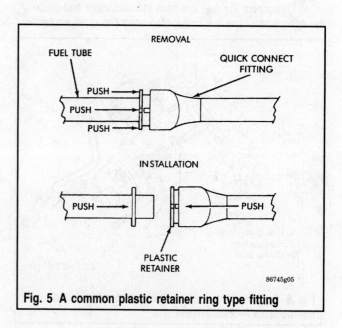

Fig. 5 A common plastic retainer ring type fitting

CARBURETED FUEL SYSTEM

Mechanical Fuel Pump

Carbureted 2.5L and 2.8L engines use a single-action stamped fuel pump that is mechanically driven by an eccentric on the camshaft.

REMOVAL & INSTALLATION

▶ See Figure 6

1. Disconnect the inlet and outlet fuel lines and, on the 2.8L engine, the fuel return line.
2. Remove the fuel pump body attaching nuts and lock washers.
3. Pull the pump and gasket or O-ring free of the engine.

➡ On the 2.8L engine, the actuating rod may fall from the engine.

To install:

4. Make sure that the mating surfaces of the fuel pump and the engine are clean.
5. Cement a new gasket to the mounting flange of the fuel pump.
6. Position the fuel pump on the engine block so that the lever of the fuel pump rests on the fuel pump cam of the camshaft.
7. Secure the fuel pump to the block with the capscrews and lock washers. tighten the capscrews to 16 ft. lbs. (21 Nm).
8. Connect the fuel lines to the fuel pump.

TESTING

Volume Check

1. Disconnect the fuel line from the carburetor and place the open end of the line into a graduated one quart container.

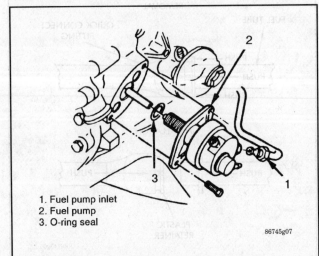

1. Fuel pump inlet
2. Fuel pump
3. O-ring seal

86745g07

Fig. 6 Exploded view of the fuel pump and related components — 2.8L engine

2. Start the engine and operate it at a normal idle speed. The pump should deliver at least one pint in 30 seconds.
3. Replace the pump if defective.

Pressure Check

1. Disconnect the fuel line at the carburetor.
2. Install a T-fitting on the open end of the fuel line and refit the line to the carburetor.
3. Plug a pressure gauge into the remaining opening of the T-fitting.
4. The hose leading to the pressure gauge should not be any longer than 6 in. (152mm). On pumps with a fuel return line, the line must be plugged. Start the engine.
5. Fuel pressures are as follows:
   • 2.5L: 4.00-5.00 psi (27-34 kPa) at idle
   • 2.8L: 6.00-7.50 psi (41-51 kPa) at idle

Carter YFA Feedback Carburetor

➡ The Carter model YFA feedback carburetor was used on the 2.5L engine.

DESCRIPTION

The Carter/Weber YFA carburetor consists of three main assemblies. The air horn contains the choke, vacuum break, choke plate duty cycle solenoid, float and assembly. The main body contains the pump diaphragm assembly, metering jet, low-speed jet, accelerator pump check ball and weight, pump bleed valve and wide open throttle switch. The throttle body contains the throttle plate, throttle shaft and lever, idle mixture screw with O-ring and a tamper-proof plug.

The duty cycle solenoid is an integral part of the YFA carburetor. The control unit operates the duty cycle solenoid to provide the proper air/fuel ratio by controlling the air flow. In open loop operation, the air supplied by the duty cycle solenoid is preprogrammed. In closed loop operation, the control unit signals the duty cycle solenoid to provide additional air to the air/fuel mixture depending upon the sensor inputs to the control unit. Air from the duty cycle solenoid is then distributed to the carburetor idle circuit and main metering circuit where it mixes with the fuel.

ADJUSTMENTS

Fast Idle Speed

▶ See Figure 7

1. Disconnect and plug the EGR valve vacuum hose at the valve.
2. Connect a tachometer to the ignition coil negative (TACH) terminal.
3. Place the automatic transmission in Park, or the manual transmission in Neutral, then start the engine and allow it to reach normal operating temperature.

4. Position the fast idle speed adjustment screw on the second step of the fast idle cam.

5. Turn the fast idle adjustment screw to obtain a fast idle speed of 2300 rpm (automatic transmission) or 2000 rpm (manual transmission). If the fast idle speed listed on the underhood emission sticker differs from the above, use the specification on the underhood sticker.

6. Allow the throttle to return to curb idle speed, then reconnect the EGR valve vacuum hose. Turn the ignition **OFF** and disconnect the tachometer.

Sole-Vac Vacuum Actuator

▶ See Figure 8

1. Connect a tachometer to the ignition coil TACH terminal.
2. Start the engine and allow it to reach normal operating temperature.
3. This adjustment is made with the automatic transmission in Drive or manual transmission in Neutral and all accessories turned **OFF**.
4. Disconnect the vacuum hose from the Sole-Vac vacuum actuator and plug. Connect an external vacuum source and apply 10-15 in. Hg (34-51 kPa) of vacuum to the actuator.
5. Adjust the idle speed to 850 rpm (auto. trans.), 950 rpm (manual trans.) using the vacuum actuator adjustment screw on the throttle lever. Use the specifications on the underhood sticker if they differ from the specifications.
6. Turn the ignition **OFF** and disconnect the tachometer and vacuum pump. The Sole-Vac curb idle speed should be adjusted following this procedure.

Curb Idle Speed

▶ See Figure 9

1. Connect a tachometer to the ignition coil TACH terminal.
2. Place the automatic transmission in Drive, or the manual transmission in Neutral.

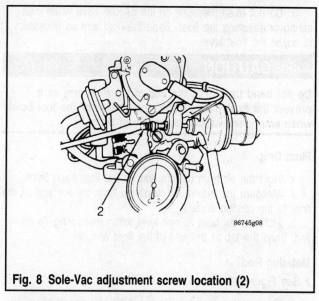

Fig. 8 Sole-Vac adjustment screw location (2)

3. Start the engine and allow it to reach normal operating temperature.
4. Disconnect and plug the vacuum hose from the actuator.
5. Adjust the hex head curb idle speed adjustment screw to 700 rpm (auto. trans.) or 750 rpm (manual trans.). Use the specifications on the underhood sticker if they differ from the above specifications.
6. Turn the ignition switch **OFF**, then disengage the tachometer and reconnect the vacuum actuator hose.

Float Level

▶ See Figure 10

1. Remove and invert the air horn assembly and check the clearance from the top of the float to the surface of the air horn with a T-scale.
2. The air horn should be held at eye level when gauging and the float arm should be resting on the needle pin.

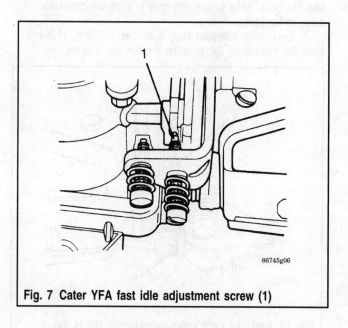

Fig. 7 Cater YFA fast idle adjustment screw (1)

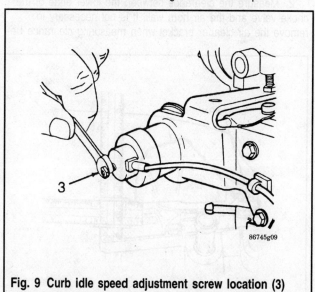

Fig. 9 Curb idle speed adjustment screw location (3)

3. Do not exert pressure on the needle valve when measuring or adjusting the float. Bend the float arm as necessary to adjust the float level.

✳✳CAUTION

Do not bend the tab at the end of the float arm as it prevent the float from striking the bottom of the fuel bowl when empty and keeps the needle in place.

Float Drop

1. Hold the air horn upright and let the float hang freely.
2. Measure the maximum clearance from the toe end of the float to the casting surface.
3. Hold the air horn at eye level when measuring To adjust, bend the tab at the end of the float arm.

Metering Rod
▶ See Figure 11

1. Remove the air horn. Back out the idle speed adjusting screw until the throttle plate is seated fully in its bore.
2. Press down on the upper end of the diaphragm shaft until the diaphragm bottoms in the vacuum chamber.
3. The metering rod should contact the bottom of the metering rod well. The lifter link at the outer end nearest the springs and at the supporting link should be bottomed.
4. Turn the rod adjusting screw until the metering rod just bottoms in the body casting. For final adjustment, turn the screw one additional turn clockwise.
5. Install the carburetor air horn and replacement gasket on the carburetor, then set the curb idle speed to specifications.

Fast Idle Cam Index
▶ See Figure 12

1. Put the fast idle screw on the second highest step of the fast idle cam, against the shoulder of the high step.
2. Measure the clearance between the lower edge of the choke valve and the air horn wall. It is not necessary to remove the air cleaner bracket when measuring clearance be-

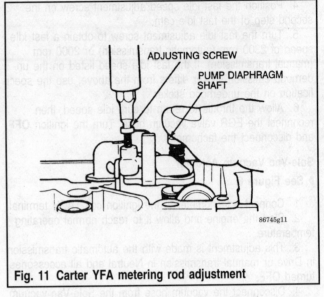

Fig. 11 Carter YFA metering rod adjustment

tween the choke valve and air horn wall, position the gauge next to the bracket.

3. Adjust by bending the choke plate connecting rod to obtain the specified clearance between the lower edge of the choke plate and the air horn wall.

Choke Unloader
▶ See Figure 13

1. Hold the throttle lever fully open and apply pressure on the choke valve toward the closed position.
2. Measure the clearance between the lower edge of the choke valve and the air horn wall. See the Specifications Chart.

➡ **DO NOT bend the unloader tang DOWN.**

3. Adjust by bending the unloader tang which contacts the fast idle cam. Bend toward the cam to increase clearance, away to decrease.
4. Ensure the unloader tang is at least 0.070 in. (1.8mm) from the main body flange when the throttle is open.

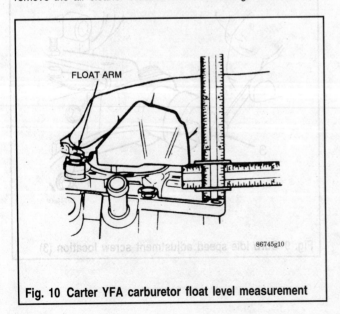

Fig. 10 Carter YFA carburetor float level measurement

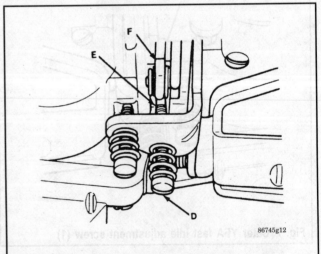

Fig. 12 Fast idle cam index adjustment. (D) is the adjusting screw; (E) is the second step of the cam (F)

5. Check for full throttle opening when throttle is operated from inside vehicle.

Automatic Choke

▶ See Figure 14

1. Loosen the choke cover retaining screws, then turn the choke cover so that the index mark on the cover lines up with the specified mark on the choke housing.

Choke Plate Pulldown

PISTON-TYPE CHOKE

▶ See Figure 15

1. Remove the air cleaner assembly.
2. Check choke cap retaining ring rivets to determine if mandrel is well below the rivet head. If mandrel appears to be at or within the rivet head thickness, drive it down or out with a $\frac{1}{16}$ in. (1.5mm) diameter punch.

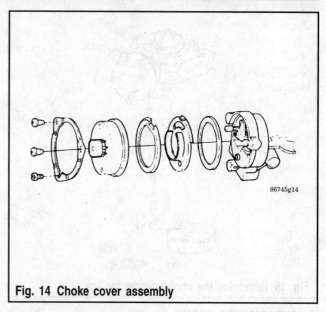

Fig. 14 Choke cover assembly

3. Use a $\frac{1}{8}$ in. (3mm) diameter drill for drilling the rivet heads. Drill into the rivet head until the rivet head comes loose from the rivet body.
4. After the rivet head is removed, drive the remaining portion of the rivet out of the hole with a $\frac{1}{8}$ in. (3mm) diameter punch.

➡ **This procedure must be followed to retain the hole size.**

5. Repeat Steps 1-4 for the remaining rivet.
6. Remove screw in the conventional manner.
7. Bend a 0.026 in. (0.66mm) diameter wire gauge at a 90° angle approximately $\frac{1}{8}$ in. (3mm) from one end. Insert the bent end of the gauge between the choke piston slot and the right hand slot in the choke housing. Rotate the choke piston lever counterclockwise until the gauge is shut in the piston slot.
8. Apply light pressure on the choke piston lever to hold the gauge in place, then measure the clearance between the lower edge of the choke plate and the carburetor bore using a drill with the diameter equal to the specified pulldown clearance.
9. Bend the choke piston lever to obtain the proper clearance.
10. Install choke cap gasket.
11. Install the locking and indexing plate.
12. Install the notched gasket.
13. Install choke cap, making certain that bi-metal loop is positioned around choke lever tang.
14. While holding cap in place, actuate choke plate to make certain bi-metal loop is properly engaged with lever tang. Set retaining clamp over choke cap and orient clamp to match holes in casting (holes are not equally spaced). Make sure retaining clamp is not upside down.
15. Place a $\frac{1}{8}$ in. diameter x $\frac{1}{2}$ in. long x $\frac{1}{4}$ in. diameter head (3mm x 12.7mm x 6mm) rivet into the rivet gun and trigger lightly to retain the rivet.
16. Press rivet fully into casting after passing through retaining clamp and pop rivet (mandrel breaks off).
17. Repeat this step for the remaining rivet.
18. Install screw in conventional manner. Tighten to 17-20 inch lbs. (1.9-2.2 Nm).

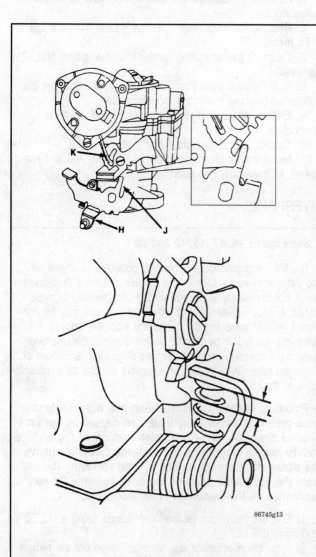

Fig. 13 Choke unloader adjustment. (H) is the throttle lever; (J) is the unloader tang; (K) is the cam; (L) is the gap

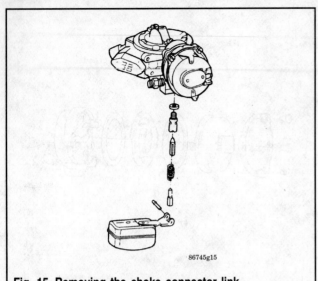

86745g15

Fig. 15 Removing the choke connector link

DIAPHRAGM-TYPE CHOKE

1. Activate the pull-down motor by applying an external vacuum source.
2. Close the choke plate as far as possible without forcing it.
3. Using a drill of the specified size, measure the clearance between the lower edge of the choke plate and the air horn wall.
4. If adjustment is necessary, bend the choke diaphragm link as required.

Choke Plate Clearance (Dechoke)

1. Remove the air cleaner assembly.
2. Hold the throttle plate fully open and close the choke plate as far as possible without forcing it. Use a drill of the proper diameter to check the clearance between the choke plate and air horn.
3. If the clearance is not within specification, adjust by bending the arm on the choke lever of the throttle lever. Bending the arm downward will decrease the clearance, and bending it upward will increase the clearance. Always recheck the clearance after making any adjustment.

Mechanical Fuel Bowl Vent

1. Start the engine and wait until it has reached normal operating temperature before proceeding.
2. Check engine idle rpm and set to specifications.
3. Check DC motor operation by opening throttle off idle. The DC motor should extend.
4. Release the throttle, and the DC motor should retract when in contact with the throttle lever.
5. Disconnect the idle speed motor in the idle position.
6. Turn engine **OFF**.
7. Open the throttle lever so that the throttle lever actuating lever does not touch the fuel bowl vent rod.
8. Close the throttle lever to the idle set position and measure the travel of the fuel bowl vent rod at point A. The distance measured represents the travel of the vent rod from where there is no contact with the actuating lever to where the actuating lever moves the vent rod to the idle set position. The

travel of the vent rod at point A should be 0.100-0.150 in. (2.5-3.8mm).
9. If adjustment is required, bend the throttle actuating lever at notch shown.
10. Reconnect the idle speed control motor.

Secondary Throttle Stop Screw

Back off the screw until it does not touch the lever. Turn the screw in until it touches the lever, then turn it an additional ¼ turn.

REMOVAL & INSTALLATION

1. Remove the air cleaner.
2. Tag and disconnect all hoses leading to the carburetor.
3. Disconnect the control shaft from the throttle lever.
4. Disengage the inline fuel filter, pullback spring and all electrical connectors.
5. Remove the carburetor mounting nuts and lift off the carburetor.
6. Remove the carburetor mounting gasket from the spacer.
To install:
7. Clean all gasket mating surfaces on the spacer and carburetor.
8. Install a new gasket on the spacer, then install the carburetor and secure it with the mounting nuts.
9. Engage all vacuum hoses, fuel lines and electrical connectors.
10. Connect the control shaft and pullback spring.
11. Install the air cleaner and adjust the curb and fast idle speed, as previously described.

OVERHAUL

▶ **See Figures 16, 17, 18, 19 and 20**

The following procedure applies to complete overhaul with the carburetor removed from the engine. A complete disassembly is not necessary when performing adjustments. In most cases, service adjustments of individual systems may be completed without removing the carburetor from the engine. A complete carburetor overhaul includes disassembly, thorough cleaning, inspection and replacement of gaskets and worn or damaged parts. When using an overhaul kit, use all applicable parts in the kit.

➡**Flooding, stumble on acceleration and other performance problems are in many instances caused by the presence of dirt, water or other foreign material in the carburetor. To help in diagnosing the problem, carefully remove the carburetor from the engine without removing the fuel from the float bowl. Examine the bowl contents for contamination as the carburetor is disassembled.**

1. Drill out the choke retainer rivet heads using a No. 30 ⅛ in. (3mm) drill bit.
2. After the rivet heads are removed, drive out the remaining portion of the rivets with a ⅛ in. (3mm) punch. This procedure must be followed exactly to retain the hole sizes.
3. Remove the screw holding the retainer.

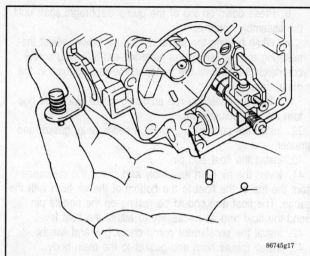

Fig. 16 Removing the accelerator pump check ball and weight

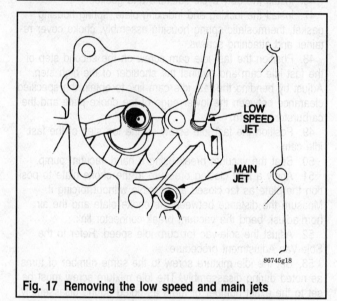

Fig. 17 Removing the low speed and main jets

4. Remove the retainer, thermostatic spring housing assembly, spring housing gasket and the locking/indexing plate.

5. Remove the vacuum break.

6. Disengage and remove the vacuum break connector link from the choke shaft lever.

7. Remove the sole-vac and the mounting bracket.

8. Remove the duty cycle solenoid from the air horn.

9. Remove the air horn attaching screws.

10. Remove the fast idle cam link.

11. Remove the air horn and gasket from the carburetor main body.

12. To remove the float from the air horn, hold the air horn bottom side up and remove the float pin and float.

13. Invert the air horn and catch the needle pin, spring and needle.

14. Remove the needle seat and gasket.

15. To remove the pump check ball and weight, turn the main body casting upside down and catch the accelerator pump check ball and weight.

16. Loosen the throttle shaft arm screw and remove the arm and pump connector link.

17. Remove the retaining screws and separate the throttle body from the main body.

18. Remove the wide open throttle switch and mounting bracket.

19. Remove the accelerator pump housing screws from the main body.

20. Lift out the pump assembly, pump lifter link and metering rod as a unit.

21. Disassemble the pump as follows:

a. Disengage the metering rod arm spring from the metering rod.

b. Remove the metering rod from the metering rod assembly.

c. Compress the upper pump spring and remove the spring retainer cup.

d. Remove the upper spring, metering rod arm assembly and pump lifter link from the pump diaphragm shaft.

e. Compress the pump diaphragm spring and remove the pump diaphragm spring retainer, spring and pump diaphragm assembly from the pump diaphragm housing.

22. Remove the low speed jet and the main metering jet.

23. Using a sharp punch, remove the accelerator pump bleed valve plug from outside the main body casting. Loosen the bleed valve screw and remove the valve.

24. Drill out and remove the tamper proof plug.

25. After removing the plug, count the number of turns required to seat the idle mixture screw lightly.

26. Remove the idle mixture screw and O-ring.

To install:

27. Thoroughly clean and inspect all components and replace any that are damaged, worn or malfunctioning. Check the idle mixture screw needle for scoring or damage and replace it if any grooves are noted.

28. Install the throttle body to the main body with the retaining screws.

29. Install the idle mixture screw.

30. Install the low speed jet and main metering jet.

31. Install the pump bleed valve and spring.

32. Install the accelerator pump assembly.

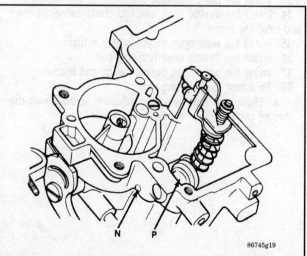

Fig. 18 Removing the accelerator pump bleed valve plug (N) and the bleed valve (P)

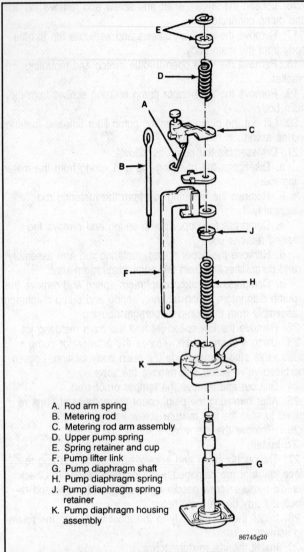

A. Rod arm spring
B. Metering rod
C. Metering rod arm assembly
D. Upper pump spring
E. Spring retainer and cup
F. Pump lifter link
G. Pump diaphragm shaft
H. Pump diaphragm spring
J. Pump diaphragm spring retainer
K. Pump diaphragm housing assembly

86745g20

Fig. 19 Exploded view of the Carter YFA accelerator assembly

33. Install the pump passage tube.
34. Install the throttle shaft arm and pump connector link and retaining screw.
35. Install the wide open throttle switch actuator.
36. Install the throttle shaft retaining bolt.
37. Install the wide open throttle switch and bracket.
38. To adjust the metering rod:
   a. Make sure the idle speed adjusting screw allows the throttle plate to close tightly in the throttle bore.

b. Press down on top of the pump diaphragm shaft until the assembly bottoms.
   c. While holding the pump diaphragm down, adjust the metering rod by turning the metering rod adjusting screw counterclockwise until the metering rod just bottoms in the main metering jet.
   d. Turn the metering rod adjusting screw clockwise one turn for final adjustment.
39. Install the needle pin, spring, needle, seat, gasket and strainer.
40. Install the float and pin.
41. Invert the air horn assembly and check the clearance from the top of the float to the bottom of the air horn with the gauge. The float arm should be resting on the needle pin. Bend the float arm as necessary to adjust the float level.
42. Install the accelerator pump check ball and weight.
43. Install the air horn and gasket to the main body.
44. Install the fast idle cam link.
45. Install the sole-vac and mounting bracket.
46. Install the duty cycle solenoid and gasket.
47. Install the locking and indexing plate, spring housing gasket, thermostatic spring housing assembly, choke cover retainer and attaching screws.
48. Position the fast idle cam screw on the second step of the fast idle cam and against the shoulder of the high step. Adjust by bending the fast idle cam link to obtain the specified clearance between the lower edge of the choke plate and the carburetor air horn.
49. Position the fast idle screw on the top step of the fast idle cam.
50. Seat the vacuum break using a hand vacuum pump.
51. Apply a light closing pressure to the choke plate to position the plate as far closed as possible without forcing it. Measure the distance between the choke plate and the air horn.adjust, bend the vacuum break connector link.
52. Adjust the sole-vac for curb idle speed. Refer to the Sole-Vac Adjustment procedure.
53. Set the idle mixture screw to the same number of turns as noted during disassembly. The idle mixture screw must be set to the exact number of turns as noted during disassembly. Install a new tamper proof plug.
54. Install the carburetor. To adjust the fast idle, turn the fast idle adjusting screw to contact the fast idle cam until the desired engine rpm is achieved. See the underhood emission control sticker for rpm specifications.

➡**Make sure the curb idle speed and mixture are adjusted to specifications before attempting the fast idle adjustment.**

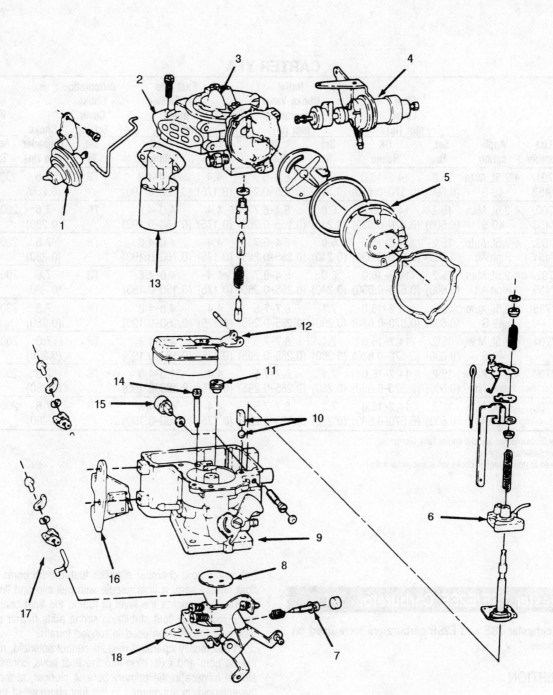

1. Vacuum break
2. Air horn
3. Choke plate
4. Sole-vac throttle positioner
5. Choke assembly
6. Accelerator pump assembly
7. Idle mixture screw with O-ring
8. Throttle plate
9. Main body
10. Accelerator pump check ball and weight
11. Main metering jet
12. Float assembly
13. Mixture control solenoid
14. Low speed jet
15. Accelerator pump vent valve
16. Wide open throttle (WOT) switch
17. Throttle shaft and lever
18. Throttle body

86745g21

Fig. 20 Exploded view of the Carter YFA carburetor components

CARTER YFA

Year	List Number	Appli-cation	Float Level mm (in)		Initial Choke Valve Clearance mm (in)		Fast Idle Cam Setting Index mm (im)		Automatic Choke Cover Setting	Choke Unloader mm (in)	Fast Idle Speed	
			Set To	OK Range	Set To	OK Range	Set To	OK Range	Set To		Set To	OK Range
1984	7701/ 7452	4-2.5L Auto 49-S	15.2 (0.600)	14.2–16.0 (0.570–0.630)	6.0 (0.240)	6.4–6.7 (0.255–0.265)	4.4 (0.175)	4.0–4.8 (0.160–0.190)	TR	7.6 (0.280)	2300*	± 100
	7700/ 7453	4-2.5L Man 49-S	15.2 (0.600)	14.2–16.0 (0.570–0.630)	6.0 (0.240)	6.4–6.7 (0.255–0.265)	4.4 (0.175)	4.0–4.8 (0.160–0.190)	TR	7.6 (0.280)	2000*	± 100
	7703/ 7454	4-2.5L Auto High Alt	15.2 (0.600)	14.2–16.0 (0.570–0.630)	6.0 (0.240)	6.4–6.7 (0.255–0.265)	4.4 (0.175)	4.0–4.8 (0.160–0.190)	TR	7.6 (0.280)	2300*	± 100
	7702/ 7455	4-2.5L Man High Alt	15.2 (0.600)	14.2–16.0 (0.570–0.630)	6.0 (0.240)	6.4–6.7 (0.255–0.265)	4.4 (0.175)	4.0–4.8 (0.160–0.190)	TR	7.6 (0.280)	2000*	± 100
1985	7705	4-2.5L Auto 49-S	15.2 (0.600)	14.2–16.0 (0.570–0.630)	7.1 (0.280)	6.7–7.5 (0.265–0.295)	4.4 (0.175)	4.0–4.8 (0.160–0.190)	TR	7.6 (0.280)	2300*	± 100
	7704	4-2.5L Man 49-S	15.2 (0.600)	14.2–16.0 (0.570–0.630)	7.1 (0.280)	6.7–7.5 (0.265–0.295)	4.4 (0.175)	4.0–4.8 (0.160–0.190)	TR	7.6 (0.280)	2000*	± 100
	7707	4-2.5L Auto High Alt	15.2 (0.600)	14.2–16.0 (0.570–0.630)	7.1 (0.280)	6.7–7.5 (0.265–0.295)	4.4 (0.175)	4.0–4.8 (0.160–0.190)	TR	7.6 (0.280)	2300*	± 100
	7706	4-2.5L Man High Alt	15.2 (0.600)	14.2–16.0 (0.570–0.630)	7.1 (0.280)	6.7–7.5 (0.265–0.295)	4.4 (0.175)	4.0–4.8 (0.160–0.190)	TR	7.6 (0.280)	2000*	± 100

*EGR Valve Disconnected and the engine fully warm.
TR—Tamper Resistant
(1) Measured at upper edge of choke valve and airhorn wall

86745c01

Rochester 2SE/E2SE Carburetor

➡The Rochester 2SE and E2SE carburetors were used on 2.8L engines.

DESCRIPTION

The Rochester Model E2SE Varajet is a two-barrel, two stage down-draft carburetor used with the Computer Command Control (CCC or C3) system of fuel control. It has three major assemblies; air horn, float bowl and throttle body; and has the following six basic operating systems:

- float
- idle
- main metering
- power
- pump
- choke

A single float chamber supplies fuel to both bores. a float, float needle seat, a float needle with pull clip and float bowl inserts, help control the level of fuel in the float chamber. On some models, a float stabilizing spring adds further control of fuel level for vehicles used in rugged terrain.

An electrically operated mixture control solenoid, mounted in the air horn and extending into the float bowl, controls the air/fuel mixture in the primary bore. A plunger, at the end of the solenoid, is submerged in the fuel chamber of the float bowl, and is controlled (or pulsed) by signals from the Electronic Control Module (ECM).

In the secondary bore, an air valve, and a tapered metering rod operating in a fixed jet, controlled the air/fuel mixture during increased engine air flow at wide open throttle.

➡The carburetor part number is stamped vertically on the float bowl in the float. Refer to this part number when servicing the carburetor.

Before checking or resetting the carburetor as the cause of poor engine performance or rough idle, check the ignition system including the distributor, timing, spark plugs and wire.

Check the air cleaner, evaporative emission system EFE system, PCV system, EGR valve and engine compression. Also inspect the intake manifold vacuum hose and connections for leaks and check the torque of the carburetor mounting bolts or nuts.

Make all adjustments with the engine at normal operating temperature, choke plate fully opened, air cleaner removed, thermac vacuum source plugged and A/C off (except if needed for a certain adjustment). Set the idle speeds only when the emission control system is in closed loop mode.

ADJUSTMENTS

Float Level

▶ See Figures 21 and 22

➡Special tools are needed for this procedure.

1. Run the engine to normal operating temperature.
2. Remove the vent stack screws and the vent stack.
3. Remove the air horn screw adjacent to the vent stack.
4. With the engine idling and the choke fully opened, carefully insert float gauge J-9789-136 or its equivalent for E2SE carburetors, or J-9789-138 or its equivalent for 2SE carburetors, into the air horn screw hole and vent hole.
5. Allow the gauge to rest freely on the float. Do not press down on the float!
6. With the gauge at eye level, observe the mark that aligns with the top of the casting at the vent hole. The float level should be within 0.06 in. (1.5mm) of the specification listed in the chart. If not, remove the air horn and adjust as follows:

   a. Hold the retainer pin firmly in place and push the float down, lightly, against the inlet needle.

   b. Using an adjustable T-scale, at a point ³/₁₆ in. (4.8mm) from the end of the float, at the toe, measure the distance from the float bowl top surface (gasket removed) to the top of the float at the toe. If the distance isn't as specified in the Chart, remove the float and bend the float arm as necessary.

Fast Idle Speed

▶ See Figure 23

1. Place the fast idle screw on the high step of the fast idle cam.
2. Disconnect and plug the EGR valve hose and the canister purge line at the canister.
3. Set the parking brake firmly and start the engine. Place the transmission in Neutral (manual) or Park (automatic).
4. Turn the fast idle screw in or out to obtain the specified fast idle speed. Refer to the underhood emission sticker for fast idle speed specifications.
5. Once all adjustments are complete, reconnect the EGR valve hose and the canister purge line at the canister.

Electric Choke Test

1. Check voltage at the choke heater connection with the engine running. If voltage is 12-15 volts, replace the electric choke unit.

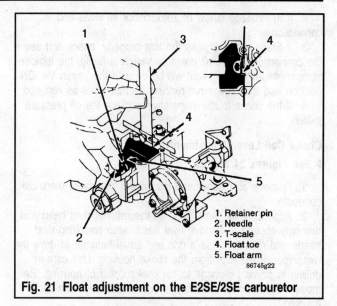

1. Retainer pin
2. Needle
3. T-scale
4. Float toe
5. Float arm

86745g22

Fig. 21 Float adjustment on the E2SE/2SE carburetor

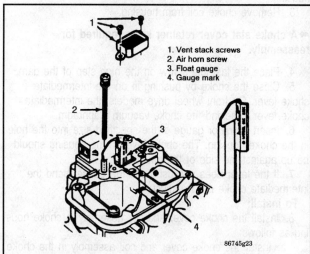

1. Vent stack screws
2. Air horn screw
3. Float gauge
4. Gauge mark

86745g23

Fig. 22 Measuring float clearance on the E2SE/2SE carburetor

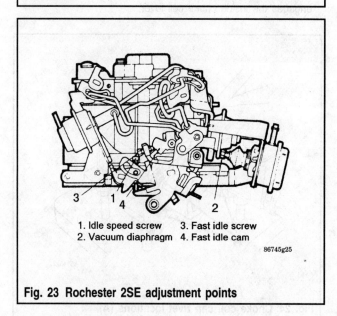

1. Idle speed screw   3. Fast idle screw
2. Vacuum diaphragm   4. Fast idle cam

86745g25

Fig. 23 Rochester 2SE adjustment points

2. If the voltage is low or zero, check all wires and connections.

3. If Steps 1 and 2 pass the test properly, check and see if the connection on the oil pressure switch is faulty, the temperature pressure warning light will be off with the key in the **ON** position and the engine not running. Repair wires as required.

4. If the choke is still inoperative, replace the oil pressure switch.

Choke Coil Lever Adjustment

▶ **See Figures 24 and 25**

1. Remove air cleaner and disconnect the choke electrical connector.

2. Align a $^5/_{32}$ in. (4mm) drill on the retainer rivet head and drill only enough to remove rivet head. After removing rivet heads and retainers, use a drift and small hammer to drive the remainder of the rivet from the choke housing. Use care in drilling to prevent damage to the choke cover or housing. Remove the three rivets and choke cover assembly from choke housing.

3. Remove choke coil from housing.

➡ **A choke stat cover retainer kit is required for reassembly.**

4. Place the fast idle screw on the high step of the dam.

5. Close the choke by pushing in on the intermediate choke lever. On front wheel drive models, the intermediate choke lever is behind the choke vacuum diaphragm.

6. Insert a drill or gauge of the specified size into the hole in the choke housing. The choke lever in the housing should be up against the side of the gauge.

7. If the lever does not just touch the gauge, bend the intermediate choke rod to adjust.

To install:

8. Install the choke cover and coil assembly in choke housing as follows:

   a. Install the choke cover and coil assembly in the choke housing, aligning notch in cover with raised casting projection on housing cover flange. Make sure coil pickup tank engages the inside choke coil lever.

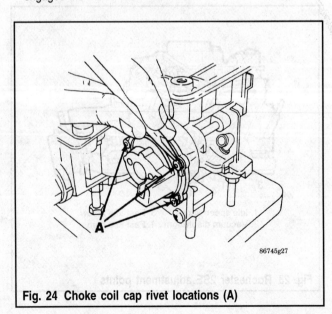

Fig. 24 Choke coil cap rivet locations (A)

86745g27

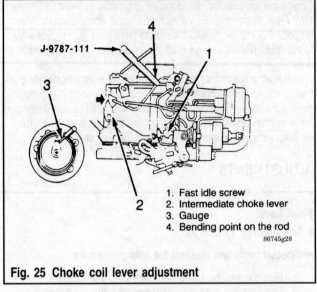

1. Fast idle screw
2. Intermediate choke lever
3. Gauge
4. Bending point on the rod

86745g28

Fig. 25 Choke coil lever adjustment

   b. A choke cover retainer kit is required to attach the choke cover to the choke housing. Install a suitable blind rivet installing tool.

9. Engage choke electrical connector.

10. Start engine, check operation of choke and then install the air cleaner.

Electric Choke Setting

This procedure is only for those carburetors with choke covers retained by screws. Riveted choke covers are preset and non-adjustable.

1. Loosen the three retaining screws.

2. Place the fast idle screw on the high step of the cam.

3. Rotate the choke cover to align the cover mark with the specified housing mark.

➡ **The specification "index" which appears in the specification table refers to the mark between "1 notch lean" and "1 notch rich".**

Secondary Lockout Adjustment

1. Pull the choke wide open by pushing out on the intermediate choke lever.

2. Open the throttle until the end of the secondary actuating lever is opposite the toe of the lockout lever.

3. Gauge clearance between the lockout lever and secondary lever should be as specified.

4. To adjust, bend the lockout lever where it contacts the fast idle cam.

Secondary Vacuum Break TVS Test

The secondary vacuum break Thermal Vacuum Switch (TVS), located in the air cleaner, improves cold starting and cold driveability by sensing carburetor air inlet temperature to control the carburetor secondary vacuum break.

1. With engine at normal operating temperature, the Thermal Vacuum Switch (TVS) must be open (air cleaner cover on).

2. Apply either engine or auxiliary vacuum to the TVS inlet port and check for vacuum at the outlet port (outlet port connects to secondary vacuum break).

3. If there is no vacuum, check air cleaner assembly for leaks, thermostatic air cleaner vacuum hoses and/or replace the TVS. Replace the TVS as follows:

    a. Remove air cleaner cover and element.

    b. Disconnect vacuum hoses.

    c. Remove clip from TVS and remove TVS.

    d. Install new TVS and replace clip.

    e. Reconnect vacuum hoses (refer to Vehicle Emission Control Information Label).

    f. Install air cleaner cover and element.

Idle Stop Solenoid Test

The solenoid should be checked to assure that the solenoid plunger extends when the solenoid is energized. an inoperative solenoid could cause stalling or a rough idle when hot, and should be replaced as necessary.

1. Turn the ignition **ON** , but do not start engine. Position transmission lever in Drive (A/T) or Neutral (M/T). On vehicles equipped with air conditioning, A/C switch must be on.

2. Open and close throttle. The solenoid plunger should retract from throttle lever. Disconnect the wire at the solenoid, the solenoid plunger should retract from the throttle lever.

3. Connect solenoid wire and the plunger should move out and contact the throttle lever. the solenoid may not be strong enough to open the throttle, but the plunger should move.

4. If the plunger does not move in and out as the wire is disconnected and connected, check the voltage feed wire:

    a. If voltage is 12-15 volts, replace the solenoid.

    b. If voltage is low or zero, locate the cause of the open circuit in the solenoid feed wire and repair.

5. If necessary to replace the idle stop, proceed as follows.

    a. Remove carburetor air cleaner.

    b. Disengage electrical connector at the solenoid.

    c. Unfasten the large retaining nut, tabbed lock washer and remove the solenoid.

    d. Install the solenoid and retaining nut, bending the lock tabs against nut flats.

    e. Engage electrical connector.

    f. Install air cleaner and adjust idle speed as necessary.

Carburetor Pre-Set Procedure

▶ See Figures 26 and 27

1. Remove the carburetor from the engine following normal service procedures to gain access to the plug covering the idle mixture needle.

2. To remove the plug, make two parallel cuts in the throttle body, one on each side of the plug, with a hacksaw. There is a locator point marking the casting at the plug. The cuts should extend down to the steel plug, but should not extend more than 1/8 in. (3mm) beyond the locator point.

3. Place a flat punch at a point near the ends of the saw cuts the throttle body. Hold the punch at a 45° angle and drive it into the throttle body until the casting breaks away and exposes the steel plug. Hold a center punch in the vertical position and drive it into the plug, then hold the punch at a 45° angle and drive the plug out of the housing. The hardened steel plug will shatter rather than remain intact. It is not necessary to remove the plug completely; instead, remove the loose pieces, then turn the idle mixture needle in until lightly seated and back out 4 turns.

4. If the plug in air horn covering the idle air has been removed replace air horn. If plug is still in place, do not remove plug.

5. Remove vent stack screen assembly to gain access to lean mixture screw. (Be sure to reinstall vent stack screen assembly after adjustment).

6. Using tool J-28696-10 BT 7928 or equivalent, turn lean mixture screw in until lightly bottomed and back out 2½ turns.

7. Reinstall the carburetor on the engine and perform the following:

    a. Do not install air cleaner and gasket.

    b. Disconnect the bowl vent line at carburetor.

    c. Disconnect the EGR valve hose and canister purge hose at the carburetor and cap the carburetor ports.

    d. Refer to Vehicle Emission Control Information Label and observe hose from sensor and secondary vacuum break TVS. Disconnect hose at temperature sensor on air cleaner and plug open hose.

    e. Connect the positive lead of a dwell meter to the mixture control solenoid test lead (green connector). Connect the other meter lead to ground. Set dwell meter to 6 cylinder position. Connect a tachometer to distributor lead (brown connector). Tachometer should be connected to the distributor side of the tach filter if vehicle is equipped with a tachometer.

    f. Block the drive wheels.

    g. Place the transmission in Park (automatic transmission) or Neutral (manual transmission) and set the parking brake.

Mixture Adjustment

▶ See Figure 28

1. Perform carburetor pre-set procedure.

2. Run engine on high step of fast idle cam until engine cooling fan starts to cycle (at least three minutes and until in closed loop).

3. Run the engine at 3000 rpm and adjust the lean mixture screw slowly in small increments allowing time for the dwell to stabilize after turning the screw to obtain an average dwell of 35°.

4. If dwell is too low, back screw out, if too high, turn it in.

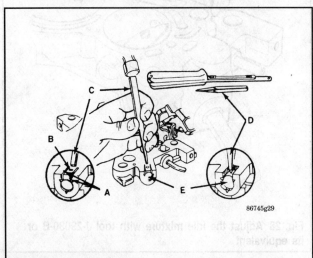

86745g29

Fig. 26 Removing the idle mixture screw cover on the 2SE/E2SE carburetor

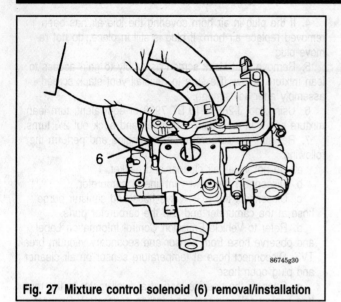

Fig. 27 Mixture control solenoid (6) removal/installation

5. If unable to adjust to specifications, inspect main metering circuit for leaks, restrictions, etc.

6. The dwell reading of the M/C solenoid is used to determine calibration and is sensitive to changes in fuel mixture caused by heat, air leaks, etc. While idling, it is normal for the dwell to increase and decrease fairly constantly over a relatively narrow range, such as 5°. However, it may occasionally vary be as much as 10-15° momentarily due to temporary mixture changes.

7. The dwell reading specified is the average of the most consistent variation. The engine must be allowed a few moments to stabilize at idle or 3000 rpm as applicable before taking a dwell reading. Return to idle.

8. Adjust the idle mixture screw to obtain an average dwell of 25° with cooling fan in off cycle.

9. If reading is too low, back screw out. If too high, turn it in. Allow time for reading to stabilize after each adjustment.

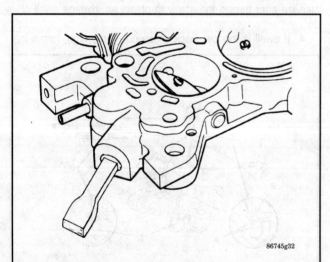

Fig. 28 Adjust the idle mixture with tool J-29030-B or its equivalent

Adjustment is very sensitive. Make final check with adjusting tool removed.

10. If unable to adjust to specifications, inspect idle system for leaks, restrictions, etc.

11. Disconnect mixture control solenoid when cooling fan is in off cycle and check for an rpm change of at least 50 rpm. If rpm does not change enough, inspect idle air bleed circuit for restrictions, leaks, etc.

12. Run engine at 3000 rpm for a few moments and note dwell reading. Dwell should be varying with an average reading of 35°. If not at 35° average dwell, reset the lean mixture screw as per Step 3. Then reset the idle mixture screw to obtain 25° dwell as per Step 5.

13. If at 35° average dwell, reconnect the systems disconnected earlier (purge and vent hoses, EGR valve, etc.), reinstall vent screen and set idle speed to specifications.

REMOVAL & INSTALLATION

Always replace all internal gaskets that are removed. Base gasket should be inspected and replaced only if damaged. Flooding, stumble on acceleration and other performance complaints are in many instances, caused by presence of dirt, water, or other foreign matter in carburetor. To aid in diagnosis, carburetor should be carefully removed from the engine without draining fuel from bowl. Contents of the fuel bowl may then be examined for contamination as the carburetor is disassembled. Be sure to check the fuel filter.

1. Remove the air cleaner and gasket.
2. Disconnect the fuel pipe and vacuum lines.
3. Disengage the electrical connectors.
4. Disconnect the accelerator linkage.
5. If equipped with automatic transmission, disconnect the downshift cable.
6. If equipped with cruise control, disconnect the linkage.
7. Remove the carburetor attaching bolts.
8. Remove the carburetor and EFE heater/insulator (if used).
9. Fill the carburetor bowl before installing carburetor. A small supply of fuel will enable the carburetor to be filled and the operation of the float and inlet needle and seat to be checked.
10. Operate throttle lever several times and check discharge from pump jets before installing carburetor.

To install:

11. Inspect EFE heater/insulator for damage. Be certain throttle body and EFE heater/insulator surfaces are clean.
12. Install EFE heater/insulator.
13. Install the carburetor and tighten the nuts alternately to the correct torque.
14. Connect the downshift cable as required.
15. Connect the cruise control cable as required.
16. Connect the accelerator linkage.
17. Engage the electrical connections.
18. Connect the fuel pipes and vacuum hoses.
19. Check the base (slow) and fast idle.
20. Install the air cleaner.

DISASSEMBLY

Air Horn

▶ **See Figures 29 and 30**

1. Invert the carburetor, then remove the plug covering the idle mixture needle as previously described.

2. Install the carburetor in a suitable holding device.

3. Remove the primary and secondary vacuum break assemblies. Be sure to take note of the linkage positions for installation.

4. Remove the three screws from the mixture control solenoid.

5. Remove the mixture control solenoid with gasket and discard the gasket.

6. Unfasten the two screws from the vent stack and remove the vent stack.

7. Remove the intermediate choke shaft link retainer at the choke lever and discard it.

8. Remove the choke link and bushing from choke lever and save the bushing.

9. Remove the retainer and bushing from the fast idle cam link and discard the retainer.

➡ **Do not remove fast idle cam screw and cam from the float bowl. If removed, the cam might not operate properly when reassembled. If needed, a replacement float bowl will include a secondary locknut lever, fast idle cam, and cam screw.**

10. Remove the retainer from the pump link. Do not remove the screw attaching the pump lever to the air horn assembly. When reassembled, the screw might not hold properly.

11. Unfasten the seven screw assemblies of various length that retain the air horn to the carburetor and remove the air horn assembly. Tilt the air horn to disconnect fast idle cam link from the slot in fast idle cam and the pump link from the hole in the pump lever.

12. Remove the cam link from the choke lever. Be sure to line up the "squirt" on the link with the slot in the lever.

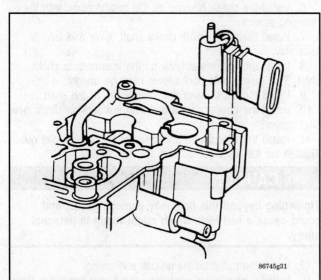

Fig. 29 Throttle position sensor removal/installation

86745g31

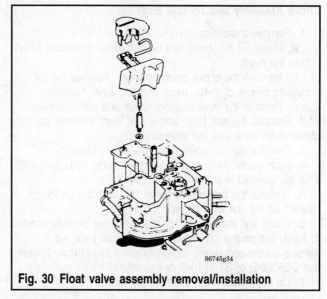

Fig. 30 Float valve assembly removal/installation

86745g34

13. Invert the air horn and remove the TPS actuator plunger. The TPS adjusting screw and plug should not be removed.

14. Remove the stakings that holds the TPS plunger seal retainer and pump stem seal retainer.

15. Remove the retainers and seals and discard them.

16. Further disassembly of the air horn is not required for cleaning purposes. The choke valve and choke valve screws, the air valve and air valve shaft should not be removed.

➡ **Do not turn the secondary metering rod adjusting screw. The rod could come out of jet and possibly cause damage.**

Float Bowl

1. Remove the accelerator pump, air horn gasket and pump return spring.

2. Remove the Throttle Position Sensor (TPS) assembly and spring. Inspect the TPS connector wires for broken insulation which could cause grounding of the TPS.

3. Remove the upper insert and the hinge pin.

4. Remove the float and lever assembly with the float stabilizing spring if used.

5. Remove the float needle and pull clip.

6. Remove the lower insert, if used.

7. Remove the float needle seat and seat gasket.

8. Remove the jet and lean mixture needle assembly.

➡ **Do not remove or change the preset adjustment of calibration needle in the metering jet unless the Computer Command Control system performance check requires it.**

9. Remove the pump discharge spring guide, using a suitable slide hammer puller only.

➡ **Do not pry the guide. Damage could occur to the sealing surfaces, and could require replacement of the float bowl.**

10. Remove the spring and check ball, by inverting the bowl and catching them as they fall out.

11. Remove the fuel inlet nut and the fuel filter spring.

12. Remove the fuel filter assembly and discard it.

13. Remove the filter gasket and discard it.

Choke Assembly and Throttle Body

1. Remove the choke cover as follows:

a. Use a $5/32$ in. (4mm) drill bit to remove the heads (only) from the rivets.

b. Remove the choke cover retainers. Remove the remaining pieces of rivets, using drift and small hammer.

c. Remove the electric choke cover and stat assembly.

2. Remove the stat lever screw, stat lever, intermediate choke shaft, lever and link assembly.

3. Remove the two screws and the choke housing.

4. Remove the four screws, and the throttle body assembly from the inverted float bowl.

5. Remove the gasket and pump link, and line up the "squirt" on the link with the slot in the lever.

6. Count and make a record of the number of turns needed to lightly bottom the idle mixture needle, then back out and remove needle and spring assembly using Idle Mixture Socket tool J-29030-B or BT-7610-B or equivalent.

7. Do not disassemble throttle body further.

INSPECTION AND CLEANING

1. Place the metal parts in immersion carburetor cleaner.

➡ Do not immerse idle stop solenoid, mixture control solenoid, throttle lever actuator, TPS, electric choke, rubber and plastic parts, diaphragms, and pump in the cleaner, as they may be damaged. Plastic bushing in throttle lever will withstand normal cleaning.

2. Blow dry the parts with shop air. Be sure all fuel and air passages are free of burrs and dirt. Do not pass drill bits or wires through jets and passages.

3. Be sure to check the mating surfaces of casting for damage. Replace if necessary. Check for holes in levers for wear or out-of-round conditions. Check the bushings for damage and excessive wear. Replace if necessary.

REASSEMBLY

▶ See Figures 31, 32, 33, 34 and 35

1. Install the mixture needle and spring assembly using Idle mixture socket tool J-29030-B or BT-7610-B or their equivalents. Lightly bottom the needle and back it out the number of turns recorded during removal, as a preliminary adjustment. Refer to idle mixture adjustment procedure in this section for the final idle mixture adjustment.

2. Install the pump link and a new gasket on the inverted float bowl.

3. Install the throttle body to the float bowl assembly and finger tighten the four retaining screws. If the secondary actuating lever engages the lockout lever, and linkage moves without binding, tighten retaining screws.

4. If the float bowl assembly was replaced, stamp or engrave the model number on the new float bowl in same location as on old bowl.

5. Place the throttle body and float bowl together on a suitable carburetor holding device.

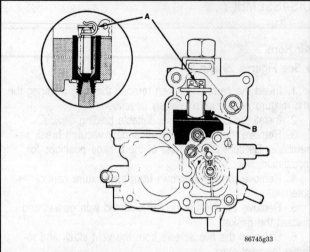

Fig. 31 Installation of the float retaining pin (A) and the float (B) on the 2SE/E2SE carburetor

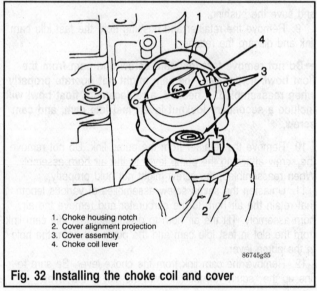

1. Choke housing notch
2. Cover alignment projection
3. Cover assembly
4. Choke coil lever

86745g35

Fig. 32 Installing the choke coil and cover

6. Install the choke housing on the throttle body, with the retaining screws.

7. Install the intermediate choke shaft, lever and link assembly.

8. Install the choke stat lever on the intermediate choke shaft. The intermediate choke lever must be upright.

9. Install the choke lever attaching screw in the shaft.

10. Install the gasket on the fuel inlet nut and install the new filter assembly in the nut.

11. Install the filter spring and then install the fuel inlet nut. Tighten the fuel inlet nut to 18 ft. lbs. (24 Nm).

❉❉CAUTION

Tightening beyond this limit may damage gasket and could cause a fuel leak, which might result in personal injury.

12. Install the pump discharge ball and spring.

13. Install a new spring guide and tap it until the top is flush with the bowl casting.

14. Install the needle seat with gasket. If used, lower the insert.

➥**Only adjust the lean mixture needle screw if it was removed or touched during disassembly.**

15. Install the jet and lean mixture needle assembly. Using lean mixture adjusting tool J-28696-10 or BT-7928 or their equivalents, lightly bottom the lean mixture needle. Back it out 2½ turns, as a preliminary adjustment.

16. Bend the float lever upward slightly at the notch.

17. If used, install the float stabilizing spring on float and the hinge pin in float lever, with ends toward the pump well.

18. Install the needle with pull clip assembly on the edge of the float lever and the float and lever assembly in float bowl.

➥**Adjust the float level using Float Level T-Scale J9789-90 or BT-8037 or equivalent.**

19. Install the upper insert over the hinge pin, with the top flush with the bowl.

20. Install the TPS spring and the TPS assembly. The parts must be below the surface of the bowl.

21. Install the gasket over the dowels.

22. Install the spring and pump assembly.

23. Install a new pump stem seal with the lip facing outside of carburetor and install the retainer. Be sure to stake it at new locations.

24. Install a new TPS actuator plunger seal with the lip facing outside of carburetor and the retainer. Be sure to stake it at new locations.

25. Install the TPS plunger through the seal in the air horn. Use lithium base grease, liberally to pin, if used, where contacted by spring.

26. Install the fast idle cam link in the choke lever. Be sure to line-up the "squirt" on the link with the slot in the lever.

27. Rotate the cam to the highest position. The lower end of the fast idle cam link goes in cam slot, and the pump link end goes into the hole in the lever.

28. Hold the pump down, and then lower the air horn assembly onto the float bowl. Be sure to guide the pump stem through the seal.

29. Install one of the air horn retaining screws finger-tight to hold the air horn in place.

30. Install the cam link in the slot of the cam. Install a new bushing and retainer to the link, with the large end of bushing facing the retainer. Check for freedom of movement.

31. Install the rest of the air horn retaining screws.

32. Install the spacer and a new seal, lightly coat the seal with automatic transmission fluid. Assemble the seal on the solenoid stem, touching the spacer.

33. Install a new retainer and a new gasket on the air horn.

34. Install the mixture control solenoid lining up the stem with the recess in the bowl.

35. Install the solenoid retaining screws.

36. Install the vent stack, with two retaining screws, (unless lean mixture needle requires on-vehicle adjustment).

37. Install a new retainer on the pump link. Adjust the air valve spring, if adjustable.

38. Install the bushing on the choke link. With the intermediate choke lever upright, install the link in the choke lever hole.

39. Install the new link retainer.

40. The following procedures is for reassembly of any small components that have been removed from the carburetor, if part replacement is necessary or for any other reason.

    a. Install the idle stop solenoid, retainer and nut to the secondary side vacuum break bracket. Bend the retainer tab to secure nut.

    b. Install the bushing to the link and the link to the vacuum break plunger. Install the retainer to the link.

    c. Rotate the assembly, insert the end of the link in the upper slot of the choke lever. Install the bracket screws.

    d. Install the idle speed device. retainer and nut to the primary side vacuum break bracket. Bend the retainer tab to secure the nut.

    e. Install the bushing to the vacuum break link.

    f. Install the link to vacuum break plunger.

    g. Install the retainer to the link and the bushing to the air valve link.

    h. Install the link to the plunger and the retainer to the link.

41. Rotate the vacuum break assembly (primary side) and insert the end of the air valve link into the air valve lever and the vacuum break link into the lower slot of the choke lever.

42. Install the bracket screws, vacuum hose between the throttle body tube and the vacuum break assembly.

43. Install the choke thermostat lever.

44. Install the choke cover and thermostat assembly in the choke housing.

45. If the thermostat has a "trap" (box-shaped pick-up tang), the trap surrounds the lever.

46. Line up the notch in the cover with projection on the housing flange. Install the retainers and rivets with rivet tool. If necessary, use an adapter. Adjust the choke as previously described.

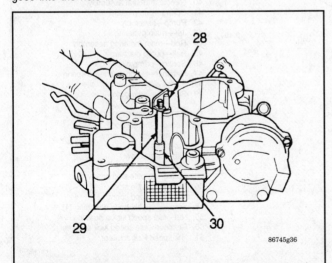

86745g36

Fig. 33 Installation of the power piston (28), metering rod (29) and metering jet (30)

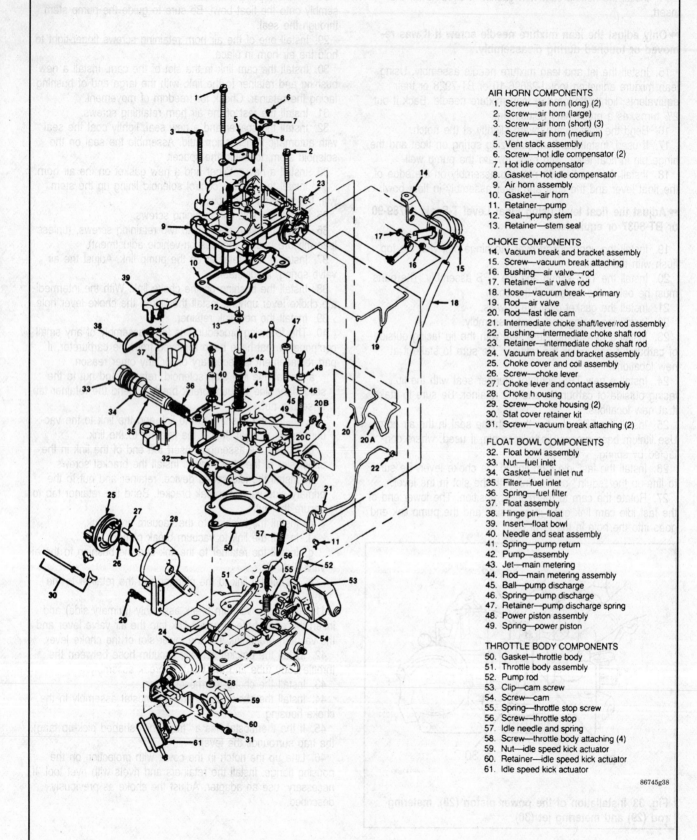

AIR HORN COMPONENTS
1. Screw—air horn (long) (2)
2. Screw—air horn (large)
3. Screw—air horn (short) (3)
4. Screw—air horn (medium)
5. Vent stack assembly
6. Screw—hot idle compensator (2)
7. Hot idle compensator
8. Gasket—hot idle compensator
9. Air horn assembly
10. Gasket—air horn
11. Retainer—pump
12. Seal—pump stem
13. Retainer—stem seal

CHOKE COMPONENTS
14. Vacuum break and bracket assembly
15. Screw—vacuum break attaching
16. Bushing—air valve—rod
17. Retainer—air valve rod
18. Hose—vacuum break—primary
19. Rod—air valve
20. Rod—fast idle cam
21. Intermediate choke shaft/lever/rod assembly
22. Bushing—intermediate choke shaft rod
23. Retainer—intermediate choke shaft rod
24. Vacuum break and bracket assembly
25. Choke cover and coil assembly
26. Screw—choke lever
27. Choke lever and contact assembly
28. Choke h ousing
29. Screw—choke housing (2)
30. Stat cover retainer kit
31. Screw—vacuum break attaching (2)

FLOAT BOWL COMPONENTS
32. Float bowl assembly
33. Nut—fuel inlet
34. Gasket—fuel inlet nut
35. Filter—fuel inlet
36. Spring—fuel filter
37. Float assembly
38. Hinge pin—float
39. Insert—float bowl
40. Needle and seat assembly
41. Spring—pump return
42. Pump—assembly
43. Jet—main metering
44. Rod—main metering assembly
45. Ball—pump discharge
46. Spring—pump discharge
47. Retainer—pump discharge spring
48. Power piston assembly
49. Spring—power piston

THROTTLE BODY COMPONENTS
50. Gasket—throttle body
51. Throttle body assembly
52. Pump rod
53. Clip—cam screw
54. Screw—cam
55. Spring—throttle stop screw
56. Screw—throttle stop
57. Idle needle and spring
58. Screw—throttle body attaching (4)
59. Nut—idle speed kick actuator
60. Retainer—idle speed kick actuator
61. Idle speed kick actuator

86745g38

Fig. 34 Exploded view of the Rochester 2SE carburetor and components

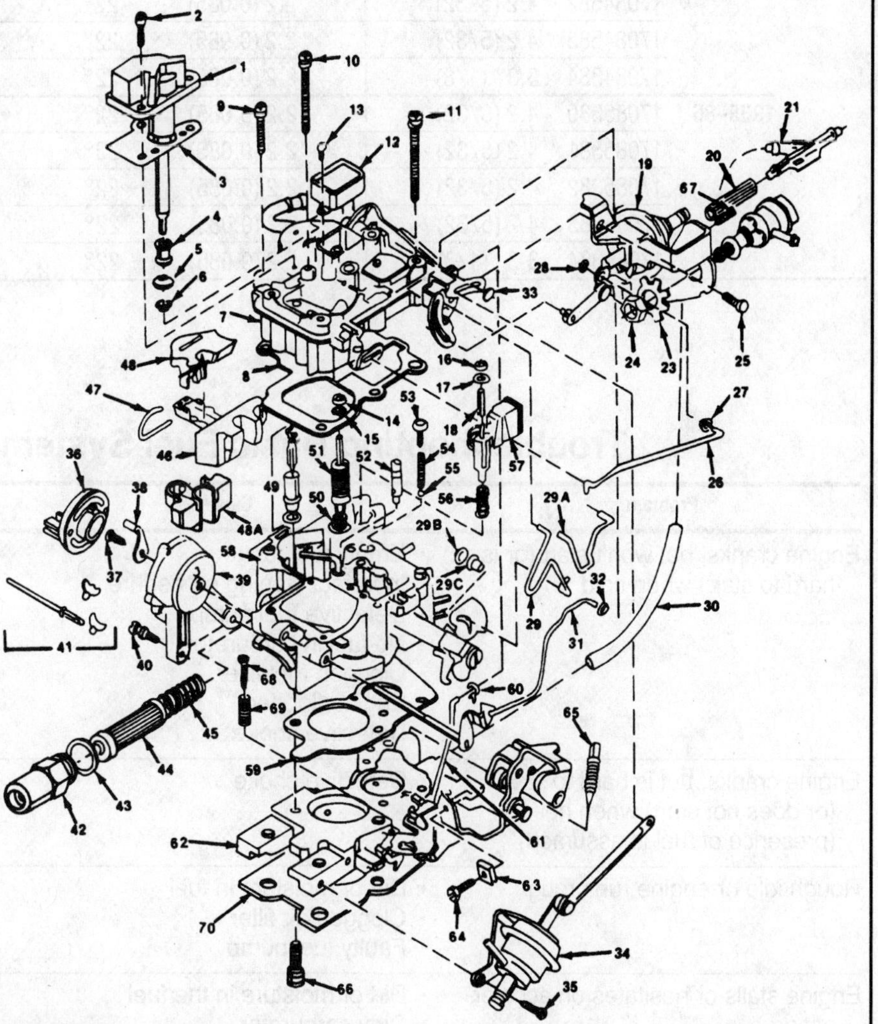

AIR HORN PARTS
1. Mixture control (M/C) solenoid
2. Screw assembly—solenoid attaching
3. Gasket—M/C solenoid to air horn
4. Spacer—M/C solenoid
5. Seal—M/C solenoid to float bowl
6. Retainer—M/C solenoid seal
7. Air horn assembly
8. Gasket—air horn to float bowl
9. Screw—air horn to float bowl (short)
10. Screw—air horn to float bowl (long)
11. Screw—air horn to float bowl (large)
12. Vent stack and screen assembly
13. Screw—vent stack attaching
14. Seal—pump stem
15. Retainer—pump stem seal
16. Seal—T.P.S. plunger
17. Retainer—T.P.S. actuator

CHOKE PARTS
19. Vacuum break and bracket assembly—primary
20. Hose—vacuum break primary
21. Tee—vacuum break
22. Solenoid—idle speed
23. Retainer—idle speed solenoid
24. Nut—idle speed solenoid attaching
25. Screw—vacuum break bracket attaching
26. Link—air valve
27. Bushing—air valve link
28. Retainer—air valve link
29. Link—fast idle cam
29A. Link—fast idle cam
29B. Link—fast idle cam
29C. Bushing—link
30. Hose—vacuum break
31. Intermediate choke shaft/lever/link assembly
32. Bushing—intermediate choke link
33. Retainer—intermediate choke link
34. Vacuum break and link assembly—secondary
35. Screw—vacuum break attaching
36. Electric choke—cover and coil assembly
37. Screw—choke lever attaching
38. Choke coil lever assembly
39. Choke housing
40. Screw—choke housing attaching
41. Choke cover retainer kit
67. Screw—vacuum break bracket attaching

FLOAT BOWL PARTS
42. Nut—fuel inlet
43. Gasket—fuel inlet nut
44. Filter—fuel inlet
45. Spring—fuel filter
46. Float and lever assembly
47. Hinge pin—float
48. Upper insert—float bowl
48A. Lower insert—float bowl
49. Needle and seat assembly
50. Spring—pump return
51. Pump plunger assembly
52. Primary metering jet assembly
53. Retainer—pump discharge ball
54. Spring—pump discharge
55. Ball—pump discharge
56. Spring—T.P.S. adjusting
57. Sensor—throttle position (TPS)
58. Float bowl assembly
59. Gasket—float bowl

THROTTLE BODY PARTS
60. Retainer—pump link
61. Link—pump
62. Throttle body assembly
63. Clip—cam screw
64. Screw—fast idle cam
65. Idle needle and spring assembly
66. Screw—throttle body to float bowl
68. Screw—idle stop
69. Spring—idle stop screw
70. Gasket—insulator flange

86745g39

Fig. 35 Exploded view of the Rochester E2SE carburetor and components

ROCHESTER 2SE/E2SE

Engine	Year	Carburetor Number	Float Level mm (in)	Air Valve Spring (Turns)	Choke Coil Lever mm (in)	Fast Idle Cam (Choke Rod) 2nd Step	Vacuum Break Primary	Air Valve Rod	Vacuum Break Secondary	Unloader
6-2.8L	1984	17084581	4.2 (5/32)	1	2.2 (0.085)	22°	26°	1°	32°	40°
		17084580	4.2 (5/32)	1	2.2 (0.085)	22°	26°	1°	32°	40°
		17084582	4.2 (5/32)	1	2.2 (0.085)	22°	26°	1°	32°	40°
		17084583	4.2 (5/32)	1	2.2 (0.085)	22°	26°	1°	32°	40°
		17084384	3.3 (1/8)	1	2.2 (0.085)	22°	25°	1°	30°	40°
	1985–86	17085380	4.2 (5/32)	1	2.2 (0.085)	22°	26°	1°	32°	40°
		17085381	4.2 (5/32)	1	2.2 (0.085)	22°	26°	1°	32°	40°
		17085382	4.2 (5/32)	1	2.2 (0.085)	22°	26°	1°	32°	40°
		17085383	4.2 (5/32)	1	2.2 (0.085)	22°	26°	1°	32°	40°
		17085384	3.3 (1/8)	1	2.2 (0.085)	22°	25°	1°	30°	40°

86745c02

Troubleshooting Basic Fuel System Problems

Problem	Cause	Solution
Engine cranks, but won't start (or is hard to start) when cold	• Empty fuel tank • Incorrect starting procedure • Defective fuel pump • No fuel in carburetor • Clogged fuel filter • Engine flooded • Defective choke	• Check for fuel in tank • Follow correct procedure • Check pump output • Check for fuel in the carburetor • Replace fuel filter • Wait 15 minutes; try again • Check choke plate
Engine cranks, but is hard to start (or does not start) when hot— (presence of fuel is assumed)	• Defective choke	• Check choke plate
Rough idle or engine runs rough	• Dirt or moisture in fuel • Clogged air filter • Faulty fuel pump	• Replace fuel filter • Replace air filter • Check fuel pump output
Engine stalls or hesitates on acceleration	• Dirt or moisture in the fuel • Dirty carburetor • Defective fuel pump • Incorrect float level, defective accelerator pump	• Replace fuel filter • Clean the carburetor • Check fuel pump output • Check carburetor
Poor gas mileage	• Clogged air filter • Dirty carburetor • Defective choke, faulty carburetor adjustment	• Replace air filter • Clean carburetor • Check carburetor
Engine is flooded (won't start accompanied by smell of raw fuel)	• Improperly adjusted choke or carburetor	• Wait 15 minutes and try again, without pumping gas pedal • If it won't start, check carburetor

86745c03

THROTTLE BODY FUEL INJECTION SYSTEM

General Information

The electronic fuel injection system is a fuel metering system with the amount of fuel delivered by the throttle body injectors (TBI) determined by an electronic signal supplied by the Electronic Control Module (ECM). The ECM monitors various engine and vehicle conditions to calculate the fuel delivery time (pulse width) of the injectors. The fuel pulse may be modified by the ECM to account for special operating conditions, such as cranking, cold starting, altitude, acceleration, and deceleration.

The ECM controls the exhaust emissions by modifying fuel delivery to achieve, as near as possible, and air/fuel ratio of 14.7:1. The injector "ON" time is determined by various inputs to the ECM. By increasing the injector pulse, more fuel is delivered, enriching the air/fuel ratio. Decreasing the injector pulse, leans the air/fuel ratio.

Relieving Fuel Pressure

The fuel system on vehicles equipped with Throttle Body Fuel Injection (TBI) is only under pressure when the fuel pump is operating. As long as the fuel pump in not operating, TBI fuel system components can be removed without the need to release system pressure.

Electric Fuel Pump

REMOVAL & INSTALLATION

▶ See Figure 36

1. Disconnect the negative battery cable.
2. Remove the fuel tank filler cap.
3. Using a siphon hose, drain the fuel tank below ¼ full.
4. Block the front wheels and raise and support the rear of the vehicle with jackstands.
5. Remove the fuel inlet and outlet hoses from the sending unit Be ready to catch any spilled fuel.
6. Remove the sending unit wires.
7. Using a brass punch and hammer, remove the sending unit retaining lockring by tapping it counterclockwise.
8. Remove the sending unit, which incorporates the electric fuel pump, along with the O-ring seal from the fuel tank. Discard the O-ring.
9. Remove and discard the pump inlet filter.
10. Disconnect the fuel pump terminal wires.
11. Remove the pump outlet hose and clamp.
12. Remove the pump top mounting bracket nut and remove the pump.

To install:

13. Install a new inlet filter on the pump.
14. Assemble the pump and bracket. Connect the hose and wiring.
15. Install the unit and new O-ring in the tank. The rubber stopper on the end of the fuel return tube must be inserted into the cup in the fuel tank reservoir.

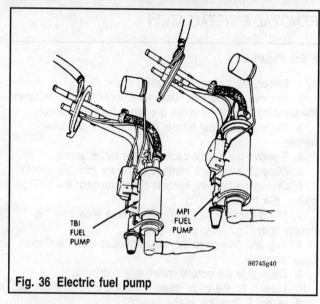

Fig. 36 Electric fuel pump

16. Install the lockring. Carefully tap it into place until it seats against the stop on the tank.
17. Connect the hoses.
18. Connect the wiring.
19. Lower the truck, fill the tank, run the engine and check for leaks.

TESTING

1. Remove the plug from the test port and engage a test port fitting in its place.
2. Connect a fuel pressure gauge to the test port fitting.
3. Start the engine and let it idle.
4. The pressure gauge should read 14-15 psi (97-103 kPa).
5. If the pressure is correct the fuel pump is operating normally.
6. If the pressure is not correct, adjust the fuel pressure regulator to obtain the correct pressure by turning the screw at the bottom of the regulator inward to increase pressure or outward to decrease pressure.
7. If the fuel pressure is considerably above specification and adjusting fails to lower it within specification, inspect the return line for an obstruction.
8. If the fuel pressure is considerably below specification and adjusting fails to raise it within specification, momentarily pinch off the return line and recheck the pressure. If pressure has risen, replace the regulator. If it has not, check the filter and supply line for an obstruction.

✳✳WARNING

Fuel pressure will rise to as much as 95 psi (655 kPa) when the return line is pinched shut. Shut the engine down immediately after pinching off the return line.

Throttle Body

REMOVAL & INSTALLATION

▶ **See Figure 37**

1. Disconnect the negative battery cable.
2. Remove the vacuum hoses from upper bonnet, unfasten the retaining clips and remove the upper bonnet assembly.
3. Remove the lower bonnet retaining bolts and lower bonnet.
4. Remove the throttle cable and the return spring.
5. Disengage the wire harness connector from the injector.
6. Disengage the wire harness connector from the WOT switch, ISA motor and TPS.
7. Disconnect the fuel supply and return lines from the throttle body.
8. Tag and disengage the vacuum hoses from the throttle body assembly.
9. Disengage the potentiometer wire connector.
10. Loosen throttle body retaining bolts and remove throttle body assembly from the intake manifold.

To install:

11. Clean the intake manifold and throttle body mating surfaces of old gasket material.
12. Install a new gasket and the throttle body assembly. Tighten the mounting bolts to 16 ft. lbs. (21 Nm).
13. Engage the potentiometer wire connector.
14. Engage the vacuum hoses to the throttle body.
15. Engage the fuel lines to the throttle body.
16. Engage the WOT switch, ISA motor, TPS, and injector electrical connections.
17. Install the return spring and throttle cable.
18. Install the lower bonnet and fasten the retainers.
19. Install the upper bonnet assembly, retaining clips and vacuum hoses.
20. Connect the negative battery cable.
21. Start the vehicle and check for fuel leaks.

Fuel Charging Assembly

REMOVAL & INSTALLATION

▶ **See Figure 38**

1. Remove the throttle body assembly from the vehicle.
2. Remove the Torx® head screws that retain the fuel body to the throttle body. Remove and discard the gasket.
3. Installation is the reverse of removal. Be sure to use a new gasket.

Fuel Injector

REMOVAL & INSTALLATION

▶ **See Figure 39**

1. Disconnect the negative battery cable.

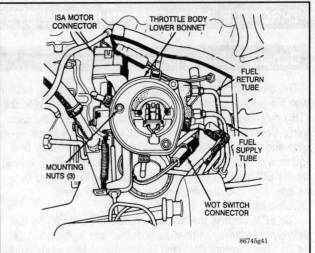

Fig. 37 Exploded view of the throttle body and related components

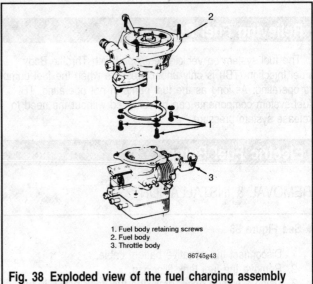

1. Fuel body retaining screws
2. Fuel body
3. Throttle body

Fig. 38 Exploded view of the fuel charging assembly

2. Remove the air cleaner and hose assembly.
3. Remove the throttle body upper and lower bonnets.
4. Remove the fuel injector wire by compressing the tabs and pulling it upwards.
5. Remove the fuel injector retainer clip screws. Remove the fuel injector retainer clip.

➡**The injector has a small locating tab that fits into a slot in the bottom of the injector bore of the throttle body. DO NOT twist the injector during removal!**

6. Using a small pair of pliers, gently grasp the center collar of the injector, between the electrical terminals, and carefully remove the injector using a lifting/rocking motion.
7. Discard the centering ring and the upper and lower O-rings.

To install:

8. Lubricate the upper and lower O-rings with transmission fluid and install them in the injector bore.
9. Install the centering ring on top of the upper O-ring and align locating ring on the injector with the slot in the housing.

10. Install the injector, retaining clip and retainer clip screws.
11. Engage the injector electrical connection.
12. Install the throttle body upper and lower bonnets and the air cleaner and hose assembly.
13. Connect the negative battery cable.

Fuel Pressure Regulator

REMOVAL & INSTALLATION

▶ See Figure 40

1. Remove the throttle body assembly from the vehicle as outlined in this section.

✳✳WARNING

To prevent spring pressure release, hold the regulator housing against the throttle body while removing the mounting screws.

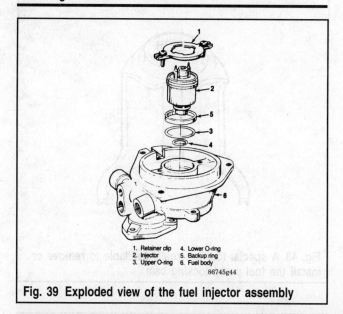

1. Retainer clip
2. Injector
3. Upper O-ring
4. Lower O-ring
5. Backup ring
6. Fuel body

86745g44

Fig. 39 Exploded view of the fuel injector assembly

2. Remove the three retaining screws that hold the pressure regulator to the fuel body.
3. Disassemble the pressure regulator assembly. Note the location of the components for reassembly. Discard the gasket.

To install:

4. Install a new gasket and the regulator assembly. Tighten the three retaining screws.
5. Install the throttle body assembly as outlined in this section.

✳✳WARNING

The pressure regulator diaphragm MUST be installed with the vent hole aligned with the vent holes in the throttle body and regulator housing!

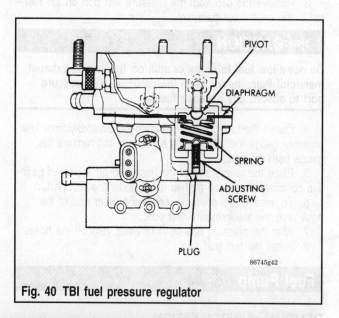

PIVOT
DIAPHRAGM
SPRING
ADJUSTING SCREW
PLUG

86745g42

Fig. 40 TBI fuel pressure regulator

MULTI-PORT FUEL INJECTION SYSTEM

General Information

The engines covered by this manual employ a Multi-Port Fuel Injection (MFI) system. The MFI system injects fuel into the intake manifold above the intake valve port of each cylinder through separate injectors.

The fuel system consists of the fuel tank, electric fuel pump, fuel filter, fuel tubes, fuel hoses, vacuum hoses, throttle body, and the fuel injectors.

A fuel return system is used on all vehicles. The system consists of the fuel tubes and hoses that route fuel back to the fuel tank.

The fuel tank assembly consists of the tank, filler vent tube, a fuel gauge sending unit/fuel pump assembly, and a pressure filler cap (on some models).

Another part of the fuel system is the evaporation control system, which is designed to reduce the emission of fuel vapors into the atmosphere. The description and function of the evaporative control system is found in Section 4.

Relieving Fuel System Pressure

▶ See Figures 41 and 42

✳✳CAUTION

Before opening any part of the fuel system, the pressure in the system must be relieved!

1. Disconnect the negative battery cable.
2. Remove the fuel filler cap.

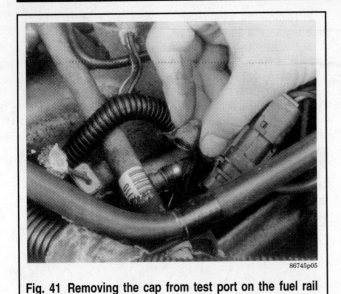

Fig. 41 Removing the cap from test port on the fuel rail

3. Remove the cap from the pressure test port on the fuel rail in the engine compartment.

✴✴CAUTION

Do not allow fuel to spray or spill on the engine exhaust manifold! Place heavy shop towels under the pressure port to absorb any escaped fuel!

---

4. Obtain the fuel pressure gauge/hose assembly from fuel pressure gauge tool 5069 or its equivalent and remove the gauge from the hose.

5. Place the gauge end of the hose into an approved gasoline container and place a shop towel under the test port.

6. To release fuel pressure, screw the other end of the hose onto the fuel pressure test port.

7. After the pressure has been relieved, remove the hose.

8. Install the test port cap.

Fuel Pump

REMOVAL & INSTALLATION

1984-95 Models

▶ See Figures 43, 44, 45, 46 and 47

1. Disconnect the negative battery cable.
2. Remove the fuel tank filler cap.
3. Relieve the fuel system pressure as outlined in this section.
4. Drain the fuel from the fuel tank.
5. Raise and support the rear end on jackstands.
6. Remove the fuel inlet and outlet hoses from the sending unit. Be ready to catch any spilled fuel.
7. Disengage the sending unit wires.
8. Using a brass punch and hammer, remove the sending unit retaining lockring by tapping it counterclockwise.
9. Remove the sending unit, which incorporates the electric fuel pump, along with the O-ring seal from the fuel tank. Discard the O-ring.

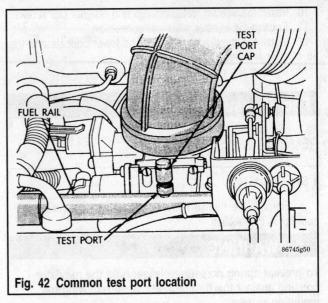

Fig. 42 Common test port location

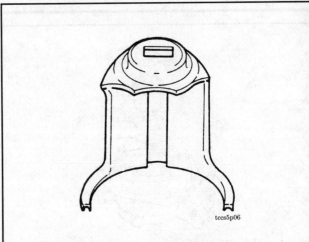

Fig. 43 A special tool is usually available to remove or install the fuel pump locking cam

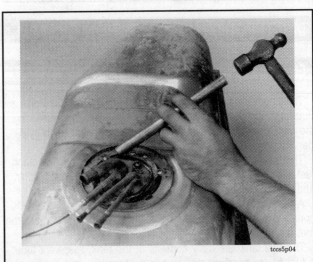

Fig. 44 A brass drift and a hammer can be used to loosen the fuel pump locking cam

10. Remove and discard the pump inlet filter.

11. Disengage the fuel pump terminal wires.

12. Remove the pump outlet hose and clamp.

13. Unfasten the pump top mounting bracket nut and remove the pump.

To install:

14. Install a new inlet filter on the pump.

15. Assemble the pump and bracket. Connect the hose and wiring.

16. Install the unit and new O-ring in the tank. The rubber stopper on the end of the fuel return tube must be inserted into the cup in the fuel tank reservoir.

17. Install the lockring. Carefully tap it into place until it seats against the stop on the tank.

18. Connect the hoses.

19. Engage the wiring.

20. Lower the vehicle, fill the tank, run the engine and check for leaks.

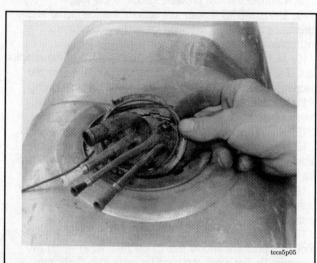

Fig. 45 Once the locking cam is released, it can be removed to free the fuel pump

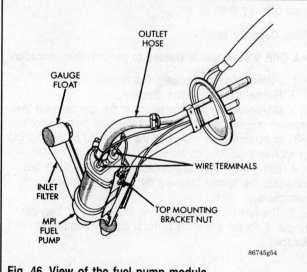

Fig. 46 View of the fuel pump module

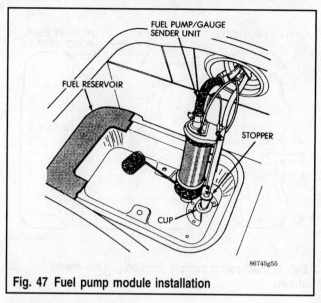

Fig. 47 Fuel pump module installation

1996 Models

▶ **See Figures 48, 49 and 50**

1. Drain and remove the fuel tank as outlined in this section.

2. Using tool 6856 or its equivalent, remove the module locknut which is threaded onto the fuel tank. The module will spring up when the nut is removed.

3. Remove the module.

To install:

4. Install a new gasket and place the module into the opening in the fuel tank.

5. Position a new locknut on top of the module and tighten the nut using tool 6856 or its equivalent to 40 ft. lbs. (54 Nm).

6. Install the fuel tank as outlined in this section.

TESTING

Fuel System Pressure

▶ **See Figures 51 and 52**

➡ **A DRB II scan tool is needed to perform this procedure.**

1. Remove the cap from the fuel rail and connect a fuel gauge capable of reading up to 60 psi (0-414 kPa) to the test port fitting.

2. Start the vehicle and note the pressure reading at idle which should be 31 psi (214 kPa).

3. Disengage the vacuum line at the pressure regulator and note the reading. The reading should be 39 psi (269 kPa).

4. The fuel pressure should be 8-10 psi (55-69 kPa) higher with the vacuum line removed. If not check the pressure regulator vacuum line for leaks, kinks or blockage. If the line is not the problem, replace the pressure regulator.

5. If the pressure exceeds 45 psi (310 kPa) check the fuel return line for kinks or obstructions.

6. If the previous tests checked out properly and fuel pressure is correct. If not proceed as follows.

7. Disengage the fuel return line at the fuel rail and install fuel line pressure test adaptor tool 6539 or its equivalent between the disconnected return line and fuel rail.

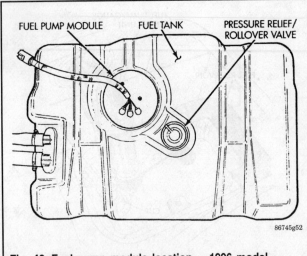

Fig. 48 Fuel pump module location — 1996 model shown

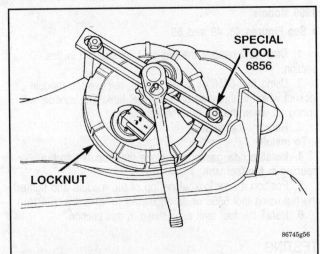

Fig. 49 Locknut removal using tool 6856 or its equivalent — 1996 model shown

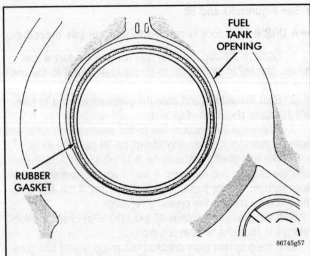

Fig. 50 Install a new gasket on the fuel tank opening — 1996 model shown

Fig. 51 Fuel pressure can be checked using an inexpensive pressure/vacuum gauge

8. Connect the fuel pressure gauge to the tool.

9. Using a DRB II scan tool activate the fuel pump and pressurize the system following the tool manufacturer's instructions.

10. Momentarily pinch the rubber hose portion of the adaptor tool. The pressure should rise 75 psi (517 (kPa) within two seconds. Do not pinch the hose for more than 3 seconds.

11. If the pressure does not rise relieve the fuel system pressure.

12. Raise the vehicle and support it safely with jackstands.

13. Disengage the fuel supply line at the inlet (fuel tank side) of the adaptor and connect fuel line pressure test adaptor tool 6631 between the fuel filter and supply line.

14. Using a DRB II scan tool activate the fuel pump and pressurize the system following the tool manufactures instructions.

15. Momentarily pinch the rubber hose portion of the adaptor tool. The pressure should rise 75 psi (517 (kPa) within two seconds. Do not pinch the hose for more than 3 seconds.

16. If the pressure does not rise, check for a restricted fuel filter and a restricted fuel supply line.

17. If the filter and line are not restricted perform the fuel pump capacity test.

Pump Capacity Test

➡ **A DRB II scan tool is needed to perform this procedure.**

1. Perform the fuel system pressure test.
2. Relieve the fuel system pressure.
3. Disengage the fuel supply line at the fuel rail near the pressure regulator and connect fuel pressure test adaptor tool 6631 or its equivalent and insert the other end of the tool into an approved gasoline container.
4. Using a DRB II scan tool activate the fuel pump and pressurize the system following the tool manufactures instructions.
5. The fuel pump should deliver 0.2642 gal. (1 liter) per minute. If not the pump the pump is defective and must be replaced.

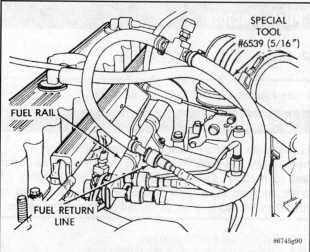

Fig. 52 Connect adaptor tool 6539 or its equivalent between the disconnected return line and fuel rail

Throttle Body

REMOVAL & INSTALLATION

▶ See Figures 53, 54, 55, 56, 57 and 58

1. Disconnect the battery ground cable.
2. Disconnect the air inlet tube from the throttle body.
3. Tag and disconnect the wiring and hoses from the throttle body.
4. Tag and disconnect all the control cables.
5. Remove the mounting bolts and remove the throttle body. Discard the gasket.

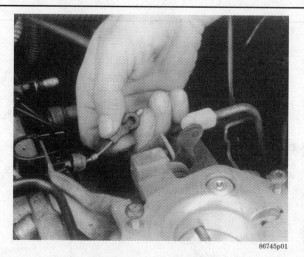

Fig. 53 Disconnect the throttle cable from the throttle body

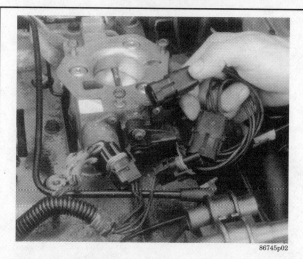

Fig. 54 Disengage the electrical connections from the throttle body

Fig. 55 Unfasten the throttle body retaining bolts

To install:

6. Install the new gasket, throttle body and mounting bolts. Tighten the bolts as follows;
   - On pre-1991 models; 23 ft. lbs. (31 Nm)
   - On 1991-1995 models; 9 ft. lbs. (12 Nm)
   - On the 1996 Grand Cherokee 5.2L engine; 200 inch lbs. (23 Nm)
   - On the 1996 Grand Cherokee 4.0L engine; 108 inch lbs. (12 Nm)
   - On the 1996 Cherokee; 108 inch lbs. (12 Nm)
7. Engage the control cables.
8. Engage the wiring and hoses to the throttle body.
9. Engage the air inlet tube to the throttle body and connect the negative battery cable.
10. Installation is the reverse of removal. Tighten the mounting bolts to 23 ft. lbs. (31 Nm) pre-1991 models and 9 ft. lbs. (12 Nm) 1991-96 models.
11. If equipped with an automatic transmission, the throttle valve cable MUST be adjusted! See Section 7.

Fig. 56 Remove the throttle body from the intake manifold

Fig. 57 Clean the old gasket from the intake manifold

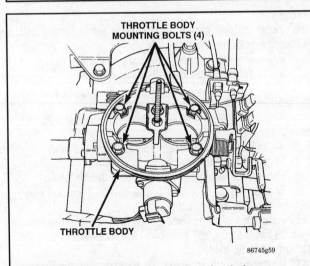

Fig. 58 Common throttle body mounting bolt locations — 1996 5.2 model shown

Fuel Injectors

REMOVAL AND INSTALLATION

◆ See Figures 59, 60, 61, 62, 63, 64 and 65

❊❊CAUTION

Fuel system pressure must be relieved before disconnecting any fuel lines. Release fuel system pressure at the test connection using a suitable pressure gauge with a pressure bleed valve. Take precautions to avoid the risk of fire whenever working on or around any open fuel system.

1. Relieve fuel system pressure.
2. Remove the air duct at the throttle body.
3. Disconnect the fuel lines at the ends of the fuel rail assembly.
4. Tag and disengage the injector wire harness connectors.
5. Remove the fuel rail assembly as outlined in this section.

➡On models with automatic transmission, it may be necessary to remove the automatic transmission throttle pressure cable and bracket to remove the fuel rail assembly.

6. Remove the clips that retain the injectors to the fuel rail and remove the injectors.
   To install:
7. Install new O-rings.
8. Install the clips that retain the injectors to the fuel rail and engage the injectors.
9. Install the fuel rail as outlined in this section.
10. Engage the injector wire harness connectors.
11. Connect the fuel lines at the ends of the fuel rail assembly.
12. Connect the air duct at the throttle body.

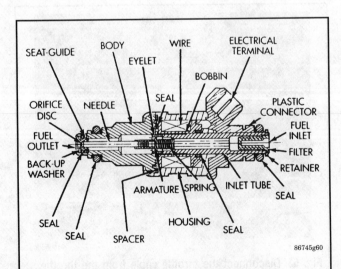

Fig. 59 Exploded view of a fuel injector internal components

Fig. 60 Remove the fuel rail, then . . .

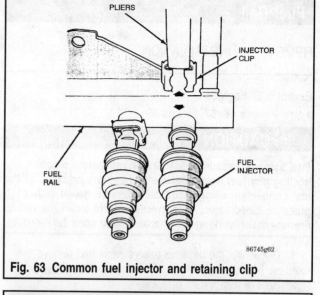

Fig. 63 Common fuel injector and retaining clip

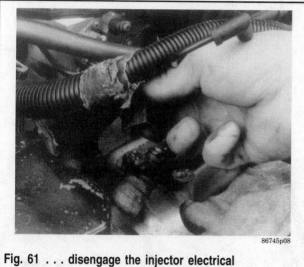

Fig. 61 . . . disengage the injector electrical connections

Fig. 64 Remove the fuel injector from the vehicle

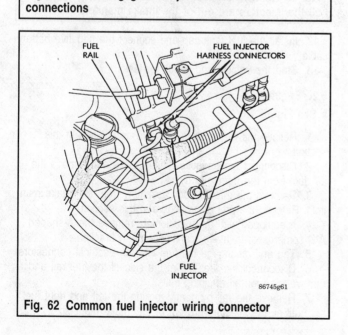

Fig. 62 Common fuel injector wiring connector

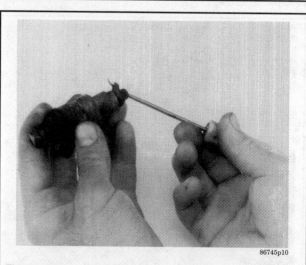

Fig. 65 Remove the old injector O-rings and replace them with new ones

Fuel Rail

REMOVAL & INSTALLATION

Except 5.2L Engines

♦ See Figures 66, 67, 68 and 69

✳✳CAUTION

Fuel system pressure must be relieved before disconnecting any fuel lines. Release fuel system pressure at the test connection using a suitable pressure gauge with a pressure bleed valve. Take precautions to avoid the risk of fire whenever working on or around any open fuel system.

1. Disconnect the negative battery cable and remove the fuel tank filler cap.
2. Relieve fuel system pressure.
3. Tag and disengage the injector wire harness connectors.

➡️On models with automatic transmission, it may be necessary to remove the automatic transmission throttle pressure cable and bracket to remove the fuel rail assembly.

4. Disengage the vacuum line from the fuel pressure regulator.
5. Disconnect the fuel supply line from the fuel rail and the fuel return line from the fuel pressure regulator.
6. Remove the fuel rail retaining bolts.
7. Remove the rail by gently rocking it until all the injectors are out of the intake manifold.

To install:

8. Position the injector tips into the correct intake manifold bore and seat the injectors.
9. Install and tighten the fuel rail retaining bolts to 20 ft. lbs. (27 Nm).
10. Engage the fuel injector wire harness connectors.
11. Connect the fuel lines and the vacuum line to the fuel pressure regulator.

Fig. 66 Remove the fuel rail retaining bolts

Fig. 67 Disengage the vacuum line from the fuel pressure regulator

Fig. 68 Remove the fuel rail by gently rocking it until all the injectors are out of the intake manifold

12. Install the fuel tank cap and connect the negative battery cable.
13. Start the vehicle and check for leaks.

5.2L Engines

♦ See Figure 70

1. Relieve the fuel system pressure as outlined in this section.
2. Disconnect the negative battery cable and remove the air duct from the throttle body.
3. Remove the throttle body assembly from the intake manifold. Refer to the proper procedure in this section.
4. If equipped with air conditioning, remove the A-shaped A/C compressor-to-intake manifold support bracket.
5. Tag and disengage the fuel injector electrical connectors.
6. Disconnect the fuel line at the side of the fuel rail and remove the fuel rail retaining bolts.
7. Remove the rail by gently rocking the left and right fuel rail until all the injectors are out of the intake manifold.

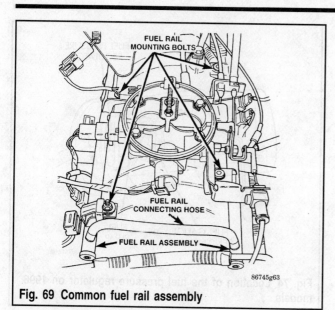

Fig. 69 Common fuel rail assembly

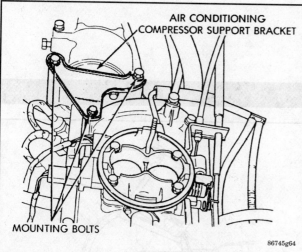

Fig. 70 If equipped, remove the A-shaped compressor bracket

To install:

8. Apply a small amount of engine oil to the injector O-rings.

9. Position the injector tips into the correct intake manifold bore and seat the injectors by pushing down on the left and right fuel rails until the injectors are firmly seated.

10. Install and tighten the fuel rail retaining bolts to 200 inch lbs. (23 Nm).

11. Engage the fuel injector wire harness connectors.

12. Install the A/C compressor bracket, if equipped.

13. Install the throttle body assembly. Refer to the proper procedure as outlined in this section.

14. Engage the fuel line at the side of the fuel rail and install the air duct.

15. Connect the negative battery cable, start the vehicle and check for leaks.

Fuel Pressure Regulator

REMOVAL & INSTALLATION

▶ **See Figures 71, 72, 73 and 74**

The fuel pressure regulator on 1996 models cannot be serviced separately. If it is found to be defective the entire fuel pump module must be replaced.

1. Relieve the fuel system pressure as outlined in this section.

2. Remove the vacuum line from the fuel pressure regulator.

3. Remove the regulator mounting clamp bolt and clamp from the fuel rail.

4. Remove the regulator and discard the O-ring seals.

To install:

5. Install the new O-ring seals.

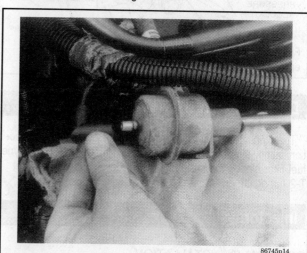

Fig. 71 Disengage the fuel pressure regulator vacuum line

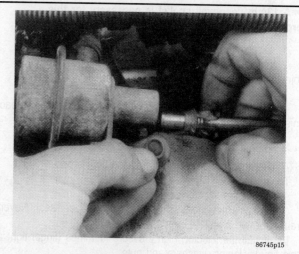

Fig. 72 Removing the fuel pressure regulator and the O-ring seals

6. Install the regulator and clamp onto the fuel rail and tighten the clamp mounting bolt.

7. Engage the vacuum line to the regulator, start the engine and check for leaks.

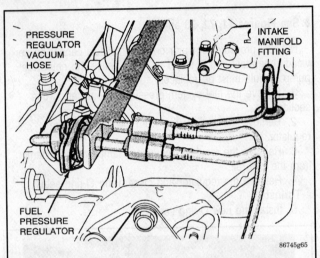

Fig. 73 A common fuel pressure regulator location on earlier model vehicles

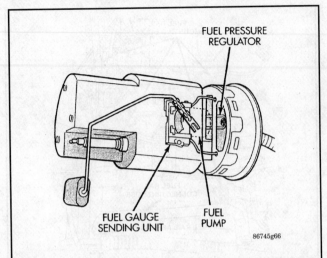

Fig. 74 Location of the fuel pressure regulator on 1996 models

DIESEL FUEL SYSTEM

The Renault-built diesel engine uses a Bosch VE4/9F injection pump, supplying Bosch KBE 48 57 injectors. A Stanadyne fuel filter cleans the system. Boost is developed by a Garret T-2 turbocharger.

Injectors

REMOVAL & INSTALLATION

▸ See Figure 75

➡ A 13mm deep-well socket is necessary for this procedure.

1. Disconnect the negative battery cable.
2. Remove the fuel return hoses and fittings from the injectors
3. Remove the high pressure lines from the injectors.
4. Remove both injector clamp nuts and washers from each injector.
5. Remove the injector clamp.
6. Pull the injector from the head.
7. Remove the copper seal and the heat shield.

To install:

8. Clean the injector bore with a brass brush.
9. Install a new heat shield and a new copper seal. Never reuse the old ones!
10. Install the injector, high pressure fuel lines (finger-tight at this time), clamps, washers and nuts.
11. Tighten the high pressure fuel lines.
12. Use new washers and install the fuel return lines. Tighten the fittings to 88 inch lbs.

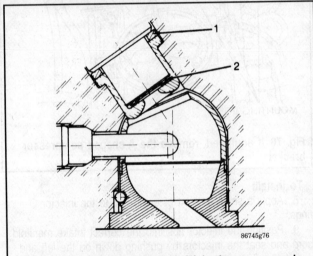

Fig. 75 Diesel injector installed. (1) is the copper seal; (2) is the heat shield

Injection Pump

REMOVAL & INSTALLATION

▸ See Figures 76, 77, 78 and 79

➡ Special tools are needed for this procedure.

1. Disconnect the negative battery cable.
2. Using heavy clamps, clamp off the coolant inlet and outlet hoses at the cold start capsule. Then, disconnect them.

3. Disconnect the throttle cable and fuel shut-off solenoid wire.

4. If so equipped, disconnect the automatic transmission throttle cable, and cruise control cable.

5. Disconnect and plug the fuel delivery and return hoses.

6. Remove the alternator drive belt.

7. Remove the power steering drive belt.

8. Remove the timing belt cover.

9. Rotate the crankshaft clockwise, as viewed from the front, until No.1 piston is at TDC compression. Make sure that the camshaft sprocket timing mark is aligned with the center boss on the cylinder head cover. Make sure, also, that the injection pump sprocket timing mark is aligned with the center of the boss on the injection pump.

10. Rotate the crankshaft counterclockwise, moving the sprocket timing marks by 3 timing belt teeth.

11. Install sprocket holding tool MOT-854 or its equivalent. It may be necessary to turn the sprocket back and forth slightly to install the tool.

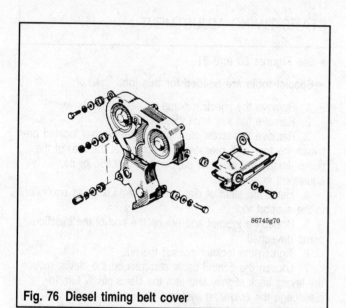

86745g70

Fig. 76 Diesel timing belt cover

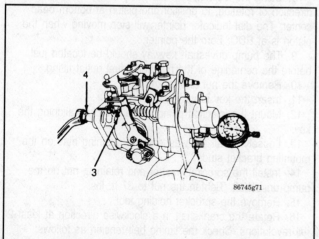

86745g71

Fig. 77 Injection pump adjustment points. (3) is the control cable screw; (4) is the injection pump shaft locknut; (A) is the fuel outlet fitting

12. Loosen the sprocket retaining nut on the end of the injection pump shaft, and turn it out just to the end of the threads.

13. Assemble the sprocket removal tool jaws, B.Vi.48 and the short screw B.Vi.859, on the sprocket removal tool, B.Vi.2801 or there equivalents.

14. Attach the tool to the injection pump sprocket.

15. Disconnect all the fuel pipe fittings from the injectors. Plug the injectors to prevent dirt from entering the fuel system.

16. Disconnect the fuel pipe fittings from the fuel injection pump. Plug the fittings to prevent dirt from entering the system.

17. Remove the fuel line fittings from the vehicle. Remove all hoses and connectors from the injection pump assembly.

18. Remove the injection pump rear bracket retaining nuts.

19. Remove the plastic shield from under the injection pump.

20. Remove the three retaining nuts located at the front of the injection pump. The lower nut is hard to get at. It may be necessary to remove the alternator to get a wrench on it.

21. Using the sprocket removal tool, separate the injection pump from the sprocket.

22. Remove the removal tool and the sprocket nut. The sprocket holding tool and the timing belt will hold the sprocket in plate. facilitating injection pump installation.

23. Remove the injection pump from the mounting brackets.

24. Remove the key from the shaft.

25. Remove the screw plug and copper washer located between the four high pressure fuel outlets, at the rear of the pump. Install dial indicator support tool Mot.856 or its equivalent in its place.

To install:

26. Install the stem of dial indicator Mot.LM in the support tool.

27. Position a locknut and nut on the end of the injection pump driveshaft.

28. Tighten the locknut against the nut.

29. Loosen the control cable set screw on the clevis, move the levers back slightly and turn the clevis pin ¼ turn to disengage the cold start system.

30. Using the locknut, turn the pump driveshaft in the normal direction of rotation, to position the piston at bottom dead

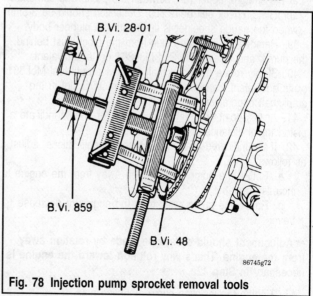

86745g72

Fig. 78 Injection pump sprocket removal tools

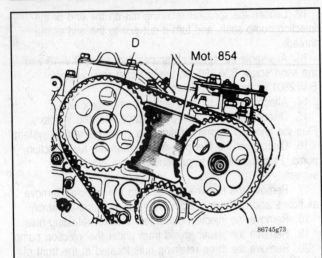

86745g73

Fig. 79 Sprocket holding tool. (D) is the camshaft sprocket bolt

center. The dial indicator pointer will stop moving when the piston is at BDC. Zero the pointer.

31. The pump driveshaft keyway should be located just before the centerline of the number 1 fuel outlet fitting.

32. Remove the nut and locknut.

33. Insert the key in its keyway.

34. Mount the injection pump in the sprocket, aligning the key.

35. Loosely install the washers and retaining nuts on the mounting bracket studs.

36. Install the sprocket washer and retaining nut on the pump driveshaft. Tighten the nut to 37 ft. lbs.

37. Remove the sprocket holding tool.

38. Rotate the crankshaft in a clockwise direction at least 2 full revolutions. Check the timing belt tension as follows:

   a. Loosen the timing belt tensioner bolts ½ turn each, maximum.

   b. The belt tensioner should, automatically, place the proper tension on the belt.

   c. Using belt tension gauge Ele.346-04 or its equivalent, at the straight, upper run, between the pump and camshaft sprockets, check belt deflection. Deflection should be 3-5mm when the gauge shoulder is flush with the plunger body.

39. Remove the threaded plug from the block, just behind the pump, and insert TDC Rod Mot.861 or its equivalent.

40. Slowly rotate the crankshaft clockwise until tool Mot.861 or its equivalent, can be inserted into the TDC slot in the crankshaft counterweight.

41. At this point, the dial indicator pointer should indicate a piston travel distance of 0.80-0.84mm.

42. If the indicated travel is not within specifications, adjust it as follows:

   a. Rotate the pump toward, then away from the engine to increase travel.

   b. Rotate the pump away from the engine to decrease travel

➡**Adjustment should always be made by rotation away from the engine. That's why rotation toward the engine is necessary in Step 42a.**

43. Tighten the injection pump mounting nuts.

44. Remove the TDC Rod from the counterweight slot.

45. Observe the dial indicator and rotate the crankshaft clockwise 2 full revolutions until the rod can, once again, be installed into the counterweight hole. The dial indicator should return to 0, then move to 0.80-0.84mm. If so, injection pump static timing is correct.

46. Remove the TDC Rod and install the plug.

47. Remove the dial indicator and install the washer and screw plug in the pump.

48. Connect the high pressure lines at the injectors.

49. Compress the timing control lever and install the clevis pin in the first position on the cable clamp.

50. With the lever against the clevis, tighten the setscrew.

51. Install and tighten the pump rear support bracket nuts.

52. Install all other parts in reverse order of removal.

➡**Don't confuse the fuel delivery and return hose banjo bolts. The delivery banjo bolt has two 4mm diameter holes; the return banjo bolt has a calibrated orifice. Never use the banjo bolts from one pump on another!**

STATIC TIMING ADJUSTMENT

◆ **See Figures 80 and 81**

➡**Special tools are needed for this job.**

1. Remove the injection pump as described above.

2. Remove the key from the shaft.

3. Remove the screw plug and copper washer located between the four high pressure fuel outlets, at the rear of the pump. Install dial indicator support tool Mot.856 or its equivalent in its place.

4. Install the stem of dial indicator Mot.LM or its equivalent in the support tool.

5. Position a locknut and nut on the end of the injection pump driveshaft.

6. Tighten the locknut against the nut.

7. Loosen the control cable setscrew on the clevis, move the levers back slightly and turn the clevis pin ¼ turn to disengage the cold start system.

8. Using the locknut, turn the pump driveshaft in the normal direction of rotation, to position the piston at bottom dead center. The dial indicator pointer will stop moving when the piston is at BDC. Zero the pointer.

9. The pump driveshaft keyway should be located just before the centerline of the number 1 fuel outlet fitting.

10. Remove the nut and locknut.

11. Insert the key in its keyway.

12. Mount the injection pump in the sprocket, aligning the key.

13. Loosely install the washers and retaining nuts on the mounting bracket studs.

14. Install the sprocket washer and retaining nut on the pump driveshaft. Tighten the nut to 37 ft. lbs.

15. Remove the sprocket holding tool.

16. Rotate the crankshaft in a clockwise direction at least 2 full revolutions. Check the timing belt tension as follows:

   a. Loosen the timing belt tensioner bolts ½ turn each, maximum.

   b. The belt tensioner should, automatically, place the proper tension on the belt.

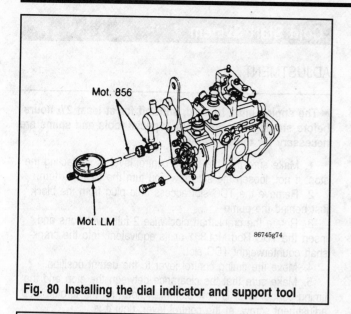

Fig. 80 Installing the dial indicator and support tool

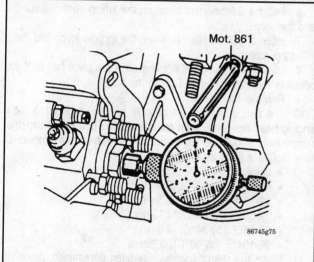

Fig. 81 Injection timing procedure using a dial indicator

c. Using belt tension gauge Ele.346-04 or its equivalent, at the straight, upper run, between the pump and camshaft sprockets, check belt deflection. Deflection should be 3-5mm when the gauge shoulder is flush with the plunger body.

17. Remove the threaded plug from the block, just behind the pump, and insert TDC Rod Mot.861 or its equivalent.

18. Slowly rotate the crankshaft clockwise until tool Mot.861 or its equivalent can be inserted into the TDC slot in the crankshaft counterweight.

19. At this point, the dial indicator pointer should indicate a piston travel distance of 0.80-0.84mm.

20. If the indicated travel is not within specifications, adjust it as follows:

a. Rotate the pump toward, then away from the engine to increase travel.

b. Rotate the pump away from the engine to decrease lift.

➡️**Adjustment should always be made by rotation away from the engine. That's why rotation toward the engine is necessary in Step 20a.**

21. Tighten the injection pump mounting nuts.

22. Remove the TDC Rod from the counterweight slot.

23. Observe the dial indicator and rotate the crankshaft clockwise 2 full revolutions until the rod can, once again, be installed into the counterweight hole. The dial indicator should return to 0, then move to 0.80-0.84mm. If so, injection pump static timing is correct.

24. Remove the TDC Rod and install the plug.

25. Remove the dial indicator and install the washer and screw plug in the pump.

26. Connect the high pressure lines at the injectors.

27. Compress the timing control lever and install the clevis pin in the first position on the cable clamp.

28. With the lever against the clevis, tighten the setscrew.

29. Install and tighten the pump rear support bracket nuts.

30. Install all other parts in reverse order of removal.

➡️**Don't confuse the fuel delivery and return hose banjo bolts. The delivery banjo bolt has two 4mm diameter holes; the return banjo bolt has a calibrated orifice. Never use the banjo bolts from one pump on another!**

Cold Start Capsule

REMOVAL & INSTALLATION

▶ **See Figures 82 and 83**

➡️**Two 6mm x 70mm threaded rods and nuts are necessary for this procedure.**

1. Using heavy clamps, clamp off the coolant lines at the cold start capsule.

✳✳CAUTION

Follow this procedure exactly when removing the cold start capsule. There is a great deal of spring tension behind the housings.

2. Remove one of the capsule retaining bolts and replace it with a 6mm diameter x 70mm long threaded rod.

3. Thread a nut down the rod and tighten it.

4. Remove the other bolt and replace it with a similar rod and nut.

5. Back off the two nuts, alternately and evenly, to release spring tension. Separate the capsule housing from the bracket and cable housing.

6. Remove the threaded rods.

7. Insert a 26mm OD section of tubing into the end of the capsule housing and hit the end sharply with a mallet to loosen the slotted retaining nut. Remove the nut, capsule and O-ring.

8. Assembly is the reverse of disassembly. Use the threaded rods to position the capsule housing, tightening them, alternately and evenly, then, replacing them, one at a time, with the bolts. Tighten the bolts securely.

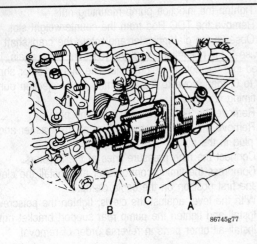

Fig. 82 Cold start capsule (A); threaded rod (B) and nut (C)

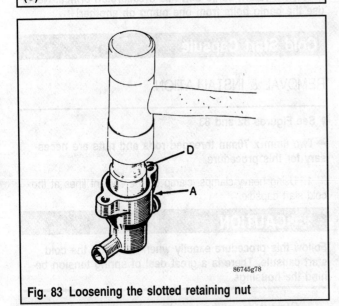

Fig. 83 Loosening the slotted retaining nut

Glow Plugs

REMOVAL & INSTALLATION

1. Disconnect the battery ground.
2. Disconnect the wire from the glow plug.
3. Unscrew the glow plug from the head.
4. Installation is the reverse of removal. Use a small amount of anti-seize compound on the glow plug threads. Tighten the glow plug to 20 ft. lbs. (27 Nm).

Cold Start System

ADJUSTMENT

➡**The engine must be cold, shut off for at least 2½ hours, before starting this procedure. Special tools and shims are necessary for this procedure.**

1. Make sure that the timing control lever is contacting the stop. If not, loosen the setscrew and turn the clevis ¼ turn.
2. Remove the TDC slot access hole plug from the block, just behind the pump.
3. Rotate the crankshaft clockwise 2 full revolutions and insert the TDC Rod Mot.861 or its equivalent, into the crankshaft counterweight TDC slot.
4. Move the timing control lever to the detent position.
5. Make sure that the clearance between the stop and the timing control lever is now 0.5mm. If not, turn the throttle stop adjustment screw, at the control lever, until it is.
6. Insert a 6.5mm shim between the timing control lever and the stop.
7. Insert a 3.0mm shim between the throttle lever and the idle stop screw.
8. Loosen the pivot ball nut and slide the pivot ball until it contacts the throttle lever. Tighten the nut.
9. Remove the shims.
10. The temperature of the capsule is now important. If the engine has been shut down for at least 2½ hours, the capsule temperature should be the same as the ambient air temperature. Select a shim as follows:

- below 66°F (19°C): 6.5mm
- 66-71°F (19-22°C): 5.9mm
- 72-76°F (22-24°C): 5.5mm
- 77-85°F (25-29°C): 4.75mm
- 86-94°F (30-34°C): 4.0mm
- 95-104°F (35-40°C): 3.25mm

11. When the shim thickness has been determined, place the shim between the timing control lever and the stop.
12. Align the clevis and the throttle cable stop so that both screw heads are in the same plane.
13. Tighten the throttle cable and position the clevis and the throttle stop so that they contact the timing control lever.
14. Tighten the throttle cable stop screw.
15. Remove the shim and make sure that the distance between the stop and the timing control lever is the same as the thickness of the shim. Correct it if necessary.
16. Start the engine and run it to normal operating temperature.
17. Make sure that the throttle lever and timing control lever are against their stops and move freely.
18. If necessary, adjust the idle with the idle adjustment screw to obtain an idle of 800 rpm.
19. Insert a 6.5mm shim between the timing control lever and its stop and measure the clearance between the throttle control lever and its stop. The clearance should be 3.0mm. If not, repeat the above adjustments.

FUEL TANK

Tank Assembly

REMOVAL & INSTALLATION

Except 1996 Grand Cherokee
▶ See Figures 84, 85, 86, 87, 88, 89 and 90

✳✳CAUTION

If the vehicle is equipped with the Multi-Point Fuel Injection, perform the fuel system pressure release sequence described earlier in this section.

1. Disconnect the negative battery cable.
2. If equipped with a fuel injection system, relieve fuel system pressure as outlined in this section.
3. Remove the fuel filler cap.
4. Drain the fuel tank.
5. Raise and support the vehicle safely.
6. On 1986-91 Comanche models, remove the rear driveshaft.
7. Tag and disengage all hoses and wires connected to the tank.

✳✳CAUTION

Wrap heavy shop towels around disconnected fuel lines to absorb spilled fuel. Be prepared to catch any fuel that is not absorbed!

8. Remove the skid plate, if equipped.
9. Remove the fuel tank shield.
10. Support the tank with a floor jack and remove the strap nuts.
11. Partially lower the tank and disconnect the tank vapor vent hoses.
12. Remove the tank.
13. Inspect for rotted or leaking fuel lines.
To install:
14. Raise the fuel tank into position and connect the vent hose to the filler neck and tighten the clamp.
15. Wrap the support straps around the fuel tank, tighten them to 100 inch lbs. (11 Nm). If 3 straps are used, tighten the center strap to 43 inch lbs. (4 Nm) and the outer straps to 65 inch lbs. (7 Nm).

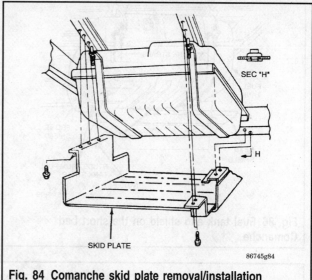

Fig. 84 Comanche skid plate removal/installation

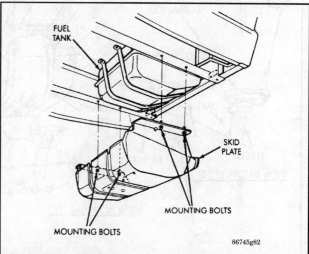

Fig. 85 Wagoneer/Cherokee skid plate removal and installation

16. Install the tank shield and skid plate.
17. Engage all wires and hoses and lower the vehicle.
18. Fill the tank and install the filler cap.
19. Connect the negative battery cable.
20. Start the vehicle and check for leaks.

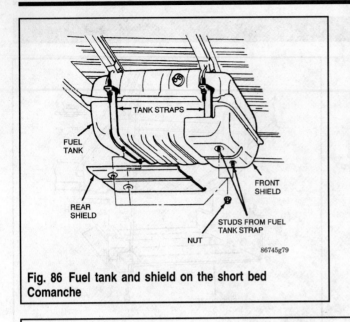

Fig. 86 Fuel tank and shield on the short bed Comanche

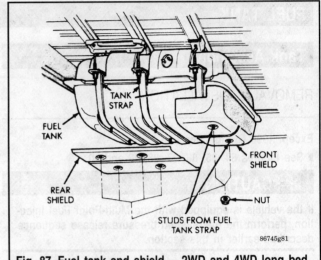

Fig. 87 Fuel tank and shield — 2WD and 4WD long bed Comanche without the skid plate

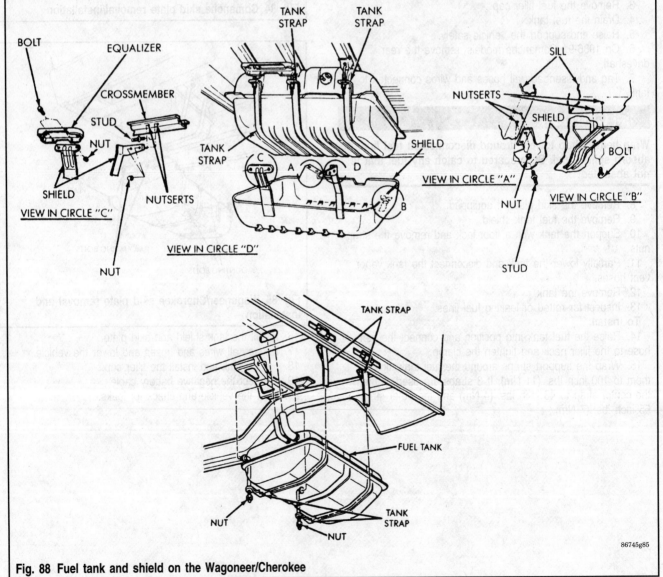

Fig. 88 Fuel tank and shield on the Wagoneer/Cherokee

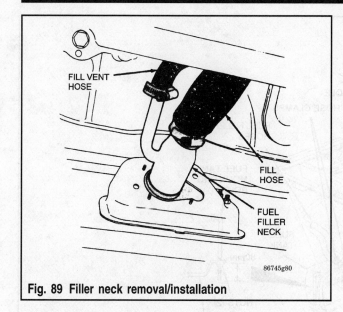

Fig. 89 Filler neck removal/installation

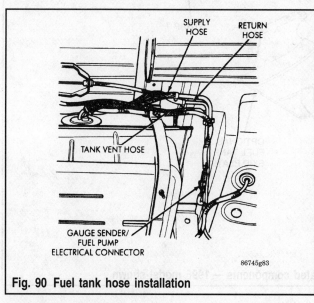

Fig. 90 Fuel tank hose installation

1996 Grand Cherokee

▶ See Figures 91 and 92

1. Disconnect the negative battery cable and relieve the fuel system pressure.

2. Raise and support the vehicle with jackstands.

3. Remove the fuel tank filler hose and vent hose clamps.

4. Remove both tubes at the filler tube.

5. If equipped remove the tow hooks and trailer hitch.

6. Remove the fuel tank skid plate retaining nuts/bolts, if equipped.

7. Unfasten the exhaust tailpipe heat shield retaining bolts and remove the shield.

8. Place a hydraulic jack under the tank.

9. Tag and disengage the fuel supply line, fuel vent line and fuel pump module electrical connection.

10. Remove the tank strap nuts and position the straps away from the tank.

11. Lower the right side of the tank while feeding the fuel hoses through the hole in the body until the filler hose clamps can be removed.

➡**Before removing the filler hoses mark their rotational position in relation to the tank**

12. Remove the hoses and clamps.

13. Insert a drain hose (from an approved draining station) into one of the hose openings and drain the tank.

14. Lower the jack and remove the tank.

To install:

15. Connect the fuel filter-to-fuel pump module supply line to the module.

16. Install the filler hoses and clamps to the tank noting their previously marked position.

17. Position the tank on the jack and raise the tank into position while guiding the fuel filler hoses through the access hole in the body.

18. Continue to raise the tank until it is in position and install the mounting straps.

19. Tighten the two mounting nuts until 3.149 in. (80mm) is attained between the end of the mounting bolt and the bottom of the strap. Do not overtighten.

20. Engage the pump module electrical connection and install the exhaust pipe heat shield.

21. Connect the fuel filter-to-fuel pump module supply line to the fuel filter.

22. Install the skid plate, trailer hitch and tow hooks, if equipped.

23. Install the fuel tank filler hose and vent hose. Tighten both clamps.

24. Lower the vehicle and connect the negative battery cable.

25. Fill the tank, start the vehicle and check for leaks.

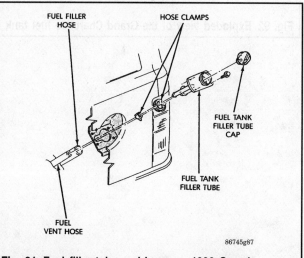

Fig. 91 Fuel filler tube and hoses — 1996 Grand Cherokee

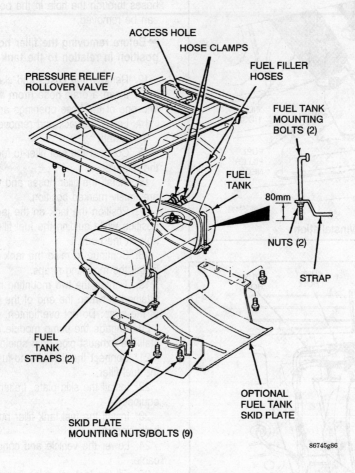

ACCESS HOLE

HOSE CLAMPS

FUEL FILLER
HOSES

PRESSURE RELIEF/
ROLLOVER VALVE

FUEL TANK
MOUNTING
BOLTS (2)

FUEL
TANK

80mm

NUTS (2)

STRAP

FUEL
TANK
STRAPS (2)

OPTIONAL
FUEL TANK
SKID PLATE

SKID PLATE
MOUNTING NUTS/BOLTS (9)

86745g86

Fig. 92 Exploded view of the Grand Cherokee fuel tank and related components — 1996 model shown

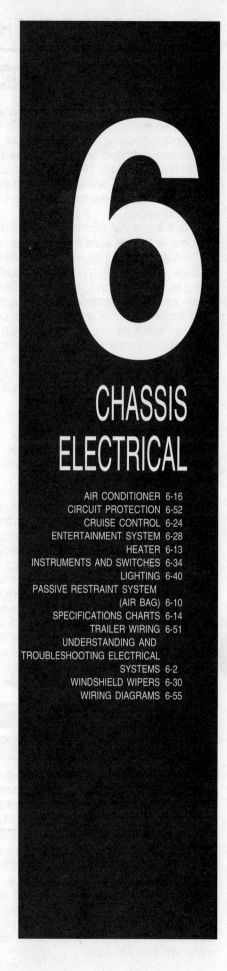

6

CHASSIS
ELECTRICAL

UNDERSTANDING AND TROUBLESHOOTING ELECTRICAL SYSTEMS

Over the years import and domestic manufacturers have incorporated electronic control systems into their production lines. In fact, electronic control systems are so prevalent that all new cars and trucks built today are equipped with at least one on-board computer. These electronic components (with no moving parts) should theoretically last the life of the vehicle, provided that nothing external happens to damage the circuits or memory chips.

While it is true that electronic components should never wear out, in the real world malfunctions do occur. It is also true that any computer-based system is extremely sensitive to electrical voltages and cannot tolerate careless or haphazard testing/service procedures. An inexperienced individual can literally cause major damage looking for a minor problem by using the wrong kind of test equipment or connecting test leads/connectors with the ignition switch **ON**. When selecting test equipment, make sure the manufacturer's instructions state that the tester is compatible with whatever type of system is being serviced. Read all instructions carefully and double check all test points before installing probes or making any test connections.

The following section outlines basic diagnosis techniques for dealing with automotive electrical systems. Along with a general explanation of the various types of test equipment available to aid in servicing modern automotive systems, basic repair techniques for wiring harnesses and connectors are also given. Read the basic information before attempting any repairs or testing. This will provide the background of information necessary to avoid the most common and obvious mistakes that can cost both time and money. Although the replacement and testing procedures are simple in themselves, the systems are not, and unless one has a thorough understanding of all components and their function within a particular system, the logical test sequence these systems demand cannot be followed. Minor malfunctions can make a big difference, so it is important to know how each component affects the operation of the overall system in order to find the ultimate cause of a problem without replacing good components unnecessarily. It is not enough to use the correct test equipment; the test equipment must be used correctly.

Safety Precautions

✳✳CAUTION

Whenever working on or around any electrical or electronic systems, always observe these general precautions to prevent the possibility of personal injury or damage to electronic components.

• Never install or remove battery cables with the key **ON** or the engine running. Jumper cables should be connected with the key **OFF** to avoid power surges that can damage electronic control units. Engines equipped with computer controlled systems should avoid both giving and getting jump starts due to the possibility of serious damage to components from arcing in the engine compartment if connections are made with the ignition **ON**.

• Always remove the battery cables before charging the battery. Never use a high output charger on an installed battery or attempt to use any type of "hot shot" (24 volt) starting aid.

• Exercise care when inserting test probes into connectors to insure good contact without damaging the connector or spreading the pins. Always probe connectors from the rear (wire) side, NOT the pin side, to avoid accidental shorting of terminals during test procedures.

• Never remove or attach wiring harness connectors with the ignition switch **ON**, especially to an electronic control unit.

• Do not drop any components during service procedures and never apply 12 volts directly to any component (like a solenoid or relay) unless instructed specifically to do so. Some component electrical windings are designed to safely handle only 4 or 5 volts and can be destroyed in seconds if 12 volts are applied directly to the connector.

• Remove the electronic control unit if the vehicle is to be placed in an environment where temperatures exceed approximately 176°F (80°C), such as a paint spray booth or when arc/gas welding near the control unit location.

Understanding Basic Electricity

Understanding the basic theory of electricity makes electrical troubleshooting much easier. Several gauges are used in electrical troubleshooting to see inside the circuit being tested. Without a basic understanding, it will be difficult to understand testing procedures.

THE WATER ANALOGY

Electricity is the flow of electrons — hypothetical particles thought to constitute the basic stuff of electricity. Many people have been taught electrical theory using an analogy with water. In a comparison with water flowing in a pipe, the electrons would be the water. As the flow of water can be measured, the flow of electricity can be measured. The unit of measurement is amperes, frequently abbreviated amps. An ammeter will measure the actual amount of current flowing in the circuit.

Just as the water pressure is measured in units such as pounds per square inch, electrical pressure is measured in volts. When a voltmeter's two probes are placed on two live portions of an electrical circuit with different electrical pressures, current will flow through the voltmeter and produce a reading which indicates the difference in electrical pressure between the two parts of the circuit.

While increasing the voltage in a circuit will increase the flow of current, the actual flow depends not only on voltage, but on the resistance of the circuit. The standard unit for measuring circuit resistance is an ohm, measured by an ohmmeter. The ohmmeter is somewhat similar to an ammeter, but incorporates its own source of power so that a standard voltage is always present.

CIRCUITS

An actual electric circuit consists of four basic parts. These are: the power source, such as a generator or battery; a hot wire, which conducts the electricity under a relatively high voltage to the component supplied by the circuit; the load, such as a lamp, motor, resistor or relay coil; and the ground wire, which carries the current back to the source under very low voltage. In such a circuit the bulk of the resistance exists between the point where the hot wire is connected to the load, and the point where the load is grounded. In an automobile, the vehicle's frame or body, which is made of steel, is used as a part of the ground circuit for many of the electrical devices.

Remember that, in electrical testing, the voltmeter is connected in parallel with the circuit being tested (without disconnecting any wires) and measures the difference in voltage between the locations of the two probes; that the ammeter is connected in series with the load (the circuit is separated at one point and the ammeter inserted so it becomes a part of the circuit); and the ohmmeter is self-powered, so that all the power in the circuit should be off and the portion of the circuit to be measured contacted at either end by one of the probes of the meter.

For any electrical system to operate, it must make a complete circuit. This simply means that the power flow from the battery must make a complete circle. When an electrical component is operating, power flows from the battery to the component, passes through the component causing it to perform it to function (such as lighting a light bulb) and then returns to the battery through the ground of the circuit. This ground is usually (but not always) the metal part of the vehicle on which the electrical component is mounted.

Perhaps the easiest way to visualize this is to think of connecting a light bulb with two wires attached to it to your vehicle's battery. The battery in your vehicle has two posts (negative and positive). If one of the two wires attached to the light bulb was attached to the negative post of the battery and the other wire was attached to the positive post of the battery, you would have a complete circuit. Current from the battery would flow out one post, through the wire attached to it and then to the light bulb, where it would pass through causing it to light. It would then leave the light bulb, travel through the other wire, and return to the other post of the battery.

AUTOMOTIVE CIRCUITS

The normal automotive circuit differs from this simple example in two ways. First, instead of having a return wire from the bulb to the battery, the light bulb return the current to the battery through the chassis of the vehicle. Since the negative battery cable is attached to the chassis and the chassis is made of electrically conductive metal, the chassis of the vehicle can serve as a ground wire to complete the circuit. Secondly, most automotive circuits contain switches to turn components on and off.

Some electrical components which require a large amount of current to operate also have a relay in their circuit. Since these circuits carry a large amount of current, the thickness of the wire in the circuit (gauge size) is also greater. If this large wire were connected from the component to the control switch on the instrument panel, and then back to the component, a voltage drop would occur in the circuit. To prevent this potential drop in voltage, an electromagnetic switch (relay) is used. The large wires in the circuit are connected from the vehicle battery to one side of the relay, and from the opposite side of the relay to the component. The relay is normally open, preventing current from passing through the circuit. An additional, smaller wire is connected from the relay to the control switch for the circuit. When the control switch is turned on, it grounds the smaller wire from the relay and completes the circuit.

SHORT CIRCUITS

If you were to disconnect the light bulb (from the previous example of a light-bulb being connected to the battery by two wires) from the wires and touch the two wires together (please take our word for this; don't try it), the result will be a shower of sparks. A similar thing happens (on a smaller scale) when the power supply wire to a component or the electrical component itself becomes grounded before the normal ground connection for the circuit. To prevent damage to the system, the fuse for the circuit blows to interrupt the circuit — protecting the components from damage. Because grounding a wire from a power source makes a complete circuit — less the required component to use the power — the phenomenon is called a short circuit. The most common causes of short circuits are: the rubber insulation on a wire breaking or rubbing through to expose the current carrying core of the wire to a metal part of the car, or a shorted switch.

Some electrical systems on the vehicle are protected by a circuit breaker which is, basically, a self-repairing fuse. When either of the described events takes place in a system which is protected by a circuit breaker, the circuit breaker opens the circuit the same way a fuse does. However, when either the short is removed from the circuit or the surge subsides, the circuit breaker resets itself and does not have to be replaced as a fuse does.

Troubleshooting

When diagnosing a specific problem, organized troubleshooting is a must. The complexity of a modern automobile demands that you approach any problem in a logical, organized manner. There are certain troubleshooting techniques that are standard:

1. Establish when the problem occurs. Does the problem appear only under certain conditions? Were there any noises, odors, or other unusual symptoms?

2. Isolate the problem area. To do this, make some simple tests and observations; then eliminate the systems that are working properly. Check for obvious problems such as broken wires, dirty connections or split/disconnected vacuum hoses. Always check the obvious before assuming something complicated is the cause.

3. Test for problems systematically to determine the cause once the problem area is isolated. Are all the components functioning properly? Is there power going to electrical switches and motors? Is there vacuum at vacuum switches and/or actuators? Is there a mechanical problem such as bent linkage

or loose mounting screws? Performing careful, systematic checks will often turn up most causes on the first inspection without wasting time checking components that have little or no relationship to the problem.

4. Test all repairs after the work is done to make sure that the problem is fixed. Some causes can be traced to more than one component, so a careful verification of repair work is important in order to pick up additional malfunctions that may cause a problem to reappear or a different problem to arise. A blown fuse, for example, is a simple problem that may require more than another fuse to repair. If you don't look for a problem that caused a fuse to blow, a shorted wire (for example) may go undetected.

Experience has shown that most problems tend to be the result of a fairly simple and obvious cause, such as loose or corroded connectors or air leaks in the intake system. This makes careful inspection of components during testing essential to quick and accurate troubleshooting.

BASIC TROUBLESHOOTING THEORY

Electrical problems generally fall into one of three areas:
• The component that is not functioning is not receiving current.
• The component itself is not functioning.
• The component is not properly grounded.
Problems that fall into the first category are by far the most complicated. It is the current supply system to the component which contains all the switches, relay, fuses, etc.

The electrical system can be checked with a test light and a jumper wire. A test light is a device that looks like a pointed screwdriver with a wire attached to it. It has a light bulb in its handle. A jumper wire is a piece of insulated wire with an alligator clip attached to each end.

If a light bulb is not working, you must follow a systematic plan to determine which of the three causes is the villain.

1. Turn on the switch that controls the inoperable bulb.
2. Disconnect the power supply wire from the bulb.
3. Attach the ground wire to the test light to a good metal ground.
4. Touch the probe end of the test light to the end of the power supply wire that was disconnected from the bulb. If the bulb is receiving current, the test light will go on.

➡**If the bulb is one which works only when the ignition key is turned on (turn signal), make sure the key is turned on.**

If the test light does not go on, then the problem is in the circuit between the battery and the bulb. As mentioned before, this includes all the switches, fuses, and relays in the system. Turn to a wiring diagram and find the bulb on the diagram. Follow the wire that runs back to the battery. The problem is an open circuit between the battery and the bulb. If the fuse is blown and, when replaced, immediately blows again, there is a short circuit in the system which must be located and repaired. If there is a switch in the system, bypass it with a jumper wire. This is done by connecting one end of the jumper wire to the power supply wire into the switch and the other end of the jumper wire to the wire coming out of the switch. If the test

light illuminates with the jumper wire installed, the switch or whatever was bypassed is defective.

➡**Never substitute the jumper wire for the bulb, as the bulb is the component required to use the power from the power source.**

5. If the bulb in the test light goes on, then the current is getting to the bulb that is not working in the car. This eliminates the first of the three possible causes. Connect the power supply wire and connect a jumper wire from the bulb to a good metal ground. Do this with the switch which controls the bulb works with jumper wire installed, then it has a bad ground. This is usually caused by the metal area on which the bulb mounts to the vehicle being coated with some type of foreign matter.

6. If neither test located the source of the trouble, then the light bulb itself is defective.

The above test procedure can be applied to any of the components of the chassis electrical system by substituting the component that is not working for the light bulb. Remember that for any electrical system to work, all connections must be clean and tight.

TEST EQUIPMENT

➡**Pinpointing the exact cause of trouble in an electrical system can sometimes only be accomplished by the use of special test equipment. The following describes different types of commonly used test equipment and explains how to use them in diagnosis. In addition to the information covered below, the tool manufacturer's instructions booklet (provided with the tester) should be read and clearly understood before attempting any test procedures.**

Jumper Wires

Jumper wires are simple, yet extremely valuable, pieces of test equipment. They are basically test wires which are used to bypass sections of a circuit. The simplest type of jumper wire is a length of multi-strand wire with an alligator clip at each end. Jumper wires are usually fabricated from lengths of standard automotive wire and whatever type of connector (alligator clip, spade connector or pin connector) that is required for the particular vehicle being tested. The well equipped tool box will have several different styles of jumper wires in several different lengths. Some jumper wires are made with three or more terminals coming from a common splice for special purpose testing. In cramped, hard-to-reach areas it is advisable to have insulated boots over the jumper wire terminals in order to prevent accidental grounding, sparks, and possible fire, especially when testing fuel system components.

Jumper wires are used primarily to locate open electrical circuits, on either the ground (-) side of the circuit or on the hot (+) side. If an electrical component fails to operate, connect the jumper wire between the component and a good ground. If the component operates only with the jumper installed, the ground circuit is open. If the ground circuit is good, but the component does not operate, the circuit between the power feed and component may be open. By moving the jumper wire successively back from the lamp toward the power source, you can isolate the area of the circuit where the open is located. When the component stops functioning, or the power is cut off, the open is in the segment of wire between the jumper and the point previously tested.

You can sometimes connect the jumper wire directly from the battery to the hot terminal of the component, but first make sure the component uses 12 volts in operation. Some electrical components, such as fuel injectors, are designed to operate on about 4 volts and running 12 volts directly to the injector terminals can cause damage.

By inserting an in-line fuse holder between a set of test leads, a fused jumper wire can be used for bypassing open circuits. Use a 5 amp fuse to provide protection against voltage spikes. When in doubt, use a voltmeter to check the voltage input to the component and measure how much voltage is normally being applied.

✳✳CAUTION

Never use jumpers made from wire that is of lighter gauge than that which is used in the circuit under test. If the jumper wire is of too small a gauge, it may overheat and possibly melt. Never use jumpers to bypass high resistance loads in a circuit. Bypassing resistances, in effect, creates a short circuit. This may, in turn, cause damage and fire. Jumper wires should only be used to bypass lengths of wire.

Unpowered Test Lights

The 12 volt test light is used to check circuits and components while electrical current is flowing through them. It is used for voltage and ground tests. Twelve volt test lights come in different styles but all have three main parts; a ground clip, a probe, and a light. The most commonly used 12 volt test lights have pick-type probes. To use a 12 volt test light, connect the ground clip to a good ground and probe wherever necessary with the pick. The pick should be sharp so that it can be probed into tight spaces.

✳✳CAUTION

Do not use a test light to probe electronic ignition spark plug or coil wires. Never use a pick-type test light to probe wiring on computer controlled systems unless specifically instructed to do so. Any wire insulation that is pierced by the test light probe should be taped and sealed with silicone after testing.

Like the jumper wire, the 12 volt test light is used to isolate opens in circuits. But, whereas the jumper wire is used to bypass the open to operate the load, the 12 volt test light is used to locate the presence of voltage in a circuit. If the test light glows, you know that there is power up to that point; if the 12 volt test light does not glow when its probe is inserted into the wire or connector, you know that there is an open circuit (no power). Move the test light in successive steps back toward the power source until the light in the handle does

glow. When it glows, the open is between the probe and point which was probed previously.

➡**The test light does not detect that 12 volts (or any particular amount of voltage) is present. It only detects that some voltage is present. It is advisable before using the test light to touch its terminals across the battery posts to make sure the light is operating properly.**

Self-Powered Test Lights

The self-powered test light usually contains a 1.5 volt penlight battery. One type of self-powered test light is similar in design to the 12 volt unit. This type has both the battery and the light in the handle, along with a pick-type probe tip. The second type has the light toward the open tip, so that the light illuminates the contact point. The self-powered test light is a dual purpose piece of test equipment. It can be used to test for either open or short circuits when power is isolated from the circuit (continuity test). A powered test light should not be used on any computer controlled system or component unless specifically instructed to do so. Many engine sensors can be destroyed by even this small amount of voltage applied directly to the terminals.

Voltmeters

A voltmeter is used to measure voltage at any point in a circuit, or to measure the voltage drop across any part of a circuit. It can also be used to check continuity in a wire or circuit by indicating current flow from one end to the other. Analog voltmeters usually have various scales on the meter dial and a selector switch to allow the selection of different voltages. The voltmeter has a positive and a negative lead. To avoid damage to the meter, always connect the negative lead to the negative (-) side of the circuit (to ground or nearest the ground side of the circuit) and connect the positive lead to the positive (+) side of the circuit (to the power source or the nearest power source). Note that the negative voltmeter lead will always be black and that the positive voltmeter will always be some color other than black (usually red).

Depending on how the voltmeter is connected into the circuit, it has several uses. A voltmeter can be connected either in parallel or in series with a circuit and it has a very high resistance to current flow. When connected in parallel, only a small amount of current will flow through the voltmeter current path; the rest will flow through the normal circuit current path and the circuit will work normally. When the voltmeter is connected in series with a circuit, only a small amount of current can flow through the circuit. The circuit will not work properly, but the voltmeter reading will show if the circuit is complete or not.

Ohmmeters

The ohmmeter is designed to read resistance (which is measured in ohms or Ω) in a circuit or component. Although there are several different styles of ohmmeters, all analog meters will usually have a selector switch which permits the measurement of different ranges of resistance (usually the selector switch allows the multiplication of the meter reading by 10, 100, 1000, and 10,000). A calibration knob allows the meter to be set at zero for accurate measurement. Since all ohmmeters are powered by an internal battery, the ohmmeter can be used as a self-powered test light. When the ohmmeter is connected, current from the ohmmeter flows through the circuit or component being tested. Since the ohmmeter's internal resistance and voltage are known values, the amount of current flow through the meter depends on the resistance of the circuit or component being tested.

The ohmmeter can be used to perform a continuity test for opens or shorts (either by observation of the meter needle or as a self-powered test light), and to read actual resistance in a circuit. It should be noted that the ohmmeter is used to check the resistance of a component or wire while there is no voltage applied to the circuit. Current flow from an outside voltage source (such as the vehicle battery) can damage the ohmmeter, so the circuit or component should be isolated from the vehicle electrical system before any testing is done. Since the ohmmeter uses its own voltage source, either lead can be connected to any test point.

➡ **When checking diodes or other solid state components, the ohmmeter leads can only be connected one way in order to measure current flow in a single direction. Make sure the positive (+) and negative (-) terminal connections are as described in the test procedures to verify the one-way diode operation.**

In using the meter for making continuity checks, do not be concerned with the actual resistance readings. Zero resistance, or any ohm reading, indicates continuity in the circuit. Infinite resistance indicates an open in the circuit. A high resistance reading where there should be none indicates a problem in the circuit. Checks for short circuits are made in the same manner as checks for open circuits except that the circuit must be isolated from both power and normal ground. Infinite resistance indicates no continuity to ground, while zero resistance indicates a dead short to ground.

Ammeters

An ammeter measures the amount of current flowing through a circuit in units called amperes or amps. Amperes are units of electron flow which indicate how fast the electrons are flowing through the circuit. Since Ohms Law dictates that current flow in a circuit is equal to the circuit voltage divided by the total circuit resistance, increasing voltage also increases the current level (amps). Likewise, any decrease in resistance will increase the amount of amps in a circuit. At normal operating voltage, most circuits have a characteristic amount of amperes, called "current draw" which can be measured using an ammeter. By referring to a specified current draw rating, measuring the amperes, and comparing the two values, one can determine what is happening within the circuit to aid in diagnosis. An open circuit, for example, will not allow any current to flow so the ammeter reading will be zero. More current flows through a heavily loaded circuit or when the charging system is operating.

An ammeter is always connected in series with the circuit being tested. All of the current that normally flows through the circuit must also flow through the ammeter; if there is any other path for the current to follow, the ammeter reading will not be accurate. The ammeter itself has very little resistance to current flow and therefore will not affect the circuit, but it will measure current draw only when the circuit is closed and electricity is flowing. Excessive current draw can blow fuses

and drain the battery, while a reduced current draw can cause motors to run slowly, lights to dim and other components to not operate properly. The ammeter can help diagnose these conditions by locating the cause of the high or low reading.

Multimeters

Different combinations of test meters can be built into a single unit designed for specific tests. Some of the more common combination test devices are known as Volt/Amp testers, Tach/Dwell meters, or Digital Multimeters. The Volt/Amp tester is used for charging system, starting system or battery tests and consists of a voltmeter, an ammeter and a variable resistance carbon pile. The voltmeter will usually have at least two ranges for use with 6, 12 and/or 24 volt systems. The ammeter also has more than one range for testing various levels of battery loads and starter current draw. The carbon pile can be adjusted to offer different amounts of resistance. The Volt/Amp tester has heavy leads to carry large amounts of current and many later models have an inductive ammeter pickup that clamps around the wire to simplify test connections. On some models, the ammeter also has a zero-center scale to allow testing of charging and starting systems without switching leads or polarity. A digital multimeter is a voltmeter, ammeter and ohmmeter combined in an instrument which gives a digital readout. These are often used when testing solid state circuits because of their high input impedance (usually 10 megohms or more).

The tach/dwell meter that combines a tachometer and a dwell (cam angle) meter is a specialized kind of voltmeter. The tachometer scale is marked to show engine speed in rpm and the dwell scale is marked to show degrees of distributor shaft rotation. In most electronic ignition systems, dwell is determined by the control unit, but the dwell meter can also be used to check the duty cycle (operation) of some electronic engine control systems. Some tach/dwell meters are powered by an internal battery, while others take their power from the vehicle battery in use. The battery powered testers usually require calibration (much like an ohmmeter) before testing.

TESTING

Open Circuits

To use the self-powered test light or a multimeter to check for open circuits, first isolate the circuit from the vehicle's 12 volt power source by disconnecting the battery or wiring harness connector. Connect the test light or ohmmeter ground clip to a good ground and probe sections of the circuit sequentially with the test light. (start from either end of the circuit). If the light is out/or there is infinite resistance, the open is between the probe and the circuit ground. If the light is on/or the meter shows continuity, the open is between the probe and end of the circuit toward the power source.

Short Circuits

By isolating the circuit both from power and from ground, and using a self-powered test light or multimeter, you can check for shorts to ground in the circuit. Isolate the circuit from power and ground. Connect the test light or ohmmeter ground clip to a good ground and probe any easy-to-reach test point in the circuit. If the light comes on or there is continuity, there is a short somewhere in the circuit. To isolate the short, probe a test point at either end of the isolated circuit (the light should be on/there should be continuity). Leave the test light probe engaged and open connectors, switches, remove parts, etc., sequentially, until the light goes out/continuity is broken. When the light goes out, the short is between the last circuit component opened and the previous circuit opened.

➡The battery in the test light and does not provide much current. A weak battery may not provide enough power to illuminate the test light even when a complete circuit is made (especially if there are high resistances in the circuit). Always make sure that the test battery is strong. To check the battery, briefly touch the ground clip to the probe; if the light glows brightly the battery is strong enough for testing. Never use a self-powered test light to perform checks for opens or shorts when power is applied to the electrical system under test. The 12 volt vehicle power will quickly burn out the light bulb in the test light.

Available Voltage Measurement

Set the voltmeter selector switch to the 20V position and connect the meter negative lead to the negative post of the battery. Connect the positive meter lead to the positive post of the battery and turn the ignition switch **ON** to provide a load. Read the voltage on the meter or digital display. A well charged battery should register over 12 volts. If the meter reads below 11.5 volts, the battery power may be insufficient to operate the electrical system properly. This test determines voltage available from the battery and should be the first step in any electrical trouble diagnosis procedure. Many electrical problems, especially on computer controlled systems, can be caused by a low state of charge in the battery. Excessive corrosion at the battery cable terminals can cause a poor contact that will prevent proper charging and full battery current flow.

Normal battery voltage is 12 volts when fully charged. When the battery is supplying current to one or more circuits it is said to be "under load." When everything is off the electrical system is under a "no-load" condition. A fully charged battery may show about 12.5 volts at no load; will drop to 12 volts under medium load; and will drop even lower under heavy load. If the battery is partially discharged the voltage decrease under heavy load may be excessive, even though the battery shows 12 volts or more at no load. When allowed to discharge further, the battery's available voltage under load will decrease more severely. For this reason, it is important that the battery be fully charged during all testing procedures to avoid errors in diagnosis and incorrect test results.

Voltage Drop

When current flows through a resistance, the voltage beyond the resistance is reduced (the larger the current, the greater the reduction in voltage). When no current is flowing, there is no voltage drop because there is no current flow. All points in the circuit which are connected to the power source are at the same voltage as the power source. The total voltage drop always equals the total source voltage. In a long circuit with many connectors, a series of small, unwanted voltage drops

due to corrosion at the connectors can add up to a total loss of voltage which impairs the operation of the normal loads in the circuit. The maximum allowable voltage drop under load is critical, especially if there is more than one high resistance problem in a circuit because all voltage drops are cumulative. A small drop is normal due to the resistance of the conductors.

INDIRECT COMPUTATION OF VOLTAGE DROPS

1. Set the voltmeter selector switch to the 20 volt position.
2. Connect the meter negative lead to a good ground.
3. While operating the circuit, probe all loads in the circuit with the positive meter lead and observe the voltage readings. A drop should be noticed after the first load. But, there should be little or no voltage drop before the first load.

DIRECT MEASUREMENT OF VOLTAGE DROPS

1. Set the voltmeter switch to the 20 volt position.
2. Connect the voltmeter negative lead to the ground side of the load to be measured.
3. Connect the positive lead to the positive side of the resistance or load to be measured.
4. Read the voltage drop directly on the 20 volt scale.

Too high a voltage indicates too high a resistance. If, for example, a blower motor runs too slowly, you can determine if perhaps there is too high a resistance in the resistor pack. By taking voltage drop readings in all parts of the circuit, you can isolate the problem. Too low a voltage drop indicates too low a resistance. Take the blower motor for example again. If a blower motor runs too fast in the MED and/or LOW position, the problem might be isolated in the resistor pack by taking voltage drop readings in all parts of the circuit to locate a possibly shorted resistor.

HIGH RESISTANCE TESTING

1. Set the voltmeter selector switch to the 4 volt position.
2. Connect the voltmeter positive lead to the positive post of the battery.
3. Turn on the headlights and heater blower to provide a load.
4. Probe various points in the circuit with the negative voltmeter lead.
5. Read the voltage drop on the 4 volt scale. Some average maximum allowable voltage drops are:
   - FUSE PANEL: 0.7 volts
   - IGNITION SWITCH: 0.5 volts
   - HEADLIGHT SWITCH: 0.7 volts
   - IGNITION COIL (+): 0.5 volts
   - ANY OTHER LOAD: 1.3 volts

➡Voltage drops are all measured while a load is operating; without current flow, there will be no voltage drop.

Resistance Measurement

The batteries in an ohmmeter will weaken with age and temperature, so the ohmmeter must be calibrated or "zeroed" before taking measurements. To zero the meter, place the selector switch in its lowest range and touch the two ohmmeter leads together. Turn the calibration knob until the meter needle is exactly on zero.

➡**All analog (needle) type ohmmeters must be zeroed before use, but some digital ohmmeter models are automatically calibrated when the switch is turned on. Self-calibrating digital ohmmeters do not have an adjusting knob, but its a good idea to check for a zero readout before use by touching the leads together. All computer controlled systems require the use of a digital ohmmeter with at least 10 megohms impedance for testing. Before any test procedures are attempted, make sure the ohmmeter used is compatible with the electrical system or damage to the on-board computer could result.**

To measure resistance, first isolate the circuit from the vehicle power source by disconnecting the battery cables or the harness connector. Make sure the key is **OFF** when disconnecting any components or the battery. Where necessary, also isolate at least one side of the circuit to be checked in order to avoid reading parallel resistances. Parallel circuit resistances will always give a lower reading than the actual resistance of either of the branches. When measuring the resistance of parallel circuits, the total resistance will always be lower than the smallest resistance in the circuit. Connect the meter leads to both sides of the circuit (wire or component) and read the actual measured ohms on the meter scale. Make sure the selector switch is set to the proper ohm scale for the circuit being tested to avoid misreading the ohmmeter test value.

✳✳WARNING

Never use an ohmmeter with power applied to the circuit. Like the self-powered test light, the ohmmeter is designed to operate on its own power supply. The normal 12 volt automotive electrical system current could damage the meter!

Wiring Harnesses

The average automobile contains about ½ mile of wiring, with hundreds of individual connections. To protect the many wires from damage and to keep them from becoming a confusing tangle, they are organized into bundles, enclosed in plastic or taped together and called wiring harnesses. Different harnesses serve different parts of the vehicle. Individual wires are color coded to help trace them through a harness where sections are hidden from view.

Automotive wiring or circuit conductors can be in any one of three forms:

1. Single strand wire
2. Multi-strand wire
3. Printed circuitry

Single strand wire has a solid metal core and is usually used inside such components as alternators, motors, relays and other devices. Multi-strand wire has a core made of many small strands of wire twisted together into a single conductor. Most of the wiring in an automotive electrical system is made up of multi-strand wire, either as a single conductor or grouped

together in a harness. All wiring is color coded on the insulator, either as a solid color or as a colored wire with an identification stripe. A printed circuit is a thin film of copper or other conductor that is printed on an insulator backing. Occasionally, a printed circuit is sandwiched between two sheets of plastic for more protection and flexibility. A complete printed circuit, consisting of conductors, insulating material and connectors for lamps or other components is called a printed circuit board. Printed circuitry is used in place of individual wires or harnesses in places where space is limited, such as behind instrument panels.

Since automotive electrical systems are very sensitive to changes in resistance, the selection of properly sized wires is critical when systems are repaired. A loose or corroded connection or a replacement wire that is too small for the circuit will add extra resistance and an additional voltage drop to the circuit. A ten percent voltage drop can result in slow or erratic motor operation, for example, even though the circuit is complete. The wire gauge number is an expression of the cross-section area of the conductor. The most common system for expressing wire size is the American Wire Gauge (AWG) system.

Gauge numbers are assigned to conductors of various cross-section areas. As gauge number increases, area decreases and the conductor becomes smaller. A 5 gauge conductor is smaller than a 1 gauge conductor and a 10 gauge is smaller than a 5 gauge. As the cross-section area of a conductor decreases, resistance increases and so does the gauge number. A conductor with a higher gauge number will carry less current than a conductor with a lower gauge number.

➡**Gauge wire size refers to the size of the conductor, not the size of the complete wire. It is possible to have two wires of the same gauge with different diameters because one may have thicker insulation than the other.**

12 volt automotive electrical systems generally use 10, 12, 14, 16 and 18 gauge wire. Main power distribution circuits and larger accessories usually use 10 and 12 gauge wire. Battery cables are usually 4 or 6 gauge, although 1 and 2 gauge wires are occasionally used. Wire length must also be considered when making repairs to a circuit. As conductor length increases, so does resistance. An 18 gauge wire, for example, can carry a 10 amp load for 10 feet without excessive voltage drop; however if a 15 foot wire is required for the same 10 amp load, it must be a 16 gauge wire.

An electrical schematic shows the electrical current paths when a circuit is operating properly. It is essential to understand how a circuit works before trying to figure out why it doesn't. Schematics break the entire electrical system down into individual circuits and show only one particular circuit. In a schematic, no attempt is made to represent wiring and components as they physically appear on the vehicle; switches and other components are shown as simply as possible. Face views of harness connectors show the cavity or terminal locations in all multi-pin connectors to help locate test points.

If you need to backprobe a connector while it is on the component, the order of the terminals must be mentally reversed. The wire color code can help in this situation, as well as a keyway, lock tab or other reference mark.

WIRING REPAIR

Soldering is a quick, efficient method of joining metals permanently. Everyone who has the occasion to make wiring repairs should know how to solder. Electrical connections that are soldered are far less likely to come apart and will conduct electricity much better than connections that are only "pig-tailed" together. The most popular (and preferred) method of soldering is with an electrical soldering gun. Soldering irons are available in many sizes and wattage ratings. Irons with higher wattage ratings deliver higher temperatures and recover lost heat faster. A small soldering iron rated for no more than 50 watts is recommended, especially on electrical systems where excess heat can damage the components being soldered.

There are three ingredients necessary for successful soldering; proper flux, good solder and sufficient heat. A soldering flux is necessary to clean the metal of tarnish, prepare it for soldering and to enable the solder to spread into tiny crevices. When soldering, always use a rosin core solder which is non-corrosive and will not attract moisture once the job is finished. Other types of flux (acid core) will leave a residue that will attract moisture and cause the wires to corrode. Tin is a unique metal with a low melting point. In a molten state, it dissolves and alloys easily with many metals. Solder is made by mixing tin with lead. The most common proportions are 40/60, 50/50 and 60/40, with the percentage of tin listed first. Low priced solders usually contain less tin, making them very difficult for a beginner to use because more heat is required to melt the solder. A common solder is 40/60 which is well suited for all-around general use, but 60/40 melts easier and is preferred for electrical work.

Soldering Techniques

Successful soldering requires that the metals to be joined be heated to a temperature that will melt the solder, usually 360-460°F (182-238°C). Contrary to popular belief, the purpose of the soldering iron is not to melt the solder itself, but to heat the parts being soldered to a temperature high enough to melt the solder when it is touched to the work. Melting flux-cored solder on the soldering iron will usually destroy the effectiveness of the flux.

➡Soldering tips are made of copper for good heat conductivity, but must be "tinned" regularly for quick transference of heat to the project and to prevent the solder from sticking to the iron. To "tin" the iron, simply heat it and touch the flux-cored solder to the tip; the solder will flow over the hot tip. Wipe the excess off with a clean rag, but be careful as the iron will be hot.

After some use, the tip may become pitted. If so, simply dress the tip smooth with a smooth file and "tin" the tip again. Flux-cored solder will remove oxides but rust, bits of insulation and oil or grease must be removed with a wire brush or emery cloth. For maximum strength in soldered parts, the joint must start off clean and tight. Weak joints will result in gaps too wide for the solder to bridge.

If a separate soldering flux is used, it should be brushed or swabbed on only those areas that are to be soldered. Most solders contain a core of flux and separate fluxing is unnecessary. Hold the work to be soldered firmly. It is best to solder on a wooden board, because a metal vise will only rob the piece to be soldered of heat and make it difficult to melt the solder. Hold the soldering tip with the broadest face against the work to be soldered. Apply solder under the tip close to the work, using enough solder to give a heavy film between the iron and the piece being soldered, while moving slowly and making sure the solder melts properly. Keep the work level or the solder will run to the lowest part and favor the thicker parts, because these require more heat to melt the solder. If the soldering tip overheats (the solder coating on the face of the tip burns up), it should be retinned. Once the soldering is completed, let the soldered joint stand until cool. Tape and seal all soldered wire splices after the repair has cooled.

Wire Harness Connectors

Most connectors in the engine compartment or that are otherwise exposed to the elements are protected against moisture and dirt which could create oxidation and deposits on the terminals.

These special connectors are weather-proof. All repairs require the use of a special terminal and the tool required to service it. This tool is used to remove the pin and sleeve terminals. If removal is attempted with an ordinary pick, there is a good chance that the terminal will be bent or deformed. Unlike standard blade type terminals, these weather-proof terminals cannot be straightened once they are bent. Make certain that the connectors are properly seated and all of the sealing rings are in place when connecting leads. On some models, a hinge-type flap provides a backup or secondary locking feature for the terminals. Most secondary locks are used to improve connector reliability by retaining the terminals if the small terminal lock tangs are not positioned properly.

Molded-on connectors require complete replacement of the connection. This means splicing a new connector assembly into the harness. All splices should be soldered to insure proper contact. Use care when probing the connections or replacing terminals in them as it is possible to short between opposite terminals. If this happens to the wrong terminal pair, it is possible to damage certain components. Always use jumper wires between connectors for circuit checking and never probe through weatherproof seals.

Open circuits are often difficult to locate by sight because corrosion or terminal misalignment are hidden by the connectors. Merely wiggling a connector on a sensor or in the wiring harness may correct the open circuit condition. This should always be considered when an open circuit or a failed sensor is indicated. Intermittent problems may also be caused by oxidized or loose connections. When using a circuit tester for diagnosis, always probe connections from the wire side. Be careful not to damage sealed connectors with test probes.

All wiring harnesses should be replaced with identical parts, using the same gauge wire and connectors. When signal wires are spliced into a harness, use wire with high temperature insulation only. It is seldom necessary to replace a complete harness. If replacement is necessary, pay close attention to insure proper harness routing. Secure the harness with suitable plastic wire clamps to prevent vibrations from causing the harness to wear in spots or contact any hot components.

➡**Weatherproof connectors cannot be replaced with standard connectors. Instructions are provided with replacement connector and terminal packages. Some wire harnesses have mounting indicators (usually pieces of colored tape) to mark where the harness is to be secured.**

In making wiring repairs, its important that you always replace damaged wires with wiring of the same gauge as the wire being replaced. The heavier the wire, the smaller the gauge number. Wires are color-coded to aid in identification and whenever possible the same color coded wire should be used for replacement. A wire stripping and crimping tool is necessary to install solderless terminal connectors. Test all crimps by pulling on the wires; it should not be possible to pull the wires out of a good crimp.

Wires which are open, exposed or otherwise damaged are repaired by simple splicing. Where possible, if the wiring harness is accessible and the damaged place in the wire can be located, it is best to open the harness and check for all possible damage. In an inaccessible harness, the wire must be bypassed with a new insert, usually taped to the outside of the old harness.

When replacing fusible links, be sure to use fusible link wire, NOT ordinary automotive wire. Make sure the fusible segment is of the same gauge and construction as the one being replaced and double the stripped end when crimping the terminal connector for a good contact. The melted (open) fusible link segment of the wiring harness should be cut off as close to the harness as possible, then a new segment spliced in as described. In the case of a damaged fusible link that feeds two harness wires, the harness connections should be replaced with two fusible link wires so that each circuit will have its own separate protection.

➡**Most of the problems caused in the wiring harness are due to bad ground connections. Always check all vehicle ground connections for corrosion or looseness before performing any power feed checks to eliminate the chance of a bad ground affecting the circuit.**

Hard-Shell Connectors

Unlike molded connectors, the terminal contacts in hard-shell connectors can be replaced. Weatherproof hard-shell connectors with the leads molded into the shell have non-replaceable terminal ends. Replacement usually involves the use of a special terminal removal tool that depresses the locking tangs (barbs) on the connector terminal and allows the connector to be removed from the rear of the shell. The connector shell should be replaced if it shows any evidence of burning, melting, cracks, or breaks. Replace individual terminals that are burnt, corroded, distorted or loose.

➡**The insulation crimp must be tight to prevent the insulation from sliding back on the wire when the wire is pulled. The insulation must be visibly compressed under the crimp tabs, and the ends of the crimp should be turned in for a firm grip on the insulation.**

The wire crimp must be made with all wire strands inside the crimp. The terminal must be fully compressed on the wire strands with the ends of the crimp tabs turned in to make a firm grip on the wire. Check all connections with an ohmmeter to insure a good contact. There should be no measurable resistance between the wire and the terminal when connected.

Add-On Electrical Equipment

The electrical system in your vehicle is designed to perform under reasonable operating conditions without interference between components. Before any additional electrical equipment is installed, it is recommended that you consult your dealer or a reputable repair facility that is familiar with the vehicle and its systems.

If the vehicle is equipped with mobile radio equipment and/or mobile telephone, it may have an effect upon the operation of any on-board computer control modules. Radio Frequency Interference (RFI) from the communications system can be picked up by the vehicle's wiring harnesses and conducted into the control module, giving it the wrong messages at the wrong time. Although well shielded against RFI, the computer should be further protected by taking the following measures:

• Install the antenna as far as possible from the control module. For instance, if the module is located behind the center console area, then the antenna should be mounted at the rear of the vehicle.

• Keep the antenna wiring a minimum of eight inches away from any wiring running to control modules and from the module itself. NEVER wind the antenna wire around any other wiring.

• Mount the equipment as far from the control module as possible. Be very careful during installation not to drill through any wires or short a wire harness with a mounting screw.

• Insure that the electrical feed wire(s) to the equipment are properly and tightly connected. Loose connectors can cause interference.

• Make certain that the equipment is properly grounded to the vehicle. Poor grounding can damage expensive equipment.

PASSIVE RESTRAINT SYSTEM (AIR BAG)

General Information

SYSTEM OPERATION

The Passive Restraint System (AIR BAG) is designed to work in concert with the seat belts to further prevent personal injury during a head-on collision with another object. The air bag system utilizes an air bag module, front impact sensors, a clockspring, and a diagnostic module.

With the battery cables connected, the air bag system system is energized and monitoring the front impact sensors and the safing sensor for collision confirmation messages. When the vehicle strikes, or is struck by, another object (such as a tree, wall, another vehicle, etc.), the front impact sensors and safing sensor send impulses to the diagnostic module, which determines the force and direction of the impact. Based on this information the diagnostic module either deploys or does not deploy the air bag.

The only time that the air bag system is completely disarmed with no chance of accidental deployment is when the battery cables have been disconnected from the battery and set aside, and at least 2 minutes have gone by to allow the system capacitor to discharge any residual energy.

SYSTEM COMPONENTS

▶ See Figure 1

Air Bag Module

The air bag module is the most visible part of the system. It contains the air bag cushion and its supporting components. The air bag module contains a housing to which the cushion and inflator are attached and sealed.

The inflator assembly is mounted to the back of the module housing. When supplied with the proper electrical signal, the inflator assembly produces a gas which discharges directly into the cushion. A protective cover is fitted to the front of the air bag module and forms a decorative cover in the center of the steering wheel. The air bag module is mounted directly to the steering wheel.

Front Impact Sensors

The impact sensors provide verification of the direction and severity of the impact. Three impact sensors are used. One is called a safing sensor. It is located inside the diagnostic module which is mounted on the floor pan, just forward of the center console. The other two sensors are mounted on the upper crossmember of the radiator closure panel on the left and right side of the vehicle under the hood.

The impact sensors are threshold sensitive switches that complete an electrical circuit when an impact provides a sufficient "g force" to close the switch. The sensors are calibrated for the specific vehicle and react to the severity and direction of the impact.

Clockspring

The clockspring is mounted on the steering column behind the steering wheel and is used to maintain a continuous electrical circuit between the wiring harness and the driver's air bag module. This assembly consists of a flat ribbon-like electrically conductive tape which winds and unwinds with the steering wheel rotation.

Diagnostic Module

The Air Bag System Diagnostic Module (ASDM) contains the safing sensor and energy reserve capacitor. The ASDM monitors the system to determine the system readiness. The ASDM will store sufficient energy to deploy the air bag for only two minutes after the battery is disconnected. The ASDM contains on-board diagnostics and will illuminate the AIR BAG warning lamp in the cluster when a fault occurs.

SERVICE PRECAUTIONS

When working on the Air Bag system or any components which require the removal of the air bag, adhere to all of these precautions to minimize the risks of personal injury or component damage:

• Before attempting to diagnose, remove or install air bag system components, you must first disconnect and isolate the negative (-) battery cable. Failure to do so could result in accidental deployment and possible personal injury.

• When an undeployed air bag assembly is to be removed from the steering wheel, after disconnecting the negative battery cable, allow the system capacitor to discharge for two minutes before commencing with the air bag system component removal.

• Replace the air bag system components only with Chrysler Mopar® specified replacement parts, or equivalent. Substitute parts may visually appear interchangeable, but internal differences may result in inferior occupant protection.

• The fasteners, screws, and bolts originally used for the Air Bag system have special coatings and are specifically designed for the Air Bag system. They must never be replaced with any substitutes. Anytime a new fastener is needed, replace with the correct fasteners provided in the service package or fasteners listed in the parts books.

Handling A Live Air Bag Module

At no time should any source of electricity be permitted near the inflator on the back of the module. When carrying a live module, the trim cover should be pointed away from the body to minimize injury in the event of accidental deployment. In addition, if the module is placed on a bench or other surface, the plastic trim cover should be face up to minimize movement in case of accidental deployment.

When handling a steering column with an air bag module attached, never place the column on the floor or other surface with the steering wheel or module face down.

Handling A Deployed Air Bag Module

The vehicle interior may contain a very small amount of sodium hydroxide powder, a by-product of air bag deployment. Since this powder can irritate the skin, eyes, nose or throat, be sure to wear safety glasses, rubber gloves and long sleeves during clean up.

If you find that the clean up is irritating your skin, run cool water over the affected area. Also, if you experience nasal or throat irritation, exit the vehicle for fresh air until the irritation ceases. If irritation continues, see a physician.

Begin the clean up by putting tape over the two air bag exhaust vents so that no additional powder will find its way into the vehicle interior. Then remove the air bag and air bag module from the vehicle.

Use a vacuum cleaner to remove any residual powder from the vehicle interior. Work from the outside in so that you avoid kneeling or sitting in an uncleaned area.

Be sure to vacuum the heater and A/C outlets as well. In fact it's a good idea to run the blower on low and to vacuum up any powder expelled from the plenum. You may need to vacuum the interior of the car a second time to recover all of the powder.

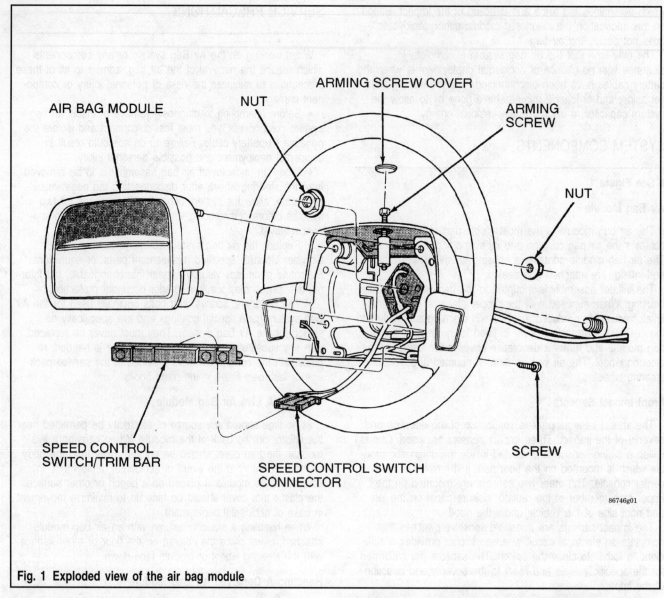

AIR BAG MODULE

NUT

ARMING SCREW COVER

ARMING SCREW

NUT

SPEED CONTROL SWITCH/TRIM BAR

SPEED CONTROL SWITCH CONNECTOR

SCREW

86746g01

Fig. 1 Exploded view of the air bag module

Check with the local authorities before disposing of the deployed bag and module in your trash.

After an air bag has been deployed, the air bag module and clockspring must be replaced, because they cannot be reused. Other air bag system components should be replaced with new ones, if damaged.

DISARMING THE SYSTEM

To disarm the Air Bag system, simply disconnect the negative battery cable from the battery. Isolate the battery cable by

taping up any exposed metal areas of the cable. This will keep the cable from accidentally contacting the battery and causing deployment of the air bag. Allow the system capacitor to discharge for at least 2 minutes, although 10 minutes is recommended, to allow for the dissipation of any residual energy.

ARMING THE SYSTEM

To arm the Air Bag system, reconnect the negative battery cable. This will automatically enable the Air Bag system.

HEATER

Blower Motor

REMOVAL & INSTALLATION

▶ See Figures 2 and 3

Except the 4.0L Engine

1. Disengage the electrical connection.
2. Remove the blower motor attaching screws.
3. Remove the blower motor.
4. Remove the blower motor fan from the motor shaft for access to the motor attaching nuts.

To install:

5. Install the blower motor fan on the motor shaft.
6. Install the blower motor and fasten the attaching screws.
7. Engage the electrical connection.

4.0L Engine

▶ See Figures 4 and 5

1. Remove the coolant overflow bottle retaining strap. Remove the coolant overflow bottle and bracket.
2. Disengage the blower motor wiring.
3. Remove the blower motor mounting fasteners.
4. Remove the blower motor.
5. Remove the blower motor fan from the motor shaft for access to the motor attaching nuts.

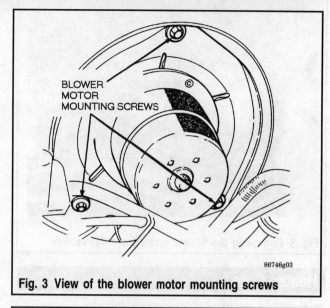

Fig. 3 View of the blower motor mounting screws

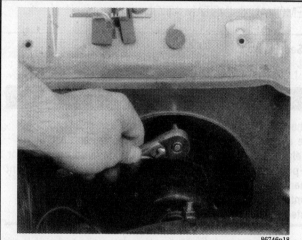

Fig. 4 Loosen and remove the blower motor retaining bolts

To install:

6. Install the blower motor fan on the motor shaft.
7. Install the blower motor and tighten the mounting fasteners.
8. Engage the electrical connection.
9. Install the coolant overflow bracket, bottle and retaining strap.

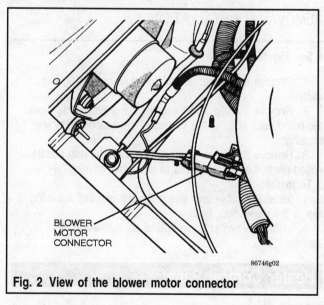

Fig. 2 View of the blower motor connector

Fig. 5 Removing the blower motor from the vehicle

Heater Core

REMOVAL & INSTALLATION

▶ See Figure 6

1. Drain the coolant.

❋❋CAUTION

When draining coolant, keep in mind that cats and dogs are attracted by ethylene glycol antifreeze, and are quite likely to drink any that is left in an uncovered container or in puddles on the ground. This will prove fatal in sufficient quantity. Always drain the coolant into a sealable container. Coolant should be reused unless it is contaminated or several years old.

2. Disconnect the heater hoses at the core tubes.
3. Remove the evaporator/blower housing as described in this section.
4. Unbolt and remove the core from the housing.
   To install:
5. Install the core in the housing.
6. Tighten the heater core retaining fasteners.
7. Connect the heater hoses at the core tubes.
8. Fill the cooling system.
9. Start the vehicle and bring it to operating temperature. Turn the heater and blower motor on and check for leakage.

Heater Control Valve

REMOVAL & INSTALLATION

➡Allow the vehicle to cool before performing this procedure.

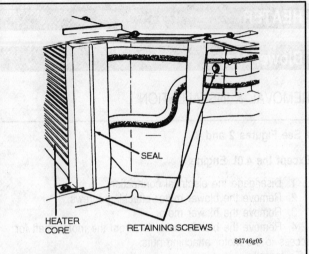

Fig. 6 When installing the heater core make sure the seal is properly installed

1. Label and disconnect all heater hoses attached to the valve.
2. Disconnect the vacuum hose which controls the valve.
3. Remove the valve.
   To install:
4. Install the valve.
5. Engage the vacuum hoses which control the valve.
6. Engage the heater hoses to the valve.

Control Cable

REMOVAL & INSTALLATION

▶ See Figures 7 and 8

1. Remove the heater control panel as outlined in this section.
2. Remove the clip and the cable self-adjusting clip from the blend door lever at the bottom of the evaporator/blower housing.
3. Remove the cable by squeezing the tabs with needle nosed pliers, being careful not to break the housing.
   To install:
4. Install the cable and attach the clip and self adjusting clip to the blend door lever.
5. Install the heater control panel as outlined in this section.

Heater Control Panel

REMOVAL & INSTALLATION

▶ See Figures 9, 10, 11 and 12

1. Disconnect the negative battery cable. Remove the ash tray.
2. Remove the instrument panel bezel fasteners and remove the bezel.
3. If necessary, remove the clock.

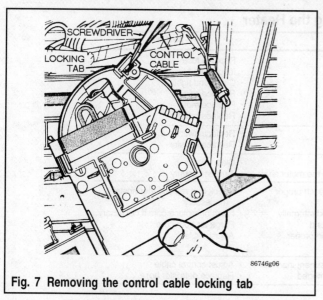

Fig. 7 Removing the control cable locking tab

Fig. 10 Remove the control panel retaining screws

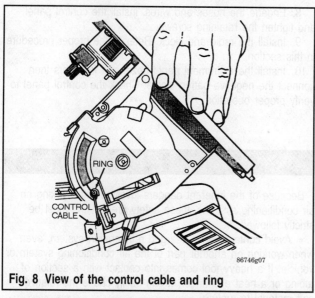

Fig. 8 View of the control cable and ring

Fig. 11 Remove the control panel from the dash

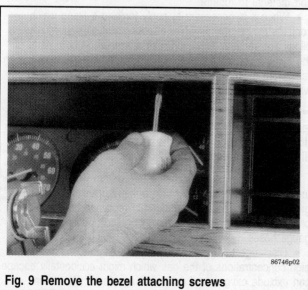

Fig. 9 Remove the bezel attaching screws

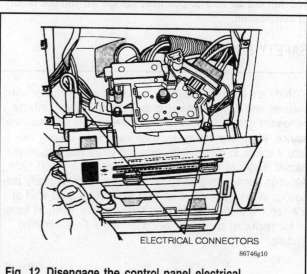

Fig. 12 Disengage the control panel electrical connectors

Troubleshooting the Heater

Problem	Cause	Solution
Blower motor will not turn at any speed	• Blown fuse • Loose connection • Defective ground • Faulty switch • Faulty motor • Faulty resistor	• Replace fuse • Inspect and tighten • Clean and tighten • Replace switch • Replace motor • Replace resistor
Blower motor turns at one speed only	• Faulty switch • Faulty resistor	• Replace switch • Replace resistor
Blower motor turns but does not circulate air	• Intake blocked • Fan not secured to the motor shaft	• Clean intake • Tighten security
Heater will not heat	• Coolant does not reach proper temperature • Heater core blocked internally • Heater core air-bound • Blend-air door not in proper position	• Check and replace thermostat if necessary • Flush or replace core if necessary • Purge air from core • Adjust cable
Heater will not defrost	• Control cable adjustment incorrect • Defroster hose damaged	• Adjust control cable • Replace defroster hose

86746c08

4. If necessary, unfasten the radio retaining screws and remove the radio. Refer to this section for the proper procedure.

5. Remove the control panel screws, pull the panel outward and disconnect and tag the hoses, wires and cable.

6. Remove the control cable locking tab by using a small prytool to release the tab.

To install:

7. Engage the control cable and fasten the retaining tab.

8. Engage the hoses and wires, install the control panel and tighten the retaining screws.

9. Install the radio and clock. Refer to the proper procedure in this section.

10. Install the instrument panel bezel and fasteners then connect the negative battery cable. Check the control panel to verify proper operation.

AIR CONDITIONER

General Precautions

➡Be sure to consult the laws in your area before servicing the air conditioning system. In most areas, it is illegal to perform repairs involving refrigerant unless the work is done by a certified technician. Also, it is quite likely that you will not be able to purchase refrigerant without proof of certification.

SAFETY PRECAUTIONS

There are two major hazards associated with air conditioning systems and they both relate to the refrigerant gas. First, the refrigerant gas (R-12 or R-134a) is an extremely cold substance. When exposed to air, it will instantly freeze any surface it comes in contact with, including your eyes. The other hazard relates to fire (if your vehicle is equipped with R-12. Although normally non-toxic, the R-12 gas becomes highly poisonous in the presence of an open flame. One good whiff of the vapor formed by burning R-12 can be fatal. Keep all forms of fire (including cigarettes) well clear of the air conditioning system.

Because of the inherent dangers involved with working on air conditioning systems, these safety precautions must be strictly followed.

• Avoid contact with a charged refrigeration system, even when working on another part of the air conditioning system or vehicle. If a heavy tool comes into contact with a section of tubing or a heat exchanger, it can easily cause the relatively soft material to rupture.

• When it is necessary to apply force to a fitting which contains refrigerant, as when checking that all system couplings are securely tightened, use a wrench on both parts of the fitting involved, if possible. This will avoid putting torque on refrigerant tubing. (It is also advisable to use tube or line wrenches when tightening these flare nut fittings.)

➡R-12 refrigerant is a chlorofluorocarbon which, when released into the atmosphere, can contribute to the depletion of the ozone layer in the upper atmosphere. Ozone filters out harmful radiation from the sun.

• Do not attempt to discharge the system without the proper tools. Precise control is possible only when using the service gauges and a proper A/C refrigerant recovery station. Wear protective gloves when connecting or disconnecting service gauge hoses.

• Discharge the system only in a well ventilated area, as high concentrations of the gas which might accidentally escape can exclude oxygen and act as an anesthetic. When leak testing or soldering, this is particularly important, as toxic gas is formed when R-12 contacts any flame.

• Never start a system without first verifying that both service valves are properly installed, and that all fittings throughout the system are snugly connected.

• Avoid applying heat to any refrigerant line or storage vessel. Charging may be aided by using water heated to less than 125°F (50°C) to warm the refrigerant container. Never allow a refrigerant storage container to sit out in the sun, or near any other source of heat, such as a radiator or heater.

• Always wear goggles to protect your eyes when working on a system. If refrigerant contacts the eyes, it is advisable in all cases to consult a physician immediately.

• Frostbite from liquid refrigerant should be treated by first gradually warming the area with cool water, and then gently applying petroleum jelly. A physician should be consulted.

• Always keep refrigerant drum fittings capped when not in use. If the container is equipped with a safety cap to protect the valve, make sure the cap is in place when the can is not being used. Avoid sudden shock to the drum, which might occur from dropping it, or from banging a heavy tool against it. Never carry a drum in the passenger compartment of a vehicle.

• Always have the system completely discharged into a suitable recovery unit before painting the vehicle (if the paint is to be baked on), or before welding anywhere near refrigerant lines.

• When servicing the system, minimize the time that any refrigerant line or fitting is open to the air in order to prevent moisture or dirt from entering the system. Contaminants such as moisture or dirt can damage internal system components. Always replace O-rings on lines or fittings which are disconnected. Prior to installation coat, but do not soak, replacement O-rings with suitable compressor oil.

Compressor

REMOVAL & INSTALLATION

▶ See Figures 13, 14 and 15

The A/C compressor may be removed and positioned aside without discharging the refrigerant system. Discharging is not normally necessary when removing the A/C compressor clutch, coil assembly, engine, cylinder head, or alternator. Simply support the compressor with strong wire from the vehicle's frame with the refrigerant lines connected.

✳✳CAUTION

Do not disconnect the refrigerant lines without having the system first discharged by a qualified professional mechanic with an approved recovery/recycling machine.

1. Disconnect the negative battery cable. Have the system discharged by a qualified professional mechanic using an approved recovery/recycling machine. Unfasten the clutch electrical connector.

2. Once the system has been discharged, unbolt the connections at the compressor and plug all of the open refrigerant fittings.

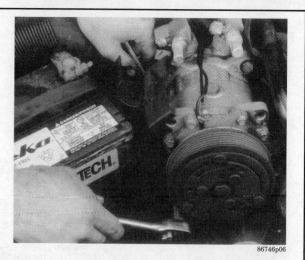

Fig. 13 Loosen the compressor-to-bracket retaining bolts

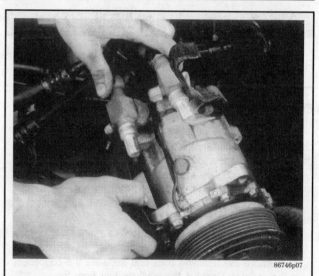

Fig. 14 Remove the compressor from the vehicle

3. Remove the compressor drive belt. Refer to Section 1 for the correct routing and adjusting procedures.

4. Support the compressor. Remove the compressor mounting bolts. Remove the compressor.

5. At this point, the compressor mounting bracket can be removed from the engine block.

To install:

6. Install the compressor mounting bracket and mounting bolts. Tighten the bolts to 20 ft. lbs. (27 Nm).

7. Position the compressor on the bracket and install the mounting bolts. Tighten the bolts and nuts to 20 ft. lbs. (27 Nm).

8. Install the drive belt. Refer to Section 1 for the correct routing and adjusting procedures.

9. Install the refrigerant lines with new O-rings to the compressor.

10. Connect the electrical wire to the compressor clutch.

11. Connect the negative battery cable.

12. Have the system evacuated and recharged by a qualified professional mechanic, utilizing the proper equipment.

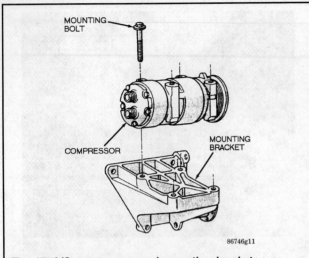

Fig. 15 A/C compressor and mounting bracket assembly

Condenser/Receiver Drier

REMOVAL & INSTALLATION

Except 1984-92 4.0L Engine

1. Disconnect the negative battery cable. Have the system discharged by a qualified professional mechanic using an approved recovery/recycling machine.
2. Drain the coolant system.
3. Disconnect the fan shroud and radiator hoses.
4. On vehicles with automatic transmissions, disconnect the transmission cooler lines.
5. Unplug the harness from the low pressure switch.
6. Remove the radiator and condenser as an assembly.
7. Remove the retaining bolts and separate the condenser from the radiator. Remove the receiver/drier from the condenser.

To install:

➡Add 1 ounce of refrigerant oil to the system when replacing the condenser.

8. Install the receiver/drier on the radiator and tighten the fasteners.
9. Install the condenser on the radiator and tighten the retaining bolts.
10. Install the radiator and condenser assembly and engage the harness to the low pressure switch.
11. On vehicles with automatic transmissions, connect the transmission cooler lines.
12. Connect the fan shroud and radiator hoses.
13. Fill the coolant system and connect the negative battery cable.
14. Have the system evacuated and recharged by a qualified professional mechanic, utilizing the proper equipment.

1984-92 4.0L Engine

1. Disconnect the negative battery cable. Have the system discharged by a qualified professional mechanic using an approved recovery/recycling machine.
2. Disconnect the fan shroud and electric fan from the radiator.
3. Remove the upper crossmember and bracket.
4. Disconnect the A/C hoses from the condenser and plug the openings.
5. Unplug the harness from the low pressure switch.
6. Remove all attaching bolts connecting the condenser to the radiator. Remove the condenser and the receiver drier as an assembly.
7. Remove the receiver/drier from the condenser.

To install:

➡Add 1 ounce of refrigerant oil to the system when replacing the condenser.

8. Install the condenser and receiver drier as an assembly. Tighten all attaching bolts connecting the condenser to the radiator.
9. Engage the harness from the low pressure switch and connect the A/C hoses to the condenser.
10. Install the upper cross member and bracket.
11. Engage the fan shroud and electric fan from the radiator and connect the negative battery cable.
12. Have the system evacuated and recharged by a qualified professional mechanic, utilizing the proper equipment.

1993-96 Models
▶ See Figures 16 and 17

1. Disconnect the negative battery cable. Have the system discharged by a qualified professional mechanic using an approved recovery/recycling machine.
2. Disconnect the air conditioning hoses from the condenser.
3. Remove the grille. Refer to Section 10 for the proper procedure.
4. Remove the upper brace bolts from the radiator braces.
5. Remove the crossmember-to-radiator bolts securing the lower part of the hood latch brace to the lower frame crossmember.

➡The radiator upper crossmember can be adjusted through the use of slotted holes. Before removal, mark the crossmember's original position.

6. Remove all the remaining bolts securing the radiator upper crossmember to the body. Lift the crossmember straight up and lay it to one side.
7. Remove the condenser upper and lower attaching bolts.
8. Carefully remove the condenser from the vehicle.

To install:
9. Install the condenser in the vehicle and tighten the retaining bolts.
10. Align the radiator upper crossmember and tighten the retaining bolts.
11. Install and tighten the bolt securing the lower part of the hood latch support brace to the lower frame crossmember.
12. Install and tighten the upper bolts securing the radiator brace to the upper radiator crossmember.

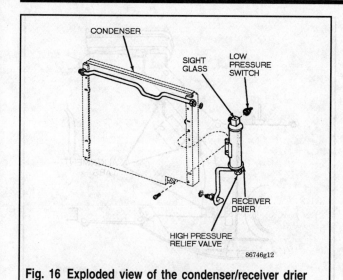

Fig. 16 Exploded view of the condenser/receiver drier mounting — 1996 2.5L model shown

13. Install the grille and connect the air conditioning hoses to the condenser.

14. Installation is the reverse of removal. Add 1 ounce of refrigerant oil to the system when replacing the condenser.

15. Have the system evacuated and recharged by a qualified professional mechanic, utilizing the proper equipment.

Evaporator/Blower Housing

REMOVAL & INSTALLATION

▶ See Figures 18, 19, 20 and 21

1. Disconnect the negative battery cable. Have the system discharged by a qualified professional mechanic using an approved recovery/recycling machine.

2. Disconnect the blower motor wires and vent tube.

3. If equipped, remove the center console as follows:

   a. On manual transmission models, remove the shift knob, boot and bezel.

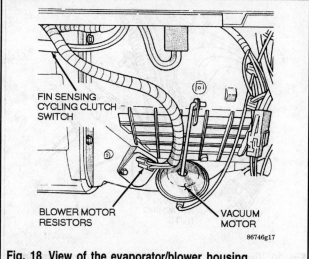

Fig. 18 View of the evaporator/blower housing components

   b. On automatic transmission models, remove the shift handle cap, plunger, spring, T-lock, shift handle and bezel.

   c. If equipped with power windows, pry the switch out of console and disconnect.

   d. Remove the console cover screws, cover and cover base.

4. Remove the lower half of the instrument panel.

5. Disconnect the wiring at the A/C relay, blower motor resistors and A/C thermostat. Disconnect the vacuum hoses at the vacuum motor.

6. Cut the plastic retaining strap that retains the evaporator housing to the heater core housing.

7. Disconnect and remove the heater control cable.

8. Remove the clips at the rear blower housing flange and remove the retaining screws.

9. Remove the housing attaching nuts from the studs on the engine compartment side of the firewall.

10. Remove the evaporator drain tube.

11. Remove the right kick panel and the instrument panel support bolt.

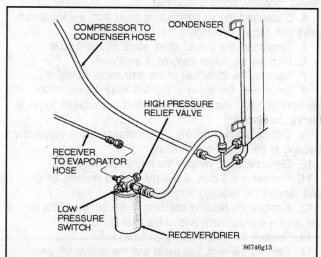

Fig. 17 Exploded view of the condenser/receiver drier connections — 1996 4.0L model shown

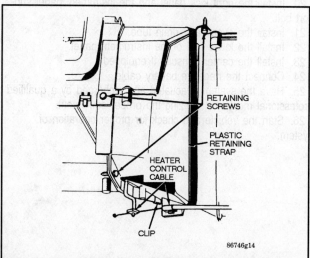

Fig. 19 View of the evaporator/blower housing control cable and retainers

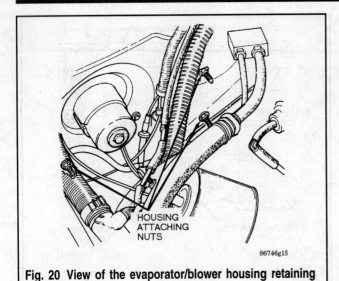

Fig. 20 View of the evaporator/blower housing retaining fasteners

12. Gently pull out on the right side of the dash and rotate the housing down and toward the rear to disengage the mounting studs from the firewall. Remove the housing.

To install:

13. Install the core in the housing. Ensure that the housing is positioned on the mounting studs on the firewall.

➡When installing the housing, care must be taken not to trap wires between the housing fresh air inlet and the dash panel on the right side of the housing.

14. Install the housing retaining screws and the rear housing clips.

15. Install the housing attaching nuts from the studs on the engine compartment side of the firewall.

16. Connect the blower motor wires and vent tube.

17. Connect the air conditioning hose at the expansion valve. Always use a back-up wrench!

18. Connect the wiring at the A/C relay, blower motor resistors and A/C thermostat.

19. Connect the heater control cable. Connect the vacuum hoses at the vacuum motor.

20. Install the right kick panel and the instrument panel support bolt.

21. Install the evaporator drain tube.

22. Install the lower half of the instrument panel.

23. Install the center console, if equipped.

24. Connect the negative battery cable.

25. Have the system evacuated and recharged by a qualified professional mechanic, utilizing the proper equipment.

26. Start the vehicle and check for proper operation of system.

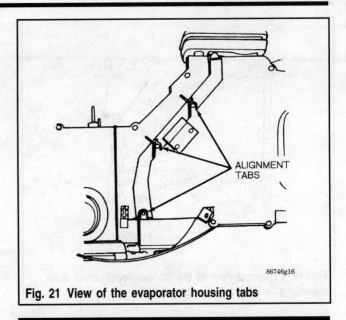

ALIGNMENT TABS

Fig. 21 View of the evaporator housing tabs

Evaporator Core

REMOVAL & INSTALLATION

1. Drain the coolant.

❋❋CAUTION

When draining coolant, keep in mind that cats and dogs are attracted by ethylene glycol antifreeze, and are quite likely to drink any that is left in an uncovered container or in puddles on the ground. This will prove fatal in sufficient quantity. Always drain the coolant into a sealable container. Coolant should be reused unless it is contaminated or several years old.

2. Disconnect the heater hoses at the core tubes.

3. Disconnect the negative battery cable. Have the system discharged by a qualified professional mechanic using an approved recovery/recycling machine.

4. Disconnect the air conditioning hose from the expansion valve and cap all openings.

5. Disconnect the blower motor wires and vent tube.

6. Remove the center console, if equipped.

7. Remove the lower half of the instrument panel.

8. Disconnect the wiring at the A/C relay, blower motor resistors and A/C thermostat. Disconnect the vacuum hoses at the vacuum motor.

9. Cut the plastic retaining strap that retains the evaporator housing to the heater core housing.

10. Disconnect and remove the heater control cable.

11. Remove the 3 clips at the rear blower housing flange and remove the retaining screws.

12. Remove the housing attaching nuts from the studs on the engine compartment side of the firewall.

13. Remove the evaporator drain tube.

14. Remove the right kick panel and the instrument panel support bolt.

15. Gently pull out on the right side of the dash and rotate the housing down and toward the rear to disengage the mounting studs from the firewall. Remove the housing.

16. Remove the top housing retaining screws and lift off the top of the housing.

17. Remove the thermostatic switch and capillary tube.

18. Remove the 2 retaining screws and lift the core from the housing.

To install:

➡If a new core is being installed, add 1 oz. of refrigerant oil to the new core.

19. Bolt the core into place in the housing.

20. Install the thermostatic switch and capillary tube.

21. Install the top of the housing.

22. Install the housing. Be careful to avoid trapping wires.

23. Install the right kick panel and the instrument panel support bolt.

24. Install the evaporator drain tube.

25. Install the housing attaching nuts on the studs on the engine compartment side of the firewall.

26. Install the 3 clips at the rear blower housing flange and install the retaining screws.

27. Connect and install the heater control cable.

28. Install a new plastic retaining strap on the evaporator housing.

29. Connect the wiring at the A/C relay, blower motor resistors and A/C thermostat. Connect the vacuum hoses at the vacuum motor.

30. Install the lower half of the instrument panel.

31. Install the center console, if equipped.

32. Connect the blower motor wires and vent tube.

33. Connect the air conditioning hose from the expansion valve and cap all openings.

34. Connect the heater hoses at the core tubes.

35. Fill the cooling system.

36. Connect the negative battery cable.

37. Have the system evacuated and recharged by a qualified professional mechanic, utilizing the proper equipment.

Air Conditioning Control Panel

REMOVAL & INSTALLATION

▶ **See Figures 22 and 23**

1. Disconnect the negative battery cable. Remove the ash tray.

2. Remove the instrument panel bezel fasteners and remove the bezel.

3. If necessary, remove the clock.

4. If necessary, unfasten the radio retaining screws and remove the radio. Refer to the this section for the proper procedure.

5. Remove the control panel screws, pull the panel outward and disconnect and tag the hoses, wires and cable.

6. Remove the control cable locking tab by using a small screwdriver to release the tab.

To install:

7. Engage the control cable and fasten the retaining tab.

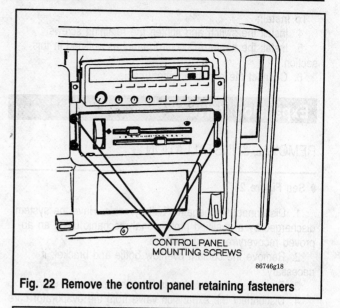

CONTROL PANEL
MOUNTING SCREWS

86746g18

Fig. 22 Remove the control panel retaining fasteners

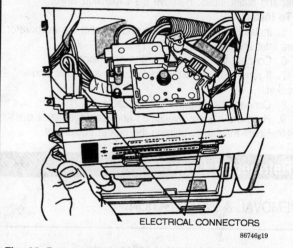

ELECTRICAL CONNECTORS

86746g19

Fig. 23 Remove the control panel and disengage the electrical connections

8. Engage the hoses, wires, install the control panel and tighten the retaining screws.

9. Install the radio and clock. Refer to the proper procedure in this section.

10. Install the instrument panel bezel and fasteners and connect the negative battery cable. Check the control panel to verify proper operation.

Blower Switch

REMOVAL & INSTALLATION

1. Disconnect the negative battery cable.

2. Remove the heater/AC control panel as outlined in this section.

3. Unfasten the screws retaining the switch to the rear of the control panel and remove the switch.

To install:

4. Install the switch and tighten the retaining screws.

5. Install the heater/AC control panel as outlined in this section.

6. Connect the negative battery cable.

Expansion Valve

REMOVAL & INSTALLATION

▶ See Figure 24

1. Disconnect the negative battery cable. Have the system discharged by a qualified professional mechanic using an approved recovery/recycling machine.

2. Remove the coolant overflow bottle and bracket, if necessary.

3. Disconnect the A/C hoses from the expansion valve.

4. Disconnect the expansion valve from the evaporator core inlet and outlet tubes. Remove the expansion valve.

To install:

5. Install the expansion valve and connect the evaporator core inlet and outlet tubes.

6. Connect the AC hoses to the expansion valve.

7. If removed, install the coolant recovery bottle and bracket.

8. Connect the negative battery cable.

9. Have the system evacuated and recharged by a qualified professional mechanic, utilizing the proper equipment.

Refrigerant Lines

REMOVAL & INSTALLATION

1. Disconnect the negative battery cable.

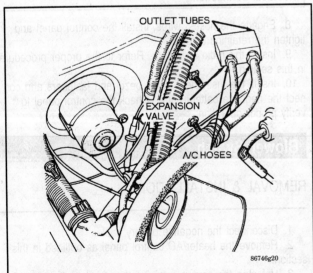

Fig. 24 View of the expansion valve location

2. Have the air conditioning system properly discharged by a qualified professional mechanic using an approved recovery/recycling machine.

3. Raise the vehicle and support safely.

4. Remove the nuts or bolts that attach the refrigerant line sealing plates to the adjoining components. If the lines are connected with flare nuts, use a back-up wrench when disassembling. Cover the exposed ends of the lines to minimize contamination.

5. Remove the support mount.

6. Remove the lines and discard the gaskets or O-rings.

To install:

7. Coat the new gaskets or O-rings with wax-free refrigerant oil and install. Connect the refrigerant lines to the adjoining components and tighten the nuts or bolts.

8. Install the support mount.

9. Have the air conditioning system evacuated and recharged by a qualified professional mechanic, utilizing the proper equipment.

10. Connect the negative battery cable and check the entire climate control system for proper operation and leaks.

Vacuum Motors

REMOVAL & INSTALLATION

Heater/Defroster/Panel Door Actuators

▶ See Figure 25

1. Remove the center console, if equipped. Refer to Section 10 for this procedure.

2. Remove the lower instrument panel. Refer to Section 10 for this procedure.

3. Disengage the vacuum hose(s) from the motor and unfasten the vacuum motor attaching nuts.

4. Remove the vacuum motor from the bracket and disengage the motor linkage retaining clip. Remove the rod from the door actuating lever.

To install:

5. Engage the rod to the door actuating lever and the vacuum motor to the bracket. Install the motor linkage retaining clip.

6. Tighten the vacuum motor retaining nuts and engage the vacuum hose(s) to the motor.

7. Install the lower instrument panel. Refer to Section 10 for this procedure.

8. If removed, install the center console. Refer to Section 10 for this procedure.

Recirculating Air Door

▶ See Figure 26

1. Remove the vacuum motor cover and disengage the vacuum hose.

2. Remove the actuating rod clip and disengage the rod from the door lever.

3. Unfasten the motor retainers and remove the motor.

4. Installation is the reverse of removal.

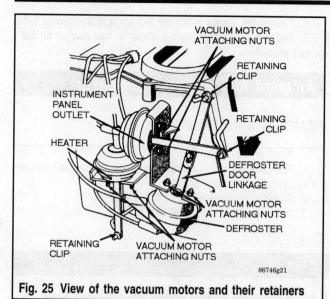

86746g21

Fig. 25 View of the vacuum motors and their retainers

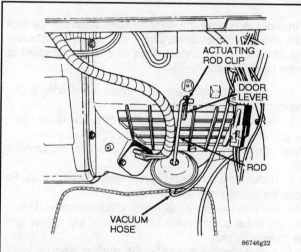

86746g22

Fig. 26 View of the recirculating air door vacuum actuator

Control Cable

REMOVAL & INSTALLATION

1. Disconnect the negative battery cable.
2. Remove the heater/AC control panel as outlined in this section.
3. Remove the lower instrument panel. Refer to Section 10 for this procedure.
4. Disengage the cable retainer from the heater housing and the push on nut attaching the cable to the blend air door. Remove the cable.
To install:
5. Engage the cable to the blend air door, install the nut and install the cable retainer.

6. Install the lower instrument panel. Refer to Section 10 for this procedure.
7. Install the heater/AC control panel as outlined in this section.
8. Connect the negative battery cable.

Cycling Clutch Switch

REMOVAL & INSTALLATION

♦ **See Figure 27**

1. Disconnect the negative battery cable.
2. Remove the center console, if equipped. Refer to Section 10 for this procedure.
3. Remove the lower instrument panel. Refer to Section 10 for this procedure.
4. Pull the wiring harness clip out of the retainer.
5. Disengage the switch electrical connection and remove the wires from the retaining clip.
6. Remove the switch probe from the evaporator fins.
To install:
7. Carefully insert the switch probe into the evaporator fins.
8. Engage the switch electrical connection and snap the wiring retainer clip into the hole in the housing.
9. Install the lower panel and the center console. Refer to Section 10 for these procedures.
10. Connect the negative battery cable.

Solar Sensor

REMOVAL & INSTALLATION

1. Pop out the defrost grille and remove the solar sensor from the grille.
2. Disengage the solar sensor from the grille.
3. Installation is the reverse of removal.

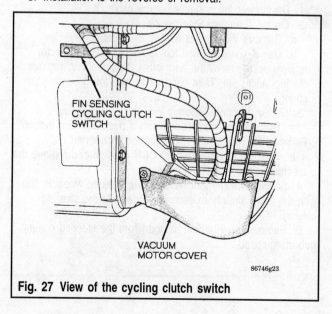

86746g23

Fig. 27 View of the cycling clutch switch

Temperature Sensor

REMOVAL & INSTALLATION

1. Remove the instrument panel. Refer to this section for the proper procedure.
2. Disengage the sensor tube from the sensor assembly and the heater/AC unit.
3. Unfasten the sensor assembly fasteners and remove the sensor assembly.
4. Disengage the sensor from the sensor assembly.
To install:
5. Engage the sensor to the assembly.

CRUISE CONTROL

General Information

The Cruise Command system is electrically actuated and vacuum operated. The turn signal lever on the steering column incorporates a slide switch which has three positions OFF, ON or RESUME. A SET button is located in the end of the lever. This device is designed to operate at speeds above approximately 35 mph (56 km/h).

The speed control module automatically controls throttle position to maintain a speed set by the operator. The vehicle will keep the set speed unless the driver presses the brake, clutch or accelerator pedal.

Control Switch

REMOVAL & INSTALLATION

1988-93 Models

1. Disconnect the negative battery cable.
2. On the Standard Steering Wheel:
   a. Remove the screws holding the front cover.
   b. Use a sharp pointed tool to depress the connector retainer and remove the horn wires. Pull gently to remove the grounding pin. Take care not to lose the grounding pin spring.
3. On the Optional Steering Wheel:
   a. Remove the horn button with a push and turn motion. Remove the rest of the horn button components.
   b. Turn ignition key to the **LOCK** position and remove the steering wheel nut and washer.
4. Scribe an alignment mark on the steering wheel in line with the mark already existing on the end of the steering column.
5. Remove the vibration damper from the steering column hub, if equipped.

6. Fasten the sensor retainers and engage the sensor tube.
7. Install the instrument panel. Refer to this section for the proper procedure.

Ambient Air Temperature Sensor

REMOVAL & INSTALLATION

1. Remove the grille and disengage the ambient air temperature sensor connection.
2. Remove the sensor from the vehicle.
3. Installation is the reverse of removal.

6. Remove the steering wheel using a steering wheel puller.

➡️**In order to remove the steering shaft snapring, the lockplate must be compressed. Use a lock spring compressor tool C4156 or its equivalent. Take care as the lockplate is under heavy tension.**

7. Compress the lockplate and remove the steering shaft snapring. Discard the snapring.
8. Remove the lockplate, cancelling cam, and upper bearing preload spring. If equipped with the optional steering wheel, remove the horn button components from the canceling cam.
9. Remove the screw and hazard warning switch knob. Remove the actuator arm attaching screw.
10. Remove the turn signal switch attaching screws. Disconnect the cruise control switch wiring harness and remove from the steering column.
11. Turn the ignition key to the **ON** position. Remove the key warning buzzer switch and retaining clip with a paper clip inserted below the retainer.

➡️**The buzzer switch and clip must be removed as a unit. If not, the clip may drop down into the steering column.**

12. Remove the ignition lock cylinder retaining screw and pull the lock out of the column.
13. Remove the screws that attach the housing and shroud assembly to the column jacket, then remove the housing and shroud assembly. DO NOT let the dimmer switch rod, lockpin or lockrack fall out.
14. Remove the turn signal/wiper lever by pulling it straight out of the column. Remove the column shift cover screw, if equipped with column shift.
To install:
15. Remove the pivot screw from the housing and remove the wiper switch. Install a new switch and switch cover.
16. Push on dimmer switch rod to make sure it is connected, then carefully position the housing and shroud assembly to column.

➡️**Ensure the nylon spring retainer on the lockpin is positioned forward of the retaining slot of the lockrack.**

17. Position the first tooth of the gear (farthest from the block tooth) with the most forward tooth of the lockrack.

18. Install the screws that attach the housing and assembly and carefully mate the housing and shroud.

19. Insert the key and lock cylinder and test that the lockpin extends fully when the key is moved to the **LOCK** position.

20. Install the buzzer switch and clip.

21. Install the turn signal switch and engage the cruise control switch electrical connection.

22. Install the hazard warning switch knob and fasten the screw.

23. If removed install the horn button components from the canceling cam.

24. Install the upper bearing preload spring, cancelling cam, and lockplate.

25. Compress the lockplate and install a new steering shaft snapring.

26. Install the steering wheel.

27. If equipped, install the vibration damper.

28. On the Optional Steering Wheel:

a. With the ignition key in the **LOCK** position, install the steering wheel nut and washer.

b. Install the horn button with a push and turn motion. Engage the rest of the horn button components.

29. On the Standard Steering Wheel:

a. Install the grounding pin and grounding pin spring.

b. Engage the horn wires.

c. Install the screws holding the front cover.

30. Connect the negative battery cable.

1994-96 Models

▶ See Figure 28

1. Disconnect the negative battery cable.
2. Remove the air bag module.
3. Remove the switch-to-steering wheel retaining screw.
4. Remove the switch from the vehicle.
5. Installation is the reverse of removal.

Vehicle Speed Sensor

REMOVAL & INSTALLATION

▶ See Figure 29

The vehicle speed sensor is usually located on the speedometer gear cable which is usually located on the extension housing of the transmission (drivers side)

1. Disconnect the negative battery cable. Raise the vehicle and safely support it with jackstands.
2. Disengage the electrical connector from the sensor and remove the sensor mounting bolt.
3. Pull the sensor straight out to remove it. Do not remove the speedometer pinon gear adaptor from the transmission.

To install:

4. Clean the inside of the pinon gear prior to installation.
5. Install the sensor into the pinon gear adaptor.
6. Install the sensor mounting bolt and tighten to 20 inch lbs. (2.2 Nm).
7. Engage the electrical connection to the sensor.
8. Connect the negative battery cable and lower the vehicle.

Speed Control Servo

REMOVAL & INSTALLATION

1. Disconnect the negative battery cable and the vacuum hose at the servo.
2. Disengage the electrical connection at the servo and remove the nuts on the servo cable sleeve.
3. Pull the speed control cable away from the servo to expose the cable retaining clip.
4. Remove the clip attaching the cable to the servo.
5. Remove the servo by pulling it away from the bracket.

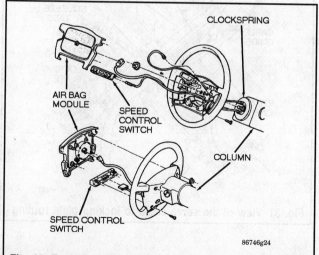

Fig. 28 Exploded view of the cruise control switch and related components

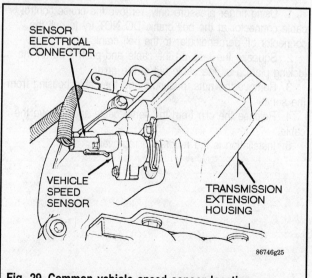

Fig. 29 Common vehicle speed sensor location

To install:

6. Insert the servo studs into the bracket and block the throttle into the full open position.

7. Align the hole in the cable sleeve with the hole in the servo pin and install the retaining clip.

8. Install the nuts on the servo cable sleeve and engage the electrical connection at the servo.

9. Tighten the mounting nuts to 50 inch lbs. (6 Nm), then engage the vacuum hose and connect the negative battery cable.

Servo Cable

REMOVAL & INSTALLATION

1988-90 Models

1. Using finger pressure only, remove the cruise control cable connector at the bell crank. DO NOT try to pull the connector off perpendicular to the bell crank.

2. Remove MAP sensor mounting nuts and slide the sensor forward off the studs.

3. Remove the attaching nuts and the cable housing from the servo.

4. Release the cable clip from the servo cable and remove the servo cable.

5. Installation is the reverse of removal.

1991-92 Models

1. Remove the lockclip and washer from the clevis pin on the bell crank.

2. Remove the chain from the clevis pin and squeeze the tabs that retain the cable housing in the bracket.

3. Remove the fasteners that secure the cable to the servo and remove the servo.

4. Installation is the reverse of removal.

1993 Models

1. Using finger pressure only, remove the cruise control cable connector at the bell crank. DO NOT try to pull the connector off perpendicular to the bell crank.

2. Squeeze the tabs on the cable and push it out of the locking plate. Pull the cable out of the guide.

3. Remove the nuts, pushnuts and the cable housing from the servo.

4. Release the clip from the servo cable and remove the cable.

5. Installation is the reverse of removal.

1994-96 Models

▶ See Figures 30 and 31

1. Using finger pressure only, remove the cruise control cable connector at the bell crank. DO NOT try to pull the connector off perpendicular to the bell crank.

2. Squeeze the tabs on the cable and push it out of the locking plate.

3. Unclip the cable from the guide at the valve cover.

4. Remove the nuts on the servo cable sleeve.

5. Pull the speed control cable away from the servo to expose the cable retaining clip.

6. Unfasten the clip attaching the cable to the servo. Remove the cable.

7. Installation is the reverse of removal.

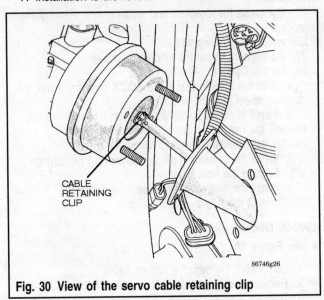

Fig. 30 View of the servo cable retaining clip

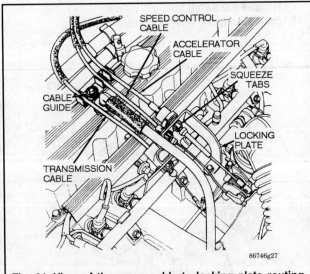

Fig. 31 View of the servo cable to locking plate routing

Cruise Control Diagnosis

CONDITION	POSSIBLE CAUSE	CORRECTION
A. System Does Not Engage in ON Position	(1) Restricted vacuum hose or no vacuum (2) Control switch defective (3) Control module defective (4) Speed sensor defective (5) Brake lamps defective (6) Brake lamp switch defective (7) Brake lamp switch wire disconnected (8) Open circuit between brake lamp switch and brake lamps (9) Mechanical vent valve position improperly adjusted	(1) Locate restriction or air leak and repair (2) Replace switch (3) Replace control module (4) Replace sensor (5) Replace brake lamp bulbs (6) Replace switch (7) Connect wire to switch (8) Adjust open circuit (9) Adjust vent valve position
B. Resume Feature Inoperative	(1) Defective servo ground connection (2) Control switch defective	(1) Check servo ground wire connection and repair as necessary (2) Replace switch
C. Accelerate Function Inoperative	(1) Accelerate circuit in control module inoperative (2) Cruise switch defective	(1) Replace control module (2) Replace switch
D. System Re-engages When Brake Pedal Or Clutch Is Released	(1) Control module defective (2) Mechanical vent valve not opening (3) Kink in mechanical vent valve hose (4) Brake lamp switch defective	(1) Replace control module (2) Adjust position or replace valve (3) Reroute hose to remove kink (4) Adjust or replace switch
E. Throttle Does Not Return To Idle Position	(1) Improper linkage adjustment (2) No slack in lost motion link	(1) Adjust properly (2) Adjust servo cable
F. Road Speed Changes More Than 2 MPH (3.2km/h) When Setting Speed	(1) Centering adjustment set wrong	(1) Adjust centering screw
G. Engine Accelerates When Started	(1) No slack in bead chain (2) Vacuum hose connections reversed at servo (3) Servo defective	(1) Adjust chain (2) Check connection and correct (3) Replace servo
H. System Disengages On Level Road Without Applying Brake Or Clutch	(1) Loose wire connection (2) Loose vacuum hose connection (3) Servo linkage broken (4) Defective brake lamp switch	(1) Repair connection (2) Check vacuum hose connection and repair as necessary (3) Repair linkage (4) Replace switch
I. Erratic Operation	(1) Reverse polarity (2) Servo defective (3) Control module defective	(1) Check position of speed sensor wires at connector (2) Replace servo (3) Replace control module
J. Vehicle Continues to Accelerate When Set Button is Released	(1) Servo defective (2) Control module defective	(1) Replace servo (2) Replace control module
K. System Engages But Slowly Loses Set Speed	(1) Air leak at vacuum hose connection or in hoses (2) Air leak at vent release valve at brake pedal	(1) Check hoses and connections and repair as necessary (2) Replace vacuum vent valve

86746c01

ENTERTAINMENT SYSTEM

Radio

REMOVAL & INSTALLATION

▶ See Figures 32, 33, 34 and 35

1. Disconnect the negative battery cable.
2. Remove the center cluster screws and bezel.
3. Remove the radio attaching screws.
4. Disconnect the radio from the instrument panel wiring harness and antenna.
5. Installation is the reverse of removal.

Speakers

REMOVAL & INSTALLATION

Instrument Panel

▶ See Figures 36 and 37

This procedure applies to all vehicles covered by this manual. Some slight differences may arise; adjust the procedure accordingly.

1. Disconnect the negative battery cable.
2. Using a trim stick or other flat-bladed tool, pry the cowl top trim panel off the instrument panel top pad.
3. Pull the cowl panel up far enough so you can disengage the solar sensor, if equipped.
4. Remove the cowl panel and unplug the speaker wires.
5. Unfasten the speaker retaining screws and remove the speakers.

To install:

6. Install the speaker, fasten the retaining screws and engage the wires.

Fig. 32 Remove the bezel retaining fasteners and the bezel

Fig. 33 Remove the radio retaining fasteners

Fig. 34 Slide the radio forward so that you may gain access to the electrical connections

7. Install the cowl trim panel, making sure you engage the solar sensor electrical connection, if equipped.
8. Connect the negative battery cable.

Door Mounted

▶ See Figures 38, 39 and 40

This procedure applies to all vehicles covered by this manual. Some slight differences may arise; adjust the procedure accordingly.

1. Disconnect the negative battery cable.
2. Remove the door trim panel. Refer to Section 10 for this procedure.
3. Remove the speaker retaining screws.
4. Pull the speaker away from the door and unplug the electrical wires from the speaker.

To install:

5. Attach the electrical wires to the speaker.

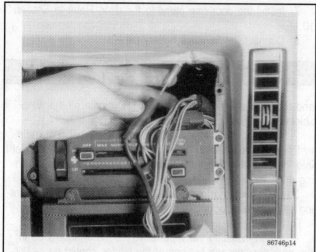

Fig. 35 Disengage the antenna and radio electrical connections

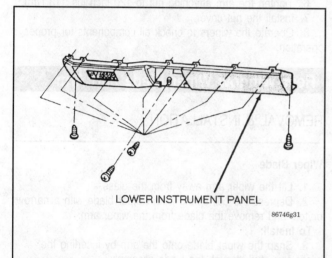

LOWER INSTRUMENT PANEL

86746g31

Fig. 36 Remove the lower instrument panel retaining fasteners

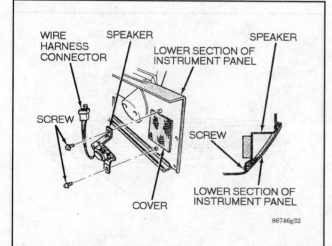

WIRE HARNESS CONNECTOR   SPEAKER   SPEAKER

LOWER SECTION OF INSTRUMENT PANEL

SCREW

SCREW

COVER

LOWER SECTION OF INSTRUMENT PANEL

86746g32

Fig. 37 Exploded view of the instrument panel speaker and related components

Fig. 38 Remove the door panel

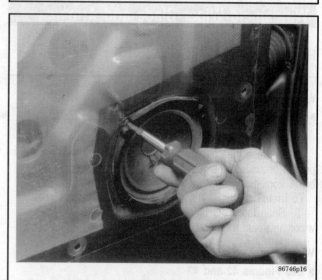

Fig. 39 Loosen the speaker retaining screws

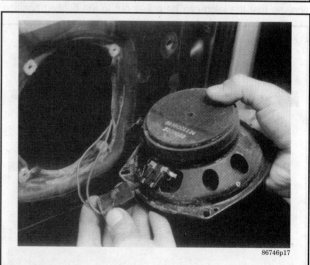

Fig. 40 Remove the speaker and disengage the electrical connection

6. Install the speaker to the door and secure in place with the retaining screws.

7. Install the door trim panel to the door. Refer to Section 10.

8. Connect the negative battery cable.

WINDSHIELD WIPERS

The windshield wipers can be operated with the wiper switch only when the ignition switch is in the Accessory or Ignition position. A circuit breaker, integral with the wiper switch, or a fuse, in the fuse box, protects the circuitry of the wiper system and the vehicle.

Wiper blades, exposed to the weather for a long period of time, tend to lose their wiping effectiveness. Periodic cleaning of the wiper blade element is suggested. The wiper blade element, arms and windshield should be cleaned with a sponge or cloth and a mild detergent or non-abrasive cleaner. If the wiper element continues to streak or smear, replace the wiper blade element or arm.

Windshield Wiper Blade and Arm

REMOVAL & INSTALLATION

Wiper Blade
▶ See Figure 41

1. Lift the wiper arm away from the glass.
2. Depress the coil spring in the wiper blade with a narrow prytool or actuate the wiper release blade and remove the blade from the wiper arm.
   To install:
3. Snap the wiper blade onto the arm by inserting the wiper arm stud through the blade assembly.

Wiper Arm Assembly
▶ See Figures 42 and 43

1. On latch release type: lift the arm (note installation position) so that the latch can be pulled out to the holding position

and then release the arm. The arm will remain off the windshield in this position.

2. On the arm attaching nut type: lift the wiper arm (note installation position) and place a ⅛ in. (3mm) pin or equivalent into the arm hole. Lift the head cover and remove the attaching nut.
3. On all types, remove the arm assembly from the mounting stud using a rocking and lifting motion.
   To install:
4. When installing the wiper arm, the motor should be in the park position and the tips of the blades should be ¾-1½ in. (19-38mm) above the bottom of the windshield moulding.
5. Position the wiper arm over the mounting stud.
6. Tighten the arm attaching nut to 120 inch lbs. (13 Nm).
7. Install the nut cover.
8. Operate the wipers to check all components for proper operation.

Rear Window Wiper Blade and Arm

REMOVAL & INSTALLATION

Wiper Blade

1. Lift the wiper arm away from the glass.
2. Depress the coil spring in the wiper blade with a narrow prytool and remove the blade from the wiper arm.
   To install:
3. Snap the wiper blade onto the arm by inserting the wiper arm stud through the blade assembly.

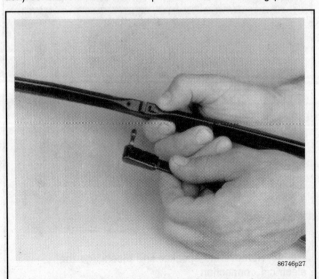

86746p27

Fig. 41 Removing the wiper blade from the wiper arm

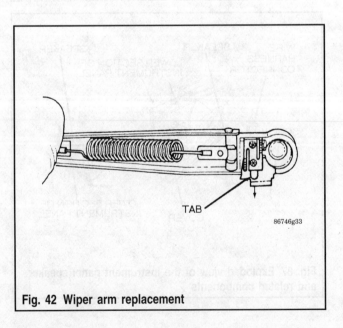

TAB

86746g33

Fig. 42 Wiper arm replacement

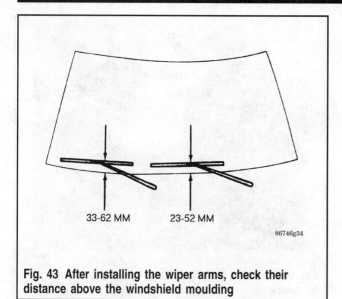

Fig. 43 After installing the wiper arms, check their distance above the windshield moulding

Wiper Arm Assembly

Refer to the procedures for the removal and installation of the windshield wiper arms, described earlier in this section.

Windshield Wiper Motor

REMOVAL & INSTALLATION

▶ **See Figures 44, 45, 46, 47, 48, 49, 50 and 51**

1. Remove the wiper arm and blade assemblies.
2. Remove the cowl trim panel.
3. Disconnect the washer hose.
4. Remove the cowl mounting bracket attaching nuts and pivot pin attaching screws.
5. Disconnect the wiring harness and unfasten the wiper motor retainers.
6. Remove the wiper motor and the plastic motor cover, if equipped.

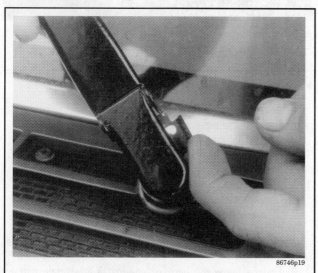

Fig. 44 Remove the wiper arms

Fig. 45 Remove the cowl panel retaining screws

Fig. 46 Remove the cowl panel

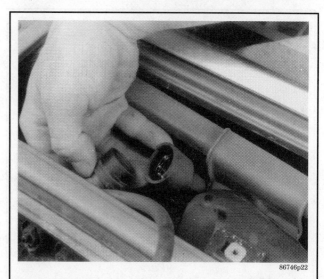

Fig. 47 Disengage the wiper motor electrical connection

7. Remove the retainers holding the motor to the linkage assembly and bracket.

To install:

8. Install the retainers holding the motor to the linkage assembly and bracket.

9. Install the wiper motor and the plastic motor cover if equipped.

10. Engage the wiring harness and fasten the wiper motor retainers. Tighten the mounting nuts to 35 inch lbs. (4 Nm).

11. Install the cowl mounting bracket attaching nuts and pivot pin attaching screws.

12. Engage the washer hose, install the cowl trim panel and the wiper arm and blade assemblies.

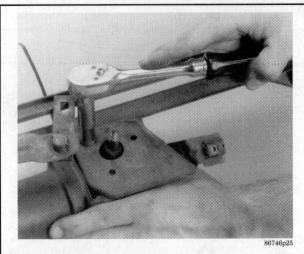

Fig. 50 Unfasten the wiper motor-to-linkage retaining fasteners

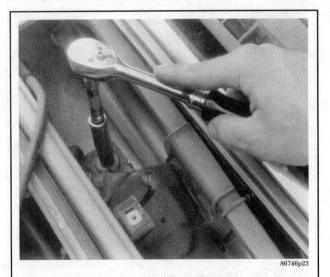

Fig. 48 Unfasten the wiper motor retainers

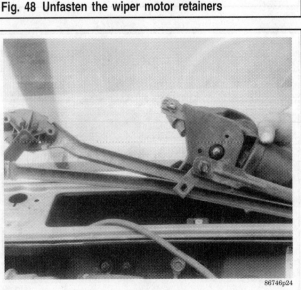

Fig. 49 Remove the wiper motor and linkage

Fig. 51 Separate the motor from the linkage

Rear Wiper Motor

REMOVAL & INSTALLATION

▶ **See Figures 52 and 53**

1. Disconnect the negative battery cable.
2. Remove the wiper arm as outlined in this section.
3. Disconnect the washer hose.
4. Remove the pivot pin retaining nut.
5. Remove the liftgate interior trim panel. Refer to Section 10 for this procedure.
6. Disconnect the wiper motor at the wiring harness.
7. Unbolt and remove the motor.

To install:

8. Install the motor and tighten the fasteners to 35 inch lbs. (4 Nm).

9. Engage the wiring harness and install the liftgate trim panel.

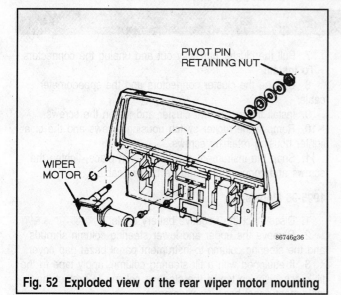

Fig. 52 Exploded view of the rear wiper motor mounting

10. Install the pivot pin retaining nut and engage the washer hose.

11. Install the wiper arm as outlined in this section.

12. Connect the negative battery cable.

Wiper Linkage

REMOVAL & INSTALLATION

1. Remove the wiper arms and pivot shaft nuts, washers, escutcheons and gaskets.

2. Disconnect the drive arm from the motor crank.

3. Remove individual links where necessary, to ease removal of the pivot shaft bodies.

4. Install in the reverse order of removal.

Windshield Washer Fluid Reservoir

REMOVAL & INSTALLATION

▶ See Figure 54

1. Disconnect the negative battery cable.

2. Drain the washer fluid from the reservoir.

3. Disengage the wiring from the fluid level sensor, if equipped.

4. Remove the reservoir retaining fasteners and disengage the hoses from the reservoir.

5. Installation is the reverse of removal.

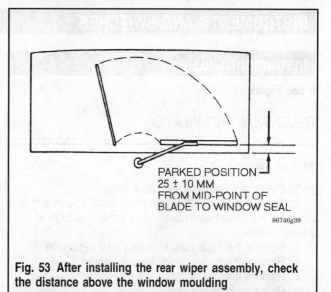

Fig. 53 After installing the rear wiper assembly, check the distance above the window moulding

Windshield Washer Motor

REMOVAL & INSTALLATION

1. Remove the windshield washer reservoir as outlined in this section.

2. Using a deep socket and an extension, remove the pump retaining fastener from inside the reservoir.

3. Remove the pump from the reservoir.

4. Installation is the reverse of removal.

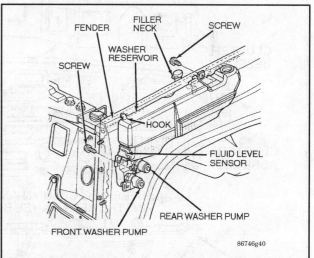

Fig. 54 Windshield washer reservoir and washer pump (motor) assembly

INSTRUMENTS AND SWITCHES

Instrument Cluster

▶ **See Figure 55**

REMOVAL & INSTALLATION

1988-94 Models

1. Disconnect the negative battery cable.
2. Remove the four instrument panel bezel screws and remove the instrument panel bezel. The bezel is snap fit at several locations.
3. Remove the cigar lighter housing retaining screws.
4. Remove the rocker switch housing screws.
5. Remove the instrument cluster screws.
6. Disconnect the speedometer cable.

7. Pull the cluster part way out and unplug the connectors.
To install:
8. Engage the cluster connectors and the speedometer cable.
9. Install the instrument cluster and fasten the screws.
10. Remove the rocker switch housing screws and the cigar lighter housing retaining screws.
11. Snap the instrument cluster bezel in place, tighten the screws and connect the negative battery cable.

1995-96 Models

1. Disconnect the negative battery cable.
2. Remove the upper and lower steering column shrouds and the steering column-to-instrument panel bezel gap cover.
3. If equipped with a tilt steering column, apply tape to the tilt mechanism on top of the steering column to protect the instrument panel bezel from damage.

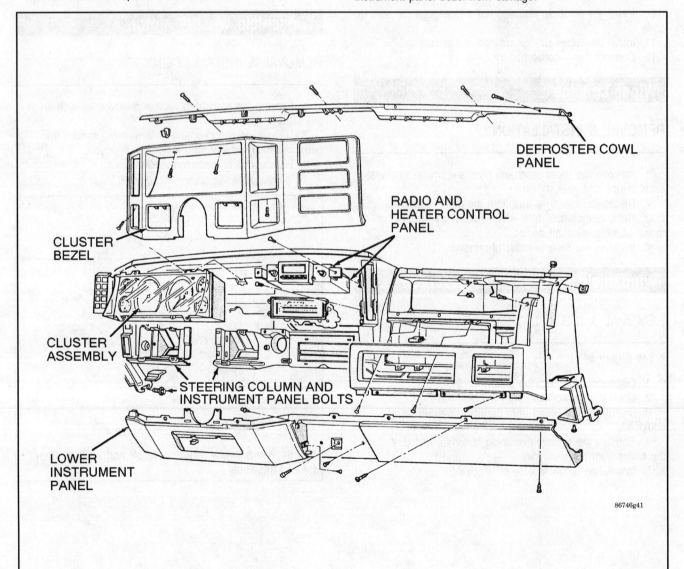

DEFROSTER COWL PANEL

RADIO AND HEATER CONTROL PANEL

CLUSTER BEZEL

CLUSTER ASSEMBLY

STEERING COLUMN AND INSTRUMENT PANEL BOLTS

LOWER INSTRUMENT PANEL

86746g41

Fig. 55 Exploded view of the instrument panel

4. Remove the four instrument panel bezel screws and remove the instrument panel bezel. The bezel is snap fit at several locations.
5. Remove the cigar lighter housing retaining screws.
6. Remove the rocker switch housing screws.
7. Remove the instrument cluster screws.
8. Disconnect the speedometer cable.
9. Pull the cluster part way out and unplug the connectors.
To install:
10. Engage the cluster connectors and the speedometer cable.
11. Install the instrument cluster and fasten the screws.
12. Remove the rocker switch housing screws and the cigar lighter housing retaining screws.
13. Snap the instrument cluster bezel in place, tighten the screws and connect the negative battery cable.

Instrument Cluster Gauges

REMOVAL & INSTALLATION

▶ See Figure 56

1. Remove the instrument cluster as outlined in this section.
2. If equipped with a trip odometer, remove the knob by gently pulling.
3. Remove the cluster lens and mask.
4. Remove the gauge attaching fasteners from the rear of the mounting bezel.
5. Remove the gauge assembly.
To install:
6. Install the gauge assembly and tighten the fasteners.
7. Install the cluster lens and mask.
8. If equipped with a trip odometer, install the knob by gently pushing.
9. Install the instrument cluster as outlined in this section.

Speedometer Cable

REMOVAL & INSTALLATION

Most vehicles from 1994 to 1996 did not utilize speedometer cables. These vehicles used a distance or vehicle speed sensor to measure the speed of the vehicle. This sensor is mounted on the transmission near the flywheel. Refer to the proper procedure in this section for the vehicle speed sensor.
1. Reach up behind the speedometer, depress the spring tab (located on the instrument cluster) in and pull the cable straight back. Pull the core from the sheath.
2. Raise and support the vehicle with jackstands and remove the cable from the transmission.
To install:
3. When installing the cable, coat it with speedometer cable lubricant before installation.
4. Engage the cable to the transmission and lower the vehicle.

5. Reach up behind the speedometer and engage the speedometer cable, making sure it firmly engages.

Printed Circuit Board

REMOVAL & INSTALLATION

▶ See Figure 57

1. Remove the instrument cluster as outlined in this section.
2. Remove all gauge attaching screws that contact the printed circuit board.
3. Remove the screw holding the cluster connector retaining strap to the bezel. Remove the strap and pivot the bezel down.
4. Remove the lamp sockets from the circuit board.
5. Remove the printed circuit board including the connector.

➡A separate printed circuit board for the warning lights is removed by removing the warning light sockets.

To install:
6. Install the printed circuit including the connector.
7. Install the lamp sockets from the circuit board.
8. Install the strap and pivot the bezel down. Fasten the screw holding the cluster connector retaining strap to the bezel.
9. Install all gauge attaching screws that contact the printed circuit board.
10. Install the instrument cluster as outlined in this section.

Windshield Wiper Switch

REMOVAL & INSTALLATION

▶ See Figure 58

The wiper switch is part of the multi-function switch. See Section 8 for replacement.

Rear Window Wiper Switch

REMOVAL & INSTALLATION

1. Remove the instrument cluster bezel.
2. Remove the switch housing panel.
3. Unplug the switch connector.
4. Installation is the reverse of removal.

Headlight Switch

REMOVAL AND INSTALLATION

▶ See Figures 59 and 60

1. Disconnect the battery ground cable.

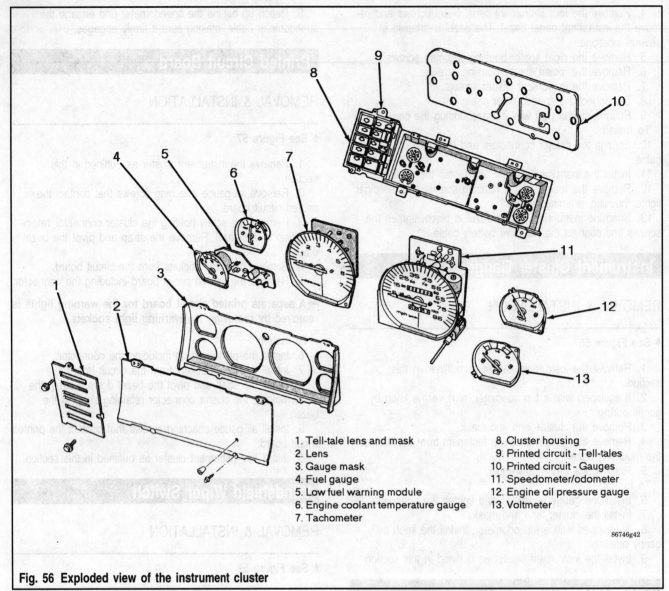

1. Tell-tale lens and mask
2. Lens
3. Gauge mask
4. Fuel gauge
5. Low fuel warning module
6. Engine coolant temperature gauge
7. Tachometer
8. Cluster housing
9. Printed circuit - Tell-tales
10. Printed circuit - Gauges
11. Speedometer/odometer
12. Engine oil pressure gauge
13. Voltmeter

86746g42

Fig. 56 Exploded view of the instrument cluster

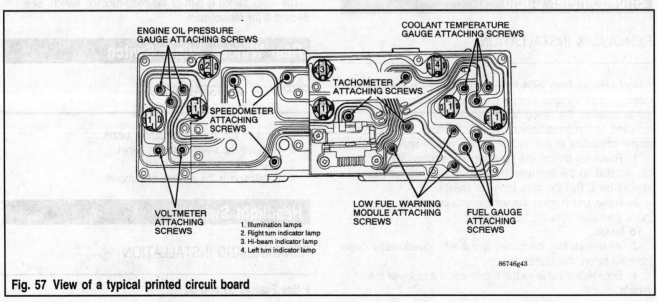

ENGINE OIL PRESSURE
GAUGE ATTACHING SCREWS

COOLANT TEMPERATURE
GAUGE ATTACHING SCREWS

TACHOMETER
ATTACHING SCREWS

SPEEDOMETER
ATTACHING
SCREWS

VOLTMETER
ATTACHING
SCREWS

LOW FUEL WARNING
MODULE ATTACHING
SCREWS

FUEL GAUGE
ATTACHING
SCREWS

1. Illumination lamps
2. Right turn indicator lamp
3. Hi-beam indicator lamp
4. Left turn indicator lamp

86746g43

Fig. 57 View of a typical printed circuit board

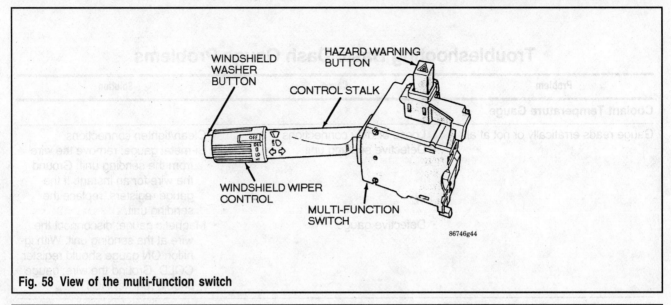

Fig. 58 View of the multi-function switch

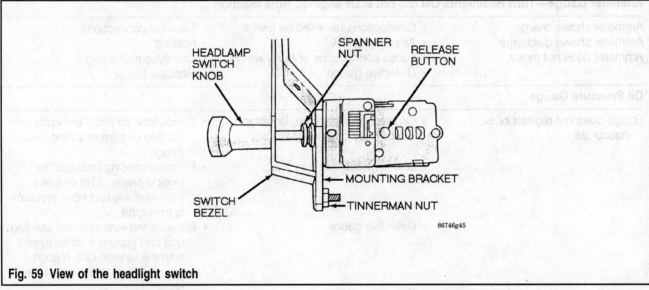

Fig. 59 View of the headlight switch

2. Pull the switch to the full ON position.

3. Reach up, under the panel and depress the switch shaft retainer button while pulling the switch control shaft straight out.

4. Remove the switch ferrule nut from the switch.

5. Disconnect the switch from the harness.

To install:

6. Connect the switch to the harness.

7. Install and tighten the switch ferrule nut on the switch.

8. Engage the switch control shaft by engaging the retainer button.

9. Turn the switch OFF and connect the negative battery cable.

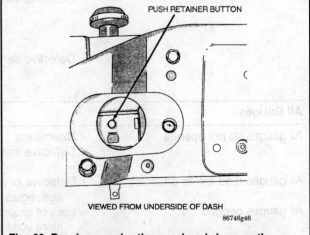

Fig. 60 Reach up under the panel and depress the switch shaft retainer button while pulling the switch control shaft straight out

Troubleshooting Basic Dash Gauge Problems

Problem	Cause	Solution
Coolant Temperature Gauge		
Gauge reads erratically or not at all	• Loose or dirty connections	• Clean/tighten connections
	• Defective sending unit	• Bi-metal gauge: remove the wire from the sending unit. Ground the wire for an instant. If the gauge registers, replace the sending unit.
	• Defective gauge	• Magnetic gauge: disconnect the wire at the sending unit. With ignition ON gauge should register COLD. Ground the wire; gauge should register HOT.
Ammeter Gauge—Turn Headlights ON (do not start engine). Note reaction		
Ammeter shows charge	• Connections reversed on gauge	• Reinstall connections
Ammeter shows discharge	• Ammeter is OK	• Nothing
Ammeter does not move	• Loose connections or faulty wiring	• Check/correct wiring
	• Defective gauge	• Replace gauge
Oil Pressure Gauge		
Gauge does not register or is inaccurate	• On mechanical gauge, Bourdon tube may be bent or kinked	• Check tube for kinks or bends preventing oil from reaching the gauge
	• Low oil pressure	• Remove sending unit. Idle the engine briefly. If no oil flows from sending unit hole, problem is in engine.
	• Defective gauge	• Remove the wire from the sending unit and ground it for an instant with the ignition ON. A good gauge will go to the top of the scale.
	• Defective wiring	• Check the wiring to the gauge. If it's OK and the gauge doesn't register when grounded, replace the gauge.
	• Defective sending unit	• If the wiring is OK and the gauge functions when grounded, replace the sending unit
All Gauges		
All gauges do not operate	• Blown fuse	• Replace fuse
	• Defective instrument regulator	• Replace instrument voltage regulator
All gauges read low or erratically	• Defective or dirty instrument voltage regulator	• Clean contacts or replace
All gauges pegged	• Loss of ground between instrument voltage regulator and car	• Check ground
	• Defective instrument regulator	• Replace regulator

86746c03

Troubleshooting Basic Dash Gauge Problems

Problem	Cause	Solution
Warning Lights		
Light(s) do not come on when ignition is ON, but engine is not started	• Defective bulb • Defective wire • Defective sending unit	• Replace bulb • Check wire from light to sending unit • Disconnect the wire from the sending unit and ground it. Replace the sending unit if the light comes on with the ignition ON.
Light comes on with engine running	• Problem in individual system • Defective sending unit	• Check system • Check sending unit (see above)

86746c04

Troubleshooting Basic Windshield Wiper Problems

Problem	Cause	Solution
Electric Wipers		
Wipers do not operate—Wiper motor heats up or hums	• Internal motor defect • Bent or damaged linkage • Arms improperly installed on linking pivots	• Replace motor • Repair or replace linkage • Position linkage in park and reinstall wiper arms
Electric Wipers		
Wipers do not operate—No current to motor	• Fuse or circuit breaker blown • Loose, open or broken wiring • Defective switch • Defective or corroded terminals • No ground circuit for motor or switch	• Replace fuse or circuit breaker • Repair wiring and connections • Replace switch • Replace or clean terminals • Repair ground circuits
Wipers do not operate—Motor runs	• Linkage disconnected or broken	• Connect wiper linkage or replace broken linkage
Vacuum Wipers		
Wipers do not operate	• Control switch or cable inoperative • Loss of engine vacuum to wiper motor (broken hoses, low engine vacuum, defective vacuum/fuel pump) • Linkage broken or disconnected • Defective wiper motor	• Repair or replace switch or cable • Check vacuum lines, engine vacuum and fuel pump • Repair linkage • Replace wiper motor
Wipers stop on engine acceleration	• Leaking vacuum hoses • Dry windshield • Oversize wiper blades • Defective vacuum/fuel pump	• Repair or replace hoses • Wet windshield with washers • Replace with proper size wiper blades • Replace pump

86746c02

LIGHTING

Headlights

REMOVAL & INSTALLATION

Sealed Beam

1988-95 MODELS

▶ See Figures 61, 62, 63, 64, 65 and 66

1. Remove the screws and the headlamp bezel.
2. Remove the screws and headlamp bulb retaining ring.
3. Disengage the headlamp bulb wire harness and remove the bulb from the socket.

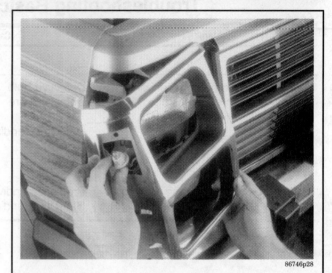

Fig. 63 Remove the headlamp bezel

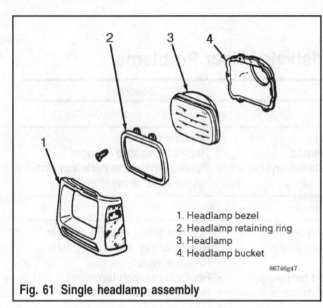

1. Headlamp bezel
2. Headlamp retaining ring
3. Headlamp
4. Headlamp bucket

86746g47

Fig. 61 Single headlamp assembly

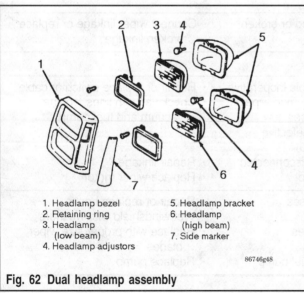

1. Headlamp bezel
2. Retaining ring
3. Headlamp (low beam)
4. Headlamp adjustors
5. Headlamp bracket
6. Headlamp (high beam)
7. Side marker

86746g48

Fig. 62 Dual headlamp assembly

Fig. 64 Remove the headlamp bulb retaining ring screws

To install:

4. Install the bulb in the bucket and engage the wire harness connector.
5. Install the retaining ring on the headlamp bulb and fasten the screws.
6. Install the bezel and tighten the screws securely.

1996 MODELS

1. Open the hood, reach into the engine compartment and locate the lock ring supporting the bulb assembly.
2. Rotate the lock ring ⅛ turn counterclockwise and pull the bulb straight out from the housing.

To install:

3. Install a new bulb and position the bulb assembly in the lamp housing.
4. Rotate the lock ring ⅛ turn clockwise to secure.

Fig. 65 Remove the headlamp bulb retaining ring and slide the bulb forward

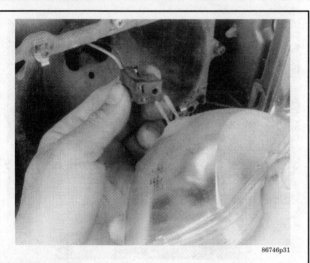

Fig. 66 Disengage the headlamp bulb electrical connector

Aero Headlamp

Aero headlamp systems use replaceable halogen bulbs that are mounted in aero dynamic, molded plastic lens reflector assemblies.

➡️**Lens fogging is a normal condition that does not require service, as moisture will vent from tubes behind the lens on aero headlamp-type systems.**

1. Grasp the lower end of the headlamp glass and pull it away from the grille opening reinforcement.
2. Disengage the lower adjuster pivots from the lens assembly.
3. Grasp the upper edge of the headlamp glass and pull it away from the grille opening reinforcement.
4. Disengage the upper adjuster pivots from the lens assembly.
5. Disengage the wire wire connector behind the headlight and rotate the bulb ring counterclockwise.
6. Remove the ring and bulb from the lens.

To install:

➡️**DO NOT handle elements with your bare hands, always handle with a clean cloth. Oil from your hands will cause the element to fail.**

7. Install the ring and the bulb in the lens and rotate the bulb ring clockwise.
8. Engage the wire connector and the upper pivots to the wire bulb assembly.
9. Engage the lower pivots and ensure the assembly is secure.

ALIGNMENT

Aiming Preparation

➡️**Headlamps should be adjusted with a special alignment tool. State regulations may vary this procedure. Use the following procedure for temporary adjustments only.**

Perform the following items before attempting to aim the headlamps:
• Verify the headlamp dimmer and high beam indicator operation
• Inspect and correct all components that could interfere with the proper headlamp alignment
• Verify proper tire inflation on all wheels
• Clean headlamp lenses and make sure that there are no heavy loads in the trunk or hatch luggage area
• The fuel tank should be full. Add 6.5 lbs. (3 kg) of weight over the fuel tank for each estimated gallon of missing fuel.

Alignment Screen Preparation

1. Position the vehicle on a level surface perpendicular to a flat wall 25 ft. (7.62m) away from the front of the headlamp lens.
2. From the floor up 5 ft. (1.3m), tape a line on the wall at the centerline of the vehicle. Sight along the centerline of the vehicle (from the rear of the vehicle forward) to verify accuracy of the line placement.
3. Rock the vehicle side to side and up and down (on front bumper assembly) a few times to allow the suspension to stabilize.
4. Measure the distance from the center of the headlamp lens to the floor. Transfer measurements to the alignment screen with tape. Use this mark for the up/down adjustment reference.
5. Measure the distance from the centerline of the vehicle to the center of each headlamp being aligned. Transfer measurements to screen with tape to each side of the vehicle centerline. Use this mark for left/right adjustment reference.

Headlight Adjustment

Horizontal and vertical aiming of each sealed beam unit is provided by two adjusting screws, which move the mounting ring in the body against the tension of the coil spring. There is no adjustment for focus; this is done during headlight manufacturing.

A properly aimed low beam headlamp will project the top edge of high intensity pattern on the alignment screen from 2 in. (50mm) above to 2 in. (50mm) below the headlamp centerline. The side-to-side outboard edge of high intensity pattern should be from 2 in. (50mm) left to 2 in. (50mm) right of the headlamp centerline.

➡**The preferred headlamp alignment is "0" for the up/down adjustment and "0" for the left/right adjustment.**

The high beams on a vehicle with aero headlamps cannot be aligned. The high beam pattern should be correct when the low beams are aligned properly. The high beam pattern on vehicles with multiple sealed beam headlamps should be aligned with the low beam lamp either disconnected or covered (do not cover illuminated headlamp for more than 15 seconds).

Signal and Marker Lights

REMOVAL & INSTALLATION

Front Parking/Turn Signal Lights
▶ **See Figures 67, 68, 69, 70, 71, 72, 73 and 74**

1. Remove the headlamp bezel screw and the side marker lamp lens/housing screw.
2. Separate the side marker lamp from the headlamp bezel and remove the screws from the headlight bezel.
3. Disengage the lamp housing from the headlamp bezel and rotate the bulb socket to remove it from the housing.
4. Remove the bulb from the socket by turning it counterclockwise.
   To install:
5. Install the new bulb, and the bulb and socket in the lamp housing.
6. Position the park/turn signal lamp housing bezel on the headlamp bezel and install the outer screws.
7. Install the side marker lamp lens/housing on the headlamp bezel and fasten the screws.

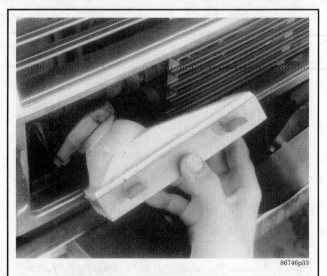
Fig. 68 Slide the turn signal lens forward

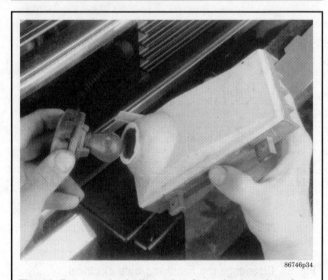
Fig. 69 Remove the bulb socket from the lens housing

Fig. 67 Remove the turn signal lens retaining screws

Fig. 70 Remove the turn signal/front parking lamp bulb from the socket

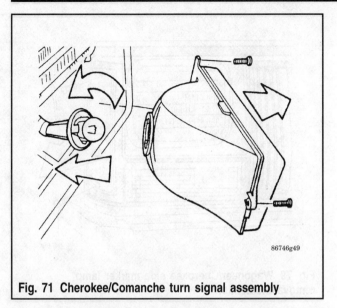

Fig. 71 Cherokee/Comanche turn signal assembly

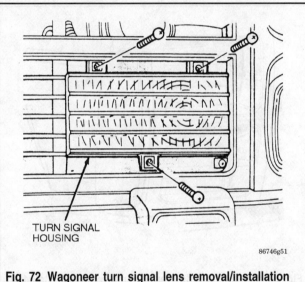

TURN SIGNAL
HOUSING

Fig. 72 Wagoneer turn signal lens removal/installation

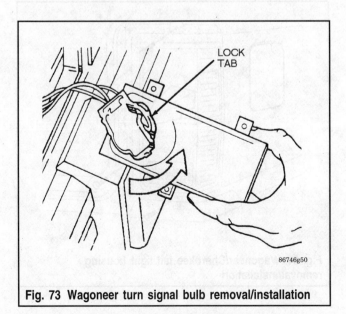

LOCK
TAB

Fig. 73 Wagoneer turn signal bulb removal/installation

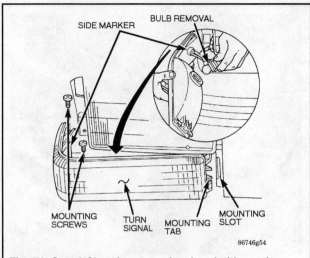

SIDE MARKER   BULB REMOVAL

MOUNTING   TURN   MOUNTING   MOUNTING
SCREWS   SIGNAL   TAB   SLOT

Fig. 74 Grand Cherokee turn signal and side marker lamp replacement

Side Marker Lights

▶ **See Figures 75, 76, 77, 78, 79 and 80**

1. Remove the screws from the side marker lamp lens and housing.
2. Separate the lens and housing from the headlamp bezel.
3. Remove the bulb from the back side of the housing.
4. Remove the bulb from the socket.

To install:

5. Install the bulb in the socket and engage the bulb and socket in the back side of the housing.
6. Position the lens and the housing on the bezel and install the screws.

Back-Up/Rear Turn Signal/Tail Lights

▶ **See Figures 81, 82, 83, 84, 85, 86 and 87**

The stop, turn signal, back-up and rear side marker lamp bulbs are incorporated into the tail lamp.

1. Remove the tail lamp retaining screws.
2. Pull the lamp away from the vehicle to gain access to the bulb socket.

Fig. 75 Remove the side marker lens retaining screws

86746p37

Fig. 76 Slide the side marker lens forward

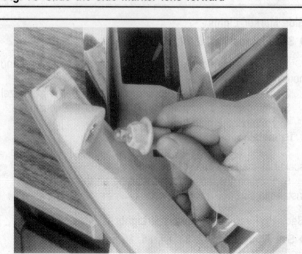

86746p38

Fig. 77 Disengage the electrical socket and bulb from the lens

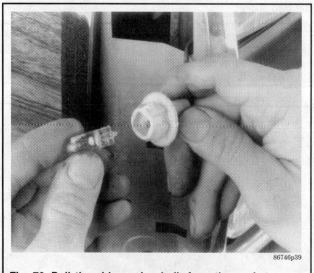

86746p39

Fig. 78 Pull the side marker bulb from the socket

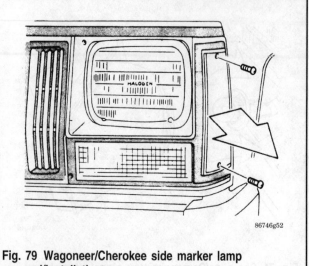

86746g52

Fig. 79 Wagoneer/Cherokee side marker lamp removal/installation

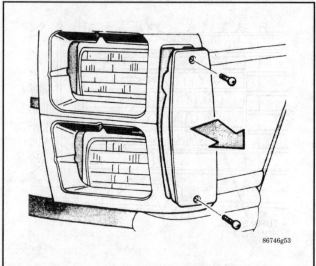

86746g53

Fig. 80 Comanche side marker lamp removal/installation

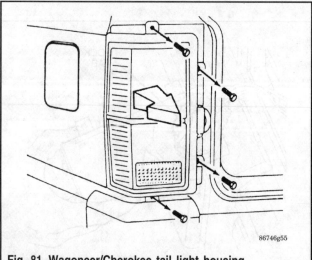

86746g55

Fig. 81 Wagoneer/Cherokee tail light housing removal/installation

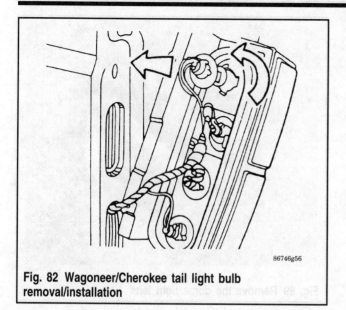

Fig. 82 Wagoneer/Cherokee tail light bulb removal/installation

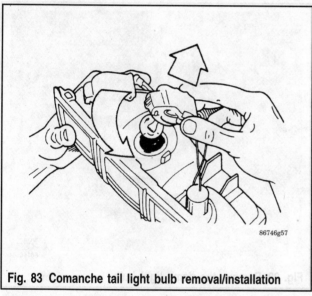

Fig. 83 Comanche tail light bulb removal/installation

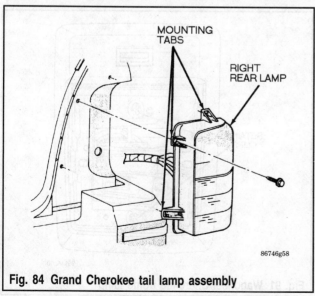

MOUNTING
TABS

RIGHT
REAR LAMP

Fig. 84 Grand Cherokee tail lamp assembly

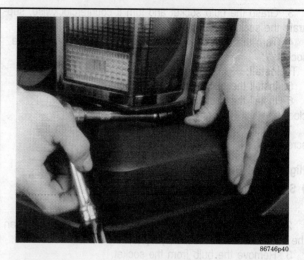

Fig. 85 Unfasten the back-up/rear turn signal/tail light lens

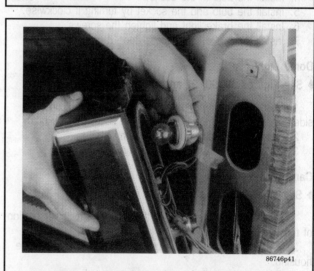

Fig. 86 Slide the back-up/rear turn signal/tail light lens forward and disengage the socket

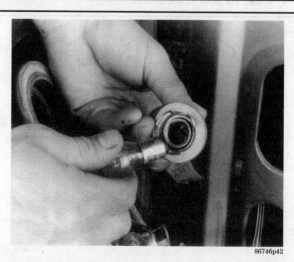

Fig. 87 Remove the bulb from the back-up/rear turn signal/tail light lens socket

3. Grasp the bulb socket and turn it counterclockwise, separate the socket from the lamp.

4. Turn the bulb counterclockwise and remove it from the socket.

To install:

5. Install the bulb in the socket and turn it clockwise.

6. Install the socket and bulb in the lamp and turn it clockwise.

7. Install the tail lamp on the vehicle and tighten the screws.

High-mount Brake Light

♦ See Figure 88

1. Remove the brake light access door, if equipped.

2. Remove the brake light lamp mounting screws and then the socket and bulb assembly by turning it counterclockwise.

3. Remove the bulb from the socket.

To install:

4. Install the bulb in the socket.

5. Install the bulb and the socket by turning it clockwise.

6. Install the brake light and tighten the screws.

7. Install the brake light access door, if equipped.

Dome Light

♦ See Figures 89, 90, 91 and 92

1. Remove the dome lamp lens by squeezing it on both sides and pulling the lens down to gain access to the bulb.

2. Remove the bulb from the assembly.

3. Installation is the reverse of removal.

Cargo Lamp

♦ See Figures 93 and 94

1. Insert a flat blade tool into the slots on the lower portion of the lens.

2. Rotate the tool upwards until the lens snaps out of the housing.

3. Remove the bulb from the socket.

To install:

4. Install the bulb in the socket.

Fig. 89 Remove the dome light lens

Fig. 90 Remove the dome light bulb

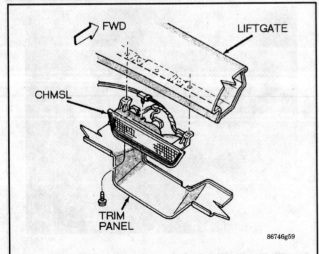

Fig. 88 Exploded view of the center high mount stop lamp

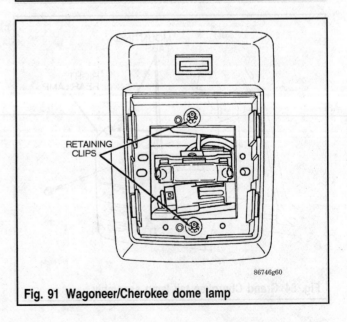

Fig. 91 Wagoneer/Cherokee dome lamp

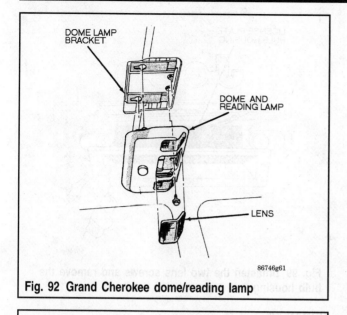

Fig. 92 Grand Cherokee dome/reading lamp

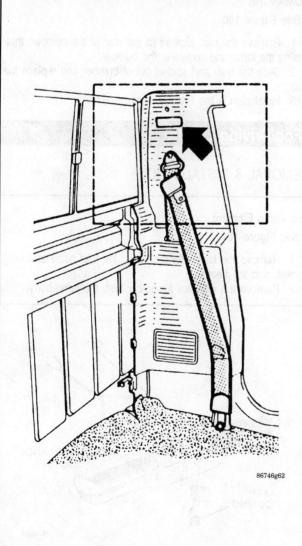

Fig. 93 The arrow points to the Comanche dome light

LIFTGATE
OPENING
UPPER PANEL

CARGO
LAMP LENS

86746g63

Fig. 94 Grand Cherokee cargo lamp

5. Insert the upper tabs of the lens in the housing and snap the lens in place.

License Plate Light

EXCEPT COMANCHE AND MODELS WITHOUT THE SWING-OUT SPARE

▶ See Figures 95, 96, 97 and 98

1. Unfasten the two lens screws and remove the bulb housing from liftgate.
2. Remove bulb from housing.
3. Installation is the reverse of removal

MODELS WITH SWING-OUT SPARE

▶ See Figure 99

1. Remove screws holding lens assembly.
2. Pry housing cover from vehicle and remove bulb.
3. Installation is the reverse of removal.

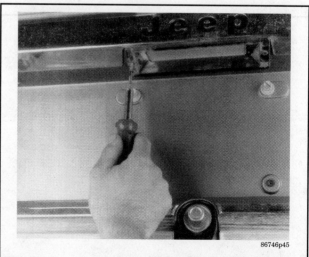

Fig. 95 Remove the license plate lamp cover retaining screws

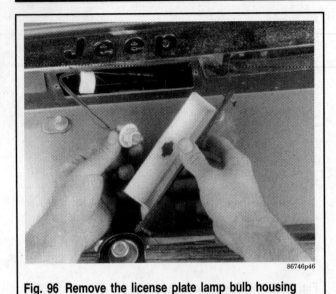

Fig. 96 Remove the license plate lamp bulb housing

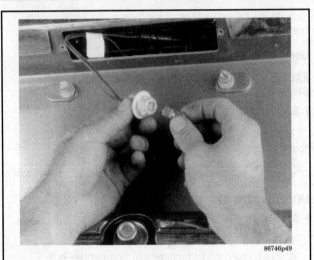

Fig. 97 Remove the license plate lamp bulb from the socket

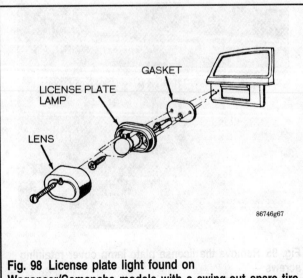

Fig. 98 License plate light found on Wagoneer/Comanche models with a swing-out spare tire

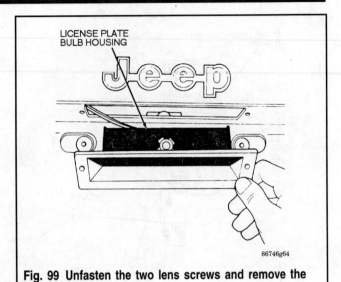

Fig. 99 Unfasten the two lens screws and remove the bulb housing

COMANCHE

▶ **See Figure 100**

1. Remove the clip, located at the rear of the bumper, that retains the lamp and socket in the bumper.
2. Slide the bulb and socket out of bumper and replace the bulb.
3. Installation is the reverse of removal.

Fog/Driving Lights

REMOVAL & INSTALLATION

Fog Lamp Element

▶ **See Figure 101**

1. Remove the lamp stone shields, the four bezel attaching screws, and the bezel.
2. Remove the reflector assembly from the lamp body.

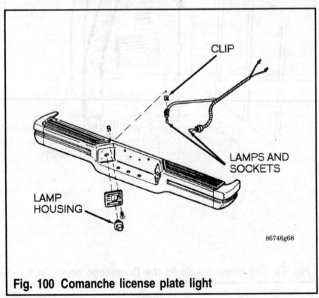

Fig. 100 Comanche license plate light

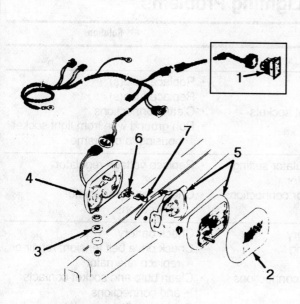

1. Instrument panel switch
2. Stone shield
3. Adjustment nut
4. Lamp body
5. Lens and reflector assembly
6. Bulb holder
7. Lamp element

86746g65

Fig. 101 Exploded view of a fog lamp assembly

3. Remove the bulb holder from the assembly. Remove the element from the bulb.

➡**DO NOT handle elements with your bare hands, always handle with a clean cloth. Oil from your hands will cause the element to fail.**

4. Installation is the reverse of removal.

FOG LAMP BEAM ADJUSTMENT

1. Position the vehicle on a level surface, facing a wall approximately 25 feet (7.62m) away. Remove the lamp stone shields and loosen the adjustment nuts.
2. Turn the fog lamps ON and adjust as follows:
  a. Distance between the light beam centers should be equal to the distance between the lamp assemblies on the bumper.
  b. Height of the light beams on the wall should be 4 in. (10.2cm) less than the center of the lamp assemblies when mounted on the bumper.
3. Install all previously removed items after turning OFF the fog lamps.

Troubleshooting Basic Lighting Problems

Problem	Cause	Solution
Lights		
One or more lights don't work, but others do	· Defective bulb(s) · Blown fuse(s) · Dirty fuse clips or light sockets · Poor ground circuit	· Replace bulb(s) · Replace fuse(s) · Clean connections · Run ground wire from light socket housing to car frame
Lights burn out quickly	· Incorrect voltage regulator setting or defective regulator · Poor battery/alternator connections	· Replace voltage regulator · Check battery/alternator connections
Lights go dim	· Low/discharged battery · Alternator not charging · Corroded sockets or connections · Low voltage output	· Check battery · Check drive belt tension; repair or replace alternator · Clean bulb and socket contacts and connections · Replace voltage regulator
Lights flicker	· Loose connection · Poor ground · Circuit breaker operating (short circuit)	· Tighten all connections · Run ground wire from light housing to car frame · Check connections and look for bare wires
Lights "flare"—Some flare is normal on acceleration—if excessive, see "Lights Burn Out Quickly"	· High voltage setting	· Replace voltage regulator
Lights glare—approaching drivers are blinded	· Lights adjusted too high · Rear springs or shocks sagging · Rear tires soft	· Have headlights aimed · Check rear springs/shocks · Check/correct rear tire pressure
Turn Signals		
Turn signals don't work in either direction	· Blown fuse · Defective flasher · Loose connection	· Replace fuse · Replace flasher · Check/tighten all connections
Right (or left) turn signal only won't work	· Bulb burned out · Right (or left) indicator bulb burned out · Short circuit	· Replace bulb · Check/replace indicator bulb · Check/repair wiring
Flasher rate too slow or too fast	· Incorrect wattage bulb · Incorrect flasher	· Flasher bulb · Replace flasher (use a variable load flasher if you pull a trailer)
Indicator lights do not flash (burn steadily)	· Burned out bulb · Defective flasher	· Replace bulb · Replace flasher
Indicator lights do not light at all	· Burned out indicator bulb · Defective flasher	· Replace indicator bulb · Replace flasher

86746c07

TRAILER WIRING

Wiring the vehicle for towing is fairly easy. There are a number of good wiring kits available and these should be used, rather than trying to design your own.

All trailers will need brake lights and turn signals as well as tail lights and side marker lights. Most states require extra marker lights for overwide trailers. Also, most states have recently required back-up lights for trailers, and most trailer manufacturers have been building trailers with back-up lights for several years.

Additionally, some Class I, most Class II and just about all Class III trailers will have electric brakes. Add to this number an accessories wire, to operate trailer internal equipment or to charge the trailer's battery, and you can have as many as seven wires in the harness.

Determine the equipment on your trailer and buy the wiring kit necessary. The kit will contain all the wires needed, plus a plug adapter set which included the female plug, mounted on the bumper or hitch, and the male plug, wired into, or plugged into the trailer harness.

When installing the kit, follow the manufacturer's instructions. The color coding of the wires is usually standard throughout the industry. One point to note: some domestic vehicles, and most imported vehicles, have separate turn signals. On most domestic vehicles, the brake lights and rear turn signals operate with the same bulb. For those vehicles without separate turn signals, you can purchase an isolation unit so that the brake lights won't blink whenever the turn signals are operated, or, you can go to your local electronics supply house and buy four diodes to wire in series with the brake and turn signal bulbs. Diodes will isolate the brake and turn signals. The choice is yours. The isolation units are simple and quick to install, but far more expensive than the diodes. The diodes, however, require more work to install properly, since they require the cutting of each bulb's wire and soldering in place of the diode.

One, final point, the best kits are those with a spring loaded cover on the vehicle mounted socket. This cover prevents dirt and moisture from corroding the terminals. Never let the vehicle socket hang loosely; always mount it securely to the bumper or hitch.

CIRCUIT PROTECTION

Fuse Panel

▶ **See Figures 102 and 103**

The fuse panel contains fuses which protect the various electrical systems. Also included are the turn signal and hazard flashers, and the chime module. The panel is usually located under the dash on the left hand side near the kick panel. There may also be an auxiliary fuse panel in the engine compartment.

The Power Distribution Center contains relays and fuses which further protect the electrical systems. It is usually located under the hood on the right side of the engine compartment.

Fuses and relays are replaced by simply unplugging the defective unit and inserting a new one. Ensure the ignition is **OFF** when replacing any fuse or relay.

❋❋CAUTION

Never replace any fuse or relay with one of a different rating (amperage). Damage to the vehicle or personal injury could result.

REMOVAL & INSTALLATION

1. Using a fuse puller remove the defective fuse from the fuse panel.
2. Install a new fuse of the proper rating (amperage) in the fuse panel.

Fusible Link

The fusible link is a short length of special, Hypalon (high temperature) insulated wire, integral with the engine compartment wiring harness and should not be confused with standard wire. It is several wire gauges smaller than the circuit which it protects. Under no circumstances should a fusible link replacement repair be made using a length of standard wire cut from bulk stock or from another wiring harness.

REMOVAL & INSTALLATION

▶ **See Figure 104**

1. Determine which circuit is damaged, its location and the cause of the open fusible link. If the damaged fusible link is one of three fed by a common No. 10 or 12 gauge feed wire, determine the specific affected circuit.
2. Disconnect the negative battery cable.
3. Cut the damaged fusible link from the wiring harness and discard it. If the fusible link is one of three circuits fed by

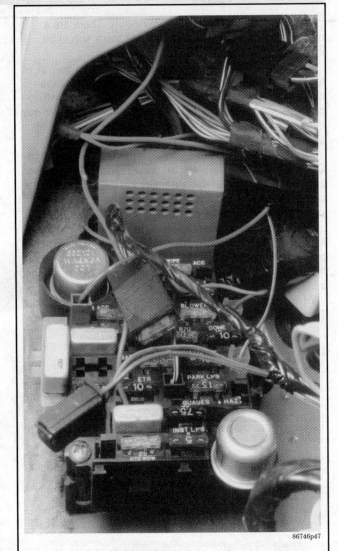

86746p47

Fig. 102 The fuse panel is usually located under the dashboard on the left-hand side near the kick panel

a single feed wire, cut it out of the harness at each splice end and discard it.

4. Identify and procure the proper fusible link and butt connectors for attaching the fusible link to the harness.
5. To repair any fusible link in a 3-link group with one feed:
   a. After cutting the open link out of the harness, cut each of the remaining undamaged fusible links close to the feed wire weld.
   b. Strip approximately 1/2 in. (13mm) of insulation from the detached ends of the two good fusible links. Then insert two wire ends into one end of a butt connector and carefully push one stripped end of the replacement fusible link into

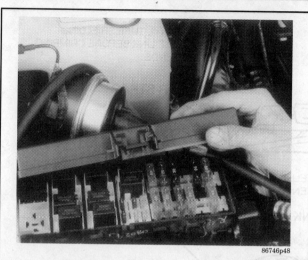

86746p48

Fig. 103 An auxiliary fuse panel may be located in the engine compartment

the same end of the butt connector and crimp all three firmly together.

➡**Care must be taken when fitting the three fusible links into the butt connector as the internal diameter is a snug fit for three wires. Make sure to use a proper crimping tool. Pliers, side cutters, etc. will not apply the proper crimp to retain the wires with the wire end of the circuit from which the blown fusible link was removed. Firmly crimp a butt connector or equivalent to the stripped wire. Then, insert the end of the replacement link into the other end of the butt connector and crimp firmly.**

   c. Using rosin core solder with a consistency of 60 percent tin and 40 percent lead, solder the connectors and the wires at the repairs and insulate with electrical tape.

   6. To replace any fusible link on a single circuit in a harness, cut out the damaged portion, strip approximately ½ in. (13mm) of insulation from the two wire ends and attach the appropriate replacement fusible link to the stripped wire ends with two proper size butt connectors. Solder the connectors and wires and insulate with tape.

   7. To repair any fusible link which has an eyelet terminal on one end such as the charging circuit, cut off the open fusible link behind the weld, strip approximately ½ in. (13mm) of insulation from the cut end and attach the appropriate new eyelet fusible link to the cut stripped wire with an appropriate size butt connector. Solder the connectors and wires at the repair and insulate with tape.

   8. Connect the negative battery cable to the battery and test the system for proper operation.

➡**Do not mistake a resistor wire for a fusible link. The resistor wire is generally longer and has print stating, "Resistor: don't cut or splice."**

Circuit Breaker

   Circuit breakers provide a similar protection to fuses. Unlike fuses most circuit breakers only have to be reset, and not replaced. Circuit breakers are used only in models equipped with power windows, and are located underneath the front seat.

REMOVAL & INSTALLATION

   1. Remove the malfunctioning circuit breaker by pulling it out of its cavity.

   2. Replace the circuit breaker with one of proper amp rating for the circuit, by pushing straight in until the fuse or circuit breaker seats itself fully into the cavity.

Flashers

REPLACEMENT

   The turn signal flasher and hazard units are usually located located under the dash either to the left or right of the steering column on most models.

   1. Remove the turn signal flasher unit or hazard unit by pulling them up from the electrical connection.

   2. To install, push the unit(s) into the electrical connector.

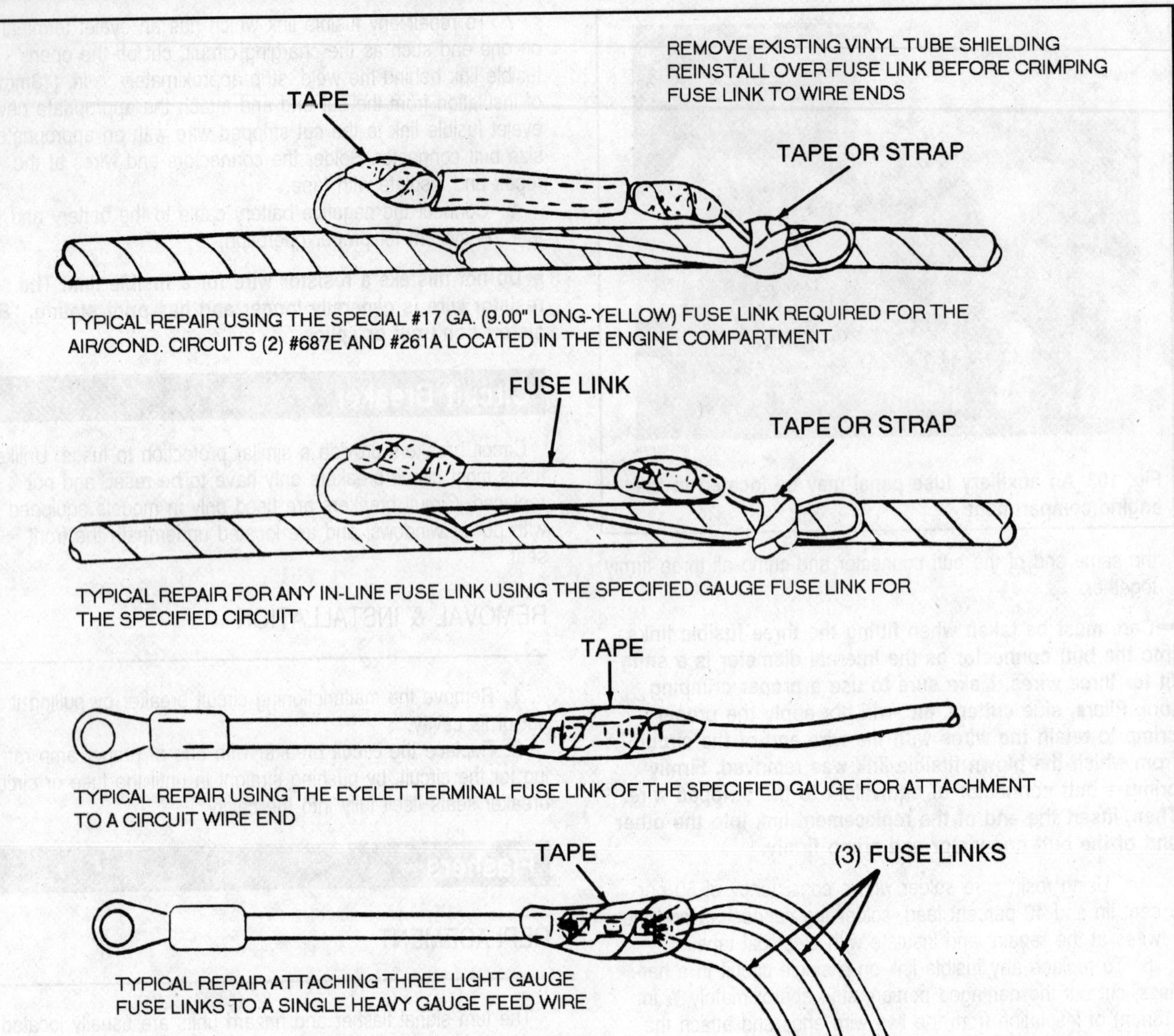

TAPE

REMOVE EXISTING VINYL TUBE SHIELDING
REINSTALL OVER FUSE LINK BEFORE CRIMPING
FUSE LINK TO WIRE ENDS

TAPE OR STRAP

TYPICAL REPAIR USING THE SPECIAL #17 GA. (9.00" LONG-YELLOW) FUSE LINK REQUIRED FOR THE
AIR/COND. CIRCUITS (2) #687E AND #261A LOCATED IN THE ENGINE COMPARTMENT

FUSE LINK

TAPE OR STRAP

TYPICAL REPAIR FOR ANY IN-LINE FUSE LINK USING THE SPECIFIED GAUGE FUSE LINK FOR
THE SPECIFIED CIRCUIT

TAPE

TYPICAL REPAIR USING THE EYELET TERMINAL FUSE LINK OF THE SPECIFIED GAUGE FOR ATTACHMENT
TO A CIRCUIT WIRE END

TAPE

(3) FUSE LINKS

TAPE

TYPICAL REPAIR ATTACHING THREE LIGHT GAUGE
FUSE LINKS TO A SINGLE HEAVY GAUGE FEED WIRE

TAPE

BUTT CONNECTOR
FOR 10 OR 12 GA. WIRE

DOUBLE WIRE CRIMPED

LIGHT GAUGE WIRE

BUTT CONNECTOR
FOR #14 OR 16 WIRE

Ⓢ

Ⓢ

FUSIBLE LINK REPAIR PROCEDURE

86746g70

Fig. 104 Fusible link repair

WIRING DIAGRAMS

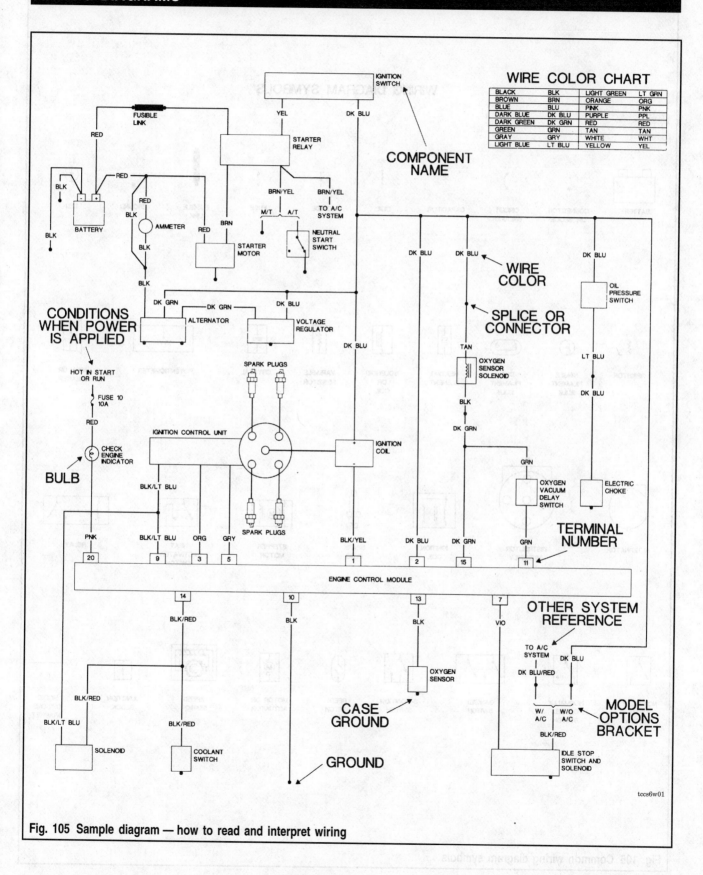

WIRE COLOR CHART

BLACK	BLK	LIGHT GREEN	LT GRN
BROWN	BRN	ORANGE	ORG
BLUE	BLU	PINK	PNK
DARK BLUE	DK BLU	PURPLE	PPL
DARK GREEN	DK GRN	RED	RED
GREEN	GRN	TAN	TAN
GRAY	GRY	WHITE	WHT
LIGHT BLUE	LT BLU	YELLOW	YEL

tccs6w01

Fig. 105 Sample diagram — how to read and interpret wiring

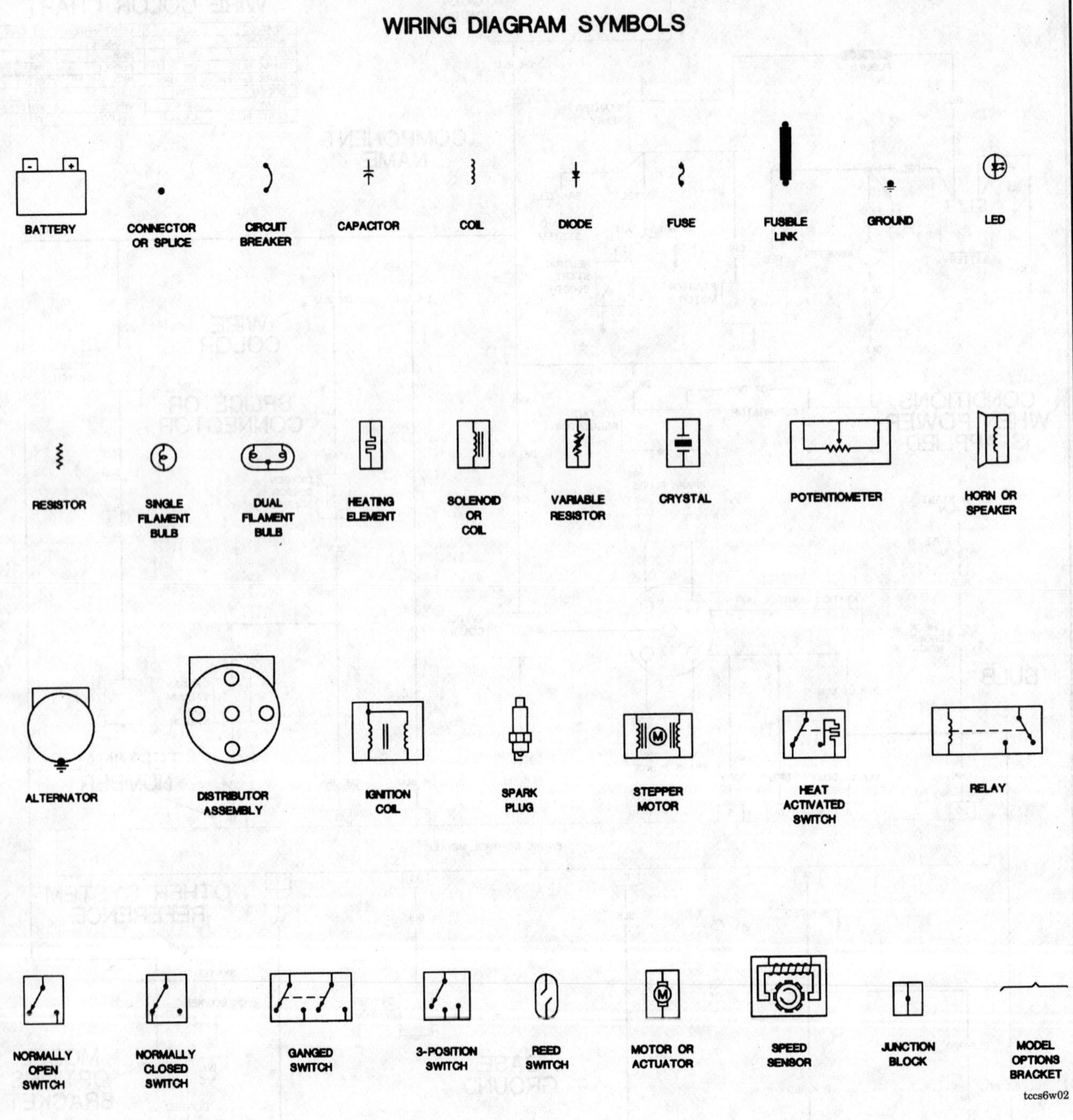

WIRING DIAGRAM SYMBOLS

BATTERY	CONNECTOR OR SPLICE	CIRCUIT BREAKER	CAPACITOR	COIL	DIODE	FUSE	FUSIBLE LINK	GROUND	LED

RESISTOR	SINGLE FILAMENT BULB	DUAL FILAMENT BULB	HEATING ELEMENT	SOLENOID OR COIL	VARIABLE RESISTOR	CRYSTAL	POTENTIOMETER	HORN OR SPEAKER

ALTERNATOR	DISTRIBUTOR ASSEMBLY	IGNITION COIL	SPARK PLUG	STEPPER MOTOR	HEAT ACTIVATED SWITCH	RELAY

NORMALLY OPEN SWITCH	NORMALLY CLOSED SWITCH	GANGED SWITCH	3-POSITION SWITCH	REED SWITCH	MOTOR OR ACTUATOR	SPEED SENSOR	JUNCTION BLOCK	MODEL OPTIONS BRACKET

tccs6w02

Fig. 106 Common wiring diagram symbols

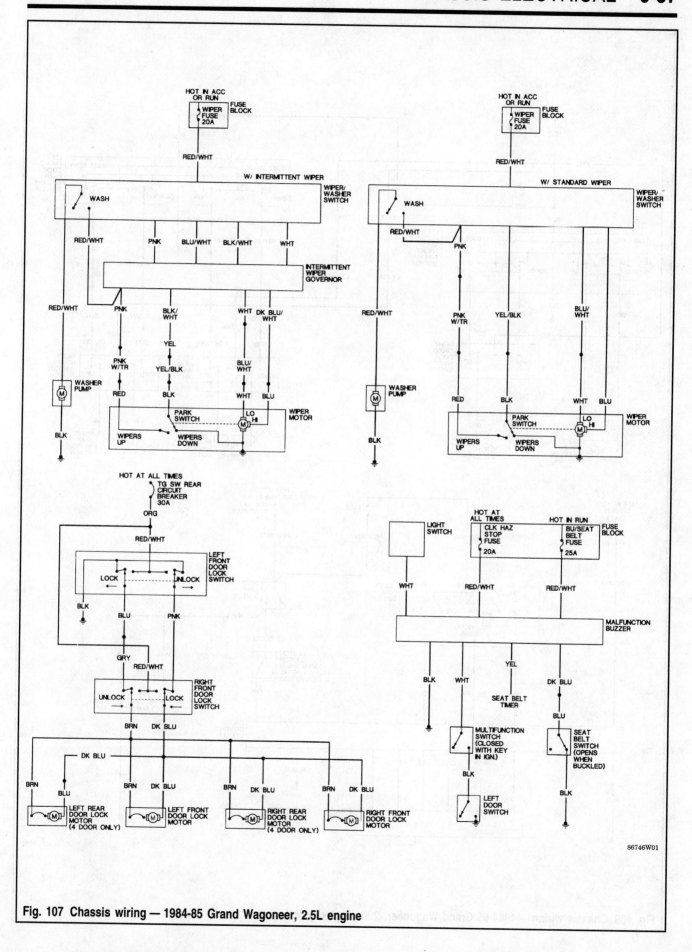

Fig. 107 Chassis wiring — 1984-85 Grand Wagoneer, 2.5L engine

86746W01

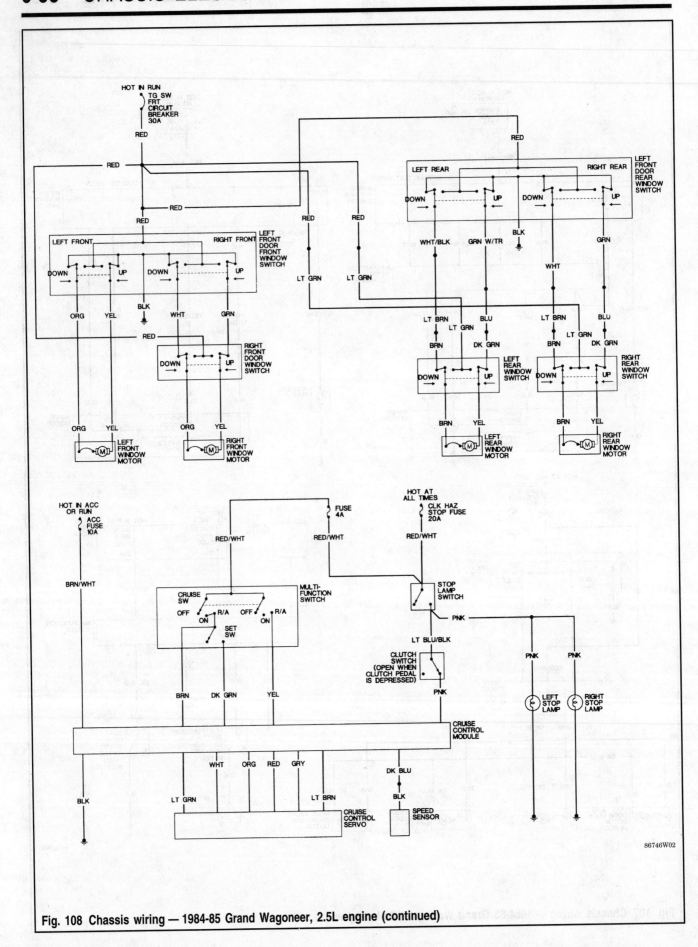

Fig. 108 Chassis wiring — 1984-85 Grand Wagoneer, 2.5L engine (continued)

86746W02

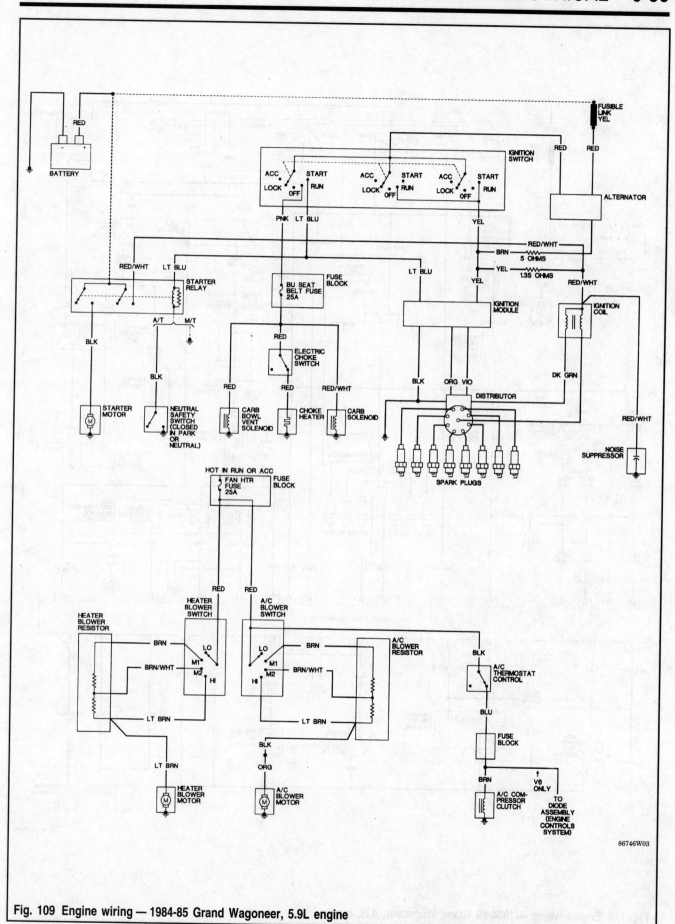

Fig. 109 Engine wiring — 1984-85 Grand Wagoneer, 5.9L engine

86746W03

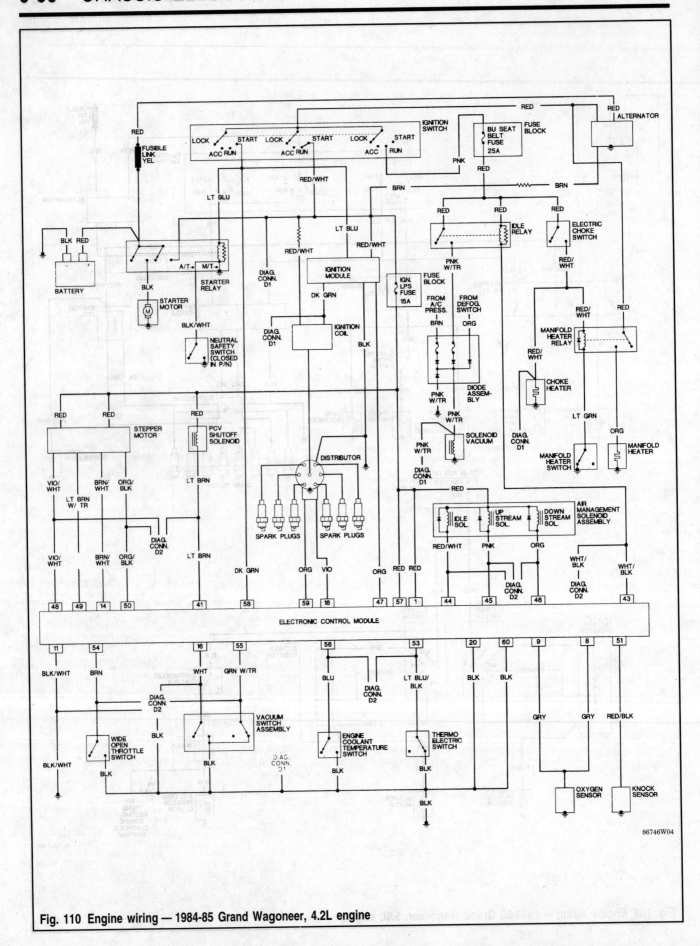

Fig. 110 Engine wiring — 1984-85 Grand Wagoneer, 4.2L engine

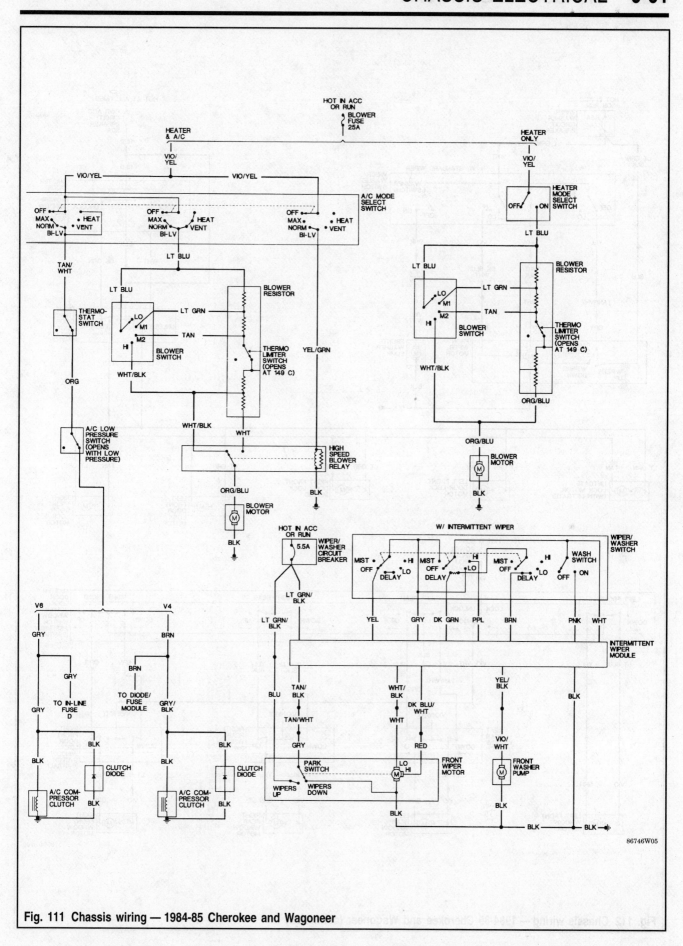

Fig. 111 Chassis wiring — 1984-85 Cherokee and Wagoneer

86746W05

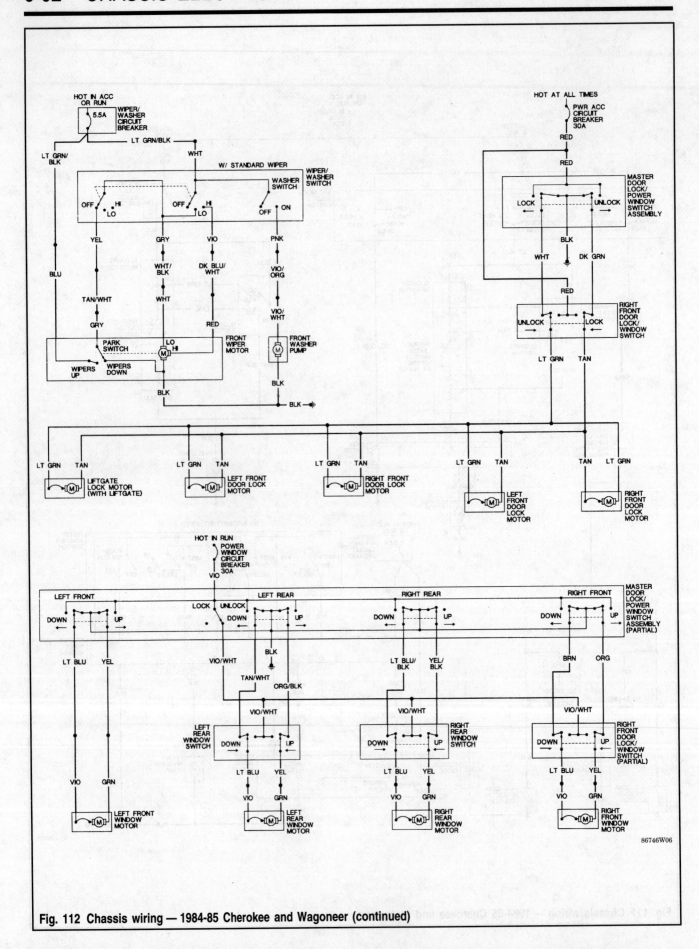

Fig. 112 Chassis wiring — 1984-85 Cherokee and Wagoneer (continued)

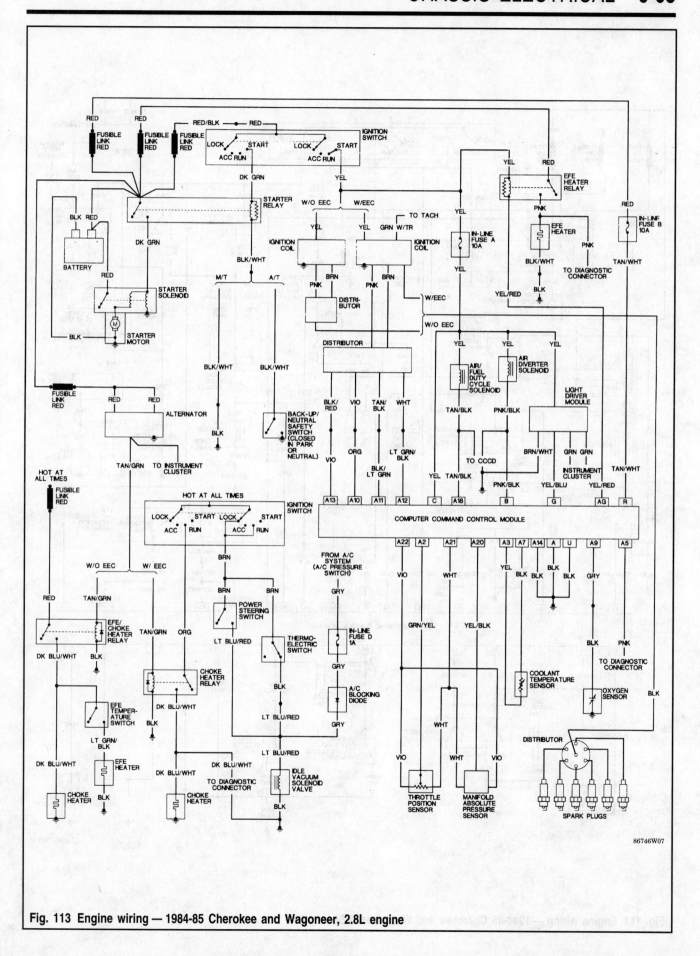

Fig. 113 Engine wiring — 1984-85 Cherokee and Wagoneer, 2.8L engine

86746W07

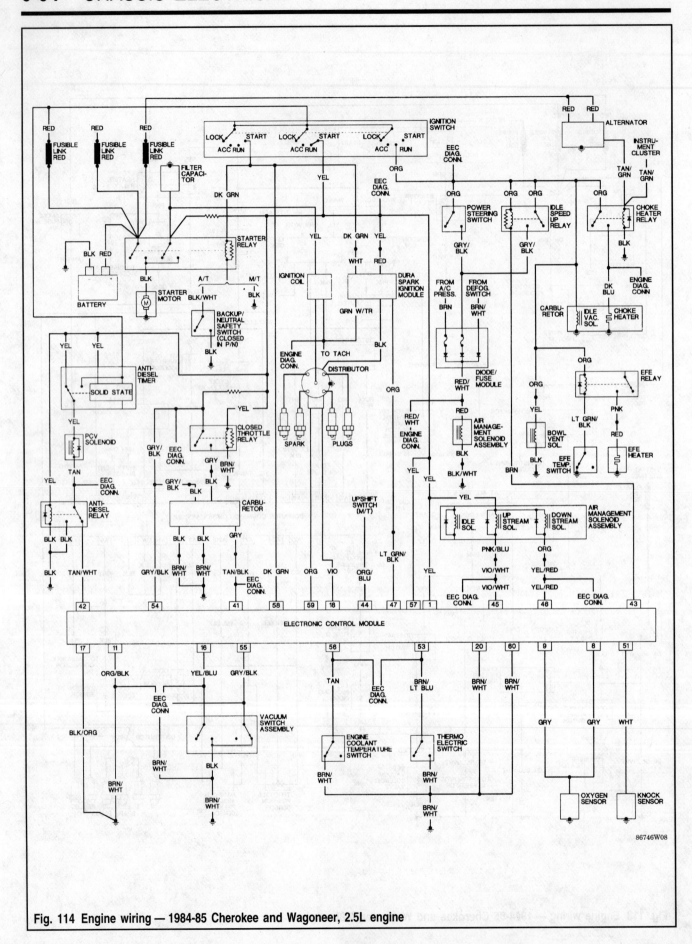

Fig. 114 Engine wiring — 1984-85 Cherokee and Wagoneer, 2.5L engine

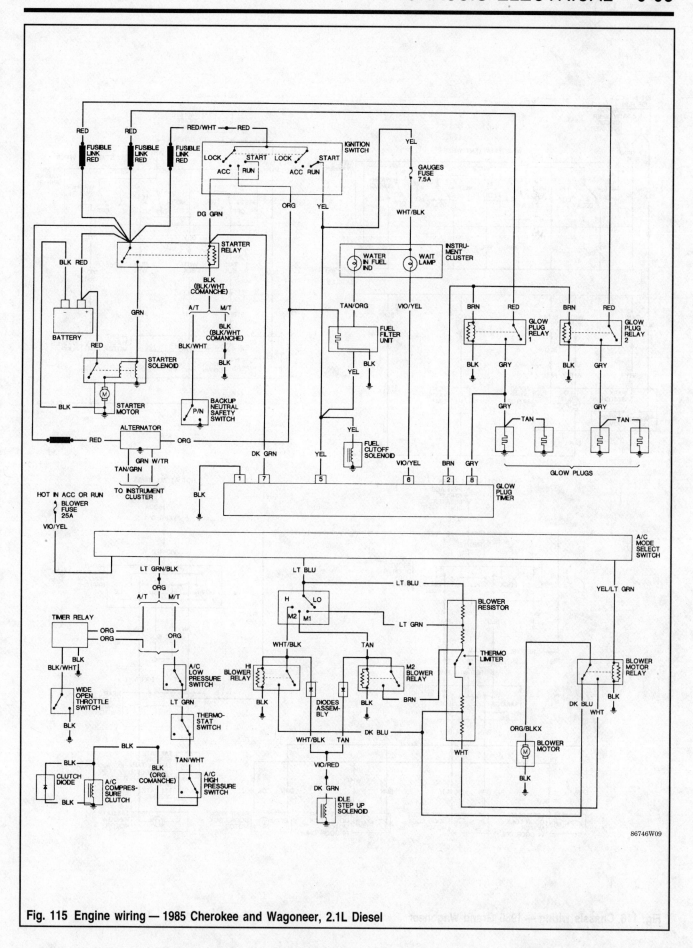

Fig. 115 Engine wiring — 1985 Cherokee and Wagoneer, 2.1L Diesel

86746W09

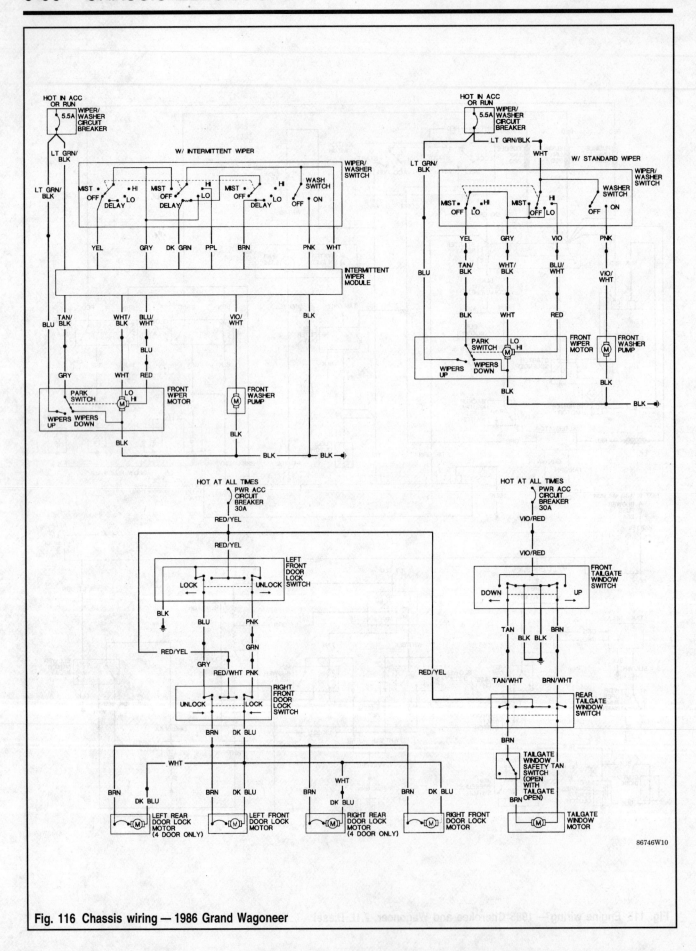

Fig. 116 Chassis wiring — 1986 Grand Wagoneer

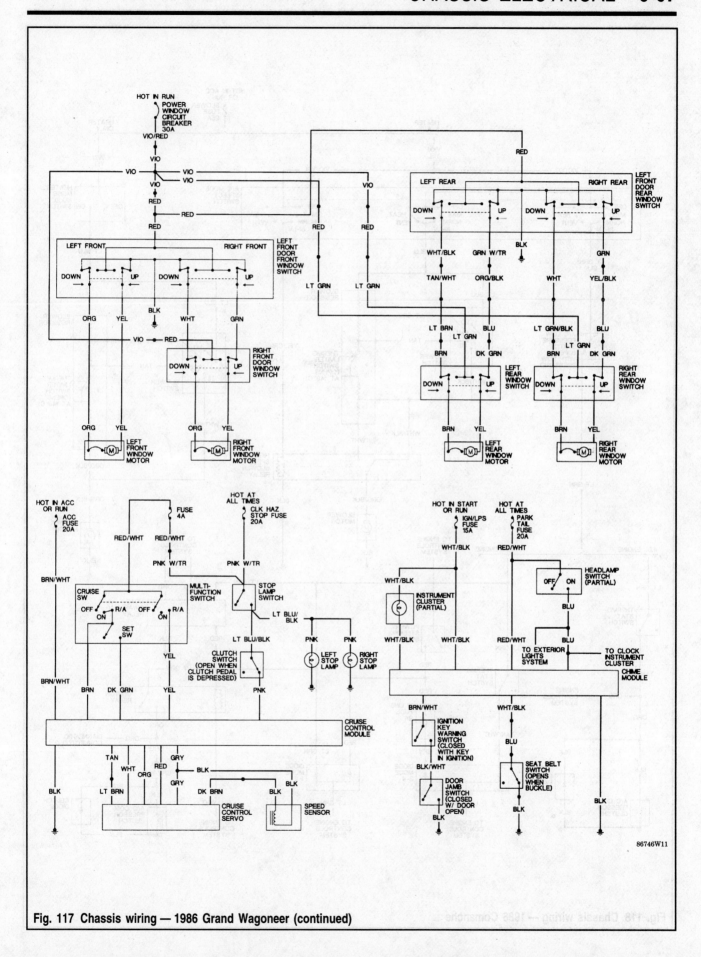

Fig. 117 Chassis wiring — 1986 Grand Wagoneer (continued)

86746W11

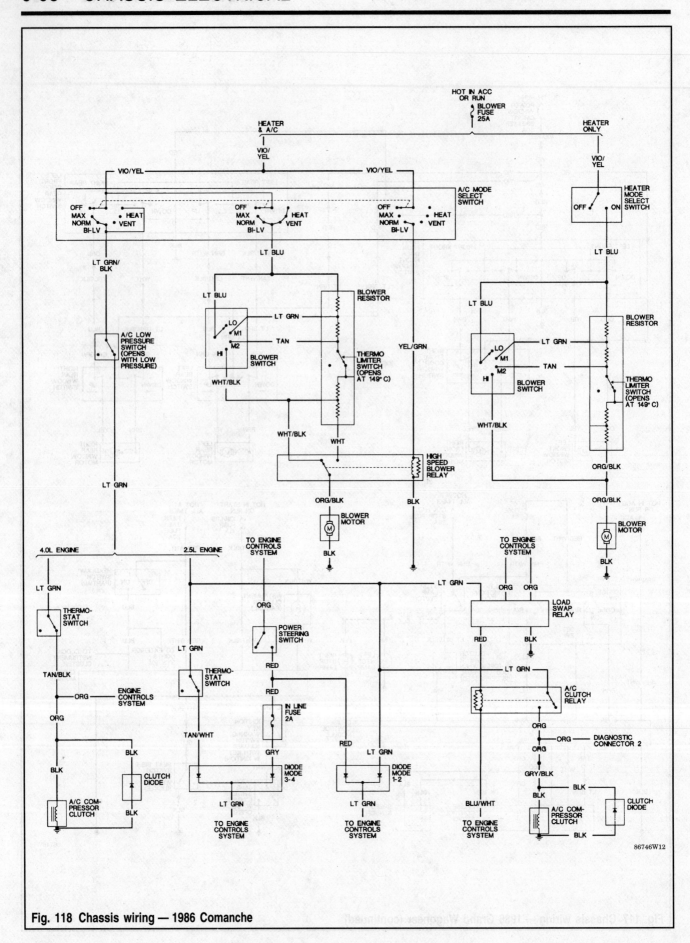

Fig. 118 Chassis wiring — 1986 Comanche

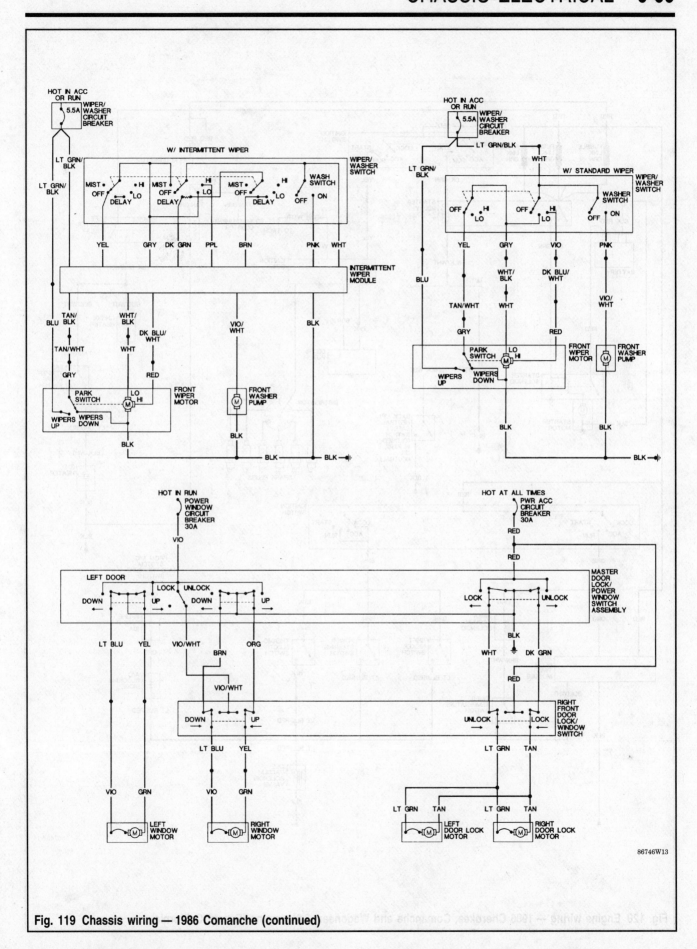

Fig. 119 Chassis wiring — 1986 Comanche (continued)

86746W13

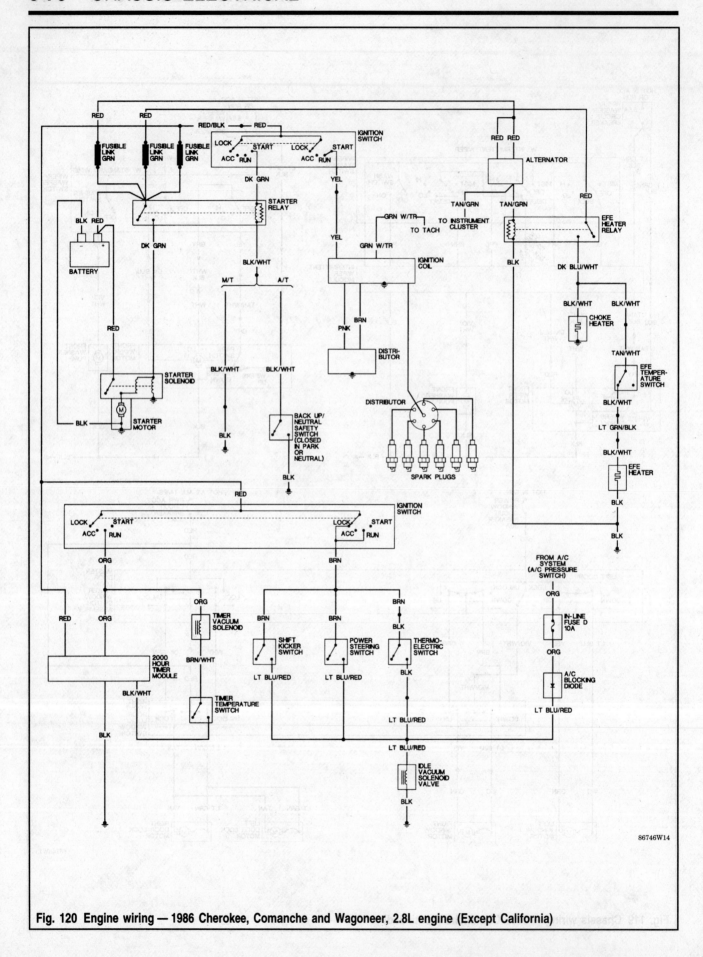

Fig. 120 Engine wiring — 1986 Cherokee, Comanche and Wagoneer, 2.8L engine (Except California)

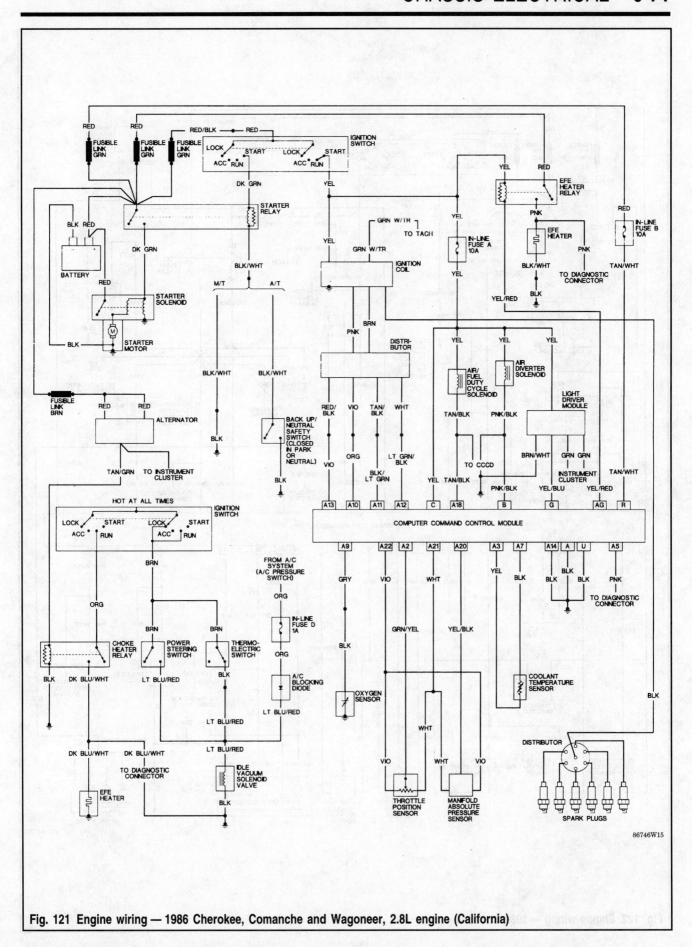

Fig. 121 Engine wiring — 1986 Cherokee, Comanche and Wagoneer, 2.8L engine (California)

86746W15

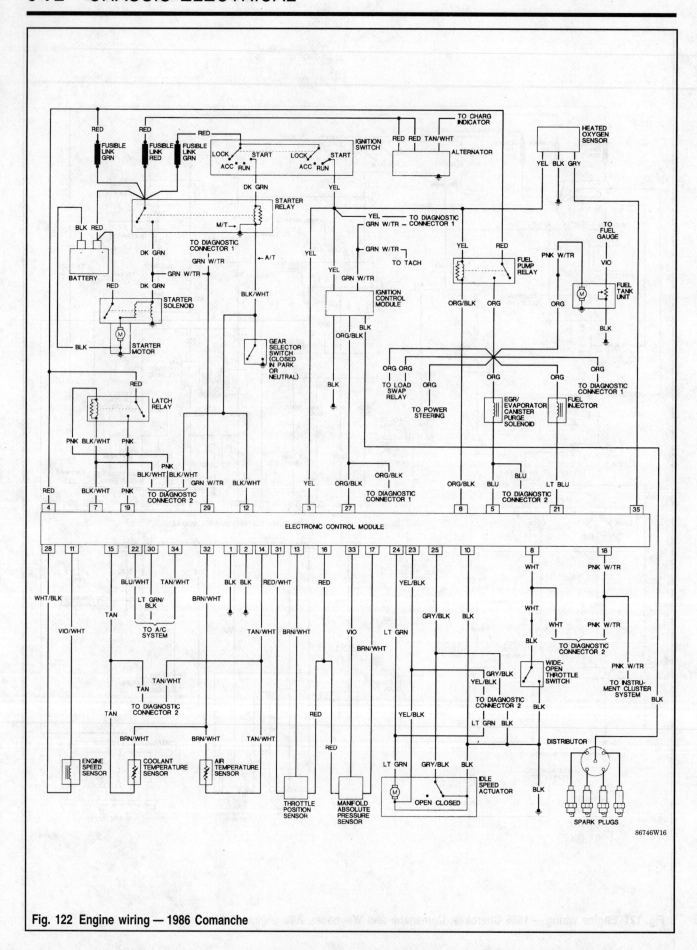

Fig. 122 Engine wiring — 1986 Comanche

86746W16

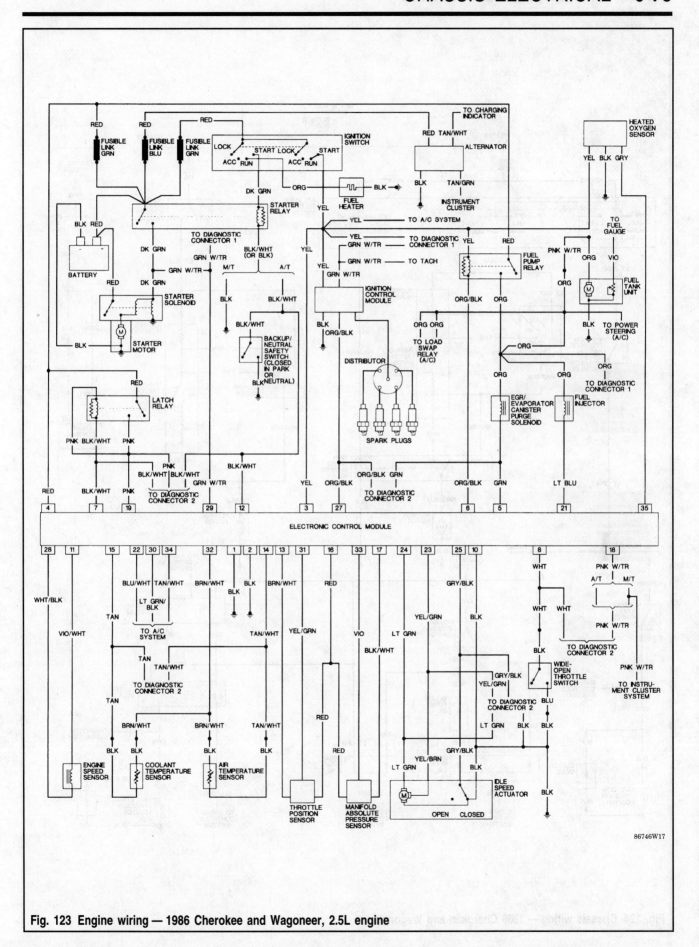

Fig. 123 Engine wiring — 1986 Cherokee and Wagoneer, 2.5L engine

86746W17

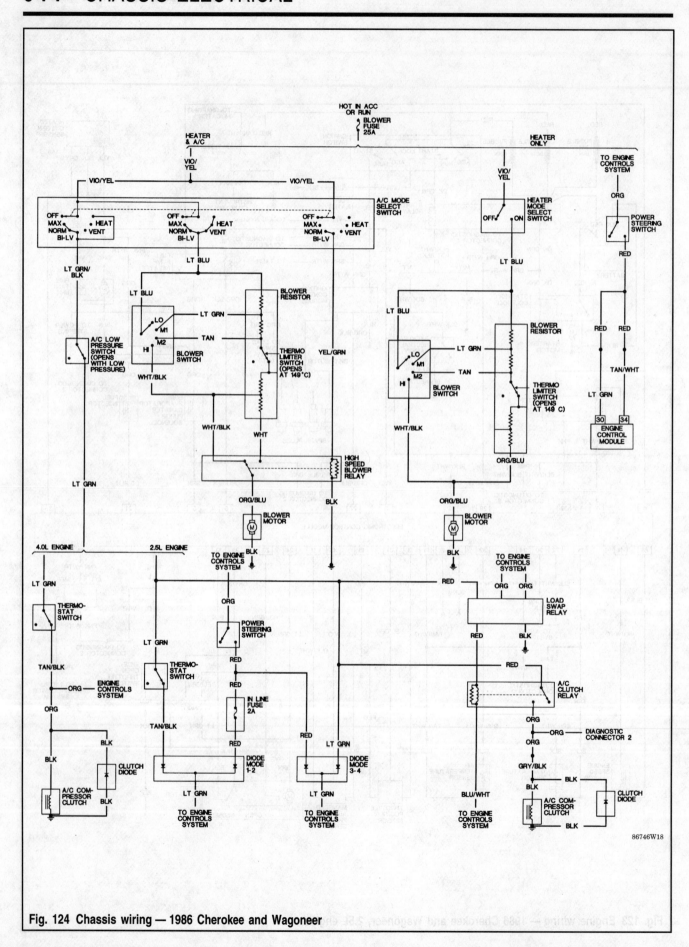

Fig. 124 Chassis wiring — 1986 Cherokee and Wagoneer

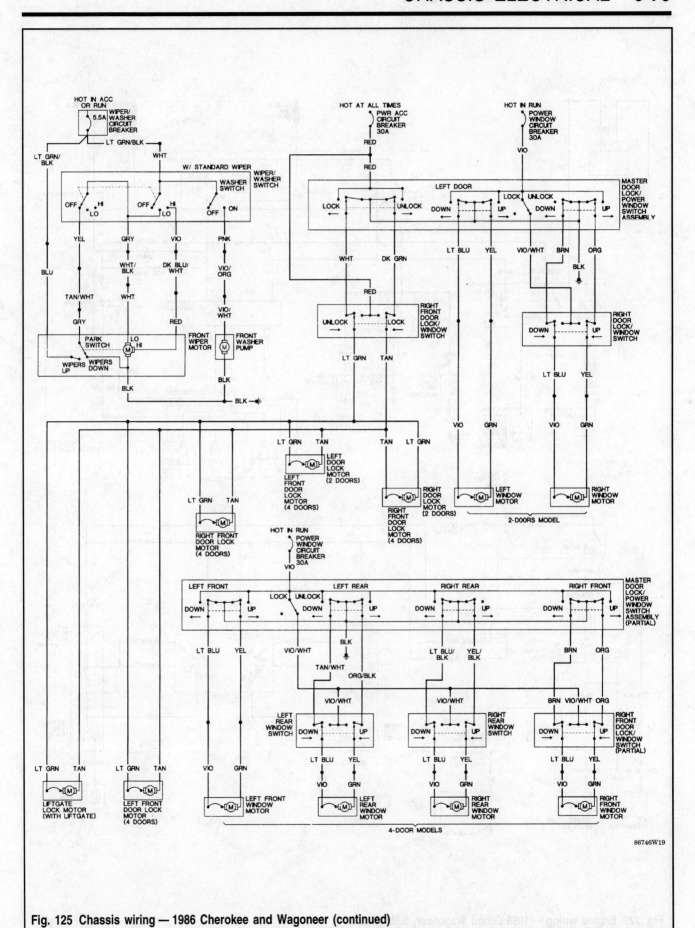

Fig. 125 Chassis wiring — 1986 Cherokee and Wagoneer (continued)

86746W19

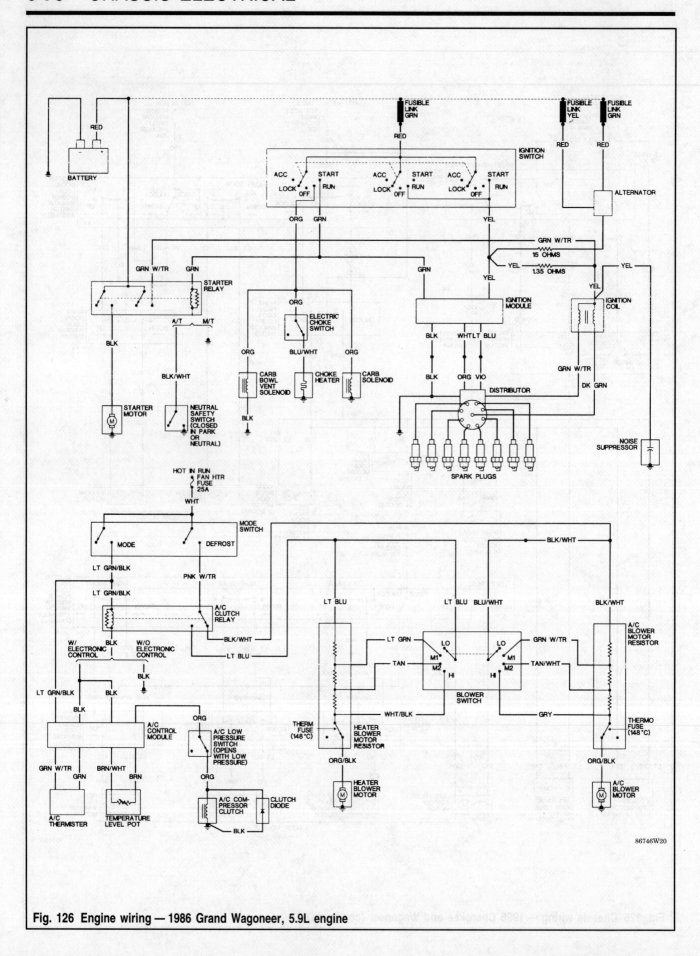

Fig. 126 Engine wiring — 1986 Grand Wagoneer, 5.9L engine

86746W20

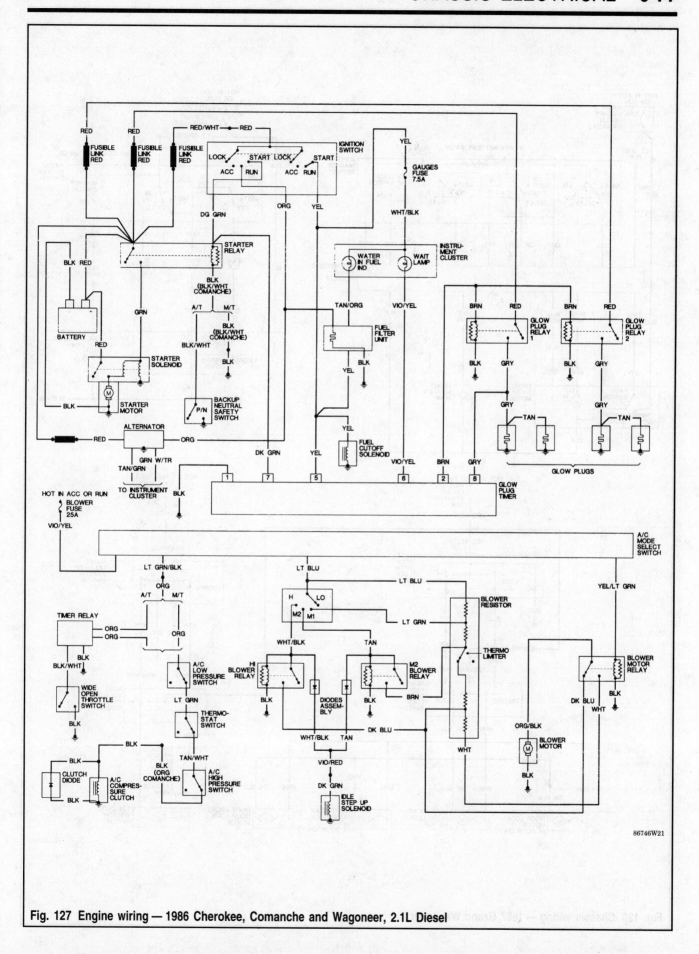

Fig. 127 Engine wiring — 1986 Cherokee, Comanche and Wagoneer, 2.1L Diesel

86746W21

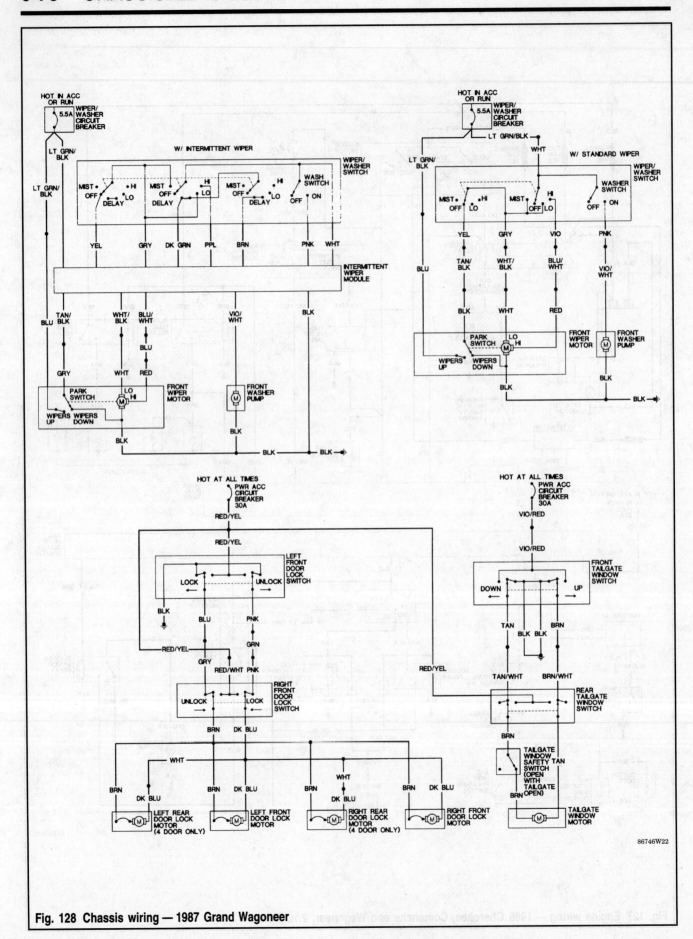

Fig. 128 Chassis wiring — 1987 Grand Wagoneer

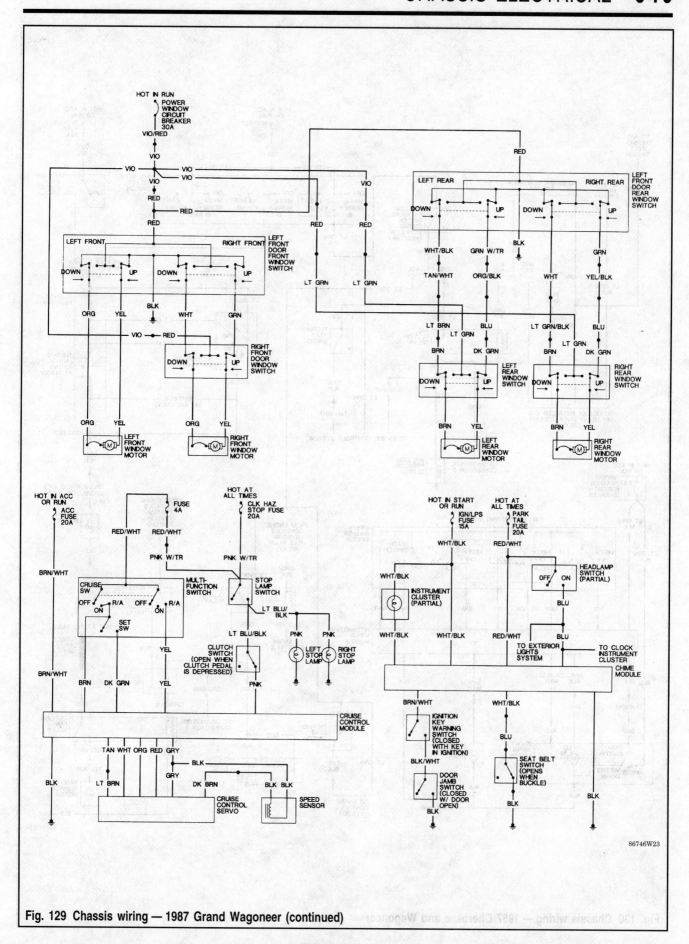

Fig. 129 Chassis wiring — 1987 Grand Wagoneer (continued)

86746W23

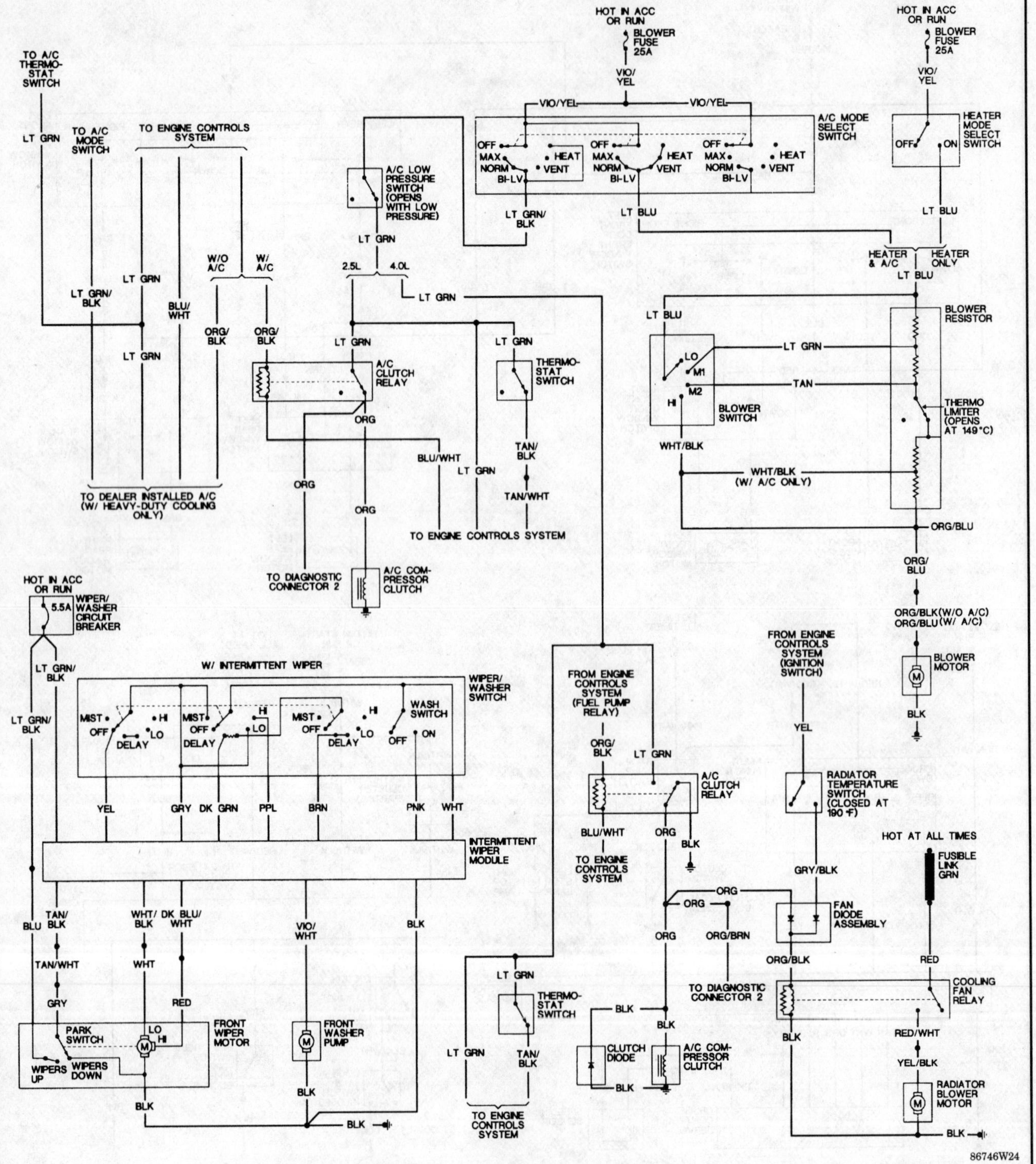

Fig. 130 Chassis wiring — 1987 Cherokee and Wagoneer

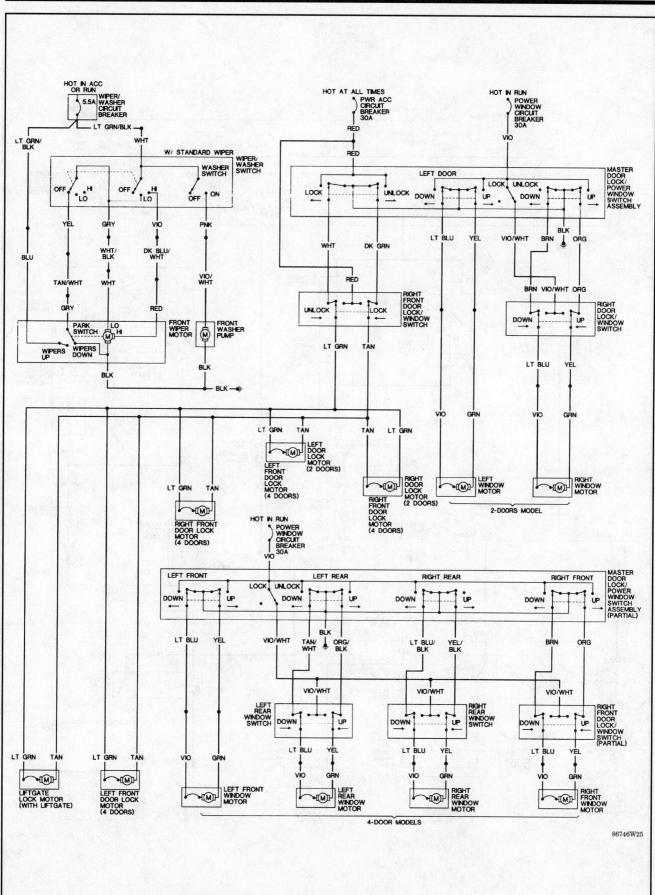

Fig. 131 Chassis wiring — 1987 Cherokee and Wagoneer (continued)

86746W25

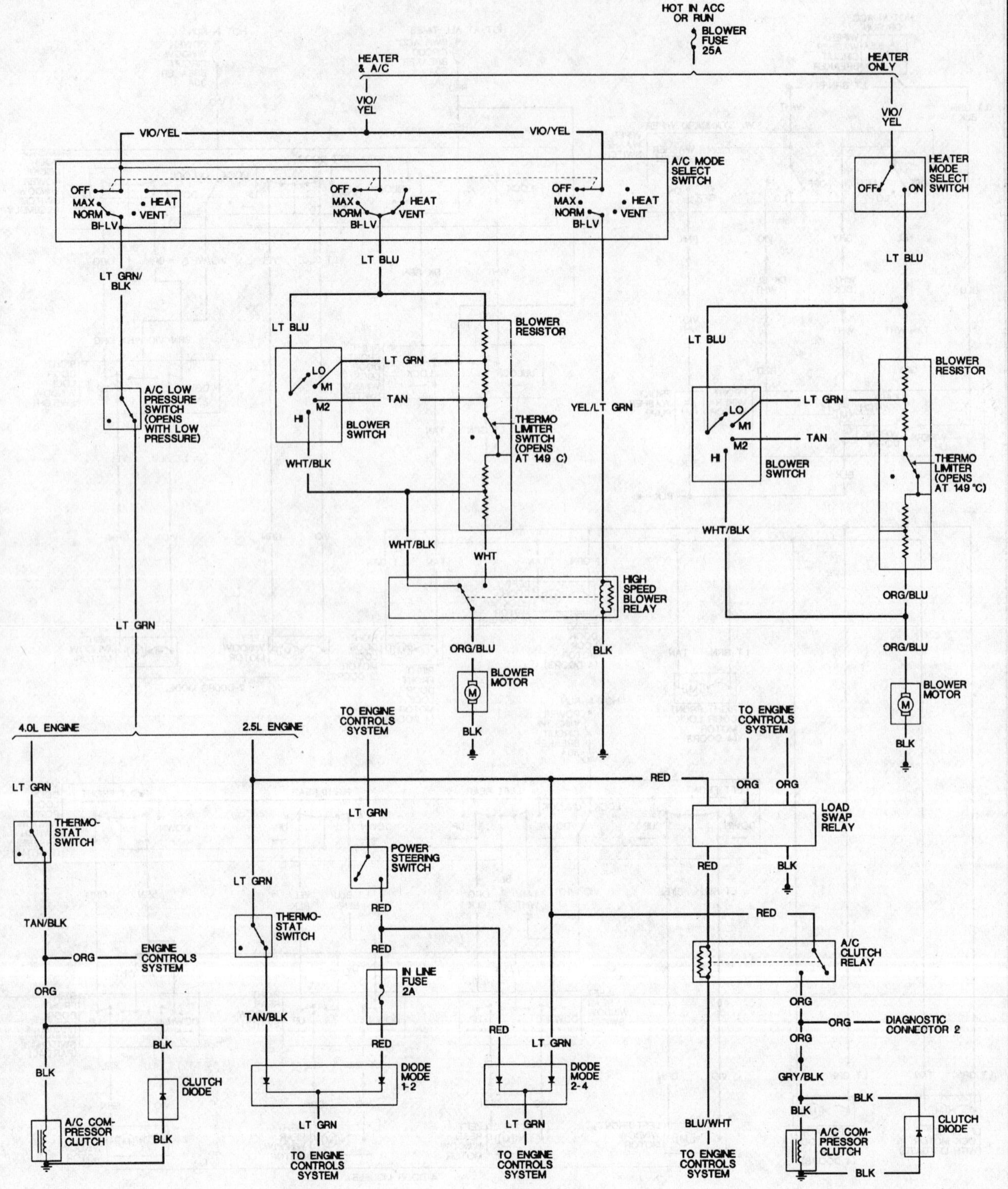

Fig. 132 Chassis wiring — 1987 Comanche

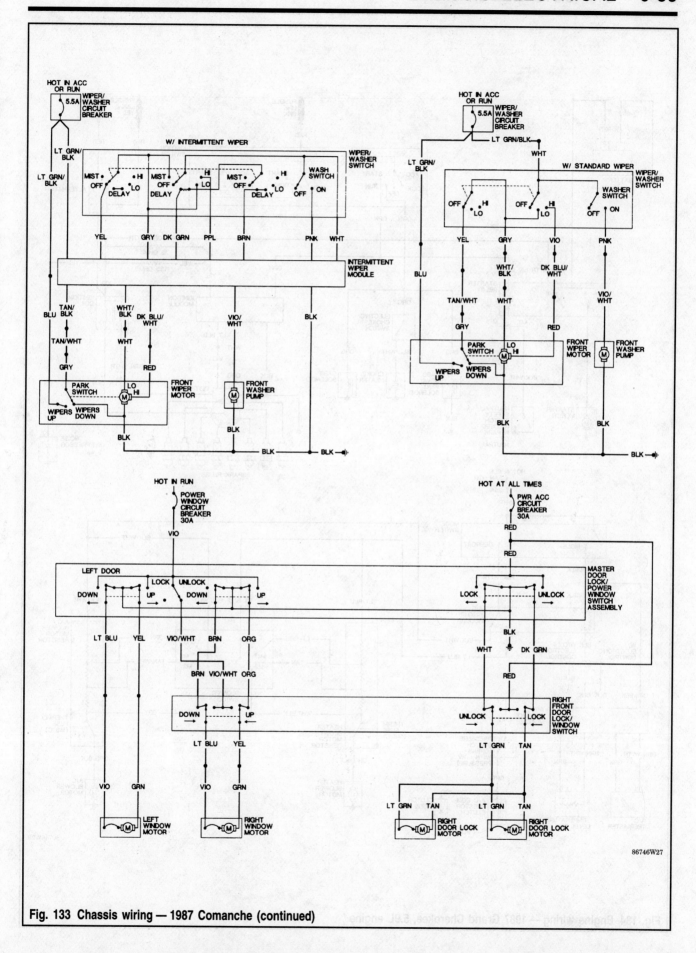

Fig. 133 Chassis wiring — 1987 Comanche (continued)

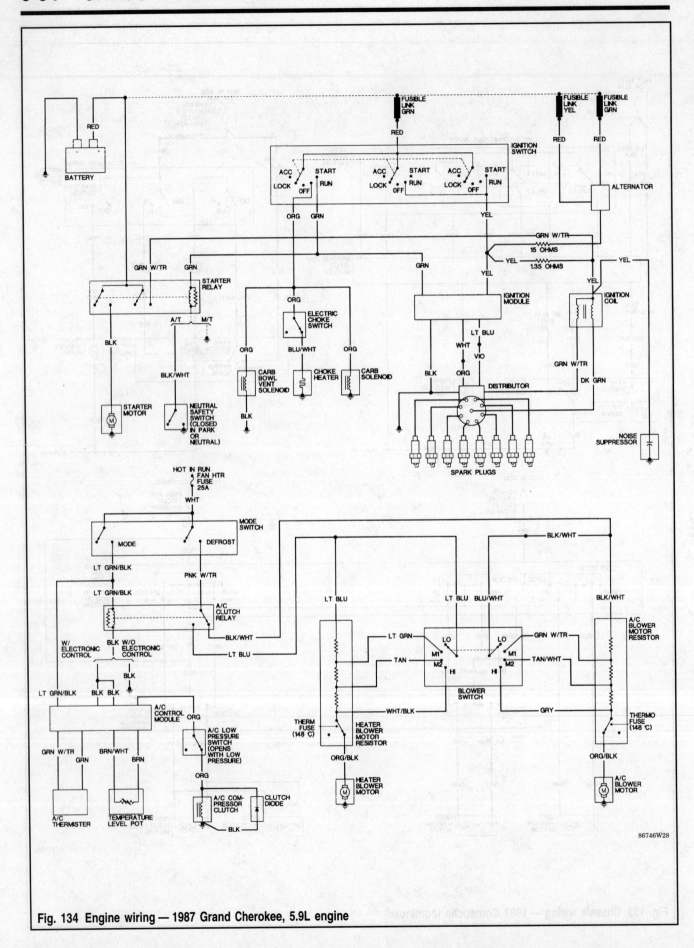

Fig. 134 Engine wiring — 1987 Grand Cherokee, 5.9L engine

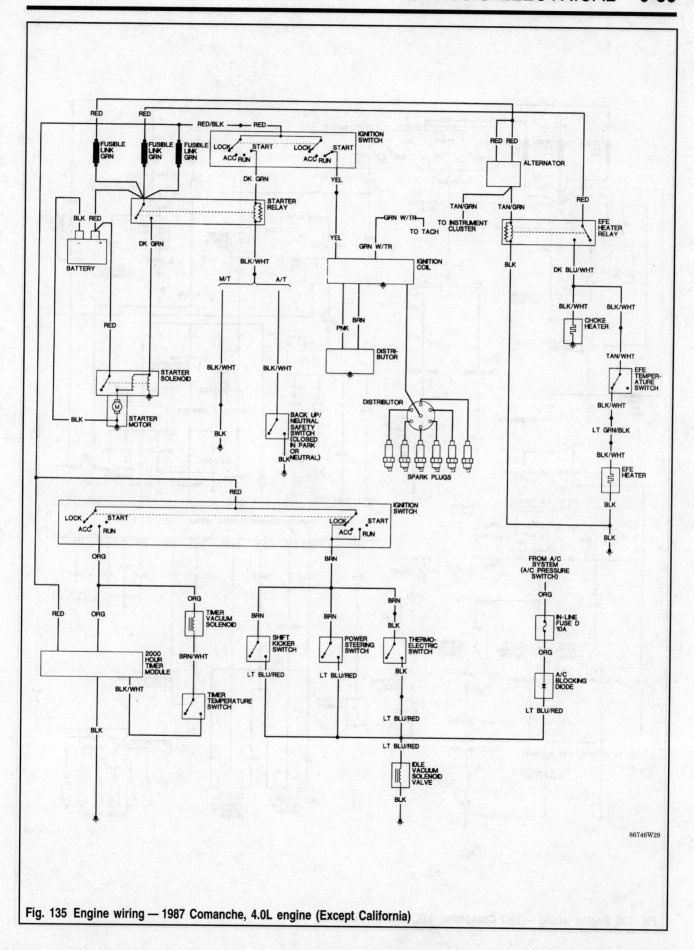

Fig. 135 Engine wiring — 1987 Comanche, 4.0L engine (Except California)

86746W29

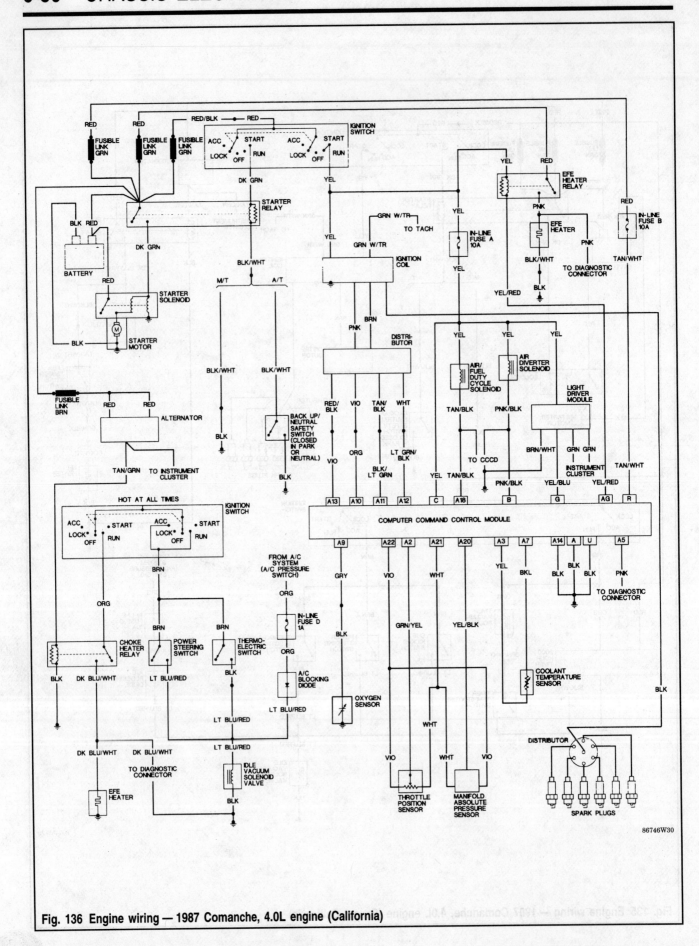

Fig. 136 Engine wiring — 1987 Comanche, 4.0L engine (California)

86746W30

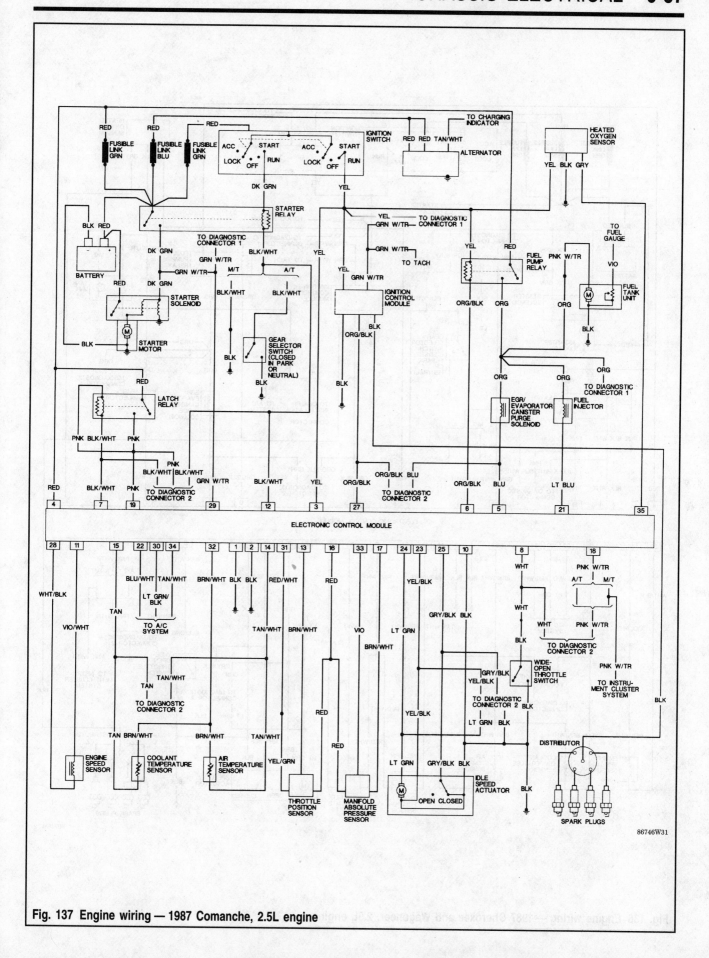

Fig. 137 Engine wiring — 1987 Comanche, 2.5L engine

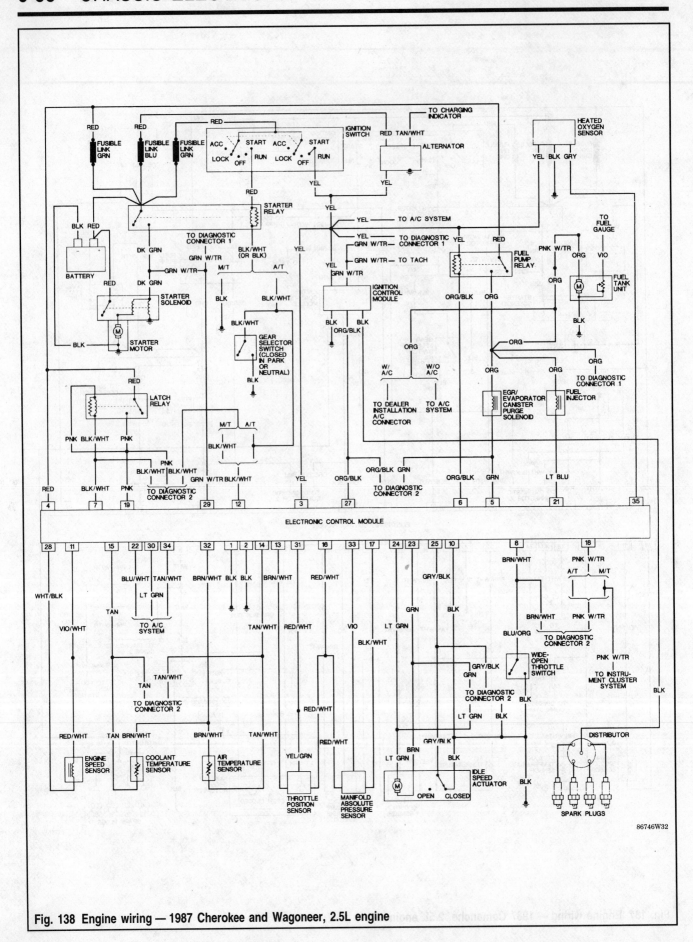

Fig. 138 Engine wiring — 1987 Cherokee and Wagoneer, 2.5L engine

86746W32

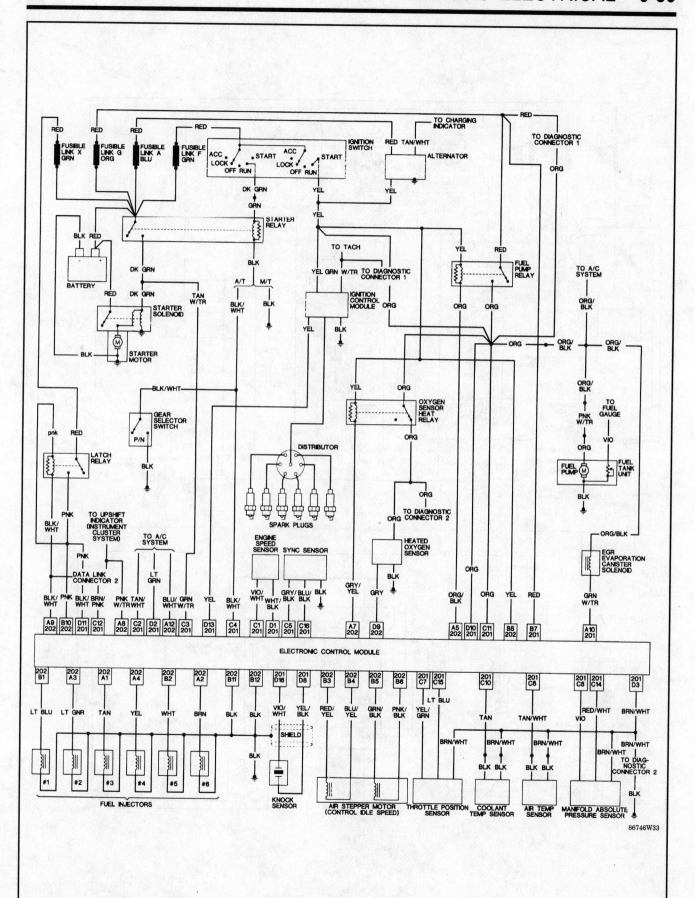

Fig. 139 Engine wiring — 1987 Cherokee and Wagoneer, 4.0L engine

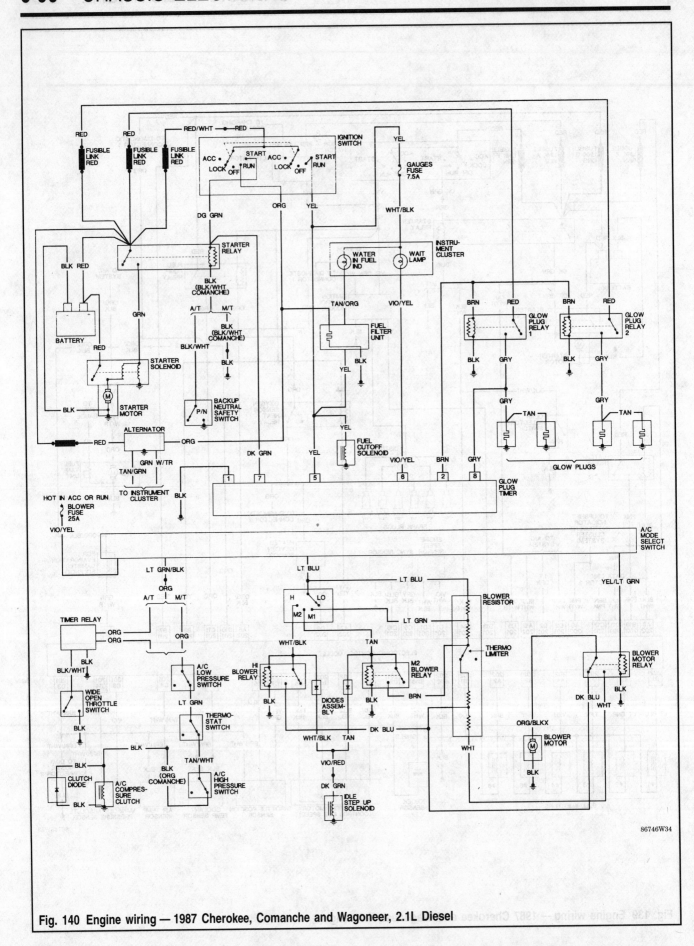

Fig. 140 Engine wiring — 1987 Cherokee, Comanche and Wagoneer, 2.1L Diesel

86746W34

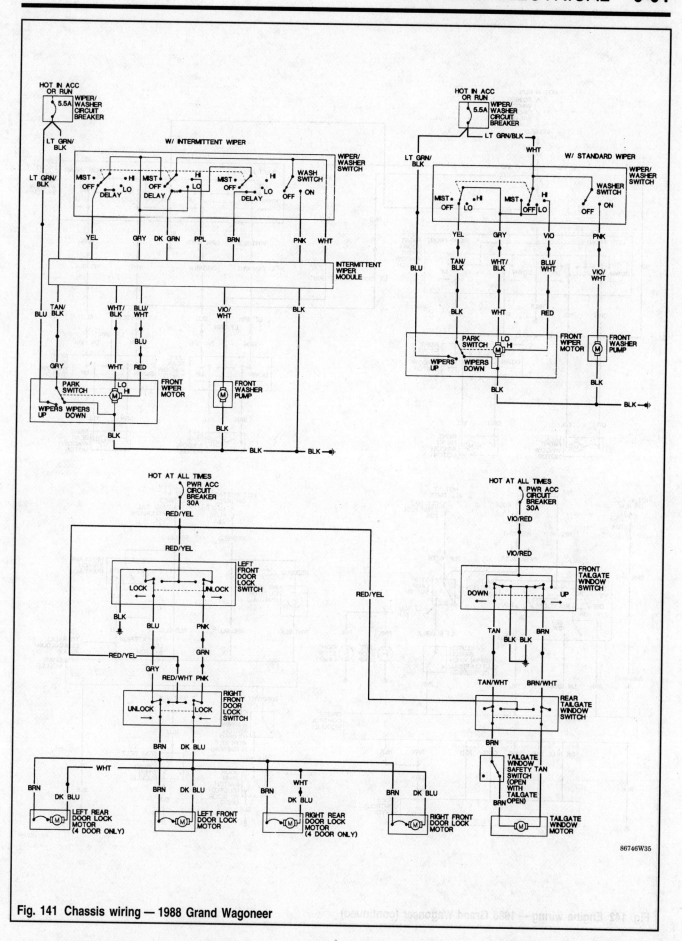

Fig. 141 Chassis wiring — 1988 Grand Wagoneer

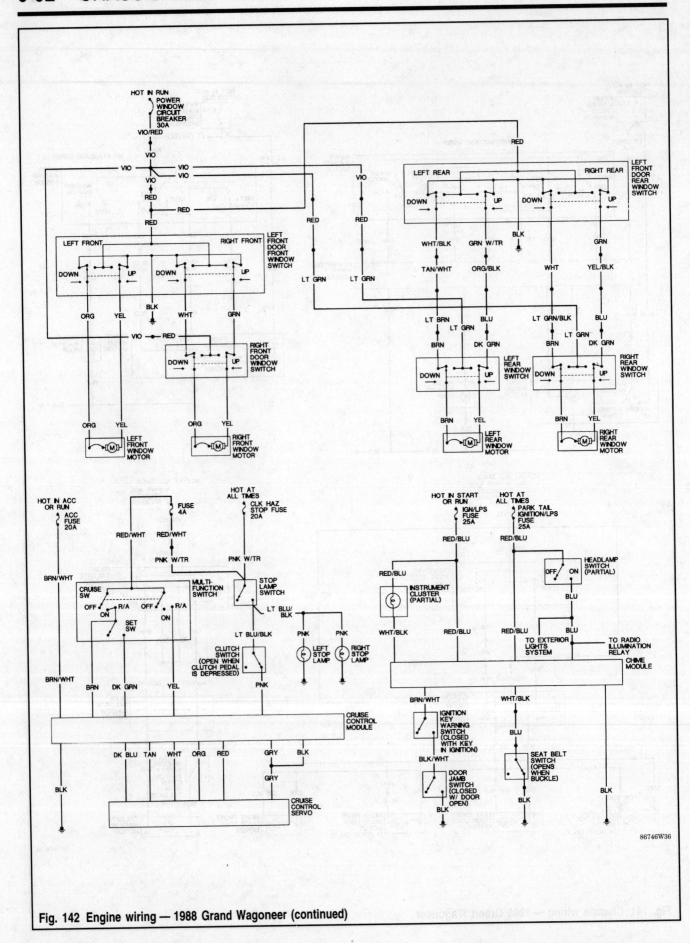

Fig. 142 Engine wiring — 1988 Grand Wagoneer (continued)

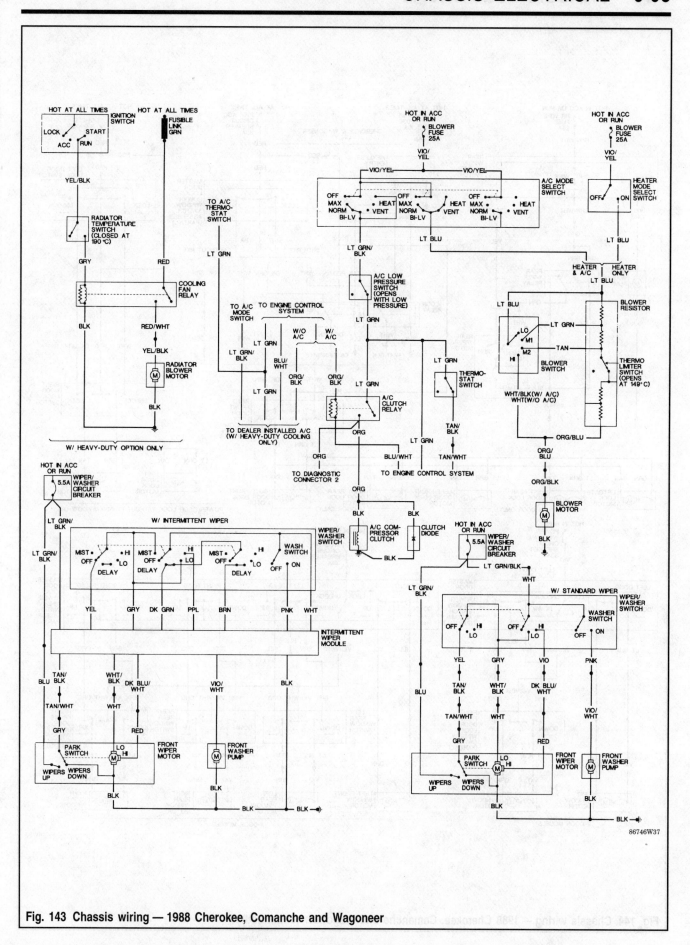

Fig. 143 Chassis wiring — 1988 Cherokee, Comanche and Wagoneer

86746W37

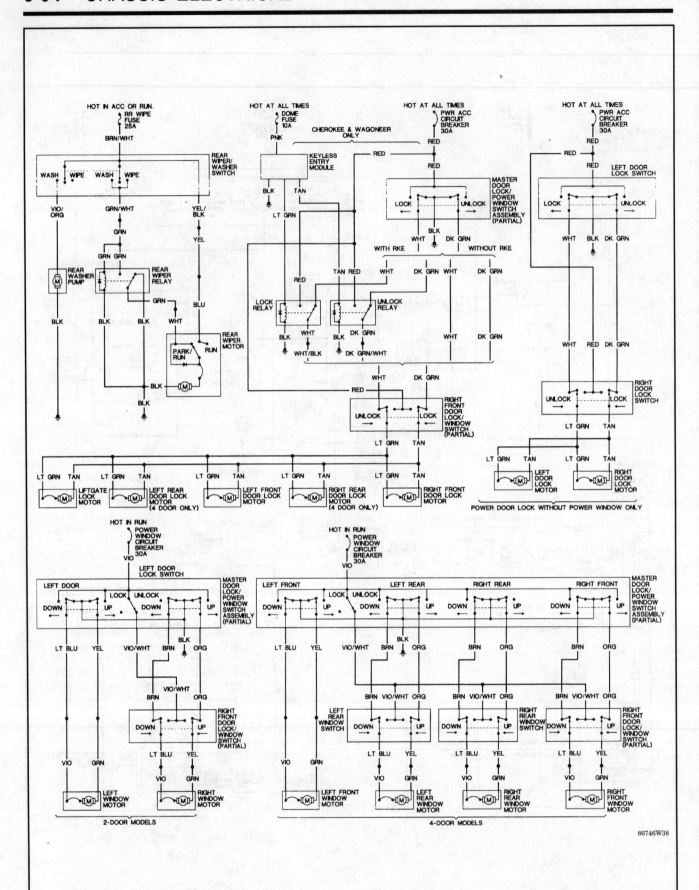

Fig. 144 Chassis wiring — 1988 Cherokee, Comanche and Wagoneer (continued)

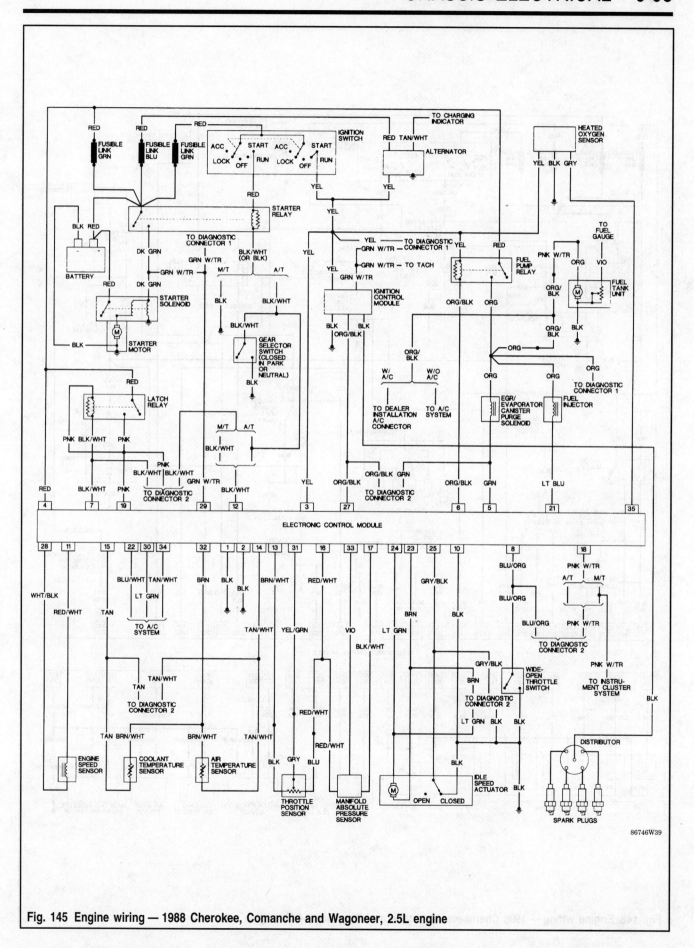

Fig. 145 Engine wiring — 1988 Cherokee, Comanche and Wagoneer, 2.5L engine

86746W39

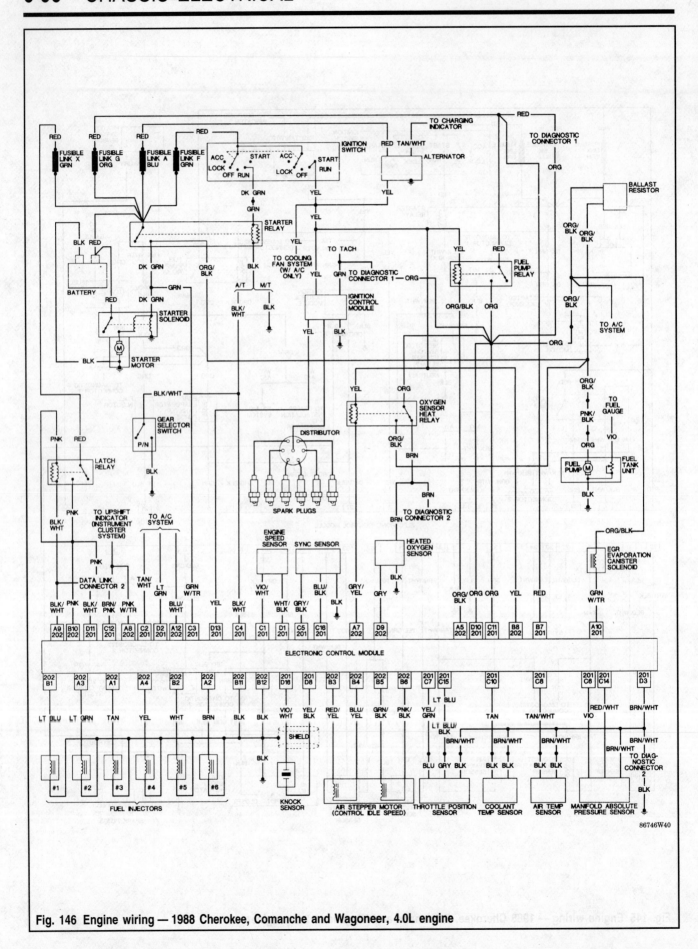

Fig. 146 Engine wiring — 1988 Cherokee, Comanche and Wagoneer, 4.0L engine

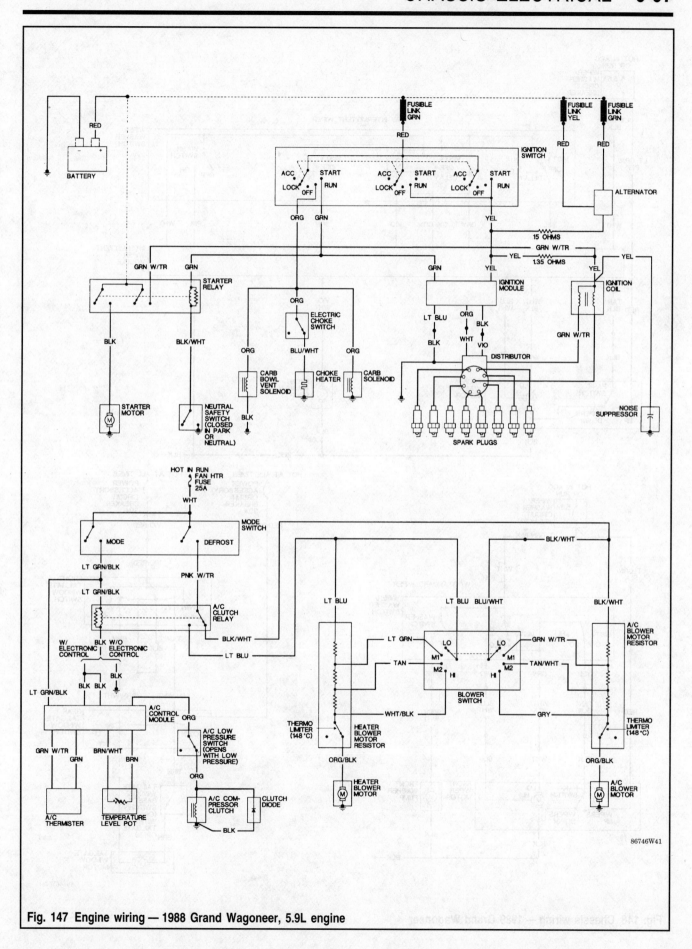

Fig. 147 Engine wiring — 1988 Grand Wagoneer, 5.9L engine

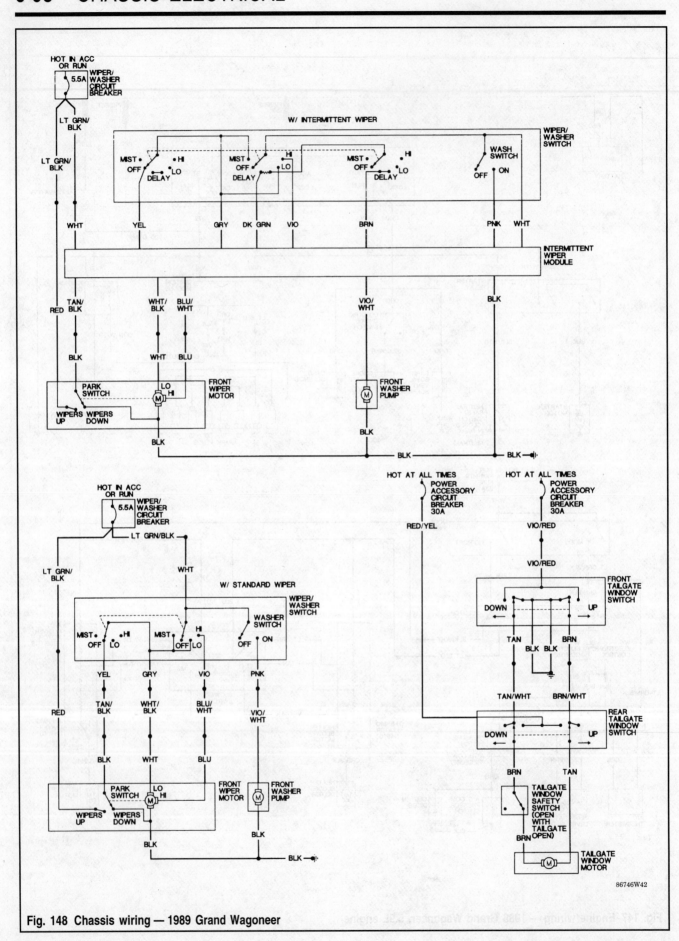

Fig. 148 Chassis wiring — 1989 Grand Wagoneer

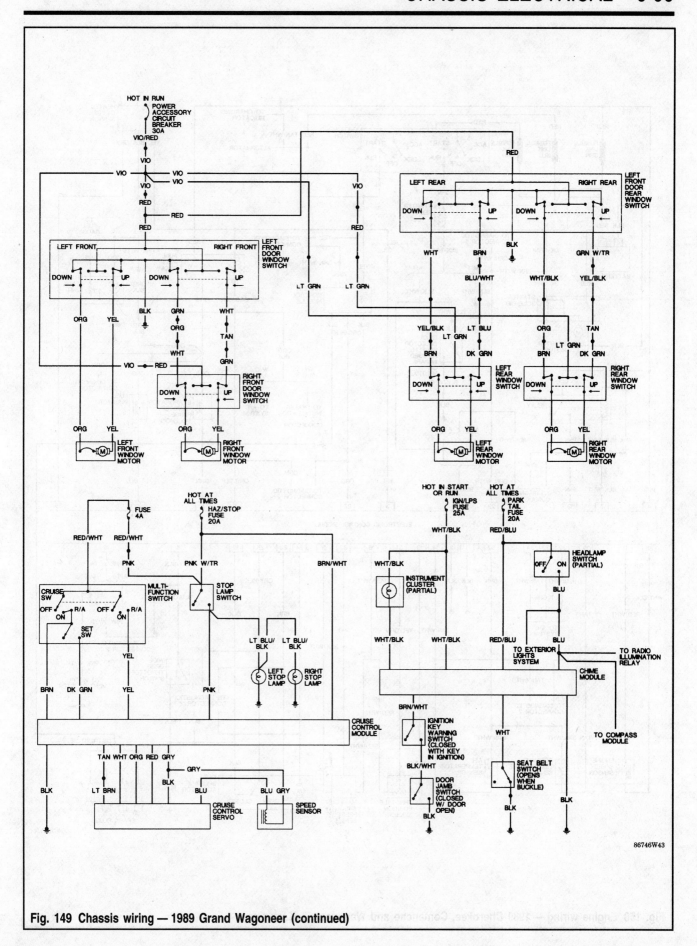

Fig. 149 Chassis wiring — 1989 Grand Wagoneer (continued)

86746W43

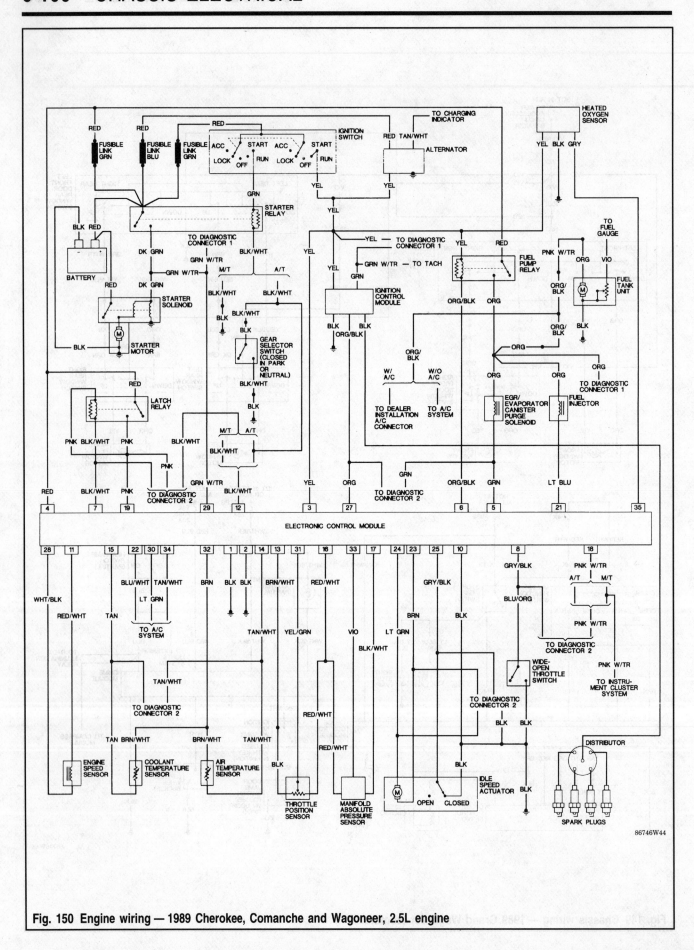

Fig. 150 Engine wiring — 1989 Cherokee, Comanche and Wagoneer, 2.5L engine

86746W44

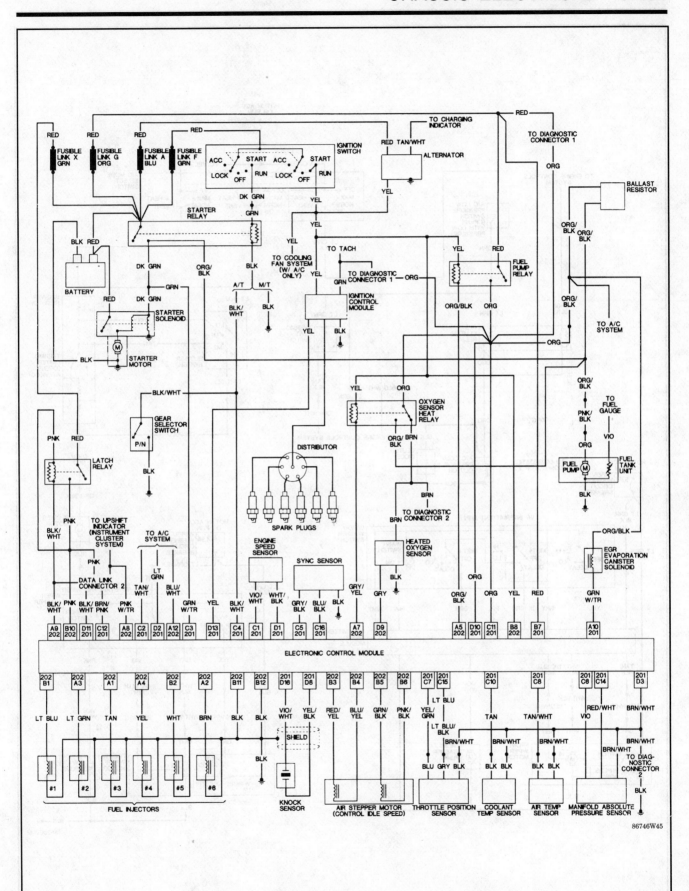

Fig. 151 Engine wiring — 1989 Cherokee, Comanche and Wagoneer, 4.0L engine

86746W45

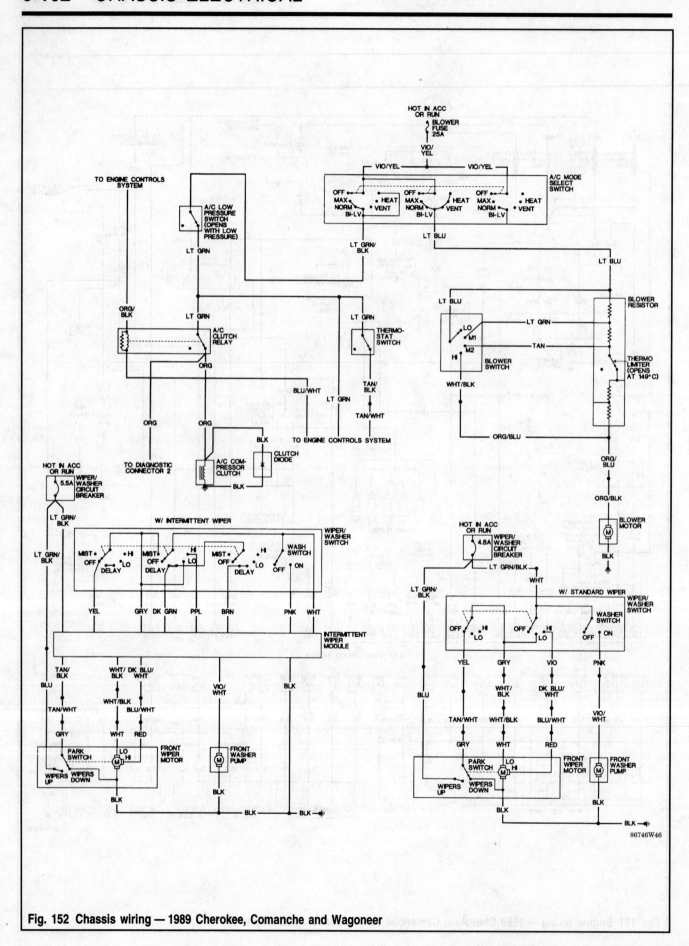

Fig. 152 Chassis wiring — 1989 Cherokee, Comanche and Wagoneer

86746W46

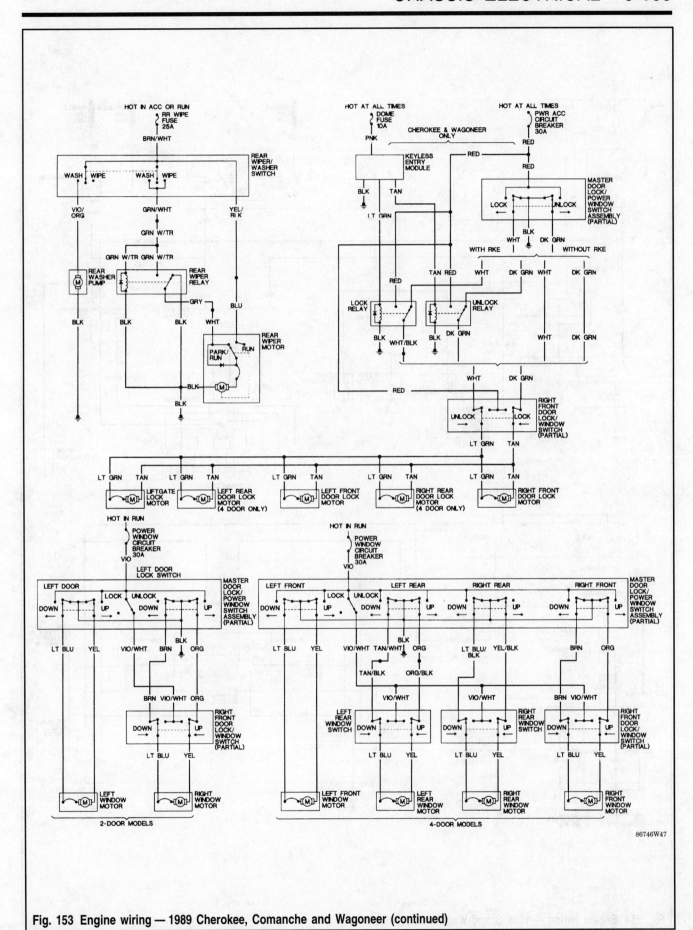

Fig. 153 Engine wiring — 1989 Cherokee, Comanche and Wagoneer (continued)

86746W47

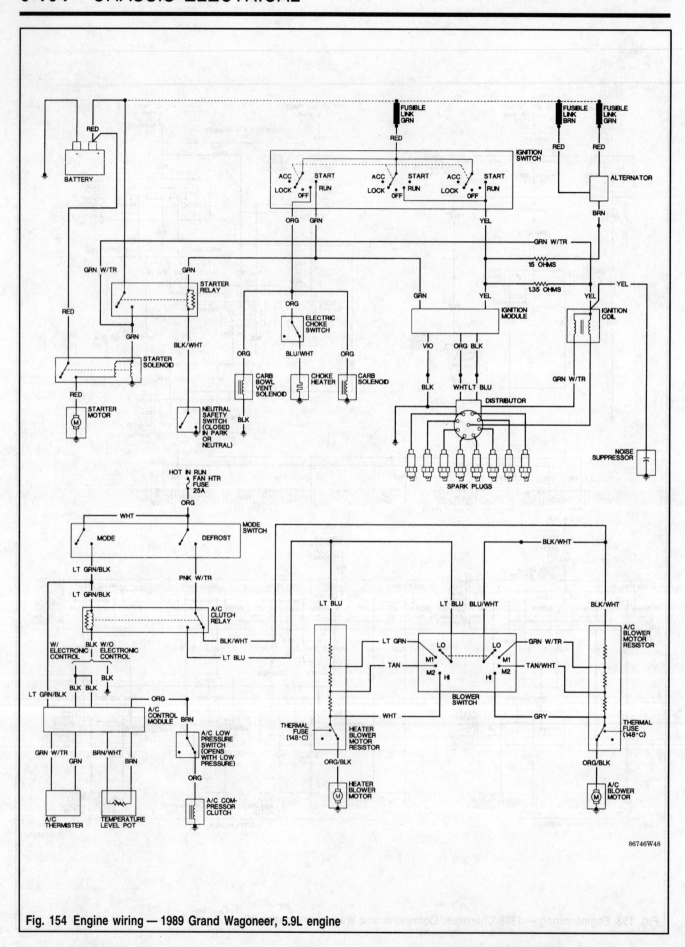

Fig. 154 Engine wiring — 1989 Grand Wagoneer, 5.9L engine

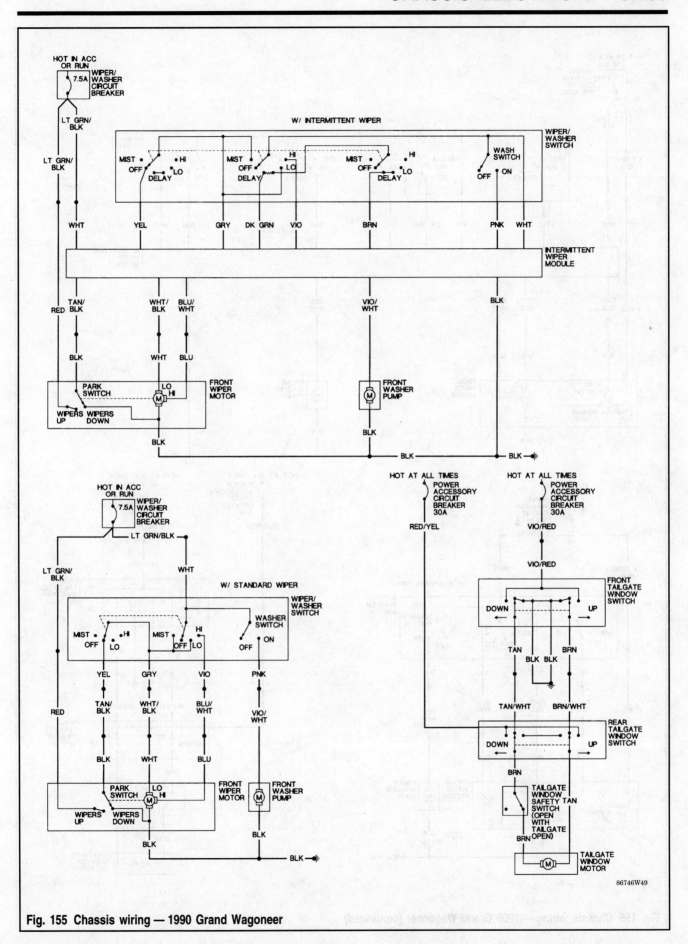

Fig. 155 Chassis wiring — 1990 Grand Wagoneer

86746W49

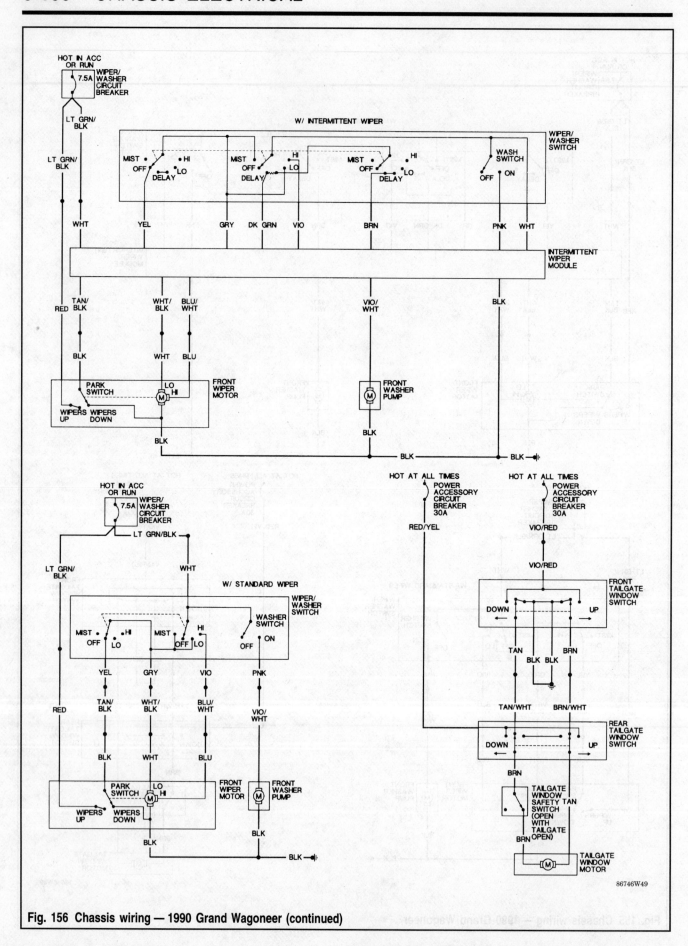

Fig. 156 Chassis wiring — 1990 Grand Wagoneer (continued)

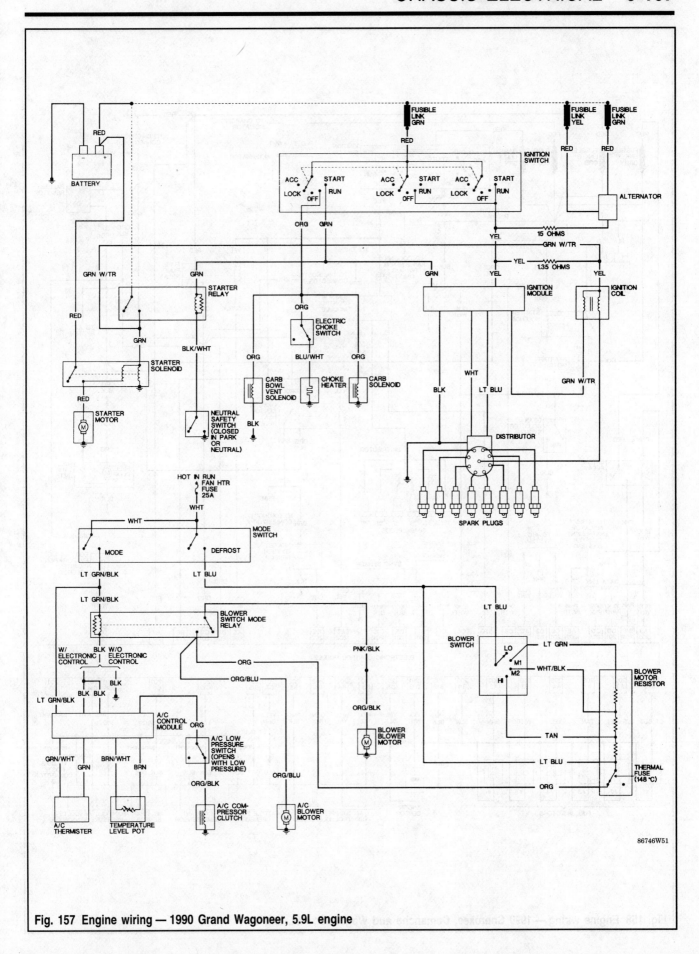

Fig. 157 Engine wiring — 1990 Grand Wagoneer, 5.9L engine

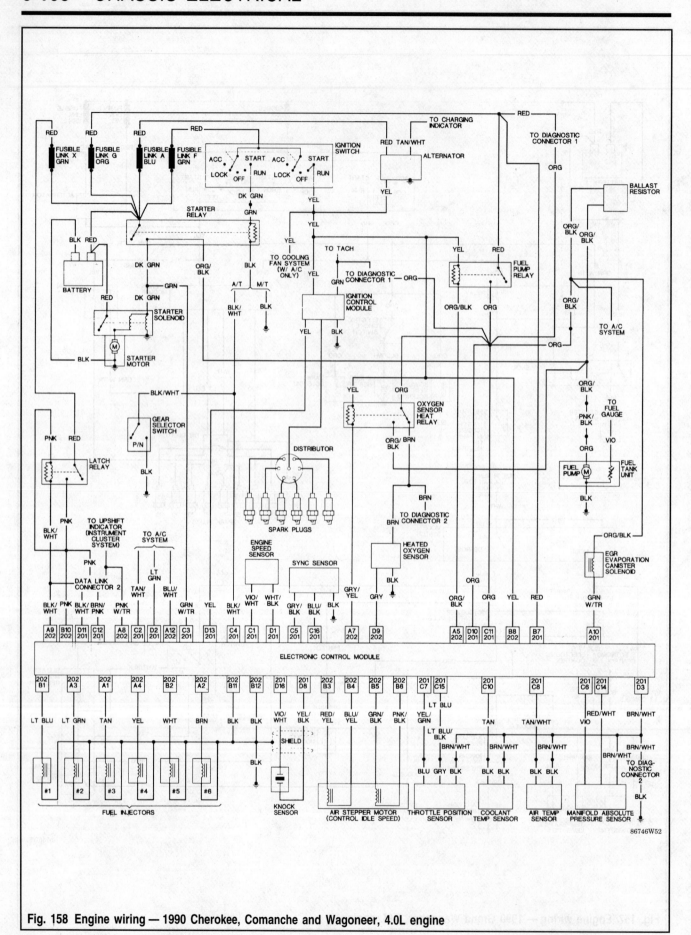

Fig. 158 Engine wiring — 1990 Cherokee, Comanche and Wagoneer, 4.0L engine

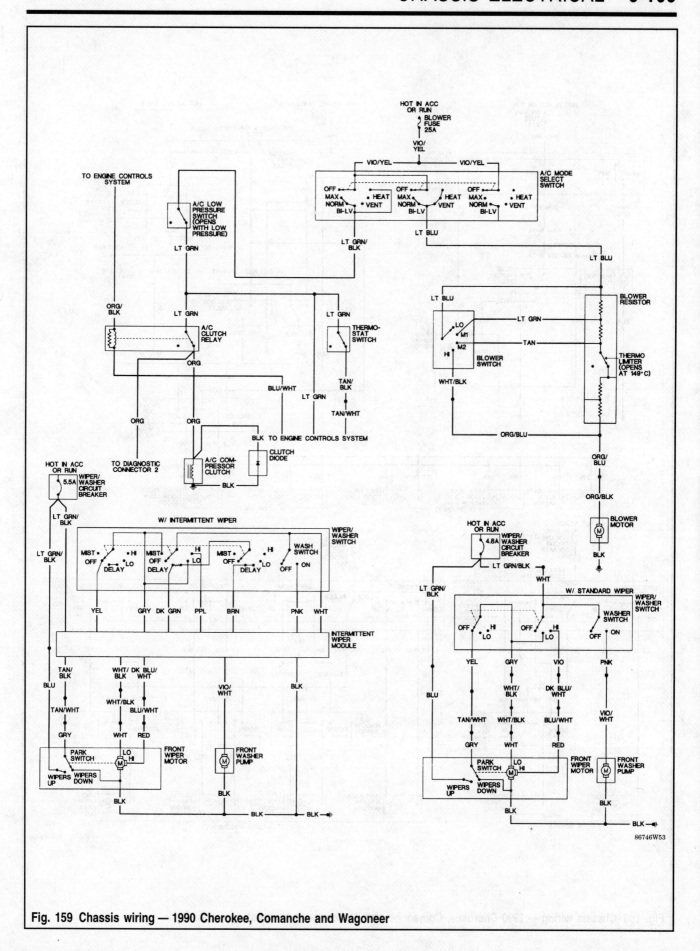

Fig. 159 Chassis wiring — 1990 Cherokee, Comanche and Wagoneer

86746W53

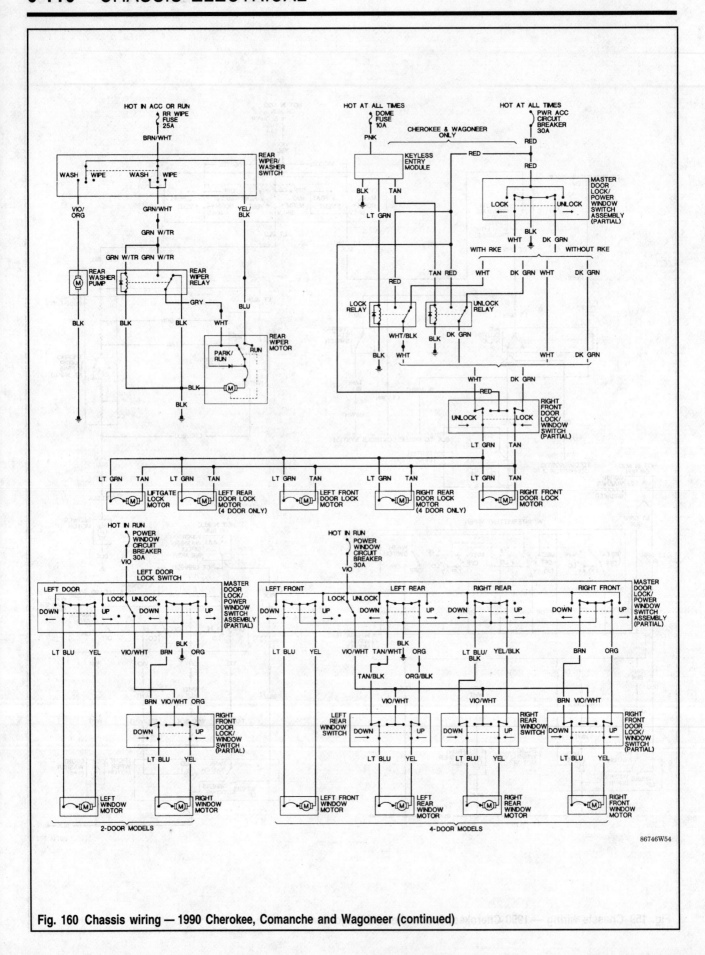

Fig. 160 Chassis wiring — 1990 Cherokee, Comanche and Wagoneer (continued)

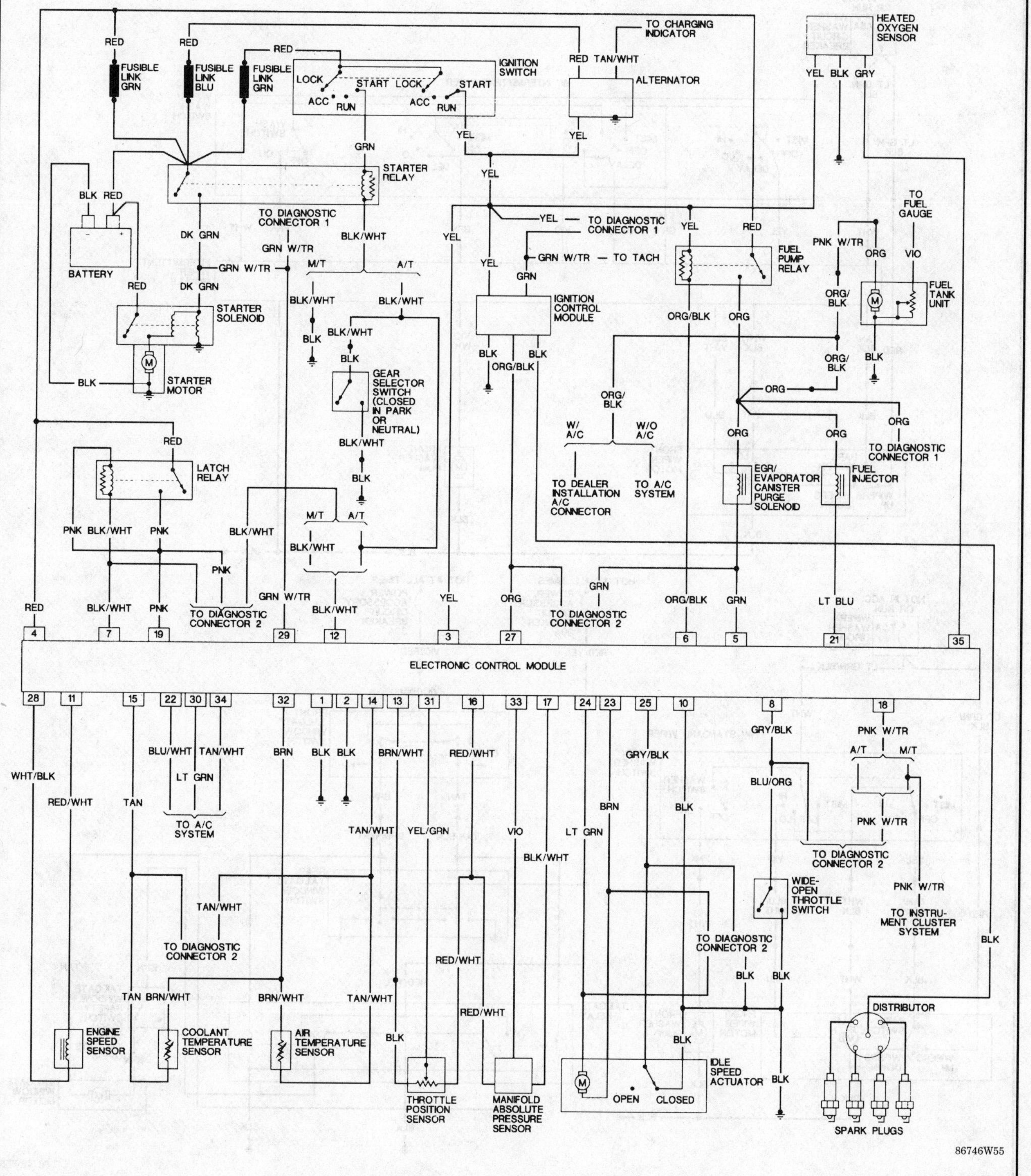

Fig. 161 Engine wiring — 1990 Cherokee, Comanche and Wagoneer, 2.5L engine

86746W55

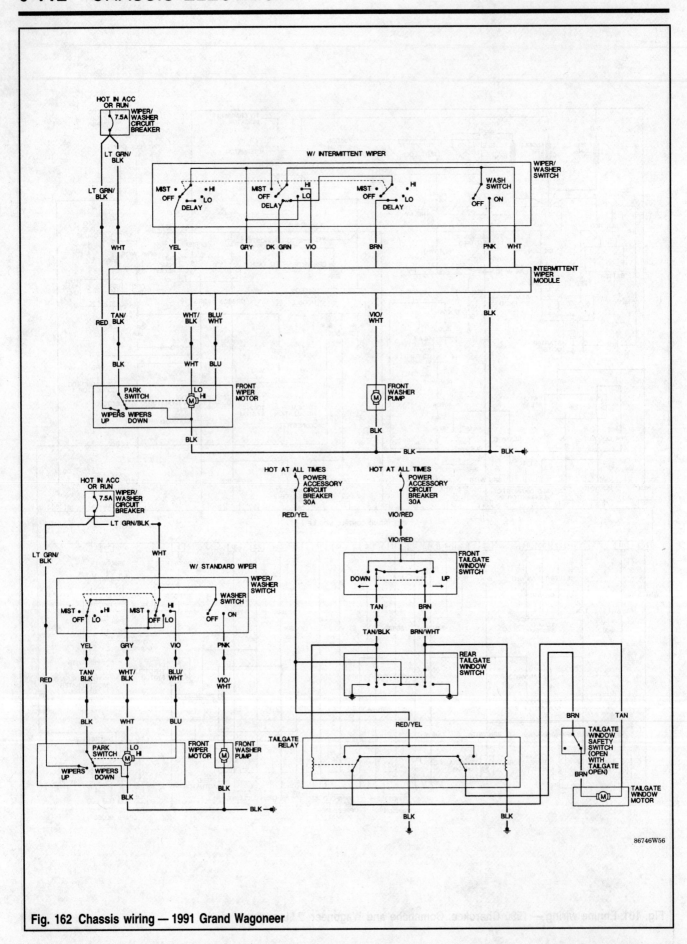

Fig. 162 Chassis wiring — 1991 Grand Wagoneer

86746W56

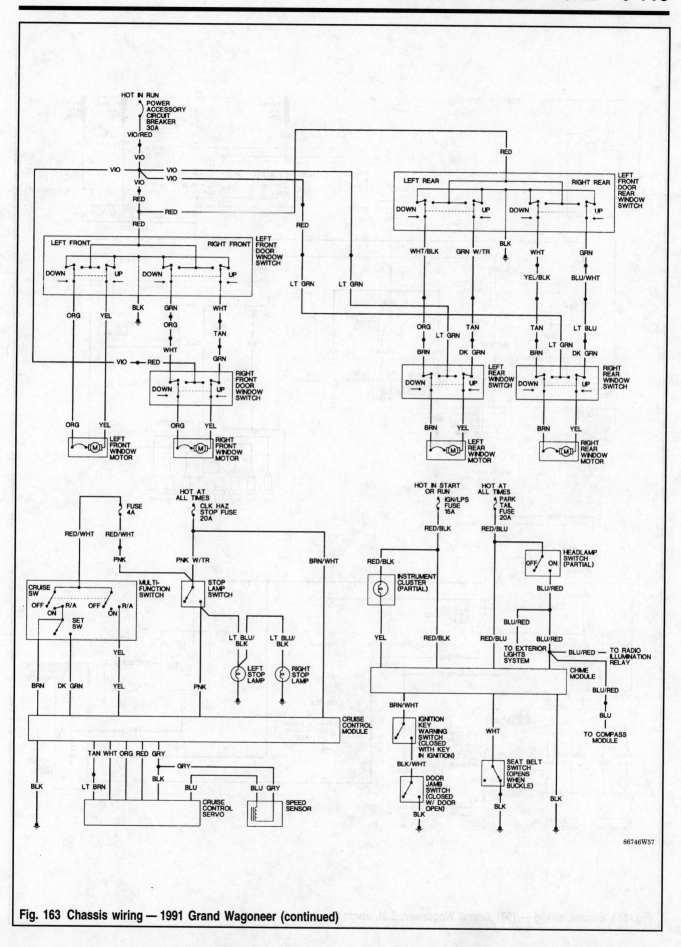

Fig. 163 Chassis wiring — 1991 Grand Wagoneer (continued)

86746W57

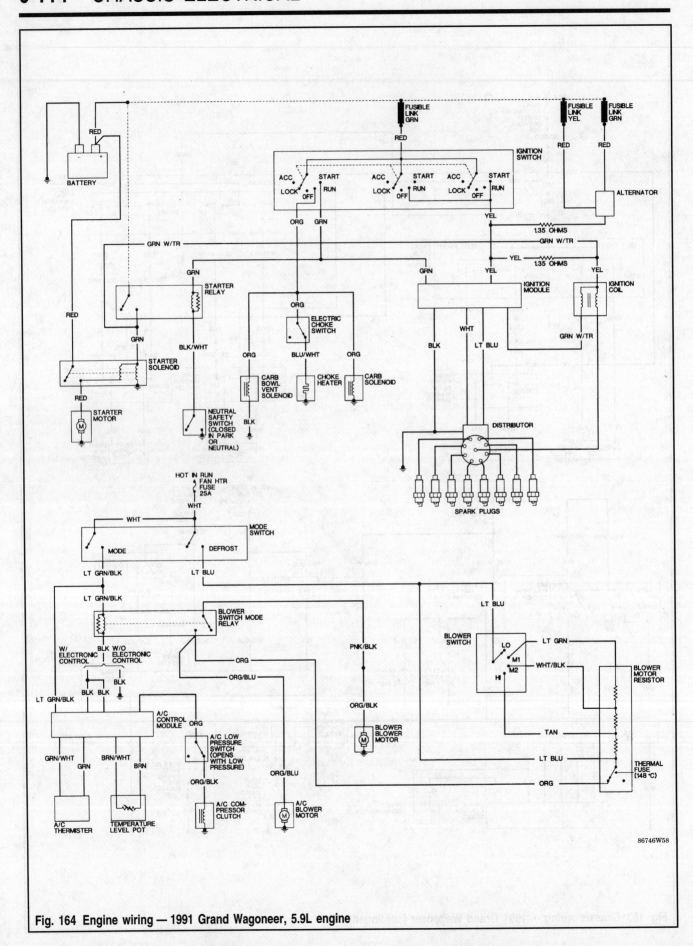

Fig. 164 Engine wiring — 1991 Grand Wagoneer, 5.9L engine

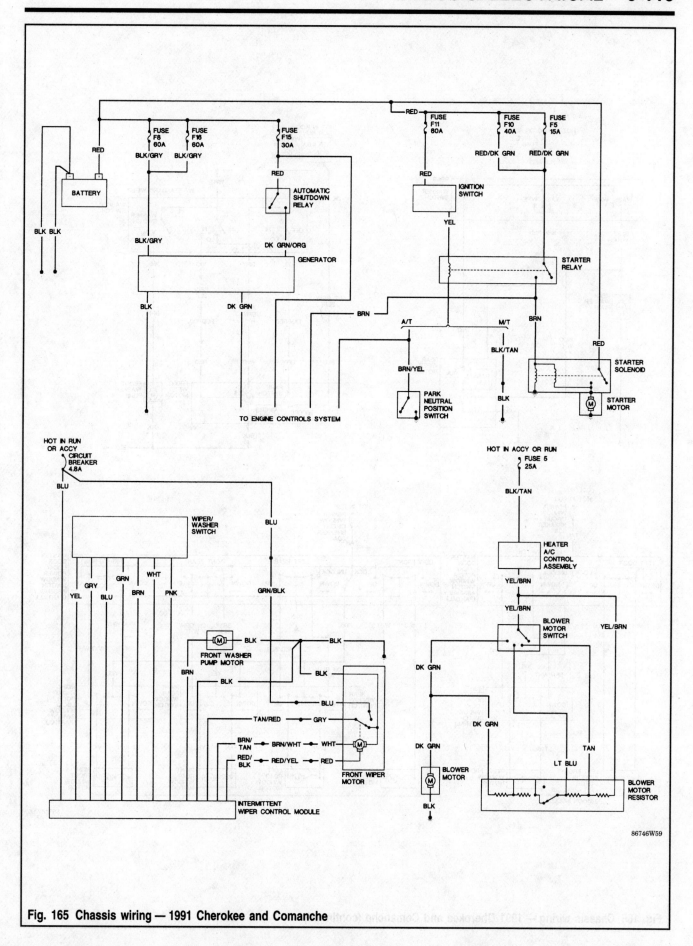

Fig. 165 Chassis wiring — 1991 Cherokee and Comanche

86746W59

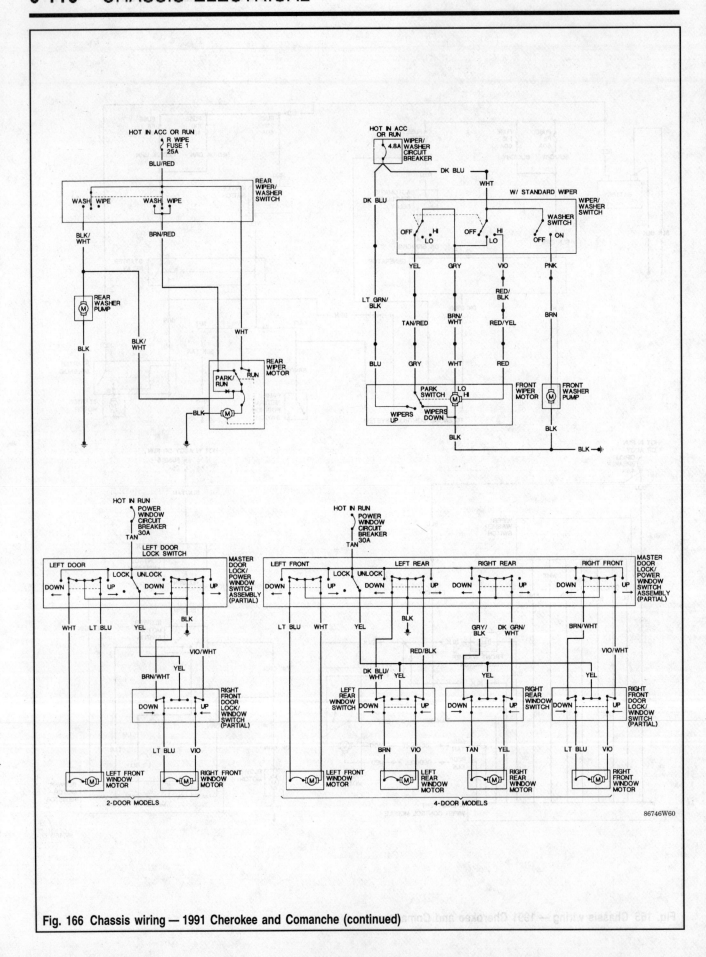

Fig. 166 Chassis wiring — 1991 Cherokee and Comanche (continued)

86746W60

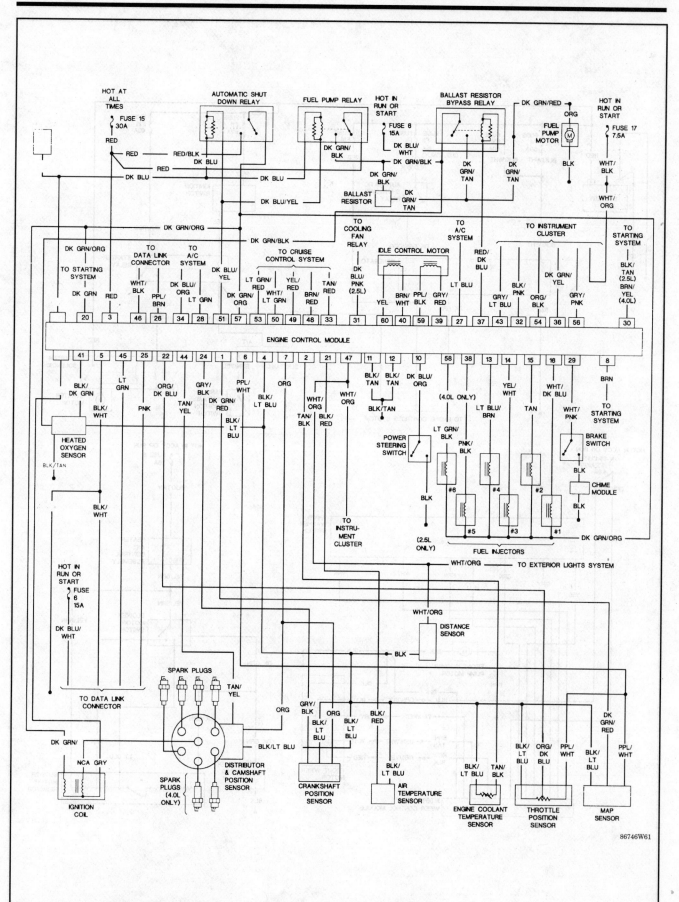

Fig. 167 Engine wiring — 1991 Cherokee and Comanche, 2.5L and 4.0L engines

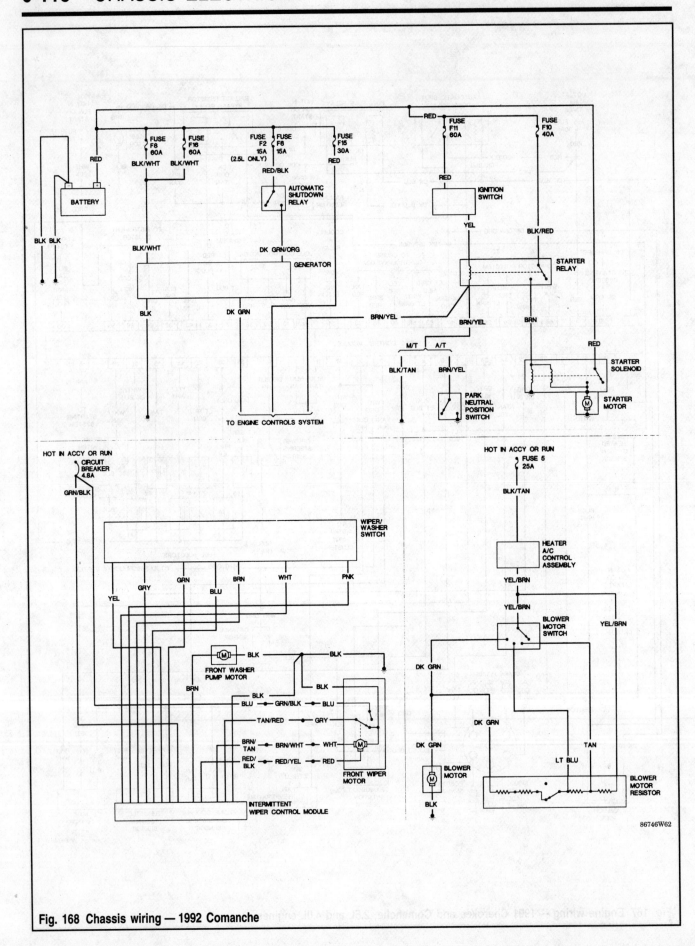

Fig. 168 Chassis wiring — 1992 Comanche

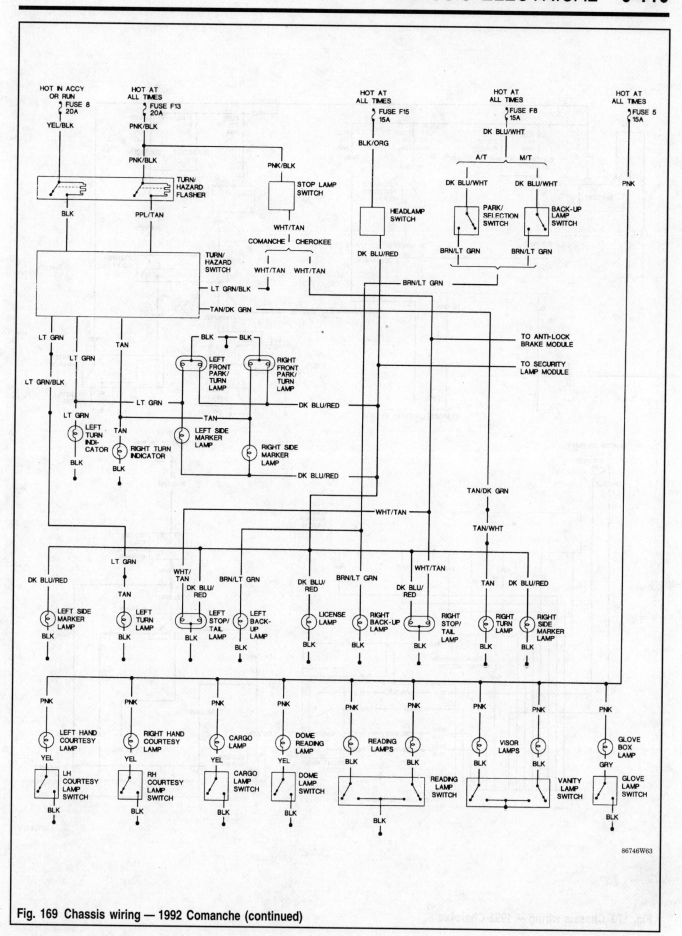

Fig. 169 Chassis wiring — 1992 Comanche (continued)

86746W63

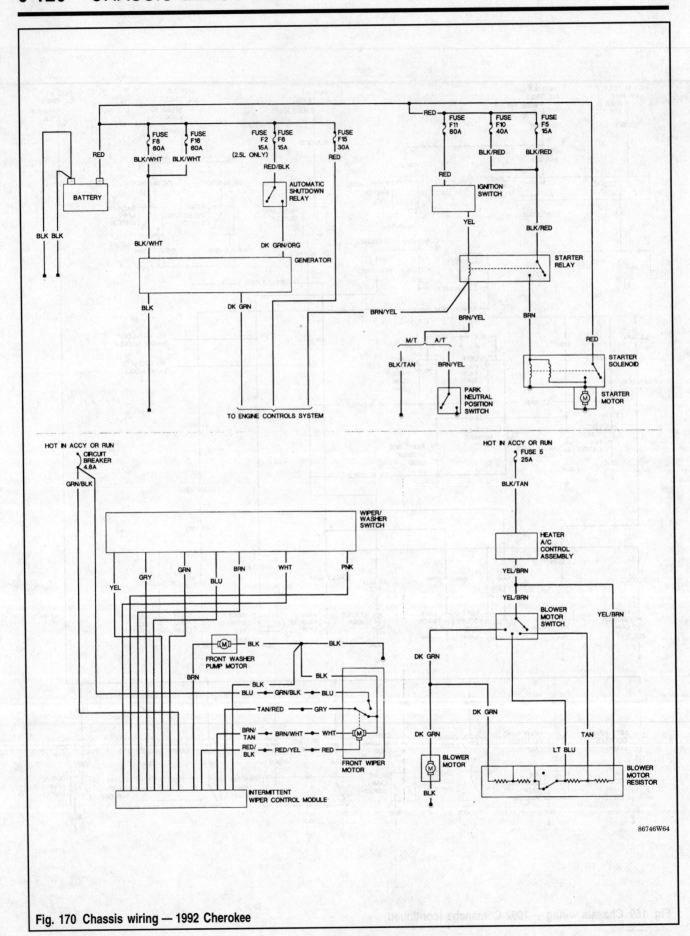

Fig. 170 Chassis wiring — 1992 Cherokee

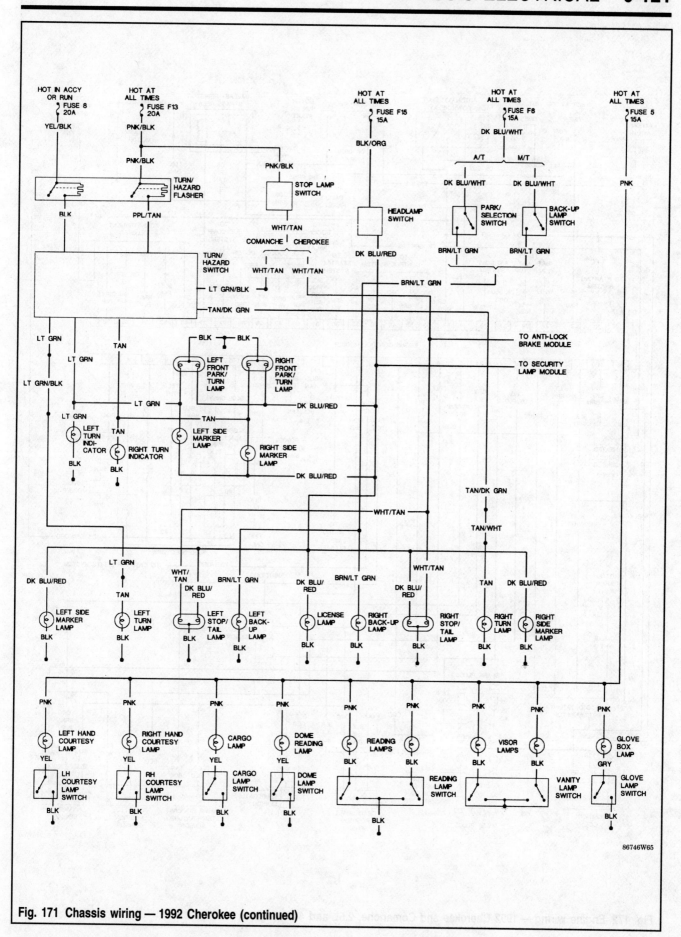

Fig. 171 Chassis wiring — 1992 Cherokee (continued)

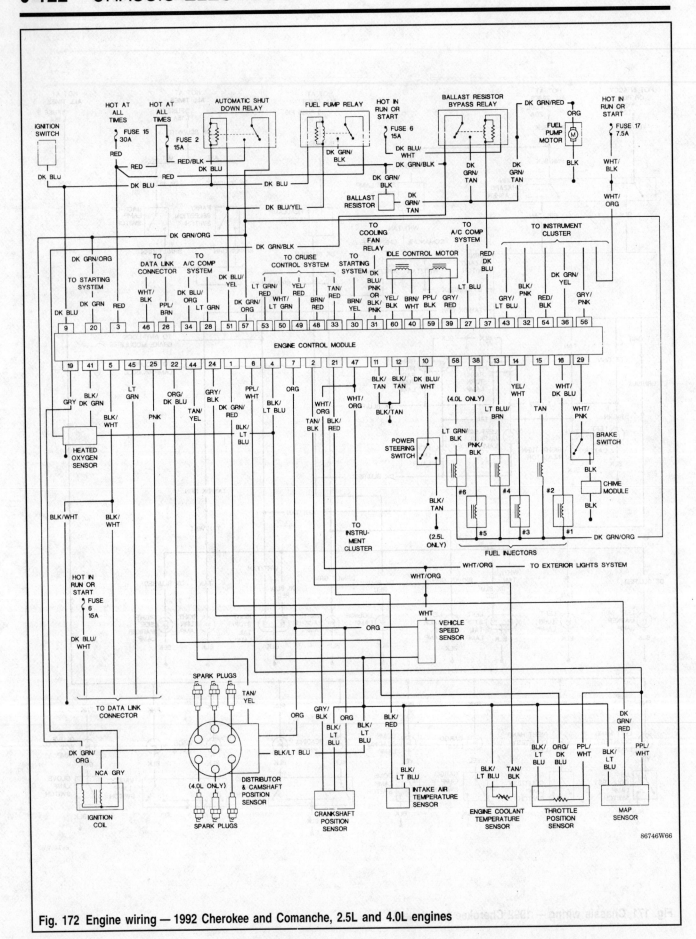

Fig. 172 Engine wiring — 1992 Cherokee and Comanche, 2.5L and 4.0L engines

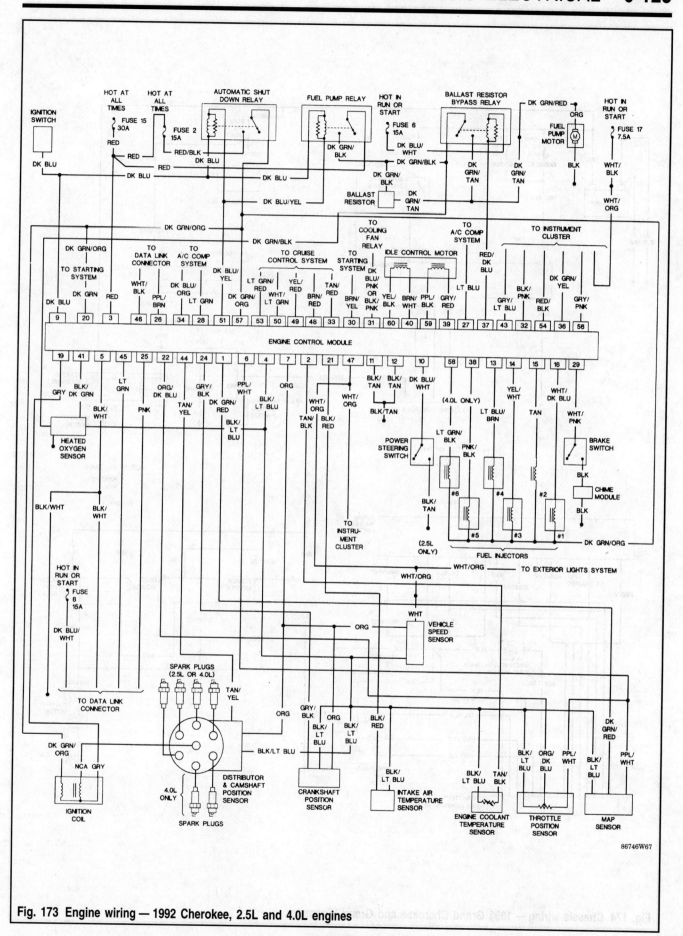

Fig. 173 Engine wiring — 1992 Cherokee, 2.5L and 4.0L engines

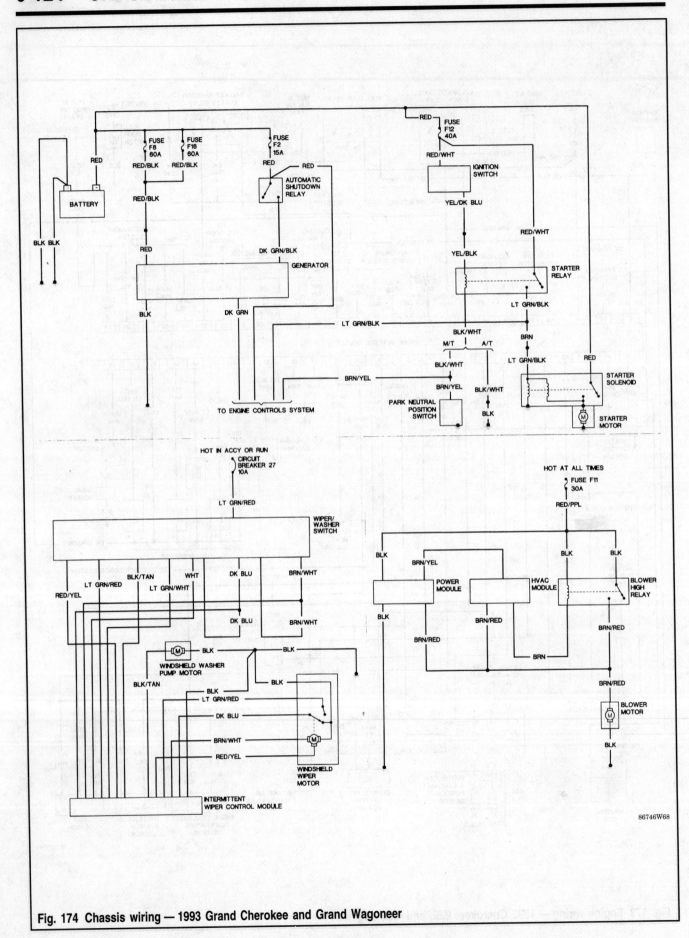

Fig. 174 Chassis wiring — 1993 Grand Cherokee and Grand Wagoneer

86746W68

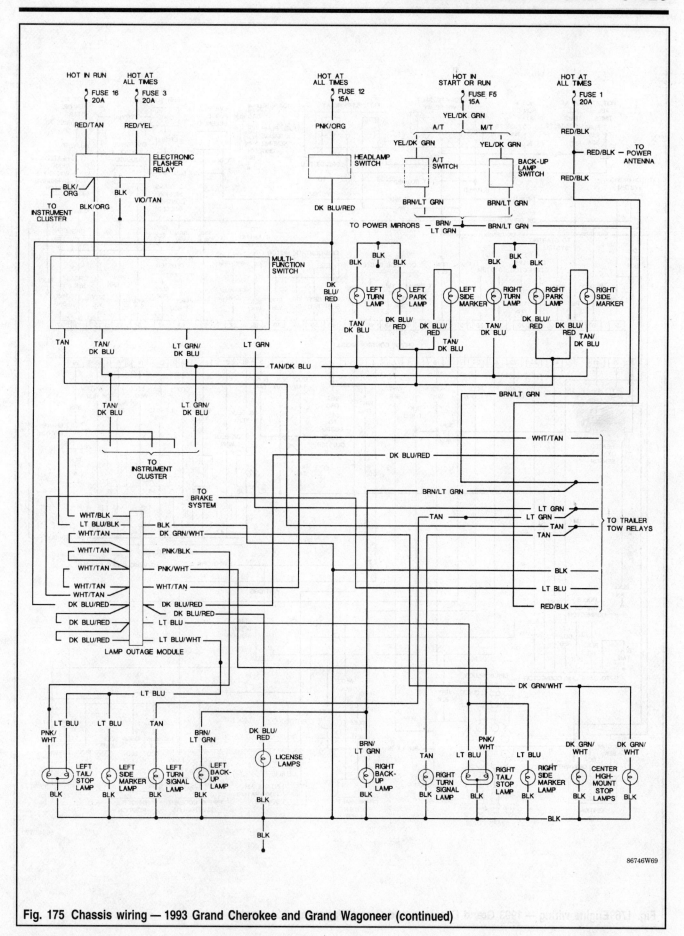

Fig. 175 Chassis wiring — 1993 Grand Cherokee and Grand Wagoneer (continued)

86746W69

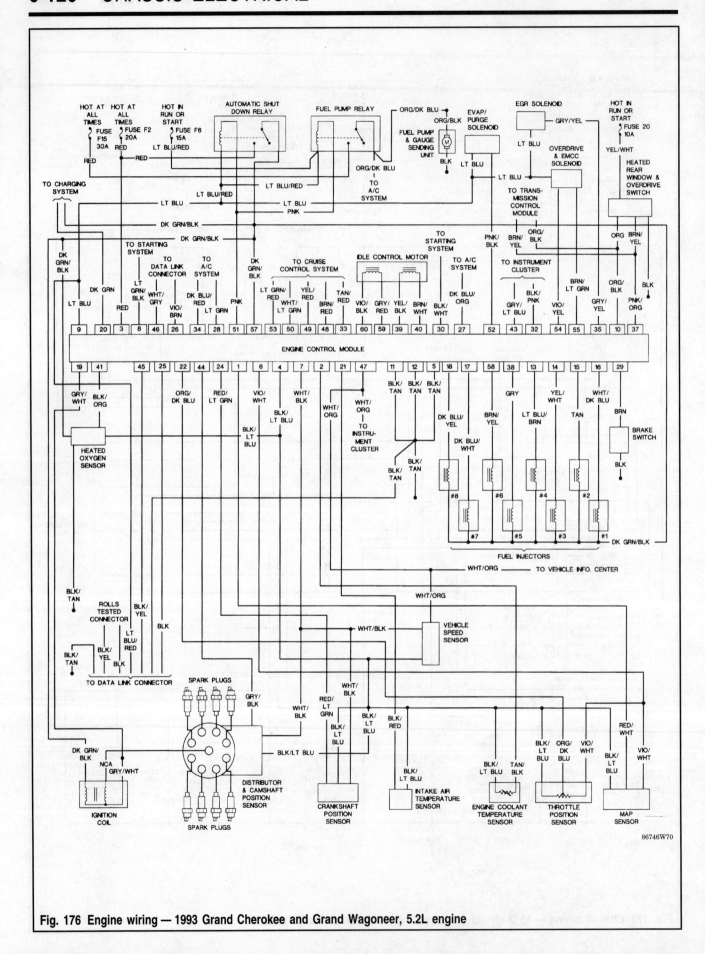

Fig. 176 Engine wiring — 1993 Grand Cherokee and Grand Wagoneer, 5.2L engine

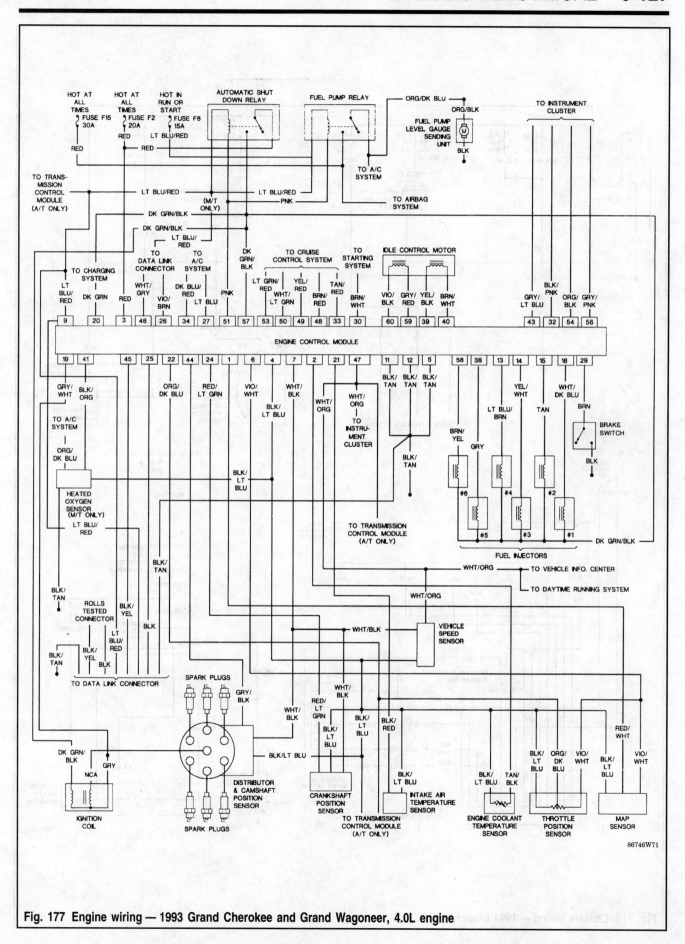

Fig. 177 Engine wiring — 1993 Grand Cherokee and Grand Wagoneer, 4.0L engine

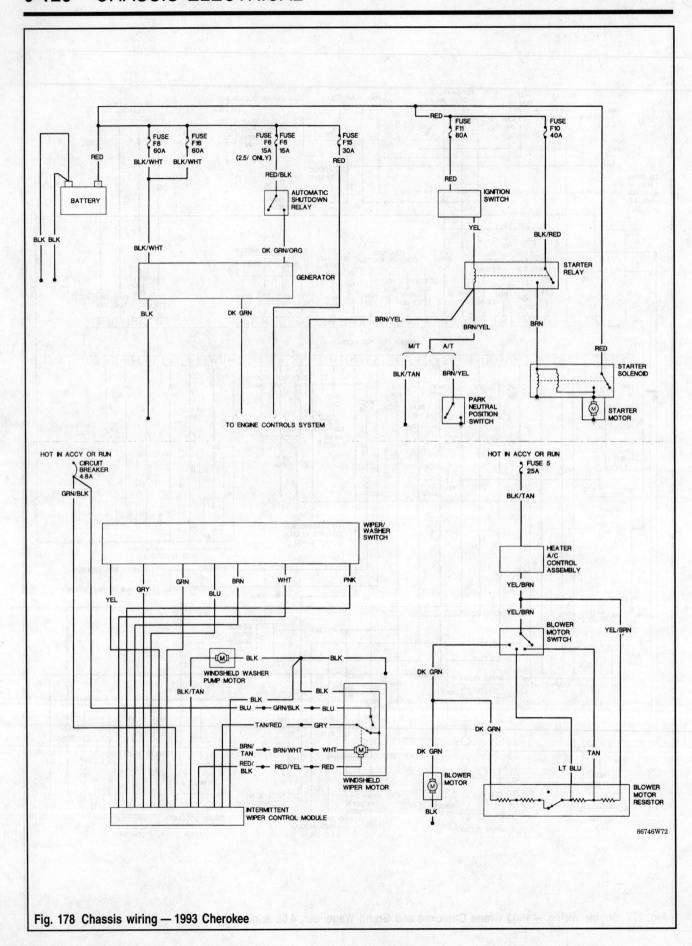

Fig. 178 Chassis wiring — 1993 Cherokee

86746W72

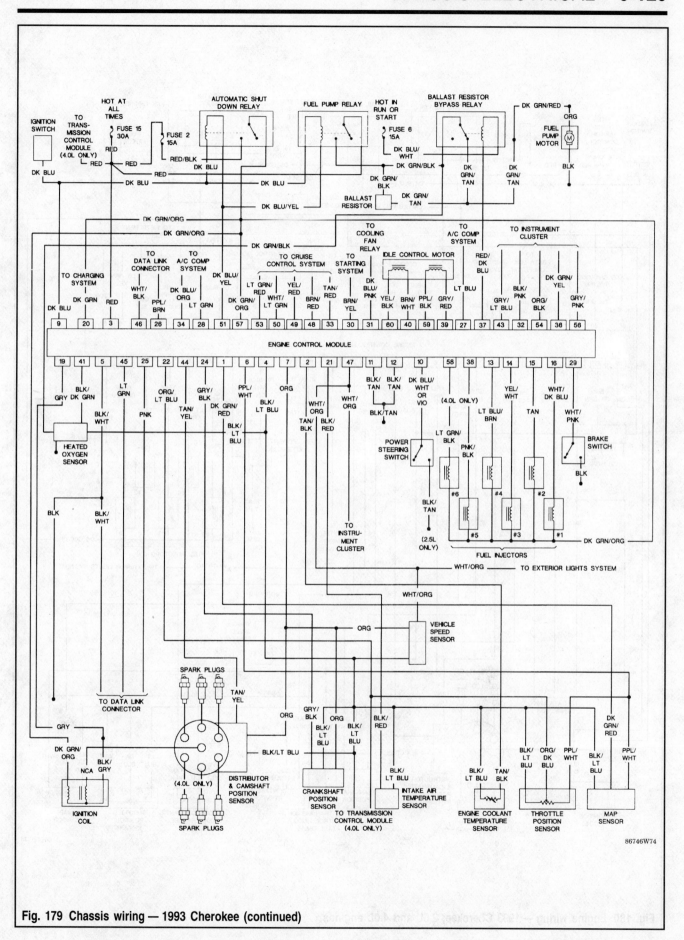

Fig. 179 Chassis wiring — 1993 Cherokee (continued)

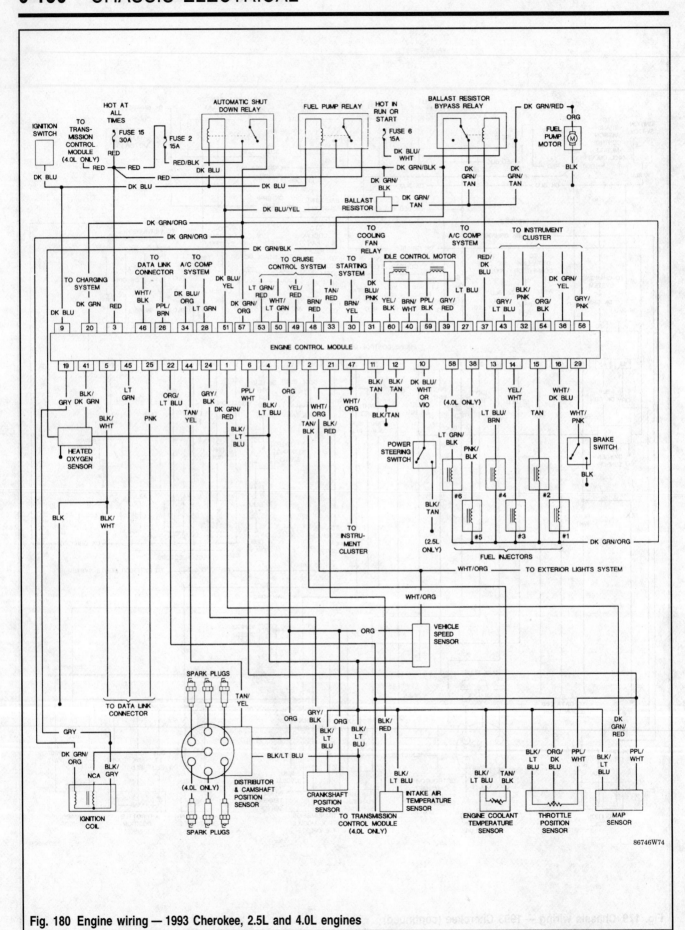

Fig. 180 Engine wiring — 1993 Cherokee, 2.5L and 4.0L engines

86746W74

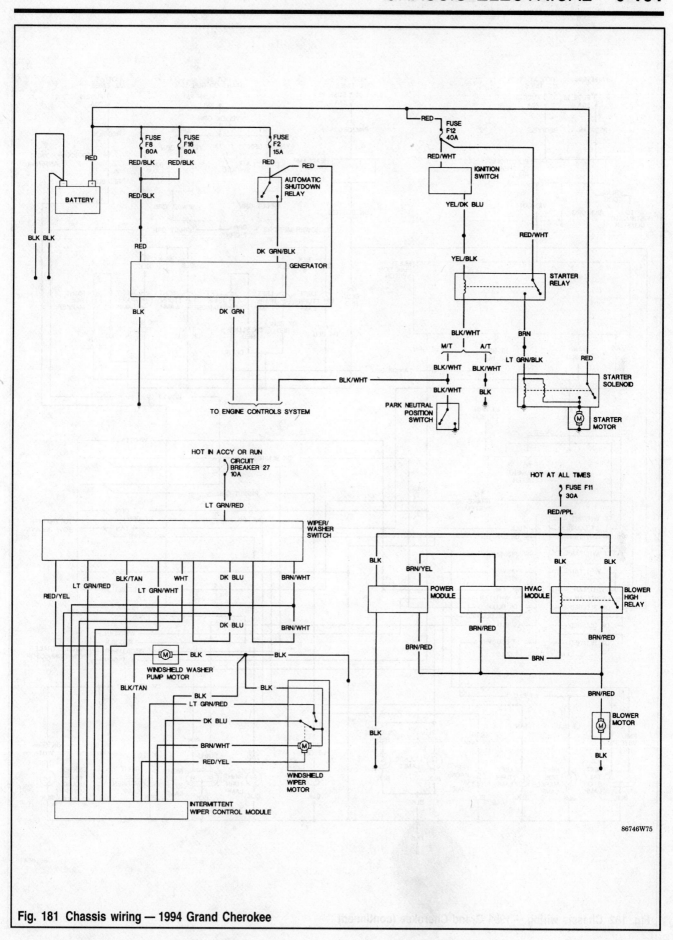

Fig. 181 Chassis wiring — 1994 Grand Cherokee

86746W75

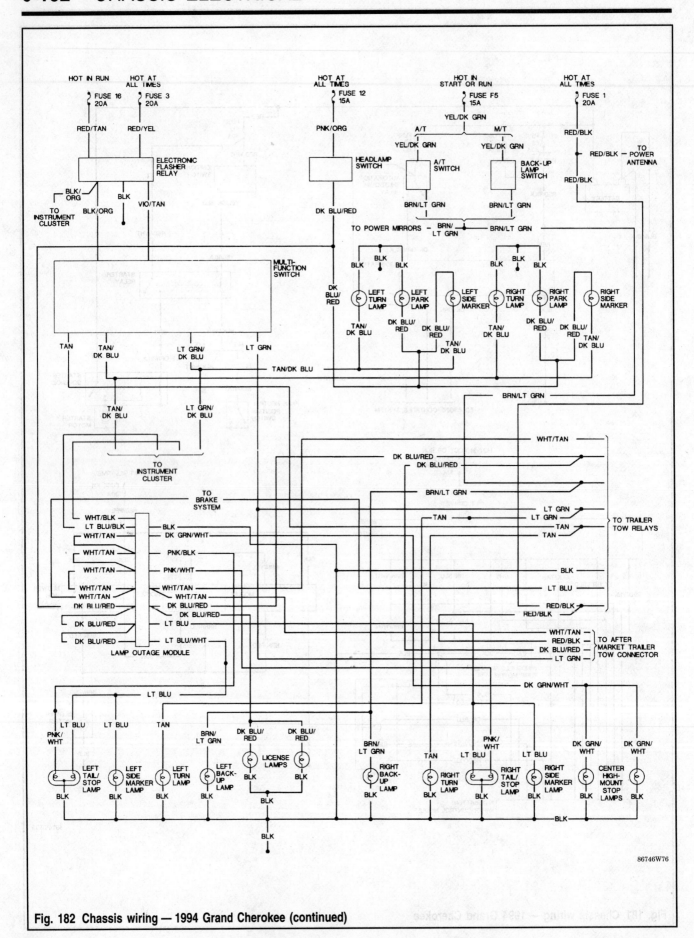

Fig. 182 Chassis wiring — 1994 Grand Cherokee (continued)

86746W76

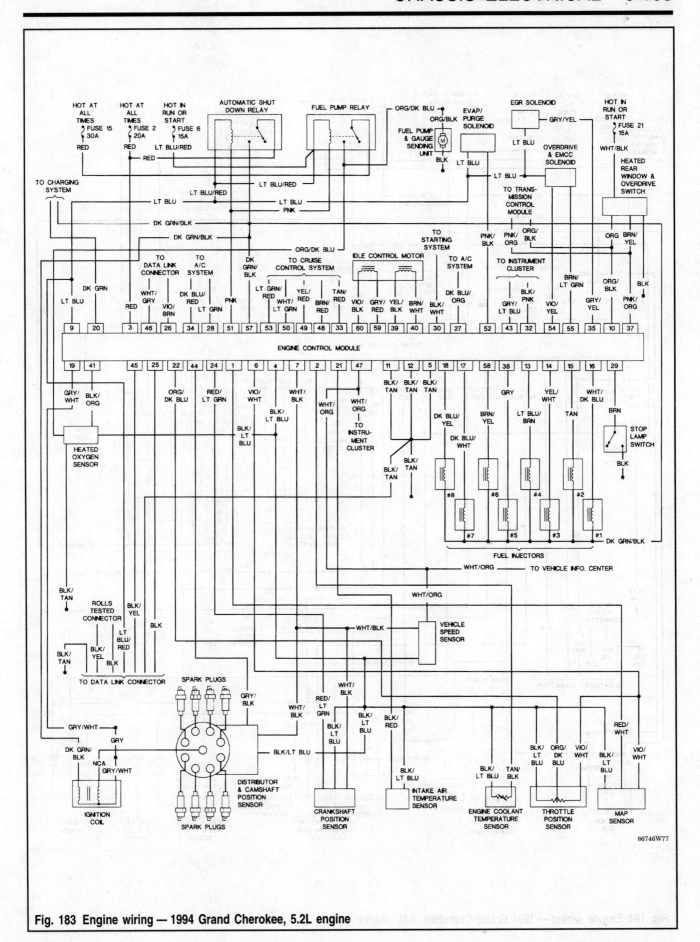

Fig. 183 Engine wiring — 1994 Grand Cherokee, 5.2L engine

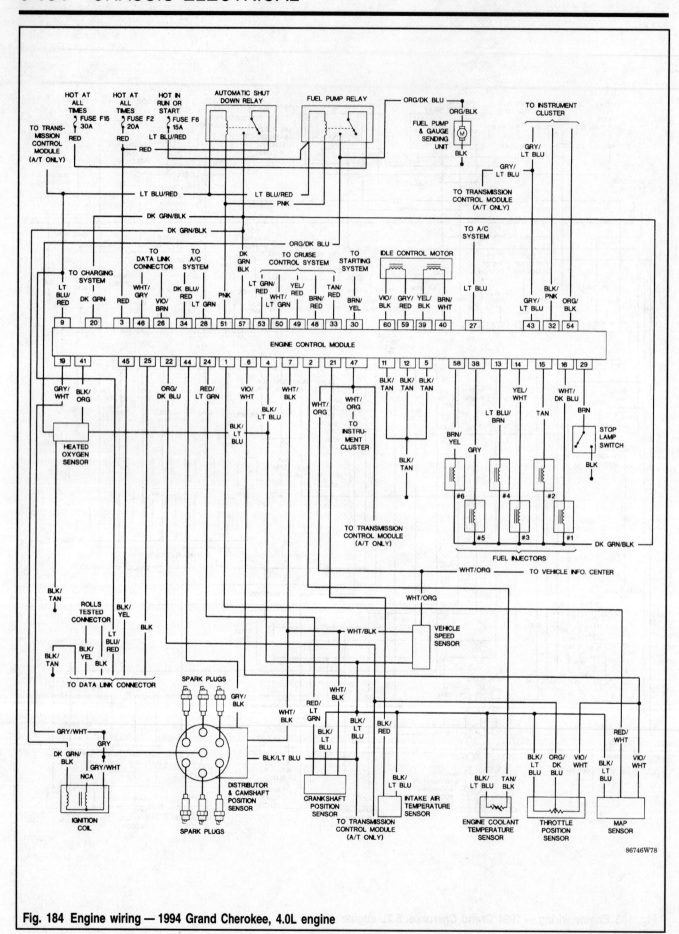

Fig. 184 Engine wiring — 1994 Grand Cherokee, 4.0L engine

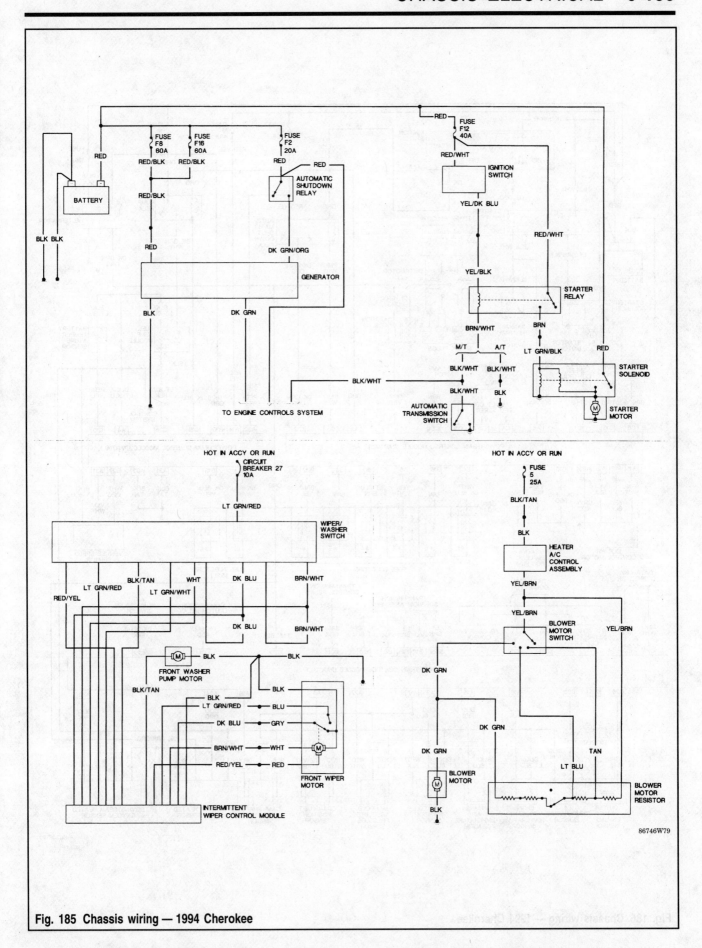

Fig. 185 Chassis wiring — 1994 Cherokee

86746W79

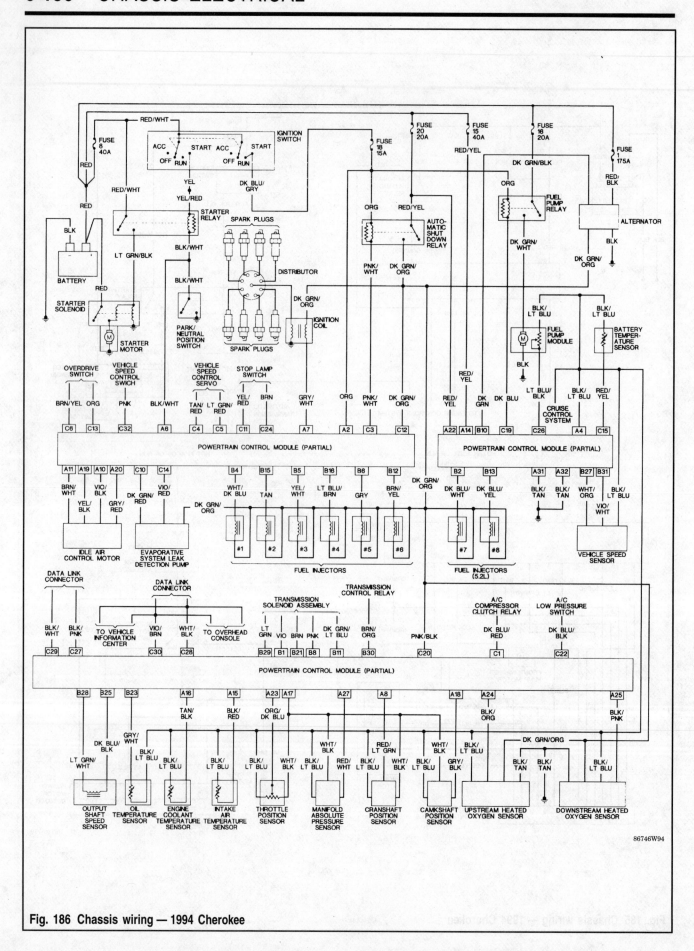

Fig. 186 Chassis wiring — 1994 Cherokee

86746W94

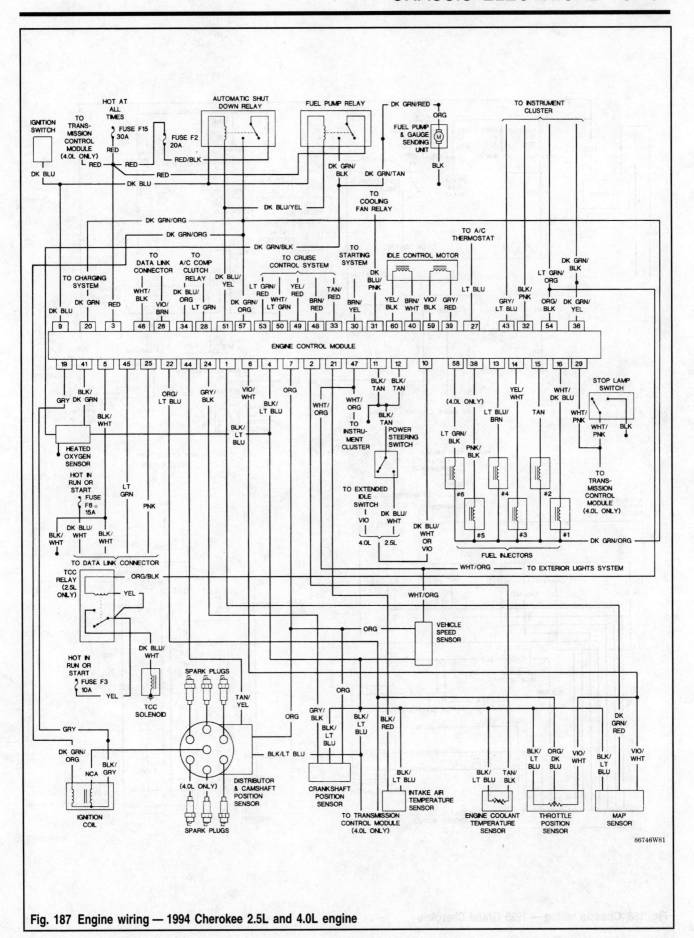

Fig. 187 Engine wiring — 1994 Cherokee 2.5L and 4.0L engine

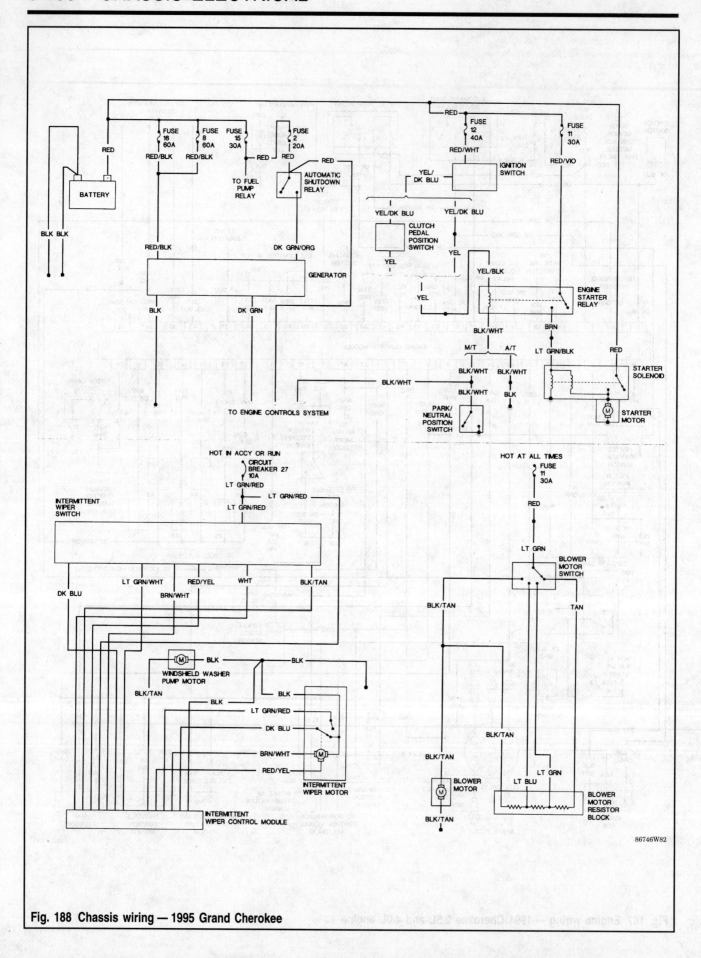

Fig. 188 Chassis wiring — 1995 Grand Cherokee

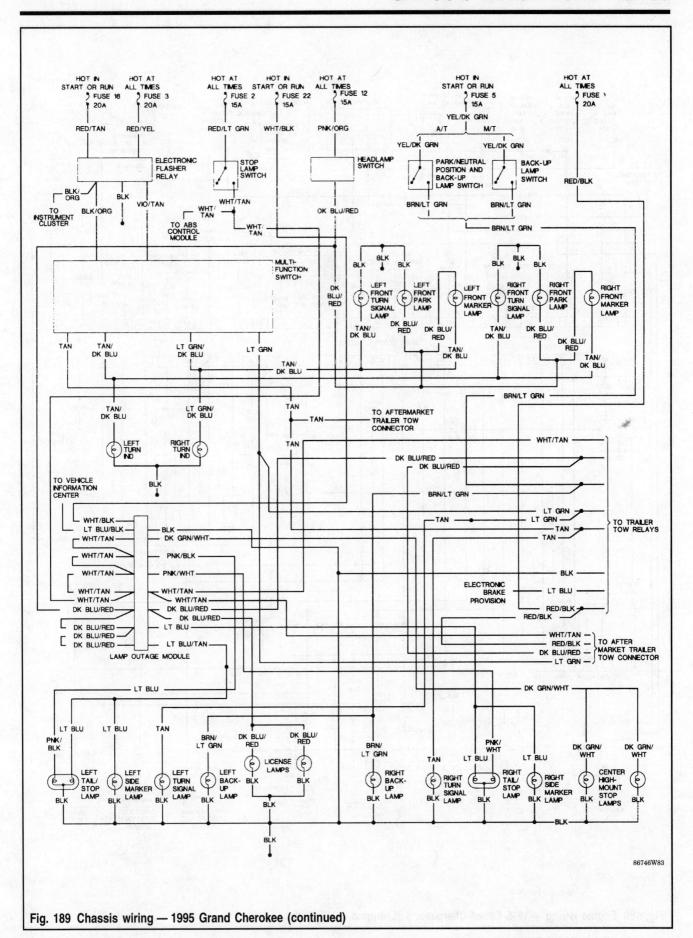

Fig. 189 Chassis wiring — 1995 Grand Cherokee (continued)

86746W83

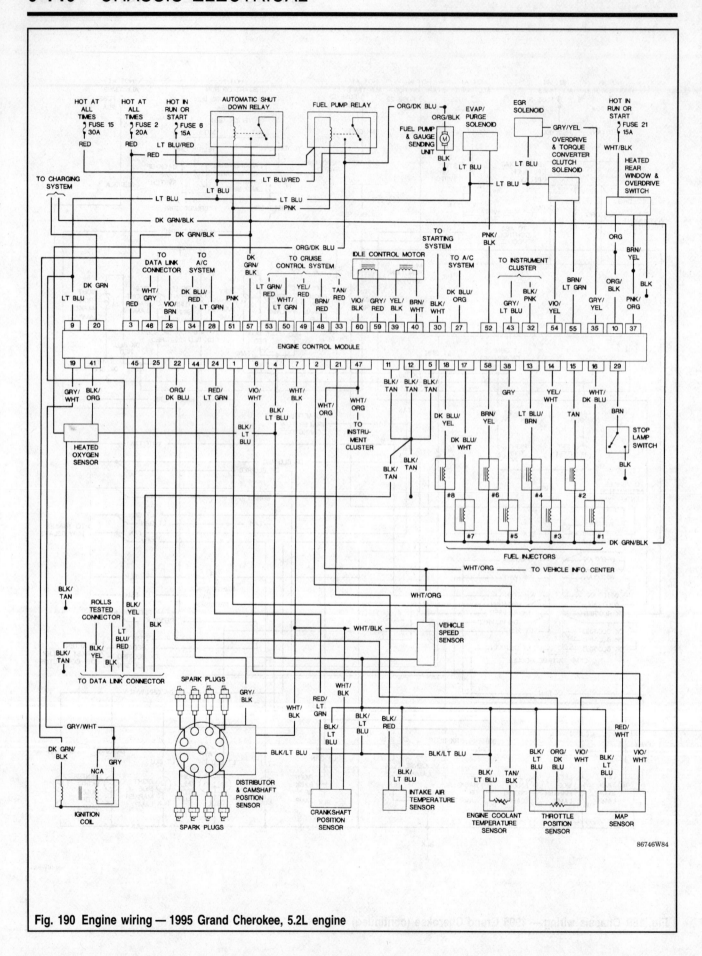

Fig. 190 Engine wiring — 1995 Grand Cherokee, 5.2L engine

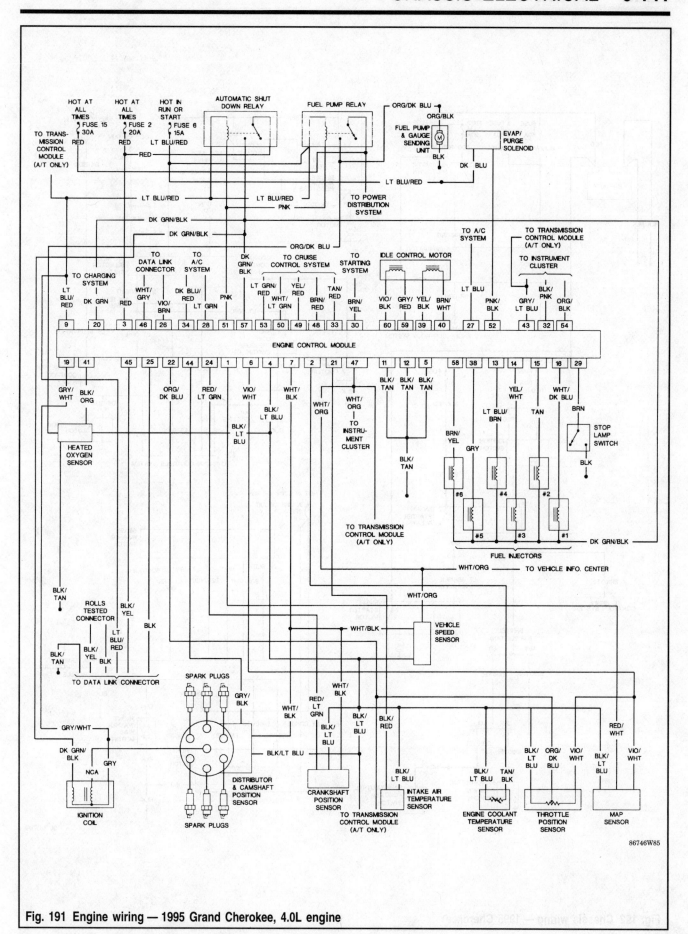

Fig. 191 Engine wiring — 1995 Grand Cherokee, 4.0L engine

86746W85

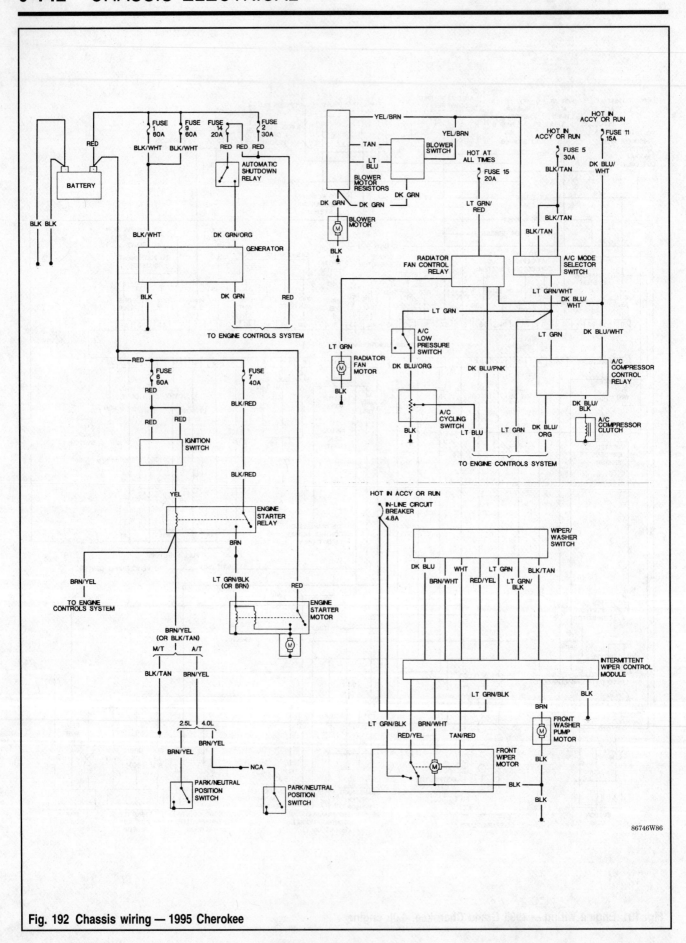

Fig. 192 Chassis wiring — 1995 Cherokee

86746W86

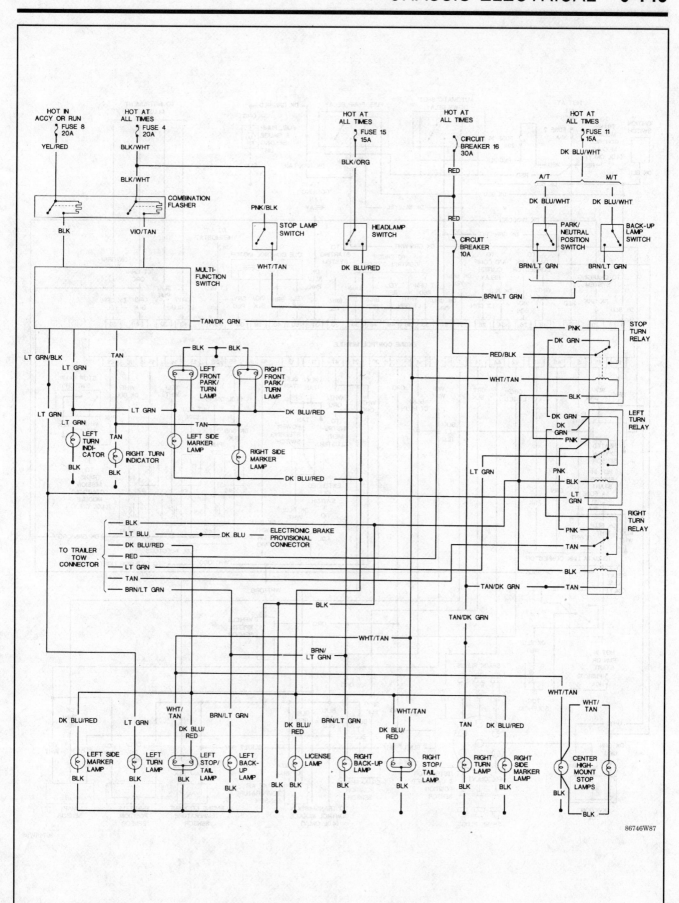

Fig. 193 Chassis wiring — 1995 Cherokee (continued)

86746W87

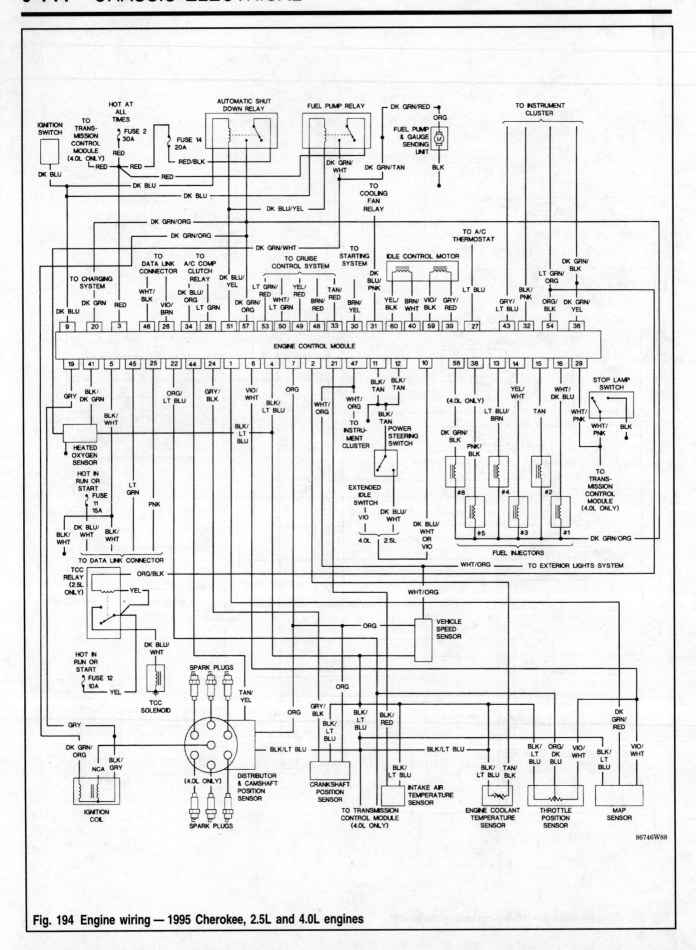

Fig. 194 Engine wiring — 1995 Cherokee, 2.5L and 4.0L engines

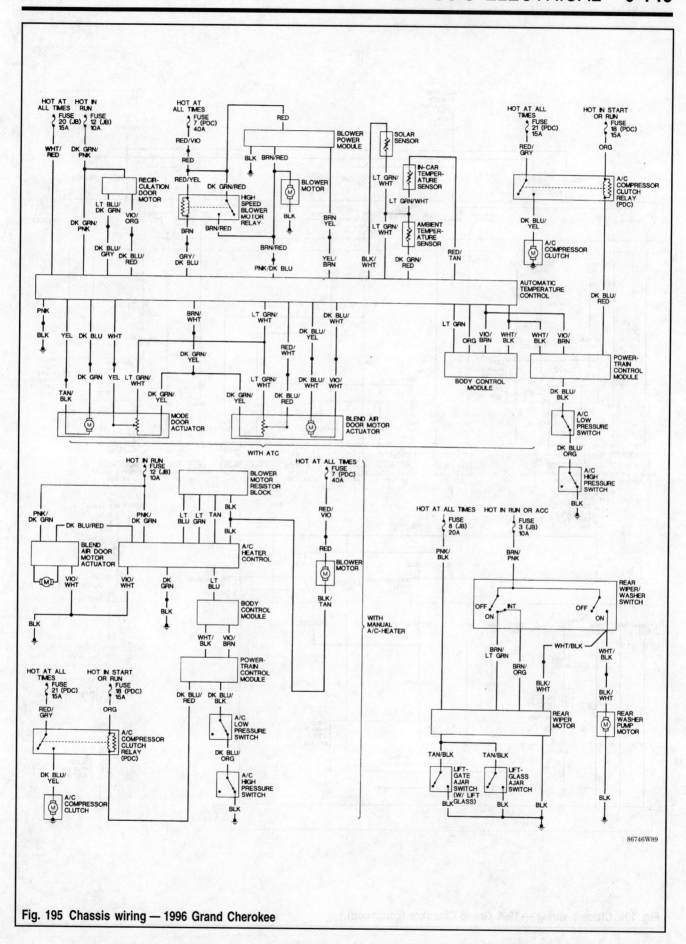

Fig. 195 Chassis wiring — 1996 Grand Cherokee

86746W89

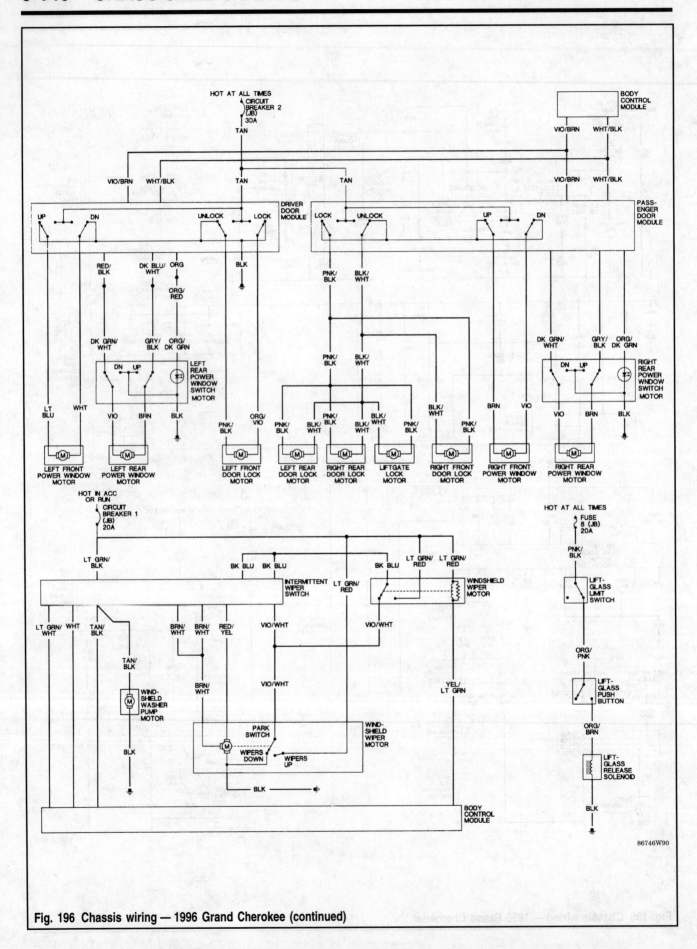

Fig. 196 Chassis wiring — 1996 Grand Cherokee (continued)

86746W90

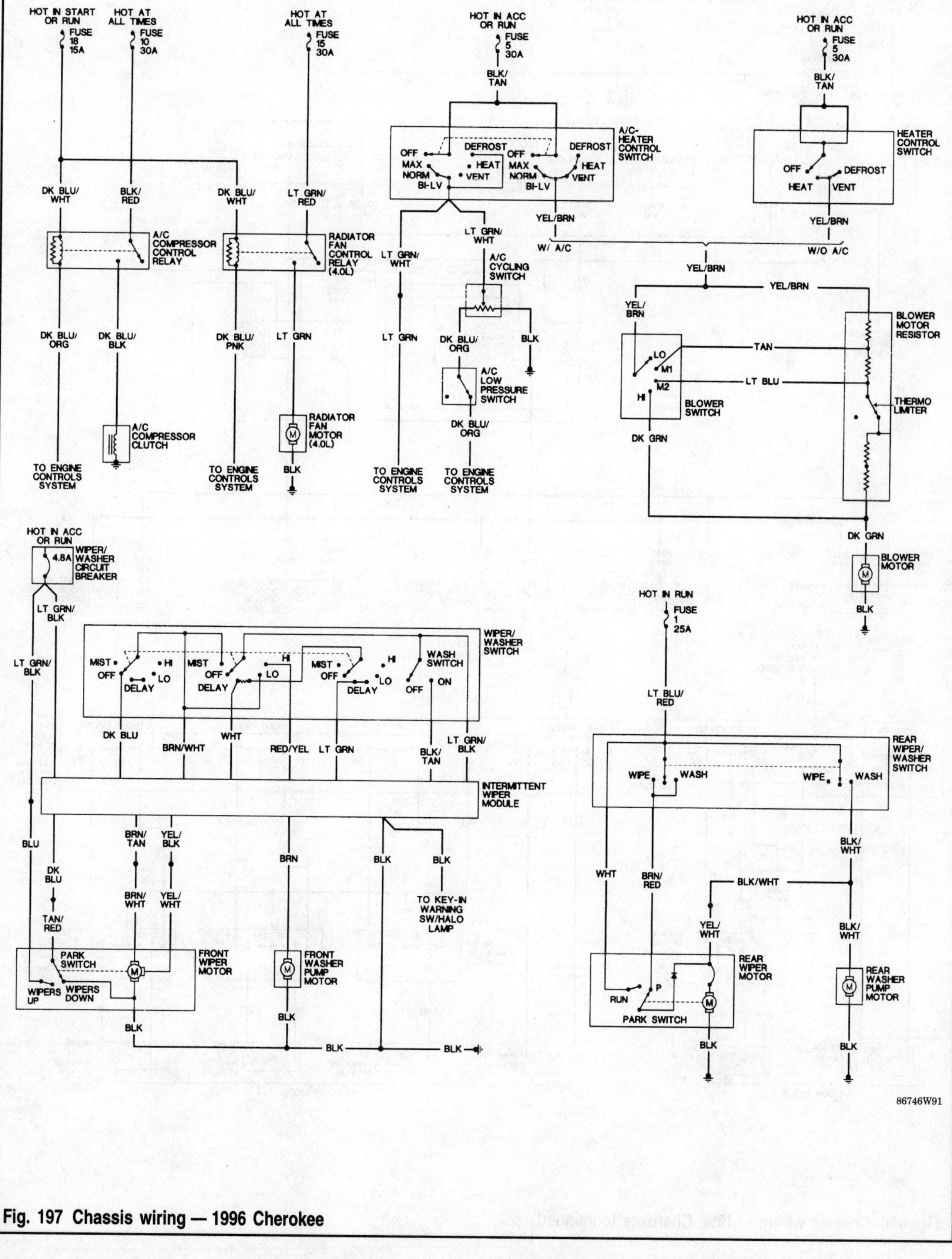

Fig. 197 Chassis wiring — 1996 Cherokee

86746W91

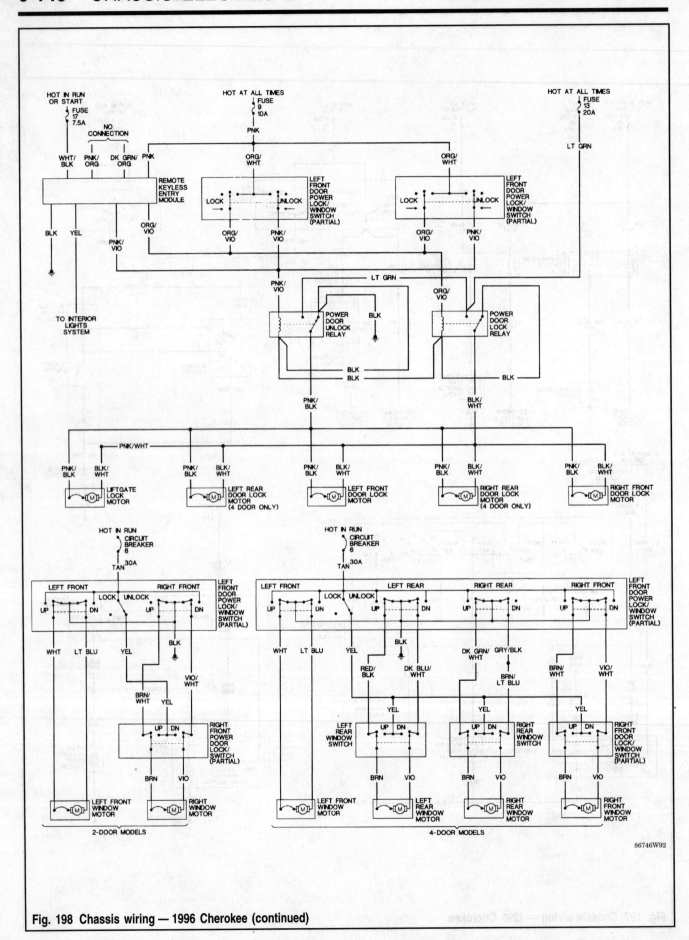

Fig. 198 Chassis wiring — 1996 Cherokee (continued)

86746W92

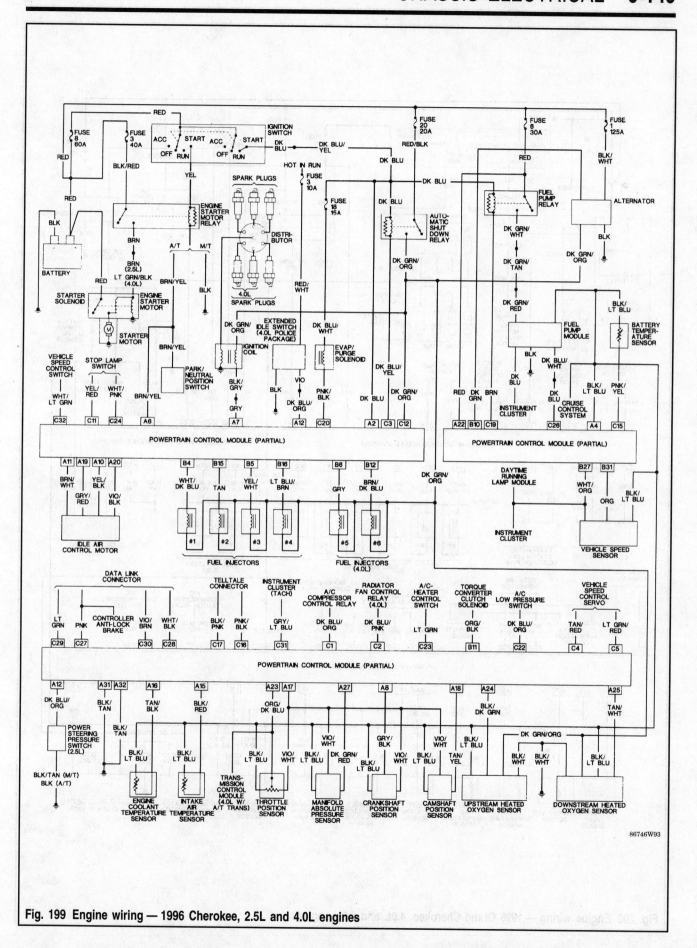

Fig. 199 Engine wiring — 1996 Cherokee, 2.5L and 4.0L engines

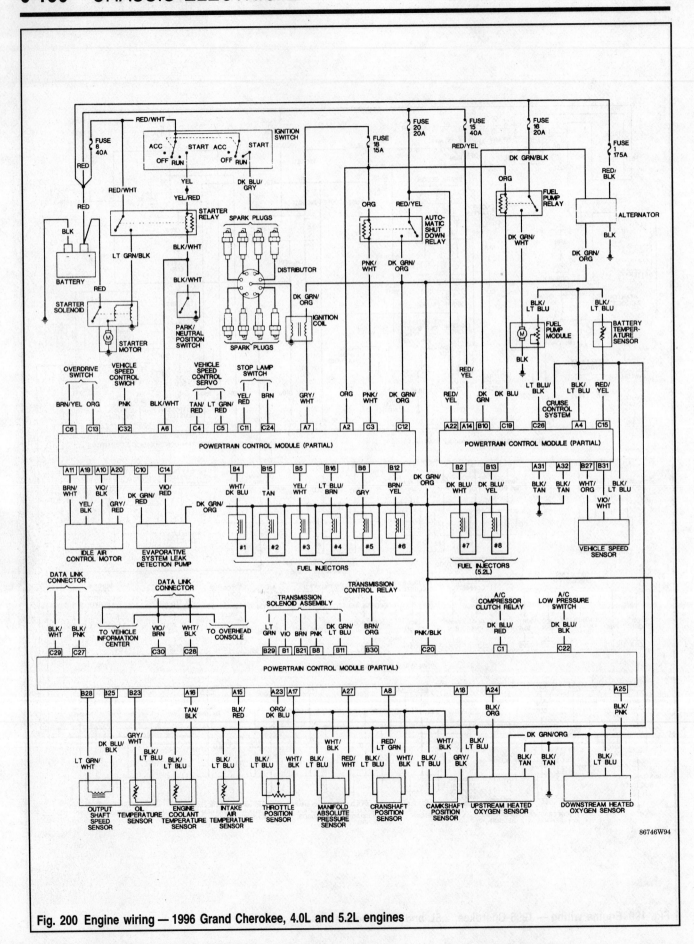

Fig. 200 Engine wiring — 1996 Grand Cherokee, 4.0L and 5.2L engines

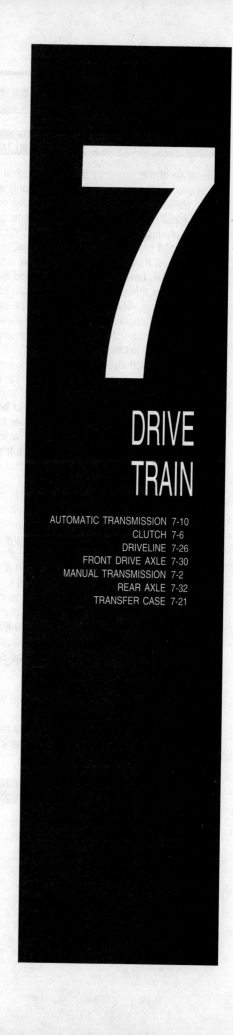

7

DRIVE TRAIN

MANUAL TRANSMISSION

Understanding Manual Transmissions

Because of the way an internal combustion engine breathes, it can produce torque, or twisting force, only within a narrow speed range. Most modern, overhead valve engines must turn at about 2500 rpm to produce their peak torque. By 4500 rpm they are producing so little torque that continued increases in engine speed produce no power increases.

The manual transmission and clutch are employed to vary the relationship between engine speed and the speed of the wheels so that adequate engine power can be produced under all circumstances. The clutch allows engine torque to be applied to the transmission input shaft gradually, due to mechanical slippage. The vehicle can, consequently, be started smoothly from a full stop.

The transmission changes the ratio between the rotating speeds of the engine and the wheels by the use of gears. On trucks, 4-speed or 5-speed transmissions are most common. The lower gears allow full engine power to be applied to the rear wheels during acceleration at low speeds.

The transmission contains a mainshaft which passes all the way through the transmission, from the clutch to the driveshaft. This shaft is separated at one point, so that front and rear portions can turn at different speeds.

Power is transmitted by a countershaft in the lower gears and reverse. The gears of the countershaft mesh with gears on the mainshaft, allowing power to be carried from one to the other. All the countershaft gears are integral with that shaft, while several of the mainshaft gears can either rotate independently of the shaft or be locked to it. Shifting from one gear to the next causes one of the gears to be freed from rotating with the shaft and locks another to it. Gears are locked and unlocked by internal dog clutches which slide between the center of the gear and the shaft. The forward gears usually employ synchronizers; friction members which smoothly bring gear and shaft to the same speed before the toothed dog clutches are engaged.

The clutch is operating properly if:

1. It will stall the engine when released with the vehicle held stationary.

2. The shift lever can be moved freely between 1st and reverse gears when the vehicle is stationary and the clutch disengaged.

Identification

Please refer to Section 1 for transmission identification.

Gear Shift Lever

REMOVAL & INSTALLATION

Warner T4/5 Models
▶ See Figure 1

1. Remove the screws attaching the the shift lever boot to the floor pan and slide the boot up.

2. Remove the bolts attaching the shift lever housing to the transmission and remove the lever and housing.

3. Installation is the reverse of removal. Make sure the lever is engaged with the shift rail before tightening the housing bolts to 18 ft. lbs. (24 Nm).

Aisin AX4/5/15 Models
▶ See Figures 2 and 3

1. Shift the transmission into first or third gear.

2. Raise and support the vehicle safely.

3. Support the transmission with a floor jack and remove the rear crossmember.

4. Lower the transmission assembly no more than 3 inches (8 cm) for access to the shift lever.

5. Reach up and around the transmission case to unseat the shifter lever dust boot from the transmission shift tower. Move the boot upward on the shift lever for access to the retainer that secures the lever in the tower.

6. Disengage the shift lever from the transmission by pressing the shift lever retainer downward and counterclockwise. Then lift the lever and retainer out of the shift tower. You can leave the shift lever in the floorpan boot for reassembly.

7. Installation is the reverse of removal. Tighten crossmember-to-frame bolts to 30 ft. lbs. (41 Nm); transmission-to-crossmember bolts to 33 ft. lbs. (45 Nm).

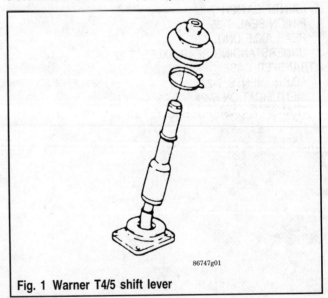

86747g01

Fig. 1 Warner T4/5 shift lever

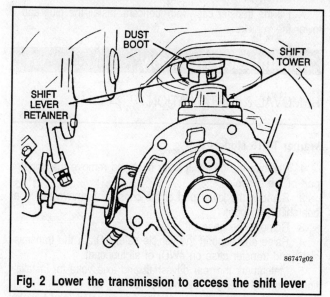

Fig. 2 Lower the transmission to access the shift lever

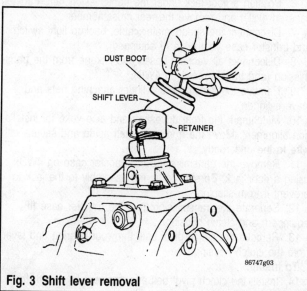

Fig. 3 Shift lever removal

BA 10/5 Models
▶ See Figure 4

1. Remove the gearshift lever boot and remove the upper part of the console.
2. Remove the lower part of the console. Remove the inner gearshift lever boot.
3. Remove the gearshift lever.

➡ **On some BA 10/5 transmissions, the shift lever may be held in place with a snapring and spring washer.**

4. Installation is the reverse of removal.

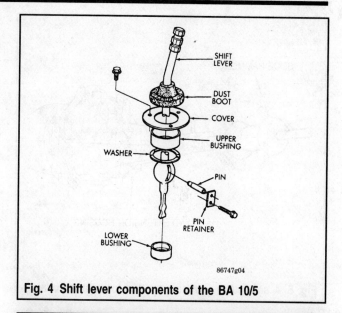

Fig. 4 Shift lever components of the BA 10/5

Backup Light Switch

REMOVAL & INSTALLATION

The backup light switch on most transmissions is located on the right side of the case.
1. Unplug the electrical connector and unscrew the switch.
2. If the switch uses a gasket (washer), replace it when installing the new switch.
3. If a gasket (washer) is not used, coat the threads of the switch with sealer before installation.
4. Tighten the switch to 27 ft. lbs. (37 Nm) and engage the electrical connector.

Extension Housing Seal

REMOVAL & INSTALLATION

2WD Models
▶ See Figures 5 and 6

The extension seal on 2-wheel drive vehicles is located at the rear of the transmission case.
1. Raise and support the vehicle safely.
2. Drain the transmission of lubricant.
3. Matchmark the driveshaft to the yoke for reassembly and remove the driveshaft.
4. Remove the old seal using a seal puller or appropriate prytool.
   To install:
5. Install a new seal, coated with sealing compound, using an appropriate seal installation tool.

➡ **Tool J-35582 or equivalent is recommended for AX4/5/15 transmissions. Tool J-21426 or equivalent is recommended for Warner T4/5 transmissions.**

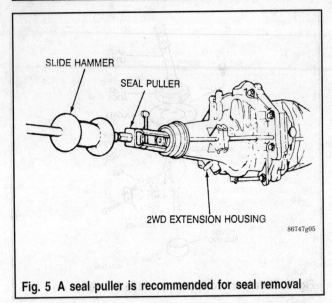

SLIDE HAMMER

SEAL PULLER

2WD EXTENSION HOUSING

86747g05

Fig. 5 A seal puller is recommended for seal removal

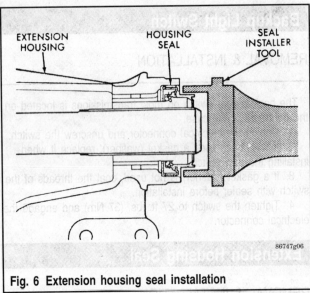

EXTENSION HOUSING

HOUSING SEAL

SEAL INSTALLER TOOL

86747g06

Fig. 6 Extension housing seal installation

6. Install the driveshaft, making certain to align the matchmark. Tighten bolts to 20 ft. lbs. (27 Nm).

7. Fill the transmission to the level of the fill plug hole. Install the plug and lower the vehicle.

4WD Models

The extension seal on 4-wheel drive vehicles is located at the rear of the transfer case.

1. Raise and support the vehicle safely.

2. Drain the transfer case of lubricant.

3. Matchmark the driveshaft to the yoke for reassembly and remove the driveshaft.

4. Remove the old seal using a seal puller or appropriate prytool.

To install:

5. Install a new seal, coated with sealing compound, using an appropriate seal installation tool.

6. Install the driveshaft, making certain to align matchmark. Tighten bolts to 20 ft. lbs. (27 Nm)

7. Fill the transfer case with lubricant. Install the plug and lower the vehicle.

Transmission Assembly

REMOVAL & INSTALLATION

Warner T4/T5 Models

1. Remove the gearshift lever boot and remove the upper part of the console.

2. Remove the lower part of the console. Remove the inner gearshift lever boot.

3. Remove the gearshift lever.

4. Raise and support the vehicle safely. Drain the transmission (and transfer case on 4WD) of all lubricant.

5. Matchmark the rear driveshaft and axle yoke for installation alignment. Remove the rear driveshaft.

6. Position a floor jack under the transmission (and transfer case on 4WD) and remove the rear crossmember.

7. Disconnect the speedometer cable, backup light switch, and transfer case vent hose (if equipped).

8. Disconnect all vacuum hoses and linkage from the transmission (and transfer case on 4WD).

9. Remove the clutch slave cylinder attaching nuts and slave cylinder.

10. Matchmark the front driveshaft and axle yoke for installation alignment. Move the front driveshaft aside and secure with wire to the underbody.

11. Remove the transmission (and transfer case on 4WD) using a floor jack. Be sure to tie the assembly to the jack to prevent it from slipping.

12. Separate the transmission from the transfer case (if equipped) and clutch housing.

13. Remove the clutch pivot ball, throwout bearing and lever from the clutch housing.

To install:

14. Install the clutch pivot ball and throwout lever with the bearing attached.

15. Shift the transmission into gear using the shift lever.

16. With the transmission supported on a floor jack, align the transmission clutch shaft with the splines in the driveplate hub. Mate the transmission to the engine and tighten the mounting bolts to 28 ft. lbs. (38 Nm).

17. Install the clutch slave cylinder and attaching nuts.

18. Install the transfer case (if equipped) using a floor jack and tighten attaching bolts to 26 ft. lbs. (35 Nm).

19. Connect the transfer case vent hose (if equipped), backup light switch, speedometer cable, transfer case vacuum hoses and all linkage.

20. Install the front driveshaft with the matchmarks aligned. Tighten the strap bolts to 14 ft. lbs. (19 Nm); and the flange-to-transfer case bolts to 35 ft. lbs. (47 Nm).

21. Install the crossmember. Tighten the crossmember-to-frame bolts to 30 ft. lbs. (41 Nm); and the crossmember-to-transmission bolts to 33 ft. lbs. (45 Nm).

22. Install the rear driveshaft with matchmarks aligned. Tighten the strap bolts to 14 ft. lbs. (19 Nm).

23. Fill the transmission (and transfer case on 4WD) with the appropriate fluid. Lower the vehicle.

24. Install the gearshift lever, lower and upper console and shift lever boot.

AX4/5/15 Models

1. Shift the transmission into first or third gear.
2. Raise and support the vehicle safely.
3. Support the transmission with a floor jack and remove the rear crossmember.
4. Disconnect the transmission shift linkage, speedometer cable, transfer case vacuum lines (on 4WD) and clutch hydraulic lines.
5. Lower the transmission assembly no more than 3 inches (8 cm) for access to the shift lever.
6. Reach up and around the transmission case to unseat the shifter lever dust boot from the transmission shift tower. Move the boot upward on the shift lever for access to the retainer that secures the lever in the tower.
7. Disengage the shift lever from the transmission by pressing the shift lever retainer downward and counterclockwise. Then lift the lever and retainer out of the shift tower. You can leave the shift lever in the floorpan boot for reassembly.
8. Matchmark the front and rear driveshafts for installation alignment and remove.
9. Disconnect the engine timing sensor, if equipped.
10. Disconnect the transmission (and transfer case on 4WD) vent hoses.
11. Disconnect the clutch master cylinder hydraulic line from the concentric bearing inlet line.
12. Secure the assembly to a floor jack with chains to prevent it from slipping during removal.

➡ **It is a good idea to place a second support (floor jack or jackstand) under the oil pan of the engine to prevent the engine from falling rearward. This second support will also ease the installation of the transmission.**

13. Remove the clutch housing brace rod.
14. Remove the clutch housing to engine attaching bolts and remove the transmission assembly.
15. Separate the transmission from the clutch housing and transfer case (on 4WD).

➡ **After separating the transmission from the clutch housing, resecure the bearing nylon straps to hold the bearing piston in place.**

To install:

16. Install the clutch housing on the transmission. Tighten the housing bolts to 27 ft. lbs. (37 Nm).
17. Install the concentric bearing. Secure the bearing to the mounting pin with a new retainer clip.
18. Mount the transmission on a floor jack, lightly lubricate the input shaft and install the transmission.
19. Install and tighten the clutch housing-to-engine bolts to 28 ft. lbs. (38 Nm).

➡ **Be sure the housing is properly seated against the engine block before tightening the attaching bolts.**

20. Lower the transmission no more than 3 inches (8 cm) to allow installation of the shifter. Insert the shift lever in the shift tower. Press the lever retainer downward and turn clockwise to lock in place. Install the lever dust boot on the shift tower.

21. Connect the concentric bearing hydraulic line and the engine timing sensor wires.
22. Mount the transfer case (if equipped) on a jack and align with the transmission shafts. Install the transfer case and tighten the transfer case-to-transmission bolts to 26 ft. lbs. (35 Nm).
23. Connect the transmission (and transfer case on 4WD) vent hoses, backup light switch, and distance sensor wires.
24. Install the rear crossmember. Tighten the crossmember-to-frame bolts to 30 ft. lbs. (41 Nm); and the transmission-to-crossmember bolts to 33 ft. lbs. (45 Nm).
25. Align and install the front and rear propeller shafts. Tighten the U-joint clamp bolts to 170 inch lbs. (19 Nm).
26. Fill the transmission (and transfer case on 4WD) with lubricant and lower the vehicle.

BA 10/5 Models

1. Shift transmission into neutral. Remove the shift knob, locknut, boot and bezel. Then remove shifter lever extension.
2. Remove the transmission shift lever dust boot.
3. Remove the shift lever cover, bushings, washer, pin and lever.

➡ **On some BA 10/5 transmissions, the shift lever may be held in place with a snapring and spring washer.**

4. Raise and support the vehicle safely. Drain the lubricant from transmission/transfer case.
5. Matchmark the rear driveshaft for reference during installation and remove.
6. Position a floor jack or support under the transmission/transfer case and remove the crossmember.
7. Disconnect the speedometer cable, backup light switch, transmission and transfer case vent hoses.
8. Disconnect the transfer case vacuum hoses. Then disconnect the transfer case range rod from the floor shift lever. Mark the hoses for assembly reference.
9. Matchmark the front driveshaft for reference during installation and remove.
10. Disconnect the clutch cylinder hydraulic line from the throwout bearing inlet line.
11. Secure the transmission/transfer case to a floor jack and remove the clutch housing bolts. Remove the transmission/transfer case assembly.
12. Separate the transmission from the transfer case, and the clutch housing from the transmission. Remove the hydraulic throwout bearing.

To install:

13. Install the clutch housing on transmission and tighten the bolts to 28 ft. lbs. (38 Nm).
14. Install the hydraulic throwout bearing. Install the shifter into the shift tower and shift the transmission into any forward gear. Then remove the shifter.
15. Raise the transmission on a floor jack. Align the input shaft and clutch disc splines and install the transmission.
16. Install the clutch housing-to-engine bolts. Tighten 12mm bolts to 55 ft. lbs. (75 Nm); the 3/8 in. bolts to 27 ft. lbs. (37 Nm); and the 7/16 in. bolts to 43 ft. lbs. (58 Nm).
17. Connect the throwout bearing to the clutch cylinder hydraulic line.

18. Mount the transfer case on a floor jack and install. Tighten the transfer case attaching bolts/nuts to 26 ft. lbs. (35 Nm).

19. Connect the transfer case vacuum hoses and linkage. Connect the transmission/transfer case vent hoses.

20. Connect the backup light switch, speedometer cable and transfer case range rod to the floor shift.

21. Install the rear crossmember and tighten the cross-member-to-frame bolts to 30 ft. lbs. (41 Nm); transmission-to-crossmember bolts to 33 ft. lbs. (45 Nm).

22. Align and install front and rear driveshafts. Tighten the bolts to 170 inch lbs. (19 Nm).

23. Fill the transmission/transfer case with lubricant. Lower the vehicle.

24. Install the transmission shift lever, lever dust boot, shift lever extension, boot, bezel and knob.

CLUTCH

The purpose of the clutch is to disconnect and connect engine power at the transmission. A car at rest requires a lot of engine torque to get all that weight moving. An internal combustion engine does not develop a high starting torque (unlike steam engines), so it must be allowed to operate without any load until it builds up enough torque to move the car. Torque increases with engine rpm. The clutch allows the engine to build up torque by physically disconnecting the engine from the transmission, relieving the engine of any load or resistance. The transfer of engine power to the transmission (the load) must be smooth and gradual; if it weren't, drive line components would wear out or break quickly. This gradual power transfer is made possible by gradually releasing the clutch pedal. The clutch disc and pressure plate are the connecting link between the engine and transmission. When the clutch pedal is released, the disc and plate contact each other (clutch engagement), physically joining the engine and transmission. When the pedal is pushed in, the disc and plate separate (the clutch is disengaged), disconnecting the engine from the transmission.

The clutch assembly consists of the flywheel, the clutch disc, the clutch pressure plate, the throwout bearing and fork, the actuating linkage and the pedal. The flywheel and clutch pressure plate (driving members) are connected to the engine crankshaft and rotate with it. The clutch disc is located between the flywheel and pressure plate, and splined to the transmission shaft. A driving member is one that is attached to the engine and transfers engine power to a driven member (clutch disc) on the transmission shaft. A driving member (pressure plate) rotates (drives) a driven member (clutch disc) on contact and, in so doing, turns the transmission shaft. There is a circular diaphragm spring within the pressure plate cover (transmission side). In a relaxed state (when the clutch pedal is fully released), this spring is convex; that is, it is dished outward toward the transmission. Pushing in the clutch pedal actuates an attached linkage rod. Connected to the other end of this rod is the throwout bearing fork. The throwout bearing is attached to the fork. When the clutch pedal is depressed, the clutch linkage pushes the fork and bearing forward to contact the diaphragm spring of the pressure plate. The outer edges of the spring are secured to the pressure plate and are pivoted on rings so that when the center of the spring is compressed by the throwout bearing, the outer edges bow outward and, by so doing, pull the pressure plate in the same direction   away from the clutch disc. This action separates the disc from the plate, disengaging the clutch and al-

lowing the transmission to be shifted into another gear. A coil type clutch return spring attached to the clutch pedal arm permits full release of the pedal. Releasing the pedal pulls the throwout bearing away from the diaphragm spring resulting in a reversal of spring position. As bearing pressure is gradually released from the spring center, the outer edges of the spring bow outward, pushing the pressure plate into closer contact with the clutch disc. As the disc and plate move closer together, friction between the two increases and slippage is reduced until, when full spring pressure is applied (by fully releasing the pedal), The speed of the disc and plate are the same. This stops all slipping, creating a direct connection between the plate and disc which results in the transfer of power from the engine to the transmission. The clutch disc is now rotating with the pressure plate at engine speed and, because it is splined to the transmission shaft, the shaft now turns at the same engine speed. Understanding clutch operation can be rather difficult at first; if you're still confused after reading this, consider the following analogy. The action of the diaphragm spring can be compared to that of an oil can bottom. The bottom of an oil can is shaped very much like the clutch diaphragm spring and pushing in on the can bottom and then releasing it produces a similar effect. As mentioned earlier, the clutch pedal return spring permits full release of the pedal and reduces linkage slack due to wear. As the linkage wears, clutch free-pedal travel will increase and free-travel will decrease as the clutch wears. Free-travel is actually throwout bearing lash.

The diaphragm spring type clutches used are available in two different designs: flat diaphragm springs or bent spring. The bent fingers are bent back to create a centrifugal boost ensuring quick re-engagement at higher engine speeds. This design enables pressure plate load to increase as the clutch disc wears and makes low pedal effort possible even with a heavy-duty clutch. The throwout bearing used with the bent finger design is $1\frac{1}{4}$ in. (31.75mm) long and is shorter than the bearing used with the flat finger design. These bearings are not interchangeable. If the longer bearing is used with the bent finger clutch, free-pedal travel will not exist. This results in clutch slippage and rapid wear.

The transmission varies the gear ratio between the engine and rear wheels. It can be shifted to change engine speed as driving conditions and loads change. The transmission allows disengaging and reversing power from the engine to the wheels.

Clutch Pedal

REMOVAL & INSTALLATION

▶ **See Figures 7 and 8**

1. Remove the instrument panel lower trim cover for needed clearance.
2. Remove the cotter pin securing the master cylinder pushrod to the pedal. Remove the flat washer and wave washer, if equipped.
3. Disconnect the pedal return spring, if equipped
4. Remove the nut securing the pedal to the pivot shaft, then slide the pedal off the shaft and remove.
5. Lubricate the clutch pedal pivot shaft and pedal bushings with chassis grease.
6. Installation is the reverse of removal.

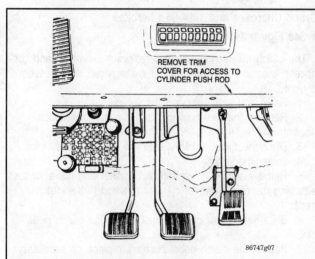

Fig. 7 Remove the lower trim cover to gain access to the clutch pedal and pushrod

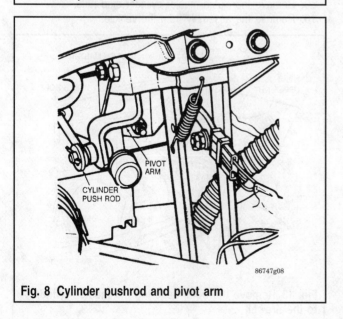

Fig. 8 Cylinder pushrod and pivot arm

Clutch Disc And Pressure Plate

REMOVAL & INSTALLATION

▶ **See Figures 9, 10, 11 and 12**

1. Raise and safely support the vehicle.
2. Remove the transmission or transmission/transfer case assembly.
3. Matchmark the pressure plate and flywheel. Loosen the pressure plate bolts, a little at a time, in rotation, to avoid warpage.
4. Remove the pressure plate and clutch disc.
5. Inspect the flywheel for scoring, cracks, warpage or other wear; resurface or replace as necessary.
6. Inspect the pilot bearing for excessive wear or damage and replace as necessary.

To install:

7. If removed, install the pilot bearing after lubricating lightly with grease. Seat the bearing in the crankshaft with a clutch alignment tool.
8. Check the clutch disc runout by installing the disc on the transmission input shaft. Runout should not exceed 0.020 in. (0.5mm) when measured ¼ in. (5mm) from the outer edge of the facing.
9. Install the clutch alignment tool in the pilot bearing.
10. Install the clutch disc on the tool.
11. Install the pressure plate and tighten the bolts finger-tight. The pressure plate bolts must be tightened a little at a time, in rotation, to avoid warpage. Tighten the pressure plate bolts as follows:

- 2.1L diesel engines — 16 ft. lbs. (22 Nm)
- 2.5L and 2.8L engines — 23 ft. lbs. (31 Nm)
- 4.0L engine — 40 ft. lbs. (54 Nm)
- 5.2L engine — 5/16 inch bolts: 17 ft. lbs. (23 Nm) and 3/8 inch bolts 30 ft. lbs. (41 Nm)

12. Install the transmission or transmission/transfer case assembly and lower the vehicle.

Fig. 9 Be sure that the flywheel surface is clean, before installing the clutch

TCCS7127

Fig. 10 Install a clutch alignment arbor, to align the clutch assembly during installation

TCCS7131

Fig. 11 Install locking agent to clutch assembly bolts

TCCS7132

Fig. 12 Install the clutch assembly bolts and tighten in steps, in an X pattern

Clutch Master Cylinder

REMOVAL & INSTALLATION

Comanche, Wagoneer and 1984-93 Cherokee
▶ See Figure 13

1. Disconnect the hydraulic line at the master cylinder. Cap the line.
2. Disconnect the pushrod at the clutch pedal. Remove the instrument panel lower trim cover for access, if necessary.
3. Unbolt the master cylinder from the firewall. One bolt is accessible from the engine compartment, the other is accessible from the passenger compartment.
4. Installation is the reverse of removal. Tighten the mounting nuts to 19 ft. lbs. (26 Nm); the hydraulic line fitting to 15 ft. lbs. (20 Nm). Refill and bleed the system.

Grand Cherokee and 1994-96 Cherokee
▶ See Figure 14

The clutch master cylinder, reservoir, slave cylinder and connecting lines are sealed units and are serviced as an assembly only.

1. Raise and safely support the vehicle.
2. Remove the slave cylinder and clip from the clutch housing.
3. Disconnect the hydraulic fluid line from the body clips.
4. Lower the vehicle.
5. Remove the retaining ring, flat washer and wave washer attaching the clutch master cylinder pushrod to the clutch pedal.
6. Slide the master cylinder pushrod off the clutch pedal pin.
7. Inspect the clutch pedal bushing, replace as necessary.
8. Remove the clutch master cylinder reservoir from the dash panel.
9. Remove the clutch master cylinder stud nuts.
10. Remove the assembly from the vehicle.

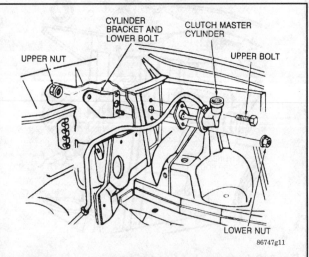

CYLINDER BRACKET AND LOWER BOLT

CLUTCH MASTER CYLINDER

UPPER NUT

UPPER BOLT

LOWER NUT

86747g11

Fig. 13 Remove the bolts securing the master cylinder to the firewall

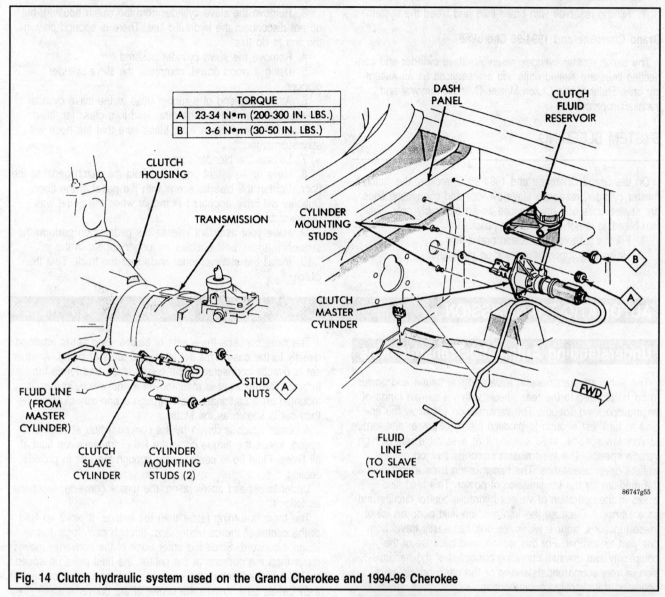

TORQUE	
A	23-34 N•m (200-300 IN. LBS.)
B	3-6 N•m (30-50 IN. LBS.)

Fig. 14 Clutch hydraulic system used on the Grand Cherokee and 1994-96 Cherokee

To install:

11. Position the assembly into the vehicle.

12. Tighten the clutch master cylinder stud nuts to 200-300 inch lbs. (24-34 Nm).

13. Position the reservoir and tighten the screws.

14. Install the clutch master cylinder pushrod on the clutch pedal pin. Secure the rod with the wave washer, flat washer and retaining ring.

15. Raise and safely support the vehicle.

16. Insert the slave cylinder through the clutch housing into the release lever. Ensure the cap on the end of the rod is securely engaged in the lever. Tighten the bolts to 200-300 inch lbs. (24-34 Nm).

17. Insert the fluid line in the body clips.

Clutch Slave Cylinder

REMOVAL & INSTALLATION

Comanche, Wagoneer and 1984-93 Cherokee

1. Raise and support the vehicle safely.

2. Disconnect the hydraulic line at the cylinder. Cap the line.

3. Unbolt and remove the slave cylinder from the clutch housing.

To install:

4. Lubricate the throwout lever socket with chassis grease.

5. Align the pushrod with the throwout lever, position the slave cylinder on the clutch cover housing and install the cylinder attaching bolts. Tighten the mounting bolts to 16 ft. lbs. (22 Nm).

6. Connect the hydraulic line to the slave cylinder. Lower the vehicle.

7. Fill the reservoir with brake fluid and bleed the system.

Grand Cherokee and 1994-96 Cherokee

The clutch master cylinder, reservoir, slave cylinder and connecting lines are sealed units and are serviced as an assembly only. Refer to the Clutch Master Cylinder removal and installation procedure.

SYSTEM BLEEDING

On the Grand Cherokee and 1994-96 Cherokee, the clutch master cylinder, reservoir, slave cylinder and connecting lines are sealed units and are serviced as an assembly only. System bleeding is not necessary or possible.

1. Fill the reservoir with clean brake fluid.
2. Raise and support the truck on jackstands.

3. Remove the slave cylinder from the clutch housing, but do not disconnect the hydraulic line. There is enough play in the line to do this.
4. Remove the slave cylinder pushrod.
5. Using a wood dowel, compress the slave cylinder plunger.
6. Attach one end of a rubber hose to the slave cylinder bleeder screw and place the other end in a glass jar, filled halfway with clean brake fluid. Make sure that the hose will stay submerged.
7. Loosen the bleeder screw.
8. Have an assistant press and hold the clutch pedal to the floor. Tighten the bleeder screw with the pedal at the floor. Bubbles will have appeared in the jar when the pedal was depressed.
9. Have your assistant release the pedal, then perform the sequence again, until bubbles no longer appear in the jar.
10. Install the slave cylinder and lower the truck. Test the clutch.

AUTOMATIC TRANSMISSION

Understanding Automatic Transmissions

The automatic transmission allows engine torque and power to be transmitted to the rear wheels within a narrow range of engine operating speeds. The transmission will allow the engine to turn fast enough to produce plenty of power and torque at very low speeds, while keeping it at a sensible rpm at high vehicle speeds. The transmission performs this job entirely without driver assistance. The transmission uses a light fluid as the medium for the transmission of power. This fluid also works in the operation of various hydraulic control circuits and as a lubricant. Because the transmission fluid performs all of these functions, trouble within the unit can easily travel from one part to another. For this reason, and because of the complexity and unusual operating principles of the transmission, a very sound understanding of the basic principles of operation will simplify troubleshooting.

THE TORQUE CONVERTER

The torque converter replaces the conventional clutch. It has three functions:

1. It allows the engine to idle with the vehicle at a standstill, even with the transmission in gear.
2. It allows the transmission to shift from range to range smoothly, without requiring that the driver close the throttle during the shift.
3. It multiplies engine torque to an increasing extent as vehicle speed drops and throttle opening is increased. This has the effect of making the transmission more responsive and reduces the amount of shifting required.

The torque converter is a metal case which is shaped like a sphere that has been flattened on opposite sides. It is bolted to the rear end of the engine's crankshaft. Generally, the entire metal case rotates at engine speed and serves as the engine's flywheel.

The case contains three sets of blades. One set is attached directly to the case. This set forms the torus or pump. Another set is directly connected to the output shaft, and forms the turbine. The third set is mounted on a hub which, in turn, is mounted on a stationary shaft through a one-way clutch. This third set is known as the stator.

A pump, which is driven by the converter hub at engine speed, keeps the torque converter full of transmission fluid at all times. Fluid flows continuously through the unit to provide cooling.

Under low-speed acceleration, the torque converter functions as follows:

The torus is turning faster than the turbine. It picks up fluid at the center of the converter and, through centrifugal force, slings it outward. Since the outer edge of the converter moves faster than the portions at the center, the fluid picks up speed.

The fluid then enters the outer edge of the turbine blades. It then travels back toward the center of the converter case along the turbine blades. In impinging upon the turbine blades, the fluid loses the energy picked up in the torus.

If the fluid were now to immediately be returned directly into the torus, both halves of the converter would have to turn at approximately the same speed at all times, and torque input and output would both be the same.

In flowing through the torus and turbine, the fluid picks up two types of flow, or flow in two separate directions. It flows through the turbine blades, and it spins with the engine. The stator, whose blades are stationary when the vehicle is being accelerated at low speeds, converts one type of flow into another. Instead of allowing the fluid to flow straight back into the torus, the stator's curved blades turn the fluid almost 90 degrees toward the direction of rotation of the engine. Thus the fluid does not flow as fast toward the torus, but is already spinning when the torus picks it up. This has the effect of allowing the torus to turn much faster than the turbine. This difference in speed may be compared to the difference in speed between the smaller and larger gears in any gear train. The result is that engine power output is higher, and engine torque is multiplied.

As the speed of the turbine increases, the fluid spins faster and faster in the direction of engine rotation. As a result, the ability of the stator to redirect the fluid flow is reduced. Under cruising conditions, the stator is eventually forced to rotate on its one-way clutch in the direction of engine rotation. Under these conditions, the torque converter begins to behave almost like a solid shaft, with the torus and turbine speeds being almost equal.

THE PLANETARY GEARBOX

The ability of the torque converter to multiply engine torque is limited. Also, the unit tends to be more efficient when the turbine is rotating at relatively high speeds. Therefore, a planetary gearbox is used to carry the power output of the turbine to the driveshaft.

Planetary gears function very similarly to conventional transmission gears. However, their construction is different in that three elements make up one gear system, and, in that all three elements are different from one another. The three elements are: an outer gear that is shaped like a hoop, with teeth cut into the inner surface; a sun gear, mounted on a shaft and located at the very center of the outer gear; and a set of three planet gears, held by pins in a ring-like planet carrier, meshing with both the sun gear and the outer gear. Either the outer gear or the sun gear may be held stationary, providing more than one possible torque multiplication factor for each set of gears. Also, if all three gears are forced to rotate at the same speed, the gearset forms, in effect, a solid shaft.

Most modern automatics use the planetary gears to provide either a single reduction ratio of about 1.8:1, or two reduction gears: a low of about 2.5:1, and an intermediate of about 1.5:1. Bands and clutches are used to hold various portions of the gearsets to the transmission case or to the shaft on which they are mounted. Shifting is accomplished, then, by changing the portion of each planetary gearset which is held to the transmission case or to the shaft.

THE SERVOS AND ACCUMULATORS

The servos are hydraulic pistons and cylinders. They resemble the hydraulic actuators used on many familiar machines, such as bulldozers. Hydraulic fluid enters the cylinder, under pressure, and forces the piston to move to engage the band or clutches.

The accumulators are used to cushion the engagement of the servos. The transmission fluid must pass through the accumulator on the way to the servo. The accumulator housing contains a thin piston which is sprung away from the discharge passage of the accumulator. When fluid passes through the accumulator on the way to the servo, it must move the piston against spring pressure, and this action smooths out the action of the servo.

THE HYDRAULIC CONTROL SYSTEM

The hydraulic pressure used to operate the servos comes from the main transmission oil pump. This fluid is channeled to the various servos through the shift valves. There is generally a manual shift valve which is operated by the transmission selector lever and an automatic shift valve for each automatic upshift the transmission provides: i.e., two-speed automatics have a low-high shift valve, while three-speeds have a 1-2 valve, and a 2-3 valve.

There are two pressures which effect the operation of these valves. One is the governor pressure which is affected by vehicle speed. The other is the modulator pressure which is affected by intake manifold vacuum or throttle position. Governor pressure rises with an increase in vehicle speed, and modulator pressure rises as the throttle is opened wider. By responding to these two pressures, the shift valves cause the upshift points to be delayed with increased throttle opening to make the best use of the engine's power output.

Most transmissions also make use of an auxiliary circuit for downshifting. This circuit may be actuated by the throttle linkage or the vacuum line which actuates the modulator, or by a cable or solenoid. It applies pressure to a special downshift surface on the shift valve or valves.

The transmission modulator also governs the line pressure, used to actuate the servos. In this way, the clutches and bands will be actuated with a force matching the torque output of the engine.

Identification

Please refer to Section 1 for transmission identification.

Adjustments

SHIFT LINKAGE/CABLE

Except 30RH/32RH, 42RE/44RE and AW4 Models
▶ **See Figure 15**

1. Raise and support the truck on jackstands.
2. Loosen the shift rod trunnion locknuts.
3. Remove the lockpin retaining the shift rod trunnion to the bellcrank and disengage the trunnion and shift rod from the bellcrank.
4. Place the shift lever in **P** and lock the steering column.
5. Move the lever on the transmission rearward to the **P** detent. Park is the last possible rearward position.
6. Check to make sure that **P** is engaged, by trying to rotate the driveshaft by hand.
7. Adjust the shift rod trunnion so that the pin fits freely in the bellcrank arm and tighten the trunnion locknuts. Prevent the shift rod from turning while tightening the locknuts.

➡**All lash in the linkage must be eliminated to provide for proper adjustment. Lash can be eliminated by pulling downward on the shift rod and pressing upward on the bellcrank.**

8. Check that the engine starts in only the **P** and **N** positions, and that all shift ranges work properly.
9. Lower the truck.

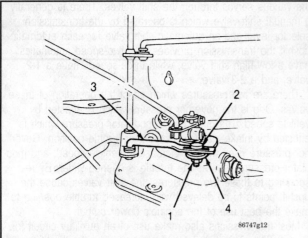

86747g12

Fig. 15 Loosen the locknut (1). Remove the lockpin retaining the shift rod. Disengage the trunnion (2) and shift rod (3) at the bellcrank (4)

30RH/32RH, 42RE/44RE and AW4 Models

▶ **See Figures 16 and 17**

1. Place gearshift lever in **P**.
2. Raise and support the vehicle safely.
3. Unlock the transmission shift control cable by prying upward on the T-shaped adjuster clamp to release.
4. Move the valve body manual lever rearward into P detent (last rearward detent). Ensure that vehicle is in **P** by attempting to rotate the driveshaft. The driveshaft should NOT rotate.
5. With the valve body manual lever in the **P** position, snap the cable into the lower reaction bracket.
6. Lock the cable by pressing the T-shaped adjuster clamp down until it snaps into place.
7. Check engine starting procedure to ensure engine will only start in **P** or **N**.
8. Lower vehicle.

PARK LOCK CABLE

▶ **See Figure 18**

Except 42RE/44RE

1. Shift the transmission into **P**.
2. Turn the ignition switch to the **LOCK** position.
3. Remove the shifter lever bezel and console screws. Raise the console for access to the cable.
4. Pull the cable lock button up to the release cable.
5. Pull the cable forward. Then release the cable and press the lock button down until it snaps in place.
6. Check the movement of the release shift handle button (floor shift) or release lever (column shift). You should not be able to press the button inward or move the column lever.
7. Turn the ignition to the **ON** position. Move the shift or column lever into **N**. If the cable adjustment is correct, ignition should not return to **LOCK** position. Recheck with the shift or column lever in the **D** position.
8. Move the shift or column lever to the **P** position. Ignition should now return to the **LOCK** position. With the ignition in the **LOCK** position, the shift or column lever should not move.

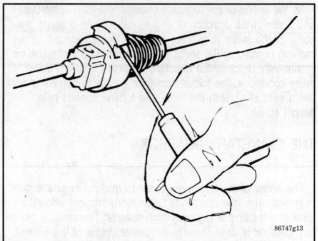

86747g13

Fig. 16 Unlock transmission shift control cable by prying upward on the T-shaped adjuster clamp to release

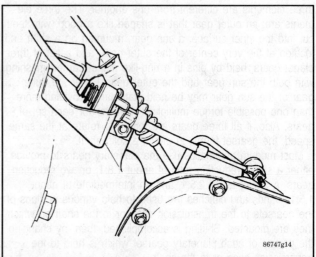

86747g14

Fig. 17 With the valve body manual lever in the P position, snap the cable into the lower reaction bracket

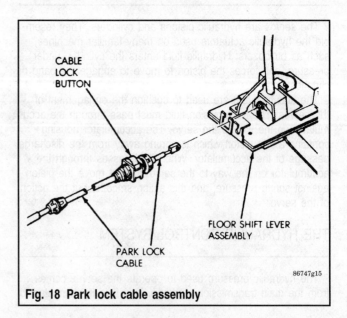

CABLE
LOCK
BUTTON

FLOOR SHIFT LEVER
ASSEMBLY

PARK LOCK
CABLE

86747g15

Fig. 18 Park lock cable assembly

42RE/44RE Models

1. Shift the transmission into **P**.
2. Turn ignition switch to the **ACC** position.
3. Remove the shifter lever bezel and console screws. Raise console for access to cable.
4. Pull the cable lock button up to release cable.
5. Pull the cable forward. Then release the cable and press the lock button down until it snaps in place.
6. With the shift lever in **P**, the ignition lock cylinder should move from **OFF** to **LOCK**. Cylinder should not rotate in any other position.
7. Turn the ignition to the **RUN** position. Press and hold the brake pedal. Check that the lever can be moved out of **P**.

THROTTLE LINKAGE

2.5L Engine with Chrysler 904 Transmission

▶ See Figures 19, 20 and 21

CARBURETED ENGINES

1. Disconnect the throttle control rod spring at the carburetor.
2. Raise and support the vehicle safely.
3. Use the spring to hold the transmission control lever forward against the stop.
4. Hook one end of another spring to the throttle control lever and the other end to the throttle linkage bellcrank bracket attached to the converter housing.
5. Lower the vehicle.
6. Block the choke open and set the throttle off of the fast idle cam.
7. Turn the ignition lock to **ON** to energize the solenoid.
8. Open the throttle halfway to allow the solenoid to lock and return the carburetor to idle.
9. Loosen the retaining bolt on the throttle control adjusting link. DO NOT REMOVE THE SPRING CLIP AND NYLON WASHER!
10. Pull on the end of the link to eliminate play and tighten the link retaining bolt.
11. Turn the ignition **OFF**.
12. Raise and support the truck on jackstands and remove the spring. Reconnect the spring in its original position.
13. Lower the truck.

TBI ENGINES

1. Place the ignition switch in the **OFF** position.
2. Raise and support the front end on jackstands.
3. Obtain a small, about 2 in. (51mm) long, coil spring. Hook one end of the spring on the throttle lever, next to the bellhousing, and the other end on the boss which projects from the side of the bellhousing.
4. Lower the truck.
5. Disconnect the Idle Speed Actuator motor (ISA) wiring harness, and connect the idle speed assembly exerciser box. When connected, the ADJUSTMENT light should go out, and the READY light should go on.
6. Press the RETRACK button. The system will, automatically, drive to the proper position with the ADJUST light on and the READY light off.

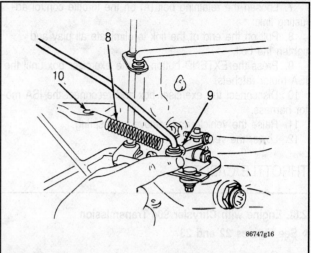

Fig. 19 Attach a spring (8) to the control lever (9) and the bellcrank bracket

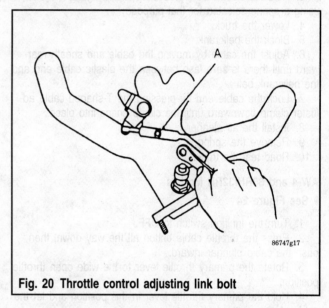

Fig. 20 Throttle control adjusting link bolt

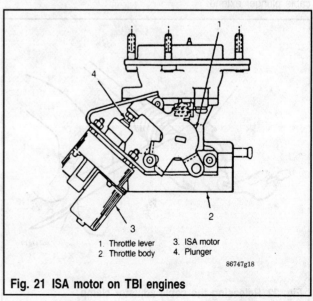

1. Throttle lever
2. Throttle body
3. ISA motor
4. Plunger

86747g18

Fig. 21 ISA motor on TBI engines

7. Loosen the retaining bolt (A) on the throttle control adjusting link.

8. Pull on the end of the link to eliminate all play and tighten the bolt.

9. Press the EXTEND button on the exerciser box until the ISA motor ratchets.

10. Disconnect the exerciser box and reconnect the ISA motor harness.

11. Raise the vehicle and remove your spring.

12. Lower the vehicle.

THROTTLE CABLE

2.8L Engine with Chrysler 904 Transmission

▶ See Figures 22 and 23

1. Remove the air cleaner.

2. Raise and support the truck on jackstands.

3. Hold the throttle control lever rearward against its stop, using a spring selected for that purpose.

4. Lower the truck.

5. Block the bellcrank.

6. Adjust the cable by moving the cable and sheath rearward until there is zero lash between the plastic cable end and the bellcrank ball.

7. Lock the cable end by pressing the T-shaped cable adjuster clamp downward until the clamp snaps into place.

8. Install the air cleaner.

9. Remove the spring.

10. Road test the truck.

AW-4 and 30RH/32RH Models

▶ See Figure 24

1. Turn the ignition switch to **OFF**.

2. Press the throttle cable button all the way down, then, push the cable plunger inward.

3. Rotate the primary throttle lever to the wide open throttle position.

4. Hold the primary throttle lever in this position and let the cable plunger extend.

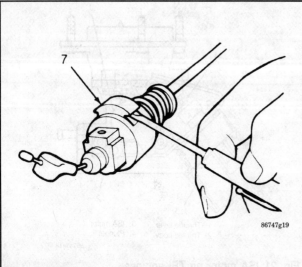

Fig. 22 Releasing the cable adjuster clamp

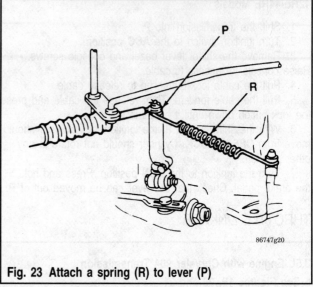

Fig. 23 Attach a spring (R) to lever (P)

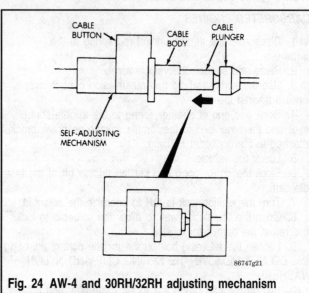

Fig. 24 AW-4 and 30RH/32RH adjusting mechanism

5. Release the lever when the plunger is fully extended.

6. The cable is now adjusted.

42RE/44RE Models

1. Turn the ignition switch to **OFF**.

2. Disconnect the cable from the stud.

3. Press the cable lock button inward to release the cable.

4. Center the end of the cable to the stud within 0.039 in. (1mm).

5. Install the cable onto the stud.

46RH Models

1. Turn the ignition switch to **OFF**.

2. Remove the air cleaner.

3. Position a 0.110-0.120 in. (2.8-3.0mm) feeler gauge between the idle stop and throttle lever.

4. Press the cable lock button to release the cable.

5. Raise the vehicle for access to the throttle valve lever.

6. Rotate the lever towards the front of the vehicle until the ratcheting sound stops.

7. Remove the feeler gauges and check the cable adjustment. The throttle lever should begin to move at the same time the lever on the throttle body moves off idle.

8. Lower the vehicle and install the air cleaner.

THROTTLE VALVE LEVER AND CABLE

2.1L Diesel Engines

▶ See Figures 25, 26 and 27

➡Special tool J-35514 and gauge J-35591 are necessary for this procedure.

1. Disconnect the throttle valve cable from the pin on the throttle valve lever.

2. Disconnect the cable from the transmission throttle lever. Remove and discard the cable.

3. Set the injection pump automatic advance lever at the curb idle position (seated against the stop).

4. Loosen the set screw and turn the cable clevis ¼ turn counterclockwise. Tighten the set screw.

5. Install the special tool as shown.

6. Loosen the thumbscrew on the tool and move the sliding legs rearward.

7. Place the notched leg of the tool on the cable bracket. Then, rest the sliding legs on the lever.

8. Move the sliding legs forward until the rear leg lightly touches the cable attaching pin. Tighten the thumbscrew.

9. Move the lever to the wide open throttle position. The cable attaching pin should now lightly touch the forward leg of the sliding legs.

10. If the cable attaching pin does not touch the forward leg, or if the pin tends to move the special tool, hold the lever in the wide open throttle position, loosen the two lever adjusting screws and move the lever to adjust the travel. Tighten the screws to 66 inch lbs. Return the lever to the curb idle position and verify that the pin is, again, lightly touching the rear leg of the sliding legs. If the pin doesn't touch the rear leg at curb idle, loosen the thumbscrew and adjust the tool so that it does, and repeat the adjustment.

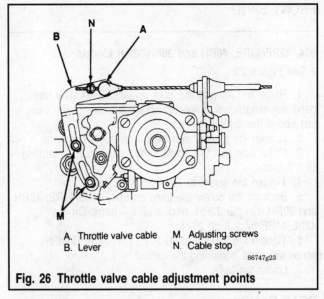

A. Throttle valve cable   M. Adjusting screws
B. Lever   N. Cable stop

86747g23

Fig. 26 Throttle valve cable adjustment points

11. Install a new throttle valve cable, part number 8953 001 796.

12. The new cable should be supplied with a cable stop, or one can be obtained from a lawn mower shop, motorcycle repair shop or small engines outlet. The throttle stop should have an inside diameter of 1.07mm.

13. The new cable has a factory installed cable stop crimped onto the end of the cable. Cut this off and slide the inner cable stop off the cable. Slide the new cable stop into place and hand tighten the set screw.

14. Connect the new cable to the throttle valve lever pin.

15. Obtain a small coil spring and use it to hold the throttle valve lever against its stop.

16. Loosen the cable stop and install gauge J-35591 between the cable stop and the retainer.

17. Remove all slack from the cable.

18. Slide the cable stop rearward against the gauge and retainer. Securely tighten the set screw and remove the gauge. Remove the spring that you used on the throttle lever. Loosen the clevis set screw and turn the clevis screw back ¼ turn.

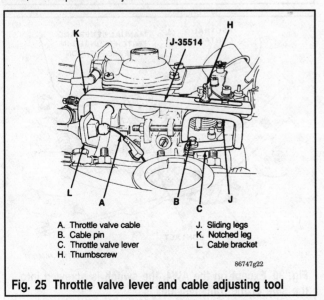

A. Throttle valve cable   J. Sliding legs
B. Cable pin   K. Notched leg
C. Throttle valve lever   L. Cable bracket
H. Thumbscrew

86747g22

Fig. 25 Throttle valve lever and cable adjusting tool

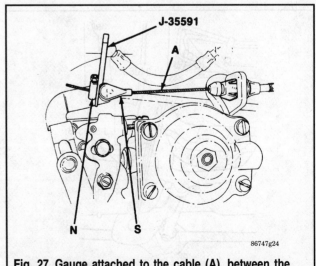

86747g24

Fig. 27 Gauge attached to the cable (A), between the cable stop (N) and retainer (S)

FRONT BAND

904, 42RE/44RE, 46RH and 30RH/32RH Models
▶ **See Figure 28**

1. Raise and support the truck on jackstands. The front band adjusting screw is located on the left side of the case, just above the control levers.
2. Loosen the locknut and back it off about five turns.
3. Make sure that the screw turns freely. Use penetrating oil if it binds.
4. Tighten the screw to 72 inch lbs. (8 Nm).
5. Back off the screw 2½ turns on 904, 42RE/44RE, 46RH and 30RH. On the 32RH, back it off 2¼ turns. On the 42RE/44RE back it off 2⅞ turns.
6. Tighten the locknut to 30 ft. lbs. (41 Nm). Hold the screw still while tightening the locknut.
7. Lower the truck.

REAR BAND

904, 42RE/44RE and 30RH/32RH Models
▶ **See Figure 29**

1. Raise and support the truck on jackstands.
2. Drain the fluid and remove the pan.
3. Remove the adjusting screw locknut.
4. Tighten the adjusting screw to 41 inch lbs. (5 Nm) on 904, 42RE/44RE and 30RH. On the 32RH, 46RH and 42RE/44RE, tighten it to 72 inch lbs. (8 Nm).
5. Back off the adjusting screw 7 turns on 904 and 30RH. On the 32RH back it off 4 turns. On the 42RE/44RE and 46RH, back it off 2 turns.
6. Hold the adjusting screw still and tighten the locknut to 35 ft. lbs. (47 Nm) on the 904. On the 30RH/32RH tighten it to 150 inch lbs. (17 Nm). On the 42RE/44RE and 46RH, tighten it to 25 ft. lbs. (34 Nm).
7. Install the pan and fill the unit with the appropriate fluid.

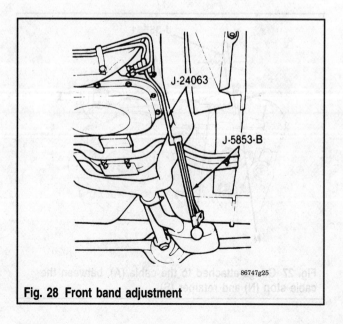

Fig. 28 Front band adjustment

Neutral Start/Back-Up Light Switch

REMOVAL & INSTALLATION

Except AW-4 Models
▶ **See Figure 30**

To replace the switch, simply unbolt it from the transmission, disconnect the wires and install a new switch.

AW-4 Models
▶ **See Figure 31**

1. Raise and support the front end on jackstands.
2. Disconnect the wiring at the switch.
3. Pry open the locktabs and remove the switch retaining nut and washer.
4. Remove the switch adjusting bolt.
5. Slide the switch off the manual valve shaft.

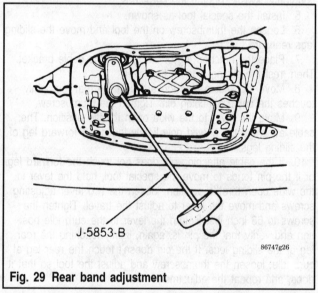

Fig. 29 Rear band adjustment

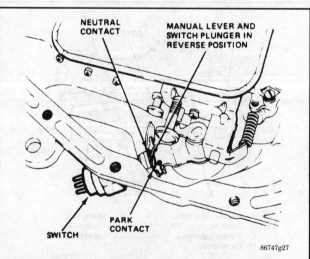

Fig. 30 Except on the AW4, the switch is screwed into the side of the transmission

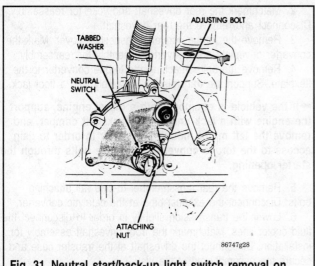

Fig. 31 Neutral start/back-up light switch removal on the AW4

To install:

6. Disconnect the shift linkage rod from the shift lever at the transmission.

7. Rotate the shift lever all the way rearward, then forward 2 detent positions to **N**.

8. Position the switch on the valve shaft and install the adjusting bolt finger-tight.

9. Install the washer and attaching nut and tighten the nut to 60 inch lbs. (7 Nm), but don't bend the tabbed washer yet.

10. Adjust the switch.

ADJUSTMENT

Except AW-4 Model

The switch is not adjustable on these transmissions.

AW-4 Models

▶ **See Figure 32**

1. Loosen the adjusting nut.

2. With the transmission in neutral, rotate the switch to align the neutral standard line with the groove on the valve shaft.

3. Hold the switch in this position and tighten the adjusting bolt to 108 inch lbs. (12 Nm).

4. Bend the tabbed washer over the retaining nut.

5. Connect the shift linkage rod.

6. Connect the switch wiring.

7. Check the switch operation. The engine should start in **P** and **N** only.

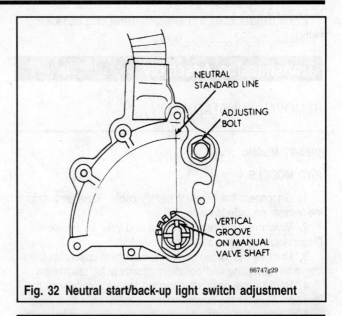

Fig. 32 Neutral start/back-up light switch adjustment

Extension Housing Seal

REMOVAL & INSTALLATION

2WD Models

The extension housing seal on 2-wheel drive vehicles is located at the rear of the transmission tail shaft.

1. Raise and support the vehicle safely.

2. Drain the transmission fluid, if necessary.

➡**In most cases it is not necessary to drain the transmission of fluid to change the seal. However, some fluid may leak out during the procedure.**

3. Matchmark the driveshaft to the yoke for reassembly and remove driveshaft.

4. Remove the old seal using a seal puller or appropriate prytool.

To install:

5. Install a new seal, coated with sealing compound, using an appropriate seal installation tool.

6. Install the driveshaft, making certain to align the matchmark. Tighten bolts to 20 ft. lbs. (27 Nm).

7. Fill the transmission fluid to the proper level.

4WD Models

The extension seal on 4-wheel drive vehicles is located at the rear of the transfer case.

1. Raise and support the vehicle safely.

2. Drain transfer case of lubricant.

3. Matchmark driveshaft to yoke for reassembly and remove driveshaft.

4. Remove old seal using a seal puller or appropriate prytool.

5. Install a new seal, coated with sealing compound, using an appropriate seal installation tool.

6. Install the driveshaft, making certain to align matchmark. Tighten bolts to 20 ft. lbs. (27 Nm).

7. Fill transfer case with lubricant. Install plug and lower vehicle.

Transmission Assembly

REMOVAL & INSTALLATION

1984-91 Models

2WD MODELS

1. Disconnect the negative battery cable. Raise and support the vehicle on jackstands.
2. Matchmark the rear driveshaft and yoke for reassembly. Disconnect and remove the rear driveshaft.
3. Remove the torque converter inspection cover. Mark the converter driveplate and converter assembly for reassembly.
4. Remove the bolts attaching the torque converter to the flexplate. Support the transmission assembly on a floor jack.
5. Remove the bolts attaching the rear crossmember to the transmission side rail. Disconnect the exhaust pipe at the catalytic converter.
6. Lower the transmission slightly in order to disconnect the fluid cooler lines.
7. Disconnect the backup light switch wire and the speedometer cable. Disconnect the transmission linkage.
8. Remove the bolts attaching the transmission assembly to the engine. Move the transmission assembly and the torque converter rearward to clear the crankshaft.
9. Carefully lower the transmission assembly from the vehicle.

To install:

10. Carefully raise the transmission into position.
11. Install the bolts attaching the transmission assembly to the engine. Tighten the bolts to 25 ft. lbs. (34 Nm) for the 904. On the AW-4, tighten the 10mm bolts to 25 ft. lbs. (34 Nm); the 12mm bolts to 42 ft. lbs. (57 Nm).
12. Connect the backup light switch wire.
13. Connect the speedometer cable.
14. Connect the transmission linkage.
15. Connect the fluid cooler lines.
16. Install the rear crossmember. Tighten the crossmember bolts to 30 ft. lbs. (41 Nm); the transmission-to-crossmember bolts to 33 ft. lbs. (48 Nm).
17. Connect the exhaust pipe at the catalytic converter.
18. Install the bolts attaching the torque converter to the flexplate. Tighten the bolts to 40 ft. lbs. (54 Nm).
19. Remove the floor jack.
20. Install the torque converter inspection cover.
21. Install the driveshaft. Tighten the nuts to 14 ft. lbs. (19 Nm).

➡**New strap bolts must be used every time the driveshaft is disconnected.**

22. Lower the truck.
23. Connect the negative battery cable.

4WD MODELS

1. Disconnect the negative battery cable. Raise and support the vehicle safely.

2. Matchmark the rear driveshaft and yoke for reassembly. Disconnect and remove the rear driveshaft.
3. Remove the torque converter inspection cover. Mark the converter driveplate and converter assembly for reassembly.
4. Remove the bolts attaching the torque converter to the flexplate. Support the transmission assembly with a floor jack.

➡**If the vehicle is equipped with a diesel engine, support the engine with a jack under the crankshaft damper, and remove the left motor mount and starter in order to gain access to the torque converter driveplate bolts through the starter opening.**

5. Remove the rear crossmember-to-side rail attaching bolts. Disconnect the exhaust pipe at the catalytic converter.
6. Lower the transmission slightly in order to disconnect the fluid cooler lines. Matchmark the front driveshaft assembly for installation. Disconnect the driveshaft at the transfer case and secure the assembly out of the way.
7. Disconnect the backup light switch wire and the speedometer cable. Disconnect the transfer case and the transmission linkage. Disconnect the vacuum lines and the vent hose.
8. Remove the bolts attaching the transmission assembly to the engine. Move the transmission assembly and the torque converter rearward to clear the crankshaft.
9. Carefully lower the transmission assembly from the vehicle. Separate the transfer case from the transmission assembly.

To install:

10. If the transmission and transfer case were separated, reassemble the components and tighten the bolts to 26 ft. lbs. (35 Nm).
11. Carefully raise the transmission into position.
12. Install the bolts attaching the transmission assembly to the engine. Tighten the bolts to 25 ft. lbs. (34 Nm) for the 904. On the AW-4, tighten the 10mm bolts to 25 ft. lbs. (34 Nm); the 12mm bolts to 42 ft. lbs. (57 Nm).
13. Connect the backup light switch wire and the speedometer cable.
14. Connect the transfer case and the transmission linkage.
15. Connect the vacuum lines and the vent hose.
16. Connect the fluid cooler lines.
17. Connect the rear driveshaft to the transfer case. Tighten the strap bolt nuts to 14 ft. lbs. (19 Nm); the flange-to-case bolts to 35 ft. lbs. (47 Nm).

➡**New strap bolts must be used everytime the driveshaft is disconnected.**

18. Install the rear crossmember. Tighten the crossmember attaching bolts to 30 ft. lbs. (41 Nm); the transmission-to-crossmember bolts to 33 ft. lbs. (45 Nm).
19. Connect the exhaust pipe at the catalytic converter.
20. Install the bolts attaching the torque converter to the flexplate. Tighten the bolts to 40 ft. lbs. (54 Nm)
21. Remove the floor jack.
22. Install the torque converter inspection cover.
23. If the vehicle is equipped with a diesel engine, install the left motor mount and starter.
24. Lower the truck.
25. Connect the negative battery cable.

1992-96 Cherokee and Comanche

2WD MODELS

1. Disconnect the negative battery cable.
2. Raise and support the vehicle safely.
3. Matchmark the rear driveshaft and yoke for reassembly.
4. Disconnect and remove the rear driveshaft.
5. Remove the torque converter inspection cover.
6. Matchmark the converter driveplate and converter assembly for reassembly.
7. Remove the bolts attaching the torque converter to the flexplate.
8. Remove the starter.
9. Support the transmission assembly using a jack.
10. Remove the bolts attaching the rear crossmember to the transmission side rail.
11. Disconnect the exhaust pipe at the catalytic converter.
12. Lower the transmission slightly in order to disconnect the fluid cooler lines.
13. Disconnect the backup light switch wire and speedometer cable.
14. Disconnect the transmission linkage.
15. Remove the bolts attaching the transmission assembly to the engine.
16. Move the transmission assembly and the torque converter rearward to clear the crankshaft.
17. Carefully lower the transmission assembly from the vehicle.

To install:

18. Carefully raise the transmission into position.
19. Install the bolts attaching the transmission assembly to the engine. Tighten the bolts to:
    - 10mm bolts: 25 ft. lbs. (34 Nm)
    - 12mm bolts: 42 ft. lbs. (57 Nm)
20. Connect the backup light switch wire.
21. Connect the speedometer cable.
22. Connect the transmission linkage.
23. Connect the fluid cooler lines.
24. Install the rear crossmember. Tighten the crossmember bolts to 30 ft. lbs. (41 Nm); the transmission-to-crossmember bolts to 33 ft. lbs. (45 Nm).
25. Connect the exhaust pipe at the catalytic converter.
26. Install the bolts attaching the torque converter to the flexplate. Tighten the bolts to 40 ft. lbs. (54 Nm).
27. Install the starter.
28. Remove the transmission jack.
29. Install the torque converter inspection cover.
30. Install the driveshaft. New strap bolts should be used every time the driveshaft is disconnected. Tighten the nuts to 14 ft. lbs. (19 Nm).
31. Lower the vehicle.
32. Connect the negative battery cable.

4WD MODELS

1. Disconnect the negative battery cable.
2. Raise and support the vehicle safely.
3. Matchmark the rear driveshaft and yoke for reassembly. Disconnect and remove the rear driveshaft.
4. Remove the torque converter inspection cover.
5. Matchmark the converter driveplate and converter assembly for reassembly.

6. Remove the bolts attaching the torque converter to the flexplate.
7. Support the transmission assembly with a jack.
8. Remove the bolts attaching the rear crossmember to the transmission side rail.
9. Disconnect the exhaust pipe at the catalytic converter.
10. Lower the transmission slightly in order to disconnect the fluid cooler lines.
11. Matchmark the front driveshaft assembly for installation.
12. Disconnect the driveshaft at the transfer case and secure the assembly aside.
13. Disconnect the backup light switch wire and speedometer cable.
14. Disconnect the transfer case and transmission linkage.
15. Disconnect the vacuum lines and vent hose.
16. Remove the bolts attaching the transmission assembly to the engine.
17. Move the transmission assembly and torque converter rearward to clear the crankshaft.
18. Carefully lower the transmission assembly from the vehicle.
19. Remove the transfer case retaining bolts from the transmission assembly.

To install:

20. If the transmission and transfer case were separated, re-attach them and tighten the bolts to 26 ft. lbs. (35 Nm).
21. Carefully raise the transmission into position.
22. Install the bolts attaching the transmission assembly to the engine. Tighten the bolts to:
    - 10mm bolts: 25 ft. lbs. (34 Nm)
    - 12mm bolts: 42 ft. lbs. (57 Nm)
23. Connect the backup light switch wire and speedometer cable.
24. Connect the transfer case and transmission linkage.
25. Connect the vacuum lines and the vent hose.
26. Connect the fluid cooler lines.
27. Connect the driveshaft at the transfer case. New strap bolts should be used whenever the driveshaft is disconnected. Tighten the strap bolt nuts to 14 ft. lbs (19 Nm); the flange-to-case bolts to 35 ft. lbs. (48 Nm).
28. Install the rear crossmember. Tighten the crossmember attaching bolts to 30 ft. lbs. (41 Nm); the transmission-to-crossmember bolts to 33 ft. lbs. (45 Nm).
29. Connect the exhaust pipe at the catalytic converter.
30. Install the bolts attaching the torque converter to the flexplate. Tighten the bolts to 40 ft. lbs. (61 Nm).
31. Remove the floor jack.
32. Install the torque converter inspection cover.
33. Install the rear driveshaft. Use new strap bolts. Tighten the strap bolt nuts to 14 ft. lbs. (19 Nm); the flange bolts to 35 ft. lbs. (48 Nm).
34. Lower the vehicle.
35. Connect the negative battery cable.

1993-96 Grand Cherokee/Wagoneer

2WD MODELS

1. Disconnect the negative battery cable.
2. Raise and support the vehicle safely.
3. If equipped, remove the skid plate.
4. If the transmission is being removed for repair, drain the fluid and reinstall the pan.

5. Matchmark the driveshaft yoke and remove the driveshaft.

6. Disconnect the vehicle speed wires, transmission solenoid wires and park-neutral position switch wires.

7. Disconnect the wires from the transmission speed sensor at the rear of the overdrive unit.

8. Remove the exhaust Y-pipe.

9. Unclip the wire harness from the transmission clips.

10. Disconnect the throttle valve and gearshift cables from the levers on the valve body manual shaft. Position the cables aside and secure them to the underbody.

11. Remove the dust cover from the transmission converter housing.

12. Remove the starter.

13. Remove the bolts attaching the converter to the driveplate.

14. Disconnect the cooler fluid lines from the transmission.

15. Support the transmission with a jack.

16. Remove the nuts and bolts securing the rear crossmember to the insulator and remove the crossmember.

17. Lower the jack to gain access to the upper portion of the transmission.

18. Remove the crankshaft position sensor.

19. Remove the transmission fill tube and discard the O-ring.

20. Remove the bolts attaching the transmission to the engine.

21. Slide the transmission back and secure a C-clamp to the converter.

22. Remove the transmission.

To install:

23. Ensure the torque converter hub and hub drive are free from sharp edges, scratches or nicks. Polish with 400 grit sandpaper if necessary.

24. Lubricate the converter hub and pump seal with high temperature grease.

25. Secure the C-clamp to the converter.

26. Ensure the dowel pins are seated in the engine block and protrude far enough to align the transmission.

27. Align the transmission with the engine dowels and converter with the driveplate. Install 2 transmission bolts to keep it in place.

28. Remove the C-clamp and install the torque converter bolts. Tighten the bolts to:
   • 3 lug converter — 40 ft. lbs. (54 Nm)
   • 4 lug converter — 270 inch lbs. (31 Nm)

29. Install and tighten the remaining transmission-to-engine bolts.

30. Install the crankshaft position sensor.

31. Install the dust cover on the converter housing.

32. Install the starter.

33. Connect the transmission shift and throttle valve cables to the transmission.

34. Fasten the wire harness to the transmission.

35. Engage the harness connectors unplugged during removal.

36. Install the transmission filler tube with a new O-ring.

37. Install the rear crossmember.

38. Connect the fluid cooler lines to the transmission.

39. Align and install the driveshaft.

40. Install the exhaust system components.

41. Lower the vehicle.

42. Connect the negative battery cable.

43. Check the transmission control cables; adjust if necessary.

44. If the transmission fluid was drained, fill the transmission with fluid to the proper level.

4WD MODELS

1. Disconnect the negative battery cable.

2. Raise and support the vehicle safely.

3. If equipped, remove the skid plate.

4. If the transmission is being removed for repair, drain the fluid and reinstall the pan.

5. Matchmark the driveshaft yokes and remove both driveshafts.

6. Disconnect the vehicle speed wires, transmission solenoid wires and park-neutral position switch wires.

7. Unclip the wire harness from the transmission clips.

8. Disconnect the transfer case shift linkage from the lever. Remove the linkage and bracket from the transfer case. Position the linkage aside.

9. Remove the nuts attaching the transfer case to the overdrive unit gear case.

10. Place a jack under the transfer case and remove the case.

11. Support the transmission with the jack.

12. Remove the rear transmission crossmember.

13. Remove the exhaust Y-pipe.

14. Remove the crankshaft position sensor.

15. Disconnect the gearshift linkage from the lever on the transmission.

16. Remove the transmission shift linkage torque shaft assembly from the transmission and frame rail. Position it aside.

17. Remove the transmission-to-engine brackets.

18. Remove the dust cover from the transmission converter housing.

19. Remove the starter.

20. Remove the bolts attaching the converter to the driveplate.

21. Disconnect the cooler fluid lines from the transmission.

22. Disconnect the solenoid and park/neutral position switch wires.

23. Remove the transmission fill tube and discard the O-ring.

24. Lower the jack to gain access to the upper portion of the transmission.

25. Remove the bolts attaching the transmission to the engine.

26. Slide the transmission back and secure a C-clamp to the converter.

27. Move the transmission rearward until it clears the engine block dowels.

➡**On some models, part of the flange joining the vehicle cab and dash panel may interfere with transmission removal. If necessary peen this part of the flange over with a mallet.**

28. Remove the transmission.

To install:

29. Ensure the torque converter hub and hub drive are free from sharp edges, scratches or nicks. Polish with 400 grit sandpaper if necessary.

30. Lubricate the converter hub and pump seal with high temperature grease.

31. Secure the C-clamp to the converter.

32. Ensure the dowel pins are seated in the engine block and protrude far enough to align the transmission.

33. Align the transmission with the engine dowels and converter with the driveplate. Install 2 transmission bolts to keep it in place.

34. Remove the C-clamp and install the torque converter bolts. Tighten the bolts as follows:
- 3 lug converter — 40 ft. lbs. (54 Nm)
- 4 lug, except 10.75 inch converter — 55 ft. lbs. (74 Nm)
- 4 lug, 10.75 inch converter — 270 inch lbs. (31 Nm)

35. Install the starter.

36. Install the strut brackets securing the transmission to the engine and front axle.

37. Install and tighten the remaining transmission-to-engine bolts.

38. Install the crankshaft position sensor.

39. Install the transmission filler tube with a new O-ring.

40. Install the exhaust system components.

41. Install the shift linkage torque bracket.

42. Connect the shift linkage to the transmission.

43. Connect the harness connectors disconnected during removal.

44. Install the rear crossmember.

45. Install the transfer case. Tighten the nuts as follows:
- ³/₈ stud nuts — 35 ft. lbs. (47 Nm)
- ⁵/₁₆ stud nuts — 26 ft. lbs. (35 Nm)

46. Install the damper on the transfer case rear retainer if removed. Tighten the nuts to 40 ft. lbs. (54 Nm).

47. Connect the transfer case shift linkage.

48. Connect the fluid cooler lines to the transmission.

49. Align and install the driveshafts. Tighten the U-joint clamp bolts to 170 inch lbs. (19 Nm).

50. Fill the transfer case to the proper level with fluid.

51. Lower the vehicle.

52. Connect the negative battery cable.

53. Fill the transmission to the proper level with the appropriate fluid.

54. Check the transmission control cables, adjust if necessary.

55. Check and adjust the transmission and transfer case shift linkage.

TRANSFER CASE

Identification

NP-207

The Model 207 transfer case is an aluminum case, chain drive, 4 position unit providing 4WD High and Low ranges, a 2WD High range and a Neutral position. The 207 is a part-time 4WD unit used with the Command-Trac® System. Range positions are selected by a floor mounted shift lever. Dexron® II automatic transmission fluid, or equivalent, is the recommended lubricant.

NP-228

The Model 228 transfer case is very similar to the Model 229 full-time transfer case used on other Jeep vehicles. The main difference in these cases is that the 228 uses a differential unit in place of a viscous coupling. It also uses modified shift collars to prevent engine run away during a delayed shift.

The 228 is used with the Selec-Trac® System. A vacuum shift motor disconnect system is connected to the transfer case to disengage the front differential. The unit operates full-time or part-time and uses Dexron® II automatic transmission fluid, or equivalent, as a lubricant.

NP-229

The Model 229 full-time transfer case has viscous torque biasing control capability. This is accomplished with a non-servicable, sealed viscous coupling, which provides a limited-slip feature for the inter-axle differential located between the front and rear output shafts.

The 229 is used with the Selec-Trac® System. It requires 3.5 qts. of Dexron® II automatic transmission fluid for lubrication.

NP-231

The Model 231 is a part-time transfer case with a built in low range gear reduction system. A front axle disconnect mechanism is used for 2-wheel drive operation. The 231 is used with the Command-Trac® System.

The 231 has three operating ranges, 2-wheel drive High and 4-wheel drive High and Low, plus Neutral. The 4-wheel drive operating ranges are undifferentiated. Dexron® II automatic transmission fluid, or equivalent, is used as a lubricant.

NP-242

The Model 242 is a full-time transfer case with four operating ranges plus a Neutral position. Used primarily on the Cherokee/Wagoneer, it provides 2-wheel drive and full-time four wheel drive operation. An inter-axle differential is used to control torque transfer to the front and rear axles.

The differential has a locking mechanism for undifferentiated 4-wheel drive in High and Low ranges. These ranges include 2-wheel drive, 4-wheel drive part-time, 4-wheel drive full-time, and 4-wheel drive Low. Dexron® II automatic transmission fluid, or equivalent, is used as a lubricant.

NP-249

The NP-249 is similar to the NP-242. The primary difference is the NP-249 uses a viscous coupling rather than an inter-axle differential.

Adjustments

RANGE CONTROL LINKAGE ADJUSTMENT

NP-207 Models
▶ See Figure 33

1. Place the range control lever in the **2WD** position.
2. Insert a ⅛ in. (3mm) spacer between the gate and the lever.
3. Hold the lever in this position.
4. Place the transfer case lever in the **2WD** position.
5. Adjust the link, at the trunnion, to provide a free pin at the case outer lever.

NP-228 and 229 Models
▶ See Figure 34

1. Place the range control lever in the **HIGH** position.
2. Insert a ⅛ in. (3mm) spacer between the shift gate and the lever.
3. Hold the lever in this position with tape.
4. Raise and support the vehicle safely.
5. Verify that the range lever is in the **HIGH** position.
6. Loosen the locknut and adjust the link, at the trunnion, to provide a free pin at the case outer lever. Tighten the locknut.
7. Lower the vehicle. Remove the spacer.

NP-231 and 242 Models
▶ See Figure 35

1. Remove the shifter lever bezel.
2. Place the range control lever in the **4 LOW** position.
3. Insert a ⅛ in. (4mm) spacer between the forward edge of the shift gate and the lever.
4. Hold the lever in this position with tape.

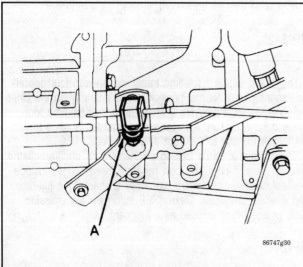

Fig. 33 NP-207 range control adjustment point (A)

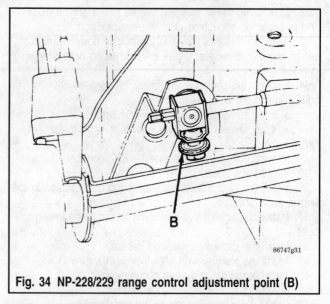

Fig. 34 NP-228/229 range control adjustment point (B)

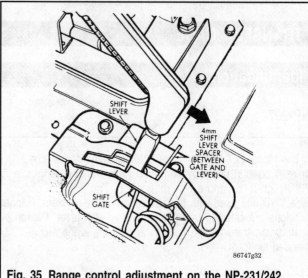

Fig. 35 Range control adjustment on the NP-231/242

5. Raise and support the vehicle safely.
6. Loosen the trunnion lock bolt. The linkage rod should now slide freely in the trunnion.
7. Position the linkage rod so it is free in the range lever. Then tighten the locknut.
8. Lower the vehicle. Remove the spacer.

NP-249 Models

1. Place the range control lever in the **N** position.
2. Raise and support the vehicle safely.
3. Loosen the trunnion lockbolt. The linkage rod should now slide freely in the trunnion.
4. Verify the shift lever on the transfer case is centered in the **N** position.
5. Tighten the lockbolt to 96-180 inch lbs. (11-20 Nm).
6. Lower the vehicle. Remove the spacer.

MODE ROD ADJUSTMENT

NP-228 and 229 Models
▶ See Figure 36

✳✳WARNING

If this adjustment is not properly made, the transfer case may not fully engage 2WD/HIGH and internal damage will result.

1. Fully engage the **2WD/HIGH** position.
2. Refer to the accompanying illustration. The range lever and the mode lever must be aligned on the same centerline.

➡**To correctly position the mode lever, it is sometimes necessary to rotate the transfer case output shaft. To do this, raise and support the rear end on jackstands and rotate the rear driveshaft, while applying a load on the mode lever. Doing this will help align the spline for full engagement of 2WD/HIGH.**

3. Adjust the length of the mode rod (4) to approximately 6 in. (152mm), to eliminate all free play.
4. Make sure all vacuum lines are secure.
5. Drive the vehicle a short distance, shifting between **4WD** and **2WD/HIGH**.
6. Check the mode lever position. The lever should be aligned as explained in Step 2. If not, repeat Steps 3 through 5, increasing the length of the mode rod one turn, until proper alignment is achieved.
7. With the transfer case vacuum motor shift rod fully extended and the transfer case in **2WD/HIGH**, adjust the mode rod so that the pin (6) moves freely in its hole.

SHIFT MOTOR REPLACEMENT

▶ See Figure 37

1. Disconnect the shift motor link from the range lever.

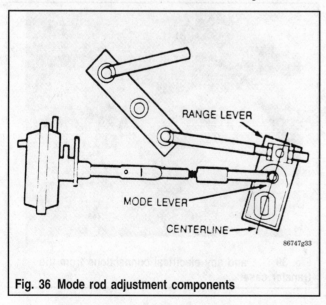

86747g33

Fig. 36 Mode rod adjustment components

2. Remove and discard the lever grommet.
3. Remove the nut and bolt attaching the shift motor bracket to the case and remove the bracket and motor as an assembly.
4. Slide the shift motor boot aside and remove the E-ring that retains the motor in the bracket.
5. Disconnect the vacuum lines from the motor. Remove the motor.

To install:

6. Position the motor in the bracket and install the E-ring.
7. Install the boot, if removed.
8. Connect the vacuum lines to the motor.
9. Position the motor and bracket assembly on the case and install the bracket attaching nut and bolt.
10. Install a new grommet in the range lever and connect the shift motor link to the lever.

Transfer Case Assembly

REMOVAL & INSTALLATION

▶ See Figures 38 and 39

New Process 207

1. Shift the case into **4H**.
2. Raise and support the vehicle safely.
3. Drain the case.
4. Matchmark the rear driveshaft and remove it.
5. Disconnect the speedometer cable, vacuum hoses and vent hose from the case.
6. Support the transmission with a floor jack.
7. Remove the crossmember.
8. Matchmark the front driveshaft and remove it.
9. Disconnect the shift lever linkage rod at the case.
10. Remove the shift lever bracket bolts.
11. Support the transfer case with a floor jack or transmission jack and remove the attaching bolts.
12. Remove the transfer case from the vehicle.

To install:

13. Raise the transfer case into position. Tighten the attaching bolts to 26 ft. lbs. (35 Nm).
14. Connect the shift lever linkage rod at the case.
15. Install the shift lever bracket bolts.
16. Install the front driveshaft. Tighten the nuts to 14 ft. lbs. (19 Nm). Tighten the flange bolts to 35 ft. lbs. (47 Nm).

➡**New strap bolts must be installed each time the driveshaft is removed.**

17. Install the crossmember. Tighten the crossmember-to-frame bolts to 30 ft. lbs. (41 Nm); the crossmember-to-transmission bolts to 33 ft. lbs. (48 Nm).
18. Remove the floor jack.
19. Connect the speedometer cable, vacuum hoses and vent hose at the case.
20. Install the rear driveshaft. Use new strap bolts, tightened to 14 ft. lbs. (19 Nm). Tighten the flange bolts to 35 ft. lbs. (47 Nm).
21. Fill the case.
22. Lower the truck.

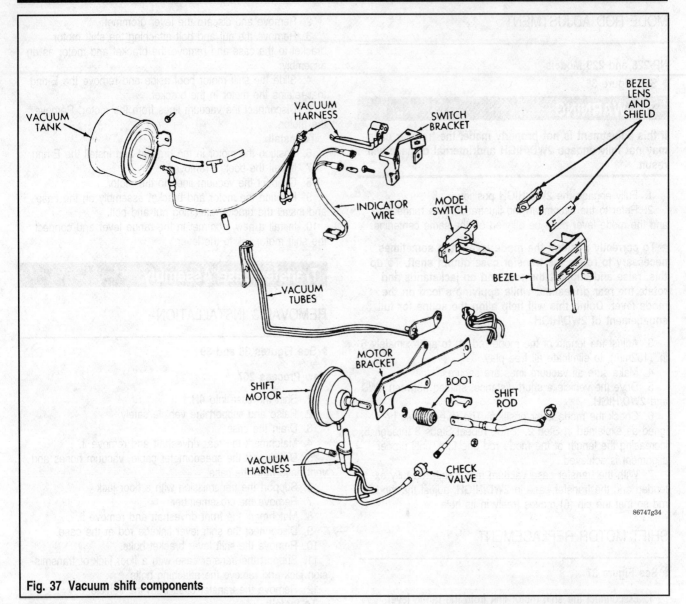

Fig. 37 Vacuum shift components

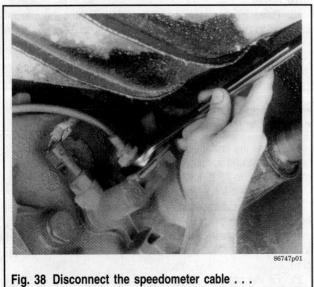

Fig. 38 Disconnect the speedometer cable . . .

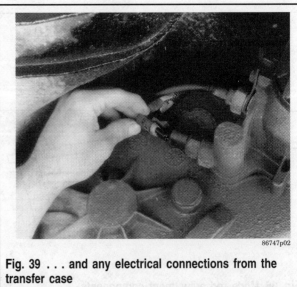

Fig. 39 . . . and any electrical connections from the transfer case

New Process 228

1. Raise and support the vehicle safely.
2. Drain the lubricant from the transfer case.
3. Disconnect the speedometer cable, vacuum hoses and vent hose from the case.
4. Disconnect the shift lever linkage rod at the case.
5. Support the transmission with a floor jack. Remove the rear crossmember.
6. Matchmark the front and rear driveshafts and remove.
7. Disconnect the shift motor vacuum hoses.
8. Remove the shift lever bracket bolts.
9. Support the transfer case with a floor jack or transmission jack and remove the attaching bolts.
10. Pull the case rearward out of the truck.
   To install:
11. Position the transfer case in the truck. Tighten the attaching bolts to 40 ft. lbs. (54 Nm).

➡ **DO NOT install any transfer case attaching bolts until the transfer case is completely seated in the transmission**

12. Install the shift lever bracket bolts.
13. Install the front and rear driveshafts. Tighten the strap bolt nuts to 14 ft. lbs. (19 Nm); the flange nuts to 35 ft. lbs. (47 Nm).

➡ **New strap bolts must be installed each time the driveshaft is removed.**

14. Install the rear crossmember. Tighten the crossmember-to-frame bolts to 30 ft. lbs. (41 Nm); the transmission-to-crossmember bolts to 33 ft. lbs. (48 Nm).
15. Connect the shift lever linkage rod at the case.
16. Connect the speedometer cable, vacuum hoses and vent hose from the case.
17. Connect the shift motor vacuum hoses.
18. Lower the truck. Fill the case with lubricant.

New Process 229

1. Raise and support the vehicle safely.
2. Drain the case.
3. Disconnect the speedometer cable and vent hose. Disconnect the shift lever link at the operating lever.
4. Support the transmission with a floor jack.
5. Remove the rear crossmember.
6. Matchmark the driveshafts and remove them.
7. Disconnect the shift motor vacuum hoses.
8. Disconnect the shift linkage at the case.
9. Support the transfer case with a floor jack or transmission jack and remove the attaching bolts.
10. Pull the case rearward and remove it.
11. Clean the gasket mating surfaces and use new gasket material for installation.
   To install:
12. Raise the transfer case into position. Tighten the bolts to 26 ft. lbs. (35 Nm).

➡ **Make certain that the case and transmission are mated without binding, before torquing the attaching bolts.**

13. Connect the shift linkage at the case.
14. Connect the shift motor vacuum hoses.

15. Install the driveshafts. Tighten the nuts to 14 ft. lbs. (19 Nm); tighten the flange nuts to 35 ft. lbs. (47 Nm).

➡ **New strap bolts must be installed each time the driveshaft is removed.**

16. Install the rear crossmember. Tighten the crossmember-to-frame bolts to 30 ft. lbs. (41 Nm); the transmission-to-crossmember bolts to 33 ft. lbs. (45 Nm).
17. Remove the transmission floor jack.
18. Connect the speedometer cable and vent hose.
19. Connect the shift lever link at the operating lever.
20. Fill the case with lubricant and lower the truck.

New Process 231

1. Shift the case into **N**.
2. Raise and support the truck on jackstands.
3. Drain the lubricant.
4. Matchmark and remove the front and rear driveshafts.
5. Support the transmission with a jackstand.
6. Remove the rear crossmember.
7. Disconnect the speedometer cable.
8. Disconnect the linkage.
9. Disconnect the vent and vacuum hoses and the indicator wire.
10. Support the transfer case with a transmission jack. Make sure that the case is secured to the jack with chains.
11. Remove the transfer case-to-transmission bolts.
12. Pull the case rearward to disengage it and lower it from the truck.
   To install:
13. Raise the transfer case into position. Make certain that the case and transmission are mated without binding, before torquing the attaching bolts. Tighten the bolts to 26 ft. lbs. (35 Nm).
14. Connect the shift linkage at the case.
15. Connect the vacuum hoses.
16. Install the driveshafts. Tighten the nuts to 14 ft. lbs. (19 Nm); tighten the flange nuts to 35 ft. lbs. (47 Nm).

➡ **New strap bolts must be used each time the driveshaft is removed.**

17. Install the rear crossmember. Tighten the bolts to 30 ft. lbs. (41 Nm).
18. Remove the transmission floor jack.
19. Connect the speedometer cable and vent hose.
20. Connect the shift lever link at the operating lever.
21. Fill the case.
22. Lower the truck.

New Process 242 and 249

1. Shift transfer case into **N**.
2. Raise and support the vehicle safely.
3. Drain the lubricant.
4. Matchmark and remove the front and rear driveshafts.
5. Raise and support the transmission with a floor jack.
6. Remove the rear crossmember.
7. Disconnect the speedometer cable.
8. Disconnect the linkage.
9. Disconnect the vent and vacuum hoses and the indicator wire.

10. Support the transfer case with a transmission jack. Make sure that the case is secured to the jack with chains.

11. Remove the transfer case-to-transmission bolts.

12. Pull the case rearward to disengage it and lower it from the truck.

To install:

13. Raise the transfer case into position. Tighten the bolts to 26 ft. lbs. (35 Nm).

➡**Make certain that the case and transmission are mated without binding, before torquing the attaching bolts.**

14. Connect the shift linkage at the case.

15. Connect the vacuum hoses.

16. Install the driveshafts. Tighten the nuts to 14 ft. lbs. (19 Nm); tighten the flange nuts to 35 ft. lbs. (47 Nm).

➡**New strap bolts must be used each time the driveshaft is removed.**

17. Install the rear crossmember. Tighten the crossmember-to-frame bolts to 30 ft. lbs. (41 Nm); the transmission-to-cross-member bolts to 33 ft. lbs. (45 Nm).

18. Remove the transmission floor jack.

19. Connect the speedometer cable and vent hose.

20. Connect the shift lever link at the operating lever.

21. Fill the case with lubricant. Lower the truck.

DRIVELINE

Front Driveshaft

Jeep vehicles may come equipped with one of two different type front driveshafts. Type one has a conventional universal joint at the axle, but a double offset joint at the transfer case. Type two has a conventional universal joint at the axle and a double cardan joint at the transfer case.

Front driveshafts on 1984 vehicles use the type one universal joint only. Front driveshafts on 1985 and later vehicles use either type one or type two.

REMOVAL & INSTALLATION

◆ **See Figures 40 and 41**

1. Matchmark the shaft ends, axle and transfer case.
2. Remove the U-joint strap bolts at the front axle yoke.
3. If equipped with a double offset U-joint, remove the double offset joint flange nuts at the transfer case.

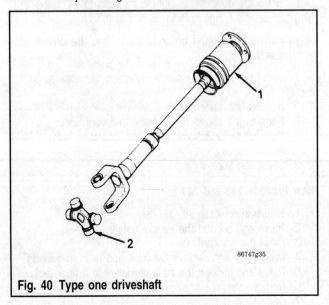

Fig. 40 Type one driveshaft

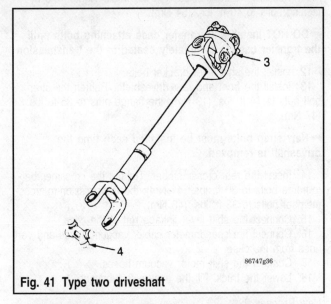

Fig. 41 Type two driveshaft

4. If equipped with a double cardan U-joint, remove the double cardan joint flange nuts at the transfer case.

5. Installation is the reverse of removal. Install new strap bolts and tighten strap bolts to 170 inch lbs. (19 Nm).

FRONT DRIVESHAFT LENGTH ADJUSTMENT

◆ **See Figure 42**

➡**The length of the front driveshaft must be checked and adjusted if the shaft has been removed or replaced.**

1. Raise the vehicle on ramps.

2. Measure from the rear edge of the groove at the transfer case end of the shaft, to the outer flange of the rubber boot on the double offset joint. The dimension should be 1½-1¾ in. (38.0-44.5mm).

3. If not, loosen the slip joint locknut and slide the shaft in or out of the double offset joint to correct the length.

4. Tighten the nut to 55 ft. lbs. (75 Nm).

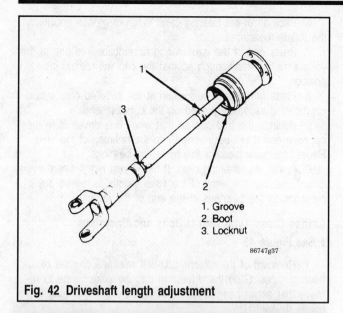

Fig. 42 Driveshaft length adjustment

1. Groove
2. Boot
3. Locknut

86747g37

Rear Driveshaft

REMOVAL & INSTALLATION

▶ See Figure 43

➡Two different driveshafts are used on these vehicles. With Command-Trac®, the driveshaft has welded yokes at each end. With Selec-Trac®, a welded yoke is used at the rear and a splined slip yoke is used at the front.

1. Raise and support the vehicle on jackstands.
2. Place the transmission in **N**.
3. Matchmark the yokes and flanges.
4. On vehicles with Command-Trac®, the driveshaft may be removed by disconnecting it at the axle and sliding it from the front yoke, leaving the front yoke attached to the transfer case. If you do this, however, you MUST matchmark the driveshaft and front yoke BEFORE separation.

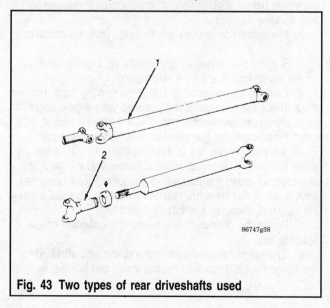

Fig. 43 Two types of rear driveshafts used

86747g38

5. On vehicles with Selec-Trac®, disconnect the yokes from the axle and transfer case. Remove the driveshaft.
6. Installation is the reverse of removal. Install new strap bolts and tighten strap bolts to 170 inch lbs. (19 Nm).

U-Joints

There are five types of universal joints used: the Cardan cross-type with U-bolts and snaprings; a Cardan cross-type with just snaprings; a double Cardan cross-type; ball and trunnion-type universal joints which serve as a combination slip-joint and universal joint. Some models have a front driveshaft which, at the transfer case end, uses a double offset joint. This unit is not repairable and must be serviced by replacement only.

Universal joints fail for numerous reasons, the primary one being lack of lubrication. Others could be structural damage incurred from hitting something, an unbalanced driveshaft, the entrance of dirt or water due to a rotted rubber seal or just plain wear from excessive mileage.

Rebuilding kits are available for both types of universal joints. The kit for a Cardan cross-type universal joint includes the entire cross assembly, the cross bearing journal, roller bearings, bearing cap with new rubber seal and new snaprings.

The rebuilding kit for the ball and trunnion-type universal joint includes a new grease cover and gasket, universal joint body, two centering buttons and spring washers, two ball and roller bearing assemblies, two thrust washers, dust cover and two dust cover clamps.

Although U-joints can be rebuilt, most procedures today call for replacement rather than rebuilding.

OVERHAUL

Cardan Cross Type with Snaprings
▶ See Figure 44

1. Remove the driveshaft from the vehicle.

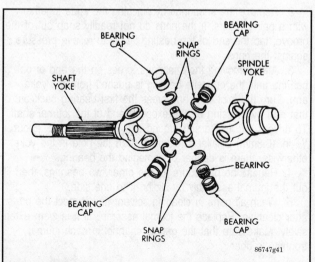

Fig. 44 Cardan cross type universal joint with snaprings

86747g41

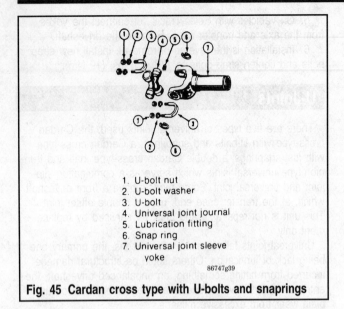

1. U-bolt nut
2. U-bolt washer
3. U-bolt
4. Universal joint journal
5. Lubrication fitting
6. Snap ring
7. Universal joint sleeve
   yoke

86747g39

Fig. 45 Cardan cross type with U-bolts and snaprings

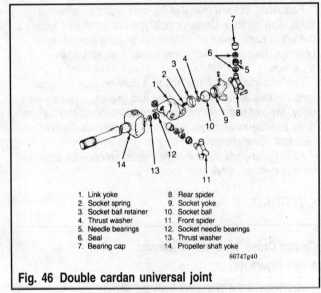

1. Link yoke
2. Socket spring
3. Socket ball retainer
4. Thrust washer
5. Needle bearings
6. Seal
7. Bearing cap
8. Rear spider
9. Socket yoke
10. Socket ball
11. Front spider
12. Socket needle bearings
13. Thrust washer
14. Propeller shaft yoke

86747g40

Fig. 46 Double cardan universal joint

2. Remove the snaprings by pinching the ends together with a pair of pliers. If the rings do not readily snap out of the groove, tap the end of the bearing lightly to relieve pressure against the rings.

3. After removing the snaprings, press on the end of one bearing until the opposite bearing is pushed from the yoke arm. Turn the joint over and press the first bearing back out of that arm by pressing on the exposed end of the journal shaft. To drive it out, use a soft ground drift with a flat face, about $\frac{1}{32}$ in. (0.8mm) smaller in diameter than the hole in the yoke; otherwise, there is danger of damaging the bearing.

4. Repeat the procedure for the other two bearings, then lift out the journal assembly by sliding it to one side.

5. Wash all parts in cleaning solvent and inspect the parts after cleaning. Replace the journal assembly if it is worn extensively. Make sure that the grease channel in each journal trunnion is open.

6. Pack all of the bearing caps $\frac{1}{3}$ full of grease and install the rollers (bearings).

7. Press one of the cap/bearing assemblies into one of the yoke arms just far enough so that the cap will remain in position.

8. Place the journal in position in the installed cap, with a cap/bearing assembly placed on the opposite end.

9. Position the free cap so that when it is driven from the opposite end it will be inserted into the opening of the yoke. Repeat this operation for the other two bearings.

10. Install the retaining clips. If the U-joint binds when it is assembled, tap the arms of the yoke slightly to relieve any pressure on the bearings at the end of the journal.

Cardan Cross Type with U-Bolts and Snaprings

▶ See Figure 45

1. Removal of the attaching U-bolt releases one set of bearing races. Slide the driveshaft into the yoke flange to remove that set of bearing races, being careful not to lose the rollers (bearings).

2. After removal of the first set of bearings, release the other set by pinching the ends of the snaprings with pliers and removing them from the sleeve yoke. Should the rings fail to snap readily from the groove, tap the end of the bearing lightly, to relieve the pressure against them.

3. Press on the end of one bearing, until the opposite bearing is pushed out of the yoke arm.

4. Turn the universal joint over and press the first bearing out by pressing on the exposed end of the journal assembly. Use a soft round drift with a flat face about $\frac{1}{32}$ in. (0.8mm) smaller in diameter than the hole in the yoke arm. Then drive out the bearing.

5. Lift the journal out by sliding it to one side.

6. Install in the reverse order of removal, using the procedures for the snapring U-joints from Step 4 on as a guide.

Double Cardan Type

▶ See Figure 46

1. Use a punch to mark the coupling yoke and the adjoining yokes before disassembly, to ensure proper reassembly and driveline balance.

2. It is easiest to remove the bearings from the coupling yoke first.

3. Support the driveshaft horizontally on a press stand, or on the workbench if a vise is being used.

4. If snaprings are used to retain the bearing cups, remove them. Place the rear car of the coupling yoke over a socket large enough to receive the cup. Place a smaller socket, or a cross press made for the purpose, over the opposite cup. Press the bearing cup out of the coupling yoke ear. If the cup is not completely removed, insert a spacer and complete the operation, or grasp the cup with a pair of slip joint pliers and work it out. If the cups are retained by plastic, this will shear the retainers. Remove any bits of plastic.

5. Rotate the driveshaft and repeat the operation on the opposite cup.

6. Disengage the trunnions of the spider, still attached to the flanged yoke, from the coupling yoke, and pull the flanged

yoke and spider from the center ball on the ball support tube yoke.

➡**The joint between the shaft and coupling yoke can be serviced without disassembly of the joint between the coupling yoke and flanged yoke.**

7. Pry the seal from the ball cavity, remove the washers, spring and three seats. Examine the ball stud seat and the ball stud for scores or wear. Worn parts can be replaced with a kit. Clean the ball seat cavity and fill it with grease. Install the spring, washer, ball seats, and spacer (washer) over the ball.

8. To assembly, insert one bearing cup part way into one ear of the ball support tube yoke and turn this cup to the bottom.

9. Insert the spider (cross) into the tube so that the trunnion (arm) seats freely in the cup.

10. Install the opposite cup part way, making sure that both cups are straight.

11. Press the cups into position, making sure that both cups squarely engage the spider. Back off if there is a sudden increase in resistance, indicating that a cup is cocked or a needle bearing is out of place.

12. As soon as one bearing retainer groove clears the yoke, stop and install the retainer (plastic retainer models). On models with snaprings, press the cups into place, then install the snaprings over the cups.

13. If difficulty is encountered installing the plastic retainers or the snaprings, smack the yoke sharply with a hammer to spring the ears slightly.

14. Install one bearing cup part way into the ear of the coupling yoke, Make sure that the alignment marks are matched, then engaged the coupling yoke over the spider and press in the cups, installing the retainers or snaprings as before.

15. Install the cups and spider into the flanged yoke as with the previous yoke.

Ball and Trunnion Type

1. Remove the driveshaft from the vehicle.
2. Position the tube of the driveshaft near the ball-type universal joint, in a bench vise; clamp tightly.
3. Bend the lugs of the grease cover away from the universal joint body and remove the cover and the gasket.
4. Remove the two clamps from the dust cover. Push the joint body toward the driveshaft tube. Remove the two center-

ing buttons and spring washers, the two ball and roller bearings and the two thrust washers from the trunnion pin.

5. Press the trunnion pin from the ball head with an arbor press.

➡**It is strongly recommended that the trunnion pin be pressed out and in by an arbor press because of the possible damage that could result from other methods such as hammer and drift. This is a critical component in the assembly and any damage could result in premature failure or even necessitate replacement of the entire driveshaft.**

6. Clean the ball head of the driveshaft with a suitable solvent and dry thoroughly.
7. Secure the larger end of the dust cover to the universal joint body with the larger of the two clamps. Install the smaller clamp at the smaller end of the dust cover, then fit the cover over the ball head shaft.
8. Push the universal joint cover toward the driveshaft tube.
9. With an arbor press, press the trunnion pin into a centered position in the ball head.

➡**The trunnion pin must project an equal distance from each side of the ball head. If it is not centered within 0.006 in. (0.15mm), driveshaft vibration may result.**

10. Hold the universal joint body toward the tube of the driveshaft to gain access to the trunnion pin. Install one thrust washer, one ball and roller bearing and one spring washer at one side of the ball head. Compress the centering buttons into the trunnion pin, then move the joint body away from the driveshaft tube, into position to surround the buttons and to hold them in place.

11. Insert the breather between the dust cover and ball head shaft, along the length of the shaft. The breather must extend no more than ½ in. (13mm) beyond the dust cover, along the shaft. Tighten the clamp screw to secure the cover to the shaft. Cut away any portion of the dust cover which protrudes from beneath either clamp.

12. Pack the raceways of the universal joint body (inner surfaces which surround the ball and roller bearings) with about 2 oz. of universal joint grease. Divide the grease equally between the raceways. Position the gasket and grease cover on the body of the universal joint and bend the lugs of the cover in place. Move the body inward and outward, toward and away from the driveshaft tube, to distribute the grease in the raceways.

13. Install the driveshaft on the vehicle.

FRONT DRIVE AXLE

Identification

Dana model 30 drive axles can be identified by a tag located on the left side of the housing cover. The tag lists part number and gear ratio. Stamped into the right side axle shaft are the production date and manufacturers identification.

Axle Shaft

REMOVAL & INSTALLATION

▶ See Figure 47

1. Raise and support the vehicle safely.

✳✳CAUTION

Brake linings may contain asbestos. Asbestos is a known cancer-causing agent. When working on brakes, remember that the dust which accumulates on the brake parts and/or in the drum may contain asbestos. Always wear a protective face covering, such as a painter's mask, when working on the brakes. NEVER blow the dust from the brakes or drum! There are solvents made for the purpose of cleaning brake parts. Use them!

2. Remove the wheels and brake assemblies.

➡ Refer to Section 9 for the proper procedures concerning brake removal.

3. Remove the cotter pin, locknut and axle hub nut.
4. Remove the hub-to-knuckle attaching bolts.
5. Remove the hub and splash shield from the steering knuckle.
6. Remove the left axle shaft from the housing.
7. If equipped with Command-Trac, disconnect the vacuum harness from the shift motor and remove the shift motor from the housing.
8. Remove the right axle shaft from the housing.
   To install:
9. Insert the left and right axle shafts into the axle tube.
10. To install the right axle shaft (with Command-Trac) first be sure that the shift collar is in position on the intermediate shaft and that the axle shaft is fully engaged in the intermediate shaft end.
11. If equipped with Command-Trac, install the shift motor, making sure that the fork engages with the collar. Tighten the bolts to 8 ft. lbs. (11 Nm).
12. On the left side, install the axle shaft in the housing.
13. Partially fill the hub cavity of the knuckle with chassis lube and install the hub and splash shield.
14. Tighten the hub bolts to 75 ft. lbs. (102 Nm).
15. Install the hub washer and nut. Tighten the nut to 175 ft. lbs. (237 Nm). Install the locknut. Install a new cotter pin.
16. Install the brake assemblies.
17. Lower the vehicle.

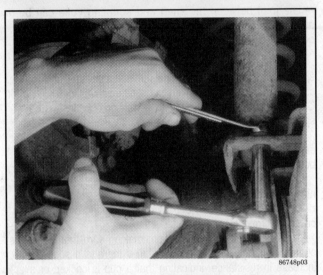

Fig. 47 Removing the axle shaft from the housing

86748p03

Command-Trac Axle Shift Motor

FUNCTIONAL TEST

▶ See Figures 48 and 49

1. Raise and support the vehicle safely.
2. Disconnect the vacuum harness and connect a hand vacuum pump to the front port. Apply 15 in. Hg (103 kPa) of vacuum to the front port and rotate the right front wheel to fully disengage axle shafts.
3. The shift motor should maintain the vacuum applied to the front port for a minimum of 30 seconds. If the motor does not maintain the vacuum, replace it. If the motor does maintain vacuum, go to Step 4.
4. Connect the vacuum pump to the rear port. Cap the port for the indicator lamp switch and apply 15 in. Hg (103 kPa).
5. The shift motor should maintain the vacuum applied to the rear port for a minimum of 30 seconds. If the motor does not maintain the vacuum, replace it. If the motor does maintain vacuum go to Step 6.
6. Remove the cap from the port for the indicator lamp switch and determine if vacuum is present. If present, the shift motor is functioning properly. If not, proceed to Step 7.
7. Apply 15 in. Hg (103 kPa) of vacuum to the shift motor rear port. Rotate the right front wheel to engage the axle shafts. The axles must be completely engaged!
8. Determine if vacuum is present at the port for the indicator lamp switch. If present, the shift motor is functioning properly. If not, replace the shift motor.

REMOVAL & INSTALLATION

▶ See Figure 50

1. Raise and support the vehicle safely. Position a drain pan under the shift motor.

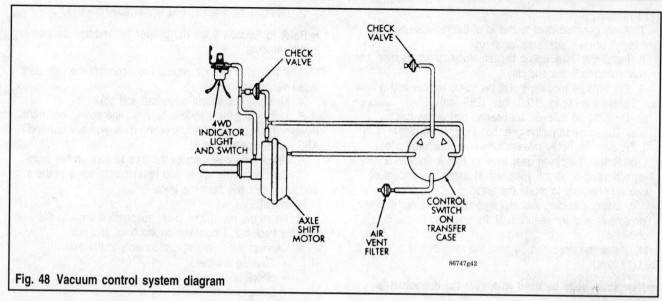

Fig. 48 Vacuum control system diagram

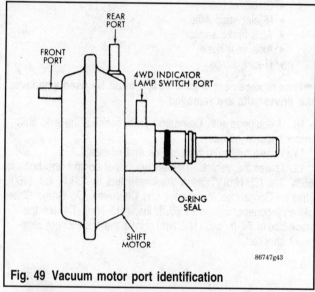

Fig. 49 Vacuum motor port identification

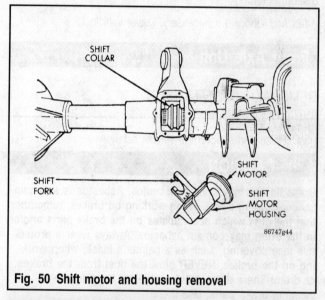

Fig. 50 Shift motor and housing removal

2. Disconnect the vacuum harness. Remove the housing attaching bolts. Remove the housing, motor and shift fork as a unit. Mark the shift fork for installation reference.

3. Rotate the shift motor and remove the shift fork and motor retaining snaprings. Remove the shift motor from the housing.

4. Remove the O-ring seal and discard.

To install:

5. Add 5 oz. of gear lubricant to the axle through the shift motor housing opening.

6. Install a replacement O-ring seal on the shift motor. Install the motor in the housing with the retaining snaprings and slide the shift fork onto the shaft with the reference marks aligned.

7. Engage the shift fork with the shift collar and install the attaching bolts. Tighten to 101 inch lbs. (137 Nm).

8. Connect the vacuum harness, lower the vehicle and road test.

Pinion Seal

REMOVAL & INSTALLATION

1. Raise and support the vehicle safely.

2. Matchmark and remove the driveshaft.

3. Rotate the pinion gear three or four times with a torque wrench attached to the yoke nut. Measure the amount of torque necessary to rotate the pinion. Note for installation reference.

4. Matchmark the pinion yoke and gear for installation reference.

5. Using a holding tool, remove the pinion yoke nut and washer. Discard the nut.

6. Punch the seal with a pin punch and pry it from the seal bore.

To install:

7. Apply gear lubricant to the lip of the replacement seal and install using a seal installation tool.

8. Install the yoke, noting the reference marks. Tighten just enough to remove the end-play.

9. On 1984-89 models, install the yoke, washer and a new nut. Tighten the nut to 210 ft. lbs. (285 Nm).

10. On 1990-96 models, set bearing preload as follows:

a. The required pinion gear bearing preload torque is ½ ft. lbs over the noted release torque as measured above.

b. Rotate the pinion gear three or four times with a torque wrench attached to the yoke nut. Measure the amount of torque necessary to rotate the pinion.

c. Using a holding tool and tighten the yoke nut in small increments and remeasure until the specified torque is obtained.

11. Install the driveshaft. Tighten the strap bolt nuts to 14 ft. lbs. (19 Nm).

➡ **New strap bolts be used whenever the driveshaft is disconnected.**

12. Add lubricant if necessary. Lower vehicle.

Front Axle Unit

REMOVAL & INSTALLATION

1. Raise and support the vehicle safely.

✳✳CAUTION

Brake linings may contain asbestos. Asbestos is a known cancer-causing agent. When working on brakes, remember that the dust which accumulates on the brake parts and/or in the drum may contain asbestos. Always wear a protective face covering, such as a painter's mask, when working on the brakes. NEVER blow the dust from the brakes or drum! There are solvents made for the purpose of cleaning brake parts. Use them!

REAR AXLE

Identification

Dana model 35/44 drive axles can be identified by a tag located on the left side of the housing cover. The tag lists part number and gear ratio. Stamped into the right side axle shaft are the production date and manufacturers identification.

The I.D. code for the AMC 7⁹⁄₁₆ in. (192mm) axle is stamped into the right hand side axle tube boss. Code "S" indicates a 3.73:1 ratio. Code "T" indicates a 3.31:1 ratio. Code "SS" or "TT" indicate the rear axle is equipped with a Trac-Lok differential.

Understanding Rear Axles

The rear axle is a special type of transmission that reduces the speed of the drive from the engine and transmission and

2. Remove the wheels, and brake assemblies.

➡ **Refer to Section 9 for the proper procedures concerning brake removal.**

3. If equipped with Command-Trac, connect the axle shift motor vacuum harness.

4. Matchmark the front driveshaft and yoke.

5. Disconnect the stabilizer bar, rod and center link, front driveshaft, shock absorbers, steering damper, track bar and ABS sensor if equipped.

6. Place a floor jack under the axle to take up the weight.

7. Disconnect the upper and lower control arms at the axle and lower the axle from the truck.

To install:

8. Install the upper and lower suspension arms to the axle and the track bar. Finger-tighten the bolts and nuts.

9. Connect the following components to the axle:

- Steering damper
- Shock absorber
- Center link-to-knuckle
- Stabilizer bar
- U-joint strap nuts
- ABS brake sensor
- Axle vent hose
- U-joint straps

➡ **New replacement U-joint straps must be used whenever the driveshafts are removed.**

10. If equipped with Command-Trac, connect the axle shift motor vacuum harness.

11. Install the brake assemblies and wheels.

12. Lower the vehicle. Tighten the upper control arm bolts to 55 ft. lbs. (75 Nm). Tighten the lower nuts to 133 ft. lbs. (180 Nm) on Comanche, Wagoneer and Cherokee. On Grand Cherokee/Wagoneer, tighten to 85 ft. lbs. (115 Nm). Tighten the track bar to 74 ft. lbs. (100 Nm). Have the front wheel alignment checked.

divides the power to the rear wheels. Power enters the rear axle from the driveshaft via the companion flange. The flange is mounted on the drive pinion shaft. The drive pinion shaft and gear which carry the power into the differential turn at engine speed. The gear on the end of the pinion shaft drives a large ring gear the axis of rotation of which is 90 degrees away from the of the pinion. The pinion and gear reduce the gear ratio of the axle, and change the direction of rotation to turn the axle shafts which drive both wheels. The rear axle gear ratio is found by dividing the number of pinion gear teeth into the number of ring gear teeth.

The ring gear drives the differential case. The case provides the two mounting points for the ends of a pinion shaft on which are mounted two pinion gears. The pinion gears drive the two side gears, one of which is located on the inner end of each axle shaft.

By driving the axle shafts through the arrangement, the differential allows the outer drive wheel to turn faster than the inner drive wheel in a turn.

The main drive pinion and the side bearings, which bear the weight of the differential case, are shimmed to provide proper bearing preload, and to position the pinion and ring gears properly.

➡The proper adjustment of the relationship of the ring and pinion gears is critical. It should be attempted only by those with extensive equipment and/or experience.

Limited-slip differentials include clutches which link each axle shaft to the differential case. Clutches may be engaged either by spring action or by pressure produced by the torque on the axles during a turn. During turning on a dry pavement, the effects of the clutches are overcome, and each wheel turns at the required speed. When slippage occurs at either wheel, however, the clutches will transmit some of the power to the wheel which has the greater amount of traction. Because of the presence of clutches, limited-slip units require a special lubricant.

Determining Axle Ratio

The drive axle is said to have a certain axle ratio. This number (usually a whole number and a decimal fraction) is actually a comparison of the number of gear teeth on the ring gear and the pinion gear. For example, a 4.11 rear means that theoretically, there are 4.11 teeth on the ring gear and one tooth on the pinion gear or, put another way, the driveshaft must turn 4.11 times to turn the wheels once. Actually, on a 4.11 rear, there might be 37 teeth on the ring gear and 9 teeth on the pinion gear. By dividing the number of teeth on the pinion gear into the number of teeth on the ring gear, the numerical axle ratio (4.11) is obtained. This also provides a good method of ascertaining exactly what axle ratio one is dealing with.

Another method of determining gear ratio is to jack up and support the car so that both rear wheels are off the ground. Make a chalk mark on the rear wheel and the driveshaft. Put the transmission in neutral. Turn the rear wheel one complete turn and count the number of turns that the driveshaft makes. The number of turns that the driveshaft makes in one complete revolution of the rear wheel is an approximation of the rear axle ratio.

Axle Shaft, Bearing and Seal

REMOVAL & INSTALLATION

Dana 44 and AMC 7⁹/₁₆ in. Models
▶ **See Figures 51, 52, 53 and 54**

➡**An arbor press is necessary for this procedure.**

1. Raise and support the vehicle safely.

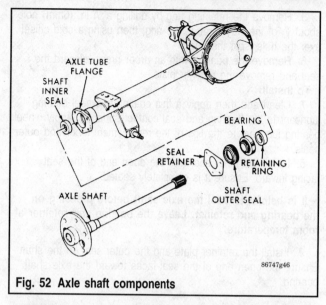
Fig. 52 Axle shaft components

2. Remove the wheel and tire and brake drum/disc assembly.

✳✳CAUTION

Brake linings may contain asbestos. Asbestos is a known cancer-causing agent. When working on brakes, remember that the dust which accumulates on the brake parts and/or in the drum may contain asbestos. Always wear a protective face covering, such as a painter's mask, when working on the brakes. NEVER blow the dust from the brakes or drum! There are solvents made for the purpose of cleaning brake parts. Use them!

3. Remove the nuts that attach the outer seal retainer (and brake backing plate) to the axle shaft tube. Discard the nuts.

Remove the axle shaft from the housing with an axle puller attached to a slide hammer.

4. Discard the inner axle seal. Position the axle shaft in a vise.

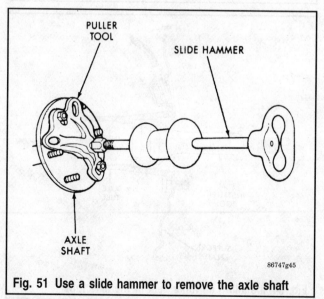
Fig. 51 Use a slide hammer to remove the axle shaft

5. Remove the retaining ring by drilling a ¼ in. (6mm) hole about ¾ of the way through the ring, then using a cold chisel over the hole, split the ring.

6. Remove the bearing with an arbor press, discard the seal and remove the retainer plate.

To install:

7. Clean and then apply a thin coating of wheel bearing lubricant to the bearing and seal contact surfaces. Apply wheel bearing lubricant to the lips of the replacement inner and outer seals.

8. Install the inner seal with the open end of the seal facing inward. Ensure it is completely seated.

➡ **It is helpful to cool the axle shaft before pressing on the bearing and retainer. Leave the bearing and retainer at room temperature.**

9. Install the retainer plate and the outer seal on the shaft. Ensure the open end of the seal faces toward the axle shaft bearing.

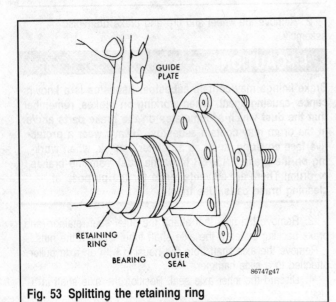

Fig. 53 Splitting the retaining ring

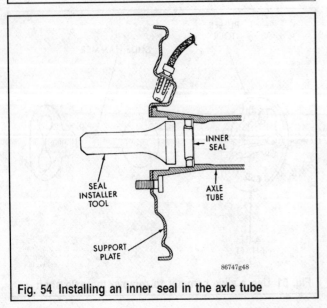

Fig. 54 Installing an inner seal in the axle tube

10. Pack the replacement bearing with wheel bearing lubricant and position on the axle shaft. Press into place.

11. Press a replacement bearing retainer on the axle shaft against the bearing.

12. Install the axle into the axle tube. Position and align the seal retainer and brake support plate and install replacement attaching nuts. Tighten nuts to 32 ft. lbs. (43 Nm).

13. Install brake assembly wheels and tires. Lower vehicle.

Dana 35 Models

▶ **See Figure 55**

1. Raise and support the vehicle safely.

✳✳CAUTION

Brake linings may contain asbestos. Asbestos is a known cancer-causing agent. When working on brakes, remember that the dust which accumulates on the brake parts and/or in the drum may contain asbestos. Always wear a protective face covering, such as a painter's mask, when working on the brakes. NEVER blow the dust from the brakes or drum! There are solvents made for the purpose of cleaning brake parts. Use them!

2. Remove the wheels and brake assemblies.

➡ **Refer to Section 9 for the proper procedures concerning brake removal.**

3. Loosen the differential housing cover and drain the lubricant. Remove the housing cover.

4. Rotate the differential so the pinion gear mate shaft lock screw is accessible. Remove the lock screw and the pinion gear mate shaft.

5. Move the axle shafts inward and remove the C-clip lock from the recessed groove in the axle shaft.

6. Remove the axle shaft from the case.

7. Remove the axle shaft seal and bearing using removal tool set 6310.

To install:

8. Wipe the bearing bore and axle shaft tube clean.

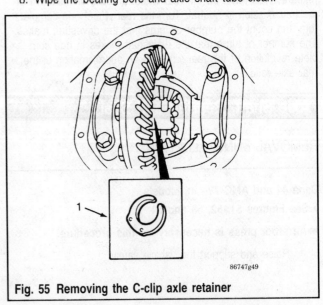

Fig. 55 Removing the C-clip axle retainer

9. Install the bearing using tools C-4171 and 6436. Seat the bearing against the shoulder in the axle tube.

10. Install the replacement axle shaft seal with tool 6437 and C-4171. When the installation tool face contacts the axle tube, the seal is at the correct depth.

11. Lubricate the bearing bore and the seal lip. Insert the axle shaft into the tube and engage its splines with the differential.

12. Install the C-clip locks and force the axles outward to seat them.

13. Insert the differential pinion gear mate shaft into the case and through the thrust washers and the pinion gears. Align the hole in the shaft with the lock screw hole. Install the lock screw and tighten to 14 ft. lbs.

14. Apply an ⅛ in. (3mm) bead of RTV to the differential cover after cleaning the differential and cover with solvent.

15. Install the cover and tighten bolts to 35 ft. lbs. (47 Nm).

16. Install the brake assemblies and wheels.

➡**For Trac-Lok differentials, a special limited slip additive is needed.**

17. Fill the differential with lubricant. Lower the vehicle and test for proper operation.

18. For vehicles equipped with Trac-Lok differentials, drive the vehicle and make 10 to 12 slow, figure-eight turns to pump lubricant through the clutch discs.

Pinion Seal

REMOVAL & INSTALLATION

▶ **See Figures 56 and 57**

1. Raise and support the vehicle.

2. Mark the driveshaft and yoke for reference during assembly and disconnect the driveshaft at the yoke.

3. Remove the pinion shaft nut and washer. Discard the nut.

4. Remove the yoke from the pinion shaft, using a puller.

5. Remove the pinion shaft oil seal with tool J-25180 on semi-floating axles, or tool J-25144 on full floating axles.

To install:

6. Install the new seal with a suitable driver.

7. On 1984-90 models, install the yoke, washer and a new nut. Tighten the nut to 210 ft. lbs. (285 Nm).

8. On 1990-96 models, set bearing preload as follows:

   a. The required pinion gear bearing preload torque is ½ ft. lbs. over the noted release torque as measured above.

   b. Rotate the pinion gear three or four times with a torque wrench attached to the yoke nut. Measure the amount of torque necessary to rotate the pinion.

   c. Using a holding tool, tighten the yoke nut in small increments and remeasure until the specified torque is obtained.

9. Align the index marks on the driveshaft and yoke and install the driveshaft. Tighten the attaching bolts or nuts to 170 inch lbs. (19 Nm).

10. Add lubricant to the rear if necessary and lower the vehicle.

Rear Axle Unit

REMOVAL & INSTALLATION

▶ **See Figure 58**

1. Raise and support the vehicle safely.

✳✳CAUTION

Brake linings may contain asbestos. Asbestos is a known cancer-causing agent. When working on brakes, remember that the dust which accumulates on the brake parts and/or in the drum may contain asbestos. Always wear a protective face covering, such as a painter's mask, when working on the brakes. NEVER blow the dust from the brakes or drum! There are solvents made for the purpose of cleaning brake parts. Use them!

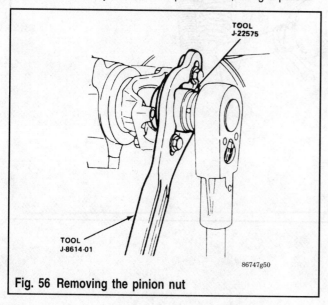

TOOL
J-22575

TOOL
J-8614-01

86747g50

Fig. 56 Removing the pinion nut

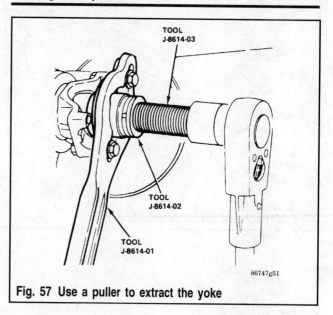

TOOL
J-8614-03

TOOL
J-8614-02

TOOL
J-8614-01

86747g51

Fig. 57 Use a puller to extract the yoke

2. Remove the wheels and brake drums/discs.

➡**For vehicles equipped with Anti-Lock Brakes (ABS), refer to Section 9 for the proper procedures concerning brake removal.**

3. Disconnect the shock absorbers.

4. Disconnect the brake hose at the frame rail and cap to prevent the entry if dirt.

➡**On Comanche models a height sensing rear proportioning valve is mounted on the rear axle. This valve must be adjusted after the axle is reinstalled. If not adjusted unsatisfactory brake action could result.**

5. Disconnect the parking brake cables at the equalizer.

6. Matchmark the driveshaft and yoke, and disconnect the driveshaft.

7. Place a floor jack under the axle to take up the weight.

8. Remove the axle-to-spring U-bolts and lower the axle.

To Install:

9. Raise the axle into place. Install the axle-to-spring U-bolts and tighten to 52 ft. lbs. (70 Nm).

10. Reconnect the driveshaft and tighten U-joint strap bolts to 170 inch lbs. (19 Nm).

11. Connect the parking brake cables at the equalizer.

12. Connect the brake hoses at the frame rail.

13. Connect the shock absorbers.

14. Install the wheels and brake drums/discs.

15. Check the differential lubricant, bleed the brakes and road test the vehicle.

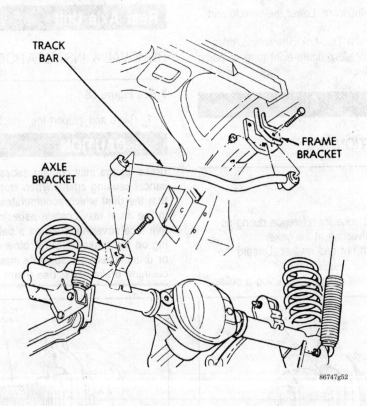

TRACK BAR

FRAME BRACKET

AXLE BRACKET

86747g52

Fig. 58 Rear axle assembly mounting

Troubleshooting the Manual Transmission and Transfer Case

Problem	Cause	Solution
Transmission shifts hard	• Clutch adjustment incorrect • Clutch linkage or cable binding • Shift rail binding • Internal bind in transmission caused by shift forks, selector plates, or synchronizer assemblies • Clutch housing misalignment • Incorrect lubricant • Block rings and/or cone seats worn	• Adjust clutch • Lubricate or repair as necessary • Check for mispositioned selector arm roll pin, loose cover bolts, worn shift rail bores, worn shift rail, distorted oil seal, or extension housing not aligned with case. Repair as necessary. • Remove, dissemble and inspect transmission. Replace worn or damaged components as necessary. • Check runout at rear face of clutch housing • Drain and refill transmission • Blocking ring to gear clutch tooth face clearance must be 0.030 inch or greater. If clearance is correct it may still be necessary to inspect blocking rings and cone seats for excessive wear. Repair as necessary.
Gear clash when shifting from one gear to another	• Clutch adjustment incorrect • Clutch linkage or cable binding • Clutch housing misalignment • Lubricant level low or incorrect lubricant • Gearshift components, or synchronizer assemblies worn or damaged	• Adjust clutch • Lubricate or repair as necessary • Check runout at rear of clutch housing • Drain and refill transmission and check for lubricant leaks if level was low. Repair as necessary. • Remove, disassemble and inspect transmission. Replace worn or damaged components as necessary.
Transmission noisy	• Lubricant level low or incorrect lubricant • Clutch housing-to-engine, or transmission-to-clutch housing bolts loose • Dirt, chips, foreign material in transmission • Gearshift mechanism, transmission gears, or bearing components worn or damaged • Clutch housing misalignment	• Drain and refill transmission. If lubricant level was low, check for leaks and repair as necessary. • Check and correct bolt torque as necessary • Drain, flush, and refill transmission • Remove, disassemble and inspect transmission. Replace worn or damaged components as necessary. • Check runout at rear face of clutch housing

86747g56

Troubleshooting the Manual Transmission and Transfer Case (cont.)

Problem	Cause	Solution
Jumps out of gear	• Clutch housing misalignment	• Check runout at rear face of clutch housing
	• Gearshift lever loose	• Check lever for worn fork. Tighten loose attaching bolts.
	• Offset lever nylon insert worn or lever attaching nut loose	• Remove gearshift lever and check for loose offset lever nut or worn insert. Repair or replace as necessary.
	• Gearshift mechanism, shift forks, selector plates, interlock plate, selector arm, shift rail, detent plugs, springs or shift cover worn or damaged	• Remove, disassemble and inspect transmission cover assembly. Replace worn or damaged components as necessary.
	• Clutch shaft or roller bearings worn or damaged	• Replace clutch shaft or roller bearings as necessary
Jumps out of gear (cont.)	• Gear teeth worn or tapered, synchronizer assemblies worn or damaged, excessive end play caused by worn thrust washers or output shaft gears	• Remove, disassemble, and inspect transmission. Replace worn or damaged components as necessary.
	• Pilot bushing worn	• Replace pilot bushing
Will not shift into one gear	• Gearshift selector plates, interlock plate, or selector arm, worn, damaged, or incorrectly assembled	• Remove, disassemble, and inspect transmission cover assembly. Repair or replace components as necessary.
	• Shift rail detent plunger worn, spring broken, or plug loose	• Tighten plug or replace worn or damaged components as necessary
	• Gearshift lever worn or damaged	• Replace gearshift lever
	• Synchronizer sleeves or hubs, damaged or worn	• Remove, disassemble and inspect transmission. Replace worn or damaged components.
Locked in one gear—cannot be shifted out	• Shift rail(s) worn or broken, shifter fork bent, setscrew loose, center detent plug missing or worn	• Inspect and replace worn or damaged parts
	• Broken gear teeth on countershaft gear, clutch shaft, or reverse idler gear	• Inspect and replace damaged part
	Gearshift lever broken or worn, shift mechanism in cover incorrectly assembled or broken, worn damaged gear train components	• Disassemble transmission. Replace damaged parts or assemble correctly.

86747g57

Troubleshooting Basic Clutch Problems

Problem	Cause
Excessive clutch noise	Throwout bearing noises are more audible at the lower end of pedal travel. The usual causes are: · Riding the clutch · Too little pedal free-play · Lack of bearing lubrication A bad clutch shaft pilot bearing will make a high pitched squeal, when the clutch is disengaged and the transmission is in gear or within the first 2″ of pedal travel. The bearing must be replaced. Noise from the clutch linkage is a clicking or snapping that can be heard or felt as the pedal is moved completely up or down. This usually requires lubrication. Transmitted engine noises are amplified by the clutch housing and heard in the passenger compartment. They are usually the result of insufficient pedal free-play and can be changed by manipulating the clutch pedal.
Clutch slips (the car does not move as it should when the clutch is engaged)	This is usually most noticeable when pulling away from a standing start. A severe test is to start the engine, apply the brakes, shift into high gear and SLOWLY release the clutch pedal. A healthy clutch will stall the engine. If it slips it may be due to: · A worn pressure plate or clutch plate · Oil soaked clutch plate · Insufficient pedal free-play
Clutch drags or fails to release	The clutch disc and some transmission gears spin briefly after clutch disengagement. Under normal conditions in average temperatures, 3 seconds is maximum spin-time. Failure to release properly can be caused by: · Too light transmission lubricant or low lubricant level · Improperly adjusted clutch linkage
Low clutch life	Low clutch life is usually a result of poor driving habits or heavy duty use. Riding the clutch, pulling heavy loads, holding the car on a grade with the clutch instead of the brakes and rapid clutch engagement all contribute to low clutch life.

86747g58

BASIC DRIVESHAFT PROBLEMS

Problem	Cause	Solution
Shudder as car accelerates from stop or low speed	• Loose U-joint • Defective center bearing	• Replace U-joint • Replace center bearing
Loud clunk in driveshaft when shifting gears	• Worn U-joints	• Replace U-joints
Roughness or vibration at any speed	• Out-of-balance, bent or dented driveshaft • Worn U-joints • U-joint clamp bolts loose	• Balance or replace driveshaft • Replace U-joints • Tighten U-joint clamp bolts
Squeaking noise at low speeds	• Lack of U-joint lubrication	• Lubricate U-joint; if problem persists, replace U-joint
Knock or clicking noise	• U-joint or driveshaft hitting frame tunnel • Worn CV joint	• Correct overloaded condition • Replace CV joint

86747g59

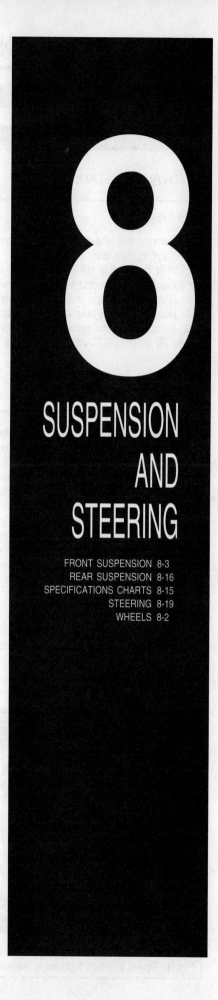

8

SUSPENSION AND STEERING

WHEELS

Wheel Assembly

REMOVAL & INSTALLATION

▶ **See Figure 1**

1. Remove the wheel cover, if equipped, by prying it off with an appropriate tool.
2. With the vehicle still on the ground loosen the lug nuts just enough to ease removal with the wheel off the ground.
3. Raise and support the vehicle safely.
4. Remove the lug nuts and remove the wheel.
5. Installation is the reverse of removal. Tighten the lug nuts to 75 ft. lbs. (102 Nm) observing the tightening sequence in the illustration.

INSPECTION

The wheels should be inspected on a frequent basis. Replace any wheel that is cracked, bent, severely dented, has excessive runout or has a broken weld. The tire inflation valve should also be inspected frequently for wear, leaks, cuts and looseness. It should be replaced if defective or its condition is doubtful.

Clean all the wheels with a mild soap and water solution only and rinse thoroughly with water. Never use abrasive or caustic materials, especially on aluminum or chrome-plated wheels because the surface will be etched or the plating severely damaged. After cleaning aluminum or chrome-plated wheels, apply a coating of protective wax to preserve the finish and luster.

➡ **DO NOT wax open pore aluminum wheels. The wax will become embedded in the pores and will be very difficult to remove.**

Wheel Lug Studs

REMOVAL & INSTALLATION

Front

▶ **See Figures 2 and 3**

1. Raise and support the vehicle safely.
2. Remove the wheel and brake caliper.

➡ **DO NOT disconnect the caliper hose. Suspend the caliper with a piece of wire.**

✴✴CAUTION

Brake linings may contain asbestos. Asbestos is a known cancer-causing agent. When working on brakes, remember that the dust which accumulates on the brake parts may contain asbestos. Always wear a protective face covering, such as a painter's mask, when working on the brakes. NEVER blow the dust from the brakes or drum! There are solvents made for the purpose of cleaning brake parts. Use them!

3. Remove the dust cap, cotter pin, nut retainer, adjusting nut and thrust washer. Remove the outer wheel bearing.
4. Remove the hub/rotor.
5. Place the hub/rotor in a shop press and remove the wheel lug stud.

To install:

➡ **Place the replacement stud in the freezer for a few minutes prior to installation.**

6. Press the replacement stud into the hub/rotor until it seats completely.
7. Install hub/rotor, outer wheel bearing, thrust washer and adjusting nut.

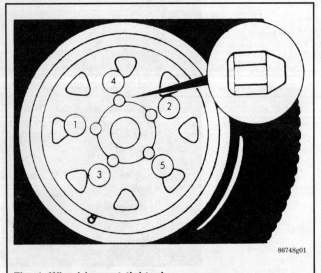

86748g01

Fig. 1 Wheel lug nut tightening sequence

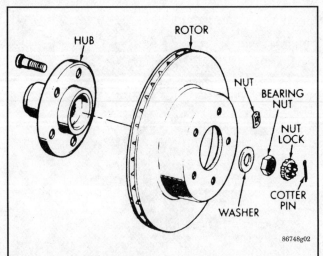

86748g02

Fig. 2 The lug studs on 4WD models is pressed into the wheel bearing hub

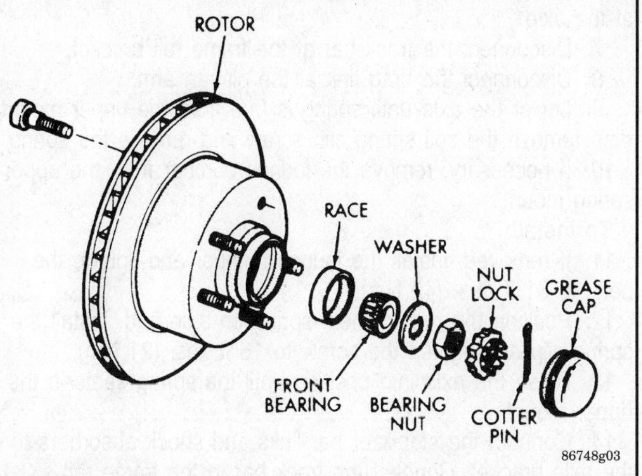

Fig. 3 On 2WD models, the studs are pressed into the rotor

8. Tighten the adjusting nut to 21 ft. lbs. (28 Nm) while spinning the rotor to seat the bearing. Loosen the adjusting nut a 1/2 turn, then retighten to 19 ft. lbs. (26 Nm).
9. Install the nut retainer, cotter pin and dust cap. Install the brake caliper.
10. Install the wheel. Lower the vehicle.

Rear

1. Raise and support the vehicle safely.
2. Remove the wheel and brake drum/disc.

**CAUTION

Brake linings may contain asbestos. Asbestos is a known cancer-causing agent. When working on brakes, remember that the dust which accumulates on the brake parts may contain asbestos. Always wear a protective face covering, such as a painter's mask, when working on the brakes. NEVER blow the dust from the brakes or drum! There are solvents made for the purpose of cleaning brake parts. Use them!

3. Using a wheel lug stud removal tool, press the damaged lug stud off the axle flange. Remove lug stud.

To install:

4. Insert the new lug stud into the axle flange. Install four to five thick washers and the lug nut on the stud.
5. Slowly tighten the nut on the lug stud until it seats completely against the axle flange. Then tighten to 80 ft. lbs. (108 Nm).
6. Remove the lug nut and washers, then install the drum/disc and wheel. Lower the vehicle.

FRONT SUSPENSION

Coil Springs

REMOVAL & INSTALLATION

Cherokee, Wagoneer and Comanche

See Figure 4

**CAUTION

Coil springs are under a great deal of tension when installed in the vehicle. Serious injury or death may result from being hit by an expanding spring. A piece of chain fastened to the frame and wrapped around the coil spring will keep the spring from flying out if it should slip before it is fully expanded.

1. Raise and support the vehicle safely.
2. Support the axle with a floor jack.
3. Remove the wheels.
4. On 4WD trucks, matchmark and disconnect the front driveshaft from the axle.
5. Disconnect the lower control arm at the axle.
6. Disconnect the stabilizer bar links and the shock absorbers at the axle.
7. Disconnect the track bar at the sill bracket.
8. Disconnect the tie rod at the pitman arm.
9. Lower the axle until tension is removed from the spring, then loosen the spring retainer and remove the spring.

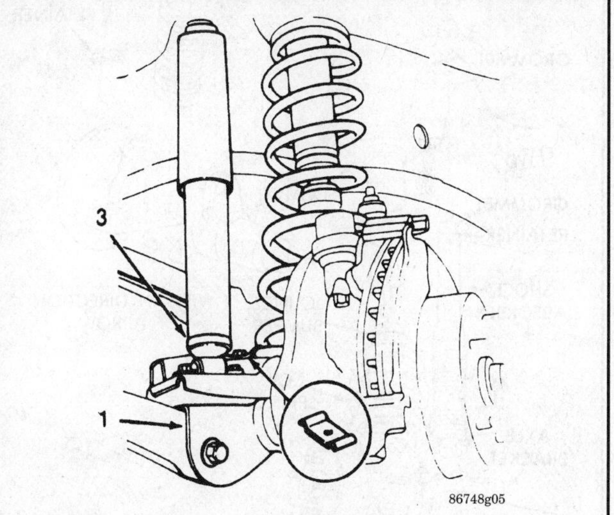

Fig. 4 Removing the coil spring retention clip

To install:

10. Position the replacement spring on the retainer, tighten the spring retainer bracket screw and lift the axle into position.
11. Connect the lower control arm to the axle. Tighten the control arm-to-axle bolt to 133 ft. lbs. (180 Nm).
12. Remove the support jack.
13. Connect the stabilizer bar links and the shock absorbers at the axle. Tighten the shock absorber-to-axle bolt to 14 ft. lbs. (19 Nm) and the stabilizer bar-to-axle bolt to 70 ft. lbs. (95 Nm).
14. Connect the track bar at the sill bracket. Tighten the track bar-to-frame rail bolt to 35 ft. lbs. (47 Nm).

15. Connect the tie rod at the pitman arm. Tighten the center link-to-pitman arm bolt to 35 ft. lbs. (47 Nm).

➡️**New strap bolts must be used each time the driveshaft is disconnected.**

16. On 4WD trucks, connect the front driveshaft. Tighten U-joint-to-axle bolt to 14 ft. lbs. (19 Nm).

17. Install the wheels and lower the vehicle.

1993-96 Grand Cherokee/Wagoneer

▶ See Figure 5

1. Raise and safely support the vehicle, allowing the front axle to hang.
2. Support the axle with a jack.
3. Paint or scribe alignment marks on the cam adjusters and axle bracket for installation reference.
4. Matchmark and disconnect the front driveshaft from the axle.
5. Disconnect the lower suspension arm nut, cam and cam bolt from the axle.

6. Disconnect the stabilizer bar links and shock absorbers at the axle.
7. Disconnect the track bar at the frame rail bracket.
8. Disconnect the drag link at the pitman arm.
9. Lower the axle until spring is free from the upper mount, then remove the coil spring clip screw and remove the spring.
10. If necessary, remove the jounce bumper from the upper spring mount.

To install:

11. If removed, install the jounce bumper and tighten the bolts to 31 ft. lbs. (42 Nm).
12. Position the replacement spring on axle pad. Install the spring clip and tighten the screw to 16 ft. lbs. (21 Nm).
13. Raise the axle into position until the spring seats in the upper mount.
14. Connect the stabilizer bar links and shock absorbers to the axle bracket. Connect the track bar to the frame rail bracket.
15. Install the lower suspension arm to the axle.
16. Connect the driveshaft to the yoke.
17. Lower the vehicle.

Shock Absorbers

REMOVAL & INSTALLATION

Cherokee, Wagoneer and Comanche

▶ See Figures 6, 7, 8 and 9

1. Remove the locknuts and washers from the upper stud.
2. Raise and support the vehicle safely.
3. If necessary for access, remove the wheels.
4. Remove the lower attaching nuts and bolts.
5. Pull the shock absorber eyes and rubber bushings from the mounting pins.

To install:

➡️**Before installing new shocks, they should be purged of air. To do this, hold the shock upright and fully extend it, then invert and compress it. Do this several times.**

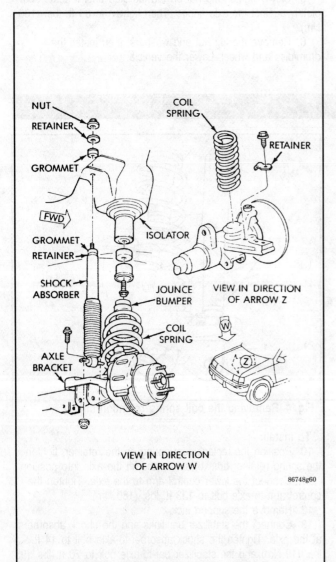

Fig. 5 Exploded view of the coil spring and shock absorber mounting

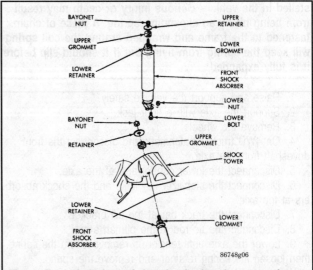

Fig. 6 Exploded view of the shock absorber mounting

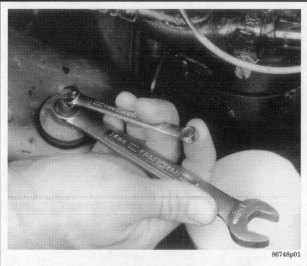

86748p01

Fig. 7 Remove the locknut from the upper stud

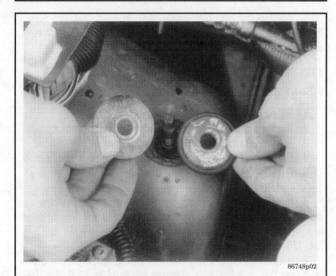

86748p02

Fig. 8 Keep all parts in the order removed

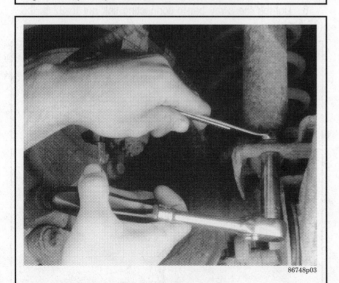

86748p03

Fig. 9 Remove the lower nuts and bolts

6. Position the shock on the vehicle and install the mounting hardware.

7. Tighten the upper end nut to 8 ft. lbs. (11 Nm) and the lower end bolts to 14 ft. lbs. (19 Nm).

8. Install the wheels and lower the vehicle.

1993-96 Grand Cherokee/Wagoneer

▶ See Figure 5

1. Remove the upper nut, retainer and grommet from the engine compartment,

2. Remove the lower bolt and nut from the mounting bracket.

3. Remove the shock absorber.

To install:

➡Before installing new shocks, they should be purged of air. To do this, hold the shock upright and fully extend it, then invert and compress it. Do this several times.

4. Position the shock on the vehicle and install the mounting hardware.

5. Tighten the upper retaining nut to 14 ft. lbs. (19 Nm) and lower bolt and nut to 17 ft. lbs. (23 Nm).

6. Install the wheels and lower the vehicle.

Upper and Lower Ball Joint

INSPECTION

To inspect the ball joints, unload the suspension and support the vehicle safely. Upper ball joints on 2WD vehicles and any ball joint on 4WD vehicles should be replaced if any play exists at all.

REMOVAL & INSTALLATION

▶ See Figures 10 and 11

➡This procedure requires the use of a special ball joint removal tool.

1. Raise and support the vehicle safely.

2. Remove the wheel. Remove the steering knuckle.

3. Position a ball joint removal tool (J-34503-1 and 34503-3 or equivalent), as illustrated, to remove the ball joint.

4. Tighten the clamp screw to remove the joint.

To install:

5. Use a ball joint installation tool (J-34503-5 or J-34503-4 or equivalent), as illustrated, to install the ball joint.

6. Install the knuckle. Tighten steering knuckle-to-ball joint nuts to 100 ft. lbs. (135 Nm).

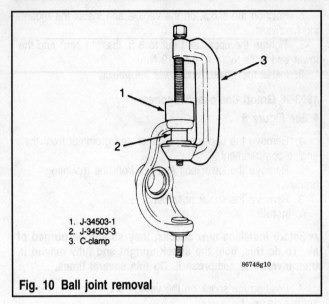

1. J-34503-1
2. J-34503-3
3. C-clamp

86748g10

Fig. 10 Ball joint removal

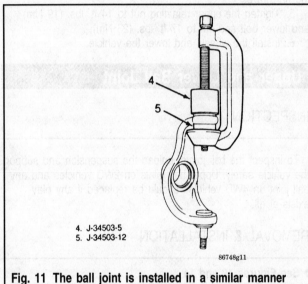

4. J-34503-5
5. J-34503-12

86748g11

Fig. 11 The ball joint is installed in a similar manner

Front Stabilizer Bar

REMOVAL & INSTALLATION

Cherokee, Wagoneer and Comanche
▶ See Figure 12

1. Raise and support the vehicle safely.
2. Disconnect the stabilizer bar at the connecting links. If necessary, disengage the connecting links from the brackets on the frame rail and steering box.
3. Remove the stabilizer bar-to-frame clamps and cushions, and remove the stabilizer bar.

To install:

4. Position the bar on the vehicle and install the clamps and cushions finger-tight.

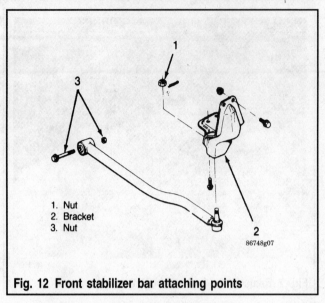

1. Nut
2. Bracket
3. Nut

86748g07

Fig. 12 Front stabilizer bar attaching points

5. Tighten the clamp-to-frame bolts to 55 ft. lbs. (75 Nm), the stabilizer bar-to-connecting link nuts to 27 ft. lbs. (37 Nm), and the connecting link-to-axle bolts to 70 ft. lbs. (95 Nm).

1993-96 Grand Cherokee/Wagoneer
▶ See Figure 13

1. Raise and safely support the vehicle.
2. Remove the sway bar links from the axle brackets.
3. Disconnect the sway bar from the links.
4. Disconnect the sway bar clamps from the frame rails.
5. Remove the sway bar.

To install:

6. Install the sway bar on the frame rail and install the clamps and bolts. Ensure the bar is centered with equal spacing on both sides. Tighten the retaining bracket bolts to 55 ft. lbs. (75 Nm).
7. Install the connecting rod link and grommets onto the stabilizer bar and brackets. Tighten the nuts to 70 ft. lbs. (96 Nm).
8. Tighten the sway bar-to-connecting link nut to 27 ft. lbs. (36 Nm).

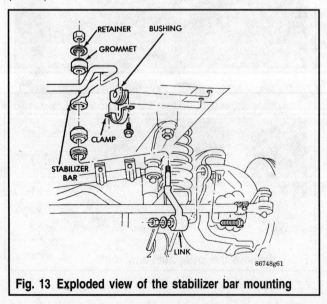

86748g61

Fig. 13 Exploded view of the stabilizer bar mounting

9. Lower the vehicle.

Track Bar

REMOVAL & INSTALLATION

▶ See Figure 14

1. Raise and support the vehicle safely.
2. Remove the cotter pin and nut securing the track bar to the frame bracket.
3. Remove the bolt and nut securing the track bar to the axle.

➡ **A puller tool may be necessary to separate the ball stud from the frame rail bracket.**

To install:

4. Position the track bar on the vehicle. Install both ends finger-tight.
5. Lower the vehicle.
6. Tighten the frame-end nut to 35 ft. lbs. (47 Nm) and the axle end bolt to 55 ft. lbs. (75 Nm).

Upper Control Arm

REMOVAL & INSTALLATION

Cherokee, Wagoneer and Comanche

▶ See Figure 15

1. Raise and support the vehicle safely.
2. On trucks with the 2.8L engine, disconnect the right engine mount and raise the engine so that the rear bolt will clear the exhaust pipe.
3. Remove the wheels.
4. Remove the control arm-to-axle bolt.
5. Remove the control arm-to-frame bolt and remove the arm.

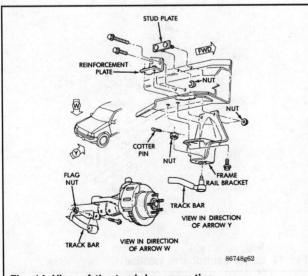

Fig. 14 View of the track bar mounting

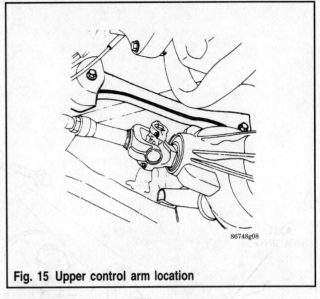

Fig. 15 Upper control arm location

To install:

6. Install the replacement control arm and all nuts and bolts finger-tight.
7. Install the wheels.
8. On 2.8L engines, connect the right engine mount.
9. Lower the vehicle.

➡ **It is important to have the front springs at their normal ride height when the upper control arm attaching nuts are tightened. Vehicle ride comfort could be adversely affected.**

10. Tighten the control arm bolts to 55 ft. lbs. (75 Nm) at the axle; 66 ft. lbs. (89 Nm) at the frame.

1993-96 Grand Cherokee/Wagoneer

▶ See Figure 16

1. Raise and support the vehicle safely.
2. Remove the upper control arm-to-axle bracket nut and bolt.
3. Remove the upper control arm-to-frame nut and bolt.
4. Remove the arm.

To install:

5. Install the upper control arm and tighten the bolts and nuts finger-tight.
6. Lower the vehicle.
7. Tighten the upper control arm bolts to 55 ft. lbs. (75 Nm).

Lower Control Arm

REMOVAL & INSTALLATION

Cherokee, Wagoneer and Comanche

▶ See Figure 17

1. Raise and support the vehicle safely.
2. Remove the wheels.
3. Remove the retainers securing the lower control arm at the axle and rear bracket.

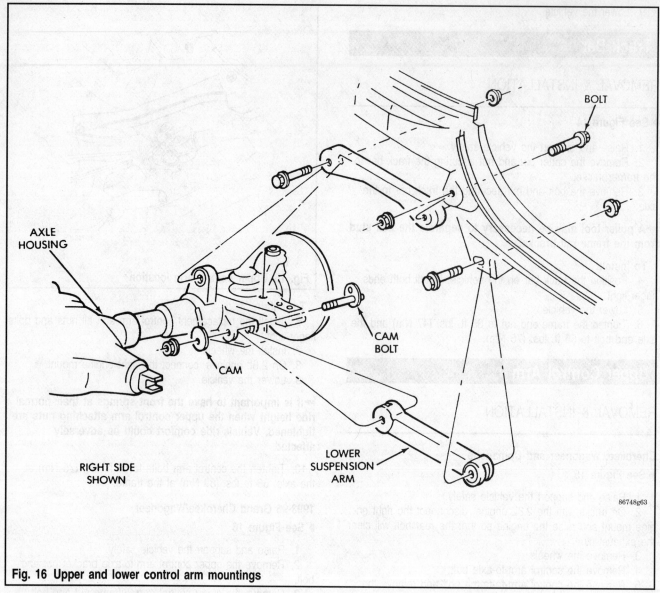

Fig. 16 Upper and lower control arm mountings

4. Remove the arm.

To install:

5. Install the replacement arm and tighten the attaching bolts finger-tight.

6. Install the wheels, then lower the vehicle.

➡️**It is important to have the front springs at their normal ride height when the lower control arm attaching nuts are tightened. Vehicle ride comfort could be adversely affected.**

7. Tighten the lower control arm attaching bolts to 133 ft. lbs. (180 Nm).

1993-96 Grand Cherokee/Wagoneer

▶ **See Figure 16**

1. Raise and safely support the vehicle, allowing the suspension to hang freely.

2. Paint or scribe alignment marks on the cam adjusters and suspension arm for installation reference.

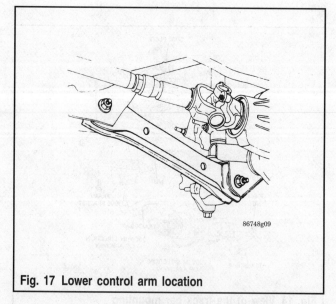

Fig. 17 Lower control arm location

3. Remove the lower control arm nut, cam and cam bolt from the axle.

4. Remove the nut and bolt from the frame rail bracket.

5. Remove the arm.

To install:

6. Install the lower control arm.

7. Tighten the rear bolts finger-tight.

8. Install the cam bolt, cam and nut in the axle while re-aligning the reference marks.

9. Lower the vehicle.

10. Tighten the nuts to 130 ft. lbs. (176 Nm).

Steering Knuckle

REMOVAL & INSTALLATION

▶ **See Figure 18**

1. Raise and support the vehicle.

2. Remove the wheels.

3. On 4WD models, remove the axle shaft.

4. Remove the disc brake caliper. See Section 9 for additional service information.

✳✳CAUTION

Brake linings may contain asbestos. Asbestos is a known cancer-causing agent. When working on brakes, remember that the dust which accumulates on the brake parts may contain asbestos. Always wear a protective face covering, such as a painter's mask, when working on the brakes. NEVER blow the dust from the brakes or drum! There are solvents made for the purpose of cleaning brake parts. Use them!

5. Remove the knuckle-to-ball joint cotter pins and nuts.

6. Drive the knuckle out with a brass hammer.

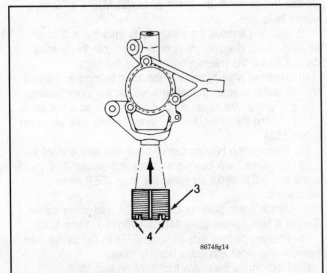

86748g14

Fig. 18 Split ring seat installation details

To install:

➡A split ring seat is located in the bottom of the knuckle. During installation, this ring seat must be set to a depth of 0.20 in. (5.23mm). Measure the depth to the top of the ring seat.

7. Position the knuckle on the vehicle. Tighten the knuckle retaining nuts to 75 ft. lbs. (102 Nm). Use new cotter pins to secure the nuts.

8. Install the brake caliper. Tighten the disc brake caliper bolts to 77 ft. lbs. (104 Nm).

9. If applicable, install the axle shaft.

10. Install the wheels and lower the vehicle.

Front Wheel Bearings

REPLACEMENT

➡Sodium-based grease is not compatible with lithium-based grease. Read the package labels and be careful not to mix the two types. If there is any doubt as to the type of grease used, completely clean the old grease from the bearing and hub before replacing.

Cherokee, Wagoneer and Comanche

2WD MODELS

▶ **See Figure 19**

1. Raise and support the vehicle safely.

2. Remove the wheels.

3. Remove the caliper without disconnecting the brake line. Suspend it out of the way using a piece of wire to prevent damage. See Section 9 for additional service information.

✳✳CAUTION

Brake linings may contain asbestos. Asbestos is a known cancer-causing agent. When working on brakes, remember that the dust which accumulates on the brake parts may contain asbestos. Always wear a protective face covering, such as a painter's mask, when working on the brakes. NEVER blow the dust from the brakes or drum! There are solvents made for the purpose of cleaning brake parts. Use them!

4. Remove the grease cap, cotter pin, nut cap, nut, and washer from the spindle. Discard the cotter pin.

5. Slowly remove the hub and rotor. Catch the outer bearing as it falls.

6. Carefully drive out the inner bearing and seal from the hub, using a wood block.

7. Inspect the bearing races for excessive wear, pitting or grooves. If they are cracked or grooved, or if pitting and excess wear is present, drive them out with a drift or punch.

8. Check the bearing for excess wear, pitting or cracks, or excess looseness.

➡If it is necessary to replace either the bearing or the race, replace both. Never replace just a bearing or a race. These parts wear in a mating pattern. If just one is replaced, premature failure of the new part will result.

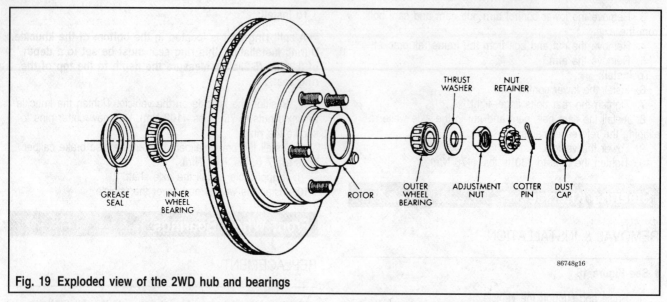

THRUST WASHER

NUT RETAINER

GREASE SEAL

INNER WHEEL BEARING

ROTOR

OUTER WHEEL BEARING

ADJUSTMENT NUT

COTTER PIN

DUST CAP

86748g16

Fig. 19 Exploded view of the 2WD hub and bearings

To install:

9. Thoroughly clean the spindle and the inside of the hub.

10. Pack the inside of the hub with high temperature wheel bearing grease. Add grease to the hub until it is flush with the inside diameter of the bearing cup.

11. Pack the bearings with the same grease. A needle-shaped wheel bearing packer is best for this operation. If one is not available, place a large amount of grease in the palm of your hand and slide the edge of the bearing cage through the grease to pick up as much as possible, then work the grease in until it squeezes through the bearing.

12. If a new race is being installed, very carefully drive it into position until it bottoms all around, using a brass drift. Be careful to avoid scratching the surface.

13. Place the inner bearing in the race and install a new grease seal.

14. Clean the rotor contact surface if necessary.

15. Position the hub and rotor on the spindle and install the outer bearing.

16. Install the washer and nut.

17. While turning the rotor, tighten the nut to 25 ft. lbs. (34 Nm) to seat the bearings.

18. Back the nut off ½ a turn. While turning the rotor, tighten the nut to 19 inch lbs. (2 Nm).

19. Install the nut cap and a new cotter pin. Install the grease cap.

20. Install the caliper.

21. Install the wheels.

4WD MODELS

▶ **See Figures 20, 21, 22, 23, 24, 25, 26 and 27**

➡ **If the hub is equipped with ball bearings, the entire unit must be replaced if defective. If the hub is equipped with tapered roller bearings, its internal components can be serviced or replaced as necessary.**

1. Raise and support the vehicle safely.

2. Remove the wheels.

3. Remove, but do not disconnect, the caliper. Suspend it out of the way. See Section 9 for additional service information.

❋❋CAUTION

Brake linings may contain asbestos. Asbestos is a known cancer-causing agent. When working on brakes, remember that the dust which accumulates on the brake parts and/or in the drum may contain asbestos. Always wear a protective face covering, such as a painter's mask, when working on the brakes. NEVER blow the dust from the brakes or drum! There are solvents made for the purpose of cleaning brake parts. Use them!

4. Remove the rotor.

5. Remove the cotter pin, nut retainer, axle nut and washer.

6. Remove the 3 hub-to-steering knuckle attaching bolts.

7. Remove the hub/bearing carrier and the rotor shield.

8. Using an arbor press, press the hub out of the bearing carrier. Special tools 5073 and 5074 are available for this job. Secure the carrier to the press plate with M12 x 1.75mm x 40mm bolts.

9. Cut and remove the plastic cage from the hub inner bearing. Using diagonal pliers or tin snips, cut the bearing cage. Discard the rollers after removing the cage.

10. Remove what remains of the inner bearing as follows:

   a. Install a bearing separator tool on the inner bearing.

   b. Position the separator tool and hub in an arbor press.

   c. Force the hub out of the inner bearing with press pin tool 5074.

11. Remove the bearing carrier outer seal and discard it.

12. Drive the inner bearing seal out and discard it. If you're using tool 5078, make sure that the word JEEP faces downward.

13. Attach press plate tool 5073 to the rear of the carrier. Secure it in the press using M12 x 1.75mm x 40mm bolts.

14. Position bearing race remover 5076 in the carrier bore between the inner and outer bearing races.

15. Position the press pin tool 5074 on tool 5076.

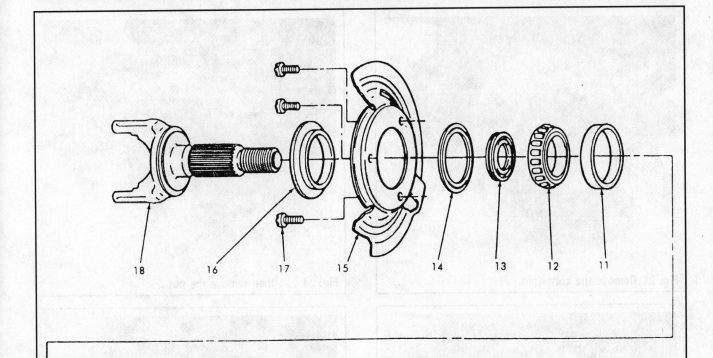

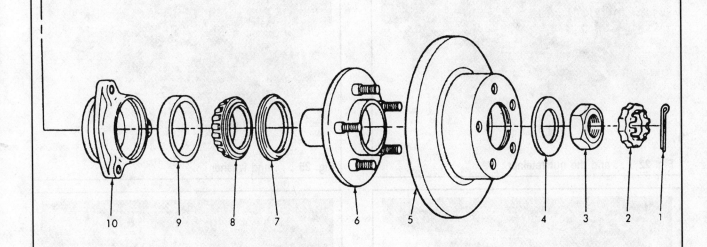

1. COTTER PIN
2. NUT RETAINER
3. NUT
4. WASHER
5. BRAKE ROTOR
6. HUB
7. OUTER BEARING SEAL
8. OUTER BEARING
9. OUTER BEARING RACE

10. BEARING CARRIER
11. INNER BEARING RACE
12. INNER BEARING
13. INNER BEARING SEAL
14. CARRIER SEAL
15. ROTOR SHIELD
16. AXLE SHAFT DUST SLINGER
17. BEARING CARRIER BOLTS
18. AXLE SHAFT

86748g15

Fig. 20 Exploded view of the 4WD hub and bearings

Fig. 21 Remove the cotter pin . . .

Fig. 22 . . . and the nut retainer

Fig. 23 Loosen . . .

Fig. 24 . . . then remove the nut . . .

Fig. 25 . . . and washer

Fig. 26 Remove the hub-to-knuckle attaching bolts . . .

86748p10

Fig. 27 . . . then remove the hub assembly and rotor shield

16. Place the bearing carrier in the press and force the inner bearing race from the carrier bore. Reverse the position of the carrier and tools and force the outer bearing race from the bore.

To assemble and install:

17. Thoroughly clean all reusable parts with a safe solvent. Discard any parts that appear worn or damaged.

18. Attach press plate tool 5073 on the bearing carrier. Secure it in the press using M12 x 1.75mm x 40mm bolts.

19. Position the new outer bearing race in the bore.

20. Position bearing race installation tool 5077 on the race. Make sure that the word JEEP faces the downward. Press the race into the bore. The race should be flush with the machined shoulder of the carrier.

21. Position the new inner bearing race in the carrier bore. Reverse the position of the carrier and tools and force the inner race into the bore.

22. Thoroughly pack the new outer bearing with wheel bearing grease. Make sure that the bearing is fully packed.

23. Coat the race with wheel bearing grease and place the bearing in the bore.

24. Place the new outer seal on the bearing and position bearing installation tool 5079 on the seal. Place the carrier in the press and force the seal into the bore. Apply wheel bearing grease to the seal lip.

25. Insert the hub through the seal and outer bearing and into the bearing carrier bore.

26. Install bearing installation tool 5078 into the rear of the bearing carrier bore and place the race installation tool 5077 on the front of the hub. Make sure that the word JEEP on 5077 is facing the hub.

27. Place the assembly in the press and force the hub shaft into the carrier bore.

28. Pack the new inner bearing with wheel bearing grease. Make sure that the bearing is thoroughly packed.

29. Coat the inner seal lip with wheel bearing grease and place it on the inner bearing.

30. Coat the inner bearing race with wheel bearing grease.

31. Place the carrier in a press along with tool 5077. The word JEEP must face the hub. Position the bearing and seal in the carrier. Place seal installation tool 5080 on the seal.

32. Force the bearing and seal into the bore and onto the hub shaft.

✷✷WARNING

Use extreme care when forcing the assembly into position! The carrier must rotate freely after installation of the bearing! Do not attempt to eliminate bearing lash with the press. Final bearing preload is attained by tightening the drive axle nut.

33. Install the new outer seal on the carrier.

34. Thoroughly clean the axle shaft and apply a thin coating of lithium-based grease to the splines and seal contact surfaces.

35. Install the slinger, rotor shield and hub/bearing assembly on the axle shaft.

36. Coat the carrier bolt threads with Loctite®. Install them and tighten to 75 ft. lbs. (102 Nm).

37. Install the rotor and caliper.

38. Install the washer and axle shaft nut. Tighten the nut to 175 ft. lbs. (237 Nm).

39. Install the nut retainer and cotter pin. NEVER back off the nut to install the cotter pin! ALWAYS advance it!

40. Install the wheel.

1993-96 Grand Cherokee/Wagoneer

1. Raise and support the vehicle safely.
2. Remove the wheel.
3. Remove the caliper and rotor.
4. Remove the cotter pin, nut retainer and axle hub nut.
5. Remove the hub-to-knuckle bolts. Remove the hub from the steering knuckle.

To install:

6. Install the hub to the steering knuckle. Tighten the bolts to 75 ft. lbs. (102 Nm).

7. Install the hub washer and nut. Tighten the nut to 175 ft. lbs. (237 Nm). Install the nut retainer and a new cotter pin.

8. Install the rotor and caliper.
9. Install the wheel and lower the vehicle.

Wheel Alignment

Alignment of the front wheels is essential if your vehicle is to go, stop and turn as designed. Alignment can be altered by collision, overloading, poor repair or bent components.

If you are diagnosing bizarre handling and/or poor road manners, the first place to look is the tires. Although the tires may wear as a result of an alignment problem, worn or poorly inflated tires can make you chase alignment problems which don't exist.

Once you have eliminated all other causes, unload everything from the trunk except the spare tire, set the tire pressures to the correct level and take the car to a reputable alignment facility. Since the alignment settings are measured in very small increments, it is impossible for the home mechanic to accurately determine the settings. The explanations that follow will help you understand the three dimensions of alignment: caster, camber and toe.

CASTER

▶ **See Figure 28**

Caster is the tilting of the steering axis either forward or backward from the vertical, when viewed from the side of the vehicle. A backward tilt is said to be positive caster while a forward tilt is said to be negative caster.

Changes in caster affect the straight line tendency of the vehicle and the "return to center" of the steering after a turn. If the camber is radically different between the left and right wheels (such as after hitting a major pothole), the car will exhibit a nasty pull to one side.

Caster can be altered by the use of shims at the rear of the lower control arms.

CAMBER

▶ **See Figure 29**

Camber is the tilting of the wheels from the vertical (leaning in or out) when viewed from the front of the vehicle. When the wheels tilt outward at the top, the camber is said to be positive. If the wheels tilt inward at the top the camber is said to be negative.

The amount of tilt is measured in degrees from the vertical. This measurement is called camber angle. This angle affects the position of the tire on the road surface during vertical suspension movement and cornering. Changes in camber affect the handling and ride qualities of the car as well as tire wear. Many tire wear patterns indicate camber related problems from misalignment, overloading or poor driving habits.

When checking wheel alignment, it is important that wheel bearings and knuckle bearings be in proper adjustment. Loose bearings will affect instrument readings when checking the camber, pivot pin inclination, and toe-in.

TOE

▶ **See Figure 30**

Toe is the turning in or out (parallelism) of the wheels. The actual amount of toe setting is normally only a fraction of an inch. The purpose of toe-in (or out) specification is to ensure parallel rolling of the wheels. Toe-in also serves to offset the small deflections of the steering support system which occur when the vehicle is rolling forward. Wheel toe-in is the distance by which the wheels are closer together at the front than at the rear. Toe-out is the distance by which the wheels are closer together at the rear than at the front.

Changing the toe setting will radically affect the overall "feel" of the steering, the behavior of the car under braking, tire wear and even fuel economy. Excessive toe (in or out) causes excessive drag or scrubbing on the tires. Toe may be roughly adjusted as follows:

1. First raise the front of the vehicle to free the front wheels. Turn the wheels to the straight ahead position.

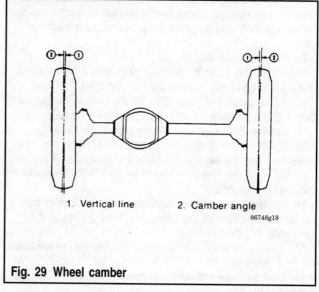

1. Vertical line   2. Camber angle

86748g18

Fig. 29 Wheel camber

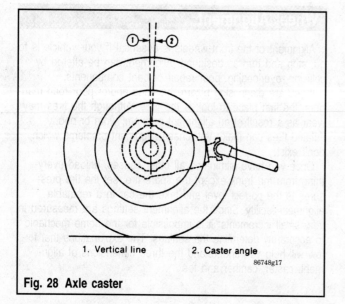

1. Vertical line   2. Caster angle

86748g17

Fig. 28 Axle caster

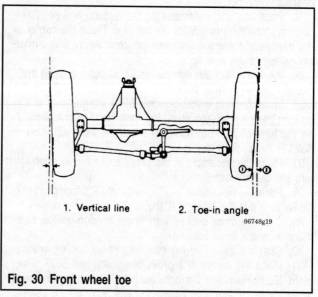

1. Vertical line   2. Toe-in angle

86748g19

Fig. 30 Front wheel toe

2. Use a steady rest to scribe a pencil line in the center of each tire tread as the wheel is turned by hand. A good way to do this is to first run a chalk stripe around the circumference of the tread at the center to form a base for a fine pencil line.

3. Measure the distance between the scribed lines at the front and rear of the wheels using care that both measurements are made at an equal distance from the floor. The distance between the lines should be within specification.

4. To adjust toe, loosen the clamp bolts and turn the tie rod with a small pipe wrench. The tie rod is threaded with right and left hand threads to provide equal adjustment at both wheels. Do not overlook retightening the clamp bolts to 15-20 ft. lbs. (20-27 Nm).

FRONT WHEEL ALIGNMENT

Year	Model	Caster Range (deg.)	Caster Preferred Setting (deg.)	Camber Range (deg.)	Camber Preferred Setting (deg.)	Toe-in (in.)	
1984	All	7P to 8P	7 1/2P	1/2N to 1/2P	0	0	1
1985	All	7P to 8P	7 1/2P	1/2N to 1/2P	0	0	1
1986	All	7P to 8P	7 1/2P	1/2N to 1/2P	0	0	1
1987	All	7P to 8P	7 1/2P	1/2N to 1/2P	0	0	1
1988	All	7P to 8P	7 1/2P	1/2N to 1/2P	0	0	1
1989	All	7P to 8P	7 1/2P	1/2N to 1/2P	0	0	1
1990	All	5P to 9P	6P	3/4N to 1/2P	0	0	2
1991	All	5P to 9P	6P	3/4N to 1/2P	0	0	2
1992	All	5P to 9P	6P	3/4N to 1/2P	0	0	2
1993	Cherokee	5P to 9P	6P	3/4N to 1/2P	0	0	2
	Grand Cherokee	6 1/2P to 7 1/2P	7P	1N to 0	1/2N	1/8P	3
	Grand Wagoneer	6 1/2P to 7 1/2P	7P	1N to 0	1/2N	1/8P	3
1994	Cherokee	5P to 9P	6P	3/4N to 1/2P	0	0	2
	Grand Cherokee	6 1/2P to 7 1/2P	7P	1N to 0	1/2N	1/8P	3
1995	Cherokee	5 1/4P to 8P	7 1/16P	3/4N to 1/2P	1/4N	0	4
	Grand Cherokee	6 1/2P to 7 1/2P	7P	1N to 0	1/2N	1/8P	3
1996	Cherokee	5 1/4P to 8P	7 1/16P	3/4N to 1/2P	1/4N	0	4
	Grand Cherokee	6 1/2P to 7 1/2P	7P	1N to 0	1/2N	1/8P	3

1: Acceptable range is 1/16 in to 1/16 out
2: Acceptable range is 1/32 in to 1/32 out
3: Acceptable range is 0 to 7/32 in
4: Acceptable range is 3/32 out to 1/8 in

86748c01

REAR SUSPENSION

Coil Springs

REMOVAL & INSTALLATION

▶ See Figure 31

➡ Coil springs are used on the 1993-96 Grand Cherokee/Wagoneer.

1. Raise and safely support the vehicle.
2. Support the axle with a suitable jack.
3. Disconnect the sway bar links and shock absorbers from the axle bracket.
4. Disconnect the track bar from the frame rail bracket.
5. Lower the axle until the spring is free from the upper mount seat. Remove the coil spring clip screw and remove the spring.

To install:

6. Position the coil spring on the axle pad, then install the spring clip and screw. Tighten the screw to 16 ft. lbs. (22 Nm).
7. Raise the axle into position until the spring seats in the upper mount.
8. Connect the sway bar links and shock absorbers to the axle bracket. Connect the track bar to the frame rail bracket.
9. Remove the supports and lower the vehicle.

Leaf Springs

INSPECTION

Leaf springs should be examined periodically for broken or shifted leaves, loose or missing clips, angle of the spring shackles, and position of the springs on the saddles. Springs with shifted leaves do not retain their normal strength. Missing clips may permit the spring leaves to fan out or break on rebound. Broken leaves may make the vehicle hard to handle or permit the axle to shift out of line. Weakened springs may break, causing difficulty in steering. Spring attaching clips or bolts must be tight. It is suggested that they be checked at each vehicle inspection.

REMOVAL & INSTALLATION

▶ See Figures 32 and 33

➡ Leaf springs are used on Cherokee, Wagoneer and Co-manche models.

1. Raise and support the vehicle safely.
2. Remove the wheels.
3. Take up the weight of the axle with a floor jack.
4. Disconnect the shock absorbers at the axle.
5. Disconnect the stabilizer bar links (if equipped) at the spring plate.
6. Remove the spring bracket U-bolts and spring plates.
7. Remove the rear spring-to-shackle bolt, then the front spring-to-shackle bolt.
8. Lower the axle and remove the spring.

To install:

9. Position the spring on the axle, then align the ends of the spring with the shackles.
10. Install the shackle bolts, then the spring bracket U-bolts. Tighten the shackle bolts to 111 ft. lbs. (151 Nm) on 1984-88 models, 105 ft. lbs. (142 Nm) on 1989 models and 65 ft. lbs. (88 Nm) on 1990 and later models. Tighten the U-bolt nuts to 52 ft. lbs. (71 Nm) for Cherokee and Wagoneer or 100 ft. lbs. (135 Nm) on Comanche.
11. Connect the stabilizer bar to the spring plate.
12. Connect the shock absorbers to the axle.
13. Install the wheels, then lower the vehicle to the ground. Double check the tightness of the fasteners.

Shock Absorbers

TESTING

Inspect each shock absorber for signs of fluid leakage (gas-charged shocks will show no signs of leaking). Replace leaking shocks.

Check the shock mounting rubber bushings for condition. The shock will rattle, pound and provide poor control if the mounting bushings are worn. Inspect the mounting brackets and fasteners. Grab the shock and try to shake it sideways, up and down.

Bounce each corner of the vehicle and compare shock action. Bounce it vigorously and quickly release at the bottom of the down stroke. Shocks in good condition will allow about one free bounce before stopping any further movement.

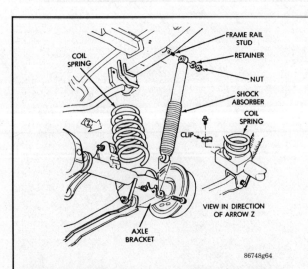

86748g64

Fig. 31 Exploded view of the coil spring and shock absorber mounting

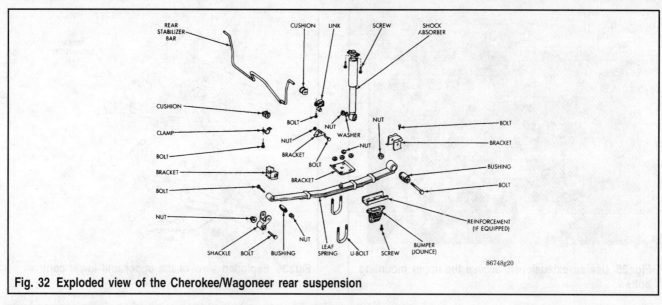

Fig. 32 Exploded view of the Cherokee/Wagoneer rear suspension

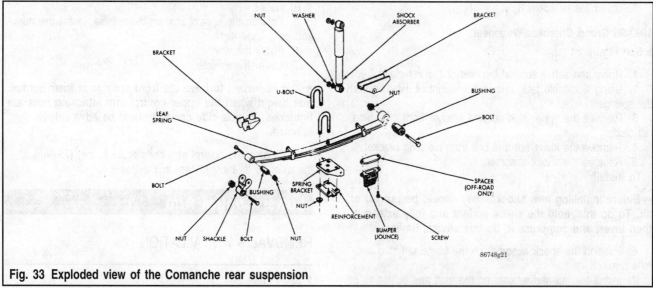

Fig. 33 Exploded view of the Comanche rear suspension

REMOVAL & INSTALLATION

Cherokee, Wagoneer and Comanche

▶ **See Figures 32, 33, 34 and 35**

1. Raise and support the vehicle safely.
2. If necessary for access, remove the wheels.
3. Remove the locknuts and washers.
4. Pull the shock absorber eyes and rubber bushings from the mounting pins.

To install:

➡ **Before installing new shocks, they should be purged of air. To do this, hold the shock upright and fully extend it, then invert and compress it. Do this several times.**

5. Position the shock on the vehicle and install the mounting hardware.
6. Tighten the nuts/bolts to 44 ft. lbs. (60 Nm). On Comanche, tighten upper bolts to 15 ft. lbs. (20 Nm).

Fig. 34 Remove the lower attaching bolt

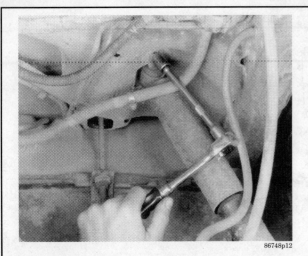

Fig. 35 Use an extension to access the upper mounting bolts

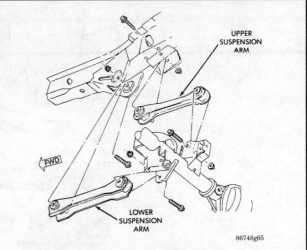

Fig. 36 Exploded view of the upper and lower control arm mountings

7. Lower the vehicle.

1993-96 Grand Cherokee/Wagoneer

▶ See Figure 31

1. Raise and safely support the rear of the vehicle.
2. Using a suitable jack, relieve the weight of the axle from the springs.
3. Remove the upper stud nut and washer from the frame rail stud.
4. Remove the lower nut and bolt from the axle bracket.
5. Remove the shock absorber.

To install:

➡Before installing new shocks, they should be purged of air. To do this, hold the shock upright and fully extend it, then invert and compress it. Do this several times.

6. Position the shock absorber on the frame rail stud and axle bracket.
7. Install the nut and retainer on the stud and tighten to 52 ft. lbs. (70 Nm).
8. Install the bolt and nut to the axle bracket and tighten to 68 ft. lbs. (92 Nm).
9. Remove the supports and lower the vehicle.

Upper Control Arm

REMOVAL & INSTALLATION

▶ See Figure 36

1. Raise and support the vehicle safely.
2. Remove the wheels.
3. Remove the control arm-to-axle bolt.
4. Remove the control arm-to-frame bolt and remove the arm.

To install:
5. Position the control arm on the vehicle. Install the nuts and bolts finger-tight.
6. Install the wheels.
7. Lower the vehicle.

➡It is important to have the front springs at their normal ride height when the upper control arm attaching nuts are tightened. Vehicle ride comfort could be adversely affected.

8. Tighten the control arm bolts to 55 ft. lbs. (75 Nm) at the axle; 66 ft. lbs. (90 Nm) at the frame.

Lower Control Arm

REMOVAL & INSTALLATION

▶ See Figure 36

1. Raise and support the vehicle safely.
2. Remove the wheels.
3. Remove the fasteners securing the lower control arm at the axle and rear bracket.
4. Remove the arm.

To install:
5. Position the arm on the vehicle. Install the attaching bolts finger-tight.
6. Install the wheels.
7. Lower the vehicle.

➡It is important to have the front springs at their normal ride height when the lower control arm attaching nuts are tightened. Vehicle ride comfort could be adversely affected.

8. Tighten the lower control arm attaching bolts to 133 ft. lbs. (180 Nm).

Rear Stabilizer Bar

REMOVAL & INSTALLATION

Cherokee, Wagoneer and Comanche

▶ See Figures 32, 33 and 37

1. Raise and support the vehicle safely.
2. Disconnect the sway bar links from the springs.
3. Disconnect the sway bar from the frame rails.
4. Remove the sway bar.

To install:

5. Install the sway bar and tighten the bar link bolts to 55 ft. lbs. (74 Nm).
6. Connect the sway bar to the frame rail and tighten the bolts to 40 ft. lbs. (54 Nm).
7. Lower the vehicle.

1993-96 Grand Cherokee/Wagoneer

▶ See Figure 38

1. Raise and support the vehicle safely.
2. Remove the wheels.
3. Disconnect the stabilizer bar links from the axle brackets.
4. Lower the exhaust by disconnecting the muffler and tail pipe hangers.
5. Disconnect the stabilizer bar from the links.
6. Disconnect the stabilizer bar clamps from the frame rails. Remove the stabilizer bar.

STEERING

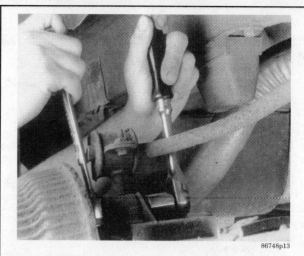

Fig. 37 Disconnecting the sway bar links from the springs

To install:

7. Position the stabilizer bar on the frame rail and install the clamps and bolts.
8. Ensure the bar is centered with equal spacing on both sides. Tighten the bolts to 40 ft. lbs. (54 Nm).
9. Install the links and grommets onto the stabilizer bar and axle brackets. Install the nuts and tighten them to 27 ft. lbs. (36 Nm).
10. Connect the muffler and tail pipe to their hangers.
11. Install the wheel and lower the vehicle.

Steering Wheel

REMOVAL & INSTALLATION

Without Air Bag

▶ See Figures 39, 40, 41, 42, 43 and 44

1. Disconnect the negative battery cable.
2. Set the front tires in the straight ahead position.
3. If equipped with the standard steering wheel:
   a. Remove the trim cover attaching screws from the underside of the wheel and remove the cover.
   b. Unplug the horn wire connectors from the contact switch.
4. If equipped with the sport steering wheel:
   a. Remove the horn button by prying outward.
   b. Remove the horn contact assembly, bushing, receiver and flex plate from the steering wheel.
5. Remove the steering wheel nut and vibration damper.
6. Scribe a line mark on the steering wheel and steering shaft if there is not one already. Release the turn signal assembly from the steering post and install a puller.
7. Remove the steering wheel and spring.

Fig. 38 Rear stabilizer bar mounting

86748g66

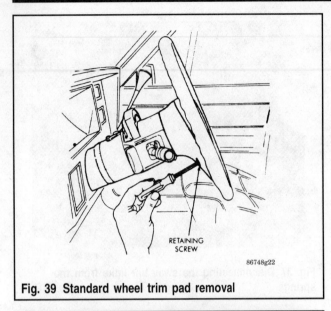

Fig. 39 Standard wheel trim pad removal

Fig. 40 Remove the horn button

Fig. 41 Remove the screws securing the horn contact assembly

Fig. 42 Loosen and remove the steering wheel nut

Fig. 43 A puller must be used to remove the steering wheel

To install:

8. Align the scribe marks on the steering shaft with the steering wheel and secure the steering wheel spring, steering wheel, and horn button contact cup with the steering wheel nut. Tighten to 25 ft. lbs. (34 Nm).

9. Install the horn assembly in the reverse order of removal.

10. Connect the battery cable and test for horn operation.

With Air Bag

▶ See Figures 45, 46 and 47

✳✳CAUTION

Before removing the steering wheel, disable the air bag system (refer to Section 6). Failure to do so could result in accidental air bag deployment and possible injury.

1. Disconnect the negative battery cable and disable the air bag system.

2. Set the front tires in a straight-ahead position.

Fig. 44 Align the scribe marks and install the wheel

86748p18

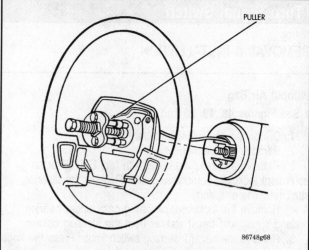

Fig. 46 Use a puller to separate the wheel from the column

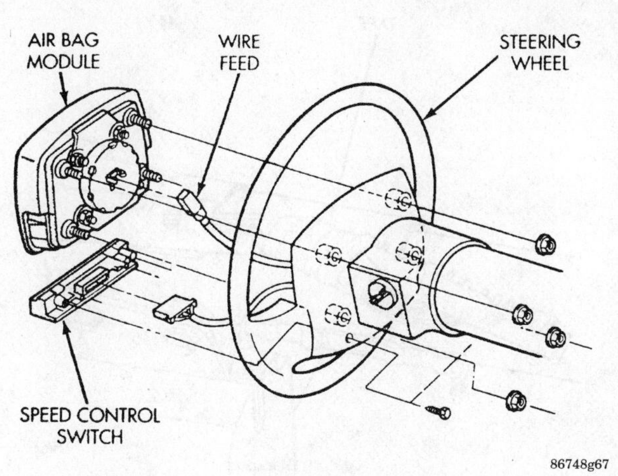

86748g68

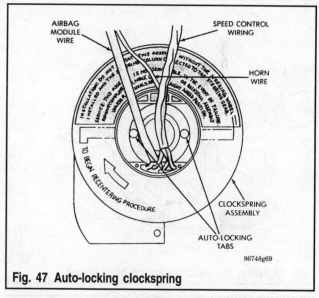

Fig. 45 Exploded view of the air bag module mounting

86748g67

Fig. 47 Auto-locking clockspring

86748g69

3. Remove the air bag module retaining nuts from behind the steering wheel.

4. Remove the air bag module.

5. If equipped, remove the cruise control switch.

6. Disconnect the horn wiring.

7. Remove the steering wheel retaining nut.

8. Scribe a line mark on the steering wheel and steering shaft if there is not one already.

9. Remove the steering wheel using a suitable puller.

To install:

10. To install, align the scribe marks on the steering shaft with the steering wheel.

11. Ensure the wheel compresses the 2 locktabs on the clockspring.

12. Pull the air bag and if equipped, cruise control wires through the larger hole and horn wire through the smaller hole. Ensure they are not pinched.

13. Install the steering wheel nut and tighten it to 45 ft. lbs. (61 Nm) while forcing the steering wheel down the shaft with the nut.

14. Connect the wire feed to the horn buttons.

15. Connect the feed wires and tighten the air bag retaining nuts to 90 inch lbs. (10 Nm). Ensure the air bag is completely seated. The latching clip arms must be visible on top of the connector housing on the module.

16. Enable the air bag system and connect the battery cable.

17. From the right side of the vehicle (in case of accidental deployment), turn the ignition switch to the **ON** position.

18. Check for proper air bag warning light operation.

Turn Signal Switch

REMOVAL & INSTALLATION

Without Air Bag
▶ See Figures 48, 49, 50 and 51

1. Disconnect the negative battery cable.
2. Remove the steering wheel.
3. Remove the lockplate cover with tool C-4156 or an equivalent lockplate compressing tool. Release the steering shaft retaining snapring.
4. Remove the lockplate, canceling cam, upper bearing preload spring and thrust washer from the steering column.
5. Remove the hazard warning switch knob. Press the knob inward and remove it from the column by turning counterclockwise.

6. If equipped with a column shift, remove the two retaining screws and the gear selector indicator cover.
7. If equipped with a column shift, remove the gear selector indicator lamp bracket retaining screw. DO NOT remove the lamp and bracket at this time.
8. Unscrew the tilt-release lever.
9. Remove the combination lever by pulling it out straight from the column. The wiper switch must be in the off position.
10. Disconnect the turn signal wiring harness located at the lower end of the steering column. Wrap it with tape to prevent it from becoming entangled.
11. Remove the plastic protector from the wire harness.
12. Remove the turn signal switch retaining screws and the dimmer switch actuator arm, then remove the switch. Guide the switch straight up out of the steering column.

To install:

13. Install the turn signal switch and wiring harness. Install the dimmer switch actuator arm and turn signal switch retaining screws. Tighten turn signal and dimmer switch attaching screws to 35 inch lbs. (4 Nm).

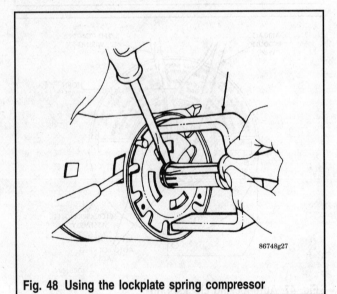

Fig. 48 Using the lockplate spring compressor

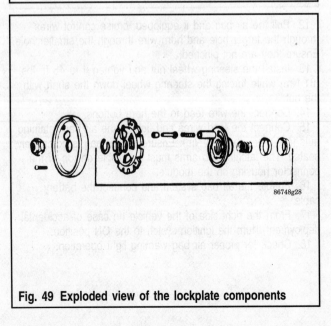

Fig. 49 Exploded view of the lockplate components

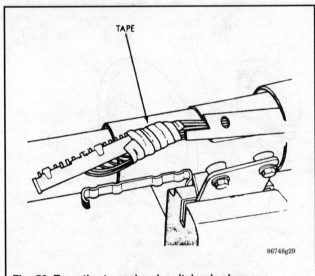

Fig. 50 Tape the turn signal switch wire harness

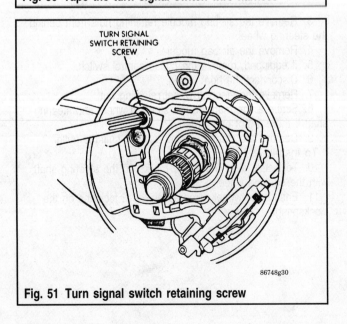

Fig. 51 Turn signal switch retaining screw

14. Install the combination lever and tilt release lever.

15. If equipped with a column shift, install the two retaining screws and the gear selector indicator cover.

16. If equipped with a column shift, install the gear selector indicator lamp bracket retaining screw.

17. Install the hazard warning switch knob. Press the knob inward and install it from the column by turning clockwise.

18. Install the lockplate, canceling cam, upper bearing preload spring and thrust washer from the steering column.

19. Install the lockplate cover and install the steering shaft retaining snapring.

20. Install the steering wheel. Tighten the nut to 25 ft. lbs. (34 Nm).

21. Connect the negative battery cable.

With Air Bag

◗ See Figures 52 and 53

❋❋CAUTION

Before performing this procedure, disable the air bag system (refer to Section 6). Failure to do so could result in accidental air bag deployment and possible injury.

1. Disconnect the negative battery cable and disable the air bag system.

2. If equipped, remove the tilt lever.

3. Remove the upper and lower steering column covers with a suitable Torx® driver.

4. Remove the steering column trim panel.

5. Remove the knee blocker.

6. Remove the steering column retaining nut and lower the column.

7. Using Snap-On® tamper-proof bit TTXR20B2 or equivalent, remove the multi-function switch screws.

8. Pull the switch away from the column, loosen the connector screw (which will remain in the connector) and unplug the electrical connector.

To install:

9. Engage the electrical connector to the multi-function switch and tighten the retaining screw.

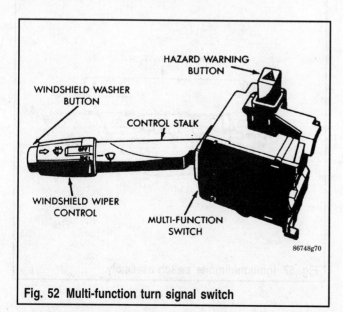

Fig. 52 Multi-function turn signal switch

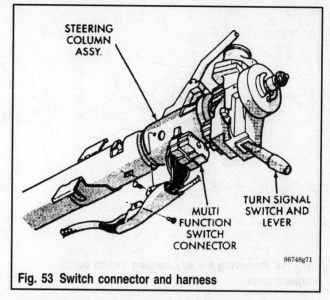

Fig. 53 Switch connector and harness

10. Mount the multi-function switch to the steering column and tighten the screws.

11. Position the steering column and tighten the retaining nuts.

12. Install the knee blocker, lower trim panel and steering column covers.

13. If equipped, install the tilt steering lever.

14. Enable the air bag system and connect the negative battery cable.

15. From the right side of the vehicle (in case of accidental deployment), turn the ignition switch to the **ON** position.

16. Check for proper air bag warning light operation.

Ignition Lock Cylinder

REMOVAL & INSTALLATION

Without Air Bag

◗ See Figures 54, 55 and 56

1. Remove the turn signal switch.

2. Insert the key in the lock cylinder and turn it to the **ON** position.

3. Remove the key warning buzzer switch and contacts AS AN ASSEMBLY using needle-nosed pliers, or a paper clip with a 90° bend.

4. With the ignition switch still in the **ON** position, insert a thin screwdriver into the slot adjacent to the switch attaching screw boss (right-hand slot). Depress the spring latch located at the bottom of the slot to release the lock cylinder.

➡**Some steering columns may have a retaining screw holding the lock cylinder in the column. When servicing this type, simply remove the retaining screw and remove the lock cylinder.**

5. Remove the lock cylinder.

To install:

6. To install the lock cylinder, turn the key to the **LOCK** position. Insert the lock cylinder in to the housing far enough to contact the drive tang. Force it inward and move the ignition

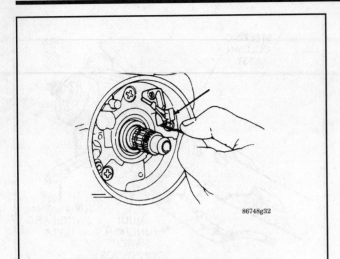

Fig. 54 Removing the key warning switch buzzer components

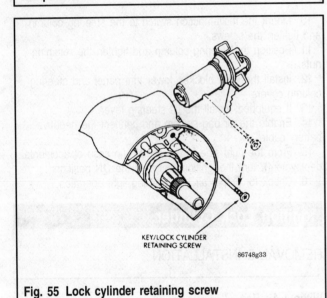

KEY/LOCK CYLINDER RETAINING SCREW

86748g33

Fig. 55 Lock cylinder retaining screw

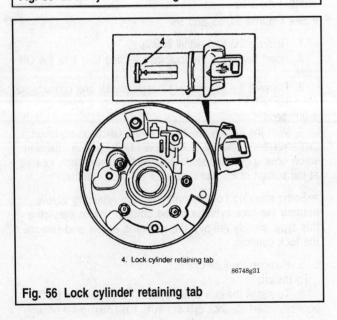

4. Lock cylinder retaining tab

86748g31

Fig. 56 Lock cylinder retaining tab

switch actuator rod up and down to align the components. When the components align, the cylinder will move inward and the spring-loaded retainer will snap into place locking the lock cylinder in the housing.

➡ **If the lock cylinder is retained by a screw, tighten the screw to 40 inch lbs. (5 Nm).**

7. Install the key warning buzzer switch.
8. Follow the ignition switch installation procedures to adjust the ignition switch.
9. Install the turn signal switch.

With Air Bag

Please refer to the ignition switch removal and installation procedure.

Ignition Switch

REMOVAL & INSTALLATION

Without Air Bag

◆ See Figures 57 and 58

The ignition switch is located on the lower part of the steering column.

1. Place the ignition in the **LOCK** position.
2. Remove any components necessary to access the switch.
3. Remove the two switch mounting screws.
4. Disconnect the switch from the rod.
5. Disconnect the wiring and remove the switch.

To install:

6. On non-tilt columns:

a. Move the ignition switch slider to the **OFF** unlocked position (move the slider all the way down, then back two clicks). The remote rod hole in the ignition switch slider should now be centered.

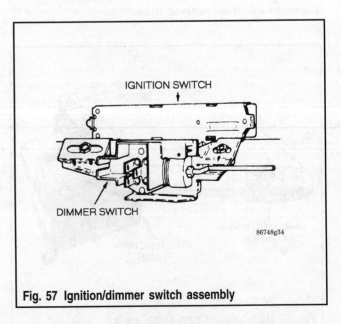

IGNITION SWITCH

DIMMER SWITCH

86748g34

Fig. 57 Ignition/dimmer switch assembly

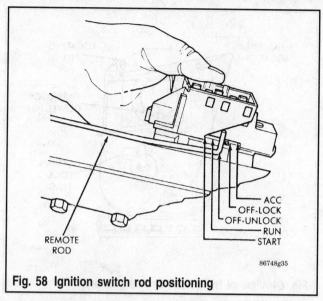

Fig. 58 Ignition switch rod positioning

b. Insert the remote rod in the ignition switch slider hole and install the ignition switch on the steering column. Tighten the attaching screws to 35 inch lbs. (4 Nm).

7. On tilt columns:

a. Insert the ignition key in the lock cylinder and turn the cylinder to the **OFF** unlocked position.

b. Move the ignition switch downward to eliminate any slack and tighten the attaching screws to 35 inch lbs. (4 Nm).

8. Install any components removed for switch access.

With Air Bag

▶ See Figures 59, 60, 61, 62, 63, 64 and 65

✳✳CAUTION

Before performing this procedure, disable the air bag system (refer to Section 6). Failure to do so could result in accidental air bag deployment and possible injury.

1. Disconnect the negative battery cable and disable the air bag system.

2. If equipped, remove the tilt lever.

3. Remove the upper and lower steering column covers with a suitable Torx® driver.

4. Using Snap-On® tamper-proof bit TTXR20BO or equivalent, remove the ignition switch screws.

5. Pull the ignition switch away from the column.

6. Release the 2 connector locks on the 7-terminal wiring connector and remove the connector from the ignition switch.

7. Release the connector lock on the key-in-switch and halo light 4-terminal connector and remove the connector from the ignition switch.

8. Insert the key into the ignition lock and ensure it is in the **LOCK** position.

9. Using a small screwdriver, depress the key cylinder retaining pin so it is flush with the key cylinder surface.

10. Turn the ignition key to the **OFF** position and the lock will release from its seated position.

➡**Do not remove the cylinder at this time.**

11. Turn the key to the **LOCK** position and remove the key.

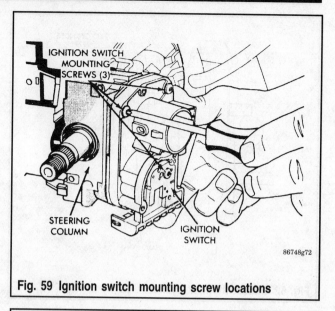

Fig. 59 Ignition switch mounting screw locations

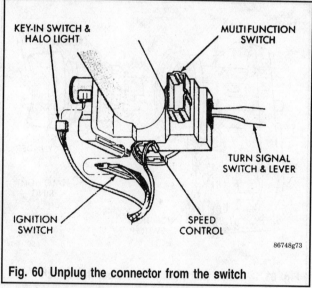

Fig. 60 Unplug the connector from the switch

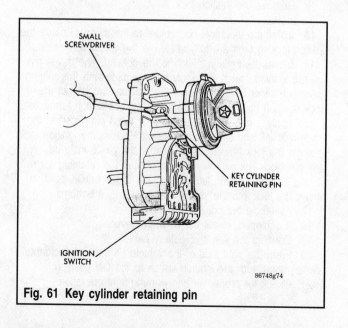

Fig. 61 Key cylinder retaining pin

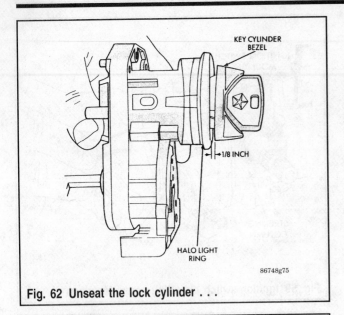

Fig. 62 Unseat the lock cylinder . . .

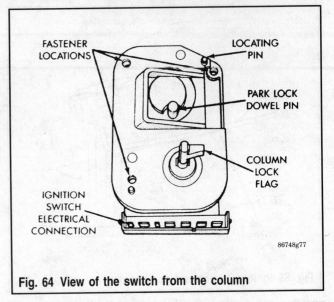

Fig. 64 View of the switch from the column

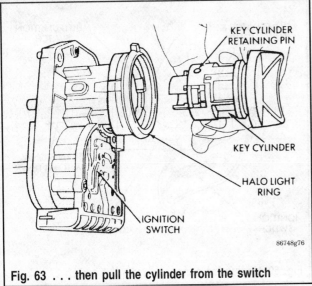

Fig. 63 . . . then pull the cylinder from the switch

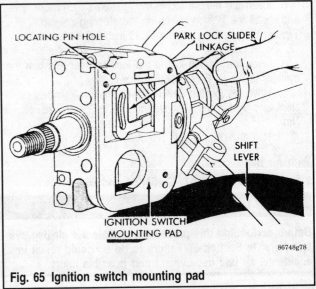

Fig. 65 Ignition switch mounting pad

12. Remove the ignition lock.

To install:

13. Install the electrical connectors to the switch. Ensure the switch locking tabs are fully seated in the wiring connectors.

14. Mount the ignition switch to the column. The dowel pin on the ignition switch assembly must engage with the column park-lock slider linkage. Ensure the ignition switch is in the lock position (flag is parallel with the ignition switch terminals).

15. Apply a dab of grease to the flag and pin. Position the park-lock link and slider to mid-travel. Position the ignition lock against the lock housing face. Ensure the pin is inserted into the park-lock link contour slot and tighten the retaining screw.

16. With the ignition lock and switch in the **LOCK** position, insert the lock into the switch assembly until it bottoms.

17. Assemble the column covers.

18. If equipped, install the tilt wheel lever.

19. Connect the negative battery cable.

20. From the right side of the vehicle (in case of accidental deployment), turn the ignition switch to the **ON** position.

21. Check for proper air bag warning light operation.

Steering Column

REMOVAL & INSTALLATION

✳✳WARNING

Hammering on, or dropping the column will damage to the plastic fasteners that maintain energy absorbing column rigidity.

Without Air Bag

1. Disconnect the negative battery cable.
2. Matchmark the intermediate shaft and steering shaft.
3. Remove the pinch bolt connecting the intermediate shaft and steering shaft.
4. Remove the lower instrument panel trim.

5. Support the column and disconnect it from the instrument panel bracket. Lower the column.

6. Disconnect the ignition switch harness, dimmer switch harness, turn signal switch harness, wiper switch harness, cruise control harness and automatic transmission park/lock cable.

7. Unbolt the column toe plate from the dash panel and pull the column from the truck.

✳✳WARNING

Use only the specified fasteners when installing the column. If any fastener must be replaced, the replacement part must meet the exact specifications of the original. The use of subgrade or overlength fasteners may cause a failure in the performance of the impact absorbing column.

To install:

➡**Install all fasteners finger-tight. Then, when all the fasteners are installed, tighten to specification. Never allow the column to hang unsupported!**

8. Position the steering column in the vehicle, align the matchmarks and connect the steering shaft to the intermediate shaft. Tighten the intermediate shaft-to-steering shaft pinch bolt to 33 ft. lbs. (45 Nm).

9. Connect the ignition switch harness, dimmer switch harness, turn signal switch harness, wiper switch harness, cruise control harness and automatic transmission park/lock cable.

10. Support the column and connect it to the instrument panel bracket. Tighten the column mounting bracket-to-instrument panel bolts to 22 ft. lbs. (30 Nm).

11. Install the column toe plate to the dash panel. Tighten the toe plate-to-dash panel bolts to 6 ft. lbs. (8 Nm).

12. Install the lower instrument panel trim.

13. Connect the negative battery cable.

With Air Bag

✳✳CAUTION

Before performing this procedure, disable the air bag system (refer to Section 6). Failure to do so could result in accidental air bag deployment and possible injury.

1. Position the wheels in the straight ahead position.

2. Disconnect the negative battery cable and disable the air bag system.

3. Remove the steering wheel.

4. Remove the column coupler upper pinch bolt.

5. Remove the trim panel column cover and support plate.

6. If equipped, remove the tilt lever from the column.

7. Remove the upper and lower lock housing shrouds.

8. Remove the heater crossover tube from under the column.

9. Loosen the panel bracket nuts and studs and allow the column to drop.

10. Remove the wiring harness from the column.

11. Remove the interlock cable from the column.

12. Remove the toe plate-to-dash panel nuts.

13. Remove the panel bracket nuts and studs. Remove the steering column from the vehicle.

To install:

14. Position the steering column into the vehicle and align the column to the coupler.

➡**Do not apply force to the top of the column.**

15. Install the interlock cable to the steering column.

16. Install the wiring harness connections to the steering column.

17. Install the shaft coupler pinch bolt finger-tight and position the column to the panel bracket.

18. Ensure both spacers are fully seated in the column support bracket and tighten the nuts and studs to 105 inch lbs. (12 Nm). Ensure the nut is installed on the short threaded side of the stud.

19. Tighten the toe plate attaching nuts to 105 inch lbs. (12 Nm).

20. Tighten the coupler pinch bolt to 35 ft. lbs. (47 Nm).

21. Install the heater crossover tube.

22. Install the upper and lower shrouds.

23. If equipped, install the tilt lever.

24. Install the trim panel column cover and support plate.

25. Install the steering wheel.

26. If installing a new column, remove the shaft shipping lock pin.

27. Enable the air bag system and connect the negative battery cable.

Steering Linkage

REMOVAL & INSTALLATION

Pitman Arm (Steering Arm)
▶ **See Figure 66**

➡**It is recommended that that front end alignment be checked after performing this procedure.**

1. Raise and support the vehicle safely.
2. Place the wheels in a straight ahead position.

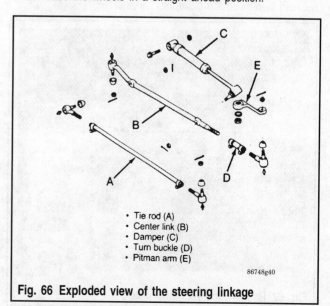

- Tie rod (A)
- Center link (B)
- Damper (C)
- Turn buckle (D)
- Pitman arm (E)

86748g40

Fig. 66 Exploded view of the steering linkage

3. Remove the cotter pin and nut, then disconnect the connecting rod from the pitman arm.

4. Matchmark the pitman arm and steering gear housing for installation alignment.

5. Remove the pitman arm nut. Some steering gears have a staked washer securing the nut. The arms of this washer must be bent out of the way to remove the nut.

6. Installation is the reverse of removal. Tighten the pitman arm nut to 185 ft. lbs. (250 Nm).

Tie Rod End

➥It is recommended that that front end alignment be checked after performing this procedure.

CHEROKEE, WAGONEER AND COMANCHE

▶ See Figures 66, 67 and 68

1. Raise and support the vehicle safely.
2. Remove the cotter pins and retaining nuts at both ends of the tie rod.
3. Remove the tie rod ends from the steering arm and center link.
4. Count the number of visible threads on the tie rod and unscrew the tie rod ends.
5. Installation is the reverse of removal. Install the tie rod ends, leaving the same number of threads exposed. Tighten the retaining nuts to 35 ft. lbs. (47 Nm).

1993-96 GRAND CHEROKEE/WAGONEER

▶ See Figure 69

1. Remove the cotter pins at the steering knuckle and drag link.
2. Loosen the ball studs using a suitable puller.
3. If necessary, loosen the end clamp bolts and remove the tie rod ends from the tube. Count the number of turns required to remove the tie rod ends so the replacement tie rod ends can be reinstalled in the same approximate position.

To install:

4. If removed, install the tie rod ends in the tube. Thread the tie rod ends into the tube the same number of turns required to remove the old ones.

Fig. 68 . . . then use a puller to separate the link

5. Position the tie rod clamps and tighten to 20 ft. lbs. (27 Nm).

6. Install the tie rod on the drag link and steering knuckle and install the retaining nuts.

7. Tighten the ball stud nuts to 55 ft. lbs. (75 Nm) and install new cotter pins. If the ball stud hole does not align with the nut castellation, further tighten the nut in order to install the cotter pin.

8. Have the wheel alignment checked.

Steering Connecting Rod (Drag Link)

➥It is recommended that that front end alignment be checked after performing this procedure.

CHEROKEE, WAGONEER AND COMANCHE

▶ See Figures 66 and 70

1. Raise and support the vehicle safely.
2. Place the wheels in a straight ahead position.
3. Remove the cotter pin and nut and disconnect the steering damper from the connecting rod.

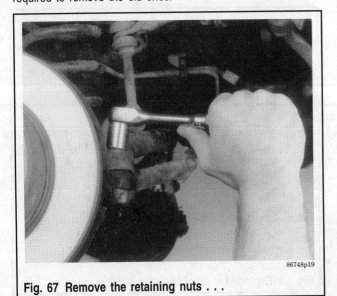

Fig. 67 Remove the retaining nuts . . .

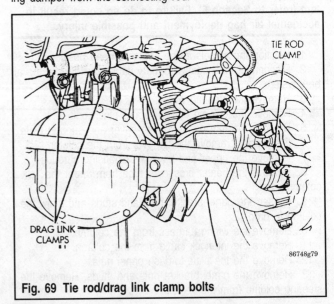

Fig. 69 Tie rod/drag link clamp bolts

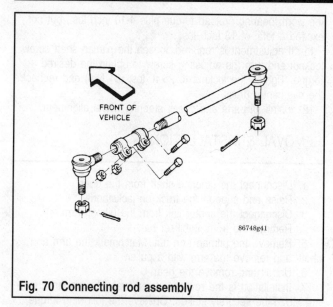

Fig. 70 Connecting rod assembly

4. Remove the cotter pins and nuts at each end of the rod, then disconnect the connecting rod from the knuckle and the pitman arm.

5. Install the connecting rod, with the wheels straight ahead and the pitman arm parallel with the vehicle centerline. Install the nuts and tighten all three to 35 ft. lbs. (47 Nm).

1993-96 GRAND CHEROKEE/WAGONEER

1. Remove the cotter pins and nuts at the steering knuckle and drag link.

2. Remove the steering dampener ball stud from the drag link using a suitable puller tool.

3. Remove the tie rod from the drag link and remove the drag link from the steering knuckle and pitman arm using a suitable puller tool.

4. If necessary, loosen the end clamp bolts and remove the tie rod end from the link. Count the number of turns required to remove the tie rod end so the replacement tie rod end can be reinstalled in the same approximate position.

To install:

5. Install the drag link adjustment sleeve and tie rod end. Thread the tie rod end and sleeve onto the drag link the same number of turns required to remove the old ones.

6. Position the clamp bolts and tighten to 36 ft. lbs. (49 Nm).

7. Install the drag link to the steering knuckle, tie rod and pitman arm. Install the nuts and tighten to 55 ft. lbs. (75 Nm). Install new cotter pins. If the ball stud hole does not align with the nut castellation, further tighten the nut in order to install the cotter pin.

8. Install the steering dampener onto the drag link and tighten the nut to 55 ft. lbs. (75 Nm). Install a new cotter pin. If the ball stud hole does not align with the nut castellation, further tighten the nut in order to install the cotter pin.

9. Have the wheel alignment checked.

Steering Dampener

♦ See Figures 66, 71, 72 and 73

➡It is recommended that that front end alignment be checked after performing this procedure.

1. Raise and support the vehicle safely.

2. Place the wheels in a straight ahead position.

3. Remove the steering dampener retaining nut and bolt from the axle bracket.

4. Remove the cotter pin and nut from the piston rod ball stud at the drag link.

5. Remove the steering dampener ball stud from the drag link.

6. Installation is the reverse of removal. Tighten retaining bolts to 55 ft. lbs. (75 Nm).

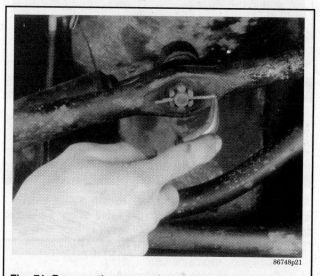

Fig. 71 Remove the cotter pin . . .

Fig. 72 . . . and nut from the drag link

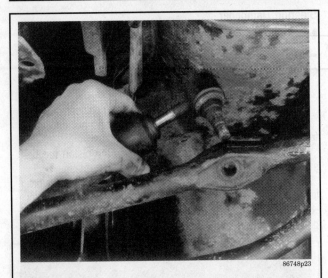

86748p23

Fig. 73 Separate the stud from the drag link

Manual Steering Gear

ADJUSTMENT

✳✳WARNING

Adjust the wormshaft bearing preload and pitman shaft overcenter drag torque in the order listed below. Failure to follow the procedures exactly may result in gear failure.

1. Raise and support the vehicle safely.
2. Check the steering gear mounting bolt torque. It should be 65 ft. lbs. (88 Nm).
3. Matchmark the pitman arm and shaft, and remove the pitman arm nut. Remove the arm with a puller.
4. Loosen the pitman adjusting screw locknut, then back off the adjusting screw 2-3 turns.
5. Remove the horn button and cover. Slowly turn the steering wheel in one direction as far as it will go, then back ½ turn.
6. Install a socket and inch-pound torque wrench on the steering wheel nut. Measure the worm bearing preload by turning the wheel through a 90° arc (¼ turn) with the wrench. Preload should be 5-8 inch lbs.
7. If preload is not within specifications, turn the adjuster screw clockwise to increase, or counterclockwise to decrease, the preload.
8. When the desired preload is attained, tighten the adjuster locknut to 50 ft. lbs. (68 Nm) and recheck the adjustment.
9. Rotate the steering wheel slowly from lock-to-lock, counting the number of turns. Turn the wheel back, ½ the number of turns to center the gear, then turn the wheel ½ turn off center.
10. Install the inch-pound torque wrench and socket on the steering wheel nut. Measure the torque required to tun the gear through the center point of travel. The drag should equal

the worm bearing preload torque plus 4-10 inch lbs., but not exceed a total of 18 inch lbs.

11. If adjustment is required, loosen the pitman shaft screw locknut and turn the adjusting screw to obtain the desired torque. Tighten the locknut to 25 ft. lbs. (34 Nm) and recheck the overcenter drag.
12. Install all parts and check steering wheel alignment.

REMOVAL & INSTALLATION

1. Disconnect the steering shaft from the gear.
2. Raise and support the truck on jackstands.
3. Disconnect the center link from the pitman arm.
4. Remove the front stabilizer bar.
5. Remove the pitman arm nut. Matchmark the arm and shaft, and remove the arm with a puller.
6. Unbolt and remove the gear.
7. Installation is the reverse of removal. The pitman arm nut MUST be securely staked. Observe the following torque specifications:

- Steering gear-to-frame: 65 ft. lbs. (88 Nm)
- Pitman arm-to-shaft: 185 ft. lbs. (250 Nm)
- Stabilizer bar-to-frame: 55 ft. lbs. (75 Nm)
- Stabilizer bar-to-link: 27 ft. lbs. (37 Nm)
- Center link-to-pitman arm: 55 ft. lbs. (75 Nm)

Power Steering Gear

ADJUSTMENT

✳✳WARNING

Adjust the wormshaft bearing preload and pitman shaft overcenter drag torque in the order listed below. Failure to follow the procedures exactly may result in gear failure.

1. Ensure the wormshaft bearing adjustment cap is seated. Score an index mark on the steering gear housing adjacent to one of the spanner wrench tightening holes.
2. Measure counterclockwise 0.19-0.23 in. (5-6mm) from the index mark and score an adjustment reference mark on the housing. Rotate the adjustment cap counterclockwise until the spanner wrench tightening hole in the cap is aligned with the adjustment reference mark on the housing.
3. Install the adjustment cap locknut and tighten to 85 ft. lbs. (115 Nm). Ensure that the adjustment cap does not rotate. Rotate the stub shaft clockwise to the stop, then rotate it counterclockwise ¼ of a turn.
4. Measure the preload torque by rotating at a constant speed with a inch pound torque wrench installed. It should be between 4-10 inch lbs.
5. Rotate the pitman shaft adjustment screw counterclockwise until it is fully extended, then rotate it 180° clockwise. Rotate the stub shaft from stop-to-stop counting the number of turns. Turn the wheel back, ½ the number of turns. Make sure the steering gear is centered. The flat area on the stub shaft should face upward and be parallel with the adjustment screw cover.

6. Measure the drag by rotating the stub shaft 45° on each side of vertical and record the highest drag torque measured at or near the steering gear center position.

7. Specifications are as follows:
- New Gears: 4-8 inch lbs. greater than wormshaft bearing preload, to a maximum of 18 inch lbs.
- Used Gears: 4-5 inch lbs. greater than wormshaft bearing preload, to a maximum of 18 inch lbs.

8. If necessary, rotate the pitman shaft adjustment screw until the correct torque is obtained. Tighten the locknut to 20 ft. lbs. (27 Nm). DO NOT allow the adjustment screw locknut to rotate.

REMOVAL & INSTALLATION

1. Place the front wheels in a straight-ahead position. Place a drain pan under the steering gear.

2. Disconnect the fluid hoses from the steering gear. Raise and secure the hoses above the level of the pump to prevent excess steering fluid loss. Plug the hoses to prevent the entry of dirt.

3. Disconnect the steering shaft from the gear.
4. Raise and support the truck on jackstands.
5. Disconnect the center link from the pitman arm.
6. Remove the front stabilizer bar.

7. Remove the pitman arm nut. Matchmark the arm and shaft, and remove the arm with a puller.

8. Unbolt and remove the gear.

9. Installation is the reverse of removal. The pitman arm nut MUST be securely staked. Observe the following torque specifications:
- Steering gear-to-frame: 65 ft. lbs. (88 Nm)
- Pitman arm-to-shaft: 185 ft. lbs. (250 Nm)
- Stabilizer bar-to-frame: 55 ft. lbs. (75 Nm)
- Stabilizer bar-to-link: 27 ft. lbs. (37 Nm)
- Center link-to-pitman arm: 55 ft. lbs. (75 Nm)

Power Steering Pump

REMOVAL & INSTALLATION

Cherokee, Wagoneer and Comanche

SERPENTINE DRIVE BELT

▶ See Figures 74 and 75

1. Loosen the alternator adjustment and pivot bolts.

2. Insert the drive lug of a ½ in. drive ratchet into the adjustment hole in the alternator bracket and move the alternator to relieve tension on the belt.

3. Remove the drive belt.
4. Remove the air cleaner.
5. Disconnect the hoses at the pump and cap the hose ends.
6. Remove the front bracket-to-engine bolts.

7. Support the pump with your hand. Remove the pump-to-rear bracket nuts.

8. Lift out the pump.

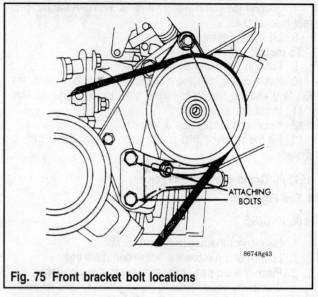

Fig. 75 Front bracket bolt locations

To install:

9. Position the pump on the engine.

10. Install and tighten the pump-to-bracket nuts to 28 ft. lbs. (38 Nm) and the bracket-to-engine bolts to 33 ft. lbs. (45 Nm).

11. Install the air cleaner.
12. Install and tension the drive belt.

13. Fill the reservoir with power steering fluid. Bleed the system.

V-TYPE DRIVE BELT

1. Loosen the power steering pump adjustment and pivot bolts.

2. Insert the drive lug of a ½ in. drive ratchet into the adjustment hole in the pump rear bracket and move the pump to relieve tension on the belt.

3. Remove the drive belt.
4. Remove the air cleaner.
5. Disconnect the hoses at the pump and cap the hose ends.
6. Remove the front bracket-to-engine bolts.

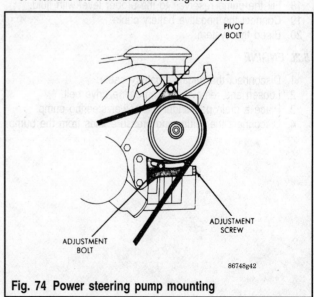

Fig. 74 Power steering pump mounting

7. Support the pump with your hand. Remove the pump-to-rear bracket nuts.

8. Lift out the pump.

To install:

9. Position the pump on the engine.

10. Install and tighten the pump-to-bracket nuts to 28 ft. lbs. (38 Nm) and the bracket-to-engine bolts to 33 ft. lbs. (45 Nm).

11. Install the air cleaner.

12. Install and tension the drive belt.

13. Fill the reservoir with power steering fluid. Bleed the system.

1993-96 Grand Cherokee/Wagoneer

▶ See Figure 76

4.0L ENGINE

1. Disconnect the negative battery cable.

2. Loosen and remove the serpentine drive belt.

3. Place a drain pan under the power steering pump.

4. Clamp the power steering pump pressure and return fluid lines and disconnect the lines from the hose from the pump.

5. Remove the rear bracket-to-pump bolts.

6. Remove the lower nut and adjustment bracket.

7. Remove the adjuster and pivot bolts.

8. Tilt the pump forward and remove the pump and front bracket assembly from the engine bracket.

9. Remove the bracket from the pump.

To install:

10. Install the bracket to the pump and tighten the bolts to 21 ft. lbs. (28 Nm).

11. Position the pump and bracket on the engine bracket.

12. Install the pivot bolt.

13. Install the adjuster bolt.

14. Install the adjuster stud nut.

15. Install the rear bracket-to-pump bolts and tighten them to 21 ft. lbs. (28 Nm).

16. Install the serpentine belt.

17. Connect the power steering lines and remove the clamps.

18. Fill the pump reservoir to the proper level with fluid.

19. Connect the negative battery cable.

20. Bleed the system.

5.2L ENGINE

1. Disconnect the negative battery cable.

2. Loosen and remove the serpentine drive belt.

3. Place a drain pan under the power steering pump.

4. Disconnect the return and pressure lines from the pump.

5. Remove the bolts attaching the pump to the bracket on the engine block.

6. If necessary, remove the bracket-to-engine block bolts.

To install:

7. Install the bracket to the engine block and tighten the bolts to 30 ft. lbs. (41 Nm).

8. Mount the pump on the bracket and tighten the bolts 20 ft. lbs. (27 Nm).

9. Install the serpentine belt.

10. Connect the fluid lines to the pump and remove the clamps.

11. Fill the power steering reservoir to the proper level with fluid.

12. Connect the negative battery cable.

13. Bleed the system.

SYSTEM BLEEDING

1. Fill the steering pump with fluid. Operate the engine until it reaches normal operating temperature, then stop the engine.

2. Turn the wheels to the full left and full right position to circulate the fluid. Add fluid to reservoir to maintain full level. Start the engine. Check the fluid level and add if necessary.

3. Purge the system of air by turning the wheels from side-to-side without going to the full left or right position.

4. Return the wheels to straight ahead position and operate the engine for 2-3 minutes, then stop the engine. Add fluid if necessary. Road test the vehicle.

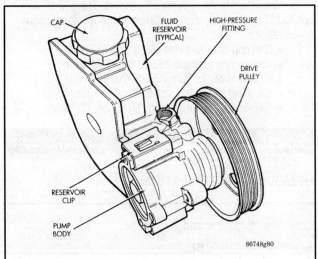

Fig. 76 Power steering pump used on the Grand Cherokee/Wagoneer

Troubleshooting Basic Steering and Suspension Problems

Problem	Cause	Solution
Hard steering (steering wheel is hard to turn)	· Low or uneven tire pressure · Loose power steering pump drive belt · Low or incorrect power steering fluid · Incorrect front end alignment · Defective power steering pump · Bent or poorly lubricated front end parts	· Inflate tires to correct pressure · Adjust belt · Add fluid as necessary · Have front end alignment checked/adjusted · Check pump · Lubricate and/or replace defective parts
Loose steering (too much play in the steering wheel)	· Loose wheel bearings · Loose or worn steering linkage · Faulty shocks · Worn ball joints	· Adjust wheel bearings · Replace worn parts · Replace shocks · Replace ball joints
Car veers or wanders (car pulls to one side with hands off the steering wheel)	· Incorrect tire pressure · Improper front end alignment · Loose wheel bearings · Loose or bent front end components · Faulty shocks	· Inflate tires to correct pressure · Have front end alignment checked/adjusted · Adjust wheel bearings · Replace worn components · Replace shocks
Wheel oscillation or vibration transmitted through steering wheel	· Improper tire pressures · Tires out of balance · Loose wheel bearings · Improper front end alignment · Worn or bent front end components	· Inflate tires to correct pressure · Have tires balanced · Adjust wheel bearings · Have front end alignment checked/adjusted · Replace worn parts
Uneven tire wear	· Incorrect tire pressure · Front end out of alignment · Tires out of balance	· Inflate tires to correct pressure · Have front end alignment checked/adjusted · Have tires balanced

Troubleshooting the Ignition Switch

Problem	Cause	Solution
Ignition switch electrically inoperative	· Loose or defective switch connector · Feed wire open (fusible link) · Defective ignition switch	· Tighten or replace connector · Repair or replace · Replace ignition switch
Engine will not crank	· Ignition switch not adjusted properly	· Adjust switch
Ignition switch wil not actuate mechanically	· Defective ignition switch · Defective lock sector · Defective remote rod	· Replace switch · Replace lock sector · Replace remote rod
Ignition switch cannot be adjusted correctly	· Remote rod deformed	· Repair, straighten or replace

86748g44

Troubleshooting the Steering Column

Problem	Cause	Solution
Will not lock	• Lockbolt spring broken or defective	• Replace lock bolt spring
High effort (required to turn ignition key and lock cylinder)	• Lock cylinder defective	• Replace lock cylinder
	• Ignition switch defective	• Replace ignition switch
	• Rack preload spring broken or deformed	• Replace preload spring
	• Burr on lock sector, lock rack, housing, support or remote rod coupling	• Remove burr
	• Bent sector shaft	• Replace shaft
	• Defective lock rack	• Replace lock rack
	• Remote rod bent, deformed	• Replace rod
	• Ignition switch mounting bracket bent	• Straighten or replace
	• Distorted coupling slot in lock rack (tilt column)	• Replace lock rack
Will stick in "start"	• Remote rod deformed	• Straighten or replace
	• Ignition switch mounting bracket bent	• Straighten or replace
Key cannot be removed in "off-lock"	• Ignition switch is not adjusted correctly	• Adjust switch
	• Defective lock cylinder	• Replace lock cylinder
Lock cylinder can be removed without depressing retainer	• Lock cylinder with defective retainer	• Replace lock cylinder
	• Burr over retainer slot in housing cover or on cylinder retainer	• Remove burr
High effort on lock cylinder between "off" and "off-lock"	• Distorted lock rack	• Replace lock rack
	• Burr on tang of shift gate (automatic column)	• Remove burr
	• Gearshift linkage not adjusted	• Adjust linkage
Noise in column	• One click when in "off-lock" position and the steering wheel is moved (all except automatic column)	• Normal—lock bolt is seating
	• Coupling bolts not tightened	• Tighten pinch bolts
	• Lack of grease on bearings or bearing surfaces	• Lubricate with chassis grease
	• Upper shaft bearing worn or broken	• Replace bearing assembly
	• Lower shaft bearing worn or broken	• Replace bearing. Check shaft and replace if scored.
	• Column not correctly aligned	• Align column
	• Coupling pulled apart	• Replace coupling
	• Broken coupling lower joint	• Repair or replace joint and align column
	• Steering shaft snap ring not seated	• Replace ring. Check for proper seating in groove.

86748g45

Troubleshooting the Steering Column (cont.)

Problem	Cause	Solution
Noise in column	• Shroud loose on shift bowl. Housing loose on jacket—will be noticed with ignition in "off-lock" and when torque is applied to steering wheel.	• Position shroud over lugs on shift bowl. Tighten mounting screws.
High steering shaft effort	• Column misaligned • Defective upper or lower bearing • Tight steering shaft universal joint • Flash on I.D. of shift tube at plastic joint (tilt column only) • Upper or lower bearing seized	• Align column • Replace as required • Repair or replace • Replace shift tube • Replace bearings
Lash in mounted column assembly	• Column mounting bracket bolts loose • Broken weld nuts on column jacket • Column capsule bracket sheared	• Tighten bolts • Replace column jacket • Replace bracket assembly
Lash in mounted column assembly (cont.)	• Column bracket to column jacket mounting bolts loose • Loose lock shoes in housing (tilt column only) • Loose pivot pins (tilt column only) • Loose lock shoe pin (tilt column only) • Loose support screws (tilt column only)	• Tighten to specified torque • Replace shoes • Replace pivot pins and support • Replace pin and housing • Tighten screws
Housing loose (tilt column only)	• Excessive clearance between holes in support or housing and pivot pin diameters • Housing support-screws loose	• Replace pivot pins and support • Tighten screws
Steering wheel loose—every other tilt position (tilt column only)	• Loose fit between lock shoe and lock shoe pivot pin	• Replace lock shoes and pivot pin
Steering column not locking in any tilt position (tilt column only)	• Lock shoe seized on pivot pin • Lock shoe grooves have burrs or are filled with foreign material • Lock shoe springs weak or broken	• Replace lock shoes and pin • Clean or replace lock shoes • Replace springs
Noise when tilting column (tilt column only)	• Upper tilt bumpers worn • Tilt spring rubbing in housing	• Replace tilt bumper • Lubricate with chassis grease
One click when in "off-lock" position and the steering wheel is moved	• Seating of lock bolt	• None. Click is normal characteristic sound produced by lock bolt as it seats.
High shift effort (automatic and tilt column only)	• Column not correctly aligned • Lower bearing not aligned correctly • Lack of grease on seal or lower bearing areas	• Align column • Assemble correctly • Lubricate with chassis grease
Improper transmission shifting—automatic and tilt column only	• Sheared shift tube joint • Improper transmission gearshift linkage adjustment • Loose lower shift lever	• Replace shift tube • Adjust linkage • Replace shift tube

Troubleshooting the Turn Signal Switch

Problem	Cause	Solution
Turn signal will not cancel	• Loose switch mounting screws • Switch or anchor bosses broken • Broken, missing or out of position detent, or cancelling spring	• Tighten screws • Replace switch • Reposition springs or replace switch as required
Turn signal difficult to operate	• Turn signal lever loose • Switch yoke broken or distorted • Loose or misplaced springs • Foreign parts and/or materials in switch • Switch mounted loosely	• Tighten mounting screws • Replace switch • Reposition springs or replace switch • Remove foreign parts and/or material • Tighten mounting screws
Turn signal will not indicate lane change	• Broken lane change pressure pad or spring hanger • Broken, missing or misplaced lane change spring • Jammed wires	• Replace switch • Replace or reposition as required • Loosen mounting screws, reposition wires and retighten screws
Turn signal will not stay in turn position	• Foreign material or loose parts impeding movement of switch yoke • Defective switch	• Remove material and/or parts • Replace switch
Hazard switch cannot be pulled out	• Foreign material between hazard support cancelling leg and yoke	• Remove foreign material. No foreign material impeding function of hazard switch—replace turn signal switch.
No turn signal lights	• Inoperative turn signal flasher • Defective or blown fuse • Loose chassis to column harness connector • Disconnect column to chassis connector. Connect new switch to chassis and operate switch by hand. If vehicle lights now operate normally, signal switch is inoperative • If vehicle lights do not operate, check chassis wiring for opens, grounds, etc.	• Replace turn signal flasher • Replace fuse • Connect securely • Replace signal switch • Repair chassis wiring as required

86748g47

Troubleshooting the Turn Signal Switch (cont.)

Problem	Cause	Solution
Instrument panel turn indicator lights on but not flashing	• Burned out or damaged front or rear turn signal bulb	• Replace bulb
	• If vehicle lights do not operate, check light sockets for high resistance connections, the chassis wiring for opens, grounds, etc.	• Repair chassis wiring as required
	• Inoperative flasher	• Replace flasher
	• Loose chassis to column harness connection	• Connect securely
	• Inoperative turn signal switch	• Replace turn signal switch
	• To determine if turn signal switch is defective, substitute new switch into circuit and operate switch by hand. If the vehicle's lights operate normally, signal switch is inoperative.	• Replace turn signal switch
Stop light not on when turn indicated	• Loose column to chassis connection	• Connect securely
	• Disconnect column to chassis connector. Connect new switch into system without removing old.	• Replace signal switch
Stop light not on when turn indicated (cont.)	Operate switch by hand. If brake lights work with switch in the turn position, signal switch is defective.	
	• If brake lights do not work, check connector to stop light sockets for grounds, opens, etc.	• Repair connector to stop light circuits using service manual as guide
Turn indicator panel lights not flashing	• Burned out bulbs	• Replace bulbs
	• High resistance to ground at bulb socket	• Replace socket
	• Opens, ground in wiring harness from front turn signal bulb socket to indicator lights	• Locate and repair as required
Turn signal lights flash very slowly	• High resistance ground at light sockets	• Repair high resistance grounds at light sockets
	• Incorrect capacity turn signal flasher or bulb	• Replace turn signal flasher or bulb
	• If flashing rate is still extremely slow, check chassis wiring harness from the connector to light sockets for high resistance	• Locate and repair as required
	• Loose chassis to column harness connection	• Connect securely
	• Disconnect column to chassis connector. Connect new switch into system without removing old. Operate switch by hand. If flashing occurs at normal rate, the signal switch is defective.	• Replace turn signal switch

Troubleshooting the Turn Signal Switch (cont.)

Problem	Cause	Solution
Hazard signal lights will not flash—turn signal functions normally	• Blow fuse • Inoperative hazard warning flasher • Loose chassis-to-column harness connection • Disconnect column to chassis connector. Connect new switch into system without removing old. Depress the hazard warning lights. If they now work normally, turn signal switch is defective. • If lights do not flash, check wiring harness "K" lead for open between hazard flasher and connector. If open, fuse block is defective	• Replace fuse • Replace hazard warning flasher in fuse panel • Conect securely • Replace turn signal switch • Repair or replace brown wire or connector as required

Troubleshooting the Power Steering Gear

Problem	Cause	Solution
Hissing noise in steering gear	• There is some noise in all power steering systems. One of the most common is a hissing sound most evident at standstill parking. There is no relationship between this noise and performance of the steering. Hiss may be expected when steering wheel is at end of travel or when slowly turning at standstill.	• Slight hiss is normal and in no way affects steering. Do not replace valve unless hiss is extremely objectionable. A replacement valve will also exhibit slight noise and is not always a cure. Investigate clearance around flexible coupling rivets. Be sure steering shaft and gear are aligned so flexible coupling rotates in a flat plane and is not distorted as shaft rotates. Any metal-to-metal contacts through flexible coupling will transmit valve hiss into passenger compartment through the steering column.
Rattle or chuckle noise in steering gear	• Gear loose on frame • Steering linkage looseness • Pressure hose touching other parts of car • Loose pitman shaft over center adjustment **NOTE:** A slight rattle may occur on turns because of increased clearance off the "high point." This is normal and clearance must not be reduced below specified limits to eliminate this slight rattle. • Loose pitman arm	• Check gear-to-frame mounting screws. • Check linkage pivot points for wear. Replace if necessary. • Adjust hose position. Do not bend tubing by hand. • Adjust to specifications • Tighten pitman arm nut to specifications

Troubleshooting the Power Steering Gear (cont.)

Problem	Cause	Solution
Squawk noise in steering gear when turning or recovering from a turn	• Damper O-ring on valve spool cut	• Replace damper O-ring
Poor return of steering wheel to center	• Tires not properly inflated	• Inflate to specified pressure
	• Lack of lubrication in linkage and ball joints	• Lube linkage and ball joints
	• Lower coupling flange rubbing against steering gear adjuster plug	• Loosen pinch bolt and assemble properly
	• Steering gear to column misalignment	• Align steering column
	• Improper front wheel alignment	• Check and adjust as necessary
	• Steering linkage binding	• Replace pivots
	• Ball joints binding	• Replace ball joints
	• Steering wheel rubbing against housing	• Align housing
	• Tight or frozen steering shaft bearings	• Replace bearings
	• Sticking or plugged valve spool	• Remove and clean or replace valve
	• Steering gear adjustments over specifications	• Check adjustment with gear out of car. Adjust as required.
	• Kink in return hose	• Replace hose
Car leads to one side or the other (keep in mind road condition and wind. Test car in both directions on flat road)	• Front end misaligned	• Adjust to specifications
	• Unbalanced steering gear valve **NOTE:** If this is cause, steering effort will be very light in direction of lead and normal or heavier in opposite direction	• Replace valve
Momentary increase in effort when turning wheel fast to right or left	• Low oil level	• Add power steering fluid as required
	• Pump belt slipping	• Tighten or replace belt
	• High internal leakage	• Check pump pressure. (See pressure test)
Steering wheel surges or jerks when turning with engine running especially during parking	• Low oil level	• Fill as required
	• Loose pump belt	• Adjust tension to specification
	• Steering linkage hitting engine oil pan at full turn	• Correct clearance
	• Insufficient pump pressure	• Check pump pressure. (See pressure test). Replace relief valve if defective.
	• Pump flow control valve sticking	• Inspect for varnish or damage, replace if necessary

86748g50

Troubleshooting the Power Steering Gear (cont.)

Problem	Cause	Solution
Excessive wheel kickback or loose steering	• Air in system	• Add oil to pump reservoir and bleed by operating steering. Check hose connectors for proper torque and adjust as required.
	• Steering gear loose on frame	• Tighten attaching screws to specified torque
	• Steering linkage joints worn enough to be loose	• Replace loose pivots
	• Worn poppet valve	• Replace poppet valve
	• Loose thrust bearing preload adjustment	• Adjust to specification with gear out of vehicle
	• Excessive overcenter lash	• Adjust to specification with gear out of car
Hard steering or lack of assist	• Loose pump belt	• Adjust belt tension to specification
	• Low oil level	• Fill to proper level. If excessively low, check all lines and joints for evidence of external leakage. Tighten loose connectors.
	NOTE: Low oil level will also result in excessive pump noise	
	• Steering gear to column misalignment	• Align steering column
	• Lower coupling flange rubbing against steering gear adjuster plug	• Loosen pinch bolt and assemble properly
	• Tires not properly inflated	• Inflate to recommended pressure
Foamy milky power steering fluid, low fluid level and possible low pressure	• Air in the fluid, and loss of fluid due to internal pump leakage causing overflow	• Check for leak and correct. Bleed system. Extremely cold temperatures will cause system aeration should the oil level be low. If oil level is correct and pump still foams, remove pump from vehicle and separate reservoir from housing. Check welsh plug and housing for cracks. If plug is loose or housing is cracked, replace housing.
Low pressure due to steering pump	• Flow control valve stuck or inoperative	• Remove burrs or dirt or replace. Flush system.
	• Pressure plate not flat against cam ring	• Correct
Low pressure due to steering gear	• Pressure loss in cylinder due to worn piston ring or badly worn housing bore	• Remove gear from car for disassembly and inspection of ring and housing bore
	• Leakage at valve rings, valve body-to-worm seal	• Remove gear from car for disassembly and replace seals

86748g51

Troubleshooting the Power Steering Pump

Problem	Cause	Solution
Chirp noise in steering pump	• Loose belt	• Adjust belt tension to specification
Belt squeal (particularly noticeable at full wheel travel and stand still parking)	• Loose belt	• Adjust belt tension to specification
Growl noise in steering pump	• Excessive back pressure in hoses or steering gear caused by restriction	• Locate restriction and correct. Replace part if necessary.
Growl noise in steering pump (particularly noticeable at stand still parking)	• Scored pressure plates, thrust plate or rotor • Extreme wear of cam ring	• Replace parts and flush system • Replace parts
Groan noise in steering pump	• Low oil level • Air in the oil. Poor pressure hose connection.	• Fill reservoir to proper level • Tighten connector to specified torque. Bleed system by operating steering from right to left—full turn.
Rattle noise in steering pump	• Vanes not installed properly • Vanes sticking in rotor slots	• Install properly • Free up by removing burrs, varnish, or dirt
Swish noise in steering pump	• Defective flow control valve	• Replace part
Whine noise in steering pump	• Pump shaft bearing scored	• Replace housing and shaft. Flush system.
Hard steering or lack of assist	• Loose pump belt • Low oil level in reservoir **NOTE:** Low oil level will also result in excessive pump noise • Steering gear to column misalignment • Lower coupling flange rubbing against steering gear adjuster plug • Tires not properly inflated	• Adjust belt tension to specification • Fill to proper level. If excessively low, check all lines and joints for evidence of external leakage. Tighten loose connectors. • Align steering column • Loosen pinch bolt and assemble properly • Inflate to recommended pressure
Foaming milky power steering fluid, low fluid level and possible low pressure	• Air in the fluid, and loss of fluid due to internal pump leakage causing overflow	• Check for leaks and correct. Bleed system. Extremely cold temperatures will cause system aeriation should the oil level be low. If oil level is correct and pump still foams, remove pump from vehicle and separate reservoir from body. Check welsh plug and body for cracks. If plug is loose or body is cracked, replace body.

86748g52

Troubleshooting the Power Steering Pump (cont.)

Problem	Cause	Solution
Low pump pressure	• Flow control valve stuck or inoperative • Pressure plate not flat against cam ring	• Remove burrs or dirt or replace. Flush system. • Correct
Momentary increase in effort when turning wheel fast to right or left	• Low oil level in pump • Pump belt slipping • High internal leakage	• Add power steering fluid as required • Tighten or replace belt • Check pump pressure. (See pressure test)
Steering wheel surges or jerks when turning with engine running especially during parking	• Low oil level • Loose pump belt • Steering linkage hitting engine oil pan at full turn • Insufficient pump pressure	• Fill as required • Adjust tension to specification • Correct clearance • Check pump pressure. (See pressure test). Replace flow control valve if defective.
Steering wheel surges or jerks when turning with engine running especially during parking (cont.)	• Sticking flow control valve	• Inspect for varnish or damage, replace if necessary
Excessive wheel kickback or loose steering	• Air in system	• Add oil to pump reservoir and bleed by operating steering. Check hose connectors for proper torque and adjust as required.
Low pump pressure	• Extreme wear of cam ring • Scored pressure plate, thrust plate, or rotor • Vanes not installed properly • Vanes sticking in rotor slots • Cracked or broken thrust or pressure plate	• Replace parts. Flush system. • Replace parts. Flush system. • Install properly • Freeup by removing burrs, varnish, or dirt • Replace part

86748g53

Troubleshooting the Manual Steering Gear

Problem	Cause	Solution
Hard or erratic steering	· Incorrect tire pressure	· Inflate tires to recommended pressures
	· Insufficient or incorrect lubrication	· Lubricate as required (refer to Maintenance Section)
	· Suspension, or steering linkage parts damaged or misaligned	· Repair or replace parts as necessary
	· Improper front wheel alignment	· Adjust incorrect wheel alignment angles
	· Incorrect steering gear adjustment	· Adjust steering gear
	· Sagging springs	· Replace springs
Play or looseness in steering	· Steering wheel loose	· Inspect shaft spines and repair as necessary. Tighten attaching nut and stake in place.
	· Steering linkage or attaching parts loose or worn	· Tighten, adjust, or replace faulty components
	· Pitman arm loose	· Inspect shaft splines and repair as necessary. Tighten attaching nut and stake in place
	· Steering gear attaching bolts loose	· Tighten bolts
	· Loose or worn wheel bearings	· Adjust or replace bearings
	· Steering gear adjustment incorrect or parts badly worn	· Adjust gear or replace defective parts
Wheel shimmy or tramp	· Improper tire pressure	· Inflate tires to recommended pressures
	· Wheels, tires, or brake rotors out-of-balance or out-of-round	· Inspect and replace or balance parts
	· Inoperative, worn, or loose shock absorbers or mounting parts	· Repair or replace shocks or mountings
	· Loose or worn steering or suspension parts	· Tighten or replace as necessary
	· Loose or worn wheel bearings	· Adjust or replace bearings
	· Incorrect steering gear adjustments	· Adjust steering gear
	· Incorrect front wheel alignment	· Correct front wheel alignment
Tire wear	· Improper tire pressure	· Inflate tires to recommended pressures
	· Failure to rotate tires	· Rotate tires
	· Brakes grabbing	· Adjust or repair brakes
	· Incorrect front wheel alignment	· Align incorrect angles
	· Broken or damaged steering and suspension parts	· Repair or replace defective parts
	· Wheel runout	· Replace faulty wheel
	· Excessive speed on turns	· Make driver aware of conditions

86748g54

Troubleshooting the Manual Steering Gear

Problem	Cause	Solution
Vehicle leads to one side	• Improper tire pressures	• Inflate tires to recommended pressures
	• Front tires with uneven tread depth, wear pattern, or different cord design (i.e., one bias ply and one belted or radial tire on front wheels)	• Install tires of same cord construction and reasonably even tread depth, design, and wear pattern
	• Incorrect front wheel alignment	• Align incorrect angles
	• Brakes dragging	• Adjust or repair brakes
	• Pulling due to uneven tire construction	• Replace faulty tire

86748g55

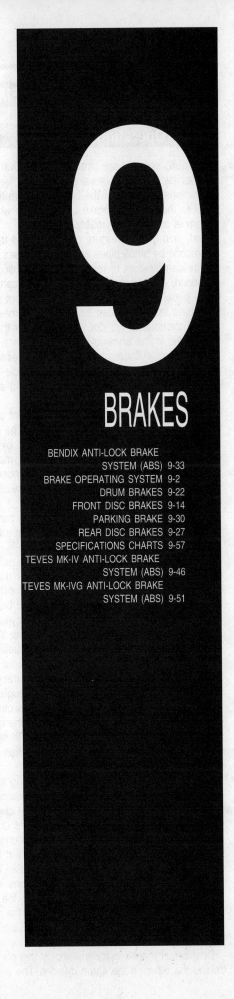

9

BRAKES

BRAKE OPERATING SYSTEM

Basic Operating Principles

Hydraulic systems are used to actuate the brakes of all automobiles. The system transports the power required to force the frictional surfaces of the braking system together from the pedal to the individual brake units at each wheel. A hydraulic system is used for two reasons.

First, fluid under pressure can be carried to all parts of an automobile by small pipes and flexible hoses without taking up a significant amount of room or posing routing problems.

Second, a great mechanical advantage can be given to the brake pedal end of the system, and the foot pressure required to actuate the brakes can be reduced by making the surface area of the master cylinder pistons smaller than that of any of the pistons in the wheel cylinders or calipers.

The master cylinder consists of a fluid reservoir and a double cylinder and piston assembly. Double type master cylinders are designed to separate the front and rear braking systems hydraulically in case of a leak.

Steel lines carry the brake fluid to a point on the vehicles frame near each of the vehicles wheels. The fluid is then carried to the calipers and wheel cylinders by flexible tubes in order to allow for suspension and steering movements.

In drum brake systems, each wheel cylinder contains two pistons, one at either end, which push outward in opposite directions.

In disc brake systems, the cylinders are part of the calipers. One cylinder in each caliper is used to force the brake pads against the disc.

All pistons employ some type of seal, usually made of rubber, to minimize fluid leakage. A rubber dust boot seals the outer end of the cylinder against dust and dirt. The boot fits around the outer end of the piston on disc brake calipers, and around the brake actuating rod on wheel cylinders.

The hydraulic system operates as follows: When at rest, the entire system, from the piston(s) in the master cylinder to those in the wheel cylinders or calipers, is full of brake fluid. Upon application of the brake pedal, fluid trapped in front of the master cylinder piston(s) is forced through the lines to the wheel cylinders. Here, it forces the pistons outward, in the case of drum brakes, and inward toward the disc, in the case of disc brakes. The motion of the pistons is opposed by return springs mounted outside the cylinders in drum brakes, and by spring seals, in disc brakes.

Upon release of the brake pedal, a spring located inside the master cylinder immediately returns the master cylinder pistons to the normal position. The pistons contain check valves and the master cylinder has compensating ports drilled in it. These are uncovered as the pistons reach their normal position. The piston check valves allow fluid to flow toward the wheel cylinders or calipers as the pistons withdraw. Then, as the return springs force the brake pads or shoes into the released position, the excess fluid reservoir through the compensating ports. It is during the time the pedal is in the released position that any fluid that has leaked out of the system will be replaced through the compensating ports.

Dual circuit master cylinders employ two pistons, located one behind the other, in the same cylinder. The primary piston is actuated directly by mechanical linkage from the brake pedal through the power booster. The secondary piston is actuated by fluid trapped between the two pistons. If a leak develops in front of the secondary piston, it moves forward until it bottoms against the front of the master cylinder, and the fluid trapped between the pistons will operate the rear brakes. If the rear brakes develop a leak, the primary piston will move forward until direct contact with the secondary piston takes place, and it will force the secondary piston to actuate the front brakes. In either case, the brake pedal moves farther when the brakes are applied, and less braking power is available.

All dual circuit systems use a switch to warn the driver when only half of the brake system is operational. This switch is located in a valve body which is mounted on the firewall or the frame below the master cylinder. A hydraulic piston receives pressure from both circuits, each circuit's pressure being applied to one end of the piston. When the pressures are in balance, the piston remains stationary. When one circuit has a leak, however, the greater pressure in that circuit during application of the brakes will push the piston to one side, closing the switch and activating the brake warning light.

In disc brake systems, this valve body also contains a metering valve and, in some cases, a proportioning valve. The metering valve keeps pressure from traveling to the disc brakes on the front wheels until the brake shoes on the rear wheels have contacted the drums, ensuring that the front brakes will never be used alone. The proportioning valve controls the pressure to the rear brakes to lessen the chance of rear wheel lock-up during very hard braking.

Warning lights may be tested by depressing the brake pedal and holding it while opening one of the wheel cylinder bleeder screws. If this does not cause the light to go on, substitute a new lamp, make continuity checks, and, finally, replace the switch as necessary.

The hydraulic system may be checked for leaks by applying pressure to the pedal gradually and steadily. If the pedal sinks very slowly to the floor, the system has a leak. This is not to be confused with a springy or spongy feel due to the compression of air within the lines. If the system leaks, there will be a gradual change in the position of the pedal with a constant pressure.

Check for leaks along all lines and at wheel cylinders. If no external leaks are apparent, the problem is inside the master cylinder.

DISC BRAKES

Instead of the traditional expanding brakes that press outward against a circular drum, disc brake systems utilize a disc (rotor) with brake pads positioned on either side of it. Braking effect is achieved in a manner similar to the way you would squeeze a spinning phonograph record between your fingers. The disc (rotor) is a casting with cooling fins between the two braking surfaces. This enables air to circulate between the braking surfaces making them less sensitive to heat buildup and more resistant to fade. Dirt and water do not affect braking action since contaminants are thrown off by the centrifugal action of the rotor or scraped off the by the pads.

Also, the equal clamping action of the two brake pads tends to ensure uniform, straight line stops. Disc brakes are inherently self-adjusting. There are three general types of disc brake:

1. A fixed caliper.
2. A floating caliper.
3. A sliding caliper.

The fixed caliper design uses two pistons mounted on either side of the rotor (in each side of the caliper). The caliper is mounted rigidly and does not move.

The sliding and floating designs are quite similar. In fact, these two types are often lumped together. In both designs, the pad on the inside of the rotor is moved into contact with the rotor by hydraulic force. The caliper, which is not held in a fixed position, moves slightly, bringing the outside pad into contact with the rotor. There are various methods of attaching floating calipers. Some pivot at the bottom or top, and some slide on mounting bolts. In any event, the end result is the same.

All the vehicles covered in this book employ the sliding caliper design.

DRUM BRAKES

Drum brakes employ two brake shoes mounted on a stationary backing plate. These shoes are positioned inside a circular drum which rotates with the wheel assembly. The shoes are held in place by springs. This allows them to slide toward the drums (when they are applied) while keeping the linings and drums in alignment. The shoes are actuated by a wheel cylinder which is mounted at the top of the backing plate. When the brakes are applied, hydraulic pressure forces the wheel cylinder's actuating links outward. Since these links bear directly against the top of the brake shoes, the tops of the shoes are then forced against the inner side of the drum. This action forces the bottoms of the two shoes to contact the brake drum by rotating the entire assembly slightly (known as servo action). When pressure within the wheel cylinder is relaxed, return springs pull the shoes back away from the drum.

Most modern drum brakes are designed to self-adjust themselves during application when the vehicle is moving in reverse. This motion causes both shoes to rotate very slightly with the drum, rocking an adjusting lever, thereby causing rotation of the adjusting screw.

❋❋WARNING

Clean, high quality brake fluid is essential to the safe and proper operation of the brake system. You should always buy the highest quality brake fluid that is available. If the brake fluid becomes contaminated, drain and flush the system and fill the master cylinder with new fluid. Never reuse any brake fluid. Any brake fluid that is removed from the system should be discarded.

Adjustments

DRUM BRAKES

These brakes are equipped with self-adjusters and no manual adjustment is necessary, except when brake linings are replaced.

DISC BRAKES

These brakes are inherently self-adjusting and no adjustment is ever necessary or possible.

BRAKE LIGHT SWITCH

▶ **See Figures 1 and 2**

1. Move the brake pedal forward by hand and note the operation of switch plunger. The plunger should extend when the pedal free-play is taken up and brake application begins. A clearance of approximately ⅛ in. (3mm) should exist between the plunger and the pedal at this point.
2. If the clearance does not meet this specification, grasp the brake pedal and pull it rearward as far as possible. The switch plunger will ratchet rearward to its correct position.
3. Check the clearance and brake light switch operation. If necessary repeat the adjustment procedure.

❋❋WARNING

Ensure that the brake pedal returns to a fully released position after the adjustment. The switch can interfere with full pedal return if it is pulled too far forward, resulting in brake drag caused by partial application.

Brake Light Switch

REMOVAL & INSTALLATION

The brake light switch is mounted in the pedal support bracket and is operated by the pedal.

1. Remove the steering column cover and lower the trim panel, if necessary.
2. Disengage the switch electrical connection.
3. Screw the switch out of the retainer, or rock the switch up and down, then pull it rearward out of the retainer.
4. Installation is the reverse of removal.

Brake Pedal

REMOVAL & INSTALLATION

1. Remove the lower trim panel and A/C duct.
2. Remove the steering column lower trim panel and bezel.

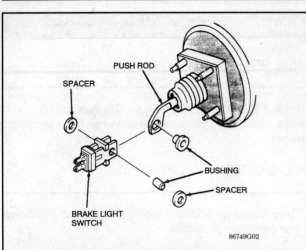

Fig. 1 Exploded view of the brake light switch mounting to the power booster pushrod — models with cruise control

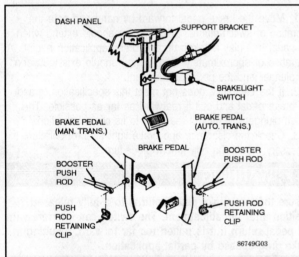

Fig. 2 Exploded view of the brake pedal and brake light switch mounting — models without cruise control

3. Remove the necessary dash panel-to-instrument panel brace rods.

4. Remove the brake light switch.

5. Remove the retaining clip securing the booster pushrod to the pedal.

6. Remove the nut securing the pedal shaft.

7. Slide the pedal shaft outward and remove the brake pedal.

8. Remove the pedal bushings, if they are to be replaced.

To install:

9. Install new bushings in the pedal and position the pedal, sleeve and bracket in the bracket.

10. Install the pivot pin and the new nut on the pivot pin. Tighten the nut to 20 ft. lbs. (27 Nm) on models with manual transmissions and 26 ft. lbs. (35 Nm) on models with automatic transmissions.

11. Install the booster pushrod on the pedal pin and secure the rod with the retainer clip.

12. Install the brake light switch and the dash brace rod.

13. Install the trim covers.

Master Cylinder

REMOVAL & INSTALLATION

Non-ABS Equipped Models

▶ **See Figures 3, 4 and 5**

1. Disconnect and plug the brake lines.

2. Remove the combination valve (if necessary).

3. Remove all attaching bolts and nuts, and lift the assembly from the vehicle.

To install:

4. Remove the protective cover from the end of the primary piston (if necessary).

5. Clean the cylinder mounting surface on the booster.

6. Install the master cylinder onto the brake booster studs.

7. Install the nuts and tighten to 220 inch lbs. (25 Nm).

8. Connect the brake lines, fill the reservoir and bleed the brake system.

ABS Equipped Models

1. Disengage the pedal travel sensor wires and remove the air cleaner.

2. Remove the clamps that secure the reservoir hoses to the Hydraulic Control Unit (HCU) pipes.

3. Drain the fluid into a container and discard the fluid.

4. Pump the brake pedal to exhaust all vacuum from the booster.

5. Disengage the brake lines and the combination valve bracket bolt at the master cylinder.

6. Unfasten the master cylinder attaching bolts and remove the master cylinder from the vehicle.

To install:

7. If installing a new master cylinder, bleed the cylinder on a bench before installation.

8. Install the master cylinder in position and engage the reservoir hoses to the HCU pipes.

9. Tighten the master cylinder retaining bolts to 25 ft. lbs. (34 Nm) and connect the brake lines.

Fig. 3 Loosening the brake lines using a backup wrench

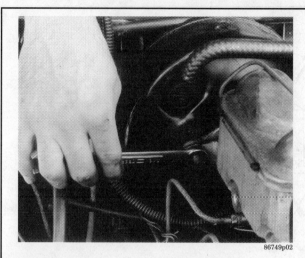

Fig. 4 Removing the master cylinder-to-booster retaining nuts

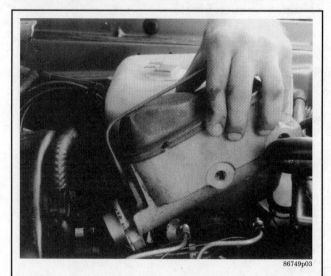

Fig. 5 Removing the master cylinder from the vehicle

10. Install the combination valve and bracket bolt (if removed).

11. Connect the sensor wires and fill the reservoir.

12. Bleed the brakes. Refer to the procedure outlined later in this section.

13. Install the air cleaner and test drive the vehicle to verify proper brake operation.

Power Boosters

▶ See Figure 6

Power brakes operate just as standard brake systems except in the actuation of the master cylinder pistons. A vacuum diaphragm is located on the front of the master cylinder and assists the driver in applying the brakes, reducing both the effort and travel he must put into moving the brake pedal.

The vacuum diaphragm housing is connected to the intake manifold by a vacuum hose. A check valve is placed at the point where the hose enters the diaphragm housing, so that during periods of low manifold vacuum brake assisting vacuum will not be lost.

Depressing the brake pedal closes off the vacuum source and allows atmospheric pressure to enter on one side of the diaphragm. This causes the master cylinder pistons to move and apply the brakes. When the brake pedal is released, vacuum is applied to both sides of the diaphragm, and return springs return the diaphragm and master cylinder pistons to the released position. If the vacuum fails, the brake pedal rod will butt against the end of the master cylinder actuating rod, and direct mechanical application will occur as the pedal is depressed.

The hydraulic and mechanical problems that apply to conventional brake systems also apply to power brakes, and should be checked for if the tests below do not reveal the problem.

Test for a system vacuum leak as described below:

1. Operate the engine at idle without touching the brake pedal for at least one minute.

2. Turn the engine **OFF**, and wait one minute.

3. Test for the presence of assistance vacuum by depressing the brake pedal and releasing it several times. Light application will produce less and less pedal travel, if vacuum was present. If there is no vacuum, air is leaking into the system somewhere.

Test for system operation as follows:

4. Pump the brake pedal (with engine **off**) until the supply vacuum is entirely gone.

5. Put a light, steady pressure on the pedal.

6. Start the engine, and operate it at idle. If the system is operating, the brake pedal should fall toward the floor if constant pressure is maintained on the pedal.

Power brake systems may be tested for hydraulic leaks just as ordinary systems are tested.

REMOVAL & INSTALLATION

▶ See Figure 7

1. Loosen, but do not remove the master cylinder retaining nuts.

2. Remove the instrument panel lower trim cover.

3. Remove the retaining clip attaching the booster pushrod to the brake pedal.

4. Loosen the vacuum hose clip and disconnect the hose from the check valve.

5. Remove the master cylinder retaining nuts and carefully move the master cylinder aside with the brake lines still attached.

6. Unfasten the booster retaining nuts/bolts and remove the booster.

To install:

7. Install the check valve and grommet in the booster.

8. Install the spacer on the booster (if equipped).

9. Position the booster on the firewall and fasten the booster mounting bolts/nuts.

10. Working inside the vehicle, install the nuts on the booster mounting studs. Tighten the bolts to 30 ft. lbs. (41 Nm) on XJ/MJ models and 25 ft. lbs. (34 Nm) on YJ models.

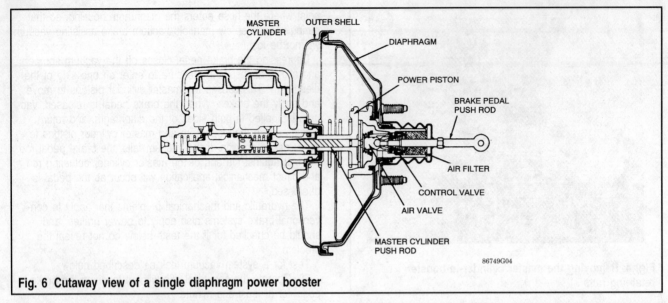

Fig. 6 Cutaway view of a single diaphragm power booster

11. Tighten the pedal pushrod bolt inner nut to 25 ft. lbs. (34 Nm) and then tighten the outer locknut to 75 inch lbs. (8 Nm).

12. Install the master cylinder and check for proper operation.

Pressure Differential Valve

▶ See Figure 8

Jeep vehicles use a pressure differential valve, mounted immediately below the master cylinder. The valve is not a serviceable part, and must be replaced if defective.

REMOVAL & INSTALLATION

1. Disconnect the brake lines at the valve and plug them.
2. Unbolt and remove the valve.

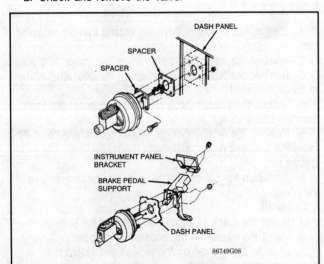

Fig. 7 Exploded view of the power brake booster mounting

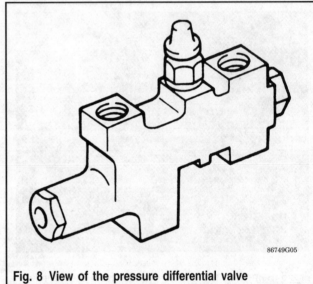

Fig. 8 View of the pressure differential valve

To install:
3. Install the valve and tighten the bolt.
4. Unplug the valve lines and connect them to the valve.
5. Bleed the system.

Height Sensing Proportioning Valve

▶ See Figures 9 and 10

In addition to the pressure differential valve, a mechanically activated height sensing proportioning valve is used on Comanche models. This valve, located above the rear axle, must be adjusted any time rear springs are replaced, or the valve is removed during service operations.

➡Any time the valve is adjusted, the lever bushing must be replaced. The adjustment must be made with the vehicle level and at curb weight. Special tools are needed for this job.

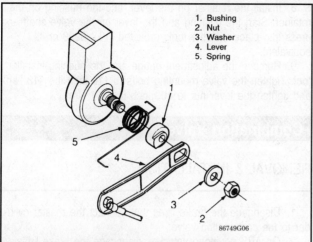

Fig. 9 Exploded view of the height sensing proportioning valve installed on the Comanche. 1990-92 models DO NOT use a spring (5)

1. Bushing
2. Nut
3. Washer
4. Lever
5. Spring

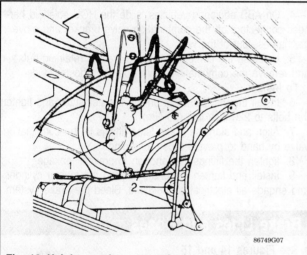

Fig. 10 Height sensing proportioning valve (1) and linkage (2)

REMOVAL & INSTALLATION

▶ See Figures 11, 12 and 13

1. Disconnect the valve lever and spring, if equipped.
2. Disconnect and cap the brake lines.
3. Unbolt and remove the valve.
4. Installation is the reverse of removal. Torque the Valve bracket-to-frame bolts to 155 inch. lbs. (17 Nm) and tighten the valve-to-bracket bolts to 118 inch. lbs. (13 Nm).
5. Perform the valve adjusting procedure outlined in this section.

ADJUSTMENT

Except 1990-96 Models

1. Remove the valve shaft nut and washer.
2. Disconnect the valve lever and remove the spring.

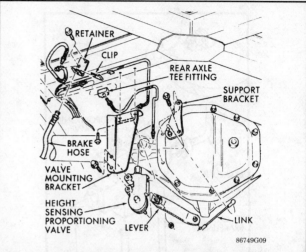

Fig. 11 Exploded view of the height sensing valve installation — Comanche with a Model 35 rear axle

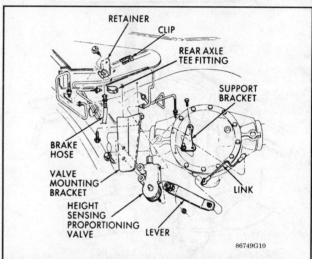

Fig. 12 Exploded view of the height sensing valve installation — Comanche with a Model 44 rear axle

3. Remove and discard the bushing.
4. Rotate the valve shaft and install adjusting gauge tool J-35853-2 or its equivalent.

➡The gauge must be properly seated on the D shape of the shaft and the valve lower mounting bolt. All linkage components, except the spring, must be connected before installing the new bushing.

5. Place the bushing in the lever, and, using bushing aligning tool J-35853-1 or its equivalent, press the bushing and lever onto the shaft.
6. Remove the lever and adjusting tool J-35853-2 or its equivalent and install the spring.
7. Install the lever, washer and nut. Tighten the nut to 100 inch. lbs. (11 Nm).
8. Connect the spring.

1990-96 Models

➡Valve adjustment requires Calibration Kit 6229 or its equivalent.

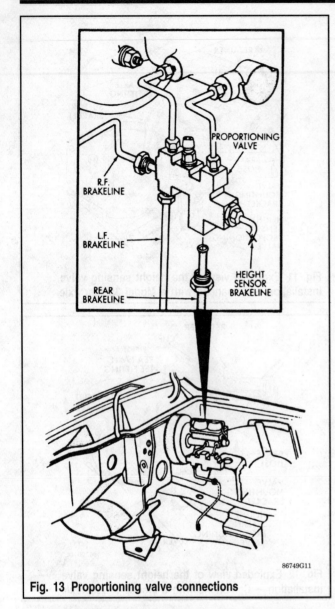

Fig. 13 Proportioning valve connections

1. Raise the vehicle and support it safely with jackstands.

2. Unload the vehicle and place on a level surface for accurate valve adjustment.

3. Remove the nut attaching lever to the valve shaft.

4. Pull the lever and retainer off the valve shaft and remove old the bushing. Discard the bushing.

5. Clean the threads and splines on the valve shaft. If valve the link was disconnected from axle the bracket or lever, reconnect the link before continuing.

6. Loosen the valve mounting bolts two full turns. Then turn valve shaft until the shaft flat is approximately between the 5 and 6 o'clock position.

7. Install the valve adjusting gauge and it position on the mounting bolts and shaft. There should be no clearance between the gauge, shaft and bolts. The gauge should be seated on the shaft flat.

8. Install the retainer on the lever, and the bushing on the retainer. Start the bushing and the lever on the valve shaft and press into place with the tools provided in kit 6229 or its equivalent.

9. Remove the adjustment gauge and the bushing installer tool. Tighten the valve mounting bolts to 118 inch lbs. (13 Nm) and tighten the lever nut to 100 inch lbs. (11 Nm).

Combination Valve

REMOVAL & INSTALLATION

1. Disengage the brake lines that connect the master cylinder to the combination valve.

2. On ABS equipped vehicles, disengage the brake lines that connect the combination valve to the Hydraulic Control Unit (HCU).

3. Disengage the electrical connection from the combination valve.

4. On ABS equipped vehicles, slide the HCU solenoid harness connectors off the combination valve bracket and move the harness out of the way.

5. Unfasten the combination valve bracket retaining nuts and remove the combination valve from the booster studs.

To install:

6. Install the valve bracket on the booster studs and tighten the bolts to 220 inch lbs. (25 Nm).

7. Align and start the brake lines fittings in the combination valve by hand to prevent cross threading.

8. tighten the fittings just enough to prevent leakage.

9. Install and tighten the brake lines to the master cylinder and engage all electrical connections. Bleed the brake system.

Brake Lines and Hoses

▶ See Figures 14 and 15

When servicing brake lines, several precautions must be taken to prevent damage to the line:

• Clean fittings of rust and road build-up before attempting to remove

• Spray fittings with penetrating oil to loosen rust and allow fitting to be removed easier

• Always use a flare nut wrench to prevent rounding the line fittings

• If possible, always use a backup wrench

• To prevent stripping, tighten fittings to the proper torque VALUE

• Plug all open lines to prevent contaminates from entering the braking system

• Always refill the system with fresh brake fluid. Never return used brake fluid to the reservoir

• When repairing damaged brake lines (hard line), it is recommended that only hard lines with double flare ends be used (some states DO NOT allow compression fittings to be used).

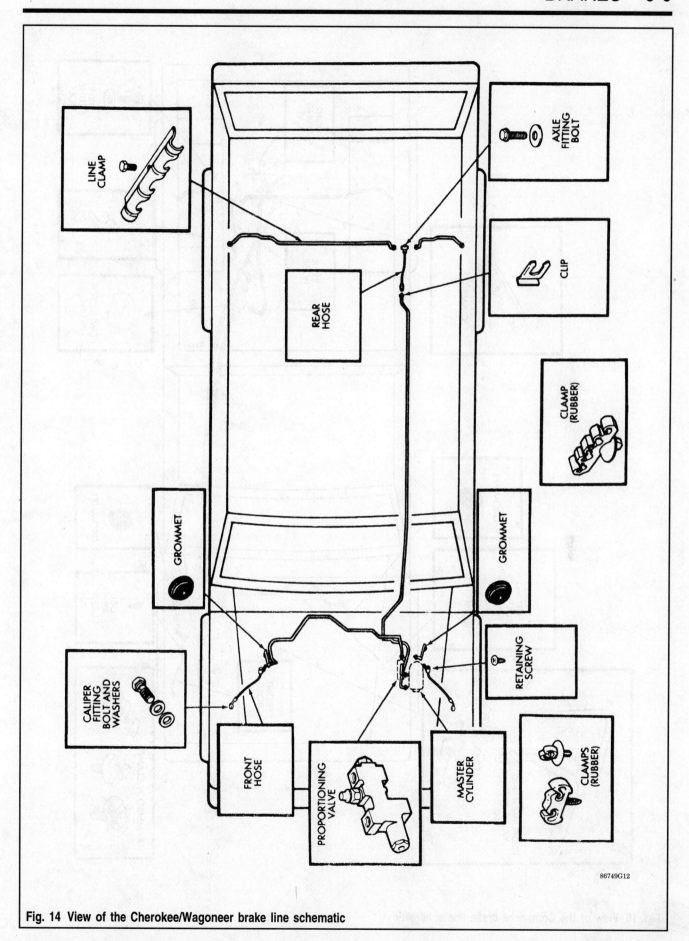

Fig. 14 View of the Cherokee/Wagoneer brake line schematic

86749G12

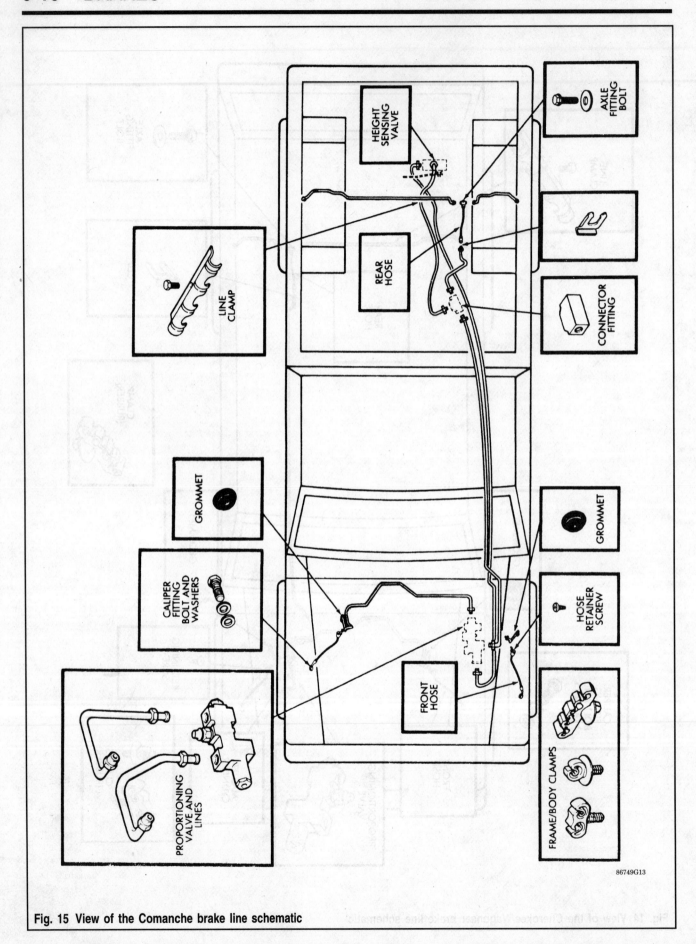

HEIGHT SENSING VALUE

AXLE FITTING BOLT

REAR HOSE

CONNECTOR FITTING

LINE CLAMP

GROMMET

GROMMET

CALIPER FITTING BOLT AND WASHERS

HOSE RETAINER SCREW

FRONT HOSE

PROPORTIONING VALVE AND LINES

FRAME/BODY CLAMPS

86749G13

Fig. 15 View of the Comanche brake line schematic

Brake Hoses and Pipes

REMOVAL & INSTALLATION

Brake Hose

▶ See Figures 16, 17, 18 and 19

1. Raise the end of the vehicle which contains the hose to be repaired, then support the vehicle safely using jackstands.
2. If necessary, remove the wheel for easier access to the hose.
3. Disconnect the hose from the wheel cylinder or caliper and plug the opening to avoid excessive fluid loss or contamination.
4. Disconnect the hose from the brake line and plug the openings to avoid excessive fluid loss or contamination.

To install:

5. Install the brake hose to the brake line and tighten to 14 ft. lbs. (19 Nm) for rear brakes or 18 ft. lbs. (24 Nm) for front brakes.
6. If installing a front brake hose, make sure the hose is routed as shown in accompanying illustration with the loop to the rear of the vehicle.
7. Install the hose to the wheel cylinder or caliper using new washers, then tighten the retainer to 36 ft. lbs. (49 Nm).
8. Properly bleed the brake system, then check the connections for leaks.
9. Remove the supports and carefully lower the vehicle.

Brake Line

▶ See Figures 18 and 19

There are 2 options available when replacing a brake line. The first, and probably most preferable, is to replace the entire line using a line of similar length which is already equipped with machine flared ends. Such lines are usually available from auto parts stores and usually require only a minimum of bending in order to properly fit them to the vehicle. The second option is to bend and flare the entire replacement line (or a repair section of line) using the appropriate tools.

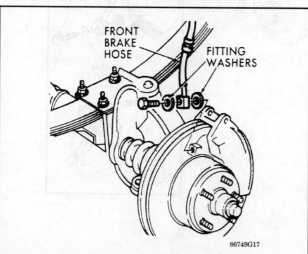

Fig. 16 Exploded view of the front brake hose-to-caliper connection

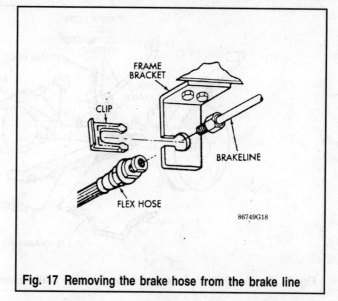

Fig. 17 Removing the brake hose from the brake line

Buying a line with machined flares is usually preferable because of the time and effort saved, not to mention the cost of special tools, if they are not readily available. Also, machined flared ends are usually of a much higher quality than those produced by hand flaring tools or kits.

1. Raise the end of the vehicle which contains the hose to be repaired, then support the vehicle safely using jackstands.
2. Remove the components necessary for access to the brake line which is being replaced.
3. Disconnect the fittings at each end of the line, then plug the openings to prevent excessive fluid loss or contamination.
4. Trace the line from one end to the other and disconnect the line from any retaining clips, then remove the line from the vehicle.

To install:

5. Try to obtain a replacement line that is the same length as the line that was removed. If the line is longer, you will have to cut it and flare the end, or if you have decided to repair a portion of the line, see the procedure on brake line flaring, later in this section.
6. Use a suitable tubing bender to make the necessary bends in the line. Work slowly and carefully; try to make the bends look as close as possible to those on the line being replaced.

➡ **When bending the brake line, be careful not to kink or crack the line. If the brake line becomes kinked or cracked, it must be replaced.**

7. Before installing the brake line, flush it with brake cleaner to remove any dirt or foreign material.
8. Install the line into the vehicle. Be sure to attach the line to the retaining clips, as necessary. Make sure the replacement brake line does not contact any components that could rub the line and cause a leak.
9. Connect the brake line fittings and tighten to 18 ft. lbs. (24 Nm), except for the rear line-to-hose fitting which should be tightened to 14 ft. lbs. (19 Nm).
10. Properly bleed the brake system and check for leaks.
11. Install any removed components, then remove the supports and carefully lower the vehicle.

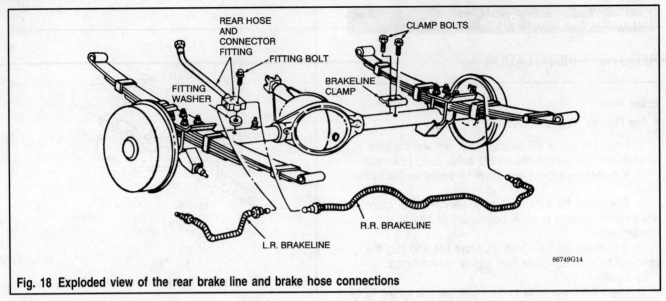

Fig. 18 Exploded view of the rear brake line and brake hose connections

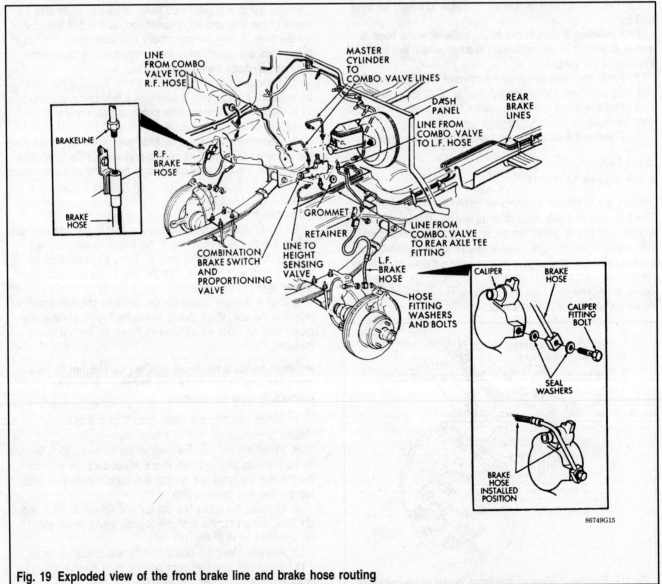

Fig. 19 Exploded view of the front brake line and brake hose routing

BRAKE LINE FLARING

Use only brake line tubing approved for automotive use; never use copper tubing. Whenever possible, try to work with brake lines that are already cut to the length needed. These lines are available at most auto parts stores and have machine made flares, the quality of which is hard to duplicate with most of the available inexpensive flaring kits.

When the brakes are applied, there is a great amount of pressure developed in the hydraulic system. An improperly formed flare can leak with resultant loss of stopping power. If you have never formed a double-flare, take time to familiarize yourself with the flaring kit; practice forming double-flares on scrap tubing until you are satisfied with the results.

The following procedure applies to the SA9193BR flaring kit, but should be similar to commercially available brake-line flaring kits. If these instructions differ in any way from those in your kit, follow the instructions in the kit.

1. Determine the length necessary for the replacement or repair and allow an additional ⅛ in. (3.2mm) for each flare, then cut the brake line to the necessary length using an appropriate saw. Do not use a tubing cutter.
2. Square the end of the tube with a file and chamfer the edges. Remove burrs from the inside and outside diameters of the cut line using a deburring tool.
3. Install the required fittings onto the line.
4. Install SA9193BR, or an equivalent flaring tool, into a vice and install the handle into the operating cam.
5. Loosen the die clamp screw and rotate the locking plate to expose the die carrier opening.
6. Select the required die set (4.75mm DIN) and install in the carrier with the full side of either half facing the clamp screw and counter bore, or both halves facing the punch turret.
7. Insert the prepared line through the rear of the die and push forward until the line end is flush with the die face.
8. Make sure the rear of both halves of the die rest against the hexagon die stops, then rotate the locking plate to the fully closed position and clamp the die firmly by tightening the clamp screw.
9. Rotate the punch turret until the appropriate size (4.75mm DIN) points towards the open end of the line to be flared.
10. Pull the operating handle against the line resistance in order to create the flare, then return the handle to the original position.
11. Release the clamp screw and rotate the locking plate to the open position.
12. Remove the die set and line, then separate by gently tapping both halves on the bench. Inspect the flare for proper size and shape as necessary.
13. If necessary, repeat Steps 2-12 for the other end of the line or for the end of the line which is being repaired.
14. Bend the replacement line or section using SA91108NE, or an equivalent line bending tool.
15. If repairing the original line, join the old and new sections using a female union and tighten.

Bleeding the Brakes

EXCEPT ANTI-LOCK BRAKES

▶ **See Figures 20 and 21**

➡**For bleeding of the Anti-lock Brake System (ABS), refer to the ABS bleeding procedure located later in this section.**

The purpose of bleeding the brakes is to expel air trapped in the hydraulic system. The system must be bled whenever the pedal feels spongy, indicating that compressible air has entered the system. It must also be bled whenever the system has been opened or repaired. You will need an assistant for this job.

➡**Never reuse brake fluid which has been bled from the brake system. It contains moisture and corrosion products and should, therefore, always be replaced with fresh fluid.**

1. The sequence for bleeding is right rear wheel, left rear wheel, right front wheel, then left front wheel for Jeep vehicles without an ABS system. Do not run the engine while bleeding the brakes.
2. Clean all the bleeder screws. You may want to give each one a shot of penetrating solvent to loosen it; seizure is a common problem with bleeder screws, which then break off, sometimes requiring replacement of the part to which they are attached.
3. Fill the master cylinder with DOT 3 or its superceding brake fluid.

➡**Brake fluid absorbs moisture from the air. Don't leave the master cylinder or the fluid container uncovered any longer than necessary. Be careful handling the fluid; spilled fluid will damage the vehicle's paint.**

Check the level of the fluid often when bleeding, and refill the reservoirs as necessary. Don't let them run dry, or you will have to repeat the process.

4. Attach a length of clear vinyl tubing to the bleeder screw on the wheel cylinder. Insert the other end of the tube into a clear, clean jar half filled with brake fluid.
5. Have your assistant slowly depress the brake pedal. As this is done, open the bleeder screw until the brake fluid starts to flow through the tube. Then, close the bleeder screw before the brake pedal reaches the end of its travel. After the bleeder valve is fully closed, have your assistant slowly release the pedal. Repeat this process until no air bubbles appear in the expelled fluid.
6. Repeat the procedure on the other three brake cylinders/calipers, checking the level of brake fluid in the master cylinder reservoir often.

After finishing, there should be no feeling of sponginess in the brake pedal. If there is, either there is still air in the line, in which case the process must be repeated, or there is a leak somewhere, which, of course, must be corrected before the vehicle is moved. After all repairs and service work is finished, road test the vehicle for proper operation.

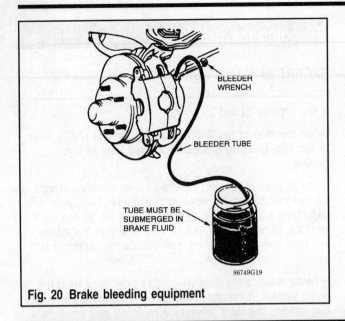

Fig. 20 Brake bleeding equipment

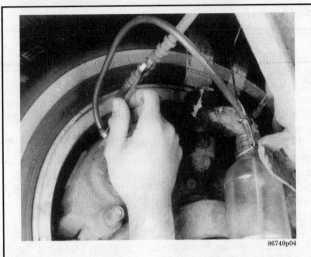

Fig. 21 Open the bleeder screw until brake fluid starts to flow through the tube

FRONT DISC BRAKES

Disc Brake Pads

REMOVAL & INSTALLATION

▶ See Figures 22, 23, 24, 25, 26, 27, 28, 29, 30, 31, 32, 33, 34, 35, 36 and 37

❋❋CAUTION

Brake shoes may contain asbestos, which has been determined to be a cancer causing agent. Never clean the brake surfaces with compressed air! Avoid inhaling any dust from any brake surface! When cleaning brake surfaces, use a commercially available brake cleaning fluid.

1. Raise and support the vehicle safely using jackstands. Remove the wheel(s) on the side to be worked on.

➡For vehicles equipped with Anti-Lock Brakes (ABS), refer to the proper procedures concerning brake system servicing.

2. Drain a small amount of the brake fluid from the front reservoir using a suction gun or a turkey baster.

3. Place a C-clamp on the caliper so that the solid end contacts the back of the caliper and the screw end contacts the metal part of the outboard brake pad.

4. Tighten the clamp until the caliper moves far enough to force the piston to the bottom of the piston bore. This will back the brake pads off of the rotor surface to facilitate the removal and installation of the caliper assembly.

5. Remove the C-clamp.

➡Do not push down on the brake pedal or the piston and brake pads will return to their original positions up against the rotor.

Fig. 22 Raise the vehicle using a hydraulic jack

6. Remove the caliper mounting bolts. Tilt the top of the caliper outward and lift it off the rotor.

7. Hold the anti-rattle clip against the caliper anchor plate and remove the outboard brake pad.

8. Remove the inboard pad and the anti-rattle clip. Be sure that the support spring is removed with the inboard pad.

9. Use a piece of wire to support the caliper so that no tension is placed on the brake hose. Do not allow the caliper to hang by the brake hose.

To install:

10. Clean all the mounting holes and bushing grooves in the caliper ears. Clean the mounting bolts. Replace the bolts if they are corroded or if the threads are damaged. Wipe the inside of the caliper clean, including the exterior of the dust boot. Inspect the dust boot for cuts or cracks and for proper

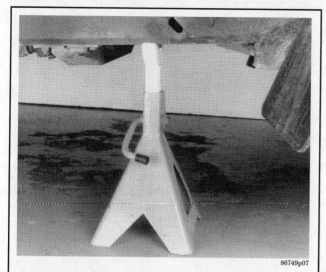

Fig. 23 Support the vehicle using safety stands

Fig. 24 A view of a common non-ABS front disc brake system

Fig. 25 Removing a small amount of brake fluid from the master cylinder using a turkey baster

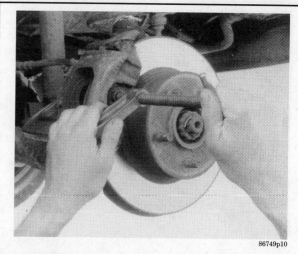

Fig. 26 Tighten the C-clamp until the piston reaches the bottom of its bore

Fig. 27 Remove the caliper mounting bolts

Fig. 28 Slide the caliper off the brake rotor

Fig. 29 Support the caliper so that no tension is placed on the brake hose

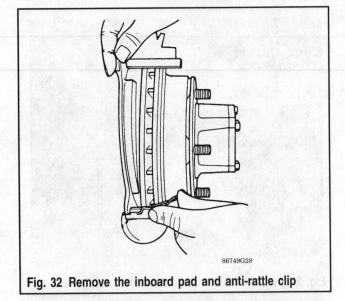

Fig. 32 Remove the inboard pad and anti-rattle clip

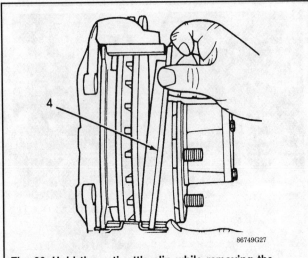

Fig. 30 Hold the anti-rattle clip while removing the outboard pad (4)

Fig. 33 Removing the inboard brake pad

Fig. 31 Removing the outboard brake pad

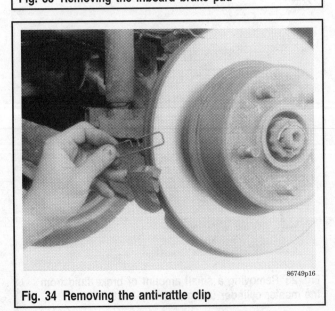

Fig. 34 Removing the anti-rattle clip

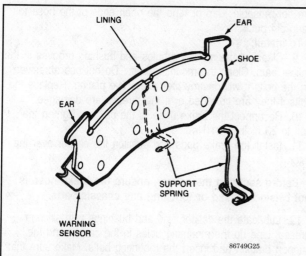

Fig. 35 Install the support spring onto the shoe of the inboard brake pad

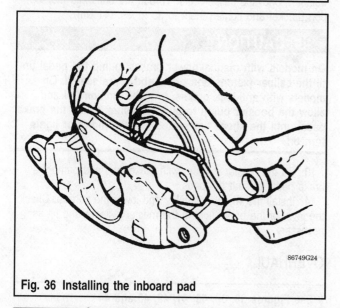

Fig. 36 Installing the inboard pad

seating in the piston bore. If evidence of fluid leakage is noted, the caliper should be rebuilt.

➡**Do not use abrasives on the bolts in order not to destroy their protective plating. You should not use compressed air to clean the inside of the caliper, as it may unseat the dust boot seal.**

11. If not already in place, attach the support spring to the inboard brake pad.

12. Install the anti-rattle clip on the trailing end of the inboard pad's anchor plate. The split end of the clip must face away from the rotor.

13. Install the inboard pad in the caliper. The pad must lay flat against the piston.

14. Install the outboard pad in the caliper while holding the anti-rattle clip.

15. With the pads installed, position the caliper over the rotor.

➡**Before securing the caliper, ensure the brake hose is not twisted, kinked or touching any chassis parts.**

16. Lubricate the caliper pins and bushings with silicone grease. Line up the mounting holes in the caliper and the support bracket and insert the mounting bolts. Make sure that the bolts pass under the retaining ears on the inboard shoes. Push the bolts through until they engage the holes of the outboard pad and caliper ears. Thread the bolts into the support bracket and tighten them to 7-15 ft. lbs. (9-20 Nm).

✳✳CAUTION

On models with manual/power brakes, pump the pedal until the caliper pistons and brake shoes are seated. On models with anti-lock brakes, turn the ignition ON and allow the booster pump to build pressure. Pump the brake pedal until the shoes are seated and the indicator lights turn off.

17. Fill the master cylinder with brake fluid and pump the brake pedal to seat the pads.

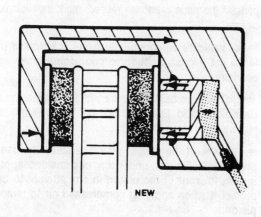
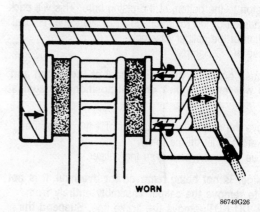

Fig. 37 Piston extension on new and worn brake pads

18. Install the wheel assembly and lower the vehicle. Check the level of the brake fluid in the master cylinder and fill as necessary.

INSPECTION

Measure lining wear by measuring the combined thickness of the pad and pad backing plate at the thinnest point. It must measure at least 5/16 in. (8mm) thick on all vehicles covered by this manual.

Always replace both front brake pad assemblies (inboard and outboard pad) on both front wheels whenever necessary. The specifications given above on front disc brake lining wear should be used as the guide for replacement.

Calipers

REMOVAL & INSTALLATION

❉❉CAUTION

Brake shoes may contain asbestos, which has been determined to be a cancer causing agent. Never clean the brake surfaces with compressed air! Avoid inhaling any dust from any brake surface! When cleaning brake surfaces, use a commercially available brake cleaning fluid.

1. Raise and support the vehicle safely using jackstands. Remove the wheel(s) on the side to be worked on.

➡**For vehicles equipped with Anti-Lock Brakes (ABS), refer to the proper procedures concerning brake system servicing.**

2. Drain a small amount of the brake fluid from the front reservoir using a suction gun or a turkey baster.

3. Place a C-clamp on the caliper so that the solid end contacts the back of the caliper and the screw end contacts the metal part of the outboard brake pad.

4. Tighten the clamp until the caliper moves far enough to force the piston to the bottom of the piston bore. This will back the brake pads off of the rotor surface to facilitate the removal and installation of the caliper assembly.

5. Remove the C-clamp.

➡**Do not push down on the brake pedal or the piston and brake pads will return to their original positions up against the rotor.**

6. Remove the caliper mounting bolts. Tilt the top of the caliper outward and lift off the rotor.

7. Remove the brake pads from the caliper.

➡**If the caliper is not being removed for overhaul, it is not necessary to remove the caliper assembly entirely from the vehicle. DO NOT remove the brake line. Suspend the caliper with a piece of wire. DO NOT allow the brake hose to support the weight of the caliper.**

8. Remove the caliper fitting bolt and disconnect the front brake line at the caliper. Discard the fitting bolt washers, they are not reusable. Cap or tape the open ends of the hose to keep dirt out.

To install:

9. Clean all the mounting holes and bushing grooves in the caliper ears. Clean the mounting bolts. Do not use abrasives on the bolts it will destroy their protective plating. Replace the bolts if they are corroded or if the threads are damaged.

10. Reconnect the brake hose to the caliper. Tighten the bolt to 23 ft. lbs. (31 Nm).

11. Install the brake pads and position the caliper over the rotor.

➡**Before securing the caliper, ensure the brake hose is not twisted, kinked or touching any chassis parts.**

12. Lubricate the caliper pins and bushings with silicone grease. Line up the mounting holes in the caliper and the support bracket and insert the mounting bolts. Make sure that the bolts pass under the retaining ears on the inboard shoes. Push the bolts through until they engage the holes of the outboard pad and caliper ears. Thread the bolts into the support bracket and tighten them to 30 ft. lbs. (41 Nm).

❉❉CAUTION

On models with manual/power brakes, pump the pedal until the caliper pistons and brake shoes are seated. On models with anti-lock brakes, turn the ignition ON and allow the booster pump to build pressure. Pump the brake pedal until the shoes are seated and the indicator lights turn off.

13. Fill the master cylinder with brake fluid and pump the brake pedal to seat the pads.

14. Install the wheel assembly and lower the vehicle. Check the level of the brake fluid in the master cylinder and fill as necessary.

OVERHAUL

▶ **See Figures 38, 39, 40, 41, 42, 43 and 44**

1. Remove the caliper assembly and remove the brake pads. If the pads are to be reused, mark their location in the caliper.

➡**For vehicles equipped with Anti-Lock Brakes (ABS), refer to the proper procedures concerning brake system servicing.**

2. Clean the caliper exterior with brake cleaning solvent or clean brake fluid. Drain any residual fluid from the caliper and place it on a clean work surface.

➡**Removal of the caliper piston requires the use of compressed air. Do not, under any circumstances, place your fingers in front of the piston in any attempt to catch or protect it when applying compressed air to remove the piston.**

3. Pad the interior of the caliper with clean cloths. Use several cloths and pad the interior well to avoid damaging the piston when it comes out of the bore.

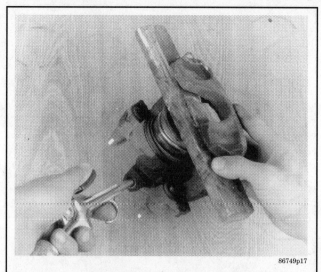

Fig. 38 Removing the piston with compressed air

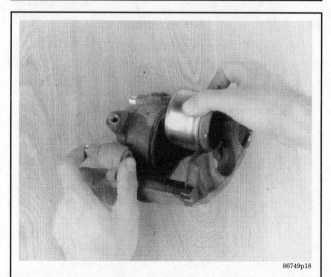

Fig. 39 Removing the piston from the caliper

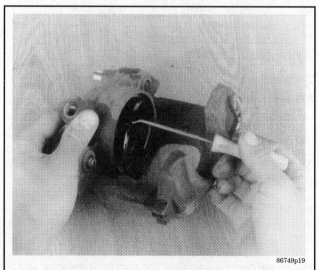

Fig. 40 Removing the O-ring from the piston bore

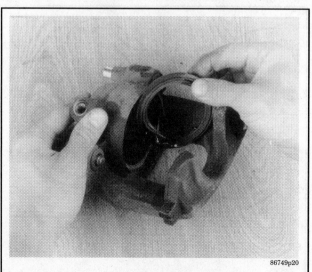

Fig. 41 Removing the dust seal from the caliper

4. Insert an air nozzle into the inlet hole in the caliper and gently apply air pressure on the piston to push it out of the bore. Use only enough air pressure to ease the piston out of the bore.

5. Pry the dust boot out of the bore with a suitable tool. Use caution during this operation to prevent scratching the bore. Discard the dust boot.

6. Remove the piston seal from the piston bore and discard the seal. Use only non-scratching implements such as a pencil, wooden stick or a piece of plastic to remove the seal. Do not use a metal tool, as it could very easily scratch the bore.

7. Remove and discard the sleeves and rubber bushings from the mounting ears.

8. Clean all the parts with brake cleaning solvent or clean brake fluid. Blow out all of the passages in the caliper and bleeder valve. Use only dry and filtered compressed air. Replace the mounting bolts if they are corroded or if the threads are damaged.

➡**Do not attempt to clean the attaching bolts with abrasives, as their protective plating may be removed.**

9. Examine the piston for defects. Replace the piston if it is nicked, scratched, corroded or the protective plating is worn off. Examine the caliper piston bore for the same defects as the piston. The bore is not plated and minor stains or corrosion can be polished with crocus cloth.

➡**Do not attempt to refinish the piston in any way. The outside diameter is the sealing surface and is made to very close tolerances. Removal of the nickel-chrome plating will lead to pitting, rusting and eventual cocking of the piston in the piston bore. Do not use emery cloth or similar abrasives on the piston bore. If the bore does not clean up with crocus cloth, replace the caliper. Clean the caliper thoroughly with brake cleaning solvent, or brake fluid if the bore was polished with crocus cloth.**

10. Lubricate the bore and new seal with clean brake fluid and install the seal in the groove in the bore.

11. Lubricate the piston with clean brake fluid and install the new dust boot on the piston. Assemble the dust boot into the piston groove so that the fold in the boot faces the open end

of the piston. Slide the metal portion of the dust boot over the open end of the piston and push the retainer toward the back of the piston until the lip on the fold seats in the piston groove. Then push the retainer portion of the boot forward until the boot is flush with the rim at the open end of the piston and snaps into place.

12. Insert the piston in the bore, being careful not to unseat the piston seal. Push the piston to the bottom of the bore.

13. Position the dust boot retainer in the counter bore at the top of the piston bore. Seat the dust boot retainer with a flat-ended punch by tapping the metal ring of the dust boot into place. Be careful not do damage the rubber portion of the dust boot. The metal retainer portion of the boot must be evenly seated in the counterbore, using tool J 33028 or J 22904 or its equivalent, and fit below the face of the caliper.

14. Connect the brake line to the caliper using new copper gaskets. Tighten to 23 ft. lbs. (31 Nm).

15. Install the brake pads, sleeves and rubber bushings.

16. Install the caliper and tighten the mounting bolts to 30 ft. lbs. (41 Nm). Bleed the hydraulic system.

Brake Rotor

REMOVAL & INSTALLATION

☀✲CAUTION

Brake shoes may contain asbestos, which has been determined to be a cancer causing agent. Never clean the brake surfaces with compressed air! Avoid inhaling any dust from any brake surface! When cleaning brake surfaces, use a commercially available brake cleaning fluid.

4-Wheel Drive

▶ See Figures 45 and 46

1. Loosen the lug nuts on the front wheels.
2. Raise and support the vehicle safely.
3. Remove the front wheels.

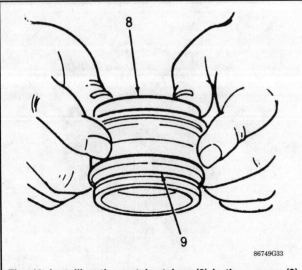

Fig. 42 Installing the metal retainer (8) in the groove (9)

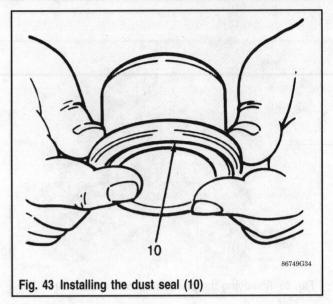

Fig. 43 Installing the dust seal (10)

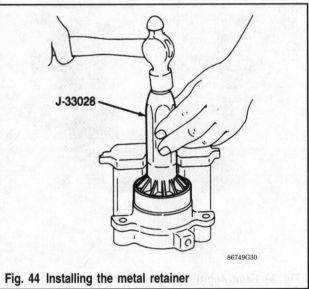

J-33028

86749G30

Fig. 44 Installing the metal retainer

4. Remove the calipers, but don't disconnect the brake lines. Suspend the calipers out of the way.

5. Remove the rotor.

6. Installation is the reverse of removal. Tighten wheel lug nuts to 75 ft. lbs. (101 Nm).

2-Wheel Drive

▶ See Figure 47

1. Raise and safely support the front end on jackstands.
2. Remove the wheels.
3. Remove the caliper without disconnecting the brake line. Suspend it out of the way. Refer to the caliper removal procedure in this section.
4. Remove the grease cap, cotter pin, nut cap, nut, and washer from the spindle.
5. Pull slowly on the hub and catch the outer bearing as it falls.
6. Remove the hub and rotor. The inner bearing and seal can be removed by prying out and discarding the inner seal.

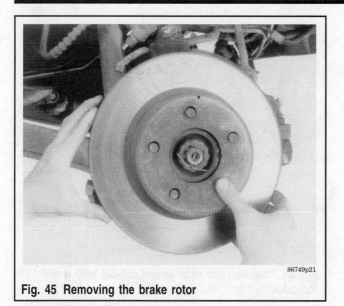

Fig. 45 Removing the brake rotor

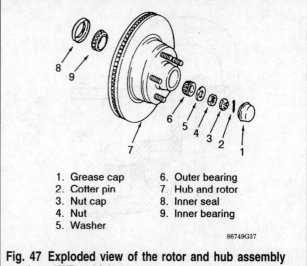

1. Grease cap
2. Cotter pin
3. Nut cap
4. Nut
5. Washer
6. Outer bearing
7. Hub and rotor
8. Inner seal
9. Inner bearing

86749G37

Fig. 47 Exploded view of the rotor and hub assembly used on 2WD vehicles

To install:

7. Clean and repack the hub and bearings, install the inner bearing and a new seal.

8. Position the hub and rotor on the spindle and install the outer bearing.

9. Install the washer and nut.

10. While turning the rotor, tighten the nut to 25 ft. lbs. (33 Nm) to seat the bearings.

11. Back off the nut ½ turn, and, while turning the rotor, tighten the nut to 19 inch lbs. (2 Nm).

12. Install the nut cap and a new cotter pin. Install the grease cap.

13. Install the caliper.

14. Install the wheels.

INSPECTION AND MEASUREMENT

▶ **See Figures 48 and 49**

Check the rotor for surface cracks, nicks, broken cooling fins and scoring of both contact surfaces. Some scoring of the

surfaces may occur during normal use. Scoring that is 0.015 in. (0.38mm) deep or less is not detrimental to the operation of the brakes.

If the rotor surface is heavily rusted or scaled, clean both surfaces on a disc brake lathe using flat sanding discs before attempting any measurements.

With the hub and rotor assembly mounted on the spindle of the vehicle or a disc brake lathe and all play removed from the wheel bearings, assemble a dial indicator so that the stem contacts the center of the rotor braking surface. Zero the dial indicator before taking any measurements. Lateral run-out must not exceed 0.005 in. (0.13mm) with a maximum rate of change not to exceed 0.001 in. (0.025mm) in 30° of rotation.

Excessive run-out will cause the rotor to wobble and knock the piston back into the caliper, causing increased pedal travel, noise and vibration.

Check the Brake Specifications Chart for rotor thickness. Discard the rotor if it is not within the specification.

➡**Remember to adjust the preload on the wheel bearings after the run-out measurement has been taken.**

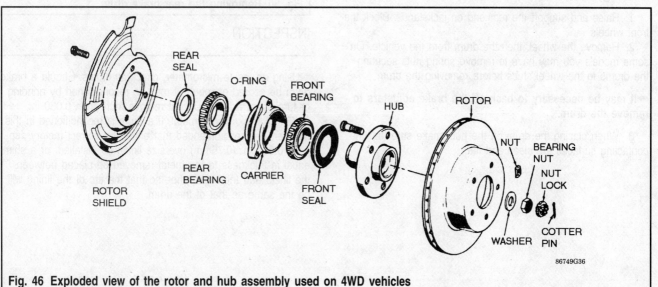

Fig. 46 Exploded view of the rotor and hub assembly used on 4WD vehicles

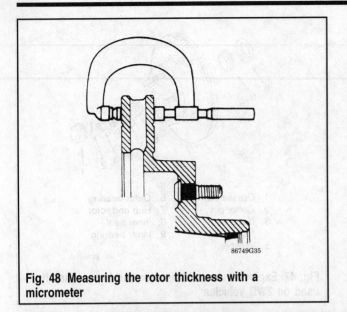

Fig. 48 Measuring the rotor thickness with a micrometer

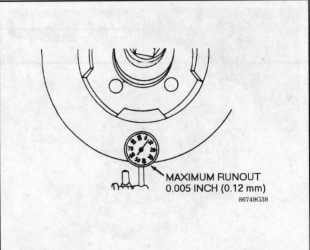

MAXIMUM RUNOUT
0.005 INCH (0.12 mm)

86749G38

Fig. 49 Checking the rotor lateral run-out with a dial indicator

DRUM BRAKES

Brake Drums

REMOVAL & INSTALLATION

▶ See Figures 50, 51 and 52

❋❋CAUTION

Brake shoes may contain asbestos, which has been determined to be a cancer causing agent. Never clean the brake surfaces with compressed air! Avoid inhaling any dust from any brake surface! When cleaning brake surfaces, use a commercially available brake cleaning fluid.

➡For vehicles equipped with Anti-Lock Brakes (ABS), refer to the proper procedures concerning brake system servicing.

1. Raise and support the rear end on jackstands. Block the front wheels
2. Remove the wheel, then the drum from the vehicle. On some models you may have to remove spring nuts securing the drums to the wheel studs before removing the drum.

➡It may be necessary to back off the brake adjusters to remove the drum.

3. When placing the drum on the hub, make sure that the contacting surfaces are clean and flat.

86749p22

Fig. 50 Removing the rear brake drum

INSPECTION

Using an inside micrometer, check all drums. Should a brake drum be scored or rough, it may be reconditioned by grinding or turning on a lathe. Do not remove more than 0.030 in. (0.76mm) thickness of metal. If a drum is reconditioned in this manner, it is recommended that either the correct factory supplied 0.030 in. (0.76mm) oversize lining be installed, or a shim equal in thickness to the metal removed be placed between the lining and the brake shoe so that the arc of the lining will be the same as that of the drum.

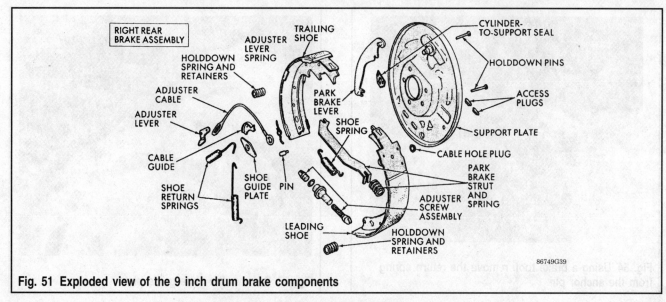

Fig. 51 Exploded view of the 9 inch drum brake components

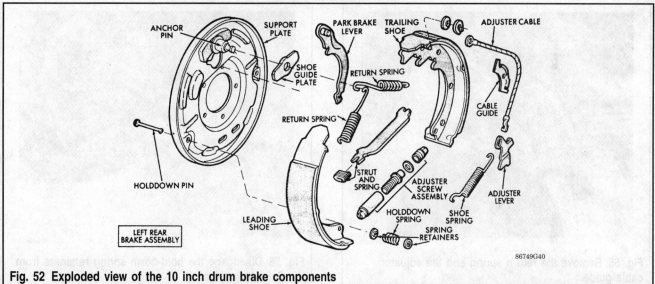

Fig. 52 Exploded view of the 10 inch drum brake components

Brake Shoes

REMOVAL & INSTALLATION

▶ See Figures 53, 54, 55, 56, 57, 58, 59, 60, 61, 62, 63, 64, 65, 66, 67, 68 and 69

❊❊CAUTION

Brake shoes may contain asbestos, which has been determined to be a cancer causing agent. Never clean the brake surfaces with compressed air! Avoid inhaling any dust from any brake surface! When cleaning brake surfaces, use a commercially available brake cleaning fluid.

➡A brake spring removal tool and a brake adjusting gauge are required for this procedure.

1. Raise and support the vehicle safely with jackstands.

Fig. 53 Using brake cleaner to clean the brake surfaces

Fig. 54 Using a brake tool, remove the return spring from the anchor pin

Fig. 57 Remove the shoe guide plate

Fig. 55 Remove the return spring and the adjuster cable guide

Fig. 58 Disengage the hold-down spring retainers from the hold-down pins

Fig. 56 Remove the adjuster cable

Fig. 59 Remove the hold-down springs and pins

Fig. 60 Pull the shoes apart and then . . .

Fig. 61 . . . remove the parking brake strut and spring

Fig. 62 Remove the shoes from the backing plate

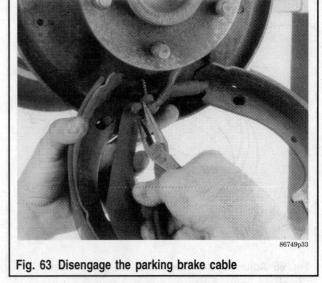

Fig. 63 Disengage the parking brake cable

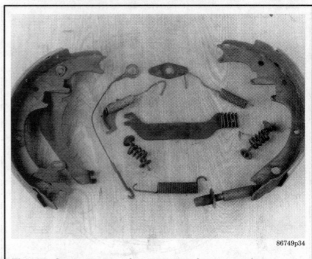

Fig. 64 Components of a common Jeep rear drum brake system

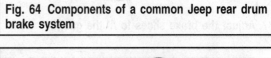

Fig. 65 Lubricate the shoe contact points — 10 inch drum brake backing plate shown

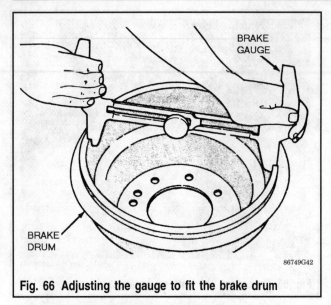

Fig. 66 Adjusting the gauge to fit the brake drum

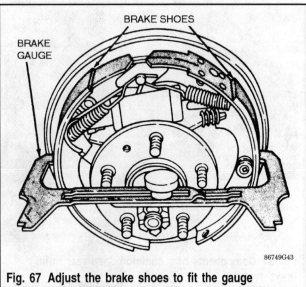

Fig. 67 Adjust the brake shoes to fit the gauge

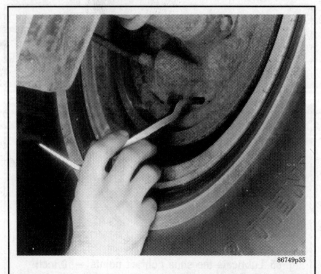

Fig. 68 Adjusting the drum brakes using a brake spoon

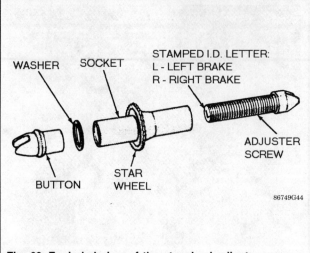

Fig. 69 Exploded view of the starwheel adjuster screw components

2. If the brakes have never been serviced before, the drums will be held on the wheel studs with spring nuts. Remove the spring nuts and discard.

3. Turn the adjustment starwheel so that the brake shoes are retracted from the brake drum and remove the brake drum.

4. Install wheel cylinder clamps to retain the wheel cylinder pistons in place and prevent leakage of brake fluid while replacing the shoes.

5. Remove the U-clip and washer securing the adjuster cable to the parking brake lever.

6. Remove the adjuster cable, cable guide, adjuster lever and adjuster springs. Remove the return springs with a brake spring remover tool.

7. Remove the hold-down retainers and springs, then remove the brake shoes.

To install:

8. Clean the backing plate with a brush or cloth. Place a dab of Lubriplate® on each spot where the brake shoes rub on the backing plate.

➡**Always replace brake linings in axle sets. Never replace linings on one side or just on one wheel.**

9. Thoroughly clean and lubricate the adjuster cable guides, adjuster screw and pivot, parking brake lever and lever pivot pin with multi-purpose grease.

10. Apply a thin coat of multi-purpose chassis lube to the mounting pads on the backing plate.

11. Transfer the parking brake actuating lever to the new secondary shoe.

12. Position the brake shoes on the backing plate, then install the hold-down springs and retainers. Don't forget to engage the parking brake lever with the cable.

13. Install the parking brake actuating bar and spring between the parking brake lever and primary shoe.

14. Install the self-adjusting cable, cable guide and upper return springs.

15. Thoroughly clean the starwheel and lightly lubricate the threads with lithium based grease.

16. Install the starwheel.

17. Install the self-adjusting cam and lower spring. A big pair of locking pliers is good for this job.

18. Check the surface of the brake shoes for any grease that may have gotten on them. If dirty, lightly clean with a piece of sandpaper.

19. Adjust the brakes, install the brake drum and wheel. Lower the vehicle and test drive.

Wheel Cylinders

REMOVAL & INSTALLATION

✳✳CAUTION

Brake shoes may contain asbestos, which has been determined to be a cancer causing agent. Never clean the brake surfaces with compressed air! Avoid inhaling any dust from any brake surface! When cleaning brake surfaces, use a commercially available brake cleaning fluid.

➡**For vehicles equipped with Anti-Lock Brakes (ABS), refer to the proper procedures concerning brake system servicing.**

REAR DISC BRAKES

Disc Brake Pads

REMOVAL & INSTALLATION

✳✳CAUTION

Brake shoes may contain asbestos, which has been determined to be a cancer causing agent. Never clean the brake surfaces with compressed air! Avoid inhaling any dust from any brake surface! When cleaning brake surfaces, use a commercially available brake cleaning fluid.

1. Raise and support the vehicle safely using jackstands. Remove the wheel(s) on the side to be worked on.

➡**For vehicles equipped with Anti-Lock Brakes (ABS), refer to the proper procedures concerning brake system servicing.**

2. Drain a small amount of the brake fluid from the front reservoir using a suction gun or a turkey baster.

3. Place a C-clamp on the caliper so that the solid end contacts the back of the caliper and the screw end contacts the metal part of the outboard brake pad.

4. Tighten the clamp until the caliper moves far enough to force the piston to the bottom of the piston bore. This will back the brake pads off of the rotor surface to facilitate the removal and installation of the caliper assembly.

1. Raise and support the vehicle safely using jackstands. Remove the wheel.

2. Disconnect the brake line at the fitting on the brake backing plate.

➡**In most cases the flare fittings that attach the brake lines to the wheel cylinders will be frozen. Clean the fittings with solvent and use penetrating oil to loosen the rust. Use the proper size flare nut wrench to avoid stripping the fitting.**

3. Remove the brake assemblies. Disconnect the brake line from the rear of the wheel cylinder.

4. Remove the screws or nuts that hold the wheel cylinder to the backing plate and remove the wheel cylinder from the vehicle.

To install:

5. Position the wheel cylinder on the backing plate and start the brake line in the cylinder fitting.

6. Install the cylinder mounting bolts and tighten to 90 inch lbs. (10 Nm).

7. To avoid stripping the fitting, tighten the brake line fitting to 132 inch lbs. (15 Nm) using a flare nut wrench.

5. Remove the C-clamp.

➡**Do not push down on the brake pedal or the piston and brake pads will return to their original positions up against the rotor.**

6. Remove the caliper mounting bolts. Tilt the top of the caliper outward and lift it off the rotor.

7. Hold the anti-rattle clip against the caliper anchor plate and remove the outboard brake pad.

8. Remove the inboard pad and its anti-rattle clip.

9. Use a piece of wire to support the caliper so that no tension is placed on the brake hose. DO NOT allow the caliper to hang by the brake hose.

To install:

10. Clean all the mounting holes and bushing grooves in the caliper ears. Clean the mounting bolts. Replace the bolts if they are corroded or if the threads are damaged. Wipe the inside of the caliper clean, including the exterior of the dust boot. Inspect the dust boot for cuts or cracks and for proper seating in the piston bore. If evidence of fluid leakage is noted, the caliper should be rebuilt.

➡**Do not use abrasives on the bolts in order not to destroy their protective plating. You should not use compressed air to clean the inside of the caliper, as it may unseat the dust boot seal.**

11. Install the inboard anti-rattle clip on the trailing end of the anchor plate. The split end of the clip must face away from the rotor.

12. Install the inboard pad in the caliper. The pad must lay flat against the piston.

13. Install the outboard pad in the caliper while holding the anti-rattle clip.

14. With the pads installed, position the caliper over the rotor.

➡**Before securing the caliper, ensure the brake hose is not twisted, kinked or touching any chassis parts.**

15. Lubricate the caliper pins and bushings with silicone grease. Line up the mounting holes in the caliper and the support bracket and insert the mounting bolts. Make sure that the bolts pass under the retaining ears on the inboard shoes. Push the bolts through until they engage the holes of the outboard pad and caliper ears. Thread the bolts into the support bracket and tighten them to 7-15 ft. lbs. (9-20 Nm).

✳✳CAUTION

On models with manual/power brakes, pump the pedal until the caliper pistons and brake shoes are seated. On models with anti-lock brakes, turn the ignition ON and allow the booster pump to build pressure. Pump the brake pedal until the shoes are seated and the indicator lights turn off.

16. Install the wheel assembly and lower the vehicle.
17. Turn the ignition **ON** and run the HCU pump until it shuts off.
18. Pump the brake pedal until the shoes are seated and the indicator lights go out. Check the brake fluid level in the master cylinder and replenish if necessary.

INSPECTION

Measure lining wear by measuring the combined thickness of the pad and pad backing plate at the thinnest point. It must measure at least $5/16$ in. (8mm) thick on all vehicles covered by this manual.

Always replace both front brake pad assemblies (inboard and outboard pad) on both front wheels whenever necessary. The specifications given above on front disc brake lining wear should be used as the guide for replacement.

Calipers

REMOVAL & INSTALLATION

✳✳CAUTION

Brake shoes may contain asbestos, which has been determined to be a cancer causing agent. Never clean the brake surfaces with compressed air! Avoid inhaling any dust from any brake surface! When cleaning brake surfaces, use a commercially available brake cleaning fluid.

1. Raise and support the vehicle safely using jackstands. Remove the wheel(s) on the side to be worked on.

➡**For vehicles equipped with Anti-Lock Brakes (ABS), refer to the proper procedures concerning brake system servicing.**

2. Drain a small amount of the brake fluid from the front reservoir using a suction gun or a turkey baster.
3. Place a C-clamp on the caliper so that the solid end contacts the back of the caliper and the screw end contacts the metal part of the outboard brake pad.
4. Tighten the clamp until the caliper moves far enough to force the piston to the bottom of the piston bore. This will back the brake pads off of the rotor surface to facilitate the removal and installation of the caliper assembly.
5. Remove the C-clamp.

➡**Do not push down on the brake pedal or the piston and brake pads will return to their original positions up against the rotor.**

6. Remove the caliper mounting bolts. Tilt the top of the caliper outward and lift off the rotor.
7. Remove the brake pads from the caliper.

➡**If the caliper is not being removed for overhaul, it is not necessary to remove the caliper assembly entirely from the vehicle. DO NOT remove the brake line. Suspend the caliper with a piece of wire. DO NOT allow the brake hose to support the weight of the caliper.**

8. Remove the caliper fitting bolt and disconnect the brake line at the caliper. Discard the fitting bolt washers, they are not reusable. Cap or tape the open ends of the hose to keep dirt out.

To install:
9. Clean all the mounting holes and bushing grooves in the caliper ears. Clean the mounting bolts. Do not use abrasives on the bolts it will destroy their protective plating. Replace the bolts if they are corroded or if the threads are damaged.
10. Reconnect the brake hose to the caliper. Tighten the bolt to 23 ft. lbs. (31 Nm).
11. Install the brake pads and position the caliper over the rotor.

➡**Before securing the caliper, ensure the brake hose is not twisted, kinked or touching any chassis parts.**

12. Lubricate the caliper pins and bushings with silicone grease. Line up the mounting holes in the caliper and the support bracket and insert the mounting bolts. Make sure that the bolts pass under the retaining ears on the inboard shoes. Push the bolts through until they engage the holes of the outboard pad and caliper ears. Thread the bolts into the support bracket and tighten them to 30 ft. lbs. (41 Nm).

✳✳CAUTION

On models with manual/power brakes, pump the pedal until the caliper pistons and brake shoes are seated. On models with anti-lock brakes, turn the ignition ON and allow the booster pump to build pressure. Pump the brake pedal until the shoes are seated and the indicator lights turn off.

13. Install the wheel assembly and lower the vehicle. Check the level of the brake fluid in the master cylinder and fill as necessary.
14. Turn the ignition **ON** and run the HCU pump until it shuts off.

15. Pump the brake pedal until the shoes are seated and the indicator lights go out. Check the brake fluid level in the master cylinder and replenish if necessary.

OVERHAUL

1. Remove the caliper assembly and remove the brake pads. If the pads are to be reused, mark their location in the caliper.

➡ **For vehicles equipped with Anti-Lock Brakes (ABS), refer to the proper procedures concerning brake system servicing.**

2. Clean the caliper exterior with brake cleaning solvent or clean brake fluid. Drain any residual fluid from the caliper and place it on a clean work surface.

➡ **Removal of the caliper piston requires the use of compressed air. Do not, under any circumstances, place your fingers in front of the piston in any attempt to catch or protect it when applying compressed air to remove the piston.**

3. Pad the interior of the caliper with clean cloths. Use several cloths and pad the interior well to avoid damaging the piston when it comes out of the bore.

4. Insert an air nozzle into the inlet hole in the caliper and gently apply air pressure on the piston to push it out of the bore. Use only enough air pressure to ease the piston out of the bore.

5. Pry the dust boot out of the bore with a suitable tool. Use caution during this operation to prevent scratching the bore. Discard the dust boot.

6. Remove the piston seal from the piston bore and discard the seal. Use only non-scratching implements such as a pencil, wooden stick or a piece of plastic to remove the seal. Do not use a metal tool, as it could very easily scratch the bore.

7. Remove and discard the sleeves and rubber bushings from the mounting ears.

8. Clean all the parts with brake cleaning solvent or clean brake fluid. Blow out all of the passages in the caliper and bleeder valve. Use only dry and filtered compressed air. Replace the mounting bolts if they are corroded or if the threads are damaged.

➡ **Do not attempt to clean the attaching bolts with abrasives, as their protective plating may be removed.**

9. Examine the piston for defects. Replace the piston if it is nicked, scratched, corroded or the protective plating is worn off. Examine the caliper piston bore for the same defects as the piston. The bore is not plated and minor stains or corrosion can be polished with crocus cloth.

➡ **Do not attempt to refinish the piston in any way. The outside diameter is the sealing surface and is made to very close tolerances. Removal of the nickel-chrome plating will lead to pitting, rusting and eventual cocking of the piston in the piston bore. Do not use emery cloth or similar abrasives on the piston bore. If the bore does not clean up with crocus cloth, replace the caliper. Clean the caliper thoroughly with brake cleaning solvent or brake fluid if the bore was polished with crocus cloth.**

10. Lubricate the bore and new seal with clean brake fluid and install the seal in the groove in the bore.

11. Lubricate the piston with clean brake fluid and install the new dust boot on the piston. Assemble the dust boot into the piston groove so that the fold in the boot faces the open end of the piston. Slide the metal portion of the dust boot over the open end of the piston and push the retainer toward the back of the piston until the lip on the fold seats in the piston groove. Then push the retainer portion of the boot forward until the boot is flush with the rim at the open end of the piston and snaps into place.

12. Insert the piston in the bore, being careful not to unseat the piston seal. Push the piston to the bottom of the bore.

13. Position the dust boot retainer in the counter bore at the top of the piston bore. Seat the dust boot retainer with a flat-ended punch by tapping the metal ring of the dust boot into place. Be careful not do damage the rubber portion of the dust boot. The metal retainer portion of the boot must be evenly seated in the counterbore, using tool J 33028 or J 22904 or its equivalent, and fit below the face of the caliper.

14. Connect the brake line to the caliper using new copper gaskets. tighten to 23 ft. lbs. (31 Nm).

15. Install the brake pads, sleeves and rubber bushings.

16. Install the caliper and tighten the mounting bolts to 30 ft. lbs. (41 Nm). Bleed the hydraulic system.

Brake Rotor

REMOVAL & INSTALLATION

✳✳ CAUTION

Brake shoes may contain asbestos, which has been determined to be a cancer causing agent. Never clean the brake surfaces with compressed air! Avoid inhaling any dust from any brake surface! When cleaning brake surfaces, use a commercially available brake cleaning fluid.

4-Wheel Drive

1. Loosen the lug nuts on the rear wheels.
2. Raise and support the vehicle safely.
3. Remove the rear wheels.
4. Remove the calipers, but don't disconnect the brake lines. Suspend the calipers out of the way.
5. Remove the rotor.
6. Installation is the reverse of removal. Tighten wheel lug nuts to 75 ft. lbs. (101 Nm).

2-Wheel Drive

1. Raise and safely support the rear of the vehicle on jackstands.
2. Remove the wheels.
3. Remove the caliper without disconnecting the brake line. Suspend it out of the way.
4. Remove the grease cap, cotter pin, nut cap, nut, and washer from the spindle.
5. Pull slowly on the hub and catch the outer bearing as it falls.

6. Remove the hub and rotor. The inner bearing and seal can be removed by prying out and discarding the inner seal.

7. Clean and repack the hub and bearings, install the inner bearing and a new seal.

8. Position the hub and rotor on the spindle and install the outer bearing.

9. Install the washer and nut.

10. While turning the rotor, torque the nut to 25 ft. lbs. (33 Nm) to seat the bearings.

11. Back off the nut ½ turn, and, while turning the rotor, torque the nut to 19 inch lbs. (2 Nm).

12. Install the nut cap and a new cotter pin. Install the grease cap.

13. Install the caliper.

14. Install the wheels.

INSPECTION AND MEASUREMENT

Check the rotor for surface cracks, nicks, broken cooling fins and scoring of both contact surfaces. Some scoring of the surfaces may occur during normal use. Scoring that is 0.015 in. (0.38mm) deep or less is not detrimental to the operation of the brakes.

If the rotor surface is heavily rusted or scaled, clean both surfaces on a disc brake lathe using flat sanding discs before attempting any measurements.

With the hub and rotor assembly mounted on the spindle of the vehicle or a disc brake lathe and all play removed from the wheel bearings, assemble a dial indicator so that the stem contacts the center of the rotor braking surface. Zero the dial indicator before taking any measurements. Lateral run-out must not exceed 0.005 in. (0.13mm) with a maximum rate of change not to exceed 0.001 in. (0.025mm) in 30° of rotation.

Excessive run-out will cause the rotor to wobble and knock the piston back into the caliper, causing increased pedal travel, noise and vibration.

Check the Brake Specifications Chart for rotor thickness. Discard the rotor if it is not within the specification.

➡**Remember to adjust the preload on the wheel bearings after the run-out measurement has been taken.**

PARKING BRAKE

Cables

REMOVAL & INSTALLATION

1984-94 Models

REAR CABLE

▶ **See Figures 70 and 71**

1. Raise and support the vehicle safely with jackstands. Fully release the parking brake.

❋❋CAUTION

Take care to support the vehicle safely. Place wheel chocks behind the wheels and use jackstands under the frame for support. Remember, the parking brake is released!

2. Remove the rear wheel and brake drum.

3. Remove the secondary (rear) brake shoe and disengage the parking brake lever from the brake shoe.

4. Compress the cable retainer with a hose clamp as illustrated.

5. Remove the cable from the backing plate, then remove the cable mounting clips.

6. Disengage the cable from the equalizer and remove the cable.

To install:

7. Install the new cable in the backing plate and engage the cable in the equalizer.

8. Install the cable mounting clips and connect the cable to the lever on the secondary brake shoe.

9. Install the secondary brake shoe and the brake drum and wheel.

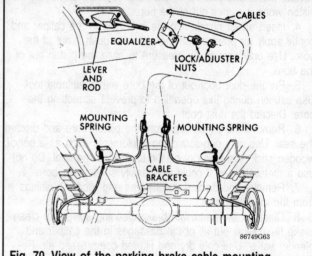

Fig. 70 View of the parking brake cable mounting — Comanche shown

10. Adjust the drum brakes and parking brakes as described in this section.

FRONT CABLE

▶ **See Figures 72, 73, 74 and 75**

1. Raise and support the vehicle safely. Fully release the parking brake.

❋❋CAUTION

Take care to support the vehicle safely. Place wheel chocks behind the wheels and use jackstands under the frame for support. Remember, the parking brake is released!

2. Remove the equalizer nuts and remove the front cable from the equalizer and cable bracket.

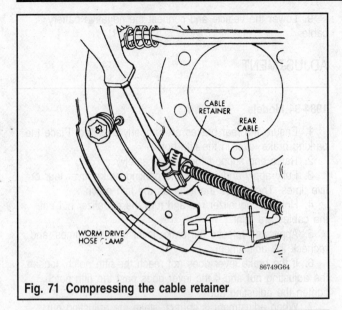

Fig. 71 Compressing the cable retainer

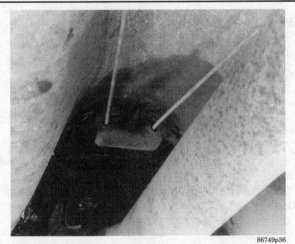

Fig. 72 View of the parking brake cable and equalizer — 1987 Wagoneer shown

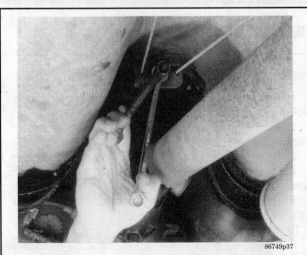

Fig. 73 Adjusting the parking brake cable — 1987 Wagoneer shown

3. Lower the vehicle.

4. Move the carpet away from the pedal assembly. Then remove the pedal mounting bolts and move the pedal assembly away from the kick panel. Disconnect the front cable from the pedal.

5. Move the carpet at the driver's side and rear of the cab to gain access to the cable floorpan clamps. Remove the clamps, unseat the cable grommet and remove the cable through the floorpan.

To install:

6. Install the pedal assembly on the kick panel.

7. Install the cable grommet and the cable floorpan clamps.

8. Install the carpet on the floorpan and raise the vehicle supporting it with jackstands.

9. Install the cable in the bracket and the equalizer.

10. Install the equalizer nuts and washer and adjust the parking brakes as described in this section.

1995-96 Models

REAR CABLE

1. Raise the vehicle and safely support it with jackstands. Release the parking brake.

2. Loosen the adjusting nut at the equalizer to provide slack in the cable.

3. Disengage the cable from the equalizer and from the chassis and body clips and retainers.

4. Slide the cable eyelet off the actuating lever. Then compress the retainer holding the cable in the bracket attached to the caliper bracket and remove the cable.

To install:

5. Install the cable eyelet on the actuating lever making sure the eyelet is seated in the lever notch.

6. Seat the cable retainer in the caliper bracket.

7. Route the cable to the tensioner and equalizer and connect the cable to the equalizer.

8. Connect the cable to the chassis and body clips and retainers.

9. Adjust the parking brake as outlined in this section.

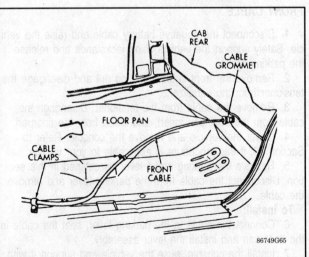

Fig. 74 View of the front cable floorpan attachment — Comanche shown

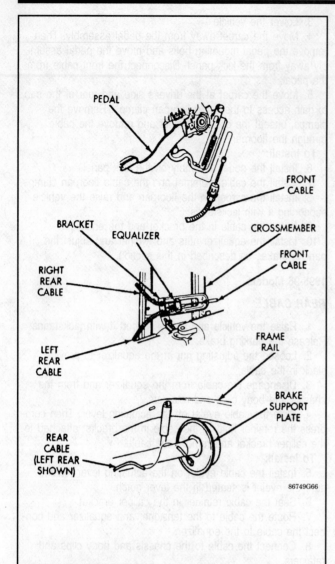

Fig. 75 View of the parking brake cable routing — Comanche shown

FRONT CABLE

1. Disconnect the negative battery cable and raise the vehicle. Safely support the vehicle using jackstands and release the parking brake.
2. Remove the front cable adjusting nut and disengage the tensioner from the equalizer.
3. Remove the cable from the tensioner. Disengage the cable from the floor pan insert, and insert from the floorpan.
4. Lower the vehicle and remove the console. Refer to Section 10, if this procedure is applicable to your vehicle.
5. Remove the parking brake lever as outlined in this section. Disconnect the cable from the parking lever and remove the cable.

To install:

6. Connect the cable to the parking lever, seat the cable in the floor pan and install the lever assembly.
7. Install the console, raise the vehicle and support it with jackstands.
8. Assemble the front cable, tensioner and equalizer. Adjust the parking cable as outlined in this section.

9. Lower the vehicle and connect the negative battery cable.

ADJUSTMENT

1984-94 Models

1. Ensure the rear brakes are properly adjusted. Place the parking brake lever in the fifth notch.
2. Raise and support the vehicle safely.
3. Fully apply and release the parking brake lever four or five times. Then place the lever on the fifth notch.
4. Hold the equalizer rod and turn the equalizer nut until the cables are tight.
5. Apply and release the brake lever fully, five times, and recheck the adjustment.
6. If the brake lever does not reach the fifth notch, loosen the adjusting nut and if the lever goes past the fifth notch, tighten the adjusting nut.
7. When adjustment is correct, stake the adjusting nut.

1995-96 Models

1. Raise the vehicle and safely support it with jackstands.
2. Back off the adjusting nut to create slack in the cables and remove the wheels and drums.
3. Ensure the rear brakes are properly adjusted and that the parking brake cables are in good condition.
4. Reinstall the wheels and drums if the brake shoe adjustment is correct.
5. Fully apply the parking brakes and leave them applied.
6. Mark the tensioner rod 1/4 in. (6.5mm) from the tensioner bracket.
7. Tighten the adjusting nut until the mark at the tensioner rod moves into alignment with the tensioner bracket.
8. Release the parking brake and verify that there is no drag on the wheels.
9. Lower the vehicle.

Brake Pedal or Lever

REMOVAL & INSTALLATION

Pedal

1. Raise the vehicle and safely support it with jackstands. Release the parking brake.
2. Loosen the adjusting nut at the equalizer to provide slack in the cable.
3. Remove the kick panel trim and release handle screws.
4. Disengage the cable retaining clip and the warning light wire.
5. Remove the pedal attaching bolts, disengage the cable from the retainer and remove the pedal.

To install:

6. Engage the pedal to the retainer, install the pedal on the panel and tighten the retaining bolts.
7. Engage the pedal retaining clip and warning light wire.
8. Install the kick panel and release handle and tighten the screws.

9. Adjust the parking brake as outlined in this section.

Lever

1. Raise the vehicle and safely support it using jackstands. Release the parking brake.
2. Remove the front cable adjusting nut and disengage the tensioner from the equalizer.
3. Remove the cable from the tensioner, then disengage the cable from the floor pan insert and the insert from the floorpan.
4. Lower the vehicle and remove the console . Refer to Section 10 for this procedure.
5. Disengage the parking brake switch and air bag control module (if equipped).
6. Unfasten the screws attaching the air bag control module to the floor pan and parking brake lever (if equipped). Move the module to one side.
7. Remove the screws attaching the parking brake lever to the bracket and lift the lever upward to access the front cable.
8. Disengage the front cable and remove the lever.

To install:

9. Connect the cable to lever and seat the cable in the floor pan.
10. Install the lever assembly and connect the parking brake switch wire.
11. Install the air bag control module and connect the wires.
12. Install the center console. Raise the vehicle and support it with jackstands.
13. Assemble the front cable, tensioner and equalizer. Adjust the parking cable as outlined in this section.

Brake Shoes

REMOVAL & INSTALLATION

1. Raise the vehicle and safely support it with jackstands. Remove the wheel.

2. Remove the caliper from the rotor and support the caliper with a piece of wire to a suspension component.
3. Remove the rubber access plug from the rear of the disc brake splash shield.
4. Retract the parking brake shoes by rotating the star wheel downwards in a clockwise direction (while facing the front of the vehicle) using a brake adjustment tool or equivalent.
5. Remove the rotor from the axle hub flange.
6. Remove the shoe hold-down clips and pins and the upper and lower springs from the shoes using needle nose pliers. Mark the adjuster screw for installation reference, then tilt the shoes outward and remove the adjuster screw.
7. Remove the shoes.

To install:

8. Install the shoes with the hold-down pins and clips making sure the shoes are properly seated in the caliper bracket and cam.
9. Install the adjuster screw assembly and the shoe upper and lower return springs. Operate the lever to verify the shoes expand and retract properly.
10. Install the rotor and caliper. Adjust the parking brake assembly as outlined in this section.
11. Install the wheel, lower the vehicle and verify that the parking brake is working properly.

Adjustment

1. Raise the vehicle and safely support it with jackstands.
2. Remove the wheel and secure the rotor with two wheel nuts.
3. Remove the rubber access plug from the rear of the splash shield and insert a brake tool.
4. Position the brake tool at the bottom of the star wheel and rotate the star wheel upward (counterclockwise) to expand the shoes.
5. Expand the shoes until a slight drag is experienced, then back off the adjuster so that the drag is barely eliminated.
6. Replace the access plug, install the wheel and lower the vehicle.

BENDIX ANTI-LOCK BRAKE SYSTEM (ABS)

General Information

The Bendix anti-lock braking system is available on 1989-92 Jeep Cherokee and Wagoneer vehicles (model designation XJ) with SelecTrac 4-wheel drive. Anti-lock Brake Systems (ABS) are designed to prevent wheel lockup under heavy braking conditions on virtually any type of road surface. The Jeep ABS limits wheel lockup by modulating the brake fluid pressure to the brakes at each wheel. A vehicle which is stopped without locking the wheels will normally stop in a shorter distance than a vehicle with locked wheels. Additionally, vehicle control can be maintained during hard braking because the front wheels do not lock. The Jeep system is an electronically operated, power assisted brake system controlled by an isolated Electronic Control Unit (ECU).

Under normal braking conditions, the ABS system functions in the same manner as a standard brake system. The primary difference is that power assistance is gained from hydraulic

pressure rather than a conventional vacuum booster. The system also prevents excessive pedal travel in the event of a hydraulic leak. Anti-lock braking is available above approximately 12 mph (19 km/h) the system disengages at approximately 4 mph (6 km/h).

There are conditions for which the ABS system provides no benefit. Hydroplaning is possible when the tires ride on a film of water, losing contact with the paved surface. This renders the vehicle totally uncontrollable until road contact is regained. Extreme steering maneuvers at high speed or cornering beyond the limits of tire adhesion can result in skidding which is independent of vehicle braking. For this reason, the system is named anti-lock rather than anti-skid.

SYSTEM OPERATION

The booster pump and accumulator provide the fluid pressure needed for power assistance. The accumulator is connected to the pump by a high-pressure feed line; a second high-pressure line connects the accumulator to the booster section of the master cylinder. The fluid reservoir is connected to the booster pump by a low-pressure line. Brake fluid from the master cylinder is sent to the calipers and brake cylinders through the pressure modulator. Each modulator channel contains 3 control solenoid valves; the valves are used to increase, decrease or maintain line pressure.

The Electronic Control Unit (ECU) receives data from the wheel speed sensors located at each wheel. Based on the sensor inputs, the ECU activates the proper solenoid valve to control braking effort at the wheels.

The ABS system is activated when the ignition switch is in the **ON** or **RUN** position. The system indicator light(s) are energized in the **START** position to serve as a bulb check. When the vehicle is motionless (no speed signal received by the ECU) and the ignition switch is in the **ON** or **RUN** position, the ECU will momentarily activate the control solenoids and operate them through full range. This allows the ECU to perform a system check. A slight whirring noise may be noticed by the operator if starting the vehicle in a quiet environment.

The main fluid supply is contained within the master cylinder reservoir and the accumulator as well as in the booster pump accumulator. The pump and the main accumulator provide the reserve fluid pressure needed for power brake assistance. The accumulator holds enough pressurized fluid for 25-30 power assisted brake applications should the pump fail.

✳✳CAUTION

The accumulator holds fluid at a normal pressure of 1,650-2,050 psi (11,376-14,134 kPa). Never attempt to work on, or around, the ABS hydraulic system without fully depressurizing the system. Severe injury may result.

Operation of the pump motor is controlled by the pump relay and by an internal line pressure switch within the pump. The pump will only operate when the ignition switch is in the **ON** or **RUN** position. The pump does not run continuously, but on demand of the line pressure switch. The pump is capable of running without connection to the ECU; thus, anti-lock function may be lost, but pressure within the system will still provide power assistance for normal braking. If, for any reason, the pump motor overheats, a thermal fuse inside the pump will blow shutting off the motor. The fuse is not serviceable and cannot be reset.

At each wheel, a fixed sensor generates an electrical signal based on the revolutions of a toothed tone wheel. This low voltage signal is sent to the ECU as wheel speed. The ECU compares the wheel speed signals to each other and to pre-programmed values; when excessive deceleration is indicated during a brake application, the system will enter ANTI-LOCK mode. During anti-lock braking, hydraulic pressure in the wheel circuits is modulated to prevent any wheel from locking. The ABS system controls pressure to the front wheels individually and to the rear wheels together. The control of the rear channel is usually based on the wheel with the greatest rate of deceleration. The system can build (increase), hold (maintain) or decay (reduce) pressure in each circuit as dictated by the ECU. Rapid changes in input data result in equally rapid changes in pressure modulation. Solenoid operation occurs in

brief rapid cycles, both front-to-rear and side-to-side. Function change and cycle times are measured in milliseconds.

As the solenoids in each channel operate to control line pressures, the operator may experience a slight pulsing sensation within the vehicle. A firmer brake pedal and/or some pedal pulsation may be noticed during anti-lock operation. The pulsing results from the rapid changes within the system and is completely normal during ABS stops.

The operator may hear a clicking or whirring sound as the booster pump and/or relay cycle on and off during normal operation. The sounds are due to normal pump motor operation and are not indicative of a system problem. Under most conditions, the sounds are only faintly audible.

Although the ABS system prevents wheel lock-up under hard braking, as brake pressure increases, wheel slip is allowed to reach as high as 30%. This means that the rolling velocity of a given wheel is 30% less than that of a free-rolling wheel at a given speed. This slip will result in some tire chirp during ABS operation. The sound should not be interpreted as lock-up, but rather as an indication of the system holding the wheel(s) just outside the point of lock-up. Additionally, since the ABS system turns off below 4 mph (6 km/h), the final few feet of an ABS-engaged stop may be completed with the wheels locked.

SYSTEM COMPONENTS

▶ **See Figures 76 and 77**

Master Cylinder/Power Booster

The integrated master cylinder and power booster is made from cast aluminum and mounted on the left side firewall within the engine compartment. A fluid reservoir is attached to the unit with rubber seals. The master cylinder portion is of the conventional split-system design. The brake pedal rod activates a ball valve at the end of the primary piston, providing boost pressure to the master cylinder and pressurized fluid to the modulator during an anti-lock stop.

The power booster only provides boost when the brake pedal is depressed. Assistance is through high pressure brake fluid supplied by an electric pump. The pump is connected to the booster unit by high-pressure brake lines.

Booster Pump and Motor
▶ **See Figure 78**

Located on the right side of the engine compartment, the booster pump is powered by an electric motor. The pump piston operates from an eccentric drive. The motor is controlled through a relay by the pressure switch located next to the pump and motor assembly. The pump and motor are equipped with an accumulator to provide additional fluid supply for working pressure.

Normal pump operating pressures are approximately 1,700-2,000 psi (11,721-13,790 kPa). The pressure switch engages the pump when the line pressure drops below 1,700 psi (11,721 kPa) once the pressure returns to 2,000 psi (13,790 kPa), the relay is de-energized and the pump shuts off. If the pump remains on for more than 4 minutes without the brakes being applied, the ECU will illuminate the red brake warning lamp on the instrument panel. If the internal pressure reaches

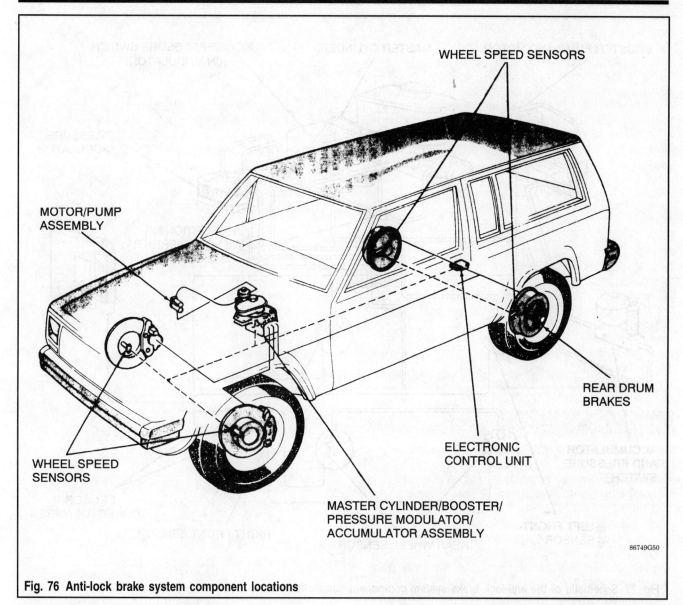

Fig. 76 Anti-lock brake system component locations

WHEEL SPEED SENSORS

MOTOR/PUMP
ASSEMBLY

REAR DRUM
BRAKES

ELECTRONIC
CONTROL UNIT

WHEEL SPEED
SENSORS

MASTER CYLINDER/BOOSTER/
PRESSURE MODULATOR/
ACCUMULATOR ASSEMBLY

86749G50

3,000 psi (20,685 kPa), an internal relief valve will open, allowing the pressure to drop.

The pump motor is also equipped with an internal thermal fuse. If operating temperature exceeds 385°F (196°C), the fuse will fail and stop operation of the motor.

Pressure Modulator

▶ **See Figure 79**

The pressure modulator is a hydro-electric unit attached to the master cylinder/power booster assembly. It provides 3-function control to each of 3 brake circuits — left front, right front and both rear wheels. The modulator contains 9 solenoids. Each brake channel has a separate isolate, build and decay solenoid assigned to it. Each solenoid performs its single task at the direction of the ECU whenever anti-lock is engaged.

Under normal brake operation, master cylinder pressure passes through the isolation solenoids to the individual wheel brake units. When ABS is engaged, the isolation solenoids block the master cylinder ports, allowing pressure to the

wheels to be controlled through the build and decay solenoids by the ECU.

The ECU activates the decay solenoid to reduce brake line pressure so the wheel can increase speed and avoid lock-up. When the ECU determines that wheel speed has increased above lock-up, the build solenoid is engaged to add braking force at the wheel. By quickly building and releasing line pressures, an individual wheel may be kept just outside the point of locking or skidding.

➡**All 3 channels operate independently. It is quite possible at any given moment, during an ABS stop, that one circuit has the build solenoid energized, while another has the decay solenoid energized.**

Electronic Control Module (ECM)

Located under the rear seat, the ECM monitors and controls the ABS system. It is connected to the wiring harness through 2 multi-pin connectors. The micro processor within the unit receives input from the a variety of sources, compares the

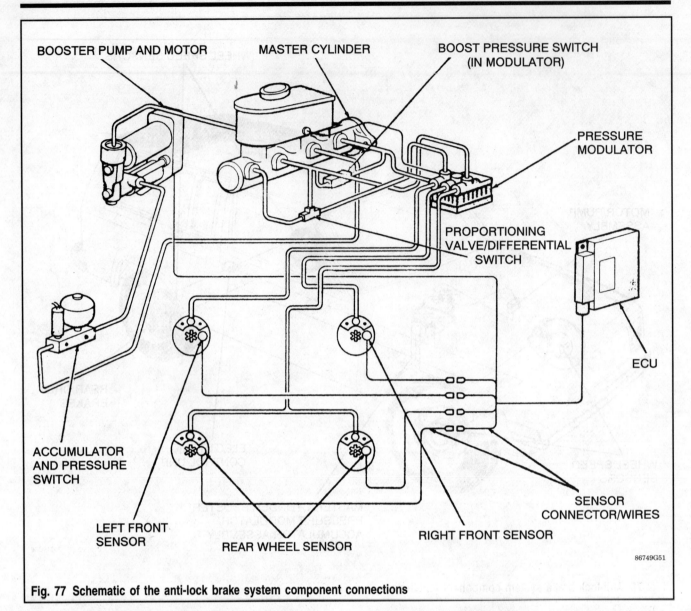

Fig. 77 Schematic of the anti-lock brake system component connections

86749G51

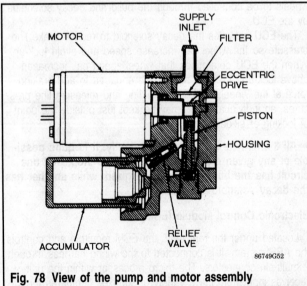

Fig. 78 View of the pump and motor assembly

86749G52

data against pre-programmed values and controls the output drivers. Sources of ECM input are:

- Speed sensors at 4 wheels
- Boost pressure differential switch
- Low fluid level switch
- Proportioning valve/pressure differential switch
- Brake pedal switch
- Parking brake switch
- Ignition switch
- Booster Pump and motor
- Modulator

The ECU contains self-check and system diagnostic capabilities. If a system fault or an internal ECU fault is detected, the ECU will assign a fault code, store it for later retrieval and turn on either or both of the dash warning lamps. There are 14 different faults that may be detected by the ECU, but only 1 fault code will be stored each time. The fault code will remain in memory until the battery is disconnected from the ECU. The stored fault code may be read with the DRB-II tester or equivalent hand-held scanner.

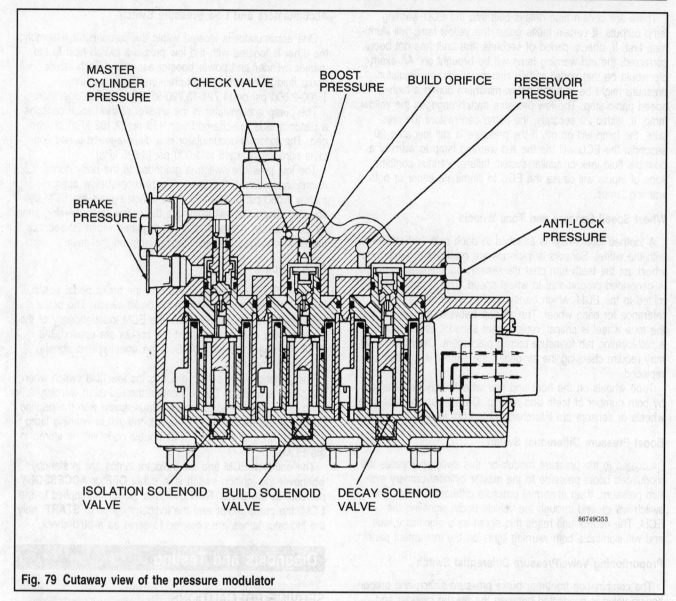

MASTER CYLINDER PRESSURE **CHECK VALVE** **BOOST PRESSURE** **BUILD ORIFICE** **RESERVOIR PRESSURE**

BRAKE PRESSURE

ANTI-LOCK PRESSURE

ISOLATION SOLENOID VALVE **BUILD SOLENOID VALVE** **DECAY SOLENOID VALVE**

86749G53

Fig. 79 Cutaway view of the pressure modulator

When the ECU is brought out of stand-by by turning the ignition switch to **ON** or **RUN**, the unit checks itself internally, as well as checking the solenoid driver circuits and certain external components. This self-check is continuously performed throughout the driving cycle. If any fault is found, the ECU will engage the yellow dash warning light and disable itself. Under these conditions, anti-lock function is disabled, but normal, power-assisted braking is still available. This provides a system fail-safe (sometimes termed default) whereby the vehicle may still be driven without the benefits of ABS.

➡The ECU contains a mercury switch which monitors the degree of vehicle deceleration to determine what type of surface the vehicle is on. The switch provides input to the ECU for improved operation when in 4WD on slippery surfaces. Proper mounting angle of the ECU is critical to the correct operation of the mercury switch.

Warning Lights

The ABS system uses 2 warning lamps on the instrument panel. Both the red and yellow lights are in circuit with the self-diagnostic program in the ECU.

The red BRAKE light serves as the normal brake system warning lamp. It warns of conditions which can affect the normal or service brakes on the vehicle. The red lamp will illuminate for low fluid level, parking brake **ON**, system pressure differential too great, and other similar conditions.

The yellow CK ANTI-LOCK light indicates conditions affecting the anti-lock brake system. The lamp is on during start up and will go out if the ECU finds no errors during the first system check. If a fault is found, the ECU will engage the yellow light until the fault is corrected, the battery is disconnected or the ignition switch is cycled **OFF** and **ON**. If the fault is still present after cycling the ignition, the ECU will re-light the lamp.

The yellow light is in circuit with the pressure modulator solenoids. When the light is on, the solenoids are disabled and ABS function is not available. If only the yellow warning lamp is lit, the vehicle will have normal braking without benefit of ABS.

There are certain time delays built into the ECU warning lamp outputs. If certain faults occur, the yellow lamp will illuminate first. If, after a period of seconds, the fault has not been corrected, the red warning lamp will be brought on. An example would be that under certain circumstances, accumulator pressure might be reduced below minimum during a high-speed panic stop. The low pressure switch engages the yellow lamp. If, within 20 seconds, the pump can restore the pressure, the lamp will go off. If the pressure is still low after 20 seconds, the ECU will trip the red warning lamp to warn of a possible fluid leak or similar system failure. Various combinations of inputs will cause the ECU to illuminate either or both warning lamps.

Wheel Speed Sensors and Tone Wheels

A toothed tone wheel is attached to each axle and rotates with the wheel. Sensors or pick-ups are mounted at each tone wheel; as the teeth turn past the sensor, an alternating current is generated proportional to wheel speed. This signal is transmitted to the ECM, which translates the signal into a digital reference for each wheel. The air gap between the sensor and the tone wheel is critical; replacement sensors usually contain a self-locating tab to insure correct placement. Diagnostic work may require checking the air gap, if the sensor is not being replaced.

Tone wheels on the front and rear wheels may be different by both number of teeth and air gap. Do not assume that tone wheels or sensors are interchangeable front to rear.

Boost Pressure Differential Switch

Located in the pressure modulator, this switch compares the modulated boost pressure to the master cylinder primary system pressure. If an abnormal pressure differential exists, the switch will ground through the vehicle body, signaling the ECM. The control unit reads this signal as a significant fault and will illuminate both warning lights on the instrument panel.

Proportioning Valve/Pressure Differential Switch

The combination front/rear brake pressure switch and proportioning valve is connected between the master cylinder and modulator. Hydraulic pressure from the master cylinder is applied through opposite ends of the valve, providing balancing forces to hold the piston centered in the bore. As long as the piston remains centered, the switch is in the **OFF** position.

If pressure loss occurs in either the front or rear circuit, a pressure differential of 70-300 psi (482-2,068 kPa), will cause the piston to move to the low pressure side, engaging the switch and grounding the red warning lamp on the dashboard.

During normal operation, the valve is positioned to allow proportional braking to the rear wheels. When ABS is engaged, the proportioning valve and the master cylinder are isolated to allow pressure modulation of the system. Continuity through the switch is checked each time the ignition switch is turned to **START** by illuminating the red warning lamp.

Fluid Level Switch

A reed switch located in the master cylinder reservoir is connected to the ECM. When a low fluid condition exists, the switch closes grounding the circuit. When the ECM senses the grounded circuit, the red dash warning lamp is lit.

Accumulators and Low Pressure Switch

One accumulator is located within the pump/motor assembly; the other is located with the low pressure switch next to the master cylinder and power booster assembly. Each stores brake fluid at extremely high pressures (approximately 1,700-2,000 psi or 11,721-13,790 kPa) for system operation.

The pump accumulator is the smaller of the two. It contains a piston and is pre-charged with 450 psi (3,102 kPa) of nitrogen. The external accumulator is a diaphragm type and contains nitrogen charged to 1,000 psi (6,895 kPa).

The low pressure switch is grounded to the body during normal operation. If the line pressure drops below approximately 1,050 psi (7,239 kPa), the switch signals the ECM by opening. The ECM will illuminate the yellow dash warning lamp for 20 seconds. If pressure is not regained within 20 seconds, the ECM engages the red warning lamp on the dash.

Switch Inputs

The ABS ECM receives input from the brake pedal switch, the ignition switch and the parking brake switch. The brake pedal switch communicates with the ECM independently of the brake lamps; once notified that the brakes are applied, the ECM is prepared to enter ABS, if the wheel speed signals indicate the need.

The parking brake switch grounds the low fluid switch when the brake is applied. This will cause the red dash warning lamp to be illuminated. If the vehicle is driven with the parking brake applied (or not fully released), the yellow warning lamp will come on and a LOW FLUID trouble code will be stored in the ECM.

The anti-lock ECM and the indicator lamps are in standby whenever the ignition switch is in either **OFF** or **ACCESSORY** position. In the **ON** or **RUN** positions, power is supplied to the ECM, the pump motor and the indicator lights. In **START**, only the indicator lamps are powered to serve as a bulb check.

Diagnosis and Testing

SERVICE PRECAUTIONS

✳✳CAUTION

This brake system uses a hydraulic accumulator which, when fully charged, contains brake fluid at very high pressure. Before disconnecting any hydraulic lines, hoses or fittings be certain that the accumulator pressure is completely relieved. Failure to depressurize the accumulator may result in personal injury and/or vehicle damage.

• Certain components within the ABS system are not intended to be serviced or repaired individually. Only those components with removal and installation procedures should be serviced.

• Both the external accumulator and the smaller accumulator within the pump contain high pressure nitrogen charges to assistance in pressurizing the system. The gas pressure is maintained even after fluid pressure in the system is reduced. Never puncture or attempt to disassemble either of these components.

- Do not use rubber hoses or other parts not specifically specified for the ABS system. When using repair kits, replace all parts included in the kit. Partial or incorrect repair may lead to functional problems and require the replacement of components.
- Lubricate rubber parts with clean, fresh brake fluid to ease assembly. Do not use lubricated shop air to clean parts; damage to rubber components may result.
- Use only DOT 3 or its superceding brake fluid from an unopened container.
- If any hydraulic component or line is removed or replaced, it may be necessary to bleed the entire system.
- A clean repair area is essential. Always clean the reservoir and cap thoroughly before removing the cap. The slightest amount of dirt in the fluid may plug an orifice and impair the system function. Perform repairs after components have been thoroughly cleaned; use only denatured alcohol to clean components. Do not allow ABS components to come into contact with any substance containing mineral oil; this includes used shop rags.
- The anti-lock ECM is a microprocessor similar to other computer units in the vehicle. Insure that the ignition switch is **OFF** before removing or installing controller harnesses. Avoid static electricity discharge at or near the controller.

DEPRESSURIZING THE SYSTEM

✳✳CAUTION

Depressurize the ABS accumulator and master cylinder assembly before performing any service operations. Failure to completely relieve the system could result in brake fluid under high pressure being sprayed on the technician and the vehicle. This can result in serious personal injury and vehicle damage.

1. Turn the ignition switch **OFF** and leave it **OFF** during repairs, unless specifically directed otherwise.
2. Firmly apply and release the brake pedal a minimum of 45-50 times.
3. The pedal feel will become noticeably harder when the accumulator is completely discharged.
4. Do not turn the ignition switch **ON** after depressurizing the system, unless service procedures specifically require it or all service operations have been performed.

➡**After the reserve pressure is depleted, the fluid level in the reservoir will rise above the MAX fill mark. This is normal; the reservoir will not overflow unless the system was originally overfilled.**

5. Always wear safety goggles when disconnecting lines and fittings.

PRE-DIAGNOSIS INSPECTION

Before diagnosing an apparent ABS problem, make absolutely certain that the normal braking system is in correct working order. Many common brake problems (dragging shoe, seepage, etc.) will affect the ABS system. A visual check of specific system components may reveal problems creating an apparent ABS malfunction. Performing this inspection may reveal a simple failure, thus eliminating extended diagnostic time. The steps should be performed in order.

1. Depressurize the system.
2. Inspect the brake fluid level in the reservoir.
3. Inspect brake lines, hoses, master cylinder assembly, brake calipers and cylinders for leakage.
4. Visually check brake lines and hoses for excessive wear, heat damage, punctures, contact with other parts, missing clips or holders, blockage or crimping.
5. Check the calipers and wheel cylinders for rust or corrosion. Check for proper sliding action, if applicable.
6. Check the caliper and wheel cylinder pistons for freedom of motion during application and release.
7. Inspect the wheel speed sensors for proper mounting and connections.
8. Inspect the tone wheels for broken teeth or poor mounting.
9. Inspect the wheels and tires on the vehicle. They must be of the same size and type to generate accurate speed signals.
10. Confirm the fault occurrence with the operator. Certain driver induced faults, such as not releasing the parking brake fully, will set a fault code and trigger the dash warning light(s). Excessive wheel spin on low-traction surfaces, high speed acceleration or riding the brake pedal may also set fault codes and trigger a warning lamp. These induced faults are not system failures but examples of vehicle performance outside the parameters of the ECM.
11. Many system shutdowns are due to loss of sensor signals to or from the ECM. The most common cause is not a failed sensor but a loose, corroded or dirty connector. Incorrect adjustment of the wheel speed sensor will cause a loss of wheel speed signal. Check harness and component connectors carefully.

DIAGNOSIS

After performing the preliminary visual checks, observe the behavior and timing of the dashboard warning lamps. Their function, when used in diagnostics, can point to possible causes and eliminate others.

Use the DRB-II with the correct cartridge to determine the specific circuit at fault. The tester with the correct adapter should be engaged to the diagnostic connector on the right side of the engine compartment. Any fault read by the tester on initial hook-up should be considered as a guide only. After initial repairs, clear the fault code, drive the vehicle and recheck for any stored code. Once the fault is identified, the DRB-II may be used to test or energize system components.

Component Replacement

✽✽CAUTION

Certain components within the ABS system are not repairable. If any fault is found with any of these components, they must be removed and replaced as a unit. Any attempt to disassemble or repair these components may result in impaired system function and/or personal injury.

The master cylinder/power booster assembly, the pressure modulator, the external accumulator, the pump and motor (with internal accumulator) and the proportioning valve are not repairable components; they must be replaced as complete assemblies. Additionally, the fluid level switch in the master cylinder and the boost pressure switch within the modulator cannot be serviced because they cannot be removed from their components.

FILLING THE SYSTEM

The only recommended brake fluid for the ABS system is fluid meeting SAE standard J-1703 and DOT 3. Use of any other fluid may result in improper function and/or component damage. Never use reclaimed fluid or fluid from a previously opened container.

The fluid level indicator mark is on the side of the plastic reservoir. Check the fluid with the engine off, after driving or running the engine. This allows the pump to charge the system and gives a true indication of fluid level. Checking the fluid when the system has not been pressurized may result in a false level within the reservoir.

Completely clean the reservoir and cap area before removing the cap. Add fluid only to the MAX mark. Overfilling may result in fluid overflow and possible reservoir damage during pump operation. Also check the reservoir filter when the cap is off; remove and clean the filter with clean brake fluid, if necessary.

BLEEDING THE SYSTEM

1. Fill the reservoir to the MAX mark with clean, fresh brake fluid.
2. The brake system must be bled in the correct order. For all vehicles, the wheel order is: right rear, left rear, right front, left front. For 1991-92 vehicles, the master cylinder/power booster must be bled before the wheels are bled.
3. For 1991-92 vehicles, bleed the master cylinder/booster assembly. Loosen and bleed the brake lines at the side of the modulator one at a time. Have a helper turn the ignition **ON** and operate the brake pedal in the usual manner while each line is loosened, bled and re-tightened. Bleed each circuit until the fluid is clear and free of air bubbles.
4. Attach a clear plastic bleed hose to the caliper or wheel cylinder fitting. Place the other end of the hose in a clear container of fresh brake fluid. Make certain the hose end is submerged in the fluid.
5. Turn the ignition switch **ON** to cycle the pump.

6. Have an assistant apply and hold brake pedal pressure to pressurize the system.
7. Open the bleed screw ½ turn. Close the bleed screw when the fluid entering the container is free of bubbles.
8. Check the reservoir level and refill to the MAX mark. Do not allow the master cylinder reservoir to run dry while bleeding. If the reservoir runs dry, air re-enters the system; the pump may be severely damaged if a constant supply of fluid is not available.
9. Repeat the bleeding procedure at the remaining wheels.

SPEED SENSORS

Removal and Installation

FRONT WHEEL

▶ See Figures 80, 81 and 82

1. Elevate and safely support the vehicle. Turn the front wheel outward for easier access to the sensor.
2. Before disassembly, note sensor wire routing including location of all clips and retainers. The sensor wire must be routed correctly during reassembly to avoid damage from moving parts.
3. Carefully remove the wire ties holding the sensor wire to the brake lines and the steering knuckle.
4. If the sensor is coated with mud, slush, etc., clean the sensor and surrounding area. This will prevent damage to the sensor and tone wheel during removal.
5. Remove the sensor attaching screw and remove the sensor from the steering knuckle.
6. Loosen the grommet holding the sensor wire from the wheel arch panel.
7. In the engine compartment, disconnect the sensor wire connector from the ABS harness. Carefully remove the sensor and harness from the car.

To install:

8. The wheel sensors have a plastic spacing strip attached to the contact face. Inspect this spacer and note the condition. If the strip is securely attached and in good condition, no

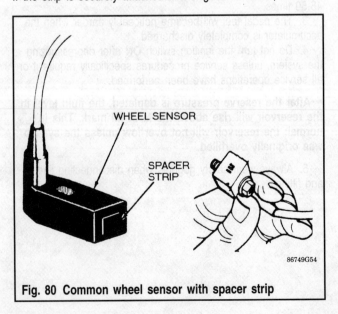

Fig. 80 Common wheel sensor with spacer strip

adjustment will be needed after installation. If the strip is damaged or not present, an air gap adjustment will be required.

9. Feed the sensor wire through the grommet hole in the wheelwell panel. Connect the sensor connector to the ABS harness and seat the rubber grommet in the panel.

10. Position the sensor on the steering knuckle and install the attaching bolt finger-tight.

11. If the spacer strip was intact and in good condition, lightly press the sensor against the tone wheel. Hold the sensor in this position and tighten the retaining bolt to 11 ft. lbs (14 Nm).

12. If the spacer was missing or damaged, clean the contacts on the sensor with a clean shop towel. Remove the spacer strip completely if loose or torn. After the sensor is loosely held in position by the retaining bolt, use a brass feeler gauge to set the air gap from the sensor to the tone wheel. Correct air gap is 0.013-0.019 in. (0.33-0.48mm). Tighten the retaining bolt to 11 ft. lbs. (14 Nm) and recheck the air gap with the feeler gauge.

➡**Use of a brass or non-magnetic gauge is required. Do not use common steel feelers; the small magnets within the sensor may be damaged. Correct air gap is critical to the proper operation of the sensor.**

13. Use new wire ties to secure the sensor wire to the brake lines and steering knuckle.

REAR WHEEL

▶ **See Figures 83 and 84**

1. Raise and fold forward the rear seat to gain access to the rear sensor connectors.

2. Disengage the sensor connector from the ABS harness; push the sensor grommet and wiring through the floor pan.

3. Elevate and safely support the vehicle.

4. Remove the wheel and brake drum.

5. Carefully remove the wire ties holding the sensor wires to the brake lines and rear axle.

6. Loosen or unseat the backing plate grommet holding the sensor wire.

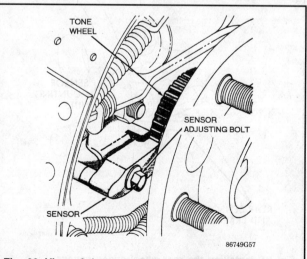

Fig. 82 Adjusting the sensor-to-tone wheel air gap

7. Remove the bolt holding the sensor to the bracket. Remove the sensor by pulling the wire through the grommet hole in the backing plate.

To install:

8. The wheel sensors have a plastic spacing strip attached to the contact face. Inspect this spacer and note the condition. If the strip is securely attached and in good condition, no adjustment will be needed after installation. If the strip is damaged or not present, an air gap adjustment will be required.

9. Feed the sensor wire through the grommet hole in the backing plate and seat the grommet in the plate.

10. If the spacer strip was intact and in good condition, lightly press the sensor against the tone wheel. Hold the sensor in this position and tighten the retaining bolt to 11 ft. lbs (14 Nm).

11. If the spacer was missing or damaged, clean the contacts on the sensor with a clean shop towel. Remove the spacer strip completely if loose or torn. After the sensor is loosely held in position by the retaining bolt, use a brass feeler gauge to set the air gap from the sensor to the tone wheel. Correct air gap is 0.030-0.036 in. (0.76-0.91mm). Tighten the

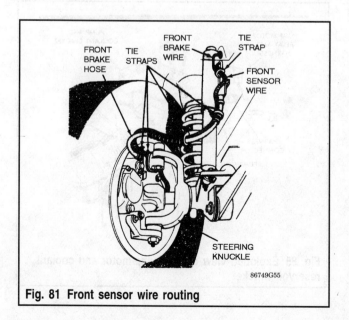

Fig. 81 Front sensor wire routing

Fig. 83 View of the rear wheel speed sensor and tone wheel

retaining bolt to 11 ft. lbs. (14 Nm) and recheck the air gap with the feeler gauge.

➡ **Use of a brass or non-magnetic gauge is required. Do not use common steel feelers; the small magnets within the sensor may be damaged. Correct air gap is critical to the proper operation of the sensor.**

12. Route the sensor wire to the rear seat area and feed through the access hole. Seat the sensor wire grommets in the floorpan.

13. Use new wire ties to secure the sensor wiring to the brake lines and rear axle. Make certain that the wiring is clear of all moving and/or hot components.

14. Install the brake drum and wheel. Lower the vehicle to the ground.

15. Within the car, connect the sensor to the ABS harness. Reposition the seat and carpet.

TONE WHEELS

Removal and Installation

The toothed tone wheels are permanently mounted to the axles and are not replaceable. In the event of damage to a tone wheel, the axle shaft assembly must be replaced with the new tone wheel attached.

PUMP AND MOTOR

Removal and Installation
♦ See Figures 85, 86 and 87

✳✳CAUTION

This brake system uses hydraulic accumulators, which, when fully charged, contain brake fluid at very high pressure. Before disconnecting any components, hydraulic lines, hoses or fittings, be certain that the accumulator pressure is completely relieved. Failure to depressurize the system may result in personal injury and/or vehicle damage.

1. Depressurize the brake system
2. Disconnect the negative battery cable.
3. Remove the strap holding the coolant reservoir bottle and move the bottle aside. The hoses may be left attached; moving the bottle allows better access.
4. Remove the bolts holding the 2-piece mounting bracket to the firewall and inner fender panels.
5. Move or rotate the bracket with the pump assembly to one side for access to the wiring and hoses. Disconnect the pump motor wiring harness from the engine harness.
6. Slowly loosen the high pressure line at the pump and allow any residual high pressure to bleed off. Wear eye protection and wrap the joint in a clean shop towel to suppress any spray. Disconnect the line from the pump.
7. Place a container or catch pan under the return line to the pump. Loosen the hose clamp and remove the line. Do not reuse the brake fluid which drains from the line.
8. Remove the pump/motor and bracket as a complete assembly.
9. Remove the screw holding the relay to the bracket. Remove the screws holding the pump and motor to the bracket and remove the bracket.

To install:
10. Position the pump assembly onto the bracket and install the assembly attaching screws. Attach the pump/motor to the mounting bracket and attach the pump relay to the mounting bracket.
11. Connect the high-pressure and return lines to the pump.
12. Connect the electrical harness from the pump to the engine harness.
13. Place the bracket with the pump/motor and relay in place and install the retaining bolts.
14. Inspect the high-pressure and return lines; make certain they are not kinked or touching the engine.
15. Fill the master cylinder to the MAX level.
16. Connect the negative battery cable.

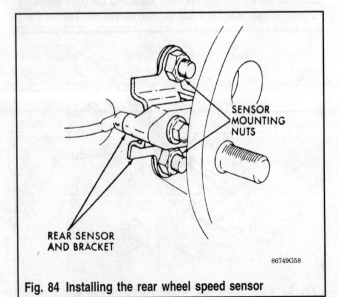

Fig. 84 Installing the rear wheel speed sensor

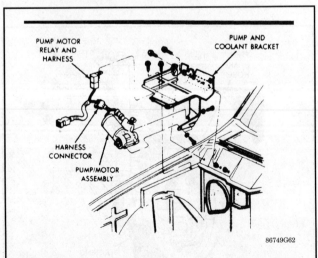

Fig. 85 Exploded view of the pump/motor and coolant reservoir bracket

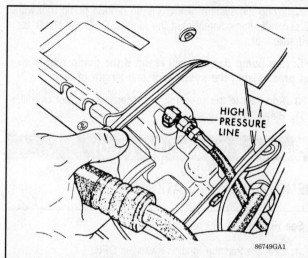

Fig. 86 Always wear eye protection when disconnecting the high pressure hose

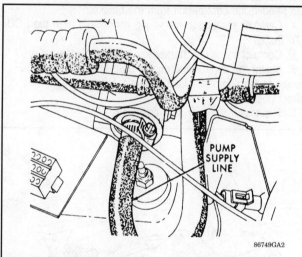

Fig. 87 Use a catch pan when disconnecting the supply/return line

17. Turn the ignition switch **ON**; the pump should start running. Listen for a drop in pump rpm; this shows the pump is pressurizing the system. If there is no drop in pump rpm within 20 seconds, immediately shut the ignition **OFF** and check for hydraulic leaks.

➡Severe pump damage will result if the pump runs without pressurizing the system for any length of time.

18. Add fluid to the reservoir as necessary. Do not overfill.
19. Reposition and secure the coolant reservoir.

Master Cylinder, Modulator and Accumulator

REMOVAL & INSTALLATION

▶ See Figure 88

✳✳CAUTION

This brake system uses a hydraulic accumulator which, when fully charged, contains brake fluid at very high pressure. Before disconnecting any hydraulic lines, hoses or fittings be certain that the accumulator pressure is completely relieved. Failure to depressurize the accumulator may result in personal injury and/or vehicle damage.

➡The master cylinder, modulator and accumulator are serviced as an assembly only. Do not attempt to disassemble or repair these components.

1. Disconnect the negative battery cable.
2. Remove the screws holding the windshield washer fluid reservoir. Disconnect the hoses and wires and remove the reservoir.
3. Remove the air cleaner assembly.
4. Disconnect the ABS ECM wiring connectors at the pressure modulator.
5. Disconnect the wiring at the proportioning valve/differential switch.
6. Disconnect the brake line at the coupling on the underside of the proportioning valve.
7. Disconnect the high pressure line at the accumulator block and immediately cap the port to prevent entry of dirt.
8. Place a catch pan below the supply line at the reservoir. Disconnect the hose at the reservoir and discard the fluid drained from the line.
9. Remove the wires from the low pressure switch on the accumulator block, the modulator boost pressure switch and the fluid level switch.
10. Disconnect the front brake lines at the outboard side of the pressure modulator.
11. Inside the car, disconnect the wiring to the brake pedal switch. It may be necessary to remove the instrument panel lower trim for access.
12. Remove the master cylinder pushrod bolt; disconnect the pushrod from the pedal. Immediately discard the nuts from the pushrod bolt; they are not reusable.
13. Remove the nuts from the brake mounting bracket studs.
14. Under the hood, carefully pull the hydraulic components and bracket forward until the studs clear the firewall. Lift the assembly up and out of the engine compartment.
   To install:
15. Install the pad onto the new bracket and place the bracket with the brake components in place against the firewall. Make certain the studs are correctly seated in the holes.
16. Position the master cylinder/modulator/accumulator on the firewall and tighten the mounting nuts to 27 ft. lbs. (31 Nm).

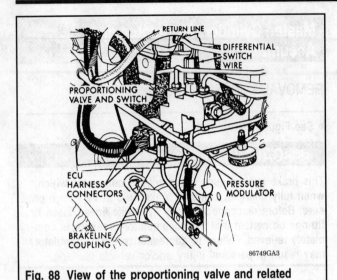

Fig. 88 View of the proportioning valve and related components

17. Connect the wiring harness to the low pressure switch, the differential switch, the pressure modulator, the low fluid and boost pressure switches.

18. Inside the vehicle, install the nuts on the mounting studs and tighten them to 31 ft. lbs (42 Nm).

19. Align the brake pedal, the brake lamp switch and the master cylinder pushrod. Install the pushrod bolt. The pushrod bolt must be correctly installed to avoid interference with the bracket. The bolt head must be on the left side of the brake pedal.

20. Use new nuts on the pushrod bolt. The inner locknut should be tightened to 25 ft. lbs. (34 Nm); the outer jam nut should be tightened to 75 inch lbs. (8.5 Nm).

21. Connect the wiring to the brake switch and install the lower dashboard trim, if it was removed.

22. In the engine compartment, connect the brake lines to the proportioning valve.

23. Connect the pressure and return lines to the accumulator.

24. Install the air cleaner assembly.

25. Connect hoses and wires to the windshield washer fluid reservoir and install it in position.

26. Inspect the high-pressure and return lines; make certain they are not kinked or touching the engine.

27. Fill the master cylinder to the MAX level.

28. Connect the negative battery cable.

29. Turn the ignition switch **ON**; the pump should start running. Listen for a drop in pump rpm; this shows the pump is pressurizing the system. If there is no drop in pump rpm within 20 seconds, immediately shut the ignition **OFF** and check for hydraulic leaks.

➡️**Severe pump damage will result if the pump runs without pressurizing the system for any length of time.**

30. Add fluid to the reservoir as necessary. Do not overfill.
31. Bleed the brake system.

Electronic Control Unit (ECU)

REMOVAL & INSTALLATION

▶ **See Figures 89, 90 and 91**

1. Confirm that the ignition switch is **OFF**.
2. Fold the rear seat cushion forward for access to the ECU.
3. Remove the bracket holding the ECU from the floorpan, then remove the control unit from the bracket.
4. Carefully disengage the wiring connectors from the ECU.
To install:
5. Connect the wiring harnesses to the replacement unit.
6. Mount the control unit on the bracket, then install the bracket to the floorpan. Make certain the bracket is in the correct position.
7. Reposition the rear seat cushion.

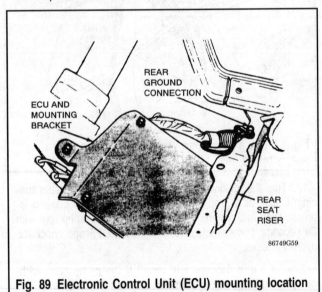

Fig. 89 Electronic Control Unit (ECU) mounting location

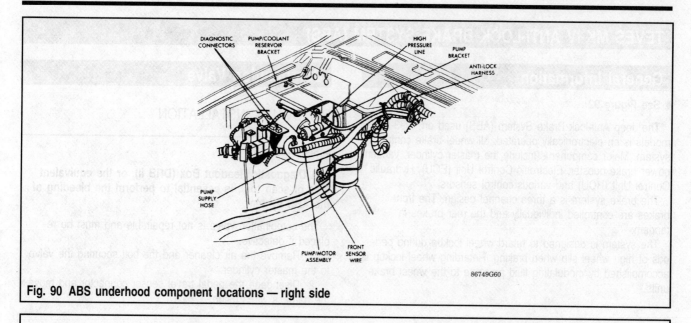

DIAGNOSTIC
CONNECTORS

PUMP/COOLANT
RESERVOIR
BRACKET

HIGH
PRESSURE
LINE

PUMP
BRACKET

ANTI-LOCK
HARNESS

PUMP
SUPPLY
HOSE

PUMP/MOTOR
ASSEMBLY

FRONT
SENSOR
WIRE

86749G60

Fig. 90 ABS underhood component locations — right side

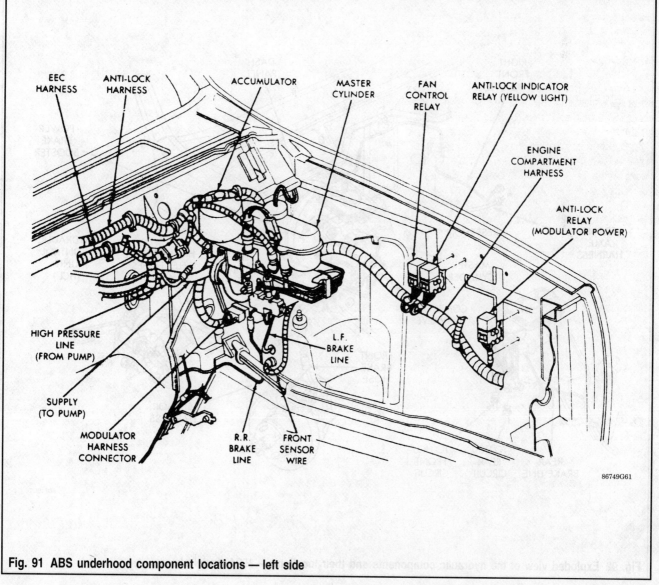

EEC
HARNESS

ANTI-LOCK
HARNESS

ACCUMULATOR

MASTER
CYLINDER

FAN
CONTROL
RELAY

ANTI-LOCK INDICATOR
RELAY (YELLOW LIGHT)

ENGINE
COMPARTMENT
HARNESS

ANTI-LOCK
RELAY
(MODULATOR POWER)

HIGH PRESSURE
LINE
(FROM PUMP)

L.F.
BRAKE
LINE

SUPPLY
(TO PUMP)

MODULATOR
HARNESS
CONNECTOR

R.R.
BRAKE
LINE

FRONT
SENSOR
WIRE

86749G61

Fig. 91 ABS underhood component locations — left side

TEVES MK-IV ANTI-LOCK BRAKE SYSTEM (ABS)

General Information

▶ **See Figure 92**

The Jeep Anti-lock Brake System (ABS) used on 1993-94 models is an electronically operated, all wheel brake control system. Major components include the master cylinder, vacuum power brake booster, Electronic Control Unit (ECU), Hydraulic Control Unit (HCU) and various control sensors.

The brake system is a three channel design. The front brakes are controlled individually and the rear brakes in tandem.

The system is designed to retard wheel lockup during periods of high wheel slip when braking. Retarding wheel lockup is accomplished by modulating fluid pressure to the wheel brake units.

Combination Valve

REMOVAL & INSTALLATION

▶ **See Figure 93**

➡**A Diagnostic Readout Box (DRB II), or the equivalent type of scan tool, is essential to perform the bleeding of the ABS system.**

The combination valve is not repairable and must be replaced if defective.
1. Remove the air cleaner and the bolt securing the valve to the master cylinder.
2. Disengage the pedal travel sensor connector and move the harness wires aside.

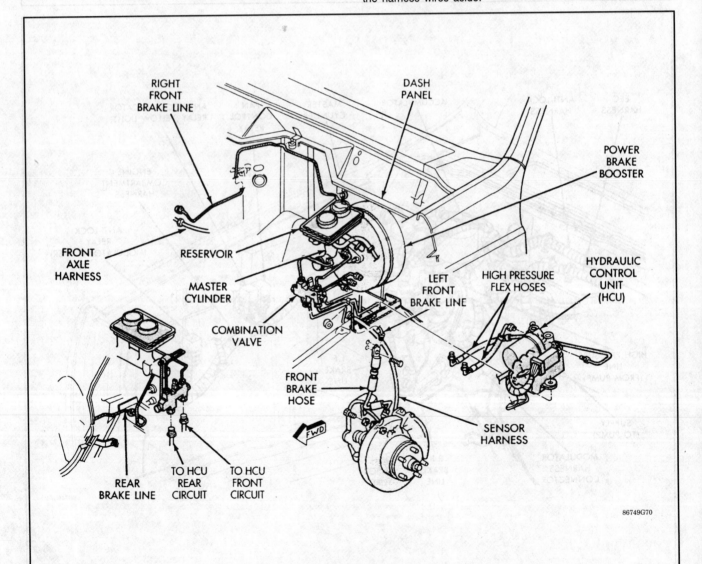

Fig. 92 Exploded view of the hydraulic components and their locations — 1994 model shown

86749G70

3. Disengage the pressure differential switch wires at the valve and disconnect the hydraulic lines. Remove the valve from the vehicle.

To install:

4. Connect the hydraulic lines and install the valve on the master cylinder. Tighten the valve to master cylinder attaching bolt to 92-112 inch lbs. (10-13 Nm).

5. Engage the pedal travel sensor and pressure differential switch electrical connections.

6. Bleed the system and test drive the vehicle to check for proper brake operation.

Hydraulic Control Unit (HCU)

REMOVAL & INSTALLATION

▶ **See Figures 94, 95 and 96**

➡**A Diagnostic Readout Box (DRB II), or the equivalent type of scan tool, is essential to perform the bleeding of the ABS system.**

1. Remove the air cleaner and the clamp that secures the air cleaner hose and pipe to the fender apron.

2. Place a suitable size drain container under the master cylinder reservoir hoses and disengage the reservoir hoses from the HCU.

3. Remove the reservoir and disengage the pump motor and solenoid harness wires at the HCU.

4. Tag and disconnect the HCU hydraulic lines at the HCU.

5. Move the HCU harness and air cleaner hose pipe aside for access to the HCU bracket fasteners and remove the fasteners.

6. Remove the HCU, being careful not to damage the brake lines or master cylinder.

To install:

7. Engage the reservoir hoses to the HCU pipes and position the HCU assembly on the bracket. Tighten the fasteners to 92-112 inch lbs. (10-13 Nm).

8. Install and tighten the HCU hydraulic lines. Check the lines and hose routing so that they are clear of engine components and have no kinks.

9. Fill the master cylinder with DOT 3 brake fluid and bleed the brake system. Refer to the bleeding procedure for this system in this section.

10. Install the air cleaner and hoses. Fasten the air cleaner hose to the fender apron with the clamp.

11. Test drive the vehicle and test for proper brake operation.

Electronic Control Unit (ECU)

REMOVAL & INSTALLATION

▶ **See Figure 97**

1. Turn the ignition **OFF** and remove the screws securing the ECU to the mounting bracket.

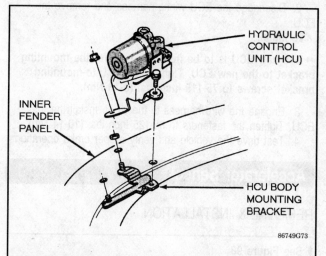

Fig. 94 Exploded view of the HCU and mounting bracket — 1994 model shown

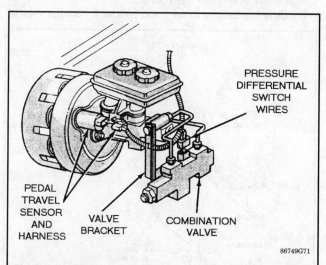

Fig. 93 View of the combination valve assembly — 1994 model shown

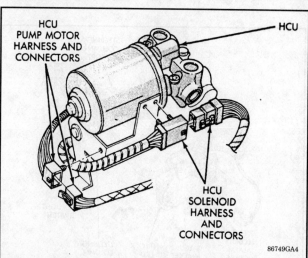

Fig. 95 Exploded view of the HCU wiring harness connections — 1994 model shown

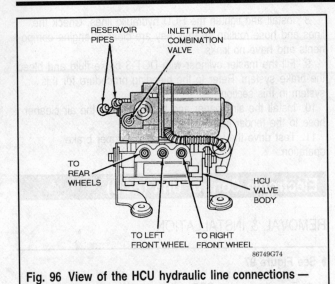

Fig. 96 View of the HCU hydraulic line connections — 1994 model shown

2. Disengage the ECU wiring harness and remove the ECU.

To install:

→**IF a new ECU is to be installed, transfer the mounting bracket to the new ECU. Tighten the ECU-to-mounting bracket screws to 75-115 inch lbs. (8-13 Nm).**

3. Engage the wire harness to the ECU. Install the the ECU. Tighten the fasteners to 85-125 inch lbs. (10-14 Nm).

4. Test drive the vehicle and verify proper brake operation.

Accelerator Sensor

REMOVAL & INSTALLATION

▶ **See Figure 98**

1. Tilt the rear seat forward to gain access to the sensor.

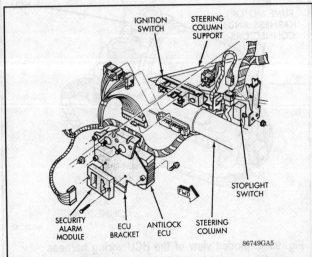

Fig. 97 Exploded view of the ECU mounting — 1994 Cherokee shown

2. Disengage the sensor harness and unfasten the screws attaching the sensor to the bracket. Remove the sensor from the vehicle.

To install:

→**Note the position of the locating arrow on the sensor. The sensor must be positioned so that the arrow faces forward.**

3. Install the sensor in the bracket and tighten the screws to 17-32 inch lbs. (2-4 Nm).

4. Engage the harness sensor and move the seat back to its normal position.

Power Brake Booster

REMOVAL & INSTALLATION

▶ **See Figure 99**

→**A Diagnostic Readout Box (DRB II), or the equivalent type of scan tool, is essential to perform the bleeding of the ABS system.**

1. Pump the brake pedal until all vacuum is expelled from the booster.

2. Disengage the pedal travel sensor and remove the air cleaner.

3. Unfasten the clamps securing the reservoir hoses to the HCU pipes. Remove the hoses from the pipes.

4. Disengage the brake lines at the master cylinder.

5. Remove the combination valve bracket bolt (if necessary).

6. Remove the nuts attaching the master cylinder to the booster mounting. Remove the master cylinder from the vehicle.

7. Tag and disconnect vacuum hose at the booster check valve.

8. Disconnect the booster pushrod from the brake pedal.

9. Remove the nuts attaching the booster to the passenger compartment side of the dash panel.

10. Slide the booster forward and remove it from the vehicle.

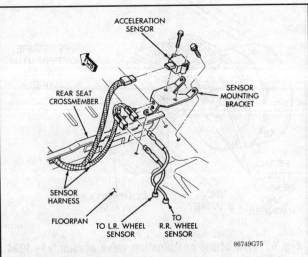

Fig. 98 Exploded view of the accelerator sensor and mounting bracket — 1994 model shown

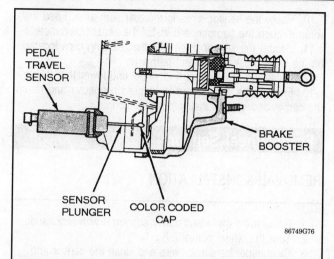

Fig. 99 Cutaway view of the booster pushrod and pedal travel sensor — 1994 model shown

To install:

11. Install the booster on the dash panel. Align the booster mounting studs with the holes in the panel and seat the booster.

12. In the passenger compartment, install the booster attaching nuts on the mounting studs. Tighten the attaching nuts to 30 ft. lbs. (41 Nm).

13. Install the seal on the master cylinder.

14. Install the pedal travel sensor and the booster pushrod.

15. Attach the vacuum hose to the booster check valve and install the master cylinder on the booster. Tighten the bolts to 18-22 ft. lbs. (25-30 Nm).

16. Engage the brake lines to the master cylinder and install the combination valve bracket bolt.

17. Engage the reservoir hoses to the HCU pipes.

18. Engage the sensor wires, bleed the brake system, install the air cleaner assembly and test drive the vehicle to verify proper brake operation.

Pedal Travel Sensor

REMOVAL & INSTALLATION

▶ See Figure 100

➡The pedal travel sensor and booster must form a matched set. The cap on the sensor and on the booster shell are color coded for identification, and to ensure that they are used as matched sets. Be sure the color of the sensor cap and the color dot on the booster shell are the same before installation.

1. Disengage the wires at the sensor and pump the brake pedal until all vacuum is depleted from the booster.

2. Unseat the sensor retaining ring and remove the sensor from the booster.

To install:

3. Check the color dot on the face of the brake booster. Then check the color cap on the sensor plunger. If the colors match, proceed with the installation. If the colors do not match, install the correct color cap on the end of the plunger.

4. Install the O-ring on the sensor.

5. Install the sensor retaining ring on the booster flange and insert the sensor in the retaining ring and booster.

6. Verify that the sensor is properly engaged, then connect the sensor wires.

Rear Wheel Sensor

REMOVAL & INSTALLATION

▶ See Figures 101, 102 and 103

1. Raise and fold the rear seat to gain access to the rear sensor connectors.

2. Disengage the sensors at the rear harness connectors and push the sensor grommets and wires through the floorpan.

3. Raise the vehicle and support it with jackstands.

4. Disengage the sensor wires at the rear axle connectors. Remove the wheels.

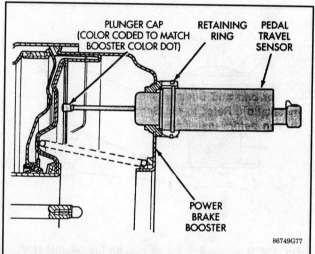

Fig. 100 Cutaway view of the pedal travel sensor and mounting — 1994 model shown

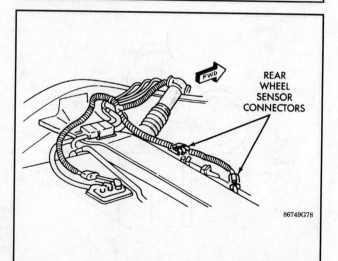

Fig. 101 View of the rear wheel sensor electrical connectors — 1994 model shown

5. Remove the brake drum and the clips securing the sensor wires to the brake lines, hoses and rear axle.

6. Unseat the sensor support plate grommet and unfasten the bolt securing the sensor to the bracket. Remove the sensor from the vehicle.

To install:

7. Insert the sensor wire through the support plate hole and seat the sensor grommet in the support plate.

8. Apply Loctite® to the bolt and install the sensor. Fasten the bolt finger-tight only at this time.

9. Set the sensor air gap as follows:

a. If installing the original sensor, remove any remaining pieces of cardboard from the pickup face. Then, using a brass feeler gauge, adjust the gap to 0.043 in. (1.1mm).

b. Tighten the sensor retaining bolt to 11 ft. lbs. (14 Nm).

c. If installing a new sensor, push the cardboard spacer on the sensor face against the tone face.

d. Tighten the sensor retaining bolt to 6 ft. lbs. (8 Nm). The correct air gap will be established as the tone ring rotates and peels the spacer off the sensor face.

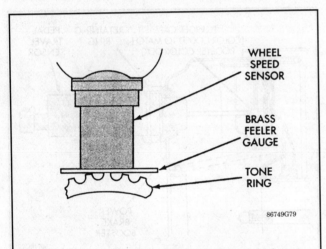

WHEEL SPEED SENSOR

BRASS FEELER GAUGE

TONE RING

86749G79

Fig. 102 When setting the air gap on the original rear sensor, use a brass feeler gauge only — 1994 model shown

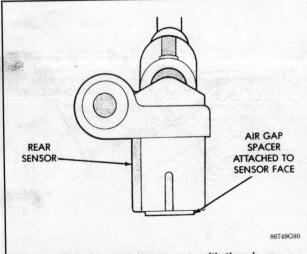

REAR SENSOR

AIR GAP SPACER ATTACHED TO SENSOR FACE

86749G80

Fig. 103 View of a new rear sensor with the air gap spacer — 1994 model shown

10. Route the sensor wires to the rear seat area. Feed the wires through the floorpan and install the sensor grommets.

11. Secure the sensor wires with the retaining clips located on the brake hoses, lines and rear axle.

12. Install the brake drum and wheel and lower the vehicle.

13. Engage the sensor wire to harness connector and return the carpet and seat to their proper position.

Front Wheel Sensor

REMOVAL & INSTALLATION

1. Raise the vehicle and safely support it with jackstands.

2. Turn the wheel outward.

3. Disengage the sensor wire and clean the sensor and surrounding area.

4. Unfasten the sensor attaching bolt

5. Remove the grommet retaining the sensor wire in the wheel house panel.

6. Disengage the sensor wire from the harness plug in the engine compartment and remove the sensor.

To install:

➡**There is no front sensor air gap adjustment. The air gap should be 0.057-0.051 in. (0.04-1.30mm). If the air gap is incorrect, the sensor is broken or loose.**

7. Install the sensor on the steering knuckle, apply Loctite® to the sensor bolt and tighten the bolt finger-tight only.

8. Tighten the bolt to 11 ft. lbs. (14 Nm) and attach the sensor wire to the steering knuckle with grommets.

9. Route the sensor wire to its original locations.

10. Seat the sensor wire grommet in the body panel and clip the wire to the brake line at the grommet location.

11. Engage the sensor wire to the harness in the engine compartment.

12. Lower the vehicle.

Bleeding The ABS System

➡**A Diagnostic Readout Box (DRB II), or the equivalent type of scan tool, is essential to perform the bleeding of the ABS system.**

The brake system must be bled any time air is permitted to enter the system through loosened or disconnected lines or hoses, or anytime the modulator is removed. Excessive air within the system will cause a soft or spongy feel in the brake pedal.

When bleeding any part of the system, the reservoir must remain as close to full as possible at all times. Check the level frequently and top off fluid as needed.

This is basically a three step process consisting of: a conventional manual bleeding procedure, a second bleeding procedure using a DRB II, followed by a repeat of the first bleeding procedure.

1. Clean around the reservoir cap and remove the cap. Fill the master cylinder with the recommended fluid.

2. The recommended bleeding sequence is: master cylinder, HCU valve body (at the fluid lines), right rear wheel, left rear wheel, right front wheel and left front wheel.

3. Clean all the bleeder screws. You may want to give each one a shot of penetrating solvent to loosen it; seizure is a common problem with bleeder screws, which then break off, sometimes requiring replacement of the part to which they are attached.

➡Brake fluid absorbs moisture from the air. Don't leave the master cylinder or the fluid container uncovered any longer than necessary. Be careful handling the fluid; spilled fluid will damage the vehicle's paint.

Check the level of the fluid often when bleeding, and refill the reservoirs as necessary. Don't let them run dry, or you will have to repeat the process.

4. Attach a length of clear vinyl tubing to the bleeder screw on the wheel cylinder. Insert the other end of the tube into a clear, clean jar half filled with brake fluid.

5. Have your assistant slowly depress the brake pedal. As this is done, open the bleeder screw until the brake fluid starts to flow through the tube. Then, close the bleeder screw when the brake pedal reaches the end of its travel. After the bleeder valve is fully closed, have your assistant slowly release the pedal. Repeat this process until no air bubbles appear in the expelled fluid.

6. Repeat the procedure on the other three brake cylinders/calipers, checking the lever of brake fluid in the master cylinder reservoir often.

7. Perform the "Bleed Brake" procedure with the DRB II scan tool:

a. Engage the DRB II scan tool to the diagnostic connector.

b. Run the test as described in the manufacturers tester manual.

8. Repeat the manual bleeding procedure as outlined in Steps 1 through 6. Check and replenish the master cylinder fluid level if necessary.

After finishing, there should be no feeling of sponginess in the brake pedal. If there is, either there is still air in the line, in which case the process must be repeated, or there is a leak somewhere, which, of course, must be corrected before the vehicle is moved. After all repairs and service work is finished, road test the vehicle to verify proper brake system operation.

TEVES MK-IVg ANTI-LOCK BRAKE SYSTEM (ABS)

General Information

The Jeep Anti-lock Brake System (ABS) used on 1995-96 models is an electronically operated, all wheel brake control system. Major components include the master cylinder, vacuum power brake booster, Electronic Control Unit (ECU), Hydraulic Control Unit (HCU) and various control sensors.

The brake system is a three channel design. The front brakes are controlled individually and the rear brakes in tandem.

The system is designed to retard wheel lockup during periods of high wheel slip when braking. Retarding wheel lockup is accomplished by modulating fluid pressure to the wheel brake units.

Combination Valve

REMOVAL & INSTALLATION

▶ See Figures 104 and 105

➡A Diagnostic Readout Box (DRB II), or the equivalent type of scan tool, is essential to perform the bleeding of the ABS system.

The combination valve is not repairable and must be replaced if defective.

1. Tag and disconnect the clean air and PCV hoses. Remove the air cleaner top cover and place a towel over the intake manifold to prevent any debris from entering.

2. Disengage the brake lines that connect the master cylinder to the combination valve.

3. Disengage the wire from the combination switch terminal and the brake lines that connect the combination valve to the HCU.

4. Slide the HCU solenoid harness off the combination valve bracket and move the harness aside.

5. Unfasten the combination valve bracket to booster studs, slide the valve off the studs and remove the valve and bracket from the vehicle.

To install:

6. Install the valve and bracket on the booster studs and hand-tighten the retaining nuts.

7. Start the brake lines in by hand to avoid crossthreading and tighten the fittings enough to prevent leaking.

8. Tighten the valve attaching nuts to 220 inch lbs. (25 Nm) and engage the wire to the pressure differential switch.

9. Bleed the brake system. Refer to the proper procedure in this section.

10. Engage the HCU solenoid wires. Install the air cleaner cover and clean air hoses.

11. Test drive the vehicle and verify proper brake operation.

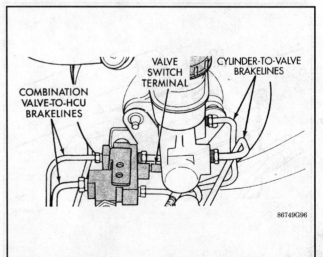

Fig. 104 Combination valve hydraulic connections — 1995 model shown

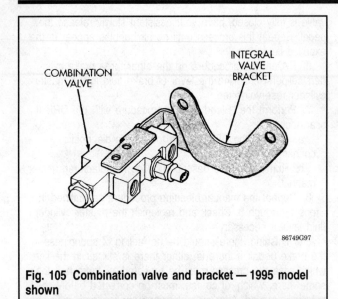

Fig. 105 Combination valve and bracket — 1995 model shown

Electronic Control Unit (ECU)

REMOVAL & INSTALLATION

▶ See Figures 106 and 107

The Electronic Control Unit (ECU) is usually located in the engine compartment, mounted on the driver's side inner fender panel.

1. Turn the ignition to the **OFF** position.
2. Remove the lower finish panel from the instrument panel.
3. Remove the ECU retaining bolts/nuts and release the metal strap that secures the ECU harness connector to the pin terminals.
4. Disengage the harness connector from the ECU. This is achieved by tilting the connector upward to disengage it from the pins and then sliding it out of the retaining tangs.
5. Remove the ECU and mounting bracket as an assembly.

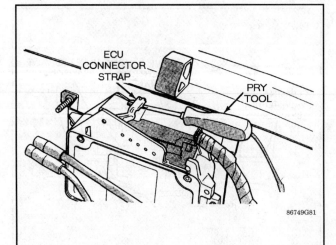

Fig. 106 Releasing the ECU harness connector strap — 1995 model shown

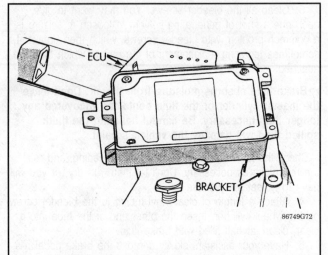

Fig. 107 Exploded view of the ECU and bracket — 1995 model shown

To install:

6. If a new ECU is to be installed, first install the mounting bracket on the ECU and tighten the fasteners to 85-125 inch. lbs (10-14 Nm).

❋❋WARNING

Use care when connecting the harness connector to the ECU, the pins may be easily damaged.

7. Engage the harness connector to the ECU making sure it is fully seated and engages the tangs on the ECU.
8. Position the ECU bracket under the dash and install the retainers. Tighten the retainers to 75-125 inch lbs. (8-14 Nm).
9. Install the finish panel on the instrument panel.

Hydraulic Control Unit (HCU)

REMOVAL & INSTALLATION

▶ See Figures 108, 109, 110, 111 and 112

➡A Diagnostic Readout Box (DRB II), or the equivalent type of scan tool, is essential to perform the bleeding of the ABS system.

1. Disengage the vent hoses and air cleaner cover.
2. Loosen the clamp securing the air cleaner hose to the intake manifold and slide the clamp out of the way.
3. Remove the air cleaner cover, hose and filter.
4. Unfasten the air cleaner housing to panel bolts and nut, then remove the air cleaner housing.
5. Disengage the flex lines at the HCU.
6. Disengage the HCU solenoid harness from the main harness and the HCU pump motor harness.
7. Disengage the brake lines at the lower left side of the HCU.
8. If removing the HCU only:
   a. Remove the HCU solenoid by squeezing the connector fasteners with needle nose pliers then pulling them out of the bracket.

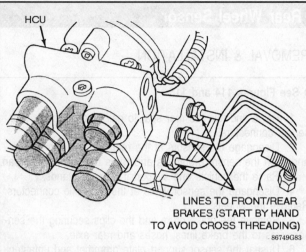

**Fig. 108 View of the HCU brake line connections —
1995 model shown**

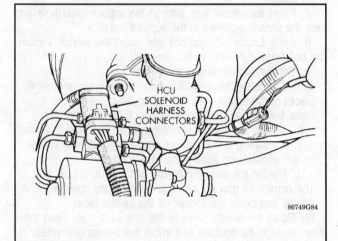

**Fig. 109 View of the HCU solenoid harness electrical
connectors — 1995 model shown**

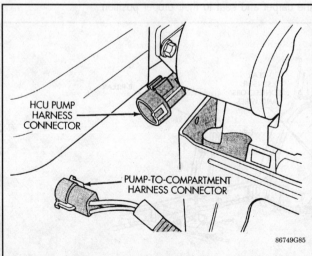

**Fig. 110 Disengage the HCU pump motor harness
connector — 1995 model shown**

b. Unfasten the shoulder bolts attaching HCU to the
bracket and remove the HCU.

9. If removing the HCU and bracket:

a. Unfasten the fasteners retaining the HCU to the
bracket and remove the HCU.

To install:

10. If only the HCU was removed:

a. Install the HCU in the bracket and tighten the shoulder
bolts.

b. Install the HCU solenoid by pressing the connector fasteners into the bracket.

11. If installing the HCU and bracket as an assembly:

a. Install the bracket on the studs and tighten the fasteners to 92-112 inch lbs. (10-13 Nm).

12. Engage the HCU pump motor and solenoid harnesses.

13. Start the brake line fittings into the HCU by hand to
avoid cross-threading and then tighten the fittings until they are
snug.

14. Start the flex line fittings into the HCU by hand to avoid
cross-threading and then tighten the fittings until they are snug.

15. Bleed the brake system. Refer to the proper procedure
in this section.

16. Tighten the brake line fittings to 130-160 inch lbs. (15-18
Nm) at the HCU and master cylinder, and 160-210 inch lbs.
(18-24 Nm) at the combination valve.

17. Install the air cleaner assembly, hoses and vacuum lines
to the manifold.

18. Check the brake pedal action before moving the vehicle
and bleed the brakes again if the pedal is not firm, (soft or
spongy).

19. Test drive the vehicle and verify proper brake operation.

Accelerator Sensor

REMOVAL & INSTALLATION

▶ See Figure 113

1. Tilt the rear seat forward to gain access to the sensor.

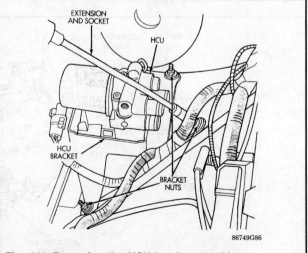

**Fig. 111 Removing the HCU bracket attaching
fasteners — 1995 model shown**

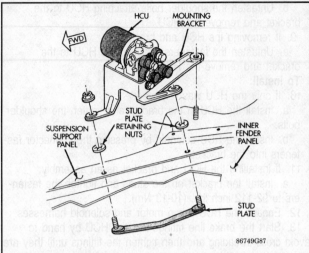

Fig. 112 Exploded view of the HCU mounting — 1995 model shown

2. Disengage the sensor harness and unfasten the screws attaching the sensor to the bracket. Remove the sensor from the vehicle.

To install:

➡️**Note the position of the locating arrow on the sensor. The sensor must be positioned so that the arrow faces forward.**

3. Install the sensor in the bracket and tighten the screws to 17-32 inch lbs. (2-4 Nm).

4. Engage the harness sensor and move the seat back to its normal position.

Rear Wheel Sensor

REMOVAL & INSTALLATION

▶ **See Figures 114 and 115**

1. Raise and fold the rear seat to gain access to the rear sensor connectors.

2. Disengage the sensors at the rear harness connectors and push the sensor grommets and wires through the floorpan.

3. Raise the vehicle and support it with jackstands.

4. Disengage the sensor wires at the rear axle connectors. Remove the wheels.

5. Remove the brake drum and the clips securing the sensor wires to the brake lines, hoses and rear axle.

6. Unseat the sensor support plate grommet and unfasten the bolt securing the sensor to the bracket. Remove the sensor from the vehicle.

To install:

7. Insert the sensor wire through the support plate hole and seat the sensor grommet in the support plate.

8. Apply Loctite® to the bolt and install the sensor. Fasten the bolt finger-tight only at this time.

9. Set the sensor air gap as follows:

a. If installing the original sensor, remove any remaining pieces of cardboard from the pickup face. Then using a brass feeler gauge adjust the gap to 0.043 in. (1.1mm).

b. Tighten the sensor retaining bolt to 11 ft. lbs. (14 Nm).

c. If installing a new sensor, push the cardboard spacer on the sensor face against the tone face.

d. Tighten the sensor retaining bolt to 6 ft. lbs. (8 Nm). The correct air gap will be established as the tone ring rotates and peels the spacer off the sensor face.

10. Route the sensor wires to the rear seat area. Feed the wires through the floorpan and install the sensor grommets.

11. Secure the sensor wires with the retaining clips located on the brake hoses, lines and rear axle.

12. Install the brake drum and wheel and lower the vehicle.

13. Engage the sensor wire to harness connector and return the carpet and seat to their proper position.

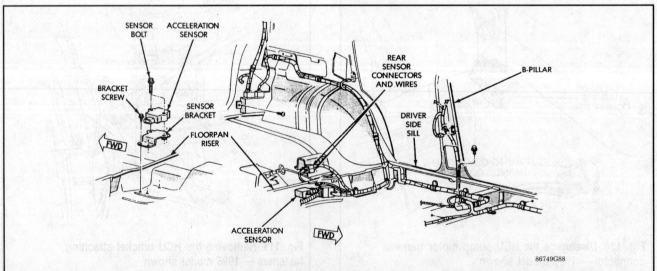

Fig. 113 Exploded view of the accelerator sensor connections and mounting locations — 1995 model shown

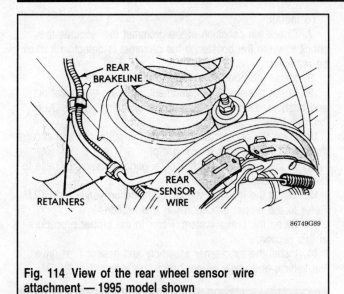

Fig. 114 View of the rear wheel sensor wire attachment — 1995 model shown

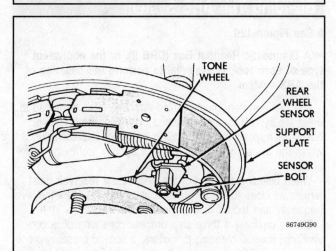

Fig. 115 View of the rear wheel sensor mounting — 1995 model shown

Front Wheel Sensor

REMOVAL & INSTALLATION

♦ See Figures 116, 117, 118 and 119

1. Raise the vehicle and support it with jackstands.
2. Turn the wheel outward.
3. Disengage the sensor wire and clean the sensor and surrounding area.
4. Unfasten the sensor attaching bolt
5. Remove the grommet retaining the sensor wire in the wheel house panel.
6. Disengage the sensor wire from the harness plug in the engine compartment and remove the sensor.

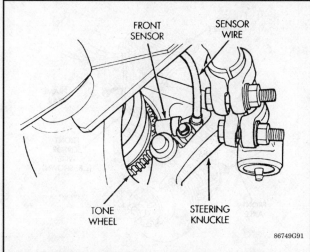

Fig. 116 View of the front wheel sensor mounting — 1995 model shown

To install:

➡There is no front sensor air gap adjustment. The air gap should be 0.057-0.051 in. (0.04-1.30mm). If the air gap is incorrect, the sensor is broken or loose.

7. Install the sensor on the steering knuckle, apply Loctite® to the sensor bolt and tighten the bolt finger-tight only.
8. Tighten the bolt to 11 ft. lbs. (14 Nm) and attach the sensor wire to the steering knuckle with grommets.
9. Route the sensor wire to its original locations.
10. Seat the sensor wire grommet in the body panel and clip the wire to the brake line at the grommet location.
11. Engage the sensor wire to the harness in the engine compartment.
12. Lower the vehicle.

Power Brake Booster

REMOVAL & INSTALLATION

➡A Diagnostic Readout Box (DRB II), or the equivalent type of scan tool, is essential to perform the bleeding of the ABS system.

1. Disconnect the negative battery cable and remove the air cleaner assembly.
2. Remove the windshield washer fluid reservoir retainers and move the reservoir to one side.
3. Remove the master cylinder, combination valve and HCU. Refer to the proper procedures in this section and disengage the vacuum hose at the booster check valve.
4. In the passenger compartment, remove the booster pushrod to pedal pin retaining clip. Then slide the pushrod off the pin.
5. Remove the locknuts that retain the booster to the dash panel.
6. In the engine compartment, remove the booster by pulling it forward and tilted slightly upward.

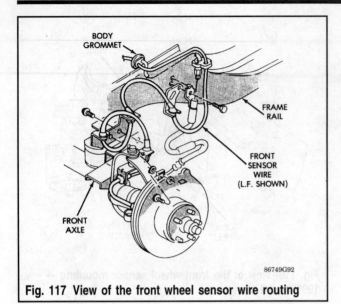

Fig. 117 View of the front wheel sensor wire routing

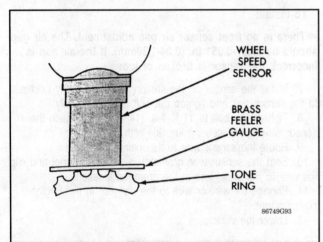

Fig. 118 When setting the air gap on the original sensor, use a brass feeler gauge only — 1995 model shown

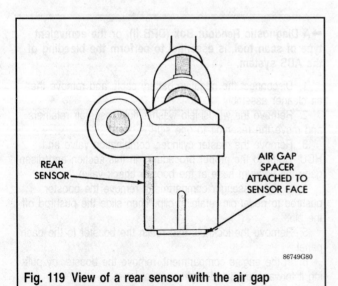

Fig. 119 View of a rear sensor with the air gap spacer — 1995 model shown

To install:

7. Check the condition of the grommet that secures the check valve in the booster. If the grommet is defective it must be replaced.

8. Install the booster on the firewall.

9. In the passenger compartment, lubricate the pedal pin and bushing, then fasten the booster attaching nuts to 30 ft. lbs. (41 Nm).

10. Slide the booster pushrod onto the pedal pin and secure the rod to pin with the retaining clip.

11. In the engine compartment, engage the vacuum hose to the booster check valve.

12. Install the master cylinder, combination valve and HCU. Refer to the proper procedures in this section.

13. Bleed the brake system. Refer to the proper procedure in this section.

14. Install the air cleaner assembly and hoses. Test drive the vehicle and verify proper brake operation.

Bleeding The ABS System

▶ See Figure 120

➡A Diagnostic Readout Box (DRB II), or the equivalent type of scan tool, is essential to perform the bleeding of the ABS system.

The brake system must be bled any time air is permitted to enter the system through loosened or disconnected lines or hoses, or anytime the modulator is removed. Excessive air within the system will cause a soft or spongy feel in the brake pedal.

When bleeding any part of the system, the reservoir must remain as close to full as possible at all times. Check the level frequently and top off fluid as needed.

This is basically a three step process consisting of: a conventional manual bleeding procedure, a second bleeding procedure using a DRB II, followed by a repeat of the first bleeding procedure.

1. Clean around the reservoir cap and remove the cap. Fill the master cylinder with the recommended fluid.

2. The recommended bleeding sequence is: master cylinder, HCU valve body (at the fluid lines), right rear wheel, left rear wheel, right front wheel and left front wheel.

3. Clean all the bleeder screws. You may want to give each one a shot of penetrating solvent to loosen it; seizure is a common problem with bleeder screws, which then break off, sometimes requiring replacement of the part to which they are attached.

➡Brake fluid absorbs moisture from the air. Don't leave the master cylinder or the fluid container uncovered any longer than necessary. Be careful handling the fluid — it will damage the vehicle's paint.

Check the level of the fluid often when bleeding, and refill the reservoirs as necessary. Don't let them run dry, or you will have to repeat the process.

4. Attach a length of clear vinyl tubing to the bleeder screw on the wheel cylinder. Insert the other end of the tube into a clear, clean jar half filled with brake fluid.

5. Have your assistant slowly depress the brake pedal. As this is done, open the bleeder screw until the brake fluid starts

to flow through the tube. Then, close the bleeder screw when the brake pedal reaches the end of its travel. After the bleeder valve is fully closed, have your assistant slowly release the pedal. Repeat this process until no air bubbles appear in the expelled fluid.

6. Repeat the procedure on the other three brake cylinders/calipers, checking the lever of brake fluid in the master cylinder reservoir often.

7. Perform the "Bleed Brake" procedure with the DRB II scan tool:

    a. Engage the DRB II scan tool to the diagnostic connector.

    b. Run the test as described in the tester manual.

8. Repeat the manual bleeding procedure as outlined in Steps 1 through 6. Check and replenish the master cylinder fluid level if necessary.

After finishing, there should be no feeling of sponginess in the brake pedal. If there is, either there is still air in the line, in which case the process must be repeated, or there is a leak somewhere, which, of course, must be corrected before the vehicle is moved. After all repairs and service work is finished, road test the vehicle to verify proper brake system operation.

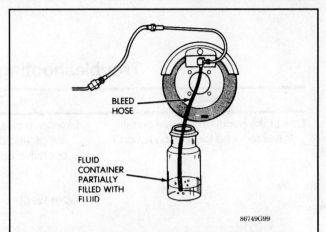

Fig. 120 Attach a length of clear vinyl tubing to the bleeder screw on the wheel cylinder. Insert the other end of the tube into a clear, clean jar half filled with brake fluid

Troubleshooting the Brake System

Problem	Cause	Solution
Low brake pedal (excessive pedal travel required for braking action.)	• Excessive clearance between rear linings and drums caused by inoperative automatic adjusters	• Make 10 to 15 alternate forward and reverse brake stops to adjust brakes. If brake pedal does not come up, repair or replace adjuster parts as necessary.
	• Worn rear brakelining	• Inspect and replace lining if worn beyond minimum thickness specification
	• Bent, distorted brakeshoes, front or rear	• Replace brakeshoes in axle sets
	• Air in hydraulic system	• Remove air from system. Refer to Brake Bleeding.
Low brake pedal (pedal may go to floor with steady pressure applied.)	• Fluid leak in hydraulic system	• Fill master cylinder to fill line; have helper apply brakes and check calipers, wheel cylinders, differential valve tubes, hoses and fittings for leaks. Repair or replace as necessary.
	• Air in hydraulic system	• Remove air from system. Refer to Brake Bleeding.
	• Incorrect or non-recommended brake fluid (fluid evaporates at below normal temp).	• Flush hydraulic system with clean brake fluid. Refill with correct-type fluid.
	• Master cylinder piston seals worn, or master cylinder bore is scored, worn or corroded	• Repair or replace master cylinder
Low brake pedal (pedal goes to floor on first application—o.k. on subsequent applications.)	• Disc brake pads sticking on abutment surfaces of anchor plate. Caused by a build-up of dirt, rust, or corrosion on abutment surfaces	• Clean abutment surfaces
Fading brake pedal (pedal height decreases with steady pressure applied.)	• Fluid leak in hydraulic system	• Fill master cylinder reservoirs to fill mark, have helper apply brakes, check calipers, wheel cylinders, differential valve, tubes, hoses, and fittings for fluid leaks. Repair or replace parts as necessary.
	• Master cylinder piston seals worn, or master cylinder bore is scored, worn or corroded	• Repair or replace master cylinder
Spongy brake pedal (pedal has abnormally soft, springy, spongy feel when depressed.)	• Air in hydraulic system	• Remove air from system. Refer to Brake Bleeding.
	• Brakeshoes bent or distorted	• Replace brakeshoes
	• Brakelining not yet seated with drums and rotors	• Burnish brakes
	• Rear drum brakes not properly adjusted	• Adjust brakes

86749c04

Troubleshooting the Brake System (cont.)

Problem	Cause	Solution
Decreasing brake pedal travel (pedal travel required for braking action decreases and may be accompanied by a hard pedal.)	• Caliper or wheel cylinder pistons sticking or seized • Master cylinder compensator ports blocked (preventing fluid return to reservoirs) or pistons sticking or seized in master cylinder bore • Power brake unit binding internally	• Repair or replace the calipers, or wheel cylinders • Repair or replace the master cylinder • Test unit according to the following procedure: (a) Shift transmission into neutral and start engine (b) Increase engine speed to 1500 rpm, close throttle and fully depress brake pedal (c) Slow release brake pedal and stop engine (d) Have helper remove vacuum check valve and hose from power unit. Observe for backward movement of brake pedal. (e) If the pedal moves backward, the power unit has an internal bind—replace power unit
Grabbing brakes (severe reaction to brake pedal pressure.)	• Brakelining(s) contaminated by grease or brake fluid • Parking brake cables incorrectly adjusted or seized • Incorrect brakelining or lining loose on brakeshoes • Caliper anchor plate bolts loose • Rear brakeshoes binding on support plate ledges • Incorrect or missing power brake reaction disc • Rear brake support plates loose	• Determine and correct cause of contamination and replace brakeshoes in axle sets • Adjust cables. Replace seized cables. • Replace brakeshoes in axle sets • Tighten bolts • Clean and lubricate ledges. Replace support plate(s) if ledges are deeply grooved. Do not attempt to smooth ledges by grinding. • Install correct disc • Tighten mounting bolts
Chatter or shudder when brakes are applied (pedal pulsation and roughness may also occur.)	• Brakeshoes distorted, bent, contaminated, or worn • Caliper anchor plate or support plate loose • Excessive thickness variation of rotor(s)	• Replace brakeshoes in axle sets • Tighten mounting bolts • Refinish or replace rotors in axle sets
Noisy brakes (squealing, clicking, scraping sound when brakes are applied.)	• Bent, broken, distorted brakeshoes • Excessive rust on outer edge of rotor braking surface	• Replace brakeshoes in axle sets • Remove rust

86749c05

Troubleshooting the Brake System (cont.)

Problem	Cause	Solution
Hard brake pedal (excessive pedal pressure required to stop vehicle. May be accompanied by brake fade.)	· Loose or leaking power brake unit vacuum hose · Incorrect or poor quality brake-lining · Bent, broken, distorted brakeshoes · Calipers binding or dragging on mounting pins. Rear brakeshoes dragging on support plate.	· Tighten connections or replace leaking hose · Replace with lining in axle sets · Replace brakeshoes · Replace mounting pins and bushings. Clean rust or burrs from rear brake support plate ledges and lubricate ledges with molydisulfide grease. **NOTE:** If ledges are deeply grooved or scored, do not attempt to sand or grind them smooth—replace support plate.
	· Caliper, wheel cylinder, or master cylinder pistons sticking or seized · Power brake unit vacuum check valve malfunction	· Repair or replace parts as necessary · Test valve according to the following procedure: (a) Start engine, increase engine speed to 1500 rpm, close throttle and immediately stop engine (b) Wait at least 90 seconds then depress brake pedal (c) If brakes are not vacuum assisted for 2 or more applications, check valve is faulty
	· Power brake unit has internal bind	· Test unit according to the following procedure: (a) With engine stopped, apply brakes several times to exhaust all vacuum in system (b) Shift transmission into neutral, depress brake pedal and start engine (c) If pedal height decreases with foot pressure and less pressure is required to hold pedal in applied position, power unit vacuum system is operating normally. Test power unit. If power unit exhibits a bind condition, replace the power unit.

86749c06

Troubleshooting the Brake System (cont.)

Problem	Cause	Solution
Hard brake pedal (excessive pedal pressure required to stop vehicle. May be accompanied by brake fade.)	• Master cylinder compensator ports (at bottom of reservoirs) blocked by dirt, scale, rust, or have small burrs (blocked ports prevent fluid return to reservoirs). • Brake hoses, tubes, fittings clogged or restricted • Brake fluid contaminated with improper fluids (motor oil, transmission fluid, causing rubber components to swell and stick in bores • Low engine vacuum	• Repair or replace master cylinder **CAUTION:** Do not attempt to clean blocked ports with wire, pencils, or similar implements. Use compressed air only. • Use compressed air to check or unclog parts. Replace any damaged parts. • Replace all rubber components, combination valve and hoses. Flush entire brake system with DOT 3 brake fluid or equivalent. • Adjust or repair engine
Dragging brakes (slow or incomplete release of brakes)	• Brake pedal binding at pivot • Power brake unit has internal bind • Parking brake cables incorrrectly adjusted or seized • Rear brakeshoe return springs weak or broken • Automatic adjusters malfunctioning • Caliper, wheel cylinder or master cylinder pistons sticking or seized • Master cylinder compensating ports blocked (fluid does not return to reservoirs).	• Loosen and lubricate • Inspect for internal bind. Replace unit if internal bind exists. • Adjust cables. Replace seized cables. • Replace return springs. Replace brakeshoe if necessary in axle sets. • Repair or replace adjuster parts as required • Repair or replace parts as necessary • Use compressed air to clear ports. Do not use wire, pencils, or similar objects to open blocked ports.
Vehicle moves to one side when brakes are applied	• Incorrect front tire pressure • Worn or damaged wheel bearings • Brakelining on one side contaminated • Brakeshoes on one side bent, distorted, or lining loose on shoe • Support plate bent or loose on one side • Brakelining not yet seated with drums or rotors • Caliper anchor plate loose on one side • Caliper piston sticking or seized • Brakelinings water soaked • Loose suspension component attaching or mounting bolts • Brake combination valve failure	• Inflate to recommended cold (reduced load) inflation pressure • Replace worn or damaged bearings • Determine and correct cause of contamination and replace brakelining in axle sets • Replace brakeshoes in axle sets • Tighten or replace support plate • Burnish brakelining • Tighten anchor plate bolts • Repair or replace caliper • Drive vehicle with brakes lightly applied to dry linings • Tighten suspension bolts. Replace worn suspension components. • Replace combination valve

BRAKE SPECIFICATIONS

All measurements in inches unless noted

Year	Model	Master Cylinder Bore	Brake Disc Original Thickness	Brake Disc Minimum Thickness	Brake Disc Maximum Runout	Brake Drum Diameter Original Inside Diameter	Brake Drum Diameter Max. Wear Limit	Brake Drum Diameter Maximum Machine Diameter	Minimum Lining Thickness Front	Minimum Lining Thickness Rear
1984	Cherokee	0.937	NA	0.815	0.004	NA	1	NA	0.031	0.031
	Comanche	0.937	NA	0.815	0.004	NA	1	NA	0.031	0.031
	Wagoneer	0.937	NA	0.815	0.004	NA	1	NA	0.031	0.031
1985	Cherokee	0.937	NA	0.815	0.004	NA	1	NA	0.031	0.031
	Comanche	0.937	NA	0.815	0.004	NA	1	NA	0.031	0.031
	Wagoneer	0.937	NA	0.815	0.004	NA	1	NA	0.031	0.031
1986	Cherokee	0.937	NA	0.815	0.004	NA	1	NA	0.031	0.031
	Comanche	0.937	NA	0.815	0.004	NA	1	NA	0.031	0.031
	Wagoneer	0.937	NA	0.815	0.004	NA	1	NA	0.031	0.031
1987	Cherokee	0.937	NA	0.815	0.004	NA	1	NA	0.031	0.031
	Comanche	0.937	NA	0.815	0.004	NA	1	NA	0.031	0.031
	Wagoneer	0.937	NA	0.815	0.004	NA	1	NA	0.031	0.031
1988	Cherokee	0.937	NA	0.815	0.004	NA	1	NA	0.031	0.031
	Comanche	0.937	NA	0.815	0.004	NA	1	NA	0.031	0.031
	Wagoneer	0.937	NA	0.815	0.004	NA	1	NA	0.031	0.031
1989	Cherokee	0.937	NA	0.815	0.004	NA	1	NA	0.031	0.031
	Comanche	0.937	NA	0.815	0.004	NA	1	NA	0.031	0.031
	Wagoneer	0.937	NA	0.815	0.004	NA	1	NA	0.031	0.031
1990	Cherokee	0.937	NA	0.860 2	0.004	NA	1	NA	0.031	0.031
	Comanche	0.937	NA	0.860 2	0.004	NA	1	NA	0.031	0.031
	Wagoneer	0.937	NA	0.860 2	0.004	NA	1	NA	0.031	0.031
1991	Cherokee	0.937	NA	0.860 3	0.004	NA	1	NA	0.031	0.031
	Comanche	0.937	NA	0.860 3	0.004	NA	1	NA	0.031	0.031
1992	Cherokee	0.937	NA	0.860 3	0.004	NA	1	NA	0.031	0.031
	Comanche	0.937	NA	0.860 3	0.004	NA	1	NA	0.031	0.031
1993	Cherokee	0.937	NA	0.860 3	0.004	NA	1	NA	0.031	0.031
	Grand Cherokee	NA	0.940 4	0.890	0.004	-		-	0.031	0.031
	Grand Wagoneer	NA	0.940 4	0.890	0.004	-		-	0.031	0.031
1994	Cherokee	0.937	NA	0.860 3	0.004	9.00	1	9.06	0.031	0.031
	Grand Cherokee	NA	0.940 4	0.890	0.004	-		-	0.031	0.031
1995	Cherokee	0.937	NA	0.860 3	0.004	9.00	1	9.06	0.031	0.031
	Grand Cherokee	NA	0.940 4	0.890	0.004	-		-	0.031	0.031
1996	Cherokee	0.937	NA	0.860 3	0.004	9.00	1	9.06	0.031	0.031
	Grand Cherokee	NA	0.940 4	0.890	0.004	-		-	0.031	0.031

1: Maximum wear limit is listed on outside of drum

2: 0.940 with 4WD

3: 0.890 with 4WD

4: Rear rotor original thickness is 0.370

86749CB1

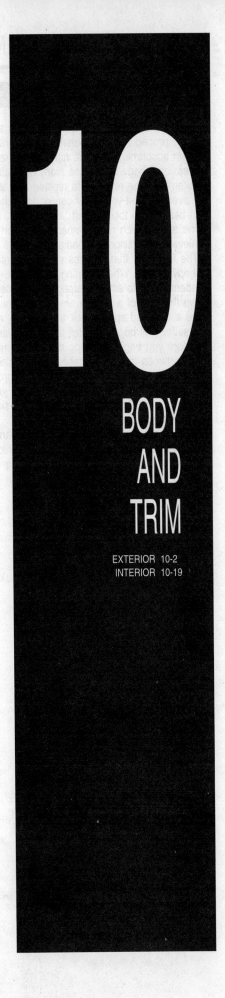

10

BODY AND TRIM

EXTERIOR

Replacement of exterior body panels is a fairly straight forward procedure. Most panels are fastened to the chassis with an assortment of bolts, nuts, screws and clips. Professional body shops use many specialty tools designed to quicken the time required to replace and align body panels but the average do-it-yourselfer can perform the same procedures with basic hand tools, it just takes longer. However, there are some areas which require special attention to detail in order to achieve a professional appearance.

The first area that requires special attention is the alignment of body panels. When aligning body panels, most of the time is spent trying to achieve straight body lines. If the body lines down the side of a vehicle are not straight, the vehicle will have a distorted appearance and anyone, even another do-it-yourselfer, will be able to tell the panel was replaced.

Before you begin replacing the panel, measure all the air gaps between the panel that is being replaced and the adjacent panels. Use this information to properly align the replacement panel. If you are repairing a vehicle that has damage on one side, measure the other side to ensure your measurements are accurate.

When installing the new replacement panel, wrap the edges with masking tape to ensure you do not nick the paint. Install all bolts in the panel loosely and then align the panel. After aligning, tighten all bolts to specification.

Doors

REMOVAL & INSTALLATION

▶ **See Figures 1, 2, 3 and 4**

1. Disconnect the negative battery cable.
2. On vehicles with power windows or locks, remove the trim panel and water shield. Disconnect the speaker wiring.
3. Matchmark the hinge-to-door position.
4. Have an assistant support the door.
5. Remove the door stop-to-pillar pin.
6. Remove the hinge-to-door bolts, catch the shims, and lift off the door.

To install:

7. Position the door and shims and install, but do not tighten the bolts.
8. Adjust the door, as described, then, tighten the bolts to 26 ft. lbs. (35 Nm).
9. Connect the wiring and install the trim panel.

ADJUSTMENT

Door adjustment is made by means of shims located between the door and the hinge. The shims are placed in shim plates. Add or remove shims as necessary to obtain proper door fit. When adjustment is complete, tighten the mounting bolts to 26 ft. lbs. (35 Nm).

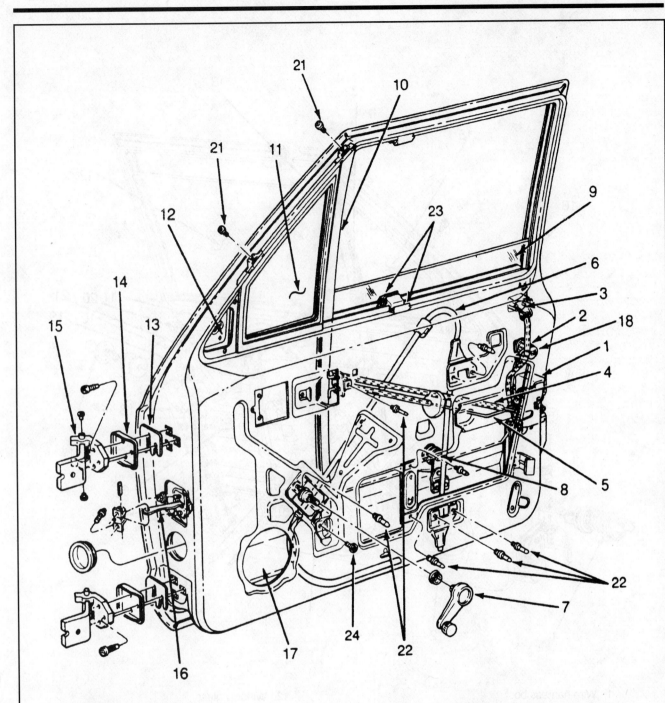

1. Latch assembly
2. Mechanical linkage
3. Exterior door release
4. Internal lock linkage
5. Internal release linkage
6. Window regulator
7. Window regulator handle
8. Window mounting surface
9. Window glass
10. Glass channel
11. Vent window

12. Side view mirror mounting surface
13. Door shims
14. Door shim mounting plate
15. Door hinge
16. Door stop
17. Speaker mounting surface
18. Door lock cylinder
21. Vent window screws
22. Window track rivets and screws
23. Weatherstrip—inner and outer
24. Glass channel screw

86740g01

Fig. 1 Front door with manual windows and locks

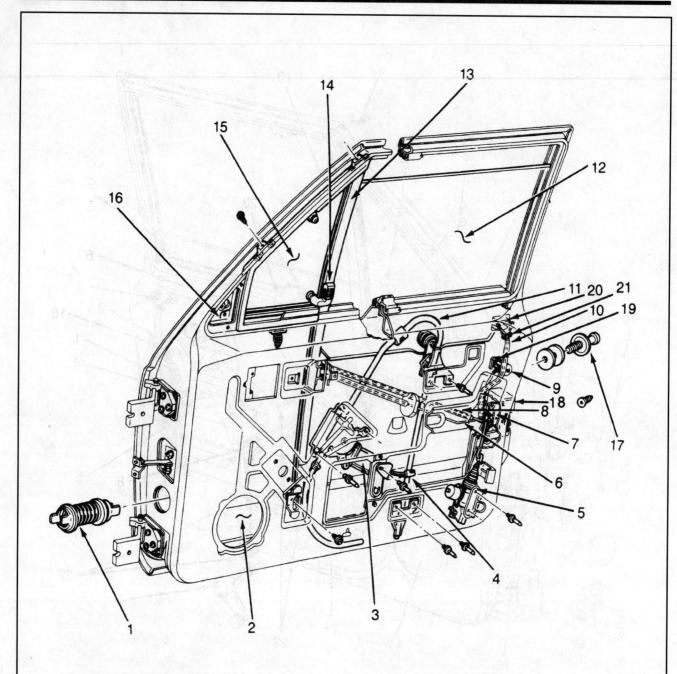

1. Wire harness boot
2. Speaker mounting surface
3. Power window motor
4. Motor wire harness connector
5. Power lock actuator
6. Internal latch release linkage
7. Door latch
8. Internal lock linkage
9. External lock
10. External latch release linkage
11. Window regulator

12. Window glass
13. Window channel
14. Vent window latch
15. Vent window
16. Side view mirror mounting surface
17. Striker
18. Latch assembly
19. External lock cylinder retainer clip
20. External door handle
21. Access plug (external door handle)

86740g02

Fig. 2 Front door with power windows and locks

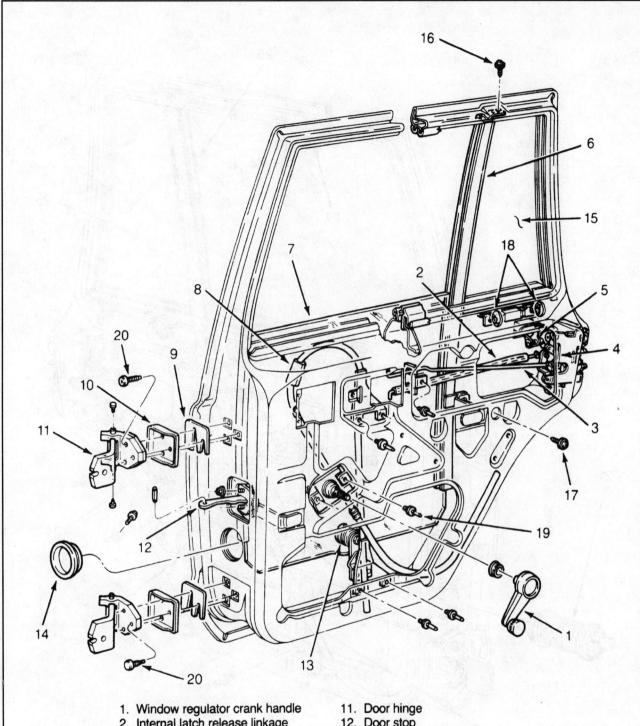

1. Window regulator crank handle
2. Internal latch release linkage
3. Internal lock linkage
4. Latch assembly
5. Exterior door handle
6. Window channel
7. Door glass
8. Window regulator
9. Shims
10. Shim retainer plate
11. Door hinge
12. Door stop
13. Glass attaching surface
14. Access plug
15. Stationary glass
16. Glass channel upper screw
17. Glass channel lower screw
18. Stationary glass frame screws
19. Regulator rivet (typical)
20. Door hinge screw

86740g03

Fig. 3 Rear door with manual window and locks

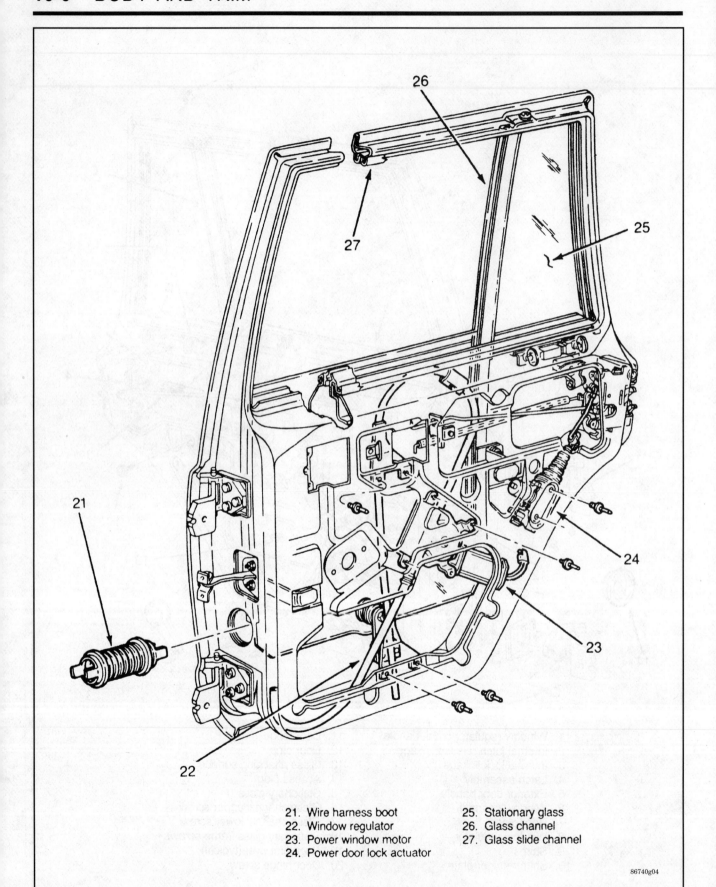

21. Wire harness boot
22. Window regulator
23. Power window motor
24. Power door lock actuator
25. Stationary glass
26. Glass channel
27. Glass slide channel

86740g04

Fig. 4 Rear door with power window and locks

Hood

REMOVAL & INSTALLATION

▶ **See Figures 5, 6, 7, 8, 9 and 10**

1. Raise the hood fully.
2. If the hood is properly aligned, prior to removal, match-mark the position of the hinges and hood reinforcement.
3. Disconnect the wiring and the release cable.
4. While your assistant supports the hood, remove the hood-to-hinge bolts and lift off the hood. Don't lose the shims, if used.
5. Installation is the reverse of removal. Tighten the bolts to 17 ft. lbs. (23 Nm).

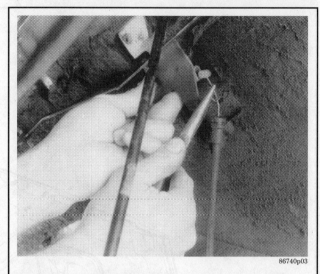

Fig. 7 . . . and the release rod

Fig. 5 Matchmark the position of the hood

Fig. 8 Loosen and remove the hinge bolts

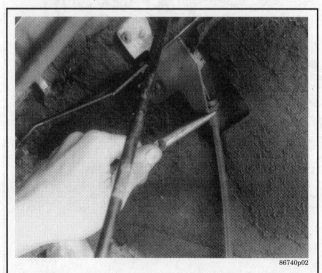

Fig. 6 Disconnect the cable from the bracket . . .

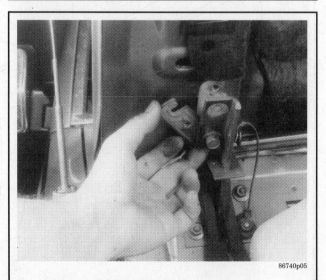

Fig. 9 Remove the shims and place them aside

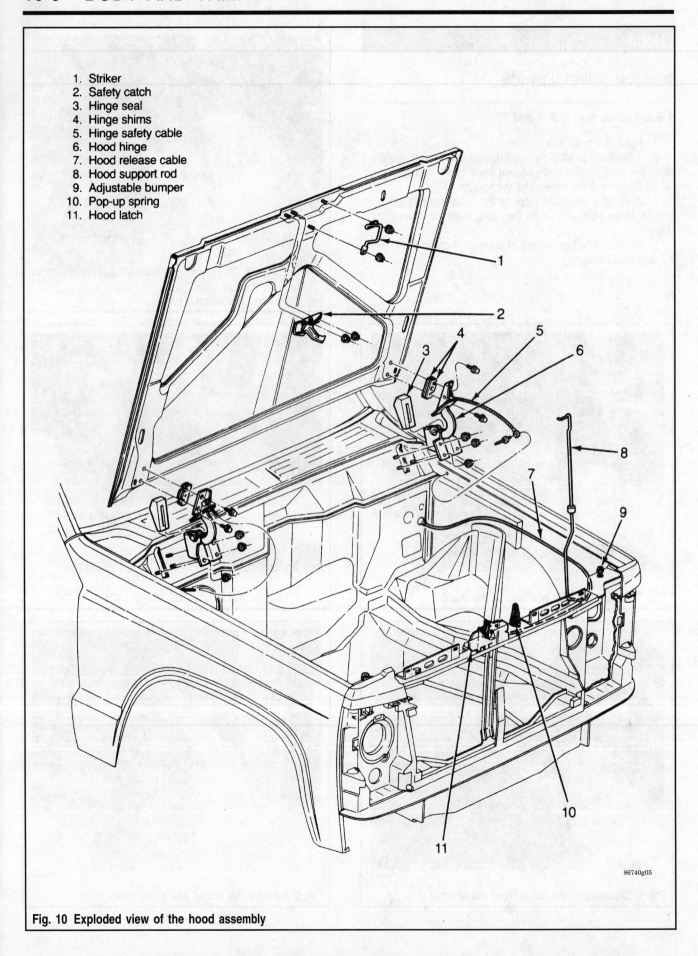

1. Striker
2. Safety catch
3. Hinge seal
4. Hinge shims
5. Hinge safety cable
6. Hood hinge
7. Hood release cable
8. Hood support rod
9. Adjustable bumper
10. Pop-up spring
11. Hood latch

86740g05

Fig. 10 Exploded view of the hood assembly

ALIGNMENT

➡**Hood hinge mounting holes are oversized to permit movement for hood alignment. If the hood is to be moved to either side, the hood lock striker, hood lever lock and safety hook assembly must first be loosened.**

1. Loosen the hinge mounting bolts slightly on one side and tap the hinge in the direction opposite to that in which the hood is to be moved.
2. Tighten the bolts.
3. Repeat this procedure for the opposite hinge.
4. Check that the lock striker, lever lock and safety hook are properly adjusted to ensure positive locking. Tighten the lockbolts to 8 ft. lbs. (11 Nm).
5. If the rear edge of the hood is not flush with the cowl, add or subtract shims (caster and camber adjusting shims will work) or flat washers between the hinge and the hood at the rear bolt (hood too low) or front bolt (hood too high).
6. Adjust the hood-to-fender height using the front bumpers, located at the left and right front corners of the vehicle.

Tailgate

REMOVAL & INSTALLATION

Comanche
▶ **See Figure 11**

1. Lower the tailgate.
2. Pull each support up at the center and force the upper end forward, then inward, to disengage it from the retaining dowel.
3. Pull the right side of the tailgate rearward to disengage the hinge.
4. Move the tailgate to the right to disengage the left hinge.
5. Installation is the reverse of removal.

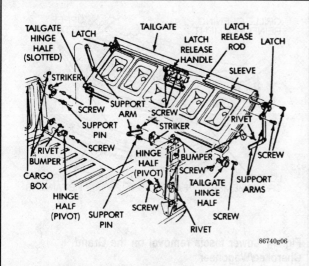

Fig. 11 Tailgate components

ADJUSTMENT

The only adjustment possible to the Comanche's tailgate is the striker adjustment. This is performed by loosening the striker plate screws and moving the striker to position it.

Liftgate

REMOVAL & INSTALLATION

▶ **See Figure 12**

1. Open the liftgate.
2. Remove the trim panel.

✳✳CAUTION

Never attempt to remove a support cylinder with the liftgate closed. The cylinders contain gas under high pressure. Severe personal injury may occur if the cylinders are disconnect with the liftgate closed!

3. Remove the retainer clips from the ball studs at the ends of the liftgate support cylinders.
4. Pull the support cylinders off of the ball studs.
5. Disconnect and remove the wiring harness.
6. Have a helper support the liftgate and remove the liftgate hinge bolts.
7. Installation is the reverse of removal. Tighten fasteners to 7 ft. lbs. (10 Nm). Check alignment.

ADJUSTMENT

The position of the liftgate can be adjusted upward or downward, and inward or outward by use of hinge shims. Liftgate stop bumpers must also be adjusted if the hinges are adjusted. The bumpers are adjusted by shims.

Front Bumper

REMOVAL & INSTALLATION

Comanche, Cherokee and Wagoneer
▶ **See Figure 13**

1. Disconnect the negative battery cable.
2. Remove the fog lamps, if equipped.
3. Disconnect the vacuum reservoir harness.
4. Support the bumper and remove the attaching bolts.
5. Installation is the reverse of removal.

Grand Cherokee/Wagoneer
▶ **See Figure 14**

1. Disconnect the negative battery cable.
2. Remove the license plate bracket.
3. Remove the 6 retainers from the fascia.

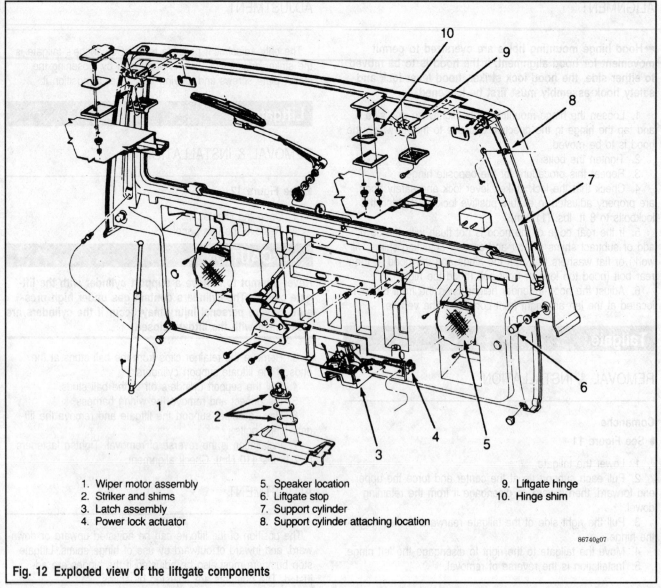

1. Wiper motor assembly
2. Striker and shims
3. Latch assembly
4. Power lock actuator
5. Speaker location
6. Liftgate stop
7. Support cylinder
8. Support cylinder attaching location
9. Liftgate hinge
10. Hinge shim

86740g07

Fig. 12 Exploded view of the liftgate components

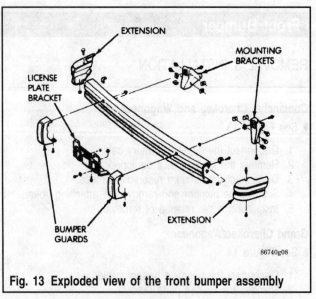

86740g08

Fig. 13 Exploded view of the front bumper assembly

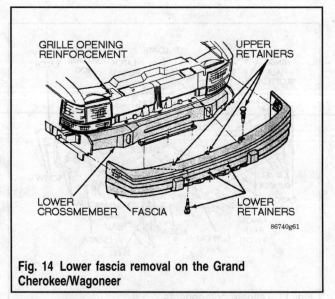

86740g61

Fig. 14 Lower fascia removal on the Grand Cherokee/Wagoneer

4. Remove the 3 plastic rivets at each front wheel well.
5. Slide the fascia off the retainer pegs.
6. Installation is the reverse of removal.

Rear Bumper

REMOVAL & INSTALLATION

▶ See Figures 15 and 16

1. On models with a rear mounted spare or trailer hitch, remove these components first.
2. Support the bumper and remove the attaching bolts.
3. Installation is the reverse of removal.

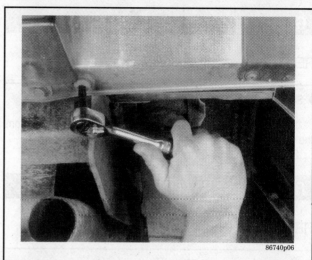

Fig. 16 Remove the bolts securing the bumper to the vehicle

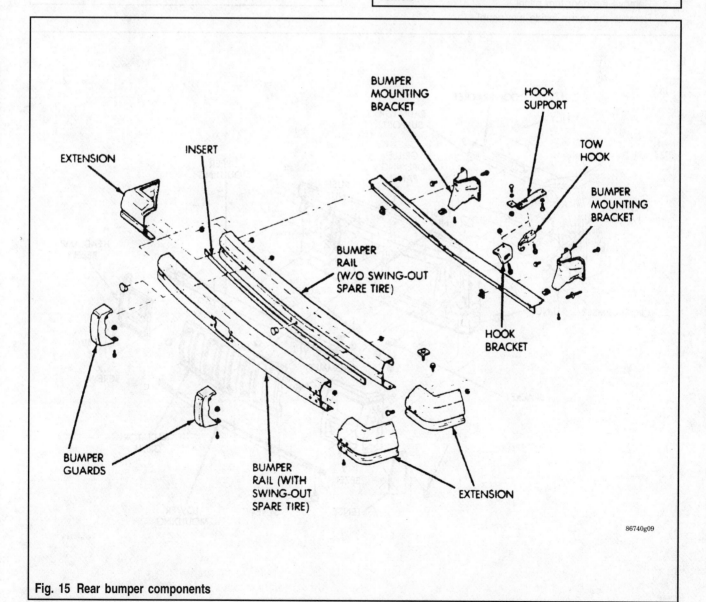

Fig. 15 Rear bumper components

Grille

REMOVAL & INSTALLATION

▶ See Figures 17, 18, 19 and 20

1. Remove the grille attaching screws and lift the grille from the grille panel.
2. Installation is the reverse of removal.

Remote and Power Exterior Mirrors

REMOVAL & INSTALLATION

▶ See Figures 21 and 22

1. Remove the door trim panel.
2. Remove the mirror inside trim panel.

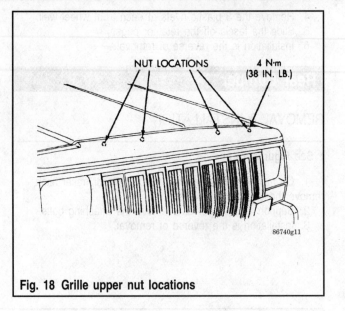

Fig. 18 Grille upper nut locations

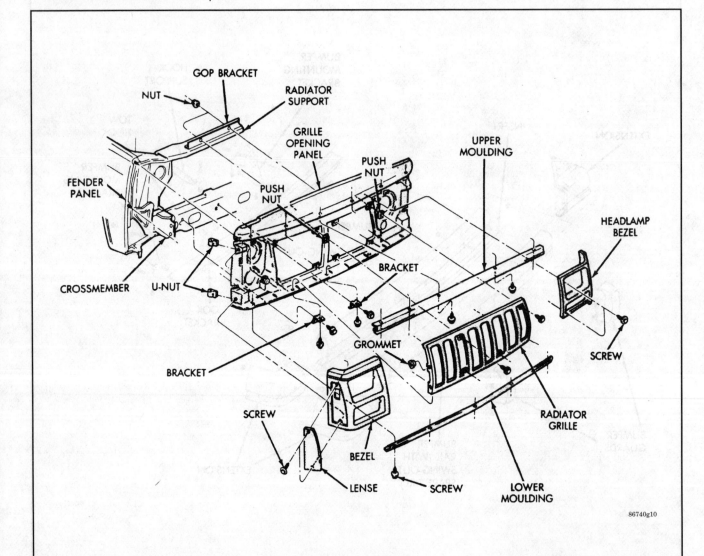

Fig. 17 Exploded view of the Cherokee/Wagoneer/Comanche front grille

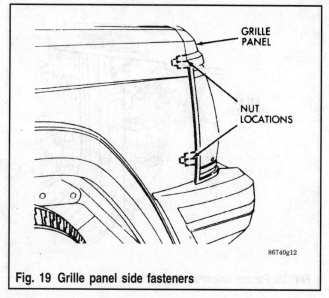

Fig. 19 Grille panel side fasteners

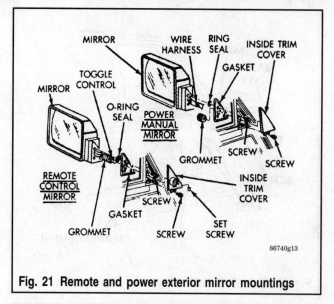

Fig. 21 Remote and power exterior mirror mountings

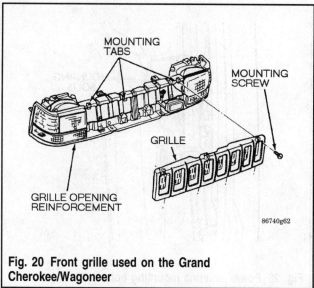

Fig. 20 Front grille used on the Grand Cherokee/Wagoneer

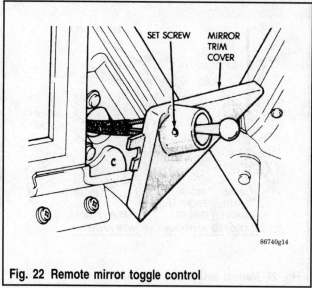

Fig. 22 Remote mirror toggle control

3. If equipped with remote mirror, loosen the set screw which holds the toggle control.

4. Remove the screws holding the window trim cover and remove.

5. If equipped with power mirrors, unplug the wire harness at the connector in the door. Pull the harness up through the door.

6. Remove the mirror retaining screws. Remove the mirror from the door.

7. Installation is the reverse of removal.

Wide-View Exterior Mirror

REMOVAL & INSTALLATION

▶ See Figure 23

1. Remove the mirror base cover.

2. Remove the mirror base attaching screws. The mirror base reinforcement is attached to the inside of the door with rivets.

3. Remove the mirror from the door panel.

4. Installation is the reverse of removal.

Antenna

REMOVAL & INSTALLATION

▶ See Figures 24, 25 and 26

1. Remove the fender inner splash shield nuts and move the panel aside far enough to get at the antenna cable and base.

2. Unscrew the antenna mast and nut, then remove the antenna pad from the top of the fender.

3. Remove the passenger side kick panel.

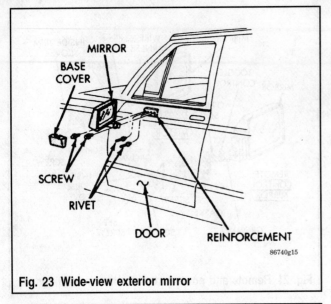

Fig. 23 Wide-view exterior mirror

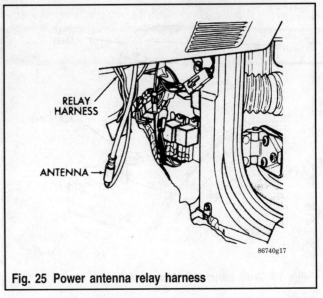

Fig. 25 Power antenna relay harness

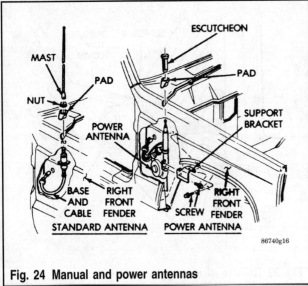

Fig. 24 Manual and power antennas

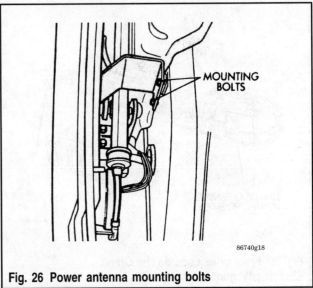

Fig. 26 Power antenna mounting bolts

4. If equipped with a power antenna:

a. Disconnect the negative battery cable.

b. Disconnect the harness from the relay. The relay is located behind the right hand side of the dash just above its lower edge.

c. Remove the antenna mounting bolts and washers.

d. Pull the antenna motor harness through the hole in the kick panel.

5. Disconnect the antenna lead by pull and twisting the metal connectors. NEVER pull on the cable!

6. Pull the rubber grommet out of the kick panel.

7. Remove the antenna assembly from the inside of the wheelhouse.

8. Installation is the reverse of removal.

Fenders

REMOVAL & INSTALLATION

▶ See Figures 27, 28 and 29

1. On Grand Cherokee/Wagoneer, remove the headlamp, side marker and turn signal lamp.

2. Remove the front bumper.

3. If removing the right side fender, remove the radio antenna.

4. Raise and support the vehicle safely.

5. Remove the front wheel, fender liner, fender flare and retainers.

6. Remove the grille and air deflector.

7. Remove the rocker panel moulding and all fender braces.

8. Remove the fender lower attaching screws.

9. Remove all other fender attaching screws.

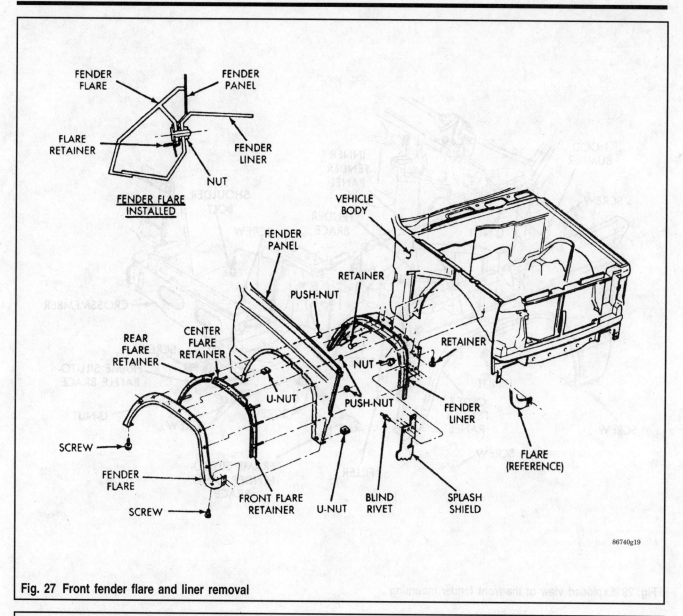

Fig. 27 Front fender flare and liner removal

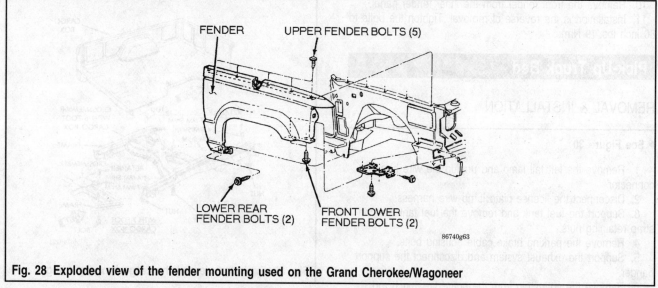

Fig. 28 Exploded view of the fender mounting used on the Grand Cherokee/Wagoneer

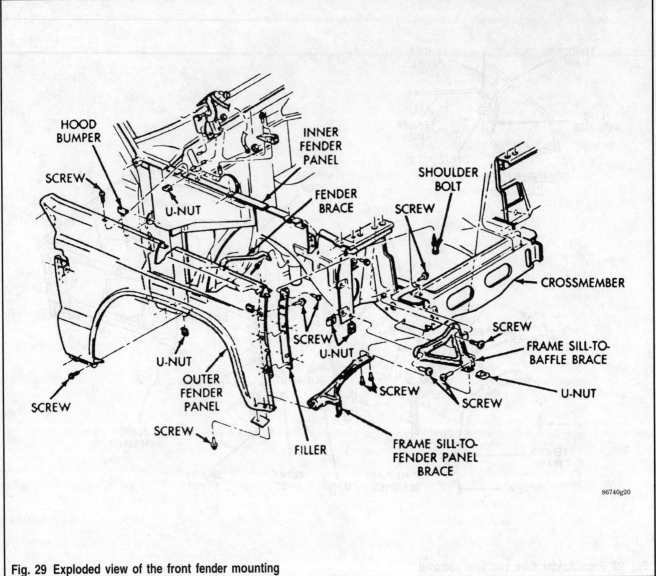

Fig. 29 Exploded view of the front fender mounting

10. Remove the front fender from the inner fender panel.
11. Installation is the reverse of removal. Tighten the bolts to 80 inch lbs. (9 Nm).

Pick-Up Truck Bed

REMOVAL & INSTALLATION

▶ See Figure 30

1. Remove the left tail lamp and unplug the wire harness connector.
2. Disconnect the license plate lamp wire harness.
3. Support the fuel tank and remove the fuel tank support strap retaining nuts.
4. Remove the parking brake cable housing bolts.
5. Support the exhaust system and disconnect the support hanger.
6. Remove the cotter pin from the spare tire winch rod.
7. Remove the cargo box retaining nuts and bolts.

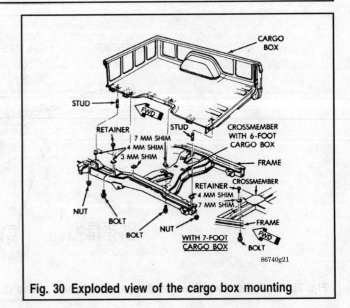

Fig. 30 Exploded view of the cargo box mounting

8. Identify, mark and retain the shims for installation.

9. Remove the cargo box from the frame using a hoist.

10. Installation is the reverse of removal.

Sunroof

REMOVAL & INSTALLATION

1. Remove the wind deflector mechanism covers.

2. Position the glass to the vent position.

3. Position the sunshade full rearward.

4. Loosen the nuts holding the glass panel to the side adjustment brackets.

5. Slide the glass panel rearward 0.50 in. (12mm) and separate the glass from the sunroof unit.

To install:

6. Position the glass panel in the opening with the logo rearward and slide the panel forward 0.50 in. (12mm).

7. Verify that the attaching nuts are below the top surface of the glass adjustment brackets.

8. Close the sunroof to center the glass in the opening.

9. Tighten the center screws to hold the adjustment.

10. Open the glass to the vent position and tighten the nuts to 71 inch lbs. (8 Nm).

11. Close the glass and check the alignment.

12. Install the mechanism covers.

13. Adjust the wind deflector if necessary.

Spare Tire Carriers

REMOVAL & INSTALLATION

Swing Away Type

▶ **See Figures 31 and 32**

1. Remove the spare tire from the carrier.

2. Detach the carrier from the liftgate with the release handle.

3. Support the carrier. Remove the retaining bolts and carrier from the carrier bracket on the rear bumper.

4. To remove the carrier bracket at the bumper:

a. Remove the rear bumper and remove the Torx® head bolts that attach the reinforcement brackets to the bumper, extension and carrier bracket.

b. Remove the Torx® head bolts that attach the carrier bracket to the bumper and the extension. Remove the bracket from the bumper.

c. Remove the bolts that attach the reinforcement brackets to the cross sill.

5. To remove the carrier bracket at the liftgate:

a. Remove the liftgate trim panel.

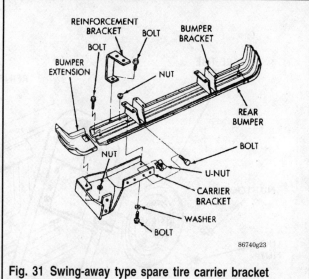

Fig. 31 Swing-away type spare tire carrier bracket

b. Remove the Torx® head bolts that attach the outer reinforcement bracket to the liftgate and the inner reinforcement bracket.

c. Remove the shoulder bolts that attach the outer reinforcement bracket.

d. Remove the reinforcement brackets from the liftgate.

6. Installation is the reverse of removal.

Interior Type

▶ **See Figure 33**

1. Remove the spare tire and wheel.

2. Remove the floor bracket retaining screws.

3. Remove the quarter trim panel.

4. Remove the retaining screws and the wheel hold-down bracket.

5. Installation is the reverse of removal.

Spare Tire Winch

▶ **See Figures 34 and 35**

The spare tire winch is located under the cargo box. On the 6 ft. cargo box it is located on a bracket attached to the cargo box crossmember and the frame rear crossmember. On the 7 ft. cargo box it is attached to the frame rear crossmember. The winch is serviced as a replacement unit only.

The winch tube is retained at the winch with a cotter pin and is supported in the rear crossmember with a snap bushing. A lug wrench is used to operate the winch.

1. Remove the spare tire.

2. Remove the cotter pin and the winch tube.

3. Remove the retaining screws and the winch from the vehicle.

4. If necessary (for 6 ft. cargo box only), remove the retaining screws and the winch bracket.

5. Installation is the reverse of removal.

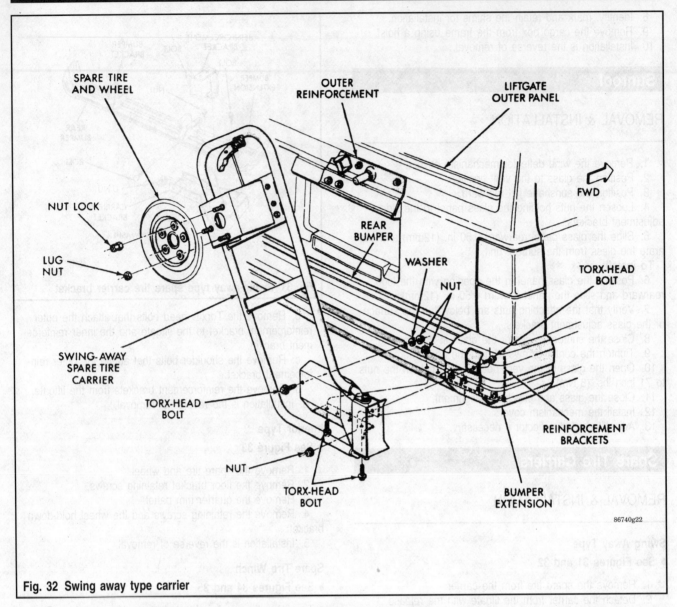

SPARE TIRE AND WHEEL

NUT LOCK

LUG NUT

SWING-AWAY SPARE TIRE CARRIER

TORX-HEAD BOLT

NUT

TORX-HEAD BOLT

OUTER REINFORCEMENT

LIFTGATE OUTER PANEL

FWD

REAR BUMPER

WASHER

NUT

TORX-HEAD BOLT

REINFORCEMENT BRACKETS

BUMPER EXTENSION

86740g22

Fig. 32 Swing away type carrier

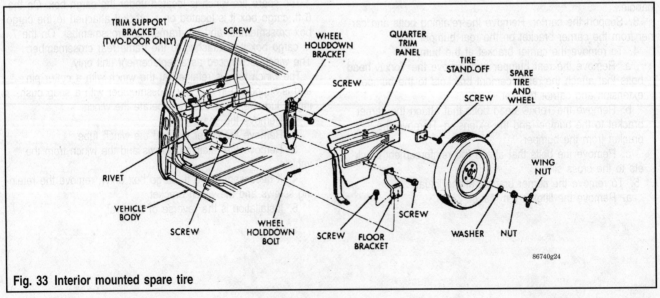

TRIM SUPPORT BRACKET (TWO-DOOR ONLY)

SCREW

WHEEL HOLDDOWN BRACKET

QUARTER TRIM PANEL

TIRE STAND-OFF

SPARE TIRE AND WHEEL

SCREW

SCREW

WING NUT

RIVET

VEHICLE BODY

SCREW

WHEEL HOLDDOWN BOLT

SCREW

FLOOR BRACKET

SCREW

WASHER

NUT

86740g24

Fig. 33 Interior mounted spare tire

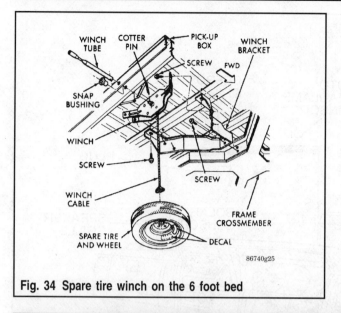

Fig. 34 Spare tire winch on the 6 foot bed

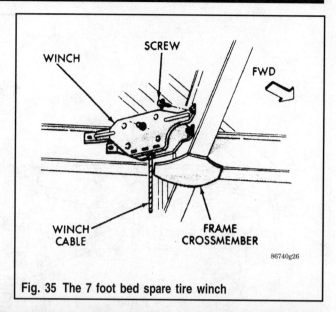

Fig. 35 The 7 foot bed spare tire winch

INTERIOR

Instrument Cluster/Panel

REMOVAL & INSTALLATION

Cherokee, Wagoneer and Comanche

▶ See Figure 36

1. Disconnect the negative battery cable.
2. Disable the air bag system, if equipped.
3. Remove the parking brake release handle.
4. Remove the lower heat-A/C duct below the steering column.
5. Remove the ashtry.
6. Remove the lower instrument panel, cluster bezel and cluster assembly.
7. Remove the radio.

Fig. 36 View of the Wagoneer instrument cluster and panel

8. Remove the climate control panel and instrument panel switches.
9. Unplug the glove box lamp.
10. Remove the defroster cowl outlet panel.
11. Remove the instrument panel attaching bolts.
12. Remove the steering column attaching bolts.
13. Remove the instrument panel assembly.

To install:
14. Position the panel on the cowl side mounting bolts.
15. Route the wiring harnesses and secure the instrument panel assembly using the mounting bolts.
16. Connect the tube to the lap cooler.
17. Reverse the removal procedures to complete the installation.
18. Connect the negative battery cable.

1993-96 Grand Cherokee/Wagoneer

▶ See Figure 37

1. Disconnect the negative battery cable and disable the air bag system.
2. Remove the defroster duct bezel from the panel.
3. Remove the speaker grilles.
4. Remove the 4 upper instrument panel retaining nuts.
5. Remove the 3 screws retaining the lower left side panel. Remove the mounting bolt for the instrument panel at the left side of the cowl through the access hole provided.
6. Remove the ashtry. Remove the mounting screw located behind the ashtray.
7. Remove the panel mounting bolt located on the right side cowl.
8. Fold down the carpet at the left side of the console. Remove the 2 mounting screws.
9. Remove the 3 screws at the lower column cover and remove the cover.
10. Remove the 6 screws at the lower knee bolster and remove the bolster.
11. Remove the tilt lever and both column covers. Disconnect the column wiring.

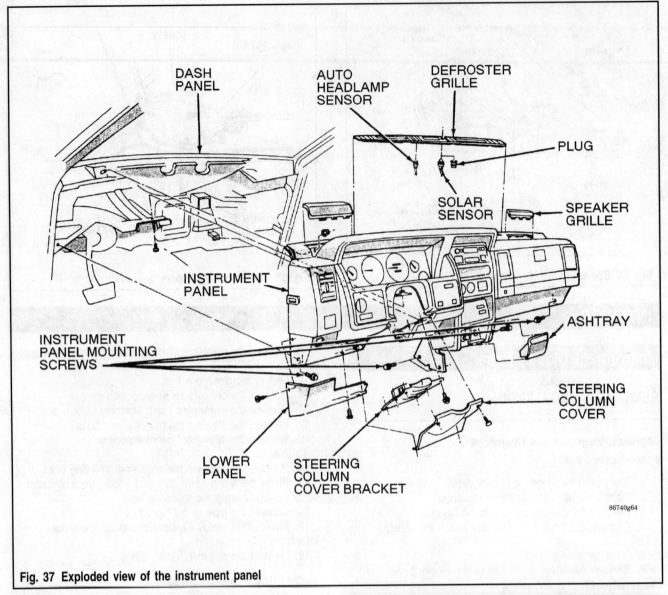

DASH PANEL

AUTO HEADLAMP SENSOR

DEFROSTER GRILLE

PLUG

SOLAR SENSOR

SPEAKER GRILLE

INSTRUMENT PANEL

ASHTRAY

INSTRUMENT PANEL MOUNTING SCREWS

STEERING COLUMN COVER

LOWER PANEL

STEERING COLUMN COVER BRACKET

86740g64

Fig. 37 Exploded view of the instrument panel

12. Remove the mounting nuts and lower the steering column.

13. Remove the panel mounting bolt located above the center of the column.

14. Unplug the bulkhead connector at the left side of the dash panel.

15. Disconnect the cluster wiring at the lower left side of the panel.

16. Remove the right side kick panel access door. Unplug the wiring at the kick panel.

17. Pull back and lower the panel. Disconnect the A/C vacuum lines and antenna.

18. Remove the panel assembly.

19. Installation is the reverse of removal.

Door Panels

REMOVAL & INSTALLATION

Front Door

▶ **See Figures 38, 39, 40, 41, 42, 43, 44, 45 and 46**

1. Unbolt and remove the inside door latch and remove the latch panel retaining screws.

2. Disconnect the door latch control linkage and, if equipped, wiring harness. Remove the control panel.

3. If equipped with manual windows, remove the window crank handles.

4. Remove the armrest lower retaining screws and swing the armrest downward to disengage the upper retaining clip. Pull the armrest straight out from the door panel.

5. Starting at the bottom of the door panel, use a flat tool, such as a wood spatula, pry out the panel-to-door frame retaining pins by levering right up against the pin. If a forked-end

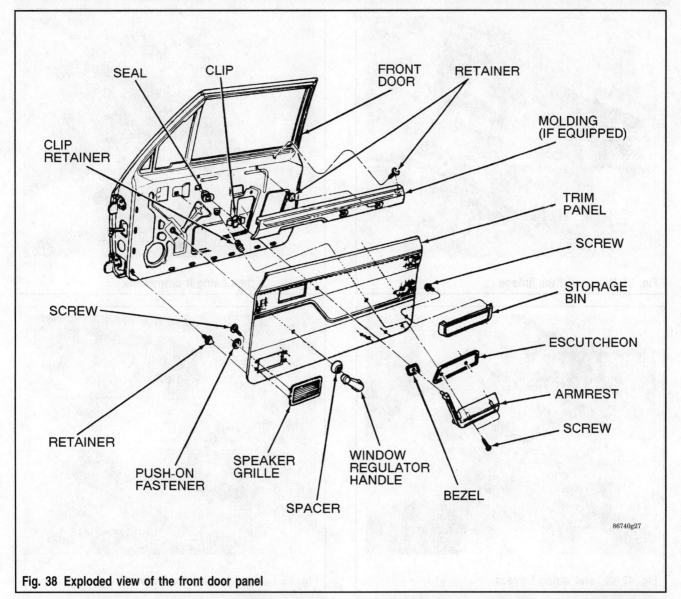

Fig. 38 Exploded view of the front door panel

Fig. 39 Remove the latch panel inner . . .

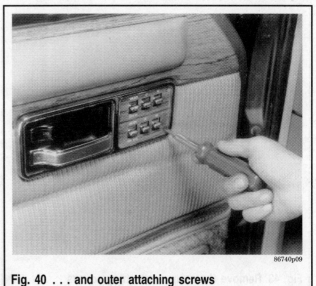

Fig. 40 . . . and outer attaching screws

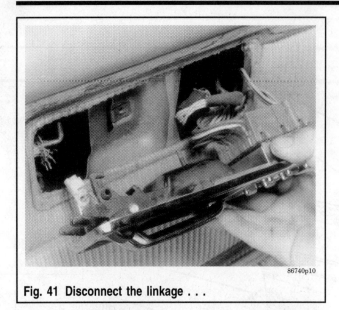

Fig. 41 Disconnect the linkage . . .

86740p10

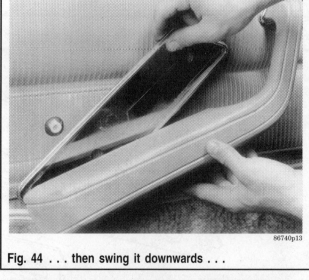

Fig. 44 . . . then swing it downwards . . .

86740p13

Fig. 42 . . . and wiring harness

86740p11

Fig. 45 . . . and pull it from the panel

86740p14

Fig. 43 Remove the armrest attaching screws . . .

86740p12

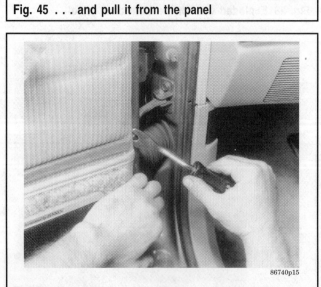

Fig. 46 A special tool is available to disengage the retaining clips

86740p15

tool is available, use one. These pins are easy to rip out of the trim panel.

6. Installation is the reverse of removal. A firm hit with the heel of your palm is usually enough to drive the retainers into the holes in the door panel. Make sure that the retainer is directly over the hole before knocking it in, or it may be damaged.

Rear Door

▶ **See Figure 47**

1. Unbolt and remove the inside door latch. Remove the latch panel retaining screws.

2. Disconnect the door latch control linkage and, if equipped, wiring harness. Remove the control panel.

3. If equipped with manual windows, remove the window crank handles.

4. Remove the armrest retaining screws and lift off the armrest.

5. Starting at the bottom of the door panel, use a flat tool, such as a wood spatula, pry out the panel-to-door frame retaining pins by levering right up against the pin. If a forked-end

tool is available, use one. These pins are easy to rip out of the trim panel.

6. Installation is the reverse of removal. A firm hit with the heel of your palm is usually enough to drive the retainers into the dooe panel holes. To prevent damage, make sure the retainer is directly over the hole before knocking it in.

Interior Trim Panels

REMOVAL & INSTALLATION

▶ **See Figures 48, 49, 50, 51, 52, 53, 54, 55 and 56**

Interior trim panels are attached to the chassis using a variety of clips and fasteners. During removal, work slowly and carefully. Most panels are plastic and can be easily damaged. DO NOT bend or attempt to remove a panel until interfering adjacent panels and components have been removed. The panels have limited flexibility. Refer to the illustrations when removing/installing trim panels.

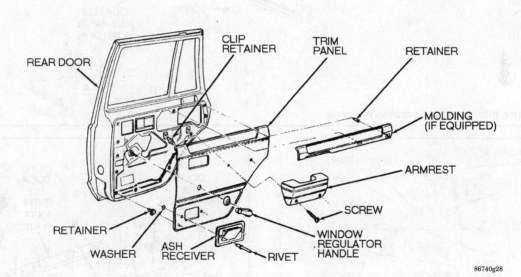

Fig. 47 Exploded view of the rear door panel

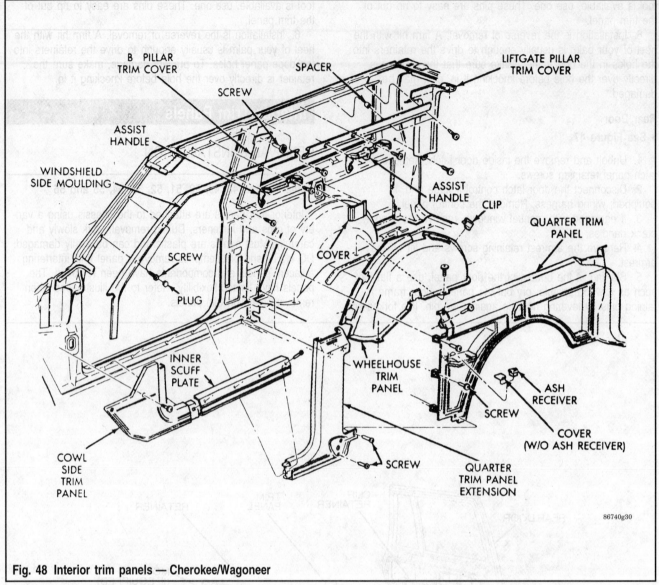

Fig. 48 Interior trim panels — Cherokee/Wagoneer

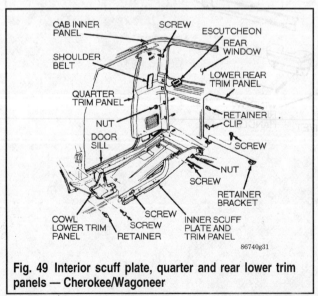

Fig. 49 Interior scuff plate, quarter and rear lower trim panels — Cherokee/Wagoneer

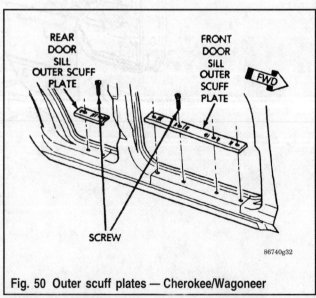

Fig. 50 Outer scuff plates — Cherokee/Wagoneer

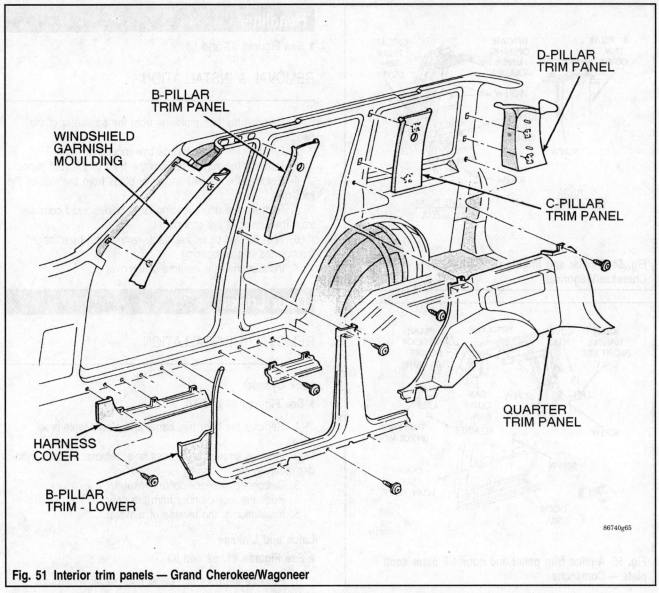

Fig. 51 Interior trim panels — Grand Cherokee/Wagoneer

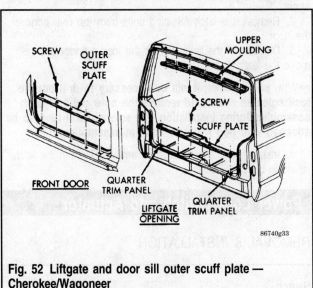

Fig. 52 Liftgate and door sill outer scuff plate — Cherokee/Wagoneer

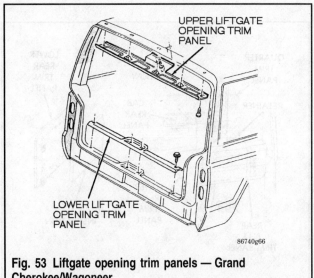

Fig. 53 Liftgate opening trim panels — Grand Cherokee/Wagoneer

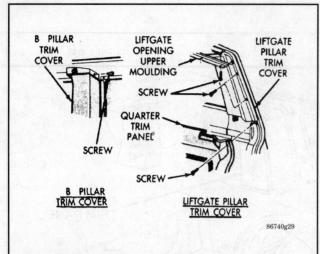

**Fig. 54 B-pillar and liftgate pillar trim covers —
Cherokee/Wagoneer**

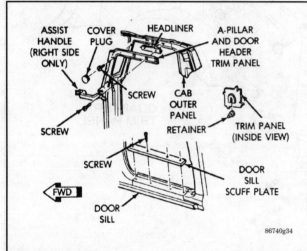

**Fig. 55 A-pillar trim panel and door sill outer scuff
plate — Comanche**

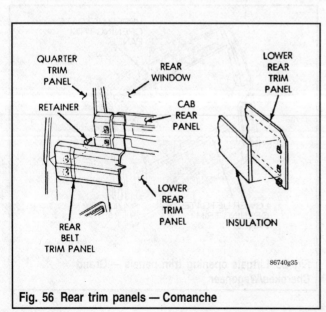

Fig. 56 Rear trim panels — Comanche

Headliner

▶ See Figures 57 and 58

REMOVAL & INSTALLATION

1. Remove the trim moldings from the perimeter of the headliner.
2. Remove the upper liftgate trim moulding.
3. Remove the sunvisors from the front of the roof panel.
4. Remove the assist handles or plugs from the side of the roof rails.
5. Remove the dome/reading lamp or overhead console from the center of the roof panel.
6. With the aid of an assistant, remove the headliner through the liftgate opening.
7. Installation is the reverse of removal.

Door Locks

REMOVAL & INSTALLATION

Lock Cylinder

▶ See Figures 59 and 60

1. Remove the door trim panel and plastic waterproof sheet.
2. Working through an access hole, remove the lock cylinder retaining clip.
3. Disconnect the lock control linkage.
4. Push the lock cylinder from the door.
5. Installation is the reverse of removal.

Latch and Linkage

▶ See Figures 61, 62 and 63

1. Remove the door trim panel and plastic waterproof sheet.
2. Remove the latch retaining bolts from the rear edge of the door.
3. Disconnect the linkage from the lock cylinder and remove the latch and linkage.

➡ **With power locks, it will be necessary to drill out the lock solenoid rivets and remove the solenoid and latch assembly. During installation, the solenoid will have to be attached with pop rivets or bolt/nut assemblies.**

4. Installation is the reverse of removal. Tighten the latch retaining bolts to 7 ft. lbs.

Power Lock Switch and Actuator

REMOVAL & INSTALLATION

Switch

1. Disconnect the battery ground.

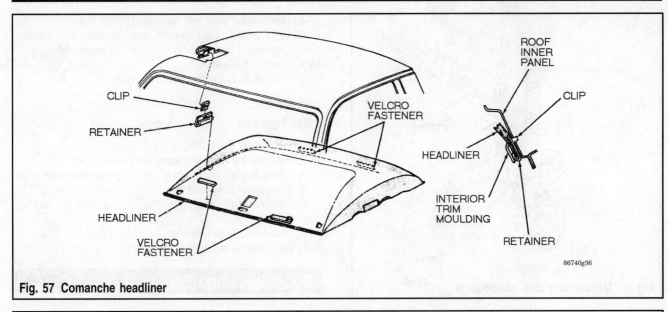

Fig. 57 Comanche headliner

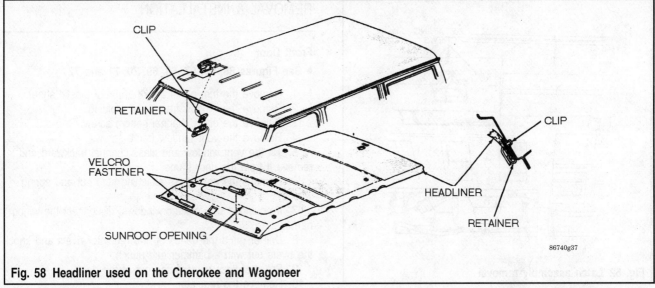

Fig. 58 Headliner used on the Cherokee and Wagoneer

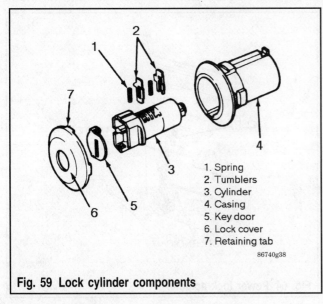

1. Spring
2. Tumblers
3. Cylinder
4. Casing
5. Key door
6. Lock cover
7. Retaining tab

Fig. 59 Lock cylinder components

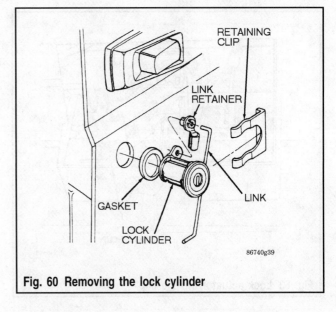

Fig. 60 Removing the lock cylinder

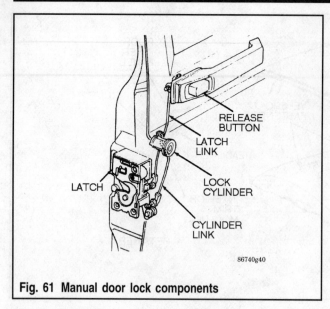

Fig. 61 Manual door lock components

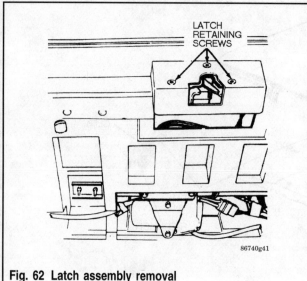

Fig. 62 Latch assembly removal

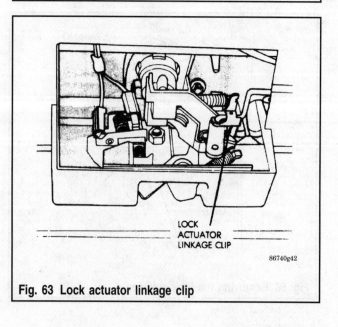

Fig. 63 Lock actuator linkage clip

2. Remove the door trim panel and watershield.

3. Remove the switch housing from the inner door panel.

4. Disconnect the wiring and pry up the switch retaining clips. Remove the switch.

5. Installation is the reverse of removal.

Actuator Motor

▶ **See Figure 64**

1. Disconnect the battery ground.

2. Remove the door trim panel and watershield.

3. Using a ¼ in. drill bit, drill out the motor mounting rivets.

4. Disconnect the motor actuator rod from the bellcrank.

5. Disconnect the wires from the motor and lift the motor from the door.

6. Installation is the reverse of removal. Use ¼ x ½ in. bolts and locknuts in place of the rivets.

Door Glass and Regulator

REMOVAL & INSTALLATION

Front Door

▶ **See Figures 65, 66, 67, 68, 69, 70, 71 and 72**

1. Remove the trim panel and waterproof plastic sheet.

2. Remove the window frame trim molding.

3. Remove the glass channel bottom screw.

4. Remove the vent window frame screws.

5. Tilt the vent window and glass channel backward and remove it from the door frame.

6. Remove the door glass attaching stud nut and spring washer.

7. If equipped with electric windows, disconnect the wiring harness.

8. Drill or grind the heads off the regulator rivets and knock the rivets out with a hammer and punch.

9. Pull the glass upward and out of the door.

10. Remove the regulator.

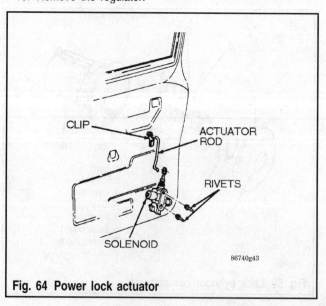

Fig. 64 Power lock actuator

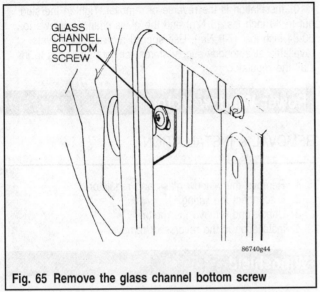

Fig. 65 Remove the glass channel bottom screw

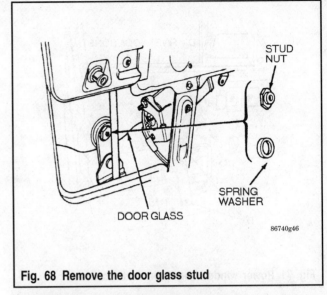

Fig. 68 Remove the door glass stud

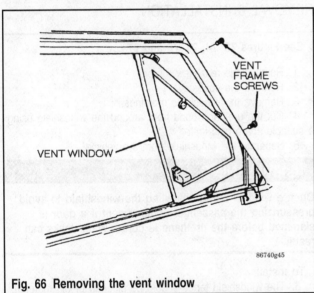

Fig. 66 Removing the vent window

Fig. 69 On power windows, unplug the wiring connector

Fig. 67 Peel the plastic sheet back

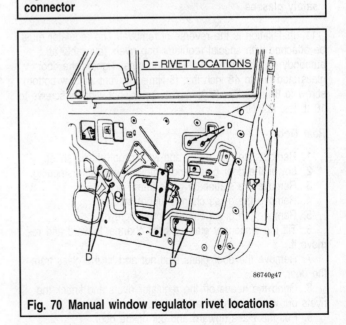

Fig. 70 Manual window regulator rivet locations

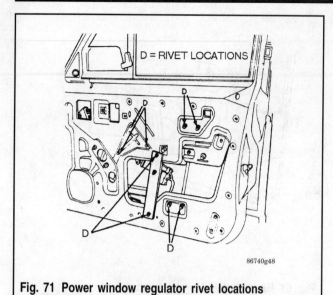

Fig. 71 Power window regulator rivet locations

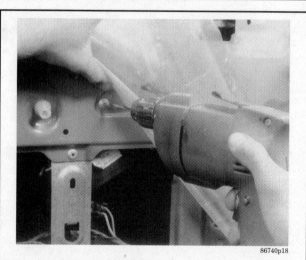

Fig. 72 Drill the heads off the rivets. Don't forget your safety glasses

11. Installation is the reverse of removal. The regulator must be attached with special regulator pop rivets (available at autobody supply stores) or bolts and nuts. Tighten the door glass stud nut to 48 inch lbs. (5 Nm); the vent window bottom screw to 84 inch lbs. (9 Nm); the upper vent window screws to 10 ft. lbs. (14 Nm).

Rear Door

1. Remove the trim panel and waterproof plastic sheet.
2. Lower the door glass and remove the weatherstripping.
3. Remove the stationary glass frame screws.
4. Remove the glass channel upper screws.
5. Remove the glass channel lower screws.
6. Tilt the stationary glass and its channel forward and remove it.
7. Remove the door glass stud nut and lift the glass from the door.
8. Grind the heads off the regulator rivets and knock the rivets out with a hammer and punch.
9. Pull the glass upward and out of the door.

10. Installation is the reverse of removal. Tighten the stud nut to 48 inch lbs. (5 Nm) and the glass channel screws to 60-84 inch lbs. (7-9 Nm). Use special regulator pop rivets (available at autobody supply stores) or nuts and bolts to install the regulator.

Power Window Motor

REMOVAL & INSTALLATION

1. Remove the window glass and regulator.
2. Disconnect the wiring.
3. Unbolt and remove the motor.
4. Installation is the reverse of removal.

Windshield

REMOVAL & INSTALLATION

▶ See Figures 73, 74, 75, 76 and 77

1. Remove the rear view mirror.
2. Remove the cowl cover.
3. Remove the windshield moldings.
4. Cut the urethane bond from around the windshield using a suitable sharp cold knife.
5. Separate the windshield from the vehicle.

❈❈WARNING

Open a window before installing the windshield to avoid pressurizing the passenger compartment if a door is slammed before the urethane is cured. Water leaks can result.

To install:
6. The windshield fence should be cleaned of old material. Support spacers should be cleaned and properly installed on

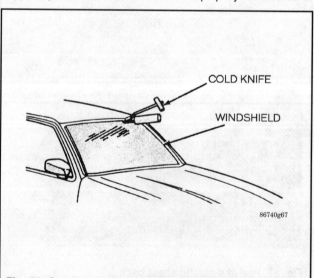

COLD KNIFE

WINDSHIELD

Fig. 73 Cut the urethane bond around the windshield

weld studs or repair screws at the bottom of the windshield opening.

7. Place the replacement windshield into the opening. Position the glass in the center of the opening against the support spacers.

8. Mark the glass at the support spacers to use as a reference for installation. Remove the replacement windshield from the opening.

9. Position the windshield inside up on a work surface on two padded blocks.

10. Clean the inside of the glass with Mopar® glass cleaner and a lint free cloth.

11. Apply clear glass primer 1 in. (25mm) wide around the windshield. wipe with a lint free cloth.

12. Apply black out primer 0.75 in. (15mm) wide on the top and sides of the glass and 1 in. (25mm) on the bottom. Allow three minutes drying time.

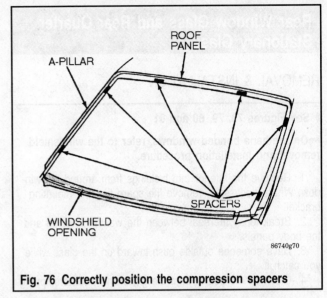

Fig. 76 **Correctly position the compression spacers**

13. Position the spacers on the lower fence above the support spacers at the edge of the opening.

14. Apply a 0.4 in. (10mm) bead of urethane around the perimeter of the windshield along the inside of the moldings.

15. With the aid of a helper, position the windshield over the opening. Align the reference marks at the bottom of the windshield with the spacers.

16. Slowly lower the glass. Guide the top molding into the proper position if necessary. Push the windshield inward to fence spacers at the bottom and until the top moulding is flush to the roof line.

17. Clean the excess urethane from the exterior with Mopar® Super Clean or equivalent.

18. Install the windshield molding. Apply 6 in. (15mm) lengths of 2 in. (50mm) masking tape spaced 10 in. (250mm) apart to hold the molding in place until the urethane cures.

19. Install the cowl cover and wipers.

20. Install the rear view mirror.

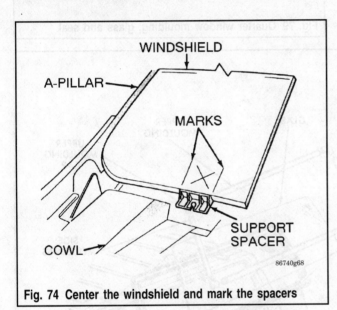

Fig. 74 **Center the windshield and mark the spacers**

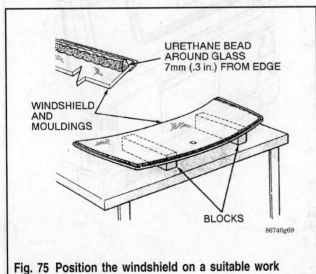

Fig. 75 **Position the windshield on a suitable work surface**

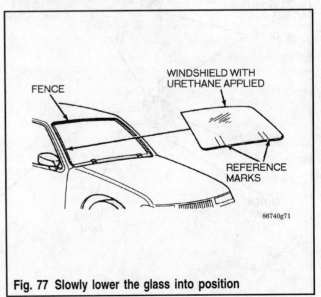

Fig. 77 **Slowly lower the glass into position**

Rear Window Glass and Rear Quarter Stationary Glass

REMOVAL & INSTALLATION

♦ See Figures 78, 79, 80 and 81

➡ On urethane bonded windows, refer to the windshield removal and installation procedure.

1. Remove the interior trim moldings from around the window. Where necessary, remove the spare tire and mounting bracket.
2. Break loose the seal between the weatherstripping and the body panels.
3. Have someone outside push inward on the glass while you catch it.
4. Clean all old sealer from the glass and weatherstripping.

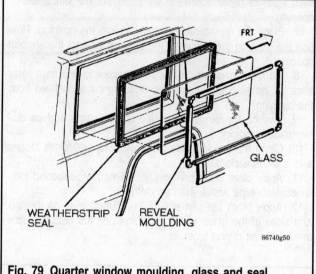

Fig. 79 Quarter window moulding, glass and seal

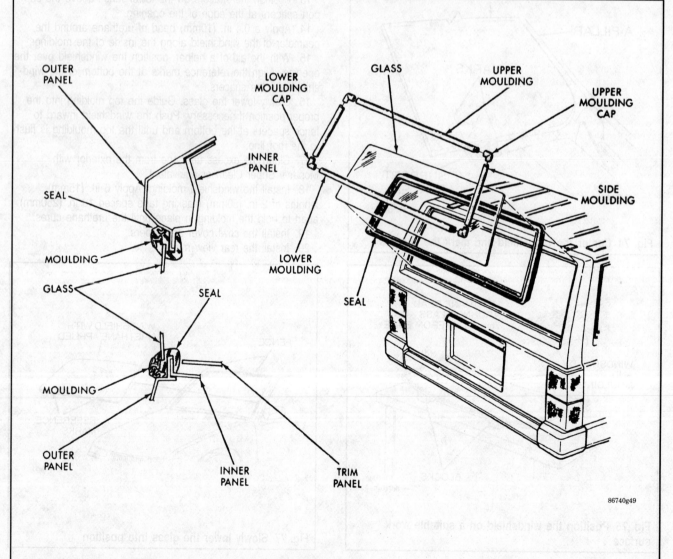

Fig. 78 Liftgate window glass revel moulding, glass and seal

To install:

5. Fill the glass cavity in the weatherstripping with a bead of sealer.

6. Fit the glass in the weatherstripping and place a cord in the frame cavity around the outside diameter of the weatherstripping. Allow the ends of the cord to hang down the outside of the glass from the top center.

7. Place the glass and weatherstripping in the vehicle opening. Pull on the cord ends to pull the lip of the weatherstripping over the body panel.

8. Install the trim molding.

Inside Rear View Mirror

REMOVAL & INSTALLATION

To replace the rear view mirror, loosen the mirror set screw and slide the mirror base up and off the retaining bracket.

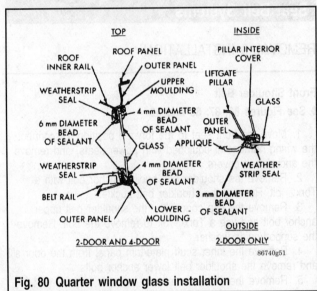

Fig. 80 Quarter window glass installation

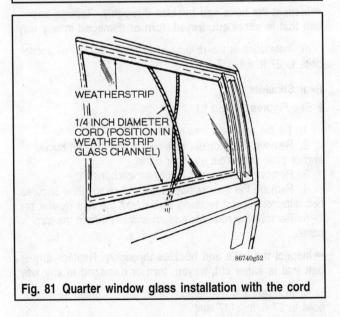

Fig. 81 Quarter window glass installation with the cord

Install the replacement mirror on to the retaining bracket and tighten the set screw. DO NOT overtighten the set screw as this will chip or break the windshield.

To replace the retaining bracket use the following procedure:

1. Mark installation reference position lines on the outside of the windshield glass with a grease pencil. Mark both horizontal and vertical reference marks.

2. If the vinyl pad remained on the windshield glass, soften and remove it with a heat gun.

3. Thoroughly clean the bracket contact surface area on the glass. Use a mild abrasive cleaning solution and final clean with isopropyl alcohol.

4. Lightly sand the contact area on the replacement bracket with fine grit sandpaper. Wipe the bracket clean with alcohol.

5. Follow the manufacturers instructions for preparing the adhesive.

6. Install the rear view mirror.

Seats

REMOVAL & INSTALLATION

Bucket Seats

▶ **See Figure 82**

Bucket seat platforms are attached to the floor panel with studs and nuts. The trim covers are attached to the platform with either push-on type fasteners or screws.

1. Remove the seat platform cover fasteners and platform cover.

2. For power seats, disconnect the wire harness connector.

3. Remove the seat retaining nuts and remove the seat from the floor panel.

4. Installation is the reverse of removal. Tighten the retaining nuts to 18 ft. lbs. (24 Nm).

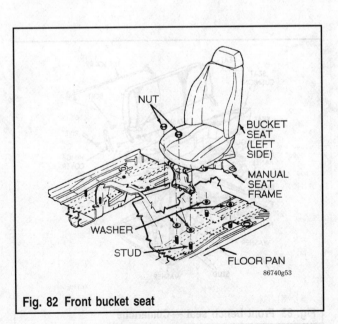

Fig. 82 Front bucket seat

Front Bench Seat

▶ See Figure 83

1. If equipped, disengage the seat frame trim cover retainers and remove the trim covers.

2. Detach the shoulder belt buckles and lap belts from the seat.

3. Remove the seat track platform retaining nuts from the studs and remove the seat.

4. Installation is the reverse of removal. Tighten the retaining nuts to 18 ft. lbs. (24 Nm).

Rear Seat

▶ See Figure 84

1. Disengage the seat cushion at the rear by pulling upward on the release strap.

2. Tilt the seat cushion forward and disengage the seat cushion latch with the release lever knob. Separate the right side latch and the left side seat bracket from the floor anchor bolts, then remove the cushion from the vehicle.

3. Remove the shoulder/lap belt buckles from the elastic straps. Release the seatback lock.

4. Remove the pivot bolts and the washers from the wheelhouse panel anchors.

5. Tilt the seatback forward, lift it upward and remove from the vehicle.

To install:

6. Position the seatback in the vehicle. Install the pivot bolts/washers and tighten to 38 ft. lbs. (52 Nm).

7. Lock the seatback in place. Insert the shoulder/lap belt buckles in the elastic straps.

8. Position the seat cushion in the vehicle. Insert the left pivot in the anchor grommet.

9. Force the tight side latch onto the anchor bolt and pivot the seat cushion to the horizontal position.

10. Lock the seat cushion in-place by pressing firmly on the center of the cushion until the latch engages.

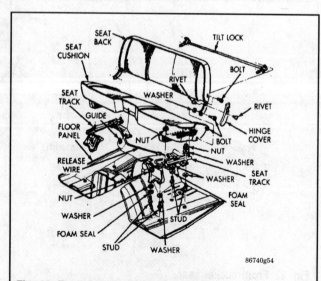

Fig. 83 Front bench seat — Comanche

86740g54

Power Seat Motor

REMOVAL & INSTALLATION

▶ See Figure 85

1. Disconnect the battery ground.

2. Remove the bolts holding the seat assembly to the floor pan.

3. Tilt the seat and disconnect the wiring harness.

4. Remove the seat assembly.

5. Invert the seat on a clean surface.

6. Remove the attaching bolts and lift out the seat motor. Disconnect the wiring and cables.

7. Installation is the reverse of removal.

➡ **If the seat transmission fails, it is not replaceable. The entire seat adjuster assembly will have to be replaced.**

Seat Belt Systems

REMOVAL & INSTALLATION

Front Shoulder Belt

▶ See Figures 86, 87, 88 and 89

1. Move the front seat to the forward position. Disconnect the wiring harness (if equipped with power seats) and remove the anchor bolt covers.

2. Remove the shoulder belt buckle anchor bolt with a Torx® bit. Remove the shoulder belt buckle.

3. Remove the cap concealing the shoulder belt upper anchor bolt and use a Torx® bit to remove the bolt. Remove the support/guide washer.

4. Remove the inner scuff plate/trim panel from the door sill and remove the shoulder belt lower anchor bolts.

5. Remove the shoulder belt and retractor.

➡ **Inspect the belts and buckles throughly. Replace any belt that is either cut, frayed, torn or damaged in any way.**

6. Installation is the reverse of removal. Tighten all anchor bolts to 27 ft. lbs. (37 Nm).

Rear Shoulder Belt

▶ See Figures 90 and 91

1. Tilt the rear seat forward.

2. Remove the shoulder belt buckle and lap belt buckle anchor plate bolts from the floor panel.

3. Remove the shoulder belt lower anchor bolt.

4. Remove the quarter trim panel and remove the shoulder belt retractor support retaining screw from the rear quarter rail.

5. Remove the retractor and shoulder belt from the trim panel.

➡ **Inspect the belts and buckles throughly. Replace any belt that is either cut, frayed, torn or damaged in any way.**

6. Installation is the reverse of removal. Tighten all anchor bolts to 27 ft. lbs. (37 Nm).

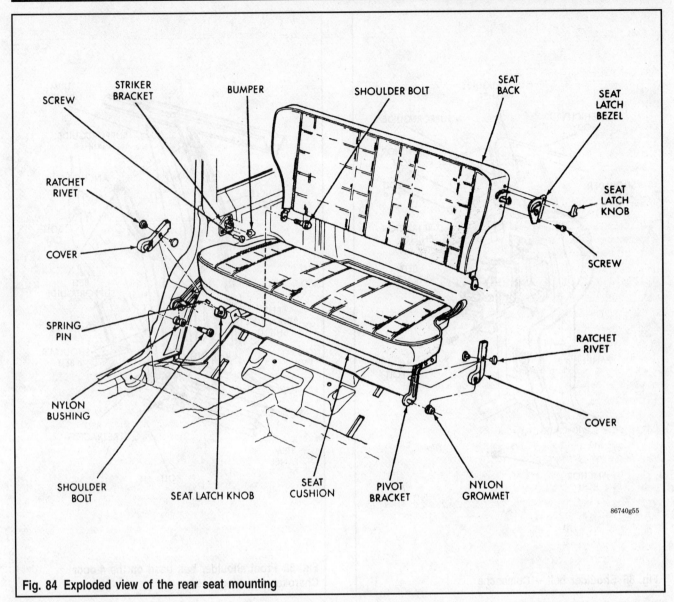

Fig. 84 Exploded view of the rear seat mounting

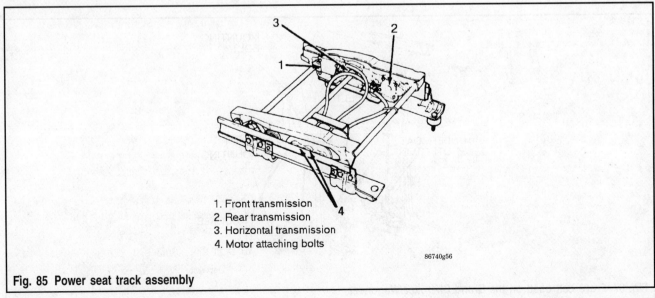

1. Front transmission
2. Rear transmission
3. Horizontal transmission
4. Motor attaching bolts

86740g56

Fig. 85 Power seat track assembly

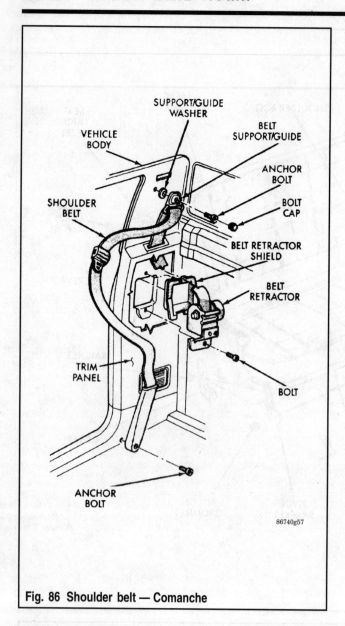

Fig. 86 Shoulder belt — Comanche

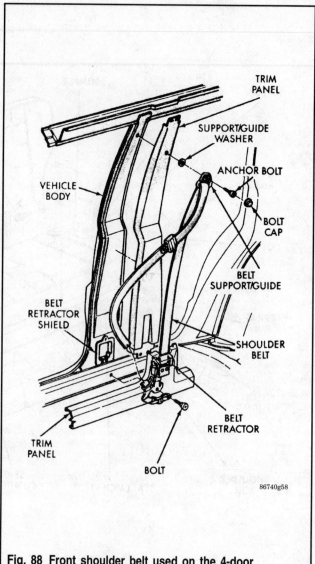

Fig. 88 Front shoulder belt used on the 4-door Cherokee and Wagoneer

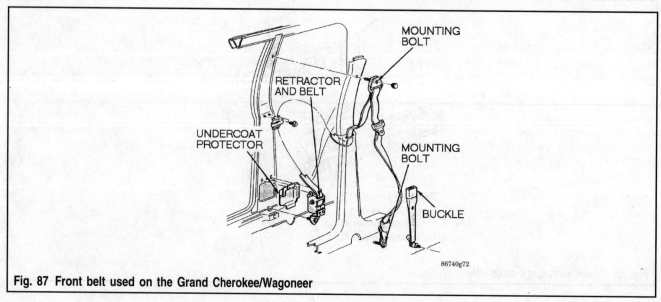

Fig. 87 Front belt used on the Grand Cherokee/Wagoneer

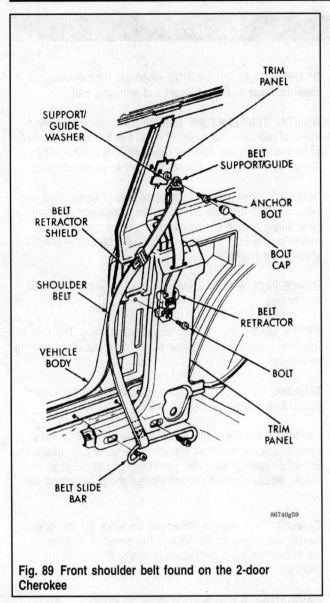

Fig. 89 Front shoulder belt found on the 2-door Cherokee

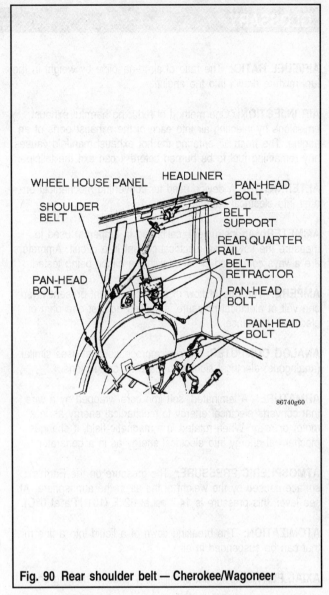

Fig. 90 Rear shoulder belt — Cherokee/Wagoneer

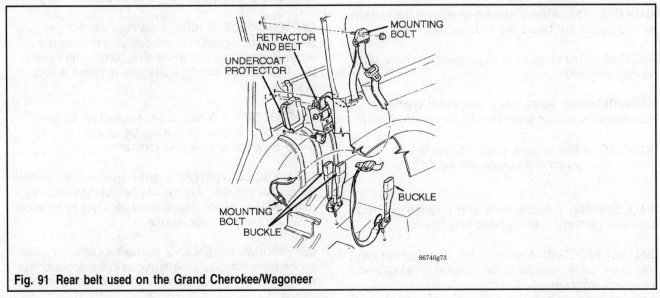

Fig. 91 Rear belt used on the Grand Cherokee/Wagoneer

GLOSSARY

AIR/FUEL RATIO: The ratio of air-to-gasoline by weight in the fuel mixture drawn into the engine.

AIR INJECTION: One method of reducing harmful exhaust emissions by injecting air into each of the exhaust ports of an engine. The fresh air entering the hot exhaust manifold causes any remaining fuel to be burned before it can exit the tailpipe.

ALTERNATOR: A device used for converting mechanical energy into electrical energy.

AMMETER: An instrument, calibrated in amperes, used to measure the flow of an electrical current in a circuit. Ammeters are always connected in series with the circuit being tested.

AMPERE: The rate of flow of electrical current present when one volt of electrical pressure is applied against one ohm of electrical resistance.

ANALOG COMPUTER: Any microprocessor that uses similar (analogous) electrical signals to make its calculations.

ARMATURE: A laminated, soft iron core wrapped by a wire that converts electrical energy to mechanical energy as in a motor or relay. When rotated in a magnetic field, it changes mechanical energy into electrical energy as in a generator.

ATMOSPHERIC PRESSURE: The pressure on the Earth's surface caused by the weight of the air in the atmosphere. At sea level, this pressure is 14.7 psi at 32°F (101 kPa at 0°C).

ATOMIZATION: The breaking down of a liquid into a fine mist that can be suspended in air.

AXIAL PLAY: Movement parallel to a shaft or bearing bore.

BACKFIRE: The sudden combustion of gases in the intake or exhaust system that results in a loud explosion.

BACKLASH: The clearance or play between two parts, such as meshed gears.

BACKPRESSURE: Restrictions in the exhaust system that slow the exit of exhaust gases from the combustion chamber.

BAKELITE: A heat resistant, plastic insulator material commonly used in printed circuit boards and transistorized components.

BALL BEARING: A bearing made up of hardened inner and outer races between which hardened steel balls roll.

BALLAST RESISTOR: A resistor in the primary ignition circuit that lowers voltage after the engine is started to reduce wear on ignition components.

BEARING: A friction reducing, supportive device usually located between a stationary part and a moving part.

BIMETAL TEMPERATURE SENSOR: Any sensor or switch made of two dissimilar types of metal that bend when heated or cooled due to the different expansion rates of the alloys. These types of sensors usually function as an on/off switch.

BLOWBY: Combustion gases, composed of water vapor and unburned fuel, that leak past the piston rings into the crankcase during normal engine operation. These gases are removed by the PCV system to prevent the buildup of harmful acids in the crankcase.

BRAKE PAD: A brake shoe and lining assembly used with disc brakes.

BRAKE SHOE: The backing for the brake lining. The term is, however, usually applied to the assembly of the brake backing and lining.

BUSHING: A liner, usually removable, for a bearing; an anti-friction liner used in place of a bearing.

CALIPER: A hydraulically activated device in a disc brake system, which is mounted straddling the brake rotor (disc). The caliper contains at least one piston and two brake pads. Hydraulic pressure on the piston(s) forces the pads against the rotor.

CAMSHAFT: A shaft in the engine on which are the lobes (cams) which operate the valves. The camshaft is driven by the crankshaft, via a belt, chain or gears, at one half the crankshaft speed.

CAPACITOR: A device which stores an electrical charge.

CARBON MONOXIDE (CO): A colorless, odorless gas given off as a normal byproduct of combustion. It is poisonous and extremely dangerous in confined areas, building up slowly to toxic levels without warning if adequate ventilation is not available.

CARBURETOR: A device, usually mounted on the intake manifold of an engine, which mixes the air and fuel in the proper proportion to allow even combustion.

CATALYTIC CONVERTER: A device installed in the exhaust system, like a muffler, that converts harmful byproducts of combustion into carbon dioxide and water vapor by means of a heat-producing chemical reaction.

CENTRIFUGAL ADVANCE: A mechanical method of advancing the spark timing by using flyweights in the distributor that react to centrifugal force generated by the distributor shaft rotation.

CHECK VALVE: Any one-way valve installed to permit the flow of air, fuel or vacuum in one direction only.

CHOKE: A device, usually a moveable valve, placed in the intake path of a carburetor to restrict the flow of air.

CIRCUIT: Any unbroken path through which an electrical current can flow. Also used to describe fuel flow in some instances.

CIRCUIT BREAKER: A switch which protects an electrical circuit from overload by opening the circuit when the current flow exceeds a predetermined level. Some circuit breakers must be reset manually, while most reset automatically.

COIL (IGNITION): A transformer in the ignition circuit which steps up the voltage provided to the spark plugs.

COMBINATION MANIFOLD: An assembly which includes both the intake and exhaust manifolds in one casting.

COMBINATION VALVE: A device used in some fuel systems that routes fuel vapors to a charcoal storage canister instead of venting them into the atmosphere. The valve relieves fuel tank pressure and allows fresh air into the tank as the fuel level drops to prevent a vapor lock situation.

COMPRESSION RATIO: The comparison of the total volume of the cylinder and combustion chamber with the piston at BDC and the piston at TDC.

CONDENSER: 1. An electrical device which acts to store an electrical charge, preventing voltage surges. 2. A radiator-like device in the air conditioning system in which refrigerant gas condenses into a liquid, giving off heat.

CONDUCTOR: Any material through which an electrical current can be transmitted easily.

CONTINUITY: Continuous or complete circuit. Can be checked with an ohmmeter.

COUNTERSHAFT: An intermediate shaft which is rotated by a mainshaft and transmits, in turn, that rotation to a working part.

CRANKCASE: The lower part of an engine in which the crankshaft and related parts operate.

CRANKSHAFT: The main driving shaft of an engine which receives reciprocating motion from the pistons and converts it to rotary motion.

CYLINDER: In an engine, the round hole in the engine block in which the piston(s) ride.

CYLINDER BLOCK: The main structural member of an engine in which is found the cylinders, crankshaft and other principal parts.

CYLINDER HEAD: The detachable portion of the engine, usually fastened to the top of the cylinder block and containing all or most of the combustion chambers. On overhead valve engines, it contains the valves and their operating parts. On overhead cam engines, it contains the camshaft as well.

DEAD CENTER: The extreme top or bottom of the piston stroke.

DETONATION: An unwanted explosion of the air/fuel mixture in the combustion chamber caused by excess heat and compression, advanced timing, or an overly lean mixture. Also referred to as "ping".

DIAPHRAGM: A thin, flexible wall separating two cavities, such as in a vacuum advance unit.

DIESELING: A condition in which hot spots in the combustion chamber cause the engine to run on after the key is turned off.

DIFFERENTIAL: A geared assembly which allows the transmission of motion between drive axles, giving one axle the ability to turn faster than the other.

DIODE: An electrical device that will allow current to flow in one direction only.

DISC BRAKE: A hydraulic braking assembly consisting of a brake disc, or rotor, mounted on an axle, and a caliper assembly containing, usually two brake pads which are activated by hydraulic pressure. The pads are forced against the sides of the disc, creating friction which slows the vehicle.

DISTRIBUTOR: A mechanically driven device on an engine which is responsible for electrically firing the spark plug at a predetermined point of the piston stroke.

DOWEL PIN: A pin, inserted in mating holes in two different parts allowing those parts to maintain a fixed relationship.

DRUM BRAKE: A braking system which consists of two brake shoes and one or two wheel cylinders, mounted on a fixed backing plate, and a brake drum, mounted on an axle, which revolves around the assembly.

DWELL: The rate, measured in degrees of shaft rotation, at which an electrical circuit cycles on and off.

ELECTRONIC CONTROL UNIT (ECU): Ignition module, module, amplifier or igniter. See Module for definition.

ELECTRONIC IGNITION: A system in which the timing and firing of the spark plugs is controlled by an electronic control unit, usually called a module. These systems have no points or condenser.

END-PLAY: The measured amount of axial movement in a shaft.

ENGINE: A device that converts heat into mechanical energy.

EXHAUST MANIFOLD: A set of cast passages or pipes which conduct exhaust gases from the engine.

FEELER GAUGE: A blade, usually metal, of precisely predetermined thickness, used to measure the clearance between two parts.

FIRING ORDER: The order in which combustion occurs in the cylinders of an engine. Also the order in which spark is distributed to the plugs by the distributor.

FLOODING: The presence of too much fuel in the intake manifold and combustion chamber which prevents the air/fuel mixture from firing, thereby causing a no-start situation.

FLYWHEEL: A disc shaped part bolted to the rear end of the crankshaft. Around the outer perimeter is affixed the ring gear. The starter drive engages the ring gear, turning the flywheel, which rotates the crankshaft, imparting the initial starting motion to the engine.

FOOT POUND (ft. lbs. or sometimes, ft.lb.): The amount of energy or work needed to raise an item weighing one pound, a distance of one foot.

FUSE: A protective device in a circuit which prevents circuit overload by breaking the circuit when a specific amperage is present. The device is constructed around a strip or wire of a lower amperage rating than the circuit it is designed to protect. When an amperage higher than that stamped on the fuse is present in the circuit, the strip or wire melts, opening the circuit.

GEAR RATIO: The ratio between the number of teeth on meshing gears.

GENERATOR: A device which converts mechanical energy into electrical energy.

HEAT RANGE: The measure of a spark plug's ability to dissipate heat from its firing end. The higher the heat range, the hotter the plug fires.

HUB: The center part of a wheel or gear.

HYDROCARBON (HC): Any chemical compound made up of hydrogen and carbon. A major pollutant formed by the engine as a byproduct of combustion.

HYDROMETER: An instrument used to measure the specific gravity of a solution.

INCH POUND (inch lbs.; sometimes in.lb. or in. lbs.): One twelfth of a foot pound.

INDUCTION: A means of transferring electrical energy in the form of a magnetic field. Principle used in the ignition coil to increase voltage.

INJECTOR: A device which receives metered fuel under relatively low pressure and is activated to inject the fuel into the engine under relatively high pressure at a predetermined time.

INPUT SHAFT: The shaft to which torque is applied, usually carrying the driving gear or gears.

INTAKE MANIFOLD: A casting of passages or pipes used to conduct air or a fuel/air mixture to the cylinders.

JOURNAL: The bearing surface within which a shaft operates.

KEY: A small block usually fitted in a notch between a shaft and a hub to prevent slippage of the two parts.

MANIFOLD: A casting of passages or set of pipes which connect the cylinders to an inlet or outlet source.

MANIFOLD VACUUM: Low pressure in an engine intake manifold formed just below the throttle plates. Manifold vacuum is highest at idle and drops under acceleration.

MASTER CYLINDER: The primary fluid pressurizing device in a hydraulic system. In automotive use, it is found in brake and hydraulic clutch systems and is pedal activated, either directly or, in a power brake system, through the power booster.

MODULE: Electronic control unit, amplifier or igniter of solid state or integrated design which controls the current flow in the ignition primary circuit based on input from the pick-up coil. When the module opens the primary circuit, high secondary voltage is induced in the coil.

NEEDLE BEARING: A bearing which consists of a number (usually a large number) of long, thin rollers.

OHM:(Ω) The unit used to measure the resistance of conductor-to-electrical flow. One ohm is the amount of resistance that limits current flow to one ampere in a circuit with one volt of pressure.

OHMMETER: An instrument used for measuring the resistance, in ohms, in an electrical circuit.

OUTPUT SHAFT: The shaft which transmits torque from a device, such as a transmission.

OVERDRIVE: A gear assembly which produces more shaft revolutions than that transmitted to it.

OVERHEAD CAMSHAFT (OHC): An engine configuration in which the camshaft is mounted on top of the cylinder head and operates the valve either directly or by means of rocker arms.

OVERHEAD VALVE (OHV): An engine configuration in which all of the valves are located in the cylinder head and the camshaft is located in the cylinder block. The camshaft operates the valves via lifters and pushrods.

OXIDES OF NITROGEN (NOx): Chemical compounds of nitrogen produced as a byproduct of combustion. They combine with hydrocarbons to produce smog.

OXYGEN SENSOR: Used with the feedback system to sense the presence of oxygen in the exhaust gas and signal the computer which can reference the voltage signal to an air/fuel ratio.

PINION: The smaller of two meshing gears.

PISTON RING: An open-ended ring which fits into a groove on the outer diameter of the piston. Its chief function is to form a seal between the piston and cylinder wall. Most automotive pistons have three rings: two for compression sealing; one for oil sealing.

PRELOAD: A predetermined load placed on a bearing during assembly or by adjustment.

PRIMARY CIRCUIT: The low voltage side of the ignition system which consists of the ignition switch, ballast resistor or resistance wire, bypass, coil, electronic control unit and pick-up coil as well as the connecting wires and harnesses.

PRESS FIT: The mating of two parts under pressure, due to the inner diameter of one being smaller than the outer diameter of the other, or vice versa; an interference fit.

RACE: The surface on the inner or outer ring of a bearing on which the balls, needles or rollers move.

REGULATOR: A device which maintains the amperage and/or voltage levels of a circuit at predetermined values.

RELAY: A switch which automatically opens and/or closes a circuit.

RESISTANCE: The opposition to the flow of current through a circuit or electrical device, and is measured in ohms. Resistance is equal to the voltage divided by the amperage.

RESISTOR: A device, usually made of wire, which offers a preset amount of resistance in an electrical circuit.

RING GEAR: The name given to a ring-shaped gear attached to a differential case, or affixed to a flywheel or as part of a planetary gear set.

ROLLER BEARING: A bearing made up of hardened inner and outer races between which hardened steel rollers move.

ROTOR: 1. The disc-shaped part of a disc brake assembly, upon which the brake pads bear; also called, brake disc. 2. The device mounted atop the distributor shaft, which passes current to the distributor cap tower contacts.

SECONDARY CIRCUIT: The high voltage side of the ignition system, usually above 20,000 volts. The secondary includes the ignition coil, coil wire, distributor cap and rotor, spark plug wires and spark plugs.

SENDING UNIT: A mechanical, electrical, hydraulic or electromagnetic device which transmits information to a gauge.

SENSOR: Any device designed to measure engine operating conditions or ambient pressures and temperatures. Usually electronic in nature and designed to send a voltage signal to an on-board computer, some sensors may operate as a simple on/off switch or they may provide a variable voltage signal (like a potentiometer) as conditions or measured parameters change.

SHIM: Spacers of precise, predetermined thickness used between parts to establish a proper working relationship.

SLAVE CYLINDER: In automotive use, a device in the hydraulic clutch system which is activated by hydraulic force, disengaging the clutch.

SOLENOID: A coil used to produce a magnetic field, the effect of which is to produce work.

SPARK PLUG: A device screwed into the combustion chamber of a spark ignition engine. The basic construction is a conductive core inside of a ceramic insulator, mounted in an outer conductive base. An electrical charge from the spark plug wire travels along the conductive core and jumps a preset air gap to a grounding point or points at the end of the conductive base. The resultant spark ignites the fuel/air mixture in the combustion chamber.

SPLINES: Ridges machined or cast onto the outer diameter of a shaft or inner diameter of a bore to enable parts to mate without rotation.

TACHOMETER: A device used to measure the rotary speed of an engine, shaft, gear, etc., usually in rotations per minute.

THERMOSTAT: A valve, located in the cooling system of an engine, which is closed when cold and opens gradually in response to engine heating, controlling the temperature of the coolant and rate of coolant flow.

TOP DEAD CENTER (TDC): The point at which the piston reaches the top of its travel on the compression stroke.

TORQUE: The twisting force applied to an object.

TORQUE CONVERTER: A turbine used to transmit power from a driving member to a driven member via hydraulic action, providing changes in drive ratio and torque. In automotive use, it links the driveplate at the rear of the engine to the automatic transmission.

TRANSDUCER: A device used to change a force into an electrical signal.

TRANSISTOR: A semi-conductor component which can be actuated by a small voltage to perform an electrical switching function.

TUNE-UP: A regular maintenance function, usually associated with the replacement and adjustment of parts and components in the electrical and fuel systems of a vehicle for the purpose of attaining optimum performance.

TURBOCHARGER: An exhaust driven pump which compresses intake air and forces it into the combustion chambers at higher than atmospheric pressures. The increased air pressure allows more fuel to be burned and results in increased horsepower being produced.

VACUUM ADVANCE: A device which advances the ignition timing in response to increased engine vacuum.

VACUUM GAUGE: An instrument used to measure the presence of vacuum in a chamber.

VALVE: A device which control the pressure, direction of flow or rate of flow of a liquid or gas.

VALVE CLEARANCE: The measured gap between the end of the valve stem and the rocker arm, cam lobe or follower that activates the valve.

VISCOSITY: The rating of a liquid's internal resistance to flow.

VOLTMETER: An instrument used for measuring electrical force in units called volts. Voltmeters are always connected parallel with the circuit being tested.

WHEEL CYLINDER: Found in the automotive drum brake assembly, it is a device, actuated by hydraulic pressure, which, through internal pistons, pushes the brake shoes outward against the drums.

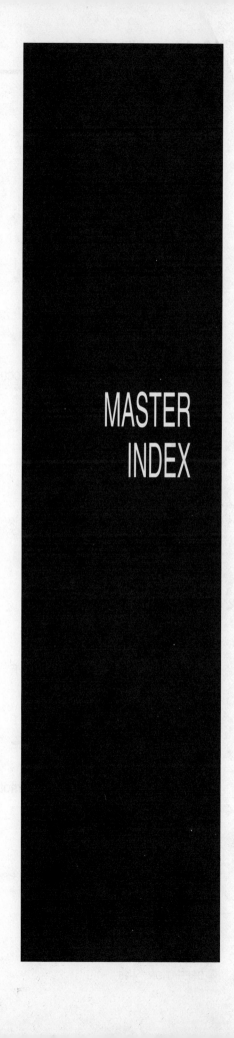

MASTER
INDEX